Selected Topics in
Communication Networks and Distributed Systems

Selected Topics in Communication Networks and Distributed Systems

Editors

Sudip Misra

Indian Institute of Technology, Kharagpur, India

Subhas Chandra Misra

Indian Institute of Technology, Kanpur, India

Isaac Woungang

Ryerson University, Canada

World Scientific

NEW JERSEY • LONDON • SINGAPORE • BEIJING • SHANGHAI • HONG KONG • TAIPEI • CHENNAI

Published by

World Scientific Publishing Co. Pte. Ltd.
5 Toh Tuck Link, Singapore 596224
USA office: 27 Warren Street, Suite 401-402, Hackensack, NJ 07601
UK office: 57 Shelton Street, Covent Garden, London WC2H 9HE

British Library Cataloguing-in-Publication Data
A catalogue record for this book is available from the British Library.

SELECTED TOPICS IN COMMUNICATION NETWORKS AND DISTRIBUTED SYSTEMS

ISBN-13 978-981-283-943-5

Typeset by Stallion Press
Email: enquiries@stallionpress.com

Printed in Singapore by World Scientific Printers.

CONTENTS

Chapter 1

MOBILITY IN WIRELESS COMMUNICATION NETWORKS

RONAN SKEHILL*, PADRAIG SCULLY, EDUARDO CANO,
JOSEPH JOHNSON, SEAN MCGRATH and JOHN NELSON
Wireless Access Research Centre,
Department of Electronic and Computer Engineering,
University of Limerick, Ireland
**ronan.skehill@ul.ie*

Underlying all wireless technologies is the fundamental principle that mobile users communicate with a base station via a wireless channel. In this chapter, a basic wireless channel is explored and the effects of distance, and thereby mobility, on the wireless channel is shown. The chapter then presents a generic wireless communication network and identifies the role and function of each component i.e., mobile device, access network and core network. The merger of new technologies and data services with mobile networks has created new issues in network management. The chapter provides a tutorial on the various mobility management methods used to mitigate and solve mobility issues. Concepts such as personal mobility, session mobility and service mobility can be viewed as high level mobility management solutions while concepts such as ad hoc mobility, mode mobility and terminal mobility are viewed as low level solutions. The chapter explores these concepts and presents current protocols/methods. A guide is provided for practitioners who may implement some of the mobility management methods. The chapter highlights research directions by presenting a range of projects and standard bodies working in the mobility management field.

1. Introduction

In every wireless network a transmitter and a receiver node is needed for communication. Radio waves start from a certain point, typically the transmitter antenna, and with a certain level of power or energy. Assuming the antenna is omni-directional, i.e., it radiates power equally in all directions, and assuming perfect conditions then radio waves continue in an ever-expanding circle. However, since the energy is finite, at any distance from the transmitter the original energy is now spread over a much larger space. The signal is said to be attenuated. If the signal is too weak, the receiver node cannot correctly receive the transmitted information. If this happens, the receiver lies outside the coverage area of the transmitter. The fundamental issue behind the coverage problem is the phenomenon of fading. Fading can be considered to be the time variation of the channel strengths due to multipath fading, as well as path loss via distance attenuation. Because receiver nodes can be mobile, the possibility of this happening increases greatly and methods to prevent out-of-coverage issues must be implemented.

A significant disadvantage of wireless networks is interference. Tse *et al.* [1] illustrate that a transmitter–receiver pair can often be thought of as an isolated point-to-point link, and that wireless users communicate over the air and there is significant interference between them. The interference can be between transmitters communicating with a common receiver (e.g., uplink of a cellular system), between signals from a single transmitter to multiple receivers (e.g., downlink of a cellular system), or between different transmitter-receiver pairs (e.g., interference between users in different cells). If the effects of interference between the isolated point-to-point link is not mitigated the signal could be completely lost.

As highlighted with fading and interference, wireless networks have some disadvantages compared to a wired network. However, the advantages of wireless networks surpass the disadvantages. The key advantage is mobility, i.e., the ability of the transmitter–receiver pair to move around and still avail of wired network functionality and services while in the coverage of the wireless network. Planning and network management techniques for fading and interference can overcome problems like coverage. Cell coverage varies as it is dependent on the wireless access technology in use. Technologies like GSM and UMTS can have large cell coverage, up to a radius of 2 km, while wireless technologies like IEEE 802.11 typically have a cell radius of less than a 100 m. Cellular systems like GSM and UMTS function on the assumption that a base station controls a limited coverage area, termed a cell. Cells can be clustered and controlled by a collection of base stations. This cluster represents a service area in which mobile users have the freedom to move/roam and gain network access simultaneously.

Movement in this service area has brought new challenges in wireless communication at all levels of the network. If relating a wireless network to the Open System Interconnected (OSI) stack, mobility primarily affects the physical

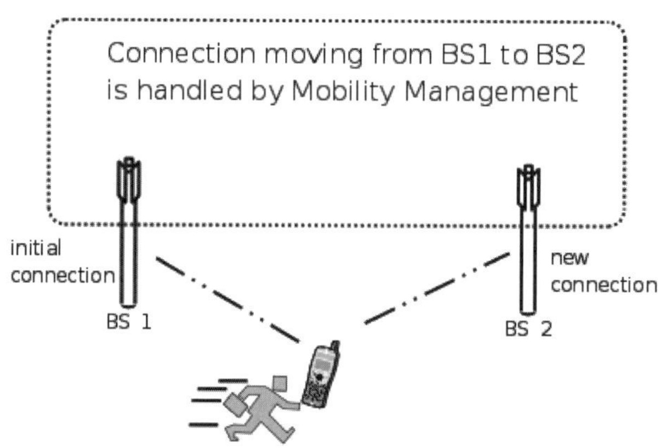

Fig. 1. Mobility management handles the connection from one base station to another.

and media access layers. Handling mobility at this level requires the network to handle mobile devices at a radio level. However, current wireless networks allow applications, including realtime and non-realtime, to run over Internet Protocol (IP) which brings issues in maintaining TCP/IP connections while the user moves from base station to base station. The Transmission Control Protocol (TCP) relies on the source and destination IP address to create a checksum; if either IP address change (which can happen if changing base station, network, etc.) then the checksum fails. If the checksum fails then the TCP connection is broken. Resolving this issue in a wireless network can be achieved by providing mobility management at the IP layer and above.

Underlying all these management techniques are the mobility characteristics of the mobile device in the wireless network. It is the movement of the mobile device that causes the management technique to be executed. Therefore, it is imperative that the movement is correctly understood. In a real-world scenario movement occurs at a multitude of levels: global movement, intercontinental, intercity, and on a smaller scale — campus, street or office. Furthermore, mobility can occur in groups or individually. Naturally, there is a speed associated with each of the movement levels; for example, in an office the speed of a mobile device is limited to walking speeds — whereas with a vehicle on a road the speed of the mobile device is now limited by road speed conditions. Associated with mobile device speed is mobile device density (measured in devices/m^2). In low speed mobility areas the mobile device density can be quite high, and with high speed mobility (cars traveling at 100 km/h) the mobile device density is low. Different wireless technologies are best suited for different mobility characteristics. For example cellular networks like GSM or UMTS are flexible and can cover high speed movements of a car on a road and pedestrians in a street, whereas IEEE 802.11 wireless LAN (WLAN) is best suited for low mobility scenarios only. Both technologies provide mobility support but ultimately the trade-off between GSM/UMTS and WLAN is data rates. WLAN can achieve data rates of over 100 Mb/s whereas GSM/UMTS networks can provide data rates up to 2 Mb/s.

Mobility management techniques must therefore be able to accommodate all these wireless technologies and be able to handle mobility speeds in all geographical areas. A single solution is not feasible so a multi-task solution is currently used. Before describing mobility management solutions, the wireless channel is explained to understand how conventional terminal mobility management works. A reference model of a generic future wireless communication network is presented that supports a multi-task mobility management technique.

2. Wireless Channel

The wireless channel is the physical medium that supports the propagation of all signals in a wireless network. In contrast with wired communications systems, the transmitted signals often do not reach their destination directly due to the presence of obstructions in the line-of-sight path. Obstacles in a communications link lead to the occurrence at the receiver of different replicas of the transmitted signal. This phenomenon, known as multipath propagation, weakens, delays and distorts the transmitted signal in a time-varying fashion. In addition to multipath propagation, the motion between the transmitter and the receiver also has a negative effect on the received signal strength. Thus, the characterization and understanding of the mobile radio channel is essential to combat these distortion effects and to acquire a desirable system performance, which in turn can satisfy the required quality of service (QoS).

An accurate estimation of multipath channel behavior allows for improving the bit error rate using equalization techniques at the receiver, optimization of the maximum capacity, and effectiveness of the shared medium access mechanisms. Furthermore, the design of a mobile radio system that satisfies the stipulated QoS metrics under realistic wireless channel conditions constitutes a major challenge, especially when service requirements demand very high data rates coupled with high-speed mobility.

2.1. *Propagation Mechanisms*

The communications path between transmitter and receiver is time, space and frequency variant. This variability of the wireless channel causes loss of signal strength at the receiver device referred to as *fading*. A good understanding of the propagation media and the circumstances that cause the fading of received signals is required for a complete characterization of the wireless channel. The variations of the channel can be roughly classified into (i) large-scale fading and (ii) small-scale fading, depending on how fast the average received power fluctuates in the distance between a receiver and a transmitter.

2.1.1. *Large-Scale Fading Effects*

Large-scale fading is predominantly caused by the path loss phenomenon. Large scale fading manifests itself as fluctuations in the voltage envelope of the received signal over relatively large distances between the transmitter and the receiver. It is common to model large scale fading effects using a path loss model that obeys some sort of power law.

Large scale fading represents the average signal power attenuation or the path loss caused by the motion of the mobile device over large areas (usually of the order of the wireless communication network cell size). This phenomenon occurs when the receiver is *shadowed* by the presence of prominent terrain contours (e.g., buildings, trees, hills, etc.).

Different approaches for modeling the path loss may be considered depending on the propagation environment. The simplest model corresponds to the direct line-of-sight transmission between transmitter and receiver, referred to as *free space loss* [2]. The principle of energy conservation establishes that the integral of the power density over any closed surface surrounding the transmit antenna must be equal to the transmit power. As the integration area is a circle of radius d centered at the transmitter position, the received power collected by the receiver antenna is obtained according to the Friis transmission equation [2] as:

$$P_{Rx}(d) = P_{Tx}G_{Tx}\frac{1}{4\pi d^2}A_{Rx} = \frac{P_{Tx}G_{Tx}G_{Rx}}{L_{FS}}, \tag{1}$$

where P_{Tx} is the transmitter power, L_{FS} is the free-space path loss and G_{Tx} is the transmit antenna gain in the direction of the receive antenna. The parameter A_{Rx} is the effective area of the receiver, which follows the relationship $A_{Rx} = \lambda^2/4\pi G_{Rx}$, with G_{Rx} being the gain of the receive antenna and $\lambda = c/f_c$ being the wavelength with c the speed of light and f_c the carrier frequency.

More realistic models take into account the effects caused by *reflections*, *scattering* and *diffraction*. A simple model that considers the reflective effect of the earth's surface is named *plane earth loss* [3]. The received power is computed for the situation where only line-of-sight ray and ground-reflected wave exists, obtaining

$$P_{Rx}(d) = \frac{P_{Tx}G_{Tx}G_{Rx}}{L_{PE}} \approx P_{Tx}G_{Tx}G_{Rx}\left(\frac{h_{Tx}h_{Rx}}{d^2}\right)^2, \tag{2}$$

where h_{Tx} and h_{Rx} are the height of the transmitter (mobile device) antenna and the receiver (base station) antenna, respectively. This path loss model is valid for distances larger than $d \geq 4h_{Tx}h_{Rx}/\lambda$. In this model, the received power decays with a factor d^{-4}, resulting in a very inaccurate measure for different types of propagation media (rural, office, etc.). The frequency dependence of the path loss is also not taken into account in this model. Thus, a more accurate model, *Egli path loss* [4], is typically employed if replacing L_{PE} by $L_{EG} = L_{PE} \cdot (40/f[\mathrm{MHz}])^2$.

More approximate models have been developed after carrying out empirical measurements. Empirical analyses confirm that the path loss can suffer significant variations in certain conditions as a function of the range, frequency and antenna heights. The empirical path loss is modeled as

$$L_E[dB] = A - B\log_{10}(d[\mathrm{km}]) - C, \tag{3}$$

where $A = f(h_{T_x}, h_{Rx}, f_c)$, $B = f(h_{R_x})$ and $C = f(f_c)$. The most commonly employed empirical model for urban areas is the Okumura–Hata [5].

2.1.2. *Small-Scale Propagation Effects*

Small-scale fading describes the rapid fluctuation in signal amplitude and phase that occurs in the received signal over a small period of time or a short traveled distance (on the order of a wavelength). These types of fluctuations are manifested in two different manners, time-spreading of the signal due to *multipath propagation* and time-variant behavior of the channel caused by the *Doppler effect*.

Multipath fading is caused by the presence of multiple replicas of the transmitted signal that occur at the receiver due to reflections against obstacles. Multiple copies of the transmitted signal sum together in either a constructive or destructive manner depending on the phase of each partial wave. These additions create fading dips in the received signal power and distort the frequency response characteristics of the transmitted signal. These distortions are linear and need to be combated at the receiver by applying equalization and diversity techniques.

The multipath wireless channels can be initially classified according to their coherence bandwidth. The coherence bandwidth represents the range of frequencies over which the channel response is flat, meaning that all the frequency components are equally attenuated. *Flat fading* occurs when the signal bandwidth is less than the channel coherence bandwidth. In this situation, the presence of deep fades due to multipath can result in deep fades in the signal over all its bandwidth. On the other hand, when the signal bandwidth is greater than the channel coherence bandwidth, the multipath fading is considered to be *frequency selective*. That is, multipath fades are unlikely to affect the signal over its entire bandwidth without experiencing fades in received energy.

The *Doppler effect* represents the variations of the observed frequency (or wavelength) of a received wave caused by the motion of the mobile device during the communications process. The Doppler effect leads to a frequency spreading of the wave. The Doppler frequency of the nth incident wave is determined by the angle of arrival α_n, which is defined by the direction of arrival of the nth incident wave and the direction of the motion of the mobile device. This Doppler frequency follows the relationship:

$$f_n = \frac{v_{Tx}}{c} f_c \cos(\alpha_n), \tag{4}$$

where v_{Tx} is the velocity of the transmitter mobile device relative to the receiver. The spectrum of the transmitted signal undergoes a frequency expansion during transmission due to Doppler effects. If the information bandwidth is smaller than the spectral broadening, given by the *Doppler spread*, the channel is *slow fading*. On the other hand, if the Doppler spread is larger than the information bandwidth, the channel is *fast fading*.

2.2. *Wireless Channel Models*

The characterization of the wireless channel requires the extraction of the main characteristics of channel sounding campaigns in order to express them in a mathematical manner. The *channel impulse response* models analytically the behavior of the channel. The relationship between the received signal $r_s(t)$, the transmitted signal $s(t)$ and the channel impulse response $h(t)$ is expressed as

$$r_s(\tau) = s(\tau) \otimes h(\tau) + n(\tau) \overset{FT\{r_s(t)\}}{\Longleftrightarrow} R(f) = S(f)H(f) + N(f), \tag{5}$$

where $\otimes$ represents the convolution operation, τ is the time variable, and $FT\{x\}$ is the Fourier transform of x. The function $n(t)$ is a thermal noise signal modeled as a zero-mean additive white Gaussian noise (AWGN) with constant power spectral density value $N_0/2$. The following channel models are classified and described in terms of their channel impulse responses.

2.2.1. *Additive Gaussian White Noise Channels*

The additive Gaussian white noise (AWGN) channel is the simplest model and mathematically describes the free-space channel without considering fading, interference, nonlinearity or dispersion phenomena. The channel impulse response is given by

$$h(t) = \sqrt{L_{FS}}\delta_D(\tau - \tau_d), \tag{6}$$

where $\delta_D(\tau)$ is the delta function and τ_d is the time taken by the transmitted wave to arrive at the input of the receiver.

2.2.2. *Narrowband Channels*

Narrowband refers to a wireless communications where the bandwidth of the transmitted signal does not significantly exceed the *coherence bandwidth* of the channel. The coherence bandwidth is a statistical measurement of the channel that accounts for the frequency interval over which two frequencies of a signal are likely to experience comparable or correlated amplitude fading. Thus, narrowband transmission uses radio signals that see flat fading. The channel impulse response of the narrowband channel can be expressed as

$$h(\tau, t) = \sqrt{L}A(t)\delta_D(\tau - \tau_d), \tag{7}$$

where $A(t)$ is the channel amplitude that varies with respect to the time t over a small area. This attenuation is typically modeled as a complex Gaussian random variable and, therefore, with an absolute value that follows a Rayleigh distribution [6].

2.2.3. *Wideband Channels*

In wideband communications systems the channel is frequency-selective since the channel's coherence bandwidth is larger than the information bandwidth. Therefore, multipath propagation effects must be taken into account in the channel impulse response, which is described as

$$h(\tau, t) = \sqrt{L}\sum_{i=0}^{N-1} A_i(t)\delta_D(\tau - \tau_i(t) - \tau_d), \tag{8}$$

where N is the total number of multipath components. The multipath amplitudes $A_i(t)$ and multipath delays $\tau_i(t)$ constitute the main parameters of the linear time-varying system.

The influence of the multipath fading on the wireless channels can be characterized by analyzing the main parameters of the *power delay profile*. The power delay profile illustrates the amount of energy collected at the receiver and the delays associated with this reception. The main channel parameters are the first moment of the power delay profile (*mean excess delay*), the variance of the power delay profile (*delay spread*) and the *number of significant paths* that accumulate most of the energy of the multipath channel [7]. The number of significant paths (N_P) is a valuable parameter to be estimated for reducing the complexity of multipath-based receiver implementations, such as RAKE receivers [8].

Several types of wideband channel models can be found in the literature. The most relevant models are the two-path fading channel [9], the Rummler channel [10] and the Saleh–Valenzuela channel [11].

Example: Bit error rate.

The bit error rate (BER) function is evaluated for two different channel scenarios in order to illustrate the effects of the wireless channel on the received information. The first environment considers the transmission of BPSK modulated signals over an AWGN channel. In the other scenario, the same modulated signal is now transmitted through a Rayleigh narrowband channel. The theoretical BER functions are computed in Ref. 12 and expressed as

$$\begin{aligned} BER_{BPSK-AWGN} &= 0.5 erfc(E_b/N_0), \\ BER_{BPSK-Ray} &= 0.5\left(1 - \frac{1}{\sqrt{1+(E_b/N_0)^{-1}}}\right), \end{aligned} \tag{9}$$

where $erfc(\cdot)$ is the complementary error function and E_b is the energy per bit. Figure 2 shows the BER performance degradation of the Rayleigh channel in comparison with that of the AWGN.

3. Background: Wireless Communication Networks

As wireless technologies evolve, the demand for better and faster communication systems also increases. Since its introduction in the 1980s, the growth of the business of commercial cellular systems has been rapid. The number of wireless communication users as well as the spectrum of the available services has increased at an unexpected rate. The main reason for this growth was the newly introduced notion of terminal, service and user mobility.

As technological enhancements in modern communication networks strive to facilitate ubiquitous connectivity, the future will be increasingly wireless. To date deployment of wireless networks such as GSM, UMTS and IEEE 802.11 has risen in

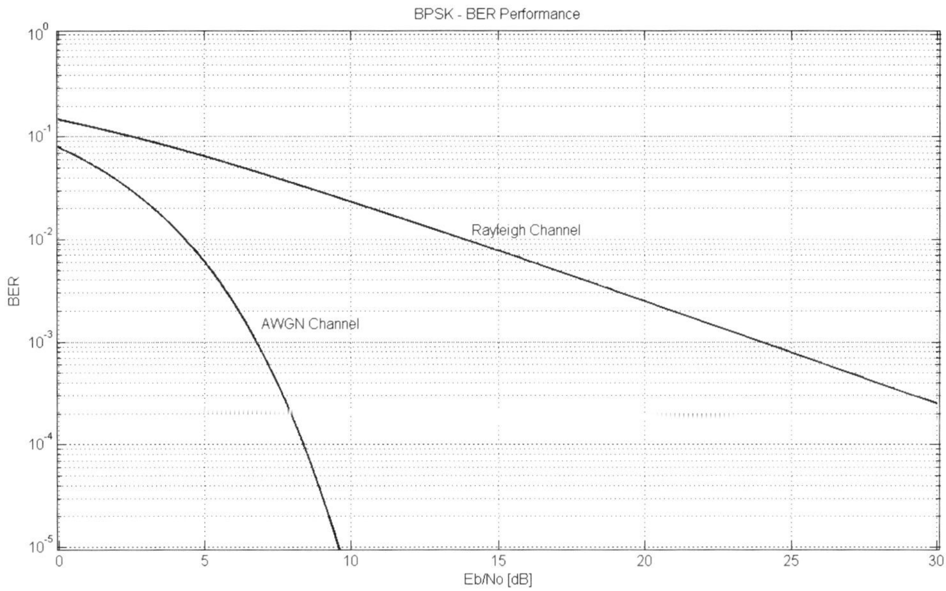

Fig. 2. BER performance for BPSK signals over AWGN and Rayleigh channels.

an effort to provide the desired pervasive access. Wireless technologies must continue to evolve in order to meet increasing demand for faster communication systems and better service availability anytime, anyplace, anywhere. It is expected that wireless communications will become the dominant mode of data access technology in the near future. With that new research challenges are arising — what services the user requires, how to provide the services effectively in the network, and how to manage the network.

Fundamental to all wireless communication systems is the mobility of the mobile device. The movement is the determinant factor in the systems' signaling, traffic and mobility management scheme. Before investigating mobility management techniques an example wireless network is illustrated in terms of architecture, cell network planning, quality of service and supported services.

3.1. *Architecture*

Existing terrestrial wireless communication networks are based on the cellular concept as outlined by MacDonald [13]. The network structure is composed of a fixed core network with wireless last hops between radio station, and mobile devices. Different cell size environments such as macrocell, microcell and picocell are grouped together as they are dependent on the wireless access technologies. The wireless communication network cell architecture is comprised of these environments tiled and layered to create a tiered cell structure. In a wireless communication service network, as illustrated by Fig. 3, three fundamental hardware

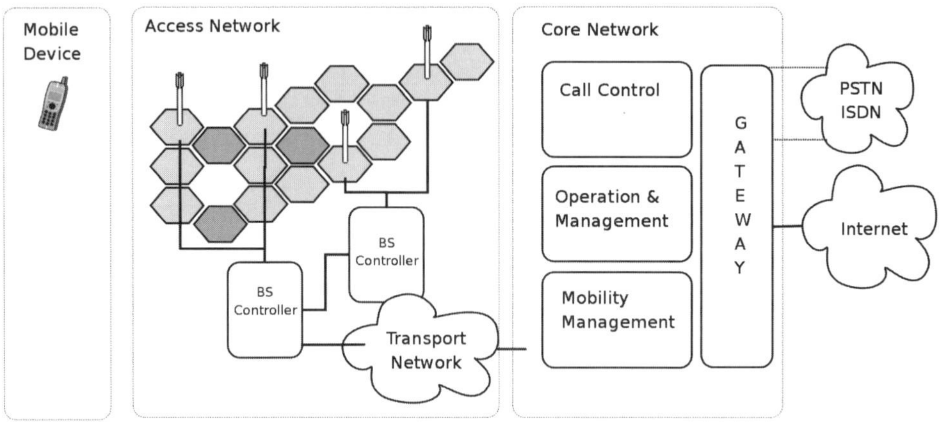

Fig. 3. Wireless communication network.

entities exist: (i) core network system, (ii) access network system and (iii) the mobile device.

The **core network system** or simply the core network (CN) is responsible for maintaining information (such as identity, location, authentication, and billing) about the users in the network. This information is stored in registers or a database. The core network provides access to other backbone networks — Internet, circuit switched, etc. When a call arrives for the mobile device, the CN interrogates its registers and processes the command request.

The **access network system** comprises base stations (BS) and base station controllers (BSC). The BS is the last fixed wired link in the wireless communication network, that is, the BS provides a radio link to the mobile device. The geographical area the BS is in provides radio coverage of an area called a cell. The size of the cell is dependent on the power of the BS and the height of the antenna. A BSC has control over several BSs and thus clusters a group of cells together; this cluster of cells forms an area known as the location area. Combining all the location areas together provides the network's service area.

The **mobile device** is carried by the user. In wireless communication networks these are small, lightweight battery powered devices. Since the mobile device is a battery powered device, the need to prolong battery life is essential. To conserve power the mobile device has two states, *active* and *idle*. When in the active state, the mobile device is actively sending and receiving information or partaking in a call. While in the active mode, its exact cell location is known. While the mobile device is in an idle state, it is passively connected to the network. Depending on the mobility management scheme used in the network, the exact location may not be known, instead the general location (that is, the location area) is known.

In essence the mobile device is any device used directly by an end user to communicate. It can be a hand-held telephone, a card in a laptop computer, or other device. It connects to the base station via a wireless link and can communicate with the core network system once the link is in place.

3.2. *Cell Planning*

When planning a location/service area for a wireless network, three main approaches exist: equilateral triangles, mesh (square or rectangle), and hexagonal coverage. Although propagation considerations recommend the circle as a cell shape, the circle is impractical for design purposes. An array of circular cells produces ambiguous areas, which are contained either in no cell or in multiple cells. On the other hand, any regular polygon approximates the shape of a circle and three types, the equilateral triangle, the square and the regular hexagon, can cover a plane with no gaps or overlaps. A service area could be designed with square or equilateral triangles, but for economical reasons the regular hexagonal shape has been adopted. The economical motivation for choosing the hexagon is as follows: Assume a base station located at the center of each cell, the center being the unique point equidistant from the vertices. The vertices are in fact the worst case points since they lie at the greatest distance from the nearest base station. Restricting the distance between the cell center and any vertex to a certain maximum value helps to assure satisfactory transmission quality at the worst case points. If an equilateral triangle, a square, and a regular hexagon all have the same center-to-vertex distance, the hexagon has a substantially larger area. Consequently, to serve a given total coverage area, a hexagonal layout requires fewer cells, therefore fewer transmitter sites [13, 14]. It is worth noting that in real wireless networks, the shape and size of the cell does vary, but for analytical modeling only homogeneous cells sizes are considered. Furthermore, in real wireless networks rectangular and sectorized cell layout is common in urban environments. However, in the scope of this chapter only hexagonal shaped homogeneous cells are considered.

Example: Available channels and cell planning.

Correct cell planning allows for a radio frequency to be reused in a different area for a completely different transmission. Second generation networks like GSM require two communication links — one link for the mobile device to communicate with the base station (uplink) and another link for the base station to communicate with the mobile device.

Consider we have a total of S duplex channels available for use with:

- k channels available per cell, and
- N total cells.

The total number of radio channels may be expressed as: $S = k \times N$.

If these N cells collectively use all the available frequencies then these group of cells are called a cluster.

If a cluster is repeated M times throughout the system then the system capacity may be roughly calculated as:

$$C = M \times k \times N = M \times S.$$

Let us assume we have 30 MHz of bandwidth.

Each voice call requires two 30 kHz channels for uplink and downlink communication, i.e., a 60 kHz duplex channel is needed. Therefore, 500 channels are available in the system. This is calculated from: 30 MHz/60 kHz. If we say that the cluster size is 7 ($N = 7$), then the total number of channels per cell $= 500/7 = 71$ approximately.

If we consider that a hexagonal cell layout ensures that each cell has six equidistant neighbors, how can we reuse a duplex channel (f_1) with causing interference to neighboring cells in the cluster?

The hexagon is an ideal choice for cellular coverage areas because it closely approximates a circle and offers a wide range of tessellating reuse cluster sizes. A cluster size of N can be constructed using:

$$N = i^2 + i \times j + j^2,$$

where i and j a positive integers.

One can find the nearest co-channel by

- moving i cells along any chain of hexagons,
- turning 60 degrees counter clockwise,
- moving j cells.

For example consider: $N = 7, i = 1, j = 2$.

The reuse distance is an important factor with this cluster size. For example consider D to be the reuse distance and r the cell radius. Then, the relationship

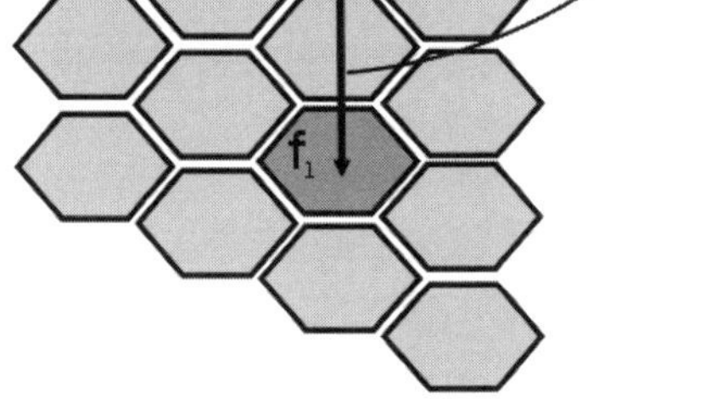

Fig. 4. Tesllated cluster.

between D and r is

$$\frac{D}{r} = \sqrt{3N}.$$

This is important when the cell size is small and when planning network topology, base station layout, etc.

3.3. *Quality of Service*

The fundamental purpose of all communication networks is to provide a connection between end users. As networks have evolved, a multitude of services have been offered to users in the form of voice, SMS, video conferencing, email and web browsing. The success or failure of that network is dependent on how the user perceives performance of the service on offer. For a user to be satisfied with a network, a number of criteria must be fulfilled. The user should be able to connect easily, the call or service should last for the intended duration without prematurely ending, and with respect to interactive data services (web browsing) download rate is a significant factor. QoS then is a measure of the perceived quality of the service being used and an indication of user satisfaction. Rather than being a single measure of a user's satisfaction, QoS is the collective term for the quantifying of network performance from an end user point of view, and for the measures taken to ensure reliable service.

To ensure that networks are performing at the desired level, one or more measurements of desired performance and priorities of a communications system are considered as part of QoS. QoS measures may include service availability, maximum bit error rate (BER), frame error rate (FER), minimum committed bit rate (CBR) and other measurements that are used to ensure quality communications service.

In heterogeneous environments, i.e., future wireless communication networks, the ability to offer end-to-end QoS while making the different radio access networks interoperate with each other is an important issue. QoS management mechanisms deal with such aspects to ensure services meet QoS requirements.

3.4. *Supported Services*

A wireless network should be designed with a diverse service environment in mind and similar to those offered on fixed networks. To realize a true mobile multimedia platform, emphasis is placed on the delivery of these services with the specification of service classes. A wireless network should have four service classes:

Conversational: The conversational class specifies realtime traffic, such as voice or voice/video conferencing. These services are bi-directional and traffic is symmetric on this link. These services have very strict timing constraints in order to preserve the integrity of the traffic, both in terms of delay and packet delivery. Thus, this class has the highest priority value associated with it.

Streaming: The streaming class represents video/audio streaming services. Streaming information is highly asymmetric traffic, as data is continuous in one direction. Streaming services are high priority services in terms of packet loss and preserving data integrity, but data is buffered so realtime delivery is not critical.

Interactive: The interactive class type refers to events such as web browsing, database queries and FTP, i.e., information being requested by the user from a remote host. Interactive traffic is asymmetric in nature because data is transferred mainly in one direction. Interactive traffic is not subject to strict timing requirements, but traffic is affected by round-trip delay and response time constraints. As with other classes, transmission errors are not tolerated. However, due to the more relaxed delay restrictions, the focus can be placed on packet delivery.

Background: Background traffic is generated by email and other applications without time constraints. The information is downloaded and assembled in the background without high priority. However, maintaining the integrity of the data is important.

Examples of traffic class applications and associated QoS characteristics (data rates, delay and FER) are presented in Table 1.

Table 1. Traffic class and associated QoS.

Traffic class	**Fundamental characteristics**	**Examples of service**	**Expected data rates**	**Delay**	**Loss (FER)**
Conversational	Preserve time variation between information entities of the stream.	Voice	4–25 Kbps	<150 ms	<3%
		Video telephony	32–384 Kbps	<150 ms	<1%
	Conversational pattern (stringent and low delay).	Video games	n/a	<250 ms	zero
Streaming	Preserve time variation between information entities of the stream.	Streaming audio	32–128 Kbps	<10 s	<1%
		Streaming video	32–128 Kbps	<10 s	<1%
Interactive	Request/ response pattern. Preserve payload content.	Web browsing	4–16 Kbps	<4 s	<3%
Background	Destination is not expecting the data within a certain time. Preserve payload.	Download of emails	4–16 Kbps	Can tolerate very high delay time	zero

4. Mobility Management

Traditionally mobility management contains two distinct but related components: location management and handover management. These tasks allow the network to track a mobile device in the wireless communication network. However, as wireless communication networks evolve towards incorporating new IP services, a multi-tier mobility management scheme is needed. The mobility of users is generally tracked through paging/registration procedures often referred to as terminal mobility. However, with increasing user requirements and QoS becoming a prerequisite in wireless communication networks, mobility management has evolved over time from terminal mobility to incorporate personal mobility, service mobility, session mobility, ad hoc and mode mobility.

These mobility management tasks can be divided into distinct levels of network tasks; *high level* and *low level* tasks. Generally low level tasks are associated with layer 1 and 2 of the OSI model, that is, the physical and media access layers. High layer tasks are executed in layer 3 and above, that is, the network, transmission, session, presentation and application layers.

4.1. *Low Level Tasks*

4.1.1. *Terminal Mobility*

Terminal mobility refers to (i) the ability of a mobile device to use telecommunication services from any location, while in motion, and (ii) the ability of the network to locate and identify the mobile device as it moves. Depending on the device design, part of the mobile device functions may reside on a removable and portable device or a smart card. According to Ref. 15, terminal mobility is associated

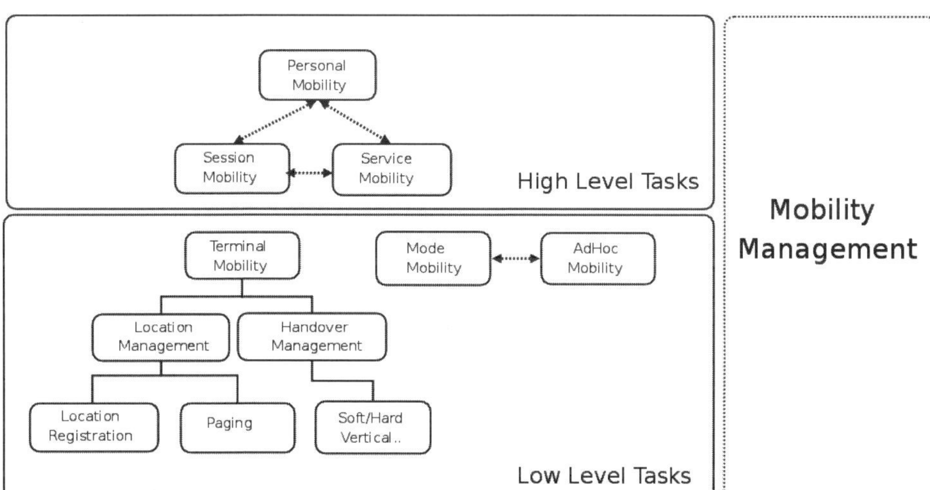

Fig. 5. Mobility management in wireless communication networks can be divided up into high level and low level tasks.

with wireless access and requires the user to carry a device and be within the radio coverage area. The coverage area is directly related to the wireless channel and thereby terminal mobility suffers from the effects of propagation and noise.

From the network point of view, terminal mobility management consists of (i) location management and (ii) handover management. These techniques correspond to the state of the mobile device. For example, with handover management, the mobile device is considered to be in an active state, the user may be partaking in a call or data session and is actively using a wireless channel. With location management, the mobile device is usually in an idle (power saving) mode, waking up periodically to determine its location and whether to update the network of its location. Location management is a twofold process. Firstly, gathering information of a mobile device's location is referred to as the location registration process. A mobile device assists in the process by updating the network of its current location by *location updating* or *registering* at certain times or events. The second process is interrogating the information gathered by the first process (which is stored in the core network) and locating the mobile device on the network. This occurs when a call arrives at the network gateway for the mobile device, a process called paging.

Registration and *paging* processes, collectively known as location management, are therefore concerned with the procedures required by a network to maintain location information about the user, or specifically, for each active user, and setting up incoming calls to non-active users. Non-active mobile devices in wireless networks conserve resources (such as radio or battery) and therefore there is no constant connection with the network. To route a call to the user, the network must find the user's location, that is, the cell in which the user resides. Terminal mobility brings fundamental problems of information management: if the network does not know exactly where the mobile device is, the amount of information stored and processed is lower than if the network knows the exact location of the user. A three-way trade-off consists of: (i) *currency*, i.e., how up-to-date the information is, (ii) *availability*, that is, the information available at all sites/locations or centrally stored, and (iii) the *precision* of the user's location. The extremes of the problem are: no up-to-date knowledge of the user location at any of the sites and up-to-date information of the user's exact cell location available to all the sites.

4.1.1.1. Handover management

Handover management enables the network to maintain a user's connection as the mobile device continues to move and change its access point to the network. According to Akyildiz *et al.* [16] the three-stage process for handover first involves initiation, where either the user, a network agent, or changing network conditions identify the need for handover — this is determined largely by the movement of the user. The second stage is new connection generation, where the network must find new resources for the handover connection and perform any additional routing operations. Under network-controlled handover (NCHO), or mobile-assisted handover (MAHO), the network generates a new connection, finding new resources for the handover and performing any additional routing operations. For mobile-controlled handover (MCHO), the mobile device finds the new resources and the network approves. The final stage is data-flow control, where the delivery of the data from the old connection path to the new connection path is maintained according to agreed-upon service guarantees.

The handover schemes can be classified according to the way the new channel is set up and the method with which the call is handed off from the old base station to the new one. At call level, there are two classes of handover schemes, namely hard handover and soft handover [17].

In **hard handover**, the old radio link is broken before the new radio link is established and a mobile terminal communicates at most with one base station at a time. The mobile device changes the communication channel to the new base station with the possibility of a short interruption of the call in progress. If the old radio link is disconnected before the network completes the transfer, the call is forced to terminate. Thus, even if idle channels are available in the new cell, a handover call may fail if the network response time for link transfer is too long. Second generation mobile communication systems based on GSM fall into this category.

In **soft handover**, a mobile device may communicate with the network using multiple radio links through different base stations at the same time. The handover process is initiated in the overlapping area between cells some short time before the actual handover takes place. When the new channel is successfully assigned to the mobile device, the old channel is released. Thus, the handover procedure is not sensitive to link transfer time. The second and third generation Code-division multiple access (CDMA) based mobile communication systems lie in this category.

Soft handover decreases call dropping at the expense of additional overhead (two busy channels for a single call) and complexity (transmitting through two channels simultaneously) [18, 19]. Two key issues in designing soft handover schemes are the handover initiation time and the size of the active set of base stations the mobile device is communicating with simultaneously.

Example: Soft handover.

Handover from one cell to the other is an important mechanism in cellular systems. Traditionally, handovers are hard: users are either assigned to one cell or the other but not both. However, CDMA enables overlapping of the repeater coverage zones, so that every mobile device is always well within range of at least one of the base stations. This enables the concept of soft handover. The soft handover process is mobile-initiated and is illustrated in Figs. 6 and 7. While a mobile device is tracking the downlink signal strength of the cell, it is currently in Cell 1; it can be searching for signal of adjacent cells (Cell 2). It is important to remember that the measurements used for the handover event are made on the downlink only.

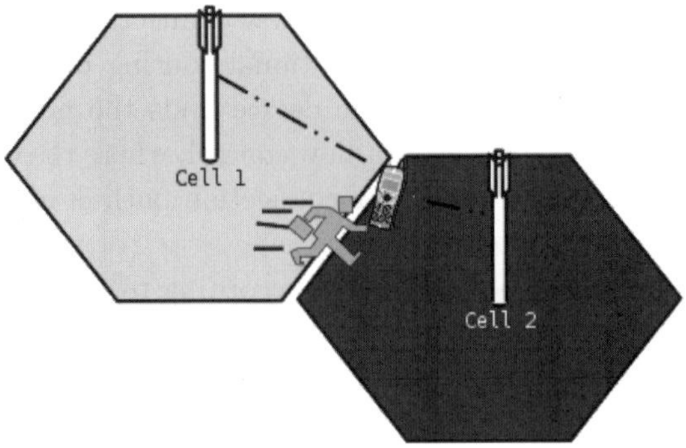

Fig. 6. Moving from Cell 1 to Cell 2 introduces handover management.

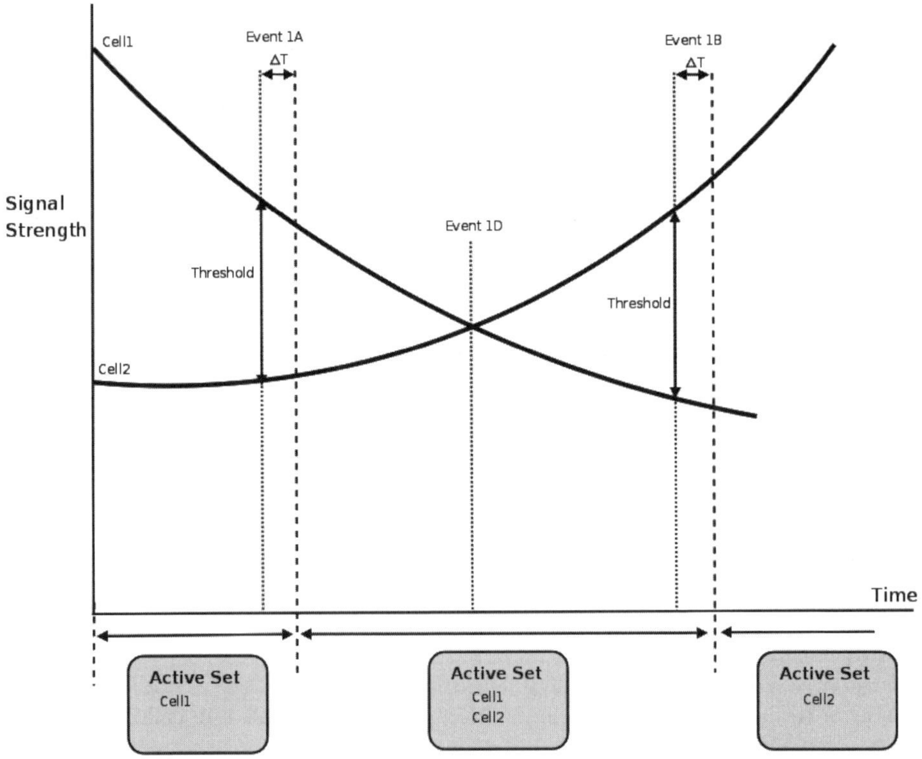

Fig. 7. Soft handover.

Idling in Cell 1 the user has Cell 1 in its active set. The active set is a set of radio links simultaneously involved in a specific communication service between the user equipment and the network. As the user moves in Cell 1 and towards Cell 2, the signal from Cell 2 increases in strength. The mobile device monitors the received the signal from Cell 2. If the measured signal of Cell 2 is greater than the best measured cell in the active set (Cell 1) minus a threshold for a period of time Δt then Cell 2 is added to the active set. This is referred to as Event 1A in WCDMA networks. In a similar manner, if the measured signal is below the best measured cell in the active set minus the threshold for a period of time Δt then Cell 1 should be removed from the active set. This is referred to as Event 1B in WCDMA networks.

The "threshold" parameter is defined as a "guard band" in order to avoid event triggering due to insignificant measurement fluctuations in the received signal.

4.1.2. *Mode and Ad hoc Mobility*

These mobility management techniques are more for the mobile device than core network functions and only a brief overview of the functions is given. Mode mobility allows a wireless user to switch between different technologies and infrastructures. For example, a device may support several different wireless technologies and thus mode mobility allows the user to switch between them [20]. Ad hoc mobility allows users to communicate with one another without any permanent infrastructure being in place. Any user can act as a router to relay a session for others. The caller and the callee can also directly establish a session if near enough.

4.2. *High Level Tasks*

4.2.1. *Introduction*

High level mobility management tasks are not concerned with underlying wireless/wired technologies and are designed to solve mobility of personal applications, services and sessions. Session Initiation Protocol (SIP) is gaining acceptance as the signaling protocol of multimedia and Internet telephony, and it is envisaged it will be used in providing mobility management solutions in next generation wireless networks. The following section defines each of the high level tasks and presents how SIP can provide mobility management.

SIP supports the concepts of personal, session and even service mobility. It is a text-based protocol similar to HTTP and defined in IETF RFC 3261 [21]. It operates between the application and transport layers and it can use reliable or unreliable transport protocols. Any transport protocol can be used but UDP and TCP support must be implemented. TCP or some other congestion-controlled transport protocol must be used when sending large SIP messages.

A SIP message consists of a header and a body like HTTP. The SIP header is used for signaling to manage the user's identity, location, authentication and authorization, etc. The body of the message is used to carry information about the session to be established or just some plain information like text or an XML document. Here is an example of a SIP message carrying a message in the

Session Description Protocol (SDP) format:

```
        INVITE sip:bob@biloxi.com SIP/2.0
        Via: SIP/2.0/UDP
pc33.atlanta.com;branch=z9hG4bKnashds8
        To: Bob <bob@biloxi.com>
        From: Alice <alice@atlanta.com>;tag=1928301774
        Call-ID: a84b4c76e66710
        CSeq: 314159 INVITE
        Max-Forwards: 70
        Contact: <sip:alice@pc33.atlanta.com>
        Content-Type: application/sdp
        Content-Length: 155

        v=0
        o=UserA 2890844526 2890844526 IN IP4 pc33.atlanta.com
        s=Session SDP
        c=IN IP4 pc33.atlanta.com
        t=0 0
        m=audio 49172 RTP/AVP 0
        a=rtpmap:0 PCMU/8000
```

The header ends with a single carriage return and the SDP parameters begin in this example with "$v = 0$". The media in the session should use the parameters described here such as the IP addresses, codecs and ports listed. The media in the session can be sent and received to any location and can be independent of the route and destination that the signaling messages follow.

SIP is an application-layer signaling protocol that solves many high level mobility management issues.

4.2.2. *Personal Mobility*

Personal mobility is the ability of a user to access services at any device based on a unique personal identifier, for example, the Universal Personal Telecommunication (UPT) number or Personal User Identity (PUI) [22]. Furthermore, personal mobility is the capability of the network to provide those services delineated in the user's service profile. Personal mobility involves the network capability to find the device associated with the user for addressing, routing and charging of the UPT user's calls. According to Chung *et al.*, personal mobility [23] is one of the key issues in realizing wireless communication networks in emerging third generation mobile communication networks such as International Mobile Telecommunication 2000 (IMT-2000). It can be realized through UPT service.

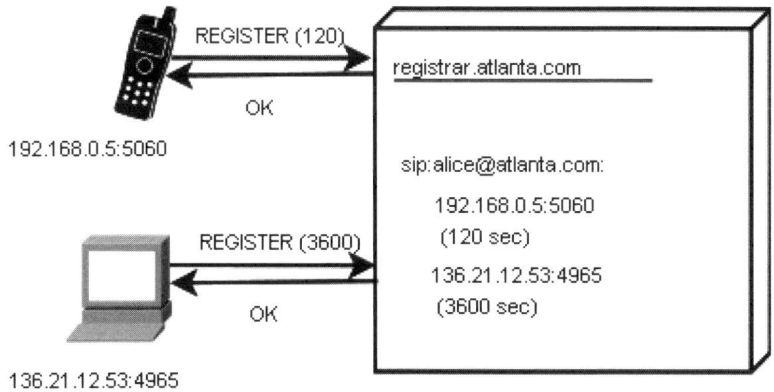

Fig. 8. SIP registration.

Example: SIP user agent registration.

SIP supports the concept of personal mobility by having a personal identifier known as the address-of-record (AOR), which takes the form of a Uniform Resource Identifier (URI). Unlike the Uniform Resource Locator (URL), the SIP URI only indicates the user's identity and is not sufficient by itself to locate the user's device. User location is achieved using a location service provided by an entity known as the "registrar." The registrar can have a list of the devices that the user is currently registered on which is kept up-to-date using the value in the "expires" parameter for each URI in the "contact" header field and if not present, the value in the "expires" header field. User agents on a device register initial values and can update them by sending additional REGISTER messages. A REGISTER message with an "expires" value of "0" is a de-registration.

The diagram in Fig. 8 shows a user called Alice being registered in the atlanta.com domain using two devices with different expiry intervals. The shorter expiry time is suited to mobile devices, which move around often and may change IP address, whereas clients such as desktops can refresh their presence less often. When someone attempts to contact Alice, both devices will "ring" and Alice can accept or reject the offer on both devices. Each device will only accept the type of media it can receive. Alice can register new devices and de-register a device at any time.

```
        REGISTER sip:registrar.atlanta.com SIP/2.0
        Via: SIP/2.0/UDP
192.168.0.5:5060;branch=z9hG4bKnashds7
        Max-Forwards: 70
        To: Alice <sip:alice@atlanta.com>
        From: Alice <sip:alice@atlanta.com>;tag=456248
        Call-ID: 843817637684230@998sdasdh09
        CSeq: 1826 REGISTER
```

```
        Contact: <sip:alice@192.168.0.5>;expires=120
        Expires: 7200
        Content-Length: 0

        REGISTER sip:registrar.atlanta.com SIP/2.0
        Via: SIP/2.0/UDP
136.21.12.53:4965;branch=z9hG4bKfdsds-ewef
        Max-Forwards: 70
        To: Alice <sip:alice@atlanta.com>
        From: Alice <sip:alice@atlanta.com>;tag=456248
        Call-ID: dav23kv3@136.21.12.53
        CSeq: 1 REGISTER
        Contact: <sip:alice@136.21.12.53>
        Expires: 3600
        Content-Length: 0
```

4.2.3. *Session Mobility*

Session mobility is ensures that active sessions are not disrupted while devices, persons or applications are moving or being relocated. For example, a caller may want to continue a session that originally began on a mobile device to a desktop PC when entering the office. A user may also want to move parts of a session, for example, if the user has specialized devices for audio and video, such as a video projector, video wall or speakerphone [24].

Example: How a SIP session is initiated and modified.

To initiate or modify a session, the invitation request must be routed to the target user agent (UA). This is done using proxies which use DNS queries and the registrars in the target domain to locate the target user.

Initially Alice is unaware of Bob's IP address and so uses her default proxy to send the request. Alice's proxy looks at the domain of Bob's URI and locates the SIP proxy for Bob's domain. This proxy then queries the registrar in that domain for Bob's location and sends the request to all the contact addresses returned. Bob's UA may start "ringing" and this is indicated to Alice via a 180 response message. If Bob accepts the session invitation, then his UA sends a 200 OK response via the proxies to Alice. In Bob's response, the location of that UA is included in the "contact" header field and Alice's location was included in the "contact" header field of the INVITE. Now both UAs know the location of each other and can send messages in a peer-to-peer fashion. The ACK confirms that Alice received the 200 OK from Bob. The session is terminated by either UA sending a BYE which is accepted with a 200 OK response.

The session can be modified to change the parameters of the session or even the address of one of the parties involved. The procedure is simply to send an INVITE again (re-INVITE) with the new parameters in the SIP header/body.

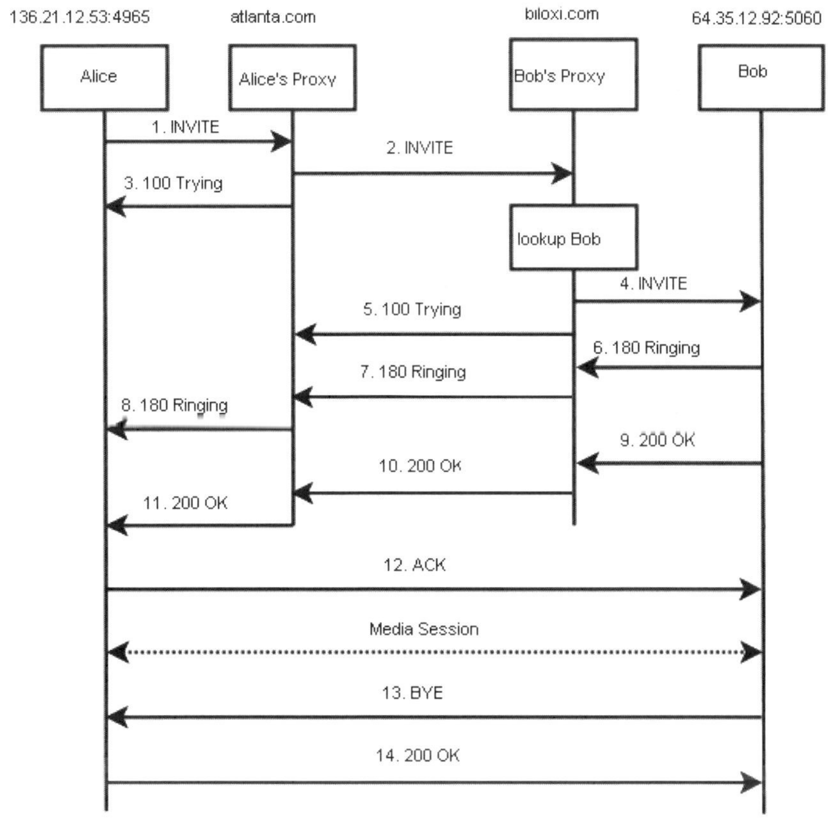

Fig. 9. SIP message sequence chart.

Parameters such as the Call-ID must remain the same so that it can be recognized as a modification to an existing session and not an entirely new session. The receiving UA can ask the user for confirmation of the change and if it is rejected, the session continues without modification. If the modification is accepted, both UAs change the parameters accordingly.

4.2.4. *Service Mobility*

Service mobility refers to the network capability to provide subscribed services at the device or location selected by the user. The services the user can invoke at the device, of course, depend on the capability of the device and the network serving the device. Service mobility is accomplished through keeping an up-to-date service profile of the user and interrogating it as necessary [15].

Example: How SIP provides service mobility.

While all the examples so far have focused on SIP providing a mechanism for setting up sessions using a SIP URI, it is also possible to register other types of contact addresses using any suitable URI. Other URIs could identify phones, fax, or email addresses. The "q" parameter also identifies a user's preference for each contact address where the highest value is the most preferred address. For example, for an AOR sip:carol@chicago.com, the "contact" header field in a REGISTER could be

```
Contact: <sip:carol@work.com>;q=0.7
Contact: <sip:carol@home.com >;q=0.3
Contact: <mailto:carol@email.com>;q=0.1
```

From the example above, we can see that Carol prefers to be contacted at her work.com SIP address. In a later registration, she can change her addresses and modify her preferences, e.g.,

```
Contact: <sip:carol@home.com>;q=0.8
Contact: <mailto:carol@webmail.com>;q=0.1
```

While each request from other users will be addressed to sip:carol@chicago.com, the destination of the request will depend on the current contact addresses and preferences registered by Carol.

5. Thoughts for Practitioners

5.1. *Implementing Quality of Service*

Supporting QoS in multi-system networks is an important issue to achieve user mobility across heterogeneous RANs with a unified service experience. Traffic management must take into account the different characteristics of each RAN to provide seamless service continuity as well as end-to-end QoS. For example, significant variation in transmission capacity can be found between RANs, etc. In addition, the traffic can cross multiple domains where each of them has its own administration, rendering end-to-end QoS provision even more complex. A mapping of the QoS services between different RANs is required to provide unified QoS traffic classes. It is also necessary to manage the QoS in each domain and to permit interaction between the different QoS management entities thanks to policy-based QoS management.

In the case of services, the traffic classes and the QoS attributes are defined as described above. As the end-to-end path in the multi-system network may include the Internet environment, the Internet QoS attributes and classes will be mapped to the classes of each RAN. There are two main QoS approaches in this area, namely, Integrated Services (IntServ) and Differentiated Services (DiffServ).

IntServ uses the per-flow approach to provide guarantees to individual streams. This approach adopts the resource reservation along the flow path using the resource reservation protocol (RSVP). The latter sets up some flow state (e.g., bandwidth reservations, accounting) in the routers that a flow goes through. An admission control is used to guarantee the QoS. It grants or rejects the flow requests, based on availability of resources and the guarantees provided to other flows. In addition to the well-known best effort service, two service classes are proposed: the guaranteed service class for the traffic requiring a firm bound on delay and the load controlled class where flow receives a quality of service closely approximating QoS that flow would receive from an unloaded network element. This is generally not seen as a scalable QoS solution for individual flows on all IP networks due to the signaling requirements.

DiffServ follows the philosophy of the aggregation of multiple flows in the edge of the DiffServ domain into a few classes of service or Per Hop Behaviors (PHBs). There is no reservation, but Differentiated Services Code Point (DSCP) etiquette has been included in the type of service (TOS) field of the IP packet header to differentiate between different PHBs. The DSCP is set at the edge of the domain where a conditioning and shaping mechanism is executed in accordance with the requirements or rules of each service. Using the DSCP, the node inside the network determines how packets are forwarded. There are two PHBs being defined with the best effort: expedited forwarding (EF) PHB and assured forwarding (AF) PHB. EF is intended to support services with tightly bounded loss, delay and jitter. AF offers different levels of forwarding assurances for packets belonging to an aggregated flow. Packets are marked with one of three drop precedences, such that those with the highest drop precedence are dropped with lower probability than those marked with the lowest drop precedence. AF gives the customer the assurance of a minimum throughput, even during periods of congestion. The per-hop basis, lack of firm reservations and statistical nature of the guarantees given by DiffServ are seen as more scalable for Internet applications.

As DiffServ and IntServ models shall be supported for PDP contexts (3GPP 23.107), the mapping between Internet QoS and UMTS QoS is under investigation. For example, when DiffServ is used in the backbone of the UMTS, the Conversational class is transported in the EF PHB; streaming is mapped to EF or AF. Interactive and background classes are mapped into AF PHBs.

When viewing multi-system networks, the minimum set of service and classes can be those as defined by 3GPP, i.e., conversational, streaming, interactive, and background. An example set of service and classes are outlined in [Ref. 25]. The latter outlines the QoS requirements that shall be provided to the end user/applications and describes them as requirements between communicating entities, i.e., end-to-end. Figure 10 summarizes the major groups of applications in terms of QoS requirements. Applications and new applications may be applicable to one or more groups. However, there is no strict one-to-one mapping between the groups of application/service defined in [Ref. 25] and the traffic classes as defined in [Ref. 26]. For instance, an Interactive application/service can very well use a bearer of the Conversational traffic class if the application/service or the user has tight requirements on delay.

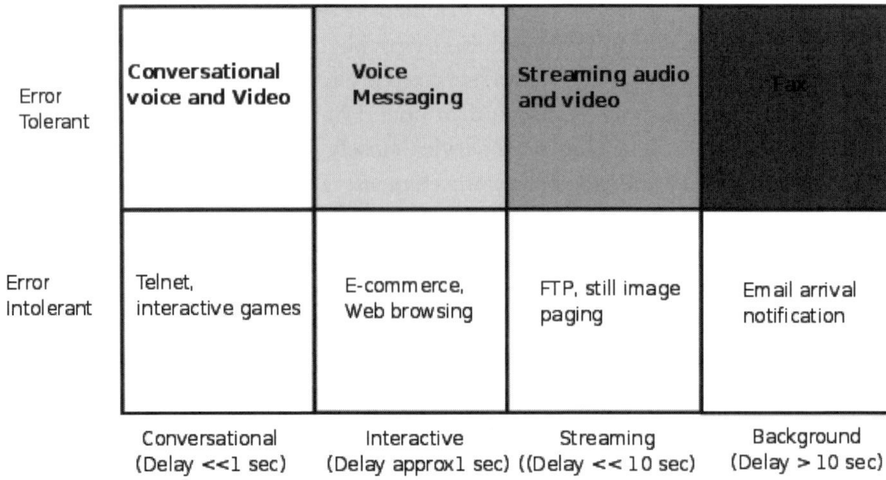

Fig. 10. Multi-system applications in terms of QoS requirements.

The reference user performance expectations are presented in Table 2 for conversational services, in Table 3 for interactive services and in Table 4 for streaming services. The QoS values in the tables represent end-to-end performance, including mobile-to-mobile calls and satellite components. Delay values represent one-way delay (i.e., from originating entity to terminating entity). The values included in the following tables are commonly accepted values from an end user viewpoint. The delay contribution within the mobile network should be kept to a minimum since there may be additional delay contributions from external networks. Note that the overall one-way delay in the mobile network (from UE to PLMN border) is approximately 100 ms.

5.2. *QoS and SIP*

SIP is not a resource reservation protocol and therefore by itself cannot guarantee a level of QoS. However, it does support QoS in conjunction with other protocols and extensions.

Example: How SIP can support QoS.

The most basic form of QoS, within SIP is the ability of a user agent to reject session requests that it cannot accept. If the invitation for a session includes a list of options, the terminating user agent has the ability to select the session description parameters that it believes are most suitable. Within a session, it is possible to renegotiate the parameters of the session to improve QoS, but it is the responsibility of the user agent application to know that change is required and what changes to make.

There is an optional extension to SIP which provides for resource management using SIP and SDP defined in [Ref. 27] and updated in [Ref. 28]. It provides for

Table 2. End user performance expectations — Conversational/realtime services.

Medium	Application	Degree of symmetry	Data rate	Key performance parameters and target values		
				End-to-end one-way delay	Delay variation within a call	Information loss
Audio	Conversational voice	Two-way	4-25 kb/s	<150 msec preferred <400 ms limit	<1 ms	<3% FER
Video	Videophone	Two-way	32-384 kb/s	<150 ms preferred <400 ms limit Lip-synch: <100 ms		<1% FER
Data	Telemetry — two-way control	Two-way	<28.8 kb/s	<250 ms	n/a	zero
Data	Interactive games	Two-way	<1 KB	<250 ms	n/a	zero
Data	Telnet	Two-way (asymmetric)	<1 KB	<250 ms	n/a	zero

Table 3. End user performance expectations — Interactive services.

Medium	Application	Degree of symmetry	Data rate	Key performance parameters and target values		
				One-way delay	Delay variation	Information loss
Audio	Voice messaging	Primarily one-way	4–13 kb/s	<1 s for playback <2 s for record	<1 ms	<3% FER
Data	Web-browsing — HTML	Primarily one-way		<4 s/page	n/a	zero
Data	Transaction services — high priority, e.g., e-commerce, ATM	Two-way		<4 s	n/a	zero
Data	E-mail (server access)	Primarily one-way		<4 s	n/a	zero

Table 4. End user performance expectations — Streaming services.

Medium	Application	Degree of symmetry	Data rate	Key performance parameters and target values		
				Start-up delay	Transport delay variation	Packet Loss at Session Layer
Audio	Speech, mixed speech and music, medium and high quality music	Primarily one-way	5–128 kb/s	<10 s	<2 s	<1% packet loss ratio
Video	Movie clips, surveillance, realtime video	Primarily one-way	20–384 kb/s	<10 s	<2 s	<2% packet loss ratio
Data	Bulk data transfer/retrieval, layout and synchronization information	Primarily one-way	<384 kb/s	< 10 s	n/a	zero
Data	Still image	Primarily one-way		<10 s	n/a	zero

a SIP "preconditions" header field and QoS parameters for SDP. Using RFC 3261 procedures alone, it would be possible for a user agent to receive an invitation to a session that it could not take part in because of a lack of network resources. The user agent would ring, and when the user answered, the session would fail. The offer from the caller can contain a list of possible session codecs and requirements, and it is necessary for the callee to answer this offer before network resources can be reserved. This extension solves the problem by requiring an exchange of a session description offer and answer before the user-agents begin to ring. If the user-agents cannot reserve the resources required, the session fails without interrupting the callee.

5.3. *Implementing SIP in a Wireless Communication Network*

SIP aims to be transport-independent and can operate on almost all IP-based networks, which makes it suitable for use as a high-level signaling protocol. It can be used to bridge ATM, UMTS and Ethernet-based networks as long as they support IP. It can also be used on both IPv4 and IPv6 networks as long as the user agents are capable of supporting the relevant IP version.

For these reasons, SIP has been chosen as a core signaling protocol by a number of standardization bodies for their next-generation network architectures. The 3GPP has defined the IP Multimedia Subsystem (IMS) [29], which defines how SIP fits into GPRS/UMTS networks. The 3GPP IMS standard has been adopted as a central part of the NGN architectures being developed by the 3GPP2, ITU-T, ETSI Telecoms & Internet converged Services & Protocols for Advanced Networks (TISPAN) and CableLabs.

They have defined the procedures and security requirements for authentication, authorization and accounting, including how to interface with existing user-information repositories within the network such as the Home Subscriber Server (HSS). The benefit of following this standard is the ability for international networks to interoperate and provide services across networks. It also allows for network operators to provide a standard interface to third party application providers. They can set trigger points based on elements in the SIP headers and provide services such as voicemail and call forwarding. They can also be contacted directly via a SIP URI to provide content services or directory lookup services. By using SIP, the aim is to simplify integration and reduce development time.

The framework also provides the interfaces and procedures required to implement QoS using SIP and SDP in conjunction with a policy decision point and a policy enforcement point using UMTS control mechanisms in 3GPP TS 23.107 [26]. Specifications for QoS specifically involving GPRS-based networks are contained in 3GPP TS 23.207 [30]. These elements can intercept session initiations to ensure that the requested QoS can be met and they can modify a session to ensure continuing QoS. ETSI and the ITU, on the other hand, define a more generic system known as the Resource and Admission Control System (RACS).

It is also possible for the SIP proxies within an IMS network to redirect the media within a session through a media gateway. This media gateway can perform functions such as transcoding to a format optimal to the end user device or the available bandwidth.

5.4. *Base station planning*

The demand for new mobile communications services has grown rapidly in recent years. Wireless networks play an important role in application areas, such as industry, medicine, personal communications, etc. To satisfy user requirements, the mobile network operators must provide these applications with a satisfactory QoS, even when the traffic increases considerably in a particular zone. Under these circumstances, the operators are obliged to increase their capacity. Since the spectral resources are finite, an option for increasing the capacity is to miniaturize and sectorize the radio zones (i.e., cells). This causes a steady increase in the number of base stations and, therefore, an increase in the network complexity. A more effective solution consists of distributing the base station within the cell and estimating its optimal antenna height taking into account the propagation conditions. Therefore, a good understanding of the wireless propagation channel is essential for cell planning strategies.

The effects on the received power of the mobile device caused by selecting different heights of the base station antennas are analyzed in the following example. The propagation model considered in this analysis is the Okumura–Hata defined for urban and suburban areas. The average received power of the mobile device is obtained from (1) in logarithmic expression as

$$P_{Rx}[dB_m] = P_{Tx}[dB_m] - G_B[dB] - G_m[dB] - L_E[dB], \tag{10}$$

where the transmitter is the base station ($G_B = G_{Tx}$) and the receiver unit is the mobile device ($G_m = G_{Rx}$). The unit dB_m is the logarithmic value of measurement related to the power in milliwatts ($dB_m = 10\log$ (power [mW]/1 mW)).

The Okumura–Hata path loss model is expressed in (3) with the following values:

$$A = 69.55 - 26.16\log_{10}(f_c) - 13.82\log_{10}(h_B) - a(h_m, f_c), \tag{11}$$

$$B = 44.9 - 6.5\log_{10}(h_B), \tag{12}$$

$$C = \begin{cases} 0, & \text{(urban)} \\ 2[\log_{10}(f_c/28)]^2 + 5.4, & \text{(suburban)} \end{cases} \tag{13}$$

where h_B and h_m are the base station and mobile antenna's heights in meters and f_c is the carrier frequency in MHz. Finally, the parameter $a(h_m)$ is defined according to the topology of the area as:

$$a(h_m, f_c) = \begin{cases} 3.2[\log_{10}(11.75h_m)]^2 - 4.97, & \text{(urban)} \\ [1.1\log_{10}(f_c) - 0.7]h_m - [1.56\log_{10}(f_c) - 0.8], & \text{(suburban)} \end{cases} \quad (14)$$

In this example, a GSM network with downlink transmissions in the 900 MHz band is considered for analyzing the effects of the path loss on the received signal strength. The following parameters are selected for this simulation analysis: $P_{Tx} = 33dB_m$, $G_B = 13dB$, $G_m = 0dB$, $f_c = 935$ MHz and $h_m = 1.75$ m. The received power values as a function of the distance between the base station and the mobile device are represented in Fig. 11 for an urban area, considering four different values of base station antenna heights ($h_B = 10$ m, $h_B = 30$ m, $h_B = 50$ m and $h_B = 75$ m). The chosen scenario considers base station coverage of microcells having a radius of about 500 m. It is important to remark that small-scale fading effects have not been considered.

Figure 11 shows the influence of the distance and the base station antenna height on the received power. In terms of distance, the received power decays approximately 25 dB when the mobile device moves from 25 m to 125 m of the base station for all antenna height values. The same power loss value is experienced when the mobile device moves from 125 m to 500 m. Therefore, the loss in power due to large-scale fading is more significant when the mobile device changes its position near to the base station.

The effects of the antenna height of the base station on the received power can be analyzed by fixing the distance value and comparing the power variations

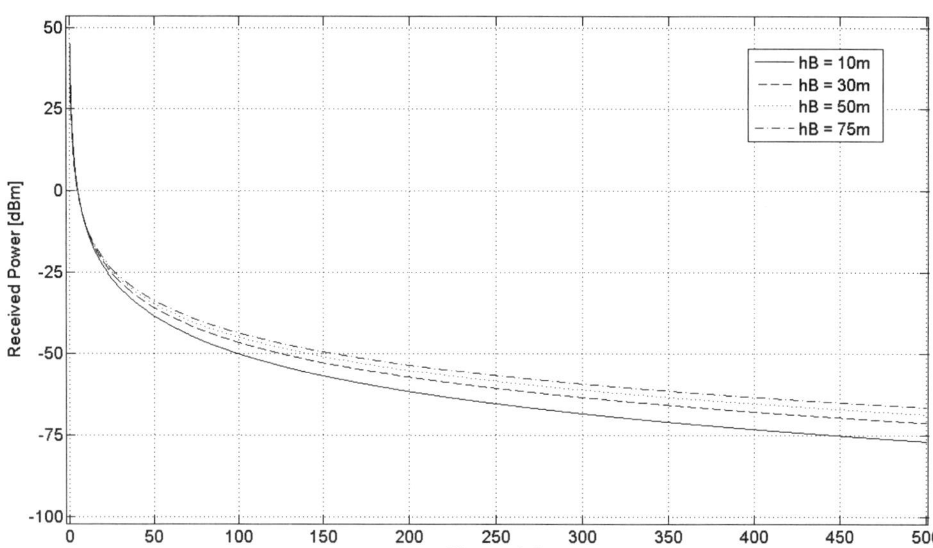

Fig. 11. Received power versus distance based on Okumura–Hata path loss model for urban areas.

when changing antenna height values. It is obvious that the received power will increase if the antenna height increases since the direct path will be less affected by obstacles. However, the improvement in the received power obtained by increasing the antenna height is not always significant, while the complexity of the base station infrastructure increases. Therefore, there is an optimum value of the base station antenna height that must be investigated for cell planning strategies. In Fig. 11, a 5 dB augmentation of the received power is observed for distance $d = 300$ when increasing the antenna height from 10 m to 30 m. However, the increase in the received power is only 2.5 dB when changing the antenna height from 30 m to 50 m.

6 Directions for Future Research

In next-generation wireless networks users will encounter both intra- and inter-system handovers. It is essential that applications running on mobile devices remain unaware of the users' movement, both intra- and inter-system, to ensure uninterrupted services with minimum QoS degradation to the end users. To achieve this continuation of upper layer sessions during handover, a new level of mobility support is required by next-generation networks. However, future mobility management brings different issues and challenges as it requires additional mobility related features such as moving networks, seamless roaming and vertical handover. Many projects and much research on mobility management within heterogeneous networks are currently ongoing with the aim of enabling seamless handover and interoperability between heterogeneous network types including both IEEE 802 and non-IEEE 802 networks. The support of multiple media types will improve the available network coverage, which can improve the user experience of mobile devices. Mobility solutions can be found by either improving existing architecture or by revising the current architecture principles to reflect the changing environment and to efficiently and easily cope with new requirements. In terms of relevance to mobility some current mobility management projects are discussed further in this section. The solutions outlined propose different addressing and packet forwarding schemes, the majority of which are IP based, allowing interoperability and easy integration with existing architectures.

The Internet Indirection Infrastructure (i3) project [31] provides mobility in a unique way by employing an overlay network with rendezvous points. These points are known servers where packets are forwarded with an identifier which is used by the receiver to obtain delivery of the packet. This level of indirection decouples the act of sending and receiving and provides natural support for mobility. However, this is not optimal as data passes via a third party during traversal from source to final destination.

Forwarding directive Association and Rendezvous Architecture (FARA) [32] is a project that aims to provide mobility by decoupling end-system names from network addresses. This flexible architecture concept separates the host identifier from location information without the introduction of a new global namespace. The FARA model allows several different forwarding mechanisms to co-exist in the network. However, it does not take into account packet forwarding issues like performance of network nodes or provide any solution for security.

The Host Identity Payload (HIP) project [33] also attempts to optimize handover performance by introducing a separation between the location and host identity information at the IP layer. It introduces a new identity, cryptographic in nature, for host identities which can be dynamically mapped to IP addresses. The host identity is basically a public key that is used to identify a related private party in the network; the separation provides a means to handle mobility and multi-homing in a secure way. However, issues arise when the host moves between IPv4 and IPv6 networks. If a mobile does not have connectivity for both versions, it may have to use a proxy node that performs the address version conversion on behalf of the mobile device.

The IST MIND project [35] is the follow up to the BRAIN project [36] and builds on the concept of an all-IP core accessible by a variety of technologies. It provides micro-mobility solutions by enabling hosts to co-operate with self-organizing wireless ad hoc networks. Among other aspects, the research considers QoS, multi-homing, multicast and security issues.

The DriVE project [36] supports the use of different access systems using flow based, host-controlled IP forwarding to enable seamless intersystem handover. The multi-access architecture handles macro-mobility with hierarchical mobile IP. Extensions for moving networks define a mobile IP based solution in OverDRiVE [37].

The ongoing research of the IETF NEMO [38] working group is concerned with managing the mobility of an entire network. The network is able to change its point of attachment to the Internet and thus its reachability in the network topology. The mobile network includes one or more mobile routers which connect the rest of the mobile network to the global Internet.

Ambient networks [39] is a new networking architecture currently under investigation, which aims at enabling the cooperation of heterogeneous networks belonging to different operator and/or technology domains. Ambient networks use the *network composition* principle, where networks form the basic building block of communication networks rather than devices. This approach is a more advanced concept than the simple inter-networking of IP. The current Internet assumes homogeneity in the environment in which to provide control. A unifying view like ambient networks has the potential to solve this issue of fragmented control.

In terms of standardization organisations such as the IEEE 802 LAN/MAN Standards Committee and the Internet Engineering Task Force (IETF) are currently working on developing a common framework to extend existing mobility protocols to facilitate and optimize seamless inter-system handover. The aim is to provide a platform for successfully addressing present challenges related with QoS, security, and seamless mobility as well as allowing for scalability for future possibilities. One such group is the IEEE 802.21.

The IEEE 802.21 standard [40] assumes mobile users are capable of supporting multiple interfaces, both wired and wireless. The goal of the project is to enable mobile users to handover between IEEE 802 networks whether or not they are of different media types and furthermore enable handover between non-802 networks. To achieve this, an abstraction layer is defined, providing Media Independent Handover (MIH) functions, with the aim of simplifying the handover management to and from IEEE 802.11, 802.16, 802.3, 3GPP2 networks and the 3GPP network family. The media-independent interface should allow higher layer network selector entities to be application specific and afford the ability of selecting the best network at a given moment for the user.

To achieve complete and seamless mobility within a pervasive infrastructure, some essential issues need to be addressed, such as the integration of different technologies, composition of networks and connectivity. The progress towards the desired uninterrupted mobility will aid in successful deployment of next-generation heterogeneous networks.

7. Conclusion

In the course of the accelerated contention of wireless technologies with wired technologies, broadband wireless service has become a reality, and wireless Internet is attainable. However, QoS and cost remain as deficiencies of wireless systems. Despite the freedom of mobility, in the data arena wireless technologies have enjoyed limited popularity to speak of. The true advantage of mobility in the context of broadband services is exemplified by the capability to deliver location specific services to the user.

Without any doubt, next-generation wireless networks will be considerably more complex than today's second/third-generation wireless systems. Global roaming and the ability to access the Internet and data resources everywhere are among the key driving factors that will have profound impact on how these networks will be managed. In this changing environment, operators will introduce new services and more powerful and efficient ways of doing business by integrating new technologies with existing ones. This is already beginning to happen with mergers of WLAN networks and cellular networks. Not only will the network elements and communication devices evolve but so too will the management systems and way of managing. Mobility management has widely been recognized as one of the most important and challenging problems for next-generation networks. New management strategies will be needed to enable seamless access to wireless networks and mobile services.

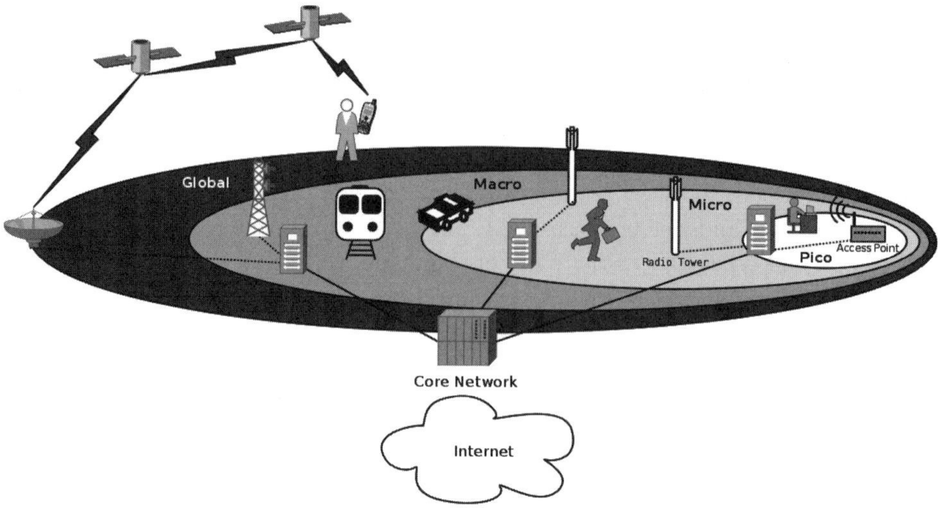

Fig. 12. Wireless communication network landscape.

The landscape of the next-generation network, as illustrated in Fig. 12, will take into consideration wireless technologies providing high-speed data access and voice in cells ranging from pico (10 m) to macro (10 km). At the same time the network must provide a seamless and transparent means of access to these services at a global level. From a service management and architectural point of view many things will be different in next-generation networks, but one fundamental concept will not change: users will be mobile.

Acknowledgments

This work was supported by the Science Federation of Ireland NCNRC project (03/CE.2/I315) and the Irish Research Council for Science, Engineering and Technology program.

Terminology

Mobility: is the ability to move or change position.

Wireless communication: The transfer of information over a distance without the use of electrical conductors or wires. The distances involved may be short (<100 m) or very long (>2 km) for radio communications. Information transmitted over distance can be affected by distortions such as fading.

Multipath fading: The propagation phenomenon that results in radio signals reaching the receiving antenna via separate paths. Causes of multipath fading include atmospheric ducting, ionospheric reflection and refraction, and reflection from terrestrial objects. As a result of multipath fading, the received signal is a sum of many reflections each with different propagation time, phase and attenuation values.

Doppler effect: The shift in frequency and wavelength of waves which results from a source moving with respect to the medium, a receiver moving with respect to the medium, or even a moving medium.

Large-scale fading: The slow variations of the mean (distance-dependent) power of the received signal over time. This phenomenon is caused by many factors including antenna losses and the presence of obstacles in the signal path, which leads to propagation losses.

Wireless Communication Network: Consists of (i) mobile devices, (ii) an access network, and (iii) a core network. A radio link between mobile devices and base stations allows the mobile devices to roam the wireless network and maintain a communications link.

Mobility management: The aim of mobility management is to track where the subscribers are, so that calls, SMS and other mobile phone services can be delivered to them. Furthermore, mobility management ensures ongoing calls are maintained as the subscriber moves.

Quality of service (QoS): Comprises all the aspects of a connection, such as time to provide service, voice quality, echo, loss, reliability, etc.

Sessions: A multimedia session is a set of multimedia senders and receivers and the data streams flowing from senders to receivers. A multimedia conference is an example of a multimedia session.

Media Independent Handover (MIH): An IEEE 802.21 function that supports algorithms enabling seamless handover between networks of the same type as well as handover between different network types. MIH may communicate with various IP protocols including SIP for signaling, mobile IP for mobility management, and DiffServ and IntServ for QoS.

Exercises

1. Name the different types of mobility management used in wireless communication networks and classify them into high and low level tasks.
2. In cell planning a frequency is placed in a cluster of N cells and reused in another cluster separated by a distance D. Using the cosine law, $[c^2 = a^2+b^2-2ab\cos(\mu)]$ show that the distance radius ratio is related to the number of cells in the cluster as $D/r = \sqrt{3N}$, where r is the radius of a cell. Let L be distance between two cell centres.

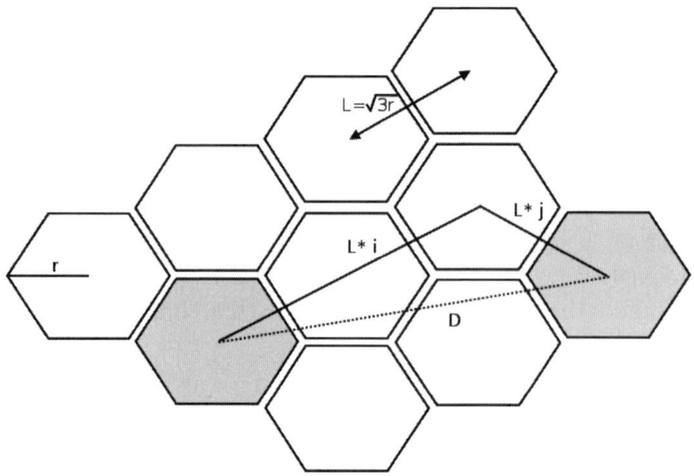

3. Name (i) the four service classes in wireless communication networks, (ii) the characteristics of the traffic, and (iii) outline the QoS requirements for each.
4. User mobility in wireless communication networks varies from low mobility (<3 m/s) to very high mobility (>100 km/h). Explain the impact mobility has on network connectivity in terms of *terminal mobility* and its subsequent functions if the user is in a cell with radius 1 km.
5. How does the network track mobile users in the network considering that 90% of the time the mobile device is in an idle state (radio off)? For the other 10% the mobile is either on a call (active state/radio on) or periodically waking up.
6. Hard handover is considered, in terms of connection, a "break before make" while soft handover is a "make before break". Briefly explain why GSM supports only hard handover while UMTS can support hard and software handover.
7. The ITU-T Y-1541 has QoS Classification of 0 to 5 with corresponding characteristics. In the *Applications* column in the table below map common wireless communication applications to the ITU-T QoS Classification.

   Common Wireless Applications: Interactive gaming, voice calls, telnet, video conferencing, FAX, network background traffic, FTP, torrent peer to peer, email, web browsing.

QoS	Characteristics	Applications
0	Realtime, jitter sensitive, highly interactive	
1	Realtime, jitter sensitive, interactive	
2	Transaction data, highly interactive	
3	Transaction data, interactive	
4	Low loss only (short data, bulk data)	
5	Traditional applications of default IP networks	

8. A base station is transmitting data to a GSM user located at a distance $d = 2$ km in a suburban area. The base station is using a channel with center frequency $f_c = 935$ MHz. Calculate the minimum height of the base station antenna that satisfies a required received power value of $P_{rx} = -85$ dBm considering the Okumura–Hata path loss model. Multipath fading and Doppler effects can be neglected for this analysis. The main parameters of the base station and the mobile device are:

$$\begin{aligned} G_B &= 12\,\text{dB (Gain of the base station antenna)},\\ G_m &= 0\,\text{dB (Gain of the mobile unit antenna)},\\ P_{tx} &= 33\,\text{dBm (Transmitted power), a–d}\\ h_m &= 1.5\,\text{m (Height of the mobile device antenna)}. \end{aligned}$$

9. How does a user agent update its location using SIP? Fill in the missing elements of the relevant SIP message sent by the user agent from its new IP of 192.168.0.35. The registrar has a domain of "registrar.altanta.com"

```
_____ sip:_______________ SIP/2.0
Via:SIP/2.0/UDP ________:5060;branch=z9hG4bKnashes7
Max-Forwards: 70
To: Alice <sip:________________>
From: Alice <sip:_______________>;tag=456248
Call-ID: 8438176384230@998sdasdh09
CSeq: 1826 ________
Contact: <sip:________________>;expires=120
Expires: 7200
Content-Length: 0
```

10. What is the function of the "expires" parameter in a "contact" header field?

References

1. D. Tse and P. Viswanath, *Fundamentals of Wireless Communication* (Cambridge University Press, 2005).
2. T. S Rappaport, *Wireless Communications Principles and Practices*, 2nd edn. (Prentice-Hall, 2002), pp. 107–110.
3. M. J. Feurstein, K. L. Blackard, T. S. Rappaport, Y. Seidel and H. H. Xia, Path loss, delay spread, and outage models as functions of antenna height for microcellular system design, *IEEE Trans. Veh. Tech.* **43**(3), 487–498 (1994).
4. E. N. Singer, *Land Mobile Radio Systems*, (PTR Prentice Hall, 1994), pp. 196.
5. T. Okumura, E. Ohmori and K. Fukuda, Field strength and its variability in VHF and UHF land mobile service, *Rev. Elect. Commun. Lab.* **16**(9/10), 825–873 (1964).
6. A. Papoulis, *Probability and Random Processes, An Introduction for Applied Scientists and Engineers* (McGraw-Hill, New York, 1965).
7. S. Lien and M. Cherniakov, Analytical approach for multipath delay spread power distribution, *IEEE Global Telecommunications Conference*, Vol. 6, Sydney, Australia (IEEE, New York, 1998), 3680–3685.
8. R.Price and P. E Green Jr., A communication technique for multipath channels, *Proc. IRE*, **46**(3), 555–570 (1958).

9. M. Guizani, *Wireless Communications Systems and Networks* (Kluwer Academic Publishers, 2004).
10. W. D. Rummler, R. P. Coutts and M. Liniger, Multipath fading channel models for microwave digital radio, *IEEE Commun. Mag.* **24**(11), 30–42 (1986).
11. A. A. M. Saleh and R. A. Valenzuela, A statistical model for indoor multipath propagation, *IEEE J. Sel. Area. Commun.* **SAC-5**(2), 128–137 (1987).
12. J. G. Proakis, *Digital Communications*, 4th edn. (McGraw-Hill, New York, 2001), pp. 257–282.
13. V. H. MacDonald, The cellular concept, *Bell Sys. Tech. J.* **58**(1), 15–41 (1979).
14. T. Tugcu, A realistic mobility model and its application to a reservation based call admission scheme for ds-cdma cellular systems, Masters thesis, Institute for Graduate Studies in Science and Engineering, Bogazii University (2001).
15. R. Pandya, Emerging mobile and personal communication systems, *IEEE Commun. Mag.* **33**(6), 44–52 (1995).
16. I. F. Akyildiz, J. Mcnair, J. S. M. Ho, H. Uzunalioglu and W. Wang, Mobility management in next-generation wireless systems, *Proc. IEEE* **87**(8), 1347–1384 (1999).
17. Y.-B. Lin and A.-C. Pang, Comparing soft and hard handovers, *IEEE Trans. Veh. Tech.* **49**(3), 792–798 (2000).
18. D. Wong and T. J. Lim, Soft handovers in CDMA mobile systems, *IEEE Pers. Commun. Mag.* **4**(6), 6–17 (1997).
19. R. Prakash and V. V. Veeravalli, Locally optimal soft handover algorithms, *IEEE Trans. Veh. Tech.* **52**(2), 231–260 (2003).
20. Q. Wang and M. A. Abu-Rgheff, Next generation mobility support, *IET Commun. Eng.* **1**(1), 16–19 (2003).
21. J. Rosenberg, H. Schulzrinne, G. Camarillo, A. Johnston, J. Peterson, R. Sparks, M. Handley and E. Schooler, *RFC 3261 — SIP: Session Initiation Protocol* (Internet Engineering Task Force 2002).
22. Telecommunication Standardization Sector of ITU, F.852: Universal personal telecommunication UPT service description (service set 2) (2000).
23. Y. Won Chung, M. Young Chung and D. Keun Sung, Effect of personal mobility management in mobile communication networks, *IEEE Trans. Veh. Tech.* **52**(5), (2003).
24. H. Schulzrinne and E. Wedlund, Application-layer mobility using SIP, *ACM SIGMOBILE Mob. Comput. Commun. Rev.* **4**(3), 47–57 (2000).
25. 3rd Generation Partnership Project, 3GPP TS 23.105 — Services and Service Capabilites, Release 7v.7.1.0 (2007).
26. 3rd Generation Partnership Project, 3GPP TS 23.107 — Quality of Service (QoS) Concept and Architecture, Release 7v.7.1.0 (2007).
27. J. Rosenberg, RFC 3312 — *Integration of Resource Management and Session Initiation Protocol (SIP)*, eds. G. Camarillo and W. Marshall (Internet Engineering Task Force, 2002).
28. G. Camarillo and P. Kyzivat, RFC 4032 — *Update to the Session Initiation Protocol (SIP) Preconditions Framework* (Internet Engineering Task Force, 2005).
29. 3rd Generation Partnership Project, TS 23.228 — IP Multimedia Subsystem (IMS) — Stage 2, Release 7v.7.9.0 (2007).
30. 3rd Generation Partnership Project, 3GPP TS 23.207 — End-to-end Quality of Service (QoS) concept and architecture, Release 7v.7.0.0 (2007).
31. I. Stoica, D. Adkins, S. Zhuang, S. Shenker and S. Surana, Internet indirection infrastructure, *IEEE/ACM Trans. Network.* **12**(2), 205–218 (2004).

32. D. Clark, R. Braden, A. Falk and V. Pingali, FARA: Reorganizing the addressing architecture, *Proc. ACM SIGCOMM FDNA Workshop*, Karlsruhe, Germany (ACM, New York, 2003), p. 313.
33. P. Jokela, P. Nikander, J. Melen, J. Ylitalo and J. Wall, Host identity protocol: Achieving IPv4–IPv6 handovers without tunneling, *Proc. Evolute Workshop 2003: "Beyond 3G Evolution of Systems and Services"*, University of Surrey, Guildford, UK (2003).
34. D. Wisely and E. Mitjana, Paving the road to systems beyond 3G — The IST MIND project, *J. Commun. Network. (JCN)*, Special issue (Korea Information and Communications Society, 2002).
35. J. Urban, D. Wisely, E. Bolinth, G. Neureiter, M. Liljeberg and T. Robles, BRAIN — an architecture for a broadband radio access network of the next generation, *Wireless Comm. Mob. Comput.* **1**(1), 55–75 (2001).
36. T. Paila, S. Alladin, M. Frank, T. Goransson, W. Hansmann, T. Lohmar, R. Toenjes and L. Xu, Flexible network architecture for future hybrid wireless systems, *IST Mobile Summit*, Barcelona, Spain (2001).
37. M. Ronai, A. Petrescu, R. Tönjes and M. Wolf, Mobility issues in OverDRiVE mobile networks, *IST Mobile Summit*, Aveiro, Portugal (2003).
38. C. Bernardos, A. de la Oliva, M. Calderon, D. von Hugo and H. Kahle, NEMO: Network mobility — Bringing ubiquity to the Internet access, *IEEE INFOCOM 2006 demonstration*, Barcelona, Spain (2006).
39. V. Typpö, J. Eisl, J. Höller, R. A. Calvo and H. Karl, Research challenges in mobility and moving networks: An ambient networks view, *Broadband Satellite Comunication Systems and the Challenges of Mobility*, IFIP International Federation for Information Processing Series, Vol. 169/2005 (Springer Boston, 2005).
40. P. Goransson and R. Greenlaw, Roaming between 802.11 and other wireless technologies, *Secure Roaming in 802.11 Networks* (Newnes, 2007), pp. 289–294.

Chapter 2

THE MULTIMEDIA BROADCAST/MULTICAST SERVICE OF THE UNIVERSAL MOBILE TELECOMMUNICATIONS SYSTEM

ANTONIOS ALEXIOU*, CHRISTOS BOURAS†,
VASILEIOS KOKKINOS‡ and EVANGELOS REKKAS§

Computer Engineering and Informatics Department,
University of Patras, Research Academic Computer Technology Institute,
N. Kazantzaki Street, University of Patras Campus,
GR26500, Greece
* *alexiua@cti.gr*
† *bouras@cti.gr*
‡ *kokkinos@cti.gr*
§ *rekkas@cti.gr*

The Universal Mobile Telecommunications System (UMTS) constitutes the premier third generation (3G) wireless technology that is dominating the global market. Multicasting is an efficient method of supporting group communication as it allows the transmission of packets to multiple destinations, using fewer network resources. The need for broadcasting and multicasting in UMTS led to the definition of the Multimedia Broadcast/Multicast Service (MBMS) framework, which targets the efficient utilization of radio and network resources of the UMTS network. This chapter introduces the key concepts of UMTS and in particular the MBMS framework of UMTS. Moreover, it investigates the power profiles of several transport channels (common and dedicated) which could be employed for the transmission of MBMS services to mobile users. Problems regarding the high power requirements for the realization of MBMS are also presented. The reader will become familiar with these problems and the proposed techniques/solutions.

1. Introduction

Due to the rapid growth of mobile communications technology, the demand for wireless multimedia communications is thriving in consumer and corporate markets. The need to evolve multimedia applications and services is at a critical point given the proliferation and integration of wireless systems. Consequently, there is a great interest in using IP-based networks to provide multimedia services. One of the most important areas in which these issues are being debated is the development of standards for UMTS.

UMTS has been specified as an integrated solution for mobile voice and data with wide area coverage. Universally standardized via the 3rd Generation Partnership Project (3GPP) and using the globally harmonized spectrum in paired and unpaired bands, 3G/UMTS in its initial phase offers theoretical bit rates of up to 384 kbps in high mobility situations, rising as high as 2 Mbps in stationary/nomadic user environments. Through 3G mobile networks, mobile users have the opportunity to run applications and realize services that are currently only offered by wired networks. Such services include mobile Internet, mobile gaming, video calls, etc.

MBMS is a novel framework, extending the existing UMTS infrastructure, that constitutes a significant step towards so-called mobile broadband. MBMS is intended to efficiently use network and radio resources, both in the core network and, most importantly, in the air interface of the UMTS Terrestrial Radio Access Network (UTRAN), where the bottleneck is placed for a large group of users. Infact, MBMS is a Point-to-Multipoint service in which data is transmitted from a single source entity to multiple destinations, allowing the network resources to be shared. MBMS is an efficient way to support the plethora of emerging wireless multimedia and application services, such as IP video conferencing and streaming video by supporting both broadcast and multicast transmission modes.

The main target of this chapter is the investigation of the selection of the most efficient radio bearers for the transmission of MBMS multicast data. MBMS services can be provided in each cell by either multiple Point-to-Point (PTP) channels or by a single Point-to-Multipoint (PTM) channel. PTM transmission uses a single channel reaching down to the cell edge, which conveys identical traffic. On the other hand, PTP transmission uses dedicated channels allocated to each user separately. Obviously, a decision has to be made on the threshold between these two approaches in order to maximize capacity and resource efficiency.

The fundamental selection criterion for channel type is the amount of base station power required to transmit multicast data to a group of users. The choice of the most efficient transport channel in terms of power consumption is a key point for MBMS since the wrong transport channel selection for the transmission of MBMS data could result in a significant decrease in the total capacity of the system. In this regard, the role of power control in MBMS multicast transmission in UMTS is extensively described and analyzed. A power control scheme for the efficient radio bearer selection in MBMS is then proposed for minimizing the power consumption and consequently maximizing network capacity.

2. Background

In UMTS, bandwidth is a limited resource since the available radio resources can support only a handful high data-rate users simultaneously. Multicasting is an efficient method of supporting group communication as it allows the transmission of packets to multiple destinations using fewer network resources. 3GPP realized the need for broadcasting and multicasting in UMTS and proposed some enhancements on the UMTS Release 6 architecture that led to the definition of the MBMS framework [1, 2].

Transmission of MBMS data may be performed over Dedicated/PTP resources [one Dedicated Channel (DCH) for each user] or Common/PTM resources [one Forward Access Channel (FACH) shared by all the users] to distribute the same content in a cell. Yet no decision has been made within 3GPP on how to optimize the MBMS data flow. However, it is proposed to avoid the duplication of data flows over the air interface and hence, only one data flow per MBMS service should be used [3, 4].

The main requirement during the delivery of MBMS services is to make an efficient overall usage of radio and network resources. This makes a common channel the favorite choice, since many users can access the same resource at the same time. The MBMS counting mechanism [5] constitutes a mechanism that decides whether it is more economic to use the PTP or PTM MBMS transmission mode. According to this mechanism the decision on the threshold between PTP and PTM bearers is operator dependent, although it is proposed that it should be based on the number of serving MBMS users. In this regard, several studies have been carried out focusing on the threshold for switching between dedicated and common resources. In certain papers [6, 7] it is claimed that for a FACH with transmission power set to 4 Watts, the threshold for switching between dedicated and common resources is around seven users per cell and five users, respectively.

However, the current MBMS counting mechanism (using a user-based switching criterion between PTP and PTM) is not always efficient and may result in significant wastage of expensive power resources since it does not take into account the base station's downlink transmission power. Power budget in UMTS networks is the scarcest resource. Thus, power control has become one of the most important aspects in MBMS. The main purpose of power control is to minimize the transmitted power, thus avoiding unnecessarily high power levels and eliminating inter-cell interference. MBMS transmission power strongly depends not only on the number of serving users but also on the cell deployment, on propagations models, quality of service (QoS) requirements, users' distributions and on mobility issues. Therefore, it has become clear that only the information regarding the number of users in a cell may not be sufficient so as to select the appropriate radio bearer (PTP or PTM) for the specific cell. The decision has to take into consideration the total downlink power required for the transmission of the multicast data in the PTP and PTM cases.

Under these assumptions, a switching point, based on power consumption, of five users between dedicated and common resources may be configured [8]. Finally, Ref. 9 presents an analysis of the factors that affect the power allocation and the switching point between multiple DCHs and FACH in micro and macro cell environments. This analysis is indicative of how complicated the determination of appropriate threshold can be.

3. Multimedia Broadcast/Multicast Service

In MBMS rich wireless multimedia data is transmitted simultaneously to multiple recipients, by allowing resources to be shared in an economical way. MBMS efficiency is derived from the single transmission of identical data over a common channel without clogging up the air interface with multiple replications of the same data.

The major factor for integrating MBMS into UMTS networks was the rapid growth of mobile communications technology and the massive spread of wireless data and wireless applications. The increasing demand for communication between one sender and many receivers led to the need for PTM transmission. PTM transmission is opposed to the PTP transmission, using the unicast technology, which is exclusively used in conventional UMTS networks (without the MBMS extension). Broadcast and multicast technologies constitute an efficient way to implement this type of communication and enable the delivery of a plethora of high-bandwidth multimedia services to a large user population.

From the service and operators' point of view, the employment of the MBMS framework involves both an improved network performance and a rational usage of radio resources, which in turns leads to extended coverage and service provision. In parallel, users are able to realize novel, high bit-rate services, currently only experienced by wired users. Such services include mobile TV, weather or sports news as well as fast and reliable data download [10].

3.1. *MBMS Operation Modes*

As the term MBMS indicates, there are two types of service mode: the broadcast mode and the multicast mode. Each mode has different characteristics in terms of complexity and packet delivery.

The broadcast service mode is a unidirectional PTM transmission type. In fact, with broadcast, the network simply floods data packets to all nodes within the network. In this service mode, content is delivered using PTM transmission to a specified area without knowing the receivers and whether there is any receiver in the area. As a consequence, the broadcast mode requires no subscription or activation from the users' point of view.

In the multicast operation mode, data is transmitted solely to users that explicitly request such a service. More specifically, the receivers have to signal their interest for the data reception to the network and then the network decides whether the user may receive the multicast data or not. Thus, in the multicast mode there is the possibility for the network to selectively transmit to cells, which contain members of a multicast group. Either PTP or PTM transmission can be configured in each cell for the multicast operation mode.[1]

Unlike the broadcast mode, the multicast mode generally requires a subscription to the multicast subscription group and then the user joining the corresponding multicast group. Moreover, due to the selective data transmission to the multicast group, it is expected that charging data for the end user will be generated for this mode, unlike the broadcast mode.

3.2. *MBMS Architecture*

The MBMS framework requires minimal modifications in the current UMTS architecture. This fact enables the fast and smooth upgrade from pure UMTS networks to MBMS-enhanced UMTS networks. MBMS consists of an MBMS bearer service and an MBMS user service. The latter represents applications, which offer for example multimedia content to the users, while the MBMS bearer service provides methods for user authorization, charging and QoS improvement to prevent unauthorized reception [1].

UMTS network is split into two main domains: the user equipment (UE) domain and the Public Land Mobile Network (PLMN) domain. The UE domain consists of the equipment employed by the user to access the UMTS services. The PLMN domain consists of two land-based infrastructures: the core network (CN) and the UTRAN (Fig. 1). The CN is responsible for switching/routing voice and data connections, while the UTRAN handles all radio-related functionalities. The CN is logically divided into two service domains: the circuit-switched (CS) service domain and the packet-switched (PS) service domain [10]. The CS domain handles voice-related traffic while the PS domain handles packet transfer. In the remainder of this chapter, we will focus on the UMTS packet-switching mechanism.

The PS portion of the CN in UMTS consists of two kinds of General Packet Radio Service (GPRS) support nodes (GSNs), namely Gateway GSN (GGSN) and Serving GSN (SGSN) (Fig. 1). SGSN is the centerpiece of the PS domain. It provides routing functionality, interacts with databases [like Home Location Register (HLR)]

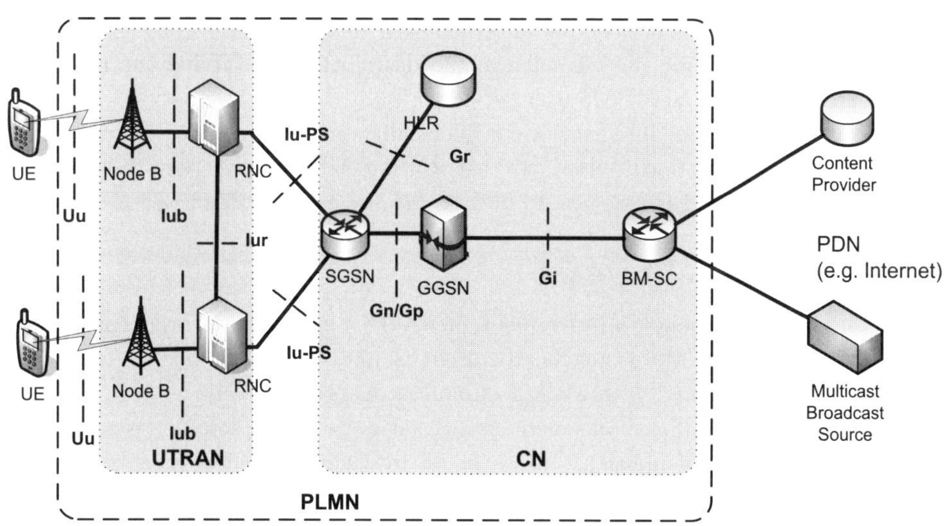

Fig. 1. UMTS and MBMS architecture.

and manages many Radio Network Controllers (RNCs). SGSN is connected to GGSN via the Gn interface and to RNCs via the Iu interface. GGSN provides the interconnection of UMTS network (through the Broadcast Multicast-Service Center) with other Packet Data Networks (PDNs), like the Internet.

UTRAN consists of two kinds of nodes: the first is the RNC and the second is Node B. Node B constitutes the base station and provides radio coverage to one or more cells (Fig. 1). Node B is connected to the UE via the Uu interface [based on the Wideband Code Division Multiple Access (WCDMA) technology] and to the RNC via the Iub interface. One RNC with all the Node Bs connected to it is called Radio Network Subsystem (RNS) [10].

The major modification in the existing UMTS platform for the provision of the MBMS framework is the addition of a new entity called the Broadcast Multicast-Service Center (BM-SC). Actually, BM-SC acts as an entry point for data delivery between the content providers and the UMTS network and is located in the PS domain of the CN. The BM-SC entity communicates with existing UMTS networks and external PDNs [1, 2].

The BM-SC is responsible for both control and user planes of an MBMS service. More specifically, the function of the BM-SC can be separated into five categories: membership, session and transmission, proxy and transport, service announcement, and security function. The BM-SC membership function provides authorization to the UEs requesting to activate an MBMS service. According to the session and transmission function, the BM-SC can schedule MBMS session transmissions and can provide the GGSN with transport associated parameters, such as QoS and MBMS service area. As far as the proxy and transport function is concerned, the BM-SC is a proxy agent for signaling over the Gmb reference point between GGSNs and other BM-SC functions. Moreover, the BM-SC service announcement function must be able to provide service announcements for multicast and broadcast MBMS user services and provide the UE with media descriptions specifying the media to be delivered as part of an MBMS user service. Finally, MBMS user services may use the security functions for integrity or confidentiality protection of the MBMS data, while the specific function is used for distributing MBMS keys (key distribution function) to authorized UEs.

3.3. *Multicast Mode of MBMS*

MBMS multicast efficiency improvement in UMTS networks can be derived from the following figures. More specifically, Figs. 2 and 3 present UMTS multicast functionality without and with MBMS enhancement, respectively.

Without the MBMS enhancement, multicast data is replicated as many times as the total number of multicast users in all interfaces. Obviously, a bottleneck occurs when the number of users increases significantly. All interfaces are heavily overloaded due to multiple transmissions of the same data. On the other hand, MBMS multicast benefits UMTS networks through the radio and network resource

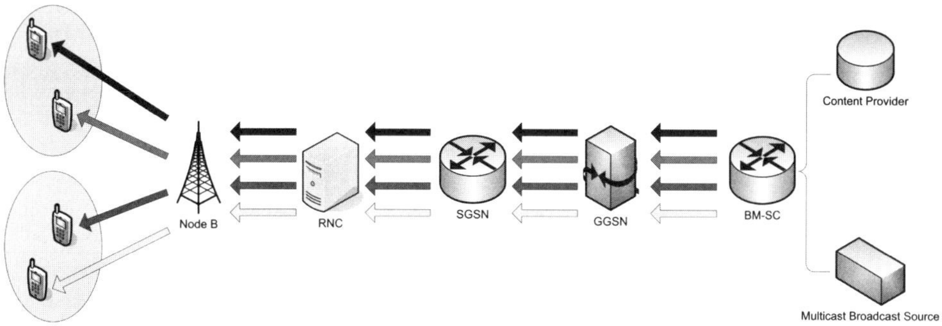

Fig. 2. UMTS multicast without MBMS enhancement.

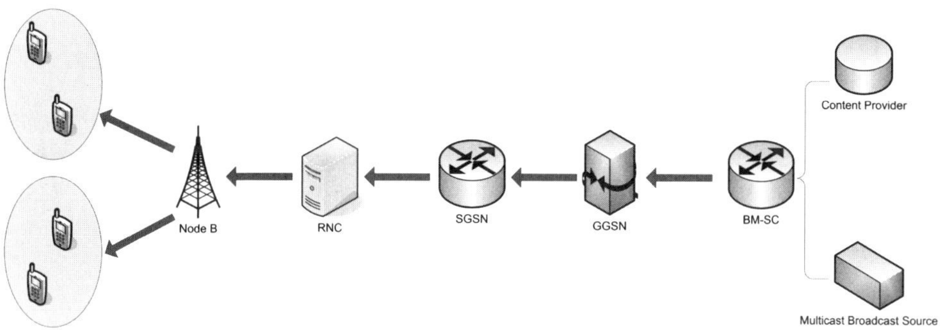

Fig. 3. UMTS multicast with MBMS enhancement.

sharing. Only a single stream per MBMS service of identical data is essential for the delivery of the multicast content, thus saving expensive resources. Consequently, MBMS multicast data distribution is optimally configured throughout the UMTS network.

3.3.1. *Packet Delivery Process*

An overview of the multicast data flow procedure during an MBMS service provision is presented in this section. Figure 4 depicts a subset of a UMTS-MBMS network. In this architecture, there are two SGSNs connected to a GGSN, four RNCs, and twelve Node Bs. Furthermore, eleven members of a multicast group are located in six cells. The BM-SC acts as the interface to external sources of traffic. In the presented analysis, we assume that a data stream that comes from an external PDN, through BM-SC, must be delivered to the 11 UEs as illustrated in Fig. 4.

The analysis presented in the following paragraphs covers the forwarding mechanism of the data packets between the BM-SC and the UEs. With multicast, the packets are forwarded only to those Node Bs that have multicast users. Therefore, in Fig. 4, the Node B2, B3, B5, B7, B8 and B9 receive the multicast

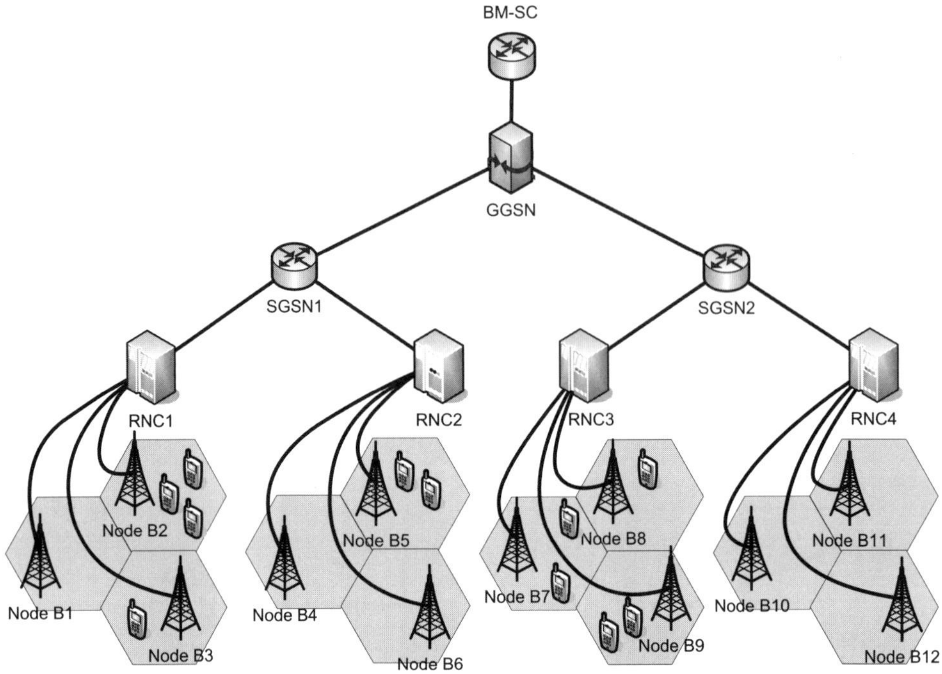

Fig. 4. Packet delivery in MBMS multicast mode.

packets issued by the BM-SC. We briefly summarize the five steps that are required for the delivery of multicast packets.

Initially, the BM-SC receives a multicast packet and forwards it to the GGSN that has been registered to receive multicast traffic. Then, the GGSN receives the multicast packet and, by querying its multicast routing lists, it determines which SGSNs have multicast users residing in their respective service areas. In Fig. 4, the GGSN duplicates the multicast packet and forwards it to SGSN1 and SGSN2 [11]. Then, both destination SGSNs receive the multicast packets and, having queried their multicast routing lists, determine which RNCs are to receive the multicast packets. The destination RNCs receive the multicast packet and send it to the Node Bs that have established the appropriate radio bearers for the multicast application. In Fig. 4, these are: Node B2, B3, B5, B7, B8, and B9. The multicast users receive the multicast packets on the appropriate radio bearers through dedicated channels transmitted to individual users separately or through common channels transmitted to all members in the cell [11].

3.3.2. *MBMS Multicast Mode Radio Bearers*

According to current MBMS specifications, the transmission of MBMS multicast packets over the Iub and Uu interfaces may be performed over common (FACH) and dedicated (DCH) transport channels. The main requirement is to make an efficient overall utilization of the radio resources. This makes a common channel the favorite choice since many users can access the same resource at the same time.

More specifically, the transport channel that 3GPP decided to use as the main transport channel for PTM MBMS data transmission is the FACH with turbo coding and quadrature phase shift keying (QPSK) modulation at a constant transmission power [2]. DCH is a PTP channel, and hence, it suffers from the inefficiencies of requiring multiple DCHs to carry the data to a group of users. However, DCH can employ fast closed-loop power control and soft handover mechanisms and is generally a highly reliable channel [3, 10].

4. Power Control in MBMS Multicast Mode

Power control is one of the most critical aspects in MBMS due to the fact that downlink transmission power in UMTS networks is a limited resource and must be shared efficiently among all MBMS users in a cell. Power control aims at minimizing the transmitted power, eliminating in this way the intercell interference. However, when misused, the use of power control may lead to a high level of wasted power and worse performance results.

On the PTP downlink transmissions, fast power control is used to maintain the quality of the link and thus to provide a reliable connection for the receiver to obtain the data with acceptable error rates. Transmitting with just enough power to maintain the required quality for the link also ensures that there is minimum interference affecting the neighboring cells. However, when a user consumes a high portion of power, more than is actually required, the remaining power allocated for the rest of the users is dramatically decreased, thus leading to a significant capacity loss in the system.

During PTM downlink transmissions, Node B transmits at a power level that is high enough to support the connection to the receiver with the highest power requirement among all receivers in the multicast group. This would still be efficient because the receiver with the highest power requirement would still need the same amount of power in a unicast link, and by satisfying that particular receiver's requirement, the transmission power will be enough for all the other receivers in the multicast group. Consequently, the transmitted power is kept at a relatively high level most of the time, which in turn increases the signal quality at each receiver in the multicast group. On the other hand, a significant amount of power is wasted and moreover intercell interference is increased.

As a consequence, downlink transmission power plays a key role in MBMS planning and optimization. This section provides an analytical description of the DCH and FACH power profiles that are employed during PTP and PTM transmission, respectively. It also presents the main characteristics of the MBMS counting mechanism. Finally, techniques for decreasing the power requirements during MBMS multicast delivery are discussed. The following analysis refers to a macrocell environment with parameters described in Table 1 [10, 12].

Table 1. Macrocell simulation assumptions.

Parameter	Value
Cellular layout	Hexagonal grid
Number of cells	18
Sectorization	3 sectors/cell
Site-to-site distance	1 km
Cell radius	0.577 km
Maximum BS Tx power	20 W (43 dBm)
Other BS Tx power	5 W (37 dBm)
Common channel power	1 W (30 dBm)
Propagation model	Okumura–Hata
Multipath channel	Vehicular A (3 km/h)
Orthogonality factor	0.5
E_b/N_0 target	5 dB

4.1. *DCH Power Profile*

The total downlink transmission power allocated for all MBMS users in a cell that are served by multiple DCHs is variable. It mainly depends on the number of serving users, their location in the cell, the bit rate of the MBMS session, and the signal quality E_b/N_0 experienced by each user. Equation (1) calculates Node B's total DCH transmission power required for the transmission of the data to n users in a specific cell [13]:

$$P_T = \frac{P_P + \sum_{i=1}^{n} \frac{(P_N + x_i)}{\frac{W}{(E_b/N_0)_i R_{b,i}} + p} L_{p,i}}{1 - \sum_{i=1}^{n} \frac{p}{\frac{W}{(E_b/N_0)_i R_{b,i}} + p}}, \tag{1}$$

where P_T is the base station's total transmitted power, P_P the power devoted to common control channels, $L_{p,i}$ the path loss, $R_{b,i}$ the ith user transmission rate, W the bandwidth, P_N the background noise, p is the orthogonality factor ($p = 0$ for perfect orthogonality), and x_i the inter-cell interference observed by the ith user given as a function of the transmitted power by the neighboring cells P_{Tj}, $j = 1, \ldots, K$ and the path loss from this user to the jth cell L_{ij}. More specifically [13]:

$$x_i \sum_{j=1}^{K} \frac{P_{Tj}}{L_{ij}}. \tag{2}$$

DCH may be used for the delivery of PTP MBMS services while it cannot be used to serve large multicast populations since high downlink transmission power would be required. Figure 5 depicts the downlink transmission power when MBMS multicast data is delivered over multiple DCHs (one separate DCH per user). Obviously, higher power is required to deliver higher MBMS data rates. In

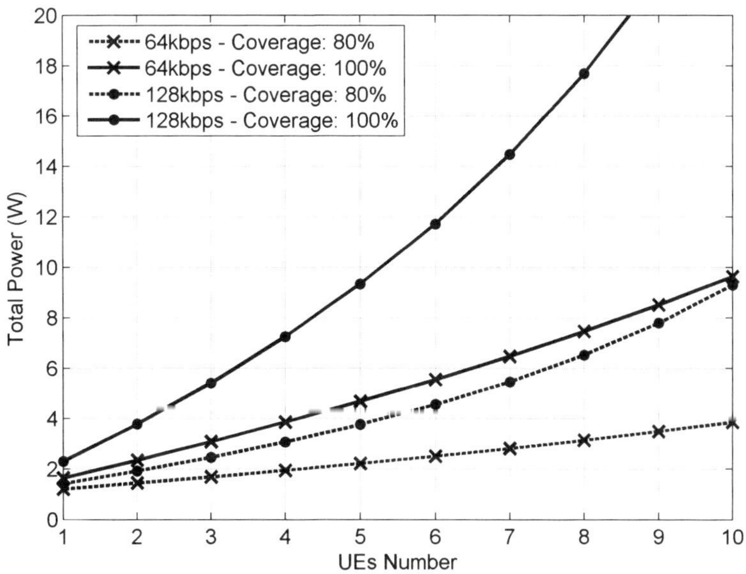

Fig. 5. DCH Tx power.

addition, increased cell coverage area and larger user groups lead to higher power consumption.

4.2. *FACH Power Profile*

A FACH essentially transmits at a fixed power level since fast power control is not supported. FACH is a PTM channel and must be received by all users throughout the cell (or the part of the cell that the users reside in). Thus, the fixed power should be high enough to ensure the requested QoS in the desired coverage area of the cell, irrespective of users' location. FACH power efficiency strongly depends on maximizing diversity as power resources are limited. Diversity can be obtained by the use of a longer transmission time interval (TTI) in order to provide time diversity against fast fading (fortunately, MBMS services are not delay sensitive) and the combining of transmissions from multiple cells to obtain macro diversity [14, 15].

Table 2 presents some indicative FACH downlink transmission power levels obtained for various cell coverage areas and MBMS bit rates, without assuming diversity techniques [8, 15]. A basic constraint is that the delivery of high data rate

Table 2. FACH Tx power levels.

Cell coverage (%)	Service bit rate (kbps)	Required Tx power (W)
50	32	1.8
	64	2.5
95	32	4.0
	64	7.6

MBMS services over FACH is not feasible since excessive downlink transmission power would be required (overcoming the maximum available power of 20 W). High bit rates can only be offered to users located very close to Node B.

4.3. *Improved MBMS Counting Mechanism*

As mentioned earlier in this chapter, MBMS multicast operation mode can employ either PTP or PTM transmission over the air interface. In general, PTP connections are established when serving a small MBMS population, while PTM transmission is preferred when the number of users is high. Figure 6a depicts MBMS multicast transmission when using PTP bearers, while Fig. 6b presents the case of PTM bearer deployment for the delivery of multicast content over the air.

A key aspect for MBMS multicast efficiency is the so-called MBMS counting mechanism. The MBMS counting mechanism allows the network to determine the switching between PTP and PTM transmission. In fact, this mechanism aims to maximize radio resource efficiency through a threshold for switching between the two different transmission modes.

However, the current MBMS counting implementation [5] uses a threshold based on the number of simultaneous users receiving the same multicast content. This scheme, though, cannot always ensure resource efficiency, since it does not consider the dynamic nature (i.e., users' mobility, etc.) of a MBMS-enabled UMTS network. Therefore, the current form of this mechanism may lead to an erroneous threshold determination that, in turn, may result in inefficient utilization of network resources.

The fundamental criterion for maximizing resource efficiency should be the Node B's total downlink MBMS transmission power [16]. The MBMS counting

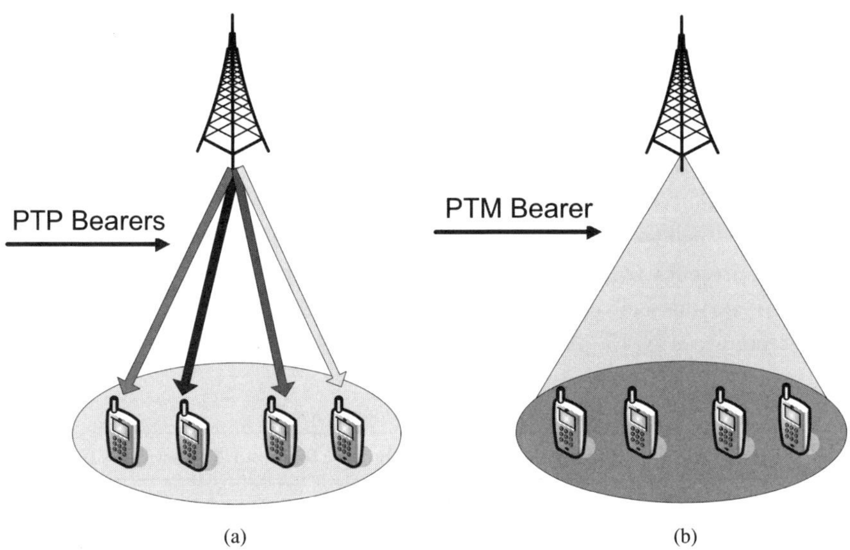

Fig. 6. MBMS bearers: (a) PTP and (b) PTM.

mechanism should adopt downlink transmission power as the optimum criterion for radio bearer selection due to the fact that any dynamic change can be reflected in the Node B's transmission power. MBMS transmission power strongly depends not only on the number of serving users but also on the QoS requirements, users distributions and on MBMS service bit rate.

The impact of the aforementioned factors on the transmission power levels when using DCH or FACH channels is depicted in the following figures. The aim of this parallel plotting is to determine the most efficient transport channel, in terms of power consumption, for the transmission of the MBMS data.

In Fig. 7a the effect of UE location throughout the cell is presented. When multiple DCHs are used, it is obvious that the further the UE is from Node B, the more power is required for successful delivery of MBMS service in a cell. Moreover, Fig. 7a depicts how the appropriate switching point between DCHs and FACH changes for different cell coverage areas. For instance, the switching point between DCHs and FACH (for a 64 kbps service) for 95% cell coverage is nine UEs. Above this number of UEs, FACH is the most appropriate channel for the transmission of multicast data in terms of power consumption. For 75% cell

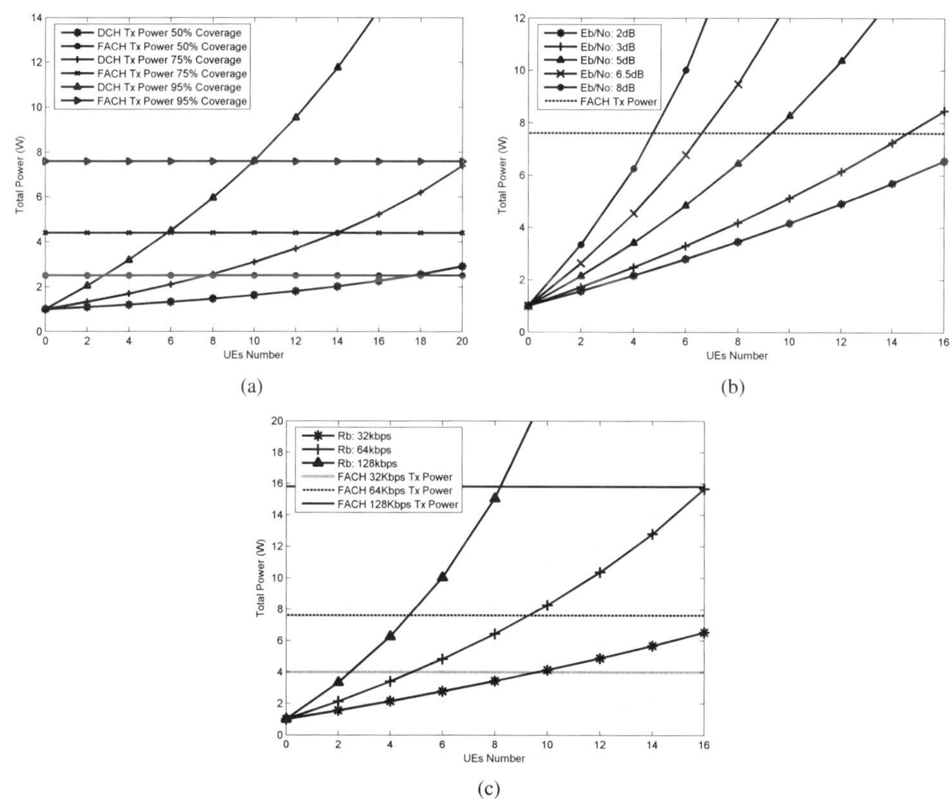

Fig. 7. DCH, FACH Tx power versus (a) cell coverage, (b) E_b/N_0 and (c) bit rate.

coverage the switching point between multiple DCHs and FACH is 14 UEs, while for 50% coverage the threshold further increases to 18 UEs. Similarly, Figs. 7b and 7c show that as E_b/N_0 and the MBMS bit rate increase, transmission power increases too. Simulation results presented in these figures correspond to the worst case scenario, where 95% coverage is assumed. Additionally, these figures depict the impact of these parameters on the switching point between DCHs and FACH.

From the preceding analysis, it is obvious that the determination of the appropriate switching point between PTP and PTM bearers is a rather complicated procedure, indicating the need for a dynamic approach.

4.4. *Power Saving Techniques*

Apart from the determination of the appropriate thresholds for switching between PTP and PTM bearers, MBMS has to confront another problem regarding the power consumption in PTM mode. More specifically, in PTM mode, multicast data is transmitted over the FACH, which requires a relatively high power allocation level. This fact may lead to increased wastage of power resources and interference in the system, especially during the provision of high bit rate MBMS services. In this section, several power saving techniques are proposed that aim to overcome this problem and substantially decrease Node B's power consumption during PTM transmission.

4.4.1. *Dynamic Power Setting (DPS)*

Setting Node B's transmission power to a level high enough so as to cover the whole cell is wasteful if not even one MBMS user is close to the cell edge. Dynamic power setting (DPS) is the technique where the transmission power of the FACH can be determined based on the "worst" user path loss. This way, FACH transmission power is allocated dynamically, and the FACH transmission power will need to cover the whole cell only if one (or more) user is at the cell boundary. To perform DPS, MBMS users need to turn on a measurement report mechanism while they are on the Cell_FACH state. Based on such measurement reports, Node B can adjust the transmission power of the FACH [17]. This is presented in Fig. 8, where Node B sets its transmission power based on the worst user path loss (i.e., distance). The information about the path loss is sent to Node B via the Random Access Channel (RACH).

Examination of Fig. 8 reveals that 4.0 W is required in order to provide a 32 kbps service to 95% of the cell. However, supposing that all the MBMS users are found near Node B (10% coverage) only 0.9 W is required. In that case, 3.1 W (4.0 W minus 0.9 W) can be saved while delivering a 32 kbps service, since with DPS Node B will set its transmission power so as to cover only 10% of the cell. The corresponding power gain increases to 6.2 W for a 64 kbps service and to 13.4 W for a 128 kbps service.

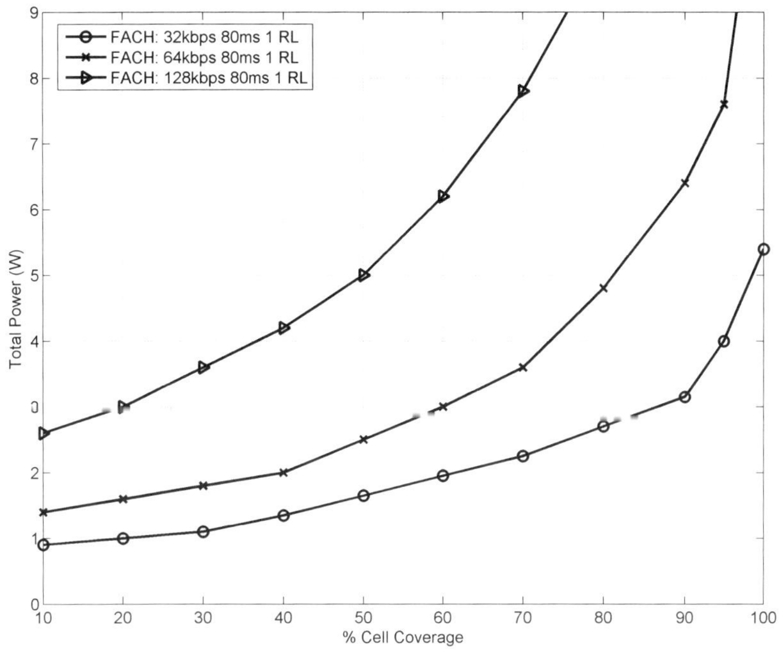

Fig. 8. FACH Tx power with DPS.

4.4.2. *Macro Diversity Combining (MDC)*

Diversity is a technique to combine several copies of the same message received over different channels. Basically, the macro diversity combining (MDC) concept consists of receiving redundantly the same information bearing signal over two or more fading channels, and combining these multiple replicas at the receiver in order to increase the overall received signal-to-noise ratio (SNR). As the user receives data from two (or three) Node Bs, simultaneously the required power of the first Node B is decreased; however, the total required power remains the same [8].

Figure 9 shows how the FACH transmission power level changes with cell coverage when MDC is applied. For the purposes of simulation we considered that a 64 kbps service should delivered, using 1, 2 or 3 Node Bs (or radio links). TTI is assumed to be 80 ms. In Table 3 we list some cases that reveal the power gains with this technique.

The main idea with regard to MDC is to decrease the power level from a Node B when it serves users near the cell edge. However, as in most cases there are three sectors per cell, this technique can also be used for distances near a Node B, where each sector is considered as one radio link. As the user receives data from two (or three) Node Bs, the required power of each Node B is decreased; however, the total required power is the same and sometimes it is higher. This technique, however, is particularly useful when the power level of a specific Node B is high, while the power level of its neighboring Node B is low.

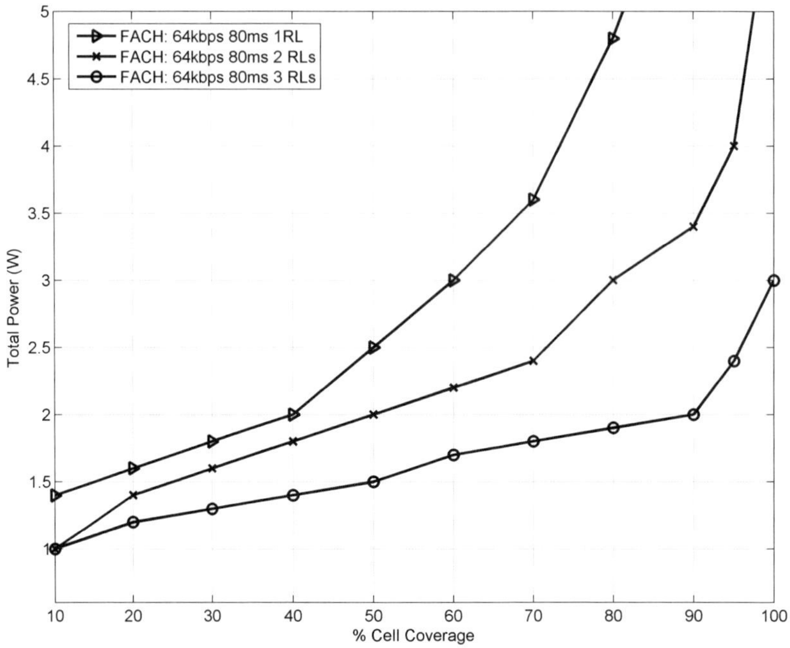

Fig. 9. FACH Tx power with MDC (1RL, 2RLs and 3RLs).

Table 3. Indicative FACH Tx power levels with MDC.

Cell coverage (%)	Radio links	Required power (W)
50	1	2.5
	2	2.0
	3	1.5
95	1	7.6
	2	4.0
	3	2.4

4.4.3. *Rate Splitting (RS)*

The RS technique assumes that the MBMS data stream is scalable and can thus be split into several streams with different QoS. Only the most important stream is sent to all the users in the cell to provide the basic service. The less important streams are sent with less power or coding protection and only the users who have better channel conditions (i.e., the users close to Node B) can receive those to enhance the quality on top of the basic MBMS stream. This way, transmission power for the most important MBMS stream can be reduced because the data rate is reduced, and the transmission power for the less important streams can also be reduced because the coverage requirement is relaxed [18].

In the scenario depicted in Fig. 10, we consider that a 64 kbps service can be split in two streams of 32 kbps. The first 32 kbps stream (basic stream of the

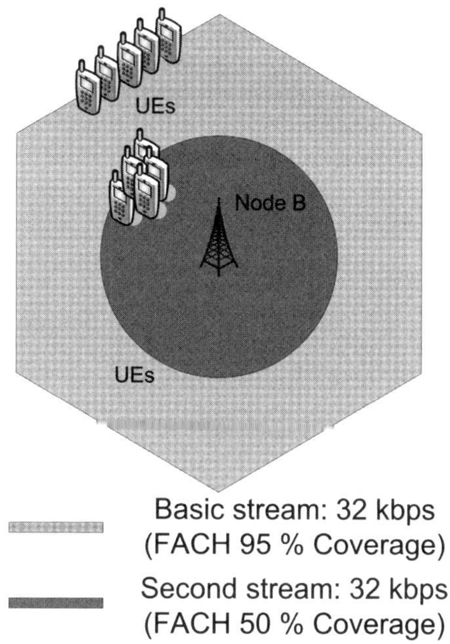

Fig. 10. MBMS provision with RS.

64 kbps service) is provided throughout the whole cell, as it is supposed to carry the important information of the MBMS service. In contrast, the second 32 kbps stream is sent only to the users who are close to Node B (50% of the cell area) providing the users in the particular region the full 64 kbps service. Figure 10 also depicts the way this technique functions, in terms of channel selection and cell coverage.

From Fig. 10 it can be seen that this technique requires 5.8 W (4.0 W for the basic stream and 1.8 W for the second). On the other hand, in order to deliver a 64 kbps service using a FACH with 95% coverage the required power would be 7.6 W. Thus, 1.8 W can be saved through the RS technique. However, it is worth mentioning that this power gain involves certain negative results. Some of the users will not be fully satisfied, as they will only receive the 32 kbps of the 64 kbps service, even if these 32 kbps have the most important information. As the observed difference will be small, Node B should weigh between the transmission power and the users' requirements.

4.4.4. *Usage of Longer TTI and Space Diversity (LTTI)*

These two methods can be employed in the physical layer to benefit every member of the MBMS group in a cell. An increment in TTI length (from 20 ms to 80 ms) can provide significant power gain. However, the use of longer TTI introduces more complexity and larger memory space requirement in the mobile station [15, 19].

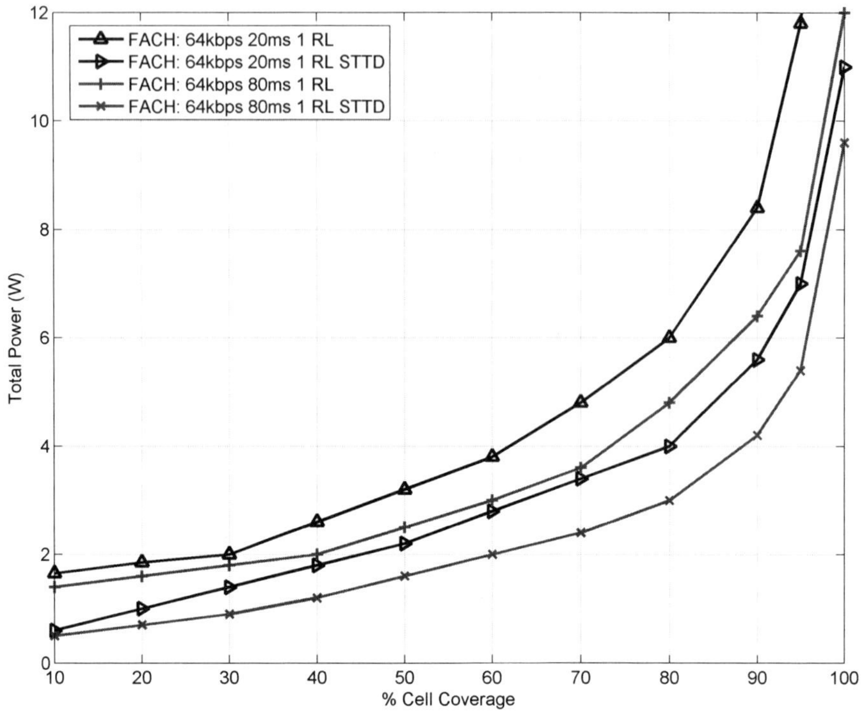

Fig. 11. FACH Tx power with LTTI.

Fortunately, MBMS services are not delay sensitive. In that case, diversity can be obtained by using a longer TTI, e.g., 80 ms instead of 20 ms, so as to provide time diversity against fast fading. Figure 11 shows the power levels that are indicative of the sums of power that can be saved by using the LTTI technique.

Table 4, on the other hand, demonstrates certain cases that reveal the sums of power that can be saved while delivering a 64 kbps service, by increasing the TTI length and obtaining STTD. The power levels are indicative of the sums of power that can be saved by using the LTTI technique.

Table 4. Indicative FACH Tx power levels with LTTI.

Cell coverage (%)	TTI (ms)	Required power (W)
50	20 — no STTD	3.2
	20 — with STTD	2.2
	80 — no STTD	2.5
	80 — with STTD	1.6
95	20 — no STTD	11.8
	20 — with STTD	7.0
	80 — no STTD	7.6
	80 — with STTD	5.4

4.4.5. *Mixed Usage of Multiple DCHs and FACH (MDF)*

MDF can significantly decrease Node B's transmission power, depending on the number and the location of the users that receive the MBMS service. In this approach, the FACH channel only covers the inner part of the sector (e.g., 50% of the sector area) and provides the MBMS service to the users that are found in this part ("inner part" users). The rest of the users are served using DCH to cover the remaining outer cell area ("outer part" users). Figure 12 shows the way of providing an MBMS service according to the MDF technique. The total downlink power consumption including FACH and dedicated channels obviously depends on the number of users who are served by DCHs and their location [20].

The main goal is to examine how the transmission power is affected by the number of users. Figure 13 represents Node B's total transmission power as a function of the number of "outer part" users. The total power in Fig. 13 includes the power that is required in order to cover the 50% of the cell with FACH (i.e., 2.5 W). Moreover, the number of "inner part" users is assumed to be high enough so as to justify the choice of FACH as the transport channel in the inner part.

Apart from the power required for the MDF technique, the power allocation level of a FACH with 95% cell coverage is depicted. This parallel plot intends to highlight the fact that a switch from MDF to a pure FACH has to be performed, or *vice versa*. For instance, in Fig. 13 when the "outer part" users exceed seven, the total power (i.e., the power to cover the inner part with FACH plus the power to cover the outer part with DCHs) exceeds the power that is required in order to cover the whole cell with a single FACH. Thereby, it is more "power efficient" to use a FACH with 95% coverage.

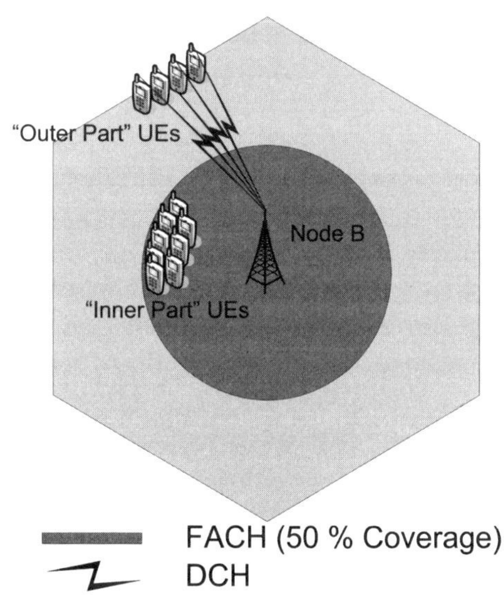

Fig. 12. MBMS provision with MDF.

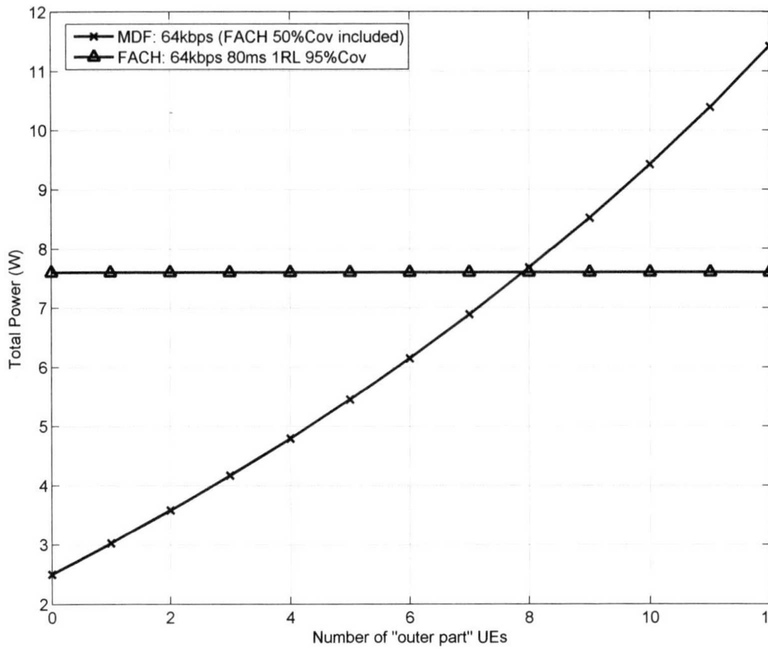

Fig. 13. Node B's Tx power with MDF.

Except for the power gain described above, the MDF technique ensures one more advantage. This advantage relies on the fact that DCH supports soft handover, while FACH does not. Since with this technique the users that are found near the cell edge are served with DCHs, their transition to another cell will be smoother, as the MBMS service will be provided uninterruptedly.

5. Thoughts for Practitioners

In the context of switching between PTP and PTM transmissions several techniques have been proposed. The MBMS counting mechanism was the prevailing approach mainly due to its simplicity of implementation and function [5]. According to this approach, a switch from dedicated to common resources occurs when the number of multicast users in a cell exceeds a predefined threshold. However, this approach suffered from much inefficiency mainly due to the difficulty of defining the appropriate threshold.

Assuming that all UEs are distributed uniformly across the cell, the MBMS counting mechanism provides an unrealistic approach because mobility and current location of the mobile users are not taken into account. On the other hand, assuming that all UEs are found near the cell borders (worst case scenario), the conventional counting mechanism may lead to misleading results, and thus to an inappropriate threshold resulting in inefficient utilization of network resources.

That the total downlink transmission power allocated for DCHs is variable and depends on several factors makes the problem even more complicated. All these factors should be taken into consideration in order to define the appropriate threshold. Moreover, the utilization of the proposed power saving techniques would lead to a multidimensional threshold scheme, making the situation even more complicated. This way, the advantage of simplicity of implementation is overshadowed by the disadvantage generated from the difficulty of determining the appropriate switching points. Summarizing, we can say that the research in the field of the MBMS counting mechanism was motivated mainly due to its simplicity of implementation. However, the difficulties regarding the determination of the switching threshold proved to be significant and in most cases insurmountable.

On the other hand, the efficiency of a power control mechanism where there is no need for *a priori* information and predefined switching thresholds has been studied in previous work [16]. In this work, the authors propose a power control scheme for efficient radio bearer selection in UTRAN. However, this approach does not take into consideration users' mobility as well as the power saving techniques. All these parameters are taken into account in the proposed power control mechanism, the description and architecture of which follows in the next section.

5.1. *Architecture of MBMS Power Control Mechanism*

This section presents and analyzes the architecture and the functionality of the proposed MBMS power control mechanism, which is used for efficient data transmission during an MBMS service. The block diagram of the mechanism is illustrated in Fig. 14.

According to Fig. 14, the mechanism consists of five distinct operation phases. These are: the initialization phase, the parameter retrieval phase, the power computation phase, the radio bearer selection phase, and the event scheduling phase. The RNC is the responsible node of the MBMS architecture for the operation of this algorithm and the decision of the most efficient bearer.

The initialization phase an launches the mechanism when one user expresses his interest in receiving an MBMS service. In other words the mechanism begins when the first user requests the MBMS service and the initialization phase is responsible for this procedure.

The parameter retrieval phase is responsible for retrieving the parameters of the existing MBMS users (through uplink channels) in each cell. These parameters are the distance of each UE from Node B and the E_b/N_0 requirement per UE. The MBMS service bit rate is assumed to be known (in BM-SC). This information is later used as input in the power computation phase.

The power computation phase substantially processes the data received from the parameter retrieval phase. During this phase, the required power to be allocated for each cell is computed. The computation is based on the assumption that the

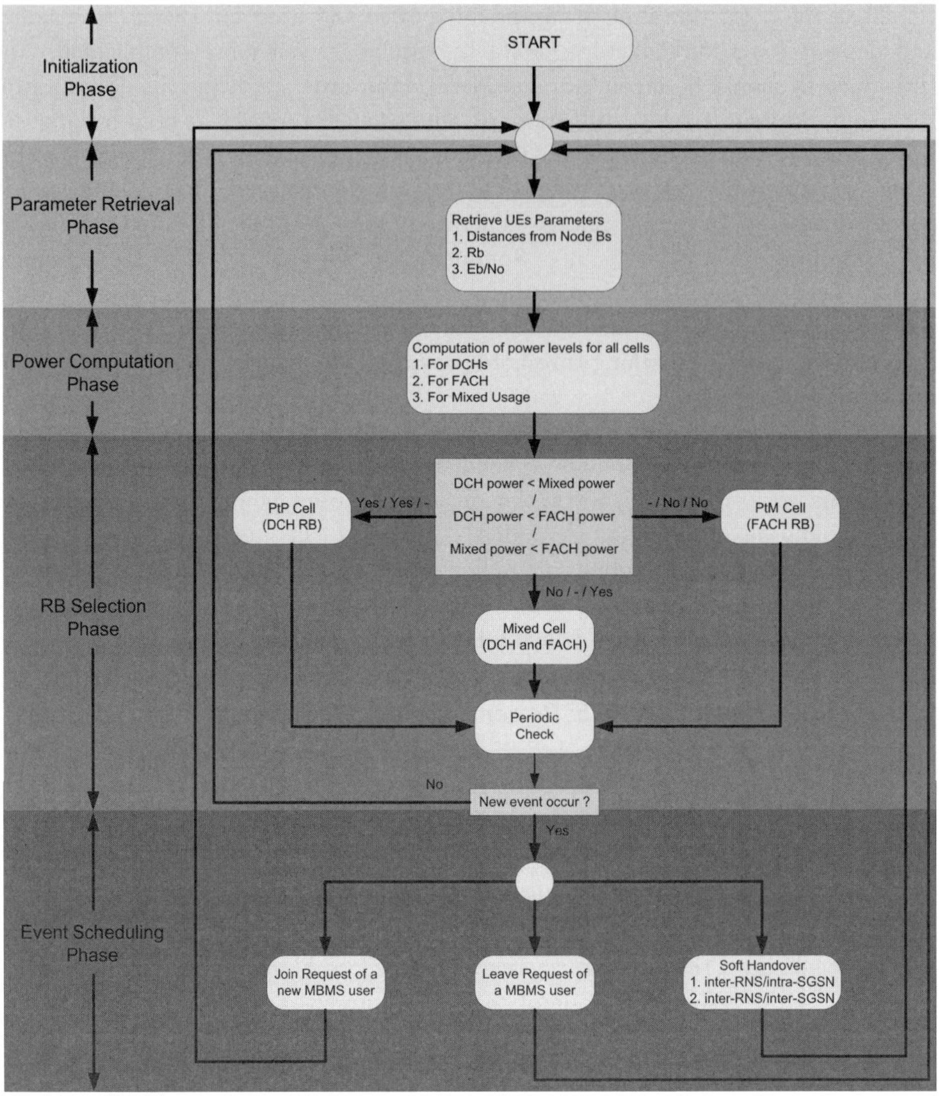

Fig. 14. Block diagram of the proposed MBMS power control mechanism.

transmission of the multicast data (for each cell separately) over the Uu interface can be performed with:

- multiple DCHs (DCHs case),
- one FACH with power so as to serve the UE that is farthest from Node B, and therefore all the UEs in the cell (FACH dynamic case), or
- one FACH with power so as to serve the UEs that reside in 50% of the cell area, while the remaining UEs are served with DCHs (mixed case).

In other words, the total Node B transmission power per cell for the given MBMS session is computed, assuming that all the UEs of the session can be served three possible ways. The computation for the DCHs case takes into account the parameters defined in the parameter retrieval phase and calculates the total required power (P_{DCH}) according to Eq. (1). For the FACH dynamic case, the total required power (P_{FACH}) is computed depending on the user with the worst path loss and according to Table 2 and Fig. 8. Finally, the mixed case assumes that if there are UEs in 50% of the cell area, they are served with one FACH (requiring 2.5 W for a 64 kbps service according to Table 2), while the power required for the rest of the UEs is calculated according to Eq. (1). The total required power for this case (P_{Mixed}) is the sum of the two mentioned power levels.

In the radio bearer selection phase, P_{DCH}, P_{FACH} and P_{Mixed} are compared in order to select the most efficient transmission method for the specific MBMS session. Thus, for each cell separately, the algorithm decides which case consumes the least power and, consequently, chooses the radio bearer that minimizes the Node B transmission power per cell. Therefore, a cell can be characterized as a PTP cell (data is carried through multiple DCHs), as a PTM cell (data is carried through the FACH channel) or as a mixed cell (data is carried through FACH and DCHs). The categorization of the cells is done for each MBMS session in the system.

The algorithm enters the event scheduling phase only if one of the following three different events occurs during an MBMS session: a Join request from a new MBMS user, a Leave request from an existing MBMS user, or a Soft Handover. The algorithm handles these three events absolutely the same way since the parameters of all the users are updated at regular time intervals. The only difference is that a Join and a Leave request influences the power of only one cell, while a Soft Handover influences the power of two different cells (the source and the destination cell).

The above description refers to a dynamic model in the sense that the UEs are assumed to be moving throughout the topology. The parameter retrieval phase is triggered at regular time intervals so as to take into account users' mobility and the three events of the event scheduling phase. Therefore, the P_{DCH}, P_{FACH} and P_{Mixed} power levels must be computed periodically at a predetermined frequency rate. This periodic computation introduces a further complexity for RNC as this information is carried in an uplink channel. This entails that a certain bandwidth fraction must be allocated for the transmission of this information in the uplink channel, thus resulting in a capacity reduction.

5.2. *Scenarios*

This section illustrates how the Node B's transmission power for an MBMS session could be reduced by selecting different transport channels for the transmission of the MBMS data over the Iub and Uu interfaces. To this end, five different scenarios are examined. The users' initial locations for the first four scenarios are presented in Fig. 15. During the simulation each UE is moving randomly throughout the

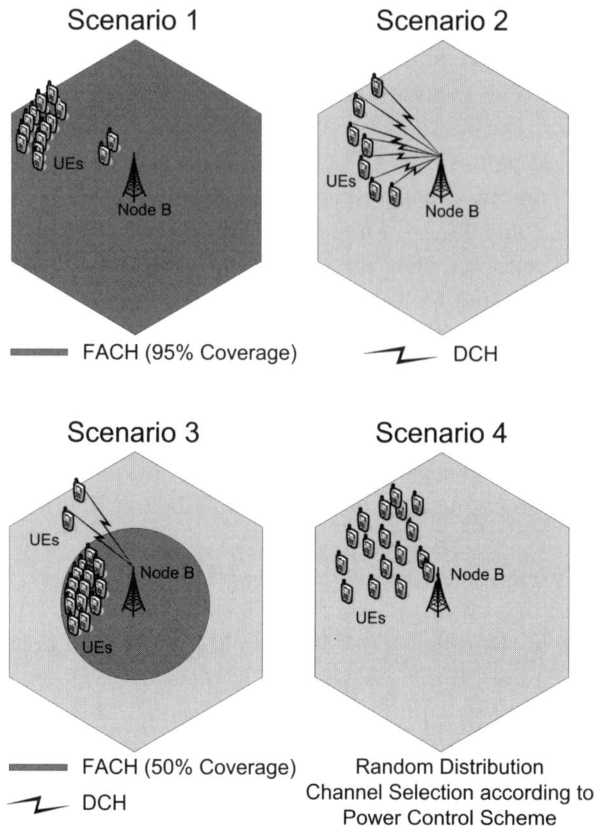

Fig. 15. UEs' initial locations for Scenarios 1–4.

topology. It is worth mentioning that in the first three scenarios the users' initial locations are selected so as to favor the transmission of the MBMS data through FACH, multiple DCHs, and the combination of these channels, respectively. Without loss of generality, these three scenarios constitute possible cases during an MBMS session in a real-world scenario. On the other hand, Scenarios 4 and 5 illustrate how the mechanism handles the three different events of the event scheduling phase.

Transmission power levels when using DCH, FACH or mixed channels are depicted in each of the following figures (Figs. 16–18, 21). These power levels constitute the overall output of the power computation phase in each scenario. In the next phase, the mechanism will force the RNC to select at each instant the radio bearer that ensures the lowest power requirements.

5.2.1. *Scenario 1: PTM Cell*

According to the first scenario, 12 UEs near the cell borders and two UEs close to Node B receive a 64 kbps MBMS service (Fig. 15). Figure 16 reveals the total power

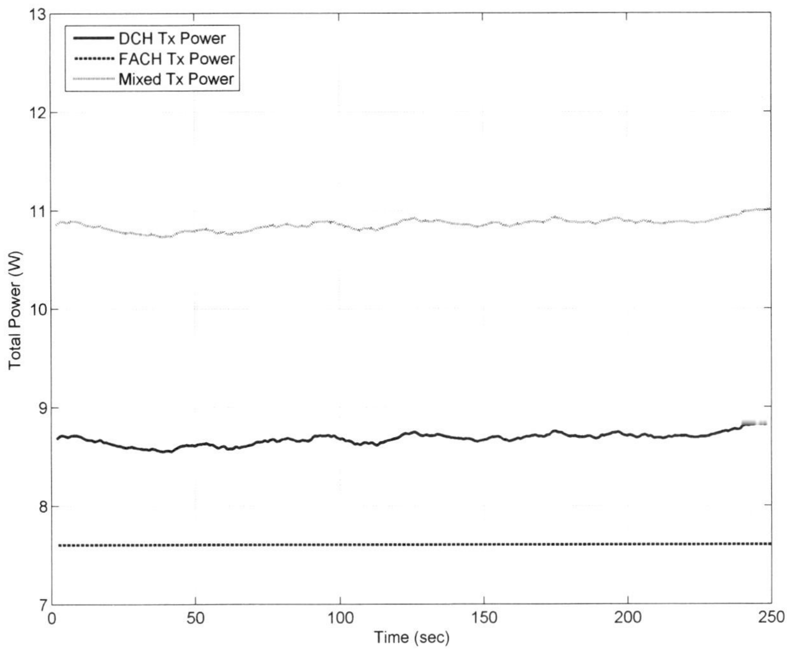

Fig. 16. Scenario 1: Tx power levels.

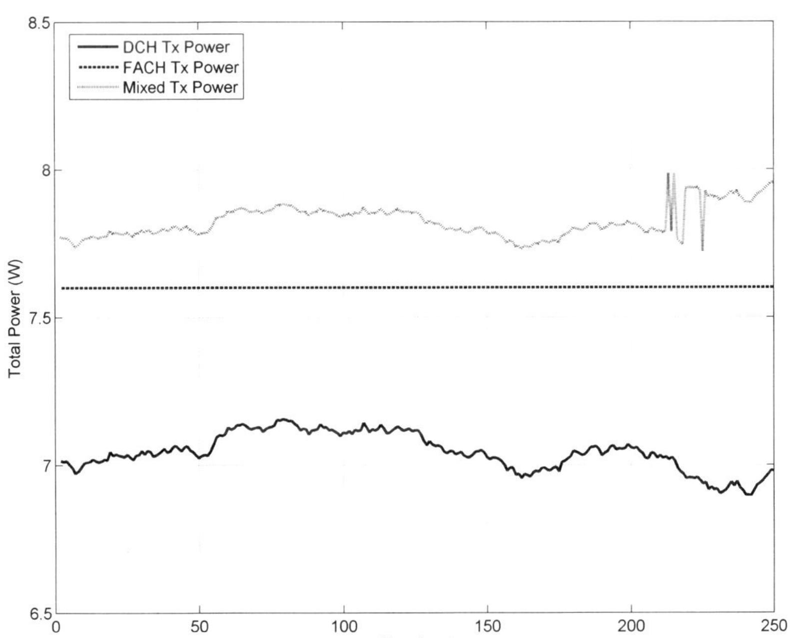

Fig. 17. Scenario 2: Tx power levels.

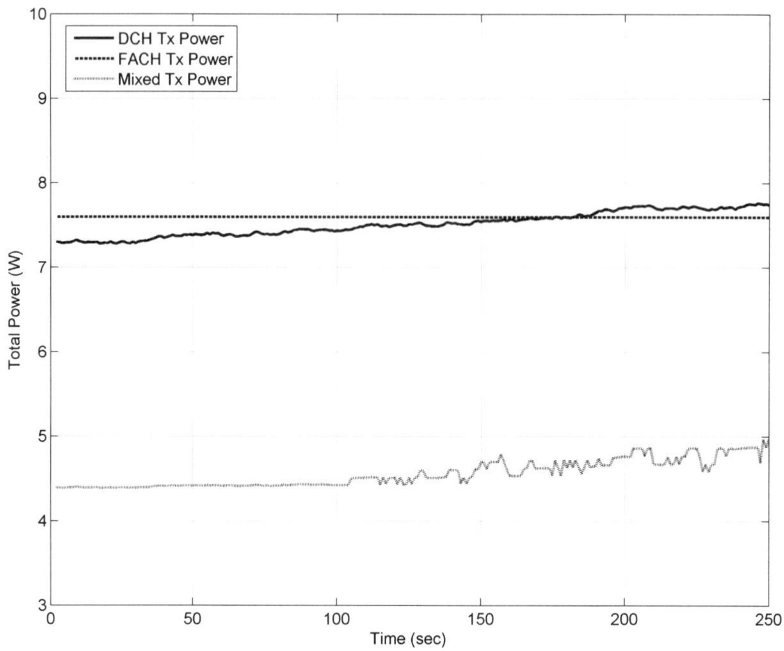

Fig. 18. Scenario 3: Tx power levels.

that is required for the successful reception of the MBMS service by all UEs, when DCHs, FACH or mixed channels are deployed.

As already mentioned this scenario favors the deployment of FACH for the transmission of MBMS data. Indeed, as presented in Fig. 16 the FACH transmission power level is lower throughout the whole simulation. More specifically, 7.6 W are required in order to cover 95% of the cell area and provide the 64 kbps MBMS service to all UEs that reside in this area (Table 2). This power level is independent of the UE population and stays constant as the user with the worst path loss remains between 90% and 95% of the cell area. If all the users moved towards Node B, the DPS technique would have forced Node B to decrease the FACH transmission power level (e.g., to 6.4 W if the user with the worst path loss remained between 80% and 90% of the cell area).

5.2.2. *Scenario 2: PTP Cell*

In the second scenario the population of the UEs that receive the MBMS service is supposed to be small. More specifically, in this scenario seven UEs with random initial locations are moving throughout the cell while receiving a 64 kbps MBMS service. The fact that the UE population is small favors the deployment of multiple DCHs. Therefore, each user should be served by one DCH.

The proposed mechanism calculates the power that is required for each user separately and calculates the total required power (for the case of DCHs) according to Eq. (1). The fact that the UEs are moving explains why the power level does not remain constant. However, even if it is not constant, the DCH power level is always lower than in the other two cases (Fig. 17).

5.2.3. *Scenario 3: Mixed Cell*

Regarding the third scenario, as depicted in Fig. 15, there are a total of 16 UEs that receive the 64 kbps MBMS service. Fourteen of the 16 UEs are found inside 50% of the cell area ("inner part" UEs), while only two UEs are outside this area ("outer part" UEs). As Fig. 18 shows, the best way to serve these UEs is to serve all the "inner part" UEs with one FACH with power so as to cover only the 50% of the cell area (2.5 W). On the other hand, each of the "outer part" UEs is served with one DCH, thereby increasing the total transmission power.

The power required with the mixed usage case is not constant, as there are UEs that are served by DCHs. Moreover, as shown in Fig. 18 the increase in the power required in this case is more obvious 100 s after the simulation starts. This occurs because some of the "inner part" UEs leave 50% of the cell area and, therefore, they are also served by DCHs. Nevertheless, the mixed usage transmission power remains lower than in the other two cases.

5.2.4. *Scenario 4: Join and Leave Requests*

All the above scenarios examine certain cases where the users appear in predefined initial positions and then move randomly throughout the cell. The UE population and the initial positions were selected in order to favor the deployment of certain channels, while simultaneously the number of UEs was kept constant during the simulation.

Scenario 4 examines a more realistic situation with main target to present how the Join and Leave requests by MBMS users are handled by the mechanism. According to this scenario, the UEs appear in random initial positions (Fig. 15) and then move randomly throughout the cell. Moreover, the number of UEs changes during the simulation. More specifically, the number of users that receive a 64 kbps MBMS service initially increases (successive Join requests by MBMS users) in order to reach 35 UEs at a simulation time of 175 s. For the following 80 s, the number of users remains constant. From a simulation time of 255 s the number of users decreases (successive Leave requests by MBMS users), and finally at the end of the simulation only six UEs receive the 64 kbps MBMS service (Fig. 19).

The transmission power levels when using DCH, FACH or mixed channels are presented in Fig. 19. The power control mechanism will force Node B to select the channel with the lowest power requirements. Thus, at the beginning of the simulation, when the number of UEs is small, the most efficient channel is DCH. The increase in the number of UEs causes a switch from DCHs to a mixed usage of DCHs and FACH (at simulation time 113 s). An additional increase in the number

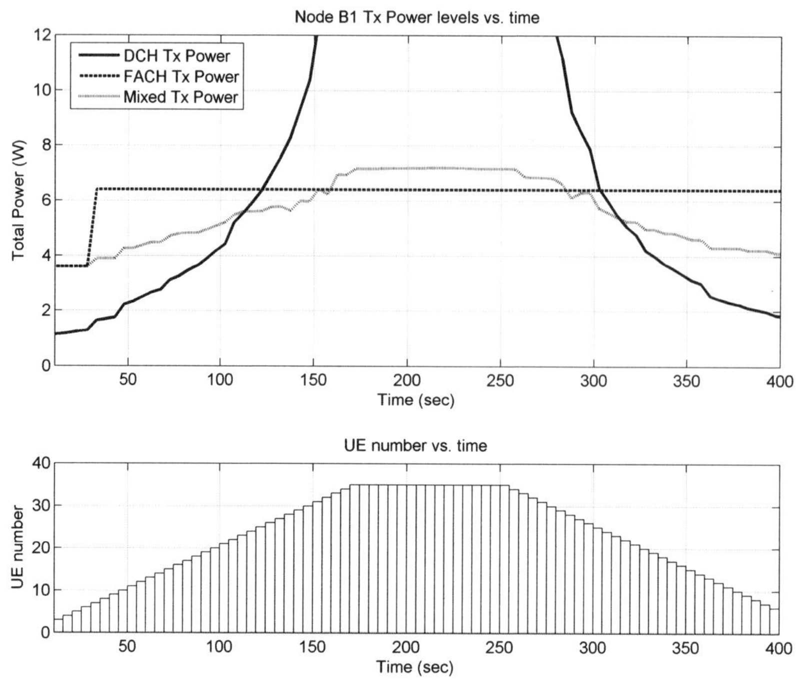

Fig. 19. Scenario 4: Tx power levels versus UE number.

of UEs results in a switch from mixed usage of DCHs and FACH to a single FACH (at a simulation time of 158 s) with transmission power high enough to cover the UE with the worst path loss. A further increase in the UE number does not involve any change, unless the user with the worst path loss moves towards the cell edge, forcing FACH to transmit at a higher power level (this case does not appear in this particular scenario). The decrease in the number of UEs causes the exact opposite results.

5.2.5. *Scenario 5: Soft Handover*

The last scenario presents the operation of the mechanism during soft handover. The UEs' initial positions according to the scenario are presented in Fig. 20. Each Node B in the topology has to serve a number of randomly moving UEs. However, Node B1 is initially serving eight UEs, four of which will follow a predefined route so that soft handover will take place. More specifically, as shown in Fig. 20, UE1 and UE2 will move towards Node B2, while UE3 and UE4 move towards Node B3.

The simulation lasts for 300 s, a time interval sufficient for the process of soft handover to be completed. Figure 21 depicts the transmission power levels of the Node Bs under study when DCH, FACH or mixed channels are used. The three Node Bs under study — in other words, the three Node Bs that participate in the process of soft handover — are: Node B1, Node B2 and Node B3.

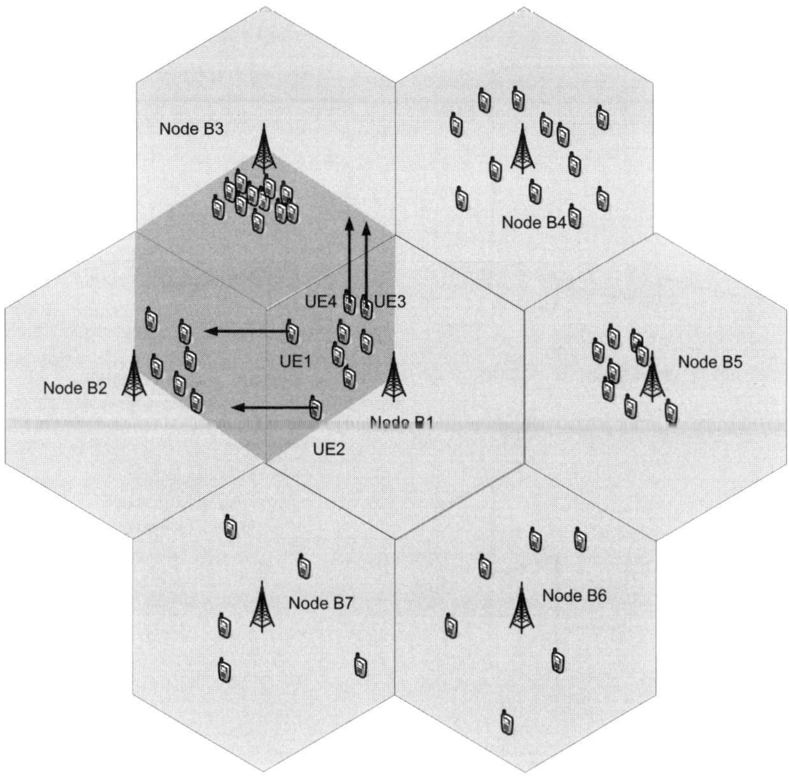

Fig. 20. Scenario 5: UEs' initial locations and routes.

More specifically, regarding Node B1, we observe that four UEs in total leave its coverage area. In Fig. 21a, this is presented by the four abrupt decrements in DCHs and mixed power level. The FACH power level remains high, until the four UEs leave the cell (about 255 s after the simulation starts), when an abrupt decrement in its power level is observed. This happens because after the UEs leave the cell the FACH will only have to serve UEs that are found at a small distance from Node B1 (Fig. 20). Nevertheless, even if the four UEs leave the cell area, multiple DCHs should be deployed as the power level in this case remains the lowest (Fig. 21a).

On the other hand, a decrement in Node B1's power levels is followed by a simultaneous increment in another Node B's power levels. For example, at simulation time 205 s, UE4 leaves the coverage area of Node B1 and enters the coverage area of Node B3 (Fig. 20). The FACH power level in Node B3 simultaneously increases because the new user (UE4) is the user with the worst path loss. The DCH and mixed power levels are also increased because in both cases Node B3 will have to serve one more user with DCH. Nevertheless, according to Fig. 21c, UE4 will force Node B3 to switch from a single FACH to mixed usage of DCHs and FACH, as the power requirements in the second case is lower.

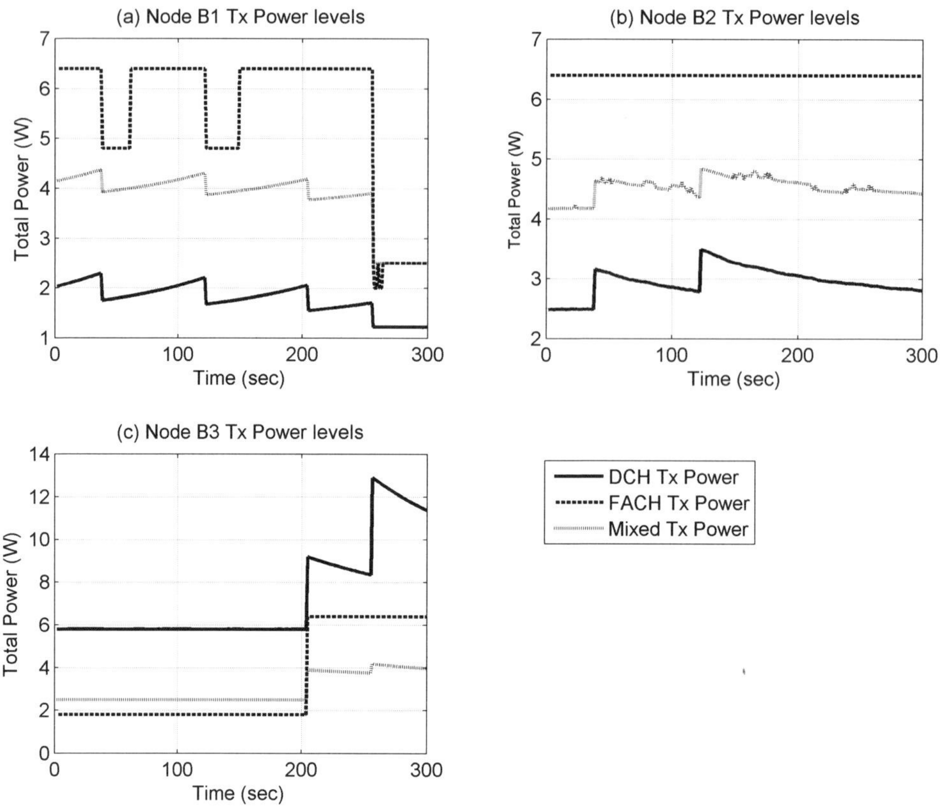

Fig. 21. Scenario 5: Tx power levels of cells under study during soft handover.

It is worth mentioning that during the whole simulation the most efficient channel was selected independently of the UE number and their location. The corresponding power levels were compared and the channel with the lowest power requirements was selected. This fact makes the mechanism much more powerful and much more resistant to changes.

6. Directions for Future Research

A power-based scheme for the efficient selection of radio bearers for the MBMS multicast transmission has been presented. This scheme aimed to switch efficiently between PTP and PTM modes. As presented, accordingly to current MBMS specifications, in PTP mode multiple DCHs can be configured, while in PTM mode a single FACH is transmitted throughout a cell. However, an interesting issue that can further improve MBMS power efficiency and capacity is the transmission of MBMS multicast data over the High Speed-Downlink Shared Channel (HS-DSCH) transport channel. HS-DSCH is characterized as a PTP channel, as well as DCH, due to its unicast nature and is envisaged as a promising radio bearer for enhanced

MBMS PTP provision. Although Release '99 transport channels (FACH, DCH) have already been investigated and standardized for the delivery of MBMS multicast sessions, MBMS over HS-DSCH is a relatively novel proposal, still in its infancy.

HS-DSCH is the main transport channel used by High Speed Downlink Packet Access (HSDPA) technology. HSDPA was introduced in the Release 5 specifications [21] of the UMTS standard in order to improve spectral efficiency and enhance radio transmission techniques and network protocol functionality in wireless networks. In fact, HSDPA is a mobile broadband extension to the UMTS radio interface, characterized as 3.5G, targeting the optimization of the air interface to support higher data rate and delay-tolerant services. The main objective of HSDPA is to increase user peak rates up to theoretically 14 Mbps for best-effort packet data services, far beyond the 3G requirement of 2 Mbps [10, 22]. Consequently, HS-DSCH can play an instrumental role in positioning MBMS services as a key enabler for true "mobile broadband".

MBMS over HS-DSCH can offer significant power savings and enhancements on total MBMS capacity, thus enabling the mass market delivery of higher bit rate multimedia services to end users [22]. In order to prove the above statement, some indicative figures are presented and discussed in the following. These figures aim to make a direct comparison between Release '99 bearers and HS-DSCH power consumption. More specifically, the following figures present MBMS power allocation for DCH, FACH and HS-DSCH transport channels when a 64 kbps MBMS service and different cell coverage areas are assumed.

For instance, in Fig. 22a (60% coverage) it can be seen that for fewer than 10 users DCHs could be used for the MBMS multicast transmission, while for 10–19 users HS-DSCH is the optimal transport channel. For even larger MBMS populations FACH should be employed. The MBMS power control mechanism proposed in Sec. 5, on the other hand, using only DCH and FACH channels (and no HS-DSCH), would use DCHs for up to 16 users and a FACH for more users. For the cases of 80% and 99% cell coverage (Figs. 22b and 22c, respectively), HS-DSCH prevails over the DCH for a small MBMS population and should be used instead of DCHs in MBMS PTP multicast transmission.

Obviously, from the above figures, the HS-DSCH employment in MBMS multicast provides a significant power saving when serving a few users. More specifically, in the PTP mode, only HS-DSCH usage (Fig. 22c) or a combination of HS-DSCH and DCH (Figs. 22a and 22b) can be used, instead of an exclusive DCH usage. This can lead to important gains in power resources as HS-DSCH requires less power compared to DCH. In this way, MBMS PTP performance is significantly improved.

Another important point emerging from these figures is that power gain can, in turn, lead to a significant capacity enhancement for MBMS operators. For most types of MBMS services, such as streaming video, 64 kbps is enough to provide good quality. MBMS can deliver 64–128 kbps MBMS content with a very good coverage probability using DCH and FACH channels. From the end user point of

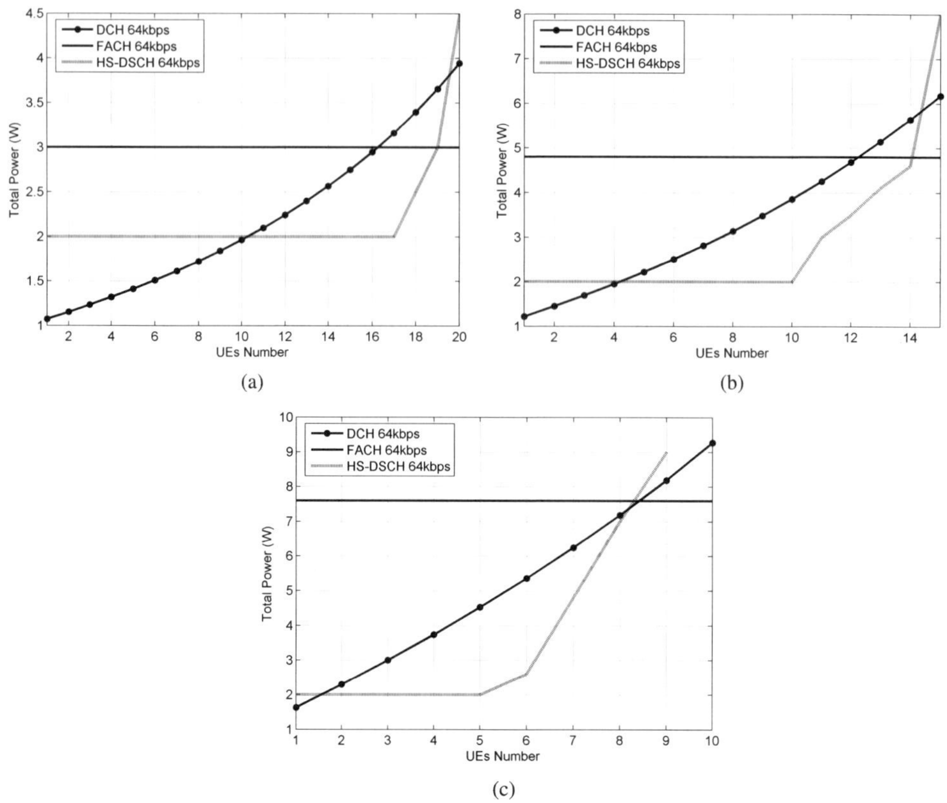

Fig. 22. DCH, FACH, HS-DSCH Tx power for (a) 60%, (b) 80%, and (c) 99% cell coverage.

view no significant improvement is expected from HS-DSCH usage at first glance. However, as can be inferred from the above figures, what HS-DSCH brings is more capacity, which, in turn, enables mass-market delivery of higher bit rate streaming to end users.

Hence, further investigation of MBMS over HS-DSCH is warranted. The preceding short analysis indicates that HS-DSCH can drastically benefit MBMS performance. An analytical dimensioning of HS-DSCH power consumption as well as the evaluation of HS-DSCH impact on MBMS capacity are considered of major importance. In addition, the integration of HS-DSCH in the architecture presented in Sec. 5 is a desirable future step. In this way, an optimal scheme that will make an efficient overall usage of radio and network resources will be realized.

7. Conclusions

This chapter introduced the key concepts of the MBMS framework of UMTS. The main target was to highlight the importance of power control and its commanding role during the delivery of MBMS multicast content, for the overall efficiency of a UMTS network. In this regard, the power profiles of several transport channels that could be employed for the transmission of MBMS services to mobile users were investigated. Moreover, the reader was introduced to certain problems that MBMS current specifications are facing and was made familiar with techniques/solutions proposed to overcome such limitations.

Finally, this chapter proposed a power control mechanism, which considers the Node B's transmission power level as the key criterion for the selection of the appropriate MBMS radio bearer. It was proved that a dynamic threshold between PTP and PTM transmission modes ensures the economic and rational usage of expensive radio and network resources. This mechanism constitutes a novel, dynamic and accurate approach for the determination of the most efficient radio bearer to deliver MBMS multicast data.

Terminology

3rd Generation Partnership Project (3GPP): The collaboration agreement that brings together a number of telecommunications standards bodies which are known as "organizational partners". The original scope of 3GPP was to produce globally applicable technical specifications and technical reports for a 3G mobile system based on the evolved global system for mobile communications (GSM) core networks and the radio access technologies that they support.

Dedicated Channel (DCH): A UMTS transport channel allocated to an individual user, initially used to support a speech channel. Additionally, it supports data transmission.

Forward Access Channel (FACH): A UMTS transport channel initially used for downlink signaling and small quantities of data. FACH is the main representative of PTM transmission.

High Speed Downlink Shared Channel (HS-DSCH): The main transport channel used by HSDPA technology.

Multimedia Broadcast/Multicast Service (MBMS): A novel framework extending the existing UMTS infrastructure. In an MBMS-enabled UMTS network data is transmitted from a single source entity to multiple destinations, allowing the network resources to be shared.

Power saving techniques: Techniques utilized in order to decrease power requirements during an MBMS session.

Point-to-Multipoint (PTM) transmission: Where a single channel is employed in order to cover the desired area of the cell. During PTM transmission, the channel conveys identical traffic and serves all the users in the area of the cell that it covers.

Point-to-Point (PTP) transmission: Where each user separately is served by a dedicated channel.

User equipment (*UE*): A portable device consisting of the mobile equipment and the USIM card. The mobile equipment is the hardware part of the portable device, while the USIM card contains all the essential information to make the access and the identification from the UMTS network possible.

Universal Mobile Telecommunication System (*UMTS*): A Code Division Multiple Access (CDMA) interface in air through which packets are exchanged, in combination with an evolved GSM/GPRS core network. The 3G system that has prevailed in Europe and is progressively extended in Northern America, with result the 3G of cellular mobile systems to be identified with this system.

Exercises

1. What is the motivation for the introduction of MBMS in UMTS networks?
2. What is the main difference between the multicast and the broadcast mode of MBMS?
3. How does the MBMS multicast framework improve network efficiency?
4. What is the main difference between DCH and FACH regarding power control?
5. What is the main scope of the MBMS counting mechanism?
6. Why is the conventional MBMS counting mechanism inefficient?
7. Name four techniques that could be utilized in order to reduce power requirements during an MBMS session.
8. Describe the dynamic power setting technique operation?
9. Name the five phases of the MBMS power control mechanism.
10. How could MBMS efficiency be further improved?

References

1. 3GPP, Technical Specification Group Services and System Aspects; Multimedia Broadcast/Multicast Service; Stage 1 (Release 8), TS 22.146, version 8.1.0.
2. 3GPP, Technical Specification Group Services and System Aspects; Multimedia Broadcast/Multicast Service; Architecture and functional description (Release 6), TR 23.846, version 6.1.0.
3. A. Boni, E. Launay, T. Mienville and P. Stuckmann, Multimedia broadcast multicast service — Technology overview and service aspects, *5th IEE Intl. Conf. 3G Mobile Communication Technologies* (*3G 2004*), London, UK, pp. 634–638.
4. J. Ogunbenkun and A. Mendjeli, MBMS service provision and its challenges, *Proc. 4th Int. Conf. 3G Mobile Communication Technologies* (*3G 2003*) (2003), pp. 128–133.
5. 3GPP, Technical Specification Group Radio Access Network; Introduction of the Multimedia Broadcast Multicast Service (MBMS) in the Radio Access Network (RAN), Stage 2 (Release 7), TS 25.346, version 7.5.0 (2006).
6. IST-2001-35125 (OverDRiVE), Deliverable of the project (D08), Spectrum efficient multicast and asymmetric services in UMTS.
7. J. de Vriendt, I. Gomez Vinagre and A. Van Ewijk, Multimedia broadcast and multicast services in 3G mobile networks, *Alcatel Telecommunication Review* (4th Quarter 2003/1st Quarter 2004).

8. IST-2003-507607 (B-BONE), Deliverable of the project (D2.5). Final results with combined enhancements of the air interface.
9. A. Alexiou, C. Bouras, V. Kokkinos and E. Rekkas, MBMS power planning in macro and micro cell environments, *2nd IEEE Workshop on Multimedia Applications over Wireless Networks* (*MediaWiN 2007*), Aveiro, Portugal (2007), pp. 33–38.
10. H. Holma and A. Toskala, *WCDMA for UMTS: HSPA Evolution and LTE*, 4th edn. (John Wiley & Sons, 2007).
11. A. Alexiou, D. Antonellis, C. Bouras and A. Papazois, An efficient multicast packet delivery scheme for UMTS, *The 9th ACM/IEEE Int. Sympo. Modeling, Analysis and Simulation of Wireless and Mobile Systems* (*MSWiM 2006*), Torremolinos, Malaga, Spain (2006), pp. 147–150.
12. 3GPP, Universal Mobile Telecommunications System (UMTS); Selection procedures for the choice of radio transmission technologies of the UMTS (UMTS 30.03 version 3.2.0), TR 101.102, version 3.2.0.
13. J. Perez-Romero, O. Sallent, R. Agusti and M. Diaz-Guerra, *Radio Resource Management Strategies in UMTS* (John Wiley & Sons, 2005).
14. S. Parkvall, E. Englund, M. Lundevall and J. Torsner, Evolving 3G mobile systems: Broadband and broadcast services in WCDMA, *IEEE Commun. Maga.* (2006).
15. 3GPP, Technical Specification Group Radio Access Network; S-CCPCH performance for MBMS, (Release 6), TS 25.803, version 6.0.0 (2005).
16. A. Alexiou, C. Bouras and E. Rekkas, A power control scheme for efficient radio bearer selection in MBMS, *The 8th IEEE 21st Int. Sympo. World of Wireless, Mobile and Multimedia Networks* (*WoWMoM*), June 17–21 (2007).
17. P. Chuah, T. Hu and W. Luo, UMTS Release 99/4 airlink enhancement for supporting MBMS Services, *2004 IEEE Conf. Communications*, Paris, France (2004), pp. 3231–3235.
18. 3GPP, MBMS Power Usage, Lucent Technologies, TSG-RAN WG1#28, R1-021239 (2002).
19. 3GPP, Evaluation of Combining Gains for MBMS (incl. STTD), Qualcomm, TSG-RAN WG1#28, R1-021234 (2002).
20. 3GPP, Power Usage for Mixed FACH and DCH for MBMS, Lucent Technologies, TSG-RAN WG1#28, R1-021240 (2002).
21. 3GPP, Technical Specification Group Radio Access Network; High Speed Downlink Packet Access (HSDPA); Stage 2 (Release 5), TS 25.308, version 5.4.0 (2002).
22. H. Holma and A. Toskala, *HSDPA/HSUPA for UMTS: High Speed Radio Access for Mobile Communications* (John Wiley & Sons, 2006).

Chapter 3

WIMAX/802.16 BROADBAND WIRELESS NETWORKS

MICHEL BARBEAU, PAUL BOONE and EVANGELOS KRANAKIS*
School of Computer Science, Carleton University,
1125 Colonel By Drive, Ottawa, ON, Canada, K1S 5B6
**kranakis@scs.carleton.ca*

WiMAX/802.16 is a kind of network providing IP-based broadband wireless access to infrastructure networks such as the Internet. The two main envisioned applications are Web access and voice over IP. Highlights of WiMAX/802.16 are secure communications and broadband access in remote areas. This chapter covers the background, physical layer, medium access control layer, mobility support, mesh mode and multihop relay operation of WiMAX/802.16. The chapter ends with a presentation of thoughts for practitioners and a discussion of directions for future research.

1. Introduction

Worldwide Interoperability for Microwave Access/IEEE 802.16 (WiMAX/802.16) is a technology for fixed or mobile and secure broadband wireless access (BWA). It is a wireless alternative to digital subscriber line (DSL). The main envisioned applications are wireless voice over IP, wireless Internet access and broadband wireless access in rural areas. Topics covered in this chapter include an overview of WiMAX/802.16, the physical (PHY) and medium access control (MAC) layers, mobility, mesh mode, multihop relay and security.

2. Background

WiMAX/802.16 was first published as the IEEE 802.16 standard that defines fixed Point-to-Multipoint (PMP) BWA in the 10–66 gigahertz (GHz) range. Amendment 802.16a adds control enhancements, mesh mode support, more frequencies in the 2–11 GHz range, non-line-of-sight communications and licensed or unlicensed operation [6]. Amendment 802.16c specifies implementation profiles [7]. This work has been combined into the 802.16-2004 standard [5]. Mobility support and improved security are introduced in 802.16e-2005 [8]. A management information base (MIB) is documented in 802.16f. Management plane procedures and services are covered in 802.16g. At this time, the latest full standard has been incorporated

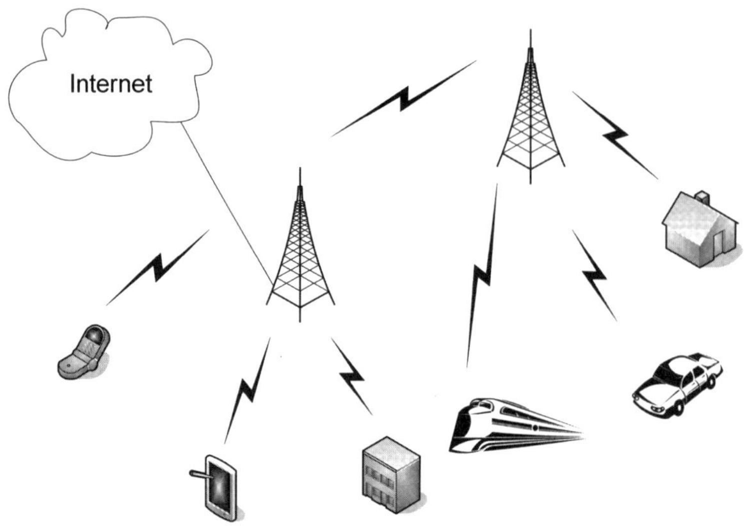

Fig. 1. A WiMAX/802.16 PMP network.

as 802.16-2008 [IEEE Standard for Local and Metropolitan Area Networks — Part 16: Air interface for fixed broadband wireless access systems, IEEE Standard 802.16-2008 (2008)]. Other IEEE standards are being drafted. The WiMAX Forum is an organization that addresses implementation certification of WiMAX/802.16 products and integration with second and third generation cellular technologies.

The main mode of operation of WiMAX/802.16 is PMP, pictured in Fig. 1. Subscriber stations (SSs), e.g., laptops, handhelds, cars or residences, get access to the network through an association with a base station (BS), pictured as a tower. The association physically takes the form of a wireless link. Logically, the WiMAX/802.16 service, at the link layer, is connection oriented. There are two categories of connections: management connections and transport connections. The former is used for control purposes while the latter is used to carry data traffic.

In contrast to WiFi/802.11, WiMAX/802.16 is designed for long-range wireless access covering several kilometers. WiFi/802.11 is designed for ranges in the order of about a hundred meters. WiMAX/802.16 is predominantly deployed by cellular or Internet service providers. Typically, WiFi/802.11 networks are used to cover smaller areas ranging from small hotspots in shops to larger areas such as an organization's campus. WiMAX/802.16 radios primarily operate in the licensed spectrum, although there is support for unlicensed operation. WiFi/802.11 operates exclusively in unlicensed spectrum ranges. The data rates of WiMAX/802.16 and WiFi/802.11 are both in the Mbps range. However, the WiFi/802.11 bandwidth is shared by all devices attached to the access point while the data rate is exclusive for WiMAX/802.16 devices. This results from WiFi/802.11 network access being contention-based. Devices in the network use carrier sense multiple access with collision avoidance (CSMA/CA) to compete for the channel and transmit. WiMAX/802.16 devices must establish a connection with a BS, competing a

Table 1. WiMAX/802.16 versus WiFi/802.11.

	WiMAX/802.16	WiFi/802.11
Regulation	Licensed and unlicensed spectrum	Unlicensed spectrum
Range	Kilometers	Meters
Rate	Exclusive Mbps	Shared Mbps
Access	FDD, TDD, TDMA	CSMA/CA
Service	Connection, QoS	Contention-based, best effort

single time during network entry. Once connected with a BS, all transmissions are scheduled by the BS. This leads to a much better quality of service (QoS) support in WiMAX/802.16 networks. A summary of the comparison can be reviewed in Table 1.

WiMAX/802.16 and WiFi/802.11 should be thought of as complementary technologies that can co-exist. WiMAX/802.16 is better suited for metropolitan area networks (MANs). WiFi/802.11 is better suited for local area networks (LANs). One possible scenario is to have WiMAX/802.16 providing the backbone Internet for WiFi/802.11 networks.

The WiMAX/802.16 network architecture is structured into two main layers: the physical (PHY) layer and the Medium Access Control (MAC) layer. The PHY is responsible for the transmission of streams of bits as electromagnetic signals. It is also responsible for the organization of the bit streams into periodic units of fixed lengths called frames. Frames are further divided into smaller units called bursts. The physical layer is a two-way mapping between MAC protocol data units (PDUs) and physical layer frames received and transmitted through coding and modulation of an RF signal. The clients of the MAC layer push data units such as IP packets or ATM cells at identified ports of the WiMAX/802.16 service interface called service access points (SAPs).

The MAC layer is subdivided into three sublayers as shown in Fig. 2. The convergence sublayer adapts data units, accepted through the SAPs, to the requirements of the MAC service data units (SDUs), and *vice versa*. That might involve, for instance, tasks such as fragmentation and reassembly. There could be several instances of the convergence sublayer according to the kind of adaptation required.

The convergence sublayer also de-multiplexes the MAC SDUs to the connections to which they belong. MAC SDUs are pushed on the common part sublayer. This layer contains the core of the WiMAX/802.16 logic. For instance, it encompasses all aspects of connection management. It creates the protocol data units (PDUs) that are mapped to frames by the PHY layer. The security sublayer addresses authentication, access control and confidentiality issues of the MAC layer traffic.

3. Physical Layer

Four choices are available at the PHY layer: WirelessMAN SC, SCa, OFDM or OFDMA. WirelessMAN-SC uses a single radio carrier. It is intended for frequencies

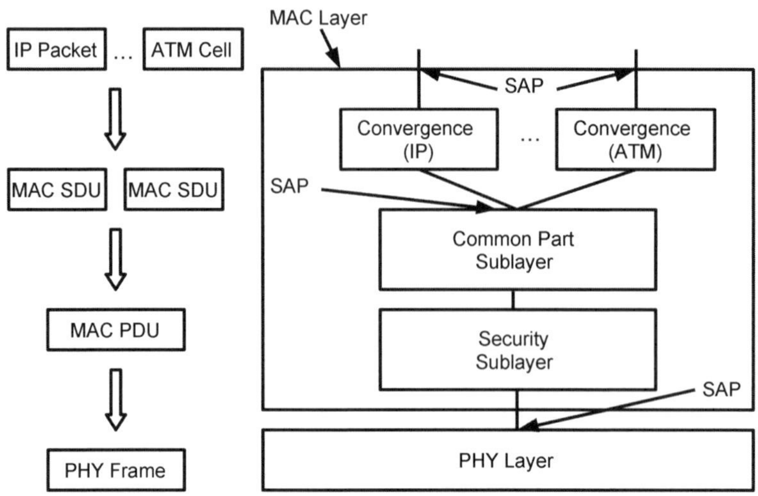

Fig. 2. Layered architecture of WiMAX/802.16.

in the range of 11–66 GHz. It requires line-of-sight (LOS). WirelessMAN-SCa uses a single-carrier at frequencies below 11 GHz and non-line-of-sight (NLOS). WirelessMAN orthogonal frequency division multiplexing (OFDM) and Orthogonal Frequency Division Multiple Access (OFDMA) are NLOS at frequencies below 11 GHz.

PMP communications consist of a BS and several SSs. The downlink, i.e., the BS to SSs channel, is determined by a frequency and a sector. The uplink, i.e., the SSs to BS channel, is determined by a frequency. If the downlink frequency and uplink frequencies are the same, then time division duplexing (TDD) is used to control the access to the channel. If the frequencies are different, then frequency division duplexing (FDD) is used. In addition, a time division multiple access (TDMA) technique is used on the uplink.

The flow of bits is structured as a sequence of frames of equal length. There is a downlink subframe and an uplink subframe. In FDD the downlink subframe and uplink subframe are simultaneous, but do not interfere because they are sent on different frequencies. In TDD, the downlink subframe and uplink subframe are consecutive and alternate. Various frame durations are supported between 2 and 20 ms in length. In TDD, the portion allocated to the downlink and portion allocated to the uplink may vary. A downlink subframe consists of a preamble, maps and data bursts (see Fig. 3). The preamble is a sequence of bits used for synchronization purposes. There are two maps. A downlink map announces the start position and transmission characteristics of the following data bursts. An uplink map announces the allocation of the bandwidth to the SSs for their transmission.

In the sequence of data bursts, each burst is transmitted according to a kind of modulation and a kind of forward error correction (FEC). They are sent in increasing

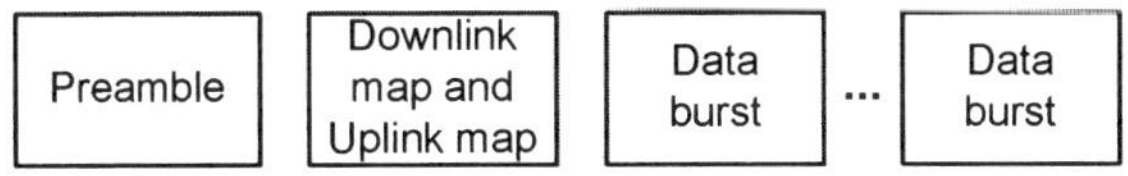

Fig. 3. A TDD downlink subframe.

Table 2. WiMAX data rates example.

	Data rate (Mbps)		
Channel bandwidth (MHz)	QPSK	16-QAM	64-QAM
20	32	64	96
25	40	80	120
30	44.8	89.6	134.4

degree of decoding difficulty, that is, in increasing level of data rate. Hence, an SS may only decode the bursts up to its reception capabilities and may ignore the bursts it cannot demodulate.

Table 2 gives the transmission characteristics of three modulation schemes. Quadrature Phase-Shift Keying (QPSK) uses four different symbols and can hence encodes two bits per symbol. 16-quadratute amplitude modulation (16-QAM) uses 16 different symbols and encodes four bits per symbol. It doubles the data rate of QPSK. 64-quadrature amplitude modulation (64-QAM) uses 64 different symbols and can encode six bits per symbol. It triples the data rate of QPSK. The degree of decoding difficulty increases with the data rate because the received signal needs to be stronger. In a downlink subframe, data bursts encoded with QPSK would be transmitted first, followed by the 16-QAM bursts and finally the 64-QAM data bursts.

An FDD downlink subframe contains a TDMA portion assigned to half duplex SSs. The TDMA portion consists of data bursts. Each data burst is assigned to a half duplex SS. A half duplex SS can transmit in a BS assigned TDMA data burst. Also, it needs to receive only when the BS transmits its data burst. A TDMA data burst on the downlink is prefixed by a preamble, transmitted by the BS, to allow the target SS to synchronize. The start position of every TDMA data burst is defined in the downlink map. QPSK is used to send the preambles.

The exact structure of an uplink subframe is determined by the BS. An uplink subframe is made of an arrangement of three kinds of bursts, which may be repeated and appear in any order. The three kinds of bursts are ranging, bandwidth requests and transmission. They are all for SS transmissions destined to the BS. A ranging burst is multiple contention-based access. When an SS initializes its attachment to the network, the SS sends range request messages to the BS with increasing power levels until reception is acknowledged by the BS, which is done by returning a range response message. The requests are sent within a ranging burst. A bandwidth request burst is multiple access contention based, but access must be in response to

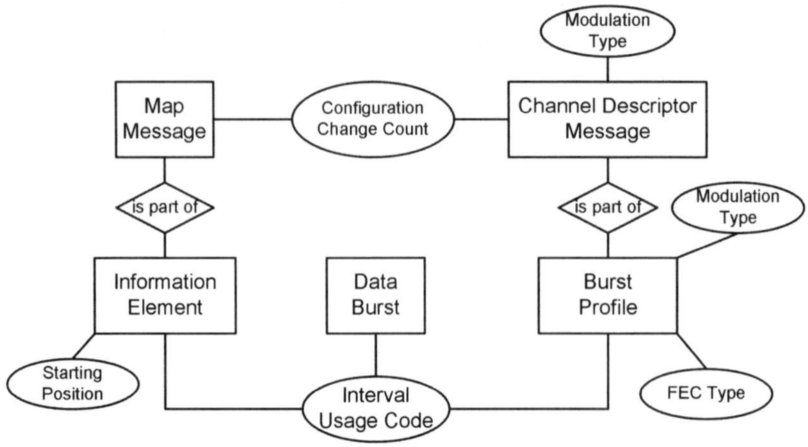

Fig. 4. Model of PHY and MAC concepts.

polling initiated by the BS. An SS may send a request for more bandwidth within such a burst. A transmission burst is a time interval granted to an SS by the BS.

The model of information of Fig. 4 represents the relationships existing among three key entities, that is, data burst, map message and channel descriptor message. Entities are represented by rectangles. Ovals represent their attributes. Lines depict relationships between entities. Data bursts are in downlink subframes and uplink subframes. A data burst is an interval of time during which data is transmitted. A data burst is identified by an interval usage code. A map message is either of type downlink or uplink and prefixes every downlink subframe. It is versioned with a number called a configuration change count. The version number matches the one of the corresponding channel descriptor message. A map message has a BS identifier. It contains a number of information elements. Each information element contains the starting position of a data burst, which is associated with the interval usage code.

A channel descriptor message is either of type downlink or uplink. It is sent periodically (maximum of 10 s between messages) in a MAC PDU. It is versioned with a number called a configuration change count. The version number matches the one of the corresponding map message. A channel descriptor message contains burst profiles. Each burst profile specifies the transmission characteristics of a data burst, which is associated to an information element with an interval usage code. The specification includes a modulation type and a FEC type.

OFDM is a transmission technique used to share the radio spectrum by several users. Another goal of OFDM is to construct communication channels using, for each of them, several segments distributed over a radio spectrum. This spreading mitigates, on the channel, the undesirable effects of fading or interference that may be stronger on some spectrum segments and weaker on others; it averages them in a sense.

The radio spectrum is divided into N adjacent subchannel elements. Each subchannel element is defined by a radio frequency that is used by a carrier. A channel consists of a number of subchannel elements. Each channel has its specific modulation parameters (rate, coding). The set of subchannel elements is divided into N_G groups. Each group contains N_E subchannel elements, i.e., N is equal to N_G times N_E. Each channel is constructed as the random selection of subchannel elements, each from different groups.

Example 1

Nine subchannel elements are used to constitute three channels. N_G is three and N_E is three. There are three groups: G_1, G_2 and G_3, each of them contains three subchannel elements. TDD is used for framing. Each frame is divided into five time slots. Each time slot on a channel can be assigned to an individual MAC layer connection. For instance, an individual connection may be assigned a sequence of time slots on a channel.

Example 2

A WiMAX/802.16 OFDMA scheme consists of 2,048 subchannel elements, i.e., N is equal to 2,048 [11]. Each subchannel occupies 187 KHz. TDD is used for framing, with TDMA on the uplink. Some subchannel elements are reserved for control purposes. For the downlink N_G is 48 and N_E is 32. For the uplink, N_G is 53 and N_E is 32.

4. Medium Access Control Layer

The PHY layer is responsible for sending bits of data from transmitters to receivers. It has no knowledge of the types of data that are transferred between parties. This is the responsibility of the MAC layer. The MAC layer controls access to the PHY layer from the higher layers in the protocol stack. The MAC layer has several other responsibilities including:

- building PDUs to be sent via the PHY layer,
- scheduling transmissions over the PHY layer,
- selecting PHY burst profiles and transmit power levels,
- providing QoS,
- retransmitting PDUs in case of error, and
- providing support for mobility.

4.1. *MAC Layer Concepts*

Figure 2 shows the three components of the MAC layer. The central element is the common part sublayer. It exchanges SDUs with the convergence sublayer. It also constructs PDUs, establishes connections and manages bandwidth. The common part is tightly integrated with the security sublayer. The security sublayer

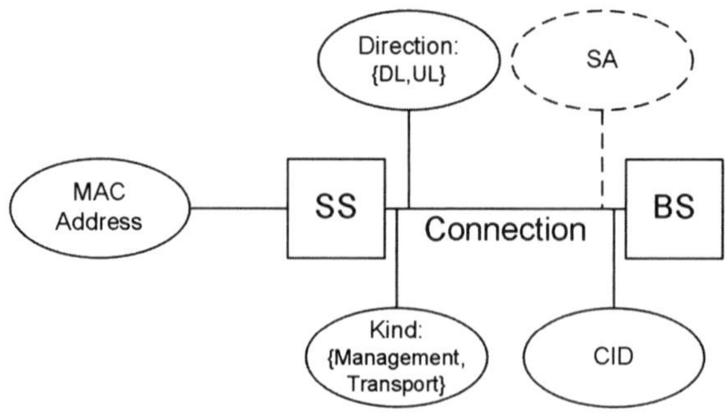

Fig. 5. Model of MAC concepts.

addresses authentication, authorization, key establishment and encryption. The security sublayer exchanges PDUs with the PHY layer.

A model of MAC concepts is shown in Fig. 5. The MAC layer is connection oriented. In order to offer services to SSs with various levels of QoS, all data communications are related to connections. An SS has a universal MAC address. A connection with a BS has a connection identifier (CID), direction [uplink (UL) or downlink (DL)], kind (management or transport) and an optional security association (SA) with the BS.

4.2. *Management Connections*

Table 3 summarizes the management connections. Following the ranging process, two pairs of management connections — one pair member for the uplink and one pair member for the downlink — are established between an SS and a BS. These are called the basic and primary uplink and downlink connections. An optional third pair of management connections, called the secondary management connections, may be created at the end of the network entry. The three pairs of connections handle the different QoS requirements of the management traffic between an SS and a BS. The basic connections are used by an SS and a BS to exchange short, time-urgent management messages, such as requests and responses for changes in burst profiles. The primary connections are used by an SS and a BS to exchange longer, delay-tolerant management messages, such as key management messages.

Table 3. Management connections.

Type	Usage
DL basic UL basic	Short and urgent management messages
DL primary UL primary	Delay tolerant management messages
DL secondary UL secondary	IP encapsulated management messages

Finally, the secondary management connections are used by an SS and a BS to transfer delay tolerant messages encapsulated in IP packets, such as DHCP, SNMP or TFP messages.

4.3. *MAC Protocol Data Units*

The common part sublayer is responsible for building PDUs with the SDUs received from the convergence sublayer. Depending on size, a SDU may be fragmented among multiple PDUs or several SDUs may be encapsulated inside a single PDU. There are two types of PDUs: the generic PDU and bandwidth request PDU.

The generic PDU carries user data and MAC layer control messages. The generic PDU contains a header, shown in Fig. 6, followed by a payload and a cyclic redundancy check (CRC) for error detection purposes. The bandwidth request PDU is used by SSs to request additional uplink bandwidth from a BS. It consists of a bandwidth request header, without payload and CRC.

The bandwidth request header is similar to the generic header shown in Fig. 6. The header is modified so that the 19 bits, starting at bit 5 and ending at the bit before the CID, holds the bandwidth request (BR) field. The BR field holds the number of bytes an SS is requesting from a BS. The header type (HT) field is set to one. The encryption control (EC) field is set to zero.

4.4. *Bandwidth Request and Allocation*

There are several messages sent by a BS in the downlink subframes. These include the downlink and uplink maps (DL-MAP and UL-MAP) and the downlink and uplink channel descriptors (DCD and UCD). The DL-MAP message defines the start time of every burst in the TDD downlink subframe and its TDMA portion. The UL-MAP message defines the structure of the uplink subframe by giving the offset of every burst. The DCD and UCD describe the PHY layer characteristics for the downlink and uplink.

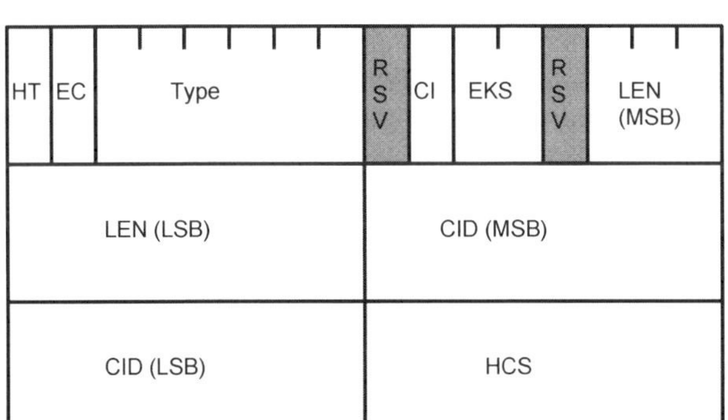

Field	Description
HT	Header type (set to 0)
EC	Encryption control (0=not encrypted, 1=encrypted)
Type	Type
CI	CRC Indicator (0=not present, 1=present)
EKS	Encryption key sequence
LEN	Length (including header)
CID	Connection ID for sending PDU
HCS	Header check sequence

Fig. 6. The generic MAC header.

Requests are sent by the SSs to ask for new uplink allocation from the BS. A request may be in the form of a standalone bandwidth request header or it may be a piggyback request, an optional feature. All bandwidth requests are made in terms of the number of bytes required to contain a MAC header and payload. The request may be transmitted during any allocated uplink slot, but not during the initial ranging interval. Bandwidth requests may be aggregate or incremental. If the BS receives an aggregate bandwidth request, then the number of bytes requested will be the new bandwidth allocation. If the BS receives an incremental bandwidth request, then the number of bytes requested will be added to the existing allocation.

A requested bandwidth is for an SS's individual connection, but the bandwidth granted by the BS is addressed to the SS's basic CID, not to individual CIDs. Since an SS does not necessarily know which request is being granted, it must either assign the bandwidth to its outstanding requests or decide to do a backoff and send additional bandwidth requests if short of bandwidth.

Polling is a mechanism where SSs are allocated bandwidth by the BS in order for them to make bandwidth requests. The allocations are not sent in an explicit message, but are contained as information elements (IEs) inside the UL-MAP. Polling may be done using unicast, multicast or broadcast. The UL-MAP and DL-MAP indicate the uplink and downlink allocations for all the SSs currently communicating with a BS.

4.5. *Service Flows*

Service flows define the parameters of transport connections. They are an important part of the bandwidth allocation process. An SS requests uplink bandwidth on a per connection basis, identifying the service flow, and the BS grants bandwidth as an aggregate of all the per connection requests. Service flows are characterized by a set of QoS parameters. These include latency, jitter and guaranteed throughput parameters. A service flow has a service flow ID (SFID).

The MAC layer maintains information about provisioned service flows that are used to create connections. This information is stored in the service provisioning tables, depicted in Fig. 7. From the provisioned service flow table, using the service class index, the QoS parameters for a flow are looked up in the service class table. These parameters include priority, minimum and peak rates, maximum burst, jitter and latency. The classifier rule table provides the rules for mapping IP packets to service flows. Their IP addresses and type of service value determine the service flow, using the service flow index.

4.6. *Quality of Service*

One of the distinguishing features of the MAC layer is the built-in QoS support for five kinds of service flows. An Unsolicited Grant Service (UGS) flow transports realtime traffic consisting of periodic fixed size packets. This is intended for T1/E1 or VoIP traffic. Bandwidth grants are of fixed size. An SS is not required to explicitly

Provisioned Service Flow Table				
Index	SS MAC Address	Direction	Service Class	State
1	00:00:00:00:00:01	DL	2	provisioned
2	00:00:00:00:00:02	UL	1	admitted

Service Class Table						
Class	Priority	Min Rate	Peak Rate	Max Burst	Jitter	Latency
1	0	2 Mbps	4 Mbps	6 Mbps	5 ms	50 ms
2	7	.5 Mbps	1 Mbps	2 Mbps	20 ms	100 ms

Classifier Rule Table			
Source IP Addr.	Dest. IP Addr.	Type of Service (TOS)	Service Flow Index
0.0.0.1		3	2
	0.0.0.3	4	1

Fig. 7. Service provisioning tables.

request bandwidth. A realtime polling service (rtPS) flow transports realtime traffic consisting of periodic variable size packets. This is suited for MPEG video traffic. To guarantee that the realtime needs are met, a BS provides realtime, periodic unicast request opportunities allowing an SS to specify the size of required bandwidth grants. An extended realtime polling service (ertPS) flow is an enhancement of both UGS and rtPS with unsolicited unicast bandwidth grants (as for UGS), while allowing variable size packets. This is intended for voice over IP services with silence suppression. A BS also allows an SS to request additional bandwidth as required. A non-realtime polling service (nrtPS) flow has unicast polls, on a regular basis, to ensure that the SS has bandwidth request opportunities even when the network is congested. It is intended for applications such as file transfers. A best-effort (BE) flow is designed for uplink traffic that has no QoS requirements.

4.7. *Network Entry*

An SS wanting to establish a connection with a BS follows the network entry procedure depicted in Fig. 8. The SS first scans to find a frequency in use by a BS. It listens to each possible frequency until it hears a frame preamble. The SS synchronizes with the BS by waiting for the DL-MAP and obtains the uplink channel characteristics from the UCD messages that are periodically broadcast by the BS. The SS then gets an Initial Ranging Interval from a DL-MAP message sent by the BS in order to perform initial ranging with the BS. Initial ranging determines the transmit power requirements and timing offsets of the SS in order to synchronize communication with the BS.

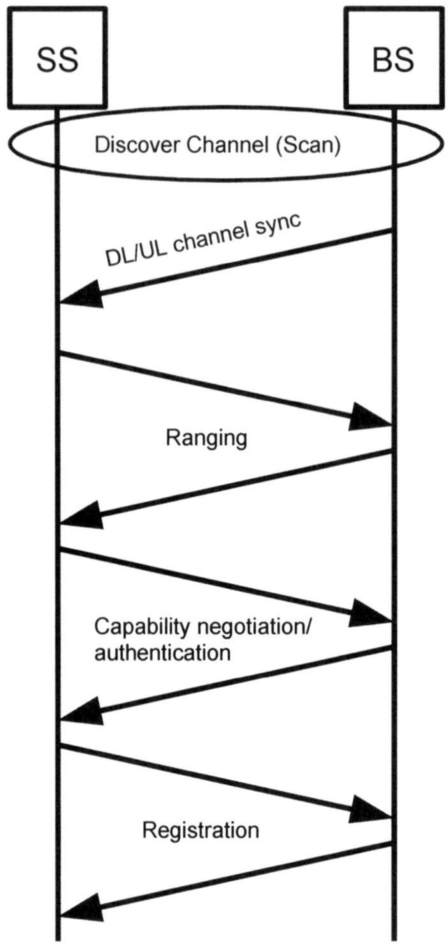

Fig. 8. Network entry procedure.

4.7.1. *Scanning*

The goal of scanning is to acquire a downlink signal from a BS. The exact number of frequencies depends on the regulatory provisioned bandwidth. It varies from one country to another. The number of frequencies is also determined by the choice of physical layer specification. Scanning continues periodically to aid SSs in the selection of suitable target BSs for a possible handover in order to maintain network connectivity in mobile WiMAX.

4.7.2. *Initial Ranging*

The initial ranging process, executed by an SS, determines the transmit power level and timing offset. The timing offset is used to synchronize each SS's transmission to a symbol marking the beginning of a minislot boundary for the SC and SCa PHY

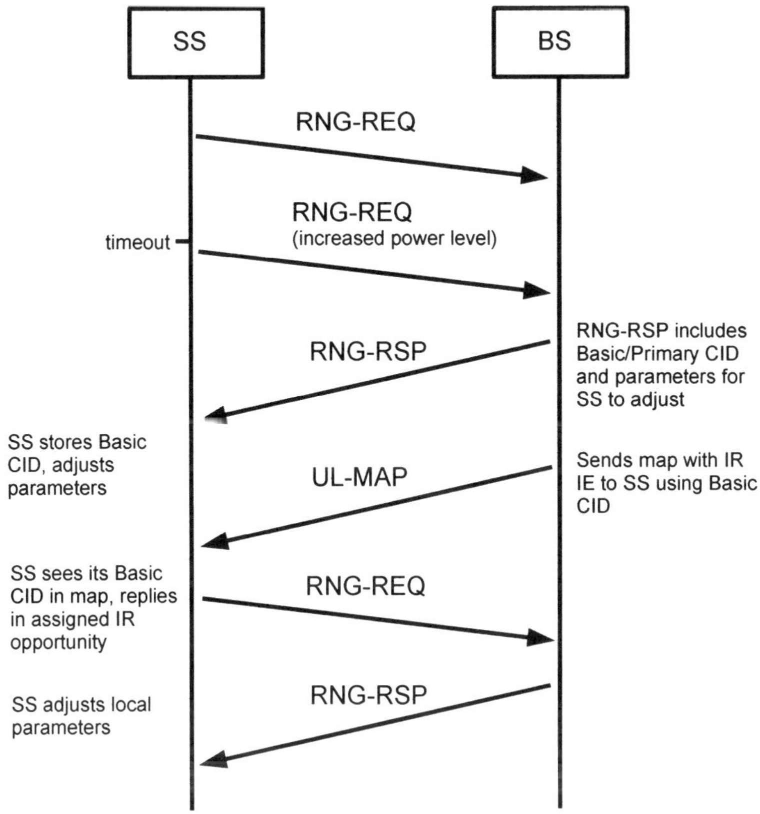

Fig. 9. Initial ranging process.

layers, or align its transmission with the BS received frame for the OFDM(A) PHY layers. Figure 9 shows the initial ranging procedure.

Once the SS has synchronized with the downlink channel and discovered the uplink channel parameters in the UCD message, it uses the UL-MAP message to determine the next initial ranging interval. Next, the SS sends a range request (RNG-REQ) message during the next interval with a CID set to zero. For OFDMA, the request is sent via code division multiple access (CDMA) using codes for initial ranging. The SS adjusts its transmission timings to account for delays, so that it appears to be collocated with the BS. The SS calculates the maximum signal strength P used for initial ranging as follows:

$$P = Max + (EIRP - RSS).$$

Max is the maximum equivalent isotropic received power for the BS receiver. $EIRP$ is the equivalent isotropic radiated power of the BS. Both are obtained from the DCD. RSS is the received signal strength measured at the SS. If the values of Max and $EIRP$ are unknown, then the SS starts sending the RNG-REQ message at a minimum power level, retransmitting and increasing power, during future ranging opportunities after a backoff period, until a BS receives the message. Once a BS has received an RNG-REQ message, it must return a range response (RNG-RSP) message with the same CID. The RNG-RSP message includes the basic and primary management CIDs assigned to the SS, as well as information on power level adjustment, offset frequency adjustment and timing offset corrections. If the status of the RNG-RSP is success, then the ranging procedure completes. If not, then the SS uses scheduled ranging intervals to complete the ranging process.

4.7.3. *Negotiating Basic Capabilities*

Negotiating basic capabilities is a necessary step because WiMAX/802.16 is broad, with core functionality that must be supported by all vendors along with optional functionality that different vendors may or may not support. In order for equipment from different vendors to operate together, they must negotiate the set of capabilities that the BS and SS both support. An example is what PHY burst profiles (e.g., 64 QAM) are supported. The negotiation is a handshake beginning with the SS sending a basic capabilities request (SBC-REQ) message to the BS indicating its capabilities. The BS replies with a basic capabilities response (SBC-RSP) message that includes the capabilities common to both the SS and BS.

4.7.4. *Registration*

Registration is the process of allowing an SS to enter the network and to receive a secondary management CID. In order to register with the network, the SS sends a registration request (REG-REQ) message to the BS. This message includes information such as uplink CID support, IP version, SS capabilities, convergence sublayer support, ARQ settings and vender specific information. The BS replies with a registration response (REG-RSP) message that includes the secondary management CID. At this point, the SS can establish IP connectivity via DHCP over the secondary management connection.

4.7.5. *Establishing a Service Flow*

Service flows can be established either from the SS or BS side depending on whether the traffic arriving is on the uplink or downlink. Figure 10 shows the creation of a service flow initiated by a BS. Here the BS checks to determine if the SS is authorized for service and if the QoS requirements can be met with the available resources. It then creates a new SFID with the required class of service and sends this information in a dynamic service addition request (DSA-REQ) message to the SS. If the SS supports the service, then it will respond using a dynamic service addition response (DSA-RSP) message. The SS also reserves the required resources and enables downlink reception. When it receives the response, the BS enables uplink reception. Finally, the BS completes the procedure by sending an

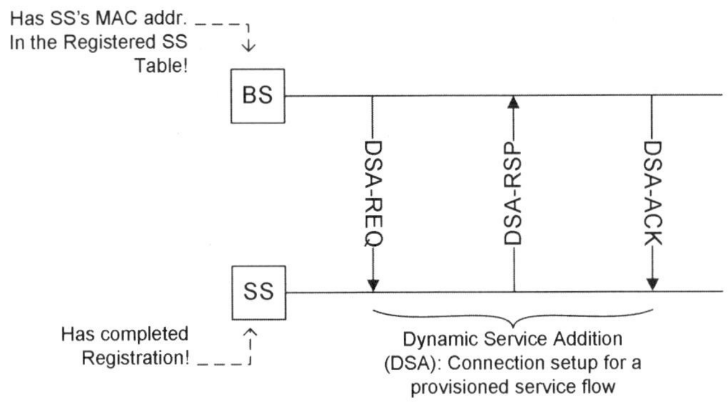

Fig. 10. Establishing a service flow: BS initiated.

acknowledgment (DSA-ACK) message. Both the BS and SS are now ready for reception and transmission can start in both directions.

When an SS wishes to establish a service flow it sends the BS a DSA-REQ message. Upon reception, the BS checks the integrity of the message and responds with a dynamic service received (DSX-RVD) message. The BS then determines if the SS is authorized for the service and if there are resources available to meet the QoS parameters. The BS then creates a new SFID with the required class of service and sends this in a DSA-RSP response message to the SS. The final step is for the SS to acknowledge the response using a DSA-ACK acknowledgment message. Both the BS and SS are now ready for reception and transmission can start in both directions.

5. Mobile WiMAX and Handovers

WiMAX/802.16 supports mobility. Mobility specific issues for the PHY layer, network support for mobility and handovers are discussed hereafter.

5.1. *Physical Layer*

For mobility support purposes, the OFDMA PHY layer has been adapted to use SOFDMA (scalable OFDMA). Here the number of subchannel elements can be chosen to optimize performance according to the channel and the radio conditions. The number of subchannel elements can be 128, 512, 1,024 or 2,048.

5.2. *Determining Network Topology*

To aid mobile stations (MSs) in discovering neighboring BSs, the BSs periodically broadcasts information about the network topology using neighbor advertisement (MOB_NBR-ADV) messages. BSs can obtain this information over the backbone network. These advertisements provide the MS with information that they would otherwise obtain by scanning.

BSs assign time for MSs to scan for neighboring BSs. The time that an MS has allocated for scanning is called the scanning interval. A BS may also schedule time to perform interleaving scanning for neighboring BSs. Interleaving scanning is the alternation of sending data and scanning. The MS requests a scanning interval by sending a MOB_SCN-REQ message to the BS including a requested amount of time. The BS responds with a MOB_SCN-RSP message either granting or denying the request. When the MS has been granted a scanning opportunity, it starts scanning for one or more neighboring BSs during the time allotted, beginning at the start frame indicated in the response message.

5.3. *Association Procedure*

Association is an optional initial ranging operation that can be done during the scanning interval. This is done between an MS and one of its neighboring BSs. There are three levels of association possible during the scanning interval.

Level 0 (scan/association without coordination): The MS performs ranging without assistance from the network. Ranging is contention based. It is successful if the MS receives the success RNG-RSP message from the neighboring BS.

Level 1 (association with coordination): The serving BS provides the MS with association parameters (ranging codes and transmission opportunity) for target BSs. This allows the MS to perform collision free ranging and succeeds when it receives the success RNG-RSP message from a neighboring BS.

Level 2 (network assisted association reporting): Similar to Level 1, but after the MS has sent its RNG-REQ message it does not need to wait for the RNG-RSP message from a BS. Instead, the RNG-RSP containing information about the PHY layer timing offsets of neighboring BSs is sent to the serving BS over the backbone network. The serving BS may send an aggregation of all this information to the MS in an association report (MOB_ASC-REP) message.

5.4. *Handovers*

As an MS moves throughout the coverage area, maintaining connectivity is done via performing handovers between neighboring BSs. An example of a handover, where an MS must choose one of six neighboring BSs, is shown in Fig. 11. In this case neighbor six is chosen. Selection of the best handover target can be complex since the MS must scan for neighboring BSs to find a suitable target based on a number of criteria such as signal strength or error rates. Since a handover is an important function, an MS should perform the scanning and determine a target BS before beginning the handover. Uplink and downlink communication can be temporarily suspended, between an MS and a BS, in order to allow the MS to perform scanning for neighboring BSs. While communication is suspended, the data streams must be buffered on either side.

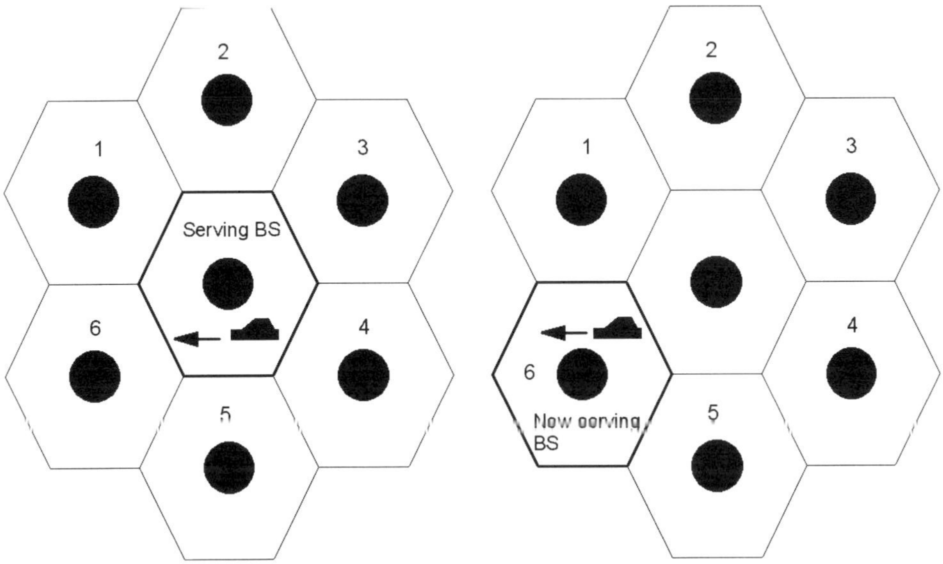

Fig. 11. A mobile station handover.

5.5. *Handover Process*

A handover is a process during which an MS changes its connections from one BS to another neighboring BS. From the perspective of an MS, the handover process is comprised of a number of steps including cell reselection, handover decision and initiation, synchronization with a target BS, ranging, negotiating capabilities, and authentication.

Network assisted handovers are supported in mobile WiMAX. Every BS obtains information about neighboring BSs over the backbone network. The BS periodically sends that information as a mobility neighbor advertisement (MOB_NBR-ADV) message to the MSs. For cell reselection, an MS may use information acquired from the MOB_NBR-ADV messages or may make a request to schedule scanning intervals to scan and perform ranging with a potential target neighboring BS. The handover decision and initiation may originate either at the MS or the serving BS. The notification of intent to handover is sent in either a mobility MS handover request (MOB_MSHO-REQ) message from the MS or a mobility BS handover request (MOB_BSHO-REQ) message from the BS. Scanning and obtaining the downlink and uplink transmission parameters of the neighboring BSs allows an MS to synchronize with the target neighbor BS. If the MS has received a MOB_NBR-ADV message including a potential target BSs identifier, frequency and channel descriptors, then this procedure can be shortened.

It is possible that a target neighboring BS has received a handover notification from the serving BS over the backbone allowing the target to assign the MS a scheduled ranging opportunity. The MS and target BS must conduct the ranging process in order to determine transmission power level and timing offsets. If the MS includes the serving BS identifier in the RNG-REQ message, then the target BS may use the backbone network to request information about the MS from the serving BS. The target BS can then decide which of the remaining network entry steps may be skipped.

6. Mesh Mode and Multihop Relay

WiMAX/802.16 has an optional fixed mesh mode, and multihop relay (MR) is being developed as part of IEEE 802.16j [9]. Mesh mode is a mechanism that increases network coverage without growing the number of BSs. MR addresses the same issue, but is it more compatible with the PMP mode and supports MSs.

6.1. *Mesh Mode*

In the PMP mode, service is established only between SSs and BSs. In mesh mode, service can be also established between SSs. Basic functions such as network synchronization and transmission scheduling are based on the neighbor information that all nodes (BSs and SSs) are required to maintain. All nodes must keep a physical neighborhood list storing information such as MAC addresses, hop counts and node IDs. This information is used to determine how to synchronize and to schedule data transmissions.

6.1.1. *Network Entry Procedure*

The mesh network configuration (MSH-NCFG) and mesh network entry (MSH-NENT) messages are used to advertise the mesh network and aid new SSs attempting to synchronize and join. MSH-NENT is sent on the basic channel by an SS wishing to join the network. MSH-NCFG is an advertisement that is broadcast to all one-hop neighbors. Nodes currently participating in a mesh must periodically send a MSH-NCFG beacon including a network descriptor that contains information on the base channel in use as well as the BS identifier. A new SS entering a mesh (called a candidate node) must scan for MSH-NCFG messages in order to synchronize and begin the network entry procedure.

An SS remains synchronized with a network as long as it is receiving MSH-NCFG messages from neighbors. The SS collects the MSH-NCFG messages until it has received one from the same neighbor twice, as well as containing the ID of an operator matching one of its own.

From all of the MSH-NCFG messages heard, a candidate node chooses a potential sponsor node. The sponsoring node is used to negotiate basic capabilities and get authorized on the network. This process, shown in Fig. 12, begins with the candidate node sending an MSH-NENT:NetEntryRequest message to the sponsor node to open a sponsor channel. If the sponsor node accepts the request, them it opens a sponsor channel by responding with an MSH-NCFG:NetEntryOpen

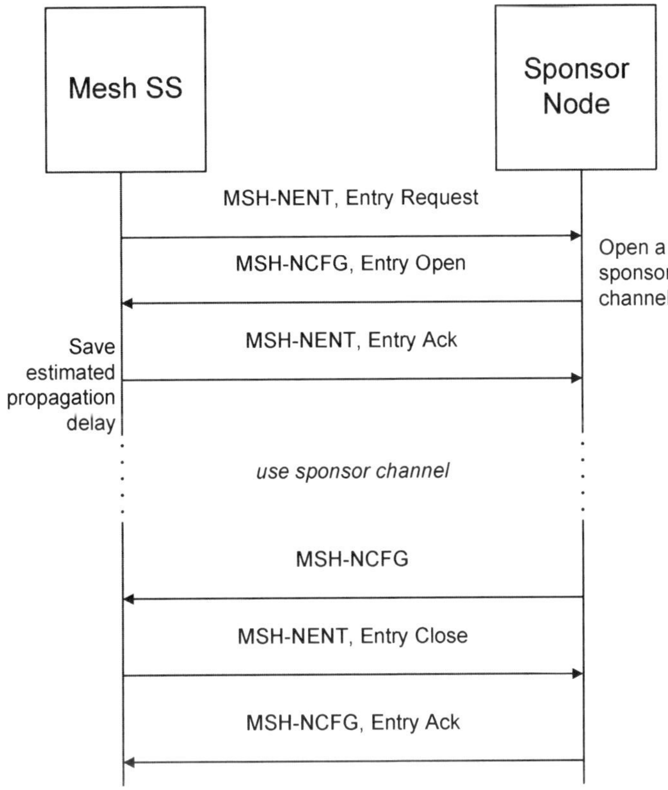

Fig. 12. Mesh mode network entry.

message including the candidate node's MAC address and scheduling information. The candidate node then acknowledges with an MSH-NENT:NetEntryAck message. The sponsor channel can now be used according to the scheduling information received from the network entry open message to negotiate basic capabilities, get authorized and register with the network, obtain an IP address, the time of day and download operational parameters. Once completed, the sponsor channel can be closed by the candidate node sending an MSH-NENT:EntryClose message to the sponsoring node and receiving an MSH-NCFG:EntryAck in response from the sponsor node. The SS is now a full member of the mesh.

Once an SS has entered the network, it is allowed to form new links with its other neighbors by using the MSH-NCFG message with the neighbor link establishment option. Figure 13 shows this in operation. When Node A wishes to establish a new link with one of its neighbors it listens for a MSH-NCFG message and obtains the frame number. Node A then sends a challenge in the form of *HMAC{Operator shared secret, frame number, NodeIDA, NodeIDB}* along with a frame number to Node B. HMAC is the hashed message authentication calculated with the secure hash algorithm SHA-1.

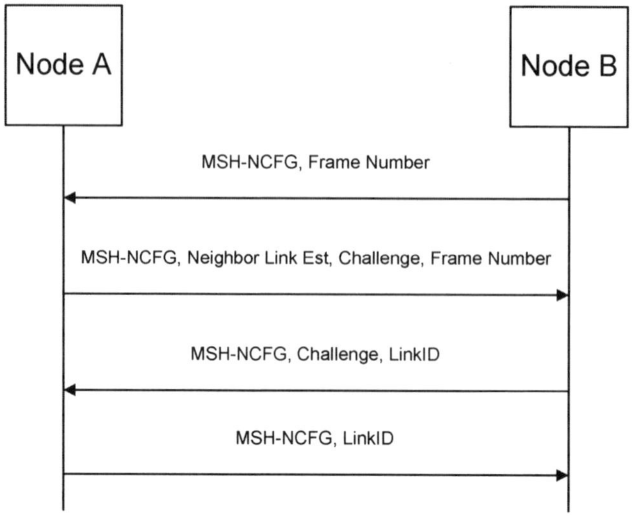

Fig. 13. Establishing new links in mesh mode.

Node B performs the same computation and compares the results to the value sent by Node A. If the values match, then Node B accepts the connection implicitly by sending a new challenge similar to the one sent by Node A. This time the frame number used in the calculation is the one sent by Node A. Node B also sends a random unused link ID with the challenge response. Node A checks validity of the challenge response and sends an MSH-NCFG:Accept along with a random unused link ID to complete the creation of a new link between A and B.

6.1.2. *Scheduling Transmissions*

Transmissions in mesh mode are TDMA based and, as such, they are coordinated and scheduled. Transmission scheduling can be done in a centralized fashion (coordinated by the mesh BS), in distributed fashion, or a combination of both. Transmissions are assigned to one of three types of logical channels: basic, broadcast or data. The basic channels are used for SS ranging and network entry messages. The broadcast channel is used for control information. The data channels are used for mostly data traffic.

6.1.2.1. Centralized scheduling

In centralized scheduling, the transmission schedule for all mesh SSs is determined by the mesh BS. The mesh BS determines the assignments of flows based on the resource requests of the mesh SSs and distributes this information to nodes in the mesh via a routing tree topology. The SSs can determine the schedule based on the assignment of flows by using a predetermined algorithm. The mesh BS acts similarly to normal PMP BSs with the exception that they may not be in direct communication with the SSs. The resource requests and assignments are sent in the control portion of the frames. Two control messages are used in establishing centralized scheduling: mesh centralized scheduling (MSH-CSCH) and mesh centralized schedule configuration (MSH-CSCF). MSH-CSCF is used to distribute a global tree topology to mesh nodes. As nodes receive MSH-CSCF messages, the multicast routing tree can be constructed (with the BS as the root), and transmission opportunities calculated. The MSH-CSCH message is created by the mesh BS and is broadcast to all its neighbors. All these neighbors with a hop count lower than a hop count threshold forward the message to neighbors further away from the mesh BS. Nodes in the mesh use MSH-CSCH messages to request bandwidth from the mesh BS by setting a grant/request flag bit and sending this message to their parents in the routing tree. All nodes report the bandwidth request of neighbors of their children in their routing subtree up to the mesh BS.

When a node receives a new schedule, it computes the time it must transmit the schedule further down the routing tree, the frame at which the last node in the tree receives the message and the mesh BS transmission time of the message. This is completed by performing the following actions:

(i) the mesh BS transmits first;
(ii) eligible children of mesh BS transmit — in the order they appear in the routing tree;
(iii) eligible children of the nodes from Step (ii) transmit — in the order they appear in the routing tree;
(iv) the process repeats until all eligible nodes in the routing tree have transmitted.

All nodes are required to compute timings of uplink requests. Uplink requests may begin in the last frame that a node has received the previous schedule. All nodes except the mesh BS are eligible to transmit and must do so starting from the bottom of the routing tree.

6.1.2.2. Distributed scheduling

Distributed scheduling may be coordinated or uncoordinated. In coordinated distributed scheduling, both the BS and SSs must coordinate their transmissions within their two-hop neighborhood to avoid interference. Every node in coordinated mode uses a portion or all of the control part of each frame to regularly send its schedule, and any schedule changes it proposes, to all its neighbors. On a given channel all neighbor stations receive the same schedule transmissions. All stations in the mesh must use this same channel. This ensures that transmissions can be scheduled in a manner independent of any BS.

Both coordinated and uncoordinated modes must use a three-way handshake:

(i) an MSH-DSCH:Request is made with an MSH-DSCH:Availabilities message indicating potential time slots for a reply as well as the current schedule;

(ii) an MSH-DSCH:Grant message is sent in reply and includes a subset of the availabilities, if any, that match the request. Any neighbor not involved in the schedule assumes that it has been approved;
(iii) an MSH-DSCH:Grant message is sent by the original node and includes a copy of the grant message from Step (ii) as a confirmation.

The main differences between coordinated and uncoordinated distributed scheduling are that in the coordinated case the MSH-DSCH messages are scheduled in the control frame while in the uncoordinated case the MSH-DSCH messages must contend for the channel. In the uncoordinated mode, any node responding to a request must wait a certain amount of time before sending a grant so that any node listed earlier in the request is able to respond. The grant confirmation is sent in the first available slot after receiving the grant message.

6.2. *Multihop Relay*

Mesh mode has a few disadvantages that need to be overcome, including a lack of compatibility with the PMP mode due to a different PHY frame structure, a different MAC network entry procedure, and no mobility support. Multihop relay (MR) addresses these disadvantages. The goal of MR is to enhance coverage, throughput and system capacity by the introduction of relay stations and enhanced protocols to support multihop relay. The specifications for MR capabilities as well as the interoperability between relay stations and BSs are currently being defined.

6.2.1. *MR Base Stations and Relay Stations*

An MR base station (MR-BS) is a BS that supports multihop relay. Unlike mesh mode, where SSs relay messages for each other in the mesh, MR introduces relay stations (RSs) to provide a path to the MR-BS. All RSs are managed by an MR-BS but have some control over relaying traffic in their neighborhood. An RS provides the following functionality:

- relays user data and/or control information between other stations, and
- maintains processes that indirectly support MR.

There are three levels of RS mobility: fixed, nomadic and mobile. Fixed RSs are deployed in a fixed position and are never moved (tower, rooftop, side of building). Nomadic RSs are portable — they can be moved about — but only operate from a stationary position. Mobile RSs operate when they are in motion. If the route is fixed, such as an RS located on a train, additional support RSs can be planned along the route. However, RSs may also move about without a predetermined path.

6.2.2. *Usage Models*

There are a number of usage models being defined to handle various multihop relay modes of operation. Topologies in MR can support routes of two or more hops and redundant routes may be maintained in order to improve network throughput and balance the network traffic.

6.2.2.1. Fixed infrastructure usage model

In this scenario, depicted in Fig. 14, a service provider deploys RSs and MR-BSs in order to enhance coverage, capacity, or throughput in areas that are not adequately serviced by a BS or to extend coverage outside the range of a BS. Fixed RSs owned by the service provider are used in this model. The provider is able to plan the deployment of RSs to provide line-of-sight conditions to other RSs or the MR-BS wherever possible. Examples of this usage model include cell edge coverage, covering holes (from shadowing) or coverage outside a cell's area.

6.2.2.2. In-building coverage usage model

In this scenario, one or more RSs are deployed to enhance coverage within a building, tunnel or underground facility. The RSs can be either provider or customer owned and typically only need to have basic functionality. The links are expected to be non-line-of-sight and the RS may have more than one antenna on the outside of a building to connect to another RS or the MR-BS. RSs may be deployed inside or outside buildings, and RSs owned by the customer may enter and leave the network at any time.

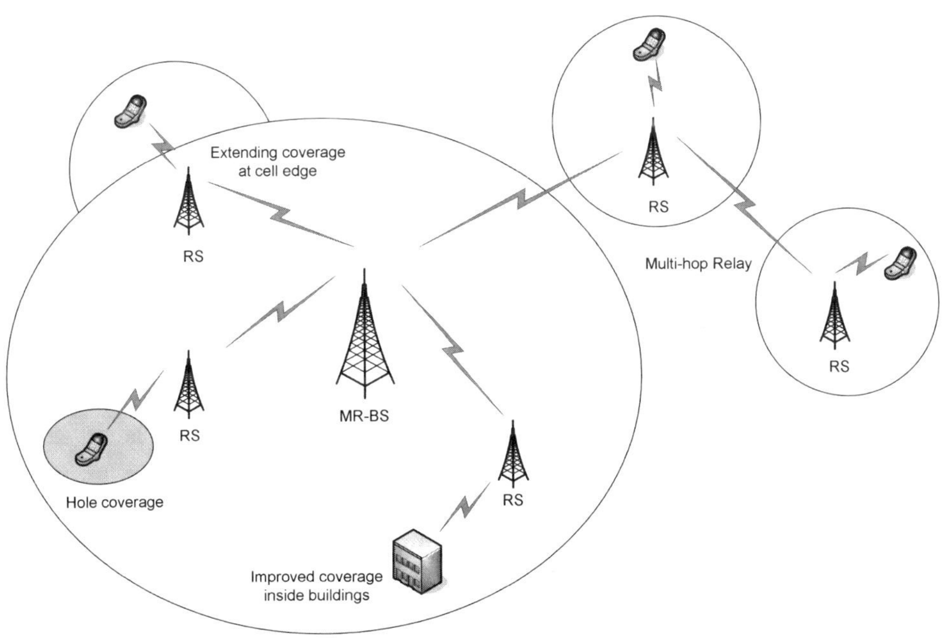

Fig. 14. MR fixed infrastructure usage model.

6.2.2.3. Temporary coverage usage model

In this scenario, nomadic RSs are deployed to provide temporary coverage to desired areas that may not have sufficient coverage by existing MR-BSs or other RSs. RSs enter the network upon deployment, and leave the network when the service is no longer required. Both line-of-sight and non-line-of-sight conditions can be expected for the RS communications with the MR-BS. Examples of this scenario include emergency, disaster recovery or special event coverage.

6.2.2.4. Mobile vehicle coverage usage model

This scenario covers situations where multiple MSs are traveling together on a vehicle such as a bus or a train. A mobile RS is located on the vehicle to connect with a MR-BS or RS. The mobile RS provides a fixed access link to MSs on the vehicle over a mobile link to the MR-BS or another RS. The mobile RS may enter and leave the network as it travels, moving in or out of the area of coverage. The mobile RS may also enter or leave the network on a fixed schedule such as the first/last run of the vehicle for the day.

7. WiMAX Security Model

Wireless LANs have attained significant commercial success because of their ease of use and deployment as well as the wider possibilities offered to users. WiFi/802.11 and WiMAX/802.16 have had a great impact on the market. They have changed the user's perception of ease and convenience in networking. Despite the obvious advantages offered by mobility to end users, drawbacks in user security and access have become evident. In this section, we focus on the security characteristics of WiMAX/802.16. We outline various security features including encryption, authentication, security associations, and key establishment and exchange. We begin with a brief introduction to WiFi/802.11.

7.1. *IEEE 802.11*

IEEE 802.11 is currently the most widespread wireless LAN standard. Recent versions allow for data rates of up to 54 Mbps. One of its major security disadvantages has been the Wired Equivalent Privacy (WEP) protocol [supporting only one encryption mechanism, the stream cipher RC4, using a pre-shared secret key and a per-packet initialization vector (IV) as input]. It was broken by the end of 2001. In addition, a cyclic redundancy check (CRC-32) is appended to a packet before it is encrypted in order to provide integrity protection. This too was shown to be ineffective by 2001. In WEP, the authentication server (AS), encryption and integrity protection endpoint (EIPE) and network access point coincide. Since the pre-shared secret key is used directly for authentication and encryption, neither key transfer from AS to EIPE nor security associations and negotiations are necessary. In fact no key agreement or key establishment is being used. Meyer gives a comprehensive introduction [15].

Many different (and sometimes incompatible) proprietary solutions were since developed until finally the new IEEE 802.11i standard was adopted in 2004. It supports additionally the Advanced Encryption Standard (AES).

7.2. *IEEE 802.16*

IEEE 802.16 was developed to address wireless access for the last mile and its working group sought from the beginning to avoid the design mistakes of IEEE 802.11 by incorporating into it a pre-existing standard. Nevertheless, Johnston and Walker in their recent article criticize the adoption of Data Over Cable Service Interface Specifications (DOCSIS) [10]. Although designed to solve the last mile problem for cable, it has an otherwise different threat model from IEEE 802.16 since the former is wired while the latter is wireless technology [13].

IEEE 802.16 defines a separate security sublayer within the MAC layer that is in charge of authentication, secure key exchange and encryption. It encrypts connections between an SS and a BS. It also provides strong protection to operators against theft of service. It uses a key management protocol whereby the BS distributes keys to the SS.

7.2.1. *Traffic Encryption Key*

Traffic encryption keys (TEKs) are used to encrypt data. Encryption of a TEK is made possible using any of the following three algorithms: (a) two-key 3-DES in EDE mode, (b) RSA and (c) 128-bit AES in ECB mode. The value fields of a TEK, in a reply message sent to a client SS by a BS, are encrypted using one of the previous three algorithms. After authorization, BSs provide separate TEK for each Security Association ID (SAID) in the authorization reply message. The TEK state machine sends key request messages to the BS periodically, requesting refreshed keying material for their respective SAIDs. The TEK is encrypted using the key exchange key derived from an authorization key. The key reply contains the TEK, a CBC initialization vector (IV), as well as the remaining lifetime of each of the two sets of keying. The BS is also generating authorization keys (AKs), TEKs and IVs using a pseudo-random number generator. AKs in authorization reply messages shall be RSA public-key encrypted using the SS's public key.

7.2.2. *Encryption*

The encryption protocol encrypts only the packet MAC PDU payload while leaving the MAC header unencrypted. Public key cryptography is used to derive a shared AK, but this key is used thereafter only as a means to derive the subsequent keying material. IEEE 802.16-2004 supports CBC-Mode 56-bit DES and CCM mode AES. The former was first supported in the IEEE 802.16-2001 to encrypt the MAC PDU payload, while the latter was first supported in the IEEE 802.16-2004, again for the encryption of the MAC PDU payload.

For DES CBC-Mode, different IVs are used for the downlink and uplink. In the downlink, the CBC initial value is calculated using the XOR of the IV included in the TEK key and content of the PHY synchronization field of the latest DL-MAP. In the uplink, the CBC initial value is calculated with XOR of the initial value in the TEK key and content of the PHY synchronization field of the DL-MAP that is in effect when the UL-MAP for the uplink transmission is created/received.

For AES in CCM mode, the MAC PDU payload is preprocessed by prepending an unencrypted four-byte packet number (PN). An eight-byte integrity check value (ICV) is appended to the payload. The PDU plaintext and ICV are encrypted and authenticated using the active TEK key.

7.2.3. *Authentication*

The basic model used is based on the IEEE 802.1X security model for authentication and access control which has been implemented in IEEE 802.11i and IEEE 802.16e networks. As depicted in Fig. 15, three entities are defined in the network: (i) the client (requesting access to the network), (ii) an access point and (iii) an authentication server (AS), i.e., a database containing the credentials needed to accept or deny access to clients. 802.1X enables port-based authentication: all stations have associated ports and traffic is blocked in the station port until an AS authenticates the client. The authentication process is summarized in Fig. 16.

The Privacy Key Management (PKM) protocol provides for secure distribution of keys between a BS and an SS whereby the former acts as a server and the latter

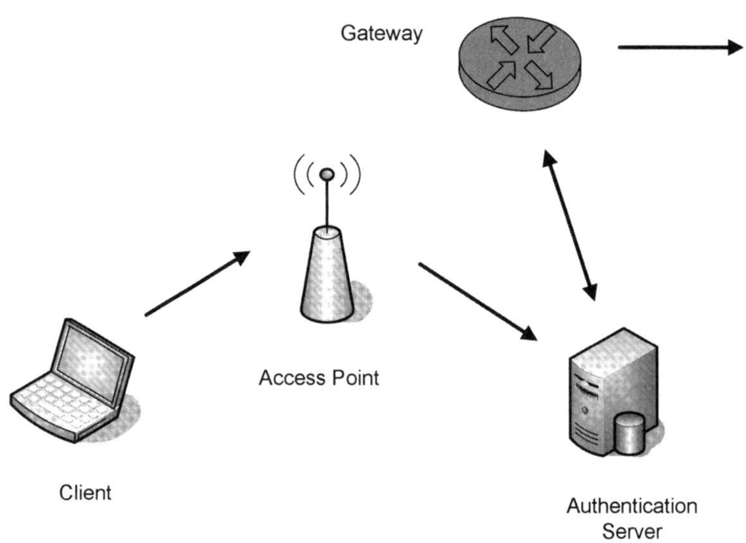

Fig. 15. Basic IEEE 802.1X scheme.

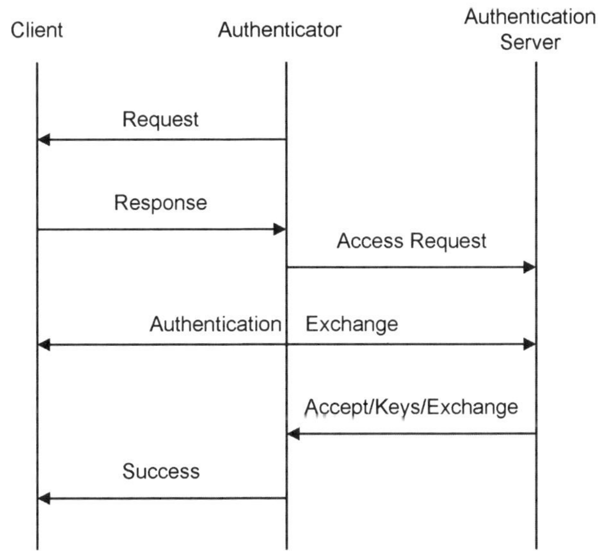

Fig. 16. Protocol authentication in the IEEE 802.1X scheme.

as a client. Information exchanged also includes how to access the several network services.

Periodic reauthorization and key refresh is also supported when the SS requests material from the BS. WiMAX/802.16 uses Public-Key Infrastructure (PKI) authentication, in which trusted authorities identify parties to a transmission via digital certificates. In addition, the PKM uses X.509 digital certificates, RSA public-key encryption algorithms and strong encryption algorithms to perform key exchanges. The digital certificate contains both the SS's public key and MAC address. Upon receipt of an authorization request from an SS, the BS verifies the digital certificate and, if valid, generates an AK which it encrypts with the SS's public key before sending it back to the SS.

7.2.4. *Security Associations*

A security association (SA) concerns the establishment of shared security information between an SS and a BS in order to support secure communications. SAs maintain the security state and keying material used to protect a connection [16]. When the two entities communicate, the subscriber may be interested in more than one service, each of which may have different service primitives like a data encryption algorithm, public key or initialization vector. Therefore an SA includes cryptographic keys, key lifetime, initialization vectors and/or digital certificates. A new authentication request is required if the SS's keying material has expired. It is the subscriber's responsibility to request this material from the BS. Service disruptions (during reauthorization) are prevented by maintaining successive generations of the authentication keys with overlapping lifetimes. SSs and BSs must be able to support up to two active authorization keys simultaneously. In response to en(dis)abling service, a BS can dynamically establish and eliminate SAs. This can be done by issuing an SA add message and further establishing a TEK.

7.3. *Other Security Issues*

As suggested by Xu *et al.*, mobility increases the vulnerability of authentication and key management protocols [18, 19]. Multicast is another issue, where authentication and key management protocols should be revised to facilitate the multicast functions. Yuksel has completed a detailed analysis of the PKM protocol [20]. An important issue also concerns secure roaming and handover procedures, which is studied by Meyer [15].

8. Thoughts for Practitioners

Wireless networks are of growing omnipresence in every facet of our lives and the threats to their security must be uncovered and addressed. Their performance must be maximized. Broadband wireless access mesh networks enable the deployment of multimedia services in rural areas and emergency situations. Applications of broadband wireless networks include emergency communications, last-mile networks and numerous Web-based services. Broadband wireless networks can provide a backup network infrastructure when the wired infrastructure is damaged and unusable. Hurricane Katrina destroyed the telecommunications infrastructure in Louisiana. WiMAX/802.16 was used after the hurricane to link to the Internet isolated rural communities of Louisiana. An important application is wireless last-mile networks that deliver data at high speed to subscribers that cannot be serviced by digital subscriber loops, because it is not economically viable. The high speed of WiMAX/802.16 addresses the needs of a wide range of subscribers, including individuals, public services, and enterprises. Potential services comprise fast Internet access, high quality audio and video communications, education and entertainment, tele-medicine, tele-metering and tele-surveillance.

Standardization organizations have established a framework for broadband wireless networks. However, several issues are intentionally left open and their solutions lead to differentiation factors between suppliers of equipment. Research is required to support this growing area.

9. Directions for Future Research

Operation in mesh modes raises security issues. Regarding authentication, authorization and accounting, the central server approach is not appropriate in the mesh mode. Mobility support uses the PKMv2 for key management, but in the mesh mode key management is limited to PKMv1, which makes subscribers theoretically vulnerable to the following attacks: sponsor node impersonation and person-in-the-middle (because of the absence of mutual authentication), message replay (because of the absence of nonce in messages) and denial of service and message modification attacks (because of the absence of authentication codes in messages, sinkhole and wormhole (because network topology information is broadcasted), security level rollback (because of the security capability negotiation process), neighbor bandwidth reduction (by faking resource allocation requests) and lack of privacy during authentication in mesh mode. Research is required to address all these security vulnerabilities.

Either a centralized or a distributed scheduling scheme is possible in the mesh mode. For distributed scheduling, the standard defines an election algorithm for the allocation of control subframes, which are used to coordinate the scheduling of data frames. In general, the scheduling problem is fairly open and can be addressed according to various and conflicting performance criteria.

10. Conclusions

In this chapter, we have given an overview of WiMAX/802.16 networking for broadband wireless access. We have discussed how it compares with other wireless technologies such as WiFi/802.11. WiMAX/802.16 operates in both PMP and mesh mode. The specifications define the PHY and MAC layers. The PHY layer is responsible for sending the individual bits across the air interface. There are multiple PHY layers depending on intended use. The MAC layer defines the access to the PHY layer from the higher layer protocols. The MAC layer has many responsibilities including network entry, scheduling transmissions and selection of burst profiles for the PHY layer, providing QoS for data flows, as well as supporting mobility.

We have described mobility support, discussing the MS association procedures, as well as handovers. We have described mesh mode operation, the mesh network entry procedure and scheduling, and we have discussed the new initiative of IEEE 802.16j, multihop relay, which aims to improve coverage and connectivity through the deployment of relay stations. Relays can be deployed based upon several usage models. Finally, we have discussed the security model, including security associations, packet encryption protocol, privacy key management protocol and authentication procedures.

Terminology

Base station (BS): A piece of equipment that provides connectivity, management and control of SSs.

Broadband Wireless Access (BWA): Wireless access providing broadband connections, typically with bandwidth greater than one MHz supporting data rates of at least 1.5 Mbps.

Burst profile: A set of parameters that describe the physical characteristics of the uplink and downlink channel. This includes such things as modulation type and forward error correction type.

Frequency Division Duplex (FDD): Transmission scheme where uplink and downlink transmissions can occur simultaneously, but on different frequencies.

Handover: The process where an MS changes its point of attachment to the network from one BS to a neighboring BS, usually due to the mobility of the MS.

Point-to-Multipoint (PMP): The typical cellular telephony model where a BS is at the center and communicates with one or more SSs that are within communications range.

Mobile station (MS): A subscriber station that is intended to be used while in motion.

Security association (SA): The set of security information that is shared between the BS and an SS in order to provide secure communications.

Service access point (SAP): The place in the protocol stack where the services of a lower level layer are accessible from the one above.

Subscriber station (SS): The piece of equipment that provides connectivity with a BS.

Time Division Duplex (TDD): A transmission scheme where uplink and downlink transmissions share a common frequency but occur at different times.

Exercises

1. QPSK, 16-QAM and 64-QAM use respectively four, 16 and 64 different pulse values. How many bits per pulse can be encoded with each modulation scheme?
2. In WiMAX/802.16, a downlink sub-frame consists of three data bursts: a QPSK burst, a 16-QAM burst and a 64-QAM burst. From first to last, in what order must these bursts be sent? Why is this ordering required?
3. In Example 2, what is the share of the bandwidth for each channel? What is the value of the bandwidth in Hertz for each channel? How much bandwidth is lost for control purposes, on the downlink? On the uplink?
4. Describe some advantages and disadvantages of centralized versus distributed scheduling in the WiMAX/802.16 mesh mode.
5. WiMAX/802.16 supports three forms of authentication: device authentication, user authentication and message authentication. Why is each form of authentication required? Explain the authentication procedure for each case.
6. Compare WiMAX/802.16 with Long Term Evolution. Consider technical criteria such as speed and radio spectrum.

7. Let Fi be the geometric region covered by frequency fi, $i = 1, 2, \ldots, k$. Given that the mobile user attempts to connect to the base station by selecting frequencies in the order $f1, f2, \ldots, fk$, the expected number of attempts until a successful connection is established is given by the formula

$$E(f1, f2, \ldots, fk) = \sum_{i=1}^{k} i \cdot \Pr[Fi \backslash (F1 \cup \cdots \cup Fi - 1)]$$
$$= \sum_{i=1}^{k} i \cdot \Pr[Fi] - \sum_{i=1}^{k} i \cdot \Pr[Fi \cap (F1 \cup \cdots \cup Fi - 1)].$$

   (a) Write the formula for the special case of two and three frequencies (i.e., $k = 2, 3$) and discuss its meaning.
   (b) Assume the three regions are the circles F_1, F_2, F_3 depicted in Fig. 17 and that frequency $fi$is available only within circle Fi. Explain what frequencies are available at the corresponding intersections. (*Hint*: There are four intersections.)
   (c) A given mobile is moving within the union of the three regions and occupies a position with the uniform distribution. Compute $\Pr[Fi]$ for $i = 1, 2, 3$. (*Hint*: Find the area delimited by the union of the three circles as well as the corresponding intersections. Observe that the desired probability is equal to the proportion of area covered by the frequency.)
   (d) What is the expected number of attempts before a frequency is found by the mobile station. [*Hint*: Compute $E(f_1, f_2, f_3)$ for the regions depicted in Fig. 17.]

8. For any permutation σ of $1, 2, \ldots, k$ let us define

$$E\sigma(f_1, f_2, \ldots, f_k) = E(f\sigma_{(1)}, f\sigma_{(2)}, \ldots, f\sigma_{(k)}).$$

   Why should we be interested in the problem of finding a permutation that minimizes the expected number of attempts $E\sigma(f_1, f_2, \ldots, f_k)$? (*Hint*: Give an example of three circles of unequal size.)

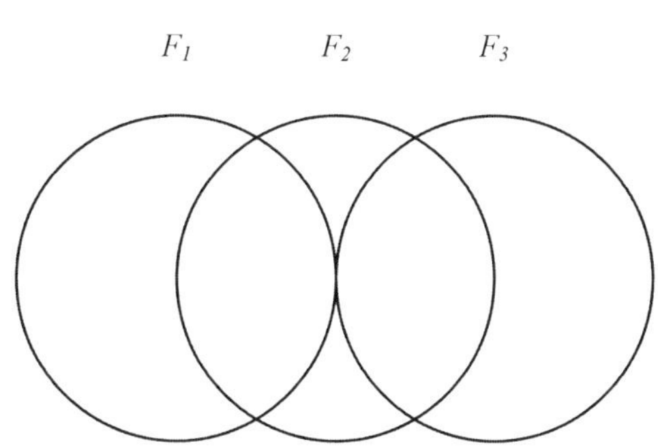

Fig. 17. Three circular regions.

9. Assume that we have two frequencies, i.e., $k = 2$. There are two possibilities for the user: either (i) to select frequencies in the order f_1, f_2 or (ii) in the order f_2, f_1. What is a good frequency selection criterion? (*Hint*: The expected number of steps until successful connection is established is

$$E(f_1, f_2) = \Pr[F_1] + 2(\Pr[F_2] - \Pr[F_2 \cap F_1]),$$
$$E(f_2, f_1) = \Pr[F_2] + 2(\Pr[F_1] - \Pr[F_1 \cap F_2])$$

in the two cases, respectively. This leads to us selecting the most likely frequency.)

10. Show that the competitive ratio of the previously described strategy is at most 2. (*Hint*: Given that $\Pr[F_1] \geq \Pr[F_2]$, we can easily find an upper bound on the competitive ratio between the worst and best choices

$$\frac{E(f_2, f_1)}{E(f_1, f_2)} = \frac{\Pr[F_2] + 2\Pr[F_1] - 2\Pr[F_1 \cap F_2]}{\Pr[F_1] + 2\Pr[F_2] - 2\Pr[F_2 \cap F_1]} \leq 2.$$

In other words, in the worst case the mobile user will take at most twice as long as the best case.)

11. Assume the regions are pairwise disjoint, i.e., $Fi \cap Fj = \emptyset$, for $i \neq j$.
    (a) Give the formula for $E(F_1, F_2, \ldots, F_k)$.
    (b) Show that for the case of k frequencies and pairwise mutually disjoint regions, a mobile user will minimize the expected number of attempts until a successful connection is established by selecting a permutation σ such that

$$\Pr[F\sigma(1)] \geq \Pr[F\sigma(2)] \geq \cdots \geq \Pr[F\sigma(k)].$$

    The permutation σ having this property defines the monotone strategy.
    (c) The mobile user cannot know the permutation that will optimize the expected number of steps (i.e., the monotone strategy). Conclude from this that the competitive ratio of the strategy in the previous exercise is at most k.

Acknowledgments

The authors gratefully acknowledge the financial support received from Mathematics of Information Technology and Complex Systems (MITACS) and Natural Sciences and Engineering Research Council of Canada (NSERC). The authors also thank Christine Laurendeau for her comments about the text of this chapter.

References

1. J. G. Andrews, A. Ghosh and R. Muhamed, *Fundamentals of WiMAX: Understanding Broadband Wireless Networking* (Prentice Hall PTR, 2007).

2. P. Djukic and S. Valaee, 802.16 mesh networking, in *WiMAX: Standards and Security*, eds. S. Ahson and M. Ilyas, (CRC Press, 2007), pp. 147–174.
3. C. Eklund, R. B. Marks, K. L. Stanwood and S. Wang, IEEE standard 802.16: A technical overview of the wirelessman air interface for broadband wireless access, *IEEE Commun. Mag.*, June, 98–107 (2002).
4. R. Fantacci, L. Maccari, T. Pecorella and F. Frosali, A Secure and Performant Token-Based Authentication for Infrastructure and Mesh 802.1X Networks IEEE Infocom Poster (2006).
5. IEEE Standard for Local and Metropolitan Area Networks — Part 16: Air interface for fixed broadband wireless access systems, October, IEEE Standard 802.16-2004, Revision of IEEE Std. 802.16-2001 (2004).
6. IEEE Standard for Local and Metropolitan Area Networks — Part 16: Air interface for fixed broadband wireless access systems, Amendment 2: Medium Access Control Modifications and Additional Physical Layer Specifications for 2–11 GHz, IEEE Standard 802.16a-2003 (2003).
7. IEEE Standard for Local and Metropolitan Area Networks — Part 16: Air interface for fixed broadband wireless access systems, Amendment 1: Detailed System Profiles for 10–66 GHz, IEEE Standard 802.16c-2002 (2002).
8. IEEE Standard for Local and Metropolitan Area Networks — Part 16: Air interface for fixed broadband wireless access systems, Amendment for Physical and Medium Access Control Layers for Combined Fixed and Mobile Operation in Licensed Bands, February, IEEE Std 802.16e-2005 and IEEE Std 802.16-2004/Cor1-2005 (Amendment and Corrigendum to IEEE Std 802.16-2004) (2006).
9. IEEE 802.16j, IEEE Standard for Local and Metropolitan Area Networks — Part 16: Air interface for fixed and mobile broadband wireless access systems, Multihop Relay Specification, Unapproved draft document, June (2007).
10. D. Johnston and J. Walker, Overview of IEEE 802.16 security, *IEEE Secur. Priv.* May/June, 40–48 (2004).
11. I. Koffman and V. Roman, Broadband wireless access solutions based on OFDM access in IEEE 802.16, *IEEE Commun. Mag.* **40**(4), 96–103 (2002).
12. H. Labiod, H. Afifi and C. De Santis, *Wi-Fi, Bluetooth, Zigbee and WiMAX* (Springer, 2007).
13. C. Laurendeau and M. Barbeau, Threats to security in DSRC/WAVE, *5th Int. Conf. Ad-hoc Networks*, Lecture Notes in Computer Science (Springer, Berlin, 2006), pp. 266–279.
14. L. Maccari, M. Paoli and R. Fantacci, Security analysis of IEEE 802.16. *IEEE Int. Conf. Communications (ICC' 07)*, 24–28 June (2007), pp. 1160–1165.
15. U. Meyer, Secure roaming and handover procedures in wireless access networks, dissertation, Fachgebiet Informatik der Technischen Universitaet Darmstadt (2005).
16. F. A. Perez, Security in Current Commercial Wireless Networks: A Survey (2006).
17. J. Sydir (ed.), *Harmonized Contribution on 802.16j (Mobile Multihop Relay) Usage Models*, June IEEE 802.16 Relay Task Group, http://www.ieee802.org/16/relay/ (2007).
18. S. Xu and C.-T. Huang, Attacks on PKM protocols of IEEE 802.16 and its later versions, *Wireless Communication Systems (ISWCS '06)*, 6–8 September (2006), pp. 185–189.
19. S. Xu, M. Matthews and C.-T. Huang, Security Issues in Privacy and Key Management Protocols of IEEE 802.16, *ACM SE06*, 10–12 March, Melbourne, Florida, USA (2006).
20. E. Yuksel, Analysis of the PKMv2 protocol in IEEE 802.16e-2005 using static analysis, thesis, Technical University of Denmark, Lyngby, February (2007).

Chapter 4

THE SYSTEM FRAMEWORK AND ITS APPLICATION IN A MOBILE RFID SERVICE NETWORK

NAMJE PARK* and RAJIT GADH†

Department of Mechanical and Aerospace Engineering, UCLA,
420 Westwood Plaza, Los Angeles, CA 90095, USA
**namjepark@ucla.com*
†rgadh@winmec.ucla.edu

SEUNGJOO KIM* and DONGHO WON†

Information Security Group, Sungkyunkwan University,
300 Cheoncheon-dong, Jangan-gu, Suwon
Gyeonggi-do, 440-746, Korea
**skim@security.re.kr*
†dhwon@security.re.kr

Mobile Radio Frequency Identification (RFID) is a newly emerging technology which uses the mobile phone as an RFID reader with a wireless technology and provides valuable new services to the user by integrating RFID and ubiquitous sensor network infrastructure with mobile communications and wireless Internet. UHF Mobile RFID technology is based on ISO/IEC 18000-6C can share UHF RFID tags used in logistics/SCM and can avoid redundant investment expected to be integrated with other frequency band RFID. Mobile RFID enables business to provide new services to mobile customers by securing services and transactions from the end user to a company's existing e-commerce and IT systems. This chapter discusses UHF based mobile RFID technology. We begin with a look at the general of a mobile RFID system anatomy, followed by a discussion of the components that make up a typical mobile RFID system framework and the underlying sub-systems that make them work.

1. Introduction

Radio Frequency IDentification (RFID) has been recognized as a key technology for ubiquitous networks, which in turn is defined as an environment in which information can be acquired anytime and anywhere through network access service [1, 9]. Currently, RFID technologies consider the environment in which RFID tags are mobile and RFID readers are stationary. However, in the future, RFID technologies could consider an environment in which RFID tags are stationary and readers are mobile. RFID based on mobile telecommunications services could be the best example of this kind of usage. RFID-based mobile telecommunications services could be defined as services that provide information access through the telecommunications network by reading RFID tags on certain objects using an RFID reader in mobile terminals such as cell phones. RFID tags play an important role as a bridge between offline objects and online information. The RFID-enabled cell phone was introduced by Nokia in 2004 [4, 8, 9, 25].

Furthermore, the RFID tags of the future will evolve as active tags with networking capabilities, which will become a key component of the ubiquitous network environment rather than the current passive RFID tags. At this stage, RFID tags need network addresses for communications. For the ubiquitous network, current RFID-related technologies need to be modified to reflect the features of mobile telecommunications services; and additional technologies for RFID-based mobile telecommunications services should be established to provide a harmonized operation of such services. In this chapter, we will explore mobile RFID technology, beginning with a discussion of the details of mobile RFID system anatomy. We then discuss the components that make up a typical mobile RFID system framework and the underlying technologies that make them work.

2. Background

In this section, we introduce the overview and basic service models of mobile RFID technology. And, we will discuss the mobile RFID technology's wireless specification, difference of EPC RFID network case.

2.1. *Mobile RFID Technology*

RFID is expected to be the base technology for the ubiquitous network and ubiquitous computing, and is likely to be associated with other technologies such as Micro Electro-Mechanical Systems (MEMS), telematics, and sensors. It is widely known that Korea is one of the countries that has established a robust mobile telecommunication's networks in the world. In particular, about 78% of the population uses mobile phones and more than 95% of those phones have Internet-enabled functions [2, 4, 9]. Korea has already recognized the potential of RFID technology and has tried to integrate it in the mobile phone. Mobile phones equipped with RFID can be expected to create new markets and provide new services to end users, and as such will be considered as an exemplary fusion of technologies. Furthermore, it may evolve its particular functions as an end-user terminal device, or a u-device (ubiquitous device), in the world of ubiquitous information technology [4, 9, 10, 23, 41].

In fact, the mobile RFID phone may represent two types of mobile phone device: one is the RFID-reader-equipped mobile phone, and the other is the RFID-tag-attached mobile phone. Each type has different application domains. On the one hand, for example, the RFID-tag-attached type can be used as a device for payment, entry control, and identity authentication, and the main feature of this application stems from the fact that RFID readers exist in fixed positions and recognize

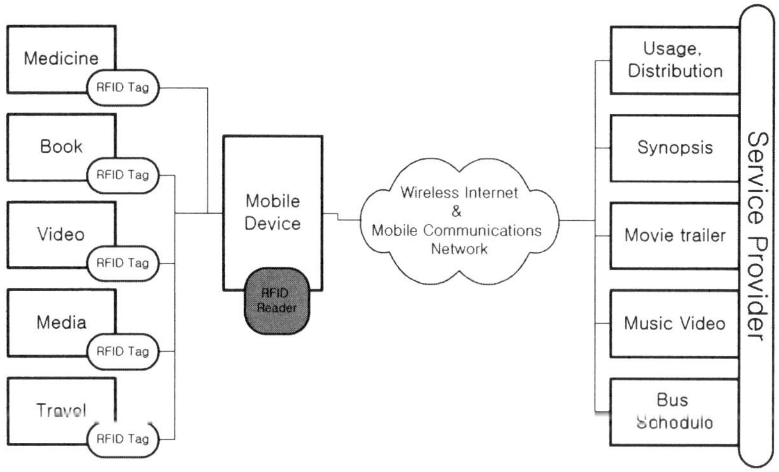

Fig. 1. Example service of mobile RFID for providing product information.

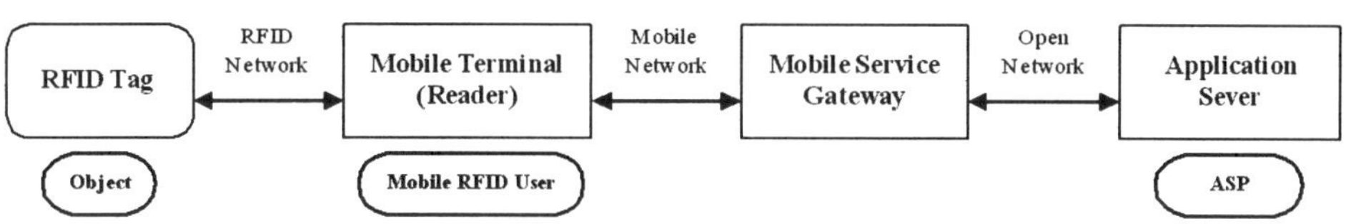

Fig. 2. Mobile RFID data communication model.

individual phones, giving the user specific services like door opening. On the other hand, the RFID-reader-equipped mobile phone, to which Korea is currently paying considerable attention, can be utilized to provide end users with detailed information about the tagged object by accessing the mobile wireless network.

The model of the mobile RFID service as shown in Fig. 2 defines three additional entities and two relationships compared to those defined in the RFID tag, the RFID access network, RFID reader, the relationship between the RFID tag and RFID reader, and the relationship between the RFID reader and the application server.

UHF (Ultrahigh Frequency) mobile RFID technology is focusing on the frequency range (860∼960 MHz), since the UHF range may enable a longer reading range and moderate data rates, as well as a relatively small tag size and lower costs [4, 9, 10]. Then, as a kind of handheld RFID reader, in the selected service domain the UHF RFID phone device can be used to provide object information directly to the end user using the same UHF RFID tags that are widespread.

2.2. *Mobile RFID Wireless Specification*

For a mobile terminal with an RFID reader embedded, the configuration of reader chip and adjacent circuitry can be illustrated as shown in Fig. 4. Inside the reader chip are two components: the digital component, which processes Host/RFID

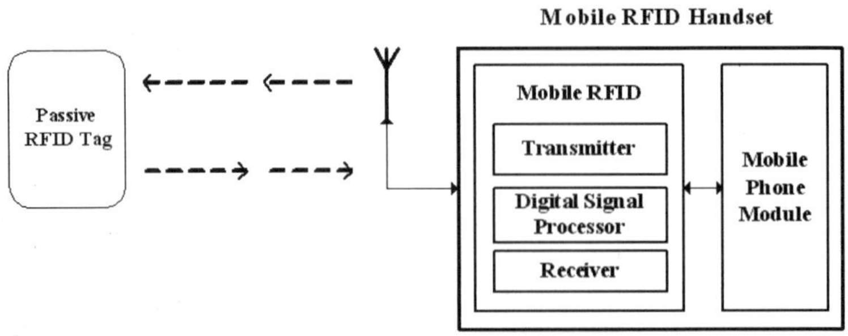

Fig. 3. Mobile RFID diagram.

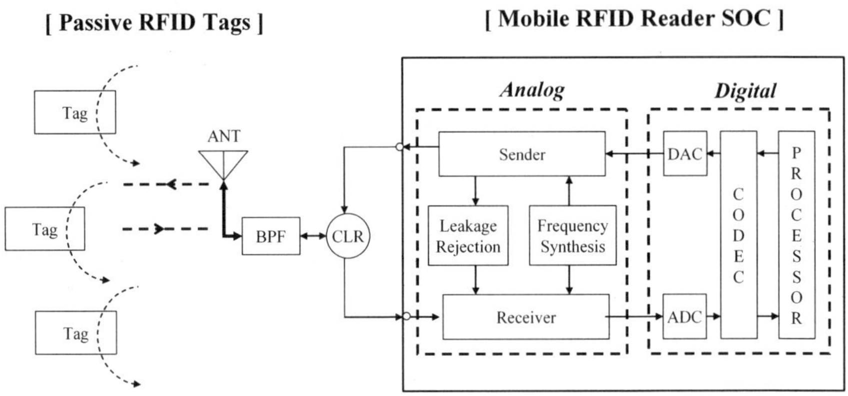

Fig. 4. Mobile RFID's soc.

protocols, and the analog component, which processes base band signals and 900 MHz RF signals.

To eliminate the analog component from the design, it is necessary to prepare the corresponding wireless specifications for it. This chapter prepared the domestic wireless specifications for mobile RFID in Korea, with reference to applicable RFID frequency, cell radius, channel allocation, and relevant radio regulation acts (ordinances), technical standards, etc.

In general, the minimum power to be delivered to a passive RFID tag is – UHF 10 dBm (100 uW). In contrast, since a mobile RFID terminal has good accessibility to tags, it can fully meet the requirements for application in mobile RFID services, if any tag can be recognized within a 1 mile radius. Accordingly, it was estimated that the signal output of a mobile RFID should be at least 20 dBm or higher, considering a link loss of -315 dB, tag antenna gain ≤ 2 dBi, built-in reader antenna gain ≤ 0 dBi, so on. However, a mobile RFID cannot emit as much output as a fixed type reader because it works only with power supplied from a mobile phone battery. Thus, our wireless specifications determined the sender output by allowing for minimum power based on link analysis, limitations of the CMOS power amplifier, and the mobile phone's battery power.

It is not necessary for mobile RFID to recognize a large number of tags at once since it is designed primarily for portability. A mobile RFID reader has to only request and send information on several tag recognition codes, so it can make any application service, if necessary, at a data rate of about 40 kbps without difficulty. For example, in Korea, the frequency band allocated for RFID ranges from 908.5 MHz to 914 MHz. The RFID device supports data rates as high as 640 kbps in this band and can communicate with other terminals only if a wide channel bandwidth is available in the restricted area. It is not appropriate for terminals like mobile RFID, which may be used by an unknown number of users. Therefore, the mobile RFID was based on a 200 kHz channel bandwidth at a data rate of about 40 kbps.

2.3. *Difference of Features*

2.3.1. *Difference of EPC RFID*

Business-to-business (B2B) RFID applications use a similar network configuration to the EPC network shown in Fig. 5. Network configurations for business-to-customer (B2C) RFID applications are illustrated in Fig. 6. There are two main differences between these B2B and B2C network models. First, the client part, that is, the RFID reader part, is completely different. The B2C model has a single RFID reader without the need to control multiple readers, but the B2B model has multiple RFID readers and controls them via a middleware host. Secondly, final service targets are different: those of the B2C model are human beings and those of the B2B model are business logistics, applications and systems. Hence, the target contents to be served are different. Such online contents as images, music, movies, news, games, information, etc., are provided by the B2C model. But online

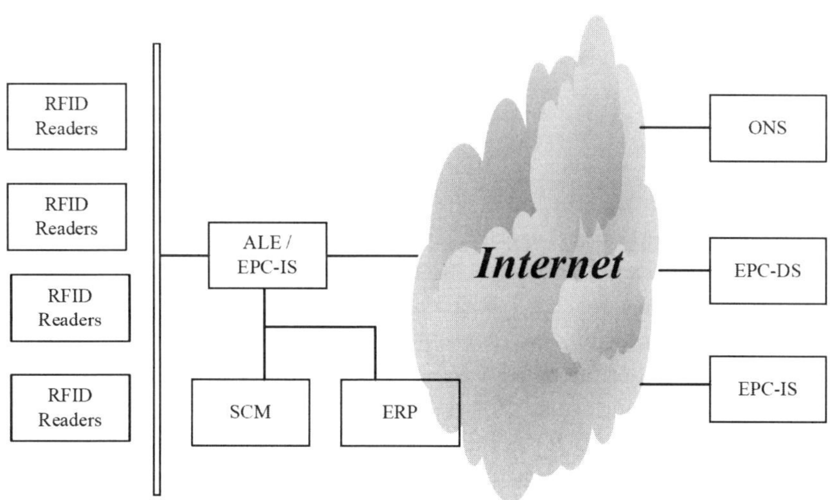

Fig. 5. EPC network configuration.

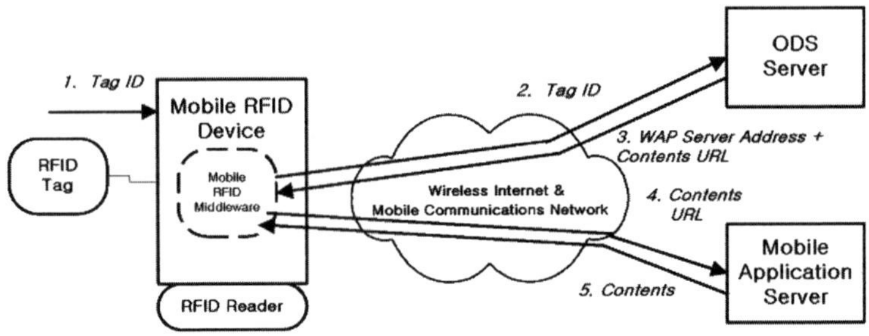

Fig. 6. Basic communication model of mobile RFID.

contents such as volume of objects, number of packaged boxes, delivery source and destination, expiry date, and so on in different properties, are provided by the B2B model. By these different characteristics, privacy management toward consumers would get important more and existing content servers should be engaged into the B2C RFID network. The following network configuration models consist of various network entities. Addition of functional features count make various networking properties for a network entity and each networking property might make different network architectures.

2.3.1.1. EPC network case

A typical RFID network model may refer to the network architecture of EPCglobal as shown in Fig. 5, where the network entities are RFID tags, readers, the ALE host, the event management server (EPC-IS), the EPC-IS service location server (EPC-DS), and the code resolution server (ONS). Business application servers such as ERP, CRM, SCM, etc. are omitted because they form part of the back-end and are associated only indirectly with the RFID network. Such a network model is for B2B applications.

2.3.1.2. Mobile RFID case

Changing the delivery target of information content to customers, rather than business applications and business logistical entities, enables B2C applications. Promising service terminals for B2C network applications are mobile handsets, that is, cell phones equipped with RFID readers. Figure 6 illustrates a basic communication models for B2C RFID applications. It consists of two network operations: code resolution and content retrieval. The design philosophy is to consider an RFID reader phone as a client node computer like a desktop PC, where a name resolution is performed first via DNS followed by a content retrieval. In the same way, a mobile RFID application client performs a code resolution first via ODS and a content retrieval thereafter. A middleware host is not necessary, unlike in the case of EPCglobal, because multiple readers are not engaged in the RFID-reader phone.

As the network connectivity expands to consumers, new network entities are installed such as the RPS, the WAP/Web server and the mobile handset, and the mobile network infrastructure is as shown in Fig. 6, where OTS is equivalent to EPC-DS, OIS to EPC-IS, and ODS to ONS, with the addition of the RPS and WAP/Web server.

2.3.2. *Classes of Mobile RFID Technology*

To realize mobile RFID services, it is necessary for RFID devices such as RFID tags or RFID readers to be installed on mobile phones. Nokia supports RFID technology based on 13.56 MHz, MIFARE ®UltraLight, and ISO 14443A. For instance, the Nokia 3220 is based on the NFC protocol, which uses a 13.56 MHz reader complying with ISO/IEC 18092. The Nokia 5140 and 5140i phones as well as 3220 the with the integrated Xpress-on^{TM} RFID reader shell are capable of launching services and accessing phone functions such as dial or send messages by touching an RFID tag. Mobile phone users can automate and initiate tasks, such as browsing service instructions or logging time-stamped data like meter readings.

KDDI in Japan has developed slide-in RFID readers that can easily be attached to the underside of a mobile phone. There are two types of RFID reader corresponding to different frequency bands: a 2.45 GHz passive type and a 315 MHz active type. Pilot tests were scheduled back in March 2005. Figure 7 describes KDDI's mobile RFID service architecture as a service broker is located. The multi-contact server provides both code resolution and the appropriate content. Table 1 shows a summary of the possible implementations of mobile RFID.

As shown above, UHF-band mobile RFID uses 908.55–913.95 MHz and complies with ISO/IEC 18000-6 Types B and C [4, 12, 41]. From the viewpoint of service

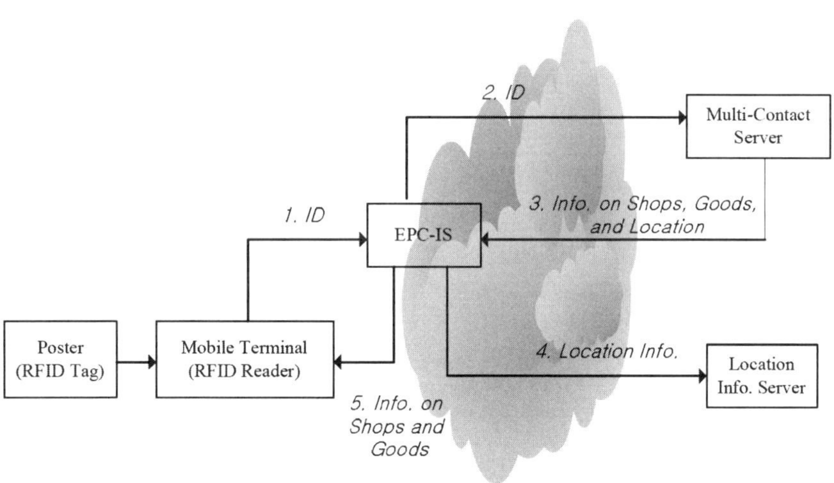

Fig. 7. Network architecture model of KDDI's mobile RFID service.

Table 1. Summary of mobile RFID implementations.

	Nokia's mobile RFID	KDDI's mobile RFID (passive)	KDDI's mobile RFID (active)	NFC near field communication	Korea's mobile RFID
Radio frequency	13.56 MHz	2.45 GHz	315 MHz	13.56 MHz	860 ~ 960 MHz
Reading range	2 × 3 cm				
Complaint standards	ISO/IEC 14443 A			ISO/IEC 18092	ISO/IEC 18000-6 B/C
Feature	HF RF Reader	RF Reader	Active RFID Reader	Tag & Reader	UHF RF Reader

deployment, the UHF-band is more viable for the following reasons:

- It has a relatively longer range of up to 100 cm.
  A longer range is favorable for most mobile RFID services, ensuring greater convenience.
- A short range of up to 2 or 3 cm is available if required; in the case of a payment system, short range may be supported by reducing the RF strength by application.
- It avoids duplicate investment for the RFID tag since most RFID tags in supply chain management (SCM) work in the 900 MHz range, i.e., ISO 18000-6 types A/B/C and EPCglobal. This means that both SCM and mobile RFID applications can share an RFID tag: a single RFID tag can provide different content according to the application.

3. UHF-band Mobile RFID Network

3.1. *An Abstract Network Architecture*

Networked RFID comprises an expanded RFID network and scope to communicate with a series of networks, inter-networks and globally distributed application systems, engendering global communication relationships triggered by RFID, for such applications as B2B, B2C, B2B2C, and G2C (government to customer). Since the provision of various services (ex, mobile RFID using compact UHF RFID chip in cellular phone) was first attempted in Korea in 2005, standardization has been ongoing. Korea's mobile RFID technology focuses on the UHF range [4, 8, 9]. Thus, as a kind of handheld RFID reader, in the selected service domain the UHF RFID phone device can be used to provide object information directly to the end-user using the same UHF RFID tags which have been distributed widely.

The mobile RFID service has been defined as the provision, through the wireless Internet network, of personalized secure services — such as searching for product information, purchasing, verifying, and paying for products — while on the move, by building the RFID reader chip into the mobile terminal [3, 11]. The

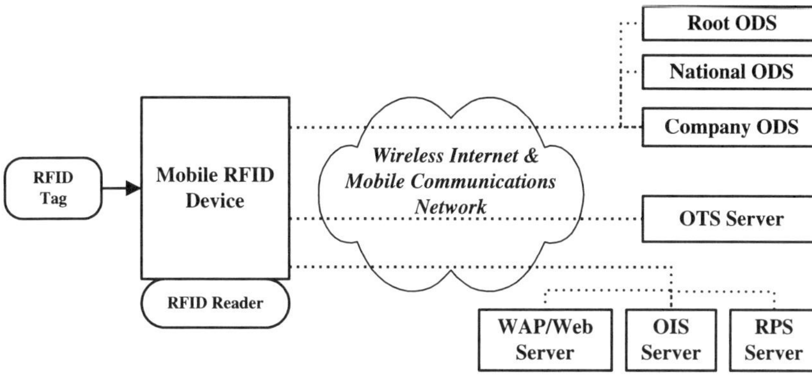

Fig. 0. Conceptual network model for mobile RFID service.

service infrastructure required for providing such an RFID-based mobile service is composed of an RFID reader, handset, communication network, network protocol, information protection, application server, RFID code interpretation, and content development.

Figure 8 shows the interface structure for the mobile RFID service's communication infrastructure and the types of relevant standards. RFID wireless access communication takes place between the RFID tag and a cellular phone, Code Division Multiple Access (CDMA) mobile communication takes place between the cellular phone and base transceiver station (BTS)/access network transceiver subsystem (ANTS), and wire communication takes place between BTS/ANTS and a networked RFID application server.

The ODS (Object Directory Service) is an information system that provides data needed to obtain an information resource over a network for a specific code expressed in numbers (or mobile RFID's Code). The Object Directory Service (ODS) server plays the role of a Directory Name System (DNS) server, which informs the mobile RFID phone of the content/service server's location, as explained above [9, 10, 24]. The ODS server may be organized in a hierarchical structure similar to that of a DNS server. The OTS (Object Traceability Service) server keeps a record of the tag throughout the lifecycle of the objects. Its main purpose is to track objects in the SCM. The Object Information Service (OIS) records the reading of the RFID tag event in the OTS server and may provide additional detailed information on an object — such as manufacturing time, manufacturer's name, expiration time, etc. The RFID Privacy Management Service (RPS) controls access to information about the object in accordance with the privacy profile put together by the owner of the object. The Wireless Application Protocol (WAP) and Web servers are content servers that provide wireless Internet content such as news, games, music, videos, stock trading, lotteries, images, and so forth.

The mobile RFID service structure is defined to support ISO/IEC 18000-6 A/B/C through wireless access communication between the tag and the reader.

However, as yet there is no RFID reader chip capable of supporting all three wireless connection access specifications and hence the communication specification for a mobile phone will be determined by the mobile communication companies [4, 24, 26]. It will also be possible to mount the RF wireless communication function on the reader chip using software defined radio (SDR) technology and develop an ISO/IEC 18000-6 A/B/C communication protocol in software to choose from the protocols when needed.

The mobile RFID middleware extends the Wireless Internet Platform for Interoperability (WIPI) software platform to provide RF code-related information obtained from an RF tag through an RFID reader installed in the mobile phone. The function of the networked terminal is concerned with the recognition distance to the RFID reader chip built into the cellular phone, transmission power, frequency, interface, technological standard, Personal Identification Number (PIN) specification, Universal Asynchronous Receiver and Transmitter (UART) communication interface, and the WIPI Application Program Interface (API) extended specification to control the reader chip. RFID reader chip middleware functions are provided to the application program in the form of the mobile platform's API. Here, the mobile RFID device driver is the device driver software provided by the reader chip manufacturer.

The function of the mobile RFID network is concerned with communication protocols such as ODS communication for code interpretation, message transportation for the transmission and reception of content between the mobile phone terminal and the application server, content negotiation that supports the mobile RFID service environment and ensures optimum content transfer between the mobile phone terminal and the application server, and session management that enables the application to create and manage the required status information while transmitting the message and the WIPI extended specification which supports these communication services [3, 8, 10, 18].

A cellular phone requires a common control interface between the various RFID readers and the application or the middleware. To that end, EPCglobal Inc. and ISO are defining the functions that an RFID reader should commonly support, as well as various common commands and standardizing message types. Mobile RFID functions will be extended continuously into standard cellular phone RFID readers, and the RFID supported WIPI extension model using WIPI — the wireless Internet standard platform — will define the API required in using the reader suitable for the mobile environment as the API extension of WIPI, while maintaining compatibility among the various devices.

The basic communication scenario for mobile RFID service is as follows. First, a mobile RFID phone reads the RFID tags on an object and fetches the code stored in it [8, 9, 12]. Second, the phone carries out the code resolution with which it obtains the location of the remote server that provides information on the product or a suitable mobile service. The code resolution protocol is identical to the DNS protocol. The ODS server in Fig. 9 as a DNS server and is similar to EPCglobal's

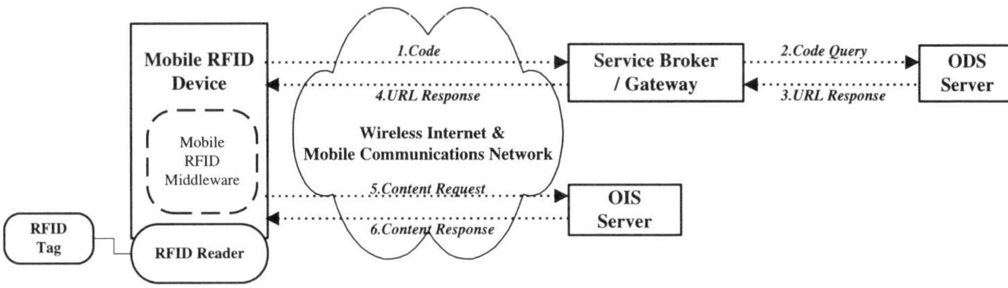

Fig. 9. Basic communication scenario for mobile RFID service.

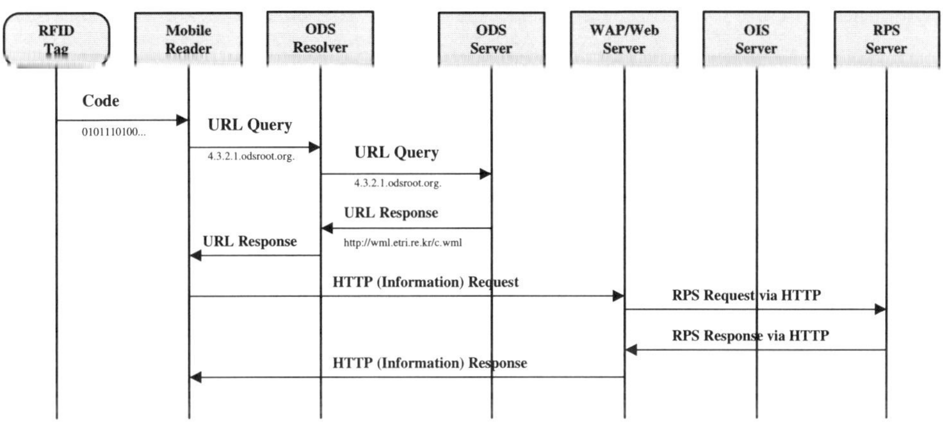

Fig. 10. Detailed schematic of the mobile RFID's code resolution process.

Object Name Service (ONS) server. The mobile RFID phone directs queries on the location of the server with a code to the ODS server, then the ODS server replies by giving the location of the server. Finally, the phone requests content or a service from the designated server whose location has been acquired from the ODS server.

Figure 10 illustrates the detailed code resolution process. The code in the RFID tag is a bit string such as '01001101110... ' and this bit string is translated into a meaningful form such as EPC, mCode (mobile RFID code), uCode, or ISO Code [9, 23, 29, 41]. If "1.2.3.4" is obtained from a bit string translation, it is converted into a uniform resource name (URN) form as "urn:mcode:cb:1.2.3.4"; the remaining code resolution process is the same as the DNS reverse lookup process. The mobile RFID reader requests content retrieval after code resolution. The RFID application in the phone requests content from the WAP or Web server returned by the code resolution.

3.2. *Data Communication Structure*

The mobile RFID service provides the requested services by using mCode, micro-mCode, and mini-mCode, defined in this standard, as well as services using the attached RFID tag based on EPC code, usually applied in distribution and logistics, and ISO/IEC 15459. This chapter describes code structures like mCode, micro-mCode, and mini-mCode for mobile RFID service and defines RFID tag data structure, where such codes can be compatible with different coding systems. Such code structure helps identify and locate online content and services with unique code structures suitable for mobile RFID service.

4. Mobile RFID System Components

Mobile RFID service systems are basically composed of the RFID tag, mobile RFID reader, ODS system, and OIS system. In this section, we discuss four key components of the mobile RFID service system and the forward/backward channel.

4.1. *Passive UHF RFID Tag and Reader*

An RFID tag consist of a microchip and a coupling element — an antenna. Most tags are only activated when they are within the interrogation zone of the interrogator; outside they "sleep". Chip tags can be both read-only (programmed during manufacture) or, at higher complexity and cost, read-write, or both. Chip tags contain memory. The size of the tag depends on the size of the antenna, which increases with the range of tag and decreases with frequency. Depending on the application and technology used, some interrogators not only read, but also remotely write to, the tags. For the majority of low-cost tags (tags without batteries, known as passive tags), the power to activate the tag microchip is supplied by the reader through the tag antenna when the tag is in the interrogation zone of the reader, as is the timing pulse. It is also convenient to classify tags by their functionality. The MIT Auto-ID center has defined five classes based on functionality, as shown in Table 2 [5, 9].

Tag readers interrogate tags for their data through an RF interface. To provide additional functionality, readers may contain internal storage, processing power or connections to back-end databases. Computations, such as cryptographic calculations, may be carried out by the reader on behalf of a tag. The channel from reader-to-tag may be referred to as the forward channel. Similarly, the tag-to-reader channel may be referred to as the backward channel.

Readers might be handheld devices or incorporated into a fixed location. One application of a fixed reader is a "smart shelf," which detects when items are added

Table 2. RFID tag functionality classes.

Class	Nickname	Memory	Power source	Features
0	Anti-shoplift tags	None	Passive	Article surveillance
1	EPC	Read-only	Any	Identification only
2	EPC	Read-write	Any	Data logging
3	Sensor tags	Read-write	Semi-passive or active	Environmental sensors
4	Smart dust	Read-write	Active	Ad hoc networking

Fig. 11. The mobile RFID reader.

or removed, and would play a key role in a realtime inventory control system. Fundamentally, readers are quite simple devices and may be incorporated into mobile devices like cellular phones or PDAs. A stand-alone, handheld reader with a wireless connection to a back-end database may cost around US$100–200. If RFID tags become ubiquitous in consumer items, tag reading may become a desirable feature in consumer electronics [37].

4.2. *Mobile Terminal Platform*

WIPI was required to come into force in Korea in the case of mobile phones from April, 2005, to support the interoperability platform for various application software and hardware. Hence, we chose the WIPI platform as our basic software development platform, and the software architecture and the relationship between the various software functions are shown as Fig. 12. The software architecture is composed of the REX OS, WIPI HAL API, WIPI runtime engine, WIPI C API, phone application, quasi-XML browser parser, and phone GUI. Most functions for mobile RFID technology are designed in the WIPI C API and they are reader

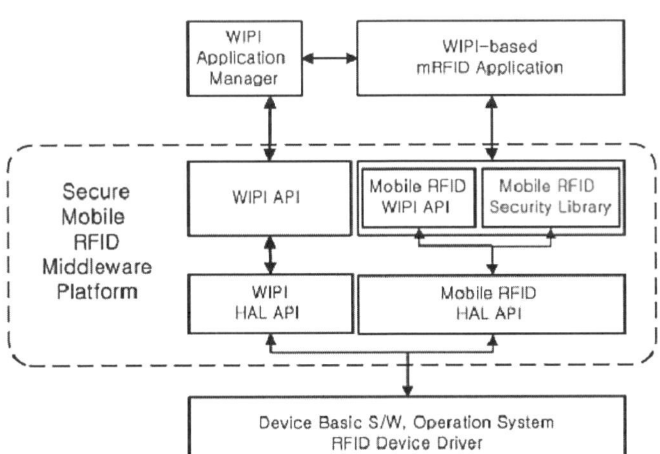

Fig. 12. Software architecture in the mobile phone.

control, tag control, buffer control and filter control for interfacing with RFID reader and code decoder, Uniform Resource Name (URN) converter, Fully Qualified Domain Name (FQDN) converter, DNS resolver and connect content server (CS) for communicating with a local ODS server and the application content web server [35].

The mobile RFID middleware extends the WIPI platform to provide RF code related information obtained from the RF tag through the RFID reader attached on a mobile phone. The functions of RFID WIPI C API [5] include RFID reader control, buffer control, tag control, filtering, and networking for code decoding, URN conversion, FQDN conversion, DNS resolving and content service. The WIPI runtime engine software for mobile RFID functions is extended to support RFID WIPI C API and RFID HAL API. The functions of RFID HAL API include RFID reader control, buffer control, tag control, filtering, and networking for configuring the IP address of the local ODS server. Figure 12 shows the middleware functions and overall software architecture. The WIPI platform is designed to minimize the side effects that may occur due to the use of different platforms.

4.3. *Back-End Service System*

The local ODS server is a DNS server using UDP port 53, and the content server is a Web server using TCP port 80 for HTTP. In the case of code resolution failure by the RFID reader in the mobile phone, the reader sends the unknown code to the local ODS to obtain the location of the content server. Local ODS function architecture as shown in Fig. 13 consists of the Multicode Decoding Module (MDM), URN/FQDN converter and DNS resolver. An operator has to insert the content server's URL information in the zone file of the local ODS server to offer the content server's location [35].

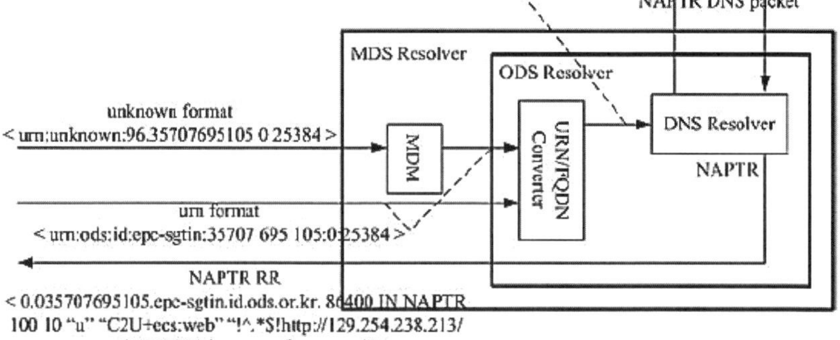

Fig. 13. Local ODS server system functions.

The content server supports B2C services and offers service environments to deliver various content to clients. The content server is able to offer application services including a delivery authentication service and tracking service. Tracking and authentication services are required after clients complete their purchases.

4.3.1. *ODS Resolver Function*

In the mobile RFID service environment, the ODS server carries out "code resolution" to look for URI information relating to an RFID code. According to the ODS communication protocol, the ODS resolver obtains the URI of the information resources relating to the code and then sends it to the mobile RFID application. The user's communication fees depend on what information system this ODS resolver contains. That is, the ODS resolver may be installed within the mobile phone or in the local ODS server of the telecom company. It is highly recommended that the mobile RFID service choose the latter.

The mobile RFID service has the least ODS resolver function within a mobile phone, the Stub ODS resolver, which sends a query on a code to the ODS server of the telecom company from the mobile phone application. The ODS server plays the role of the ODS resolver, performing code resolution with the root ODS first and other ODS servers according to the ODS hierarchy. The ODS resolver of the telecom company transmits the final URI information to the Stub ODS resolver within the mobile phone and in turn the information is delivered to the application. Through this mechanism, the mobile RFID application within a mobile phone calls for code resolution through a one-time ODS query and receives a response message; communication traffic occurs much less than when the ODS resolver of the phone carries out the function itself.

4.3.2. *Selecting the ODS Resolver*

The address of the ODS resolver or local ODS server should be set in a mobile phone like setting the DNS server address. The port number of TCP and UDP is 53, the same as that of DNS. The basic network information stored in a mobile phone includes the DNS server address, which the user may change. Likewise, the ODS server address should initially be set by the manufacturer according to the telecom company and the user should be allowed to change it. The purpose of this is to comply with the requirements for open networks and services.

4.3.3. *ODS NAPTR Record*

Once the RFID coding system is decided, it has a great influence on the overall service infrastructure. If it is a unique coding system, objects might need several tags. For example, since it is impractical to trace and manage individual beer bottles, a refrigerator may become an object for management and tracing. Since a refrigerator may become a target not only for management and tracing in logistics and distribution but for the mobile RFID service, it would need tags for both services.

If the mobile RFID service adopts the EPC coding system, because information resources for the mobile handset-based RFID service differ from those for PDAs, desktop PCs, and business systems for logistics and distribution, there may be more than two information resources relating to one EPC code (herein information resources refer to content). Since a single code may be related to many information resources, a method should be considered to identify the URI information of each information resource and to ask the content server for the desired information with a specific URI. To resolve this issue, the ODS NAPTR record regarding a code has to retain information indicating its service kind.

4.3.4. *Content Negotiation*

A mobile phone has a variety of software operation environments. They involve screen size and shape, resolution, color, software implementation platform, browser, input/output interface, and available languages, etc. It may be impossible for users to know these details about their mobile phone, but even if they do, it would be inconvenient to choose their favorite content for their particular environment by communication with content servers, causing the associated communication charges. Instead, a mobile phone should ensure the delivery of the optimal content for its environment through prior negotiation with content servers by using efficient negotiation parameters.

5. Selection Criteria for Mobile RFID

The mobile RFID Service Application Requirements Profile (ARP) describes the requirements for an RFID tag, the RFID reader, handset, the wireless Internet, network, content server, ODS server, etc. that the mobile RFID service, content, and technical infrastructure should be equipped with, from the application service perspective, when the mobile RFID service provides, by means of the B2C method, specific application services such as movie trailers, ticket bookings for movies, trains, express buses, and flights, etc.

The mobile RFID service Common Requirements Profile (CARP) refers to requirements for RFID tags, readers, handsets, wireless Internet, networks, content servers, ODS servers, service application programs, etc. that the mobile RFID service, content, and technical infrastructure should be equipped with when the B2C-based mobile RFID service offers common application services as well as specific application services. In other words, this refers to common requirements for all mobile RFID service applications or common requirements defined in every ARP. The ARP for an application service should contain common application requirements, and if a specific ARP exceeds common requirements, the common requirements should be modified or nullified, otherwise the application service should be announced to be unfeasible.

This section includes the common requirements for mobile RFID services such as application service requirements, code system requirements, RFID tag requirements, RFID reader requirements, test requirements, network environment requirements, and security requirements.

5.1. *Mobile RFID Service Range*

5.1.1. *Frequency Conditions*

The mobile RFID service standard supports only 900 MHz UHF communication based on ISO/IEC 18000-6. That is, mobile RFID reader chips and tags are communication devices working in the 900 MHz frequency range. Table 3 gives the radio frequencies for RFID applications according to the ISO/IEC 18000 standard.

5.1.2. *Network Conditions*

The mobile RFID service operates based on the TCP/IP and online communication conditions and does not rely on wireless communication network technologies like CDMA2000 1x, 1x EV-DO, 1x EV-DV, WLAN, WCDMA, and WiBro. This implies that once the wireless or mobile communication technologies support TCP/IP, the mobile RFID service would be accessible under any wireless network.

5.1.3. *On-line Communication*

Portable mobile RFID readers are not always able to handle online communication. The infrastructure components and data flows of mobile RFID services depend on the circumstances. After reading an RFID tag, a mobile RFID reader can carry out a batch work later over a network. Alternatively, an RFID reader can process the tag data immediately through a network connection. The mobile RFID service provides an environment wherein tag data can be processed immediately through wireless Internet because an RFID reader module is installed within a portable handset.

5.1.4. *Application Software Platform Conditions*

The mobile RFID service based on the TCP/IP communication environment uses a reader chip working at 900 MHz on the WIPI-based platform. The mobile RFID service would also be available when a WLAN-based handset with a 900 MHz built-in RFID reader and the WIPI application platform is backed by TCP/IP

Table 3. ISO/IEC 18000-x wireless access standard.

Specifications	Description
ISO/IEC 18000 1	Reference architecture and definition of parameters to be standardized
ISO/IEC 18000 2	Parameters for air interface communications below135 kHz
ISO/IEC 18000 3	Parameters for air interface communicaitons at 13.56 MHz
ISO/IEC 18000 4	Parameters for air interface communicaitons at 2.54 GHz
ISO/IEC 18000 6	Parameters for air interface communicaitons at 860 MHz to 960 MHz
ISO/IEC 18000 7	Parameters for active air interface communications at 433 MHz

network communication. In other words, because a PDA handset supported by TCP/IP can run WIPI application programs with its 900 MHz reader chip and WIPI platform, mobile RFID services would be accessible under the WIBRO mobile Internet communication environment.

5.2. *Application Service Requirements*

Application service requirements do not necessarily rely on mobile RFID technologies in order to be supported by the mobile RFID service infrastructure. Some of them may need technical solutions, but they can also be acquired through the procedure of software system design when a content server creates the content. For such cases, this standard does not suggest the solutions for the application service requirements, regarding but regards them as achieved. Yet this standard specifies the requirements for mobile RFID tags, readers, mobile phones, wireless Internet, networks, content servers, and services that need mobile RFID technologies and specifications.

5.2.1. *Active Application Software Operation*

When the user selects the relevant application software for a tag code, it should be downloaded for installation and implementation. If it is already downloaded, the user is able to use it. Different application software may be used depending on the tag code.

5.2.2. *Identical Code Multiple Application Service Model*

A specific tag code should not be limited to one single application service. One product can access multiple service models because each service model may choose an individual tag, or one single tag may involve all related services. Therefore, there can be multiple services (WAP site, application software) for a certain tag code, and the user should be able to access the desired service from among them.

In the music domain, for instance, a record company wants to promote the record, a record store to sell the record, and customers to listen before buying. They could diverge from a single service, but they might each need different service models because they are distinct service providers. For example, the record store might want its own bargain sale event for a certain record. Therefore, a tag code should be able to access multiple services.

5.2.3. *Variable Multiple Application Service Model*

The service relating to a tag code should provide the user with different content depending on the circumstances. For example, during an event period, the tag code might connect to services like the event introduction and contests to win prizes. After the event, it may announce prize winners or provide other services. In another example, the user might be provided with product information before buying, but manuals, repair services, and maintenance information after buying. The service also varies depending on place. A refrigerator in a shop is for promotion or sale, while one at home is for use. A record is for promotion or sale in a shop, but at home it might be an item requiring maintenance.

5.2.4. *Independent "Read" and "Implementation"*

Reading the tag code and using the application services associated with the code should be separate operations. That is, the user may access services immediately after reading the tag code or later using a stored tag code.

5.2.5. *Manual Code Input*

If a reader fails to read a tag due to tag/reader problems or some unknown reason, application programs should support a user interface to input the tag code by hand. This is an optional requirement.

5.2.6. *Save Application Program Status*

The commencement or termination of a mobile RFID application service is not necessarily performed only when the mobile phone is on. Even if a mobile phone happens to turn off in the middle of an application service, the service should remain as it is. When mobile shopping, the user should be able to see previous purchasing information when a cell phone is turned on again, and the payment should be completed after buying all desired items even if the phone happens to turn on and off several times during the procedure. This is an optional requirement because not all application service models require this.

5.3. *Code System Requirements*

This section is not for describing requirements. Instead, it aims to define the characteristics of coding systems to help decide which one should be used for a given RFID service. There are three standards of coding for RFID application services. They are EPC by EPCglobal, ISO/IEC 15963 and 15459 by ISO/IEC, and ucode by the Ubiquitous ID center. It has to be decided whether to choose one from among them or whether to create one's own unique coding structure.

In the mobile RFID application service model, a real object serves as a medium between information resources on a network and a user. The RFID code performs functions of the medium, and the physical tag can be compared to a bowl containing a code. Information resources conveyed to humans need to be expressed in a way that human senses can recognize through a mobile phone that has a limited data input/output environment.

Since mobile RFID services are supposed to target people sharing the same culture and language and constitute an exclusive wireless Internet content environment, a country can choose its own unique coding structure instead of adopting the coding system promoted by international organizations or market leading institutions. Therefore, selecting a unique coding structure could be a feasible alternative.

5.4. *Tag, Reader Requirements*

5.4.1. *Single Code Storage*

The mobile RFID service must store only a single code as UII in a tag. In the case that there are more than two codes, the first read code is accepted and any others are ignored.

5.4.2. *User Data Field*

There are various kinds of tags including a tag that contains just code information or that can store application data in its user data field for the application service. The mobile RFID service should be able to employ two such kind. The latter tag is used as follows. The user data field is used by a content service provider or the mobile RFID application within a mobile phone. The former is optional and the latter required. Therefore, in mobile RFID application programs or WIPI API, the user data field must be available as described in Sec. 4.2.

Since a content provider optionally uses the user data field, it saves data there when necessary. For the mobile RFID service, the process explained in Sec. 3.1 should be carried out before code resolution and other procedures. Code resolution can take place after the process described in Sec. 2.1; otherwise the service may terminate without code resolution.

5.4.3. *Mobile RFID Reader Module*

When constructing the infrastructure for application services, reader functionality is an important element in defining overall data flows and mutual interface because the reader functionality determines whether a specific task will be performed by the reader or other systems.

For the mobile RFID service infrastructure, only one RFID reader is mounted within a mobile phone, which does not require a host system to manage multiple readers. Some functions of the ALE host system on the EPC network are integrated into a mobile phone with application programs, and the mobile RFID phone would become the integrated RFID reader system. The integrated RFID reader system of the mobile RFID service can serve as an assumed service broker between a handset and content servers by diminishing communication traffic and processing information for additional services. Yet the service broker is not considered a common requirement for the mobile RFID service, and it would not affect the requirements for constructing the reader system. As for the service broker, its network structure and relevant standards are discussed in separate documents.

6. Enforcing Security in a Mobile RFID Environment

Mobile RFID is a technology designed to allow an RFID reader to be embedded in a mobile terminal and to provide various application services over wireless networks. Robust mobile RFID security must both protect service networks against security threats and shield consumers from privacy intrusions. The keys to robust mobile RFID security are simplicity and a fundamentally secure foundation. This section looks at these security issues and recommends an alternative approach to achieving robust mobile RFID security. It aims at providing secure mobile RFID services, and analyzing secure mobile RFID service models to solve security issues like security among domains, personal privacy profiles, authentication, end-to-end security, and tracking prevention.

There are many ways to interfere with RFID services and various issues have been tackled theoretically, but also proved to be possible practically. The vulnerabilities in RFID security include passive signal interception attacks on tags and readers, reading of tags by unauthorized readers, falsifying tag or reader identities, use of attack tools against tags, neutralization of tags, and elaborate attacks on tags with cryptographic hacking methods. There are similar vulnerabilities and issues of possible infringement of privacy with regard to mobile RFID technology. Proper security technologies are required. Furthermore, we also require information protection service models that ensure security and privacy protection and management for service providers in compliance with present RFID specifications and mobile RFID standards even when tags do not use coding algorithms. This chapter suggests and analyzes these mobile RFID information protection service models considering the situations mentioned above. The provision of secure mobile RFID services needs a combined security framework resolving many security issues like security among domains, personal privacy profile, authentication, end-to-end security, and tracking prevention.

7. Conclusions

As mentioned above, mobile RFID is an emergent and promising application that uses RFID technology. However, the mobility of readers and its service model — which differs from the RFID service in the retail and supply chain — will give rise to additional security threats.

To address these issues, while both are important tools, neither killing nor recoding is the final answer in RFID privacy. Killing alone is not enough, and new mechanisms are needed for building privacy-preserving RFID architectures. In this chapter, we have tried to introduce the concept of mobile RFID and some of the additional security threats involved. The frequency band to support the air protocol is allocated from 908.5 MHz to 914 MHz in Korea in order to comply with ISO 18000-6 for air interface communications at 860 MHz to 960 MHz. We also describe a way of incorporating the new technology to work with cell phones in particular, both as an external security reading device (replacing 900 MHz) and as an added security service to manage all RFID mobile device mediums. With this purpose in mind, the application areas of this service platform are also briefly presented. By doing so, customized security and privacy protection can be achieved. In this regard, the suggested technique is an effective solution for security and privacy protection in a networked mobile RFID service system.

Acknowledgments

This work was supported by the Korea Research Foundation Grant funded by the Korean Government (KRF-2008-357-D00255). The authors thank the members of the RFID/USN research team at ETRI for formulating many of the concepts discussed in this chapter. The authors also thank to all members of Wireless Internet for Mobile Entertainment Consortium (WINMEC http://winmec.ucla.edu/) and the UCLA RFID Lab (http://winmec.ucla.edu/rfid/), University of California at Los Angeles. Due to the introductory character of this chapter, some of the material that provides detailed information relevant to the topic of the chapter is not included. Readers interested to know more about matter described here are directed to conference papers and more technical information on mobile RFID's security are Namje Park's website: http://www.security.re.kr/~njpark.

Terminologies

Code: This refers to the number given to an on-line or off-line object in the mobile RFID service. It is a structured number like a phone number and points to the number system stored in the tag, especially in the mobile RFID service. This code is a mean to identify each object. The mobile RFID service supports multiple code systems like EPC, ucode, mCode and micro-mCode. A service provider can choose any one of them as a basic code system for its mobile RFID service.

Mobile RFID: This refers to general activities that provide information services to users by integrating RFID into the mobile communication environment, introduced by the mobile RFID forum. Its abbreviation is 'mRFID'.

Mobile RFID Tag/Transponder (*Mobile RFID Tag*): This refers to the RFID tag used for the mobile RFID service. This tag is available in three types: ISO/IEC 18000-6 B, ISO/IEC 18000-6 C and EPC C1-Gen2. The tag of the mobile RFID service adopts the ISO/IEC 18000-6 C standard for basic and ISO/IEC 18000-6 B for options; the EPC C1Gen2 standard can also be used for the RFID tag because it is equal to or compatible with ISO/IEC 18000-6 C.

mCode: This refers to a code system that the mobile RFID Forum defined for the mobile RFID service. This code was designed for on-line contents, but it is also available for off-line objects since an RFID tag is attached to them.

Object Directory Service (*ODS*): ODS is an information system that provides data needed to obtain an information resource over a network for a specific code expressed in numbers (or mCode).

Object Information Service (*OIS*): This server retains details about a certain object, and they could be any information. In this regard, OIS is similar to the WAP/web content server that offers common contents.

Object Traceability Service (*OTS*): This refers to an information system that reads a tag and records its history in order to trace information when the tag-attached product was rolled out, how it was distributed, and what processes it went through.

Radio Frequency Identification (*RFID*): RFID is a generic term for technologies that use radio waves to remotely store and retrieve data. In other words, it is a combined term with RF and ID where RF means a wireless communication technology and ID means identification information of a tag. So it is said that RFID is theoretically a wireless networking technology to transmit identification information stored in an electronic memory space.

RFID Privacy Management Service (*RPS*) *Server*: This refers to a policy-based privacy management service that enables decision-making and adoption of privacy protection policy so that tag information can be applied to the policy within the mobile RFID network infrastructure.

Tag: Consisting of chip and antenna, tag is a device analyzing the command sent from mobile RFID service reader and backscattering response to the reader.

Uniform Resource Identifier (*URI*): URI is classified into "locator" and "name" URI consists of URL and URN.

Uniform Resource Name (*URN*): URN enables identification of a specific information resource by its name.

User Memory Bank: In the memory structure of the ISO/IEC 18000-6C standard, "Bank 11" field is called the "User Memory Bank".

Exercises

1. Where would you use a Mobile RFID network?

   A. B2C application cases
   B. Luggage tracking
   C. ERP, CRM *etc.*
   D. Retail store supply chain

2. You are a Korean manufacturer and have a contract to ship goods to U.S. Will the tags you are currently using be able comply with the Wal-Mart mandate?

   A. Yes.
   B. No. The Korea uses the 902–928 MHz frequency, whereas U.S. uses 865–868 (870) MHz. Two tags would have to be used.
   C. Yes, if the tags are made to operate on both frequencies.
   D. Yes, if the U.S. customer used the Korea readers.

3. Which types of RFID tags carry a battery? (Select two options)

   A. Active tags
   B. Passive tags
   C. Semi-passive tags
   D. All of the above

4. Which of the following are major air interface standards for UHF RFID? (Select TWO)

   A. ISO/IEC 15961
   B. ISO/IEC 18000, Part 6
   C. EPC Class 1 Gen 2
   D. European Article Numbering. Uniform Code Council Global Tag (EAN.UCC GTAG)

5. What could be a reason to use a read-only RFID tag?

   A. There is no reason to use them; they are not even manufactured anymore.
   B. They have better performance than read–write tags.
   C. They are more secure.
   D. They are smaller.

6. Which types of tags can use near-field as well as far-field communication?

   A. Passive UHF
   B. Passive LF
   C. Passive microwave
   D. All passive tags

7. What standard does the ISO ratification of the EPC Gen 2 protocol create?

   A. ISO/IEC 18000 Part 6C
   B. ISO/IEC 18000 Part 8
   C. ISO/IEC 19000 Part 1
   D. FCC Part 15.103

8. Mobile Terminal Platform can control which of the following reader functionalities?

   A. Data filtering
   B. Light stack functionality

C. Motion detectors
D. Manual triggering of reads

9. Which standard applies to 900 MHz mobile RFID tags?

A. EPC Generation 2
B. ISO/IEC 18000 Part 3
C. ISO/IEC 18000 Part 7
D. ANSI INCITS 256

10. What does Terminal Platform as Mobile RFID middleware do?

A. Filter and smoothen data
B. Provide a GUI to end users
C. Print to RFID labels
D. Monitor the health of the RFID network

References

1. T. Tsuji, S. Kouno, J. Noguchi, M. Iguchi, N. Misu and M. Kawamura, Asset management solution based on RFID, *NEC J. Adv. Technol.* **1**(3), 188 (2004).
2. K. Finkenzeller, *RFID Handbook: Fundamentals and Applications in Contactless Smart Cards and Identification* (Wiley, 2003).
3. L. Sullivan, Middleware enables RFID tests, *Information Week*, no. 991 (2004).
4. J. Chae and S. Oh, Information Report on Mobile RFID in Korea, ISO/IEC JTC1/SC 31/WG4 N0922, Information paper, ISO/IEC JTC1 SC31 WG4 SG 5 (2005).
5. S. E. Sarma, S. A. Weis and D. W. Engels, RFID systems, security and privacy implications, Technical Report, MIT-AUTOID-WH-014, AutoID Center, MIT (2002).
6. S. Weis *et al.*, Security and privacy aspects of low-cost radio frequency identification systems, *1st Int. Conf. Security in Pervasive Computing* (2003).
7. M. Ohkubo, K. Suzuki and S. Kinoshita, Cryptographic approach to "privacy-friendly" tags, RFID Privacy Workshop (2003).
8. W. Park and B. Lee, Proposal for participating in the Correspondence Group on RFID in ITU-T, Information Paper, ASTAP Forum (2004).
9. S. Yoo, Mobile RFID Activities in Korea, Contribution Paper to the APT Standardization Program (2005).
10. Y. Kim and N. Koshizuka, Review Report of Standardization Issues on Network Aspects of Identification Including RFID, ITU-T, Paper TD315 (2006).
11. M. Tsukada and A. Narita, Development Models of Network Aspects of Identification Systems (Including RFID) (NID) and Proposal on Approach for the Standardization, ITU-T, JCA-NID Document 2006-I-014 (2006).
12. B. Park, S. Lee and H. Youm, A Proposal for Personal Identifier Management Framework on the Internet, ITU-T, COM17-D165 (2006).
13. N. Park, J. Kwak, S. Kim, D. Won and H. Kim, *WIPI Mobile Platform with Secure Service for Mobile RFID Network Environment*, Lecture Notes in Computer Science, Vol. 3842 (Springer-Verlag, 2006), p. 741.
14. N. Park, S. Kim, D. Won and H. Kim, *Security Analysis and Implementation Leveraging Globally Networked Mobile RFIDs*, Lecture Notes in Computer Science, Vol. 4217 (Springer-Verlag, 2006), p. 494.

15. G. Avoine and P. Oechslin, RFID traceability, A multilayer problem, in *Financial Cryptography — FC'05*, Lecture Notes in Computer Science, Vol. 3570, eds. A. Patrick and M. Yung (Springer-Verlag, 2005), p. 125.
16. Y. Yutaka and K. Nakao, A Study of Privacy information Handling on Sensor Information Network, Technical Report of IEICE (2002).
17. ITU-T TSAG RFID CG Deliverable, Review Report of Identification Based Business Models and Service Scenarios (2006).
18. B. Chug *et al.*, Proposal for the Study on a Security Framework for Mobile RFID Applications as a New Work Item on Mobile Security, ITU-T, COM17D116E, Q9/17, Contribution 116, Geneva (2005).
19. D. Choi, H. Kim and K. Chung, Proposed Draft of X.rfidsec-1: Privacy Protection Framework for Networked RFID Services, ITU-T, COM17C107E, Q9/17, Contribution 107, Geneva (2007).
20. J. Kwak, K. Rhee, S. Oh, S. Kim and D. Won, *RFID System with Fairness within the Framework of Security and Privacy*, Lecture Notes in Computer Science, Vol. 3813 (Springer-Verlag, 2005), p. 142.
21. S. Garfinkel, A. Juels and R. Pappu, RFID privacy: An overview of problems and proposed solutions, *IEEE Secur. Priv.* **3**(3), 34 (2005).
22. MIC (Ministry of Information and Communication) of Korea, RFID Privacy Protection Guideline, MIC Report Paper (2005).
23. J. Lee and H. Kim, RFID code structure and tag data structure for mobile RFID services in Korea, *Proc. ICACT* (2006).
24. Y. Sakurai and H. Kim, Report for Business Models and Service Scenarios for Network Aspects of Identification (Including RFID), ITU-T, TSAG TD 314 (2006).
25. Nokia, RFID Phones — Nokia Mobile RFID Kit, http://europe.nokia.com/nokia.
26. TU-T TSAG, A Proposed New Work Item on Object/ID Associations (2005).
27. Mobile RFID Forum of Korea, WIPI C API Standard for Mobile RFID Reader, Standard Paper (2005).
28. Mobile RFID Forum of Korea, WIPI Network APIs for Mobile RFID Services, Standard Paper (2005).
29. Mobile RFID Forum of Korea, Mobile RFID Code Structure and Tag Data Structure for Mobile RFID Services, Standard Paper, http://www.mrf.or.kr (2005).
30. Mobile RFID Forum of Korea, Access Right Management API Standard for Secure Mobile RFID Reader, MRFS-4-03, Standard Paper, http://www.mrf.or.kr (2005).
31. Mobile RFID Forum of Korea, HAL API Standard for RFID Reader of Mobile Phone, Standard Paper (2005).
32. Mobile RFID Forum of Korea, WIPI API for Mobile RFID Reader Device, Standard Paper (2005).
33. F. Thornton *et al.*, RFID Security (Andrew Williams, 2006).
34. K. J. Strandburg and D. S. Raicu, *Privacy and Technologies of Identity: A Cross-Disciplinary Conversation* (Springer, 2005).
35. M. Son, Y. Lee and C. Pyo, Design and implementation of mobile RFID technology in the CDMA networks, *Proc. ICACT* (2006).
36. H. Lee and J. Kim, Privacy threats and issues in mobile RFID, *Proc. 1st Int. Conf. Availability, Reliability and Security*, Vol. 1 (2006).
37. S. A. Weis, S. E. Sarma, R. L. Rivest and D. W. Engels, Security and privacy aspects of low-cost radio freguency identification systems, *Proc. 1st Int. Conf. Security in Pervasive Computing* (2003).
38. B. Lee, H. Kim and K. Chung, The design of dynamic authorization model for user centric service in mobile environment, Vol. 3, *Pro. ICACT 2006*, 20 (2006).

39. D. M. Konidala and K. Kim, Mobile RFID security issues, *Proc. Symp. Cryptography and Information Security* (2006).
40. Y. Kim, J. Lee, S. Yoo and H. Kim, A network reference model for B2C RFID applications, *Proc. ICACT* (2006).
41. S. Garfinkel and B. Rosenberg, *RFID: Applications, Security and Privacy* (Addison-Wesley, 2005).
42. S. Shepard, *RFID: Radio Frequency Identification* (McGraw-Hill, 2005).
43. Xiaoyong Su, Chi-Cheng Chu, B. S. Prabhu and Rajit Gadh, On the identification device management and data capture via WinRFIO edge-server, *IEEE Systems Journal* **1**(2), 95–104 (2007).
44. B. S. Prabhu, Xiaoyong Su, Harish Ramamurthy, Chi-Cheng Chu and Rajit Gadh, WinRFID — A Middleware for the enablement of Radio Frequency Identification (RFID) based Applications, Invited chapter in Mobile, Wireless and Sensor Networks: Technology, Applications and Future Directions, Rajeev Shorey, Chan Mun Choon, Ooi Wei Tsang, A. Ananda (eds.), John Wiley & Sons, Inc., 331–336 (2006).

Chapter 5

USING NEURAL NETWORKS IN WIRELESS MAN QoS ARCHITECTURES

MANJUNATH RAMACHANDRA
Philips Innovation Campus, Bangalore, India
manjunath.ramachandra@philips.com

Wireless metropolitan networks support the mobility of subscribers over a wide range by associating them to the access points or base stations in the vicinity. The base stations together with the mobile users form an ad hoc network. Dynamic allocation of resources in such a network is challenging as the infrastructure is not fixed and the topology keeps changing fast. To make matters worse, each application, such as network gaming, file transfer, video streaming and online advertising, require different bandwidths, buffering and different levels of service quality. Maintenance of the agreed quality of service is difficult owing to the frequent handoffs, mobility of the users, and fading and synchronization issues.

1. Introduction

In a wireless metropolitan network (WMAN), there is a large number of pico base stations to support the mobility. This results in frequent handoffs with the effect that the issues of fading, multipath and synchronization creep in, incurring a quality of service (QoS) penalty. Accurate timing of these hand offs is essential to ensure satisfactory call completion and QoS. These network impairments translate into delay, jitter and packet loss in the received content. The issues call for effective transmission management by controlling the rate of transmission over the channel.

2. Background

A wireless ad hoc network with multi-hop transmissions and Rayleigh fading suffers from a range of issues that drastically reduce throughput if not addressed properly. Unlike a fixed infrastructure network, in a mobile ad hoc network, every bit transmission is costly in terms of power. In addition, realtime multimedia transmission over the network poses serious challenges in terms of attainable throughput after considering the losses and the predominant issues of a time varying channel.

2.1. *Example: Fading*

Fading is a prime concern in QoS testing. Base-station coverage and range are both victims of fading. A building or a hill situated between base station and phone can attenuate the signal, causing fading. This effect is predictable and can be mitigated by strategic base-station placement.

Wireless phone fading results when one or more reflected signals, delayed because their indirect path is longer, meet the directly transmitted signal as it arrives at the receiver. Because of the delay, the reflected signals are slightly out of phase. The signals combine with the direct transmission additively one moment and subtractively the next, depending on the phase relationship, resulting in signal level fluctuation. The other outcome of fading is the long-range dependency in the signal.

The task is to optimize both QoS and system throughput. The solution scheme is based on fast adaptive modulation and scheduling of the IP traffic that adapts to short-term fading, i.e., during fading the bit rates need to be controlled. For this a neural network may be used to predict the future channel quality, in the form of loss rates, for all active mobile terminals.

2.2. *Example: Synchronization*

The increasing quantity and diversity of mobile communication traffic is creating greater network loading. Mobile network operators are installing micro and pico base stations as a means to open the network to a larger subscriber base. As a result cellular calls have to be handed off more frequently and accurate timing of these handoffs is essential to ensure satisfactory call completion and QoS, such as cell loss probability or throughput, delay, etc.

Service providers will have differing approaches to network synchronization where issues range from periodical reconfiguration of facilities, causing a staggered hit to mobile services, to free running network elements, causing dropped calls. The staggered hits result in frequency shifts well beyond the prescribed synchronization guidelines. They ultimately result in problems with voice and data transmissions.

A base station needs synchronization to ensure stable frequencies for the on air wireless channels. If these channel frequencies drift, the result is co-channel interference. Mobile switching centers and base station controllers also require accurate time signals to assure a smooth handover when the user crosses cells. As experienced by the end user, lack of synchronization can result in low voice quality, poor call setup and even dropped calls. In non-voice applications it creates serious QoS issues such as failed data downloads, jerky video, skipped lines in faxes and loss of location-based services.

3. Thoughts for Practitioners

Controlling the loss rate by increasing the buffer size is much less efficient as it increases delay and jitter. Statistical multiplexing and source traffic control are

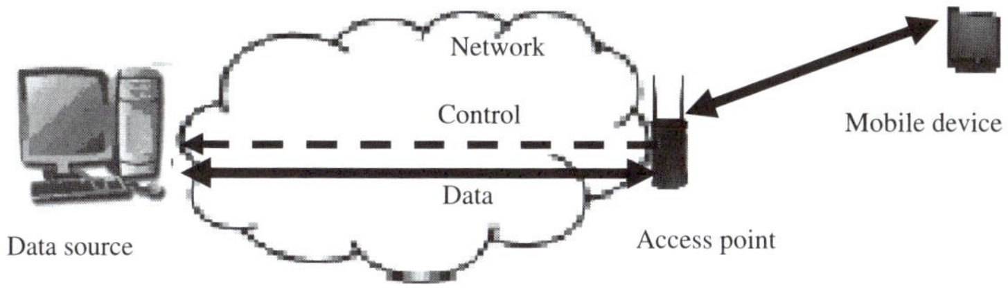

Fig. 1. Illustration of the feedback signal as it is transferred to the data source. The feedback signal takes wireless as well as fixed infrastructure paths.

two efficient ways to handle this, and to achieve high utilization while keeping loss low. Based on received statistics, packet loss rates are predicted, and this predicted information is used as feedback to the source. The sources then reduce the transmission rates or signal out busy mode or reduce the activities as applicable. The prediction makes it possible to adjust the rates well in advance and fully utilize the underlying network. The predicted signal traverses over the network and reaches the data source as shown in Fig. 1.

The condition of the network as seen by the resources would be measured. Base on this, the future state of the network may be predicted with the help of an intelligent element, a differentially fed neural network. The predicted value would then be transferred to the source through an existing asynchronous operation and maintenance (OAM) protocol. The source would change the data rate depending on the network status, preventing the already congested network from getting overloaded with packets.

In addition, based on the predicted parameters and the presence of appropriate messages, new users may be added or existing users may be deleted to optimally manage the network resources. The prediction would help to guarantee service quality over a time window.

4. Artificial Neural Networks

Artificial neural networks (ANN) are extremely useful for relating nonlinearly dependent outputs with inputs. Various ANN architectures have been proposed to speed up the training period and reduce the square error. Here we present new classes of neural networks with differential feedback. The output y of a neural network but for the nonlinearities can be written as

$$y = \sum w_i x_i, \tag{1}$$

where x_i are the inputs and w_i are the corresponding weights. The space spanned by the weight vector for different inputs is a hyper plane. Again the linearity of the output (1) may be viewed as a particular case of auto regressive moving average (ARMA):

$$y(n-1) = b_0 y(n) - b_1 y(n-1) - \cdots - a_0 x_n - \cdots, \tag{2}$$

where b_0 and a_0 are constants. The auto regressive terms $b_0, \ldots, b_n$ may be realized using an implied differential feedback. With differential feedback it has been found that the number of iterations required for training is reduced. With first order different feedback, the output reduces to $\Sigma w_i x_i + b_1 y_1$.

5. Wireless QoS Architecture

Time scales are very important in providing effective control. There is much experimental evidence that network traffic processes exhibit ubiquitous properties of self-similarity and long-range dependence (LRD), i.e., of statistical properties over a wide range of time scales. It is interesting to see that the fading and multipath data transfers are manifested as LRD. The observed LRD may be due to stationarity in the data caused by the superposition of signals from multiple paths. LRD will remain a salient feature of network traffic even as network characteristics such as bandwidth and topology evolve over time. At much larger time scales one can expect LRD to break down.

5.1. *The Multi-Channel Superposition*

A signal is typically the superposition of bursts occurring on many different time scales. Although rare, long radio frequency bursts having very large amplitude provide much of the energy content of the signal, while short bursts with small amplitude, although very frequent, provide a small contribution to the energy of the signal. The energy is therefore fairly well localized in time and the signal is non-stationary. By providing appropriate shifts to the feedback signal to the source, the long-range dependency introduced by the multi-channel fading path can be reduced. This will have improvement over throughput and cell loss rates.

6. Performance with Multiple Scales of Congestion Control in WMAN

The dynamics of a network congestion control strategy can span multiple time scales. On the fastest time scale, congestion control should provide protection against sudden surges of traffic by quick reaction to buffer overloads. The reaction time in this type of control is, at best, on the order of one round-trip time since that is how fast news of congestion can reach a source node and the response to it propagate back to the trouble spot. This type of congestion control is referred as dynamic and the corresponding time scale is referred to as *short term*. On a slower time scale, congestion control could mean gradual but more steady reactions to the build-up of congestion, as perceived over a period involving tens or hundreds of round-trip times. It is on this time scale that notions such as the *average transmission rate* of a session, *rate allocation*, and *fairness* become meaningful.

The terms *quasi-static* and *medium term* are used to refer to this type of congestion control and the corresponding time scale, respectively. Still, on slower time scales, congestion control can include longer-term activities such as service scheduling on network switches and network reconfiguration, where possible.

Next, a window scheme for end-to-end congestion control is considered. A window scheme keeps the amount of outstanding data for a given session limited to a maximum, called the window size. The window size may be changed in response to changing network conditions. It is important to see what type of congestion control can be accomplished by a window scheme if the window size is held constant.

Let S be a session with a window size w_S. An infinite source for the session is assumed, so that the window is always fully utilized. Denoting by θ_s and ρ_s the round-trip time and the transmission rate of this session, averaged over some short-term interval, Little's formula gives

$$\rho_s \approx \frac{\omega_s}{\theta_s}. \tag{3}$$

Even with a fixed ω_s as the traffic increases and network links approach congestion, the round-trip time θ_s will increase, resulting in a proportional reduction in the rate ρ_S.

The reaction to increased queuing delay takes place within one round-trip time. Therefore, a window scheme provides a form of dynamic congestion control even if the window size is not adjusted according to network conditions. If the window size is modified in response to *quasi-static* network conditions, then the window scheme combines dynamic and quasi-static congestion control.

Allocation rates play an important role in traffic shaping. These allocated rates, once computed (e.g., by the sessions themselves), may be applied in two ways: directly by controlling the instantaneous transmission rate, or indirectly by a window scheme with the window size set in accordance with the allocated rate.

Let r_s denote the average rate allocated to session S. In the direct (i.e., rate-based) approach, in order to apply r_s, the minimum spacing between packet transmission times may be either set to $1/r_s$ or, more generally, determined through a leaky bucket mechanism. Alternatively, to apply r_s by means of a window scheme, the window size ω_s should be set to $\omega_s = r_s. \tau_s$, where τ_s is the average round-trip time of session S.

The above approach combines the fast dynamics of a window scheme with the quasi-static rate adjustments, provided that τ_s is the *medium term* average round-trip time of session S. To see why the *medium term* qualification in τ_s is necessary, consider θ_s and ρ_s, respectively the round-trip time and the transmission rate of session S, averaged over some *short-term* interval. It follows that

$$\rho_s \approx \frac{\omega_s}{\theta_s} = r_s \frac{\tau_s}{\theta_s}, \tag{4}$$

clearly showing that with the increase of short-term round-trip time θ_s, the short term rate ρ_s decreases, providing the quick reaction to congestion that was discussed. If instead τ_s is allowed to be dominated by short-term fluctuations of round-trip time, then we get $\tau_s \approx \theta_s$, and $\rho_s \approx r_s$, in effect neutralizing the dynamic component of window congestion control. Use an exponentially weighted running average algorithm to update the estimation of τ_s upon observing round-trip time $\theta^{(\rho)}$ of each new packet p from S:

$$\tau_s \leftarrow (1-\beta)\tau_s + \beta \cdot \theta^{(p)}. \tag{5}$$

If β is on the order of $1/\omega_s$, then the averaging interval in (5) is roughly one round-trip time (i.e., the time it takes to send ω_s packets), which is not what is required. For averaging to take place over the medium term, β in (5) should be at least one or two orders of magnitude smaller than $1/\omega_s$.

The quasi-static allocation of session rates is formulated as a global optimization problem. The solution algorithms are initially expressed in terms of the session rates r_s and later use (4) to convert them to algorithms for directly updating the window sizes ω_s.

The basic principle of the proposed active queue management scheme is to avoid congestion within a network by predicting the future input rate via the predictability of LRD processes. The first goal is to maintain an upper bound on average queue size and reduce jitter as much as possible even in the absence of cooperation from transport protocols by keeping the aggregated input rates at or just below the service rate at a congested router all the time. The second goal is to protect well-behaving flows from poorly-behaving ones by allocating bandwidth among flows in an approximately fair manner. The additional goals include the avoidance of global synchronization and of a bias against bursty traffic.

The first goal of a congestion avoidance mechanism at a gateway is to detect incipient congestion. A congestion avoidance mechanism maintains the network in a region of low delay and high throughput. The proposed scheme uses the predicted future input rate to detect incipient congestion on a large time scale. If it detects an incipient congestion, it marks incoming packets randomly according to the corresponding marking probabilities that are determined as a function of the severity of an incipient congestion. By considering input rate variations, the proposed scheme can adjust to rapid input rate variations.

Because the proposed scheme detects an incipient congestion on a large time scale, senders can react to network conditions more rapidly. They can receive the congestion signal and reduce their sending rates before the network gets severely congested. As a result, the aggregated input rate at a congested router is kept at or just below the service rate. So, the amount of buffer space required, accommodating an applied load greater than the link capacity, can be reduced. This also reduces end-to-end delay and delay jitter.

The second key component of a congestion avoidance gateway is to decide which flows to notify about congestion at the gateway. If congestion is detected before the gateway buffer becomes full, it is not necessary for the gateway to drop packets to notify sources of congestion.

In this case, gateways can notify sources to reduce the sending rate without packet drops. Thus, the proposed scheme can support various congestion control mechanisms at end systems and can be easily combined with gateway mechanisms. Because the packet marking probability is set in proportion to the predicted input rate, the more a flow sends packets in the case of congestion the more packets from the flow are marked. Thus, the probability of marking a packet from a particular flow becomes roughly proportional to that flow's share of the bandwidth through the gateway. By doing so, the proposed mechanism can protect well-behaving flows from poorly-behaving ones and will not have bias against bursty traffic.

The proposed scheme uses randomization in choosing which arriving packets to mark to avoid global synchronization. The scheme is scalable because it can provide a QoS mechanism without maintaining per-flow states. It is evolutionary because it can be easily deployed in current routers merely by upgrading software, and it is economic in that it does not require large buffer space.

7. Multiple Time Scale Traffic Control

Self-similarity and long-range dependence implies predictability structure at large time scales that may be exploitable for traffic control purposes. Most feedback traffic controls are impervious to this information, principally due to the fact that the time scale of the feedback loops, i.e., roundtrip time, is an order of magnitude (or more) smaller than the time scale at which long-range correlation structure, in practice, manifests itself: a millisecond versus second range.

The multiple time scale traffic control framework is effective at yielding significant performance improvement when large time scale correlation is exploited for traffic control. Multiple time scale traffic control may be extended to adaptive redundancy control where adaptive packet level FEC is used for endtoend QoS control of realtime traffic. An important benefit of multiple time scale traffic control is the mitigation of performance cost of reactive controls in broadband wide area networks with a large delay bandwidth product due to outdated feedback.

The mechanism for exploiting large time scale structure couples the feedback traffic control (i.e., short time scale module) with the large time scale module via a well-defined modular interface, and is called selective aggressiveness control (SAC). Two methods are distinguished: selective slope control and selective level control. In selective slope control, used in rate-based and window-based congestion control, the slope of the linear increase phase is varied as a function of expected contention level during large time intervals (e.g., 2 s), increasing the slope if the contention level is predicted to be low (thereby amplifying aggressiveness), and *vice versa* if the opposite is true.

In selective level control, used in adaptive redundancy control, a DC level, which is held constant during a large time scale interval, is shifted from high to low (and *vice versa*) across successive time intervals as a function of predicted contention level. Selective aggressiveness control is but one approach to engaging large time scale predictability structure for traffic control.

There may be other approaches and mechanisms, equally or perhaps even more effective, which can be used to harness long-term predictability for traffic control. Their identification and evaluation are subjects for continued exploration.

7.1. *Congestion Control Algorithm and Time Scale*

Recent studies have shown that the long-range dependency in traffic originates because of congestion control mechanisms and the round-trip delays. In an active queue management scheme, incipient congestion is detected on a large time scale by using the predictability of the self-similar aggregated input traffic process. The approach is unique in that it uses the characteristics of input traffic on a large time scale. In the proposed scheme, an average input traffic rate for the next interval is predicted based on the history of traffic activity at the end of the current interval.

The predicted average input traffic rate is used to determine incipient congestion. If an incipient congestion is detected, the primary packet marking probability is calculated considering the predicted average input rate and link capacity. By doing so, the proposed scheme can react quickly to the large variation in the input traffic level. The time scale of a congestion detection interval is larger than typical round-trip time of a flow detected using the queue length trigger at the instant in time that the applied load decreases at the bottleneck link in response to congestion notification. Because the proposed scheme decides the incipient congestion on a large time scale, sources can react to network conditions more rapidly.

A source can receive the congestion signal and reduce its sending rate before the network becomes severely congested. As a result, the aggregated input rate at a congested router is kept at or just below the service rate. So, the required buffer space, accommodating an applied load greater than the link capacity, can be reduced. This means that average delay and delay jitter can be reduced when using the proposed scheme. Moreover, the number of marked packets of a flow is approximately proportional to the share of the flow because the packet marking probability is determined based on the predicted average input rate. This means that the proposed active queue management scheme can allocate bandwidth among flows that share the bottleneck gateway in an approximately fair manner.

7.1.1. *Congestion Detection Interval T*

The congestion detection interval is a critical point in the design of the proposed congestion avoidance algorithm. If the interval is too long, the gateway cannot adapt to rapid changes of the traffic input rate and the difference between the predicted input rate and the actual input rate becomes large. Therefore, the gateway may unduly drop many packets. Because the scaling property of WAN traffic appears on a time scale larger than a few hundred of milliseconds, if the interval is too short, the predictability characteristics of the LRD process that is used to predict future input rate cannot be applied. In general, the scaling region of the input rate process appears on a time scale that exceeds the maximum round-trip time of flows which go through the gateway. In general, the maximum round-trip time of a flow does not exceed a few hundred of milliseconds, and Internet traffic shows burstiness over a time scale that is larger than a few hundred seconds. Therefore, for adaptability of the prediction process and effectiveness of the predicted input traffic rate, the congestion detection interval can be set to an arbitrary value which is in a range from a few hundred milliseconds to a few hundred seconds.

Thus, the addition of self-similar traffic makes the resulting traffic self similar unless channel capacity is exceeded. As the load increases, variance increase when reaches equal to capacity, congestion control holds aggregate throughput steady at the network capacity so the variance falls. If increased further, the feedback signal dominates and reduces the rate. Again the variance increases.

When round-trip time is small, the source transmission rate quickly increases to its former level, possibly allowing the congestion to continue. Hence, the phase transition of a network where everybody has short round-trip time tends to occur at a lower load. In other words, traffic exhibits self-similarity at lower load when round-trip time is small. Thus better predictable.

At a given arrival rate, streams with different round-trip times may be in different phases. In particular, if L is the load as *stream* n moves from the phase to the next, L is smaller if the other streams that *stream* n competes with have shorter round-trip times. This makes the frequency of limit cycles higher and amplitude lower, i.e., the variance is reduced.

The variance of the aggregate traffic, on the other hand, is a function of the variance of all the individual streams and is dominated by the stream with the highest variance.

7.2. *Scaling with Shifts*

Shift changes the self similarity because shift implies a different order. In central interpolation, $(d^n y/dt^n)$ is replaced by $(d^{n+1}y/dt^{n+1})$, i.e., the time scale is different. This is as though the number of sources increases. Increasing the number of sources is equal to changing t to at, equivalent to multiplying the differential by a. This changes $(d^n y/dt^n)$ to $(d^{n+1}y/dt^{n+1})$. This is because differentials and shifts are related by central interpolation, i.e., $y = A(dy/dt)$ becomes

$$y = B\frac{d^2y}{dt^2} \tag{6a}$$

$$= C\frac{d^3y}{dt^3}. \tag{6b}$$

The outputs of DANN are central differences which are generated with shifts. Shift for predicted samples amounts to generating samples with future and past values.

The derivative action generally reduces oscillations. So the proportional derivative with prediction may be used to reduce q variance. These derivatives are realized with DANN. The idea here is to use the near future prediction of loss probability as the control signal that is fed back to the input. This works because of the round-trip time. The controller will not react immediately on drop decision.

In advanced technique, instead of present values of the marking probability, its predicted value is used one step in advance. This predicted value is generated with a DANN and makes use of several previous values. The usage of several previous values is equivalent to sieving the traffic through multiple time scales. Hence, when DANN is used, it is equivalent to scaling the time by a factor function of the exponential power of the order of the feedback. DANN produces the same results of scaling. Consider the traffic equation

$$w(t) = \frac{1}{R(t)} - \frac{w(t)w(t-R(t))}{2R(t-R(t))}p(t-R(t)) \tag{7}$$

and

$$q(t) = \frac{w(t)}{R(t)}N(t) - C \tag{8}$$

where

$w =$ Expected data window size (packets),
$q =$ Q length packets,
$R =$ Round-trip time,
$C =$ Link capacity,
$N =$ Load,
$p =$ Drop probability.

Replace $p(t - R(t))$ with $p(t)$. Again the same scaling effect or equivalent is obtained by passing through multiple windows. This is because the equation may be thought of as a backward prediction starting from $p(t)$ and up to $p(t - RTT)$. ANN works the same way for the backward prediction.

A shift in the feedback signal amounts to scaling the network. One effect of scaling is that the number of events gets reduced. In any case, the bandwidth-delay product remains the same and is governed by the capacity of the network. It represents the capacity of the pipe. Specifically, let B and D denote, respectively, the available bandwidth and delay along a path in the original network, and P_{BDP} the bandwidth-delay product along the path. For notational convenience, the corresponding variables in the downscaled network are denoted by a prime, i.e., B', D', and P'_{BDP} . The following constraint is used in the down/up scaling operations:

$$P_{BDP} = B \cdot D = B' \cdot D' = P'BDP \tag{9}$$

From Eq. (9), a scaling parameter α, where $\alpha > 1$, is determined as follows:

$$B' = \alpha \cdot B \tag{10}$$

and

$$D' = \frac{D}{\alpha}. \tag{11}$$

8. QoS Architecture with Neural Networks

In the network, packet loss probability is fed back to the source as an indication of the channel state. At the intermediate switching nodes, the packet loss rates are predicted. This predicted information is used as feedback to the source. The sources then reduce the transmission rates or signal out busy mode or reduce the activities as applicable. The prediction makes it possible to adjust the rates well in advance and prevent congestion on an overloaded network. The effect of the prediction step on the performance is indicated in the simulation that follows.

8.1. *Handling the Fading Issue*

There is much experimental evidence that mobile ad hoc network traffic processes exhibit the ubiquitous properties of self-similarity and LRD wherein the traffic is correlated over a wide range of time scales. However, there is still considerable debate about how to model such processes and about their impact on network and application performance.

Many systems of interest in the physical world exhibit a property of correlation over many different time scales, often referred to as LRD or long memory. The higher the order of the differential feedback in DANN, the greater will be the dependency. It accurately models LRD as well as the implied self-similarity.

The signals taking multiple paths and faded channels suffer self-similarity and LRD, where the shape of the autocorrelation remains invariant when observed over different time scales. This kind of dependency reduces the performance. An effective way of handling this issue is to predict the traffic and fading channel characteristics in advance and adjust the data rate so that the source does not further compound the fading effects. It is possible to control the impact of LRD by adjusting the prediction step in terms of time units. The prediction can be carried out using a differentially fed artificial neural network.

The prediction information in terms of packet loss probability is provided to data source at appropriate intervals as an indication of the channel state. The sources then reduce the transmission rates or signal out busy mode or reduce the activities as applicable. The prediction makes it possible to adjust the rates well in advance and prevent the pumping of packets over faded channels at a higher rate. The effect of the prediction step on the performance is indicated in the following simulation.

The buffer size of the gateway is 200 packets. One hundred twenty sources are considered in the experiment. The simulation is carried out using Simulink Version 6 Release 12. Traces up to 70 ms are considered. Prediction is performed

Table 1. Performance with different prediction steps.

Sl. no.	Shift	Loss probability	Peak delay	Delay variance
1	0	0.5	0.5989	0.0964
2	1	0.14	0.5920	0.0874
3	2	0.1065	0.5920	0.0821
4	4	0.1009	0.5920	0.0724
5	8	0.1009	0.5920	0.0672

Table 2. Performance with max buffer size = 200, traffic = 20 ftps.

Sl. no.	Shift	Loss probability	Peak delay	Delay variance
1	0	0.34	0.5989	0.0926
2	1	0.09796	0.5937	0.0856
3	2	0.08957	0.5937	0.0808
4	4	0.07792	0.5937	0.0739
5	8	0.07795	0.5920	0.0706
6	12	0.07795	0.5920	0.0827

Table 3. Performance with max buffer size = 250, traffic = 20 ftps.

Sl. no.	Shift	Loss probability	Peak delay	Delay variance
1	0	0.5	0.5989	0.0964
2	1	0.14	0.5920	0.0874
3	2	0.1065	0.5920	0.0821
4	4	0.1009	0.5920	0.0724
5	8	0.1009	0.5920	0.0672
6	12	0.1009	0.5920	0.0720

with a DANN. The results are shown in Table 1. As seen in the table, the loss rate reduces with an increase in prediction step or order of feedback.

Fading falls into two classes: large-scale or long-term effects and small-scale or short-term effects. Large-scale fading lasts for a few seconds while small-scale fading is of the order of milliseconds. Large-scale effects originate due to distance-related attenuation involving the terrain, buildings, and other obstacles between the transmitter and receiver. It may be seen as a relatively constant term when seen over a shorter time scale.

Small-scale effects originate due to the scattering or reflections of the transmitted signals from surrounding objects. They impart and rapid large fluctuations to the signal strength. They are modeled as a Gaussian distribution. A better estimation of these parameters is required to prevent rapid transmissions that result in more losses.

In general, estimation over multiple scales, each representing a particular communication scenario, would be more helpful. However, merging the information from these estimators meaningfully is a difficult task. The time scales in which rate control and admission control decisions may be taken will be of importance.

8.2. *Handling Synchronization Issues*

With prediction feedback in place, throughput improves. It may be seen that the QoS also improves resulting in a better tolerance for synchronization constraints. Prediction makes it possible to adjust the rates well in advance providing sufficient time and fully utilizing the underlying network. The mismatch in synchronization will be reflected as a variation in the prediction step. Hence, its impact on the QoS can be limited by adjusting the prediction step. For our simulation, reduction in the delay is shown in Fig. 2 for a shift or prediction step of 8. Twenty sources have been considered.

In ad hoc network traffic, buffer control significantly influences the effect of cell loss. A simple ANN can be used for resource allocation. The neural network.

9. Adaptive Learning

In a wireless network, there is very little data and time for a neural networks to learn. Topology changes rapidly make it useless to work with fixed weights and necessitate unsupervised learning.

A self-organizing system basically makes decisions using "past experience." It aims to optimize job specific parameters as well as resource utilization. The scheduling system is able to dynamically learn and cluster information in a large dimensional parameter space and at the same time to explore new regions in the

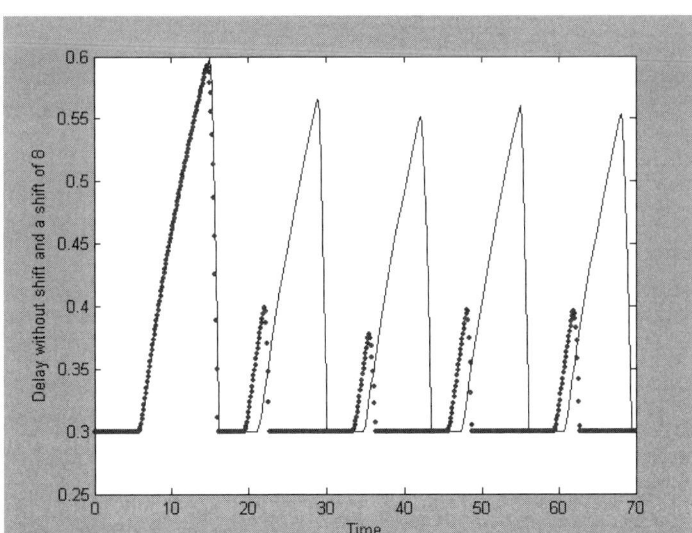

Fig. 2. Delay versus time graph. The solid line indicates delay without shift. The points indicate delay with a shift of 8.

parameter space. The issues of congestion control and of scheduling the activation of links in ad hoc networks are highly interdependent.

Conventional networks have the advantage of fixed infrastructure whereby the positions of routers are fixed and a minimal amount of user support is made available. The only random parameter is the load applied on the network, which a conventional network can handle conveniently in all management problems with mechanisms such as routing, scheduling, congestion control, QoS control, etc. However, in an ad hoc network scenario, the network has to be self-dependent and the infrastructure is also not fixed. Here the network has to handle two types of randomness. So, fixed neural networks may not be of much help as their performance on untrained data is less satisfactory. Self-organized neural networks are explored here to see the untrained regions of the parameter space. A new self-organizing neural network concept based on differential feedback is described.

Compared to conventional neural network structures, this organization greatly reduces the interconnections in the neural network by using local interconnection based on statistical analysis, and eliminates the need to store a large number of synaptic weights. The network is characterized by an evolvable hardware structure and adjustable threshold values based on selection criteria, which use mutual information.

With the very high speeds of emerging switches and time-varying traffic, different scheduling policies may have to be adaptively used catering to different QoS requirements. It will be shown that such a scheme would result in a reduced burden on the buffer and would reduce cell loss probability.

9.1. *Traffic Shaping Through Unsupervised Learning*

An ANN is a massively parallel distributed processor made up of simple processing units, which has a natural ability for storing experimental knowledge and making it available for use. In general, there are many different classes of network architectures. All of them require extensive interconnections between source nodes and neurons, and/or between neurons. The knowledge acquired through a learning process is stored as synaptic weights for every connection. Since the numbers of interconnections and synaptic weights increase quickly as the numbers of input nodes and neurons increase, it is difficult to build a neural network with a large number of neurons, even with the most advanced VLSI fabrication technology. To overcome this difficulty, a new reconfigurable ANN organization using a learning algorithm based on the maximum mutual information principle (MMIP) and statistical analysis was developed for data classification application. This organization also uses a multi-layer feed forward network, but the experimental knowledge is stored in the form of the evolved circuit structure instead of the synaptic weights like in conventional neural networks. Only the threshold values to activate the neurons are stored for every neuron; the output signals of the preceding layer of neurons are processed through logical circuits before being feed-forwarded to the next layer of neurons. Further, by statistical analysis performed during the learning process, only those features important for classification are selected and grouped as subsets to feed into the neural networks and only those outputs of the most useful neurons are forwarded to the next layer. After decisions are made for every subset of features, these results are combined together to get a more accurate final decision.

The final organization of the network is reconstructed and fully arrived at through the learning process. The final network structure looks more like a multiplayer combinational circuit rather than a conventional neural networks. The interconnections between neurons are greatly reduced and the memory needed is much smaller, especially for those networks with a large number of input nodes and neurons.

A "classical" neural network learns a set of rules or functions by training. After a job is executed based on this decision, a performance evaluation can be done to quantify it, i.e., the weights are updated. However, a self-organizing model makes use of the "past experience" from jobs that have been executed to create a dynamic decision-making scheme. A competitive learning algorithm is used to "cluster" correlated information in the multi-dimensional input space defined by the parameters describing the systems, jobs, decisions and results.

In the area of competitive learning quite a large number of models exist which may have similar goals but differ considerably in the way they work or how the implementation is done to solve certain problems. One among them has to be selected optimally subjected to the context. In our case, a feature mapping architecture able to identify correlation and cluster data distributed in a high-dimensional input space is carried out using a growing self-organizing network. Incremental network models do not have a predefined structure (as in the case of self-organizing maps) and the addition and removal of neurons from the structure are done as part of the learning procedure.

The addition and deletion of neurons is achieved by changing the orders of differentiation. A higher order differential obviously covers the entire learning process. The strategies for modifying the network topology during the learning process (adding, deleting and clustering neurons) are to improve the pattern identification in the data and at the same time to try to increase the overall entropy. Entropy increases with the increase in the order of feedback and reaches a maximum when the order is infinite.

In the presence of congestion, the schedulers have to discard some cells or send the feedback information to the transmitter, which may not be possible in mobile ad hoc networks as the resource management (RM) cells and the message cells do not necessarily pass through the same nodes that sense the decision. Though a separate path may be set aside for RM cells, i.e., somehow make the feedback cells reach the source, they do not carry network status as they travel by a different path and at a different time, which no way reflects the traffic suffered by message cells. Hence, a separate open loop control system, making use of intelligent elements like self-organizing systems, is advisable.

Some cells may be discarded to overcome congestion. Continuing to discard cells will not help as this results in the retransmission of packets since the source would not have received the acknowledgments. This is one of the reasons why the Transmission Control Protocol (TCP) is not recommended for ad hoc networks. This calls for an optimal discard policy, which learns adaptively. Hence, a decision has to be taken as to whether the cells should be discarded or the source rate retarded. If cell discard is allowed, that option may be tried again to meet a specified cell discard rate and also maintaining a specified data rate. This forces the ANN to explore unseen corners of the parameter space.

9.2. *Learning Algorithm for a Self-Organizing Neural Network*

During the training process the network is presented with each input pattern in turn, and all the nodes calculate their activation levels. The winning node and some of the nodes around it are then allowed to adjust their weight vectors to match the current input vector more closely. The nodes included in the set which are allowed to adjust their weights are said to belong to the "neighborhood" of the winner. The size of the winner's neighborhood is varied throughout the training process. Initially all of the nodes in the network are included in the neighborhood of the winner, but as training proceeds the size of the neighborhood is decreased linearly after each presentation of the complete "training set" (all the mass spectra being analyzed), until it includes only the winner itself. The amount by which the nodes in the neighborhood are allowed to adjust their weights is also reduced linearly throughout the training period.

The adjustments to each item in the weight vector are made in accordance with the following equation:

$$\delta w_i = \alpha(w_i - i_i), \tag{12}$$

where α = learning rate, δw = incremental change in the weight. The neuron with the weight vector closest to a given input pattern will win for that pattern and for any other input patterns that it is closest to. Input patterns which allow the same node to win are then deemed to be in the same group, and when a map of their relationship is drawn, a line encloses them.

However, self-learning networks have some drawbacks such as the large quantity of good quality representative training data required; possibly misleading visualization; neurons close together in output space represent similar input patterns, but it does not *necessarily* follow that those far apart will be very different; no generally accepted measure of "quality" of a self-organizing map (SOM); average quantization error.

Since the exact input output pattern for an ad hoc network cannot be learnt as it restricts the network to a small region of parameter space, self-organized neural networks are more relevantly used.

9.2.1. *Superposition of Hyper Planes*

Bayesian learning is a probability distribution function (PDF) over hypothesis (parameterized) space, expressing degree of belief in a specific hypothesis. A neural network trained with Bayesian learning algorithm outputs an entire distribution of probabilities over a hypothesis set rather than a single hypothesis. Such a distribution is Bayes' aposterior and depends up on the training data and on the prior distribution. This dependency on the prior distribution makes it a memory system where previous outputs have a role in deciding the present output. In the present context each hypothesis corresponds to one hyper plane, i.e., different orders of feedback.

An alternative perspective is that each hyperplane may be thought of as a classifier with an associated probability density function. The degree of belief is 0 for no feedback and approaches 1 for infinite feedback or when all classifiers merge. In such a classifier the actual output may be thought of as superposition of beliefs, i.e., addition of different feedbacks. As the order of differential feedback increases, the number of estimators considered in the sum increases by the same amount and hence the degree of belief approaches 1. The addition is not simple but weighted by belief or PDF. It has been proved that the number n of differential terms with a feedback of degree n may be replaced by a single nth degree differential term. It follows that a single equivalent or effective distribution will be emerge with nth degree differential feedback. The equations show that learning algorithms with differential feedback do indeed resemble Bayesian learning algorithms and are hence resistant to over fitting. This may be attributed to the hidden auto regression associated with differential feedback.

Simulation results have shown that the weighted sum of the zero order feedback and first order feedback data with their corresponding PDFs is found to be identical to the weighted second order differential feedback with the corresponding PDF, i.e., the classifier represented by a certain hyper plane is the weighed sum of the hyper planes of classifiers below. In this way, the ideal classifier is the weighted sum of all the classifiers.

9.2.2. *Differentially Fed ANN as Self-organized Neural Network*

Each of these self-organized neural networks may be thought of as an estimator. It has been shown that a large number of estimators can be replaced by a single one with differentially fed ANN. Thus, a bunch of self-organized neural networks forming the feature space can be replaced by a differentially fed neural network to get similar performance.

10. Differential Feedback Based Schedulers

The optimal performance of the network is achieved as a weighted average of the performance under the different absolute priority rules. Given this solution, the optimal performance can be obtained either exactly or as closely as desired by determining a suitable combination of absolute priority rules to use. Differential feedback networks can approximate this type of ideal estimators. Optimal performance measure is a weighted combination of the performance under different absolute priority rules. The performance under this procedure can be made as close to the optimal solution as desired. Each rule may be learnt individually by an ANN. The same setup may be replaced by a single differentially fed ANN.

This scheme reduces hardware requirements since the weighted sum of all estimators turns out to be an ideal estimator which can be realized through differential feedback. It can be shown that the minimization of cost function boils down to maximization of mutual information. This in turn calls for maximization of the cross entropy, which is readily achieved through differentially fed ANNs.

The simulation is carried out in MATLAB version 6. IP traffic is taken as the example. Two four-input, four-output switches are considered. One among them is used at random to simulate vanishing/added nodes of the ad hoc network. The traffic from these four sources is destined randomly for any of the four outputs. The addresses are uniformly distributed. The cells from the second input are buffered and the properties of this buffer are studied. The growth of buffer size is a reflection of the algorithm followed in routing of the cells. When the differential feedback concept is applied, the maximum buffer occupancy gets reduced. In Case 1, the decision is made at two levels. The first level ANN is used to select one among the rules while the rules themselves are implemented with two ANNs. The first ANN, based on instantaneous maximum buffer utilization (here 400 is taken as the maximum or reference), selects one of the rules. The ANNs are used to learn the rules, which are as follows. A differentially fed neural network takes the buffer utilization as additional input.

Rule 1: Permission 1 = 1 if there is no blocking head for input 1. For input 2 cells of input 1 are blocking heads and so on.

Rule 2: Same as rule 1 with input 2 given the highest priority.

Here, ANNs are trained separately according to the rule and then used. In another architecture, a single differentially fed ANN is used to learn both rules.

For self-organized learning, 16 neurons are considered each with four weights. Four neurons are taken neighboring each survivor, and the different patterns are applied in each case. One hundred packets are used for training, as this covers all 16 cases.

It is clear from Table 4 that the differentially fed ANN can efficiently replace the two ANNs, reducing the hardware as well as improving the switching efficiency

Table 4. Buffer occupancy in different scheduling techniques.

Method	Total cycles to flush all cells	Maximum buffer utilization with two switches together
ANN without differential feedback	953	599
ANN with differential feedback	927	423
ANN with self-organization	936	447

in routing the cells. It also outperforms the self-organizing neural network as well as multiple scheduling schemes.

11. Future Research

MANs increasingly make use of the access points of the subscribers as the pico base stations in an attempt to support seamless mobility. This sits well with the paradigms of grid computing and mesh networking that are becoming popular. With this it supports peer-to-peer networking. As a result, the base stations of subscribers have to support the data of other subscribers. This throws open at least two issues. Firstly, the support of the wireless communication of other users impacts power consumption and at the same time is likely to reduce the available bandwidth. Secondly, in addition to the possible intrusion of privacy, significant security issues must be overcome.

12. Summary

With differential feedback from output to input, an ANN, begins exhibiting interesting properties. These properties are correspondingly mapped onto the one observed in an ad hoc mobile network. The missing characteristics of this network as a result of the manifestation of these properties have been deduced providing effective solutions for issues such as fading and synchronization. A feedback to the source to alter the transmission is to be provided based on the channel characteristics. Here, it has been shown that by providing appropriate shifts to the feedback signal to the source, the long-range dependency introduced by the multi-channel fading path can be reduced. This will result in improvements in throughput and cell loss rates. In addition, the hazardous effects of mismatch in the synchronization in ad hoc networks can be minimized with appropriate time shifts given to the feedback signal.

A set of ANNs, each learning a different algorithm, may be used for cell scheduling. Conventionally, any of them may be triggered based on the cost function, once again decided by another ANN. Each scheduling algorithm is an estimator. In the place of many estimators, a single differentially fed ANN may be used since a number of Bayesian estimators can be replaced by an ideal estimator. Also, in an ad hoc network, usage of a self-organized network can be conveniently replaced by a DANN by providing appropriate shifts to the feedback signal to the source, and the impairments introduced by the fluctuations in the sampling frequency can be reduced. This will result in improvements in loss rate and delay performance.

Acknowledgments

The authors are grateful to their colleagues at Philips Innovation Campus, Bangalore for providing effective review comments and encouragement.

Terminology

Access point: A micro base station.

Ad hoc network: A network where there is no centralized server or controller.

Artificial neural network (ANN): A nonlinear signal processing system with learning capabilities that produces appropriate output for unforeseen inputs.

DANN: A differentially fed ANN; differentials of the output serve as additional inputs.

Quality of service (QoS): Represent the guaranteed parameters such as packet loss, delay and jitter.

Supervised learning: A learning network provided with the sample data sets or training patterns.

Traffic shaping: Altering the traffic characteristic features and parameters through intelligent routing, data rate control, scheduling or otherwise.

Wireless metropolitan area network (WMAN): A wireless network spanning a region or city.

Self-similarity: A signal or process is said to be self-similar if its statistical properties are invariant when observed over different time scales.

Long-range dependency (LRD): The dependency of the present state or output on previous states.

Exercises

1. Show that the output of a DANN but for nonlinearity represent set of hyper planes parallel to each other.
2. What is the relevance of differential feedback?
3. How do time scales impact QoS?
4. How does a DANN represent a multipath channel?
5. Where should the DANN sit in the traffic shaping loop?
6. How is LRD related to multipath?
7. Why are neural networks required for traffic shaping in a WMAN?

8. What is the effect of shifted prediction?
9. Why is simulation of network traffic important?
10. Why is unsupervised learning preferred in ad hoc networks?

References

1. E. H. L. Aarts and J. H. M. Korst, *Simulated Annealing and Boltzmann Machines* (Wiley, Chichester, 1989).
2. S. Amari, Information geometry of the EM and em algorithms for neural networks, *Neural Networks* **8**(9), 1379–1408 (1995).
3. S. Amari, Differential geometry of curved exponential families — curvatures and Information loss, *Ann. Stat.* (1982).
4. S. Amari, Information Geometry of Neural Networks — New Bayesian Duality Theory.
5. S. Amari, Natural gradient works efficiently in learning, *Neural Comput.* **10**, 251–276 (1998).
6. S. Amari and H. Nagaoka, *Methods of Information Geometry* (AMS and Oxford University Press, 2000).
7. S. Amari, Mathematical foundations of neurocomputing, *Proc. IEEE* **78**, 1446–1463 (1990).
8. D. R. Figueiredo, B. Liu, V. Misra and D. Towsley, On the autocorrelation structure of TCP traffic, *COMNET2002* (2002).
9. N. C. Ericsson, Adaptive modulation and scheduling over fading channels, *Globecom99*, Rio de Janeiro, 5–9 December, pp. 2668–2672 (1999).
10. N. C. Ericsson, On adaptivity in wireless IP communications, Licentiate thesis, Signals and Systems, Uppsala University (2001).
11. M. Frazier and B. Jawerth, Decomposition of Besov spaces, *Indiana Uni. Math. J.* **34**(4), 777–779 (1985).
12. B. Jawerth and G. Peters, Wavelets on non smooth sets of Rn. Reprint (1993).
13. J. Zhan *et al.*, Unified spatial diversity combining and power allocation for CDMA systems in multiple time-scale fading channels, *IEEE J. Sel. Area. Comm.* **19**(7), (2001).
14. L. Zhang, Synchronisation techniques for high efficiency coded wireless systems, PhD thesis, Department of Electronics University of York (2003).
15. R. Manjunath and K. S. Gurumurthy, System design using differentially fed artificial neural networks, *TENCON'02* (2002).
16. D. J. C. MacKay, The evidence framework applied to classification networks, *Neural Comput.* **4**, 720–736 (1992).
17. D. J. C. MacKay, A practical Bayesian framework for back propagation networks, *Neural Comput.* **4**, 448–472 (1992).
18. S. Mallat and W. L. Hwang, Singularity detection and processing with wavelets, Preprint Courant Institute of Mathematical Sciences, New York University (1991).
19. M. Grossglauser and D. N. C. Tse, Mobility increases the capacity of ad hoc wireless networks, *IEEE Trans. Network* **10**(4), 477 (2002).
20. P. McKenzie and M. Alder, Initializing the EM algorithm for use in Gaussian mixture modeling, in *Pattern Recognition in Practice IV*, eds. E. S. Gelsema and L. N. Kanal (Elsevier, Amsterdam, 1994), pp. 91–105.
21. P. R. Morin, The impact of self-similarity on network performance analysis, PhD dissertation, Carleton University (1995).

22. P. Meinicke and H. Ritter, Resolution based complexity control for Gaussian mixture models, Technical report, Faculty of Technology, University of Bielefeld (1999).
23. N. Radford, *Bayesian Learning in Neural Networks* (Springer Verlag, 1996).
24. C. R. Rao, Efficient estimates and optimum inference procedures in large samples, *J. R. Stat. Soc. B* **24**, 46–72 (1962).
25. T. Tuan and K. Park, Multiple time scale redundancy control for QoS sensitive transport of real-time traffic, *Proc. IEEE INFOCOM '00* (2000).
26. H. Zhu and R. Rohwer, Bayesian invariant measurements of generalization for continuous distributions. Technical report NCRG/4352, Aston University. ftp://cs.aston.ac.uk/neural/zhuh/continuous.ps.Z (1995).

Chapter 6

USING A STATISTICAL LEARNING MODEL AND SVM FOR LOCATION MANAGEMENT IN WLANS

ABHISHEK SISODIA, AMIT GUPTA, KUNAL KAPOOR
and SHASHIKALA TAPASWI*
Indian Instiute of Information Technology and Management,
Gwalior (M.P), India
* *stapaswi@hotmail.com*

Determining the location of a wireless device by measuring the signal strengths from a set of various access points (location fingerprinting) is an important issue. This work analyzes and applies the support vector machine (SVM) methodology under the framework of a statistical learning model to attain the objective of location estimation. SVMs are a set of related supervised learning methods that can be used for classification and regression. A special property of SVMs is that they simultaneously minimize the empirical classification error and also maximize the geometric margin. Received signal strength (RSS) along with the corresponding location information forms a training dataset for the experiment. As RSS is a part of the normal operating mode of wireless equipment, in particular Wi-Fi, no custom hardware is required. On a given dataset, tests are performed based on the SVM paradigm, with the results obtained being comparable to other approaches being used.

1. Introduction

Location detection management is rapidly becoming a crucial issue in wireless environments. Location management refers to the problem of updating and searching the current locations of multiple mobile nodes in a wireless network [6]. Knowledge about the user's position has many applications in civil, commercial, military and emergency environments, from helping a tourist through a town to advertising a restaurant to nearby people who are looking for a meal.

The location of a user gives information about one of the context in which it works. Context refers to the physical and social situation in which computational devices are embedded. All this contextual information is studied by context aware computing, which is also known as sentinel computing. It refers to all techniques by which an electronic device may obtain information about the context in which it operates, so that applications can take advantage of this information. Three important aspects of context are: (i) where you are (location, as already stated), (ii) who you are with, and (iii) what resources are nearby. Although location is a primary capability, location awareness does not necessarily capture things of interest that are mobile or changing. One goal of context aware computing is to acquire and utilize information about the context of a device to provide services that are appropriate to a particular user, place, time, event, etc. For example, a cell phone should always vibrate and never beep in a concert, if the system knows the location of the cell phone and the concert schedule. However, this is more than simply a question of gathering more and more contextual information about complex situations. More information is not necessarily more helpful. Further, gathering information about a user's activities raises privacy issues. Context information is useful only when it can be usefully interpreted, and it must be treated with sensitivity.

The wireless Ethernet standard IEEE 802.11b, also known by the more business-friendly name of Wi-Fi (wireless fidelity), is an important research target for context aware computing. A Wi-Fi network is characterized by a number of base stations, also called access points, placed throughout the networked environment and connected to a wired LAN.

In mobile computing systems, where wireless networking is used to distribute content and services to mobile users, a significant and useful piece of context information is location or position. To detect the position of a device, the intrinsic properties of wireless networks can be used, namely, their use of radio signals. Propagation of radio signals is complex, and in most real-world cases deriving the signal strength from a model of the environment and of the electromagnetic signal propagation is extremely complex. The intensity of a radio signal at a given point can be obtained by measurement, and it usually varies with time due to many independent causes. For this reason, the functional dependence between the signal strength from an access point [received signal strength intensity (RSSI)] and the physical position is not deterministic, but a statistical law connecting signal strength and position can be investigated.

Here a support vector machine (SVM) is used for determining the location of a wireless device by using the intensity of the RSSI from wireless access points in a Wi-Fi network.

2. Background

Location fingerprinting systems are an integral component of probabilistic plan-recognition systems in artificial intelligence (AI). In general, they operate in two phases: an *offline training phase* and an *online localization phase*. During the offline phase, a *radio map* is built which tabulates the signal strength received from the access points at selected locations in the area of interest. During the localization phase, the signal strength samples received from the access points are used to search the radio map to estimate a user's location. In building the radio maps, two techniques have been attempted: deterministic and probabilistic. Deterministic techniques rely on radio propagation models which take into account such environmental factors as path loss functions. When this is possible to do where certainty is relatively low, signal distribution models can be derived with a relatively small number of samples using knowledge on propagation channels. This also enables nearest neighbor or triangulation techniques to be used.

For example, the RADAR system by Microsoft Research uses nearest neighbor heuristics and triangulation methods to infer a user's location. Each signal strength sample is compared against the radio map and the coordinates of the best matches are averaged to give location estimation. The accuracy of RADAR is about 3 m with 50% probability. An online procedure based on feedback from users was employed to correct the location estimation of the system. A similar technique for sensor networks has been applied; for example, the LANDMARC system utilizes the concept of reference tags to alleviate the effects caused by the fluctuation in RF signal strength. The method first computes the distance between the signal strength vectors received from the tracking tags and those from different reference tags, respectively. It then uses k nearest reference tags' coordinates to calculate the approximate coordinate of the tracking tag.

Probabilistic techniques confront uncertainty in an indoor wireless environment by constructing the signal strength distributions over different locations in the radio map and use probabilistic inference methods for localization using a joint clustering technique to group locations together in order to reduce the computational cost of the system. The method first determines a most likely cluster within which to search for the most probable location, then applies the maximum likelihood estimation (MLE) method to infer the most probable location within the cluster.

More recently, intense research efforts have been directed towards boosting the accuracy of the location determination systems. For example, to handle the sequential characteristic of user traces, a sensor fusion model has been suggested, which shows a strong correlation between consecutive samples. The robotics-based location sensing system applies Bayesian inference to compute the conditional probabilities over locations based on received signal-strength samples from various access points. Then, a post-processing step, which utilizes the spatial constraints of a user's movement trajectories, refines the location estimation and rejects the estimates that show significant changes in the location space. Depending on whether the post-processing step is used or not, the accuracy of this method is 83% or 77% within 1.5 m. The dynamic features of the signal strength are studied and a regression model to adapt the change of radio map with reference points is constructed. A radio map is formed using data-mining methods in an effort to reduce the samples collected for calibration.

3. Learning Theory

3.1. *Machine Learning*

As a broad subfield of AI, machine learning is concerned with the design and development of algorithms and techniques that allow computers to learn [1]. At a general level, there are two types of learning: inductive and deductive. Inductive machine learning methods extract rules and patterns out of massive datasets. Deductive machine learning works on existing facts and knowledge and deduces new knowledge from them. Arguably, deductive learning does not generate "new" knowledge at all; it simply memorizes the logical consequences of what is known already.

The major focus of machine learning research is to extract information from data automatically by computational and statistical methods. Hence, machine learning is not only closely related to data mining and statistics but also to theoretical computer science. Machine learning algorithms are organized into taxonomy, based on the desired outcome of the algorithm. Common algorithm types include the following.

(*a*) *Learning*

Imagine that there is a function f and the task of the learner is to guess what it is. Our hypothesis about the function to be learned is denoted by h. Both f and h are functions of a vector valued input $X = (x_1, x_2, \ldots, x_6, \ldots, x_n)$, which has n components. We think of h as being implemented by a device that has X as input and $h(X)$ as output. Both f and h themselves may be vector valued. We assume *a priori* that the hypothesized function h is selected from a class of functions $\mathcal{H}$. Sometimes, we know that f also belongs to this class or to a subset of this class. We select h based on a training set S of m input vector examples.

(*b*) *Supervised learning*

In supervised learning, we know (sometimes only approximately) the values of f for the m samples in the training set S. We assume that if we can find a hypothesis h that closely agrees with f for the members of S, then this hypothesis will be a good guess for f, especially if S is large.

(*c*) *Unsupervised learning*

In unsupervised learning, we simply have a training set of vectors without function values for them. The problem in this case, typically, is to partition the training set into subsets $S_1, \ldots, S_R$ in some appropriate way. We can still regard the problem as one of learning a function; the value of the function is the name of the subset to which an input vector belongs.

3.2. *Statistical Learning*

The main goal of statistical learning theory is to provide a framework for studying the problem of inference, that is, of gaining knowledge, making predictions, making decisions or constructing models from a set of data. This is studied in a statistical framework [7] in which there are assumptions of a statistical nature about the underlying phenomena (in the way the data is generated).

While a functional dependency of physical coordinates from received signal strengths does not exist (the same radio measurements could be received in two different locations, while in the same location different values can be detected in two subsequent measurements), a statistical relation can be investigated.

The search for a statistical dependency starts with data collection, where signal strengths from all access points are monitored from a set of known physical positions. Let us call $\mathcal{L}$ the set of location information, i.e., the space of tuples representing information about physical location. Two cases shall be considered:

(a) *Regression problem*: Location data can be expressed as a d-uple of real coordinates where d, the dimension of physical space, may vary from 1 (e.g., position along a corridor) to 5 (position in three-dimensional space and orientation expressed in spherical coordinates), $\mathcal{L} = R^d$.

(b) *Decision or classification problem*: Location data is a single variable from a two-valued set, usually $\{-1,1\}$, the values meaning "outside" and "inside" a given area; in this case, $d = 1$ and $\mathcal{L} = \{-1, 1\}$. In both cases, r independent radio access points are located in the working area and send continuous beaconing signals. The collected data can be seen as a sequence of tuples, each tuple representing the measurement of all radio signals from a single location.

$$(y_1, x_1), \ldots, (y_1 x_1) \in \mathcal{L} \times R^r, \tag{1}$$

where x_i represents the radio component, and y_i the spatial component of the measurement. This set of tuples shall be called the training set. A training set consists of an input vector and an *answer* vector, and is used together with a supervised learning method to *train* a knowledge database (e.g., a neural net or a naive Bayes classifier) used by an AI machine.

In general, the intelligent system consists of a function taking one or more arguments and results in an output vector, and the learning method's task is to run the system once with the input vector as the arguments, calculating the output vector, comparing it with the answer vector, and then changing somewhat in order to get an output vector more like the answer vector next time the system is simulated.

The purpose of statistical learning theory is to investigate the probabilistic dependency of a random variable Y on a random variable X by inferring as much information as possible from the training set. In a general way, this amounts to looking for the unknown conditional probability distribution $P(y|x)$, In most practical cases, the target of the investigation is the functional dependency of the expected value of Y from X:

$$E(Y|X = x) = \int_{\mathcal{D}Y} \mathcal{X} P(\mathcal{X}|x) d\mathcal{X}, \tag{2}$$

where $\mathcal{D}Y$ is the domain of the random variable Y, i.e., its value set. Usually, an approximation can be identified within a large family of functions of the form $y = f_\lambda(x)$, where $\lambda \in \Lambda$ is an abstract parameter, in some cases a real vector. Λ is the set of abstract parameters. The parametric set of functions $\mathcal{H} = (f_\lambda)_{\lambda \in \Lambda}$ is usually called the *hypothesis space.* A hypothesis is a function on the sample space giving a value for each point in the sample space. If the possible values are $\{0, 1\}$ then we can identify a hypothesis with the subset of those points that are given a value one. The error of a hypothesis is the probability of that subset where the hypothesis disagrees with the true hypothesis. Learning from example is the process of making independent random observations and eliminating those hypotheses that disagree with your observations.

A measure of how much a function result differs from the experimental value is called a *loss function* $L(y, f_\lambda(x))$. The choice of the loss function influences the metric of the problem, and different results can be expected with different choices of L. In the regression problem, examples of L are the absolute value of the difference, or its square for classification. A simple expression for L is

$$L(y, f_\lambda(x)) = \begin{cases} 0 & \text{if } y = f_\lambda(x), \\ 1 & \text{otherwise.} \end{cases} \tag{3}$$

Once the loss function is given, its expected value is called the *risk function*:

$$R(\lambda) = \int_{R^\tau \times \mathcal{L}} L(y, f_\lambda(x))P(y, x)dxdy, \tag{4}$$

where $P(y, x)$ is the joint probability distribution of x and y. While this probability distribution is unknown, the training set can be used to approximate the true risk function through its *empirical* version.

The goal is to find the function $f_\lambda(x)$ which minimizes the risk function $R(\lambda)$ over the class of functions of $f_\lambda(x)$, $\lambda \in \Lambda$ in the situation where the joint probability distribution $P(x, y)$ is unknown and the only available information is contained in the training set.

3.3. *The Empirical Risk Minimization Induction Principle*

In order to minimize the risk function, for an unknown probability measure, the following induction principle is usually used.

The expected risk function $R(\lambda)$ is replaced by

$$R_{\text{smp}}(\lambda) = \frac{1}{n}\sum_{i=1}^{n} L(y_i, f_\lambda(x_i)), \tag{5}$$

the *empirical risk* function constructed on the basis of training set.

The empirical risk minimization (ERM) principle is quite general. The classical methods for solving a specific learning problem, such as the least squares method in the problem of regression estimation or the maximum likelihood method in the problem of density estimation, are realizations of the ERM principle for the specific loss functions considered above. Indeed, in order to specify the regression problem, one introduces an $(n+1)$-dimensional variable $z = (x, y) = (x^1, \ldots, x^n, y)$ and uses loss function

$$L(y, f_\lambda(x)) = (y - (f_\lambda(x)))^2. \tag{6}$$

Using this loss function in the functional

$$R_{\text{smp}}(\lambda) = \frac{1}{n}\sum_{i=1}^{n} L(y_i, f_\lambda(x_i)) \tag{7}$$

yields the functional

$$R_{\text{smp}}(\lambda) = \frac{1}{n}\sum_{i=1}^{n}(y_i - f_\lambda(x))^2, \tag{8}$$

which one needs to minimize in order to find the regression estimate (i.e., the least squares method).

In order to estimate a density function from a given set of functions $p(x, \lambda)$, one uses the loss function

$$L(P_\lambda(x)) = -\ln p_\lambda(x). \tag{9}$$

Putting this loss function into

$$R_{\text{smp}}(\lambda) = \frac{1}{n}\sum_{i=1}^{n} L(y_i, f_\lambda(x_i)), \tag{10}$$

one obtains the maximum likelihood method: the functional

$$R_{\text{smp}}(\lambda) = \frac{1}{n}\sum_{i=1}^{n} \ln p_\lambda(x_i), \tag{11}$$

which one needs to minimize in order to find the approximation of the density.

Since the ERM principle is a general formulation of these classical estimation problems, any theory concerning the ERM principle applies to the classical methods as well.

4. Structural Risk Minimization

The goal of supervised learning of a global model is to find a function g, given a set of points of the form $(x,\ g(x))$. It is assumed that the set of points for which the behavior of g is known is an independent and identically distributed (*i.i.d.*) sample drawn according to an unknown probability distribution p of a larger, possibly infinite population. Furthermore, one assumes the existence of a task-specific loss function L of type

$$L : Y \times Y \to R^+, \tag{12}$$

where Y is the co-domain of g, and L maps onto the non-negative real numbers (further restrictions may be placed on L). The quantity $L(z, y)$ is the loss incurred by predicting z as the value of g at a given point when the true value is y.

The *risk* associated with a function f is then defined as the expectation of the loss function, as follows:

$$R(f) = \sum_i L(f(x_i), g(x_i))p(x_i), \tag{13}$$

if the probability distribution p is discrete (the analogous continuous case employs a definite integral and a probability density function).

The goal is now to find a function f^* among a fixed subclass of functions for which the risk $R(f^*)$ is minimal. However, since the behavior of g is generally only known for a finite sequence of points $(x_1, y_1), \ldots, (x_n, y_n)$, one can only approximate the true risk, for example with the *empirical risk*:

$$\widetilde{R_n}(f) = \frac{1}{n} \sum_{i=1}^{n} L(f(x_i)y_i). \tag{14}$$

Selecting the function f^* that minimizes the empirical risk is known as the principle of *empirical risk minimization.* Statistical learning theory investigates the conditions under which empirical risk minimization is admissible and how good the approximations can be expected to be.

Structural risk minimization (SRM) [2] is an inductive principle for model selection used for learning from finite training datasets. It describes a general model of capacity control and provides a trade-off between hypothesis space complexity (the VC dimension of approximating functions) and the quality of fitting the training data (empirical error).

SRM is primarily used for preventing overfitting of data. In statistics, overfitting is fitting a statistical model that has too many parameters. An absurd and false model may fit perfectly if the model has enough complexity in comparison to the amount of data available. Overfitting becomes an important issue as dimensions are increased. This is called the "curse of dimensionality," which can be explained as the problem caused by the exponential increase in volume associated with adding extra dimensions to a (mathematical) space. For example, 100 evenly-spaced sample points suffice to sample a unit interval with no more than a distance of 0.01 between points. An equivalent sampling of a 10-dimensional unit hypercube with a lattice with a spacing of 0.01 between adjacent points would require 10^{20} sample points. Thus, in some sense, the 10-dimensional hypercube can be said to be a factor of 10^{18} larger than the unit interval [3].

The procedure for SRM is outlined below:

- Using *a priori* knowledge of the domain, choose a class of functions, such as polynomials of degree n, neural networks having n hidden layer neurons, a set of splines with n nodes or fuzzy logic models having n rules.

- Divide the class of functions into a hierarchy of nested subsets in order of increasing complexity. For example, polynomials of increasing degree.
- Perform empirical risk minimization on each subset (this is essentially parameter selection).
- Select the model in the series whose sum of empirical risk and VC confidence is minimal.

By a *structure* we mean a set $S = \{H_1, \ldots, H_s\}$ of s hypothesis spaces. The idea behind SRM is to *a priori* define a structuring of the hypothesis space $\mathcal{H}$ into nested subsets of $\mathcal{H}_0 \subset \mathcal{H}_1 \subset \cdots \subset \mathcal{H}_n$ increasing complexity. Then, in each hypothesis space $\mathcal{H}_i$ empirical risk minimization is performed. Based on results from statistical learning theory, an SRM algorithm returns the classifier with the smallest *guaranteed risk*.

Vapnik [4] shows that there is a function $\Phi(.,.)$ such that, given a hypothesis space $\mathcal{H}$ and an arbitrarily small probability η, it is possible to determine a constant h so that, however small the probability η is, the bound

$$R(\lambda) \leq R_{\text{smp}}(\lambda) + \Phi\left(\frac{l}{h}, \frac{\ln \eta}{l}\right) \tag{15}$$

is valid with probability $1 - \eta$. The rightmost term $\Phi(l/h, \ln \eta/l)$ is the amplitude of the confidence interval, and for every value of the probability parameter it has the following properties:

$$\lim_{t \to 0^+} \Phi(t,.) = +\infty, \quad \lim_{t \to \infty} \Phi(t,.) = 0. \tag{16}$$

The constant h is called the Vapnik–Chervonenkis dimension (VC dimension for short) of the function set. When considering classification problems (so that the hypothesis space is a set of indicator functions), the VC dimension of a hypothesis space is the largest number h of examples that can be shattered, i.e., functional dependence must be known in advance so that only a small number of parameters must be determined. Moreover, although consistency results are proved, a large number of training tuples must be provided to have a valid estimate.

5. Support Vector Machines

Linear separating functions, however, generalized with an error minimization rate, are not suitable for real-world applications. The idea of the SVM [4, 5, 8] is to map the input vectors onto a *feature space* with a higher number of dimensions, and to find an optimal separating hyperplane in the feature space. For example, points in a two-dimensional space $(x_1, x_2) \in R^2$ may be mapped onto the five dimensional plane $(x_1, x_2, x_1x_2, x_1^2, x_2^2) \in R^5$; a separating hyperplane in this larger space will correspond to a conic separator in R^2.

A mapping onto high-dimensional feature space is constructed by the use of reproducing kernels. The idea of the kernel function is to enable operations to be

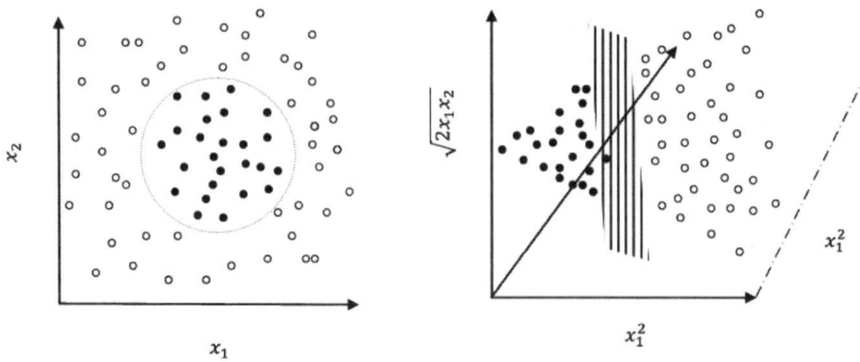

Fig. 1. A separating hyperplane in higher dimensions.

performed in the input space rather than the potentially high-dimensional feature space. Hence, the inner product does not need to be evaluated in the feature space. This provides a way of addressing the curse of dimensionality. However, the computation is still critically dependent upon the number of training patterns, and providing a good data distribution for a high-dimensional problem will generally require a large training set.

The kernel function $F\langle .,. \rangle$ is a convolution of the canonical inner product in the feature space. Common kernels for use in an SVM are the following:

(i) Dot product: $K(x, y) = x.y$; in this case no mapping is performed, and only the optimal separating hyperplane is calculated.
(ii) Polynomial functions: $K(x, y) = (x \cdot y + 1)^d$, where the *degree* d is given.
(iii) Radial basis functions (RBF): $K(x, y) = e^{-\gamma\|x-y\|^2}$ with parameter γ.
(iv) Sigmoid (or neural) kernel: $K(x, y) = \tanh(ax.y + b)$ with parameters a and b.
(v) ANOVA kernel: $K(x, y) = (\sum_{i=1}^{n} e^{-\gamma(x_i - y_i)})^d$, with parameters γ and d.

5.1. *SVM for Regression*

5.1.1. *Basic Idea*

Suppose we are given training data $\{(x_1, y_1), \ldots, (x_1, y_1)\} \subset X \times R$, where X denotes the space of input patterns (e.g., $X = R^d$) [5, 12–14]. In $\varepsilon - SV$ regression, our goal is to find a function $f(x)$ such that it has at most ε deviation from the actually obtained targets y_i for all the training data, and at the same time is as flat as possible. In other words, we do not care about errors as long as they are less than ε, but we will not accept any deviation larger than this. This may be important if we do not want errors in location in the context of wireless networks to be more than ε. We begin by describing the case of linear functions f taking the form

$$f(x) = \langle w, x \rangle + b \quad \text{with} \quad w \in X, \; b \in R, \tag{17}$$

where $\langle .,. \rangle$ denotes the dot product in X. *Flatness* in this case means that one seeks a small w. One way to ensure this is to minimize the norm, i.e., $\|w\|^2 = \langle w, w \rangle$.

We can write this problem as a convex optimization problem:

$$\text{minimize } \frac{1}{2}\|w\|^2 \tag{18}$$

$$\text{subject to } \begin{cases} y_1 - \langle w, x_1 \rangle - b \leq \varepsilon, \\ \langle w, x_i \rangle + b - y_i \leq \varepsilon. \end{cases} \tag{19}$$

Here, the assumption is that such a function f actually exists that approximates all pairs (x_i, y_i) with ε precision, or in other words, the convex optimization problem is really possible. Sometimes, however, this may not be the case, or we may also want to allow for some errors. Analogously to the soft margin loss function, one can introduce slack variables ξ_i, ξ_i^* to cope with otherwise infeasible constraints of the optimization problem. Hence, we have a formulation stated by Vapnik:

$$\text{minimize } \frac{1}{2}\|w\|^2 + C\sum_{i=1}^{\ell}(\xi_i + \xi_i^*) \tag{20}$$

$$\text{subject to } \begin{cases} y_1 - \langle w, x_i \rangle - b \leq \varepsilon + \xi_i, \\ \langle w, x_i \rangle + b - y_i \leq \varepsilon + \xi_i^*, \\ \xi_i, \xi_i^* \geq 0. \end{cases} \tag{21}$$

The constant $C > 0$ determines the trade-off between the flatness of f and the amount up to which deviations larger than ε are tolerated. This corresponds to dealing with a so-called ε-sensitive loss function $|\xi|_\varepsilon$ described by

$$|\xi|_\varepsilon := \begin{cases} 0 & \text{if } |\xi| \leq \varepsilon, \\ |\xi| - \varepsilon & \text{otherwise.} \end{cases} \tag{22}$$

It turns out that in most cases the optimization problem can be solved more easily in its dual formulation. Dual formulation provides the key for extending the SVM to nonlinear functions. Hence, the standard dualization method using Lagrange multipliers is used.

5.1.2. *Dual Problem*

The Lagrange function is constructed from the objective function and the corresponding constraints. It can be shown that this function has a saddle point with respect to the primal and dual variables at the solution.

$$\begin{aligned} L := {} & \frac{1}{2}\|w\|^2 + C\sum_{i=1}^{\ell}(\xi_i + \xi_i^*) - \sum_{i=1}^{\ell}(\eta_i\xi_i + \eta_i^*\xi_i^*) \\ & - \sum_{i=1}^{\ell} a_i(\varepsilon + \xi_i - y_i + \langle w, x_i \rangle + b) - \sum_{i=1}^{\xi} a_i^*(\varepsilon + \xi_i^* + y_i - \langle w, x_i \rangle - b). \end{aligned} \tag{23}$$

Here L is the Lagrangian and $\eta_i, \eta_i^*, \alpha_i, \alpha_i^*$ are Lagrange multipliers. Hence, the dual variables in (23) have to satisfy positive constraints

$$\alpha_i^{(*)}, \eta_i^{(*)} \geq 0. \tag{24}$$

Note that by $\alpha_i^{(*)}$ we refer to α_i and α_i^*.

Saddle point condition: partial derivatives of L with respect to primal variables (w, b, ξ_i, ξ_i^*) have to vanish for optimality:

$$\partial_b L = \sum_{i=1}^{\ell} (\alpha_i^* - \alpha_i) = 0, \tag{25}$$

$$\partial_w L = w - \sum_{i=1}^{\ell} (\alpha_i - \alpha_i^*) x_i = 0, \tag{26}$$

$$\partial_{\xi_i^{(*)}} L = C - \alpha_i^{(*)} - \eta_i^{(*)} = 0. \tag{27}$$

The dual optimization problem reduces to

$$\text{maximize} \begin{cases} -\dfrac{1}{2} \displaystyle\sum_{i,f=1}^{\ell} (\alpha_i - \alpha_i^*)(\alpha_j - \alpha_j^*)\langle x_i, x_j \rangle, \\ -\varepsilon \displaystyle\sum_{i=1}^{\ell} (\alpha_i + \alpha_i^*) + \sum_{i=1}^{\ell} y_i(\alpha_i + \alpha_i^*), \end{cases} \tag{28}$$

$$\text{subject to} \sum_{i=1}^{\ell} (\alpha_i + \alpha_i^*) = 0 \quad \text{and} \quad \alpha_i, \alpha_i^* \in [0, C].$$

In deriving (28), we already eliminated the dual variables η_i, η_i^* through condition (27), which can be reformulated as $\eta_i^{(*)} = C - \alpha_i^{(*)}$.

Equation (26) can be rewritten as

$$w = \sum_{i=1}^{\ell} (\alpha_i - \alpha_i^*) x_i$$

thus

$$f(x) = \sum_{i=1}^{\ell} (\alpha_i - \alpha_i^*)\langle x_i, x \rangle + b. \tag{29}$$

This is support vector expansion, i.e., w can be completely described by a linear combination of the training patterns x_i. In a sense, the complexity of a function's representation by SVs is independent of the dimensionality of the input space X, and depends only on the number of SVs.

5.2. *SVM in Context of Location Fingerprinting*

A location fingerprinting localization system consists of two phases: offline (training phase) and online (location phase) [9–11]. During the offline phase, a site survey is performed by measuring the received signal strength (RSS) values from multiple access points (APs). The floor is divided into predefined grid points. The RSS values are measured at predefined locations on the grid. Multiple measurements are taken and the average values are stored in a database. RSS is the simplest and most effective RF measurement technique as its values are easily accessible with WLAN cards. RSS was chosen over signal-to-noise ratio (SNR) as the radio signature because it is more location dependent. Noise can vary considerably from location to location and variation may also occur due to external factors, but this is not the case for the received signal strength. Since the RSS values fluctuate over time for a given location, it can be considered a random variable, and hence should be described in a statistical fashion, estimating its distribution parameters.

In the online phase, the system simply measures the RSS values and matches the measured value to the closest location in the database. The drawback here is the extensive training values that have to be predetermined, depending on the indoor environment.

Let us consider a training dataset of ℓ tuples where each tuple is of the form $(y_i, x_i), i = 1, \ldots, \ell$, with x_i being an array of r radio signal intensity values and y_i the location information, either a pair of coordinates (regression problem) or ± 1 (classification problem). Now, for each input x, y is determined on the basis of SVM for regression/classification on the training dataset.

6. Other Approaches

To evaluate the efficiency and accuracy of SVMs, other approaches are also examined.

(*a*) *K-nearest neighbor*

K-nearest neighbors (KNN) is a memory-based method that, in contrast to other statistical methods, requires no training (i.e., no model to fit). It falls into the category of prototype methods. It functions on the intuitive idea that close objects are more likely to be in the same category. Thus, in KNN, predictions are based on a set of prototype examples that are used to predict new (i.e., unseen) data based on the majority vote (for classification tasks) and averaging (for regression) over a set of k-nearest prototypes.

In this method, an object is classified by a majority vote of its neighbors, with the object being assigned the class most common among its k nearest neighbors. k is a positive integer, typically small. If $k = 1$, then the object is simply assigned the class of its nearest neighbor. In binary (two class) classification problems, it is helpful to choose k to be an odd number as this avoids difficulties with tied votes.

The same method is used for regression by simply assigning the property value for the object to be the average of the values of its k nearest neighbors. It can be useful to weight the contributions of the neighbors such that the nearer neighbors contribute more to the average than the more distant ones.

The neighbors are taken from a set of objects for which the correct classification (or, in the case of regression, the value of the property) is known. This can be thought of as the training set for the algorithm, though no explicit training step is required. In order to identify neighbors, the objects are represented by position vectors in a multidimensional feature space.

(b) Linear regression

The linear regression method is a regression method that analyzes the relationship between Y (dependent variable), X (independent variable) and a random term ϵ (error). The model can be written as:

$$Y = \beta_1 + \beta_2 X_2 + \cdots + \beta_p X_p + \epsilon,$$

where β_1 is the intercept (constant term), the β_is are the respective parameters of independent variables, and p is the number of parameters to be estimated in the linear regression.

In general, the goal of linear regression is to find the line that best predicts Y from X. Linear regression does not test whether the data is linear (except via the runs test). It assumes the data is linear, and finds the slope and intercept that make a straight line that best fits the data.

There are various sorts of linear regression methods, which are as follows:

- *Least squares analysis*: The goal of this method is to adjust the values of slope and intercept to find the line that best predicts Y from X. More precisely, the goal is to minimize the sum of the squares of the vertical distances of the points from the line.
- *Modification of least squares analysis*: The least squares analysis method can be modified as weighted least squares, which is a generalization of the least squares method, or as polynomial fitting, which involves fitting a polynomial to the given data.
- *Polynomial fitting*: A polynomial fit is a specific type of multiple regression. The simple regression model (a first-order polynomial) can be trivially extended to higher orders. The regression model is a system of polynomial equations of order with polynomial coefficients.
- *Robust regression*: A host of alternative approaches to the computation of regression parameters are included in the category known as robust regression. One technique minimizes the mean absolute error, or some other function of the residuals, instead of mean squared error as in linear regression. Robust regression is much more computationally intensive than linear regression and is somewhat more difficult to implement as well.

7. Implementation Outline

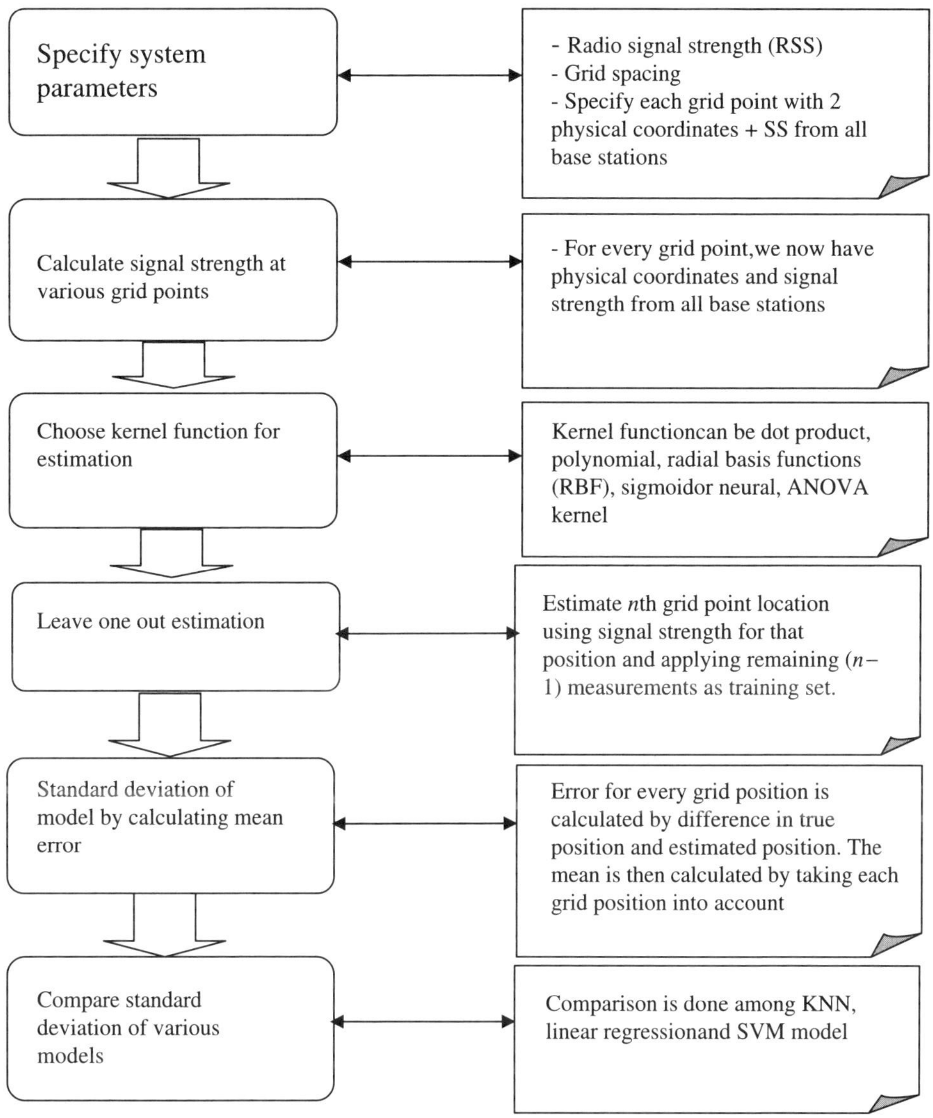

Fig. 2. Implementation outline chart.

8. Experimental Results

We have described the functioning of the SVM and some other approaches for regression analysis. The performance and efficiency of the SVM model is judged on the following criteria:

(i) mean absolute error,
(ii) root mean squared error, and
(iii) time taken.

In order to optimize the results obtained from the SVM regression model, the following were closely observed: variations in trends in the value of C (C denotes the trade-off between margin and the amount up to which deviation larger than are tolerated), γ (γ denotes the radial basis function parameter) and ε (ε denotes the permissible error). The optimum values of C, γ and ε were then chosen for which the root mean squared error was minimum. Observations for the optimization problem based on the dataset provided by the authors of Refs. 9–11 are shown in Appendix B. Figures 3–5 show the variations observed in the above-mentioned parameters.

Based on the above variations, the optimized values of C, γ and ε are 9.0,0.00275 and 0.0001, respectively. Table 1 shows a comparison of mean absolute error and root mean squared error for the default and optimized cases.

The SVM model was then applied to the dataset provided by the authors of Refs. 9–11. The results for the whole dataset are shown in Table 2.

The set of results shown in Appendix B were generated on the basis of the training sets.

Figure 6 illustrates the true positions of nodes along with their estimated positions. The estimated positions are observed to be in close proximity to true positions. However, some vacant spaces are observed near the boundary walls of the room. This is because estimated signals are found to be detected away from the boundary wall of the room, whereas their corresponding true signals are closer

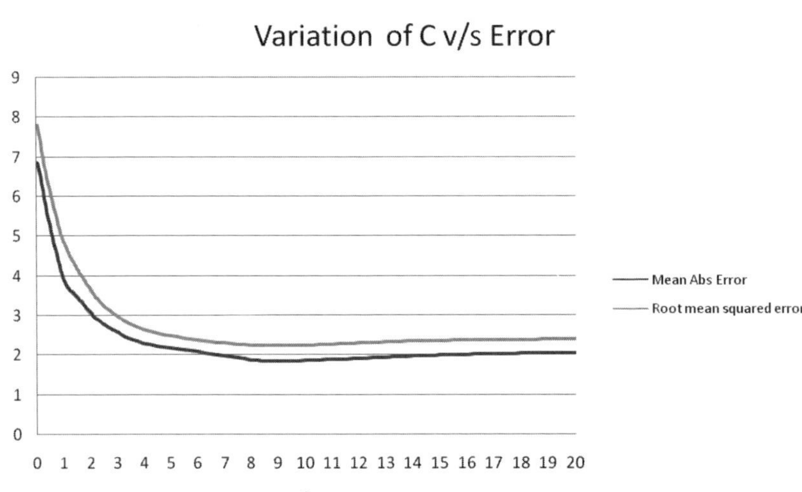

Fig. 3. Variation of error in estimated position with C.

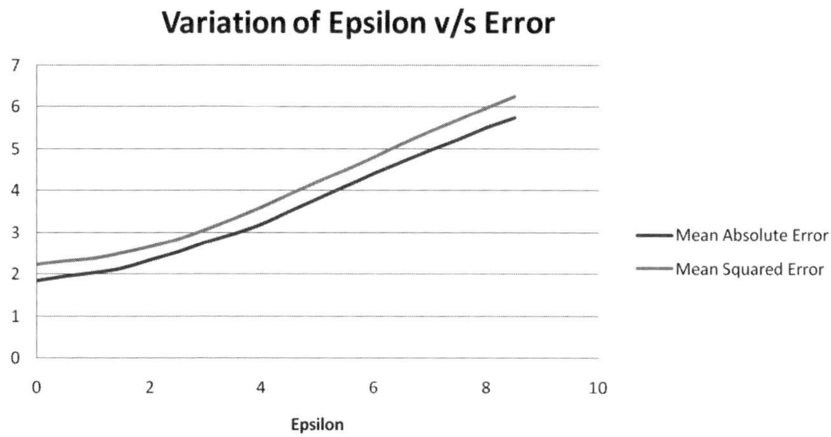

Fig. 4. Epsilon versus mean absolute error and mean squared error.

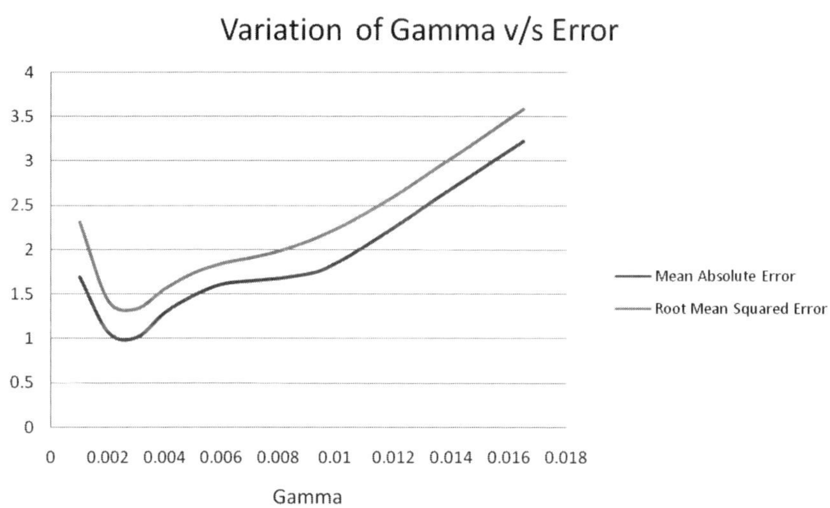

Fig. 5. Gamma versus mean absolute error and root mean squared error.

Table 1. Comparison between optimized and default cases.

	SVM (RBF Kernel) (Un-optimized)		SVM (RBF Kernel) (Optimized)		SVM (Linear Kernel) (Un-optimized)		SVM (Linear Kernel) (Optimized)	
	X	Y	X	Y	X	Y	X	Y
Mean abs. error	3.9458	4.3452	0.9695	1.2952	1.6839	1.5273	1.6846	1.559
RMS error	4.8842	5.8716	1.3185	1.6743	2.2904	1.854	2.2907	1.847

Table 2. Comparison between different models.

	SVM (RBF Kernel)		SVM (Linear Kernel)		K-Nearest Neighbor		Linear Regression	
	X	Y	X	Y	X	Y	X	Y
Mean abs. error	0.9695	1.2952	1.6846	1.559	1.4745	1.5905	1.699	1.4719
RMS error	1.3185	1.6743	2.2907	1.847	1.7652	1.8337	2.212	1.6684

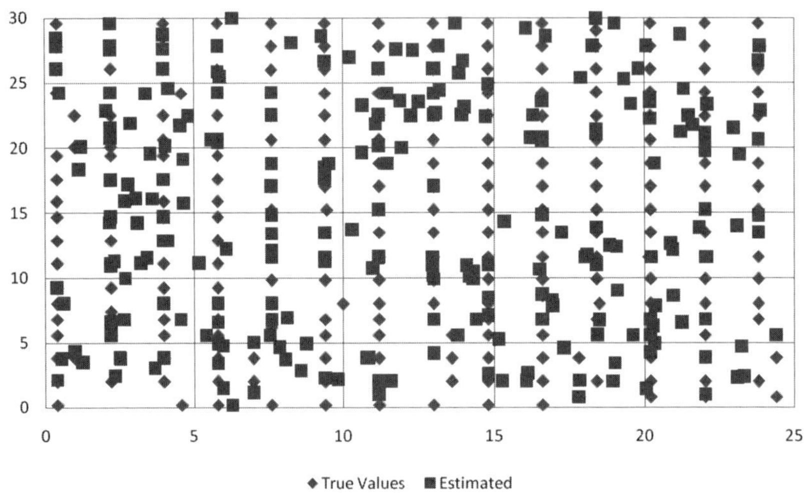

Fig. 6. True and estimated positions.

to the walls. The map for which the above experiments were conducted is shown in Fig. 7. The dataset and map were provided by Mauro Brunato and Roberto Battiti [9–11].

9. Conclusions

The SVM paradigm essentially utilizes the fundamental principles of statistical learning theory. This technique can be used in its regression version to estimate the location of a mobile user, and as a classification engine to decide the area, for example, of the room the user is currently in. The same techniques, discussed in this chapter, can be applied in principle to any wireless mobile transceiver, such as a cellular phone or a bluetooth device, provided that data about the signals received from multiple fixed stations can be accessed.

In this work, location information of a wireless device is estimated based on the previously trained datasets for a particular grid system which was set up for the experiment. Estimated locations are in close agreement with the true locations with a distance error of nearly 1 unit.

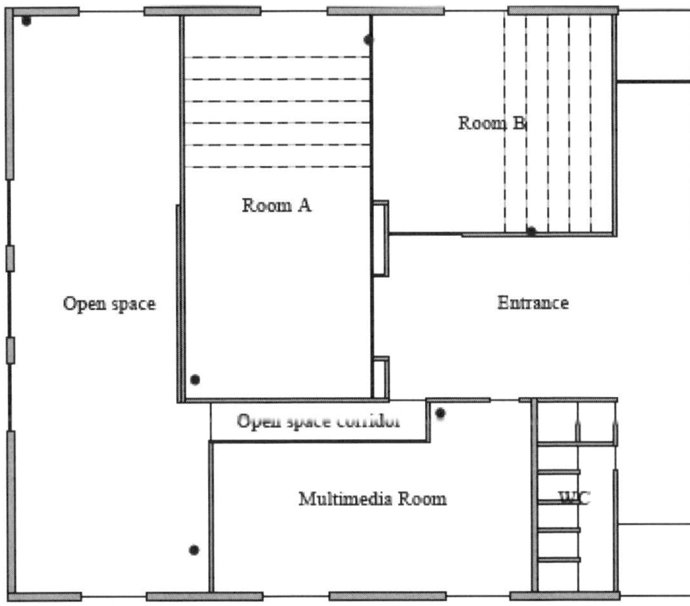

Fig. 7. Experimental setup used by Brunato [11] to collect dataset.

10. Future Research Work

An SVM can be made to estimate location information with far more accuracy by introducing the concept of area-based probability and altered input vectors. Area-based probability can be applied along with the location metric. Location or area under investigation has to be divided into grids for classification or regression and these grids can then be assigned different probabilities based on the observed trends. Altered input vectors based on received signal strength may take into account information based on various environmental factors, boundary conditions and noise associated with signals.

Appendix A

A.1. *Convex Sets*

A convex set is a set of elements from a vector space such that all the points on the straight line between any two points of the set are also contained in the set. If a and b are points in a vector space, the points on the straight line between a and b are given by

$$x = \lambda a + (1 - \lambda)b \quad \text{for all } \lambda \text{ from 0 to 1.}$$

The above definition can be restated as: A set S is convex if for any two points a and b belonging to S there are no points on the line between a and b that are not members of S. Another restatement of the definition is: A set S is convex if there are no points a and b in S such that there is a point on the line between a and b that does not belong to S. The point of this restatement is to include the empty set within the definition of convexity. The definition also includes singleton sets where a and b have to be the same point and thus the line between a and b is the same point.

A.2. *Glivenko–Cantelli Class*

Consider a set $\mathcal{S}$ with sigma algebra of Borel subsets A and a probability measure P. For a class of subsets $\mathcal{C} \subset \{c : c \textit{ is measurable subset of } \mathcal{S}\}$ and a class of functions $\mathcal{F} \subset \{f : \mathcal{S} \to \mathbb{R}, f \textit{ is measurable}\}$ define random variables

$$\|P_n - P\|_{\mathcal{C}} = \sup_{c \in \mathcal{C}} |P_n(c) - p(c)|,$$

$$\|P_n - P\|_{\mathcal{F}} = \sup_{f \in \mathcal{F}} |P_n f - \mathbb{E} f|,$$

where $P_n(c)$ is the empirical measure, $P_n f$ is the corresponding map, and $\mathbb{E}f = \int_{\mathcal{S}} f dP$, assuming that it exists.

In the theory of probability, the Glivenko–Cantelli theorem determines the asymptotic behavior of the empirical distribution function as the number of *i.i.d.* observations grows. This uniform convergence of more general empirical measures becomes an important property of the Glivenko–Cantelli classes of functions or sets.

A.3. *Definitions*

A class $\mathcal{C}$ is called a Glivenko–Cantelli class (or GC class) with respect to a probability measure P if any of the following equivalent statements is true:

$$\|P_n - P\|_{\mathcal{C}} \to 0 \text{ almost surely as } n \to \infty,$$

$$\|P_n - P\|_{\mathcal{C}} \to 0 \text{ in probablity as } n \to \infty,$$

$$\mathbb{E}\|P_n - P\|_{\mathcal{C}} \to 0 \text{ as } n \to \infty \text{ (convergence in mean)}.$$

The Glivenko–Cantelli classes of functions are defined similarly. A class is called a universal Glivenko–Cantelli class if it is a GC class with respect to any probability measure P on (S, A).

A class is called uniformly Glivenko–Cantelli if the convergence occurs uniformly over all probability measures P on (S, A):

$$\sup_{P \in \mathcal{P}(\mathcal{S}, A)} \mathbb{E}\|P_n - P\|_{\mathcal{C}} \to 0,$$

$$\sup_{P \in \mathcal{P}(\mathcal{S}, A)} \mathbb{E}\|F_n - F\|_{\mathcal{F}} \to 0.$$

Appendix B: The Result Obtained by Applying the SVM Model with the RBF Kernel

S. No.	Y (true)	X (true)	SS0	SS1	SS2	SS3	SS4	SS5	Y (esti.)	X (esti.)	Error in X	Error in Y
1	29	18.4	22	38	30	18	34	11	28.562	16.704	−1.696	−0.438
2	29.6	0.4	14	5	23	8	0	16	28.504	0.4	0	−1.096
3	29.6	5.8	17	31	31	15	24	17	29.992	6.338	0.538	0.392
4	29.6	4	19	30	32	12	10	17	28.674	3.999	−0.001	−0.926
5	29.6	2.2	12	24	29	9	11	18	29.6	2.2	0	0
6	29.6	14.8	28	39	24	29	35	16	24.834	14.8	0	−4.766
7	29.6	16.6	18	41	25	16	25	18	29.6	13.753	−2.847	0
8	29.6	20.2	10	37	27	23	33	11	28.699	21.175	0.975	−0.901
9	29.6	22	18	[illegible]	27	19	32	10	29.6	18.98	−3.02	0
10	29.6	23.8	12	34	16	12	35	11	26.674	23.799	−0.001	−2.926
11	29.6	9.4	26	36	39	24	28	16	26.701	9.401	0.001	−2.899
12	29.6	7.6	11	37	34	20	25	24	28.107	8.295	0.695	−1.493
13	29.6	11.2	26	44	39	28	36	19	23.502	12.529	1.329	−6.098
14	29.6	13	21	39	29	21	34	17	29.168	16.051	3.051	−0.432
15	24.2	4.6	14	23	42	14	9	27	24.607	4.164	−0.436	0.407
16	24.2	3.4	7	26	38	3	3	23	24.199	3.4	0	−0.001
17	24.2	14.8	21	38	40	24	34	23	24.199	11.479	−3.321	−0.001
18	24.2	16.6	30	51	33	25	44	17	22.514	16.282	−0.318	−1.686
19	24.2	9.4	23	40	34	27	28	15	27.477	12.319	2.919	3.277
20	24.2	11.2	24	46	34	26	35	20	25.725	13.873	2.673	1.525
21	24.2	13	28	53	25	27	31	20	24.201	13	0	0.001
22	24.267	0.4	14	10	44	13	14	27	24.266	0.475	0.075	0
23	24.267	5.8	8	31	41	12	23	35	24.267	5.8	0	0
24	24.267	2.2	11	16	41	11	2	32	24.267	2.2	0	0
25	24.267	18.4	19	43	35	26	41	12	25.41	17.889	−0.511	1.143
26	24.267	20.2	23	50	28	22	42	13	23.379	19.52	−0.68	−0.888
27	24.267	22	23	39	31	25	51	14	19.821	22.001	0.001	−4.446
28	24.267	23.8	14	40	28	25	50	20	19.468	23.184	−0.616	−4.799
29	24.267	7.6	10	34	44	17	22	35	24.267	7.6	0	0.001
30	26	5.8	6	21	46	11	11	31	25.869	5.799	−0.001	−0.131
31	26	7.6	13	31	47	14	20	31	25.459	5.9	−1.7	−0.541
32	26.067	0.4	9	9	40	6	6	30	26.067	0.4	0	0
33	26.067	4	8	26	39	13	19	29	26.067	4	0	0.001
34	26.067	2.2	9	16	34	12	6	21	27.535	2.199	−0.001	1.468
35	26.067	14.8	31	43	38	21	33	27	22.415	12.273	−2.527	−3.651
36	26.067	16.6	13	51	37	28	44	16	23.576	16.601	0.001	−2.49
37	26.067	18.4	18	44	33	26	42	14	25.227	19.294	0.894	−0.84
38	26.067	20.2	20	46	25	36	46	11	23.512	20.2	0	−2.555
39	26.067	22	13	43	29	29	38	20	26.067	19.778	−2.222	0.001
40	26.067	23.8	14	49	27	26	42	15	24.538	21.291	−2.509	−1.529
41	26.067	9.4	25	38	38	22	37	16	26.066	13.03	3.63	0
42	26.067	11.2	23	42	38	25	29	21	26.066	11.201	0.001	0
43	26.067	13	28	41	33	17	34	19	26.067	13.02	0.02	0.001
44	22.4	16.6	25	50	30	34	50	19	20.815	16.6	0	−1.585
45	22.4	18.4	27	43	22	27	47	11	21.217	21.221	2.821	−1.183
46	22.4	20.2	19	42	25	29	50	8	21.453	22.979	2.779	−0.947

(*Continued*)

(*Continued*)

S. No.	Y (true)	X (true)	SS0	SS1	SS2	SS3	SS4	SS5	Y (esti.)	X (esti.)	Error in X	Error in Y
47	22.4	22	23	38	21	30	48	5	20.822	22	0	−1.578
48	22.4	23.8	19	43	26	15	41	16	22.4	21.479	−2.321	0
49	22.467	5.8	22	37	48	19	20	37	22.396	4.802	−0.998	−0.07
50	22.467	4	24	40	56	18	18	41	21.684	4.567	0.567	−0.782
51	22.467	2.2	22	27	51	13	16	34	21.447	2.2	0	−1.02
52	22.467	1	20	30	44	15	24	33	22.815	2.059	1.059	0.348
53	22.467	14.8	23	56	37	21	36	26	22.467	13.952	−0.848	0
54	22.467	9.4	23	47	45	20	39	22	21.825	11.073	1.673	−0.642
55	22.467	7.6	23	46	54	18	25	28	22.466	7.6	0	−0.001
56	22.467	11.2	22	49	41	23	33	29	22.466	11.2	0	0
57	22.467	13	25	53	38	21	32	19	22.467	13.001	0.001	0
58	27.8	0.4	10	10	26	14	5	11	27.8	0.4	0	0
59	27.8	5.8	19	36	35	11	26	17	27.801	5.8	0	0.001
60	27.8	4	15	18	37	12	20	19	27.639	4	0	−0.161
61	27.8	2.2	11	16	28	16	7	18	27.8	2.2	0	0
62	27.8	14.8	23	40	33	26	28	20	27.529	11.797	−3.003	−0.271
63	27.8	16.6	21	41	32	27	27	16	27.8	13.179	−3.421	0
64	27.8	18.4	17	36	28	20	32	11	29.877	18.401	0.001	2.077
65	27.8	20.2	14	41	30	21	36	14	27.8	20.036	−0.164	0
66	27.8	22	7	32	25	22	29	13	27.8	18.285	−3.715	0
67	27.8	23.867	14	34	21	22	35	9	27.801	23.866	0	0.001
68	27.8	9.4	20	41	31	21	34	23	26.647	13.969	4.569	−1.153
69	27.8	7.6	20	39	34	20	28	23	28.548	9.281	1.681	0.748
70	27.8	11.2	26	40	36	20	30	23	26.937	10.234	−0.966	−0.863
71	27.8	13	25	45	35	26	35	23	24.351	13.2	0.2	−3.449
72	15.2	14.8	34	33	26	38	46	23	10.646	16.515	1.715	−4.554
73	15.2	16.6	30	37	27	38	43	18	14.807	16.601	0.001	−0.393
74	15.2	18.4	31	39	21	33	48	22	13.872	18.4	0	−1.328
75	15.2	20.2	28	41	27	40	57	23	12.569	20.872	0.672	−2.631
76	15.2	22	26	43	26	33	63	20	15.2	22	0	0
77	15.2	23.8	22	41	21	36	60	17	14.721	23.801	0.001	−0.479
78	15.2	9.467	44	33	24	42	42	23	13.627	10.31	0.843	−1.573
79	15.2	7.6	27	32	54	30	33	30	14.778	7.601	0.001	−0.422
80	15.2	11.2	38	33	18	30	38	16	15.201	11.199	−0.001	0.001
81	15.2	13	39	34	32	39	41	26	10.989	12.999	−0.001	−4.211
82	14.667	0.4	28	30	45	28	22	38	14.199	3.11	2.71	−0.468
83	14.667	5.8	24	24	40	28	22	45	9.971	2.677	−3.123	−4.696
84	14.667	4	28	26	46	21	29	44	14.667	3.999	−0.001	0.001
85	14.667	2.2	26	26	42	23	20	39	14.667	2.2	0	0.001
86	13.467	14.8	35	38	29	33	48	30	10.891	14.083	−0.717	−2.576
87	13.467	16.6	30	36	27	41	44	15	13.467	17.216	0.616	0
88	13.467	18.4	28	40	23	38	48	28	11.705	18.086	−0.314	−1.761
89	13.467	20.2	24	34	23	35	54	15	13.903	23.092	2.892	0.436
90	13.467	22	30	41	16	34	56	10	13.769	21.804	−0.196	0.303
91	13.467	23.8	23	37	17	31	56	18	13.467	23.793	−0.007	0
92	13.467	9.4	47	38	32	36	35	32	13.467	9.4	0	0
93	13.467	11.2	40	35	35	31	37	33	11.529	11.158	−0.042	−1.938
94	13.467	13	33	37	32	45	45	32	9.917	13.001	0.001	−3.55
95	13.4	7.6	37	34	54	24	32	36	13.4	7.6	0	0

(*Continued*)

(Continued)

S. No.	Y (true)	X (true)	SS0	SS1	SS2	SS3	SS4	SS5	Y (esti.)	X (esti.)	Error in X	Error in Y
96	12.867	0.4	25	29	42	31	24	46	11.208	2.297	1.897	−1.659
97	12.867	5.8	30	29	39	26	28	46	12.867	4.144	−1.656	0
98	12.867	4	32	27	48	28	23	50	12.867	4	0	0.001
99	12.867	2.2	29	27	44	19	24	45	16.053	3.04	0.84	3.186
100	11.6	14.8	39	32	34	39	48	24	10.936	14.8	0	−0.664
101	11.6	16.6	33	38	30	37	53	23	11.6	18.033	1.433	0
102	11.6	18.4	25	31	29	37	45	22	10.977	18.399	−0.001	−0.623
103	11.6	20.133	35	39	26	36	45	20	14.252	15.354	−4.779	2.652
104	11.6	22	26	38	21	44	57	14	11.599	21.999	−0.001	−0.001
105	11.6	23.8	27	27	29	39	55	24	11.6	20.218	−3.582	0
106	11.6	9.4	48	31	33	32	45	34	11.6	9.399	−0.001	0
107	11.6	7.6	32	34	46	32	33	39	11.601	7.6	0	0.001
108	11.6	11.2	39	39	28	33	44	33	11.601	11.2	0	0.001
109	11.6	13	38	35	33	30	41	28	11.599	12.999	−0.001	−0.001
110	11.067	0.4	25	23	46	20	22	52	14.296	2.18	1.78	3.23
111	11.067	5.8	30	22	41	24	27	45	11.067	3.226	−2.574	0.001
112	11.067	4	29	24	44	25	32	45	11.066	5.185	1.185	−0.001
113	11.067	2.2	22	24	37	24	24	51	10.887	2.2	0	−0.18
114	9.867	14.8	26	35	27	43	46	32	7.78	16.953	2.153	−2.087
115	9.867	16.6	27	38	32	39	45	31	9.866	14.33	−2.27	−0.001
116	9.867	18.4	27	33	30	37	47	20	12.427	18.813	0.413	2.56
117	9.867	20.2	28	40	34	40	53	18	12.409	19.037	−1.163	2.543
118	9.867	22	29	42	25	43	55	20	12.083	20.916	−1.084	2.216
119	9.867	23.8	26	32	23	42	48	21	8.627	20.962	−2.838	−1.239
120	9.8	9.4	54	35	36	33	43	29	11.203	9.4	0	1.403
121	9.8	7.6	26	25	50	25	36	38	12.013	7.599	−0.001	2.213
122	9.8	11.2	45	35	33	38	41	27	11.669	11.199	−0.001	1.869
123	9.8	13	35	35	31	31	45	29	10.419	14.319	1.319	0.619
124	9.2	0.4	23	28	40	34	27	56	9.201	0.4	0	0.001
125	9.2	5.8	32	30	34	29	25	36	12.164	6.093	0.293	2.964
126	9.2	4	23	25	38	25	22	41	11.501	3.408	−0.592	2.301
127	9.2	2.2	25	24	49	31	22	43	11.112	2.2	0	1.912
128	20.6	5.8	22	27	59	14	24	39	20.43	5.8	0	−0.17
129	20.6	4	20	31	61	24	16	39	19.126	4.634	0.634	−1.474
130	20.6	14.8	17	45	37	24	37	26	23.065	14.049	−0.751	2.465
131	20.6	16.6	20	55	33	19	48	23	20.521	16.6	0	−0.079
132	20.6	18.4	21	45	28	26	44	22	21.437	18.401	0.001	0.837
133	20.6	20.2	20	47	27	26	48	14	21.757	21.621	1.421	1.157
134	20.6	22	15	51	13	22	47	13	20.6	21.999	−0.001	0
135	20.6	23.8	15	40	17	30	48	11	20.6	23.8	0	0
136	20.6	9.4	26	49	45	32	35	27	18.436	9.401	0.001	−2.164
137	20.6	7.6	22	27	60	16	19	35	20.6	5.577	−2.023	0
138	20.6	11.2	20	47	40	26	32	23	23.558	11.901	0.701	2.958
139	20.6	13	32	47	42	25	35	25	20.02	11.96	−1.04	−0.58
140	8.6	16.6	32	35	24	46	45	28	8.674	16.599	−0.001	0.074
141	8	0.4	26	16	34	27	21	58	8	0.622	0.222	0
142	8	5.8	34	27	21	37	34	46	8.001	5.8	0	0.001
143	8	4	35	20	24	38	33	47	8	4	0	0
144	8	14.8	34	31	29	37	43	29	8.496	14.801	0.001	0.496

(Continued)

(*Continued*)

S. No.	Y (true)	X (true)	SS0	SS1	SS2	SS3	SS4	SS5	Y (esti.)	X (esti.)	Error in X	Error in Y
145	8	18.467	21	28	25	48	51	31	6.697	18.467	0	−1.303
146	8	20.2	27	36	24	47	50	34	8.181	16.903	−3.297	0.181
147	8	22	28	32	25	45	45	18	9.023	19.066	−2.934	1.023
148	8	23.8	19	38	25	47	59	18	11.598	22.073	−1.727	3.598
149	8	7.6	38	22	45	27	35	34	8	7.599	−0.001	0
150	8	10	39	32	28	35	37	29	10.688	11.002	1.002	2.688
151	8	11.2	38	37	34	38	47	29	10.131	12.975	1.775	2.131
152	8	13	26	39	32	40	48	32	10.094	14.214	1.214	2.094
153	7.4	2.2	21	20	29	31	25	55	3.717	0.533	−1.667	−3.683
154	6.8	0.4	32	22	31	38	22	46	6.8	2.651	2.251	0
155	6.8	5.8	31	16	33	39	34	41	6.599	5.799	−0.001	−0.201
156	6.8	4	40	17	36	35	32	31	6.8	4.546	0.546	0
157	6.8	2.2	33	20	29	36	34	54	6.548	2.199	−0.001	−0.252
158	6.8	14.8	28	29	22	41	34	26	7.037	14.799	−0.001	0.237
159	6.8	16.6	26	22	10	53	42	26	6.8	16.6	0	0
160	6.8	18.4	19	35	20	56	39	25	6.222	20.282	1.882	−0.578
161	6.8	20.2	16	31	4	46	44	18	6.801	20.199	−0.001	0.001
162	6.8	22	15	35	10	47	42	25	6.8	21.999	−0.001	0
163	6.8	23.8	13	31	12	41	44	26	6.502	21.251	−2.549	−0.298
164	6.8	9.4	28	25	22	33	31	40	4.6	7.858	−1.542	−2.2
165	6.8	7.6	26	23	45	46	27	37	6.8	7.6	0	0
166	6.8	11.2	28	30	12	47	38	31	6.8	14.395	3.195	0
167	6.8	13	30	27	15	34	36	25	6.8	13	0	0
168	6.2	7.6	34	18	32	39	37	36	6.942	8.104	0.504	0.742
169	5.6	0.4	28	19	27	32	27	46	3.717	2.498	2.098	−1.883
170	5.6	5.8	27	20	29	37	19	44	5.601	5.4	−0.4	0.001
171	5.6	4	29	23	30	31	30	40	4.785	5.968	1.968	−0.815
172	5.6	2.2	32	18	30	33	34	53	5.601	2.2	0	0.001
173	5.6	14.8	26	21	15	42	34	22	5.6	13.823	−0.977	0
174	5.6	16.6	19	29	14	40	44	22	4.891	20.336	3.736	−0.709
175	5.6	18.4	22	31	15	39	45	19	7.79	20.369	1.969	2.19
176	5.6	20.2	24	31	16	56	38	20	5.6	20.2	0	0
177	5.6	22	21	25	11	44	48	17	5.6	19.58	−2.42	0
178	5.6	24.4	13	27	6	57	37	25	5.601	24.4	0	0.001
179	5.6	9.4	33	18	28	35	34	34	5.601	7.537	−1.863	0.001
180	5.6	11.2	27	21	28	40	35	39	4.862	8.785	−2.415	−0.738
181	5.6	13.6	24	24	16	48	35	29	5.231	15.136	1.536	−0.369
182	3.8	0.4	26	22	24	37	30	48	3.8	2.472	2.072	0
183	3.8	5.8	27	24	33	31	33	44	4.866	5.8	0	1.066
184	3.8	7	22	22	42	37	26	32	5.043	7	0	1.243
185	3.8	4	21	16	24	40	31	44	3.8	4	0	0
186	3.8	1	26	20	28	27	30	54	4.275	0.999	−0.001	0.475
187	3.8	14.8	27	21	30	38	31	36	3.673	8.05	−6.75	−0.127
188	3.8	16.6	20	25	10	49	37	27	3.426	18.989	2.389	−0.374
189	3.8	17.8	25	31	11	39	43	28	4.53	17.313	−0.487	0.73
190	3.8	20.2	20	25	23	46	38	30	2.598	16.129	−4.071	−1.202
191	3.8	22	18	29	8	51	46	20	3.8	22	0	0
192	3.8	24.4	15	26	6	51	35	21	4.722	23.233	−1.167	0.922

(*Continued*)

(Continued)

S. No.	Y (true)	X (true)	SS0	SS1	SS2	SS3	SS4	SS5	Y (esti.)	X (esti.)	Error in X	Error in Y
193	3.8	9.4	22	23	26	36	33	26	3.799	10.856	1.456	−0.001
194	3.8	11.2	21	23	21	38	39	39	1.847	11.199	−0.001	−1.953
195	3.8	13.6	22	24	20	34	31	27	3.801	10.805	−2.795	0.001
196	20.067	2.2	20	28	52	13	18	36	21.892	2.882	0.682	1.826
197	20.067	1	22	27	49	17	21	37	20.066	1.187	0.187	0
198	2	0.4	21	17	27	34	30	55	2.145	0.399	−0.001	0.145
199	2	5.8	23	21	28	32	23	41	3.43	5.799	−0.001	1.43
200	2	7	17	18	30	38	34	38	1.109	7	0	−0.891
201	2	4	23	18	28	36	24	48	2.37	2.344	−1.656	0.37
202	2	2.2	27	19	28	30	32	46	2.976	3.673	1.473	0.976
203	2	14.8	20	27	20	41	40	35	2.001	15.252	0.452	0.001
204	2	16.6	21	26	14	42	45	26	2.018	18.935	2.335	0.018
205	2	18.4	17	21	16	40	47	32	2	16.053	−2.347	0
206	2	20.2	15	26	19	47	42	28	1.357	20.056	−0.144	−0.643
207	2	22	24	32	17	55	39	30	5.574	18.424	−3.576	3.574
208	2	23.8	15	30	13	55	44	27	2.326	23.328	−0.472	0.326
209	2	9.4	22	23	30	36	37	32	2.001	11.604	2.204	0.001
210	2	11.2	22	19	17	41	38	31	2	11.199	−0.001	0
211	2	13.6	25	19	27	35	38	37	2.123	9.813	−3.787	0.123
212	2	13.6	25	23	25	35	38	37	1.999	11.543	−2.057	−0.001
213	0.8	17.8	18	24	19	45	41	28	0.799	17.801	0.001	−0.001
214	0.8	20.2	19	32	12	47	38	28	4.224	20.2	0	3.424
215	0.8	22	12	23	17	55	40	24	1.006	22	0	0.206
216	0.8	24.4	15	26	16	56	36	23	2.248	23.096	−1.304	1.448
217	0.2	0.4	22	20	26	41	24	52	3.467	1.264	0.864	3.267
218	0.2	5.8	16	17	29	39	32	39	1.423	5.977	0.177	1.223
219	0.2	4.6	17	19	24	35	30	34	0.2	6.291	1.691	0
220	0.2	14.8	17	22	24	46	42	33	2.539	14.799	−0.001	2.339
221	0.2	16.6	19	24	20	48	45	31	2.091	17.823	1.223	1.891
222	0.2	9.4	25	19	26	36	35	29	2.291	9.4	0	2.091
223	0.2	7.6	22	21	15	30	32	29	2.785	8.559	0.959	2.585
224	0.2	11.2	19	21	14	37	35	28	0.952	11.2	0	0.752
225	0.2	13	20	30	22	33	34	35	4.133	13.001	0.001	3.933
226	19.4	0.4	25	30	46	24	23	36	17.157	2.795	2.395	−2.243
227	19.4	5.8	19	35	56	22	18	36	20.584	5.8	0	1.184
228	19.4	4	21	30	55	21	22	39	19.504	3.524	−0.476	0.104
229	19.4	2.2	23	28	52	14	20	38	20.724	2.201	0.001	1.324
230	18.8	14.8	30	42	39	22	37	21	22.595	13.104	−1.696	3.795
231	18.8	16.6	17	44	21	20	45	23	18.801	20.328	3.728	0.001
232	18.8	18.4	19	52	28	24	47	20	21.069	18.401	0.001	2.269
233	18.8	20.2	25	46	26	28	47	14	22.255	20.2	0	3.455
234	18.8	22	16	47	27	28	53	14	19.706	22	0	0.906
235	18.8	23.8	17	44	25	18	42	10	22.833	23.888	0.088	4.033
236	18.8	9.4	26	48	45	25	38	30	18.801	9.541	0.141	0.001
237	18.8	7.6	17	34	73	24	27	38	18.8	7.6	0	0
238	18.8	11.2	27	47	35	34	41	26	18.8	11.477	0.277	0
239	18.8	13	28	49	43	29	37	25	19.58	10.614	−2.386	0.78
240	17.6	0.4	16	20	44	18	14	38	18.291	1.15	0.75	0.691

(Continued)

(*Continued*)

S. No.	Y (true)	X (true)	SS0	SS1	SS2	SS3	SS4	SS5	Y (esti.)	X (esti.)	Error in X	Error in Y
241	17.6	5.8	27	35	47	21	24	37	20.12	4.041	−1.759	2.52
242	17.6	4	20	38	48	27	21	42	17.601	4	0	0.001
243	17.6	2.2	24	23	47	16	13	43	17.488	2.199	−0.001	−0.112
244	17	14.8	20	39	44	26	30	22	23.218	10.658	−4.142	6.218
245	17	16.6	26	48	37	20	39	23	22.362	14.714	−1.886	5.362
246	17	18.4	26	42	31	24	42	23	20.72	16.232	−2.168	3.72
247	17	20.2	14	47	32	24	42	12	23.742	20.2	0	6.742
248	17	22	18	45	28	22	46	17	21.167	22	0	4.167
249	17	23.8	23	42	24	28	46	7	23.273	22.094	−1.706	6.273
250	17	9.4	28	45	44	29	34	31	17.641	9.4	0	0.641
251	17	7.6	32	44	51	24	34	29	17	7.603	0.003	0
252	17	11.2	30	45	44	27	36	21	20.12	11.201	0.001	3.12
253	17	13	35	44	39	24	39	28	17	13.001	0.001	0
254	15.867	0.4	24	19	54	24	27	38	15.865	2.687	2.287	−0.002
255	15.867	5.8	27	28	45	22	14	39	16.098	3.63	−2.17	0.231
256	15.867	4	30	31	44	23	28	42	15.775	4.671	0.671	−0.092

Appendix C: Tool Used

WEKA v3.4: Weka (Waikato Environment for Knowledge Analysis) is a popular suite of machine learning software written in Java, developed at the University of Waikato. WEKA is free software available under the GNU General Public License.

Weka supports several standard data mining tasks, more specifically, data preprocessing, clustering, classification, regression, visualization, and feature selection. All of Weka's techniques are predicated on the assumption that the data is available as a single flat file or relation, where each data point is described by a fixed number of attributes (normally, numeric or nominal attributes, but some other attribute types are also supported). Weka provides access to SQL databases using Java database connectivity and can process the result returned by a database query. It is not capable of multirelational data mining, but there is separate software for converting a collection of linked database tables into a single table that is suitable for processing using Weka.

Terminology

Access Points: In computer networking, a wireless access point (WAP or AP) is a device that allows wireless communication devices to connect to a wireless network using Wi-Fi, Bluetooth or related standards. The WAP usually connects to a wired network, and can relay data between the wireless devices (such as computers or printers) and wired devices on the network.

Feature Space: A feature space is an abstract space where each pattern sample is represented as a point in n-dimensional space. Its dimension is determined by

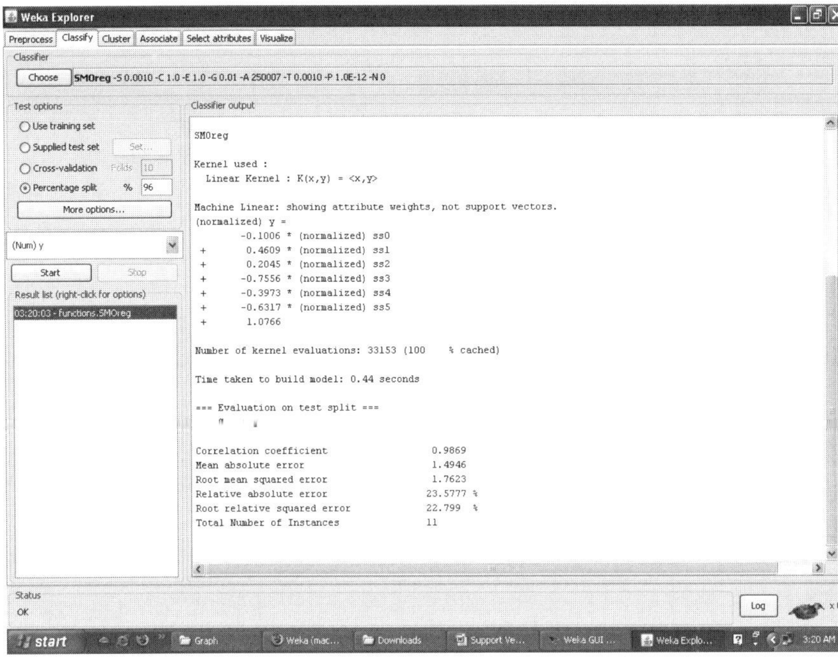

Fig. 8. Execution of SVM with 96% training dataset and remaining as test set.

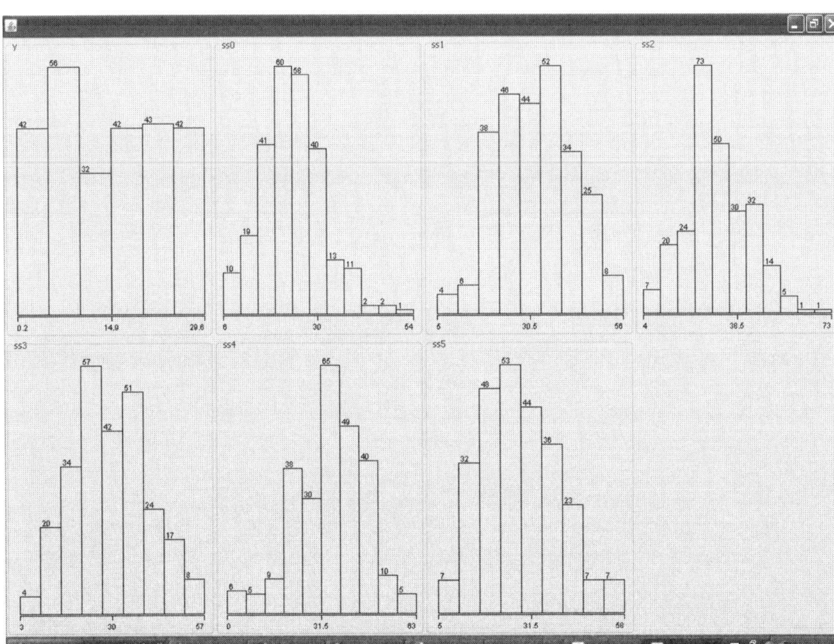

Fig. 9. Visualization of dataset.

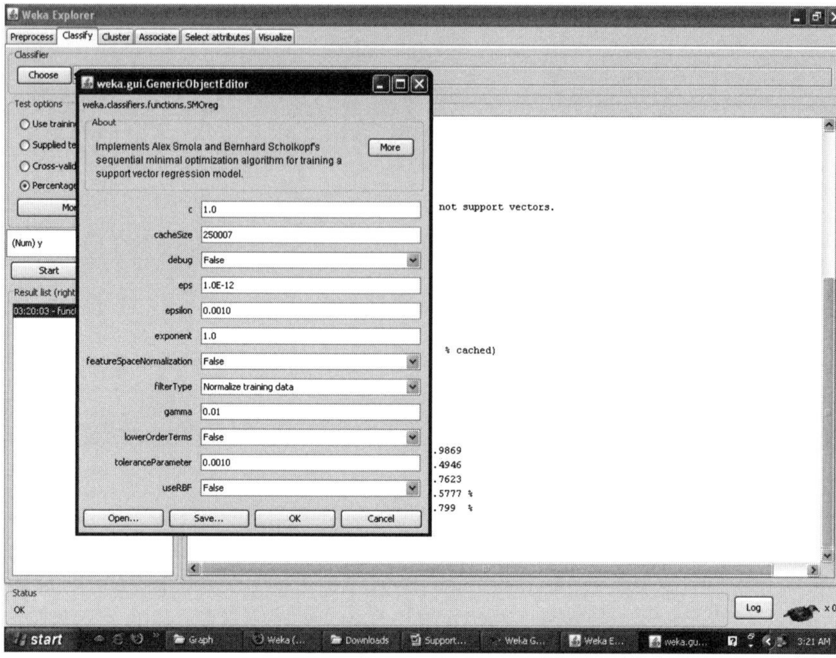

Fig. 10. Modifying parameters of SVM.

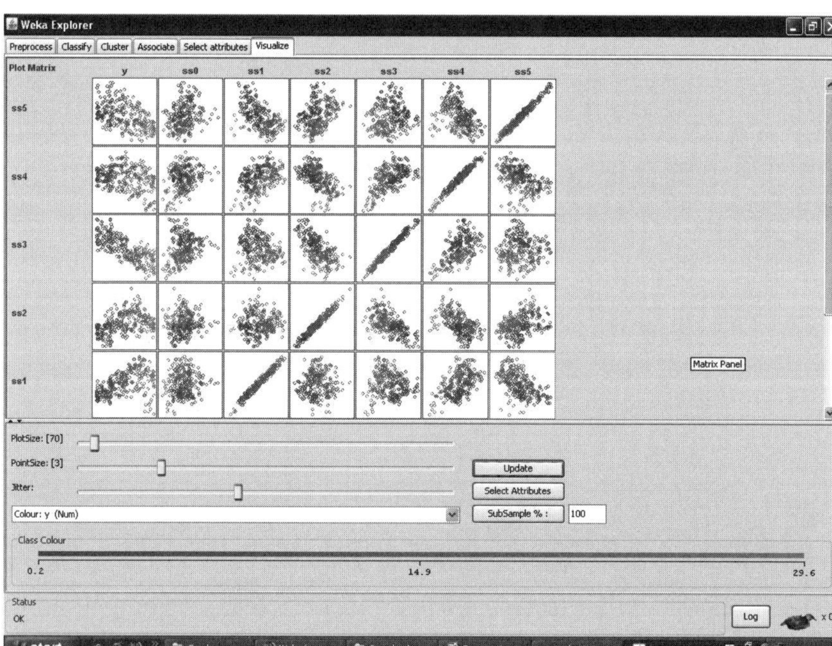

Fig. 11. Plot matrix of data.

the number of features used to describe the patterns. Similar samples are grouped together, which allows the use of density estimation for finding patterns.

Hypothesis: A hypothesis is a function on the sample space, giving a value for each point in the sample space. If the possible values are $\{0, 1\}$ then we can identify a hypothesis with the subset of those points that are given value 1. The error of a hypothesis is the probability of that subset where the hypothesis disagrees with the true hypothesis. Learning from examples is the process of making independent random observations and eliminating those hypotheses that disagree with your observations.

Convex Sets: A convex set is a set of elements from a vector space such that all the points on the straight line between any two points of the set are also contained in the set. If a and b are points in a vector space the points on the straight line between a and b are given by $x = \lambda a + (1 - \lambda)b$ for all λ from 0 to 1.

Hyperplane: A hyperplane is higher-dimensional generalization of the concepts of a line in the plane and a plane in three-dimensional space. The most familiar kinds of hyperplane are affine and linear hyperplanes; less familiar is the projective hyperplane. In a one-dimensional space (a straight line), a hyperplane is a point; it divides a line into two rays. In two-dimensional space (such as the xy plane), a hyperplane is a line; it divides the plane into two half-planes. In three-dimensional space, a hyperplane is an ordinary plane; it divides the space into two half-spaces. This concept can also be applied to four-dimensional space and beyond, where the dividing object is simply referred to as a "hyperplane".

Saddle Point: A saddle point is a point in the domain of a function of two variables which is a stationary point but not a local extremum. At such a point, in general, the surface resembles a saddle that curves up in one direction, and curves down in a different direction (like a mountain pass).

Exercises

1. Differentiate between supervised and unsupervised learning on the basis of hypothesis space.
2. How statistical learning theory helps to study the problem of inference and how it is applied in case of Location Fingerprinting?
3. How Support Vector Machine can be used for summarization of information?
4. Explain the concept of kernels and list some of the common kernels used by SVM.
5. How can you apply SVM for location fingerprinting?
6. How overfitting of test data lead to "Curse of Dimensionality"?
7. Why do we need to use Structural Risk Minimization over Empirical Risk Minimization?
8. Why VC dimension is needed in Statistical Learning Theory?
9. Enumerate the procedure required for SRM.

References

1. N. J. Nilsson, *Introduction to Machine Learning*, drafts of incomplete notes.
2. Vapnik and Chervonekis, *Structural Risk Minimization* (1974).
3. R. Bellman, *Dynamic Programming* (Princeton University Press, 1957).
4. S. R. Gunn, Support vector machines for classification and regression, Technical report, School of Electronics and Computer Science, University of Southampton, Southampton, U.K. (1998).
5. A. J. Smola and B. Schölkopf, A tutorial on support vector regression, NeuroCOLT technical report NC-TR-98-030, Royal Holloway College, University of London, UK (1998).
6. T. Kohno, A. Broido and K. C. Claffy, Remote physical device fingerprinting, *IEEE Trans. Depend. Sec. Comput.* **2**(2), 93–108 (2005).
7. V. N. Vapnik, An overview of statistical learning theory, *IEEE Trans. Neural Network.* **10**(5), 988–999 (1999).
8. C. Cortes and V. Vapnik, Support vector networks, *Mach. Learn.* **20**, 273–297 (1995).
9. R. Battiti, T. Le Nhat and A. Villani, Location-aware computing: A neural network model for determining location in wireless LANs. Technical report DIT-5, Universitá di Trento, Dipartimento di Informatica e Telecomunicazioni (2002).
10. M. Brunato and R. Battiti, Statistical learning theory for location fingerprinting in wireless LANs, *Comput. Network. ISDN Syst.* **47**(6), (2005).
11. M. Brunato and C. Kiss Kalló, Transparent location fingerprinting for wireless services, *Proc. Med-Hoc-Net, Cagliary, Italy*, September (2002).
12. C. J. C. Burges, A tutorial on support vector machines for pattern recognition, *Data Mining Knowl. Discov.* **2**(2), 121–167 (1998).
13. www.support-vector-machines.org.
14. http://en.wikipedia.org/wiki/Support_vector_machine.

Chapter 7

TRANSMISSION POWER CONTROL FOR MOBILE AD HOC NETWORKS

BASEL ALAWIEH* and CHADI ASSI
Faculty of Engineering and Computer Science
Concordia University, Montreal, Quebec, Canada
** b_alawi@encs.concordia.ca*

HUSSEIN MOUFTAH
School of Information Technology and Engineering
University of Ottawa, Ottawa, Ontario, Canada
mouftah@site.uottawa.ca

The IEEE 802.11 distributed coordination function standard has gained global acceptance and popularity both in wireless LANs and the wireless multi-hop ad hoc environment. In IEEE 802.11, all packets (RTS/CTS/DATA/ACK) are sent with maximum power. It has been shown that this type of handshake communication decreases spatial reuse and thus decreases capacity throughput, which additionally may yield unnecessary energy consumption. Hence, enhancing spatial reuse and conserving energy consumption have been perhaps the two most vital issues in designing IEEE 802.11-based multi-hop ad hoc networks. Transmission power control has been adopted as an efficient technique to reduce the total energy consumed in packet delivery and/or enhance network throughput by increasing the channel spatial reuse by allowing concurrent transmissions to occur at the same time. Judiciously controlling the transmit power is far from easy. Improper control may result in performance that is poorer than without such control. For instance, reducing the power too much may leave the network unconnected, or produce excessive delays. In this chapter, we present an overview of the research done in the area of transmission power control. The main theme of this chapter is to provide the reader with an understanding of the problems encountered in the exploitation of power control, approaches to solving these problems and their performance benefits.

1. Introduction

Mobile ad hoc networks (MANETs) have emerged as a new platform for delivering telecommunication services for areas where a fixed infrastructure is difficult to deploy [1]. MANET systems attempt to form multi-hop networks in which mobile nodes communicate over a wireless channel in a peer-to-peer fashion to sustain network connectivity and perform routing functions [2]. Such a platform has enabled the existence of various applications ranging from the monitoring of herds of animals to supporting communication in military battlefields and civilian disaster recovery scenarios.

Nodes in MANETs are usually powered by batteries. Therefore, energy conservation is a crucial issue in the design of MANETs. There have been attempts to conserve energy by enabling nodes to have self-power capabilities and employing techniques to extract energy from the environment. However, these attempts have been unsuccessful since the energy dissipation level attained by these attempts is still above $100\,\mu$W, which necessitates frequent battery replacement. Given the fact that the amount of energy required by a node to execute around 3,000 instructions is the same as the energy needed to transmit a bit a distance of 100 m through wireless radio, techniques to reduce the energy consumption in wireless interfaces are of particular interest.

One approach to conserving the energy of wireless interfaces is to use power saving mechanisms. Normally, a wireless node can be in the awake state, the doze (low-power) state or the off state. In the off state, a node consumes no power but is not able to communicate with other nodes. There are three modes, namely, transmit, receive and idle, for a node in the awake state. A node in the doze state is unable to transmit or receive. A node in the transmit mode consumes slightly more power than in the receive mode, which in turn consumes slightly more power than in the idle mode. This is because a node in the idle mode has to continuously listen to the wireless medium for potential communication. The power consumption in the doze state is, in general, an order of magnitude lower than that in the awake state. Moreover, the transition from the doze state to the awake state takes much less time than the transition from the off state to the awake state. These observations suggest that energy conservation is achieved by putting a node in the doze state for as long as possible to reduce power consumption caused by overhearing without scarifying the throughput performance of an ad hoc wireless network.

Another approach to reducing energy consumption is by using variant transmission power levels mechanisms; additionally, transmission power control (TPC) enhances the network throughput. TPC schemes are divided into two classes: topology-based and per-packet basis. In the topology-based class, the TPC determines the network topology based on specific policies, and thus impacts the subsequent routing decisions taken by the transmitter [3]. There after, the same transmit power will be used by any node for transmitting its packets. The second class of TPC is the per-packet basis, i.e., the power values are agreed upon between the transmitter and the receiver for each packet transmitted. The per-packet basis is further divided into two categories: energy-oriented and throughput-oriented. The former aims at conserving the energy consumption while the latter enhances the throughput by enhancing the spatial reuse. Moreover, TPC can be performed using either the network layer or the medium access control layer; in this chapter, we use the latter to study transmission power control.

The goal of this chapter is to provide the reader with an understanding of the problems encountered in the exploitation of transmission power control from the perspective of the MAC layer, specifically the per-packet basis. It is targeted towards students and researchers working on mobile ad hoc networking protocols, providing the necessary background, design tools, ideas and insights for ex-ploiting transmission power control schemes. The rest of this chapter is organized as follows. We survey the IEEE 802.11 distributed coordination function (DCF) and the motivation behind doing power control. In Sec. 3, we discuss topology control and list its deficiencies. Section 4 presents BASIC [4], a power control scheme. The BASIC scheme has triggered the starting point for several possible enhancements in the area of power control. Section 4 presents solutions to the existing problems encountered in BASIC. Finally, we give thoughts for researchers in Sec. 5 and summarize the chapter and overview interesting areas of research in Sec. 6.

2. Background

2.1. *IEEE 802.11 DCF*

The IEEE 802.11 DCF standard [5] is currently the dominant medium access control for multi-hop networks. IEEE 802.11 DCF relies on carrier sensing multiple access with collision avoidance (CSMA/CA). DCF employs two different channel access modes for data packet transmission: the default two-way (basic access) and the optional four-way handshaking (RTS/CTS) access scheme [5]. Here, the optional (RTS/CTS) scheme assumes the transmission of short request-to-send (RTS) and clear-to-send (CTS) control packets prior to the data packet transmission. In the (RTS/CTS) access scheme, a node with packets to transmit first senses the medium through physical carrier sensing (PCS). If the medium is idle for at least a certain period DIFS (distributed interframe space), it will immediately request the channel by sending a short control frame RTS to the receiver node. If the receiver correctly receives the RTS, it will reply with a short control frame CTS after waiting a SIFS (short interframe space) period. Once the sender receives the CTS, it will start to transfer DATA. After the successful reception of DATA, the receiver sends an ACK to the sender. The SIFS duration is the shortest of the interframe spaces and is used after the RTS, CTS, and DATA frames to give the highest priority to CTS, DATA and ACK, respectively. Nodes implementing IEEE 802.11 maintain a network allocation vector (NAV), which shows the remaining time of the ongoing transmission sessions. Using the duration information in the RTS, CTS, and DATA packets, nodes adjust their NAVs whenever they receive a packet. This is shown in Fig. 1. For the basic scheme, upon sensing the DATA or ACK packet nodes will refrain from transmitting any packet for EIFS.

Moreover, if the channel is sensed busy, the station has to wait until the channel is sensed idle for a DIFS time. At this point, the station generates a random backoff time interval before transmission, in order to minimize the probability of collisions

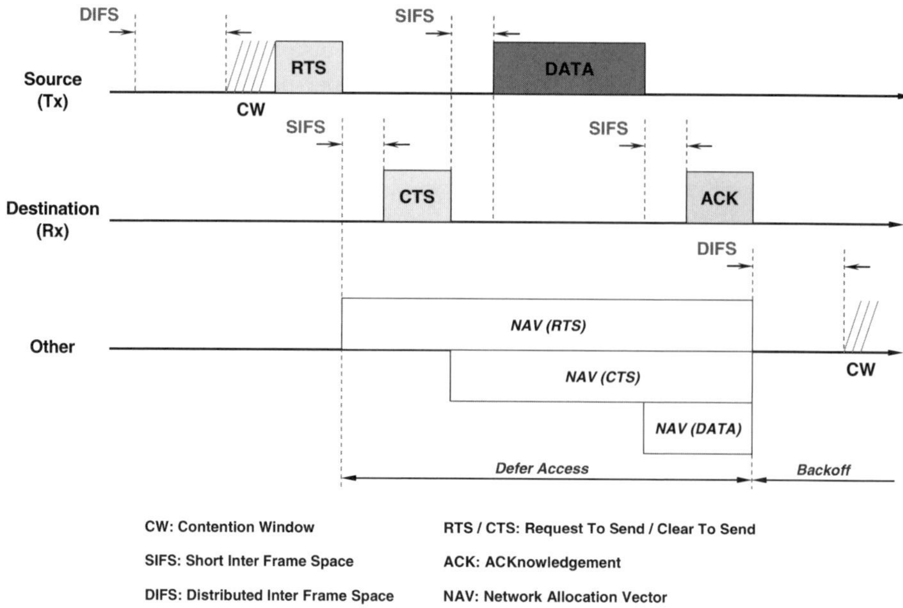

Fig. 1. IEEE 802.11 DCF.

with packets being transmitted by other stations. DCF adopts an exponential backoff scheme. At each packet transmission, the backoff time is uniformly chosen in the range $[0, CW]$. The value CW is called the contention window, and depends on the number of failed transmissions for the packet. At the first transmission attempt, CW is set to $CW_{\min}$. After each retransmission, CW will be exponentially increased until the maximum value $CW_{\max}$. Upon successful transmission, CW will be reset to $CW_{\min}$.

2.2. *Communication Model*

Assume a sender A transmits to its receiver B and another node F (hidden node), unaware of the transmission of A, may start to transmit to its intended receiver as shown in Fig. 2. Here, the two signals from A and F may overlap in time at the receiver B. Whether the signal from sender A can be correctly decoded depends on the so-called capture effect, i.e., the stronger signal will be captured by the receiver modem, while the weaker signal will be rejected as noise.

While in the literature there exist various models that characterize the capture effect [6–9], in this survey we present the most widely adopted model. A receiver B can correctly decode the signal if the signal-to-interference plus noise ratio (SINR) exceeds a certain predetermined threshold denoted by ζ. This results in the following constraint:

$$P_r \geq \zeta \times (P_n), \tag{1}$$

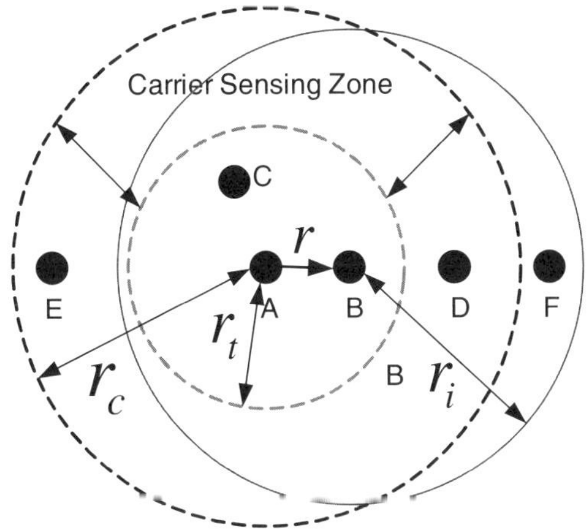

Fig. 2. Different ranges according to IEEE 802.11.

where P_n is the total allowed interference power which consists of interference power from interfering nodes and background thermal noise. Here, the value of ζ is determined according to the rate at which a packet is received at the receiver.

Moreover, due to the path loss constraints, a receiver B is able to receive and correctly decode a packet when the received power (P_r) of a frame from a transmitter (with a transmission power P_t) is higher than or equal to κ (the receiver sensitivity). Accordingly, adopting the two-ray model with antenna heights and gains equal to one, the transmission range (r_t) is

$$r_t = \left(\frac{P_t}{\kappa}\right)^{\frac{1}{4}}, \tag{2}$$

where κ is dependent on the rate the packet is received at the receiver; note that the higher the rate, the smaller κ is [5]. Note that the circular range is an idealized assumption and that no ideal circular ranges exist in reality.

Furthermore, a transmitter cannot initiate any communication if it senses a signal with a power level larger than a predefined CS_{th}. Hence, the CS_{th} specifies the signal strength above which a node determines the medium is busy and will not attempt transmission. Let the carrier sense set of a transmitter A (denoted as CS_A) be defined as the set of nodes such that if any of them transmits, node A will sense the medium busy [10]. Formally,

$$CS_A = \left\{ A' \middle| \frac{P_{A'}}{d^4} \geq CS_{th} \right\},$$

where d is the distance between the sender A and node A′ (in the carrier sense set), and $P_{A'}$ is the transmission power of A′. If all nodes use the same transmission power, P_t, then the carrier sense range r_c, defined as the maximum value of d such that the above constraints hold, can be expressed as

$$r_c = \left(\frac{P_t}{CS_{th}}\right)^{\frac{1}{4}}, \tag{3}$$

Note, however, that if nodes use different powers, the carrier sense region (CS_A) will have an arbitrary shape (not circular).

Another acronym of interest is the silence area that results from the transmission of node A. The silence set of a transmitter A (denoted as SL_A), assuming fixed CS_{th} for all nodes, is the set of nodes that will detect the channel to be busy if A transmits [10]. Formally,

$$SL_A = \left\{ A' \middle| \frac{P_A}{d^4} \geq CS_{th} \right\}.$$

Clearly, $SL_A \equiv CS_A$ if all nodes use the same transmission power.

2.3. *Power Control*

Extensive research has been done to address the throughput and energy deficiencies in the IEEE 802.11 DCF implementation in multi-hop networks [3, 11, 12]. Namely, research efforts have focused on (i) transmit power control [3] (ii) data rate adaptation [13, 14], (iii) physical carrier sensing threshold tuning [14], and (iv) optimizing the binary exponential backoff mechanisms [15, 16]. Different variants of access methods have been proposed to optimize the operation of DCF by helping nodes to select either optimal contention windows or optimal transmission probabilities which may yield to a decrease in collision among hosts, ultimately minimizing both the collision and idle periods. On the other hand, physical carrier sensing [17, 18] is another effective mechanism to detect simultaneous transmissions, and thus tuning the carrier sensing threshold may have an impact on eliminating or reducing future interference, thereby reducing collisions in wireless networks. Data rate adaptation can also be a good candidate for improving the throughput. The basic idea behind data rate adaptation [14] is to exploit good channel conditions by using higher rates for improved efficiency (i.e., throughput), and improve the transmission reliability by lowering the rate in the presence of channel impairments. Finally, controlling the transmit power [3] is one of the most efficient mechanisms used to exploit both spatial reuse and power conservation opportunities (reducing power consumption).

In 802.11, all packets (RTS/CTS/DATA/ACK) are sent with maximum power. It has been shown that this kind of handshake communication decreases spatial reuse and thus decreases capacity throughput and additionally yields unnecessary energy consumption [19]. To illustrate, consider the scenario in Fig. 3, where node A uses its maximum transmission power (TP) to send packets to node B and nodes C and F will try to initiate a communication with nodes D and E, respectively. Nodes C and F will not be able to do that since they lie in the transmission vicinity

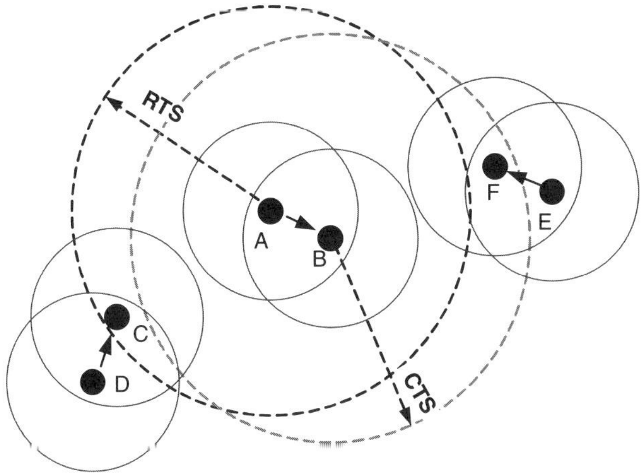

Fig. 3. Power control merits.

of nodes A and B, respectively. Here, nodes C and F are termed exposed terminals. However, it is easy to show that the three transmissions A → B, D → C, and E → F can overlap in time if nodes are able to select their transmission power appropriately as shown in Fig. 3. As a consequence, there is an increase in network throughput, possibly reducing the overall energy consumption. Adjusting the transmitted power is extremely important in ad hoc networks for three principal reasons:

- The transmitted power of the mobile node determines the network topology. The network topology in turn has considerable impact on the throughput performance of the network [20].
- Mobile nodes in ad hoc networks are usually energy constrained, and hence have to be as energy efficient as possible. Thus, the power control should adjust the transmitted power to be the least power required to send the data packet to meet the required signal-to-interference and noise ratio (SINR) threshold.
- Transmitting at high power can degrade other ongoing transmissions and in the meantime can prevent future transmission, as illustrated in Fig. 3. Thus, reducing the transmission power will reduce interference on other nodes and may enhance the overall network throughput as well as energy consumption.

While the idea of power control is simple, achieving this in an IEEE 802.11 based multi-hop network is challenging. When reducing the transmission power, the number of nodes included within the transmission range of the sender and competing for wireless channel access is reduced and hence the number of collisions from contending nodes is reduced. Moreover, although it is intuitive that using reduced power minimizes the interference level between neighboring nodes, there is an increase in the number of concurrent transmissions because the transmission range of each node is reduced. Consequently, the overall signal-to-interference ratio (SIR) might degrade when using a lower transmission power and this may lead to an increase in frame error rate. While reducing the transmit power may indeed decrease the energy consumption, the likelihood of packet corruptions (error or collisions) during packet reception goes up, and hence retransmissions of the same packet could result in a power consumption higher than the maximum power.

We classify power control schemes into two classes, topology-based and per-packet based, and we survey them in the next section.

3. Topology Control

Reducing the transmission power may have a great impact on network connectivity. This is due to the fact that the number of active links may be reduced and the network may become partitioned. Thus, applying transmission power control to determine the network topology should be performed with the objective of determining the minimal possible transmission power while maintaining the network connectivity.

A topology control protocol COMPOW, which requires that all nodes use a common minimum transmission power, was developed in Ref. 21. The authors showed that spatial reuse can be enhanced and energy is conserved if nodes agree on the minimum common power that maintains network connectivity. In COMPOW, each node tries to find the best minimum power by locating the route entry that maximizes the throughput among other entries. This is accomplished by running several routing daemons in parallel, one for each power level. However, COMPOW suffers from overhead problems due to link-state messages exchanged by nodes. Moreover, it is inefficient in cluster topologies since it tends to use higher power. Finally, COMPOW is highly affected by mobility; if a node moves away from the topology, redetermination of the common power is triggered, and thus global reconfiguration is required.

A cone-based topology control scheme was proposed in Ref. 22. Here, each node determines the minimum power that preserves its connectivity with at least one neighbor existing in every cone of degree ϕ. In order to find its neighbors, a node broadcasts a Hello message at the lowest power and gradually increases its power. Thereafter, the node stores the direction in which replies are received for every Hello packet transmitted at a certain power level. Based on the saved directions, the node is able to determine whether its neighbor lies in a cone of degree ϕ. The algorithm has been analytically proven to maintain network connectivity for $\phi = 5\pi/3$.

A distributed position-based topology control algorithm is proposed in Ref. 23. Through this algorithm, each node (e.g., node i) periodically broadcasts its position information and builds a sparse graph called an enclosure graph with the position information contained in the broadcasting packets from its neighbors. Then node i assigns a cost metric respectively for each neighbor node j included in the enclosure graph. Here, the cost metric is defined as the minimum required power to establish a link between node i and j, and this is also broadcast by node i. Afterwards, all nodes are able to select an optimal link on the enclosure graph using the distributed Bell Ford shortest path algorithm.

One common limitation of the above topology control mechanisms is finding the minimum power to determine the links to node neighbors. Transmitting at low power yields the so-called hidden terminal, which will be elaborated upon in the coming section. Accordingly, the study of per-packet TPC is more beneficial since it is more flexibly and efficiently deployed in dynamically changing environments.

4. BASIC

BASIC [4] is a simple per-packet power control mechanism proposed for IEEE 802.11-based networks and is based on power information during the RTS, CTS, DATA and ACK frame transmissions. This technique is based on the idea of transmitting the RTS and CTS frames at the maximum transmit power level. Based on the received RTS signal strength, a receiver node will be able to determine the channel gain and accordingly the minimum power needed for DATA and ACK packets to be received successfully. This information is relayed to the sender via the CTS packet. The operation of BASIC is illustrated as follows. Assume two nodes A and B that are a distance r apart, as shown in Fig. 4. Node A transmits an RTS packet with power P_t, and node B receives the RTS packet accordingly with power P_r. The channel gain loss is simply

$$\text{Gain} = \frac{P_r}{P_t}. \tag{4}$$

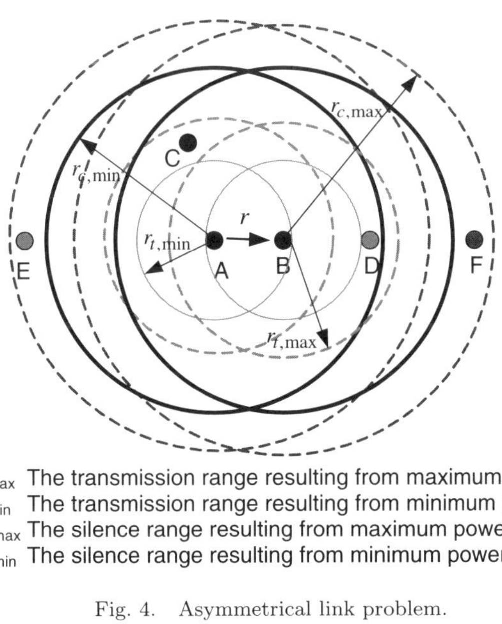

Fig. 4. Asymmetrical link problem.

The minimum received power required to correctly receive and decode the packet correctly is κ. Thus, the minimum transmitted power $P_{t,\min}$ is

$$P_{t,\min} = \frac{\kappa}{\text{Gain}}. \tag{5}$$

Clearly, this method does not utilize any advantages of the potential spatial channel reuse as the reservation of the channel is always done at the maximum power level. Thus, BASIC suffers from exposed terminals. On the other hand, significant energy is saved as the DATA and ACK frames are transmitted at lower power levels. However, this reduction in the transmit power of the DATA and ACK frames may cause collisions at the receiver (with the DATA frame) as well as at the transmitter (with the ACK frame). This is due to the introduction of asymmetric links between the communicating nodes and other potential transmitters that cannot sense the medium busy during the ongoing low power transmission. Such collisions result in frame retransmission and hence increased energy consumption, eliminating any possible gain obtained from power control. A simple power control MAC protocol that allows nodes to vary transmission power on a per-packet basis is presented in Ref. 4. The main idea is to allow nodes to use different power levels for RTS/CTS and DATA/ACK frames. More specifically, a maximum transmission power is used for sending the RTS/CTS frames and a lower power level, necessary to communicate, is used for DATA/ACK packets. This protocol is referred to as the BASIC protocol and the authors of Ref. 4 have pointed out its deficiencies. BASIC was proposed to enhance the energy efficiency; however, it suffers severely from high collision rates from hidden terminals due to asymmetrical link problems. This, in turn, increases the energy consumption and deteriorates the throughput. Elaborating more on the asymmetrical link problem, consider two nodes A and B, which are a distance r away from each other, exchanging their RTS and CTS frames at the maximum power (Fig. 4); nodes E and F back off for EIFS since they lie in the silence range of the RTS and CTS frames. Now, nodes A and B exchange their DATA and ACK packets at the minimum transmission power. Hence, nodes E and F are no longer inside the silence zone of both nodes. After an EIFS duration, they will contend for the channel if they have a packet to transmit. If the duration of the DATA packet (from A to B) is long, node F may corrupt the frame reception at the receiver, B. Similarly, node E may also corrupt the ACK packet reception.

5. Power Control Solutions

The design of transmission power control to achieve energy efficiency and/or throughput gains is especially challenging in an IEEE 802.11-based multi-hop network. This is due to the existence of the hidden and the exposed terminals, as is the case with BASIC. In this section, we survey the many TPC proposals that aimed to solve the problems associated with BASIC.

5.1. *PCM: Power control MAC*

In order to address this problem, the authors in Ref. 4 proposed transmitting the DATA packet periodically at maximum power. Here, every 190 μs the transmitter raises the DATA power level to its maximum for a period of 15 μs so that potential interfering nodes will be able to detect the transmission and accordingly defer their future transmissions and prevent collisions with the current transmission. The receiver then transmits an ACK frame using the minimum required power to reach the source node, similar to the BASIC scheme. The calculation of the periodic time for increasing the power is dependent on the duration of EIFS. Here, EIFS = SIFS + DIFS + [(8 ∗ ACKsize) + PreambleLength + PLCPHeader − Length]/BitRate, where ACKsize is the length (in bytes) of an ACK frame, and BitRate is the physical layer's lowest mandatory rate. PreambleLength is 144 bits and PLCPHeaderLength is 48 bits. Using a 2 Mbps channel bit rate, EIFS is equal to 212 μs. Here, the 15 μs should be adequate for carrier sensing, with 5 μs to power up and down the power level. So the time will be 210 μs, which is less than 212 μs. In this way, the ACK packet is well protected and the energy is assumed to be conserved. However, the spatial reuse is not improved since the RTS and CTS packets, which are sent at maximum power, may still unnecessarily silence future concurrent transmissions.

5.2. *Distributed Power Control Scheme*

It was suggested in Ref. 11, as another enhancement to the BASIC scheme, that a node should be aware of the success and failure of its own transmissions. To achieve this, a node maintains a table that keeps a record of all the previous RTS-CTS-DATA-ACK transmission power levels used to communicate with each of its neighbors. Given this information, a transmitter would be able to adjust adaptively the transmission power of its future communication according to a predefined policy. Here, the policy dictates that each transmitter increases/decreases its transmission power to its receiver if the last transmission to the same receiver fails/succeeds. As opposed to the BASIC scheme, a node uses the reduced power level for all its transmissions (i.e., RTS-CTS-DATA-ACK). This algorithm yields higher throughput because of the enhanced spatial reuse and lower energy consumption compared with the IEEE 802.11 MAC protocol. Here, the channel reuse is enhanced since the RTS/CTS packets are exchanged at a reduced power level, allowing for simultaneous transmissions to exist. Nevertheless, this mechanism still suffers from hidden terminals since it does not provide an efficient protection for the DATA packet. Moreover, the asymmetric link problem is not completely addressed here.

5.3. *ALCA: Asymmetric Link Collision Avoidance*

Another enhancement to BASIC was proposed in Ref. 24. The authors argued that through knowing the received signal pattern, a node can predict if the signal belongs to a transmitted CTS packet. Upon recognizing the CTS packet, the node accordingly sets its NAV so as not to interfere with the upcoming DATA packet reception. A solution has been proposed in Ref. 25 to overcome the asymmetric link problem of the BASIC scheme by allowing nodes in the carrier sensing zone of an RTS/CTS transmission to acknowledge the transmission duration information of the upcoming DATA packet. Although these nodes are not able to correctly decode the RTS/CTS packet, they can still detect the time duration when the physical carrier is sensed or not. The physical duration of the RTS/CTS frames is increased by simply adding a few bits to them. Thus, the ALCA protocol provides a discrete set of N different carrier durations (CD) for RTS/CTS frames, and each CD is mapped to different durations for the DATA packet transmission duration. A node in the carrier sensing zone of the RTS/CTS transmission senses the physical carrier of RTS/CTS duration and can extract the CD for the RTS/CTS frame. Correspondingly, it can acknowledge the transmission duration for the DATA packet and set its NAV to this value, instead of setting the NAV to the standard EIFS value.

5.4. *Correlative Power Control Scheme*

In Ref. 26, the authors investigated the correlations that exist between the required transmission power of RTS, CTS, DATA and ACK frames to guarantee a successful four-way handshake. Based on these correlations, they proposed Core-PC (a class of correlative power control schemes). The scheme argues that all the packets should be transmitted at the same power value to achieve the best throughput performance. In their scheme, they considered the accumulated interference from all interfering nodes. Moreover, they protected the CTS or the ACK packet from collisions by forcing the transmission range of the RTS or DATA packet to be equal to the interference range of the CTS or ACK packet. Furthermore, they proposed localized heuristics to determine the average power of the accumulative interference.

Consider an ongoing communication between two nodes A and B and adopt the two-ray channel model with antenna heights and gains set to one. The path loss constraint requires that the received power should be greater than κ, the receiver sensitivity. Moreover, given that the RTS packet is successfully received, the received power $P_{r,CTS}$ of the CTS also needs to fulfill the SIR requirement. Thus, we have

$$P_{r,CTS} \geq P_{\text{Noise},A} \cdot \zeta \tag{6}$$

where $P_{\text{Noise},A}$ and ζ are the SIR threshold and worst case interference level. Moreover, we have $P_{T,CTS} \geq P_{\text{Noise},A} \cdot \zeta \cdot r^4$, where $P_{T,CTS}$ is the required transmit power of CTS. The worst case interference level $P_{\text{Noise},A}$ after transmitting the RTS packet, as shown in Fig. 5, is calculated based on the assumption that all nodes outside the transmission range of the RTS packet potentially interfere (those

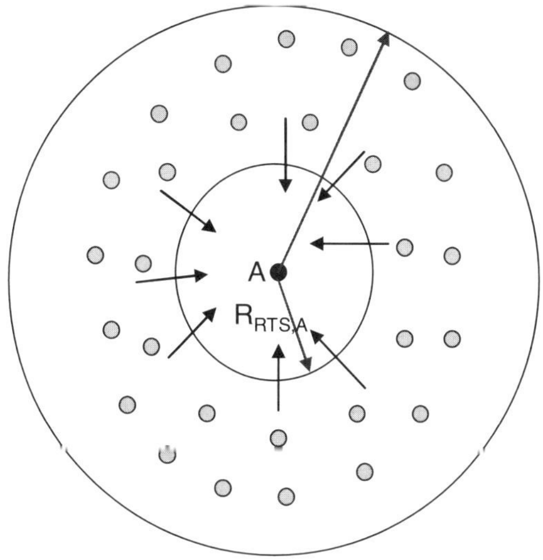

Fig. 5. Interference model.

nodes will interfere with the CTS packet reception) with an average radius R_{avg} and average transmission power P_{avg}. Here, $R_{\text{avg}} = P_{\text{avg}}/R_{\text{avg}}$. If one of these interfering nodes transmits, none of the nodes lying in its transmission range will transmit, and accordingly the active node density Δ is bounded by $1/R^2_{\text{avg}}$. Hence, $P_{\text{Noise},A}$ is derived as follows:

$$P_{\text{Noise},A} = \int_{R_{\text{RTS},A}}^{\infty} \frac{2 \cdot \pi x \cdot P_{\text{avg}} \cdot dx}{{R_{\text{avg}}}^2 \cdot x^4} \leq \pi \cdot \sqrt{\frac{P_{\text{avg}}}{P_{RTS,A}}} \cdot \kappa. \tag{7}$$

The power of CTS becomes

$$P_{T,CTS} = \min\left(P_{\min}, \pi \cdot \kappa \cdot \zeta \cdot r^4 \cdot \sqrt{\frac{P_{\text{avg}}}{P_{RTS,A}}}\right), \tag{8}$$

where $P_{RTS,A}$ is the transmitted power of the RTS packet and $P_{\min} = \kappa \cdot r^4$. Repeating the same analysis, we get the transmission power of the DATA packet ($P_{t,DATA}$) and ACK packet ($P_{t,ACK}$):

$$P_{T,DATA} = \min\left(P_{\min}, \pi \cdot \kappa \cdot \zeta \cdot r^4 \cdot \sqrt{\frac{P_{\text{avg}}}{P_{T,CTS}}}\right), \tag{9}$$

$$P_{T,ACK} = \min\left(P_{\min}, \pi \cdot \kappa \cdot \zeta \cdot r^4 \cdot \sqrt{\frac{P_{\text{avg}}}{P_{T,DATA}}}\right). \tag{10}$$

The only unknowns are the transmission power of the RTS packet and P_{avg}. Three alternatives for assigning a transmit power for the RTS packet have been considered. In a simple scenario, the RTS is transmitted at the maximal transmission power. In the symmetric scenario, the RTS is transmitted at a power level such that the RTS, CTS, DATA and ACK are all transmitted at the same power. In such a scenario, spatial reuse is maximized since the maximal value of the transmission power of the control and DATA packets is minimized. In the minimum scenario, the RTS frame is transmitted at a power such that the power of the DATA packet is minimized. In this manner, energy consumption is minimized since a long DATA packet is sent at the minimum power. Similarly, three different ways of finding P_{avg} are proposed. In the worst case scenario, consider that P_{avg} is always equal to the maximum power. In the adaptive scenario, P_{avg} equals the maximum power and then increases when one frame is lost and decreases when N consecutive frames are successfully received. In another adaptive scenario, P_{avg} is estimated as a moving average from the network performance. Then the value of $P_{\text{avg}} \leftarrow 0.9P_{\text{avg}} + 0.1P_t$ is determined as at each node, where P_t is the average of all transmitted powers of the packets captured at a node. Considering all the above scenarios and schemes, we can induce 12 power control schemes. Performance evaluation for all schemes shows that sending all packets at the same reduced power with P_{avg} determined from the node performance with initial value not equal to the maximum power yields the best throughput and reduced energy values. Determining P_{avg} in such schemes is a key design parameter since the initial condition P_{avg} may lead to dramatically different results as shown in Ref. 26. Moreover, the concept of carrier sensing range is not considered when deriving the interference model, which does not resemble the real scenario of the IEEE 802.11 implementation.

5.5. *Power Control using Prediction Filter*

In Ref. 27, a Kalman filter is deployed to perform power control. A node measures the interference around its transmission zone, and based on this measured interference, the node makes use of a Kalman filter to predict future interference. By predicting future interference, a node can assign the transmission power of its CTS, DATA and ACK packets accordingly to meet a target SINR. Before transmitting an RTS packet, a node measures the interference in its surroundings and accordingly predicts the future interference (I) when receiving the CTS packet. The node then encapsulates this information in the RTS message initiated towards the destination, which is sent at the maximum power. Upon receiving the RTS message, the destination makes use of the included predicted interference to assign a power value to the ensuing CTS message. Before sending the CTS message, the destination node repeats the same procedure of measuring the surrounding interference and then predicting the interference in the future (I^+). This information is sent within the CTS message towards the source node and used for assigning a power value to the DATA packet. The same criteria is carried again by the source node A (I^{++}) and used by the destination node B for assigning a power value to the ACK frame. Therefore, assuming a two-ray model, the channel gain equals one and assuming nodes A and B are a distance r apart, the power values assigned for the CTS, DATA and ACK packets become:

$$P_{T,CTS} = \min\left(P_{\min}, \frac{\zeta \cdot I}{\text{Gain}}\right), \tag{11}$$

$$P_{T,DATA} = \min\left(P_{\min}, \frac{\zeta \cdot I^{+}}{\text{Gain}}\right), \tag{12}$$

$$P_{T,ACK} = \min\left(P_{\min}, \frac{\zeta \cdot I^{++}}{\text{Gain}}\right), \tag{13}$$

where $P_{\min} = \kappa \cdot r^4$ is the minimum required transmitted power, adopting a two-ray channel model with antenna height and gain set to one. ζ is the SIR threshold. The parameter Gain is the channel gain loss, which is equal to the received power over the transmitted power. The performance of the proposed scheme is dependent on the predictions of the kalman filter and more its convergence to the network changes. Throughput and energy efficiency gains are enhanced in this scheme. Nevertheless, RTS is sent at maximum power, which may still affect the spatial reuse.

5.6. *Multiple Channel Power Control Protocols*

A power controlled multiple access protocol (PCMA) is proposed in Ref. 28. In PCMA, the receiver advertises its tolerable interference margin on an out-of-band channel and the transmitter selects the transmission power that does not disrupt any ongoing transmissions. To elaborate more, each receiver transmits busy-tone pulses over a separate channel to inform its neighbors (potential interferers) of its interference margin. A potential interfering node, upon receiving the pulse, determines its signal strength and accordingly takes a decision to bound its future transmission or not. Specifically, a potential interfering node first senses the busy-tone channel to calculate an upper bound on its transmission power, for all of its control and data packets complying to the most sensitive receiver in its transmission zone. This potential interfering node, upon determining this upper bound value, will transmit an RTS packet and wait for the CTS from the receiver. If the receiver is able to correctly decode the RTS packet (i.e., it lies within the RTS range of the transmitter node) and the power needed to send back the CTS packet is below the power bound at the receiver, the receiver then transmits back a CTS allowing the DATA packet transmission to begin. Implementation of PCMA shows significant throughput gain (more than twice) over the IEEE 802.11. Nevertheless, the collision resulting from contention among busy tones is not addressed.

Performing TPC with the use of a separate control channel for (RTS, CTS, ACK) in conjunction with a busy-tone scheme was proposed in Ref. 29. A transmitter sends the DATA packets and busy-tones at reduced power, while the receiver transmits its busy-tones at the maximum power. Upon receiving the busy-tone, a potential interfering node estimates the channel gain and decides to transmit if the interference value from its future transmission does not add more than a fixed interference on the ongoing reception. The protocol is shown to achieve considerable throughput enhancements. Nevertheless, the assumptions made in the design of the protocol are not realistic — specifically, that the antenna system neglects the interfering power of a signal that is less than the power of the "desired" signal (i.e., they assume perfect capture) and that there is no requirement for any interference margin. Moreover, when addressing the energy consumption, the power utilized in transmitting busy tones is not considered. The collision from contention among busy tones is also not addressed. Although these algorithms claim to achieve good throughput and less energy consumption, the implementation of dual or multiple channels in the framework of IEEE 802.11 faces both technical difficulties and market resistance — as such algorithms would require a complete change of the standards.

The authors in Ref. 3 extended the work on PCMA, in Ref. 28 to a single channel power controlled MAC protocol named POWMAC. Instead of delivering the interference margin information on a second channel, POWMAC exchanges the interference information and DATA packet using only one channel. To achieve this, POWMAC employs an access window (AW) to allow for a series of RTS/CTS exchanges to take place before several concurrent DATA packet transmissions can commence. Thus, during the AW, each node is aware of the interference margin of its neighboring nodes and accordingly bounds its transmission power as in PCMA such that DATA transmissions can proceed simultaneously as long as collisions are prevented.

5.7. *Collision Avoidance Power Control*

The authors of Ref. 30 introduced a collision avoidance power control (CAPC) MAC protocol to protect the transmission of DATA and ACK packets by appropriately selecting their power values. For example, a DATA packet may be protected if the interference range r_i (to be derived later) at its receiver is set to be equal to the transmission range r_t of the ensuing CTS packet, as shown in Fig. 6. Here, the authors assumed that an interfering node always sends at maximum power to

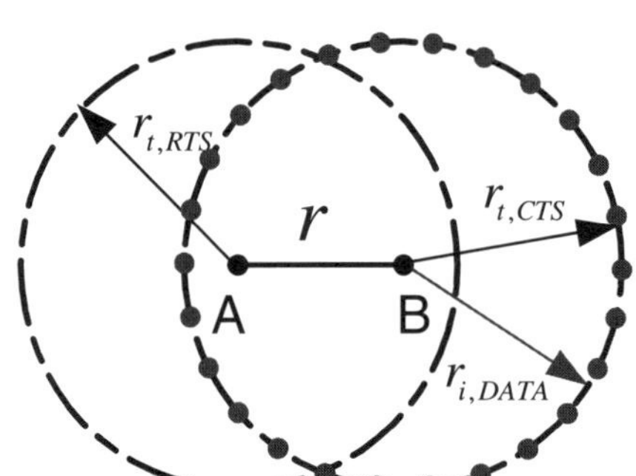

Fig. 6. Transmission range of CTS protects DATA.

derive the interference range. Similar to BASIC, RTS and CTS frames are sent at maximum power and that may impact the spatial reuse in the network.

Consider an ongoing communication between nodes A and B that are a distance r apart. If node A transmits with power P_t, node B receives this signal with a received power $P_r = P_t/r^4$. Moreover, if we neglect thermal noise, P_n in Eq. (1) can be expressed as $P_n = P_{cn} + P_{tn}$. Here, P_{cn} is the current measured interference at node B and P_{tn} is the maximum remaining interference that node B can tolerate while it is still able to decode correctly the packet it receives from node A. Accordingly, and making use of Eq. (1), we can express P_{tn} as

$$P_{tn} \leq \frac{P_t}{r^4 \cdot \zeta} - P_{cn}. \tag{14}$$

Now assume an interfering node F (Fig. 2 which is a distance d away from node B initiates a communication with a power P_i while node B is receiving a packet from node A. The received power $P_{ri} = P_i/d^4$ at node B from node F should satisfy the condition that $P_{ri} \leq P_{tn}$ such that node B is still able to receive and correctly decode the packet from node A. Accordingly, we define the interference set of a receiver B (denoted as IN_B) as the set of nodes whose transmission, if overlapping with the transmission of a sender, will cause collision at the receiver. Specifically, if node F transmits,

$$IN_B = \left\{ F \middle| \frac{P_i}{d^4} \geq \frac{P_t}{r^4 \cdot \zeta} - P_{cn} \right\}. \tag{15}$$

With the condition of the interference set from Eq. (15), we define the interference range r_i as the maximum value of d such that the inequality in Eq. 15 holds:

$$r_i = \left(\frac{P_i}{\frac{P_t}{r^4 \cdot \zeta} - P_{cn}} \right)^{\frac{1}{4}}. \tag{16}$$

In CAPC, P_i is assumed equal to the maximum power $P_{\max}$ under the worst case scenario. In CAPC, as stated earlier RTS and CTS packets are transmitted at maximum power; thus, we have

$$r_t = \left(\frac{P_{\max}}{\kappa} \right)^{\frac{1}{4}} = r_i = \left(\frac{P_{\max}}{\frac{P_{t,DATA}}{r^4 \cdot \zeta} - P_{cn}} \right)^{\frac{1}{4}}. \tag{17}$$

The data packet power $P_{t,DATA}$ is then calculated as follows:

$$P_{t,DATA} = \zeta \cdot r^4 \cdot (P_{cn} + \kappa). \tag{18}$$

5.8. *Adaptive Range-Based Power Control for Collision Avoidance*

More recently, the authors of Ref. 31 extended the work in Ref. 30 and proposed an adaptive range-based power control (ARPC) MAC protocol for avoiding collisions and conserving energy consumption. They derived four mechanisms and studied their performances: carrier-sensing range cover mechanism (SCRC), receivers carrier-sensing range cover mechanism (RCRC), senders transmission range cover mechanism (STRC), and receivers transmission range cover mechanism (RTRC), to adapt the transmission power for a node. In SCRC, the RTS and CTS packets are transmitted at maximum power and the transmission power of DATA and ACK packets are calculated such that the carrier sensing range of the DATA packet covers the entire interference range of the DATA packet, as shown in Fig. 7. In RCRC, the RTS packet is also transmitted at maximum power and the DATA packet is transmitted at minimum power while the transmission power of the CTS frame is determined such that the carrier sensing range of the CTS equals the interference range of the DATA packet given that the size of the DATA packet is small. Moreover, in RCRC, the ACK packet is transmitted at a maximum power. In the other two mechanisms, STRC and RTRC, RTS and CTS packets are transmitted at maximum power while the DATA or ACK packet is transmitted at adapted power such that the interference range of the DATA packet is protected by the transmission range of the RTS or CTS packets (as shown in Fig. 6), respectively. The authors further derived an adaptive algorithm that selects between the proposed mechanisms based on the distance between the sender and the receiver. Performance evaluation has shown that the proposed scheme has completely eliminated the hidden terminal problem and thus the DATA collision rate becomes negligible. Additionally, in the proposed mechanisms, the interference range is always calculated under the worst case scenario, in which the potential interfering node is considered to transmit at maximum power, which does not reflect the real channel conditions. However, in their methods, the RTS (and most of the time CTS) frame is always

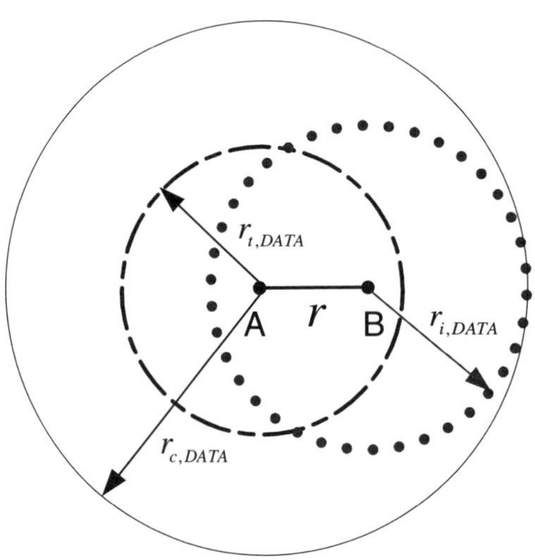

Fig. 7. Carrier sensing range of DATA protects DATA.

transmitted at maximum power, which, as mentioned earlier, affects the channel spatial reuse.

6. Open Issues

Table 1 shows a protocol design comparison between all the per-packet TPC schemes discussed. As can be viewed from Table 1, most of the schemes do use discrete power level values. Usually, in practice wireless interface cards have some specific discrete power values among which a node can select a value while per-forming power control. For example, the Cisco Aironet 350 series cards (IEEE 802.11b compliant) allow the transmission power level to be set to one of 1, 5, 20, 30, 50 and 100 mW, while the Cisco Aironet 1200 series cards (IEEE 802.11a compliant) allow the power level to be set to one of 5, 10 and 20 mW. Thus, a key issue when designing TPC is to test using available discrete power values.

The exposed terminal problem has shown itself to be more dominant in determining the throughput of the system. Although the CTS protects the DATA packet, and in some instances the power value of the CTS packet may reach the maximum value in order to protect the DATA packet, the RTS packet should not be sent at maximum power in order not to affect the spatial reuse. Heuristic schemes for controling the transmit power of RTS should be carried separately from the other packets (CTS, DATA and ACK).

Currently, most wireless devices implement the IEEE 802.11b standard. Some of the existing TPCs in the literature make use of multiple channels as shown in Table 1, but the implementation of these schemes face cost challenges, technical difficulties and market resistance as such schemes would require a complete change of the standards. Thus, ideally, when considering a TPC design, it should be compatible with single channel IEEE 802.11 from the hardware and software perspectives. Hence, the implementation of such a TPC design should be very easy to deploy with the current standards.

Table 1. Protocol design comparison.

Protocol	RTS-max	CTS-max	Discrete power	Channel	Category
BASIC	Yes	Yes	Yes	1	Energy
PCM	Yes	Yes	Yes	1	Energy
DPS	Yes	Yes	Yes	1	Energy
ALCA	Yes	Yes	Yes	1	Energy
Core PC	No	No	No	1	Throughput
Kalman	Yes	No	No	1	Throughput
PCMA	No	No	No	2	Throughput
Busy	No	No	No	3	Throughput
CAPC	Yes	Yes	No	1	Throughput
SCRC	Yes	Yes	No	1	Throughput
RCRC	Yes	No	No	1	Throughput
STRC	Yes	Yes	No	1	Throughput
RTRC	Yes	Yes	No	1	Throughput

7. Summary and Future Work

The control of transmit power by medium access control (MAC) provides a real opportunity to enhance both spatial reuse and energy efficiency. Nevertheless, translating this potential into real performance gain is not a trivial task and requires essential modifications to existing mechanisms. In this chapter, we have considered mechanisms for the exploitation of transmission power control for increased spatial reuse and energy efficiency. Specifically, we targeted collision avoidance schemes.

Data rate adaptation can also be a good candidate for improving the throughput. Currently, the enhanced versions of IEEE 802.11 — IEEE 802.11a and the 802.11b — provide multi-rate capability at the physical layer. The set of possible data rates that are being supported by IEEE 802.11a are 6, 9, 12, 18 and 54 Mbps, while those supported by IEEE 802.11b are 1, 2, 5.5 and 11 Mbps. The basic idea behind data rate adaptation [14] is exploiting good channel conditions by using higher rates for improved efficiency (i.e., throughput), and improving the transmission reliability by lowering the rate in the presence of channel impairments. As can be seen from Eq. (7), data rate selection is a key factor in determining the interference range. Judiciously combining DATA rate with TPC may therefore have more benefits than only considering transmission power control.

Prior research has noted the impact of tuning PCS threshold on the network throughput [32]. That is, the larger the carrier sensing threshold, the better the spatial reuse; but the more the hidden nodes tend to exist and hence the higher the collision probability becomes, and *vice versa*. Thus, there exists an optimal PCS that balances the trade-off between spatial reuse and probability of collision [10]. Combining tuning carrier sensing threshold with power control would be a step forward in enhancing the spatial reuse, although such a combination would be a challenging task to achieve.

Usually, a node is unable to determine whether the collision occurring is due to nodes contending for the channel (i.e., transmitting at the same time slot) or due to packet reception error (collision from hidden nodes). If this information is provided to the transmitter, the true potential of transmission power control schemes will be realized. There have been proposals addressing the use of directional antennas to save energy and enhance throughput. Nevertheless, the use of directional antennas faces operational challenges such as deafness. The capabilities of directional antennas have not yet been utilized in the current literature.

The theoretical limits of ad hoc network capacity with power control have been investigated in Ref. 33. Nevertheless, this model had several deficiencies. For instance the model did not include the effects of the carrier sensing range. Thus, a more realistic model to measure the benefits of power control for ad hoc networks should take into consideration physical attributes such as the interference range and the carrier sensing range.

Terminology

MANET: Mobile ad hoc networks.

TPC: Transmission power control.

IEEE 802.11: The adopted MAC standard for wireless LAN.

SINR: Signal-to-interference plus noise ratio.

Transmission range: A node inside a transmission range will be able to correctly receive and decode a packet.

Carrier sensing range: A node existing in this range is able to sense a transmission.

Carrier sensing zone: A node inside a carrier sensing zone will be able to correctly receive but is unable to decode a packet.

Interference range: A node inside the interference range of a receiver; if it transmits, it will corrupt any packet reception at the receiver.

Kalman filter: A filter used to predict a value in the future; this value can be a voltage, power, etc.

Spatial reuse: Allowing simultaneous transmissions to take place in the same vicinity.

Exercises

1. What are the two techniques used to save energy in the MANET environment?
2. How is the power management technique is performed?
3. What are the types of transmission power control (TPC)?
4. How does a node using IEEE 802.11 DCF RTS/CTS transmit a packet?
5. What are the two major problems associated with the implementation of TPC in an IEEE 802.11 based ad hoc network?
6. Consider the network of four nodes A, B, C, D shown in Fig. 8. Node A is communicating with node B and node C is communicating with node D. The distances between terminals are $d(\text{A},\text{B}) = 95\,\text{m}$, $d(\text{A},\text{D}) = 98\,\text{m}$,

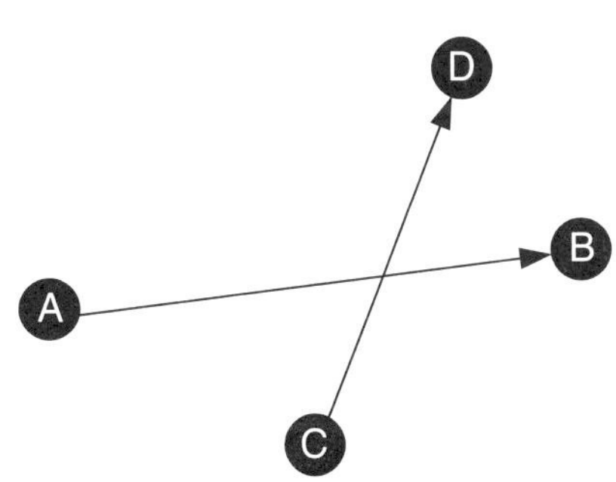

Fig. 8. Interference model.

$d(\mathrm{C},\mathrm{B}) = 65\,\mathrm{m}$, and $d(\mathrm{C},\mathrm{D}) = 57\,\mathrm{m}$. The target SINR for both connections is 10 dB. Assume that the target SINR is defined as the minimum required SINR when receiving a packet so that the node will be able to correctly receive and decode a packet. The additive average noise power is $-90\,\mathrm{dBw}$ ($10^{-10}\,\mathrm{mW}$). The transmitted power is 24 dB (250 mW) for both transmitting nodes A and C. Moreover, each node is equipped with a transceiver of processing gain, $G = 10$. The height and the antenna gains are assumed equal 1. The channel model is a two-ray model.

(i) Assume no power control is applied; check if the transmission from node A to B and from node C to node D will be successful.
(ii) Repeat (i) but now applying power control. Assume that the transmitted power of node A is 20 mW and that of node C is 100 mW.

7. Assume the network with six homogenous nodes (A, B, C, D, E and F) in a chain topology shown in Fig. 9. The distances between nodes are given as $d(\mathrm{A},\mathrm{B}) = d(\mathrm{C},\mathrm{D}) = d(\mathrm{E},\mathrm{F}) = 70\,\mathrm{m}$, $d(\mathrm{B},\mathrm{E}) = 500\,\mathrm{m}$, $d(\mathrm{C},\mathrm{A}) = 450\,\mathrm{m}$. The target SINR for both connections is 10 dB. The receiver sensitivity and the carrier sensing threshold are $7.1936 \times 10^{-12}\,\mathrm{W}$, and $3.0708 \times 10^{-13}\,\mathrm{W}$ respectively. The maximum power is 0.0281 W and assume a 2 Mbps channel rate. Assume node A has a packet to send to node B, node C has a packet to send to node D, and node E has a packet to send to node F. The antenna gain and height of a node are both equal to one. The additive average noise power is 10^{-16} W. The two-ray model is adopted for channel modeling. Assuming node A starts the RTS/CTS handshake; all nodes apply the BASIC power control scheme. DATA packet size = 1,000 bytes. Check if the communication from A to B will be successful.
8. Consider an ongoing communication between nodes A and B, which are a distant r apart. Using an equation, derive the worst case scenario for the interference range for the DATA packets for nodes implementing BASIC. Assume the current noise equals zero and the distance covered by RTS or the CTS packets is $r_{\max}$. The SINR threshold = 10 dB.

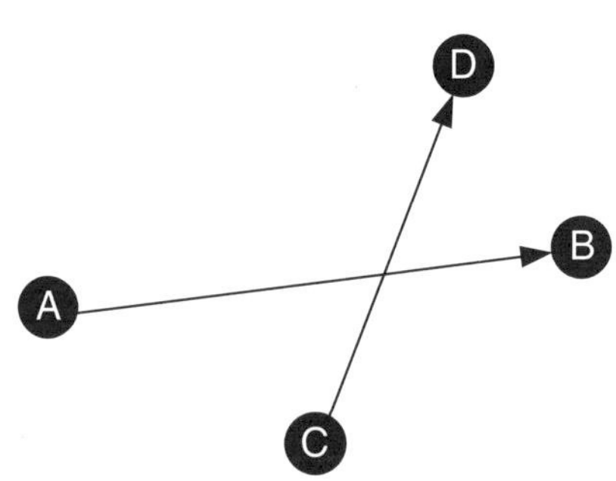

Fig. 9. Interference model.

9. Consider an ongoing communication between nodes A and B, which are 50 m distant apart. The antenna gain and height of a node are both equal to one. The receiver sensitivity is 3.652×10^{-12} W. The SIR threshold is 10 dB. The maximal transmission power is 0.02818 W. Assume a successful RTS/CTS handshake between nodes A and B, and interfering node C, which is 180 m away from node initiates a communication to node D. Check if the transmission from C will corrupt the DATA packet receptions assuming the current noise equals zero if the nodes implement (a) IEEE 802.11 without power control, (b) BASIC (c) CAPC. The DATA packet size = 1,000 bytes and the channel rate = 2 Mbps.
10. What are other techniques to enhance spatial reuse in an IEEE 802.11 based multi-hop ad hoc networks?

References

1. R. Ramanathan and J. Redi, A brief overview of ad hoc networks: Challenges and directions, *IEEE Commun. Mag.* **40**(5), 20–22 (2002).
2. S. Kumar, V. S. Raghavan and J. Deng, Medium access control protocols for ad-hoc wireless networks: A survey, *Elsevier Ad-Hoc Network. J.* **4**(3), 326–358 (2006).
3. A. Muqattash and M. Krunz, A single-channel solution for transmit power control in wireless ad hoc networks, *Proc. ACM MobiHoc*, Tokyo, Japan, May (2004), pp. 276–283.
4. E. Jung and N. H. Vaidya, A power control MAC protocol for ad hoc networks, *Proc. ACM MOBICOM*, Atlanta, USA (September, 2002), pp. 36–47.
5. IEEE 802.11 wireless LAN media access control (MAC) and physical layer (PHY) specifications (1999).
6. C. Lau and C. Leung, Capture models for mobile packet radio networks, *IEEE Trans. Commun.* **40**(5), 917–925 (1992).
7. C. Ware, J. Chicharo and T. Wysocki, Modelling of capture behaviour in IEEE 802.11 radio modems, Invited paper, *IEEE Int. Conf. Telecommunications* (2001).
8. H. Chang, V. Misra and D. Rubenstein, Fairness and physical layer capture in random access networks, *Proc. IEEE SECON*, 18–21 June (2007), pp. 381–390.
9. A. Kochut, A. Vasan, A. U. Shankar and A. Agrawala, Sniffing out the correct physical layer capture model in 802.11b, *Proc. IEEE ICNP* (2004), pp. 252–261.
10. Y. Yang, J. C. Hou and L.-C. Kung, Modeling the effect of transmit power and physical carrier sense in multi-hop wireless networks, *Proc. IEEE INFOCOM*, Alaska, USA, May (2007), pp. 2331–2335.
11. S. Agarwal, R. Katz, S. Krishnamurthy and S. Dao, Distributed power control in ad-hoc wireless networks, *Proc. IEEE PIMRC*, San Diego, USA, October (2001), pp. 59–66.
12. S. Yi, Y. Pei and S. Kalyanaraman, On the capacity improvement of ad hoc wireless networks using directional antennas. *Proc. ACM Mobihoc*, Annapolis, Maryland, USA, May (2003), pp. 108–116.
13. T. Lin and J. Hou, Interplay of spatial reuse and SINR-determined data rates in CSMA/CA-based, multi-hop, multi-rate wireless networks, *Proc. IEEE INFOCOM 2007*,Anchorage, Alaska, USA, May (2007), pp. 803–811.
14. T. Kim, J. Hou and H. Lim, Improving spatial reuse through tuning transmit power, carrier sense threshold, and data rate in multihop wireless networks, *Proc. ACM Mobicom*, California, USA, October (2006), pp. 366–377.

15. K. Medepalli and F. Tobagi, On optimization of CSMA/CA based wireless LANs: Part I — Impact of exponential backoff, *Proc. IEEE ICC*, Istanbul, Turkey, June (2006), pp. 2089–2094.
16. K. Medepalli, F. Tobagi, D. Famolari and T. Kodama, On optimization of CSMA/CA based wireless LANs: Part I — Mitigating efficiency loss, *Proc. IEEE ICC*, Istanbul, Turkey, June (2006), pp. 4799–4804.
17. J. Fuemmeler, N. Vaidya and V. V. Veeravalli, Selecting the transmit powers and the carrier sensing thresholds for CSMA protocols, *Proc. WICON*, Boston, USA, August (2006), pp. 1321–1329.
18. H. Ma, H. Alazemi and S. Roy, A stochastic model for optimizing physical carrier sensing and spatial reuse in ad hoc networks, *Proc. IEEE MASS*, Washington, USA, November (2005), pp. 615–622.
19. A. Arora and M. Krunz, Interference-limited MAC protocol for MANETs with directional antennas, *Proc. IEEE WoWMoM*, Taormina, Italy, June (2005), pp. 2–10.
20. R. Ramanathan, On the performance of ad hoc networks with beamforming antennas, *Proc. MobiHoc*, October (2001).
21. S. Narayanaswamy, V. Kawadia, R. Sreenivas and P. Kumar, Power control in ad-hoc networks: Theory, architecture, algorithm and implementation of the COMPOW protocol, in *Proc. European Wireless Conf.* (2002).
22. V. Rodoplu and T. H. Meng, Minimum energy mobile wireless networks, *IEEE J. Sel.Area. Commun.* **17**(8), 1333–1344 (1999).
23. R. Wattenhofer, L. Li, P. Bahl and Y. Wang, Distributed topology control for wireless multihop ad-hoc networks, *Proc. IEEE INFOCOM* (2001).
24. J. Rao and S. Biswas, Transmission power control for 802.11: A carrier-sense based NAV extension approach, *Proc. ACM GLOBECOM*, Vol. 6, 28 November–2 December (2005), p. 6.
25. A. A. Pires, J. F. de Rezende and C. Cordeiro, Alca: A new scheme for power control on 802.11 ad hoc networks, *Proc. IEEE WoWMoM*, June (2005), pp. 475–477.
26. J. Zhang, Z. Fang and B. Bensaou, Adaptive power control for single channel ad hoc networks, *Proc. IEEE ICC*, May (2005).
27. C. A. Basel Alawieh and W. Ajib, Distributed correlative power control scheme for MANET, *Proc. AINA*, Niagara Falls, Canada, May (2007), pp. 23–31.
28. J. P. Monks, V. Bharghavan and W. W. Hwu, A power controlled multiple access procotol for wireless packet networks, *Proc. IEEE INFOCOM*, Anchorage, USA, April (2001), pp. 219–228.
29. S. Wu, Y. Tseng and J. Sheu, Intelligent medium access for mobile ad hoc networks with busy tones and power control, *IEEE J. Sel. Area. Commun.* **18**(9), 1647–1657 (2000).
30. K. P. Shih and Y. D. Chen, CAPC: A collision avoidance power control MAC protocol for wireless ad hoc networks, *IEEE Commun. Lett.* **9**, 859–861, September (2005).
31. K. P. Shih, Y. D. Chen and C. C. Chang, Adaptive range-based power control for collision avoidance in ad hoc networks, *Proc. ICC 2007*, Glasgow, Scotland, June (2007), pp. 3672–3677.
32. J. Zhu, X. Guo, L. L. Yang, W. S. Conner, S. Roy and M. Hazra, Adapting physical carrier sensing to maximize spatial reuse in 802.11 mesh networks, in *Wireless Communications and Mobile Computing*, Vol. 4 (2004), pp. 933–946.
33. S. Gobriel, R. Melhem and D. Moss, A unified interference/collision analysis for power-aware adhoc networks, *Proc. IEEE INFOCOM*, Hong Kong, China, March (2004), pp. 608–620.

Chapter 8

COLLISION AVOIDANCE AWARE MAC PROTOCOLS FOR MULTI-HOP AD HOC NETWORKS: CHALLENGES, SOLUTIONS AND OPEN ISSUES

BASEL ALAWIEH* and CHADI ASSI
Faculty of Engineering and Computer Science,
Concordia University, Montreal, Quebec, Canada
** b_alawi@encs.concordia.ca*

HUSSEIN MOUFTAH
School of Information Technology and Engineering,
University of Ottawa, Ottawa, Ontario, Canada
mouftah@site.uottawa.ca

Energy efficiency and spatial reuse have been the key design constraints for evaluating the performance of IEEE 802.11-based multi-hop ad hoc networks. Energy efficiency is crucial because mobile nodes are equipped with short-range lightweight radios operating with limited energy, while efficient spatial reuse is needed to increase the network capacity. The performance of IEEE 802.11 DCF in multi-hop networks suffers from more collisions due to the existence of hidden nodes. The increase in the number of collisions will deteriorate the network throughput and increase energy consumption. Collision avoidance MAC protocols for multi-hop ad hoc networks have addressed this challenge. Three physical attributes are of importance to avoid collisions and hence enhance throughput, namely, physical carrier sensing threshold, transmission data rate, and transmit power. In this chapter, we identify the challenges and open issues involved in designing protocols for better spatial reuse in multi-hop ad hoc networks. Specifically, we survey the research aimed at resolving these challenges and propose future work to address open issues.

1. Introduction

The rapid evolution of mobile Internet technology has provided incentives for building efficient multi-hop wireless networks [1]. A wireless ad hoc network precludes the use of a wired infrastructure and allows hosts to communicate either directly or indirectly over radio channels. These networks are applicable to environments in which a prior deployment of network infrastructure is not possible. Wireless ad hoc networks have enabled the existence of various applications ranging from the monitoring of herds of animals to supporting communication in military battlefields and civilian disaster recovery scenarios as well as providing an emergency warning system for vehicles on the road. Due to the scarce wireless channel resources, an effective medium access control (MAC) protocol which regulates the nodes access to the shared channels is required. Thus, recently the development of efficient MAC protocols for multi-hop ad hoc networks has been the focus of extensive research [2, 3].

The IEEE 802.11 distributed coordination function (DCF) standard [4] has gained global acceptance and popularity both in wireless LANs and wireless multi-hop ad hoc environments. The DCF employs two different channel access modes for data packet transmission: the default two-way (basic access) and the optional four-way handshaking (RTS/CTS) access scheme [4]. The optional (RTS/CTS) scheme assumes that the transmission of short request-to-send (RTS) and clear-to-send (CTS) control packets prior to the data packet transmission will reduce the vulnerability duration, i.e., the time interval in which hidden nodes can interfere with data packet transmission.

While the multi-hopping technique can potentially maximize channel spatial reuse by allowing multiple simultaneous transmissions separated in space [2] to co-exist, the performance of IEEE 802.11 DCF in multi-hop networks suffers, however, from more collisions due to the existence of hidden nodes. The increase in the number of collisions will deteriorate the network throughput and definitely increase energy consumption.

Stations running the IEEE 802.11 DCF MAC basic access protocol use physical carrier sensing (PCS) to determine if the air medium is idle before transmitting a data packet to avoid collisions. This is accomplished by monitoring the channel radio frequency (RF) energy level and data packet transmission is initiated only if the power of the detected signal is below a PCS threshold [4, 5]. Meanwhile, nodes implementing the RTS/CTS access scheme contend for a channel if both the PCS and VCS (virtual carrier sensing) conditions are satisfied. Nodes using VCS are typically those in the transmission range of the RTS or CTS control packet sender and they will refrain from transmission for a duration of the whole communication that is updated in their network allocation vector (NAV) table upon hearing the RTS or CTS message.

Extensive research has been done to address the throughput and energy deficiencies in the IEEE 802.11 DCF implementation in multi-hop networks [6–8]. In particular, research efforts have focused on (i) transmit power control [6] (ii) data rate adaptation [9, 10], (iii) physical carrier sensing threshold tuning [10] (iv) optimizing binary exponential backoff mechanisms [11, 12]. Different variants of access methods have been proposed to optimize the operation of DCF by helping nodes to select either optimal contention windows or optimal transmission probabilities, which may yield to a decrease in collision among hosts and ultimately minimize both the collision and idle periods. On the other hand, physical carrier sensing [13, 14], is another effective mechanism to detect simultaneous transmissions, and thus tuning the carrier sensing threshold may have an impact on eliminating or reducing future interference and thereby reducing collisions in wireless networks. Data rate adaptation can also be a good candidate for improving the throughput. The basic idea behind data rate adaptation [10] is to exploit good channel conditions by using higher rates for improved efficiency (i.e., throughput), and improve the transmission reliability by lowering the rate in the presence of channel impairments. Finally, controlling the transmit power [6] is one of the most efficient mechanisms used to exploit both spatial reuse and power conservation opportunities (reducing power consumption).

In this chapter, we focus on physical carrier sensing threshold, power control and rate adaptation to avoid collisions. Specifically, we survey key elements of DCF and discuss challenges for tuning the physical attributes when used in a multi-hop ad hoc environment. Moreover, we survey the existing mechanisms that aim at resolving these challenges. The organization of this chapter is as follows. In Sec. 2, a general description of IEEE 802.11's key elements and the challenges its physical attributes pose are discussed. Section 3 surveys solutions to these challenges. Finally, Sec. 4 presents future work to address open issues.

2. Background

2.1. *IEEE 802.11 DCF*

The IEEE 802.11 DCF standard [4] is currently the dominant MAC for multi-hop networks. IEEE 802.11 DCF relies on carrier sensing multiple access with collision avoidance (CSMA/CA). DCF employs two different channel access modes for data packet transmission: the default two-way (basic access) and the optional four-way handshaking (RTS/CTS) access scheme [4]. Here, the optional (RTS/CTS) scheme assumes the transmission of short request-to-send (RTS) and clear-to-send (CTS) control packets prior to the data packet transmission. In the (RTS/CTS) access scheme, a node with packets to transmit first senses the medium through physical carrier sensing (PCS). If the medium is idle for at least a certain period DIFS (distributed interframe space), it will immediately request the channel by sending a short control frame RTS to the receiver node. If the receiver correctly receives the RTS, it will reply with a short control frame CTS after waiting a SIFS (short interframe space) period. Once the sender receives the CTS, it will start to transfer DATA. After the successful reception of DATA, the receiver sends an ACK to the sender. The SIFS duration is the shortest of the interframe spaces and is used after the RTS, CTS, and DATA frames to give the highest priority to CTS, DATA and ACK, respectively. Nodes implementing IEEE 802.11 maintain a network allocation vector (NAV), which shows the remaining time of the on-going transmission sessions. Using the duration information in the RTS, CTS, and DATA packets, nodes adjust their NAVs whenever they receive a packet. This is shown in Fig. 1. For the basic scheme, upon sensing the DATA or ACK packet nodes will refrain from transmitting any packet for EIFS.

Moreover, if the channel is sensed busy, the station has to wait until the channel is sensed idle for a DIFS time. At this point, the station generates a random backoff time interval before transmission, in order to minimize the probability of collisions

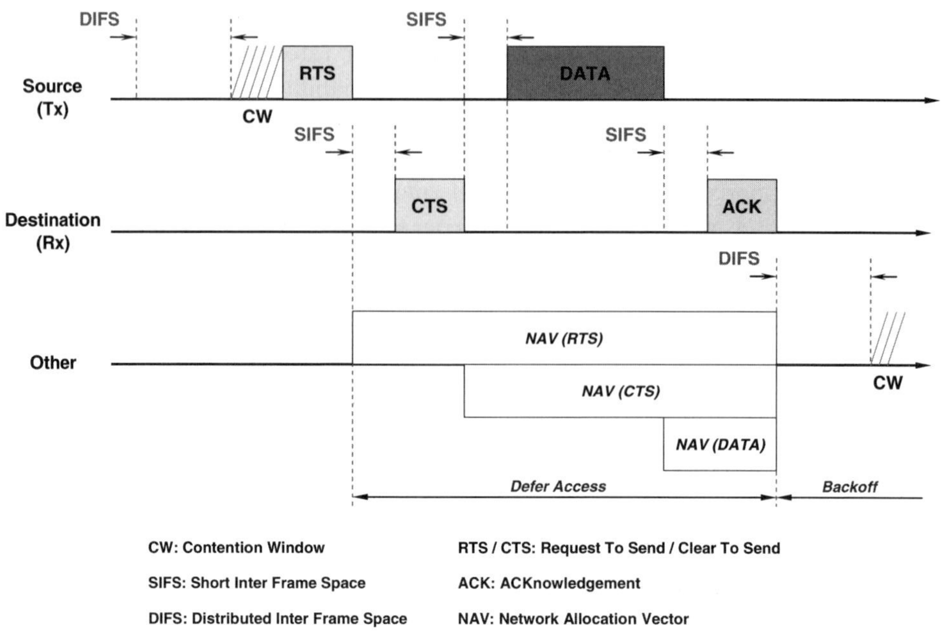

Fig. 1. IEEE 802.11 DCF.

with packets being transmitted by other stations. DCF adopts an binary exponential backoff scheme (BEB).

2.2. *Backoff Algorithm*

The main purpose of the backoff algorithm is to reduce the probability of collision among contending nodes. In the IEEE 802.11 DCF, the transmitter of the colliding packet needs to refrain from immediate retransmissions in order to avoid repeated collisions. Thus, each competing node sets up a backoff timer according to a randomly selected backoff time period and enters the backoff state. This backoff time period is selected uniformly between 0 and the contention window (CW). In the BEB algorithm, the contention window is doubled every time a node experiences a packet collision, i.e., when the CTS packet or the ACK reply are not received before a timeout occurs. If a node is successful in its packet transmission, the contention window is reset to the minimum value $CW_{\min}$. In order to avoid the contention window from growing too large or shrinking too small, two bounds on CW are defined: the maximum contention window $CW_{\max}$ and the minimum contention window $CW_{\min}$.

2.3. *Communication Model*

Assume a sender A transmits to its receiver B, and another node F (hidden node) unaware of the transmission of A may start to transmit to its intended receiver as

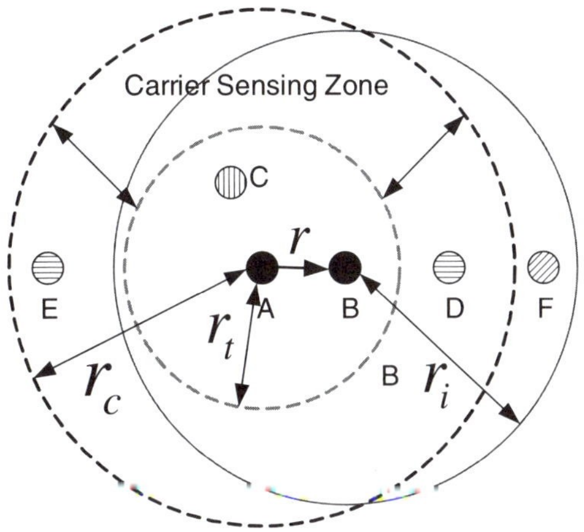

Fig. 2. Different ranges according to IEEE 802.11.

shown in Fig. 2. The two signals from A and F may overlap in time at the receiver B. Whether the signal from sender A can be correctly decoded depends on the so-called capture effect, i.e., the stronger signal will be captured by the receiver modem, while the weaker signal will be rejected as noise.

While in the literature there exist various models that characterize the capture effect [15–18], in this survey we present the most widely adopted model. A receiver B can correctly decode the signal if the signal-to-interference plus noise ratio (SINR) exceeds a certain predetermined threshold denoted by ζ. This results in the following constraint:

$$P_r \geq \zeta \times (P_n), \tag{1}$$

where P_n is the total allowed interference power, which consists of interference power from interfering nodes and background thermal noise. Here, the value of ζ is determined according to the rate at which a packet is received at the receiver.

Moreover, due to path loss constraints, a receiver B is able to receive and correctly decode a packet when the received power (P_r) of a frame from a transmitter (with a transmission power P_t) is higher than or equal to κ (the receiver sensitivity). Accordingly, adopting the two-ray model with antenna heights and gains equal to one, the transmission range (r_t) is

$$r_t = \left(\frac{P_t}{\kappa}\right)^{\frac{1}{4}}, \tag{2}$$

where κ is dependent on the rate the packet is received at the receiver; note that the higher the rate, the smaller κ is Ref. 4. Note that a circular range is an idealized assumption and that no ideal circular ranges exist in reality.

Furthermore, a transmitter cannot initiate any communication if it senses a signal with a power level larger than a predefined CS_{th}. Hence, the CS_{th} specifies the signal strength above which a node determines that the medium is busy and will not attempt transmission. Let the carrier sense set of a transmitter A (denoted as CS_A) be defined as the set of nodes, if any of them transmits, node A will sense the medium busy [19]. Formally,

$$CS_A = \left\{ A' \middle| \frac{P_{A'}}{d^4} \geq CS_{th} \right\},$$

where d is the distance between the sender A and node A′ (in the carrier sense set), and $P_{A'}$ is the transmission power of A′. If all nodes use the same transmission power, P_t, then the carrier sense range r_c, defined as the maximum value of d such that the above constraints hold, can be expressed as

$$r_c = \left(\frac{P_t}{CS_{th}} \right)^{\frac{1}{4}}. \tag{3}$$

Note however, that, if nodes use different powers, the carrier sense region (CS_A) will have an arbitrary shape (not circular).

Another acronym of interest is the silence area that results from the transmission of node A. The silence set of a transmitter A (denoted as SL_A), assuming fixed CS_{th} for all nodes, is the set of nodes that will detect the channel to be busy if A transmits [19]. Formally,

$$SL_A = \left\{ A' \middle| \frac{P_A}{d^4} \geq CS_{th} \right\}.$$

Clearly, $SL_A \equiv CS_A$ if all nodes use the same transmission power.

2.4. *Power Control*

In IEEE 802.11, all packets (RTS/CTS/DATA/ACK) are sent with maximum power. It has been shown that this kind of handshake communication decreases spatial reuse and thus decreases capacity throughput and additionally yields unnecessary energy consumption [20]. To illustrate this, consider the scenario in Fig. 3, where node A uses its maximum transmission power (TP) to send packets to node B and nodes C and F will try to initiate a communication with nodes D and E, respectively. Nodes C and F will not be able to do that since they lie in the transmission vicinity of nodes A and B, respectively. Nodes C and F are termed exposed terminals. However, it is easy to show that the three transmissions A → B, D → C, and E → F can overlap in time if nodes are able to select their transmission power appropriately as shown in Fig. 3. Consequently, the network throughput is increased and possibly the overall energy consumption is reduced. Adjusting the transmitted power is extremely important in ad hoc networks for three major reasons:

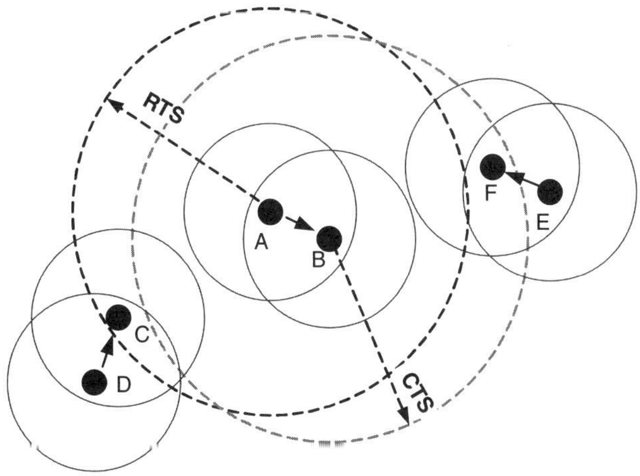

Fig. 3. Power control merits.

- The transmitted power of the mobile node determines the network topology. The network topology in turn has considerable impact on the throughput performance of the network [21].
- Mobile nodes in ad hoc networks are usually energy constrained, and hence they have to be as energy efficient as possible. Thus, the power control should adjust the transmitted power to be the least power required to send the data packet to meet the required SINR threshold.
- Transmitting at high power can degrade other ongoing transmissions and in the meantime can prevent future transmission, as illustrated in Fig. 3. Thus, reducing the transmission power will reduce interference on other nodes and may enhance the overall network throughput as well as energy consumption.

While the idea of power control is simple, achieving this in an IEEE 802.11 based multi-hop network is challenging. When reducing the transmission power, the number of nodes included within the transmission range of the sender and competing for wireless channel access is reduced and hence the number of collisions from contending nodes is reduced. Moreover, although it is intuitive that using reduced power minimizes the interference level between neighboring nodes, there is an increase in the number of concurrent transmissions because the transmission range of each node is reduced. Consequently, the overall signal-to-interference ratio (SIR) might degrade when using a lower transmission power and this may lead to an increase in frame error rate. While reducing the transmit power may indeed decrease the energy consumption, the likelihood of packet corruptions (error or collisions) during packet reception goes up, and hence retransmissions of the same packet could result in a power consumption higher than the maximum power.

2.5. *Physical Carrier Sensing Threshold*

Physical carrier sensing is essentially used to determine whether or not a node may access the medium. Typically, a node senses the medium, before initiating any communication, and defers its transmission if the channel is sensed busy, that is, if the strength of the received signal exceeds the carrier sensing threshold (CS_{th}). The PCS method reduces the likelihood of collision by preventing nodes in the vicinity of one another from transmitting simultaneously, while allowing nodes that are separated by a safe margin (termed the carrier sensing range r_c) to engage in concurrent transmissions. The former is referred to as collision avoidance while the latter is known as spatial reuse. Thus, the selection of the carrier sensing threshold is key for enhancing spatial reuse by avoiding anticipated collisions.

2.6. *DATA Rate Adaptation*

Data rate adaptation can also be a good candidate for improving the throughput. Currently, the enhanced versions of IEEE 802.11, IEEE 802.11a and IEEE 802.11b, provide multi-rate capability at the physical layer. The set of possible data rates that are being supported by IEEE 802.11a are 6, 9, 12, 18 and 54 Mbps, while those supported by IEEE 802.11b are 1, 2, 5.5 and 11 Mbps. We note that a higher rate does not necessarily yield a higher throughput. Here, increasing the rate increases the SINR threshold requirements for the correct reception of the packet. For instance, a packet transmitted at 2 Mbps is correctly received and decoded at the receiver with a SINR threshold equal to 9 dB whereas if transmitted at 11 Mbps, the SINR threshold required for successful reception may be 15 dB. Only when the channel condition is good does a higher rate give a higher throughput. This is due to the fact that in IEEE 802.11 based ad hoc multi-hop networks, the channel conditions suffer from collisions due to interference from hidden terminals.

2.7. *Interference Model*

We now explain the interference range [22]. Consider an ongoing communication between nodes A and B, which are a distance r apart. If node A transmits with power P_t, node B receives this signal with a received power $P_r = (P_t/r^4)$. Moreover, if we neglect the thermal noise, P_n in Eq. (1) can be expressed as $P_n = P_{cn} + P_{tn}$. Here, P_{cn} is the current measured interference at node B and P_{tn} is the maximum remaining interference that node B can tolerate while it is still able to decode correctly the packet it receives from node A. Accordingly, making use of Eq. (1), we can express P_{tn} as

$$P_{tn} \leq \frac{P_t}{r^4 \cdot \zeta} - P_{cn}. \tag{4}$$

Now assume an interfering node F, which is d meters away from node B, initiates a communication with a power P_i while node B is receiving a packet from node A. The received power $P_{ri} = (P_i/d^4)$ at node B from node F should satisfy the condition that $P_{ri} \leq P_{tn}$ such that node B is still able to receive and correctly decode the packet from node A. Accordingly, we define the interference set of a receiver B (denoted as IN_B) as the set of nodes whose transmission, if overlapping with the transmission of a sender, will cause collision at the receiver. Specifically, if node F transmits,

$$IN_B = \left\{ F \middle| \frac{P_i}{d^4} \geq \frac{P_t}{r^4 \cdot \zeta} - P_{cn} \right\}. \tag{5}$$

With the condition of the interference set from Eq. (5), we define the interference range r_i as the maximum value of d such that the inequality in Eq. (5) holds:

$$r_i = \left(\frac{P_i}{\frac{P_t}{r^4 \cdot \zeta} - P_{cn}} \right)^{\frac{1}{4}}. \tag{6}$$

Based on the above equation, we can see that both ζ (whose value depends on physical transmission rate) and the power value (P_t) of an ensuring packet determines the interference range at the receiver.

According to the definition of the interference range and silence range, we distinguish two types of collisions for IEEE 802.11 based multi-hop ad hoc networks:

- A collision may occur due to simultaneous transmission (i.e., during the first time slot of the packet is started to be transmitted) by one or more nodes that are located in the intersection of the interference range area of the receiver and the silence range of the transmitter.
- A collision may occur if there are one or more transmissions initiated during the vulnerable interval (the duration of the packet transmission) from nodes located in the hidden area (part of the interference zone that is not covered by the silence zone). These nodes are termed the hidden terminals, since they are unaware of the sender's transmission, and they can interfere any time during the packet reception at the receiver. Accordingly, we define the *hidden terminal* as a node that neither senses the transmission of a transmitter nor correctly receives the reservation packet from a corresponding receiver.

Additionally, in a multi-hop wireless network, frame loss may occur due to the accumulative interference resulting from nodes lying outside the silence range of the transmitter. Several accumulative interference models have been proposed in Refs. 23–25; the most commonly used is the honey grid model, which was first introduced in Ref. 23. In a honey grid model, as shown in Fig. 4, the nodes are uniformly distributed and form concentric hexagons, called rings, around the sender. When a node is transmitting, there are at most six nodes which can transmit concurrently with the transmitter. Thus, those six nodes form the first ring tier of interfering nodes. The second and other tiers are similarly constructed. Accordingly, the jth ring tier has $6j$ nodes. Furthermore, the authors of Ref. 5 adopted the worst case scenario interference model [24] derived for cellular networks, where the receiver

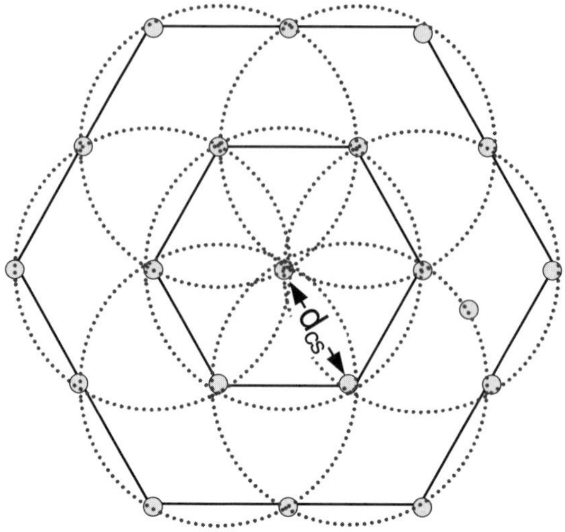

Fig. 4. Honey grid model.

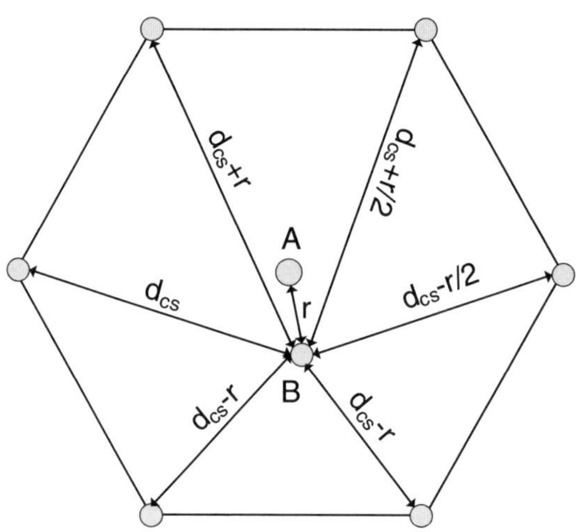

Fig. 5. Accumulated interference calculation.

lies on the edge of the transmission range of the sender. The adopted model as shown in Fig. 5 assumes the observations in Refs. 26 and 27, that is the interference from the first tier (six nodes) dominates and the interference from other tier rings is negligible. In a worst case scenario, the receiver node, which is a distance r away from the transmitter, is positioned such that the six first-tier[a] interfering nodes are

[a]Recently, the author in Ref. 28 pointed out that the number of interfering nodes at the first ring are fewer than six.

respectively $d_{cs} - r$, $d_{cs} - r$, $d_{cs} - \frac{r}{2}$, d_{cs}, $d_{cs} + \frac{r}{2}$ and $d_{cs} + r$ away from it. Hence, assuming all nodes use the same transmission power P_t, and adopting the two-ray model, the maximum interference $I_{\max}$ can be expressed as

$$I_{\max} = \frac{2P_t}{(d_{cs} - r)^4} + \frac{P_t}{(d_{cs} - \frac{r}{2})^4} + \frac{P_t}{(d_{cs} + \frac{r}{2})^4} + \frac{P_t}{(d_{cs} + r)^4} + \frac{P_t}{(d_{cs})}. \quad (7)$$

From the above definitions we can observe that the size of the carrier sensing range decides the number of concurrent transmissions, and hence the level of spatial reuse. On the other hand, the size of the interference range decides the number of potential interfering nodes, and hence the transmission quality of a single link. Therefore, the network capacity is jointly determined by the size of the interference range and the carrier sensing range (silence range). Now in order to enhance the network capacity, one can appropriately adjust the size of the interference range by tuning transmission power and data rate, according to Eq. (6), or adjust the size of the carrier sensing range by tuning transmission power and CS_{th}, according to Eq. (3). Considering the interplay between these parameters would be of interest in the area of enhancing the performance of ad hoc networks. For instance, performing power control with data rate adaptation enhances spatial reuse from the perspective of avoiding collisions, or always transmitting at the highest rate while performing power control is more advantageous.

2.8. *Challanges*

The challenges facing the triggering of physical attributes can be summarized as follows:

- Increasing the rate does not enhance the throughput in some cases, and as the rate increases the interference range increases.
- Decreasing the rate adds more overhead and as such decreases the throughput.
- Increasing the power will decrease the interference range but will add more interference to other ongoing communication.
- Decreasing the power will increase the interference range and accordingly there is a higher likelihood for DATA packet corruption.
- Decreasing the carrier sensing threshold to avoid collisions will hinder nodes from transmission and accordingly will decrease the spatial reuse.
- Increasing the carrier sensing threshold provides more opportunities for nodes to transmit but spatial reuse may decrease due to anticipated collisions.
- Solving the hidden terminal problem will increase the possibility of the exposed terminals and *vice versa*.

In what follows, we survey a list of proposals aimed at enhancing the system throughput by improving the spatial reuse through tuning one or more of the physical attributes listed above.

3. Solutions

3.1. *Tuning the Carrier Sensing Threshold*

Recently, tuning the physical carrier sensing threshold (CS_{th}) has been proposed as an efficient mechanism to enhance the network throughput in an IEEE 802.11 based multi-hop ad hoc network. The physical carrier sensing method reduces the likelihood of collision by preventing nodes in the vicinity of one another from transmitting simultaneously, while allowing nodes that are separated by a safe margin (carrier sensing range) to engage in concurrent transmission.

The authors of Ref. 29 introduced the concept of tuning the CS_{th} for throughput enhancement. By setting the physical silence range, r_c, such that it covers the interference range (i.e., $r_c = r_i + d$), the interference impact from hidden terminals is eliminated. Accordingly, they derived the optimal CS_{th} for several grid topologies to achieve maximum network throughput (via enhancing the spatial reuse) given a predetermined transmission rate and SINR; the work did not, however, consider the MAC overhead.

The ECHOS architecture [30] improved the network capacity in hotspot wireless networks by dynamically tuning the CS_{th} to allow more flows to co-exist. Here, hot spot deployment operates in infrastructure where an access point (AP) services connectivity to multiple clients. ECHOS adjusts CS_{th} based on interference measured at both the AP and client side. The clients report the measured interference to their APs. Then each AP estimates the maximum tolerable future interference for the clients and set its CS_{th} to avoid hidden terminals.

In contrast, the authors of Refs. 14, 31 and 32 studied analytically the effect of CS_{th} on the performance of ad hoc networks and showed through theoretical analysis, and verified later via simulations, that the optimum CS_{th} that maximizes the throughput allows hidden terminals to exist.

The authors of Ref. 5 further explored the interactions between the MAC and PHY layers and studied the impact of MAC overhead on the choice of optimal carrier sense range and the aggregate throughput. They concluded that the optimal CS_{th} depends on the degree of channel contention, packet size and MAC overhead.

In Ref. 33, the transmitter collects the RTS/CTS success ratio and the signal strength, and builds a mapping table between the two. This mapping table is updated after every access request. Before each transmit attempt, the sender looks up the mapping table with the current sensed signal strength to obtain the estimated success ratio. If the obtained success ratio is higher than a certain threshold, the transmitter starts transmission. Otherwise, it blocks itself until it decides the channel is clear.

In Ref. 34, the authors first claim through an analytical study that the CS_{th} which allows a certain number of hidden terminals to exist can enhance the network capacity. Moreover, they propose that the number of contending nodes (n_c) is determined by CS_{th} and they derive an optimal value of n_c that can maximize the throughput. They also present an algorithm that adjusts n_c through tuning

CS_{th}. In this algorithm, a node first estimates n_c from the measured information, such as the time that the node senses the channel as idle, busy and captured for receiving; then the node adjusts its CS_{th} in order to achieve an optimal n_c.

4. Power Control Solutions

4.1. *Power Control Solutions*

The authors of Ref. 35 introduced a collision avoidance power control (CAPC) MAC protocol to protect the transmission of DATA and ACK packets by appropriately selecting their power values. For example, a DATA packet may be protected if the interference range r_i (to be derived later) at its receiver is set to be equal to the transmission range r_t of the ensuing CTS packet, as shown in Fig. 6. Here, the authors assumed that an interfering node always sends at maximum power to derive the interference range. The RTS and CTS frames are sent at maximum power and that may impact the spatial reuse in the network. Making use of (3) and (6), as stated earlier are transmitted at maximum power. Thus, we have

$$r_t = \left(\frac{P_{\max}}{\kappa}\right)^{\frac{1}{4}} = r_i = \left(\frac{P_{\max}}{\frac{P_{t,DATA}}{r^4 \cdot \zeta} - P_{cn}}\right)^{\frac{1}{4}}. \tag{8}$$

The data packet power $P_{t,DATA}$ is then calculated as follows:

$$P_{t,DATA} = \zeta \cdot r^4 \cdot (P_{cn} + \kappa). \tag{9}$$

More recently, the authors of Ref. 36 extended the work in Ref. 35 and proposed an adaptive range-based power control (ARPC) MAC protocol for avoiding collisions and conserving energy consumption. They derived four mechanisms and studied their performances: carrier-sensing range cover mechanism (SCRC), receivers carrier-sensing range cover mechanism (RCRC), senders transmission range cover mechanism (STRC), and receivers transmission range cover mechanism (RTRC), to adapt the transmission power for a node. In SCRC, the RTS and CTS packets are transmitted at maximum power and the transmission power of DATA

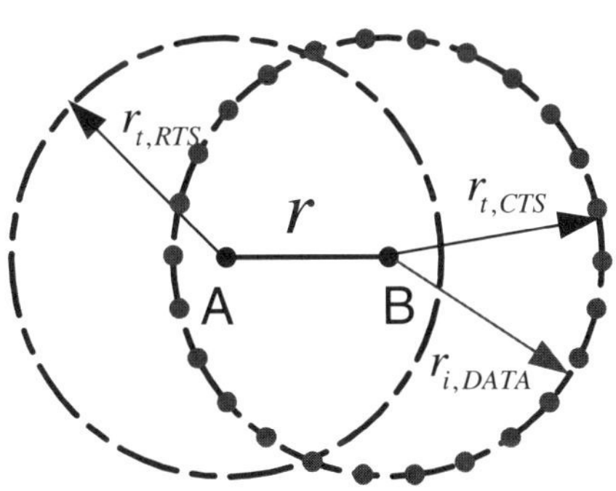

Fig. 6. Transmission range of CTS protects DATA.

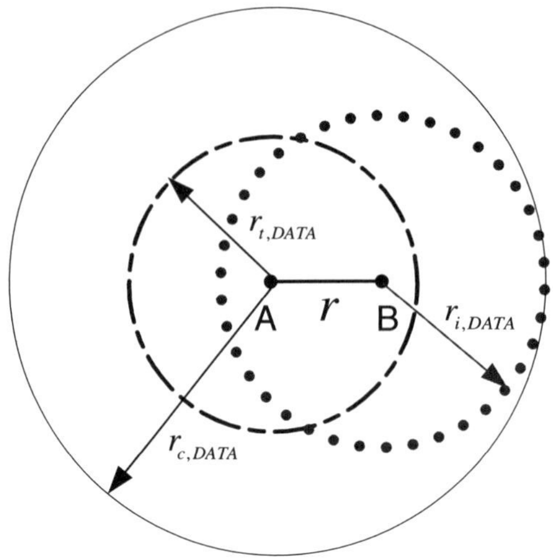

Fig. 7. Carrier sensing range of DATA protects DATA.

and ACK packets are calculated such that the carrier sensing range of the DATA packet covers the entire interference range of the DATA packet, as shown in Fig. 7. In RCRC, the RTS packet is also transmitted at maximum power and the DATA packet is transmitted at minimum power while the transmission power of the CTS frame is determined such that the carrier sensing range of the CTS equals the interference range of the DATA packet given that the size of the DATA packet is small. Moreover, in RCRC, the ACK packet is transmitted at a maximum power. In the other two mechanisms, STRC and RTRC, RTS and CTS packets are transmitted at maximum power while the DATA or ACK packet is transmitted at adapted power such that the interference range of the DATA packet is protected by the transmission range of RTS or CTS packets (as shown in Fig. 6), respectively. The authors further derived an adaptive algorithm that selects between the proposed mechanisms based on the distance between the sender and the receiver. Performance evaluation has shown that the proposed scheme has completely eliminated the hidden terminal problem and thus the DATA collision rate becomes negligible. Additionally, in the proposed mechanisms, the interference range is always calculated under the worst case scenario, in which the potential interfering node is considered to transmit at maximum power, which does not reflect the real channel conditions. However, in their methods, the RTS (and most of the time CTS) frame is always transmitted at maximum power, which, as mentioned earlier, affects the channel spatial reuse.

4.2. *Joint Power and Rate Adaptation*

In an IEEE 802.11 based multi-rate wireless network, a transmission failure can be caused by either collisions or channel errors. Thus, a transmitter node decreases its transmission rate only when it faces transmission failures that are due to channel errors. On the other hand, if the transmission failures are due to collisions, there is no need to decrease the transmission rate. Based on this observation, a collision aware rate adaptation (CARA) [37] uses adaptively the RTS/CTS exchange to differentiate packet collisions from packet transmission failures caused by channel errors in order to avoid unnecessary rate decrements. Two assumptions have been made:

- All the RTS transmission failures are due to collisions. This assumption is based on the fact that the transmission error probability of an RTS packet is negligible due to its small size (20 bytes) and its lower robust transmission rate (and corresponding lower SINR requirement).
- The RTS/CTS exchange can cover the entire interference range of the DATA packet. Namely, the RTS/CTS exchange can completely eliminate all hidden terminals.

Based on the assumptions stated above, it can be concluded that a DATA packet transmission failure following a successful RTS/CTS exchange must be due to channel errors. Because the successful RTS/CTS exchange has already re-served, the transmission floor guarantees no collision to the subsequent DATA packet transmission. Therefore, if the RTS/CTS exchange is applied before each data transmission, there will be no DATA packet frame collisions, and hence no misinterpretation of a DATA packet collision as a channel-error-caused DATA frames transmission failure. As a result, unnecessary rate decrements are completely avoided.

However, one side effect of this approach is the added RTS/CTS overhead, which wastes precious wireless bandwidth. To address this problem, a scheme which dynamically switches RTS/CTS exchange ON/OFF was proposed. More specifically, a node first transmits a DATA packet without RTS/CTS exchange. If the transmission fails, the node treats this transmission failure as a collision and does not decrease its transmission rate. Then, the RTS/CTS exchange will be activated for the next retransmission attempt. If the retransmission fails again, the node concludes that this failure is due to channel errors and it accordingly decreases its transmission rate.

In general, CARA is aimed at differentiating collisions from channel errors. However, it only applies for specific scenarios which do not have hidden terminals. When hidden terminals exist, CARA may incorrectly identify the collisions from hidden terminals as channel errors. Moreover, CARA fails to reduce the bandwidth overhead of the RTS/CTS exchange in a crowded network due to frequent collisions.

In Ref. 38, the authors proposed an energy efficient scheme (MiSer) by jointly controlling both transmit power and PHY transmission rate. They compute offline an optimal rate-power combination table, and then at runtime, a wireless station determines the most energy efficient transmission strategy for each data frame.

A link adaptation scheme called ILARI (Integrated Link Adaptation with Rate selection and Interference avoidance) was presented in Ref. 39. Here, ILARI adopts the RTS/CTS access mechanism for the purposes of both probing the channel quality and preventing the interference from hidden terminals. Moreover, ILARI adaptively performs a dynamic switch between the RTS/CTS access scheme and the basic scheme based on a predefined policy in order to avoid the additional overhead caused by the RTS/CTS exchange. When operating using the basic access scheme, ILARI utilizes physical carrier sensing (PCS) to protect DATA packet reception from the interference from hidden terminals. This is based on the fact that when a hidden node lies inside the physical sensing zone of the transmitter, the reception of the DATA packet transmission is guaranteed even without the RTS/CTS access mechanism. Furthermore, given a fixed power, transmitting at a lower data rate decreases the interference range of the receiver since the required SINR for successful transmissions decreases. Given this fact, and based on the receiver's channel quality and the size of the data frame, ILARI chooses lower data rates such that the physical carrier sensing range covers the interference range of the receiver so that the RTS/CTS handshake is not required.

To summarize, ILARI bases its transmission strategy on the following criteria:

$$r_i = \min\left(\frac{r_c}{1+\zeta^{0.25}}, r_t\right), \tag{10}$$

where r_i, r_c, r_t, and ζ are the interference range, carrier sensing range, transmission range of the CTS packet and signal-to-interference-noise ratio threshold, respectively.

Accordingly, ILARI chooses two transmission strategies S_1, S_2. S_1 adopts PCS with the lowest rate that satisfies $r_t > d$, whereas S_2 adopts VCS with the highest rate that satisfies $r_i > d$ (d being the distance between the transmitter and receiver). Then, S_2 follows the same principles of RBAR (receiver-based auto-rate). In RBAR, the channel conditions are exchanged through the RTS/CTS packets and accordingly the receiver selects the data rate. Thus, the following policy is constructed:

$$\text{Transmission Strategy} = \begin{cases} S_1 \mapsto w/oRTS \\ \quad \Rightarrow \text{if } \left\lceil \dfrac{l+0.375}{bps_{rate_1}} \right\rceil \cdot 4 \le \left\lceil \dfrac{l+0.375}{bps_{rate_2}} \right\rceil \cdot 4 + 128, \\ S_2 \mapsto wRTS \Rightarrow \text{otherwise}, \end{cases} \tag{11}$$

where $\lceil \frac{l+0.375}{bps_{rate}} \rceil$ is the transmission time of the data packet with l being the packet size, bps is the data rate and $128\,\mu$sec is duration of the RTS/CTS handshake overhead, i.e., $2T_{SIFS} + T_{RTS} + T_{CTS} + T_{PCLP} = 128$. Here, T_{RTS}, T_{CTS} and T_{PCLP} are the times to transmit the RTS packet, CTS packet, and their physical headers, whereas T_{SIFS} is the SIFS time. Figure 8 demonstrates the effectiveness of ILARI. Here, the packet size = 100 bytes, S_1 = 18 Mbps, S_2 = 54 Mbps. It is

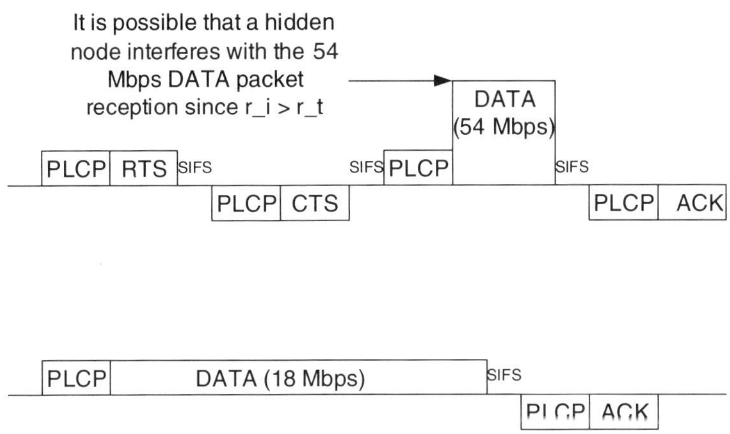

Fig. 8. ILARI scenario example.

noticeable that the transmission at 18 Mbps is more efficient than 54 Mbps due to the fact that the DATA packet can be corrupted in the latter case.

4.3. *Tuning CS_{th} and Rate Adaptation*

In Ref. 40 the authors observed that the space occupied by each transmission can be adjusted by tuning some protocol parameters (e.g., CS_{th} and transmission rate) and accordingly they proposed the concept of spatial backoff. More specifically, in order to allow more concurrent transmission to be initialized, CS_{th} should be increased. On the other hand, in order to make sure that these transmissions can take place simultaneously without corrupting one another, one should reduce the size of the interference range by lowering the transmission rate. To conclude, a lower rate and higher CS_{th} result in smaller occupied space. Accordingly, the authors proposed an algorithm for improving spatial reuse by dynamically adjusting CS_{th} and the transmission rate as shown in Fig. 9. The y-axis represents the different transmitting rate levels, which are in increasing order, while the x-axis represents the different CS_{th} levels in decreasing order. A node at point ($CS[i]$, $Rate[j]$) means the node is using carrier sensing threshold $CS[i]$ and transmitting rate $Rate[j]$.

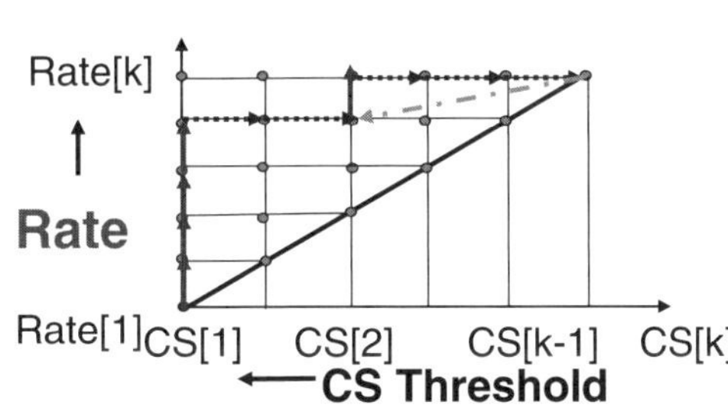

Fig. 9. Spatial backoff.

Assuming that the interference at the transmitter equals the interference at the receiver, the authors derived a minimum CS_{th} associated with each transmission rate, represented by the diagonal in the figure. A node adjusts its transmitting rates and CS_{th} based on the network performance. More specifically, when a node faces a certain number of consecutive transmission successes, it increases its transmitting rate by one level and CS_{th} remains the same. This action is presented by the solid arrow in Fig. 9. When the node faces a certain number of consecutive transmission failures and the CS_{th} threshold does not reach the minimum value for the current transmission rate, the node decreases the CS_{th} by one level, and the transmitting rate remains the same, as represented by the dotted arrows in the figure. When the transmission fails and the CS_{th} has already reached the minimum value for the current rate, the node decreases the transmission rate by one level, and increases the CS_{th} to the one it used with the lower rate before, represented by the dashed arrows in the figure.

4.4. *Power Control, Rate Adaptation and Tuning* CS_{th}

The authors in Ref. 41 argued that for the CSMA protocols the product of the transmit power and the carrier sensing threshold should be kept constant. That is, the lower the transmit power, the higher the carrier sensing threshold and hence the smaller the carrier sensing range and *vice versa*. Further, the authors proposed a heuristic algorithm to improve spatial reuse by incorporating this proposition.

Similarly, the authors of Ref. 10 studied the impact of spatial reuse on network capacity and derived the network capacity as a function of both transmission power and CS_{th}. They showed that in the case where discrete data rates are available, tuning the transmission power offers several advantages that tuning CS_{th} cannot, provided there is a sufficient number of power levels available. The merits of power control is elaborated in the following example shown in Fig. 10. Here, both nodes A and D are transmitting concurrently to their intended receivers B and C. Let $r[1]$, $r[2]$ and $r[3]$ denote the available transmission rates with SINR thresholds $SINR_{th}[1]$, $SINR_{th}[2]$ and $SINR_{th}[3]$, respectively. Moreover, let P_A and P_D denote the initial transmission power for node A and D and we assume that $P_A = P_D$ and the same transmission rate $r[2]$ is adopted for both senders. With transmission power control, node A can increase its transmission power P_A up to the appropriate value P'_A, where it sustains a higher data rate $r[3]$ with SINR threshold $SINR_{th}[3]$, while not disturbing the other concurrent transmission from D to C with data rate $r[2]$. Here, the increase in interference at node C from the increase in transmission power of node A does not make the SINR value at node C fall below $SINR_{th}[2]$. In contrast, when tuning the carrier sensing threshold of node A to achieve the rate $r[3]$, then node A should decrease its CS_{th} such that node D is included within its carrier sense range. As a result, the two transmissions cannot take place at the same time. Furthermore, the authors also pointed out that in the case that the achievable

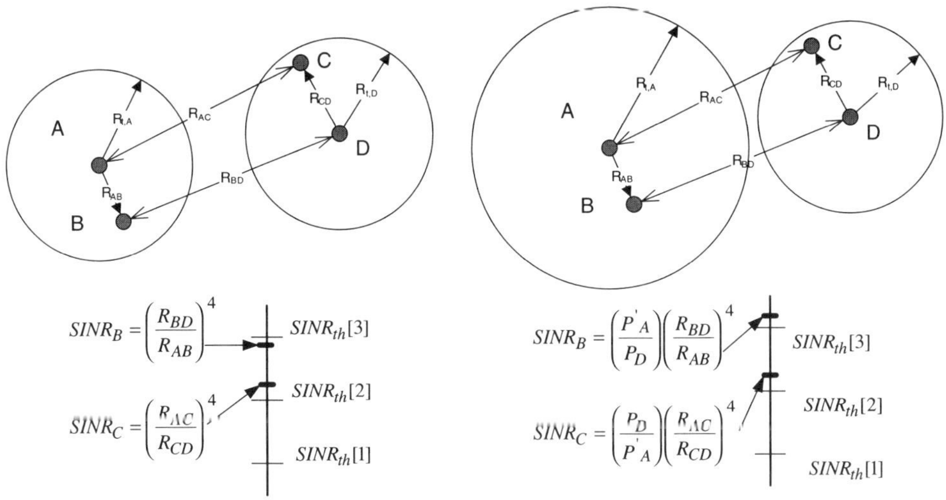

Fig. 10. Illustrative example to show when power control is more beneficial than tuning CS_{th}.

channel rate follows the Shannon capacity, spatial reuse depends only on the ratio of transmission power and CS_{th}. This is contrary to the work of Ref. 41, where it was shown that transmitters should keep the product of transmission power and CS_{th} fixed at a constant. Accordingly, a localized heuristic algorithm was proposed that adjusts the space occupied by a node by dynamically jointly tuning transmission power and rate.

In Ref. 19, the authors proposed an analytical model to investigate the impact of transmit power and carrier sense threshold on network throughput in the basic access mechanism; they extended both Bianchi's [42] and Kumar's [43] models to derive the single node's throughput. Through their model, the authors argued that an optimum throughput can be achieved for a specific carrier sensing threshold. Moreover, they concluded that a higher system throughput can be achieved with the use of smaller transmit power (subject to network connectivity) and carrier sense threshold.

In Ref. 9 the authors investigated the interaction between the carrier sensing threshold, contention window size CW, and discrete data rates for the IEEE 802.11 DCF. To accomplish this, they adopted and extended Cali's [44] model to derive the capacity of the network as a function of the carrier sensing threshold and SINR. The theoretical analysis verified that the throughput can be maximized at various transition points of the carrier sensing threshold. Thus, the capacity is strictly not a monotonically increasing/decreasing function of the carrier sensing threshold. Moreover, the throughput can be further enhanced by tuning the contention window size. A spatial reuse optimization mechanism is considered in Ref. 45 for multi-hop wireless networks, where the authors considered variable transmission power and different receiver sensitivities.

More recently, the authors in Ref. 28 proposed a model to study analytically the impact of CS_{th} on the network capacity in wireless multi-hop networks. In their model, the effect of collisions caused by accumulative interference is considered. Additionally, they claimed that the transmission attempt probability is a function of both contention window size and CS_{th}, and accordingly they showed that in order to enhance throughput the attempt probability should remain large, allowing some collisions to exist. To achieve high attempt probability, the size of the contention window should be fixed to smaller values while higher CS_{th} should be used.

4.5. *Other Avoidance Schemes*

Another category of alternative collision avoidance schemes that do not consider all the above proposed techniques have been proposed in Refs. 46 and 47. Both schemes embed extra information regarding the upcoming transmission in the physical layer convergence procedure (PLCP) header so that a larger group of potential interferers become aware of the transmission. The information can be the locations of the transmitter and receiver as in Ref. 47 or the interference range as in Ref. 46. Upon receiving the PLCP header, a neighboring node is able to determine whether it lies inside the interference range of the receiver and accordingly decide whether to block its own transmission or not. However, mandating extra information in the PLCP header of every control or data packet adds extra overhead.

Another enhanced carrier sensing (ECS) scheme was proposed in Ref. 48. Here, the MAC frame type is encapsulated into the PLCP header. Upon receiving the PLCP header, neighboring nodes can distinguish the type of transmitted frame and accordingly back off for a specific duration that is assigned based on the MAC frame type information.

An aggressive virtual carrier sense mechanism is presented in Ref. 49. The basic idea is that a node which overhears either an RTS packet or a CTS packet, but not both, would not consider the media as busy and accordingly may attempt transmission.

5. Conclusion, Open Issues and Future Directions

In this chapter, we have addressed spatial reuse enhancement from the perspective of avoiding collisions. Three physical attributes are of importance: carrier sensing threshold, transmission power, and data rate. We surveyed a list of proposals that study the interplay between these attributes to achieve throughput enhancement. Some areas that are open issues and offer exciting research opportunities include:

- The integration of other physical layer parameters such as modulation, spreading codes, etc. that can also be exploited and integrated with power control, carrier sensing threshold, and rate adaptation for improving collision avoidance.
- Note that the schemes studied in this chapter do not completely avoid collisions from hidden terminals. Specifically those mechanisms based on tuning the

physical carrier sensing threshold. This is due to the fact that a node adjusts its CS_{th} only in order to improve its own performance (i.e., based on the success/failure history) without considering whether such an adjustment may severely impact the transmission of neighboring nodes. Thus, a complete solution for tuning the CS_{th} has to be explored. Moreover, the fairness issue should also be addressed.

- How the physical carrier sensing threshold affects the contention among nodes has not yet been addressed in literature.
- Exploitation of the interplay between physical carrier sensing threshold, data rate and power control for routing.

Terminology

MANET: Mobile ad hoc networks.

TPC: Transmission power control.

IEEE 802.11: The adopted MAC standard for wireless LAN.

SINR: Signal-to-interference plus noise ratio.

Transmission range: A node inside a transmission range will be able to correctly receive and decode a packet.

Carrier sensing range: A node existing in this range is able to sense a transmission.

Carrier sensing zone: A node inside a carrier sensing zone will be able to correctly receive but is unable to decode a packet.

Interference range: A node inside the interference range of a receiver; if it transmits, it will corrupt any packet reception at the receiver.

Data rate adaptation: Exploits good channel conditions by using higher rates for improved efficiency (i.e., throughput), and improves the transmission reliability by lowering the rate in the presence of channel impairments.

Physical carrier sensing (*PCS*): Reduces the likelihood of collision by preventing nodes in the vicinity of each other from transmitting simultaneously, while allowing nodes that are separated by a safe margin (termed the carrier sensing range) to engage in concurrent transmissions.

Spatial reuse: Allows simultaneous transmissions to take place in the same geographical vicinity.

Exercises

1. What are the three most important physical attributes used for throughput enhancement in IEEE 802.11?
2. What are the two kinds of collisions that a node usually encounters?

3. How does one avoid each kind of collisions in Question 2?
4. Which physical attributes save energy?
5. How does a node tune its physical carrier sensing threshold in order to avoid collisions from hidden nodes?
6. Consider the network of four nodes A, B, C, D shown in Fig. 11. Node A is communicating with node B and node C is communicating with node D. The distances between terminals are given as $d(A,B) = 95\,\mathrm{m}$, $d(A,D) = 98\,\mathrm{m}$, $d(C,B) = 65\,\mathrm{m}$ and $d(C,D) = 57\,\mathrm{m}$. The target SINR for both connections is 10 dB. Assume that the target SINR is defined as the minimum required SINR when receiving a packet so the node will be able to correctly receive and decode a packet. The additive average noise power is -90 dBw (10^{-10} mW). The transmitted power is 24 dB (250 mW) for both transmitting nodes A and C. Moreover, each node is equipped with a transceiver of processing gain, $G = 10$. The height and the antenna gains are assumed equal 1. The channel model is a two-ray model.

   (i) Assume no power control is applied; check if the transmission from node A to B and from node C to node D will be successful.
   (ii) Repeat (i) but now applying power control. Assume that the transmitted power of node A is 20 mW and that of node C is 100 mW.

7. Two flows are shown in Fig. 12: node A is transmitting to node B and node C is transmitting to node D. The distance between A and B equals that between C and D (= 100 m), while the distance between C and D is 180 m. Assume all the nodes are using the same power and the basic handshake of the IEEE 802.11b. Calculate the optimum data rate such that collision is avoided if

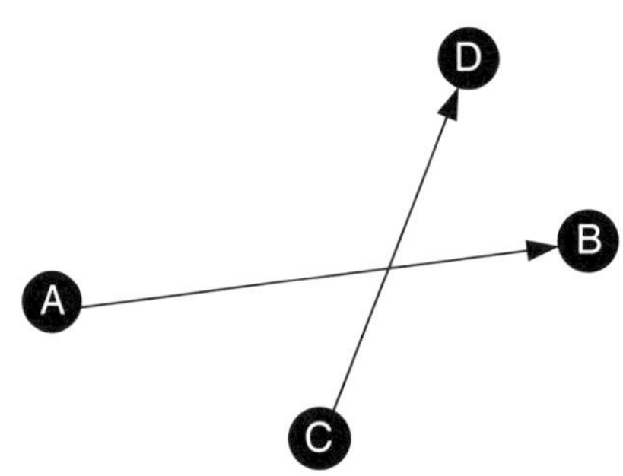

Fig. 11. Interference model.

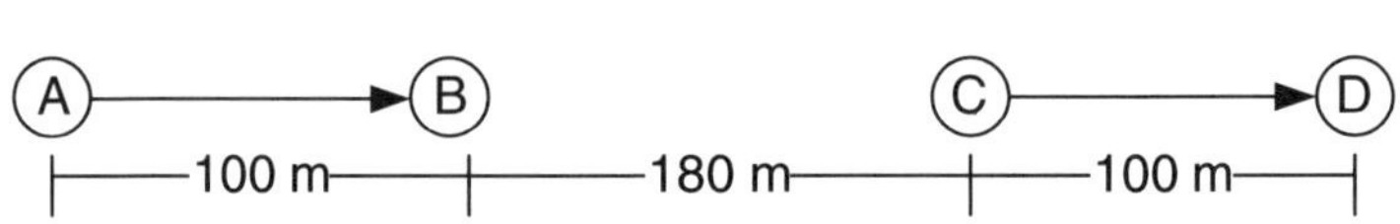

Fig. 12. Interference model.

both flow transmissions are occurring simultaneously. The SINR thresholds for the data rates 1, 2, 5.5 and 11 Mbps are 6 dB, 10 dB, 12 dB and 15 dB, respectively.

8. Consider the same topology as in Question 7, but the distance between B and C is 230 m, the transmission range of the node is 250 m, and the carrier sensing range of the node is 550 m. The SINR thresholds for the data rates 1, 2 , 5.5 and 11 Mbps are 6 dB, 10 dB, 12 dB and 15 dB, respectively. Which scheme will ILARI implement, given the packet size is 512 bytes?
9. Which one of the four schemes in adaptive power range control will be adopted if the following is given: data rate = 11 Mbps; transmitter-receiver distance = 200 m; carrier sensing range of a node is 550 m while the transmission range is 250 m; packet size = 128 bytes; SINR threshold is 15 dB.
10. Consider an ongoing communication between nodes A and B, which are 50 m apart. The antenna gain and height of a node both are equal to one. The receiver sensitivity is set to 3.652×10^{-12} W. The SIR threshold is set to 10 dB. The maximal transmission power is set to 0.02818 W. Assuming a successful RTS/CTS handshake between nodes A and B, and that an interfering node C which is 180 m away from node starts initiating a communication to another node D. Check if the transmission from C will corrupt the DATA packet receptions, assuming the current noise equals zero, if the nodes implement: (a) IEEE 802.11 without power control or (b) CAPC. Here, the DATA packet size = 1000 bytes and the channel rate = 2 Mbps.

References

1. R. Ramanathan and J. Redi, A brief overview of ad hoc networks: Challenges and directions, *IEEE Commun. Mag.* **40**(5), 20–22 (2002).
2. S. Kumar, V. S. Raghavan and J. Deng, Medium access control protocols for ad-hoc wireless networks: A survey, *Elsevier Ad-Hoc Network. J.* **4**(3), 326–358 (2006).
3. H. Dai, K.-W. Ng and M.-Y. Wu, An overview of MAC protocols with directional antennas in wireless ad hoc networks, *IEEE Int. Multi-Conf. Comput. Global Information Technology (ICCGI)*, Washington, DC, USA, July (2006), pp. 84–90.
4. IEEE 802.11 wireless LAN media access control (MAC) and physical layer (PHY) specifications (1999).
5. X. Yang and N. H. Vaidya, On the physical carrier sense in wireless ad-hoc networks, *Proc. IEEE INFOCOM*, Miami, USA, March (2005), pp. 2525–2535.
6. A. Muqattash and M. Krunz, A single-channel solution for transmit power control in wireless ad hoc networks, *Proc. ACM MobiHoc*, Tokyo, Japan, May (2004), pp. 276–283.
7. S. Agarwal, R. Katz, S. Krishnamurthy and S. Dao, Distributed power control in ad-hoc wireless networks, *Proc. IEEE PIMRC*, San Diego, USA, October (2001), pp. 59–66.
8. S. Yi, Y. Pei and S. Kalyanaraman, On the capacity improvement of ad hoc wireless networks using directional antennas, *Proc. ACM Mobihoc*, Annapolis, Maryland, USA, May (2003), pp. 108–116.

9. T. Lin and J. Hou, Interplay of spatial reuse and SINR-determined data rates in CSMA/CA-based, multi-hop, multi-rate wireless networks, *Proc. IEEE INFOCOM 2007*, Anchorage, Alaska, USA, May (2007), pp. 803–811.
10. T. Kim, J. Hou and H. Lim, Improving spatial reuse through tuning transmit power, carrier sense threshold, and data rate in multihop wireless networks, *Proc. ACM Mobicom*, California, USA, October (2006), pp. 366–377.
11. K. Medepalli and F. Tobagi, On optimization of CSMA/CA based wireless LANs: Part I — Impact of exponential backoff, *Proc. IEEE ICC*, Istanbul, Turkey, June (2006), pp. 2089–2094.
12. K. Medepalli, F. Tobagi, D. Famolari and T. Kodama, On optimization of CSMA/CA based wireless LANs: Part I — Mitigating efficiency loss, *Proc. IEEE ICC*, Istanbul, Turkey, June (2006), pp. 4799–4804.
13. J. Fuemmeler, N. Vaidya and V. V. Veeravalli, Selecting the transmit powers and the carrier sensing thresholds for CSMA protocols, *Proc. WICON*, Boston, USA, August (2006), pp. 1321–1329.
14. H. Ma, H. Alazemi and S. Roy, A stochastic model for optimizing physical carrier sensing and spatial reuse in ad hoc networks, *Proc. IEEE MASS*, Washington, USA, November (2005), pp. 615–622.
15. C. Lau and C. Leung, Capture models for mobile packet radio networks, *IEEE Trans. Commun.* **40**(5), 917–925 (1992).
16. C. Ware, J. Chicharo and T. Wysocki, Modelling of capture behaviour in IEEE 802.11 radio modems, Invited paper, *IEEE Int. Conf. Telecommunications* (2001).
17. H. Chang, V. Misra and D. Rubenstein, Fairness and physical layer capture in random access networks, *Proc. IEEE SECON*, 18–21 June (2007), pp. 381–390.
18. A. Kochut, A. Vasan, A. U. Shankar and A. Agrawala, Sniffing out the correct physical layer capture model in 802.11b, *Proc. IEEE ICNP* (2004), pp. 252–261.
19. Y. Yang, J. C. Hou and L.-C. Kung, Modeling the effect of transmit power and physical carrier sense in multi-hop wireless networks, *Proc. IEEE INFOCOM*, Alaska, USA, May (2007), pp. 2331–2335.
20. A. Arora and M. Krunz, Interference-limited MAC protocol for MANETs with directional antennas, *Proc. IEEE WoWMoM*, Taormina, Italy, June (2005), pp. 2–10.
21. R. Ramanathan, On the performance of ad hoc networks with beamforming antennas, *Proc. MobiHoc*, October (2001).
22. K. Xu, M. Gerla and S. Bae, Effectiveness of RTS/CTS handshake in IEEE 802.11 based ad hoc networks, *Elsevier Ad-Hoc Network J.* **1**(1), 107–123 (2003).
23. R. Hekmat and P. Mieghem, Intereference in wireless multihop ad hoc networks, *Proc. Med-hoc-net*, Sardegna, Italy, September (2002).
24. W. C. Y. Lee, Elements of cellular mobile radio systems, *IEEE Trans. Veh. Tech.* **35**(2), 48–56 (1986).
25. J. Zhang, Z. Fang and B. Bensaou, Adaptive power control for single channel ad hoc networks, *Proc. IEEE ICC*, May (2005).
26. B. Hajek, A. Krishna and R. O. LaMaire, On the capture probability for a large number of stations, *IEEE Trans. Commun.* **45**(2), 254–260 (1997).
27. M. Grossglauser and D. Tse, Mobility increases the capacity of ad-hoc wireless networks, *Proc. IEEE INFOCOM* (2001).
28. Z. Zeng, Y. Yang and J. Hou, How physical carrier sense affects system throughput in IEEE 802.11 wireless networks, *Proc. IEEE INFOCOM* (2008).
29. J. Zhu, X. Guo, L. Yang and W. Conner, Leveraging spatial reuse in 802.11 mesh networks with enhanced physical carrier sensing, *Proc. IEEE ICC*, Paris, France, June (2004), pp. 4004–4011.

30. A. Vasan, R. Ramjee and T. Woo, ECHOS: Enhanced capacity 802.11 hotspots, *Proc. IEEE INFOCOM*, Miami, USA, March (2005), pp. 1562–1572.
31. E. Wong and R. Cruz, A spatio-temporal model for physical carrier sensing wireless ad-hoc networks, *Proc. IEEE SECON*, Reston, VA, USA, September (2006), pp. 276–285.
32. J. Deng, B. Liang and P. K. Varshney, Tuning the carrier sensing range of IEEE 802.11 MAC, *Proc. IEEE GLOBECOM*, Texas, USA, December (2004), pp. 2987–2991.
33. C. C. Chen, E. Seo, H. Kim and H. Luo, Self-learning collision avoidance for wireless networks, *Proc. IEEE INFOCOM*, Barcelona, Spain, April (2006), pp. 2987–2991.
34. Y. Zhu, Q. Zhang, Z. Niu and J. Zhu, On optimal physical carrier sensing: Theoretical analysis and protocol design, *Proc. IEEE INFOCOM*, Alaska, USA, May (2007).
35. K. P. Shih and Y. D. Chen, CAPC: A collision avoidance power control MAC protocol for wireless ad hoc networks, *IEEE Commun. Lett.* **9**, 859–861 (2005).
36. K. P. Shih, Y. D. Chen and C. C. Chang, Adaptive range-based power control for collision avoidance in ad hoc networks, *Proc. ICC 2007*, Glasgow, Scotland, June (2007), pp. 3672–3677.
37. J. Kim, S. Kim, S. Choi and D. Qiao, CARA: Collision-aware rate adaptation for IEEE 802.11 WLANs, *Proc. IEEE INFOCOM*, Barcelona, Spain (2006), pp. 1–11.
38. D. Qiao, S. Choi, A. Jain and K. G. Shin, MiSer: An optimal low-energy transmission strategy for IEEE 802.11a/h, *Proc. ACM MobiCom*, San Diego, USA, September (2003), pp. 161–175.
39. Y. Eunho, C. J. Kim, C. Kwon and L. Jaewha, An enhanced link adaptation strategy for IEEE 802.11 wireless ad hoc networks, *Proc. IEEE WiCom*, Dalian, China, September (2007), pp. 1672–1676.
40. X. Yang and N. Vaidya, A Spatial backoff algorithm using the joint control of carrier sense threshold and transmission rate, *Proc. IEEE SECON*, San Diego, USA, June (2007), pp. 501–511.
41. J. A. Fuemmeler, N. H. Vaidya and V. V. Veeravalli, Selecting transmit powers and carrier sense thresholds in csma protocols for wireless ad hoc networks, *Proc. ACM WICON*, August (2006), p. 15.
42. G. Bianchi, Performance analysis of the IEEE 802.11 distributed coordination function, *IEEE J. Selected Area Commun.* **18**, 535–547 (2000).
43. A. Kumar, E. Altman, D. Miorandi and M. Goyal, New insights from a fixed point analysis of single cell IEEE 802.11 WLANs, *Proc. IEEE INFOCOM*, Miami, USA, April (2005), pp. 1550–1561.
44. F. Cali, M. Conti and E. Gregori, Dynamic tuning of the IEEE 802.11 protocol to achieve a theoratical throughput limit, in *IEEE/ACM Transactions on Networking*, Vol. 8 (2000), pp. 785–799.
45. H. Zhai and Y. Fang, Physical carrier sensing and spatial reuse in multirate and multihop wireless ad hoc networks, *Proc. IEEE INFOCOM*, Barcelona, Spain, April (2006), pp. 1–12.
46. L. Song and C. Yu, Improving spatial reuse with collision-aware DCF in mobile ad hoc networks, *Proc. IEEE ICPP*, Columbus, USA, August (2006), pp. 219–228.
47. T. Nadeem, L. Ji, A. Agrawala and J. Agre, Location enhancement to IEEE 802.11 DCF, *Proc. IEEE INFOCOM*, Miami, USA, March (2005), pp. 651–663.
48. Z. Li, S. Nandi and A. Gupta, Improving MAC performance in wireless ad hoc networks using enhanced carrier sensing (ECS) *Proc. Network.* **3042**, 600–612 (2004).
49. F. Ye, S. Yi and B. Sikdar, Improving spatial reuse of IEEE 802.11 based ad hoc networks, *Proc. IEEE GLOBECOM* (2003), pp. 1013–1017.

Chapter 9

A CROSS LAYER DOA ROUTING PROTOCOL FOR MOBILE AD HOC NETWORKS

C. MALA*, S. VIKRAM† and N. P. GOPALAN‡
Department of Computer Science and Engineering
National Institute of Technology, Tiruchirappalli, India
**mala@nitt.edu*
†sc.vikram@gmail.com
‡gopalan@nitt.edu

Waypoint routing is a lightweight hierarchical routing model in which the route from source to destination is divided into a number of segments by waypoint nodes. Routing is then done at intersegment and intrasegment levels. A major difficulty in waypoint routing is the metric by which a route is divided into segments. There are a few ad hoc methods such as dividing the route based on the number of hops, or dividing by selecting high speed nodes as waypoints. But a better approach would be one which considers wireless environment characteristics for dividing the route into segments, i.e., considering cross layer (link and physical layer) parameters like packet loss rate, bandwidth, interference, etc. to divide the route into segments. Such a waypoint routing protocol, called cross layer DOA (dynamic source routing over ad hoc on-demand distance vector) routing protocol, is proposed and discussed in this chapter.

1. Introduction

A mobile ad hoc Network (MANET) consists of a set of mobile nodes connected by wireless links. The network topology in an ad hoc network changes randomly. Traditional routing protocols which are used for wired networks cannot be used for ad hoc networks directly, due to their highly dynamic network topology, absence of established infrastructure for centralized administration (like base stations or access points), bandwidth constrained wireless links, and energy constrained nodes.

Many routing protocols have been proposed for MANETs [1, 8, 10, 17]. Based on routing information update mechanism, routing protocols are classified as proactive (table driven), reactive (on demand) and hybrid.

In proactive routing protocols, every node maintains network topology information in the form of a routing table by periodically exchanging routing information. The Destination Sequenced Distance Vector (DSDV) routing protocol is an example of a proactive routing protocol. Reactive routing protocols do not maintain topology information: they try to establish a path whenever it is required, i.e., on demand. These routing protocols do not require periodic exchange of routing information as in proactive routing protocols. Dynamic Source Routing (DSR) [5, 6] and ad hoc on-demand distance vector (AODV) routing [3, 4] are examples of reactive protocols. Hybrid protocols have the best features of both proactive and reactive routing protocols. The network is divided into a number of zones or clusters. For routing within a zone, a table-driven approach is used. For nodes among different zones, an on-demand routing approach is used. The Zone Routing Protocol (ZRP) is an example of a hybrid routing protocol.

Proactive routing protocols may flood the network with control packets which are required for periodic updating of routing information. The routing table size becomes very large with increasing network size. Thus, they are not scalable. Reactive routing protocols being on-demand routing protocol avoid the control packet overhead but connection setup delay on link failure is very large. Hybrid routing protocols avoid these two problems by performing routing operations using both proactive and reactive approaches.

Based on routing topology, routing protocols are classified into flat and hierarchical types. Flat routing protocols use a flat addressing scheme and all nodes are assigned the same functionalities. Flat routing protocols work fine for small networks containing hundreds of nodes. However, their performance degrades rapidly as the network grows because of routing overhead. Hierarchical routing protocols use logical hierarchy in the network. Hierarchical routing reduces the state information maintained at core routers in the network. The network is divided into groups and a subset of nodes is assigned special functionalities, typically coordinating roles between groups. Clustered Gateway Switch Routing (CGSR) is a typical hierarchical routing protocol. After the network is divided into zones or clusters, the route maintenance activity will only affect a few neighboring clusters, while other clusters remain untouched and scalability is achieved. However, the overhead to dynamically maintain the hierarchy may be high in mobile environments.

As the network grows the routes between source and destination become longer. When routes break due to mobility or node failure, flat routing protocols like DSR and AODV will discard the entire original route and begin new route discovery from source to destination. Whenever a route breaks, usually only a few hops are broken, while others are still intact.

2. Background

As the network size grows, it becomes difficult to maintain longer routes between source and destination. If the routes are maintained end-to-end (like the path from source to destination), then the route gets discarded even if a single hop is broken on this path. If the route maintenance is done at each node on the path from source to destination then the maintenance becomes costly. These two problems,

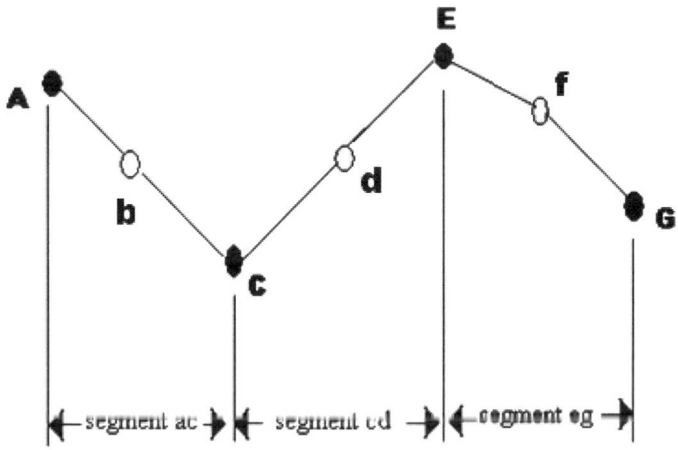

Fig. 1. Path divided into segments in WPR.

can be avoided by the waypoint routing (WPR) approach [13]. In WPR, a few intermediate nodes on the route from source to destination are picked up for doing route maintenance. Such nodes are generally called waypoint nodes. These nodes perform route maintenance whenever the path is broken. Consider the example shown in Fig. 1, which shows a route A-b-C-d-E-f-G in a network where A and G are the source and destination nodes and b, C, d, E, f are the intermediate nodes on the route. Traditionally, if a path fails between nodes d and E, then the complete route from source A to destination G is discarded and new route discovery is started by source A. Let C and E be the intermediate nodes on the route which also do route maintenance tasks along with source A and destination G on the route. Nodes C and E are called waypoint nodes. Now if a link E-f fails, the waypoint node E gets the failure message and it starts route discovery to node f and its next consecutive node G. If it finds a new route, which is not much longer than the original distance from node C, then this new route will be used for sending data to destination G. Since the time to find a route between nodes C and f or nodes C and G is much less than the time to find a route between nodes A and G, the failed routes get connected faster, reducing the route maintenance cost in the network.

Flat routing protocols like DSR and AODV do route maintenance either end-to-end or on every node in the network, respectively. In DSR routing, complete route information is stored for every destination. In AODV routing, each node stores the complete network information. These two protocols work fine for small networks. If the network size grows, in DSR the routes fail every now and then because of interference, which leads to a higher maintenance cost. In AODV, as the network grows, there is an overflow in the size of the routing table information. The alternative approach to these two routing protocols is the DOA routing protocol (DSR over AODV), which uses the WPR approach. The waypoint nodes in DOA use DSR routing and the other nodes use the AODV routing approach. As DSR discovers routes quickly compared to AODV, the waypoint nodes run the DSR routing protocol. AODV routing does a fast recovery in the case of single hop failure and so this routing approach is used at the intermediate node level.

The WPR approach requires a method for selecting these waypoint nodes. DOA routing selects waypoint nodes based on the some constant integer value, e.g., selecting a node as a waypoint node after every two nodes. A better approach would be to select these nodes based on wireless network parameters like the bandwidth, interference, etc.

A routing approach that uses wireless network characteristics for routing is generally termed a cross layer routing approach. CDOA routing is a cross layer DSR over AODV routing protocol, which uses the waypoint and cross layer routing approach, required for supporting large networks.

Flat routing protocols like DSR and AODV maintain routes end-to-end, which leads to higher route maintenance cost. The DSR routing protocol, which is an on-demand routing protocol, maintains complete route information for every destination to which it is sending the data. AODV is thus a waypoint routing approach that fits better for wireless networks, where the chances of failing links between two nodes is very high.

Hop count is the most commonly used metric to choose a path during route discovery [13]. But this metric fails to choose paths with high throughput and leads to poor performance. Hence, another metric, expected transmission count (ETX), is used in this protocol.

Example 1. Figure 1 gives an example of how a route from node A, to node G is divided into segments. Nodes C and E are selected as waypoint nodes. Source A and destination G are also waypoint nodes and the other nodes are forwarding nodes. Waypoint nodes C and E divide the route into three segments: AC, CE and EG. A segment can be simply identified by its start and end nodes. The nodes between the start and end nodes of a segment are forwarding nodes. For example, segment A-b-C can be referred to as segment AC. If there is a break in any link, then a new route discovery is started by the intermediate waypoint nodes instead of the start node, thus reducing the time required for route repair.

A major difficulty in the WPR approach is selection of waypoint nodes. The following section outlines a set of approaches which have been proposed for WPR routing.

3. Selection of Waypoint Nodes

There are many policies for selecting waypoint nodes on a route. A few of these along with their drawbacks are given in the following.

Select a waypoint node on the route after every n node, where n is a non-negative constant and should be less than the total path length. In Example 1, the value of n is 1, and a waypoint is selected after every node on the route. Thus A, C,

E and G are the waypoint nodes. The value of n is arbitrarily chosen here. Thus, we need some basis on which a value of n can be decided.

Waypoint nodes can also be selected based on node speed (or mobility). Using slow-speed mobile nodes as waypoint nodes apparently makes routes last longer. But finding the speed of the node requires GPS, which is costly to implement.

Thirdly, waypoint nodes can be selected based on their security association. Using nodes from the same security association makes routes more secure. But finding nodes with the same security requirement is again an important issue here.

A major disadvantage of the above methods is that they are unaware of the wireless link characteristics. A wireless network is dynamic in nature. A link between any two nodes in a wireless network is not determined by the distance and bandwidth between the nodes as in a wired network. There are other factors like interference, mobility of nodes, natural disturbances like lightening, etc. which make wireless links more prone to error. They all adversely affect the transmission capacity of wireless links. In Example 1, it may be that link AB is less susceptible to error compared to link DE. Similarly, a segment is characterized by the characteristics of all the links within a segment.

Let $E(\cdot)$ be a function representing the wireless link characteristics. Assume a wireless link xy. Then $E(x, y)$ denotes the link characteristic. For a segment, *Eseg*$(\cdot)$ denotes the wireless characteristic of the whole segment, which is a function of all the links in the segment. For segment AC in Example 1, *Eseg*(A, C) denotes a link characteristic which is a function of the links AB and BC denoted as E(A, B) and E(B, C), respectively. Similarly, *Eseg*(E, G) denotes the characteristics of segment EF and segment FG.

An ideal waypoint node selection policy would be one in which all the segments on the route require the same time to repair whenever any link is broken. A policy nearest to such an ideal approach would be one that selects waypoint nodes based on wireless link characteristics link bandwidth, link error rate, etc. In an ideal waypoint node selection policy, *Eseg*(A,C) and *Eseg*(E, G) have similar characteristics. Then the time required to repair any of these segments is almost the same.

Such a policy requires the routing layer to select waypoint nodes based on link characteristics bandwidth, interference, etc., which have to be obtained from the lower layers such as the link and physical layers. Hence, some sort of dependency between routing layer and its lower layers is required. This new technique is called cross layer design.

4. Thoughts for Practitioners

Current wireless networks are based on the traditional layered-design concept. They ignore the dependencies between layers and the dynamicity of mobile ad hoc networks. As a result, the resulting protocols are not adaptive and far from optimal.

Cross layer design for wireless networks [2, 9], on the other hand, allows information to be exchanged among protocol layers, such that each layer responds

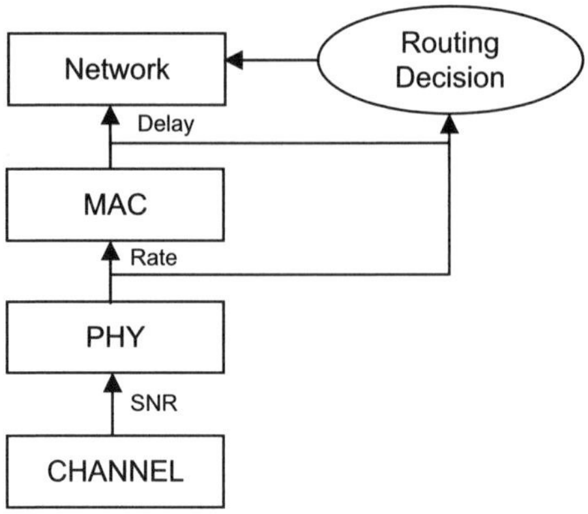

Fig. 2. Cross layer routing.

appropriately to the changes in other layers as well as in the layer itself, facilitating global considerations.

Figure 2 gives an example of the link layer and physical layer parameters used for routing decisions in cross layer routing. Network layer routing decisions are based on the link delay obtained by the MAC layer and data rate obtained by the physical layer. In turn, the data rate at the physical layer requires the signal-to-noise ratio (SNR), which is obtained from the channel. This is how a routing decision is made based on link delay and data rate, ensuring routing protocols are more adaptive to an ad hoc network environment.

4.1. *Cross Layer Design Technique for Selecting Best Path*

Routing in wireless networks is a challenging issue because of the unpredictable behavior of the wireless medium. In order to exploit all its advantages, a routing metric should come from a cross layer approach to make the routing layer aware of the local issues of the underlying layers.

One such cross layer routing metric is called cumulative expected transmission time (CETT). Each link is assigned a transmission time that is equal to the expected amount of time it would take to successfully transmit a packet of some fixed size S on that link. This time depends on bandwidth and loss rate.

One of the simplest metrics used in ad hoc networks is ETX [7, 14]. This metric estimates the number of retransmissions needed to send unicast packets by measuring the loss rate of broadcast packets between pairs of neighboring nodes. To compute ETX, every node broadcasts a probe packet every second. The probe contains the count of probes received from each neighboring node in the previous 10 s. Based on these probes, a node can calculate the loss rate of probes on the links to and from its neighbors.

Consider a wireless link between two nodes A and B. Both nodes are sending probe packets every second. Assume node A has received nine packets from node B and node B has received seven packets from node A in 10 s. After 10 s node A receives an acknowledgment packet containing the number of probes B has received from A. Based on these count values, node A calculates the forward and backward link loss rate as $(10 - 9)/10$ and $(10 - 7)/9$.

Let the loss rates in the forward and reverse directions be p_f and p_r, respectively. Then the probability p with which these packets are transmitted successfully from node A to B is given by

$$p = (1 - p_f) \times (1 - p_r).$$

A successful unicast data transfer in IEEE 802.11 involves sending the data packet and receiving a link layer acknowledgment from the receiver. If the losses are assumed to be independent, the expected number of retransmissions (i.e., ETX) before the packet is successfully delivered is given by

$$\text{ETX} = \frac{1}{p}.$$

Node A calculates a new ETX value for the link from A to B every time it receives a probe from B. But the limitation with ETX is that it may not necessarily select paths with high bandwidths. If either the data or the acknowledgment is lost, the IEEE 802.11 ARQ mechanism retransmits unicast packets.

Expected transmission time (ETT) [7] is a metric which takes bandwidth of the link and uses ETX for measuring the link quality. ETT is calculated as

$$\text{ETT} = \text{ETX} \times \frac{S}{B},$$

where S is the size of the probe packet and B is the bandwidth of the link.

The routing protocol finds the path that minimizes the sum of expected transmission times over the path. The cost of the entire path (of length n) from source to destination is given by CETT which is the cumulative ETT over the entire path:

$$\text{CETT} = \sum_{i=1}^{n} \text{ETT}_i$$

CETT is used for selecting the best paths between source and destination.

4.2. *Cross Layer Technique for Selecting Waypoint Nodes*

Waypoint nodes are selected using a cross layer technique such that the selection policy becomes more adaptive to the dynamic nature of MANETs. The selection of waypoint nodes is explained using the following example.

Example 2. Consider the path A-B-C-D-E in Fig. 1. Each node regularly calculates ETT values in the network, as explained in Sec. 4.1. Let E_a, E_b, E_c, E_d, E_f and E_e, be the calculated ETT values at the respective nodes. Let

SEGMENT_THRESHOLD_ETT be the threshold ETT of a segment. If CETT of the path is larger than SEGMENT_THRESHOLD_ETT, then a node is selected as a waypoint node, creating a segment. Segmenting a path based on the ETT value helps in dividing a path into segments of nearly equally expected transmission time.

The length of the segment shows the quality of the link. If the links are bad (i.e., more prone to failures) then the ETT values of the links are higher, thus forming a segment with very few hops. This helps in repairing segments quickly on link failures. If the links are good (i.e., less prone to failures) then the ETT values of links are small, thus forming segments with a large number of hops, which avoids the overhead of having more smaller segments. Such a criterion leads to an efficient selection of waypoint nodes since it considers link layer and physical layer parameters reflecting the wireless link characteristics.

4.3. *Deciding on the Value of SEGMENT_THRESHOLD_ETT*

As explained in Sec. 4.1, each node in the network calculates forward and reverse probabilities (p_f and p_r, respectively) for all the neighbors in its range. Based on these loss probabilities, probability p with which probes are transmitted successfully between two nodes is calculated.

If the maximum reverse or forward loss probability allowed is 0.5, then based on these values, probability p is calculated. Using this value, the ETX between two nodes is calculated. The ETT value obtained from ETX gives the threshold ETT over the link. Similarly, the loss probability allowed over a segment can be decided, from which the SEGMENT_THRESHOLD_ETT value can be calculated.

Example 3. Consider a network with links of bandwidth 2 Mbps using 20-byte probes for calculating ETT. Let p_f and p_r allowed over the segment be 0.5. Then the probability p with which the probes are transmitted successfully is 0.25. The ETX is 4. Using this ETX the ETT value obtained is 76.3 μs. This can be taken as the SEGMENT_THRESHOLD_ETT, which decides the amount of maximum delay that should be borne by a packet. If the ETT value of the segment (CETT) is larger than this, then the number of retransmissions is higher (as the ETX value is higher). Thus, loss probabilities are high, which indirectly indicates that the links in this segment are bad.

5. CDOA Routing

Cross layer DOA (CDOA) routing is a linearly hierarchical waypoint routing protocol which uses the cross layer technique for the selecting best paths and waypoint nodes. DSR is used for the global intersegment routing [13]. The AODV is used for the local intrasegment routing [13], hence the suffix DOA in CDOA. There are three basic components of a routing protocol: route discovery, data forwarding, and route maintenance.

Accordingly, four types of control messages are defined for CDOA routing: route request (RREQ), route reply (RREP), route error (RERR) and route activate (RACT). For route discovery from the source to destination, RREQ and RREP control messages are used. An RERR message is used to signify problems like failure at a certain point on the route. To set up a reverse path from the end node to the start node of a segment, the RACT message is used. Two tables, namely routing cache and routing table, are maintained by each node in the CDOA protocol. Routing cache is used for storing global intersegment routing information while routing table is used for storing local intrasegment routing. In CDOA the path contains only waypoint nodes. The routing table has two entries: the address of the end node of the segment and the next hop node address which points towards the end node of the segment.

5.1. *Route Discovery*

The route discovery process in CDOA comprises two parts, namely intersegment route discovery and intrasegment route discovery. Each route discovery process involves two phases: the route request phase and the route reply phase.

5.1.1. *Intersegment Route Request*

The RREQinter control message is used for intersegment route discovery. When a new route is to be found from a source node to a destination node then a RREQinter message is broadcast by the source node. This RREQinter message is unique as it carries with it the address of the source node and its broadcast ID number. Further, the RREQinter message also records the list of nodes it has traversed as in the DSR routing protocol.

When the RREQinter message is received by an intermediate node, it discards it if it is a duplicate by checking the request seen table. If RREQinter is new then the intermediate node appends its address to the path recorded in RREQinter.

5.1.2. *Intersegment Route Reply*

The intersegment route reply is done based on the CETT value. If the cost (or CETT) of the path recorded in RREQinter exceeds the threshold value (SEGMENT_THRESHOLD_ETT), the destination divides the path into segments by selecting waypoint nodes from the path. The cost of each segment is nearly equal to SEGMENT_THRESHOLD_ETT.

Example 4. Let the path from source A to destination G be A-B-C-D-E-F-G (refer Fig. 1). Table 1 shows the ETT values calculated at the nodes.

Table 1. Nodes and their ETT values.

Nodes	A	B	C	D	E	F	G
ETT (in μs)	10	8	6	4	15	10	7

Suppose the value of DEFAULT_SEGMENT_COST is $30\,\mu s$. A possible path division would be A-b-C-d-E-f-G, where the upper case letters indicate waypoint nodes and the lower case letters indicate forwarding nodes. (The same convention is followed in remaining chapter, whenever a path consists of both upper and lower case letters). There are three segments: segment AC, segment CE, and segment EG with CETT values 24, 25 and 32, respectively. Nodes A, C, E and G are waypoint nodes. The length of each segment varies according to the CETT of that segment. From this example it is inferred that, if the links are bad in a segment, the segment length is short; otherwise it is long. Consider the segment DF. Since the ETT values over links EF and FG are very large, the segment is of only two hops. Thus, in the case of link failure, it has to repair a segment of smaller length.

Once the path has been divided, the destination generates an RREPinter message which holds the path with both the waypoint nodes and forwarding nodes. When a waypoint node receives an RREPinter message, it updates both its route cache and its routing table, whereas when a forwarding node receives an RREPinter message, it updates only its routing table.

A RACT message with two values, namely start_seq and start hop_count, is sent by the start node to the end node to make the forwarding nodes and the end node aware of the sequence number and the hop count of the start node.

When the RREPinter message reaches the source node that initiated the intersegment route discovery, the source updates both its route cache and routing table. Figure 3 shows the overall message exchanges required for the intersegment route discovery process.

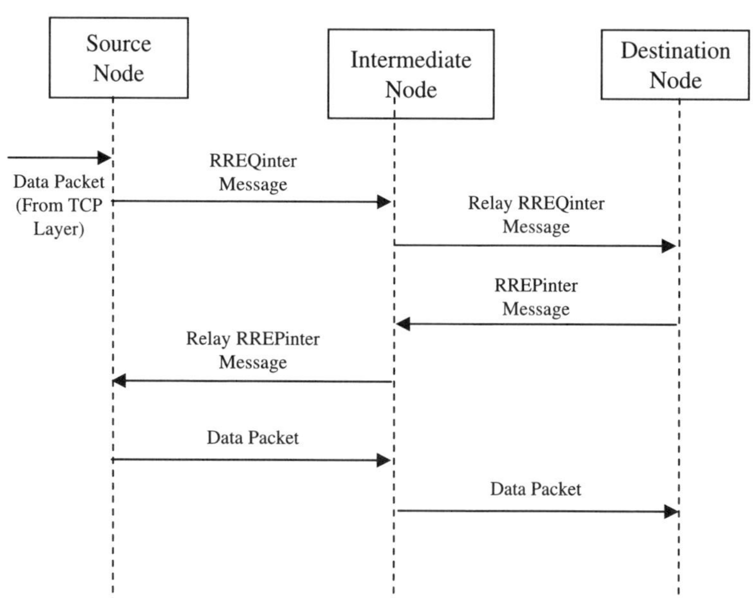

Fig. 3. Control message exchanges in intersegment route discovery.

5.2. *Data Forwarding*

In the CDOA protocol, to transmit a data packet, the source gets the source route, which comprises only waypoint nodes from its route cache. It then inserts this source route into the header of the data packet. The source node then processes intrasegment routing for the first segment on the route. It gets the next hop to the end node of the current segment and after that the packet is sent to the next hop node, which is a forwarding node.

In intersegment routing, the current_ seg field in the source route option of a data packet is used. The value of this field is maintained by the waypoint nodes. This field is incremented by one whenever a data packet leaves an upstream segment and enters a downstream segment at a waypoint node.

5.3. *Route Maintenance*

In CDOA, a route is composed of segments. Any route which is broken can be repaired either at the broken segment level or at the level of a few segments near the broken segment. There are two levels of route repair, namely intrasegment route repair (range is one segment) and intersegment route repair (range is multiple segments).

5.3.1. *Intrasegment Route Repair*

This works on the AODV routing approach. An RERRintra message which has information about the broken link and the end nodes is sent by the node which finds that its next hop is unreachable to its precursor nodes. If the node that receives this RERRintra message is not a start node of a broken segment, then it invalidates the entry of the node from which it received the RERRintra message in its routing table. If it is a start node, it becomes the initiator of an intrasegment route repair and broadcasts the RREQintra message looking for the end node of the broken segment.

The time to live (TTL) value of this RREQintra is set to SEGMENT_THRESHOLD_ETT. When a node receives the RREQintra message, it calculates its ETT value based on lower layer parameters. Then, the information regarding the ETTs of the nodes the RREQintra message has traveled and the ETT of the current node is used to generate THRESHOLD_ETT. THRESHOLD_ETT is compared with the SEGMENT_THRESHOLD_ETT available in the TTL field. The node will forward the RREQintra message if the message is not a duplicate and the SEGMENT_THRESHOLD_ETT of the message is greater than the calculated THRESHOLD_ETT. When the target node receives the first RREQintra message, it sends the RREPintra message to the initiator. The RREPintra message is relayed as a unicast message along the reverse path from the target to the initiator. Upon receiving the RREPintra message, the initiator updates its route cache and route table, buffering the data packets it received, which go through the broken segment. On receiving the RREPintra message it forwards all the buffered packets.

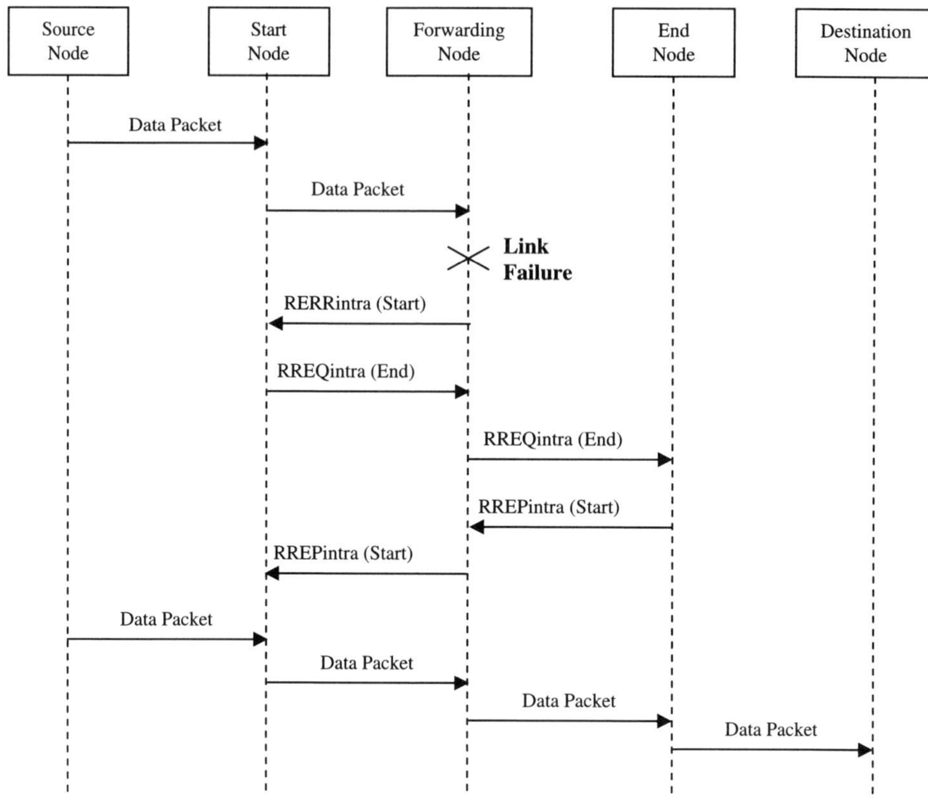

Fig. 4. Control message exchanges in intrasegment route repair.

If the intrasegment route repair succeeds, the data packets can be forwarded along the same waypoint nodes and so the source node will not be notified about the repair. If it fails, then the initiator will try the intersegment route repair. The intrasegment route repair is shown in Fig. 4 using a sequence diagram showing various control message exchanges.

5.3.2. *Intersegment Route Repair*

The Intersegment route repair is initiated if no route was discovered even after the expiry of a timer Intra_CheckReplied, which is set at the start of the repair. In this intersegment route repair, the routes to downstream waypoint nodes on the route are discovered by repairing the broken routes if required and sending back to the source node. When an intermediate node receives an RREQinter message, it handles it in the same way as in the route discovery phase.

When the target receives the RREQinter, it divides the path recorded in it into segments if the path has a CETT value greater than SEGMENT_THRESHOLD_ETT. The target sends an intersegment route reply (RREPinter) to the initiator.

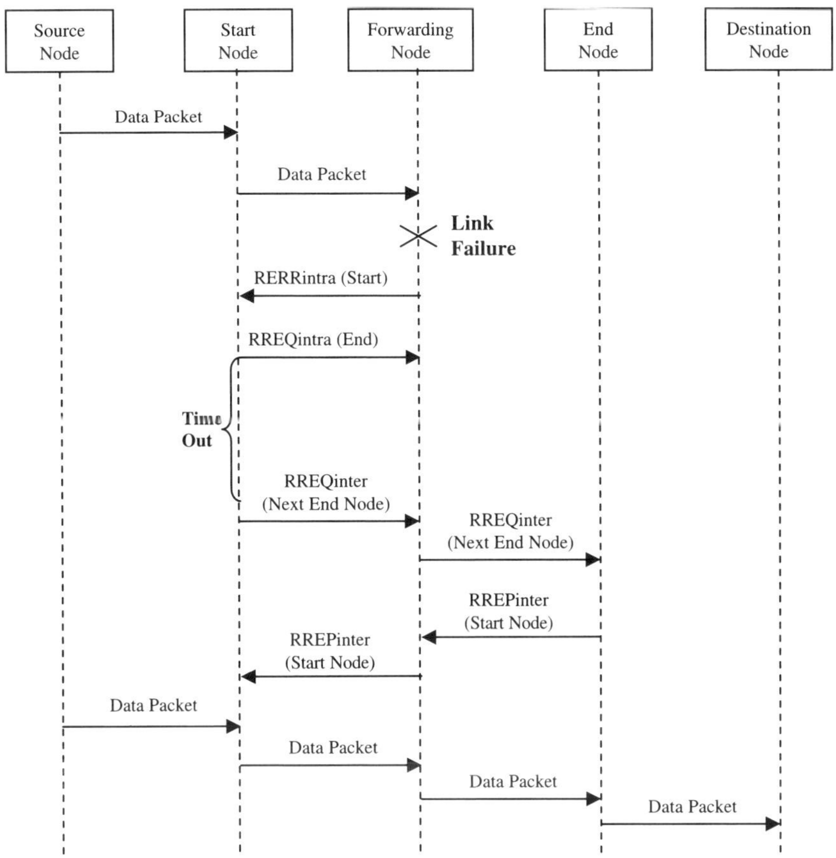

Fig. 5. Control message exchanges in intersegment route repair.

The initiator, after receiving the RREPinter message replaces the broken segment and a few unused old downstream segments with the new segment returned by RREPinter. It then updates its route cache, sends RERRinterRepair message with the new route through upstream waypoint nodes to the source, which in turn transmits the buffered data packets using the repaired route. The intersegment route maintenance process for route repair is shown in Fig. 5 with all the various control message exchanges.

6. Performance of CDOA Routing

The CDOA routing algorithm is simulated using GloMoSim 2.03 [11], a scalable simulation environment for wireless networks developed using PARSEC [12]. The simulation uses the two-ray propagation model, 2 MB/s bandwidth, and 250 m radio range. The MAC layer used in simulation is the standard IEEE 802.11 distributed coordinated function (DCF). The traffic is constant bit rate (CBR). The mobility

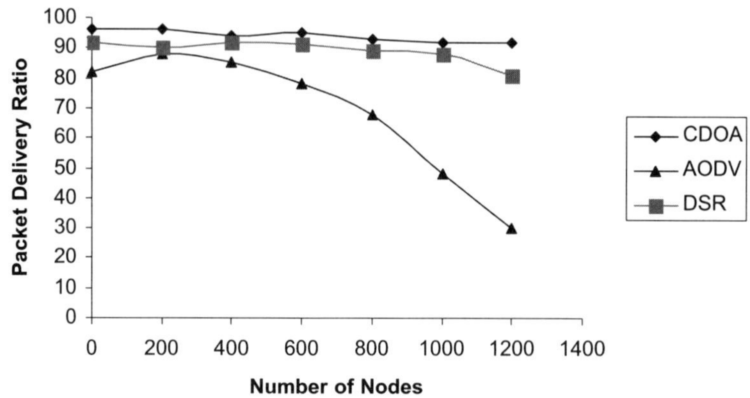

Fig. 6. Packet delivery ratio.

model used is random waypoint with speeds ranging from 0 m/s to 10 m/s and a pause time of 30 s. Simulation time was 600 s.

Packet Delivery Ratio: The packet delivery ratio is calculated based on many simulations with each simulation having a different number of nodes. The number of successful packet transmissions to the total number of packets transmitted calculated over the entire nodes gives the packet delivery ratio. Figure 6 shows that CDOA performs better than DOA, AODV and DSR.

7. Directions for Future Research

Further research may be directed towards incorporating security in the WPR routing model, using heuristic methods in the selection of waypoint nodes, and testing with other protocols for intra- and intersegment routing in WPR. Further work should assess the performance of the protocol by analysis using other metrics such as network allocation vector count (NAVC), modified expected number of transmissions (mETX), metric of interference and channel switching (MIC), blocking metric, etc., while varying the network size, the number of flows and the packet size.

8. Conclusions

CDOA routing finds better routes using cross layer parameters, divides route into segments using link layer parameters, and gives segment sizes proportional to the segment cost. The method proves to be one of the best ways to divide a route into segments compared to previous ad hoc methods. Simulation shows that CDOA routing is also more scalable compared to the DSR and AODV routing protocols. Further, the packet delivery ratio in CDOA is better than the DSR, AODV and DOA routing protocols.

Terminology

Keywords

1. MANET
2. MAC layer
3. Waypoint routing
4. DOA
5. DSR
6. Cross layer routing
7. Route repair
8. Intrasegment Routing
9. Intersegment Routing
10. ETX

Mobile ad-hoc network (MANET): Consists of a set of mobile nodes connected by wireless links whose network topology changes dynamically.

Media access control (MAC) layer: A sublayer of the data link layer which provides addressing and channel access control mechanisms to enable several nodes to communicate in a network.

Waypoint routing: A lightweight hierarchical routing model in which the route is divided into segments by the waypoints.

DOA (DSR over AODV): A routing protocol in which a number of intermediate nodes on a route are selected as waypoints and the route is divided into segments by the waypoints.

Dynamic source routing (DSR) protocol: A routing protocol for wireless mesh networks which provides routes on demand.

Cross layer routing: A routing protocol in which the routing decision is based not only on the input from network layer parameters but also on physical layer parameters and link layer parameters.

Route repair: Repairing a broken route locally, at the level of the broken segment or at the level of a few segments near the broken segment.

Intrasegment routing: Occurs only at waypoint nodes. Intermediate nodes get the next hop to the end node of the current segment from their routing tables and send the data packet to the next hop.

Intersegment routing: A routing between segments, done at both waypoint and forwarding nodes.

Expected transmission count (ETX): Estimates the number of retransmissions needed to send unicast packets by measuring the loss rate of broadcast packets between pairs of neighboring nodes.

Exercises

1. Why is control packet overhead less in the waypoint routing approach compared to hierarchical routing protocols?
2. Explain how CDOA considers cross layer issues like interference, bandwidth and queuing delay for routing decisions at the network layer.
3. What are the advantages of the CDOA routing protocol over AODV and DSR routing protocols?
4. CDOA routing is an adaptive routing scheme. How does CDOA routing adapt itself to highly mobile environments?
5. Consider two nodes A and B. Both nodes transmit probe packets every second for calculating ETX. Node A has received 10 probes from node B in the previous 10 s, and the last probe from B reported that it had received nine probe packets from A in the previous 10 s. Answer the following:

   (a) What are the forward and reverse loss probabilities between A and B?
   (b) What is the expected transmission count value calculated at node A?

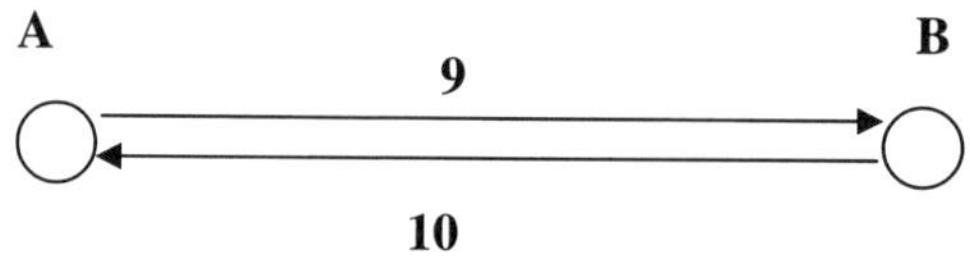

6. Consider a small ad hoc network of three nodes A, B and C. The nodes use ETT as their routing metric. Node A receives eight probes from node B and 10 probes from C in the previous 10 s. The last probe from B reported that it had received six probes from A and the last probe from C reported that it had received five probes from A in the previous 10 s. Let the bandwidth over all the links in network be 2 Mbps. The size of the probe packets is 20 bytes. Find out the ETT between links AB and AC and compare them.

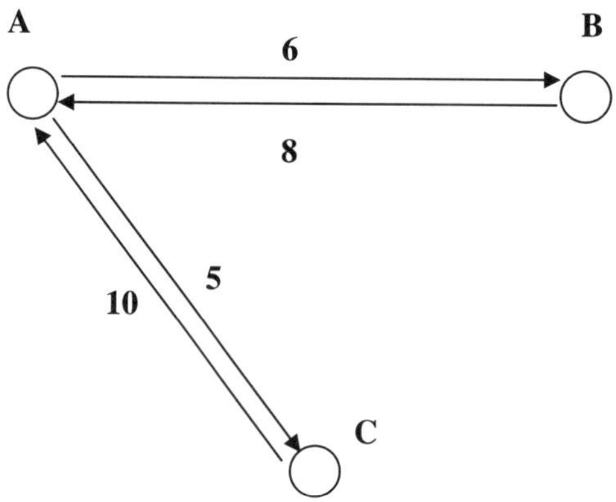

7. Node X has received a RREQinter control message from source node A. The path stored in the RREQinter message is A-B-C-D-E-F-G-H-I-J-K-L-M and the

list of ETT values of these nodes is: 7, 5, 7, 5, 8, 6, 8, 4, 10, 6, 4, 9 and 6 μs. The threshold value of the ETT for a segment is calculated based on the forward and reverse packet loss probability of 0.5 each. Assume that the bandwidth over all the links is 2 Mbps. Let the size of the probes be 10 bytes. Find the waypoints in the route received from the RREQinter message at node X.

8. Node A has received an RREPinter message from source node K. The path in the RREPinter message is A-B-C-D-E-F-G-H-I-J-K, where A, D, F and K are waypoint nodes and the others are forwarding nodes. The cost (ETT values) list in the RREPinter message is: 7, 8, 3, 6, 10, 5, 6, 2, 2 and 5 μs, respectively. The node maintains both routing cache and routing table as follows:

   Routing cache:

Destination	Source Route	Cost
F	X-Y	30

   Routing table:

Destination	Next Hop Node	Hop Count
F	B	5

   What will the routing table and routing cache contents be when node D receives the RREPinter message and updates the table accordingly?

9. What does the source node do whenever it receives the following control messages in the CDOA routing protocol:

   (a) RERRinterRepair
   (b) RERRinterLoop
   (c) RERRinterBroken
   (d) RERRintra

10. What is the need for the route activate (RACT) control message in the CDOA routing protocol?

References

1. A. Iwata, C.-C. Chiang, G. Pei, M. Gerla and T.-W. Chen, Scalable routing strategies for ad hoc wireless networks, *IEEE J. Sel. Area. Commun.* (Special Issue on ad-hoc Networks), 1369–1379 (1999).
2. B. Zhou, A. Marshall, J. Wu, T.-H. Lee and J. Liu, Cross layer design for wireless ad-hoc networks, *EURASIP J. Wireless Commun. Network.* **5**(5), 645–660 (2005).
3. C. E. Perkins and E. M. Royer, Ad-hoc on-demand distance vector routing, *Proc. Workshop Mobile Computing Systems and Applications* (*WMCSA '99*), February (1999).
4. C. E. Perkins, E. M. Belding-Royer and I. D. Chakeres, Ad hoc on demand distance vector (AODV) routing, *IETF Internet Draft*, October (2003).
5. D. B. Johnson and D. A. Maltz, Dynamic source routing in ad hoc wireless networks, in *Mobile Computing*, Vol. 353 (Kluwer Academic, 1996).

6. D. B. Johnson, D. A. Maltz and Y.-C. Hu, The dynamic source routing protocol for mobile ad hoc networks (DSR), Internet draft, draft-ietf-manet-dsr-09.txt, April (2003).
7. D. S. J. De Couto, D. Aguayo, J. Bicket and R. Morris, A high throughput metric for multi-hop wireless networks, *Int. Conf. Mobile Computing and Networking* (2003), pp. 134–146.
8. E. Royer and C. Toh, A review of current routing protocols for ad hoc mobile wireless networks, *IEEE Pers. Comm.* (1999), pp. 46–55.
9. L. Iannone, R. Khalili, K. Salamatian and S. Fdida, Cross-layer routing in wireless mesh networks, *Wireless Communication Systems, 2004, 1st Int. Symp.* September (2004), pp. 319–323.
10. J. Broch, D. A. Maltz, D. B. Johnson, Y.-C. Hu and J. Jetcheva, A performance comparison of multi-hop wireless ad hoc network routing protocols, *Proc. MobiCom* (1998), pp. 85–97.
11. L. Bajaj, M. Takai, R. Ahuja, R. Bagrodia and M. Gerla, GloMoSim: A scalable network simulation environment, Technical report 990027 (1999).
12. R. Bagrodia, R. Meyer, M. Takai, Y. Chen, X. Zeng, J. Martin and H. Y. Song, Parsec: A parallel simulation environment for complex systems, *Computer* **31**(10), 77–85 (1998).
13. R. Bai and M. Singhal, DOA: DSR over AODV routing for mobile ad hoc networks, *IEEE Trans. Mob. Comput.* **5**(10) (2006).
14. R. Draves, J. Padhye and B. Zill, Comparison of routing metrics for static multi-hop wireless networks, *Proc. 2004 Conf. Applications, Technologies, Architectures, and Protocols for Computer Communications* (2004), pp. 133–144.
15. S.-J. Lee, E. M. Belding-Royer and C. E. Perkins, Scalability study of the ad hoc on-demand distance vector routing protocol, *Int. J. Network Management* **13**(2), 97–114 (2003).
16. S. R. Das, C. E. Perkins and E. E. Royer, Performance comparison of two on-demand routing protocols for ad hoc networks, *Proc. INFOCOM* (2000), pp. 3–12.
17. X. Hong, K. Xu and M. Gerla, Scalable routing protocols for mobile ad-hoc networks, communication networks/systems, *IEEE Commun. Soc.* **16**(4), 11–21 (2002).

Chapter 10

PERVASIVE SERVICE DISCOVERY PROTOCOL FOR POWER OPTIMIZATION IN AN AD HOC NETWORK

C. MALA*, S. SANDEEP KUMAR† and N. P. GOPALAN‡

Department of Computer Science and Engineering,
National Institute of Technology, Tiruchirappalli, India
**mala@nitt.edu*
†san_1385@yahoo.co.in
‡gopalan@nitt.edu

Usage of wireless devices give rise to interesting spontaneous networking scenarios *viz.* service discovery, self-organization, etc. In service discovery, devices automatically discover network services and may advertise their existence in a dynamic way. In an ad hoc network, where users are organized in groups, the management procedures are introduced to support such dynamic spontaneous groups. The proposed spontaneous group management is based on the concept of group leader, in which a terminal is responsible for the location update of a group of terminals. As energy is a scarce resource, novel schemes to reduce the search time and power consumption of all the devices in the ubiquitous environment are required. These are proposed and discussed in this chapter.

1. Introduction

"Ubiquitous computing," "pervasive computing," "invisible computing," or "anytime, anywhere, any device computing" all largely mean the same: computation embedded in an environment and available everywhere to assist users in accomplishing their tasks.

A service is a functional element provided by an application or a device to other applications or devices in the network. Service discovery is composed of the ability to describe, select and use a service [3, 11, 17, 18]. Service discovery is important to ubiquitous computing because services in this environment may not always be discernable to users through conventional means, including physical senses and virtual location. Service description is a key component of the service discovery process. Providing the foundation of a service discovery protocol description determines the information available about a service. Without an appropriate description scheme, a service discovery protocol cannot accurately describe and, consequently, locate desired services. This chapter describes how a service discovery protocol handles various issues such as finding a service in a dynamically changing network (i.e., since the ad hoc network is composed of one or more groups, the device can move to any of its groups and it can also go out of the network), management of the cache memory, the energy of a device, and finally how it handles the situation when a device goes out of the network — in a group, the group leader is responsible for communication among the groups. When a service advertisement or service request or any other message comes to a group from other groups, the group leader has to forward the message or request to all the group members. When all devices leave the network and this is unknown to the group leader, then these transmissions are wasted, accessing power and leading to power consumption.

2. Background

Pervasive computing emerged in the late 1980s and early 1990s as the brainchild of Mark Weiser of Xerox Palo Alto Research Center (PARC). Weiser talks of computing and technology offering the computational services we already enjoy in addition to new services, all while being integrated into the world around us. This goal of distraction free technology services is what the pervasive computing community strives for in research and development. While the actual definition and scope of pervasive computing are highly debated and continually expanding, the goal throughout the community remains unchanged: building unobtrusive technology and services to aid in tasks. A key component of pervasive computing is communication. Communication is important because it provides a medium not only for direct control but also for information dissemination and acquisition. Collaboration between devices in pervasive computing environments means distribution of responsibilities, better understanding of the environment through greater context awareness, and combined efforts in accomplishing tasks. Service discovery provides the means for location awareness and interaction between devices, services, and users.

3. Thoughts for Practitioners

The ad hoc network connection method is often associated with wireless devices. The connection is established for the duration of a session and requires no base station. Alternatively, devices discover others within range to form a network. Devices may search for target nodes that are out of range by flooding the network with packets that are forwarded by each node. Connections are possible over multiple nodes (multi-hop ad hoc network). Routing protocols provide stable connections even if nodes are moving around.

This section discusses the major issues and challenges that must be considered in the design of an ad hoc network. They are: self-organization, routing, multicasting, addressing, service discovery, energy management, and scalability.

3.1. *Self-organization*

An important property that an ad hoc network should exhibit is the ability to organize and maintain the network by itself [15]. The major activities that an ad hoc network is required to perform for self-organization include neighbor discovery, topology organization, and topology reorganization. During neighbor discovery, every node in the network gathers information about their neighbors and maintains that information in appropriate data structures. This may require periodic transmission of short packets called beacons. Certain MAC protocols permit varying transmission power to improve the spectrum reusability. In the topology organization phase, every node in the network gathers information about the entire network or a part of the network in order to maintain topological information.

During the topology reorganization phase, an ad hoc network updates the topology information by incorporating the topological changes occurring in the network due to the mobility and failure of nodes. The reorganization consists of two major activities: first, the periodic or aperiodic exchange of topological information, and second, the adaptability (recovery from major topological changes in the network). An ad hoc network should be able to self-organize quickly and efficiently in a way that is transparent to the user and the applications.

3.2. *Routing*

The responsibilities of a routing protocol [7, 9, 16] include exchanging the route information and finding a feasible path to a destination based on criteria such as hop length, minimum power required, and lifetime of the wireless link. The major challenges for a routing protocol with respect to "pervasive service discovery protocols for an ad hoc network" are:

- *Mobility*: One of the most important properties of ad hoc networks is the mobility [6] associated with the nodes. The mobility of nodes results in frequent path breaks, packet collisions, transient loops, stale routing information, and resource reservation problems.
- *Location-dependent contention*: The load on a wireless channel varies with the number of nodes present in a given geographical region. This makes the contention for the channel high when the number of nodes increases. The high contention for the channel increases the number of collisions. A good routing protocol should have a built-in mechanism for distributing the network load uniformly across the network so as to avoid the formation of regions with high channel contention.

The major requirements of a routing protocol in an ad hoc network are the following:

- *Minimum route acquisition delay*: The route acquisition delay for a node that does not have a route to a particular destination node should be minimal. This delay may vary with the size of the network and the network model.

- *Quick route reconfiguration*: Unpredictable changes in the topology of the network require that the routing protocol be able to quickly perform route reconfiguration in order to handle path breaks and subsequent packet losses.
- *Loop-free routing*: This is a fundamental requirement of any routing protocol to avoid unnecessary wastage of network bandwidth. In ad hoc networks, due to the random movement of nodes, transient loops may be formed in the routes that are established. A routing protocol should detect such transient routing loops and take corrective action.
- *Distributed routing approach*: An ad hoc wireless network is a fully distributed wireless network and the use of centralized routing approaches in such a network may consume a large amount of bandwidth.

3.3. *Multicasting*

Multicasting of information is required in certain applications using ad hoc wireless networks, namely, emergency search-and-rescue operations and military communication. In such environments, nodes form groups to carry out certain tasks that require point-to-multipoint and multipoint-to-multipoint voice and data communication. The arbitrary movement of nodes changes the topology dynamically in an unpredictable manner. The mobility of nodes, with the constraints of power source and bandwidth, makes multicast routing very challenging. Traditional wired network multicast protocols such as Core Based Tress (CBT), Protocol Independent Multicast (PIM) and the Distance Vector Multicast Routing Protocol (DVMRP) do not perform well in ad hoc networks as all these involve a tree-based multicast structure, which is highly unstable and needs to be frequently readjusted to include broken links. The use of any global routing structure such as the link-state table results in a high control overhead. The use of single-link connectivity among nodes in a multicast group results in a tree-shaped multicast routing topology which provides high multicast efficiency. The major issues in designing multicast routing protocols are as follows:

- *Robustness*: Multicast routing protocols must be able to recover and reconfigure quickly from link break, thus making them suitable for highly dynamic environments.
- *Efficiency*: A multicast protocol should make a minimum number of transmissions to deliver a data packet to all the group members.
- *Efficient group management*: Group management refers to the process of accepting multicast session members and maintaining the connectivity among them until the session expires. This process of group management needs to be performed with a minimal exchange of control messages.
- *Scalability*: A multicast routing protocol should be able to scale to a network with a large number of nodes.

3.4. *Addressing*

Addressing is significant in ad hoc networks due to the absence of any centralized coordinator. An address that is globally unique is required for a node in an ad hoc network in order to participate in communication. Auto-configuration of addresses is required to allocate non-duplicate addresses to the nodes. In networks where the topology is highly dynamic, frequent partitioning and merging of network components require duplicate address-detection mechanisms in order to maintain unique addressing in the connected components of the network.

3.5. *Service Discovery*

A service is an interface to an application of a device which a client may access. Services present in pervasive computing environments may vary among devices. While these services are diverse in kind, they share a common requirement. The end devices (requesting and requested) need to have some way for a user to locate and interact with them. Locating and interacting with services is the job of *service discovery*. This can be broken down into the tasks of description, dissemination, selection, and interaction. Each component has a unique set of responsibilities in the service discovery process. The goal of service discovery is to provide the best service options among the many that may be available to the entity desiring the services and aid in communication with them.

A variety of service discovery protocols is currently under development. The most well known so far are:

- Service Location Protocol (SLP), developed by the IETF,
- Jini, Sun's Java-based approach to service discovery [17],
- salutation,
- Microsoft's Universal Plug and Play (UPnP) [18], and
- Bluetooth Service Discovery Protocol (SDP).

3.6. *Energy Management*

Energy management is defined as the process of managing the sources and consumption of energy in a node or in the network as a whole for enhancing the lifetime of networks [1, 10, 13]. Some of the functions of energy management are: shaping the energy discharge pattern of a node's battery to enhance the battery life, finding routes that result in minimum total energy consumption in the network, using distributed scheduling schemes to improve battery life, and handling the processor and interface devices to minimize power consumption. Energy management can be classified into the following categories:

- transmission power management,
- processor power management,

- battery energy management, and
- device power management.

In the following we concentrate on transmission and processor power management.

3.6.1. *Transmission Power Management*

The transmission power is determined by the reachability requirement of the network, the routing protocol, and the MAC protocol employed. Power conservation responsibility lies across the data link, network, transport, and application layers.

Designing a data link layer that reduces unnecessary retransmissions, prevents collisions, switches to standby or sleep mode whenever possible, and reduces the transmit/receive switching are some of the techniques used in power management at the data link layer.

The network layer routing protocol considers the battery life and load balancing across the network while selecting paths.

At the transport layer, issues such as reducing the number of retransmissions, and recognizing and handling the reason behind packet losses locally should be incorporated into the protocols.

Power consumption varies with application. In a mobile computer, image/video processing/playback software and 3D gaming software consume more power than other applications. Hence, the application software developed for mobile computers should also take into account the power consumption, and this is done in the application layer.

3.6.2. *Processor Power Management*

The CPU can be put into different power-saving modes under low processing load conditions. Power can be completely turned off if the machine is idle for a long time. In such cases, interrupts can be used to turn on the CPU upon detection of user interaction or other events. Processor power management mainly depends on the clock speed and the numbers of instructions executed per unit time as these are some of the processor parameters that affect power consumption.

3.7. *Scalability*

Even though the number of nodes in ad hoc networks is not growing by the same magnitude as today's Internet, the operation of a large number of nodes in the ad hoc mode is not far off. Traditional applications such as military uses emergency operations and crowd control may not lead to such a large ad hoc network [19].

The latency of path-finding involved in an on-demand routing protocol for a large ad hoc wireless network may be unacceptably high. Similarly, the periodic routing overhead involved in a table-driven routing protocol may consume a significant amount of bandwidth in a large network.

A large ad hoc network may not have homogeneous nodes. A hierarchical topology-based system with the relevant addressing may be more suitable for large ad hoc wireless networks. Hybrid architectures that combine the multi-hop radio relaying may improve scalability.

4. Design and Implementation of the Service Discovery Protocol

Consider an ad hoc network composed of N devices each offering S services. Each device has a user agent (UA) and a service agent (SA). A UA is a process working on behalf of the user to search for information about the services offered in the network. An SA is a process working to advertise the services offered by the device. Each device has a cache containing the list of services that have been heard from the network.

In a network an enabled device will broadcast its services as shown in Fig. 1. These services are advertised through the service URL [2, 8, 14] and a service template. The service URL contains the IP address of the service, the port number, and the path. Service templates [5] specify the attributes that characterize the service and their default values. A service template associated with a network printer, for example, may be given by:

Service:printer://ij1385.tum.de:1000/queue1,
Printer-name = ij1385,
Printer-model = HPIJ1385N,
Printer-location = Room 0138,
Color-supported = True,
Pages-per-minute = 9.

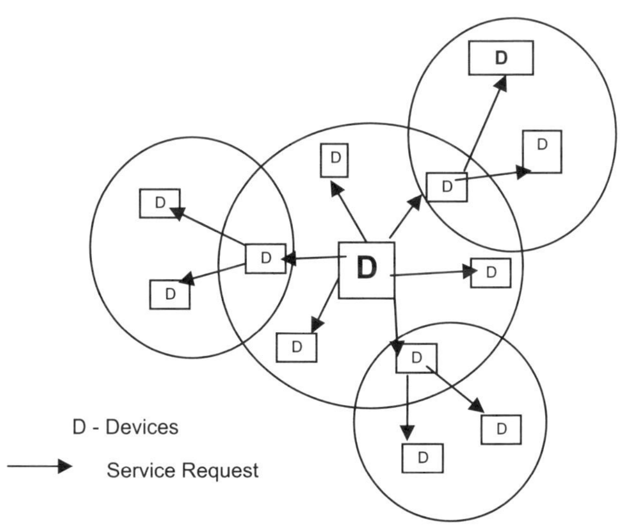

Fig. 1. A device multicasting its services.

The devices present in the network will register the services which are advertised in their cache. The cache is organized into two levels, namely, local cache and remote cache. The services present in the device are stored in local cache, and in remote cache the services present in the network and not in the current device are stored. The idea of having different levels of cache is to reduce the search time for service request (*sdp_service_request*) and reply (*sdp_service_reply*) messages. If device_1 wants to access a service on device_2 (device_2 can be present in any region), and the information is present in its remote cache, device_1 will directly access the remote service by sending a request, as shown in Fig. 2.

Each element of the cache has a service description [4, 12]. As the device cache memory is very small and if the number of devices is high, then the information about all the services will not fit in the cache, and the service information that is already present may not be useful for the device. To overcome this problem, the cache memory should be refreshed and this permits any other new device's services to be available for registering in the cache. This is done using the least recently used (LRU) algorithm. A situation may arise when device_1, which wants to use a service of device_2 to perform its task, just deregistered (i.e., the service was overridden and in the next moment the device needs that service to perform its task). Then, device_1 will broadcast its service request message using an *sdp_service_request* to all the devices in the network; the devices that matched their services with the service request will unicast the replies to device_1 using an *sdp_service_reply* message, as shown in Fig. 3. The management of communication between regions will be handled by a multicasting agent as discussed in Sec. 2.

Consider two working scenarios:

Case 1: When device_X needs a service offered by device_Y, device_X can search in its remote cache directly, get the required information and send a request

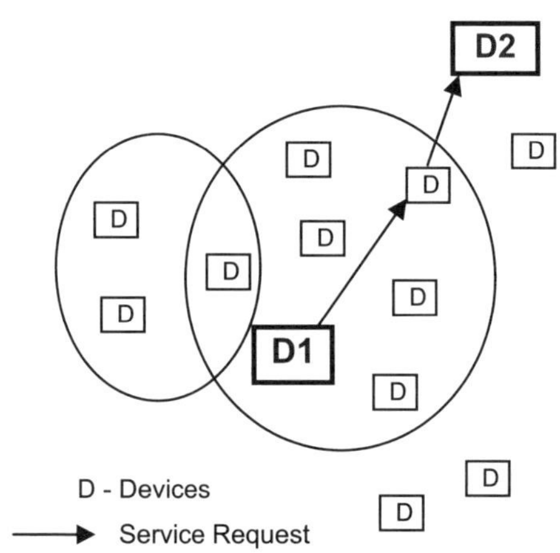

Fig. 2. Multicasting a service request message.

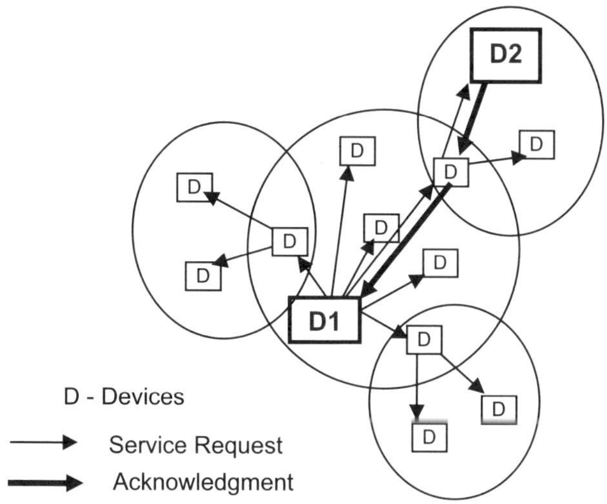

Fig. 3. Devices unicast their reply.

message to device_Y. Therefore, searching is done at only one level, i.e., in remote cache and not the whole cache memory. This reduces the search time.

Case 2: When the information about a service of device_Y has expired, its content will be deregistered in the cache memory of device_X. Later, when device_X broadcasts an *sdp_service_request* message to all the devices in the network, all the other devices compare the request message with their local cache. As the remote cache is not searched, this reduces the search time.

Overload is of concern in any protocol. Let there be n devices, all requesting to one device for a service. Overload arises in conditions when there are many devices offering a particular service and all other devices requesting only one particular device, as shown in Fig. 4. For example, let there be three printers (P1, P2, P3) in a network offering the same service and n other devices requesting to P2. Though P1 and P3 also offer the same service as P2, the workload is more on P2. As P2 is doing more work, power consumption by the device will be greater. This problem of overloading can be solved by load sharing, as shown in Fig. 5.

The process of load sharing is explained using algorithm 1.

Algorithm 1. Load sharing algorithm.

Step 1. If P1.Q_len > P1.Threshold && P3.Q_len < P3.Threshold
Select service P3;
Step 2. if P1.Q_len < P1.Threshold && P3.Q_len > P3.Threshold
Select service P1;
Step 3: if P1.Q_len < P1.Threshold && P3.Q_len > P3.threshold
Select services P1 and P3;

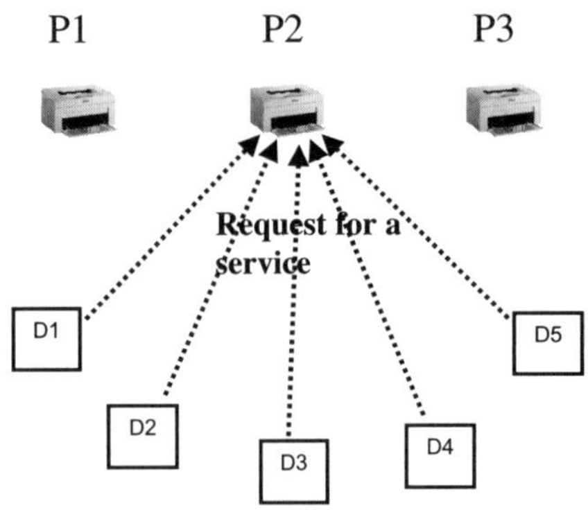

Fig. 4. n devices requesting for same service.

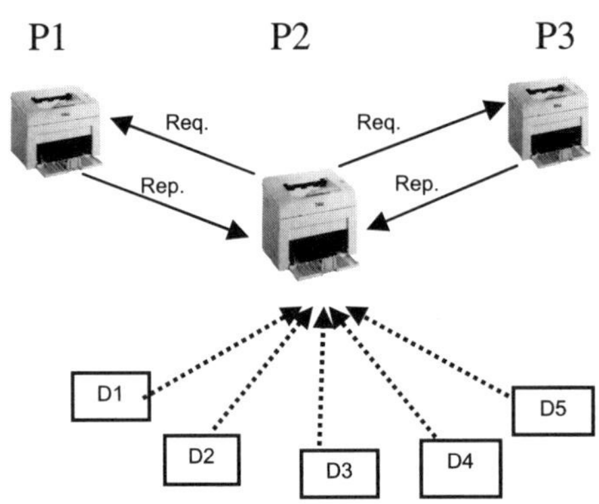

Fig. 5. Load sharing.

Step 4. wait for a random time, say t seconds, and repeat the process;
    if P2.Q_len < P2.Threshold
        Stop load sharing
        else
            repeat from Step 1.

Consider the situation shown in Fig. 5. Printer P2 is overloaded and it wants to share the work with other printers offering the same service. It will multicast the request, the Printers P1 and P3 will respond by unicasting to P2. Then P2 will send a unicast request message (*sdp_load_req*) to know the load of the device. The device will respond by sending its length of the process queue. Then, P2 will transfer the work to the device whose queue length is lower.

There may be a situation when some or all the devices may leave the group or region and the information about the devices which are not present in the group must be deregistered. If the information about the device is not deleted, devices waste their time searching for every request and trying to access the service of devices not present in the network. Then, the requesting device will be waiting for a reply which will degrade performance as it increases the traffic by sending unnecessary messages and hence the power consumption also increases. To overcome this issue, the entry of a device must be removed from the remote cache when the device is not present in the network.

Now, two scenarios are to be considered: one is the device being present within the network, and the other is when the device has changed its region or group. Consider an example that demonstrates this scenario. (The solution is given for a group and it can be extended to the whole network.) To know whether device_x (assume the device can be in any group) is present in the network or not, all the devices have to send a signal once every 30 seconds to its own group. All the devices must respond by sending an acknowledgment of the signal. After receiving the acknowledgment the device will check with its internal registry that stores the information about all the devices within the group and mark the entry of the device which responded to the signal. The device then sends one more signal to all other devices which are unmarked in its registry and waits for the response for T time units. If the acknowledgment is not received from device_x within the T units, the device that sent the signal will conclude that the device is not present in the network and its information will be deregistered in its remote cache. The same process is performed by all other devices in the group or the whole network.

5. Performance Analysis

The proposed protocol has been simulated using NS2. A set of N devices each having M number of services are used in the simulation, and the results of the simulation are shown using time variant, energy consumption and performance graphs. Figure 6 depicts the relation between the number of mobile devices (x-axis) and the search time (y-axis) in finding the service. From the results it can be inferred that in the present SDP if a service is available in the cache memory, the search time is less and it is the same with an increase in the number of mobile devices. If the required

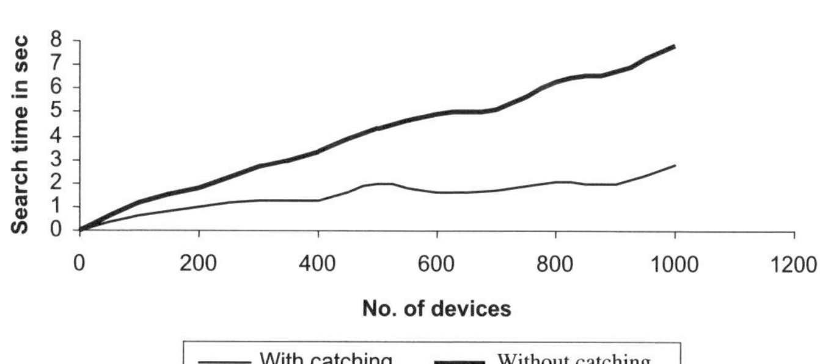

Fig. 6. Time variance.

service is not present, then it multicasts as in Fig. 2 and hence the search time increases. Without effective use of cache, it is not possible to handle the information about the services of all the devices and the time required to find a service increases quickly. This in turn increases the processing power of the device and the power consumption goes up accordingly. This would not be suitable for realtime environments.

All the factors for saving energy, i.e., reducing the power consumption of a device, should be considered, including reducing search time and access time, and balancing the load among compatible devices. In Fig. 7, the relation is shown between the power utilization (y-axis) and workload (x-axis). When the number of devices increases in the network, there is a direct increase in the workload.

The overall performance of the protocol is also simulated and tested, taking into account various factors such as cache management, reducing the search time, load balancing, group management, group communication and number of transmissions. Figure 8 shows the relation between the performance (y-axis) and the number

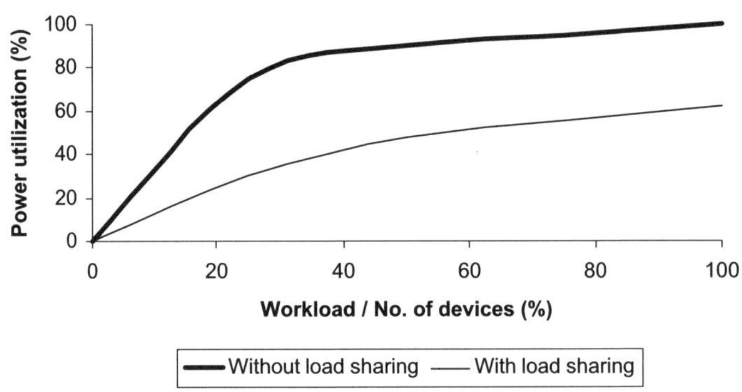

Fig. 7. Energy consumption.

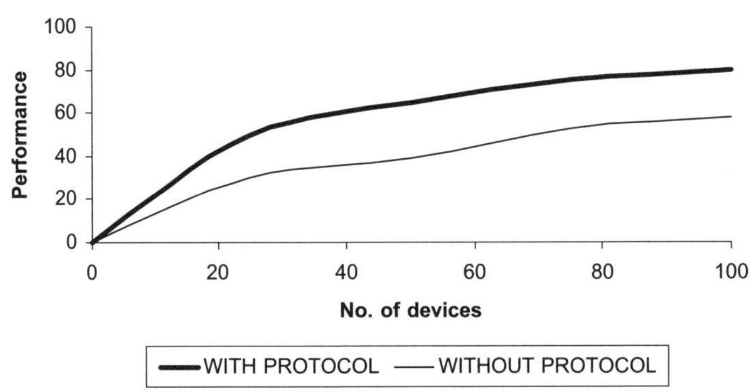

Fig. 8. Performance comparison.

of devices (x-axis). It can be seen from the figure that there is a significant improvement in the performance of the devices with the proposed SDP.

6. Directions for Future Research

Further research may be directed towards analyzing the performance of the protocol for a multi-tier environment, incorporating security features in the protocol, and suggesting novel methods to further reduce the energy consumption and memory requirement of the devices.

7. Conclusions

We have proposed a novel service discovery protocol mechanism for highly dynamic ubiquitous environments (i.e., that do not depend on any existing infrastructure) which considers the power constraints of devices. It takes into account the frequent interactions with close devices and unusual interactions with distant devices. The protocol also exploits cooperation between devices to achieve the best performance with the least effort. Our simulation results show that there is a significant improvement in the performance of devices in terms of load sharing and search time with the use of this protocol.

Terminology

Service discovery: A service is an interface to an application of a device which a client may access. Services present in pervasive computing environments may vary among devices. While these services are diverse in kind, they share a common requirement. The end devices (requesting and requested) need to have some way for an user to locate and interact with them. Locating and interacting with services is called *service discovery.*

Ad hoc network: A network with wireless or temporary plug-in connections in which the network devices (mobile or portable devices which are in some close proximity to the rest of the network) are part of the network only for the duration of a communication session and require no base station.

Routing: The process of determining and prescribing the path for establishing one or more connections and/or for forwarding messages.

Unicasting: A communication between a single sender and a single receiver over a network, or point-to-point communication.

Multicasting: A single stream of data (i.e., a set of packets) that is transmitted simultaneously to selected multiple hosts in the appropriate multicast group.

Signal: The short messages (used in network terminology) transmitted over the network.

Pervasive or ubiquitous computing: Computation embedded in an environment that is available everywhere to assist users in accomplishing tasks.

LRU algorithm: A page replacement algorithm which replaces the page that has not been used for the longest period of time.

Load sharing (*LS*): Uneven task arrivals may temporarily overload some nodes while leaving others underloaded. This problem can be solved or alleviated by load sharing (LS), i.e., some of the tasks arriving at overloaded nodes, called overflow tasks, are transferred to underloaded nodes. One important issue in LS is locating the underloaded nodes to which the overflow tasks can be transferred. This is termed *location policy*.

Beacons: Signals used to indicate the presence of a device or access point.

Exercises

1. What is pervasive computing?
2. What is service discovery?
3. How is group management done in an ad hoc network?
4. Explain the major requirements of a routing protocol in an ad hoc network.
5. What are the major issues in designing a multicasting routing protocol?
6. Name the various energy management techniques.
7. How are beacons useful?
8. What is load sharing and when and why is it implemented in a service discovery protocol?
9. Each device consists of two different memories, $L1$ and $L2$, where $L1$ is used to store the services present in the device and $L2$ is used to store the services present in the network other than its own services. Explain the situation when the service requested by the device is not present in $L1$.
10. The device consists of two caches, $L1$ and $L2$, where $L1$ is local cache and $L2$ is remote cache. Let $h1$, $a1$, $h2$ and $a2$ be the hit ratio and access time for two cache memories $L1$ and $L2$, respectively. Based on the previous history, $X\%$ of requests by devices are for local data and $Y\%$ of requests by devices are for remote data.
    (a) What is the service access time for a device to locate a service?
    (b) Assume the ad hoc network comprises three hop networks. suppose $a1 = 5\,\text{ns}$, $a2 = 10\,\text{ns}$, $h2 = 0.65$, $x = 30\%$, $y = 70\%$ and the transmission delay for one hop is 15 ms.
        (i) What is the service access time to find a local service for the device?
        (ii) What is the service access time to find a remote service for the device?

    (*Hint*: If the device finds its request service in $L1$, then $h1 = 1$.)

References

1. B. Chen, K. Jamieson, H. Balakrishnan and R. Morris, Span: An energy-efficient coordination algorithm for topology maintenance in ad hoc wireless networks, *Proc. 7th Annual Int. Conf. Mobile Computing and Networking*, Rome, Italy, July (2001), pp. 85–96.
2. C. E. Perkins and E. Guttman, DHCP options for service location protocol, Internet RFC 2610, June (1999).
3. C. Lee and S. Helal, A multi-tier ubiquitous service discovery protocol for mobile clients, *1st ACM Int. Conf. Mobile Clients*, Vol. 4, March (2001), pp. 3443–3456.
4. C. Lee and S. Helal, Context attributes: An approach to enable context-awareness for multicasting, *Proc. Symp. Applications and the Internet* (*SAINT*) (2003), pp. 22–30.
5. E. Guttman, C. E. Perkins and J. Kempf, Service templates and service schemes, Internet RFC 2609, June (1999).
6. I. F. Akyildiz, J. Y. McNair, J. S. M. Ho, H. Uzunalioglu and W. Wang, Mobility management in next generation wireless systems, *IEEE Proc.* **87**(8), 1347–1385 (1999).
7. I. F. Akyildiz, W. Yen and B. Yener, A new hierarchical routing protocol for dynamic multihop wireless networks, *Proc. INFOCOM '97, 16th Annual Joint Conf. IEEE Computer and Communications Societies, Driving the Information Revolution*, April 9–11 (1997), p. 1422.
8. J. Bound, M. Carney and C. E. Perkins, Dynamic host configuration protocol for Ipv6 (DHCPv6), Internet draft, draft-ietf-dhc-dhcpv6-14txt, May (2000).
9. J. Broch, D. A. Maltz, D. B. Johnson, Y.-C. Hu and J. Jetcheva, A performance comparison of multi-hop wireless ad hoc network routing protocols, *Proc. 4th Annual ACM/IEEE Int. Conf. Mobile Computing and Networking*, Dallas, Texas, October 25–30 (1998), pp. 85–97.
10. L. M. Feeney and M. Nilson, Investigating the energy consumption of a wireless network interface in an ad hoc networking environment, *IEEE INFOCOM* (2001), pp. 1548–1557.
11. M. S. Thompson and S. F. Middkiff, A framework for evaluating service discovery protocols, unpublished manuscript (2005).
12. M. S. Thompson and S. F. Middkiff, Service description for pervasive service discovery, *Proc. 1st Int. Workshop Services and Infrastructure for the Ubiquitous and Mobile Internet*, Vol. 3, June (2005), pp. 273–279.
13. S. Agarwal, R. H. Katz, S. Krishnamurthy and S. K. Dao, Impact of group movement on energy consumption in ad hoc wireless networks, *Proc. IEEE INFOCOM'01*, Anchorage, AK, April (2001).
14. S. Cheshire and M. Krochmal, Dns-based service discovery, IETF internet draft, available at http://files.dns-sd.org/draft-cheshire-dnsext-ulticastdns.txt (2004).
15. S. Rafaeli and D. Hutchison, A survey of key management for secure group communication, *Proc. ACM Comput. Survey.* 35(3), 309–329 (2003).
16. S. Basagni, I. Chlamtac, V. R. Syrotiuk and B. A. Woodward, A distance routing effect algorithm for mobility (DREAM), *Proc. 4th Annual ACM/IEEE Int. Conf. Mobile Computing and Networking*, Dallas, Texas, October 25–30 (1998), pp. 76–84.
17. Sun technical white paper, Jini Architectural Overview.
18. Universal Plug and Play Device Architecture, http://www.upnp.org/download/UpnPDA10_20000613.htm.
19. Y. Kim, A. Perrig and G. Tsudik, Simple and fault-tolerant key agreement for dynamic collaborative groups, *Proc. 7th ACM Conf. Computer and Communications Security*, Athens, Greece, November 1–4 (2000), pp. 235–244.

Chapter 11

AREA COVERAGE PROBLEMS IN WIRELESS SENSOR NETWORKS

BANG WANG, CHENG FU, HOCK BENG LIM,
MINGHUI LI and DI MA
Intelligent Systems Centre,
Nanyang Technological University, Singapore

Coverage, which reflects how well a sensor field is monitored or observed, is an important performance metric for distributed sensor networks. The individual sensor coverage model is closely related to the sensing functions of different sensor types while the network coverage is a collective measure from geographically distributed sensor nodes. In the literature, the coverage problems in distributed sensor networks have been formulated in various ways with different assumptions, constraints and objectives. This chapter surveys recent research progress made to address area coverage problems. We first provide detailed discussions on the sensor coverage model and the design issues. We then classify three main types of area coverage problems in different network operation phases. Before network deployment, the main coverage problem is to determine the least number of nodes that is needed to completely cover the sensor field. After network deployment, sensing activity scheduling decides how to activate sensors alternatively in order to prolong network operation time. Network redeployment is possible if sensor nodes are equipped with a mobility unit. The node movement strategy determines how to move nodes to desired positions while guaranteeing coverage. We review representative approaches in the literature for each type of problem. We also outline some variants each with different assumptions, constraints or objectives for these problems, which we list as further reading.

1. Introduction

Generally speaking, a sensor is a device which responds to physical stimulus such as heat, light, sound, pressure and magnetism by converting the stimulus into a recordable impulse such as an electrical signal. A sensor node encapsulates one or more sensors, a power supply, data processing, and storage and transmission units. In a distributed sensor network, a number of sensor nodes are deployed in

Correspondence to: B. Wang, Intelligent Systems Centre, Research Techno Plaza, Nanyang Technological University, 50 Nanyang Drive, Singapore 637553, wangbang@ntu.edu.sg, wangbang@ieee.org.

different geographical locations to collectively monitor certain physical phenomena in an area of interest (called a *sensor field* hereafter).[a] Sensor nodes equipped with radio transceivers are able to transmit and receive data via radio channels. A *wireless sensor network* (WSN) may consist of hundreds or thousands of such wireless capable sensor nodes and can be deployed in remote, harsh environments. Applications of distributed sensor networks are diverse, including battlefield surveillance, environmental monitoring, biological detection, smart spaces and industrial diagnostics [1].

Coverage is one of the fundamental issues in WSNs, which reflects how well a sensor field is monitored or observed by the deployed sensor nodes.[b] The coverage problem is heavily dependent on the coverage model of individual sensors and the locations of the deployed sensor nodes. A *sensor coverage model* can be considered as a measure of the quality of service of a sensor's sensing function and is subject to a wide range of interpretations due to a large variety of sensors and applications. *Network sensing coverage* on the other hand, can be considered as a collective measure of the quality of service provided by sensor nodes of different geographical locations. In many cases, we may interpret the coverage concept as a non-negative mapping between the *space points* (of a sensor field) and the sensor nodes (of a deployed sensor network).

Coverage problems have also been researched in other fields, for example, the Art Gallery problem [2] and the Circle Covering problem [3]. Computational geometry is applied to solve such coverage problems. The solutions to these problems provide some theoretical background; however, they may not be directly applied to the coverage problems in WSNs due to some specific properties of WSNs such as limited energy and ad hoc topology. In the literature on WSNs, coverage problems have been formulated in various ways with different assumptions and objectives. The sensor coverage model may need to take into consideration the specific signal processing technique for a sensor as well as the cooperative signal processing technique for multiple sensors. In the design stage, one may want to know the least number of nodes that is needed such that every point in a sensor field can be covered. In the deployment stage, sensor nodes may be deterministically placed into the sensor field or simply randomly scattered. Also mobile sensor nodes may move to more preferable positions after the initial deployment to improve network coverage. In the operation stage, one may want to schedule different sensor nodes to work alternatively in order to prolong network operation time while still preserving network coverage. Some other network performance metrics such as energy consumption and network connectivity may need to be integrated with coverage problems in the context of WSNs.

[a] In this chapter, we assume that mainly consider those sensor fields within a 2D plane.

[b] In this chapter, we assume that one sensor node is equipped only with one sensor and we use "sensor" and "sensor node" equivalently and interchangeably throughout.

There has been a lot of coverage related research work as well as some recent surveys [4–6]. In this chapter, we present a tutorial-like survey of coverage problems by providing canonical yet detailed problem formulation and solutions. We first classify different types of coverage problems and generalize the key issues behind these problems. Among the different coverage types, we choose area coverage as the context to introduce and compare some typical solutions. We also provide brief reviews on other coverage types and list related references as further reading.

This chapter is structured as follows. Section 2 introduces some sensor coverage models and generalizes the basic design issues. According to the network operation scenario, three types of area coverage problems are reviewed. Section 3 discusses the critical sensor density problem for network pre-deployment. Section 4 summarizes the sensing activity scheduling problem for network operation after network deployment. Section 5 reviews the node movement strategy for network redeployment. The chapter ends with some concluding remarks in Sec. 6.

2. Background

2.1. *Sensor Coverage Model*

Coverage problems in WSNs are dependent on the coverage model of individual sensors and their locations in the sensor field. Simply put, the coverage model of a sensor specifies the geometric relationships between space points and the sensor. In many cases, the sensor coverage model is simplified as a 0-1 model (Boolean model), where a point is either covered (1) or not covered (0) by this sensor. For example, consider a camera used as a sensor to capture photos of its nearby environment. If an object on a point can be identified from the photos, then this point can be considered to be covered by this camera. In this case, the resolution and the angle of the camera determine the area it can cover. In the WSN literature, the most commonly used sensor coverage model is a *sensing disk model*: all points within a disk centered at a sensor node with a certain disk radius are considered to be covered by this sensor. The disk radius is called the *sensing range*, R_s, of a sensor. Due to the variety of sensing modalities and applications, a sensor coverage model of course can adopt other definitions. For example, Wang *et al.* [7] recently proposed the concept of *information coverage* based on estimation theory. In what follows, we try to explain both models from the viewpoint of signal processing, which is the basis for most applications in WSNs.

The basic functionality of a sensor is sensing (or monitoring), i.e., to record some information of its nearby environment such as measurements of environmental temperature, or acoustic, or seismic signal amplitude. A sensor can process its measurements locally and send only the processed results to the sink. This needs a decision-making model at each individual sensor node, which can be based on the theory of signal detection. For example, suppose that a seismic sensor has a corrupted measurement $x(t)$ at time t. It can apply a *likelihood ratio test* to tell whether an event had occurred (or a target had appeared). Further suppose that the detection model has only two hypothesis H_0 and H_1, and the conditional probability distribution of $x(t)$ given the hypothesis is $P(X \mid H_i), i = 0, 1$. If the ratio $P(x \mid H_1)/P(x \mid H_0)$ is larger than some threshold, it decides an event has occured and reports 1 to the sink. Otherwise, it sends 0. Under some assumptions about the signal decay model and statistical distributions of event signals and background noise, a sensor may determine its sensing range such that the detection probability of the events within the sensing range is maximized. As commented in [Ref. 8], the sensing range based on such a signal detection model does not imply a hard boundary between the area where an event is *always* detected and the area where an event is *never* detected. In the literature on WSNs, however, many assume a fixed sensing range and an *isotropic* detection capability of the sensor, i.e., a disk coverage model. From the viewpoint of signal detection, the most commonly used sensing disk model can be interpreted as a sensor detecting an event that occurred within its covered disk area; or in other words, such a disk is covered by the sensor. Another implication of this sensing disk model is that each sensor node makes decisions independent of other sensors. In some applications, different geographically distributed sensor nodes actually measure the same event/target source but each with a noise corrupted copy. Their measurements therefore are correlated and can be processed together (or *fused*) to improve signal processing.

The definition of information coverage, on the other hand, considers measurement correlations to exploit *sensing spatial diversity* from geographically distributed sensors. Suppose that an event with some parameter θ occurs on a space point with the Euclidean distance d to a sensor s_k. For example, θ can be the acoustic amplitude due to a motor engine or due to leakage from a gas barrel. For a magnetic wave such as an acoustic wave, amplitude is attenuated when propagating. We can thus assume that the parameter θ decays with distance, and at distance d it is θ/d^α, where $\alpha > 0$ is the decay exponent. The measurement of the parameter x_k, at a sensor may also be corrupted by an additive noise n_k. Thus,

$$x_k = \frac{\theta}{d_k^\alpha} + n_k, \quad k = 1, 2, \ldots, K. \tag{1}$$

A parameter estimator, e.g., a *best linear unbiased estimator* (BLUE) [9], can be used to estimate θ based on the measurements x_k, $k = 1, 2, \ldots, K$. Let $\hat{\theta}$ and $\theta = \hat{\theta} - \theta$ denote the estimate and the estimation error, respectively. If the estimation error is small, an event/target can be claimed to be detected and its parameter can be obtained within a certain confidence level. We define *information exposure* as the probability that the absolute value of the estimation is less than or equal to a predefined constant A, i.e., $\Pr\{|\theta_K| \leq A\}$, to measure how well a point is monitored [10]. When it is equal to or larger than a predefined threshold $\varepsilon(0 \leq \varepsilon \leq 1)$, i.e., $\Pr\{|\theta_K| \leq A\} \geq \varepsilon$, this point is said to be *information covered* [or (K, ε)-covered] by these K sensors [7]. When all noise is assumed to be independent

Gaussian with zero mean and σ^2 variance, then

$$\Pr\{|\theta_K| \leq A\} = 1 - 2Q\left(\frac{A}{\sigma\sqrt{C_K}}\right), \tag{2}$$

where $C_K = \left(\sum_{k=1}^{K} d_k^{-2\alpha}\right)^{-1}$ and $Q(x) = \frac{1}{\sqrt{2\pi}}\int_x^\infty \exp(-t^2/2)\,dt$. The information coverage model can be reduced to a sensing disk model if only $(1, \varepsilon)$ coverage is considered for an isotropic sensor. When higher order information coverage is considered, e.g., $(K = 2, \varepsilon)$ coverage, the area covered by these K sensors is no longer a simple union of these K sensors' sensing disks but larger than that.

Figure 1 illustrates the concept of the sensing disk coverage model and the concept of the information coverage model when putting sensor nodes at the vertices of a triangle and a rectangle. In the left column, the area that can be covered is the union of the sensors' sensing disks. Note that there are some areas covered by more than one sensor node. In the right column, some points that are not within the sensing disk can still be information covered, and the covered area is larger than the union of the sensing disks.

Both the sensing disk coverage model and the information coverage model assume an isotropic sensor with the same sensing ability in all directions.

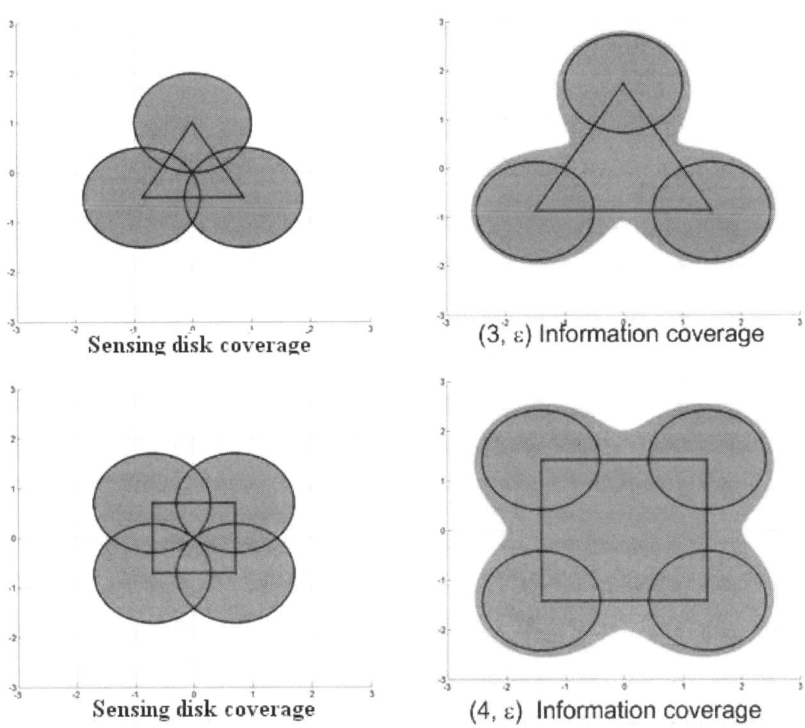

Fig. 1. Comparison of sensing disk coverage and information coverage ($\alpha = 1.0, \varepsilon = 0.683$).

Furthermore, they are both 0-1 coverage models and specify the geometric relationship between a space point and one sensor or more. In the literature, the isotropic sensing assumption and the 0-1 coverage model are the most commonly used for coverage problems. Here, we mainly focus on such coverage problems based on the isotropic sensing and 0-1 coverage model. Given the sensor coverage model of individual sensors, the coverage statistics of a sensor field is also dependent on the locations of the deployed sensor nodes. Furthermore, the operations of the deployed sensors, e.g., active/sleep, will also impact on coverage. In the next subsection, we introduce some design issues for the coverage problem in the context of WSNs.

2.1.1. *Further Reading*

There are also some other sensor coverage models. The *directional sensor coverage model* assumes that a sensor can only cover a sector of a disk, for example, a camera sensor. The area covered by a directionional sensor is dependent on the sector angle, node orientation and the sensing range. Some coverage problems based on the directional coverage model have been studied in Refs. 11–13.

Besides the 0-1 coverage model, there are also some other coverage models that use a positive number to indicate how a space point is covered. Meguerdichian *et al.* [14] consider an *attenuated coverage density model.* A space point x is said to receive a sensing density

$$\frac{C}{d^{\alpha}(s,x)}$$

from a sensor s, where C and α are constants and $d(s,x)$ is the Euclidean distance between x and s. In this model, every space point is subject to a certain amount of coverage density.

Some definitions of the coverage model also exploit sensing spatial diversity based on the overall detection probability. The detection probability of a target by a single sensor may be modeled as distance dependent. For example, Zou and Chakrabarty [15, 16] adopt an attenuated detection model for a single sensor. The detection probability of sensor s on a space point x is given by

$$p_s(x) = \begin{cases} 1 & d(s,x) < R_1, \\ e^{-\alpha d^{\beta}(s,x)} & R_1 \le d(s,x) < R_2, \\ 0 & d(s,x) > R_2, \end{cases}$$

where α, β, R_1 and R_2 are constants. The overall detection probability of point x by its S surrounding sensors is given by $P(x) = 1 - \prod_{s=1,\ldots,S}(1 - p_s(x))$. The point x is said to be covered by these S sensors if $P(x)$ is no smaller than a threshold. Some similar coverage definitions from this approach can also be found in Refs. 17 and 18.

2.2. *Thoughts for Practitioners*

A sensor node which is normally designed for some specific sensing task (e.g., sensing temperature, acoustic or seismic signals) in general has a small size, low weight and limited (and non-rechargeable) battery energy. For example, the temperature and relative humidity sensor MEP510 by Crossbow Technology Inc. is $6.35 \times 4.13 \times 3.81$ cm in size and weight 89.8 g including a battery [19]. The expected lifetime of such a device is six months when a default sampling rate is used. Although a single sensor node may only have limited sensing, processing and communication capabilities, a large number of geographically distributed sensors can form networks and collaborate to achieve a high performance for most applications in a large field of interest. Due to different application requirements, the subject to be covered by a WSN can be the whole field of interest or only some particular discrete points/targets within the sensor field.

Sensor nodes may be deterministically placed or randomly scattered into a sensor field. In a random deployment, the number of scattered sensor nodes is in general larger than the optimum to compensate for the lack of exact positioning. Roughly speaking, a sensor node can be in one of the following three states: the transmit and receive state, the sensing and processing state, or the sleep state. Although different types of sensor nodes may have different energy consumption models, the most energy intensive state in general is the transmit and receive state and the least is the sleep state. Since replacing the node battery is not feasible in many applications, it is desirable to schedule sensor states to save battery life. Besides the sensing task, it is often required in many applications that sensor nodes can deliver their sensed data to a sink for further processing. A *coverage hole*, an area not covered by any sensor, may happen due to node death or due to fewer than required nodes in a randomly deployed sensor field. In such cases, mobile sensors can be used to recover coverage holes. Sensor nodes can also be assumed to have different sensing, processing and communication capabilities, which also have an impact on the coverage problems. In this chapter, we classify the following design issues for coverage problems: *coverage type*, *coverage degree*, *coverage ratio*, *deployment method*, *sensor heterogeneity*, *activity scheduling*, *network connectivity* and *performance metric*.

- *Coverage type:* According to Cardei *et al.* [4], the coverage can be classified into three types according to the subject to be covered, namely, *area coverage*, *target coverage* and *barrier coverage*. The most frequently considered coverage type is the area coverage, which addresses how a sensor field is covered. Recently, target coverage, addressing how to cover a set of discrete targets with known locations, has also been researched. Barrier coverage is different from area and point coverage in that the subjects to be covered are not known before node deployment. Instead, it is concerned with finding a penetration path across the sensor field with some desired property. For example, the maximal breach path problem presented in Ref. 20 is a kind of barrier coverage which tries to find a path such that each point on the path has the maximal Euclidean distance to its closest sensor.

- *Coverage degree:* In the sensing disk coverage model, coverage degree refers to a point being covered by however many sensor nodes. In area and target coverage, a space point within an area or a target is called k-covered if it is within k distinct nodes' sensing disks. Using more than one sensor to cover a point can improve the coverage robustness in the case of node failure. A similar definition can also be applied to information coverage by defining k distinct sensor sets (the intersection of any of them is an empty set), each providing the required information coverage. For brevity, in what follows a point/target is said be to covered if it is within the sensing disk of at least one sensor, i.e., 1-covered. k-coverage and information coverage of points will be explicitly stated.
- *Coverage ratio:* Coverage ratio measures how much of an area or how many targets are covered. *Complete coverage* is an important performance metric for area and target coverage. Complete area (target) coverage means that the coverage degree of every point within the sensor field (every target) should be no less than a threshold. *Sensor density* is defined as the number of sensor nodes per unit area. Complete area coverage is a very strict requirement in terms of very high sensor density and sometimes may be relaxed by using *percentile coverage* in which only the ratio between the covered area and the whole sensor field is not less than some threshold.
- *Deployment method:* Deterministic sensor deployment is the placement of sensors in desired locations such that certain objectives can be achieved, such as the minimum number of sensors deployed. Deterministic sensor placement can be applied to a small to medium sensor network in a friendly environment. When the network size is large and/or the sensor field is remote and hostile, random sensor deployment is most often used. There are two commonly used random deployment models. One is the *random uniform deployment* of λ sensors such that each of the sensors to be deployed has an equal likelihood of falling at any location in the sensor field, independently of the other sensors. The other is the *random Poisson deployment* with density λ, where the process for deploying sensors is a stationary Poisson point process and the number of sensors in any subregion is Poisson distributed and mutually independent of each other in different disjoint subregions [21]. In a randomly deployed sensor network, *critical sensor density* is an important performance metric indicating *the least* number of sensors per unit area required for complete area coverage.
- *Sensor heterogeneity:* Sensor nodes may have different sensing, processing and communication capabilities, i.e., sensors are heterogeneous. For example, some sensor nodes may be resource rich nodes that have a larger power supply and/or are equipped with better sensing, processing and communication units. In the context of the sensing disk coverage model, some nodes may cover a disk with a larger radius than those of others. A heterogeneous sensor network may also consist of both stationary and mobile sensor nodes. Stationary sensor nodes will

be at fixed locations once deployed, while mobile nodes can move around after the initial deployment. A mobile node is in general more expensive than a stationary one and is normally assumed to be resource rich. Mobility can be well exploited to maximize coverage of a mobile sensor network since mobile nodes can move to fix coverage holes. A good moving strategy for mobile nodes can help a network to quickly respond to coverage holes, to reduce signaling and moving cost, and to prolong network operation time.

- *Activity scheduling:* Scattered sensor nodes may be more numerous than the optimum in a randomly deployed sensor network. If the area covered by one sensor can also be covered by other sensors, such a sensor is considered to be redundant and can temporarily transit to an energy-saving sleep state without sacrificing coverage. Hence, *activity scheduling* mainly concerns how to decide which sensors should be in which states for how long such that certain coverage requirements can be guaranteed and network lifetime can be prolonged. In the context of coverage problems, *network lifetime* is often defined as the period from the network setup time to the time that the deployed network cannot provide adequate coverage (e.g., complete or percentile coverage). Many *distributed algorithms* and *centralized algorithms* have been proposed for scheduling sensor activity based on different assumptions and objectives. In distributed algorithms, the decision process is decentralized and in many cases localized in each individual sensor node by using information only from a few neighboring nodes. In centralized algorithms, a central controller makes all the decisions and distributes the results to sensor nodes. For large sensor networks with dynamic topologies, distributed algorithms are more often preferred than centralized ones.
- *Network connectivity:* Wireless sensor nodes communicate via their radio transceivers. Two wireless nodes are directly connected if they can transmit and receive the data to and from each other via a radio channel. Two nodes can also be connected by multi-hop transmissions with some other nodes serving as *relays*. *Complete connectivity* ensures that the sensed data of any sensor node can be transmitted to all other sensor nodes in the sensor field as well as to the sink possibly via multi-hop transmissions. In much of the WSN literature, an *omni-antenna* is assumed in the transceiver unit such that a node can reach other nodes (without error) within an area of a disk centered at itself with the radius of its *communication range*, denoted by R_c. In this case, a unit disk graph can be used to describe the network connectivity. Furthermore, the radio transmission of a sensor may be power controlled such that different communication ranges can be achieved by using different transmission powers and the maximum transmission range is referred to as the distance when the maximum transmission power is used. Sensor nodes may also be equipped with *directional antennas*, where only sensors within the radio transmission sector are connected. The transceiver unit is in general independent of the sensing unit in a sensor node, and the sensing range and the communication range of a sensor can be

with different distances. Scheduling sensor activity may also impact the network connectivity.

- *Performance metric:* With different problem settings, the performance metric may also be different for different coverage problems. The most commonly used performance metrics include the critical sensor density for complete coverage, the number of selected active nodes and the coverage ratio by these active nodes. Sometimes the *coverage intensity*, which is defined as the average time ratio between covered and uncovered periods for a point, is also used to measure how a point is covered. In energy constrained sensor networks, the network lifetime is often used to measure how well an activity scheduling algorithm performs. Network connectivity, though independently controlled by a radio transceiver, is sometimes used as a performance metric for activity scheduling. Low message overhead is often desired for distributed algorithms. Some other aspects in general algorithm design such as computation and complexity, and the difference between the optimal solution and an approximate one are also used for evaluating an algorithm.

2.3. *Area Coverage Problems*

The most studied coverage type in the literature is area coverage, where the basic research problem is how to cover every point or as many points as possible in a sensor field. Coverage ratio and the number of nodes to achieve such a coverage ratio are the two main performance metrics for area coverage. In the following sections, we take area coverage as our context to study how some classical coverage problems are formulated and solved, especially addressing their assumptions, objectives, and approaches. We classify area coverage problems into three groups:

(i) *Critical sensor density (CSD) for network deployment.* Before network deployment, one may want to know how many nodes are needed to cover all the points in a sensor field. For deterministic deployment, the basic objective is to use the least number of nodes possible. For random deployment, the basic objective is to determine the critical sensor density: whenever the number of deployed nodes is equal to or larger than this critical density times the area of the sensor field, all points in the sensor field can be covered almost surely in every random deployment.

(ii) *Sensor activity scheduling for network operation.* In a randomly deployed network, there may be some redundant nodes. This is the case when the number of deployed nodes is larger than that required by the critical density. This may also be the case in a random deployment even if its deployment density is less than the critical sensor density. One may want to determine the nodes' redundancy and to schedule their activity to prolong the network lifetime. With different assumptions — such as with or without node location information — different algorithms operate differently and have different performances.

(iii) *Node movement strategy for network redeployment.* In a sensor network with some or all nodes being mobile, one may want to move the mobile nodes to improve network coverage after the initial deployment. The moving strategy needs to consider not only the coverage ratio but also the cost of moving the mobile nodes.

In the following sections, we will present and compare some representative algorithms and protocols for each group of area coverage problems. For some problem variants, we provide brief discussions and references to these problems as further reading for interested readers.

3. Critical Sensor Density

Before network deployment, one may want to know how many sensor nodes are needed such that every point in the sensor field can be covered. Although the field of interest is normally with finite area, many mathematical analyses for the critical sensor density are carried out for an infinite area (or asymptotical analysis). When the sensing range is very small compared with the size of the sensor field, boundary effects may be neglected. We review some CSD analyses for both deterministic and random network deployment in this section.

3.1. *Deterministic Node Placement*

For deterministic sensor deployment, the most important objective is to use the least number of sensors to completely cover a sensor field when sensors can be placed at any point in the field. It is well known that putting sensor nodes at the vertices of an equilateral triangle lattice requires the least number of nodes to provide complete coverage for a plane [22]. This is illustrated in Fig. 2, where the side length of an equilateral triangle is equal to $\sqrt{3}R_s$. Obviously, if the communication range is equal to or larger than the side length, i.e., $R_c \geq \sqrt{3}R_s$, then all the nodes form a connected network. Wang *et al.* [7] compare the sensor density requirement for complete coverage based on the information coverage model and that based on the sensing disk coverage model, when using equilateral triangles/squares/hexagons (simplified as t/s/h hereafter) with nodes placed on their corners to tile a sensor field (c.f., Fig. 1). Accordingly, $(3, \varepsilon)/(4, \varepsilon)/(6, \varepsilon)$ coverage is examined for regular t/s/h tiling. When the sensing disk coverage model is used, it is very easy to show that if the center point of a regular t/s/h is covered, then all points inside the t/s/h are also covered. The corresponding sensor density requirements are therefore

$$\frac{2}{3\sqrt{3}} \times \frac{1}{R_s^2}, \quad \frac{1}{2} \times \frac{1}{R_s^2}, \quad \text{and} \quad \frac{4}{3\sqrt{3}} \times \frac{1}{R_s^2}$$

for regular triangle, square and hexagon tiling, respectively. However, how to prove the same property for high order information coverage is still an open question. Instead, we can use a grid approach to examine complete information coverage.

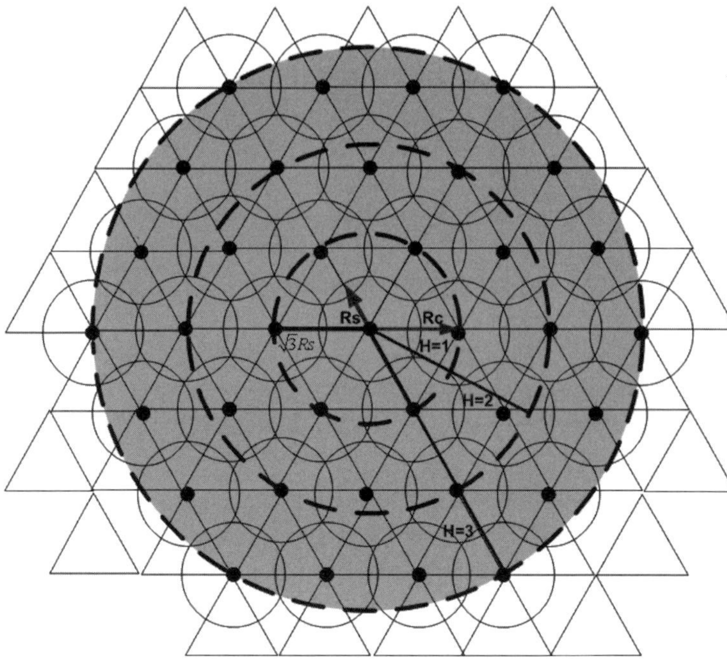

Fig. 2. Illustration of triangle tessellation for complete coverage.

A t/s/h is sampled into a grid with granularity 0.01 and if all vertices of the grid have information coverage, then complete information coverage is claimed for the t/s/h. Based on the computations, we conjecture the following.

Conjecture: *When using regular triangle, square and hexagon tiling, the sensor densities for complete* $(3, \varepsilon)/(4, \varepsilon)/(6, \varepsilon)$ *coverage are*

$$\frac{2}{3\sqrt{3}} \times \frac{1}{\sqrt[\alpha]{3}} \times \frac{1}{R_s^2}, \quad \frac{1}{2} \times \frac{1}{\sqrt[\alpha]{4}} \times \frac{1}{R_s^2}, \quad \text{and} \quad \frac{4}{3\sqrt{3}} \times \frac{1}{\sqrt[\alpha]{6}} \times \frac{1}{R_s^2}, \text{ respectively.}$$

Lyengar *et al.* [23] propose using a strip-based pattern (c.f., Fig. 3) to provide connected complete coverage: the placed nodes not only completely cover the sensor field but also form a connected network. Bai *et al.* [24] show that such a strip-based deployment is asymptotically optimal for achieving complete coverage and 1-connectivity when $R_c < \sqrt{3}R_s$ and also provide an optimal deployment to achieve complete coverage and 2-connectivity. 2-connectivity refers to being there at least two node-disjoint paths between every pair of nodes. A horizontal strip (as illustrated by the transparent disks) of nodes is formed by putting together nodes at a regular separation of $a = \min\{R_c, \sqrt{3}R_s\}$. These strips are deployed horizontally with alternate rows shifted to the right by a distance of $\alpha/2$. The vertical separation between the neighboring strips is $b = R_s + \sqrt{R_s^2 - a^2/4}$. When $R_c < \sqrt{3}R_s$, these horizontal strips are not connected and some additional nodes are placed as the vertical strips (as illustrated by the shaded disks) to connect

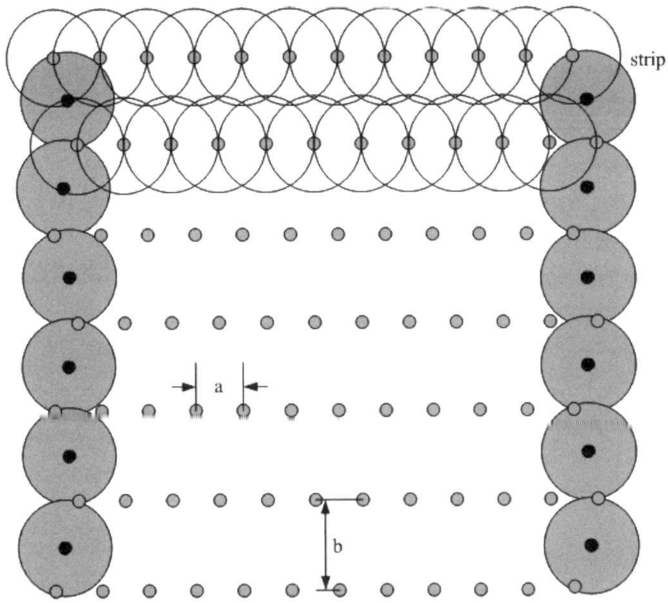

Fig. 3. Strip-based deployment pattern to achieve complete coverage and two-connectivity.

these horizontal strips. When $R_c \geq \sqrt{3}R_s$, such vertical strips are not needed. Bai *et al.* [24] also provide an analysis on connected coverage for regular t/s/h tessellations and rhombus tessellation with general values of R_c/R_s and establish the following claims. In terms of the number of nodes for providing connected coverage, when $R_c/R_s \leq 1.14$, hexagon tessellation is the best among the four; when $1.14 \leq R_c/R_s \leq \sqrt{2}$, the square pattern is the best; when $\sqrt{2} \leq R_c/R_s \leq \sqrt{3}$, rhombus tessellation is the best; and when $\sqrt{3} \leq R_c/R_s$, triangle tessellation is the best.

3.1.1. *Further Reading*

Alam and Haas [25] investigate the minimum number of nodes for complete coverage in 3D space. They suggest that the use of truncated octahedral tessellation to completely cover a 3D space requires the least number of nodes compared to that using hexagonal prism, rhombic dodecahedron and cube tessellations.

Sen *et al.* [26] introduce another constraint for the minimum number of nodes: the distance between any two nodes should be no less than a certain threshold. This constraint is motivated from work on the health sensing applications since nodes may emit heat and invalidate temperature measurement is from a human body sensor network.

Wang *et al.* [27] consider the problem of node placement for arbitrary-shaped fields possibly with obstacles. Such scenarios often occur in indoor environments. Their approach is to partition the sensor field into smaller subfields based on

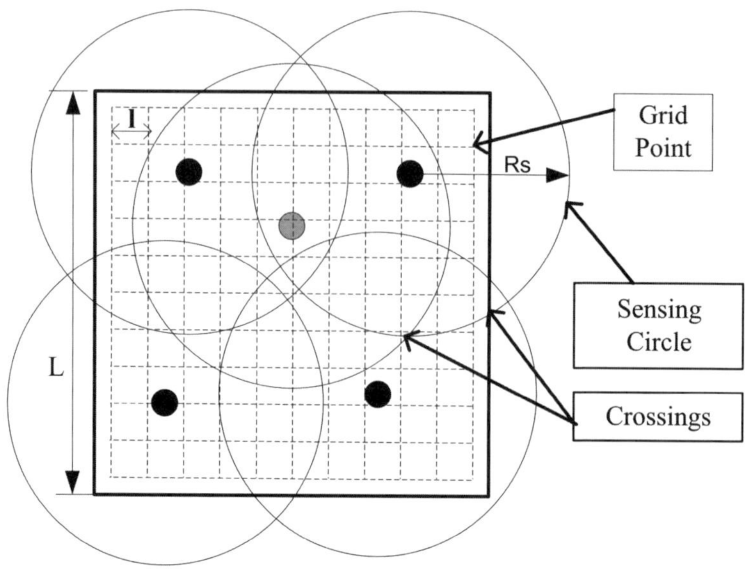

Fig. 4. Illustration of using crossing and grip approaches in CSD analysis.

the shape of the field and the obstacles in the field and to apply the strip-based deployment for each subfield.

3.2. *Random Node Deployment*

Random node deployment is often needed when the sensor field is remote and/or hostile. For example, sensor nodes can be scattered from an aircraft. Given the area of the sensor field, the critical sensor density helps to decide the least number of nodes that are needed to completely cover the sensor field for every random deployment. The analysis of CSD normally starts by providing bounds for the complete coverage probability of a square region $\Re$ with finite area (i.e., $\|\Re\|$ is finite) and then using asymptotical analysis to provide the relationship between the CSD and the area (or the side length) of the square.

For a point z within the square $\Re$, let $\aleph(z)$ denote a function that indicates whether the point z is covered, i.e.,

$$\aleph(z) = \begin{cases} 1 & \text{if } z \text{ is not within at least one sensing disk,} \\ 0 & \text{otherwise.} \end{cases} \tag{3}$$

The vacancy V within $\Re$ is defined to be the area that is not covered:

$$V = V(\Re) \equiv \int_{\Re} \aleph(z)\, dz. \tag{4}$$

As shown by Hall (see Theorem 3.3 and remarks in Ref. 21), no vacancy within $\Re$ [i.e., $V(\Re) = 0$] implies the complete coverage of $\Re$. Therefore, it is desirable to provide bounds for the probability of no vacancy, i.e., to bound $\Pr\{V = 0\}$.

To do so, the first step is to establish the probability that an arbitrary point is not covered, i.e., $\Pr\{\aleph(z) = 1\}$, and then to bound the probability of no vacancy based on $\Pr\{\aleph(z) = 1\}$ from some special points in the field. In the literature, two approaches have been used to bound $\Pr\{V = 0\}$ (or $\Pr\{V > 0\}$). One is to exploit the property of the sensing disk model [21, 28]; the other is based on a grid approach [29].

In the first approach, a *crossing* is defined as the intersection point of the outmost circles of two sensing disks (called the *sensing perimeter*) or the intersection point of a sensing perimeter and the boundary of the sensor field $\Re$. A crossing is said to be covered if it is an interior point of at least one disk. Note that a crossing is not considered to be covered by its driving sensing perimeters. Hall claims that the probability of a vacancy can be divided into three parts (Theorem 3.11 in Ref. 21):

$$\Pr\{V > 0\} = p_1 + p_2 + p_3,$$

where

$$\begin{aligned} p_1 &\equiv \Pr\{\text{no disks centered within } \Re\}, \\ p_2 &\equiv \Pr\{\text{at least one disk centered within } \Re, \\ &\quad \text{but none of these disks intersects any other disk}\}, \\ p_3 &\equiv \Pr\{\Re \text{ not covered, at least one disk centered within } \Re, \\ &\quad \text{and at least one of these disks intersects with another disk}\}. \end{aligned}$$

It is easy to give upper bounds for p_1 and p_2. To upper bound p_3, the Markov inequality (see e.g., Ref. 30, page 263) can be applied. Note that p_3 is based on the property of disk coverage. By such decomposition, complete area coverage is connected with only a few discrete crossings. Let $\Re$ be a unit square and suppose that the random deployment is a Poisson point process with intensity λ. Hall provides both the lower and upper bounds for $\Pr\{V > 0\}$ as follows:

Theorem 1 (Hall [21], Theorem 3.11). *Let $\alpha = \pi R_s^2$. For each $\lambda \geq 1$ and $0 < R_s \leq 1/2$,*

$$0.05 \min\{1, (1 + a\lambda^2)e^{-a\lambda}\} < \Pr\{V > 0\} < 3 \min\{1, (1 + a\lambda^2)e^{-a\lambda}\}. \tag{5}$$

Wang et al. (see Ref. 31 Theorem 4) propose an extended counterpart of Hall's decomposition: a convex field is complete k-covered if (i) there exist crossings within the field and (ii) all these crossings are k-covered. Zhao and Hou [28] follow the same decomposition method by Hall to provide bounds for the probability of k-vacancy (i.e., the probability that there exists a point that is not k-covered). Mo et al. [32] also consider the randomness of the sensing range by modeling it as a random variable with mean R_s and with some variance.

In the grid-based approach to bound $\Pr\{V > 0\}$, a grid with side length denoted by l is created within the sensor field. Complete area coverage is connected to completely cover all grid points. The justification for using the grid approach is based on the following claim: *If all grid points can be covered by disks with radius R_s, then complete area coverage can be achieved by using disks with radius $R' \geq R_s + l/\sqrt{2}$.* This claim is also valid for k-coverage (see e.g., Ref. 29, Lemma 3.1). After creating the grid, the probability that all grid points are covered can be lower bounded by using Janson's Inequality (see, e.g., Ref. 33, Theorem 8.1.1) as follows. Let Z denote the set of grid points. The probability that all grid points are covered is lower bounded by the product of all grid point coverage probabilities:

$$\Pr\{\wedge_{z\in Z}(\aleph(z)=0)\} \geq \prod_{z\in Z} \Pr\{\aleph(z)=0\}.$$

After providing bounds for $\Pr\{V > 0\}$, asymptotical analysis can be applied to provide the relationship between the sensor density λ and a scaling factor of the sensor field (e.g., the square side length L). When doing such asymptotical analysis, care must be taken to account for the *boundary effect.* The *torus convention* assumes that each disk protruding one side of the square enters the square again from the opposite side (see e.g., Ref. 21, page 23) and can be used to eliminate considerations of boundary effects. Zhang and Hou [28] apply the torus convention to derive the asymptotic k-coverage. Without boundary effects, the asymptotic k-coverage requires that the sensor density λ grows with the side length according to

$$\lambda = \log(L^2) + (k+1)\log\log(L^2) + c(L)$$

with $\lim_{L\to\infty} c(L) = \infty$. With boundary effects, Wan and Yi [34] derive the asymptotic k-coverage requirement:

$$\lambda = \log(L^2) + 2k\log\log(L^2) + c(L)$$

with $\lim_{L\to\infty} c(L) = \infty$. Kumar *et al.* [29] take the asymptotic analysis further by considering the case that each sensor is active with a certain probability independent of the others, and arrive at results similar to those in Refs. 28 and 34.

The above CSD analysis provides the required sensor density to achieve complete coverage. In some cases, one would also like to know the average vacancy of a given sensor density. To find the expected value of vacancy, we can use Fubini's theorem and exchange the order of integral and expectation, i.e.,

$$E[V] = \int_{\Re} E[\aleph(z)]dz = \int_{\Re} \Pr\{\aleph(z)=1\}dz = \|\Re\| \Pr\{\aleph(z)=1\}.$$

Compared to the probability of no vacancy $\Pr\{V=0\}$, the average vacancy $\mathrm{E}[V]$ is easy to obtain. For example, in a random Poisson deployment, an arbitrary point is not covered if there is no sensor in the disk area centered at this point with radius R_s, i.e., $\Pr\{\aleph(z)=1\} = e^{-\lambda\pi R_s^2}$. Furthermore, the average vacancy can reflect the coverage in a finite area well, and $E[V=0]$ also implies $V=0$ with a probability of one. Liu and Towsley [35] argue that the derivation of the average vacancy is

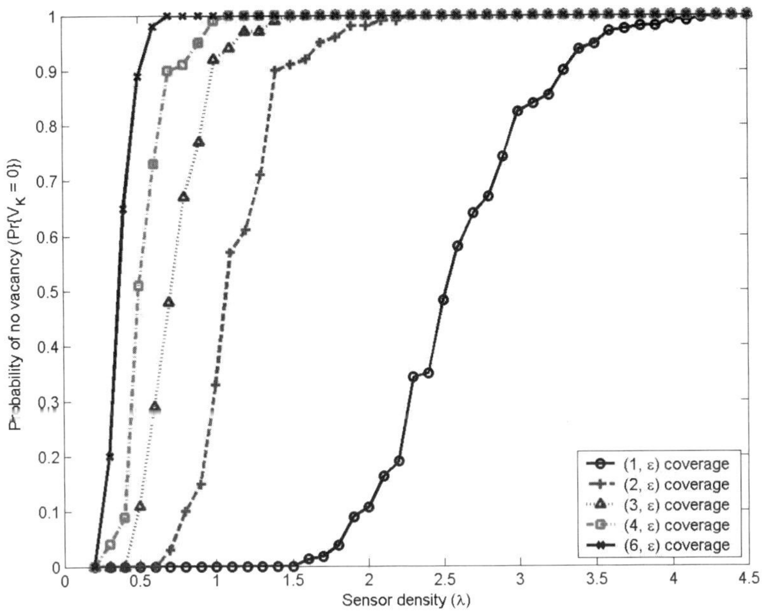

Fig. 5. Comparison of sensor density and average probability of vacancy.

independent of $\Re$ and hence the average area coverage ratio can be simply obtained by $1 - e^{-\lambda \pi R_s^2}$. Wang *et al.* [36] provide an upper bound for the probability that an arbitrary point is not (K, ε)-covered based on the property of information coverage. They also define the critical density for average (K, ε) coverage as the smallest λ such that the average (K, ε) vacancy [the area not (K, ε)-covered] is equal to a predefined threshold.

Figure 5 plots simulation results comparing the sensor density and the average probability of vacancy. It can be observed that there is a *phase transition* gap determined by two density values, λ_l and λ_h. λ_l denotes the largest sensor density such that for any sensor density $\lambda \leq \lambda_l$ the probability of no vacancy is zero almost surely; and λ_h denotes the smallest sensor density such that for any $\lambda \geq \lambda_h$ the probability of no vacancy is one almost surely, i.e., the critical sensor density for complete coverage. In other words, if the area of the sensor field is $\|\Re\|$ and at least $\lambda_h \|\Re\|$ sensor nodes are randomly scattered, then the sensor field can be completely covered almost surely in every random deployment. Note that this does not exclude the situation that $\Re$ may also be completely covered in some deployments when the number of deployed nodes is less than $\lambda_h \|\Re\|$ but larger than $\lambda_l \|\Re\|$.

3.2.1. *Further Reading*

Besides the above CSD analysis for complete coverage based on the sensing disk coverage model and the information coverage model, there are also other CSD analyses [35, 37, 38] based on other sensor coverage models. Liu and Towsley [35] and Adlakha and Srivastava [37] consider the critical sensor density required to achieve a certain detection probability based on the attenuated sensor coverage intensity model [14]. Liu and Towsley [35] claim the existence of a critical sensor density above which the detection probability is one almost surely. According to Adlakha and Srivastava [37], the number of sensors to be deployed in a field $\Re$ is of the order $O(\|\Re\|/R_s^2)$ such that the detection probability for a moving target along a straight line is 98% or above. Ma and Liu [38] consider the coverage problem in a directional sensor network and derive the minimal number of directional sensors in a sensor field required to achieve a predefined coverage ratio.

Lazos and Roovendran [39] study a counterpart of the CSD problem: Given an arbitrary sensor field $\Re$ of finite size and with N deployed sensors each with an arbitrary shape sensing area, what is the fraction of $\Re$ being k-covered? This is equivalent to computing the probability that an arbitrary point P in $\Re$ is covered by at least k sensors, $\Pr(P \text{ is } k\text{-covered})$, which is computed by applying the results from *integral geometry* [40]. Since $\Pr(P \text{ is } k\text{-covered})$ is only dependent on the volume of each individual sensor's sensing area and the sensing field area as well as their perimeters, their analytical method can be applied to arbitrary node deployment distributions and arbitrary individual sensing shapes.

4. Sensor Activity Scheduling

As discussed in the previous section, if the number of deployed sensor nodes in one random deployment is higher than that required by the critical sensor density, then this deployment can achieve complete coverage almost surely. In some cases, the number of deployed sensor nodes may even be much higher than the optimum to provide a certain robustness for the deployed network. After sensor nodes have been deployed, there might be some redundant sensors whose covered area can also be covered by other sensors. Node activity scheduling can thus be used to schedule nodes to be activated alternatively such that the network operation time may be prolonged and certain area coverage requirements can still be met. Sensor activity scheduling has been intensively researched in the literature. Although these scheduling schemes are different from the point of view of their assumptions, objectives and approaches, they all need to answer the following question: *How does not determine which sensors should be active at what time and for how long?*

The first part of the question is the focus of this section and we will review some representative schemes. The second part of the question can be approached in two ways. One is to let each active sensor operate until it depletes its energy. After that, selection of active sensors is performed again. The other way is to let each active sensor operate for a fixed time interval and re-selection of active sensors is then performed at the beginning of each interval.

The basic objective of sensor activity scheduling is to guarantee a certain coverage ratio by the selected active sensors. Two types of activity scheduling can be classified. One is to preserve complete coverage by the selected active sensors. Obviously, this normally requires the assumption that the deployed sensor nodes can provide complete coverage for a given sensor field. The other allows that the area of the sensor field covered by the selected active sensors can be less than that by all the deployed sensors. Let $S = \{s_1, s_2, \ldots\}$ and $S_a \subseteq S$ denote the set of all the deployed sensors and the set of selected active sensors, respectively. The set of active sensors is also called a sensor *cover*. Let $A(s)$ denote the area covered by a sensor s. Let $R(S) = \bigcup_{s \in S} A(s)$ and $R(S_a) = \bigcup_{s \in S_a} A(s)$ denote the area of the sensor field covered by all the deployed sensors and by the selected active sensors, respectively. Then preserving complete coverage requires that $R(S_a) = R(S)$, while preserving percentage coverage requires that $R(S_a)/R(S) \geq \delta$, where $0 < \delta \leq 1$.

Another objective of sensor active scheduling is to select the least possible number of active sensors. If the grid approach to approximate complete coverage is used (c.f., Fig. 4 and Sec. 3.2) and preserving complete coverage is required, then the problem of selecting the least number of active nodes is the Set Covering Problem (see e.g., Ref. 41, page 1033), which is NP-complete: every grid point is covered by at least one element in S and all grid points are covered by S. Preserving complete coverage requires that all grid points should also be covered by $S_a \subseteq S$ and the problem of finding such an S_a with the minimum size is the Set Covering Problem. A greedy heuristic with polynomial time (see Ref. 41, page 1035) can be used to find a subset of S to completely cover all grid points with bounded approximations compared to an optimal solution. In the literature, simulations are often used to compare the number of selected active sensors using different algorithms. Many sensor activity scheduling algorithms also exploit sensing disk properties to determine a redundant sensor.

There may be some other objectives when designing a sensor activity scheduling algorithm. For example, selected active sensors may also be required to form a connected network; the network lifetime can be maximized by the scheduling algorithm; and computation complexities, communication overhead and distributed algorithms are also desirable design objectives. The network lifetime in our context is defined as the time from the network setup time to the time that a certain coverage requirement cannot be satisfied. Generally speaking, selecting the minimum number of sensing active nodes helps to prolong the network lifetime. But care must be taken since data processing and dissemination also consume energy and impact network lifetime. Furthermore, when preserving complete coverage is required, sensor activity scheduling may not lead to an extension of the network lifetime. For example, consider the case that a small area in a completely covered sensor field is only covered by one sensor. To preserve complete coverage, this sensor has to be active all the time and the network lifetime in this example cannot be prolonged via activity scheduling. This may be addressed by using the percentile coverage requirement. In the following subsections, we review some representative scheduling schemes.

4.1. *Preserving Complete Coverage*

An important issue in designing a scheduling algorithm for preserving complete coverage is to determine whether the area covered by one sensor can also be completely covered by its neighboring active nodes. If so, then this node is redundant and can go into an energy-saving sleep state. Either the grid approach or the properties of the sensing disks can be used for redundancy checking.

In the grid approach, the *greedy set cover* algorithm (see e.g., Ref. 41, page 1035) is a rather canonical algorithm: at first, all nodes are set to the sleep state and all grid points are not covered. At each selection step, a node is selected as active if it covers the maximum number of uncovered grid points among all unselected nodes. The algorithm ends when all grid points are covered. Obviously, the objective of this algorithm is to select the least number of active sensors in each selection process. Yan *et al.* [42] consider the problem of how to determine the active duration for each sensor such that all grid points can be covered in any time instant by active sensors. They divide the time line into consecutive intervals of equal length. Each sensor first randomly determines the starting time and the duration of its active duration in one interval for its covered grid points. It then adjusts its active schedule based on the schedules broadcast from its neighboring nodes such that every grid point within its sensing disk can be covered by at least one sensor in each interval.

When taking network lifetime into design consideration, one may want to select a series of disjoint sensor covers, each providing complete coverage and these covers are activated alternatively. Two sensor covers S_1 and S_2 are disjoint if $S_1 \cap S_2 = \phi$. When only sensing energy consumption is considered, the network lifetime can be computed as the sum of the operation times of each such sensor cover. Slijepcevic and Potkonjak [43] propose a heuristic to find such a series of disjoint sensor covers. They divide the sensor field into some subfields such that every point of a subfield is covered by the same set of sensors. A heuristic called the most-constrained and least-constraining is used to select active sensors to form a cover according to their priorities. A sensor has higher priority if it covers the critical subfield (the grid points in such a subfield are covered by a minimal number of sensors), covers a high number of uncovered subfields, covers sparsely covered subfields; and does not cover subfields redundantly. Cardei and Du [44] look at the problem of finding the maximum number of such disjoint covers as a maximum-flow problem which is then formulated as mixed integer programming. They propose a heuristic based on the results from the mixed integer programming and show their algorithm can generate more disjoint covers than that generated by using the Slijepcevic and Potkonjak heuristic [43].

Using a grid to approximate area coverage is a general method as it does not restrict the sensing coverage model used by individual sensors. Instead, it is necessary to specify the coverage relationship between each grid point and each sensor, which, however, may be computationally complicated, time consuming and storage intensive. For the sensing disk coverage model, some of its geometric properties can be exploited and computation complexity and storage requirements may be greatly reduced.

Tian and Georganans [45] propose a concept of *sponsored sector* for checking redundancy. A sensor s_2 is called a sponsor to sensor s_1 if $d(s_1, s_2) \leq R_s$, where $d(s_1, s_2)$ denotes the Euclidean distance between s_1 and s_2. The sponsored sector by sensor s_2 to sensor s_1 is the sector area of s_1 within the intersection lens of the two sensing disks, as shown by the shaded sector in Fig. 6. If the sensing disk of sensor s can also be covered by the sponsored sectors from its sponsors, then sensor s is eligible to be inactive. In Fig. 6, sensor s_1 is eligible to go into a sleep state.

Huang *et al.* [46] propose using *perimeter coverage* to check field complete coverage and sensor redundancy. Two sensing disks intersect each other and have two crossings if $d(s_1, s_2) < 2R_s$ and each is called a sensing neighbor to the other. As illustrated in Fig. 7, sensor s_1 has three sensing neighbors. The arc p_1p_2 is the segment of s_2's sensing perimeter within s_1's sensing disk and is covered by sensors s_3 and s_4. For all sensing neighbors of sensor s, if their respective arcs within s's sensing disk are also covered by s's sensing neighbors other than s, then s's sensing disk is covered and s is eligible to go into a sleep state. In Fig. 7, sensor s_1 is eligible to go into a sleep state.

Xing *et al.* [31] propose a Coverage Configuration Protocol (CCP) which applies *crossing coverage* to determine redundant sensors (c.f., Sec. 3.2 for definition of crossing). As shown in Fig. 8, the crossing p_1 within s_1's sensing disk is created by

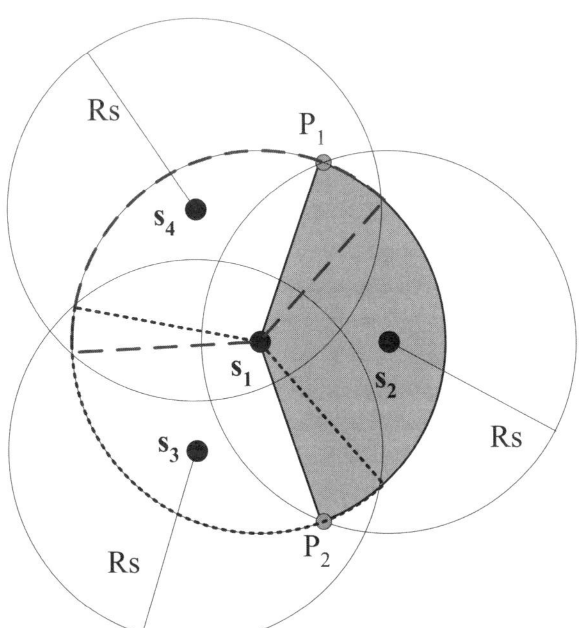

Fig. 6. Sponsored coverage for checking redundancy.

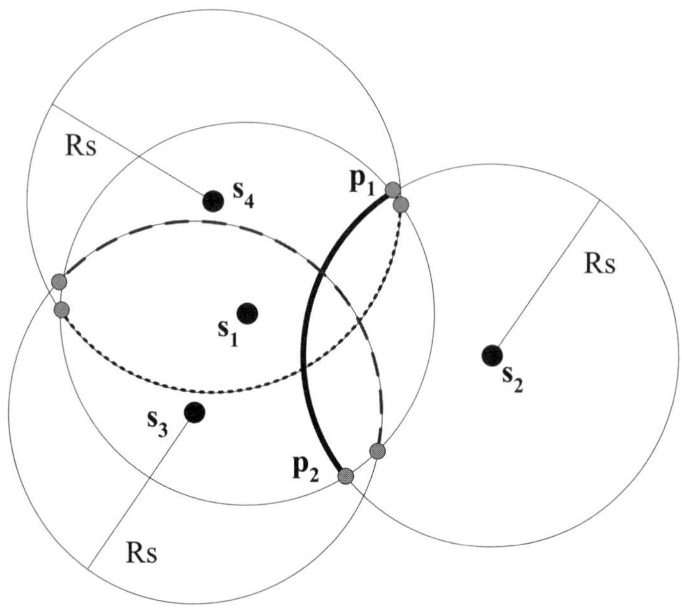

Fig. 7. Perimeter coverage for checking redundancy.

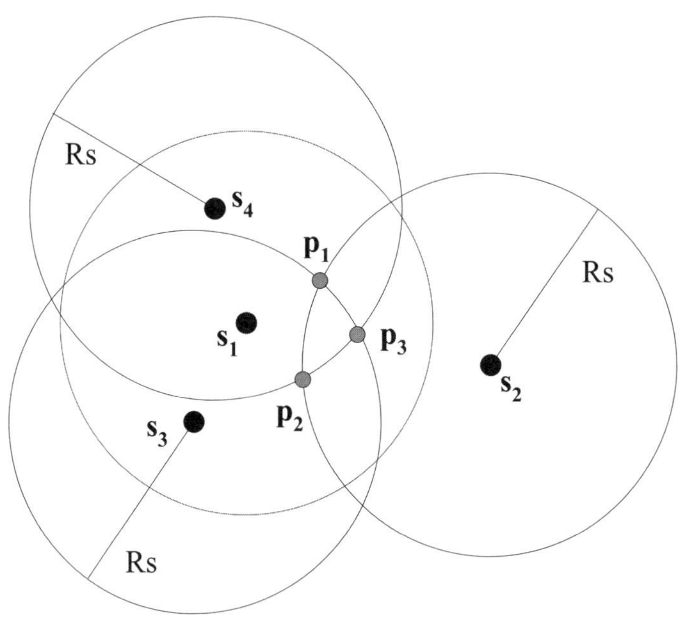

Fig. 8. Crossing coverage for checking redundancy.

s_2's sensing perimeter and s_3's sensing perimeter, and is covered by s_4's sensing disk. If all crossings within sensor s's sensor disk are covered, then s's sensing disk is covered and s is eligible to be inactive. In Fig. 8, sensor s_1 is eligible.

Carbunar [47] propose using *Voronoi diagram vertices and intersections* to check redundancy. A Voronoi diagram for N sensors $s_1, s_2, \ldots, s_N$ in a plane is defined as the subdivision of the plane into N cells for each sensor, such that the distance between any point in a cell and the sensor of the cell is closer than that between this point and other sensors. When checking sensor s redundancy, a Voronoi diagram is first constructed for it from other sensors other than itself, i.e., sensor s is excluded when constructing his Voronoi diagram. Given the constructed Voronoi diagram for sensor s, the points for checking its redundancy are those Voronoi vertices within s's sensing disk (point VV_1 in Fig. 9) and the intersection points between those Voronoi edges and s's sensing perimeter (points $VIP_{1,2,3}$ in Fig. 9). If these points are covered by s's neighbors, then sensor s is redundant and is eligible to enter a sleep state. In Fig. 9, sensor s_1 is eligible.

Based on a given redundancy check, a distributed sensor activity scheduling protocol can be established. For example, one can let all sensors be active initially and then let each sensor perform its redundancy check. After a sensor has determined its own redundancy, it may choose to go into a sleep state. When this

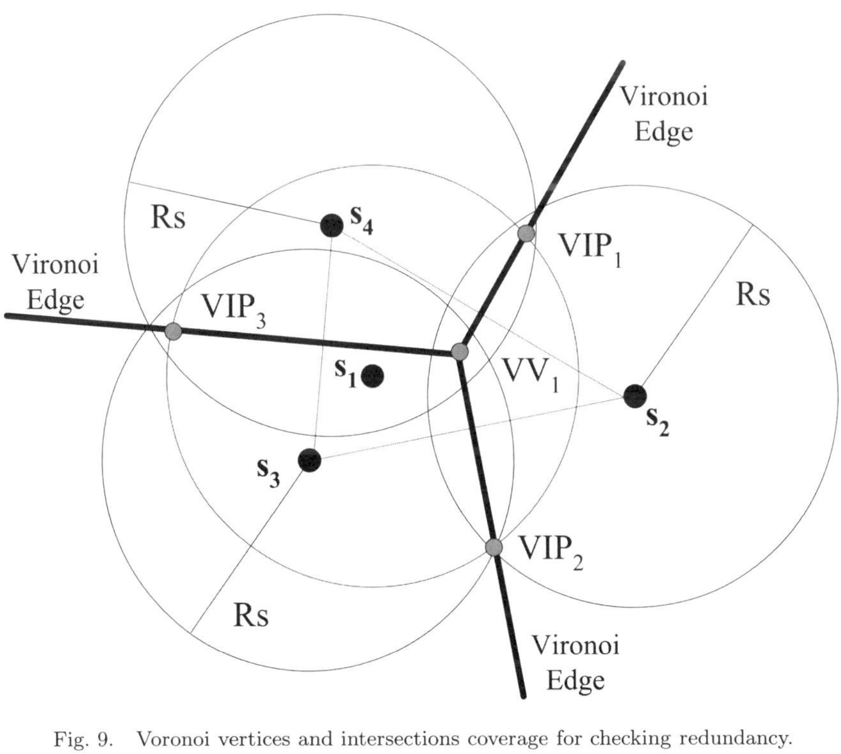

Fig. 9. Voronoi vertices and intersections coverage for checking redundancy.

is done in a distributed manner, care must be taken to avoid creating a coverage hole. Since a sensor's activity state is dependent on its neighboring node's state, a coverage hole may appear if two activity dependent sensors sleep at the same time. For example, in Fig. 6, if s_2 is also redundant, then s_1 and s_2 cannot both be in the sleep state; otherwise, some points only covered by s_1 or s_2 will not be covered. This problem can be mitigated or avoided by using a random backoff mechanism with fine-tuned parameters for asynchronous state decisions and carefully designed message exchanges.

The counterpart to letting redundant sensors sequentially become inactive is activating proper sensors sequentially. Zhang and Hou [48] propose an Optimal Geographical Density Control (OGDC) scheduling scheme based on a triangle tessellation process. As discussed previously and shown in Fig. 2, the optimal distance between two sensors is $\sqrt{3}R_s$ if a sensor field is tiled by equilateral triangles. In OGDC, the time line is divided into consecutive rounds with a decision phase at the beginning of each round. In the decision phase, a residual energy based random volunteer selection is first performed and then the starting active node broadcasts its information. Among nodes having received such a message, the one that is not redundant and with the minimum deviation to the desired direction and angle required by the already active nodes will have the largest chance of becoming active next. The desired distance and angle are computed to approximate the optimal triangle tessellation as much as possible. The redundancy check in OGDC may be based on either a grid approach or a crossing coverage approach.

Using triangle tessellation to sequentially activate sensors can also be applied to other sensing models (e.g., the sensing attenuation model [15, 16]). The main challenge is to determine the maximum side length of an equilateral triangle such that every point within such a triangle satisfies the coverage requirement, which Hefeeda and Ahmadi [49] call the maximum separation between any two active nodes. They derive the maximum separation for the sensing attenuation model. Furthermore, they also propose letting a newly active node activate six of its surrounding nodes to form a hexagon to speed up the triangle tessellation process.

The above redundancy check techniques and sequential activation require that each node knows its own location coordinates as well as those of its neighbors. Wu and Ssu [50], Zhang *et al.* [51] and Younis *et al.* [52] propose using the nodes' distance information instead of their locations to select active nodes. The nodes' distance information can be obtained from the received signal strength based on an attenuation radio transmission model [50] or estimated from the number of neighboring nodes given that the deployment density is known to every node [51]. The basic idea is to guarantee that all points within a triangle are covered by the three active sensors on the triangle vertices. An inactive node needs to perform a triangle self-test to determine whether its surrounding triangle (formed by three active sensors) contains an uncovered point. If so, then this inactive sensor becomes active in order to fix the coverage hole.

4.1.1. *Further Readings*

Variants of the greedy set cover heuristic use sophisticated cost or profit functions besides using the number of newly covered grid points. For example, Kalidindi and Kannan [53] include the residual energy and Wang *et al.* [54] include not only residual energy but also transmission energy consumption into a profit function to select the next node with maximum profit.

Sanli and Cam [55] propose a scheduling scheme based on a hexagonal grid approach where the side length of a hexagon is set to $R_s/2$. If any one of the sensors within a hexagon is active, then all points within the hexagon are covered.

Du and Lin [56] propose an active schedule allocation scheme similar to Yan *et al.* [42] for heterogeneous networks, where resource rich nodes form clusters and decide active durations based on the grid point coverage degree. Huang *et al.* [57] extend the work of Yan *et al.* [42] to set the nodes' active schedule. They reduce the computation complexity by only considering activity schedules for crossings other than for all grid points.

Boukerche *et al.* extend the idea of using sponsored coverage for the redundancy check to be energy aware [58] and to the case of irregular polygon sensing coverage model [59].

Huang and Tseng [60] propose using a *parameter test* to determine whether a sensor field is completely k-covered: the sensor field is k-covered if and only if the sensing perimeter of each sensor is k-covered by its neighbors. Note that the problem of complete area coverage checking is different from the problem of complete sensor coverage checking. The parameter test cannot guarantee that a sensor is also k-covered. Tezcan and Wang [61] introduce two more tests together with a parameter test for redundancy checking.

Huang *et al.* [62] extend their work on perimeter coverage for checking node redundancy in 2D space to 3D space. Ahmed *et al.* [17] extend the idea of checking perimeter coverage to locally determine complete coverage based on their probabilistic coverage model (c.f., Sec. 2.1.1).

Using crossing coverage for redundancy checking may not be valid when sensors have different sensing ranges. Lu *et al.* [63] propose including sampling points for the redundancy check for sensors with different sensing ranges. A sampling point for sensor s is selected from a sensing perimeter that is within the s's sensing disk but does not intersect with any other sensing perimeters.

So and Ye [64] propose a higher order Voronoi diagram based algorithm to check complete k-coverage, which is more computation efficient than the perimeter coverage based algorithm [60]. A kth order Voronoi diagram $V_k(S)$ for the deployed sensor set S is first created. So and Ye prove that it is sufficient to only check (i) the vertices of $V_k(S)$, (ii) the intersections between $V_k(S)$ and the field boundaries, and (iii) the corners of the sensor field to answer the yes/no question of complete k-coverage.

Shang and Shi [65] propose several scheduling schemes to improve the OGDC by relaxing the coverage requirements by replacing location requirements with distance requirements alone and by considering adjustable sensing ranges. Wu and Yang [66] also consider improving the OGDC by using adjustable sensing ranges to further minimize the overlapped area.

4.2. *Preserving Percentile Coverage*

As discussed previously, preserving complete coverage is a very strict requirement and may not lead to an increase in the network lifetime. Sometimes, designing a scheduling algorithm to preserve statistical percentile coverage may be of practical interest; although coverage ratio may be at the cost of some slight loss, the network lifetime may be significantly improved [28]. Furthermore, when complete coverage is not enforced, a sensor may not be required to check its redundancy and hence computation complexity and storage requirements can also be greatly reduced.

Random Independent Sleeping (RIS) might be the simplest sensor activity scheduling scheme where a sensor schedules its activities independent of other sensors (see e.g., Refs. 67 and 68). One approach to implementing an RIS scheme is to use asynchronous decisions as follows [67]. The time line is divided into rounds of equal length T for each sensor node but the beginning time of the very first round is different across nodes, i.e., the round is not synchronized across nodes. At the beginning of a round, a sensor decides its active state with the duration given by $p \times T$ and the remainder of the round is in the sleep state. Suppose that N nodes are uniformly deployed in the sensor field. The expected number of active nodes at any time in RIS is $p \times N$ and they are distributed uniformly. Although RIS may lead to a low coverage ratio (when p is small) or select more active sensors (when p is large), its simplicity may still lend it a lot of practical usage: it requires no node location information, no computation, no time synchronization, and no message overhead. Tian and Georganas [68] also analyze the relationship between p and the coverage loss.

Another approach to implementing an RIS scheme is using synchronous decisions as follows. The time line is divided into rounds of equal length and the starting time of every round is considered to be synchronized across nodes. Two versions can be implemented following this synchronized decision approach. One is to, at the beginning of each round, let each node decide its active state for one round with probability p [69]. This method produces non-disjoint sets of active nodes in different rounds, that is, the intersection between the active node set produced in round T and that produced in round $T + 1$ is not an empty set. Choi and Das [69] analyze the relationship between the average active nodes $p \times N$ and the expected coverage ratio to determine how many nodes are required to be active in each round. Another version is to divide the deployed nodes into K disjoint sets to be activated alternatively [70]. Each node randomly generates an integer between 1 and K to decide which set it belongs to. Abrams *et al.* [70] show that given K, the average covered area by the random cover selection is a $1 - 1/e$ approximation of an optimal one.

RIS can only provide statistical sensing coverage. In RIS, a point that is within n sensors' sensing disks may be covered for some time interval (t_1, t_2) and not covered at all for another time interval (t_2, t_3). This can be modeled as an *alternative renewal process* with two states: k-covered and not k-covered. The probability or the distribution of such a point being k-covered is important in detection and tracking applications. Let $Y^{(k)}$ and $Z^{(k)}$ be two random variables denoting the length of the k-covered and not k-covered period s, respectively. Hua and Yum [71] derive the expectations for $Y^{(k)}$ and $Z^{(k)}$ as follows:

$$E[Y^{(k)}] = \frac{1 - \sum_{i=0}^{k-1}(n/i)p^i(1-p)^{n-i}}{n(n/k-1)p^k(1-p)^{n-k+1}}, \quad k = 1, \ldots, n,$$

and

$$E[Z^{(k)}] = \frac{\sum_{i=0}^{k-1}(n/i)p^i(1-p)^{n-i}}{n(n/k-1)p^k(1-p)^{n-k+1}}, \quad k = 1, \ldots, n.$$

Hsian and Liu [72] analyze the tail distribution of the probability that a point within n sensors' sensing disks cannot be covered by any active sensor.

Besides completely random self-scheduling like RIS, a sensor can schedule its activity based on some knowledge about its neighbors such as their activity states. Ye *et al.* [73] propose a *Probing Environment and Adaptive Sleeping* (PEAS) scheduling scheme where the basic idea is letting a sensor decide to become active if no other sensors are active within its probing area. In PEAS, each sensor sleeps for an exponentially distributed duration. When a sensor wakes up, it probes whether there exists any other active sensor within a disk centered at itself with a radius of its *probing range*. Any active sensor that hears this probe should reply. And if at least one reply is received by this probing sensor, then it enters the sleep mode again for another random period of time. Otherwise, it enters the active state till its death. Evidently, the probing range controls the density of the active nodes and the higher the probing range, the less the coverage.

Wang *et al.* [74] propose a *Layered Diffusion based Coverage Control* (LDCC) scheduling scheme where the hop count is exploited to schedule node activity. As shown Fig. 2, hop count is a relative distance measure to a hop count originator, normally the sink. Layered diffusion refers to a message exchange process in which messages of particular types are likely to be the first generated by the hop count originator or the nodes with small hop count to the nodes in a ring farthest from the originator. The basic idea of LDCC is that the node with hop count zero first activates itself and then broadcasts an active message. Any node sets a timer when receiving such a message and a node becomes inactive if it receives two active messages from nodes with the same hop count as itself.

The number of active neighbors can also be exploited for sensor activity scheduling [68, 75]. If the number of active neighbors of a sensor exceeds a given threshold value, then this sensor enters an inactive state. Gao *et al.* [75] analyze the problem of how many *sensing neighbors* [defined by $d(s, s_i) \leq R_s$] are needed for a sensor s to completely cover its sensing disk. They show that at least three sensing neighbors are needed to completely cover a sensing disk. In a uniformly random sensor network, the probability of no vacancy within a sensing disk is bounded above and below according to

$$1 - n0.609^{n-1} \leq \Pr\{V = 0\} \leq 1 - n0.609^{n-1} + \frac{n(n-1)}{2}(0.276)^{n-1},$$

where n is the number of sensing neighbors. Furthermore, the average percentage of a sensing disk covered by the sensing neighbors is not smaller than $1 - 0.609^n - (n.6 - 0.109)0.109^{n-1}$. Wu *et al.* [76] also propose a Lightweight Deployment Aware Scheduling (LDAS) scheme based on their analysis.

Some scheduling schemes approximate area coverage by node coverage [77–79]. The basic idea behind these schemes is that if deployed sensors are dense enough, area coverage may be approximated by guaranteeing that all deployed sensors are covered. One reason to do so is to exploit the graph properties of the sensor network. Suppose that the sensor network is represented by an undirected unit disk graph $G = (S, E)$, where S is the set of deployed sensors and E is the set of edges. A *dominating set* is a subset $S_{ds} \subseteq S$ such that all vertices not in S_{ds} have at least one neighbor in S_{ds}. Two dominating sets S^1_{ds} and S^2_{ds} are disjoint if $S^1_{ds} \cap S^2_{ds} = \phi$. A *minimal dominating set* is a dominating set which cannot be a dominating set any longer if any vertex is removed from it. Cardei *et al.* [77] convert activity scheduling to the problem of finding the maximal number of disjoint dominating sets. Yang *et al.* [78] define the k-coverage set problem to find a subset $S_{kds} \subseteq S$ such that each sensor in S is dominated (covered) by at least k different sensors in S_{kds} and the number of sensors in S_{kds} is minimized. They further formulate it as an integer programming problem and provide a cluster-based heuristic to solve it. Zheng *et al.* [79] analyze the coverage property of minimal dominating sets. Let $R(S)$ and $R(S_{mds})$ denote the size of the area covered by the sensors in S and the sensors in a minimum dominating set, respectively. Zheng *et al.* [79] show that

$$\frac{R(S)}{R(S_{mds})} \geq \frac{R_s^2}{(R_s + R_c)^2},$$

and provide the condition for the minimum communication range such that a minimal dominating set can achieve the same coverage by all the deployed sensors with a probability close to one. Note that the sensors in a (minimal) dominating set may not form a connected network. A (minimum) dominating set is connected if any two sensors in the set can reach each other, possibly via multi-hop communications.

Some scheduling schemes apply the connected dominated set to address network connectivity and to approximate area coverage, which will be introduced in the next subsection.

4.2.1. *Further reading*

Deng *et al.* [80, 81] study how to compute the activity probability p in RIS to prolong network lifetime for a clustered network: each node may have a different value of p based on its distance to the cluster head and the residual energy. Lu and Suda [82] study a counterpart of RIS for the sensing attenuation model and provide a method to compute the activity probability.

Gui and Mohapatra [67] extend PEAS and propose a Probing Environment and Collaborating Adaptive Sleeping (PECAS) scheduling scheme by modifying the continuously working mode in PEAS such that any active sensor will only be active for some time and then reenter the sleep state.

Hefeeda and Bagheri [83] consider approximating area k-coverage by node k-coverage, i.e., each sensor node is covered by k active nodes. They apply the concepts of set system and hitting set and propose a randomized k-coverage scheme which iteratively selects nodes to form a qualified hitting set based on their cumulatively assigned weights.

4.3. *Preserving Coverage and Connectivity*

The communication unit (radio transceiver) in a sensor is in general independent of the sensing unit of the sensor [1]. The activity scheduling schemes discussed in the previous subsection do not necessarily imply that an inactive sensor shall also shut off its communication unit and cannot serve as an intermediate relay for forwarding data. In some cases, it might be desirable for an inactive sensor to turn off its communication unit. However, network connectivity may not be guaranteed if only active sensor nodes are used for data transport. Hence, in these cases activity scheduling should ensure both network connectivity and coverage requirements.

One can first schedule sensor activity for coverage and then try to ensure network connectivity based only on the selected active sensor nodes with an appropriate transmission range [31, 48, 84]. Xing *et al.* [31] and Zhang and Hou [48] provide a sufficient condition for the connectivity of sensing active nodes. If a sensor field is completely covered by a set of sensors and the communication range is at least twice the sensing range, $R_c \geq 2R_s$, then these sensor nodes also form a connected network. This result suggests that in the case of $R_c \geq 2R_s$, one can focus on scheduling sensors for complete coverage without loss of network connectivity. Furthermore, this result can also be extended to higher degree network connectivity and k-coverage preservation. Tian and Georganas [84] further this result in a more general scenario. Suppose that a set of sensors S can form a connected network and cover an area $R \equiv \bigcup_{s \in S} A(s)$. If a subset of sensors $S_a \subseteq S$ can also preserve the same coverage, i.e., $R' \equiv \bigcup_{s \in S_a} A(s) = R$, and $R_c \geq 2R_s$, then sensors in

S_a also form a connected network. The difference between the work of Tian and Georganas [84] and that of Xing *et al.* [31] and Zhang and Hou [48] is that although all sensor nodes in S form a connected network, they may not be able to provide complete area coverage.

In the case that $R_c \geq 2R_s$ or preserving complete coverage is not enforced, one approach is to address both coverage and connectivity at the same time by only selecting connected nodes as sensing active nodes. Gupta *et al.* [85, 86] provide greedy algorithms to sequentially select connected sensor nodes. Let S_a be the set of selected sensor nodes and let $N(S_a)$ denote the set of sensors that are neighbors of at least one sensor node in S_a but not in S_a. In each stage, the greedy algorithm selects a node in $N(S_a)$ such that a profit function (e.g., the size of the covered area) can be maximized. The greedy algorithm stops if complete area coverage is achieved. Since only nodes in $N(S_a)$ are considered, network connectivity can be guaranteed. Obviously, this is a variant of the greedy set cover heuristic discussed in Sec. 4.1 with a connectivity constraint. By using different profit functions, different objectives such as minimal energy consumption and optimal balance between energy consumption and coverage requirements can also be achieved. Gupta *et al.* [85] also provide an upper bound on the number of the selected connected active nodes related to that by an optimal solution.

Another approach to providing connected coverage is to first select sensing active nodes and then activate mode nodes if only the sensing active nodes cannot form a connected network. Liu *et al.* [87] use RIS to first select active sensors and then apply an extra-on rule to further activate inactive nodes to ensure network connectivity. They use the synchronous decision approach of RIS to randomly produce k disjoint set of covers (c.f., Sec. 4.2). The extra-on rule is as follows: if a node s in a cover k is active in slot t but has no neighboring nodes in another cover k' that is active in slot t as determined by the RIS, then an extra node in k' neighboring s should also be activated in this slot.

Zou and Chakrabarty [15] propose a token-based coverage-centric active node selection (CCANS) algorithm by using token passing to sequentially decide node state. In the first stage, a starting sensor locally determines its active state if its sensing disk is not fully covered by its neighbors and then passes the token to one of its neighbors such that this neighbor can make its decision. The first stage ends if all sensors have decided their states. In the second stage, those inactive sensors in the first stage become active if they have active neighbors that are not connected. Zou and Charkrabarty [15] also provide a rigorous analysis to show that their algorithm can ensure complete coverage and network connectivity.

Some scheduling schemes consider approximating area coverage by node coverage and maintaining both coverage and connectivity by using a connected dominating set (CDS) [88, 89]. A CDS is a dominating set whose nodes are connected (c.f., Sec. 4.2 for the definition of a dominating set). The problem of finding a minimum connected dominating set (MCDS) has been extensively studied in the literature. For example, Dai and Wu [90] propose a distributed dominant-pruning algorithm to find an MCDS by first using a marking process to find a strongly connected dominating and absorbent set and then applying a rule-k pruning process to further remove those redundant nodes. Carle *et al.* [88] modify their pruning algorithm to find a connected area dominating set by further imposing a constraint. Initially, the marking process is performed as in Ref. 90 and a marked sensor is also considered active. Then, a marked active sensor can choose to be inactive only if it can do so by the pruning algorithm and its covered area is also covered by its active neighbors.

4.3.1. *Further Reading*

Zhou *et al.* extend the basic idea of using greedy connected node selection to consider k-coverage and k-connectivity with or without variable sensing ranges in Refs. 91 and 92. Liu and Liang [93] propose a greedy algorithm with the similar idea of finding connected sensors to provide percentile area coverage.

5. Node Movement Strategy

As discussed in Sec. 3.2, a large number of sensors is required to provide complete coverage in a randomly deployed sensor network. After an initial random deployment, coverage holes may exist if the number of deployed sensors is not larger than that required by the critical sensor density. Besides using more sensors to improve coverage, we can also use mobile sensor nodes which are equipped with mobile platforms [94] to adjust their positions to improve network coverage after the initial deployment. A mobile sensor node is normally more expensive than its stationary counterpart. Although movement is not for free, using mobile nodes may greatly reduce sensor density. Wang *et al.* [95] provide a detailed analysis on the tradeoffs between using mobile nodes and using more stationary sensor nodes. In this section, we review the network redeployment enabled by a fraction of or all mobile nodes in a deployed sensor network. Sensor redeployment mainly focuses on how to efficiently move mobile sensors to improve coverage. Two network scenarios are often considered in the literature. One is a hybrid sensor network that consists of both stationary and mobile sensors. The other is pure mobile sensor networks.

5.1. *Hybrid Sensor Networks*

In a hybrid network, one objective of using mobile sensor nodes is to heal coverage holes created by only stationary sensors after initial sensor deployment. Although the price of mobile sensors may be higher than stationary sensors, such costs are justifiable since the number of sensors required for complete coverage can be greatly reduced. When designing a hole healing algorithm, two issues are to be addressed. First, the positions and the sizes of coverage holes need to be carefully estimated. Second, movements of mobile sensors need to be coordinated in order to minimize both the uncovered area and moving cost (e.g., the distance to be traversed).

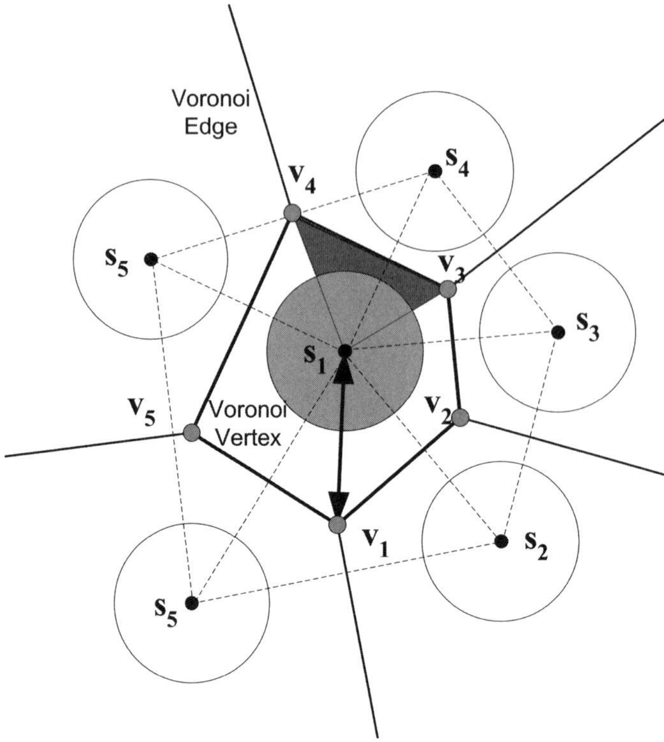

Fig. 10. Voronoi diagram to decide hole size.

Wang *et al.* [96] propose using a Voronoi diagram for hole detection and hole size estimation. As shown in Fig. 10, sensor s_1 can determine the existence of coverage holes by examining whether there are uncovered Voronoi vertices in its own Voronoi cell. Furthermore, they propose using the distance between the sensor to its farthest uncovered Voronoi vertex to estimate the size of a coverage hole and that vertex is also considered the target position for a mobile sensor to reside. In Fig. 10, the target position is the Voronoi vertex v_1. Ghosh [97] proposes an exact hole size estimation method also based on the use of Voronoi diagrams. The hole size of a sensor is that uncovered area within its Voronoi cell. As shown in Fig. 10, the uncovered area in one Voronoi triangle $\Delta s_1 v_3 v_4$ can be exactly computed when the coordinates of the triangle vertices are known and the hole of sensor s_1 is the sum of those uncovered areas of its Voronoi triangles.

After determining coverage holes and target positions, efficient mobility algorithm are needed to maximize network coverage. Wang *et al.* [96] show that the problem of maximizing network coverage through a given number of mobile sensors is NP-hard. They propose a distributed bidding protocol which uses the size of an estimated coverage hole for a sensor as its bidding price. Each mobile sensor maintains a base price which is set as the hole size it is currently covering.

If the highest bid it receives is larger than its base price, it will move to the target position of the corresponding coverage hole to heal it. A *duplicate healing* occurs when two mobile sensors move to heal the same coverage hole. They propose a self-detection algorithm to solve this problem. Wang *et al.* [98] further improve this mobility algorithm to reduce energy consumption. Instead of actually moving to the target position, mobile sensors first move logically in their proxy-based sensor deployment protocol. After the logical move, one-time physical movements are then carried out to fix coverage holes.

5.1.1. *Further Reading*

Ahmed *et al.* [99] provide a survey not only on coverage hole problems but also routing hole problems and other types of hole problems in WSNs. Ghrist and Muhammad [100] use an algebraic topological method utilizing homology theory to detect coverage holes without coordinates. Li *et al.* [101] propose a distributed triangle mesh self-healing (3MeSH) algorithm also based on homology theory.

5.2. *Mobile Sensor Networks*

In a pure mobile sensor network, all sensor nodes are mobile and can adjust their positions any time after initial deployment. Since all nodes are mobile, coverage holes may be created if the nodes' movements are not coordinated. Furthermore, in some event observation applications, the places closer to the event source may need more sensors for observation and may require a concentrated coverage distribution centered on the event source and with a higher coverage degree than other subareas. Therefore, one important objective in a mobile sensor network is to coordinate the nodes' movement such that a high coverage ratio or the desired coverage distribution can be achieved after the mobiles reach their respective new positions.

Zou and Chakrabarty [16] propose a virtual force algorithm (VFA) to calculate the desired position for each mobile node to move to. Each sensor behaves like a source of force to all other sensors. This force can be either positive (attractive) or negative (repulsive). For example, if the distance between two sensors is smaller than a predetermined threshold, then they exert negative forces on each other, which moves them farther away. On the other hand, if the distance is larger than another threshold, then they exert positive forces on each other, moving them closer. The thresholds are set according to the triangle tessellation and the tolerance to coverage hole. A mobile sensor determines its desired new position based on the forces from its neighbors. To further reduce energy consumption, logical movements are first performed and then followed by one-time physical movement. Wang *et al.* [102] propose three mobility algorithms to redistribute mobile sensors, namely vector-based (VEC), voronoi-based (VOR) and Minimax. The VEC algorithm is similar to VFA and the VOR and the Minimax algorithms are based on the Voronoi diagram. The VOR moves a sensor node towards the farthest uncovered Voronoi vertex of itself. The Minimax algorithm moves a sensor to the point where the distance to the farthest Voronoi vertex is minimized.

Khan *et al.* [103] study the interesting problem of how to move three mobile nodes to provide area coverage in a time-multiplexed way. The three mobile nodes form an equilateral triangle to provide coverage (to perform some operations) for such a triangular area for some time and then move to other positions to form a new triangle. The sensor field is covered in a time-multiplexed way with many such small triangles as the nodes move from one triangle to another. The objective is to minimize the total traveling distance or time required to completely cover the sensor field. Figure 11 illustrates the basic traversal patterns between two consecutive triangle formations. The whole sensor field is divided into horizontal and vertical strips of such triangles. The mobile nodes move either left or right till the end of each horizontal strip and then move vertically to the next horizontal strip and repeat the horizontal movement again. Khan *et al.* [103] also provide detailed analysis for the upper and lower bound on total transverse distance and time for a given rectangle sensor field.

The aforementioned movement schemes require that each node computes its exact target location and this demands high computation requirements. When the sensor network is of a large scale and also the sensor field, the grid approach, which partitions the sensor field into smaller cells, can be used to reduce communications overheads and unnecessary movements. If there is no sensor (e.g., due to sensor death) in a cell, sensor nodes from other cells need to move to this cell to re-cover the cell. Wang *et al.* [104] propose a grid-quorum solution which organizes grid cells into quorums to quickly locate the closest redundant sensor with low message complexity. They also propose a *cascaded movement* strategy to move redundant sensors. In the cascaded movement, a redundant mobile node may not need to travel a large distance to re-cover a cell. Instead, several cascading (intermediate) mobile nodes are first identified and then move in a cascaded way (one replaces another). By using cascaded movement, movement delay can be reduced and energy consumption can be more balanced. Wu and Yang [105] propose a scan-based movement-assisted sensor deployment (SMART), which uses scan and dimension exchange to obtain the information about sensor distributions. The SMART algorithm first calculates the average load (e.g., the number of sensors) of each cell and then determines the

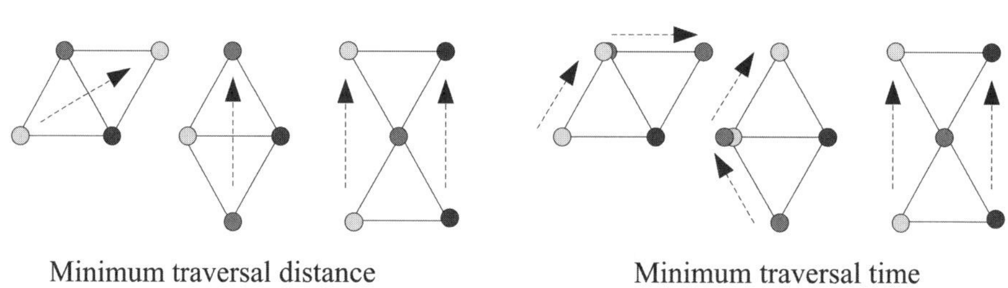

Fig. 11. Traversal patterns between formations [103].

amount of overload and underload in all cells. Mobile nodes can then move from overload cells to under-load cells to achieve a balanced state.

All the above mobility schemes assume a uniform coverage distribution where all points of a sensor field have the same importance. Hence, the main objective of a mobility algorithm is to evenly distribute sensors in the field. In event-driven applications, some portions of the field may become more important than others. For example, in animal monitoring applications, it would be better to put more sensors near the water pool since the probability of finding animals around the pool might be much higher. Therefore, the objective of a mobility algorithm in such event-driven applications is to move nodes such that the sensor distribution can match the event's distribution.

Cortes *et al.* [106] propose a distributed mobility algorithm based on the classic Lloyd algorithm (also known as Voronoi iteration/relaxation). The algorithm first constructs a Voronoi diagram for all mobile nodes. It then uses the mass centroid (weighted by event density function) of the Voronoi cell of a sensor to determine its desired new location. Mobile nodes then iteratively move towards the mass centroid such that more sensors will move to locations where event density is high. The resulting distribution of using the Lloyd algorithm has *blue noise* characteristics.

5.2.1. *Further Reading*

Liu *et al.* [107] study the area coverage during a time interval and target the detection time of a mobile sensor network with randomly moving nodes. Random mobility does not impact on the average area coverage at any given time instant, but can help to increase the area covered in a time interval which helps to reduce target detection time. Bisnik *et al.* [108] investigate coverage dynamics in terms of the stochastic event capturing capability of a mobile sensor network. An event is modeled as occurring at any point in the sensor field with finite lifetime.

Howard *et al.* [109] apply the concept of potential field, which is similar to virtual force, to control the velocity and position of each movement step. Poduri and Sukhatme [110] also apply the concept of virtual force to redeploy mobile sensors with an additional constraint that each sensor needs to have at least k neighbors. Heo and Varshney [111] propose a mobility algorithm similar to VFA [16]. Besides distance between nodes, they also include the expected sensor density for uniform coverage in the desired position calculation.

Wang *et al.* [112] propose a crystal-lattice permutation (CLP) mobility algorithm whose basic idea is to coordinate node movement to emulate a hexagon tessellation process. Chellappan *et al.* [113] adopt a grid approach to evenly distribute mobile nodes into each cell but with a limited mobility constraint, i.e., a mobile can only move a small distance. Yang and Cardei [114] study the problem of how to prolong network lifetime by redistributing mobile nodes with different densities according to the distances to the sink. Since nodes closest to the sink normally consume more energy for transmission and are bottleneck nodes with respect to network lifetime, it is desirable to redistribute more nodes closest to the sink.

Manoj *et al.* [115] study an interesting movement problem in a dying network where one or more nodes die from time to time. Dead nodes may cause coverage vacancy which can be partly/fully recovered by its neighboring mobile nodes. On the other hand, the moving of a mobile node may also cause coverage vacancy. Hence, a mobile node needs to move to a position to balance the two vacancies.

Butler and Rus [116] propose a local incremental movement strategy: a mobile node moves toward the event source position a small distance in a step. They also provide a Voronoi diagram based algorithm to redistribute mobiles uniformly after the end of an event. Balam and Gibson [117] also apply a distributed Lloyd algorithm for mobile nodes to move to an event source and study the effect of the communication constraint: a mobile is allowed to communicate with its H-hop neighbors to calculate its next position.

6. Conclusions

In this chapter, we have surveyed recent contributions on coverage problems in wireless sensor networks. The sensor coverage model determines the coverage between space points and individual sensors, which together with the geographical locations of the deployed nodes determine network coverage. Coverage problems may be classified into three types according to the network operation phase. For each type, canonical coverage problems and representative approaches to solving these problems have been reviewed. Some variants for each type of problem have also been included as further reading.

Terminology

Wireless sensor node: Consists of, at least, a sensing unit, a power unit, a radio communication unit and a computation and storage unit, and is used to sense and process physical phenomena, and transmit the processed data wirelessly.

Wireless sensor network: Consists of, normally, a large number of spatially distributed sensor nodes to cooperatively monitor and report physical phenomena in an area, such as the temperature or pressure of a room, or a target moving in an open space.

Sensor coverage model: Reflects the sensing capability of a sensing modality which is dependent on the hardware design of this sensor modality such as the sampling rate, A/D conversion and signal processing unit. Different sensor types may have different sensing/coverage models. To study the coverage problem, a sensor coverage model can be considered as a mapping function stating the relationship between the space points and the sensor location.

Sensing disk model: A commonly used model for modeling sensor capability. It states that a disk area centered at the sensor location with a radius of the sensing range can be sensed (or covered) by a sensor.

Network sensing coverage: Describes how a sensor field is covered by geographically distributed sensors. It describes the relationship between the space points and the networked sensors.

Coverage types: According to the subject to be covered, coverage types can be grouped into area coverage, target coverage and barrier coverage. Area coverage discusses how a sensor field (2D/3D) is covered; target coverage focuses on how to cover a set of discrete targets; barrier coverage is normally used to find a penetration path in a sensor field.

Coverage degree: In the sensing disk coverage model, coverage degree refers to the number of sensor nodes a point is covered by. In area and target coverage, a space point within the area or a target is called k-covered if it is within k distinct nodes' sensing disks. Using more than one sensor to cover a point can improve the coverage robustness in the case of node failure.

Coverage ratio: Measures how much of an area or how many targets are covered. Complete coverage is an important performance metric for area and target coverage. Complete area (target) coverage means that the coverage degree of every point within the sensor field (every target) should be no less than a certain threshold.

Critical sensor density: Before network deployment, one may want to know how many nodes are needed to cover all points in a sensor field. For deterministic deployment, the basic objective is to use in the least number of nodes as possible. For random deployment, the basic objective is to determine the critical sensor density: whenever the number of the deployed nodes is equal to or larger than this critical density times the area of the sensor field, all points in the sensor field can be covered almost surely in every random deployment.

Sensing activity scheduling: Scattered sensor nodes may be more than the optimum in a randomly deployed sensor network. If the area covered by one sensor can also be covered by other sensors, such a sensor is considered to be redundant and can temporarily transit into an energy-saving sleep state without sacrificing the coverage requirement. Hence, activity scheduling is mainly concerned with deciding which sensors are in which states for how long such that certain coverage requirements can be guaranteed and network lifetime can be prolonged.

Sensing-oriented mobility: In a sensor network with some or all nodes as mobile nodes, one may want to move the mobile nodes to improve network coverage after the initial deployment. The moving strategy needs to consider not only the coverage ratio but also the cost of moving the mobile nodes.

Exercises

1. Compare the sensor coverage model and network sensing coverage.
2. Explain the sensing disk model and the information coverage from a signal processing viewpoint.
3. List the design issues when studying coverage problems.
4. What is the critical sensor density?
5. List the approaches to determining the critical sensor density in randomly deployed networks.
6. What is sensing activity scheduling used for?
7. List several approaches to sensing activity scheduling.
8. List several existing algorithms to determine a redundant sensor.
9. How does node mobility help to improve network coverage?
10. List the methods used to determine a coverage hole.

References

1. I. F. Akyildiz, W. Su, Y. Sankarasubramaniam and E. Cayirci, Wireless sensor networks: A survey, *Comput. Network.* **39**, 393 (2002).
2. J. O'Rourke, *Art Gallery Theorems and Algorithms* (Oxford University Press, 1987).
3. R. Williams, *The Geometrical Foundation of Natural Structure: A Source Book of Design* (Dover, New York, 1979), pp. 51,52.
4. M. Cardei and J. Wu, Coverage in wireless sensor networks, in *Handbook of Sensor Networks*, eds. M. Ilyas and I. Mahgoub (CRC Press, 2004).
5. C. F. Huang and Y.-C. Tseng, A survey of solutions to the coverage problems in wireless sensor networks, *J. Internet Tech.* **6**, 1 (2005).
6. L. Wang and Y. Xiao, A survey of energy-efficient scheduling mechanisms in sensor networks, *Mob. Network. Appl.* **11**, 723 (2006).
7. B. Wang, W. Wang, V. Srinivasan and K. C. Chua, Information coverage for wireless sensor networks, *IEEE Commun. Lett.* **9**, 967 (2005).
8. X. R. Wang, G. L. Xing, Y. F. Zhang, C. Y. Lu, R. Pless and C. Gill, Integrated coverage and connectivity configuration in wireless sensor networks, *Proc. ACM Int. Conf. Embedded Networked Sensor Systems* (2003), p. 28.
9. J. M. Mendel, *Lessons in Estimation Theory for Signal Processing, Communications and Control* (Prentice Hall, 1995).
10. B. Wang, K. C. Chua, W. Wang and V. Srinivasan, Worst and best information exposure paths in wireless sensor networks, *Proc. Int. Conf. Mobile Ad-hoc and Sensor Networks, Lecture Notes in Computer Science, Vol. 3794* (2005), p. 52.
11. J. Ai and A. A. Abouzeid, Coverage by directional sensors in randomly deployed wireless sensor networks, *J. Comb. Optim.* **11**, 21 (2006).
12. H. D. Ma and Y. H. Liu, Some problems of directional sensor networks, *Int. J. Sensor Network.* **2**, 44 (2007).
13. Y. L. Cai, W. Lou, M. L. Li and X. Y. Li, Target-oriented scheduling in directional sensor networks, *Proc. IEEE Infocom* (2007), p. 1.
14. S. Meguerdichian, F. Koushanfar, G. Qu and M. Potkonjak, Exposure in wireless ad hoc sensor networks, *Proc. ACM Int. Conf. Mobile Computing and Networking* (2001), p. 139.

15. Y. Zou and K. Chakrabarty, A distributed coverage- and connectivity-centric technique for selecting active nodes in wireless sensor networks, *IEEE Trans. Comput.* **54**, 978 (2005).
16. Y. Zou and K. Chakrabarty, Sensor deployment and target localization in distributed sensor networks, *ACM Trans. Embed. Comput. Syst.* **3**, 61 (2004).
17. N. Ahmed, S. S. Kanhere and S. Jha, Probabilistic coverage in wireless sensor networks, *Proc. IEEE Conf. Local Computer Networks* (2005), p. 672.
18. W. Wang, V. Srinivasan, K. C. Chua and B. Wang, Energy-efficient coverage for target detection in wireless sensor networks, *Proc. 6th Int. Conf. Information Processing in Sensor Networks* (2007), p. 313.
19. Crossbow Technology Inc., MEP 510 Datasheet, www.xbow.com (2005).
20. S. Meguerdichian, F. Koushanfar, M. Potkonjak and M. B. Srivastava, Coverage problems in wireless ad-hoc sensor networks, *Proc. IEEE Infocom*, Vol. 3 (2001), p. 1380.
21. P. Hall, *Introduction to the Theory of Coverage Processes* (John Wiley and Sons, 1988).
22. R. Kershner, The number of circles covering a set, *American J. Math.* **61**, 665 (1939).
23. R. Lyengar, K. Kar and S. Banerjee, Low coordination topologies for redundancy in sensor networks, *Proc. ACM 6th Int. Symp. Mobile Ad Hoc Networking and Computing* (2005), p. 332.
24. X. L. Bai, S. Kumar, D. Xuan, Z. Q. Yun and T. H. Lai, Deploying wireless sensors to achieve both coverage and connectivity, *Proc. ACM 7th Int. Symp. Mobile Ad Hoc Networking and Computing* (2006), p. 131.
25. S. M. N. Alam and Z. J. Haas, Coverage and connectivity in three-dimensional networks, *Proc. ACM 12th Int. Conf. Mobile Computing and Networking* (2006), p. 346.
26. A. Sen, N. Das, L. Zhou, B. H. Shen, S. Murthy and P. Bhattacharya, Coverage problem for sensors embedded in temperature sensitive environments, *Proc. IEEE 4th Communications Society on Sensor and Ad Hoc Communications and Networks* (2007), p. 1.
27. Y. C. Wang, C. C. Hu and Y. C. Tseng, Efficient deployment algorithms for ensuring coverage and connectivity of wireless sensor networks, *Proc. IEEE Int. Conf. Wireless Internet* (2005), p. 114.
28. H. H. Zhang and J. Hou, On deriving the upper bound of α-lifetime for large sensor networks, *Proc. ACM Int. Symp. Mobile Ad Hoc Networking and Computing* (2004), p. 121.
29. S. Kumar, T. H. Lai and J. Balogh, On k-coverage in a mostly sleeping sensor network, *Proc. ACM Int. Conf. Mobile Computing and Networking* (2004), p. 114.
30. R. D. Yates and D. J. Goodman, *Probability and Stochastic Processes: A Friendly Introduction for Electrical and Computer Engineers* (John Wiley and Sons, 1999).
31. G. L. Xing, X. R. Wang, Y. F. Zhang, C. Y. Lu, R. Pless and C. Gill, Integrated coverage and connectivity configuration for energy conservation in sensor networks, *ACM Trans. Sensor Network.* **1**, 36 (2005).
32. W. Mo, D. J. Qiao and Z. D. Wang, Mostly-sleeping wireless sensor networks: Connectivity, k-coverage, and α-lifetime, *Proc. 43rd Annual Allerton Conf. Communication, Control, and Computing* (2005).
33. N. Alon and J. Spencer, *The Probabilistic Method* (John Wiley and Sons, 2000).
34. P. J. Wan and C. W. Yi, Coverage by randomly deployed wireless sensor networks, *IEEE Trans. Inform. Theory* **52**, 2658 (2006).

35. B. Y. Liu and D. Towsley, A study of the coverage of large-scale sensor networks, *Proc. IEEE Int. Conf. Mobile Ad-hoc and Sensor Systems* (2004), p. 475.
36. B. Wang, K. C. Chua, V. Srinivasan and W. Wang, Information coverage in randomly deployed wireless sensor networks, *IEEE Trans. Wireless Commun.* **6**, 2994 (2007).
37. S. Adlakha and M. Srivastava, Critical density thresholds for coverage in wireless sensor networks, *Proc. IEEE Wireless Communications and Networking Conference* (2003), p. 1615.
38. H. D. Ma and Y. H. Liu, On coverage problems of directional sensor networks, *Proc. Int. Conf. Mobile Ad-hoc and Sensor Networks* (2005), p. 721.
39. L. Lazos and R. Poovendran, Stochastic coverage in heterogeneous sensor networks, *ACM Trans. Sensor Network.* **2**, 325 (2006).
40. L. A. Santalo, *Integral Geometry and Geometric Probability*, 2nd Edn. (Cambridge University Press, 2004).
41. T. H. Cormen, C. E. Leiserson, R. L. Rivest and C. Stein, *Introduction to Algorithms* (MIT Press, 2001).
42. T. Yan, T. He and J. A. Stankovic, Differentiated surveillance for sensor networks, *Proc. ACM Int. Conf. Embedded Networked Sensor Systems* (2003), p. 51.
43. S. Slijepcevic and M. Potkonjak, Power efficient organization of wireless sensor networks, *Proc. IEEE Int. Conf. Communications* Vol. 2 (2001), p. 472.
44. M. Cardei and D. Z. Du, Improving wireless sensor network lifetime through power aware organization, *Wireless Network.* **11**, 333 (2005).
45. D. Tian and N. D. Georganas, A node scheduling scheme for energy conservation in large wireless sensor networks, *J. Wireless Commun. Mob. Comput.* **3**, 271 (2003).
46. C. F. Huang, Y. C. Tseng and H. L. Wu, Distributed protocols for ensuring both coverage and connectivity of a wireless sensor network, *ACM Trans. Sensor Network.* **3**, 1 (2007).
47. B. Carbunar, A. Grama, J. Vitek and A. Octavian, Redundancy and coverage detection in sensor networks, *ACM Trans. Sensor Network.* **2**, 94 (2006).
48. H. H. Zhang and J. C. Hou, Maintaining sensing coverage and connectivity in large sensor networks, *J. Ad Hoc Sensor Wireless Network.* **1**, 89 (2005).
49. M. Hefeeda and H. Ahmadi, A probabilistic coverage protocol for wireless sensor networks, *Proc. IEEE Int. Conf. Network Protocols* (2007), p. 1.
50. T. T. Wu and K. F. Ssu, Determining active sensor nodes for complete coverage without location information, *Int. J. Ad Hoc Ubiquit. Comput.* **1**, 38 (2005).
51. M. Zhang, M. C. Chan and A. L. Ananda, Coverage protocol for wireless sensor networks using distance estimates, *Proc. IEEE 4th Annual Communications Society on Sensor and Ad Hoc Communications and Networks* (2007), p. 1.
52. O. Younis, M. Krunz and S. Ramasubramanian, Coverage without location information, *Proc. IEEE Int. Conf. Network Protocols* (2007), p. 51.
53. R. Kalidindi and R. Kannan, Energy and deployment aware sensing for wireless sensor networks, *Proc. IEEE Int. Conf. Wireless and Mobile Computing, Networking and Communications* (2005), p. 446.
54. B. Wang, S. Vikram, K. C. Chua and W. Wang, Information coverage and network lifetime in energy constrained wireless sensor networks, *Proc. IEEE 32nd Conf. Local Computer Networks* (2007), p. 512.
55. H. O. Sanli and H. Cam, Energy efficient differentiable coverage service protocols for wireless sensor networks, *Proc. IEEE Int. Conf. Pervasive Computing and Communications* (2005).
56. X. J. Du and F. J. Lin, Maintaining differentiated coverage in heterogeneous sensor networks, *EURASIP J. Wireless Commun. Network.* **4**, 565 (2005).

57. C. F. Huang, L. C. Lo, Y. C. Tseng and W. T. Chen, Decentralized energy-conserving and coverage-preserving protocols for wireless sensor networks, *Proc. Int. Symp. Circuits and Systems* (2005).
58. A. Boukerche, X. Fei and R. B. Araujo, An optimal coverage-preserving scheme for wireless sensor networks based on local information exchange, *Elsevier Comput. Commun.* **30**(14–15), 2708 (2007).
59. A. Boukerche and X. Fei, A coverage-preserving scheme for wireless sensor network with irregular sensing range, *Elsevier Ad Hoc Network.* **5**(8), 1303 (2007).
60. C. F. Huang and Y. C. Tseng, The coverage problem in wireless sensor networks, *Mob. Network. Appl.* **10**(4), 519 (2005).
61. N. Tezcan and W. Y. Wang, Effective coverage and connectivity preserving in wireless sensor networks, *Proc. IEEE Wireless Communications and Networking Conf.* (2007), p. 3388.
62. C. F. Huang, Y. C. Tseng and L. C. Lo, The coverage problem in three-dimensional wireless sensor networks, *Proc. IEEE Global Telecommunications Conf.* (2004), p. 3182.
63. J. Lu, J. S. Wang and T. Suda, Scalable coverage maintenance for dense wireless sensor networks, *EURASIP J. WCN*, 1 (2007).
64. A. M. C. So and Y. Y. Ye, On solving coverage problems in a wireless sensor network using voronoi diagrams, *Proc. 1st Workshop on Internet and Network Economics* (2005).
65. Y. Shang and H. C. Shi, Flexible energy efficient density control on wireless sensor networks, *Int. J. Distrib. Sensor Network.* **3**(1), 5 (2007).
66. J. Wu and S. H. Yang, Energy-efficient node scheduling models in sensor networks with adjustable ranges, *Int. J. Found. Comput. Sci.* **16**(1), 3 (2005).
67. C. Gui and P. Mohapatra, Power conservation and quality of surveillance in target tracking sensor networks, *Proc. ACM Int. Conf. Mobile Computing and Networking* (2004), p. 129.
68. D. Tian and N. D. Georganas, Location and calculation-free node-scheduling schemes in large wireless sensor networks, *Ad Hoc Network.* **2**(1), 65 (2004).
69. W. Choi and S. K. Das, Trade-off between coverage and data reporting latency for energy-conserving data gathering in wireless sensor networks, *Proc. IEEE Int. Conf. Mobile Ad-Hoc and Sensor Systems* (2004), p. 503.
70. Z. Abrams, A. Goel and S. Plotkin, Set k-cover algorithms for energy efficient monitoring in wireless sensor networks, *Proc. ACM Int. Symp. Information Processing in Sensor Networks* (2004), p. 424.
71. C. Q. Hua and T. S. P. Yum, Asynchronous random sleeping for sensor networks, *ACM Trans. Sensor Network.* **3**(3), 1 (2007).
72. C. F. Hsin and M. Y. Liu, Randomly duty-cycled wireless sensor networks: Dynamics of coverage, *IEEE Trans. Wireless Commun.* **5**(11), 3182 (2006).
73. F. Ye, G. Zhong, J. Cheng, S. W. Lu and L. X. Zhang, Peas: A robust energy conserving protocols for long-lived sensor networks, *Proc. Int. Conf. Distributed Computing Systems* (2003), p. 28.
74. B. Wang, C. Fu and H. B. Lim, Layered diffusion based coverage control in wireless sensor networks, *Proc. IEEE 32nd Local Computer Networks* (2007).
75. Y. Gao, K. Wu and F. L. Li, Analysis on the redundancy of wireless sensor networks, *Proc. ACM Int. Conf. Wireless Sensor Networks and Applications* (2003), p. 108.
76. K. Wu, Y. Gao, F. L. Li and Y. Xiao, Lightweight deployment aware scheduling for wireless sensor networks, *Mob. Network. Appl.* **10**(6), 837 (2005).

77. M. Cardei, D. Maccallum, X. Y. Cheng, M. Min, X. H. Jia, D. Y. Li, D. Z. Du and D. Du, Wireless sensor networks with energy efficient organization, *J. Interconn. Network.* **3**(3–4), 213 (2002).
78. S. H. Yang, F. Dai, M. Cardei and J. Wu, On multiple point coverage in wireless sensor networks, *Proc. IEEE Int. Conf. Mobile Ad-Hoc and Sensor Systems* (2005), p. 757.
79. R. Zheng, G. H. He and X. Liu, Location-free coverage maintenance in wireless sensor networks, Technical Report, Department of Computer Science, University of Houston (2005).
80. J. Deng, Y. H. S. Han, W. D. B. Heinzelman and P. K. Varshney, Scheduling sleeping nodes in high density cluster-based sensor networks, *ACM Mob. Network. Appl.* **10**(6), 825 (2005).
81. J. Deng, Y. H. S. Han, W. D. B. Heinzelman and P. K. Varshney, Balanced-energy sleep scheduling scheme for high-density cluster-based sensor networks, *Comput. Commun.* **28**(14), 1631 (2005).
82. J. Lu and T. Suda, Coverage-aware self-scheduling in sensor networks, *Proc. IEEE Workshop on Computer Communications* (2003), p. 117.
83. M. Hefeeda and M. Bagheri, Randomized k-coverage algorithms for dense sensor networks, *Proc. InfoCom* (2007), p. 1.
84. D. Tian and N. D. Georganas, Connectivity maintenance and coverage preservation in wireless sensor networks, *Ad Hoc Network.* **3**(6), 744 (2005).
85. H. Gupta, S. R. Das and Q. Y. Gu, Connected sensor cover: Self-organization of sensor networks for efficient query execution, *Proc. ACM Int. Symp. Mobile Ad Hoc Networking and Computing* (2003), p. 189.
86. H. Gupta, Z. H. Zhou, S. R. Das and Q. Y. Gu, Connected sensor cover: Self-organization of sensor networks for efficient query execution, *IEEE/ACM Trans. Network.* **14**(1), 55 (2006).
87. C. Liu, K. Wu, Y. Xiao and B. Sun, Random coverage with guaranteed connectivity: Joint scheduling for wireless sensor networks, *IEEE Trans. Parallel Distrib. Syst.* **17**(6), 562 (2006).
88. J. Carle and D. Simplot-Ryl, Energy-efficient area monitoring for sensor networks, *IEEE Comput.* **37**(2), 40 (2004).
89. J. Carle, A. Gallais and D. Simplot-Ryl, Preserving area coverage in wireless sensor networks by using surface coverage relay dominating sets, *Proc. IEEE Symp. Computers and Communications* (2005), p. 347.
90. F. Dai and J. Wu, Distributed dominant pruning in ad hoc networks, *IEEE Proc. Int. Conf. Communications* (2003), p. 353.
91. Z. H. Zhou, S. Das and H. Gupta, Connected k-coverage problem in sensor networks, *Proc. IEEE Int. Conf. Computer Communications and Networks* (2004), p. 373.
92. Z. H. Zhou, S. Das and H. Gupta, Fault tolerant connected sensor cover with variable sensing and transmission ranges, *Proc. IEEE Communications Society Conf. Sensor and Ad Hoc Communications and Networks* (2005), p. 594.
93. Y. Z. Liu and W. F. Liang, Approximate coverage in wireless sensor networks, *Proc. IEEE Conf. Local Computer Networks* (2005), p. 68.
94. G. T. Sibley, M. H. Rahimi and G. S. Sukhatme, Robomote: A tiny mobile robot platform for large-scale ad-hoc sensor networks, *Proc. IEEE Int. Conf. Robotics and Automation* (2002), p. 1143.
95. W. Wang, V. Srinivasan and K. C. Chua, Trade-offs between mobility and density for coverage in wireless sensor networks, *Proc. ACM 13th Annual Int. Conf. Mobile Computing and Networking* (2007), p. 39.

96. G. L. Wang, G. H. Cao and T. LaPorta, A bidding protocol for deploying mobile sensors, *Proc. IEEE Int. Conf. Network Protocols* (2003), p. 315.
97. A. Ghosh, Estimating coverage holes and enhancing coverage in mixed sensor networks, *Proc. IEEE Int. Conf. Local Computer Networks* (2004), p. 68.
98. G. L. Wang, G. H. Cao and T. LaPorta, Proxy-based sensor deployment for mobile sensor networks, *Proc. IEEE Int. Conf. Mobile Ad-Hoc and Sensor Systems* (2004), p. 493.
99. N. Ahmed, S. S. Kanhere and S. Jha, The holes problem in wireless sensor networks: A survey, *ACM SIGMOBILE Mob. Comput. Commun. Rev.* **9**(2), 4 (2005).
100. R. Ghrist and A. Muhammad, Coverage and hole-detection in sensor networks via homology, *Proc. Int. Symp. Information Processing in Sensor Networks* (2005), p. 254.
101. X. Y. Li, D. K. Hunter and Y. Kun, Distributed coordinate free hole detection and recovery, *Proc. IEEE Global Telecommucations Conference* (2006), p. 1.
102. G. L. Wang, G. H. Cao and T. LaPorta, Movement-assisted sensor deployment, *Proc. IEEE Infocom* (2004), p. 2469.
103. A. Khan, C. M. Qiao, P. Sharma and S. K. Tripathi, An energy-efficient mobile triangulation-based coverage scheme, *Proc. IEEE Int. Conf. Communications* (2007), p. 3527.
104. G. L. Wang, G. H. Cao, T. LaPorta and W. S. Zhang, Sensor relocation in mobile sensor networks, *Proc. IEEE Infocom* (2005), p. 2302.
105. J. Wu and S. H. Yang, Smart: A scan-based movement-assisted sensor deployment method in wireless sensor networks, *Proc. IEEE Infocom* (2005), p. 2313.
106. J. Cortes, S. Martinez, T. Karatas and F. Bullo, Coverage control for mobile sensing networks, *IEEE Trans. Robot. Autom.* **20**(2), 243 (2004).
107. B. Y. Liu, P. Brass, O. Dousse, P. Nain and D. Towsley, Mobility improves coverage of sensor networks, *Proc. ACM Int. Symp. Mobile Ad Hoc Networking and Computing* (2005), p. 300.
108. N. Bisnik, A. Abouzeid and V. Isler, Stochastic event capture using mobile sensors subject to a quality metric, *Proc. ACM the 12th Annual Int. Conf. Mobile Computing and Networking* (2006), p. 98.
109. A. Howard, M. J. Matarijäc and G. S. Sukhatme, Mobile sensor network deployment using potential fields: A distributed, scalable solution to the area coverage problem, *Proc. 6th Int. Symp. Distributed Autonomous Robotics Systems* (2002), p. 1.
110. S. Poduri and G. S. Sukhatme, Constrained coverage for mobile sensor networks, *Proc. IEEE Int. Conf. Robotics and Automation* (2004), p. 165.
111. N. Heo and P. K. Varshney, A distributed self spreading algorithms for mobile wireless sensor networks, *Proc. IEEE Wireless Communications and Networking Conf.* (2003), p. 1597.
112. P. C. Wang, T. W. Hou and R. H. Yan, Maintaining coverage by progressive crystal-lattice permutation in mobile wireless sensor networks, *Proc. IEEE Int. Conf. Systems and Networks Communication* (2006), p. 1.
113. S. Chellappan, W. J. Gu, X. L. Bai, D. Xuan, B. Ma and K. Z. Zhang, Deploying wireless sensor networks under limited mobility constraints, *IEEE Trans. Mob. Comput.* **6**(10), 1142 (2007).
114. Y. Y. Yang and M. Cardei, Movement-assisted sensor redeployment scheme for network lifetime increase, *Proc. ACM 10th Int. Symp. Modeling Analysis and Simulation of Wireless and Mobile Systems* (2007), p. 13.

115. B. S. Manoj, A. Sekhar and C. S. R. Murthy, On the use of limited autonomous mobility for dynamic coverage maintenances, *Elsevier Comput. Network.* **51**(8), 2126 (2007).
116. Z. Butler and D. Rus, Event-based motion control for mobile sensor networks, *IEEE Pervas. Comput. Mag.* **2**(4), 34 (2003).
117. J. Balam and J. D. Gibson, Adaptive event coverage using high power mobiles over a sensor field, *Proc. IEEE Vehicular Technology Conf.*, Vol. 7 (2004), p. 4611.

Chapter 12

COGNITIVE NETWORKS

MANUEL PERALTA* and SUPRATIK MUKHOPADHYAY†
Utah State University, USA
**m.peralta@usa.edu*
†*supratik.mukhopadhyay@usa.edu*

RAMESH BHARADWAJ
Naval Research Laboratory, USA
ramesh@itd.nrl.navy.mil

KRISHNA SHENAI
University of Toledo, USA
kshenai@utnet.utoledo.edu

In this chapter, we study how combinations of knowledge processing techniques with networking technologies can help develop *cognitive networks* that involve heterogeneous devices connected through wireless/wired media which are context-aware, can sense and adapt their environment(s), make intelligent decisions and effect changes in their environment(s), can self-manage, self-heal, and self-protect. They can be profitably applied to make a difference in areas that include soil and water management in agriculture, intelligent management and optimization of power systems, reliable and smart control of fermentation processes and bio-reactors, management of environmental hazards and disasters, optimized modulation of communication antennas, precise management of hospitals and assisted living premises, and control of space and defense systems. We will study two applications: soil and water management in agriculture, and intelligent management and optimization of power systems.

1. Introduction

Cognitive networked systems will play the same role in the 21st century that the Internet played in the 20th century. A cognitive networked system is one that can perceive its environment and can adapt to it, make intelligent decisions based on its knowledge that effect changes in its environment, self-manage, and self-heal.

In recent years, heterogeneous networks involving sensors, actuators, access points, and control stations connected through wired/wireless media have been widely deployed in healthcare, military, automobile and space sectors. Because of their deployment in mission-critical sectors, reliable delivery of service as well as secure and trustworthy exchange of information between the elements of such networks are issues of utmost importance. Such issues are complicated by realtime, fault-tolerance and security requirements put forward by clients and service providers. Service providers and clients may be forced to run in meager-resource environments (e.g., on PDAs) with bandwidth limitations, and shortage of space and other critical resources and communicate different types of data (e.g., voice, multimedia) through highly unreliable and possibly eavesdropped communication channels that conform to different standards (e.g., IEEE 802.11, Zigbee, etc.). Individual nodes in such a network may monitor physical processes and/or generate appropriate reactions, in response to changing contexts, that get actuated through actuators. Information exchange in such a network involves passing messages between elements that include semi-structured data whose integrity can get compromised due to the presence of possible faults/breaches in the network.

Heterogeneous networks as mentioned above are now being deployed in mission-critical areas such as the military, space research, nuclear power plants, patient monitoring systems, etc. Any malfunction in such applications can result in catastrophic consequences. In many situations such networks have to operate without any human intervention. Hence, it is of utmost importance that they perform reliably and intelligently in accordance with the user's requirements. In order to provide service autonomously in a harsh rapidly-changing environment, such networks need to be context-aware, self-managing, self-healing, and self-reconfiguring.

Tremendous advances have been made in knowledge-based (distributed) software systems technology over the last 30 years. Today, such software systems are embedded in almost every device that we can think of ranging from X-ray machines, pacemakers and MRI machines to cell phones and GPS devices. These software systems process knowledge obtained from diverse sources and can make (hopefully smart) decisions based on this knowledge. They can receive percept streams from the environment, adapt to them, and make intelligent decisions based on their knowledge that effect changes in the environment, self-manage, and self-heal. During the past 20 years the artificial intelligence community has done a tremendous amount of research on providing knowledge-processing capabilities to computer and communication systems. The results of that research are bearing fruit today in diverse areas of human endeavor such as robotics, intelligent networks, smart buildings, and intelligent traffic management systems. In this chapter we study how combinations of knowledge processing techniques with networking technologies can help develop *cognitive networks* [48] that involve heterogeneous devices connected through wireless/wired media, which are context-aware, can sense and adapt to their environment(s), make intelligent decisions and effect changes in their environment(s), can self-manage, self-heal, and self-protect. They should be profitably applied to make a difference in areas that include soil and water management in agriculture, intelligent management and optimization of power systems, reliable and smart control of fermentation processes and bio-reactors, management of environmental hazards and disasters, optimized modulation of communication antennas, precise management of hospitals and assisted living premises, and control of space and defense systems.

2. Background

Fred Dretske's book "Knowledge and the Flow of Information" [49] is a classic work on knowledge and cognitive information processing. Dretske attempts to differentiate between ordinary information processing structures and cognitive structures. He argues that classical information theory, on which modern communication systems and networks are based, deals with the amount of information transmitted and not with its content. He goes on to state that the reason why an ordinary sensor that receives and transmits sensory information cannot be called a cognitive system is that such a system lacks an internal semantic belief state that controls its external behavior. In particular, an ordinary sensor receives information in "analog" form and does not have the capability to "digitalize" [49] that information. For instance, a camera does not have the capability to deduce the presence of raging ire from the picture of a forest fire. In this chapter, we study next-generation networked and communication systems in which elements have epistemic (or belief) states that are formed and changed based on the content of the information received and affect their external behavior and that have the capability of digitalizing analog information received from the environment. We examine how such elements can improve the functionality and reliability of sensor network-based mission-critical networked control systems. In this chapter we will study two particular networked control applications: soil and water management in agriculture, and intelligent management and optimization of power systems.

3. Soil and Water Management in Agriculture

World demand for fresh water is increasing, and competition for allocation of water between the urban and agricultural sectors is rapidly growing in arid and semi-arid climates. This has brought an emphasis on intensive water management to achieve greater system efficiencies, especially in irrigated agriculture in arid regions such as the western US. Further, studies by the Food and Agricultural Organization (FAO) and others predict that, in the coming 20 years, this competition for water will present potentially serious economic, political, and social problems for much of the population in both urban and rural areas of developing countries, especially in the arid and semi-arid regions of the world. The most cost-effective solution to these emerging problems lies in (i) the development and implementation of better technologies to acquire data at various spatial and temporal scales, (ii) the translation of such data into decision-relevant management information, and (iii) the empowerment of social institutions to take advantage of this information stream to improve the management of water resources. Current state-of-the-art irrigation control involves dumb wired sensors collecting data and reporting to costly data loggers that communicate with a gateway through RF, which in turn reports to a database through the Web [26]. The collected data is only used for informational purposes; control of actuators is not done in a reactive way [47]. Sprinklers are generally controlled by timers that can turn them on and off at specific times of the day without any regard to the current state of the soil, the weather forecast, and other factors. As a result, there is a tremendous wastage not only of water but also of energy. Wired sensors are affected by soil moisture content and salinity and are susceptible to damage due to the passage of tractors, etc. The fault proneness of such sensors is a big bottleneck for the application of sophisticated sensor technology to agricultural irrigation problems. Application of cognitive wireless sensor and networking technologies can potentially address these informational needs in the context of the achievement of greater water and energy efficiency in irrigated agriculture.

We present a novel irrigation control system to intelligently and reliably manage large soil and water ecological systems for environmental and agricultural applications. The control system is based on a cognitive wireless sensor network that can intelligently make control decisions and modulate the actuators precisely in realtime based on data about the soil parameters such as moisture content and salinity, and information about external factors such as the weather forecast. The system integrates intelligent sensor coordination and data fusion techniques to access, retrieve, process, and communicate with disparate wireless sensors in an ad hoc manner to deliver dynamic decisions and provide adequate information management. Our approach drastically reduces the hardware cost almost by a factor of 10 and removes the main bottleneck in irrigation control arising from wired sensors. Apart from this, it provides a smart control mechanism with formal reliability guarantees that is reconfigurable at runtime in response to changing requirements.

4. Intelligent Management and Optimization of Power Systems

Wall street guru George Gilder says "Information quality power is one of the greatest business opportunities of our time." However, over the last 30 years, neglect as well as lack of investment has resulted in the sorry state of our current infrastructure for generating and delivering power. Currently, over 60% of equipment needs replacing [32]. Despite significant advances in electronics and information technology during this time, the North American power grid (as well as power grids in other continents) still continues to use technology from the 19th and the early 20th century. Electromechanical relays (e.g., Buchholz relays) and other devices are still the order of the day. On the one hand, such an obsolete grid presents significant challenges in transmitting power reliably and efficiently; on the other, the demands of consumers have kept on increasing — demands for the provision of more energy more efficiently and reliably and at a lower cost. It is also notable that reliability is a major concern in managing an expansive power system (consider the 2003 US blackout). Today, energy is one of the principal driving forces of the global information economy. Failure to deliver power reliably and efficiently can have disastrous consequences. With the proliferation of digital and analog devices being used in mission-critical environments, the need for delivery of high quality power is even more critical.

By a *cognitive power system* we mean an electric power system in which generation, transmission and distribution are managed intelligently and adaptively by smart distributed communication networks whose elements may consist of wireless or wired sensors (e.g., power factor meters, thermometers), actuators (e.g., static VAR compensators, variable voltage transformers), simulators, and other services orchestrated by a network software layer. Such systems are modulated by a distributed closed-loop control system; apart from transforming our obsolete power grid into a self-managing, self-protecting, self-healing, and enduring one, these control systems attempt to optimize the operation of a power system with objectives including but not limited to minimization of line loss, voltage fluctuations, illegal usage, and peak time load imbalance. Today, smartly-managed power grids are still in their infancy. According to Morgan Stanley [32], "Silicon will reconfigure the grid. ... will make the electric grid a smart, efficient, and adaptive system — just as Web and telecommunication systems are." In North America alone, the power system market is US$275 billion [32]; out of that the market for electronics, communication networks, and software for intelligently controlling the grid amounts to US$81 billion. Power systems today are characterized by distributed generation, one of the main reasons for this being the increasing incorporation of renewable sources of energy into the grid photovoltaics such as photovoltaics and biogas. Today's power system is thus a hybrid one (see Fig. 1) consisting of different kinds of energy sources, different types of transmission systems, along with different kinds of customers. As a result, such systems require decentralized, rather than centralized, management.

Merely replacing vintage equipment with new ones without embracing modern technology will not help meet today's energy challenges. Of course, advances in power electronics over the last 30 years have resulted in better devices, which are cheaper, smaller, and more efficient than previous generations. For example, power electronics-based transformers today are not only more efficient than their old-generation counterparts with copper winding, they can be programmed to step up or step down with different ratios. However, installing such next-generation equipment is not only extremely capital intensive, it also solves only a part of the problem. Even with such costly state-of-the-art equipment, power systems will continue to be inefficient unless they are intelligently managed. Smartly managing a grid as expansive as the North American power grid calls for integration of state-of-the-art sensing and networking technologies with knowledge-processing capabilities.

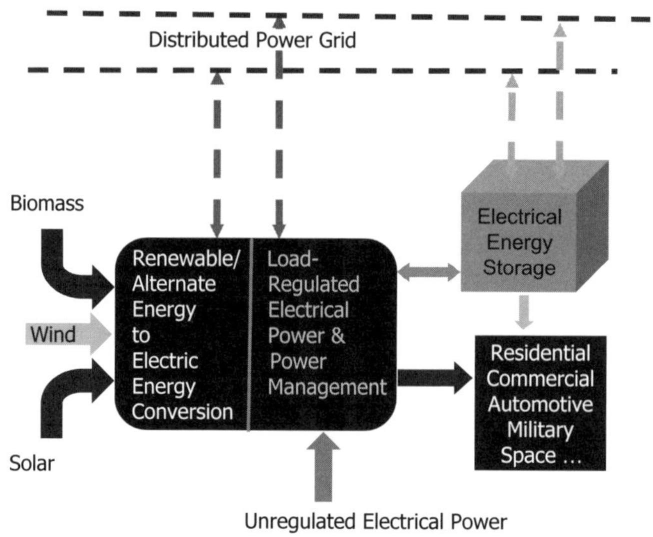

Fig. 1. Today's distributed hybrid power system.

In this chapter, we aim to integrate fundamental principles from formal methods, engineering, and information sciences to develop novel techniques and tools and for intelligent and reliable management of power systems. More precisely, we develop a novel distributed wireless sensor network-oriented knowledge-based control system to intelligently and reliably manage the operation of large power systems. Our controller combines techniques from knowledge-based systems with state-of-the-art distributed information integration and networking technologies. It integrates intelligent sensor coordination and data fusion techniques to access, retrieve, process, and communicate with disparate wireless sensors in an ad hoc manner to deliver dynamic decisions and provide adequate information management. The system provides formal guarantees that the policies and requirements of the customer will be met and quality of service (QoS) guarantees such as security, fault-tolerance and timeliness will be respected even in rapidly changing environments. The system is amenable to dynamic reconfiguration in response to changing requirements without incurring any system downtime. It is integrated with state-of-the-art provenance management techniques to prevent false triggers of actuating devices, and it uses state-of-the-art data structures from distributed computing to ensure scalability over an expansive grid.

4.1. *An Example Management Scenario*

Figure 2 describes a sample scenario for controlling the power factor and voltage fluctuation in a power grid. Low power factors can result in increased losses while voltage fluctuations can damage equipments. Low power factors are generally caused by inductive or capacitive loads, e.g., furnaces, fluorescent lamps, etc. Today,

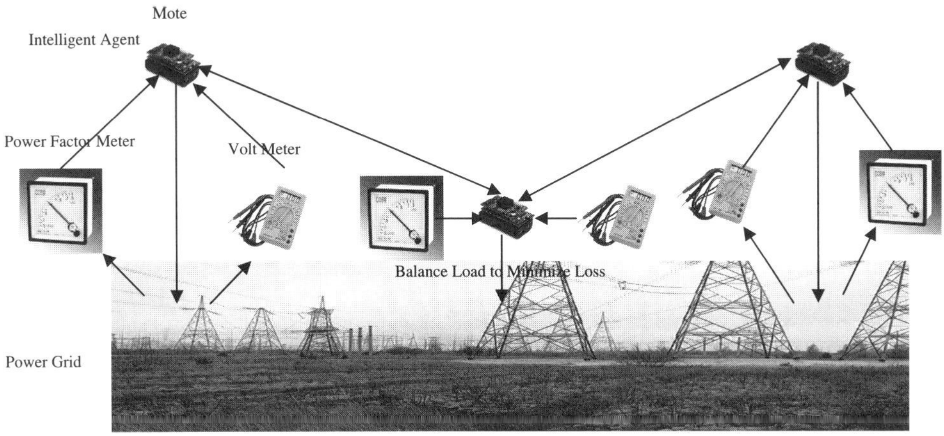

Fig. 2. A power factor and voltage control scenario.

energy companies impose penalty surcharges on customers (e.g., steel plants) that operate loads such as furnaces. This increases the electricity bills of manufacturing industries by millions of dollars every year. Given the current off-shoring trend of manufacturing industry, such penalty surcharges will not result in a business friendly atmosphere. Intelligent management of power systems and loads can alleviate the problem.

The voltage as well as the power factor across the power system are sampled by installing power factor meters and voltmeters distributed spatially at different loads. These meters locally report to motes running knowledge-based distributed intelligent software agents that make intelligent control decisions based on the data. Motes can communicate among one another as well as with control stations. If the power factor is significantly below unity in a particular area, the control action might be switching on a static VAR compensator (capacitive or inductive, depending on whether the power factor is lagging or leading) to correct the power factor. This action is actuated through a driver. Switching on a static VAR compensator may result in voltage fluctuations (with voltage increasing for a capacitive compensator and decreasing for an inductive compensator). The software agent, in response to such data from the local voltmeter, will order the automatic switching on of a transformer (step up or step down) depending on the situation. Depending on the stability characteristics of the power system, the transient effects will reduce over time resulting in stabilization of the voltage and power factor at the respective set points.

5. Related Work

Significant research has been done in massively distributed environment-aware computing (also known as "swarm computing" [1–3]), in particular on creating and reasoning about swarm programs. Most of these works have been focused on developing programming paradigms, tools, and languages for swarm computing.

EnviroTrack [3], an object-based distributed middleware system, raises the level of programming abstraction for distributed sensor networks by providing a convenient and powerful interface to the application developer geared towards tracking the physical environment. Menezes *et al.* [2] study different abstractions in the field of swarms. In Ref. 39, the authors develop an agent-based framework for simulating power and communication systems. In Refs. 16, 40 and 41, techniques and languages for programming sensor networks are developed. In Ref. 42, the authors describe the problems in the monitoring and control of large scale power systems and offer the Astrolabe framework [43] as a robust solution. The author of Ref. 44 estimates that power systems failure affects 700,000 customers every year. He suggests multi-agent systems as a way of ameliorating the problem.

None of these works, however, are concerned with the problem of using formal methods for building distributed reliable knowledge-based sensor-oriented systems that provide provable guarantees of meeting users' requirements.

6. A Framework for Cognitive Networks

Figure 3 describes the conceptual framework for our approach. Data from different sources (sensors, weather stations, reports from observers, voltmeters, ampere meters, energy meters, power factor meters, power system simulators, etc.) are received by distributed knowledge-based intelligent software agents (a software agent is a program that can sense its environment and can effect changes in it) running in motes (small devices having embedded processors) that can be situated at different locations (typically these motes will be physically located close to loads

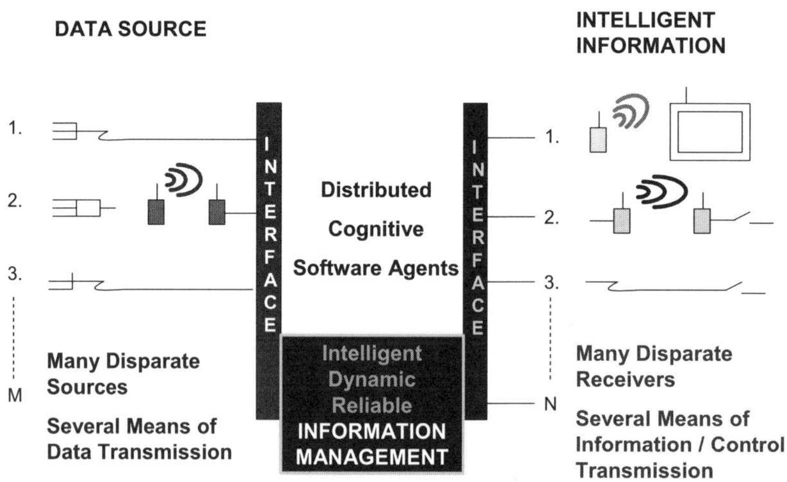

Fig. 3. Information management in cognitive networks.

in power systems or on the surface in irrigated agricultural land; several such motes can be installed in a steel plant for example). Deployed software agents provide naming, discovery, routing, identity, and security for the motes. Agents in different motes are able to communicate among themselves as well as with base stations and can interact with physical devices through drivers for actuation and for receiving alerts. The communication among agents and with data sources and actuators (e.g., sprinklers, static VAR compensators, and circuit breakers) is managed through a reliable software infrastructure. The infrastructure provides an event-driven publish-subscribe framework for sending and receiving alerts. The agents, based on their collective knowledge (shared through communication), make smart decisions that are actuated through drivers.

Location of all the individual motes can be tracked using wireless communication within a range of 350 ft ($\sim$100 m). A reliable communication medium between the diverse elements of the network is provided by the Secure Infrastructure for Networked Systems (SINS), a formally verifiable middleware framework developed by Dr. Bharadwaj and Dr. Mukhopadhyay as part of the SINS project [14]. SINS uses the Spread [17] group communication tool from Johns Hopkins University as a transport layer. We have built a distributed hash table [33] on top of the SINS platform to ensure scalability. SINS has data provenance mechanisms built in to prevent spurious triggers of actuators.

Figure 4 shows an architecture for generating and deploying software agents in our framework. Given a set of services and devices available in a network (in this case, sensors, probes, meters, base stations, and software and hardware services running on them or on the Internet), their formal interface specifications are stored in the cognitive information management (CIM) directory (see Fig. 4) as logical formulas in CIM logic. CIM logic is an intuitionistic hybrid modal logic [29] suitable for knowledge representation for our domain (see below). The CIM directory is a database that provides an interface for querying and updating records. The CIM logic interface specifications of services and devices can be obtained by automatically compiling UPnP [18] specifications (available as a UPnP database from the manufacturers) to CIM logic using a compiler. The CIM directory is replicated for fault-tolerance with standard techniques used to maintain consistency.

The agent generator (see Fig. 4) is the heart of our architecture. It is a deductive engine that uses knowledge represented declaratively as CIM logic sentences to automatically generate distributed intelligent software agents that are guaranteed to meet the application requirements. It can interact with the CIM directory. It implements natural deduction-based proof systems for the CIM logic. The agents synthesized from the knowledge use the inputs of the sensors/meters/probes and the management policies of the customer to generate realtime control decisions for managing the system. The control decisions can either be delivered to appropriate personnel for manual intervention or directly actuated through wireless actuators. The agents can be deployed automatically on a distributed

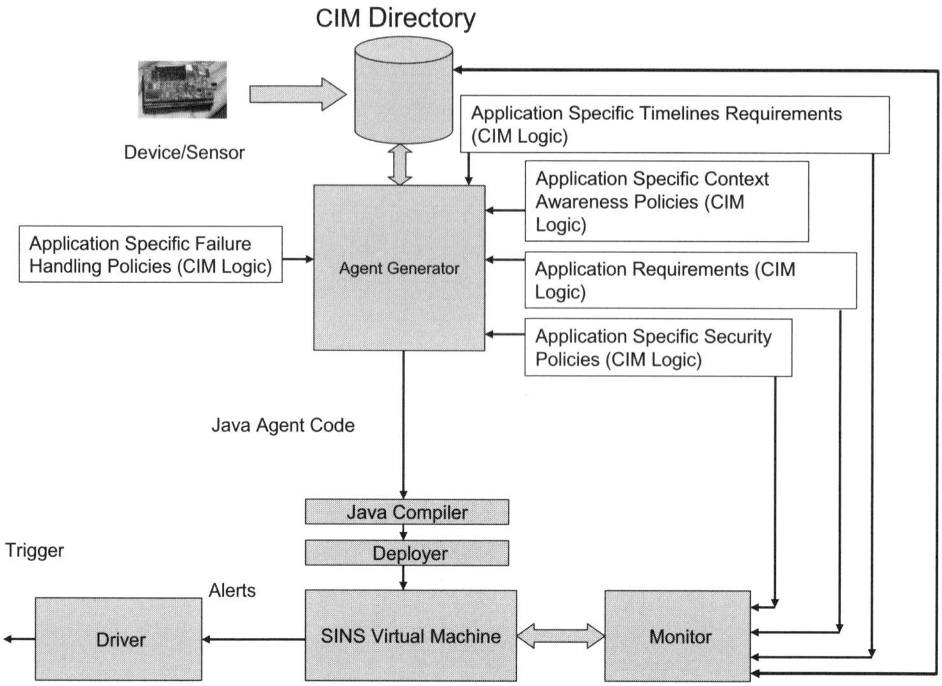

Fig. 4. Agent generation and deployment architecture.

network involving sensors'/meters'/probes' tracking system parameters, actuators' controlling devices, sprinklers, relays, breakers, and valves, and diverse computing and communication elements such as PDAs, etc. Our approach provides formal guarantees that the policies of the customer are respected and the QoS goals specified by them are met even in changing conditions like sensors failing, actuators changing their configuration or network nodes getting compromised. Changing environments are handled by a dynamic reconfiguration of the agents by a monitoring agent. Reconfiguration may include substituting new services/devices for existing ones and can be used to provide new functionalities in response to changing requirements.

The agent generator takes as input application-specific policies for security, context-awareness, failure handling [19], and realtime response as CIM logic sentences (see Fig. 4). In order to hide the formal logic from an untrained user, a SCR table-like [34] intuitive graphical user interface can be provided. The graphical user interface can be readily assembled using Adobe's flex [35]. In addition, the agent generator takes as input the management objectives (application requirements) of the customer as CIM logic formulas. It tries to constructively prove the management objectives of the customer using the logical formulas in the CIM directory as axioms and the application-specific policies input by the user as constraints. The proof shows how the data from the different sources are integrated under the application constraints to make decisions for meeting management objectives. From the proof, distributed agents in Java can be synthesized automatically using a Curry–Howard style correspondence [38].

The agents are then compiled to Java byte-code and automatically wirelessly deployed on SINS virtual machines (SVMs) running on different hosts in the network (base stations, motes) using specified deployment information. We use Xito [36] for automatically deploying the agents over the network. SVMs have a small footprint allowing deployment on resource-constrained motes. Monitoring agents running in SVMs can detect possible violations of policies and take action for immediate recovery. Monitoring agents are also automatically synthesized from the knowledge base. They ensure fault tolerance and guard against cyber attacks.

7. Knowledge Representation with CIM Logic

Table 1 shows a fragment of the syntax of CIM logic. CIM logic is a normal hybrid modal logic. It is hybrid in the sense that it allows terms (called nominals) denoting states to be used as formulas. CIM logic specifications can express QoS requirements like context-awareness and timeliness. The logic is equipped with a sometime/eventually modality for temporal evolution, and a somewhere modality for spatial location. It has nominals standing for state. There are atomic formulas (with a typed signature; note that every variable is typed; for the sake of readability, we do not provide the types in Table 1) for describing relations among variables. We provide a constructive/intuitionistic interpretation of the logic, that is, classical

Table 1. Syntax of a fragment of CIM logic.

$\phi 1, \phi 2$ ::-	Formula
F	false
U	nominal
n	name
pred$(x_1, \ldots, x_n)$	atomic formula
$x \sim c$	atomic constraint
$//\sim ::= > \mid < \mid \leq \mid \geq$, c is a natural number	
$\phi 1 \rightarrow \varphi 2$	implication
$\phi 1 \wedge \phi 2$	conjunction
φ	sometime or eventually
$\Theta\phi$	somewhere
Sense$(u;\ \phi;\ loc)$	senses u
serv$(u;\ v;\ \phi 1;\ \phi 2;\ I)$	service invocation returning u
@T$(I,\ \sigma)$	constraint σ becomes true
@F$(I,\ \sigma)$	constraint σ becomes false
@C$(I,\ x)$	variable x becomes changes
PREV(x)	previous value of variable
INIT$(x,\ u)$	initial value of x is u
$\exists t\phi$	existential quantification on time
$\exists I\varphi$	quantification over nominals

negation is not allowed and for any formula φ, the formula ($\varphi \vee (\varphi \rightarrow$F)) is not a tautology. This is done with the aim of generating constructive proofs of formulas from which distributed Java agents will be synthesized. We assume a finite set of nominals (the participants in a computation). We provide a brief explanation of important formulas of the logic below with examples. The formula serv(u; v; φ1; φ2; I) describes the properties of a software/hardware service on the network declaratively. Basically, it describes a service to which an object u is passed as parameter, returns object v, satisfies the pattern φ1, can be invoked by a process that matches the pattern φ2, and is exported by the entity with nominal I (that includes the location of the entity). The formula Sense(u; φ; *loc*) states that the object u is sensed from a sensor that matches the pattern φ and is located at location *loc*. We limit ourselves to regular patterns here. The formulas @T(I, σ), @F(I, σ), and @C(I, x) stand for, respectively, the entity with nominal I comes to know that the truth value of constraint σ has changed from false to true, the truth value of constraint σ has changed from true to false, and the value of variable x has changed. The formula PREV(x) (a term used as a formula since this is a hybrid logic) denotes the previous value of the variable x while the formula INIT(x, u) states that the initial value of x is u. Let us provide some examples of specifications in CIM logic. A meter "met" sensing voltage would be specified as

$$(\text{Sense}(\textit{voltage}; \text{"met"}; \textit{loc}) \rightarrow @C(S, \textit{voltage}).$$

Several things to note here. First, instead of using material implication, we use Lewis-style strict implication [31] to avoid vacuous truth; here ? is the dual of $\Diamond$. Second, S is a nominal and not a constant. The specification states that if any entity S subscribes to the voltage variable published by "met", it will see a change in voltage every time "met" samples a new voltage. Additionally, we have the axiom that @T(I, φ) $\rightarrow$ @C(I, x), where φ is an expression involving the variable x. The specification fragment for a simple voltage factor controller is

$$
\begin{array}{l}
(\text{INIT}(\textit{alert}, \textit{off}) \rightarrow \\
\quad (\text{PREV}(\textit{alert}) = \textit{off} \\
\quad \rightarrow (@\text{T}(\text{VoltageController}, \textit{voltage} >= 1000) \\
\qquad \rightarrow \textit{High}) \\
\qquad \wedge (\neg(@\text{T}(\text{VoltageController}, \textit{voltage} >= 1000) \\
\qquad \rightarrow \\
\text{PREV}(\textit{alert}))))
\end{array}
$$

Let us call this specification *spec1*. It says that *alert* should be initially *off* and thereafter if *voltage* changes to 1000 or more then a *High* alert should be sent.

The CIM logic is equipped with a sound and complete proof system based on natural deduction. The proof rules, which we do not provide here, involve introduction and elimination rules for the various logical constants.

7.1. *Synthesis of Java Agents*

Java agents are synthesized by a natural deduction [30] of the management objectives using the axioms contained in the CIM directory under the constraints provided as policies by the customer. From the proof, Java agents are synthesized using a Curry–Howard-style correspondence. For example, consider the specification *spec1* above. From the presence of the variable *voltage* in it, as well as the presence of the specification of the meter "met" in the CIM directory that publishes the variable *voltage* (using the Sense modality), the proof system will conclude that the *VoltageController* will subscribe to a variable voltage that is published by the meter "met". This will lead the agent generator to generate the following Java code fragment for the Voltage Controller for indicating that voltage is the variable that it monitors:

```
public HashMap<String, HashMap<String, Object>> getMonVars()
                     throws Exception {
HashMap<String, HashMap<String, Object>> ht = new HashMap<String,
HashMap<String, Object>>();
                                HashMap<String, Object> prop = null;
                                prop = new HashMap<String, Object>();
                                prop.put("value", Voltage);
                                ht.put("Voltage", prop);
            return ht;
       }

                                                                    }
```

The rest of the specification *spec1* would be translated to the following Java code.

```
import java.util.*;
import sins.*;
public class VoltageController implements Deterministic, Reactive{
enum YAlert { Off,High };
int Voltage, PREV_Voltage;
YAlert Alert, PREV_Alert;

public void init(){
Alert=YAlert.Off;
}

public YAlert Alert(){
switch(PREV_Alert){
case Off:
```

```
    if((Voltage>=1000) && !(PREV_Voltage>=1000)) return YAlert.High;
    return PREV_Alert;
}
return
 YAlert.Off;
}
}
```

The theoretical computational complexity of agent synthesis is $O(d^N \times F^C \times P)$ where d is the number of disjuncts in the knowledge base, P is the number of nominals involved, F is the size of the set of axioms in CIM directory, c is the maximal constant in the knowledge base supplied, and N is the number of conjuncts in the knowledge base. The parameters N and C are usually not too large for real examples.

8. Hardware Infrastructure

8.1. *Agricultural Deployment*

A high-level view of the smart irrigation control system described in this chapter is illustrated in Fig. 5. It employs a novel method for underground communication in a wireless sensor network using magnetic induction [4]. The wireless, fully-buried soil moisture sensing node is equipped with one or more ferromagnetic coils which

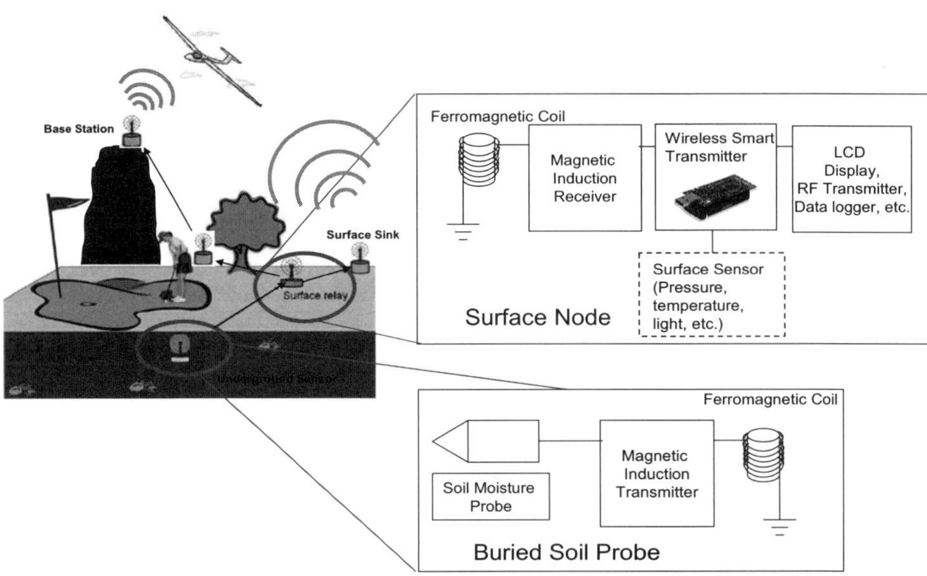

Fig. 5. High level view of agricultural deployment (the left-hand side scenario is adapted from Ref. 5).

are stimulated by a current oscillating at a certain carrier frequency. A time-varying magnetic field will result, propagating from the buried node to the surface relay. The sensor data is transmitted via the resulting magnetic field by modulation of the carrier signal. The time-varying magnetic flux density incident on a second coil onboard the receiving node induces a modulated voltage from which the data is recovered.

Communication is configured for peer-to-peer ad hoc networking and uses multi-hopping to pass data from node to node and eventually to a local area surface node where data is analyzed and transmitted through the air using conventional RF methods. The magnetic field used to transmit the sensor data has very little sensitivity to soil type, composition (excepting soils containing magnetites), compaction, or moisture content, unlike existing RF transmission technologies [5]. Magnetic induction transmission also requires less power than short-range RF transmitters due to simpler circuitry and lower operating frequencies [6–8]. A ferromagnetic coil may also be used as a recharging device for the buried node, eliminating the need to unearth the sensor for battery replacement. Periodic recharging transmissions from a surface node to a buried node will occur, using the voltage induced in the buried coil to charge the sensor node battery.

9. Sensor Network

A schematic diagram of the sensor network is provided in Fig. 6. Although only two sensor nodes are shown, experimental results have indicated that the network can efficiently handle a large number of nodes. The underground buried sensors transmit a signal wirelessly through magnetic induction to the surface relays, which are configured to accept this type of signal, manipulate it and then transmit it to a surface sink or to other surface relays.

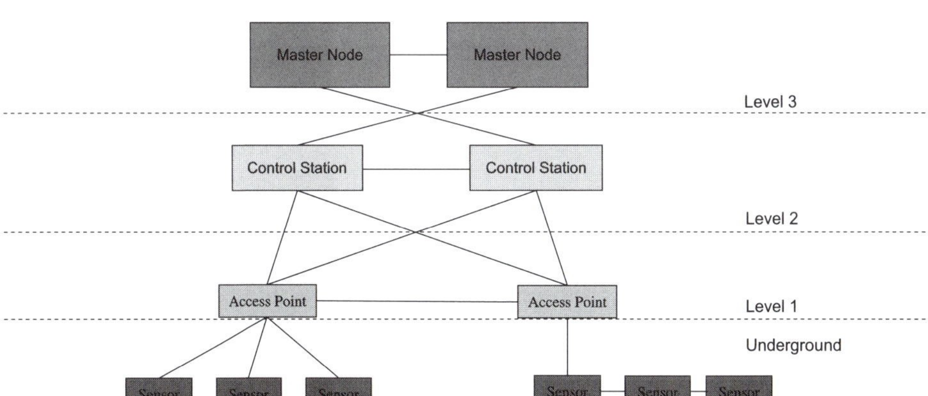

Fig. 6. Irrigation control sensor network.

A surface relay is a wireless mote [21] that is programmed to accept input, analyze it and transmit the signal to another surface relay or base station depending on the set of instructions given to it. The surface sinks are also wireless motes, but with different configurations, and are assigned to different tasks. The surface sink accepts data from the surface relays in order to bridge a connection between the surface relays and the base stations. The base stations can be considered as workstations where data is collected and analyzed for decision-making or to transmit a signal to another data collector device such as an unmanned aerial vehicle (UAV).

The input to the surface relay contains critical information regarding several different soil properties. A novel multifunction sensor probe that provides frequency-dependent measures of complex permittivity for soil volumetric water content (VWC) determination in addition to soil temperature and soil electrical conductivity is deployed. The sensor output voltage is digitally sampled, processed, and used to power the transmitting ferromagnetic coil using a specially designed ultra low-power CMOS mixed signal magnetic induction receiver module with embedded power management, thus minimizing the overall power consumption and increasing the battery life [9]. The surface nodes in state-of-the-art instruments used today utilize sensors that detect soil properties wired serially to a data logger, which is used for data collection and communication between base stations, as shown in Fig. 7.

The data logger measures sensor signals, provides non-volatile data storage, initiates measurement and control functions based on time or event, and controls

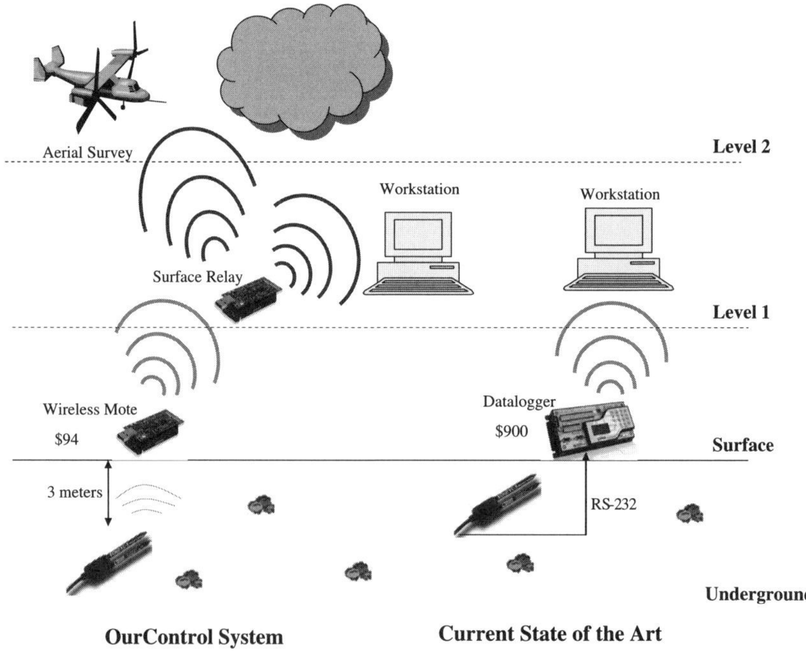

Fig. 7. Novelty of our irrigation controller.

external devices such as pumps, motors, alarms, etc. Moreover, it can interface with on-site and telecommunication devices such as transceivers, satellite transmitters, and Ethernet interfaces. The data logger is configured to issue and read control signals from the sensors using a serial connection between the data logger and sensors such as RS-232 or CS I/O ports [10]. All sensors are serially connected to the data logger in order to transmit the data from the data logger to a base station via an RF communication. This poses serious limitations for the use of state-of-the-art technology for large-scale integration. For example, to measure soil properties at several locations in a large field or watershed, long wires need to be installed to establish a connection between the sensors and the data logger. Although this can be achieved by routing the wires on the surface or underground, this approach is expensive and not commercially viable especially in applications where wired architecture is impractical. The current controller solves this problem with less expensive instrumentation and in a wireless architecture.

In our controller, shown in Figs. 6 and 7, costly data loggers are replaced with novel surface relay nodes that are wirelessly connected to a central server which handles data collection and manipulation while providing a web interface to schedule jobs or tasks on the network via Java Runtime Environment. The wireless module nodes (TelosB and Mica2 motes) can act as base stations or wireless sensors depending on the way in which they are programmed. The main building blocks of these motes are the low-power microcontroller and the digital spectrum radio. The low-power microcontroller (TI MSP430), designed by Texas Instruments, consumes very little power during operation and can be programmed easily via a USB interface to perform several simultaneous tasks depending on the signal received. The digital-spectrum radio (CC2420), designed by Chipcon Inc., is compliant with IEEE 802.15.4, and can transmit a signal across a 100-m range at a frequency up to 2.4 GHz. The motes contain a 10 kb memory that is used to install the programming instructions on in order to sample, transmit or process data. Due to the low power consumption of these motes, they can last for several months using two AA batteries [11].

The motes interface with several devices such as sensor boards (MTS400, used in agriculture to sense ambient light, barometric pressure, temperature and humidity) and data acquisition boards (MDA320, used for precision data collection and analysis) through a serial I/O interface. To further reduce the cost of the surface relay, we replace TelosB and Mica2 motes with a novel, specially designed mote consisting of a commercial low-power RF transceiver interfaced between a Java smart-card [27] and a magnetic induction receiver chip. The net result is a cost reduction from US$94 to US$10 per surface relay. We provide a connection between the surface magnetic induction receiver and the Java card through a serial I/O by placing electric contacts on the Java card processor and connecting them to the output port of the receiver. During this stage, the Java application downloaded on the processor will receive incoming signals and will act accordingly by initiating commands to send data and the status of received signal to a transceiver, which will transmit the signal via RF.

In our controller, data on soil properties are collected initially from underground using a commercial soil probe (ECH20 EC-5 soil probe) and communicated to the surface relay via magnetic induction. This commercial probe will be subsequently replaced with a novel multi-function soil moisture sensor. The motes interact with one another and all the data are sent simultaneously in realtime to a central server where all the information is stored. This gives the user access to vital data anytime and from anywhere by accessing the server thorough the Internet. The server is used to synthesize and deploy software agents on all these motes and set the infrastructure of the wireless network.

10. Thoughts for Practitioners

Next-generation networked systems will consist of smart elements such as intelligent routers and motes that form and change epistemic states or beliefs based on the content of the information that they receive from the environment as well as other elements. The behavior of the network will depend on these epistemic states. We envision that the next generation networks will be adaptive with adaptability stemming from changing epistemic states. We believe that next-generation networks will be controlled and managed by software that will be automatically synthesized and deployed on demand and will be agnostic to the communication media. Because such networks will be deployed in mission-critical systems, the reliability of such software is an important issue.

11. Directions for Future Research

There remain several open problems that need to be solved before cognitive networks can become part of mainstream practice. Some future research directions are:

(i) Developing techniques and tools for verifying and validating the correctness of software controlling complex networked systems. The techniques need to scale up in order to verify software controlling networks comprising hundreds of thousands of nodes.
(ii) Developing techniques and tools for performance analysis of cognitive networks. New performance measures are needed that can characterize adaptability, context-awareness, etc.

12. Conclusions

Our approach has the following benefits:

(i) *Formal guarantees*: Our approach is unique in that it formally guarantees that the goals of the user are met, QoS constraints are respected and none of the policies imposed by the individual services/devices or the application are violated even in changing environments. Satisfaction of non-functional safety specifications is also guaranteed.

(ii) *Automatic synthesis of agents*: Our technique allows the synthesis of intelligent distributed agents from declarative specification of the business logic, QoS goals, and formal models of available devices and services.

(iii) *Automatic deployment*: Our approach allows automatic deployment of the bytecode obtained by compiling an agent to run on an SVM specified by the deployment information.

(iv) *Security and other QoS goals*: The modeling approach as well as the implementation of SINS encompasses an in-built security model for providing security guarantees, which are essential for deployment in a multi-zone implementation.

(v) *Maintaining data provenance*: Our approach provides a mechanism for certifying the provenance/pedigree of the data exchanged between agents and helps in preventing the generation of spurious triggers for activating services/devices.

(vi) *Reconfigurability*: It is possible in our approach to reconfigure an agent at runtime. Such reconfiguration may include substituting new services/devices for existing ones and can be used to provide new functionalities in response to changing requirements.

(vii) *Underground wireless transmission*: Wireless transmission of data on soil properties from underground sensors solves a bottleneck in irrigation monitoring and control.

Finally, our magnetic induction based innovative communication technology not only reduces the cost of a sensor network by a factor of 10 but also improves water and energy efficiency substantially in irrigated agriculture.

Terminology

Cognitive structure: A structure that has a semantic epistemic state.

Sensor network: Networks consisting of sensors, actuators, etc. that interact with the physical world.

Formal methods: Techniques based on mathematical logic for reasoning about the correctness of hardware and software systems.

Software agent: A software program that can sense its environment and can effect changes in it.

Mote: A small device having an embedded processor.

Adaptable system: A system that changes its behavior in response to changing environment.

Context awareness: A concept that connects computer systems with changes in the environment.

Curry–Howard correspondence: A correspondence between proofs in mathematical logic and programs.

Middleware: Software that glues together different software components.

Mission-critical system: A computer system whose malfunction can cause loss of life, property, etc.

Exercises

1. Suppose that you are programming a mote that can use different means of communication (i.e., different communication protocols) depending on the situation (e.g., Bluetooth for short range, RF for long range, etc.). What design pattern(s) [45] would you use for programming a software agent for controlling communication in such a mote? Write Java code for such a software agent.
2. Write a Java program for controlling the water level in a swimming pool. Annotate your code with assertions. Use ESC/Java [46] to verify your program.
3. Write a program to control a sensor network corresponding to the voltage and power factor modulation scenario of Fig. 2 in nesC [16].
4. Consider the temporal logic CTL [50]. Is the formula $(\phi \wedge \psi)$ logically equivalent to the formula $\phi \wedge \psi$?
5. Is the formula $\sigma \rightarrow$@T(I, σ), where σ is a constraint, valid?
6. In propositional logic, is the formula $p \rightarrow p \rightarrow p \rightarrow p$, where p is an atomic proposition, valid? If so, provide a natural deduction proof for the formula.
7. Is it possible to frame the problem of automatically synthesizing a program (a state machine) from a CTL specification as the problem of finding the winning strategy for a two-player game?
8. Draw an interaction diagram for the voltage and power factor control system in Fig. 2.
9. Draw an interaction diagram for the irrigation management system in Fig. 5.
10. Use the Spread group communication tool [17] to develop a program for transferring small files from one computer to another in a wireless network.

References

1. D. Evans, Programming the Swarm, NSF C. A. Proposal.
2. R. Menezes and R.Tolksdorf, A new App. to scalable Linda-systems based on Swarms, *SAC* 375–379 (2003).
3. T. Abdelzaher, B. Blum B, Q. Cao, Y. Chen, D. Evans, J. George, S. George, L. Gu, T. He, S. Krishnamurthy, L. Luo, S. Son, J. Stankovic, R. Stoleru and A. Wood, EnviroTrack: Towards an environmental computing paradigm for distributed sensor networks, *24th Int. Conf. Distributed Computing Systems*, Tokyo, Japan, March 23–26 (2004).

4. K. Shenai and N. Jack, Device and method for wireless communication using magnetic induction, US Provisional Patent Document (in file), Technology Commercialization Office, Utah State University, Logan, UT.
5. I. F. Akyildiz and E. P. Stuntebeck, Wireless underground sensor networks: Research challenges, *Science Direct — Ad Hoc Networks 4* (Elsevier, 2006), pp. 669–686.
6. J. J. Sojdehei, P. N. Wrathall and D. F. Dinn, Magneto-inductive (MI) communications, *IEEE MTT-S Digest*, MTS 0-933057-28-9, pp. 513–519.
7. C. Bunszel, Magnetic induction: A low-power wireless alternative, *RF Design*, November (2001), pp. 78–80.
8. C. Bunszel, Linking home devices with magnetic induction, CommsDesign, Freescale Semiconductors, available at www.commsdesign.com/showArticle.jhtml?articleID=16503424.
9. R. N. Simons, D. G. Hall and F. A. Miranda, RF telemetry system for an implantable bio-MEMS sensor, *IEEE MTT-S Digest* (2004), pp. 1433–1436.
10. Campbell Scientific, Inc., www.campbellsci.com/dataloggers.
11. Division of Engineering and Applied Sciences, Harvard University, Cambridge, MA, www.eecs.harvard.edu/~mdw/proj/codeblue/.
12. S. S. Yau, *et al.*, Automated synthesis of workflows for service-based systems, *Int. J. Web Ser. Res.* (2007).
13. S. S. Yau, H. Davulcu, S. Mukhopadhyay, D. Huang and Y. Yao, Adaptable situation-aware secure service-based (AS^3) systems, *ISORC 2005*, 308–315 (2005).
14. R. Bharadwaj, Verifiable middleware for secure agent interoperability, *Proc. 2nd IEEE Workshop on Formal Approaches to Agent-Based Systems (FAABS II)*, 126–132 (2002).
15. H. Abelson, D. Allen, D. Coore, C. Hanson, G. Homsy, T. F. Knight, R. Nagpal, E. Rauch, G. J. Sussman and R. Weiss, *Amorphous Comput. Commun. ACM* **43**(5), 74–82 (2000).
16. D. Gay, P. Levis, R. von Behren, M. Welsh, E. Brewer and D. Culler, The nesC language: A holistic approach to networked embedded systems, *Proc. Programming Language Design and Implementation (PLDI)*, June (2003).
17. Y. Amir, C. Danilov, M. Miskin-Amir, J. Schultz and J. Stanton, The Spread toolkit: Architecture and performance, Technical report, Johns Hopkins University.
18. http://www.upnp.org.
19. S. S. Yau, S. Mukhopadhyay and R. Bharadwaj, Specification, analysis and implementation of architectural patterns for dependable software systems, *WORDS 2005*, 197–204 (2005).
20. R. Bharadwaj, S. Mukhopadhyay and N. Padh, Service composition in a secure agent-based architecture. *EEE 2005*, 787–788 (2005).
21. http://www.xbow.com
22. A. Benveniste, P. Caspi, S. A. Edwards, N. Halbwachs, P. Le Guernic and R. de Simone, The synchronous languages 12 years later, *Proc. IEEE* **91**(1), 64–83 (2003).
23. R. Bharadwaj and S. Mukhopadhyay, From synchrony to SINS, Technical report, Utah State University (2006).
24. R. Bharadwaj and S. Sims, Salsa: Combining constraint solvers with BDDs for automatic invariant checking, *Proc. 6th Int. Conf. Tools and Algorithms for the Construction and Analysis of Systems (TACAS'2000), ETAPS 2000*, Berlin, March (2000).
25. P. Maier, A Lattice-theoretic framework for circular assume guarantee reasoning, PhD thesis, MPI (2005).
26. www.campbellsci.com/index.cfm.

27. Wikipedia, available at http://en.wikipedia.org/wiki/Java_Card [Accessed September 11, 2007].
28. A. Appel, *Compiling with Continuations* (Cambridge University Press, 1992).
29. P. Blackburn, M. de Rijke and Y. Venema, *Modal Logic* (Cambridge University Press, 2002).
30. D. Prawitz, *Natural Deduction: A Proof-Theoretical Study* (Dover Publications, 2006).
31. E. W. Dijkstra, *A Discipline of Programming* (Prentice Hall, 1976).
32. http://www.globalenvironmentfund.com/Emerging_Smart_Grid.pdf.
33. http://en.wikipedia.org/wiki/Distributed_hash_table.
34. 34. C. L. Heitmeyer, R. D. Jeffords and B. G. Labaw, Automated consistency checking of requirements specifications, *ACM Trans. Softw. Eng. Methodol.* **5**(3), 231–261 (1996).
35. www.adobe.com/products/flex/.
36. http://www.xito.org.
37. G. Priest, *An Introduction to Non-Classical Logic* (Cambridge University Press, 2001).
38. H. Barendregt, *The Lambda Calculus, Its Syntax and Semantics* (North-Holland, 1984).
39. K. Hopkinson *et al.*, EPOCHS: Integrated cots software for agent-based electric power and communication simulation, *IEEE Trans. Power Systems.*
40. A. Awan, S. Jagannathan and A. Grama, Macroprogramming heterogeneous sensor networks using cosmos, *EuroSys*, 159–172 (2007).
41. R. Newton, G. Morrisett and M. Welsh, The regiment macroprogramming system, *IPSN*, 489–498 (2007).
42. K. P. Birman, J. Chen, K. Hopkinson, B. Thomas, J. Thorp, R. van Renesse and W. Vogels, Overcoming communications challenges in software for monitoring and controlling power systems, *IEEE Trans. Power Eng.* (2002).
43. R. van Renesse, K. P. Birman and W. Vogels, Astrolabe: A robust and scalable technology for distributed system monitoring, management, and data mining, *ACM Trans. Comput. Syst.* **21**(2), 164–206 (2003).
44. M. Amin, Towards self-healing energy infrastructure systems, *IEEE Comput. Appl. Power* (2001).
45. E. Gamma. R. Helm, R. Johnson and J. Vlissides, *Design Patterns: Elements of Reusable Object-Oriented Software* (Addison-Wesley, 1995).
46. http://kind.ucd.ie/products/opensource/ESCJava2/.
47. R. Bharadwaj, M. Peralta, S. Mukhopadhyay, K. Shenai and S. Majumder, Cognitive distributed networks in environmental e-science, *Proc. IEEE Int. Workshop on Future Trends in Distributed Computing Systems* (2008).
48. K. Shenai and S. Mukhopadhyay, Cognitive sensor networks, *Proc. IEEE MIEL* (2008).
49. F. I. Dretske, *Knowledge and the Flow of Information* (CSLI Press, 1999).
50. E. A. Emerson, *Temporal and Modal Logic*, Handbook of Theoretical Computer Science, Vol. B.

Chapter 13

ROUTING AND TRAFFIC MANAGEMENT

EL-SAYED M. EL-ALFY
College of Computer Sciences and Engineering,
King Fahd University of Petroleum and Minerals, Saudi Arabia
alfy@kfupm.edu.sa

We begin by providing an overview of communication networks and discussing their differences from a routing/switching perspective. Subsequently, we focus on both wired and wireless packet-switched communication networks and explain various features of routing techniques. Since routers are essentially an indispensable component in building high-performance communication networks, we briefly examine the different architectures and design issues. We then describe the fundamental routing techniques used in today's networks for unicast, multicast and broadcast communication. After that, we explore advances in routing to provide quality of service support and enforce administrative policies while making the best of the network resources. To see how theory is put into practice, we look at routing protocols for two important communication networks: the Internet and the mobile ad hoc network. We then show how traffic management techniques can help in improving the performance of routing and forwarding of network traffic while optimizing the utilization of network resources. At the end of this chapter, we highlight some directions for future research related to routing and traffic management.

1. Introduction

With the proliferation of communication networks and distributed systems technologies and applications, several challenges have emerged in their design and operation. Many of these challenges are related to two core networking tasks, namely *routing* and *traffic management*. The aim of routing is to determine end-to-end routes/paths to be followed by packets as they flow from a sender to a receiver. What makes it difficult is the limited network bandwidth, the increasing volume of network traffic and the diverse requirements for quality of service (QoS) support for emerging network applications. For example, while some applications have stringent requirements on timely delivery, others put more emphasis on error-free delivery within reasonable time. To help in managing network resources efficiently under such conditions, traffic management plays a crucial role in high-performance communication networks. It encompasses a set of functions for monitoring traffic and optimizing the allocation of network bandwidth and buffers to satisfy acceptable quality-of-service levels for individual network users.

Routing and traffic management have attracted considerable attention of several network researchers and engineers. As a result, several routing algorithms and protocols as well as traffic management techniques have been proposed and extensively studied for various network environments. However, providing cost-effective scalable solutions to satisfy the demand for high bandwidth and QoS support for emerging network applications is still an active area of research. Due to the importance of routing, the Internet Engineering Task Force (IETF) established several working groups within the routing area to guide discussions and proposals on various routing topics [1].

In the following sections, we explore the details of these two important related networking tasks: routing and traffic management.

2. Background

2.1. *Classification of Communication Networks*

A communication network provides delivery services for communicating end systems (network hosts) independent of the underlying network and transmission technologies. There are several types of communication networks as shown in Fig. 1. Based on the type of connectivity provided, communication networks can be subdivided into two broad classes: *broadcast networks* and *switched networks.* In broadcast networks, such as local area networks (LANs) and wireless networks, a single transmission medium is shared among several devices. Thus, they can communicate directly, i.e., a message sent by some source will be received by all other devices but only the intended destination(s) will process it. In such networks, no routing is needed but instead a medium access control mechanism is used

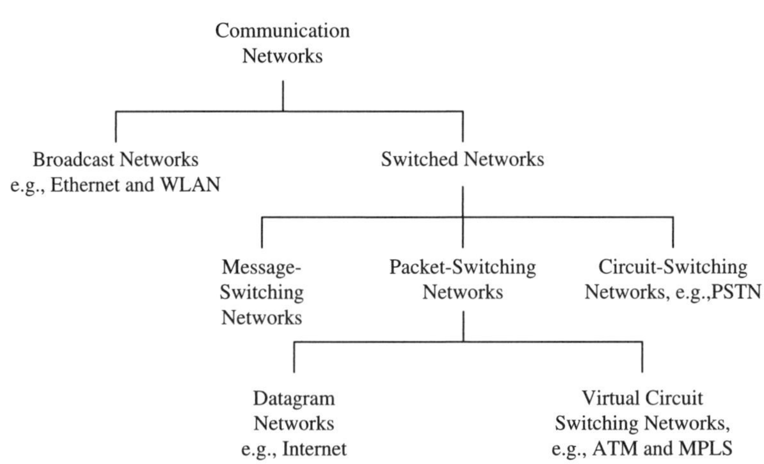

Fig. 1. Classification of communication networks based on the type of connectivity.

to coordinate the allocation of the shared medium and reduce/avoid collisions. However, broadcast networks have serious limitations in terms of geographic coverage and number of attached end systems. For example, an Ethernet LAN typically covers no more than 2,500 m and the number of attached hosts cannot exceed 1,024. Another example is wireless networks (WLANs), which are limited by their radio frequencies and coverage. On the other hand, a switched network consists of a set of interconnected switches/routers. It allows communication between hosts even if they are not directly connected. Consequently, larger and complex networks can be built to cover wider areas and serve more end systems.

Switched networks are further classified into three categories: *circuit-switching networks*, *message-switching networks* and *packet-switching networks*. In a circuit-switching network, such as the traditional public switched telephone network (PSTN), a connection (circuit) setup precedes the actual transfer of voice signals. Hence, this type of service is called *connection-oriented* service. Figure 2(a) illustrates the three phases in circuit-switching networks, where s is the source node,

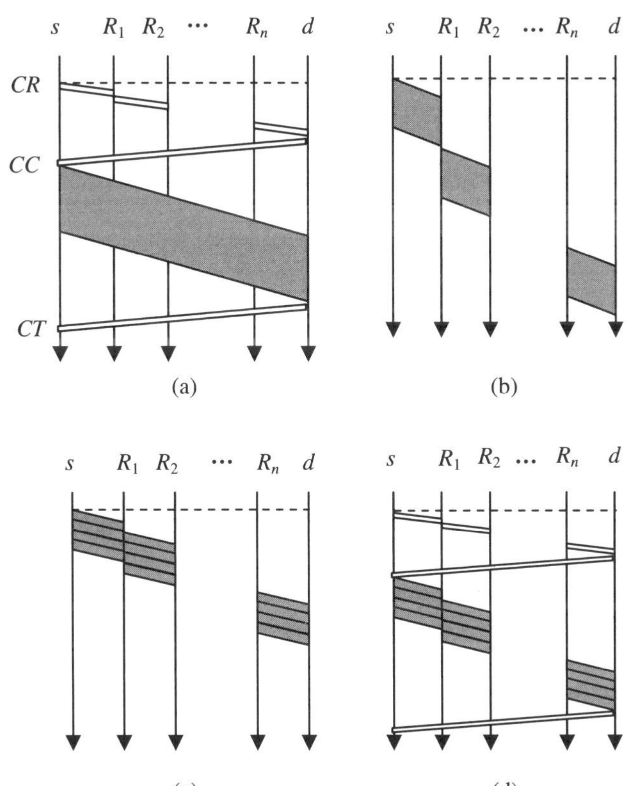

Fig. 2. Total delay in various types of communication networks: (a) circuit-switching networks, (b) message-switching networks, (c) packet-switching networks, and (d) virtual circuit-switching networks.

d is the destination node and $(R_1, R_2, \ldots, R_n)$ are the intermediate nodes on the path from the source s to the destination d. The connection setup is initiated once a connection request (CR) is received. During the connection setup phase, resources are reserved along the entire path from the source to the destination and are not allowed to be used by other users for the whole duration of this call. The data transfer phase can only start if the source receives a connection confirmation (CC). At the end of the call, the connection is terminated (CT) and allocated resources are released and thus can be used by other calls. Although it may take some time to get a connection (especially during rush hours), circuit switching has low delay for data transfer. In addition, the desired level of service quality for ongoing sessions can be guaranteed through the reservation of enough resources and the utilization of admission control procedures that reject new connection requests if the remaining resources are not adequate to support the new requests. This kind of communication can waste a lot of network resources especially when the data is generated in bursts, which is usual in many network applications (such as transferring a huge file, which may only happen rarely).

To enhance the utilization of network resources, message switching (store-and-forward) networks allow resources to be shared on demand. However, because messages need to be stored completely in intermediate nodes before forwarding, they can significantly experience large end-to-end delays in addition to requiring a huge buffer to be allocated in each intermediate node; see Fig. 2(b). Also messages typically vary widely in length; hence the delay variation (or jitter) will be large. Furthermore, it can lead to unfair allocation of network resources to different sources. To address many of these problems, datagram networks, of which the Internet is a popular example, have been developed. Datagram networks are similar to message-switching networks but they use shorter messages by encapsulating data in independent units called packets or datagrams; see Fig. 2(c). They avoid dedicating links for transferring long messages and enhance fairness for sharing resources among different sources. Packet switches also do not need to wait long before starting to forward the packet. Even before receiving the whole packet, a node can start forwarding the packet once the packet header is received. Moreover, several packet switches on the path from the source to the destination can simultaneously process different packets. This *pipelining* process can radically reduce the overall delay for transferring the message. One of the critical tasks in such networks is routing, which is responsible for determining the routes/paths to be followed by packets as they flow from a source to a destination. Routers maintain *routing tables* and use them to direct packets towards their destinations. The entries in routing tables are determined through the interaction of routers collectively according to a specific *routing protocol* that implements some *routing algorithm*. In real networks, several routing protocols can be deployed. But network administrators can configure routers to use them as they desire. A drawback of datagram networks is that they have no guarantee on the delivery time, which can be unreasonably large during congestion periods since it depends on the network load. This type of service, which is known as *connectionless* service, may be suitable for elastic traffic that has flexible requirements on the delay, such as transferring large files, but it may not be acceptable for realtime traffic such as audio traffic in Internet telephony.

Another related packet-switching approach that uses concepts of datagram networks as well as circuit-switching networks is known as virtual circuit switching. Similar to circuit switching, it has three phases: connection setup, data transfer and connection tear down; see Fig. 2(d). During connection setup, a virtual circuit from the source to the destination is set up. During the data transfer phase, the message is transferred as a sequence of packets similar to packet switching. However, unlike packet switching, each packet contains a virtual circuit identifier (VCI) or label in its header instead of the destination address.

The VCI/label in each packet will be checked by each packet switch on its way to the destination against a lookup table to determine the outgoing interface on which the packet is forwarded. Virtual circuit switching shares the benefits of circuit switching networks as well as datagram networks. Two popular examples of circuit switching networks are Asynchronous Transfer Mode (ATM) and Multi-Protocol Label Switching (MPLS) networks. For a detailed discussion on these networks, see Refs. 2–5. In this chapter, we mainly focus on routing techniques and traffic management mechanisms for datagram networks. However, some of the concepts discussed are general and are applicable to other types as well.

2.2. *Routing Performance Criteria*

A variety of performance criteria has been used to assess routing algorithms including correctness/reliability, overhead/complexity/efficiency, optimality, adaptability, robustness/resilience, stability and QoS support. These criteria are briefly explained in Table 1. Some of these criteria may conflict with each other and a compromising solution depends on the particular environment and specific goals of network operator and users.

2.3. *Routing Taxonomy*

Routing algorithms can be classified in various dimensions as shown in Fig. 3. For example, based on the number of recipients, they can be subdivided into *unicast*, *multicast* or *broadcast*. In unicast routing, a packet is routed from the source to a single destination. Broadcast routing sends the packet to all recipients whereas multicast routing sends the packet to a particular set of recipients that form a group. In broadcast and multicast, the data is sent over a tree that is rooted either at the source (source-specific tree) or at a common node (group-shared tree).

Routing techniques can be classified also based on the way routing tables are determined as *centralized* or *distributed*. In centralized routing techniques, a single node that has complete knowledge of the network topology will first determine

Table 1. Routing performance criteria.

Criterion	Description
Correctness/reliability	A routing algorithm should find correct paths for packets to their intended destinations.
Complexity/efficiency	A good routing algorithm must have low overhead in terms of the number of control messages exchanged among routers, size of routing tables, and processing time. The bottom line is to use resources efficiently.
Optimality	A good routing algorithm must have the ability to determine optimal routes in reasonable time based on some routing metric which is determined to optimize the objectives of a network operator.
Adaptability	In real networks, unexpected things can happen such as link and/or router failure. A good routing algorithm must have the ability to quickly adapt to changes in the network topology. Also it must have the capability to adapt to fluctuations in traffic loads.
Robustness/resilience	A good routing algorithm must be capable of rerouting packets away from heavily overloaded and/or failed links or routers. The routing tables need to be updated automatically and quickly when there is a link/node failure without the need to reboot the router.
Stability/convergence	A good routing must be stable, i.e., ensure loop-free paths to avoid routing loops or oscillation. This also requires quick convergence of routing table update when there is change in the network.
Scalability	A good routing must be capable of being used in complex and heterogeneous networks that have a large number of nodes.
QoS support	A good routing must be capable of supporting QoS required by different applications or individual users.

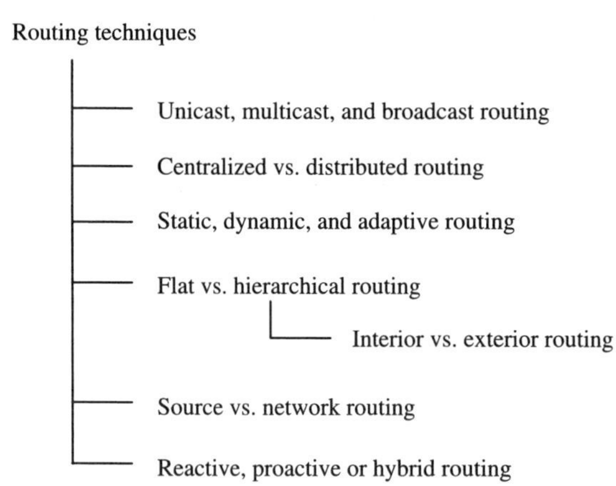

Fig. 3. Taxonomy of routing techniques.

all the routes and upload them to other nodes. However, in distributed routing techniques, nodes cooperatively determine the routing tables in a decentralized fashion. Depending on the frequency of changing the entries in the routing tables, routing techniques can be classified as *static*, *dynamic* or *adaptive*. In static routing, routes are pre-calculated; then routing tables are populated and remain unchanged. This approach assumes the network topology remains fixed for relatively long periods of time. Static routing table entries can also be manually configured by a network administrator. However, in real networks, the situation is different. Topological changes can happen frequently due to router or link failures. Hence, dynamic routing is used to update tables to reflect these changes. This can be achieved either periodically (as in the distance vector routing algorithm) or triggered when some event happens (as in the link state routing algorithm). When the network size is small, tables can be updated manually or calculated at a central controller and then uploaded to other routers. However, in large networks, routers continuously discover the state of the network and automatically update routing tables in a distributed fashion. Thus, the routing algorithm can adapt to changes in the network topology and load as well. Hence, if certain parts of the network are congested, packets can be re-routed over other paths. This makes the network more resilient in case of failures and/or congested links.

Another way to classify routing techniques is *flat* versus *hierarchical*. In contrast to flat routing, hierarchical routing scales well and can handle complexity in large networks. For example, the Internet is divided into a set of interconnected autonomous systems (domains) and routing is performed in a hierarchical manner: *interior* routing (also called intra-domain routing) and *exterior* routing (also called inter-domain routing). When the source and the destination hosts belong to the same autonomous system, interior routing will take care of forwarding the packet over a path from the source to the destination. Thus, for interior routing each node will have an entry for each other node in the same autonomous system. However, when the source and the destination hosts are in two different autonomous systems, then the source sends the packet to an appropriate border router which knows how to reach the border router at the destination autonomous system. Interior routing and exterior routing typically have different goals. While interior routing is looking for shortest (least-cost) paths, exterior routing requires certain administrative policies to be applied even if this results in using suboptimal paths from the source to the destination.

Routing techniques can also be classified as *proactive*, *reactive* or *hybrid*. In proactive approaches, routing tables are pre-computed and maintained at all times regardless of whether a source needs them or not. This separation between route computation and data delivery allows more powerful techniques to be used for route optimization and can significantly reduce the delivery time. On the other hand, in reactive approaches, routes are computed only if needed. This allows constructing viable routes that take the current network status into account. It also reduces the overhead required to store and maintain routing tables but at the expense of slower response times. Since reactive techniques and proactive techniques complement each other, a better approach may be combining them to gain the merits of both. For example, some nodes may use a reactive technique while others use a proactive technique. Another way is to run a proactive technique first. Then, when there is a need, a reactive technique is called. Another possibility is similar to hierarchical routing, where reactive techniques are used in interior routing and proactive techniques are used for exterior routing. All techniques discussed in this chapter for the Internet are reactive while those used in mobile ad hoc networks are either reactive, proactive or hybrid. For a comparative study between reactive and proactive protocols in mobile ad hoc environments, see Ref. 6.

Finally, routing techniques can be classified as *source* (explicit) routing versus *network-assisted* routing. Source routing puts burdens on end systems and can be used in datagram or virtual circuit-switching networks. Before a source host sends a packet, it has to determine the sequence of nodes to be visited on the path to the destination and include it in the packet header. Intermediate network nodes just forward the packet to their next node on the path toward the destination using the path information contained in the packet header. Thus, the intermediate nodes only need to have information about their neighboring nodes and no routing tables are needed. The number of nodes on the path from the source to a destination can vary and thus the packet size will change. Besides wasting the network bandwidth, including the whole path in the packet header increases the processing overhead and delay. On the other hand, in network-assisted routing the source node does not know which path should be followed by a packet to a destination and only includes the destination address in the packet header. Now it is the job of network routers to determine the paths and set up routing tables. On receiving a packet, the router extracts the destination address from the packet header and consults the forwarding table to determine its outgoing interface. This process is repeated at each router on the path to the destination until eventually the packet reaches its destination.

2.4. *Network Model*

A communication network consists of a set of end systems (called hosts) and an interconnection network (also called network core) composed of a set of routers (or packet switches). The core has two types of routers: edge routers (also called ingress/egress routers, or gateway routers) and transit routers. Hosts belong to different local area networks, which are connected to the core through one or more gateway routers. Local area networks are broadcast networks and hence a packet sent by a host will be received by the gateway router without routing.

Similarly, the gateway router can send a packet to a host in its local area network by broadcasting. For routing purposes, the ingress/egress routers act as sources/destinations. Now, the interconnection network can be abstractly viewed as a graph $G = (N, L)$, where N is the set of nodes representing routers, and L is the set of edges representing communication links between routers/switches regardless of their physical nature (e.g., coaxial cables, twisted pairs, optical fiber, or wireless). Nodes can be either stationary or mobile (as in a mobile ad hoc network where moving hosts act as routers). We use the notation *link*(a, b) to mean that node a can directly communicate with node b. If two nodes, a and b, are communicating in both directions, then we have two links *link*(a, b) and *link*(b, a). When communication between two nodes is bidirectional and symmetric, it will be represented by an undirected edge. In most real networks, the communication between two nodes is asymmetric, and hence it will be represented by two directed edges in the opposite directions. Figure 4 shows an example network and its graph representation of the interconnection network, where R_1, R_2, R_3 and R_4 are ingress/egress routers and router R_5 is a transit router. The graph has five nodes representing R_1, R_2, R_3, R_4 and R_5, and six undirected edges representing communication links between routers.

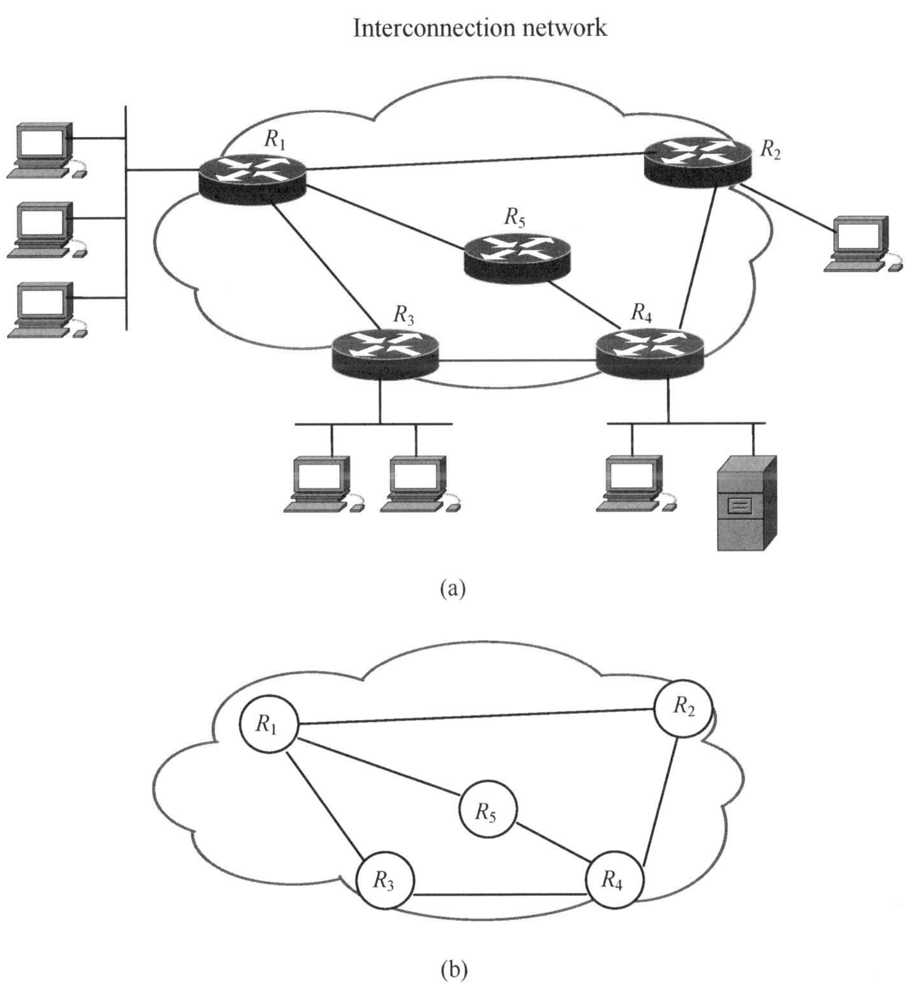

Fig. 4. (a) An example network and (b) its representation by a graph.

3. Router Duties and Architectures

Large datagram communication networks are built using dedicated internetworking devices called routers (packet switches) to connect a collection of isolated networks. To build high-performance networks, a special attention has been given to the implementation of routers. Reference 7 presents an overview and a detailed discussion of router design issues, traditional and new powerful router architectures, and challenges facing the next generation of routers. Primarily, a router performs two functions: routing and forwarding. Routing procedures are responsible for constructing and maintaining routing tables whereas forwarding functions are responsible for switching each incoming packet (within the router) to the port/interface (as dictated by forwarding tables extracted from the routing tables) that is connected to its next hop on the path toward its destination. Forwarding functions include routing table lookup to determine the next hop for each incoming packet, time-to-live (TTL) control to decrement nonzero TTL and discard the packet if TTL becomes zero, recalculation of checksum and packet validation. Besides these basic functions, a router may have additional features for security such as authentication, encryption and packet filtering as well as traffic management such as packet classification and traffic prioritization, packet scheduling, traffic shaping and policing, etc. A router also has network management components such as the simple network management protocol (SNMP) agent and management information bases (MIBs). A generic architecture of a router is depicted in Fig. 5. Obviously, a router is composed of several modules: line cards [including network interfaces, traffic manager (TM), and ingress/egress port buffers], forwarding engines, a routing processor, an interconnection unit, routing/forwarding tables, and management components.

Due to its demanding role in network performance, router design has gone through several generations [7]. Several categories of routers have been identified based on the type of interconnection unit (e.g., bus, shared memory, or switch fabric) and whether the forwarding operations are centralized or distributed. Early implementations of routers were purely in software running on a single general-purpose computer. However, due to its architectural limitations, achieving routing at high speeds was difficult. Improvement over this simple architecture was introduced by using multiple processors and distributing packet forwarding operations over the network interface cards. Moreover, using route caches for frequently seen addresses allows network interface cards to process packets locally some of the time [7]. With the recent advances in current technologies, it becomes possible to build efficient routing solutions that incorporate both hardware and software. Current improvements in network transmission speeds have fueled parallel improvement in router technology to keep pace [8]. Router architectures with multiple network interfaces interconnected by a high-speed switch fabric with multiple forwarding engines have allowed switching speeds in the range of multi-gigabit and terabit per second. This in turn dramatically improves network performance. Partridge *et al.*

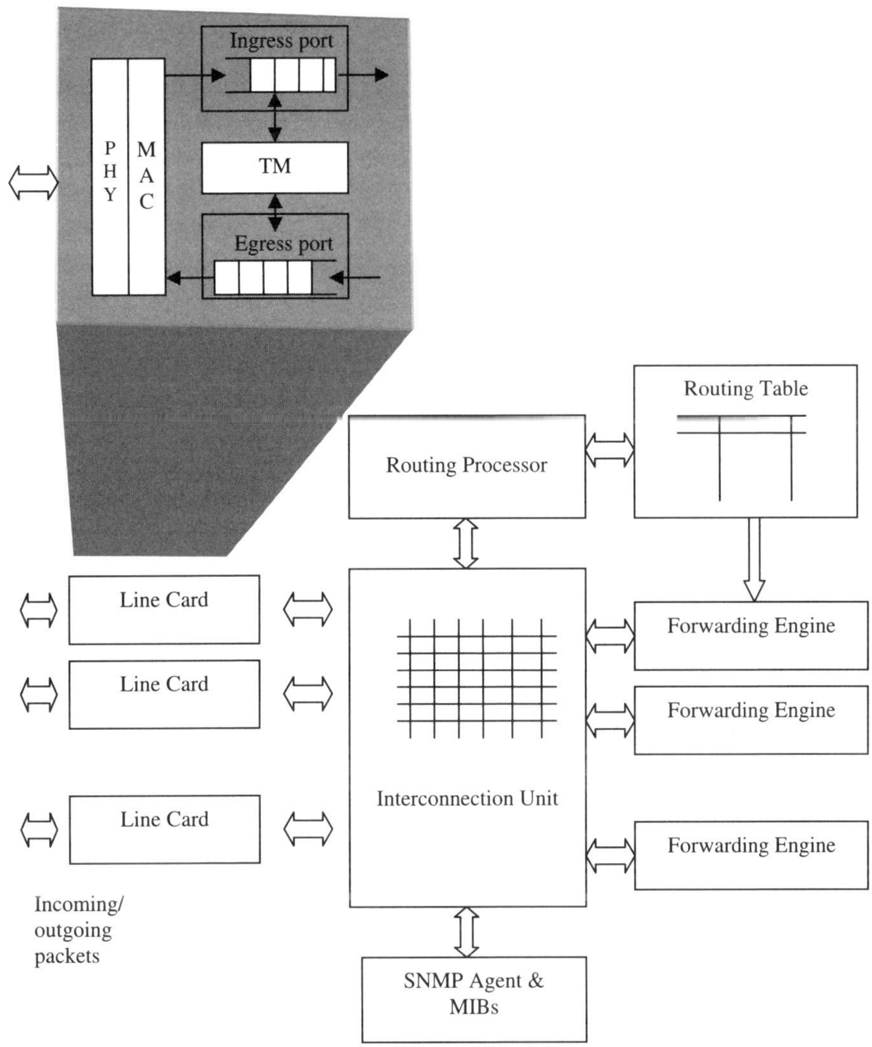

Fig. 5. A generic router architecture.

[8] describes a router which is more than fast enough to keep up with the latest transmission technologies. The router has a backplane speed of 50 Gb/s and can forward tens of millions of packets per second. Once these large capacity scalable routers become available in the market, they are going to replace clusters of mid-size core routers that are interconnected with numerous links and expensive line cards and hence avoid unnecessary intra-cluster traffic [9–15].

Routers cooperatively find paths between different nodes and set up their forwarding tables. This process is known as routing. Each row of a forwarding table maps a destination address to a next hop. The forwarding table should be implemented (as a data structure or a specialized hardware) so as to speed up the process of looking up a destination address. For a comparison on different hashing schemes for address lookup in routers, see Ref. 16. Arriving packets are forwarded by examining an identifier in their headers and consulting a forwarding table (sometimes called routing table with minor differences between them) to determine on which outgoing links the packets should be forwarded. For datagram networks, the identifier included in the packet header represents its destination addresses whereas in virtual circuit-switching networks it represents a label/VCI. In packet switching (whether datagram or virtual circuit network), the decision is made for each packet (although the processing time is different). Another important component is input/output buffers. Arriving packets may need to be buffered before the router starts to process. Similarly, outgoing packets may need to be buffered before transmission due to the limited capacity of outgoing links. Since buffers (whether at the input or output) are of limited size, packets can be dropped at the router. Hence, buffer management is very essential to enhance router performance.

4. Basic Routing Algorithms

Several routing algorithms have been proposed and deployed in various network protocols for unicast, multicast and broadcast communication. In this section we review basic routing procedures. We begin with a flooding technique that is simple but robust and still applied in some unicast, multicast and broadcast protocols. Then, we assume the network topology and link costs are completely known and solve an optimization problem to determine minimum cost paths. Then, we will see how routers in a real network cooperate to dynamically compute optimal routes by discovering the topology and link costs either gradually as in distance vector routing or in full as in link state routing. After that, we discuss hierarchical routing and techniques for routing broadcast and multicast packets.

4.1. *Flooding*

A simple routing approach that does not require routers to do much is flooding. Once a packet is received, the router forwards copies of the packet on all outgoing interfaces except the one on which the packet has been received (see Fig. 6). Eventually, the packet will reach its destination as long as at least one path exists between the source and the destination. It sounds simple and easy to implement since no routing tables are needed and the processing at each router is minimal. However, if the network has loops, the amount of traffic on the network grows rapidly and can overwhelm the network which in turn can severely degrade the performance and cause the network to go down. Still flooding is an effective approach in several situations: for example, when a router receives a packet for which no routing information is available in the routing tables (e.g., during system startup), when

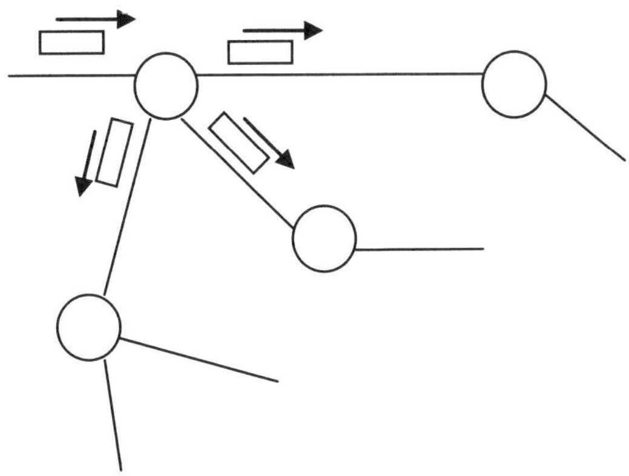

Fig. 6. Routing by flooding.

providing a highly reliable solution is of high demand (e.g., in military applications), or when a router receives a broadcast packet (e.g., in distributing link-state packets in link state routing).

One way to improve this uncontrolled flooding approach and avoid cycling packets is to make each router keep track of packets using the source addresses and packet identifiers. Upon receiving a packet, the router checks if it has been seen before and hence discards it. For example, the Gnutella protocol uses sequence number controlled flooding, at the application layer, to broadcast queries in its overlay network [17]. In Sec. 4.6, we will see other techniques for further improvement of the flooding algorithm.

4.2. *Optimal Routing*

In optimal routing, routes are selected according to some cost metric. Each link is assigned a cost. If *link*(a, b) and *link*(b, a) are symmetric, they can be represented by a single undirected arc. For asymmetric links, a cost is assigned to each direction. The cost of the path from a source to a destination is the sum of the costs of links along the path. Various cost functions can be used based on the objective of a network operator such as physical distance, delay, bandwidth, traffic load, reliability, output queue length, etc. When link costs are all equal, the optimal route is the path with the minimum number of hops. When delay is used as a routing metric, the optimal route is the path with the minimum delay. When traffic load is used, the optimal path is the least congested link. When bandwidth is used, the optimal route is the path with the highest bandwidth available, which in turn can balance load distribution on the network and thus minimize congestion. Now, having complete knowledge of the network topology and link costs, one can determine an optimal path from a specific source to a specific destination (single-pair problem), determine optimal paths from a specific source to all destinations (single-source problem), or determine optimal paths from each source to each destination (all-pairs problem). For a given source-destination pair, there may be several possible paths between them. In practice, the single-pair problem is solved as the single-source problem. The single-source shortest path problem can be solved using Dijkstra's algorithm or Bellman–Ford's algorithm. The all-pairs shortest path problem can be solved using Floyd-Warshall's algorithm or Johnson's algorithm. For routing in real network applications, only the single-source shortest path problem is of interest. In the following, we will focus on the Dijkstra and Bellman–Ford algorithms.

4.2.1. *Dijkstra's Algorithm*

When link costs are non-negative and completely known, Dijkstra's algorithm can be used to determine the shortest (minimum cost) paths from a given source node to all others nodes in the network. This algorithm is a greedy approach. Its output is a tree rooted at the source such that the path through the tree from the root node to each other node is the shortest (or least cost) path. It starts from the source node and iteratively expands a tree that ultimately spans all nodes reachable from that source. Nodes are added to the tree based on the cost of the path from the source. The pseudo-code is given in Table 2 in which S maintains the set of nodes for which the shortest paths from the source have been already determined. The minimum distance from the source to node j is denoted as d_j. Initially, S includes only the source node s whose shortest path cost is $d_s = 0$. Let c_{ij} be the link cost from node i to node j. If two nodes are not allowed to directly communicate, then the cost of the link between these two nodes is infinity, i.e., $c_{ij} = \infty$ if j is

Table 2. Optimal routing using Dijkstra's algorithm.

```
procedure dijkstra
S = {s};  // initialize the set S to have the source node s
d_s = 0;  // initialize the minimum cost of the source node s
for (each node j ≠ s) // initialize the minimum cost of nodes other than s
  if (j is a neighbor of s)
      d_j = c_sj;
  else
      d_j = ∞;  // not directly reachable
while (S does not contain all nodes) {
      i ← arg min_{j∉N} {d_j}
      S = S ∪ {i}  // add node i to S
      for (each neighbor j of node i that is not in S)
         d_j ← min{d_j, d_i + c_ij} // update minimum costs for nodes not in S
}
```

not a neighbor of node i. The link cost from a node to itself is zero, i.e., $c_{ii} = 0$ for all i.

The complexity of this algorithm depends on the data structure used and the sparseness of the network. For example, if the network is represented by an adjacency matrix, the running time is $O(N^2)$, where N is the number of nodes in the network. If a binary heap is used to keep track of nodes not included in S, then the running time will be reduced to $O(L \cdot \log_2 N)$, where L is the number of links [18]. To illustrate how Dijkstra's algorithm is applied, let us consider the following step-by-step example (In addition, there are several interactive Java applets that can be found in Ref. 19).

Example 1. Consider a network represented by the graph shown in Fig. 7; determine the shortest paths from the source node s to all other nodes.

Table 3 summarizes the steps to determine the shortest paths, also illustrated graphically in Fig. 8. Initially, the permanent list S has only one node s and the cost to all other nodes from s is initialized as shown in step 0. Since node b has the shortest path among nodes not in S, it is moved next to the permanent set S and all costs to other nodes are updated if a better path through b exists. The procedure is repeated until all nodes are moved to S. Finally, the routing table at node s is as follows:

Destination	Next-Hop	Cost
s	s	0
a	b	6
b	b	2
c	b	7
d	b	5
e	b	8

4.2.2. *Bellman–Ford's algorithm*

Similar to Dijkstra's algorithm, Bellman–Ford's algorithm solves the single-source shortest path problem. But unlike Dijkstra's algorithm, it allows links to have negative weights as long as no negative cycles exist in the network. To explain

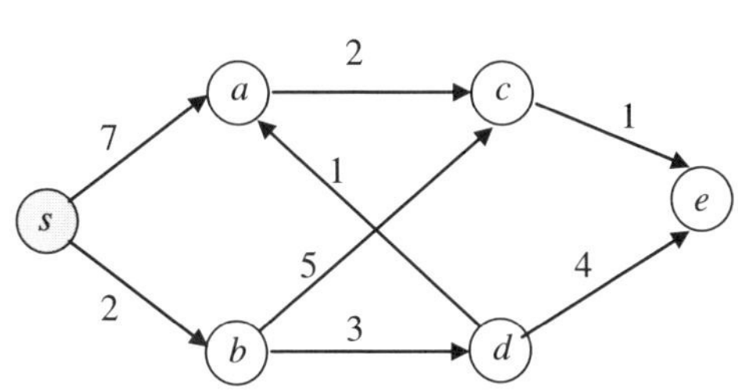

Fig. 7. An example of Dijkstra's algorithm.

Table 3. Step-by-step execution of Dijkstra's algorithm for the example shown in Fig. 7.

Step	S	a	b	c	d	e
0	s	7, s	2, s	∞, s	∞, s	∞, s
1	sb	7, s		7, b	5, b	∞, s
2	sbd	6, d		7, b		9, d
3	$sbda$			7, b		9, d
4	$sbdac$					8, c
5	$sbdacd$					

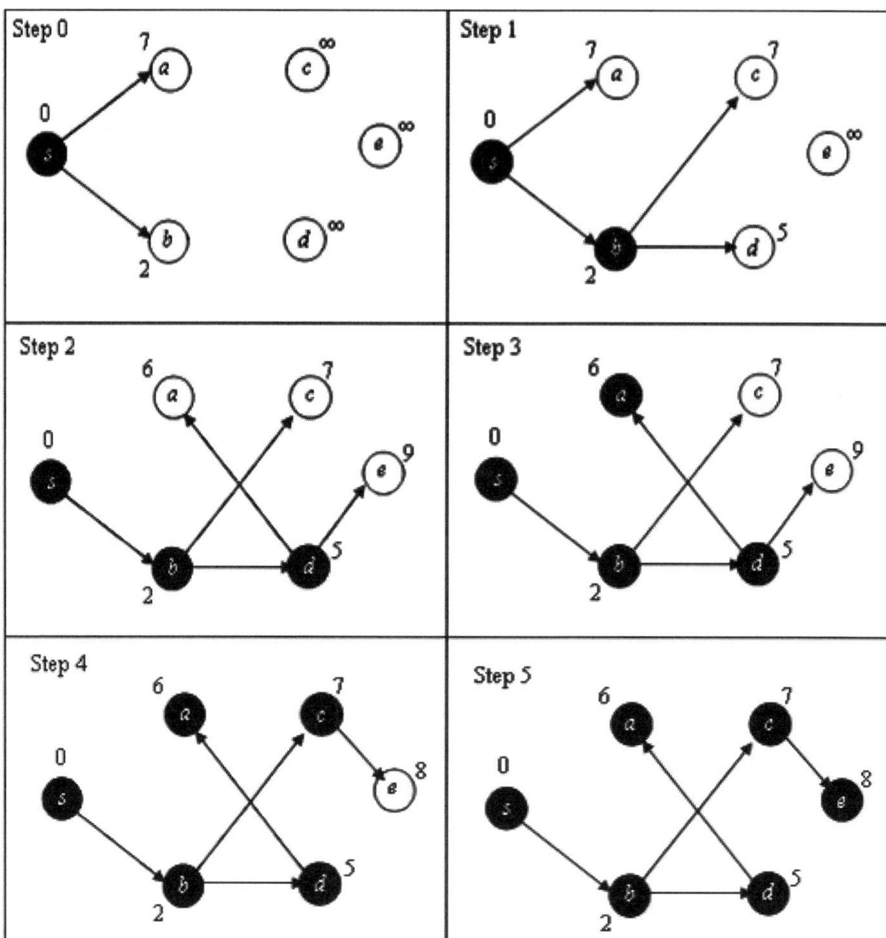

Fig. 8. Step-by-step illustration of Dijkstra's algorithm for the example shown in Fig. 7.

the steps of this algorithm, assume node i has a set of neighboring nodes N_i and the optimal cost from the sources to each one of them is known to be d_j for all $j \in N_i$. Then, the cost of the optimal path from s to i is given by the following equation:

$$d_i = \min_{j \in N_i} \{c_{ij} + d_j\}$$

This equation is known as the Bellman–Ford equation, which is based on Bellman's optimality principle. The solution of this set of equations for all nodes will generate the optimal routes. Also, instead of using the greedy approach to determine shortest paths, this algorithm uses the dynamic programming approach. Table 4 illustrates the steps of Bellman–Ford's algorithm. Its running time is worse than Dijkstra's algorithm. The Bellman–Ford algorithm complexity is $O(L \cdot N)$, where L is the number of links and N is the number of nodes [18]. When all link weights are positive, Dijkstra's algorithm provides a more efficient alternative. However, Dijkstra's algorithm needs global information about the network topology. As we will see in distance vector routing, a distributed version of Bellman–Ford's algorithm is applied to allow each node to asynchronously update its routing table.

To illustrate how Bellman–Ford's algorithm is applied, consider the following example. (For an interactive Java applet demonstration, see the website in Ref. 20.)

Example 2. Consider the simple network shown in Fig. 9(a). Find the shortest path from node s to each other node. The distance of each node from the source is initially as shown in Fig. 9(b). Then, after the first iteration of the outer loop, the distances will be updated as shown in Fig. 9(c). In the next iteration, distances are updated as shown in Fig. 9(d). Finally, the solution is given in Fig. 9(e). It may happen that the intermediate steps have different values depending on the order in which the links are considered. However, the final solution will always remain the same unless there are multiple optimal solutions of equal cost.

Table 4. Bellman–Ford's algorithm.

```
procedure bellman–ford
// input: a weighted graph with no negative weight cycles
d_s = 0;  // initialize the minimum cost of the source node s
for (each node j ≠ s)
      d_j = ∞; p_j = j; // initialization for other nodes

for (i = 1 to N − 1)
      for (each link(j, k))
            if (d_j + c_jk < d_k) then
                  d_k = d_j + c_jk; p_k = j;
```

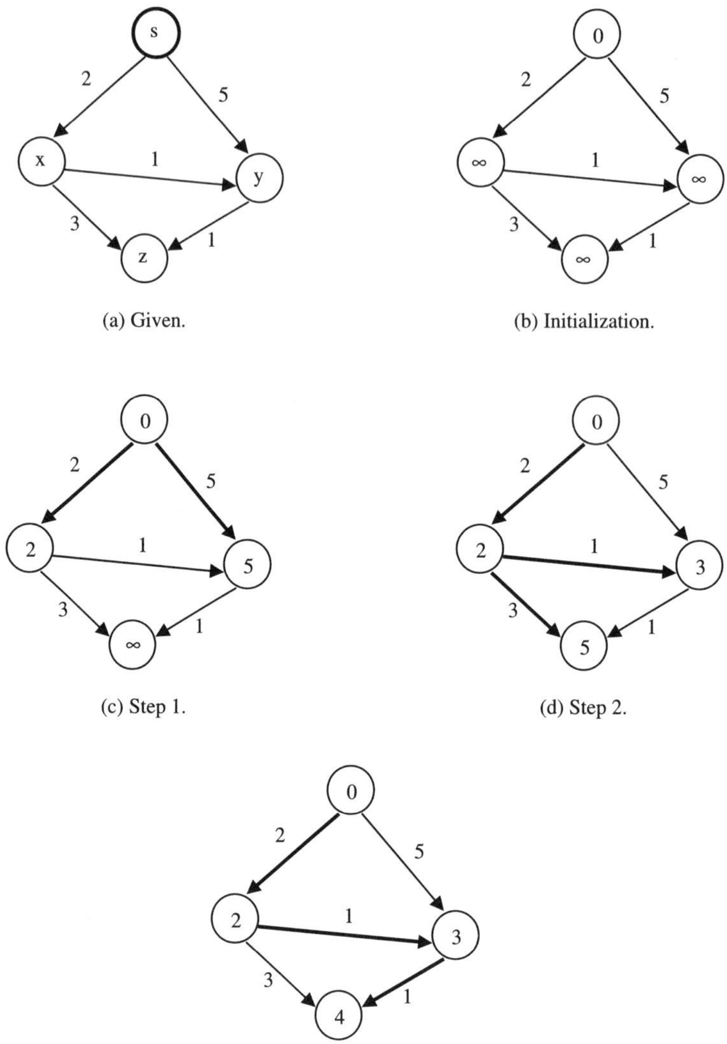

(a) Given. (b) Initialization.

(c) Step 1. (d) Step 2.

(e) Step 3.

Fig. 9. Step-by-step illustration of Bellman–Ford's algorithm.

In practice, the assumption of complete knowledge of network topology and link costs restricts the benefit of the discussed optimal routing approaches in their current form. Furthermore, the network topology can change more often as a result of turning on/off new network components or as a result of changes in link costs due to variation in the network load. To cope with these dynamic changes in the network, the network topology and link costs should be quickly discovered online. Also a distributed implementation of the route calculation algorithm will make it scale well for large networks. This can be accomplished in two different approaches, which will be discussed next: *distance vector routing* and *link state routing*.

4.3. *Distance Vector Routing*

Distance vector routing is one of the earliest routing techniques that has been used in the original ARPANET, RIP1, RIP2, Cisco IGRP, and BGP protocols. In this algorithm a distributed version of Bellman–Ford's algorithm is used to dynamically update routing tables at regular intervals (e.g., 30 seconds as implemented in the RIP) or when there is a change in some routing table. All links are assumed to have equal costs (weights) of one (i.e., one hop). Thus, the best path from a source to a destination is the minimum hop path. Other metrics can be used such as delay or available bandwidth; in that case, each router is assumed to be able to estimate the distance to each of its neighbors. For example, if the metric is delay, the router can ping each neighbor to measure the round trip time. However, the current implementation of this algorithm in Internet protocols (such as RIP) uses the number of hops as the path cost.

Distance vector routing solves the set of Bellman–Ford equations asynchronously (see Table 5). Each router first constructs a distance vector giving the best known distance to each other node in the network. For example node i will keep $DV_i = [\langle j, d_{ij} \rangle : j \in N]$. When the algorithm starts, each node i initializes its distance vector such that $d_{ij} = c_{ij}$ if j is a neighbor of i; otherwise $d_{ij} = \infty$. Then, periodically each router exchanges this information with its neighbors. When a node receives information from its neighbors, it assumes that these are the best known paths through the neighbors and compares them with what it currently has. To illustrate this update operation, consider the example shown in Fig. 10 in which node A adds one hop to each hop count in its distance vector then advertises this information to its neighbors. Assume node B receives the advertisement from node A, then node B will run the update procedure (as shown in Table 5) and the resulting routing table will be as shown in Fig. 10. This node will then advertise to all its neighbors again the best routes. If the network topology and link costs are fixed, and if routers continuously exchange distance vectors and run the update procedure, then each node's distance vector will finally converge to the optimal values.

Although distance vector routing is simple and easy to implement, it does not scale well and has poor convergence properties as changes propagate node by node. Distance vector routing suffers from count-to-infinity and routing loop problems. To illustrate these problems, consider the example shown in Fig. 11. Initially assume the network is working fine and the routing table at B has one entry for reaching A in one hop and similarly the routing table at C has one entry for reaching A via B in two hops. Then, assume either the link between A and B or node A has failed. After failure, B knows immediately that it cannot reach A directly and updates its table. However, depending on the exact timing of events, it may happen that

Table 5. Distance vector routing procedures.

procedure distance-vector-routing

1. each node calculates the distances between itself and all other nodes in the network and runs the initialize procedure
2. each node constructs a distance vector from the information gained in step 1
3. periodically each node advertises its DV to its neighboring nodes by running the advertise procedure
4. upon receiving an advertisement from a neighboring node, call the update procedure

procedure initialize

```
for (each node j ∈ N)
if (j ∈ N_i)
    d_ij = c_ij;
else
    d_ij = ∞;
```

procedure advertise

```
add one hop to each hop count in the DV_i.
send DV_i to all each node j ∈ N_i;
```

procedure update-table

```
update = false;
 for (each advertised destination node x)
   if (x is not in the current routing table)
      add one entry for x to the routing table (x, sender, advertised cost);
else if (the current next hop to reach x is the same as the sender)
   update the current hop count with the advertised one;
   update = true;
else if (advertised hop count for x is smaller than one in the current routing table)
   update the next hop and cost by the sender and the advertised cost;
   update = true;
if (update = true)
   call the advertise procedure
```

C's advertisement reaches B before B's advertisement reaches C. Thus, B would know that it can reach A via C in three hops and re-advertise the update. Then, C will update its table to reach A via B in four hops. This process will be repeated and the cost to reach A will gradually increase. Finally, both B and C will know that A is unreachable. Thus, the approach suffers from slow convergence when bad news occurs such as a node failure, a link failure or even when the link cost increases. During this time, the traffic from one node may loop back and forth between B and C.

To lessen the severity of these problems and allow faster convergence, some protocols set an approximate value for infinity (e.g., 16). This sets an upper bound on the hop count and a node will be considered unreachable if the hop count reaches this value. Another solution for this problem is known as split horizon. It prevents a node from advertising routes that it has learned from another node back to it during the routing update. In the previous example (in Fig. 11), node C has an entry to reach A via B. Hence, when C advertises to B, it will not include this entry in the distance vector. A third solution is called split horizon with poisoned reverse.

Destination	Cost
A	1
B	2
D	4
E	3
F	2

(Received advertisement from node *A*)

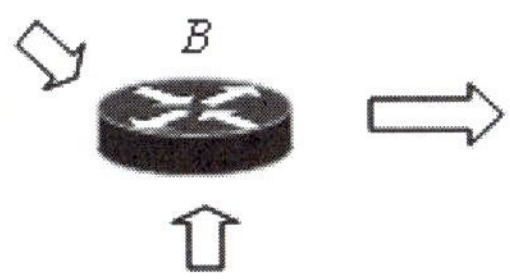

Destination	Next-Hop	Cost
A	*A*	1
B	*B*	0
D	*A*	4
C	*C*	1
E	*A*	3
F	*A*	2

(Updated routing table at node *B*)

Destination	Next-Hop	Cost
A	*A*	1
B	*B*	0
D	*C*	5
C	*C*	1
E	*A*	2

(Current routing table at node *B*)

Fig. 10. Routing update at node B on receiving advertisement from node A.

Applying this approach, node C will advertise its entry about A back to B but after poisoning it with negative information, i.e., C will advertise to B that it can reach A in infinite number of hops. Thus, B will never use C to reach A as long as C is reaching A via B. Neither solution is perfect for the count-to-infinity problem. When loops have three or more nodes, the problem is not resolved (for example, when C's entry to A is via D but in fact D reaches A via B).

These severe drawbacks limit the usefulness of distance vector routing in large-scale networks. To tackle the convergence problem, link state routing has been developed. However, link state routing suffers from the additional complexity in configuration that makes it undesirable for small-scale networks. Relatively recently, the Cisco Enhanced Interior Gateway Routing Protocol (EIGRP) applied a loop-free version of distance vector routing. It converges as quickly as the current link state routing protocols while avoiding counting to infinity and without creating routing table loops [21].

4.4. *Link State Routing*

Link state routing is another popular unicast routing technique in datagram communication networks. It has been implemented in several Internet routing protocols including OSPF and IS-IS. Recently, an optimized version of link state routing (named OSLR) is deployed in mobile ad hoc networks (MANETs). Link state routing has a number of advantages over distance vector routing that allow it to scale better to handle complexity in communication networks. It can react quickly to changes in the network and thus provides more stable routing than distance vector routing. It reduces the broadcast overhead and allows different routing metrics to be taken into consideration such as delay, bandwidth, and reliability in addition

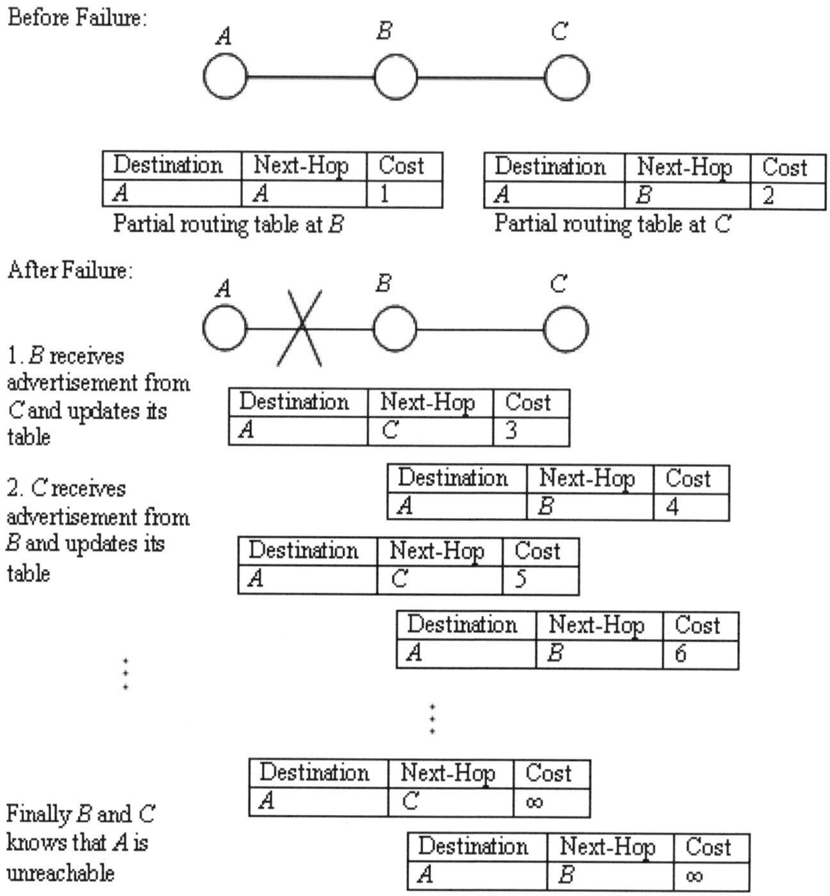

Fig. 11. The count-to-infinity problem.

to distance or hop count. The operation of link state routing depends mainly on two procedures: one to construct a network map and another to calculate optimal routes. Before optimal routes can be calculated, link costs and network topology need to be discovered, from which a network map is constructed at each node. This information is gained through the exchange of link state advertisements (LSAs). Each node forms a link-state packet summarizing costs of directly attached links and advertises it by flooding throughout the network. The collection of information in all link-state packets gives a global view of the network. With this information, each node can now independently run Dijkstra's algorithm to determine optimal paths to all other nodes. The resulting routing information is populated in its routing table. The steps of the link state routing algorithm are summarized in Table 6. The differences between distance vector routing and link state routing are summarized in Table 7. For a quantitative comparison between the performance of link state routing and distance vector routing, see Ref. 22.

Table 6. Distance vector routing procedures.

procedure link-state-routing

1. discover neighboring nodes
2. estimate the cost of the link to each neighbor node
3. construct LSP containing neighbor node identifier and link cost
4. advertise LSP by flooding to all nodes in the network
5. construct a network map from the collection of received LSPs
6. run Dijkstra's algorithm to find least-cost paths to all other nodes

Table 7. A comparison of distance vector and link state routing algorithms.

Distance vector routing	Link state routing
Optimal route calculation is decentralized using distributed Bellman–Ford algorithm	Optimal route calculation is centralized by running Dijkstra's algorithm at each node
Does not require a global map of the network	Global map is needed before calculating optimal paths
Advertise to neighbors only known distances to all other nodes (i.e., distance vector)	Advertise to all nodes (by flooding) the cost to its neighbors only (i.e., LSPs)
Use hop count as a cost metric	Allows other more sophisticated metrics to be used including delay, load, reliability, bandwidth, etc.
Share information at regular intervals if an update occurs	Share information only if there is a change in the network (update triggered)
Suffers from routing loop problem	Loop-free routing
Suffers from count-to-infinity problem	Quick convergence

4.5. *Hierarchical Routing*

As we have seen, large networks create problems either for distance vector routing or for link state routing. These approaches assume that the whole network is controlled by a single administration. In addition, neither distance vector nor link state scale well. They can be used in small and medium-size networks that are made of few nodes (probably not more than a hundred). Distance vectors can suffer from instability and poor convergence (due to the count-to-infinity problem) and link state can produce huge traffic (due to flooding) on the network and requires more computing power to determine optimal paths. One approach to simplify dealing with complex networks is hierarchical routing. The idea of this approach is simple: the whole network is divided into a set of regions interconnected at different levels. Then, routing is accomplished within each region or from one region to another through other levels. Each level hides the details of lower levels when performing routing from one level to another. For example, the Internet is divided into a set of interconnected autonomous systems (ASs) then routing is performed in the same autonomous system (called intra-AS routing) or between autonomous systems (called inter-AS routing). Another example is the OSPF protocol that is used in the Internet for intra-AS routing; it divides the autonomous system into a set of interconnected areas and then routing is achieved within an area or between different areas (this adds a third level to the routing hierarchy in the Internet). In many large-scale networks, this division sounds natural since a large-scale network is in fact made of various networks that may have different administrative authorities or are running different routing protocols for internal routing. For example, although the Internet keeps changing, its architecture is mostly hierarchical. Internet users are connected through Internet Service Providers (ISPs), who provide service at various levels; for example, local service providers, regional service providers, national service providers and international service providers. Thus, routing can be done at a macroscopic level (aggregate traffic), i.e., all traffic submitted to users attached to an ISP will be sent to their local ISP router (gateway), which in turn forwards this traffic to the right destination. Routers outside a local ISP only need to keep only one entry in routing tables on how to forward traffic to each local ISP. This can greatly reduce the routing table size and overhead. Moreover, routing in each level may have different objectives. Network operators can independently plan and operate their networks to achieve their own objectives while enforcing certain policies for traffic passing through other networks.

4.6. *Broadcast Routing*

First, recall that broadcast is the basic mode of operation of broadcast networks, such as wireless and local area networks, where each transmitted packet will be received by all neighbors located within one hop in the coverage range from the sender. In this section, we discuss techniques for broadcasting in communication networks that are inherently non-broadcast. There are many situations in which it is required to send the same message to all other nodes. For example, it is often required to distribute link state packets by routing protocols for topology discovery. Another example is updating software automatically on all machines. The straightforward approach to broadcasting a message is to construct duplicate packets at the source, one for each destination, and send them independently using unicast routing. However, the source may not know the addresses of all destinations. Moreover, several copies of the same message may traverse the same link, which wastes network resources such as bandwidth, buffer, and processing time — in addition to escalating congestion in the network and increasing the delivery time.

A more efficient solution is to use a broadcast address and send only one copy of the message to the gateway router. Now the router should use a broadcast routing procedure to forward the datagram to each destination. Flooding is the direct solution to achieve this goal. Nevertheless, flooding can generate a traffic storm just to send one packet (you can imagine the situation to send many packets by flooding); a solution becomes a problem! Thus, to achieve the goal with minimal overhead, two other practical procedures have been developed. These are reverse path forwarding (RPF) and spanning tree forwarding (ST).

4.6.1. *Reverse Path Forwarding*

Reverse path forwarding [23] is a practical approach that can be used to deliver broadcast packets. RPF ensures loop-free forwarding and thus prevents endless loops of broadcast packets. When a router receives a packet, unlike flooding, it has to decide whether to send it over all other outgoing links or block it. The decision is made based on the interface on which the packet arrives. If the packet has arrived over the same link used to send unicast packets to the source of the received packet, the packet is forwarded to all outgoing links. Otherwise, the router silently drops the incoming packet. When this approach is used in a network that has symmetric links and uses distance vector routing, it ensures that the packet will be forwarded if it is traversing the shortest path from the source. Figure 12 shows an example to demonstrate how RPF works. Assume routers are using hop count as the routing metric for constructing unicast routing tables. Also assume that router A generates a broadcast packet and sends it to router B and C. Router C checks its routing table to find out that the received packet is traveling over the shortest path from A to C, thus router C sends it out to B. Now, router B finds that this packet (the empty one in the figure) is not coming over the shortest path; thus, router B blocks this packet. However, router B sends the shaded packet out through all interfaces except the one on which it has arrived. Similarly, router C blocks the gray packet because it is not coming over the shortest path. Obviously, RPF prevents loops but it does not guarantee that each subnet receives a single copy of the broadcast packet. For example, if a subnet is attached to routers C and D, it will receive one copy through C and another copy through D. To resolve this problem, if a subnet is connected through several routers to the rest of the network, only one of these routers is named as a designated router and will be responsible for sending broadcast packets to this subnet. This approach is sometimes called reverse path broadcast (RPB).

4.6.2. *Spanning Tree Forwarding*

Another solution for broadcast routing that minimizes bandwidth consumption is the spanning tree approach. However, this is achieved at the expense of having each

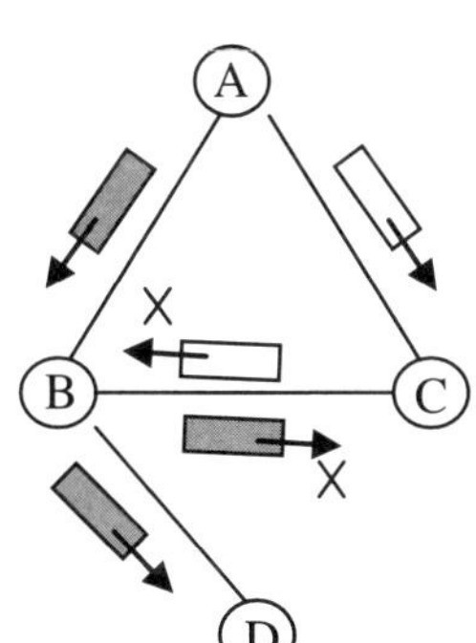

Fig. 12. Reverse path forwarding.

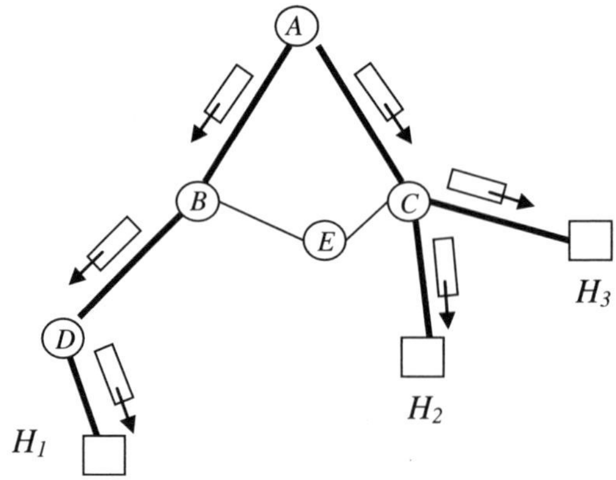

Fig. 13. Spanning tree forwarding.

router maintain additional information to be used solely for broadcast routing [24]. Before sending a broadcast packet, a spanning tree needs to be constructed. Once a spanning tree is constructed, any node receiving a broadcast packet will forward it to all its neighbors in the spanning tree except the one from which the packet is received. Thus, each node does not need to have complete knowledge of the spanning tree but only needs to know its neighbors in the spanning tree. Figure 13 shows an example of spanning tree forwarding. An advantage of the spanning tree is that once it is constructed, it can be used regardless of the source, i.e., any node can use it to broadcast to others.

Formally, a spanning tree is defined as the smallest set of links that provides connectivity between all switching nodes with attached hosts in the network [24]. Thus, if the network is represented by a graph $G = (N, L)$, the spanning tree T is defined as a sub-graph $T = (N, L')$, where $L' \subseteq L$ such that T is a tree connecting all nodes (i.e., with no cycles). Moreover, if there are several spanning trees and links are assigned some routing costs, the minimum-cost spanning tree can be used. Several algorithms such as Kruskal's algorithm and Prim's algorithm [18] can be used to construct a minimum-cost spanning tree (MST). However, the complexity associated with these approaches restricts their applications in dynamic routing. Numerous distributed spanning tree algorithms have been developed [25–28].

4.7. *Multicast Routing*

Unlike unicast, which sends a packet to a single destination, and broadcast, which sends a broadcast packet to all nodes, multicast delivers a multicast packet only to a subset of nodes (that form a group). Besides the need for a group identifier and a protocol to dynamically manage joining/leaving of group members, a multicast routing algorithm is required to efficiently forward multicast packets from the source to group members only. In this chapter, we focus on routing rather than addressing or group management. Again as mentioned in discussing broadcast, a multicast packet can be encapsulated in a unicast packet of which one copy is sent separately to each member in the group. Another approach is to broadcast the multicast packet; the packet will eventually be received by all nodes including group members. Neither of these two solutions is efficient. A third approach is to use algorithms developed specifically for multicast routing. One can identify two general solutions for this problem: source-based tree and group-shared tree. These algorithms mainly differ in the tree that they use to deliver multicast packets. In the source-based tree approach, a tree rooted at the source and having group members as leaves is constructed then used to send multicast packets from the source to all group members. An advantage of this approach is that a shortest path tree rooted at the source can be used. However, if there are many source nodes and groups, then one tree must be constructed for each source node and for each group. The complexity of this approach is $O(N \cdot M)$, where N is the number of source nodes and M is the number of groups per source. Alternatively, a group-shared tree approach has only one tree per group regardless of the number of sources. This tree is rooted at a designated router, called a core router or rendezvous point (RP). In this approach, the source first encapsulates the multicast packet in a unicast packet and sends it to the core router, which in turn forwards it over the multicast tree.

One way to construct a multicast tree is to have the source or the core router send a tree construction message by broadcast routing. This will create a spanning tree covering all routers. Then, if a gateway router does not have hosts participating in this group communication, it will send a prune message to its upstream router to inform it not to forward anymore multicast packets to it. In the same way, if a router does have any of its children willing to receive multicast packets, it will send a prune message to its upstream router, which will then take it off the tree. Similarly, if a host join the group, its network gateway will send a graft message which will inform the upstream router to resume sending multicast packets to it. Another issue in group-shared tree construction is the selection of core routers or rendezvous points; see Ref. 29 for details.

5. QoS Routing

As communication networks evolve, new routing paradigms are required to consider packet content, support diverse QoS requirements, handle service requirements between service providers and users, and to impose policies. QoS routing is at present an active and remarkable research area since most emerging network services require specialized QoS functionalities that cannot be provided by the existing routing protocols [30–32]. For example, Internet telephony, video conferencing, video on demand, and other multimedia applications have strict requirements on the timely delivery of audio and video traffic which is hard to achieve using the best-effort service provided by the current Internet. QoS-unaware routing techniques suffer from several limitations. They are primarily driven by network topology and base their routing decisions on destination addresses. Hence, these techniques are no longer adequate for networks that provide integrated services with diversified QoS requirements. For example, the current Internet routing protocols such as RIP or OSPF use shortest (or least-cost) path routing. Using a single routing metric for path computation such as hop count or delay can cause congestion on the same links and incur significant delay if the path has no sufficient capacity to accommodate the traffic. These techniques do not allow traffic to be routed over alternative paths when the current path to a destination is overloaded while others are not used or are lightly used. Several other severe problems can result as well. If a better path is found, traffic will be routed over the new path even if the existing path can meet the service requirements of this traffic. This problem becomes even worse when routing is based on a frequently changing metric such as available bandwidth. In this case, routing updates can become frequent and thus consume network bandwidth and router processing time and introduce routing oscillations. Frequently changing routes can increase the delay variation (or jitter) experienced by end users. The main objectives of QoS-based routing are [31]: dynamic determination of feasible paths, optimization of resource usage and graceful performance degradation. QoS routing must be able to select a path, from possibly many choices, that has a good chance of accommodating the QoS of the given flow. Feasible path selection may be subject to policy constraints, such as path cost, provider selection, etc. This has many advantages compared to a state-insensitive routing scheme. This includes efficient utilization of network resources by improving the total network throughput, efficient network engineering, and giving more graceful performance degradation [33].

However, these benefits of QoS routing also incur the cost of developing new routing protocols and/or extending existing ones. Moreover, it potentially increases communication, processing and storage overheads. QoS routing raises several issues, e.g., which metrics are used and how QoS-accommodating paths are computed for unicast and for multicast flows. In addition, a router must be able of determining the QoS capability of each outgoing link and reserve link resources as needed.

Over the past decade several approaches and architectures have been proposed. For example, IntServ (or Integrated Services) is an architecture that has been developed by the Internet community to provide QoS at the flow level. IntServ is described in RFC 1633 [34], RFC 2212 [35], and RFC 2215 [36]. In flow routing, all packets belonging to an application session follow the same path, allowing bandwidth to be reserved along that path, in order to ensure high quality of service. Because many thousands or even millions of packets are typically sent during a single application session, flow routing occurs far less often than datagram routing, making it practical to apply more complex decision procedures than can be used in datagram routing. One serious drawback of IntSrev is that it requires routers to maintain per-flow information, which can become overwhelming in the Internet. Due to this scalability problem of IntServ, another architecture called DiffServ was introduced by IETF. DiffServ resolves some of the problems of IntServ to provide differentiated services based on the class of service defined in the packet header. DiffServ is described in RFC 2474 [37] and RFC 2475 [38]. A more recent architecture that expedites packet forwarding while facilitating traffic engineering to support QoS routing is Multi-Protocol Label Switching (MPLS) [39–42], which is defined in RFC 3031 [43]. Also several protocol extensions have been proposed to accommodate QoS, e.g., OSPF QoS-routing extensions in RFC 2676 [44, 45].

QoS routing calculates routes based on some knowledge of resource availability in the network and the QoS requirement of traffic flows. QoS routing allows alternate paths and prevents shifting a traffic flow to a better alternate path if the existing path meets its service requirements. The problem of QoS routing can be solved as a constrained optimization problem using constraint based routing (CBR) algorithms that base path selection decisions on a set of requirements or constraints in addition to the destination. Constraints imposed by QoS requirements include bandwidth, delay and loss. In addition to satisfying QoS constraints, the routes are selected to reduce costs, balance network load, increase security, or impose administrative policies. For a discussion on several constraint-based routing approaches and their requirements, complexities, and recent research proposals, see Ref. 46.

According to Ref. 30, the QoS unicast routing problem is defined as follows: given a source s, a destination t, a set of QoS constraints C, and possibly an optimization goal, find the best feasible path from$s$ to t which satisfies C. This routing problem can be divided into subclasses according to the QoS metrics. For metrics based on bandwidth and residual buffer space, the routing problem is divided into two subclasses: link-optimization routing and link-constrained routing. An example of link-optimization routing is to find a path that has the largest bandwidth on the bottleneck link. An example of link-constrained routing is to find a path whose bottleneck bandwidth is above a required value. For other metrics such as delay, delay jitter and cost, routing problems can be divided into two subclasses: path-optimization routing and path-constrained routing. Many composite routing problems can be derived from the above four basic problems. Unfortunately, there are two NP-complete problem classes, that is, path-constrained path-optimization routing (PCPO) and multi-path constrained routing (MPC) [47]. An example of PCPO is delay-constrained least-cost routing, which finds a least-cost path with bounded delay. An example of MPC is delay delay-jitter constrained routing, which is to find a path with both bounded delay and bounded delay jitter. In contrast, the QoS multicast routing problem is defined as follows: given a source s, a set R of destination nodes, a set C of QoS constraints, and possibly an optimization goal, find the best feasible tree covering s to all nodes in R which satisfies C. Multicast routing is different from unicast routing as an optimization or a constraint must be applied to the entire tree instead of a single path. There are several well-known multicast routing problems. The Steiner tree problem is to find the least-cost tree, i.e., a tree covering a group of destinations with the minimum total cost over all links. The constrained Steiner tree problem is to find the least-cost tree with bounded delay. The delay delay-jitter constrained multicast routing problem belongs to the multi-tree constrained routing problem class. The above multicast routing problems are all NP-complete. Several heuristic approaches have been proposed to solve some of these hard problems, including evolutionary algorithms, simulated annealing and Tabu search.

6. Internet Routing Protocols

The Internet is an example of a large-scale and complex network; in fact, it is a network of networks. Although the topology of today's Internet is much more complex, it can be conceptually viewed as an approximate hierarchical structure (see Fig. 14). At the lowest level customers are connected to local ISP networks, such as universities, enterprises, or local ISPs networks. These networks are usually connected to regional or national ISPs, which are then connected to international ISPs. Several routing protocols have been proposed and deployed over the Internet since its early days. They are defined by IETF in various RFCs [48]. Routing protocols specify how routers collect information about their neighbors, share the collected information with other routers, and select routes from each source to each destination. A routing protocol will also specify the metric used in determining best routes and the routing algorithm used in selecting best routes. In this section, we review some popular protocols for unicast and multicast routing in the Internet.

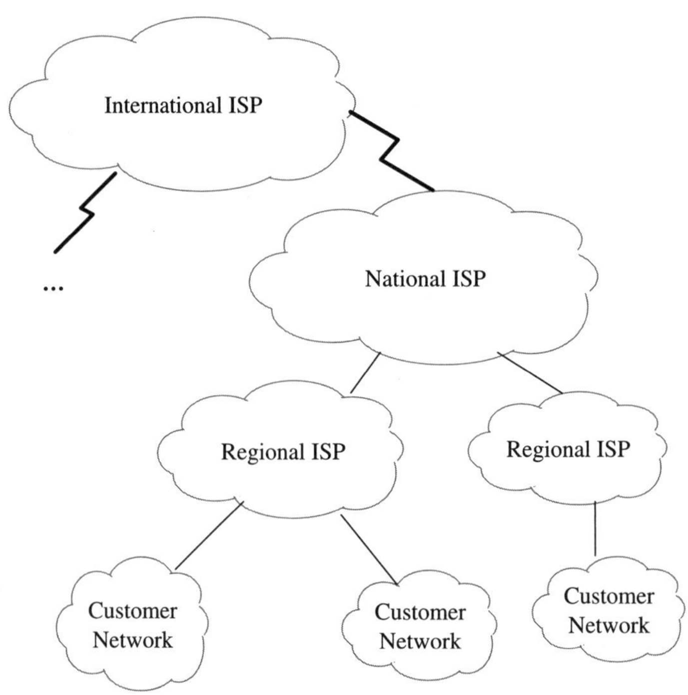

Fig. 14. The Internet hierarchical structure.

6.1. *Unicast Routing Protocols*

Simplifying its routing complexity, the Internet, uses hierarchical routing. The Internet is divided into a set of interconnected autonomous systems (ASs). Each autonomous system is a homogenous network consisting of a collection of networks and routers that are under the same administration (e.g., a university campus network, an enterprise network, or an Internet service provider network). Figure 15 shows an example illustrating three interconnected autonomous systems. Routing is achieved in two phases: routing inside an autonomous systems and routing between autonomous systems. A routing protocol used inside an autonomous system is referred to as an intra-AS, intra-domain, or interior gateway routing protocol (IGP). On the other hand, a routing protocol used between autonomous systems is called an inter-AS, inter-domain, or exterior gateway routing (EGP).

Several protocols have been developed for intra-domain and inter-domain routing. In this section, we briefly review the salient features of RIP and OSPF as examples of intra-domain protocols, and BGP as an example of inter-domain routing protocols. RIP uses distance vector routing whereas OSPF uses link state routing. But BGP uses a technique called path vector routing to enforce policies set by the network administrators since different autonomous systems may have different policies. Figure 16 shows a classification of unicast routing protocols used over the Internet. All these routing protocols are considered as part of the network although they are in different layers as shown in Fig. 17. For example, RIP runs over the UDP transport layer protocol using port 520 whereas BGP runs over TCP on port 179.

6.1.1. *Routing Information Protocol*

The routing information protocol (RIP) is one of the earliest developed intra-domain routing protocols for IP networks and is still widely used in internal networks and

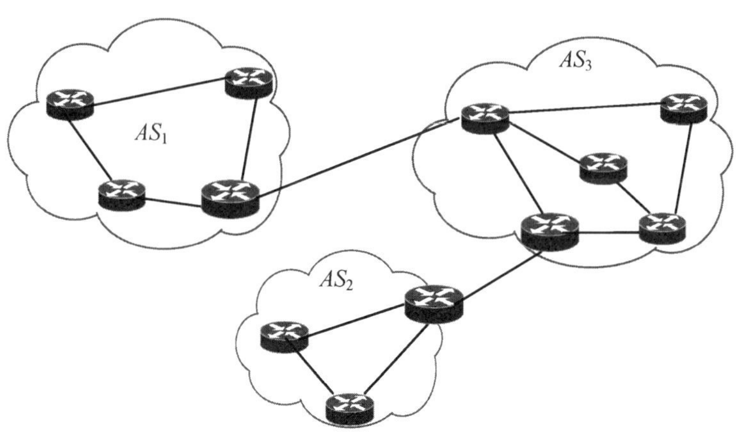

Fig. 15. An example of autonomous systems.

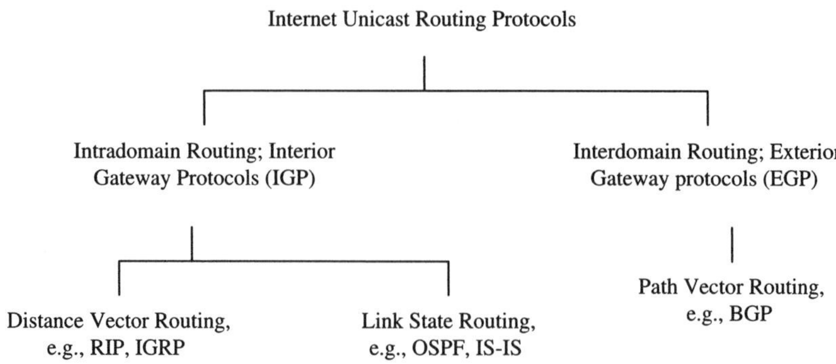

Fig. 16. Classification of the Internet unicast routing protocols.

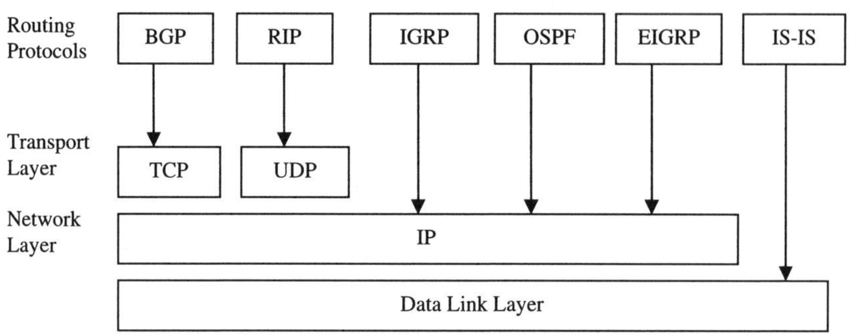

Fig. 17. An example illustrating autonomous systems.

inside autonomous systems. Its earliest version was developed at Xerox Parc as part of the Xerox Network Services protocol suite. It was implemented and distributed as part of the Berkeley Software Distribution (BSD) version of the Unix operating system. Currently, there are three versions defined by IETF; namely, RIP1 defined in RFC 1058 [49], RIP2 defined in RFC 2453 [50] for IPv4 networks, and RIPng defined in RFC 2080 [51] for IPv6 networks. RIP2 expands the amount of useful information carried in RIP1 messages. Hence, it provides support for variable length subnetting and router authentication. RIP is also easier to configure since it requires minimal parameter settings and is simpler than other intra-domain routing protocols such as OSPF, IS–IS and EIGRP. It has acceptable performance in small to mid-size networks. However, due to its poor convergence and scalability, its use is limited. RIP implements a distance vector routing algorithm to adapt to changes in the network topology. It uses hop count (i.e., number of subnets traversed to reach a destination) as a routing metric and thus all links are assigned an equal cost of one unit. RIP limits the maximum hop count to 15 hops to prevent routing loops from continuing indefinitely. It also implements split horizon to prevent incorrect routing information from being propagated as explained previously. As also mentioned each router shares its routing table (distance vector) with its neighbors via RIP advertisements. The assumption was that RIP will be used in networks that are no more than 15 hops in diameter and have no more than 25 subnets in the routing table. RIP update messages are exchanged every 30 seconds or whenever a router updates its distance vector upon receiving an advertisement from another router. According to Ref. 52, this ensures that the routing tables are kept up-to-date even if routing update messages are occasionally lost. However, when there are many routers on a single network, there is a tendency for them to synchronize with each other such that they all issue updates at the same time. This problem occurs whenever the 30-second timer is affected by the processing load on the system. It is undesirable for the update messages to become synchronized since it can lead to unnecessary collisions on broadcast networks. This can be avoided either by a clock whose rate is not affected by the system load or by adding a small random value in the range of −5 to +5 seconds to the update interval [53]. For a detailed discussion of the synchronization problem of periodic routing messages with proposals for methods to avoid it, see Ref. 52. Recent implementations of RIP introduce deliberate time variation into the update timer at each router to avoid synchronization.

6.1.2. *Open Shortest Path First*

Initially the network size was not that big and hence RIP was appropriate and had acceptable performance. Due to its simplicity, it had widespread deployment. However, to handle the complexity in today's Internet, other Internet routing protocols have been developed. Perhaps the most widely deployed intra-domain routing protocol for enterprise networks is open shortest path first (OSPF). It is defined in RFC 1131 (OSPF1) [54], RFC 2328 (OSPF2) [55] and RFC 2740 (OSPF3) [56]. The latest version OSPF3 supports both IPv4 and IPv6. It is intended to be used within a single autonomous system. However, it divides the OSPF domain (or autonomous system) into areas and uses hierarchical routing in the OSPF domain (see Fig. 18). This helps in significantly reducing the overhead due to routing traffic and thus improving its scalability for use in larger networks. Like some versions of RIP, OSPF also provides support for variable length subnetting, classless inter-domain routing (CIDR) and authentication of routing updates. In contrast, OSPF has more features than RIP. For example, it allows using multiple link metrics and supports load balancing via equal cost multi-path routing, which facilitates better distribution of traffic over several equal cost paths to a destination [57–60].

Routers inside each area use link state routing to discover the area topology and compute a shortest path tree using Dijkstra's algorithm. OSPF updates routing tables quickly when there is a change in the network topology or link cost. Each area has an area number and one of the areas acts as a backbone/core that is connected (either directly or through a virtual link) to all other areas. The backbone area has area number 0 by convention. Inter-area routing is achieved through routers connecting the backbone area to the other areas. OSPF defines various types of

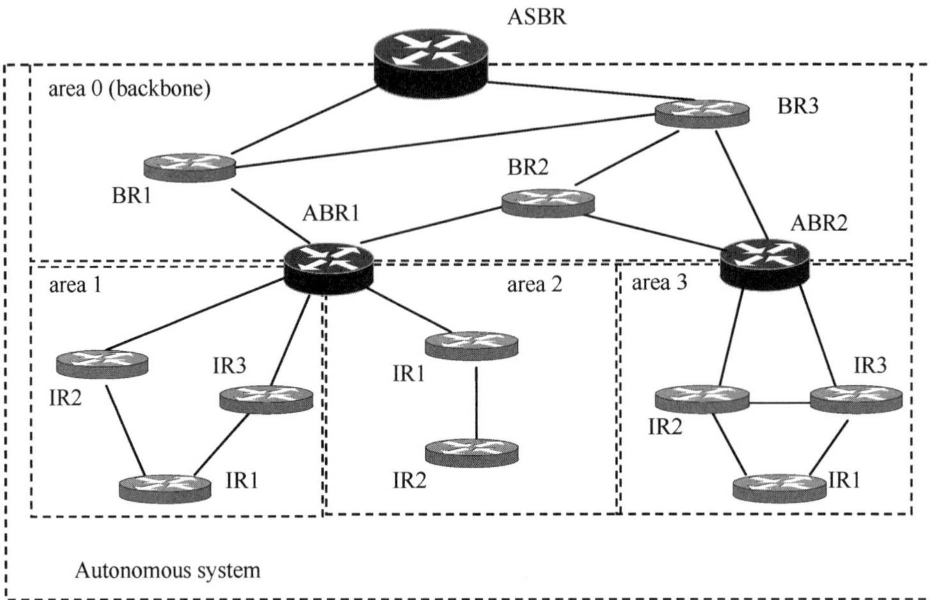

Fig. 18. An example illustrating hierarchical routing inside an autonomous system using OSPF.

routers: backbone routers (BRs), area border routers (ABRs), internal routers (IRs), and AS border routers (ASBRs). Backbone routers are routers that belong to the backbone area. Area border routers are backbone routers that connect the backbone to non-backbone areas. Internal routers are routers inside a non-backbone area. An AS border router is a backbone router that connects an autonomous system to other autonomous systems. Thus, the same physical router can have different roles based on its position in the topology and thus keeps multiple copies of routing information. Also, an ASBR runs OSPF for intra-domain routing besides an inter-domain routing protocol such as BGP. Figure 18 shows an illustrative example of OSPF division of an autonomous system into areas and different router types.

6.1.3. *Border Gateway Protocol*

In today's Internet, the most popular inter-domain routing protocol is the border gateway protocol (BGP). Typically, customer networks are connected to ISPs and the BGP is used for exchanging routing information between ISPs. The BGP is based on path vector based routing, which enforces the application of administrative policies while selecting the best route between autonomous systems. Under BGP, a path is defined as a sequence of intermediate domains between source and destination routers. The BGP is defined by IETF and its latest version is BGP4 defined in RFC 4271 [61]. Routers connecting ASs exchange reachability information among autonomous systems to construct a network map of AS connectivity and achieve routing in a fully decentralized fashion. The internal topology of an autonomous system is hidden at this level. BGP4 supports CIDR and allows route aggregation to decrease the size of routing tables.

To enable BGP to select the best path to a particular destination when multiple paths exist, BGP paths have associated properties known as path attributes. These attributes include weight, local preference, multi-exit discriminator (MED), origin, AS path, and next hop. The path selection is achieved by applying the following criteria in the order presented [62]:

- If the path specifies a next hop that is inaccessible, drop the update.
- Prefer the path with the largest weight.
- If the weights are the same, prefer the path with the largest local preference.
- If the local preferences are the same, prefer the path that was originated by BGP running on this router.
- If no route was originated, prefer the route that has the shortest AS path.
- If all paths have the same AS path length, prefer the path with the lowest origin type.
- If the origin codes are the same, prefer the path with the lowest MED attribute.
- If the paths have the same MED, prefer the external path over the internal path.
- If the paths are still the same, prefer the path through the closest IGP neighbor.
- Prefer the path with the lowest IP address, as specified by the BGP router ID.

6.2. *Multicast Routing Protocols*

Many modern applications over the Internet require multicast communication to send messages from one sender to multiple receivers including online video conferencing, video on demand, software update distribution, distance learning and distributed interactive simulation. Multicast routing protocols allow such applications to efficiently distribute data from one point to multi-points among members of a multicast group by avoiding sending multiple copies over shared links on various paths. Today, there are many multicast routing protocols developed to allow sending data from a single source to a multicast group over the Internet [63]. There are three essential components in multicast communication: group management, delivery tree construction and data forwarding. Multicast-enabled routers use the Internet Group Management Protocol (IGMP) to dynamically manage group membership; new members can join and existing members can leave at any time. The latest version of IGMP is IGMP-3 and is defined in RFC 3376 [64]. Multicast groups are identified by class D IP addresses. Multicast routing protocols differ in the way they construct and use distribution trees. While some protocols use source-based trees, others use group-shared trees (see Fig. 19). Examples of the first category includes Distance Vector Multicast Routing Protocol (DVMRP), Multicast OSPF (MOSPF), and Protocol Independent Multicast-Dense Mode (PIM-DM). Examples of the other category are Core Based Tree (CBT) and Protocol Independent Multicast-Sparse Mode (PIM-SM). Group-shared tree

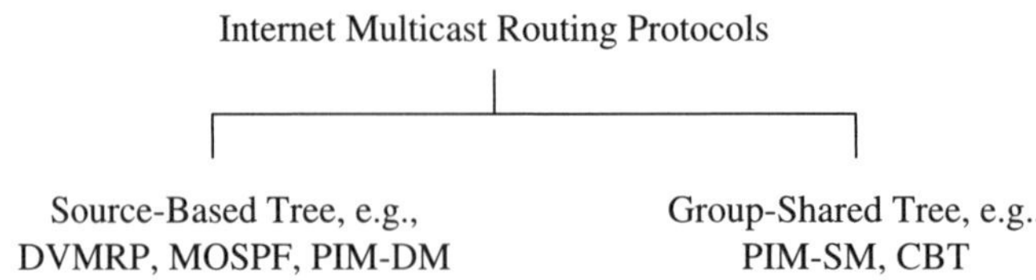

Fig. 19. Classification of the Internet multicast routing protocols.

protocols are more scalable since they reduce the state information stored at each router. However, it has higher delay time than source-specific tree multicast routing protocols. For a succinct discussion of multicast routing protocols over the Internet, we refer the reader to Ref. 65 and 66.

6.2.1. *Distance Vector Multicast Routing Protocol*

The Distance Vector Multicast Routing Protocol (DVMRP) is a multicast routing protocol that provides an efficient mechanism for connectionless datagram delivery to a group of hosts across an inter-network. DVMRP can be used only within an autonomous system. DVMRP is a distance vector multicast routing protocol derived from RIP. It is described in RFC 1075 [67]. DVMRP uses RPF with pruning/grafting to dynamically build a shortest path spanning tree rooted at the source and having group members as terminal nodes. All branches that do not lead to active members are pruned from the tree and new members can join using graft messages. DVMRP suffers from poor scaling because of the necessity to flood frequently. DVMRP has been used to build MBONE (a virtual backbone network across the public Internet that allows multicast packets by building tunnels between DVMRP-capable routers to go across non-multicast routers).

6.2.2. *Multicast Open Shortest Path First*

Multicast Open Shortest Path First (MOSPF) is a multicast extension to OSPF version 2 and is intended to be used within an autonomous system. The current version of MOSPF is defined in RFC 1584 [68]. MOSPF works only in inter-networks that use OSPF for unicast routing. MOSPF includes multicast information in OSPF link state advertisements so that an MOSPF router learns which multicast groups are active on which LANs. MOSPF constructs a shortest path distribution tree rooted at the source for each source-group pair. This tree is cached and will be recomputed when there is a change or when the cache expires. MOSPF works well in environments that have relatively few source-group pairs active at any give time. Its performance becomes less accepted when there are many active sources or unstable links. MOSPF also suffers from poor scaling when there are multiple sources or many groups. It is best used when relatively few sources or groups are active at any given time. It does not work well in the presence of unstable links as it leads to frequent state updates. MOSPF does not support tunneling either.

6.2.3. *Core Based Tree Protocol*

The Core Based Tree Protocol (CBT) version 2 is described in RFC 2189 [69]. CBT builds a bidirectional shared tree for each group and is used by any active source to send data to that group. This tree is rooted at a selected node called a core node or rendezvous point. Members in the group can join and leave at any time during the life time of the group. A host that wants to join a group sends a join message to its designated router (DR) using the IGMP. Then, the DR sends a join message hop-by-hop toward the core until it is received by the core or any node on the shared tree, which sends back a join acknowledgment message toward the sender node. Once a shared tree is constructed, any active source that wants to send a message for group members will send its message hop-by-hop toward the core until again it is received by the core or any node on the shared tree, at which it will be redistributed to the group members along the constructed shared tree. The source may or may not be a member in the group. Similarly, any node that wants to leave a group sends a prune message hop-by-hop toward the core. Then, the core or any member node on the path from the sender to the core that sees the request sends back a prune acknowledgment message toward the sender node.

In CBT, the membership information is stored at the core node. Since all sources use the same shared tree to deliver their messages, this eliminates the need for explicit source lists or member lists, thus resulting in good scalability of the protocol. Although the shared tree protocol results in traffic concentration near the core, which can lead to congestion on the shared links, it has a number of advantages when the number of sources is large. CBT is also independent of the unicast routing protocols, which means that it can work with any unicast routing protocol to send messages between the sources and the core.

6.2.4. *Protocol Independent Multicast*

Protocol Independent Multicast (PIM) is another very popular multicast routing protocol that works independent of the existing unicast routing protocol [70]. It has two modes of operation: dense mode (PIM-DM) and sparse mode (PIM-SM). The recent revisions of PIM-DM and PIM-SM are defined in RFC 3973 [71] and RFC 4601 [72], respectively. The dense mode is used when the multicast traffic is high and constant and when there are few senders and many receivers which are close to each other. PIM-DM resembles DVMRP since both use RPF with pruning to build source-based distribution trees. The sparse mode is used when there are few receivers in a group and they are far from each other and from the source. Also, the traffic pattern is low. Thus, under such conditions the use of RPF in PIM-DM is not justified since it wastes network bandwidth. In contrast, PIM-SM is optimized for such environments. PIM-SM is similar to CBT; it builds a group-shared tree rooted at a rendezvous point (RP). Initially, it assumes that no node wants to receive multicast traffic. When a node wants to participate in the group, it registers at the rendezvous point by sending a join message. Similarly, when a node wants to leave a group, it sends a prune message to the RP. When a source wants to send a multicast packet, it first sends it to unicast the rendezvous point, which in turn distributes it to registered members. PIM-SM also has the capability to switch to source-specific tree when the group size increases and/or the source sends many messages.

7. Mobile Ad Hoc Network Routing

A MANET [73–80] is a dynamic multi-hop wireless network established by a group of mobile stations that can move freely. It is a multi-hop network since network nodes act as routers and cooperate to forward packets from a source to a destination that are not directly within the wireless transmission range of each other over multiple hops through other nodes. Routes are dynamically established between sources and destinations by forwarding the messages over a chain of intermediate stations. This network is infrastructure-less in the sense that nodes are equal peers without having a special central node, such as a base station, to coordinate communication between them. Stations in the vicinity of a transmitting host will receive the transmitted packet and can forward it to other stations in the network that may be far from the transmitting node. This transitive closure of the neighborhood of all stations forms the ad hoc network.

MANETs have their own distinguishing features from wired networks. Besides the issues resulting from the characteristics of the wireless channel, the highly dynamic nature of nodes in MANET increases the complexity of routing among nodes. Due to the changes of the wireless transmission conditions and the arbitrary move of nodes in the network, the MANET topology changes very often and in an unpredictable manner. To keep the MANET network completely self-organizing and self-configuring, routes are automatically determined and maintained by the routing protocol. Routing in MANET has been and is still an active research area and several ad hoc routing protocols have been proposed [73–75]. Many of these protocols are extensions of the distance vector and link state routing protocols that are used in wired networks. Typically, ad hoc routing protocols are subdivided into two main categories: reactive and proactive. The difference between these two categories is principally based on when routes (and hence routing tables) are established. While routes in reactive routing protocols are established on demand, they are pre-computed and stored in routing tables before needed in proactive routing protocols. In other words, proactive routing protocols are table-driven, where each node tries to maintain routing information about every other node in the network at all times. The reactive approach eliminates the need to periodically flood the network with table update messages, which are required in a table-driven (a.k.a. proactive) approach. For a detailed list and classification of different ad hoc routing protocols, see the Wikipedia website in Ref. 81 and the survey in Ref. 82. In the following subsections, we briefly discuss two popular ad hoc routing protocols: AODV (a reactive approach) and OLSR (a proactive approach).

7.1. *Ad Hoc on Demand Distance Vector*

A routing protocol designed for MANET is the Ad hoc On Demand Distance Vector (AODV) routing algorithm that is capable of unicast, multicast and broadcast routing [83–86]. The current description is in IETF RFC 3561 [84]. Because nodes are mobile in MANET, the topology very often changes. This protocol is an example of a reactive approach in which a route is established only on demand, i.e., only if a source node requests it. Also, it is based on a variant of the Bellman–Ford distance vector algorithm. The AODV protocol consists of two main mechanisms: route discovery and route maintenance. The protocol automatically discovers routes in a decentralized fashion.

When a source node wants to send a packet to a destination node for which a route does not currently exist, it broadcasts a route request (RREQ) message. Nodes that receive the RREQ message update their information for the source node and set up backward pointers to the source node in their routing tables. If a node receiving RREQ is a destination node or has a route to the destination node with corresponding sequence number greater than or equal to that contained in the RREQ, it sends a route reply (RREP) message unicast back to the source. Otherwise, the node re-broadcasts the RREQ. To limit traffic due to flooding, nodes keep track of the RREQ sequence numbers and if a RREQ has been processed before, it is discarded and not forwarded. Sequence numbers also ensure the route freshness. As the RREP message moves back to the source, nodes set up forward pointers to the destination. Once the source node receives the RREP, it has a route to the destination and can start sending data to it. If any node on the route later receives another RREP with a greater sequence number or with the same sequence number but a smaller hop count, then the node may update its routing table accordingly for that destination. The route remains active as along as the source is sending data on that route; otherwise, it will time out and will eventually, be deleted from the routing tables of intermediate nodes. AODV is resilient in the case of link breakages, which are very likely in ad hoc networks due to the mobility of nodes. If a link breaks while the route is active, the upstream node sends back a route error (RERR) message to the source, which in turn can reinitiate a route discovery if still wanted to communicate with the same destination. The RREQ packets flooding in AODV is illustrated in Fig. 20.

7.2. *Optimized Link State Routing Protocol*

Another routing protocol for MANETs is the Optimized Link State Routing Protocol (OLSR) [87–91]. The current version of OLSR is now defined by the IETF MANET working group in RFC 3626 [92]. Several implementations of OLSR are publicly available from Ref. 93. OLSR is a proactive table-driven routing protocol that regularly exchanges topology information between nodes. OLSR uses a technique called multipoint relaying [94–96] for optimized message flooding. In this technique, each node selects a set of its neighbor nodes as multi-point relays

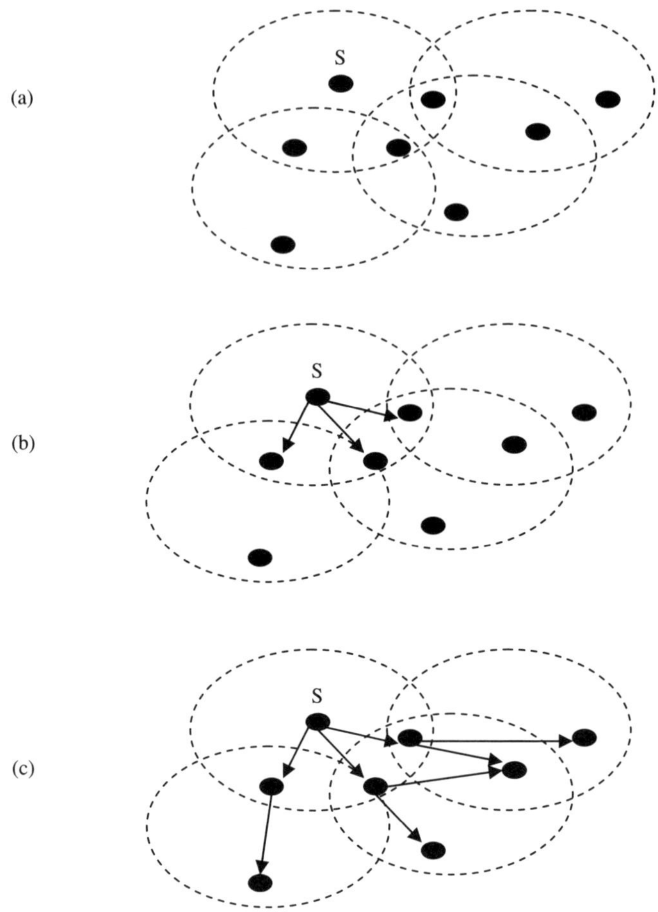

Fig. 20. Route request (RREQ) packets flooding in AODV: (a) illustrates the range of each node broadcast, (b) after a single hop broadcast, and (c) after two-hop broadcast.

(MPRs); see Fig. 21. The nodes which are selected as MPRs periodically announce reachability information about nodes which have selected them as MPRs to the network in their control messages. Thus, unlike pure link state protocols, the technique declares only a subset of links and reduces flooding of control messages using only nodes within the MPR set (instead of the entire network).

8. Traffic Management Mechanisms

With the evolution of communication networks, increasing network traffic, and limited available resources, supporting the required QoS for emerging applications is becoming very difficult. Different applications vary in their requirement for QoS. While some applications have stringent requirements for timely delivery, others put more emphasis on assuring loss-free and error-free delivery. Under such conditions,

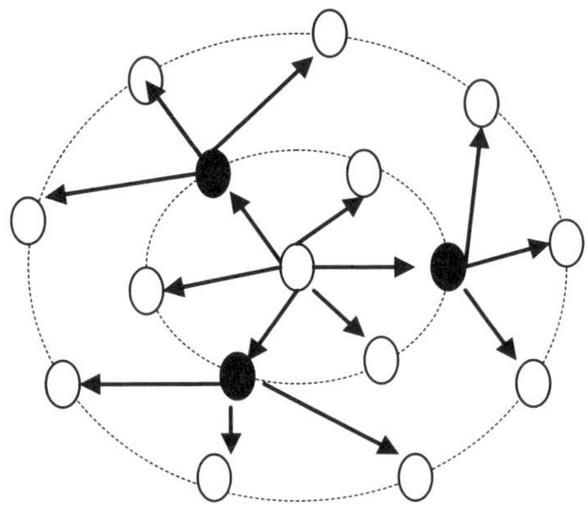

Fig. 21. Illustration of multi-point relays.

network providers want to achieve high utilization of their network resources while meeting the required QoS levels for individual users. Traffic management is very critical in achieving these goals in high-performance networks [97]. It can be implemented at the flow level or at the packet level. For example, the InterServ architecture in the Internet deals with traffic flows whereas ATM and DiffServ deal with packets of different classes. Some traffic management mechanisms can be implemented at the source node while others can be implemented in each network node. For example, admission control is implemented at the network edge (gateway router) whereas buffer management is implemented at each network node. Some techniques can be implemented at the source as well as in each router, such as traffic policing and shaping. In this section, we discuss four traffic management mechanisms:

- Resource reservation and admission control — To deny access for new flows if the required QoS cannot be guaranteed for the new arrival and ongoing flows.
- Traffic policing — To monitor the adherence of incoming traffic characteristics to the service contract specifications and take appropriate responses accordingly, e.g., discard, delay, or mark packets/flows violating the contract.
- Traffic shaping/conditioning — To regulate the traffic rate that enters the network, thereby, smoothing out bursty traffic.
- Buffer management — To set the packet drop policy that decides which packet is discarded when the buffer is filled or is about to be filled.
- Packet scheduling — To determine the order of transmission at which buffered packets will be processed/transmitted.

8.1. *Resource Reservation and Admission Control*

One way to satisfy the required QoS is through a resource reservation mechanism. When a source makes a reservation, it sends the specifications of its potential traffic (e.g., delay, delay variation, bandwidth and reliability) and its need for resources (e.g., bandwidth, buffer size and CPU time) to the router beforehand. Before the router accepts the flow for processing, it first checks the flow characteristics. Then, the router decides to accept or reject the flow based on incoming flow specifications, its current commitment for ongoing flows and the availability of resources. These mechanisms are currently used as part of the IntServ model in the Internet.

8.2. *Traffic Policing and Shaping (Rate Control)*

Traffic policy checks the adherence of incoming traffic to the service agreement between the customer and the network provider. However, bursty traffic creates many problems and temporarily leads to congestion. The aim of traffic shaping is to regulate the rate at which the traffic enters the network or leaves a network node. If the traffic is bursty, it will be smoothed out. The commonly used techniques for traffic shaping are: leaky bucket and token bucket [98–101]. While leaky bucket poses a hard limit on the traffic rate, token buckets allows some variability but imposes a limit on the average rate.

8.2.1. *Leaky Bucket Algorithm*

This approach operates using an analogy to a bucket with a hole at the bottom [102]. The water enters the bucket and leaks through the hole at a constant rate as long as the bucket is not empty, i.e., the output rate remains fixed even if the input rate is varying (see Fig. 22). A simple leaky bucket implementation in a network router is through a finite buffer FIFO queue discipline that holds arriving packets and then processes them at a constant rate, as shown in Fig. 23. If the arriving packets exceed the buffer size, the extra packets will be dropped. Otherwise, packets are buffered and served/transmitted out from the queue at a constant rate. This approach works

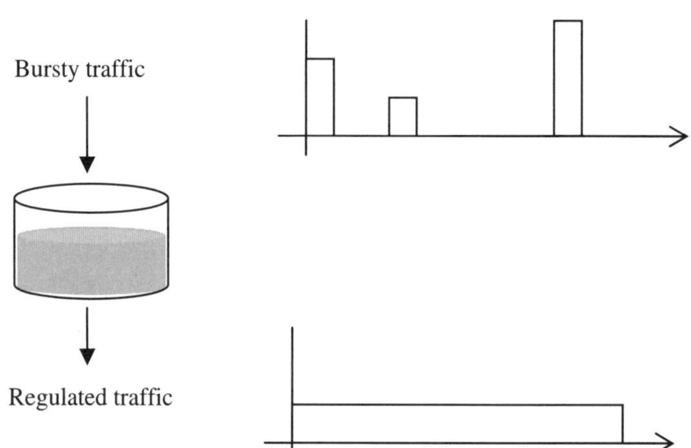

Fig. 22. Traffic regulation using leaky bucket algorithm.

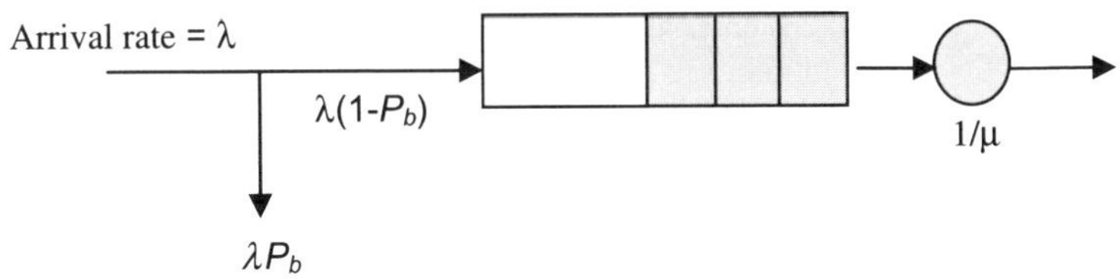

Fig. 23. Simple illustration of leaky bucket algorithm.

perfectly if packets have a fixed size and as long as the rate of incoming packets does not exceed the peak rate specified in the service level agreement between the source node and the network provider. A continuous-state version of this approach called the generic cell rate algorithm (GCRA) is used in ATM networks to effectively police realtime traffic at the ingress router. For variable-length packets, a byte counter is used. At regular intervals the counter is initialized to n bytes and one or more packets are transmitted from the buffer as long as their size is less than the byte counter. The counter is decreased by the size of each transmitted packet.

8.2.2. *Token Bucket Algorithm*

Another traffic shaping algorithm is the token bucket algorithm. Unlike the leaky bucket algorithm, it allows some burstiness in the outgoing traffic but limits the maximum burst size. The bucket holds tokens instead of packets. Each token represents a credit used to grant permission to transmit a packet or L bytes. They are added at a fixed rate to the bucket but when the bucket fills up, additional tokens are discarded. An arriving packet will be transmitted if enough tokens exist in the bucket to cover its size. Otherwise, it is discarded or buffered until the next period. Tokens are removed from the bucket for each transmitted packet. The token bucket algorithm is described by three parameters r, b and T, which represent the rate (bytes/s) that tokens are added to the bucket, bucket depth (maximum burst size) and the time interval, respectively. The operation of the token bucket algorithm is illustrated in Fig. 24.

8.3. *Buffer/Queue Management Mechanisms*

As mentioned, packets often arrive at the router in bursts. Buffers in the router are used to smooth out burstiness in incoming traffic rates by absorbing fluctuations in traffic. When the incoming rate is higher than the outgoing rate, the queue size will increase and eventually the buffer overflows and packets are dropped (since the available buffer space is finite). In order to avoid high packet loss rate during congestion, a large queue size can be used. However, this will also undesirably increase the delay. Hence, the buffer management policy that decides on how packets are dropped plays a crucial role in keeping the average queue size low, avoiding congestion and controlling the required QoS.

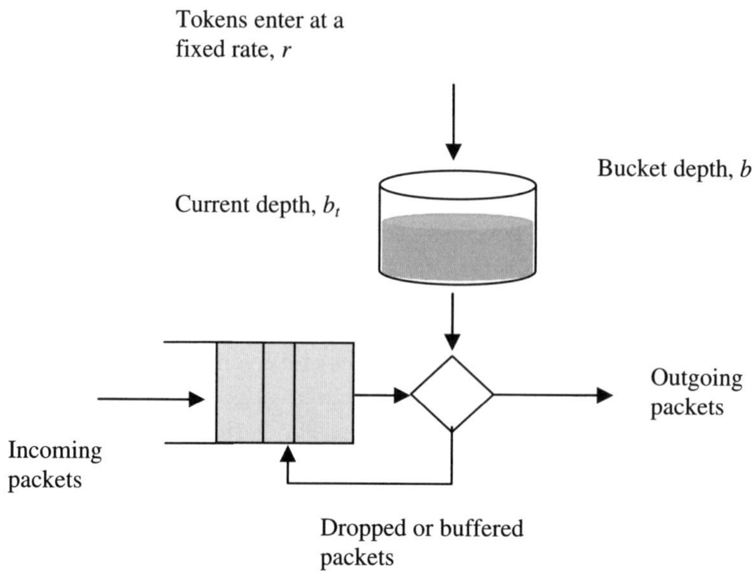

Fig. 24. Traffic regulation using token bucket algorithm.

8.3.1. *Tail Drop*

Under a tail drop policy, when a packet arrives and the buffer is full, the arriving packet is dropped (see Fig. 25). Although it is a simple approach, it has two drawbacks. First, few traffic flows can monopolize the buffer leaving no space for other flows. In addition, it can reduce the link utilization and overall throughput of the network. This is because an arriving burst causes multiple packets to be dropped (which in turn notifies the congestion control to throttle the sources) leading to a sustained period of low traffic.

Instead of dropping the arriving packet, two other implementations are possible. When a new packet arrives and the buffer is full, drop the packet at the front of the queue or drop a packet randomly selected from the queue. This can only resolve the first drawback, i.e., monopolization.

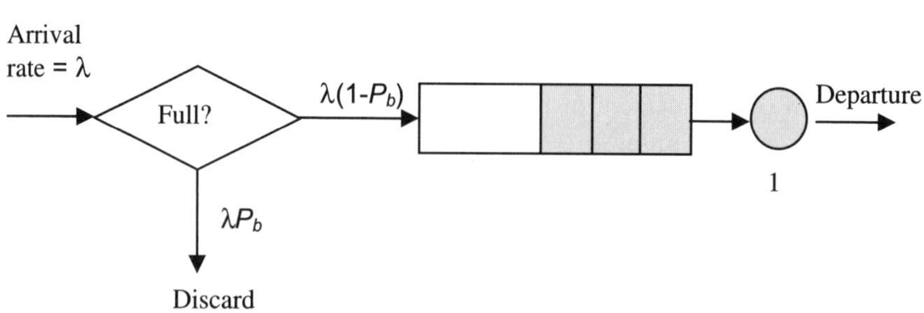

Fig. 25. Tail drop buffer management.

8.3.2. Random Early Detection

To keep the average queue size low while improving the packet drop rate, Floyed and Jacobson [103] proposed an active queue management technique called Random Early Detection (RED), which drops packets probabilistically; see the flowchart in Fig. 26. The RED algorithm keeps the average queue length low while allowing occasional bursts of packets in the queue. It detects congestion early before the queue overflows by computing the average queue length (Q_{avg}) at each packet arrival. Then, it compares the average queue length with two pre-specified thresholds: minimum threshold (th_{min}) and maximum threshold (th_{max}). If the average queue length is below the minimum threshold, the arriving packet is admitted to the queue. However, if the average queue length is greater than the maximum threshold, the packet is dropped or marked. This ensures that the average queue length does not significantly exceed the maximum threshold. Finally, when the average queue length is between the minimum and maximum thresholds, then the packet is dropped or marked with probability p, which is a function of the average queue size, th_{min} and th_{max}. The performance of RED depends on how the average queue length and the dropping probabilities are computed. The algorithm for computing the average queue length determines the degree of burstiness that will be allowed in the queue. The algorithm for calculating the packet-marking probability determines how frequently the gateway marks packets, given the current level of congestion. The RED algorithm calculates the average queue length using a low-pass filter

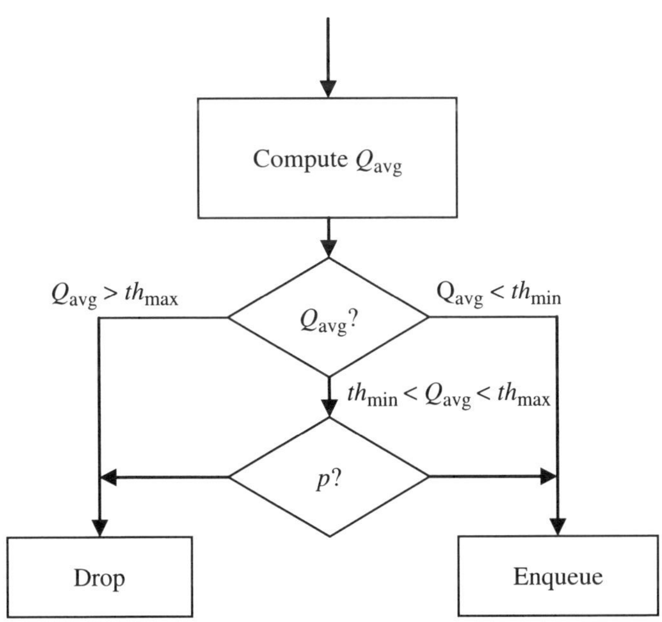

Fig. 26. Random early detection buffer management.

with an exponential weighted moving average. During congestion, the probability that the gateway notifies a particular connection to reduce its window is roughly proportional to that connection's share of the bandwidth through the gateway. RED gateways are designed to accompany a transport-layer congestion control protocol such as TCP. The RED gateway has no bias against bursty traffic and avoids the global synchronization of many connections decreasing their window at the same time. The goal is for the gateway to mark packets at fairly evenly spaced intervals, in order to avoid biases and to avoid global synchronization, and to mark packets sufficiently frequently to control the average queue size. Several variations of RED have been proposed. For example, Weighted Random Early Detection (WRED) is a queue management extension of RED which allows QoS differentiation. It assigns different buffer thresholds and different dropping probabilities for different queues. Packets are classified into these queues according to priority information such as IP precedence or DSCP (for DiffServ). In this way, packets in queues with higher buffer occupation thresholds or lower dropping probabilities are effectively prioritized. Another example is adaptive RED (ARED) [104], which changes the probability of dropping or marking packets based on how aggressive or conservative RED is, by observing the average queue length. If the average queue length oscillates around the minimum threshold, then RED is too aggressive. On the other hand, if the average queue length oscillates around the maximum threshold, then RED is being too conservative.

While active queue management techniques, including RED, are certainly an improvement over traditional tail-drop queues, they suffer from several shortcomings [105, 106]. For example, RED uses the average queue length as an indication of congestion, but this gives little information about the severity of congestion, i.e., the number of competing connections sharing the link. For example, in a busy period, a single source transmitting at a rate greater than the bottleneck link capacity can cause a queue to build up just as easily as a large number of sources can. From queueing theory, only when the packet inter-arrival times are exponentially distributed does the average queue length directly relate to the number of active sources. While RED can achieve an ideal operating point, it can only do so when it has a sufficient amount of buffer space and is correctly parameterized. Based on these observations, Feng *et al.* [106] proposed a fundamentally different active queue management algorithm, called BLUE, which uses packet loss and link utilization history to manage congestion. BLUE maintains a single probability, which it uses to mark (or drop) packets when they are queued. If the queue is continually dropping packets due to buffer overflow, BLUE increments the marking probability, thus increasing the rate at which it sends back congestion notification. Conversely, if the queue becomes empty or if the link is idle, BLUE decreases its marking probability. Through simulation and experimentation, the author demonstrates the superiority of BLUE to RED in reducing packet losses even when operating with a smaller buffer.

8.4. Scheduling Techniques

Another important traffic management function is deciding how to serve packets in the queue. Several approaches have been proposed and intensively studied in the literature for different queueing disciplines. In the following, we briefly describe only four approaches (although there are many other variants); these include first come first served (FCFS), priority queueing (PQ), weighted fair queueing (WFQ), and deficit weighted round robin (DWRR).

8.4.1. *First Come First Served Queueing*

FCFS queueing is the most popular queue scheduling discipline and has been extensively examined in the literature. It also serves as a baseline for comparing the performance of other queue scheduling disciplines. In FCFS queueing, all packets are placed into a single queue and then served in the same order in which they arrived. Hence, it is also known as first-in-first-out (FIFO) queueing. Although it is simple and has predictable behavior and an extremely low computational load on the system, it has some severe limitations for multimedia traffic. It is incapable of providing differentiated services and can not isolate the effect of ill-behaved flow on other flows. A bursty flow can consume the entire buffer space and causes all other flows to be denied service until after the burst is serviced. This can result in increased delay, jitter and loss for the other well-behaved flows traversing the queue. To reduce the impact of ill-behaved sources, other queue disciplines have been proposed to isolate traffic flows into separate queues. These queues can be serviced according to some scheduling scheme. Among these are priority queueing, fair queueing, weighted fair queueing, weighted round robin or class-based queueing, and deficit weighted round robin.

8.4.2. *Priority Queueing*

PQ is a simple approach to providing differentiated services to different packet flows. Packets of different flows are assigned a priority level according to their QoS requirements. When packets arrive at the output link, they are first put into different classes and enqueued separately based on their priorities. Then, queues are served in the order of the assigned priorities. The highest priority queue is served first before serving lower priority queues. However, packets in the same priority class are still served in an FCFS manner. As soon as high priority packets are served, serving packets from a lower priority class can start. But if a higher priority packet arrives while serving a lower priority packet, the server waits until completing the service of the current packet before going back to serve the higher priority queue (non-preemptive PQ). The limitation of PQ is that lower priority packets may receive little attention when a higher priority class has a continuous stream of packets. This is known as the starvation problem. Also, it lacks fairness.

8.4.3. *Weighted Fair Queueing*

WFQ is another attractive technique that plays a central role in integrated and differentiated services architectures. WFQ was inspired by work on fair queueing by Nagle in 1987 to resolve some of the limitations when mixing several flows of different packet sizes on a shared link. Arriving packets are first classified on the basis of different flows or service classes and assigned to one of multiple queues (see Fig. 27). Each queue is assigned a weight based on the required bandwidth. Then, queues are served in round robin such that the number of packets served from each queue is proportional to its weight. WFQ has several advantages. It can provide a weighted, fair allocation of resources to each flow (or service class) independent of the behavior of other flows (or classes) when combined with traffic shapers at the edges of the network. However, it is computationally complex and the supported delay bounds can still be large. Also, it cannot handle ill-behaved flows within the same service class. Several attempts to balance complexity and performance of WFQ have been proposed and implemented for differentiated services [107].

8.4.4. *Deficit Weighted Round Robin*

DWRR was proposed to guarantee QoS with respect to delay and bandwidth for realtime bursty traffic. DWRR was proposed by Shreedhar and Varghese in 1995 [108] to address the limitations of WFQ and an earlier algorithm known as weighted round robin (WRR). Similar to WFQ, packets are first classified into various service classes and assigned to separate queues and then serviced in a round robin order. However, each queue maintains a deficit counter that specifies the total number of bytes that the queue is permitted to transmit. Each time a queue is visited by the scheduler, the deficit counter is first increased by a quantum of service proportional to its weight. Then, the scheduler transmits the packets at the head of the queue and decrements the deficit counter by the size of the transmitted packet as long as

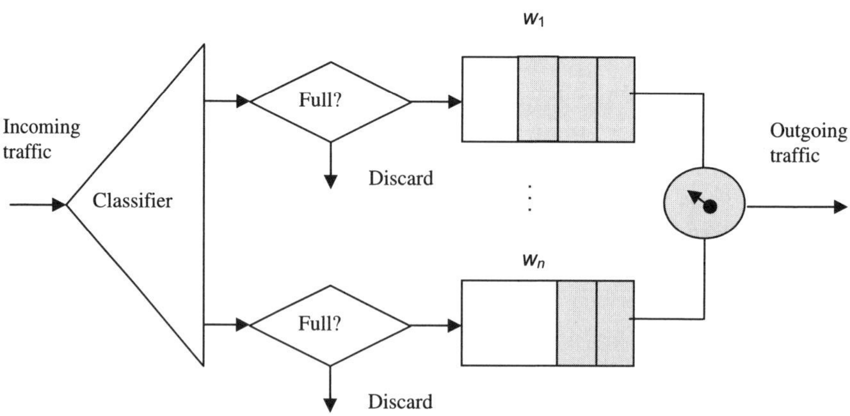

Fig. 27. Weighted fair queueing.

the size of the packet is not greater than the deficit counter. If the queue becomes empty, the deficit counter is set to zero. Then, the scheduler moves to the next non-empty queue. DWRR has several strengths over other queue disciplines such as lower complexity and better control of network resources especially when serving variable size packets. For a detailed discussion of DWRR, we refer the reader to Ref. 109.

9. Directions for Future Research

As the communications network grows and more applications that generate intense traffic appear, providing solutions with minimum computation cost and low overhead for updating routing tables is becoming more crucial. In this section, we highlight some ongoing research efforts and open issues related to routing and traffic management that still need to be addressed.

Many open research issues are related to QoS-aware routing that can cope with imposed requirements of emerging network services and technologies [46]. Routing decisions can contribute to provisioning of QoS but this problem is extremely complex. The challenge is to provide affordable and practical solutions that are tractable, scalable and robust. For example, dynamic QoS routing requires accurate information about resource availability (residual bandwidth, buffers, *etc.*) to make routing decisions. However, frequent exchange of state updates increases the routing overhead and thus does not scale well. Some researchers have studied the impact of inaccurate information on routing [44, 110–112]. Three important outcomes of these studies are [46]: (i) inaccuracies have a minimum impact if only bandwidth requirements are given; (ii) inaccuracies can have a high impact on end-to-end delay requirements, and the path selection problem becomes intractable; and (iii) triggering policies for updates (that do not result in pruning of links and advertised values) and randomization approaches for path selection can perform well in periods of high inaccuracy in the perceived link information. Although QoS routing with multiple constraints is known to be NP-hard, some attempts are trying to provide approximate solutions using heuristics for dynamic selection among multiple paths while meeting QoS constraints [113, 114].

Numerous routing protocols and algorithms have been proposed for mobile ad hoc networks. However, few attempts have been done to take QoS information into account. For example, Munaretto and Fonseca [115] extend the standardized OLSR to deal with QoS parameters. Three variants are introduced using heuristics designed for the selection of MPRs based on QoS parameters.

Another evolving area is providing scalable solutions for multimedia content distribution (e.g., web documents, audio and video streams) over the Internet from content providers to a large community of geographically distributed clients. Content routing aims at efficiently delivering a user request to a nearby replicated content site that can serve them quickly. This approach moves the route selection functionality to the application layer. Ni *et al.* [116] proposes a hierarchical content routing architecture for large-scale content delivery networks (CDN) based on a two-level hierarchical overlay network.

Recently, building dense wireless networks of heterogeneous nodes that collect and disseminate environmental data has drawn considerable research attention. Routing between a large number of low-power mobile nodes is a challenging problem. Current research focuses on developing solutions that are scalable and robust to find the minimum energy path to optimize energy usage at each node. See for example the work by Shah and Rabaey [117], Toh [118], and Heinzelman *et al.* [119].

10. Conclusions

A communication network provides connectivity between end systems so that they can communicate. There are several types of communication networks. In this chapter we have mainly focused on datagram networks that move messages from a source to a destination in separate packets. The main building blocks of datagram networks are routers or packet switches. Routers maintain routing information and forward packets from their sources towards their destinations. Several routing algorithms have been proposed and deployed. For large-scale networks, routing tables are automatically determined and maintained in a decentralized manner. Routing updates allow routers to keep up-to-date routing information that reflects changes in the network topology or link metrics. We have discussed several algorithms at the network layer for unicast, multicast, and broadcast routing. We have also discussed some advanced issues that impose constraints on selected routes to support QoS requirements by various applications or enforce administrative policies in various networks. To see how theory is put into practice, we have looked at two real networks. We first reviewed a bunch of routing protocols deployed over the Internet for both unicasting and multicasting. We then explored issues related to mobility and looked at two routing techniques for mobile ad hoc networks. After that, we discussed several issues related to traffic management and how these can help in getting the most out of the available network resources while meeting acceptable QoS levels. Finally, we presented some directions for ongoing and future research.

Acknowledgments

The author would like to thank King Fahd University of Petroleum and Minerals (KFUPM), Dhahran, Saudi Arabia for providing computing facilities and support during this work.

Terminology

Autonomous system: A homogenous network consisting of a collection of networks and routers that are under the same administration (e.g., a university campus network, an enterprise network, or an Internet service provider network).

Flooding: A simple routing approach that does not require routers to do much. Once a packet is received, the router forwards copies of the packet on all outgoing interfaces except the one on which the packet has been received.

Inter-domain routing: Routing between different autonomous systems; also called *exterior routing* or *inter-AS routing*.

Intra-domain routing: Routing within a single autonomous system; also called *interior routing* or *intra-AS routing*.

Mobile ad hoc network: A dynamic multi-hop wireless network established by a group of mobile stations that can move freely. This network is infrastructure-less in the sense that nodes are equal peers without having a special central node, such as a base station, to coordinate communication between them.

Multicast routing: A routing mechanism that sends multicast packets to a particular set of recipients that form a group.

Multipoint relaying: A technique used in OLSR to limit flooding of control messages by restricting the set of nodes that retransmit the packet to a subset of nodes called multi-point relays (MPRs).

Random Early Detection (RED): An active queue management technique that starts to drop or mark packets before the buffer gets full (also known as *Random Early Drop or Discard*).

QoS routing: A routing procedure that determines the paths from the source to the destination while taking into consideration the constraints imposed on various quality measures required by network applications and the resources available.

Traffic policing: A traffic management technique that monitors the adherence of incoming traffic characteristics to the service contract specifications and takes appropriate responses accordingly (e.g., discard, delay, or mark packets/flows violating the contract).

Traffic shaping: A traffic management technique that regulates the traffic rate that enters the network and thus smoothes out bursty traffic.

Exercises

1. Mention and briefly explain various performance measures that can be used to evaluate routing techniques.
2. Compare distance vector routing and link state routing.
3. What is the count-to-infinity problem and how can it be resolved?
4. Explain how OLSR determines the path from a source to a destination.
5. Explain the operation of each of the following: random early detection, leaky bucket, and deficit weighted round robin.

6. Describe and sketch the main components of a router.
7. Mention two techniques for controlling the traffic generated during flooding.
8. What is the difference between traffic shaping and traffic policy?
9. Mention the main difference(s) between AODV and OLSR.
10. Give five examples of applications for multicast routing.
11. Verify that the complexity of Dijkstra's algorithm is $O(N \cdot L)$.
12. Assume the traffic that enters a switching node with differentiated service belongs to three classes with arrival rates 10 packets/s, 20 packets/s and 30 packets/s. Also assume the average service time for packets of each class is 100 ms, 200 ms and 300 ms, respectively. What is the total rate of packets that enter the switch? What is the overall average packet service time? What is the average number of packets that will be in the switch?
13. Consider the network shown in the following figure. Determine the shortest paths from node a to all other nodes using Dijkstra's algorithm.

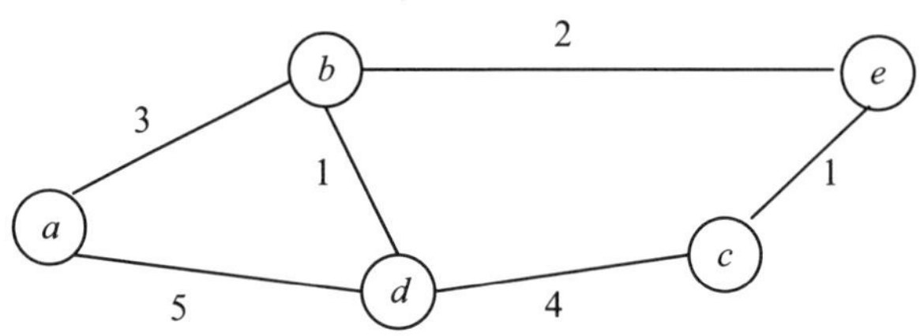

References

1. http://www.rtg.ietf.org.
2. D. E. McDysan and D. L. Spohn, *ATM: Theory and Applications* (McGraw-Hill, 1995).
3. H. G. Perros, *An Introduction to ATM Networks* (Wiley, 2001).
4. W. Stallings, *High-Speed Networks TCP/IP and ATM Design Principles* (Prentice Hall, 1998).
5. E. Osborne and A. Simha, *Traffic Engineering with MPLS* (Cisco Press, 2002).
6. C. Mbarushimana and A. Shahrabi, Comparative study of reactive and proactive routing protocols performance in mobile ad hoc networks. *21st Int. Conf. Advanced Information Networking and Applications Workshops (AINAW'07)* (2007).
7. J. Aweya, IP router architectures: An overview, *Int. J. Commun. Sys.* **14**(5), 447–475 (2001).
8. C. Partridge, P. P. Carvey, E. Burgess, I. Castineyra, T. Clarke, L. Graham, M. Hathaway, P. Herman, A. King, S. Kohalmi, T. Ma, J. Mcallen, T. Mendez, W. C. Milliken, R. Pettyjohn, J. Rokosz, J. Seeger, M. Sollins, S. Storch, B. Tober, G. D. Troxel, D. Waitzman and S. Winterble, A 50-Gb/s IP router, *IEEE/ACM Trans. Network.* **6**(3), 237–248 (1998).
9. H. J. Chao and B. Liu, *High Performance Switches and Routers* (John Wiley and Sons, 2007).
10. Q. Ye and M. H. Macgregor, Cluster-based IP router: Implementation and evaluation, *IEEE Int. Conf. Cluster Computing* (2006).
11. J. Wang and K. Nahrstedt, Parallel IP packet forwarding for tomorrow's IP Routers, *IEEE Workshop on High Performance Switching and Routing*, May (2001).

12. N. Miyaho, A. Yamazaki, T. Sakurai and K. Miyahara, Next generation IP router architecture using SFQ technology, *Asia-Pacific Conf. Communications (APCC '06)*, August (2006).
13. J. Aweya, On the design of IP routers part 1: Router architectures, *J. Syst. Archit.* **46**(6), 483–511 (2000).
14. H. J. Chao and T.-S. Wang, An optical interconnection network for terabit IP routers, *J. Lightw. Tech.* **18**(12), 2095–2112 (2000).
15. A. Singhal and R. Jain, Terabit switching: A survey of techniques and current products, *Compu. Commun.* **25**(6), 547–556 (2002).
16. R. Jain, A comparison of hashing schemes for address lookups in computer networks, *IEEE Trans. Commun.* **40**(10), 1570–1573 (1992).
17. J. Kurose and K. Ross, *Computer Networking: A Top-Down Approach Featuring the Internet*, 3rd edn. (Addison Wesley, 2005).
18. T. H. Cormen, C. E. Leiserson, R. L. Rivest and C. Stein, *Introduction to Algorithms*, 2nd edn. (MIT Press and McGraw-Hill, 2001).
19. http://en.wikipedia.org/wiki/Dijkstra's_algorithm.
20. http://en.wikipedia.org/wiki/Bellman-Ford_algorithm.
21. R. Albrightson, J. J. Garcia-Luna-Aceves and J. Boyle, EIGRP — A fast routing protocol based on distance vectors, *Proc. Networld/Interop 94*, Las Vegas, Nevada, May (1994).
22. A. U. Shankar, C. Alaettinoglu, I. Matta and K. Dussa-Zieger, Performance comparison of routing protocols using MaRS: Distance–vector versus link-state, *Proc. ACM SIGMETRICS and PERFORMANCE '92 Int. Conf. on Measurement and Modeling of Computer Systems* (1992).
23. Y. K. Dalal and R. M. Metcalfe, Reverse path forwarding of broadcast packets, *Commun. ACM* **21**(12), 1040–1048 (1978).
24. T. Saadawi, M. Ammar and A. ElHakeem, *Fundamentals of Telecommunication Networks* (John Wiley and Sons, 1994).
25. R. G. Gallager, P. A. Humblet and P. M. Spira, A distributed algorithm for minimum weight-spanning trees, *ACM Trans. Program. Lang. Syst.* **1**(5), 66–77 (1983).
26. F. C. Gartner, A survey of self-stabilizing spanning-tree construction algorithms, Technical report IC 2003/38, Swiss Federal Institute of Technology (EPFL), School of Computer and Communication Sciences (2003).
27. Y. K. Dalal, A distributed algorithm for constructing minimal spanning trees, *Trans. Softw. Eng.* **13**(3), 398–405 (1987).
28. S. Liu, D. Epley and W. Decker, An incremental distributed minimum directed spanning tree algorithm, *Proc. (466) Parallel and Distributed Computing and Systems* (2005).
29. F. Font and D. Mlynek, Choosing the set of rendezvous points in shared trees minimizing traffic concentration, *Proc. IEEE Int. Conf. on Communications (ICC'03)*, May (2003).
30. S. Chen and K. Nahrstedt, An overview of quality of service routing for next-generation high-speed networks: Problems and Solutions, *IEEE Network Mag.* **12**(6), 64–79 (1998).
31. E. Crawley, R. Nair, B. Rajagopalan and H. Sandick, A framework for QoS-based routing in the Internet, RFC 2386, August, http://www.ietf.org/rfc/rfc2386.txt (1998).
32. X. Masip-Bruin, M. Yannuzzi, J. Domingo-Pascual, A. Fonte, M. Curado, E. Monteiro, F. Kuipers, P. Van Mieghem, S. Avallone, G. Ventre, P. Aranda-Gutiérrez, M. Hollick, R. Steinmetz, L. Iannone and K. Salamatian, Research challenges in QoS routing, *Compu. Commun.* **29**(5), 563–581 (2006).

33. J. M. Akinpelu, The overload performance of engineered networks with non-hierarchical routing, *AT&T Tech. J.* **63**, 1261–1281 (1984).
34. R. Braden, D. Clark and S. Shenker, Integrated Services in the Internet architecture: An overview, RFC 1633, June, http://www.ietf.org/rfc/rfc1633.txt (1994).
35. S. Shenker, C. Partridge and R. Guerin, Specification of guaranteed quality of service, RFC 2212, September, http://www.ietf.org/rfc/rfc2212.txt (1997).
36. S. Shenker and J. Wroclawski, General characterization parameters for integrated service network elements, RFC 2215, September, http://www.ietf.org/rfc/rfc2215.txt (1997).
37. K. Nichols, S. Blake, F. Baker and D. Black, Definition of the differentiated services field in the IPv4 and IPv6 headers, RFC 2474, December, http://www.ietf.org/rfc/rfc2474.txt (1998).
38. S. Blake, D. Black, M. Carlson, E. Davies, Z. Wang and W. Weiss, An architecture for differentiated services, RFC 2475, December, http://www.ietf.org/rfc/rfc2475.txt (1998).
39. D. Awduche, MPLS and traffic engineering in IP Networks, *IEEE Commun. Mag.* **37**(12), 42–47 (1999).
40. X. Xiao, A. Hannan, B. Bailey and L. Ni, Traffic engineering with MPLS in the Internet, *IEEE Network Mag.* **14**(2), 28–33 (2000).
41. A. Elwalid, C. Jin, S. Low and I. Widjaja, MATE: MPLS adaptive traffic engineering, *Proc. IEEE Infocom* (2001).
42. K. Kar, M. Kodialam and T. Lakshman, Minimum interference routing of bandwidth guaranteed tunnels with MPLS traffic engineering applications, *IEEE J. Sel. Areas Commun.* **18**(12), 2566–2579 (2000).
43. E. Rosen, A. Viswanathan and R. Callon, Multiprotocol label switching architecture, RFC 3031, January, http://www.ietf.org/rfc/rfc3031.txt (2001).
44. G. Apostolopoulos, D. Williams, S. Kamat, R. Guerin, A. Orda and T. Przygienda, QoS routing mechanism and OSPF extensions, RFC 2676, August, http://www.ietf.org/rfc/rfc2676.txt (1999).
45. D. Katz, K. Kompella and D. Yeung, Traffic Engineering (TE) Extensions to OSPF Ver. 2, RFC 3630, Technical report, September (2003).
46. O. Younis and S. Fahmy, Constraint-based routing in the internet: basic principles and recent research, *IEEE Commun. Surv. Tuto.* **5**, (2003).
47. H. Abrahamsson, B. Ahlgren, J. Alonso, A. Andersson and P. Kreuger, A multi-path routing algorithm for IP networks based on flow optimization, *Int. Workshop on Quality of Future Internet Services* (2002).
48. http://www.ietf.org.
49. C. Hedrick, Routing information protocol, RFC 1058, June, http://www.javvin.com/protocol/rfc1058.pdf (1988).
50. G. Malkin, RIP Ver. 2, RFC 2453, November, http://www.javvin.com/protocol/rfc2453.pdf (1998).
51. G. Malkin and R. Minnear, RIPng for IPv6, RFC 2080, January http://www.javvin.com/protocol/rfc2080.pdf (1997).
52. S. Floyd and V. Jacobson, The synchronization of periodic routing messages, *IEEE/ACM Trans. Network.*, Apr (1994).
53. http://www.faqs.org/rfcs/rfc2453.html.
54. J. Moy, The OSPF specification, RFC 1131, October, http://www.faqs.org/rfcs/rfc1131.html (1989).
55. J. Moy, OSPF Ver. 2, RFC 2328, April, http://www.javvin.com/protocol/rfc2328.pdf (1998).

56. R. Coltun, D. Ferguson, J. Moy, OSPF for IPv6, RFC 2740, December, http://www.ietf.org/rfc/rfc2740.txt (1999).
57. I. Cidon, R. Rom and Y. Shavitt, Multi-path routing combined with resource reservation, *Proc. IEEE INFOCOM*, April (2000).
58. B. Fortz and M. Thorup, Internet traffic engineering by optimizing OSPF weights, *Proc. IEEE Infocom*, March (2000).
59. B. Fortz and M. Thorup, Optimizing OSPF/IS–IS weights in a changing world, *IEEE J. Sel. Areas Commun.* **20**(4), 756–767 (2002).
60. Y. Bejerano, S.-J. Han and A. Kumar, Efficient load-balancing routing for wireless mesh networks, *Comput. Network.* **51**(10), 2450–2466 (2007).
61. Y. Rekhter, T. Li and S. Hares (eds.), A Border gateway protocol 4 (BGP-4), RFC 4271, January, http://www.rfc-editor.org/rfc/rfc4271.txt (2006).
62. http://www.cisco.com/univercd/cc/td/doc/cisintwk/ito_doc/bgp.htm.
63. P. Paul and S. V. Raghavan, Survey of multicast routing algorithms and protocols, *Proc. 15th Int. Conf. on Computer Communications*, Mumbai, India, August (2002), pp. 902–926.
64. B. Cain, S. Deering, I. Kouvelas and A. Thyagarajan, Internet group management protocol, Ver. 3, RFC 3376, October, http://www.ietf.org/rfc/rfc3376.txt (2002).
65. M. Capan, Survey of different multicast routing protocols, *MIPRO'98*, May, http://cn.carnet.hr/materijali/1998/ (1998), pp. 130–137.
66. M. Ramalho, Intra- and inter- domain multicast routing protocols: A survey and Taxonomy, *IEEE Commun. Surv. Tutor.* **3**(1), 2–25 (2000).
67. http://www.faqs.org/rfcs/rfc1075.html.
68. http://www.ietf.org/rfc/rfc1584.txt.
69. A. Ballardie, Core-based trees (CBT Ver. 2) multicast routing: Protocol specification, RFC 2189, September, http://www.ietf.org/rfc/rfc2189.txt (1997).
70. S. Deering, D. L. Estrin, D. Farinacci, V. Jacobson, C.-G. Liu and L. Wei, PIM architecture for wide-area multicast routing, *IEEE/ACM Trans. Network.* **4**(2), 153–162 (1996).
71. A. Adams, J. Nicholas and W. Siadak, Protocol independent multicast — dense mode (PIM-DM): Protocol specification (revised), RFC 3973, January, http://www.ietf.org/rfc/rfc3973.txt (2005).
72. B. Fenner, M. Handley, H. Holbrook and I. Kouvelas, Protocol independent multicast — sparse mode (PIM-SM): Protocol specification (revised), RFC 4601, August, http://www.ietf.org/rfc/rfc4601.txt (2006).
73. E. Belding-Royer and C. Toh, A review of current routing protocols for ad hoc mobile wireless networks, *IEEE Pers. Commun.* 46–55 (1999).
74. C.-K. Toh, *Ad Hoc Mobile Wireless Networks: Protocols and Systems* (Prentice Hall, 2001).
75. C. S. R. Murthy and B. S. Manoj, *Ad Hoc Wireless Networks: Architectures and Protocols* (Prentice Hall, 2004).
76. S. Basagni, M. Conti, S. Giordano and I. Stojmenovi (eds.), *Mobile Ad Hoc Networking* (Wiley-IEEE Press, 2004).
77. O. K. Tonguz and G. Ferrari, *Ad Hoc Wireless Networks: A Communication-Theoretic Perspective* (John Wiley and Sons, 2006).
78. L. Layuan, L. Chunlin and Y. Peiyan, Performance evaluation and simulations of routing protocols in ad hoc networks, *Comput. Commun.* **30**(8), 1890–1898 (2007).
79. P. Jacquet and L. Viennot, Overhead in mobile ad hoc network protocols, Research report-3965, INRIA, June (2000).

80. P. Jacquet and A. Laouiti, Analysis of mobile ad hoc protocols in random graph models, Research report RR-3835, INRIA, December (1999).
81. http://en.wikipedia.org/wiki/Ad_hoc_routing_protocol_list.
82. C. Liu and J. Kaiser, A survey of mobile ad hoc network routing protocols, University of Ulm, Technical report series, Nr. 2003–08 (2005).
83. C. E. Perkins and E. M. Royer, Ad hoc on-demand distance vector routing, *Proc. 2nd IEEE Workshop Mobile Computing Systems and Applications*, New Orleans, LA, February (1999).
84. C. E. Perkins, E. M. Belding-Royer and S. R. Das, Ad hoc on demand distance vector (AODV) routing, RFC 3561, July, http://www.ietf.org/rfc/rfc3561.txt (2003).
85. E. M. Royer and C. E. Perkins, Multicast operation of the ad hoc on-demand distance vector routing protocol, *Proc. MobiCom '99*, Seattle, WA, August (1999).
86. E. M. Royer and C. E. Perkins. An implementation study of the aodv routing protocol, *Proc. IEEE Wireless Communications and Networking Conf.*, Chicago, IL, September (2000).
87. T. H. Clausen, G. Hansen, L. Christensen and G. Behrmann, The optimized link state routing protocol, evaluation through experiments and simulation, *IEEE Symp. Wireless Personal Mobile Commun.*, September (2001).
88. http://www.olsr.org.
89. P. Jacquet, A. Laouiti, P. Minet and L. Viennot, Performance analysis of OLSR multipoint relay flooding in two ad hoc wireless network models, Research report 4260, INRIA, September (2001).
90. A. Laouiti, P. Muhlethaler, A. Najid and E. Plakoo, Simulation results of the OLSR routing protocol for wireless network, *1st Mediterranean Ad Hoc Networks Workshop (Med-Hoc-Net)*, Sardegna, Italy (2002).
91. M. Benzaid, P. Minet and K. Al Agha, Analysis and simulation of fast-OLSR, *Proc. 57th IEEE Semiannual Vehicular Technology Conf. (VTC'03)*, Jeju, Korea, April (2003).
92. T. Clausen and P. Jacquet (eds.), Optimized link state routing protocol (OLSR), RFC 3626, October, http://hipercom.inria.fr/olsr/draft-ietf-manet-olsr-11.txt (2003).
93. http://hipercom.inria.fr/olsr/.
94. A. Qayyum, L. Viennot and A. Laouiti, Multipoint relaying: An efficient technique for flooding in mobile wireless networks, Research report RR-3898, INRIA, February (2000).
95. A. Qayyum, Analysis and evaluation of channel access schemes and routing protocols for wireless networks, Ph.D. Thesis, November (2000).
96. A. Laouiti, A. Qayyum and L. Viennot, Multipoint relaying: An efficient technique for flooding in mobile wireless networks, *35th Annual Hawaii Int. Conf. System Sciences (HICSS'02)* (2002).
97. A. R. Bashandy, E. K. P. Chong and A. Ghafoor, Generalized quality-of-service routing with resource allocation, *IEEE J. Sel. Areas Commun.* **23**(2), 450–463 (2005).
98. J. Zhigang and L. Lemin, Analysis of the leaky bucket algorithm for priority services, *J. Electron.* **13**(4), 333–338 (1996).
99. R. J. McEliece, J. Murphy, M. Jennings and Z. Yu, On simplified modelling of the leaky bucket, *Proc. IEE 13th UK IEE Teletraffic Symp.*, Strathclyde, March (1996).
100. T. Ozawa, Performance characteristics of a packet-based leaky-bucket algorithm for ATM Networks, http://www.komazawa-u.ac.jp/~toshi/research/papers/leaky_bucket.pdf (1996).

101. J. Rexford, F. Bonomi, A. Greenberg and A. Wong, A scalable architecture for fair leaky-bucket shaping, *IEEE Infocom'97* (1997), pp. 1056–1064.
102. J. S. Turner, New directions in communication, or which way to the information age, *IEEE Commun. Mag.* **24**, 8–15 (1986).
103. S. Floyd and V. Jacobson, Random early detection gateways for congestion avoidance, *IEEE/ACM Trans. Network.* **1**(4), 397–413 (1993).
104. S. Floyd, R. Gummadi and S. Shenker, Adaptive RED: An algorithm for increasing the robustness of RED's active queue management, August (2001).
105. E. Hashem, Analysis of random drop for gateway congestion control, Report LCS TR-465, Laboratory of Computer Science, MIT (1989).
106. W.-C. Feng, K. G. Shin, D. D. Kandlur and D. Saha, The BLUE active queue management algorithms, *IEEE/ACM Trans. Network.* **10**(4) (2002).
107. C. Semeria, Supporting differentiated service classes: Queue scheduling disciplines, White Paper, Juniper Networks, Inc (2001).
108. M. Shreedhar and G. Varghese, Efficient fair queueing using deficit round robin, *ACM SIGCOMM Comput. Commun. Rev.* **25**(4), 231–242 (1995).
109. T. Kwon, S. Lee and J. Rho, Scheduling algorithm for real-time burst traffic using dynamic weighted round robin, *Proc. IEEE Int. Symp. Circuit. Syst.* **6**(31), 506–509 (1998).
110. G. Apostolopoulos, R. Guerin, S. Kamat and S. K. Tripathi, Quality of service based routing: A performance perspective, *ACM SIGCOMM'98*, Vancouver, B.C. (1998).
111. G. Apostolopoulos, R. Gurin, S. Kamat and S. K. Tripathi, Quality of service based routing: a performance perspective, *ACM Comput. Commun. Rev.* **28**(4), (1998).
112. G. Apostolopoulos, R. Guerin, S. Kamat and S. Tripathi, Improving QoS routing performance under inaccurate link state, *Proc. 16th Int. Teletraffic Congress (ITC'16)*, Edinburgh, United Kingdom, June (1999).
113. A. Sridharan, R. Guerin and C. Diot, Achieving near-optimal traffic engineering solutions for current OSPF/IS–IS networks, *IEEE/ACM Trans. Network.* **13**(2), 234–247 (2005).
114. M. Ericsson, M. Resende and P. Pardalos, A genetic algorithm for the weight setting problem in OSPF routing, *J. Comb. Optim.* **6**(3), 299–333 (2002).
115. A. Munaretto and M. Fonseca, Routing and quality of service support for mobile ad hoc networks, *Comput. Network.* **51**, 3142–3156 (2007).
116. J. Ni, D. H. K. Tsang, I. S. H. Yeung and X. Hei, Hierarchical content routing in large-scale multimedia content delivery network, *IEEE Int. Conf. Communications (ICC '03)*, May (2003).
117. R. C. Shah, J. M. Rabaey, Energy aware routing for low energy ad hoc sensor networks, *IEEE Wireless Communications and Networking Conf. (WCNC'02)*, Orlando, FL, March (2002).
118. C. K. Toh, Maximum battery life routing to support ubiquitous mobile computing in wireless ad hoc networks, *IEEE Commun. Mag.* 138–147 (2001).
119. W. Heinzelman, A. Chandrakasan and H. Balakrishnan, Energy-efficient communication protocols for wireless microsensor networks, *Proc. Hawaaian Int. Conf. Systems Science*, January (2000).

Chapter 14

NETWORK MANAGEMENT: A TUTORIAL AND SURVEY

HUI XU* and DEBAO XIAO
Institute of Computer Network and Communication,
Huazhong Normal University, Wuhan, 430079, China
**xuhui_1004@hotmail.com*

Since its research and standardization started in late 1980s, network management has become more and more crucial for keeping pace with the changing management requirements of ever-developing networks. After briefly describing some background, this chapter respectively discusses network management standards (since the development of management technology is always coupled with protocol standardization) and methodology (including both techniques and strategies), and evaluates these solutions from the OSI perspective using its proposed network management model. This chapter then examines present-day challenges in the network management domain and illuminates current trends. Finally, this chapter points out directions for future research, which may be utilized to build management solutions for next-generation networks.

1. Introduction

Since network management research and standardization started in late 1980s, several solutions have been proposed, from protocol-based ones (mainly including CMIP and SNMP), to policy-based ones, and to distributed ones with the use of COBRA and Web technologies. Meanwhile, with COBRA, mobile agent rapid development of the Internet, the complexity of computer networks has greatly increased, and more and more network resources need to be effectively managed. Hence, new techniques have been employed by either various commercial network management solutions or research communities, such as XML-based network management (possibly using of Web services technologies), cooperative network management, improved root cause analysis (RCA) techniques, semantic network management, active network management, predictive network management, autonomic network management with intelligent self-managing devices, and so on. The aim of this chapter is then to give an overview of network management, including the challenges faced, the state-of-the-art solutions and future perspectives.

2. Background

With their rapid development, computer networks have become increasingly popular and important in daily life. Crash or even low efficiency may lead to discuption of network users, delays receiving emergent databases, loss of commercial revenue, etc. Hence, maintaining smoothly running networks is essential and this is where the concept of network management came into being.

2.1. *Definition*

In this chapter, our focus is on network and systems management. We consider network management as a management of the network comprising nodes and links, and systems management as management of a system's resources. And as an extension of network and systems management, service management deals with services provided by organizations to customers [1].

The definition of network management differs as management requirements from users change. Different organizations also use various definitions. Based on a widely accepted definition, network management refers to the activities, methods, procedures and tools that pertain to the operation, administration, maintenance and provisioning of networked systems [2]. That is to say, it is a process that controls a complex computer network and aims to ensure that it possesses the highest efficiency and productivity possible. According to the network management system used, this process always involves data collection (automatically or through a manager's manual work), data processing, data analysis, and so on.

2.2. *Importance*

The importance of modern network management mainly concerns the following facets.

Firstly, the complexity of network devices is making network management more and more complicated. The reasons for this are (a) the increasingly intricate functionality of network devices, (b) the increasing number of device manufacturers and (c) the large diversity of product specifications, make, standardization more and more difficult. Due to the complexity of network devices, it is usually not possible to use the traditional manual network management style; advanced automatic management approaches become increasingly necessary.

Secondly, the economic benefits of networks is gradually becoming dependent on the efficient management of networks. Modern computer networks have become large and complex systems, while their operation, administration, maintenance and provisioning have gradually evolved as a special subject. Without the support of an effective network management system, it is quite difficult to implement traffic control and enhance connectivity, both of which may make network operators lose money if not sufficiently well handled.

Finally, advanced and dependable network management is an inevitable result of the development of networks themselves. Since people increasingly depend on networks, network management has become a necessity to guarantee their network reliability.

2.3. *Goal*

The goal of network management is to meet the following requirements from network managers and users:

- availability,
- reliability,
- compatibility,
- integration,
- security,
- cost.

2.4. *Basic Features*

Network management mainly involves the following basic features:

- traffic control
- routing strategy
- security protection
- fault diagnosis
- account management

2.5. *Development*

Several solutions have been developed for network management researches and standardizations. However, existing solutions have not kept pace with the changing requirements of the industry and none of them seem to completely satisfy the needs of network management since they have limitations of some degree in terms of performance, scalability, flexibility, maintainability and reliability, all of which hinder their further application in the ever-evolving network management domain.

Among the trends that have then been observed in both academia and industry, the main focus is standardization, automation and integration. And future development needs to focus on the following topics [3]:

- *Management for new networks*: On the one hand, management for novel networks based on grid and P2P requires more attention. On the other hand, these novel networks are also greatly impacting conventional network management patterns. As a result, management for new networks has become a hot issue.
- *Next-generation network management solutions*: With the rapid development of next-generation networks, corresponding management solutions must be seriously considered, including:
  - P2P-based network management,
  - predictive network management,
  - autonomic networks with intelligent self-managing devices.

- *Research on management information models*: New information models should provide support for object-oriented objects and services, an ontology repository that contains management information and strict semantic information for the extension of the information model and the design of management strategy.

3. Network Management Standards and the OSI Model

3.1. *Network Management Standards*

There is still no framework and technology satisfying the needs of network management entirely. Initial protocol-based approaches, such as Open System Interconnection Systems Management (OSI-SM) and Simple Network Management Protocol (SNMP), have become the main standards within the scope of network management [4, 5].

Both OSI-SM and SNMP adopt the manager-agent model, as depicted in Fig. 1, which defines the principles of operations for protocol-based management solutions, and these managed resources are then modeled as management objects (MOs) [6].

At one end of the spectrum, OSI-SM is considered as the most powerful management technology in theoretical terms. However, it is complicated and expensive to implement, and relies on OSI protocols, which have gone out of fashion. At the other end of the spectrum, SNMP has been the most widely deployed management framework in practice, particularly in IP environments. However, since its information modeling capabilities are rudimentary and it does not support configuration management well due to its lack of transaction capabilities, its simplicity is its biggest weakness [7].

3.2. *OSI Network Management Model*

The OSI network model is an ISO standard and may be the best of all the model proposed. The model is well-structured and addresses all aspects of management. An OSI network management architecture comprises four models: (a) the organization model, (b) the information model, (c) the communication model, and (d) the functional model.

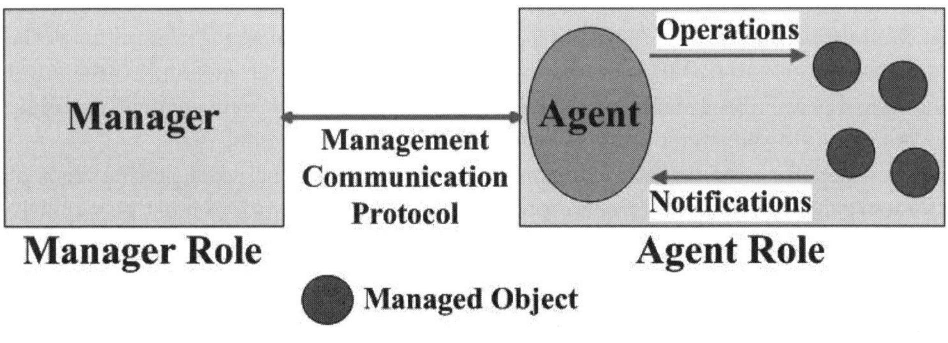

Fig. 1. The manager-agent model.

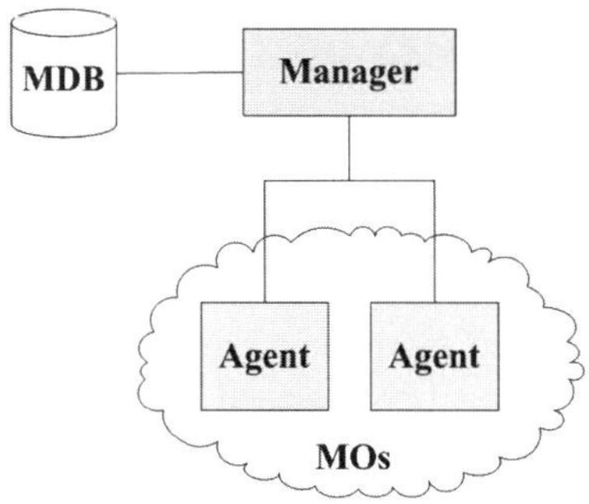

Fig. 2. Two-tier network management organization model.

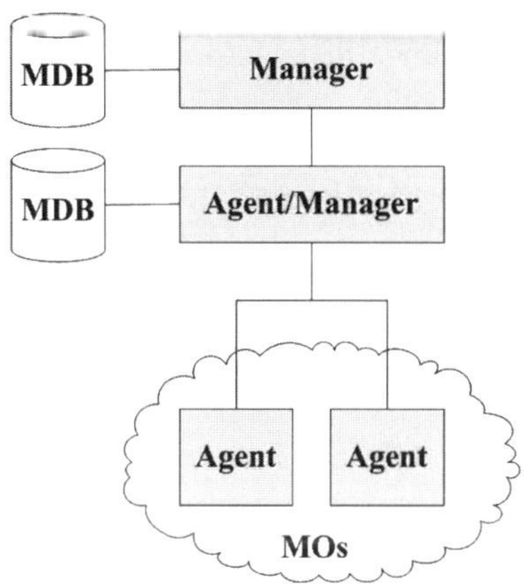

Fig. 3. Three-tier network management organization model.

3.2.1. *Organization Model*

The organization model describes the components of the network management architecture and their relationships.

Figure 2 shows a two-tier model. The manager manages the MOs, which have management processes running in them, called agents. Figure 3 provides a three-tier model in which the intermediate layer has two roles, acting as both agent and manager.

3.2.2. *Information Model*

The key specifications related to the OSI-SM information model are standards, and the model is based on the following object-oriented principles [8–11]:

- encapsulation,
- inheritance,
- allomorphism.

For naming purposes, a containment relationship is used, which may represent either a physical resource containment hierarchy or a logical containment hierarchy.

The containment hierarchy has a tree structure, which is dynamic and grows as MOs are instantiated [11].

Important concepts for the information model include *attribute* (a characteristic that is visible at the OSI MO boundary and has a value), *notification* (sent spontaneously by an OSI MO to report an internal or external event of significance), and *behavior* (description of the dynamic characteristics of an OSI MO). These characteristics are grouped into modular constructs called *packages*, which can be mandatory or optional and must be possessed by every object of the class [11].

3.2.3. *Communication Model*

The OSI-SM communication model is based on a seven-layer OSI stack with a connection-oriented transport layer. The first six layers are not specific to management. At the same time, it is important to stress the role played by the presentation layer, which offers mechanisms for converting between different representations of information. The seventh layer, the application layer, is composed of the following application service elements (ASEs):

- Common Management Information Service Element (CMISE),
- Association Control Service Element (ACSE),
- Remote Operation Service Element (ROSE).

Among these ASEs, only CMISE is specific to management [12]. Common Management Information Services (CMIS) are the services offered by CMISE, while Common Management Information Protocol (CMIP) is the protocol for realizing these services, which uses the services of ROSE and the connection-oriented services of the transport layer [13, 14].

3.2.4. *Functional Model*

OSI-SM offers numerous standard management functions for use across management applications as follows:

- object management,
- state management,
- alarm reporting,
- log control,
- workload monitoring.

The workload monitoring function [11] provides tools for monitoring the performance characteristics of resources. It defines three models: (a) the resource utilization model, which monitors the resources used, (b) the rejection rate model, which monitors the service request rejection rate, and (c) the resource request model, which monitors the requests for usage of resources. These three models rely on six supporting metric MO classes.

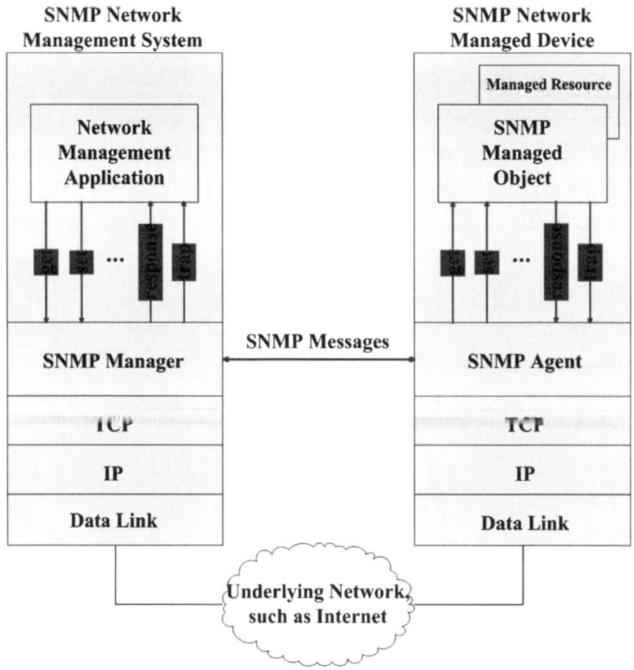

Fig. 4. SNMP-based network management organization model.

3.3. *Evaluation of Network Management Standards*

Using the OSI network management model discussed above, network management standards such as SNMP, currently the most popular one used in the industry, can be evaluated.

SNMP adopts a manager-agent organization model, as illustrated in Fig. 4.

Since its introduction in late 1980s, SNMP has been used mostly in fault and performance monitoring, but has hardly been used for configuration management. The reason lies in the fact that the SNMP management framework has some weaknesses related to configuration management in managing large networks. First, SNMP Structure of Management Information (SMI) or even Structure of Management Information next generation (SMIng) is insufficient to represent hierarchical network configuration data. Second, with SNMP it is difficult to support several high-level management operations required by network configuration tasks. Third, SNMP over UDP is insufficient for bulk and reliable configuration data transfers.

4. Network Management Methodology

4.1. *Policy-Based Network Management*

The term "policy" in Policy-Based Network Management (PBNM) refers to the rules governing choice in the behavior of the managed element. It seems that policies may act as the language for controlling autonomic systems or the guidance for decision-making. Thus, in comparison with traditional network management approaches, such as SNMP, the policy-based approach offers a more flexible management solution.

The Common Open Policy Service (COPS) and its extension for policy provisioning (COPS-PR) have been developed as the protocols to implement PBNM [15, 16]. The COPS protocol is a simple query and response protocol that can be used to exchange policy information between a policy server, policy decision point (PDP), and its clients, policy enforcement points (PEPs). Each PEP may support one or more clients of different client-types that exist for different policing areas. COPS-PR is one of those client-types. In COPS-PR, policy requests describe the PEP and its configurable parameters. If a change occurs in these basic parameters, an updated request is sent. Decisions are not necessarily mapped directly to requests and are issued mostly when the PDP responds to external events or PDP events.

A Policy Information Base (PIB) is used, to some extent, as a conceptual tree namespace in which the branches of the tree represent structures of data or provisioning classes (PRCs), while the leaves represent various instantiations of provisioning instances (PRIs) [17] PIBs are defined using the Structure of Policy Provisioning Information (SPPI) specification, and the SPPI and PIB modules are in fact based on SNMP's SMI and Management Information Base (MIB) modules [18].

4.2. *COBRA-Based Network Management*

The application of distributed object technology to increasingly complicated network management is inevitable, and CORBA is a key technology in this field.

The CORBA standard, which provides the software infrastructure to develop distributed object-oriented applications, is driven by the Object Management Group (OMG) [19] CORBA is independent of language implementations, providing the concept of a distributed object that can be called in a network environment. A distributed object is specified using the Interface Definition Language (IDL) [20]. An IDL specification is a set of interfaces containing operations. An interface corresponds to an object class and an operation to a class function member.

Using this IDL specification, a client is able to execute remotely an object as if it were located in the same process. An IDL compiler takes as input the IDL specification to produce a stub that allows a client to use a particular object. It also produces a skeleton for implementation of the object at the server side.

CORBA has been applied to network management, and the static translations between CORBA and SNMP are analyzed in detail including features, architecture and implementation.

4.3. *Mobile Agent-Based Network Management*

The emergence of mobile agent frameworks has led many researchers to examine their applicability to network management and control environments [21]. Given the large amount of data that needs to be transferred in respective solutions based on traditional approaches, it is believed that mobile agents can provide better solutions to performance and fault management problems [22].

Mobile agent frameworks are currently addressed by two standard bodies. The Foundation of Intelligent Physical Agents (FIPA) looks at high-level, semantically-rich interactions between software agents that deploy some form of intelligent adaptability [23]. It has its roots in Distributed Artificial Intelligence (DAI). OMG looks mostly at the issue of mobility according to a standard interoperable framework through its Mobile Agent System Interoperability Facility (MASIF).

4.4. *Web-Based Network Management*

With the development of Web technology and its wide application to the Internet, Web-Based Management (WBM), which integrates Web functions with network management techniques, has been attracting interest especially in distributed network management.

A typical example of WBM solutions is Web-Based Enterprise Management (WBEM), which is an initiative of the Distributed Management Task Force (DMTF) and includes a set of technologies that enable the interoperable management of an enterprise, in order to unify the management of distributed computing environments [24]. The set of management and Internet standard technologies developed by WBEM consists of a Common Information Model (CIM), a representation of CIM in XML, and a specification for CIM operations over HTTP [25–27]. CIM provides a data modeling environment in the form of object-oriented design diagrams and a language-neutral description of the model known as Managed Object Format (MOF), which is also object-oriented.

4.5. *XML-Based Network Management*

XML-based network management, which applies XML technologies to network management, is regarded as an alternative to existing network management, especially to SNMP. eXtensible Markup Language (XML) is a meta-markup language standardized by the World Wide Web Consortium (W3C) for document exchange in the Web [28], and is supported and accepted by thousands of vendors as well as many related technologies and tools [29] (Fig. 5).

XML-based specifications such as XML Schema, the Document Object Model (DOM), Simple API for XML (SAX), XML Path language (XPath), eXtensible Stylesheet Language (XSL), XSL Transformations (XSLT), Simple Object Access Protocol (SOAP), and Web Services Description Language (WSDL) are widely applied in network management.

The main advantages offered by the use of XML in network management are as follows [29]:

- Management data can be represented as XML documents.
- The structures of management data can be expressed as XML Schemas.

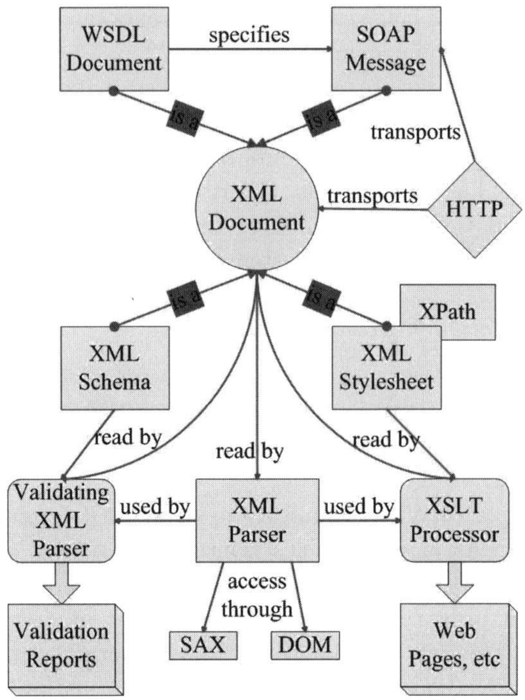

Fig. 5. XML technologies and tools.

- The DOM and SAX APIs can be used to access management data from applications.
- XSLT can be used to process management data.
- Widely deployed protocols, such as HTTP, can be used to ship management data.
- High-level management operations can be defined through WSDL and called via SOAP.

4.6. *Event Correlation Techniques*

An event is an instantaneous occurrence at a time point, and typically it is associated with an MO in which it occurs. One class of events is alarms, which are directly generated in the object, while another class consists of events that are considered to occur when there is a change in the state of the object. Event correlation works by establishing relationships between network events. Event correlation systems aid in detection or isolation of faults, filtering events, and performance tuning [30].

In event correlation, the relationships between events can be classified as being causal, temporal or spatial. As the simplest relationship between events that can be considered, a causality relation or a cause-effect relation is the problem of determining root causes of faults by using this causality relationship among events. And since events happen at particular time instants, richer correlations between events based on the specific instants of their occurrence can be established by defining temporal relationships between them. Additionally, spatiality-based correlation correlates events from multiple observation spaces or sensors at the same time to detect attack scenarios [31].

Large amounts of event-based data that are produced by networks can be collected and used for the purpose of security management. Thus, a critical challenge has become how to correlate these events across causality of components in the networks as well as observation space and time to detect and track various attack scenarios.

Obviously, it is not sufficient to use a single event as the signature to detect attacks; this would always lead to a high false alarm rate. Networks are dynamic in nature and at each time interval their components produce large amounts of event-based data. Theoretically, various network security products can collect all these events, and the trace of an attack is often scattered in extraordinary events. Thus, an efficient event correlation is urgently required to identify the trace of an attack in this large and noisy event environment.

Event correlation is, in essence, a pattern recognition problem, in which an attack scenario signature (also called a pattern) must be identified to distinguish one attack from other attacks as well as normal network activities. Thus, instead of using a single event as the signature, we can use a joint scenario signature combined with causal, spatial and temporal patterns to characterize and distinguish various attacks. The correlation accuracy then depends on the accuracy of both attack scenario signatures (patterns) and collected events. Therefore, a chief problem lies in how to characterize various attack scenarios.

Causal relationships are the basic types of rules for correlation, describing the case of some coinstantaneous phenomena in event data. In the case of event correlation, a causal correlation rule can be defined as follows.

Definition 1. If an attack has some scenario signatures, then it has some other particular scenario signatures [32].

This correlation rule can be formalized as "$X \Rightarrow Y$", where X and Y are sets of event data. For example, SNORT records that HOST P has produced a lot of events about an IIS attack to other servers (labeled as event set $Y1$). With only this kind of event, we may simply judge that it is indeed an IIS attack. But at the same time, the router also records that HOST P accesses ports 139 and 445 of other hosts largely (labeled as event set Y2). Using causal rule "$X \Rightarrow Y1$ and $Y2$", where X represents the fact that the host has been infected by a worm virus, we can correlate these two event sets $Y1$ and $Y2$ and argue that HOST P has been infected by a worm virus and that this is a worm virus attack.

How the evidence of an attack is distributed over space and time is illustrated as follows [31]:

(a) Based on the cause-effect relationship, an attack could affect the events of multiple observation spaces at the same time.

(b) An attack affects events across time.

A temporal rule definition in the case of event correlation is as follows.

Definition 2. If a set of event data happens during a period of time, then another set of event data will happen during another period of time [32].

As is implied in Definition 2, a temporal operator is always needed in defining a temporal event correlation rule. Note that since event correlation can be computed in real time, there are no temporal operators whose value needs "to look into the future"; in other words, in the temporal case we take the correlation relation to be between histories of events time-stamped with their instants of occurrence.

5. Current Challenges and Trends

5.1. *Current Challenges*

5.1.1. *Shortcomings of Existing Network Management Solutions*

Initial network management solutions were mostly protocol-based, such as SNMP. Then, policy-based solutions were investigated, but they were not applied well in the industry. Recently, more attention is being paid to distributed solutions, and in particular, Web-based ones seem to be quite appropriate for distributed network management. At the same time, XML has emerged as another widely used technology. Furthermore, event correlation techniques are being intensively studied, but they are still limited due to the large number of events generated by network devices.

The following summarizes what we have said concerning existing network management solutions. SNMP-based manager-agent management solutions are the *de facto* standard that is still widely used in the industry, but it provides inadequate coverage of the five functional areas of network management (fault, configuration, accounting, performance and security management) specified by OSI and has a scalability problem as the network size increases. Policy-based solutions offer a more flexible management concept than traditional ones, but they are still not widely applied due to their complexity. Distributed network management such as CORBA-based solutions and mobile agent-based solutions, has emerged as a promising approach while Web-based solutions are a new direction for distributed network management. However, distributed technologies and network management technologies are still far from perfectly combined [3]. XML-based solutions focus on the improvement of SNMP in configuration management and integration with SNMP, but they still lack adequate standardization. A promising way forward is an integrated application of NETCONF and Web services. Event correlation techniques are limited in capability due to the large number of events generated by network devices. Thus, verification techniques to reduce false positives have become an important prerequisite to gaining good correlation results.

5.1.2. *Summary of Current Challenges*

As a specialized field, network management has developed greatly over the past few years. However, as mentioned above, existing solutions have limitations of some degree in terms of performance, scalability, flexibility, maintainability and reliability, and thus have not kept pace with the ever-changing requirements of the industry. Hence, current challenges in network management are as follows:

- *Requirements of inter-domain cooperative management for highly distributed networks.* When dealing with highly distributed networks, current network management systems fail to provide proper support for inter-domain cooperative management, since they were designed to operate in the limited environment of local domains [33].
- *Requirements of integration for multiple network management solutions.* Many network management solutions have been proposed but not widely applied in the industry. Hence, the compatibility of multiple solutions in network management domain must be carefully considered in order to integrate new solutions with old ones.
- *Requirements of vendor-proprietary network management solutions.* With a plethora of vendor-specific network devices and proprietary protocols, existing network management solutions are not vendor agnostic in the truest sense leading to difficulties in management of heterogeneous networks [34]. Hence, vendor-proprietary solutions are urgently required.
- *Requirements of mature technologies for convenient application in network management domain to promote automation.* A mature network management solution should not only be sound in theory but also feasible in practice. That is just one of the important reasons for SNMP's success. With the rapid development of networks, there is an urgent need for mature technologies to be applied to network management, especially to promote automation, which is one of main goals for future management solutions.

We may conclude that a "merge and map" concept can be used to describe the challenges for present-day network management. That is to say, future network management solutions needs to work in a manner that supports not only collaboration and integration ("merge") but vendor-proprietary requirements ("map"), possibly using mature technologies for automation.

5.2. *Current Trends*

NETCONF and Web services are now under study with a view to improving the standardization process of XML-based network management. Meanwhile, semantic approaches with the use of ontologies seem to be promising in the field of automatic network management. Other approaches have also been applied, typical ones of which are integrated network management, improved RCA techniques, and active network management.

5.2.1. *Web Services-Based Network Management*

As an integration of the Web and XML, Web services have emerged as one of the promising technologies in the field of network management, since they can provide a distributed processing environment with the advantage that they are based on widely used technologies.

(i) *XML-based network management using Web services*: The use of XML-based technologies makes Web services platform-, programming language-, and vendor-independent. In order to better use Web services for network management, WSDL and SOAP over HTTP provide the capability for standardizations of management information definition and access [35, 36]. In this way, Web services provide a distributed management capability for monitoring the services of applications on the Internet or an Intranet using standard XML protocols and formats. These factors have allowed Web services to become one of the dominant technologies in the development of network management to access and perform operations on managed resources.

A Web service is described in a WSDL document. In order to easily use Web services for standardization of network, management information definition is needed. On the other hand, with the mechanism provided by WSDL to describe a Web service in a modular manner using the elements <import> or <include>, modularization can be achieved.

With regard to the division of WSDL documents, some attempts have been made. The Universal Description, Discovery and Integration (UDDI) Technical Committee recommended "two separate WSDL definitions" containing an interface part and an implementation part [37]. Aiko Pras *et al.* suggested "Three separate WSDL definitions", comprising an abstract part, messages and interfaces (the *what* part), and two concrete parts, a binding (the *how* part) and a service (the *where* part) with the WSDL import mechanism [35]. And the latter one seems more reasonable according to the functionalities of each element.

Currently, the use of Web services in XML-based network management becomes a trend. As an example, an XML-based configuration management system using web services (XCMS-WS) has been proposed, which consists of a manager, an agent and a private UDDI registry [38].

(ii) *Application of Web services-based SOA to network management*: The word "services" in Web services refers to service-oriented architecture (SOA) [39]. In SOA, functionality is "published" on a network where two important capabilities are also provided: (a) "discovery", the ability to find the functionality, and (b) "binding", the ability to connect the functionality. So when considering SOA, three parts must be taken into account: "publish," "find," and "bind." In the Web services architecture, three important roles are Web service provider, Web service requester, and Web service register, which correspond to the "publish," "find," and "bind" aspects of SOA. The Web services-based SOA, combined with related technologies, is shown in Fig. 6.

Fig. 6. Web services-based SOA.

The Web services-based SOA can effectively improve current network management systems [40]. On one side, flexibility is always quite important in the applications related to network management. Loosely coupled services in the Web services-based SOA are typically more flexible than tightly coupled applications. On the other side, the objective of SOA is to allow applications and services to communicate and understand each other no matter what platforms they run on. This interoperability provided by Web services-based SOA makes it much easier to manage more and more complicated networks.

5.2.2. *Semantic Network Management and Application of Ontologies*

Recently, Semantic Web and ontology (the main component in the Semantic Web) have emerged as promising candidates for the use in network management domain.

As the "next-generation Internet," the Semantic Web is a vision of a new architecture for the World Wide Web (WWW), characterized by adding machine-accessible formal semantics to traditional Web content. Tim Berners-Lee has stated that the Semantic Web is not a separate Web but an extension of the current one, in which information is given a well-defined meaning, better enabling computers and people to work in cooperation [41].

Ontology plays an important role in Semantic Web for it is much more powerful than XML in expressing semantics. Although there are already many definitions of ontology, the most commonly accepted one may be that ontologies are explicit and formal specifications of shared conceptualization [42].

Since current management information languages can be seen as lightweight ontologies, a framework has then been established to compare those languages from an ontology viewpoint [43]. Using this ontology-based approach, management information definition languages are analyzed and compared based on their semantic expressiveness [44].

Ontology languages that have been developed include: DARPA Agent Markup Language (DAML) and Ontology Inference Layer (OIL), DARPA Agent Markup

Language + Ontology Inference Layer (DAML + OIL), and recently the Web Ontology Language, called OWL not an acronym [45–47].

The main difference between ontology languages and management information definition languages, such as SMI and SMIng, is that the semantics of the former has been formalized, which may explain their predominance in network management domain. Thus, ontology languages may be used as information definition languages in the field of network management. Recently, the use of OWL has been proposed to specify management information, describing a set of mapping rules with constructions of management languages [48].

5.2.3. *Integrated Network Management*

Network management has developed in a way that generic technologies are widely used, and next-generation network management calls for a collaboration of these technologies. Hence, integration plays a significant role in the evolution of network management. An example of this is to integrate XML-based network management with SNMP, since at present XML should be seen as an accompaniment to conventional SNMP management rather than a replacement. Semantic Web services-based management is a new trend within the scope of integrated network management, and the formalization of OWL-S has provided one way to realize this [49].

(i) *Case study: Applying Semantic Web services to integrated network management.* As a new research paradigm, Semantic Web services is generally defined as the augmentation of Web service descriptions through Semantic Web annotations, to facilitate the higher automation of service discovery, composition, invocation, and monitoring in an open, unregulated, and often chaotic environment (that is, the Web) [50].

In fact, Semantic Web services represent an important step toward a new vision of Web services with the application of Semantic Web, in terms of utilizing, managing, and creating semantic markup languages for services. From this point of view, Semantic Web services can greatly enhance the semantics that Web services provide, thereby improving current Web services-based network management. In order to easily use Semantic Web services in network management domain to promote automation, there should be an agreement on or standardizations for the definitions of management information and operations. To accomplish this, an appropriate markup language is in great demand.

WSDL only provides a mechanism to describe a Web service in a modular manner. This means that a WSDL document can only be used when services are not automated. But considering the semantic capabilities added into Web services, we need a markup language particularly for Semantic Web services. In particular, OWL-S, an application of OWL, has evolved into a semantic markup language for Web services [51]. OWL-S complements WSDL descriptions by supporting a richer semantics, including logical constraints between the input and output parameters of services. Moreover, WSDL documents can specify data types using XML Schema, whereas OWL-S uses OWL classes, which provides a better semantics [52].

(ii) *OWL-S: A semantic markup language for Web services.* The four tasks which OWL-S is expected to be able to accomplish are:

- automatic Web services discovery,
- automatic Web services invocation,
- automatic Web services composition and interoperation,
- automatic Web services execution monitoring.

Note that versions of OWL-S developed so far have not ventured into the area of the fourth task. However, this task may be quite useful for management of the Web service where a user wants to know the state of a request.

The ontology of services in OWL-S is depicted in Fig. 7. This ontology is composed of several classes, the main one being the *Service* class. In fact, it is the *Resource* class that "provides" a *Service.* In order to construct the ontology of services, it is necessary to provide following three essential types of knowledge about a service:

- The *ServiceProfile* class expresses what the service requires of the user(s), or other agents, and provides for them. Thus, the *Service* "presents" a *ServiceProfile.*
- The *ServiceModel* class expresses how the service works and details the semantic content of each request. Thus, the *Service* is "described by" a *ServiceModel.*
- The *ServiceGrounding* class expresses how the service is used and defines a mapping with a WSDL document of the Web service. Thus, the *Service* "supports" a *ServiceGrounding.*

As explained above, we argue that the semantic description of Web services in OWL-S can be separated into three parts: two abstract parts containing the *ServiceProfile* (the *what* part) and the *ServiceModel* (the *abstract how* part), and one concrete part, which is the *ServiceGrounding* (the *concrete how* part).

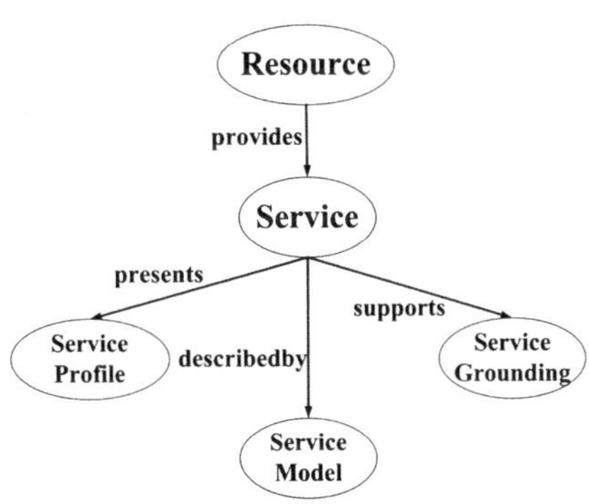

Fig. 7. The ontology of services in OWL-S.

(iii) *Applying OWL-S to network management.* Now that OWL-S, the ontology for Web services, has been presented, a related approach can be applied to network management at the Semantic Web services level.

First of all, management information exchanged between managers and managed network devices by means of Web services can now directly be instances of ontology classes, since OWL-S specifies data types using OWL classes in order to provide a better semantics. Thus, a manager that can deal with the ontology language may be very useful in this case.

Then, in OWL-S we can use the *Process* class to indicate the operations of different granularities. The *Process* collects three types of processes: atomic, simple and composite. The main entity of the *Process* class is, unsurprisingly, a process. A process can often be viewed at different levels of granularity, either as a primitive or as a composite process. Using different processes provided by OWL-S, we can easily realize the operation granularities. However, the choice of one certain operation granularity will be a tradeoff between simplicity and expressiveness.

In addition, a process produces a data transformation from a set of inputs to a set of outputs, while the use of parameter binding notation in OWL-S enables the parameter transmission in a specialized process as a data flow. In this way, related problems can be solved, which guarantee an effective data exchange between managers and managed network devices.

What is more, the definition of processes includes a set of preconditions and effects that can be expressed as formal logic rules in order to model the behavior of the processes. The main processes are composite ones, which specify the behavior that the client can perform by sending and receiving a set of messages, with the use of control constructs (sequence, split, join, choice, if-then-else, iterate, repeat-while, and repeat-until).

Overall, due to the formality of OWL-S, a semantic description of a Web service including both the definition of the required processes and their mappings to Web service operations, as well as the formal logical rules about those processes, can be obtained by the manager, which can then manage those network devices easily.

5.2.4. *Improved Root Cause Analysis Techniques*

RCA is now a prime focus area of all the current network management solutions, aiming to provide to the network administrator the source of network problems. Since network devices are interconnected, sometimes in complex ways, RCA is not always straightforward, and the fact is that there is high likelihood of one network fault causing a cascading effect, resulting in other network faults. Some of the advanced RCA techniques being employed by some of the solutions available today are [34]:

- Advanced event correlation,
- probes and agents,
- advanced analysis techniques.

5.2.5. *Active Network Management*

A new breed of network management solutions are based on monitoring the network by actively participating in the network operations/protocols, thereby greatly improving the fault reporting time. Such solutions are named active network management [34].

Active network management solutions have hardware as well as software components and involve physically connecting the hardware device to existing network infrastructure, such as routers. The hardware device acts as a dummy router and receives all the routing table information and exchanges of router connectivity/configuration messages. In this way, these devices help in building real-time network topology and are able to detect outages as fast as the devices that are participating in the routing infrastructure.

6. Thoughts for Practitioners

6.1. *Management Data Modeling*

Though data modeling is currently a hot research area, it is still at an inchoate stage in network management research. There is a growing need to establish an evaluation framework for data modeling languages (DMLs) with a view to leveraging their capabilities in adapting to the requirements of network management. We argue that a well-designed framework for evaluation will play an important role in studying data modeling for network management.

6.1.1. *Proposed Framework for Evaluation*

Our proposed evaluation framework is based on the following set of criteria [53].

(i) *Modeling approaches.* Four main modeling approaches must be considered: the data-oriented approach, the command-oriented approach, the object-oriented/object-based approach and the document-oriented approach. The data-oriented approach models all management aspects through data objects, and at least two operations ("get" and "set") must be defined. The command-oriented approach defines a large number of management operations, specifying not the details but the commands to get/set the selected information. The object-oriented/object-based approach combines the data-oriented approach and the command-oriented approach in the view of integration. The document-oriented approach represents both state information and configuration information of a device as a structured document.

(ii) *Interoperability.* With the development of next-generation networks, management in an environment with a heterogeneous set of devices has become a trend. Hence, the standardization of data models (DMs) for network management should work at a higher level, making them closer to information models (IMs). Thus, DMLs should accordingly provide interoperability, which is consistent with the understanding of MOs already learned by network operators.

- *Protocol independence*: The language should define management data supporting any protocol instead of belonging to some specific protocol. In other words, DM defined by this language can be implemented on any platform that installs different protocols.
- *Naming independence*: Naming independence is a desirable mechanism provided by the DML that specifies how name collisions are handled, and thus uniquely identifies attributes, groups of attributes, and events.

(iii) *Readability.* It is desirable that DMLs for network management should be easily understood by both operators and computers. Human readability is necessary for convenient study and use; machine readability is required to accelerate the automatic process of network management, since both DMs and IMs are now being complemented by semantic models, where the meaning of concepts used in network management and relationships existing between them are made explicit [54].

- *Human readability*: Administrators should be able to directly read and understand both input and output representations (requirements, responses, error messages, etc).
- *Machine readability*: Descriptions of the corresponding DM should be easily read and understood by computers, and thus related applications can be quickly developed and efficiently implemented. Its implementation largely depends on semantic expressiveness, and its speed also has a close relation to the parseability of machines. Note that each DML has a different level of semantic expressiveness, which includes several facets like concepts, relations and behaviors, and it is not easy to measure semantic expressiveness. This problem can temporarily be reduced to a problem of integrating different languages.

(iv) *Conformance.* Traditional network management solutions are often not strong in configuration management, mostly as a result of modeling problems related to data representation, such as configuration objects not being easily identified. Consequently, the level of data representation ability should be included.

- *Backward compatibility*: New versions of the DML can be used to define the corresponding DML for the sake network management as older versions used to do.
- *Versioning*: Each version of the DML is complete, and thus easy to control.
- *Definition of event notification messages*: This is a feature that needs to be ensured by the DML to allow a single definition of notification content to be sent either asynchronously or synchronously.
- *Definition of error messages*: Error messages generated by network management applications must be identified by the DML.

(v) *Data representation.* When defining MOs, it is also necessary to describe machine-readable conformance for the DM.

- *Support of hierarchical data*: Hierarchical data should be clearly described by the DML so that it can be easily understood by both operators and computers.
- *Specification of configuration data, state data and statistics data*: Configuration data are the read-write data, and state data and statistical data are the read-only data. The corresponding DM specified for a device must identify what state data are and what configuration data are without the need for separating container elements.

(vi) *Extensibility.* With the increase of complexity of the Internet, there is a great need for DMLs to have the ability to extend data structures, data types, elements and attributes easily in order to facilitate the development of related software or systems to manage future heterogeneous networks.

- *Extensibility of data structures*: The DML should have the capability to add new data structures without affecting the available ones, and thus express the relations among data effectively and operate on data easily.
- *Extensibility of data types*: Extensibility of data types means that data types defined by the DML can be extended easily, so that the language can support various kinds of data simply and clearly.
- *Extensibility of elements and attributes*: Types of element nodes and attributes defined by the DML should not be too fixed to allow extension. That is to say, adding new types of elements or new attributes for existing elements is desired to be easy.

(vii) *Security considerations.* Security cannot be ignored by DMLs to ensure the confidentiality and integrity of management data.

- *Granularity of access control*: This refers to the precision with which data are accessed from the corresponding model. There are mainly two levels of granularity: coarse and fine. Using coarse granularity, large amounts of the data can be retrieved and edited from the DM, such as getting the whole data from MIB while a fine granularity refers to a detailed operation to a small part of data, such as elements.
- *Lock mechanism*: This should be considered by DMLs in order to guarantee the security of the configuration.

6.1.2. *Comparison*

The languages being measured are:

(i) Guidelines for the Definition of Managed Objects (GDMO) for CMIP,
(ii) SMI with its different versions for SNMP,

(iii) Management Information Format (MIF) for Desktop Management Interface (DMI),
(iv) Managed Object Format/Common Information Model (MOF/CIM) for WBEM,
(v) SMIng for both SNMP and COPS-PR.

Table 1 shows which modeling approach each language adopts for the purpose of network management [53]. As implied by Table 1, the object-based approach is especially distinguished from the object-oriented approach, since the former one is an incomplete version of the latter one.

Table 2 compares the different data modeling languages in terms of the criteria detailed in Sec. 6.1.1 [53].

Note that our evaluation is classified according to the following four levels:

- A minus sign (−) means that the language does not have such a capability.
- An asterisk (*) denotes that the language has little of the capability.
- A plus sign (+) is used when the language has much of the capability

Table 1. Modeling approach adopted by each language.

	Data modeling languages				
Modeling approaches	GDMO	SMI	MIF	MOF/CIM	SMIng
Data-oriented		√			
Command-oriented					
Object-based			√		√
Object-oriented	√			√	
Document-oriented					

Table 2. Comparison of languages.

	Data modeling languages				
Criteria	GDMO	SMI	MIF	MOF/CIM	SMIng
Protocol independence	−	−	+	−	*
Naming independence	−	−	−	−	−
Human readability	*	*	*	*	+
Machine readability	+	*	*	+	+
Support of hierarchical data	−	*	−	−	−
Specification of configuration data, state data and statistics data	−	−	−	−	−
Backward compatibility	−	+	*	*	−
Versioning	−	−	−	+	*
Definition of event notification messages	−	++	−	−	++
Definition of error messages	−	−	−	−	−
Extensibility of data structures	−	−	−	−	−
Extensibility of data types	−	+	−	+	+
Extensibility of elements and attributes	−	−	−	−	+
Granularity of access control	−	+	−	−	+
Lock mechanism	−	−	−	−	−

- Two plus signs (++) signify that the language completely possesses the capability.

The following conclusions can be drawn from Table 2:

(i) Almost all the existing DMLs are weak in terms of features related to data representation, security considerations and extensibility. This indicates that these three features are quite important when modeling management data and need to be taken into consideration as a priority.
(ii) Only a few facets of both interoperability and conformance are involved in particular languages, one example of which is SMIng, which only focuses on few of these facets. Taking management data modeling into consideration, this level is far from the aim.
(iii) All the languages attach some importance to readability, especially machine readability, in which they adopt different methods to promote their semantic expressiveness. The fact is that current languages are towards the automatic requirements of network management.

From the viewpoint of the languages themselves, it can also be concluded from Table 2 that SMIng is the language with the best implementation of most criteria, while SMI and MOF/CIM are close to achieving the capabilities of SMIng.

6.2. *Standardizations for Network Management*

Since generic technologies are widely used, standardization has played an important role in the implementation of network management systems. An example is the standardization of XML-based network management using NETCONF, which is briefly discussed in the following.

XML-based configuration management is currently a hot research area. In particular, NETCONF has emerged as a promising approach to standardizing XML-based network management for the purpose of automation, although NETCONF-based data modeling is still under review, since the specification of NETCONF content depends on the implementations adopted [55–58].

NETCONF defines a simple mechanism, through which a network device can be managed, configuration information can be retrieved, and new configuration data can be uploaded and manipulated. It uses a paradigm named Remote Procedure Call (RPC), and permits the functionality of this management protocol to closely monitor the native functionality of the device. Additionally, it allows a client to discover the set of protocol extensions supported by a server. These so called "capabilities" guarantee the client to adjust its behavior to take advantage of the features exposed by the device.

In addition, as mentioned above, Web services provide a distributed management capability for monitoring the services of applications on the Internet or an intranet using standard XML protocols and formats. Current research includes

Web services-based configuration management and management performance comparison between Web services and SNMP [7, 38].

It seems that the application of an integrated approach based on NETCONF and Web services may be a promising way towards standardization of XML-based network management.

7. Directions for Future Research

7.1. *Management of New Networks*

Since novel network technologies are constantly appearing, overlay networks based on grid and P2P require much attention, and this in turn influences conventional network management patterns. Hence, developing new network management organization models, information models, communication protocols and realizing new management functions have become important research issues [3].

7.2. *Next-Generation Network Management Solutions*

7.2.1. *P2P-based Network Management Solutions*

P2P networks are overlay networks composed of peers located at the edges of the Internet. P2P characteristics include self-organization, symmetric communications and distributed control [59]. Leveraging P2P technologies seems to be a very promising solution, enabling both distributed and scalable techniques in the scope of network management.

P2P systems and network management are usually related to each other because the traffic loads of P2P systems have to be controlled to avoid regular network services becoming unavailable due to network congestion [33].

Using the Management by Delegation (MbD) approach, a P2P-based network management usually contains the following three entities [60, 61]:

(i) top-level manager (TLM), which is a peer that is responsible for both reacting to the requests from human operators and communicating with other management peers in order to accomplish a particular management task;
(ii) mid-level manager (MLM), which is a peer that is responsible for reacting to the requests from the TLM and other MLMs;
(iii) agent, which is software that is responsible for treating requests and responding to them.

Thus, from the analysis above, we argue that P2P technologies make inter-domain network management possible and sensible, while they motivate the development of cooperative management when tackling heterogeneous networks. This point distinguishes P2P-based solutions from traditional solutions in the field of network management.

Of course, P2P technologies may do more than that. The application of P2P technologies to reliable management message exchange (how a P2P-based application layer routing can improve connectivity between management entities) and load balancing of management tasks (how groups of peers can be used to process management tasks in a balanced way) has been already discussed [33].

All these characteristics of P2P technologies are indicative of a promising future for network management.

Furthermore, a P2P-based network management solution is not quite like most of current solutions since P2P technologies aim to improve existing network management technologies rather than replace them. This has the advantage of allowing a P2P-based network management solution to integrate conveniently with other solutions.

Integration with SNMP is a case in point. Today, SNMP-based manager-agent network management solutions are still widely used, and each SNMP-based agent usually manages a single domain. With the use of P2P technologies, managing SNMP-based agents from different domains becomes possible, as demonstrated in Fig. 8.

7.2.2. *Predictive Network Management*

It is known that one major objective of a network management solution is to help reduce the mean time to restoration (MTTR) for network faults [34]. However, most of current solutions fail to report faults before they occur. Predictive network management is thus a promising solution for implementing active network management. On the one hand, active network management aims at monitoring networks by active participation in operations, so as to greatly reduce the fault response time. On the other hand, as an improvement of active network

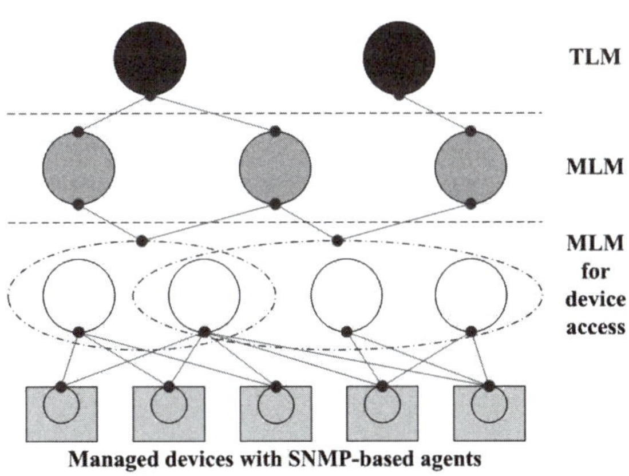

Fig. 8. Application of P2P technologies to manage SNMP-based agents from different domains.

management, predictive network management focuses on analyzing past network behaviors to ascertain spatial and temporal relationships between network faults and the elements involved.

At present, research work is limited to predicting network source usage [62, 63]. In particular, researchers have created an architecture named Atropos, which provides a network prediction service utilizing the capability of active networks to inject fine-grained models into communication networks, and aims at reducing the management burden caused by growing complexity through integrating management support into the inherent function of network operation. Note that the definition of proactive network management is also provided for the precise projection of faults as soon as possible before they occur [62]. This attempt is just towards the very goal of solutions that can predict specific network faults.

7.2.3. *Autonomic Networks with Intelligent Self-Managing Devices*

Traditionally, one or more operators must be involved in the whole process of network management, defining high-level policies, executing low-level commands for immediate problem resolution, and so on. But this form of management through human intervention has become increasingly inappropriate for the ever-evolving development of networks. Autonomic networks are thus designed to have the ability to dynamically adapt to changes in their environments with little or no human intervention. Self-management technologies have been introduced to help networks autonomously control themselves. According to the IBM autonomic computing initiative, self-management can be divided into four functional areas: self-configuration, self-healing, self-optimization and self-protection [64].

7.3. *Research on Management Information Models*

Since the complexity of computer networks has greatly increased, as more and more network resources need to be effectively managed, the definition of IM and DM must be seriously considered for network management. DMs are different from IMs, which manage objects at a conceptual level and are thus protocol-neutral. In contrast, DMs are defined at a concrete level, and are implemented in different ways and are protocol-specific. In other words, multiple DMs can be derived from a single IM [65].

Note that the main difference between these two concepts is the level of abstraction [54]. DMs are closer to the underlying protocols used to transport the management information and the particular implementation in use. In fact, they are intended for implementers. Working at a conceptual level, IMS are intended to be independent of any particular implementation or management protocol and usually provide more expressiveness to designers.

As mentioned above, both DMs and IMs are now being complemented by semantic models, where the meaning of concepts used in the network management field and relationships existing between them are made explicit, as shown in Fig. 9.

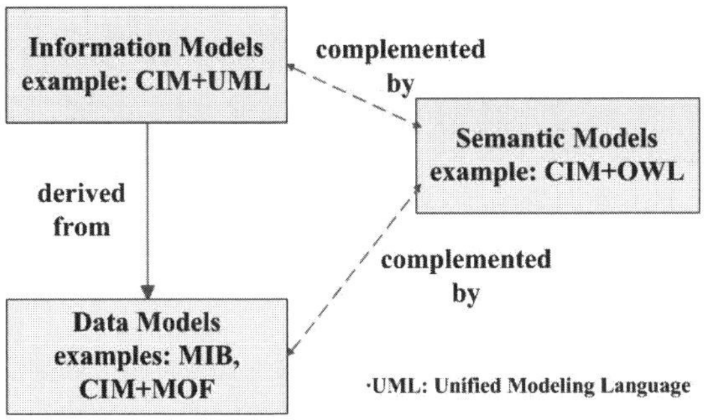

Fig. 9. Relationships among DMs, IMs and semantic models.

Additionally, this meaning is defined in a machine-readable format, thus making it accessible to both software management components and humans [54].

On the other hand, the objects described by current IMs only focus on network facilities. And in response to the rise of various network services, the components in network management must be reorganized and extended.

8. Conclusions

In this chapter we have presented a tutorial and survey of network management.

First of all, this chapter briefly described some background on network management. Since the development of management technology is always coupled with network management protocol standardization, this chapter went on to discuss network management standards including OSI-SM and SNMP. At the same time, the OSI network management model comprising the organization model, information model, communication model and functional model was described and also used for evaluating SNMP-based network management.

This chapter then considered network management methodology (including both techniques and strategies): policy-based network management, distributed network management with the use of COBRA, mobile agent and Web technologies, XML-based network management, and event correlation techniques. During this process, some solutions were specially evaluated from the OSI perspective using its proposed network management model.

This chapter also examined the present-day challenges in the network management domain and illuminated current trends, including standardization, automation and integration. Various approaches were discussed, such as Web services-based network management, semantic network management, integrated network management, improved RCA techniques, and active network management.

In order to help practitioners, this chapter focused on the evaluation of DMLs in network management domain and standardization issues for implementing network management systems.

Finally, this chapter pointed out directions for future research, which may possibly be utilized to build management solutions for next-generation networks, including topics such as management for new networks, P2P-based network management, predictive network management, autonomic networks with intelligent self-managing devices, and research on IM for network management.

Acknowledgments

This work was supported by the Key Scientific and Technological Project of Hubei Province, P. R. China under Grant No. 2008BAB012.

Terminology

Network management: The activities, methods, procedures and tools that pertain to the operation, administration, maintenance and provisioning of computer networks.

Systems management: Management of a system's resources, such as central processor usage, disk usage and application processes.

Service management: Treatment of services provided by organizations to customers as an extension of network and systems management.

OSI network management model: An ISO standard and the most superior of all the models, which is structured and addresses all aspects of management, comprising four models: organization model, information model, communication model and functional model.

Organization model: Description of the components of network management and their relationship.

Manager: Used to manage network elements, or in other words, managed objects in network management domain.

Agent: Defined as a management process running in managed objects in network management domain.

Information model: Used to model managed objects at a conceptual level.

Data model: Defined at a concrete level, thus implementing in different ways and being protocol-specific.

Communication model: Demonstration of how management data is exchanged between managers and agents, based on a seven-layer OSI stack with a connection-oriented transport layer.

Functional model: Used to address user-oriented applications, which are formally specified in the OSI model.

Exercises

1. What is network management? Explain how it differs from systems management and service management.
2. Compare the OSI-SM and SNMP network management standards.
3. Explain the OSI network management model.
4. Analyze the shortcomings of existing network management solutions.
5. Summarize present-day network management challenges.
6. Illuminate current trends in network management domain.
7. Share your understanding of data modelling issues for network management.
8. Provide an example to interpret how standardization plays an important role for the implementation of network management systems.
9. Point out directions for future research which may possibly be utilized to build management solutions for next-generation networks.
10. Note down all your thoughts during your study of this chapter.

References

1. M. Subramanian, *Network Management: Principles and Practice* (Addison Wesley Longman Press, Boston, 1999).
2. A. Clemm, *Network Management Fundamentals* (Cisco Press, Indianapolis, 2006).
3. G. Gu and J. Luo, Some issues on computer networks: Architecture and key technologies, *J. Comput. Sci. Technol.* **21**(5), 708–722 (2006).
4. ISO/IEC 10040, Information Technology — Open Systems Interconnection — Systems Management Overview, ITU-T Recommendation, X. 701 (1998).
5. J. Case, M. Fedor, M. Schoffstall and J. Davin, A simple network management protocol (SNMP), *RFC*, 1157 (1990).
6. L. Raman, OSI systems and network management, *IEEE Commun. Mag.* **36**(3), 46–53 (1998).
7. G. Pavlou, P. Flegkas, S. Gouveris and A. Liotta, On management technologies and the potential of web services, *IEEE Commun. Mag.* **42**(7), 58–66 (2004).
8. ISO/IEC 10165-1, Information Technology — Management Information Services — Open Systems Interconnection — Structure of Management Information: Management Information Model, CCITT Recommendation, X.720 (1993).
9. ISO/IEC 10165-2, Information Technology — Open Systems Interconnection — Structure of Management Information: Definition of Management Information, ITU-T Recommendation, X.721 (1992).
10. ISO/IEC 10165-4, Information Technology — Open Systems Interconnection — Structure of Management Information — Part 4: Guidelines for the Definition of Managed Objects, ITU-T Recommendation, X.722 (1992).
11. R. H. Glitho, Contrasting OSI systems management to SNMP and TMN, *J. Net. Syst. Manag.* **6**(2), 113–133 (1998).
12. L. Raman, CMISE functions and services, *IEEE Commun. Mag.* **31**(5), 46–51 (1993).
13. ISO/IEC 9595, Information Technology — Open Systems Interconnection — Common Management Information Service, ITU-T Recommendation, X.710 (1998).
14. ISO/IEC 9596-1, Information Technology — Open Systems Interconnection — Common Management Information Protocol: Part I: Specification, ITU-T Recommendation, X.711 (1998).

15. D. Durham (ed.), The COPS (Common Open Policy Service) Protocol, *RFC*, 2748 (2000).
16. K. Chan *et al.*, COPS usage for policy provisioning (COPS-PR), *RFC*, 3084 (2000).
17. R. Sahita (ed.), Framework policy information base, *RFC*, 3318 (2003).
18. K. McCloghrie *et al.*, Structure of Policy Provisioning Information (SPPI), *RFC*, 3159 (2001).
19. OMG, Common Object Request Broker Architecture (CORBA), www.corba.org.
20. OMG, Interface Definition Language (IDL), www.omg.org/gettingstarted/omg_idl.htm.
21. FMA, Mobile Agent, fma.sourceforge.net/index2.htm.
22. C. Bohoris, G. Pavlou and H. Cruickshank, Using mobile agents for network performance management, *Proc. 6th IEEE/IFIP Network Operations and Management Symp.* (IEEE, New York, 2000), pp. 637–652.
23. IEEE, Foundation for Intelligent Physical Agent (FIPA), www.fipa.org.
24. DMTF, Web-Based Enterprise Management (WBEM), www.dmtf.org/standards/wbem.
25. DMTF, Common Information Model (CIM), www.dmtf.org/standards/cim.
26. DMTF, Specification for the Representation of CIM in XML Version 2.2 (2004).
27. DMTF, Specification for CIM Operations over HTTP Version 1.2 (2004).
28. T. Bray, J. Paoli, C. M. Sperberg-McQueen, E. Maler and F. Yergeau (eds.), Extensible Markup Language (XML) 1.0 (Fifth Edition), *W3C Recommendation* (2008).
29. F. Strauss and T. Klie, Towards XML oriented Internet management, *Proc. 8th IFIP/IEEE Int. Symp. Integrated Network Management* (IEEE, New York, 2003), pp. 505–518.
30. M. Hasan, B. Sugla and R. Viswanathan, A conceptual framework for network management event correlation and filtering systems, *Proc. 6th IFIP/IEEE Int. Symp. Integrated Network Management* (IEEE, New York, 1999), pp. 233–246.
31. G. Jiang and G. Cybenko, Temporal and spatial distributed event correlation for network security, *Proc. American Control Conf.* (IEEE, New York, 2004), pp. 996–1001.
32. H. Xu, Z. Liu, Y. Bai and D. Xiao, Applying an integrated approach of data fusion and data mining to event correlation for network security, *Proc. 2nd Int. Conf. Computer Science & Education* (2007), pp. 1309–1314.
33. L. Z. Granville *et al.*, Managing computer networks using peer-to-peer technologies, *IEEE Commun. Mag.* **43**(10), 62–68 (2005).
34. A. Gupta, Network management: Current trends and future perspectives, *J. Net. Sys. Manage.* **14**(4), 483–491 (2006).
35. J. Sloten, A. Pras and M. Sinderen, On the standardisation of web service management operations, *Proc. 10th Open European Summer School (EUNICE 2004) and IFIP WG 6.3 Workshop* (2004), pp. 143–150.
36. T. Drevers, R. Meent and A. Pras, Prototyping web services based network monitoring, *Proc. 10th Open European Summer School (EUNICE 2004) and IFIP WG 6.3 Workshop* (2004), pp. 135–142.
37. OASIS, Universal Description, Discovery and Integration (UDDI), uddi.xml.org.
38. S. Yoo, H. Ju and J. W. Hong, *Web Services Based Configuration Management for IP Network Devices*, in *Lecture Notes in Computer Science*, Vol. 3754 (Springer, Berlin, 2005), pp. 254–265.
39. Wikipedia, Service-Oriented Architecture (SOA), en.wikipedia.org/wiki/ Service-oriented_architecture.

40. E. Ort, Service-Oriented Architecture and Web Services: Concepts, Technologies, and Tools, java.sun.com/developer/technicalArticles/WebServices/soa2.
41. T. Berners-Lee, J. Hendler and O. Lassila, The semantic web, *Scientific American* **284**(5), 34–43 (2001).
42. R. Studer, V. R. Benjamins and O. Fensel, Knowledge Engineering: Principle and Methods, *Data & Knowledge Engineering*, **25**(1–2), 161–197 (1998).
43. H. Wache *et al.*, Ontology-based integration of information — A survey of existing approaches, *Proc. IJCAI-01 Workshop: Ontologies and Information Sharing* (2001), pp. 108–117.
44. J. E. López de Vergara, V. A. Villagrá, J. I. Asensio and J. Berrocal, Ontologies: Giving semantics to network management models, *IEEE Network* **17**(3), 15–21 (2003).
45. DARPA, DARPA Agent Markup Language, www.daml.org.
46. Ontology Inference Layer (OIL), www.ontoknowledge.org/oil.
47. P. E. Patel-Schneider, P. Hayes and I. Horrocks (eds.), OWL Web Ontology Language Semantics and Abstract Syntax, *W3C Recommendation* (2004).
48. J. E. López de Vergara, V. A. Villagrá and J. Berrocal, Applying the web ontology language to management information definitions, *IEEE Commun. Mag.* **42**(7), 68–74 (2004).
49. H. Xu and D. Xiao, Applying semantic web services to automate network management, *Proc. 2nd IEEE Conf. Industrial Electronics and Applications* (IEEE, New York, 2007), pp. 461–466.
50. T. Payne and O. Lassila, Semantic web services, *IEEE Intelli. Sys.* **19**(4), 14–15 (2004).
51. D. Martin (ed.), OWL-S: Semantic Markup for Web Services, *W3C Member Submission* (2004).
52. J. E. López de Vergara, V. A. Villagrá and J. Berrocal, Application of OWL-S to Define Management Interfaces Based on Web Services, in *Lecture Notes in Computer Science*, Vol. 3754 (Springer, Berlin, 2005), pp. 242–253.
53. H. Xu, D. Xiao, Evaluation on Data Modeling Languages for NETCONF-Based Network Management, *Proc. 11th IEEE/IFIP Network Operations and Management Symp.* (IEEE, New York, 2008), pp. 674–677.
54. A. Pras *et al.*, Key research challenges in network management, *IEEE Commun. Mag.* **45**(10), 104–110 (2007).
55. R. Enns (ed.), NETCONF Configuration Protocol, *RFC*, 4741 (2006).
56. M. Wasserman and T. Goddard, Using the NETCONF Configuration Protocol over Secure SHell (SSH), *RFC*, 4742 (2006).
57. T. Goddard, Using NETCONF over the Simple Object Access Protocol (SOAP), *RFC*, 4743 (2006).
58. E. Lear and K. Crozier, Using the NETCONF Protocol over the Blocks Extensible Exchange Protocol (BEEP), *RFC*, 4744 (2006).
59. D. S. Milojicic *et al.*, Peer-to-peer computing, HP Laboratories Technical Report, HPL-2002-57 (2002).
60. G. Goldzmidt and Y. Yemini, Distributed management by delegation, *Proc. 15th Int. Conf. Distributed Computing Systems* (1995), pp. 333–340.
61. A. Panisson *et al.*, Designing the architecture of P2P-based network management systems, *Proc. 11th Symp. Computers and Communications* (2006), pp. 69–75.
62. S. F. Bush and S. Goel, An active model-based prototype for predictive network management, *IEEE J. Sel. Areas Commun.* **23**(10), 2049–2057 (2005).

63. S. F. Bush and S. Kalyanarman, Management of active and programmable networks, *J. Net. Sys. Manage.* **14**(1), 1–5 (2006).
64. A. G. Ganek and T. A. Corbi, The dawning of the autonomic computing era, *IBM Sys. J.* **42**(1), 5–18 (2003).
65. A. Pras and J. Schoenwaelder, On the difference between information models and data models, *RFC*, 3444 (2003).

Chapter 15

THE PRINCIPLES OF NETWORK MONITORING

MONICA BROCKMEYER
Department of Computer Science, Wayne State University,
5143 Cass Avenue, 431 State Hall,
Detroit, MI 48202, USA
mbrockmeyer@wayne.edu

JAWWAD SHAMSI*
National University of Sciences and Technology,
Islamabad, Pakistan
jawwadshamsi@gmail.edu

Efficient and cost-effective measurement of network characteristics is pivotal for distributed systems deployed on the Internet. The network characteristics are utilized by Internet-based distributed systems to provide better services to users and enhanced performance for applications. This chapter provides a detailed analysis of existing techniques for the measurement of the four important network characteristics: latency, bandwidth, path detection and loss rate. The chapter describes key concepts related to network measurements, including techniques for clock synchronization, strategies for time stamping of probes, methods for network analysis, difference between active and passive measurements, and comparison of round trip times versus one-way delay measurements. It elaborates on the usefulness of different transport and network layer protocols (i.e., Transmission Control Protocol (TCP), User Datagram Protocol (UDP) and Internet Control Message Protocol (ICMP) for obtaining network measurements and describes some important measurement tools such as Ping, Traceroue, Pathchar, Sting, Scriptroute, Spruce and Paris Traceroute. The chapter explains the effectiveness and limitations of these tools with respect to the measurement of network characteristics.

1. Introduction

The effectiveness of a distributed application providing service to its end users depends largely on the characteristics of the underlying network. A web server is of no use if its immediate router fails and all the paths leading to the web server become unavailable. Similarly, a Voice over Internet Protocol (VoIP) service has restricted functionality if the available bandwidth is limited.

*Corresponding author.

The two examples mentioned above are not infrequent. Internet-based systems exhibit enough uncertainty and unpredictability to affect the quality and effectiveness of distributed systems. This uncertainty underlines the need for monitoring of various network characteristics, both at the level of the service provider and the application. An Internet Service Provider (ISP) may monitor the bandwidth used by its customers, in order to allow a fair share of the bandwidth usage, while an application could periodically measure latency to its servers in order to detect congestion and failure.

1.1. *Which Network Characteristics are Relevant for Measurements?*

The significance and relevance of network characteristics vary with application. A content distribution network may be interested in measuring latency from its clients to the application server, whereas a load balancing application may find available bandwidth as a useful criterion to adjust the load on the servers. Other network characteristics such as congestion, queuing delay, network failure, topology discovery, and bottleneck determination also have great significance. However, there are four network characteristics that constitute the basic paradigm of network measurements and that could be utilized in the computation of other related network characteristics:

- *Latency*: Latency refers to the time taken by the message to traverse from the sending host to the destination host. It is usually measured in milliseconds (ms). The latency of a path has a great significance for many applications. In many cases, latency is used to determine the availability of servers and select the nearest available server in terms of latency, specifically in content distribution networks. Further, variation in latency (i.e., the deviation between successive latency measurements) is used to determine the quality of the path and detect network congestion.
- *Loss rate*: If the rate of packets sent from the source host is not equal to the rate of packets received at the destination host then the path experiences packet loss. The loss rate of a path is the rate (in percentage) at which packets are being lost while traversing through the network path. Lost packets affect the performance of the application as they are often required to be retransmitted. When packets cannot be retransmitted (for example, such as the live transmission of audio or video streams), a high packet loss could lead to low application performance. For these reasons it is always desirable to select paths with low loss rate.
- *Path detection*: When a message is sent across the Internet, it traverses through various intermediate routers to reach the destination. Path detection is the process of determining the actual path taken by the message in going from source to destination. Since there are many possibilities for a path from one host to another, path detection enables an application to determine the actual path taken by the message during transmission. Path changes are possible on the

Internet; therefore path detection also facilitates in determining a change in the path between two nodes. It can also be used as a sanity check to determine or isolate network failure.

- *Bandwidth*: Bandwidth refers to the capacity of the path to transfer data in a unit time. It is measured in bits per second (bps). Bandwidth has great implication for multimedia applications. Such applications generally have high bandwidth requirements. If the available path has limited bandwidth then the multimedia application suffers with degraded performance. Bandwidth detection tools can be used to infer the path quality and select the appropriate path.

The purpose of this chapter is to develop the reader's skills and proficiency related to network measurements. The chapter elucidates basic concepts about network monitoring and explains several approaches and tools for the measurement of the four basic network characteristics. The chapter also discusses practical issues related to the development of network monitoring tools. The chapter assumes that the reader has an understanding of basic networking terms such as the seven layer OSI model and familiarity with transport layer protocols such as TCP and UDP.

2. Background Information

Network monitoring is a vast and rigorous topic. In order to thoroughly explain the concepts, some background information is provided in this section. The information includes a description of different types of network monitoring and an explanation of the underlying protocols used for monitoring. Readers may also refer to the terminology section of this chapter, which explains some key terms associated with network monitoring.

2.1. *Types of Network Monitoring*

There are two basic approaches for network monitoring: active monitoring and passive monitoring.

- *Active monitoring*: Active monitoring involves injecting probes into the network, specifically for the purpose of monitoring. Active monitoring bears the cost of sending additional traffic in the network; however, under most scenarios, the packet size is relatively small compared to the actual capacity of the network, and therefore the cost of injecting additional traffic is minimal. The cost of injecting traffic can be reduced by decreasing the probing rate; however, this may reduce the quality of the measured characteristics. Active monitoring provides full control with respect to monitoring interval, packet size, and the path to be monitored. Further, the data obtained is not specific to any particular application.
- *Passive Monitoring*: Passive monitoring is the process of observing the existing network traffic and collecting information from it without injecting additional monitoring probes into the network. In a passive measurements based system, network measurement information is retrieved through packets that are sent as a

part of another application. Packets are captured by the monitoring application, which is deployed either at the source and the destination hosts or along the path through a *tap*.[a] The passive mode of monitoring avoids the overhead of introducing measurement traffic in the network and also evades the use of stale data for measurements. However, in passive mode the monitoring application has little or no control over probing interval, packet size or the path to be monitored. Further, due to the increase in the capacity of the core links, it is expensive to identify and measure a packet of a particular flow. Passive monitoring could also raise privacy concerns.

The preference for the type of monitoring varies with application. For instance, an application measuring the performance of an existing application such as an intrusion detection system might prefer a passive approach, whereas an application employing performance enhancement measures such as load balancing may desire an active scheme. An application may also employ a combination of the passive and active schemes for higher efficiency. The Wren grid monitoring system utilizes such a scheme, in which the passive mode is used when an application is sending messages, while the active mode is used when the application is silent [18].

2.2. *Network Protocol*

For passive monitoring, the measurement system cannot choose the underlying protocol for network measurement, i.e., the monitoring application monitors packets that are sent as part of another application. However, in the active mode, the measurement system has to decide about the underlying protocol used for sending probes. Many choices are available and they are discussed below.

- *ICMP*: Internet Control Message Protocol (ICMP) is the underlying protocol for the famous ping utility. It operates at the networking layer. The principle advantage of ICMP-based measurement tools is simplicity and ease of use. ICMP-based schemes do not require connection setup or handshake. Further, they do not require any specific implementation at the recipient end, i.e., only the host sending the active probes implements the mechanism for sending the ICMP probes. Since ICMP messages are control messages, an ICMP request is automatically replied by the destination host. However, the automatic response capability of the host could be exploited by attackers and is seen as a security vulnerability. ICMP will be discussed further when we analyze the ping utility.
- *TCP*: The Transmission Control Protocol (TCP) is the underlying protocol for many Internet applications including World Wide Web (WWW) and File Transfer

[a]A tap is a hardware device which provides a way to capture data along a path. A tap usually has three connection points. Two connection points are connected to each end of the path, while the third point is connected to a monitor which listens for the information. A tap is not a sink, i.e., it copies all the information to the monitor and the communication between the two ends of the path remains uninterrupted.

Protocol (FTP). It operates at the transport layer. Unlike ICMP-based tools, TCP-based utilities bear the overhead of the TCP handshake.[b] TCP-based tools also require that the destination host runs a service on a designated port. The sending host establishes a TCP connection to the destination through the TCP handshake and sends probes to the destination host at the server port. The server at the destination replies with a response, which is used for network measurement.

An important limitation of TCP-based tools is that since TCP is not a packet-based protocol, it makes its own decisions about sending packets. By using various optimizations, including the Nagle algorithm [34], TCP coalesces packets of small sizes. Since TCP has a large overhead including a 40-byte header (20-bytes for IP and 20 for TCP), these optimizations allow TCP to conserve bandwidth. At the user level, it is difficult to force TCP to send packets at a specific interval [44].

In some cases, the requirement of a running service at the destination can be eliminated using TCP ACK and RST. According to RFC 793 [33], if a sender sends a TCP ACK packet to a closed[c] TCP port, then the TCP at the destination will reply with the TCP RST packet and the same sequence number as the TCP ACK packet in the request. In such a case, the TCP RST can be used as a response. However, this type of request-response method can be used only if the response from the destination host is not specific to the request, i.e., the response is not generated based on the contents in the request.

- *UDP*: The User Datagram Protocol (UDP) is a datagram-based protocol that operates at the transport layer. Unlike TCP, UDP does not require a handshake. Additionally, UDP has an 8-byte header (plus a 20-byte IP header) that results in lower overhead than TCP. Since UDP is a packet protocol, it allows the sending of probe packets at controlled intervals. Moreover, UDP is a connectionless protocol in which a lost request (or a response) can be effectively used to detect packet loss.

  Like TCP, UDP can also eliminate the need to run a service at the destination port. If a UDP request is received at a port at which the service is not running, then it responds by sending an "ICMP destination unreachable" message to the sender.

  Many other choices such as the Datagram Congestion Control Protocol (DCCP) and the Stream Control Transmission Protocol (SCTP) also exist. The selection of underlying protocol for network monitoring is based on the requirements and restrictions of an application.

3. Network Characteristics

Having identified the basic principles of monitoring, this section describes various approaches for the measurement of network characteristics. Each of the four network characteristics, latency, loss rate, path detection and bandwidth, are discussed in a

[b]TCP handshake is a three-way process. In the first step, the host initiating the connection sends a TCP SYN packet. The recipient host responds with an ACK packet. Finally, the original host sends a SYN ACK packet. All three packets contain sequence numbers for proper identification.
[c]A port that is not running any TCP service.

subsection which explains the basic concepts about the characteristic and various approaches for its measurement.

3.1. *Latency*

Latency has been the most widely measured network characteristic. It refers to the time (in ms) taken by the packet to traverse from the sending host to the destination host. The latency between two hosts could vary for two reasons. First, variation is possible due to changes in queuing delay or congestion, and second, due to route changes. When a packet is sent from sender to receiver, it traverses through multiple intermediate routers, each of which has variable queuing delay. Therefore, two successive packets could follow different routes, resulting in a different latency for each. Route changes are quite common due to congestion or network failure. Therefore, the variation in latency can be utilized to depict congestion between the two end points, where paths with low congestion observe more consistency in latency.

The notion of latency mentioned here represents the one-way latency from the sender to the receiver, commonly referred to as one-way delay (OWD). It is measured by subtracting the time the packet is sent by the sending host from the time the packet is received at the recipient host.

Besides OWD, the word latency is also sometimes used to refer to the Round Trip Time (RTT) between the two hosts. This involves the time taken by the packet to reach the recipient host from the sending host and the reply from the recipient host to the sending host. Fig. 1 shows the difference between OWD and RTT.

Example 1: Assume the RTT between two Internet hosts is 200 ms. What is the OWD between them?

Solution: Unknown. The Internet is asymmetric, i.e., the forward and backward routes between two hosts are not necessarily the same. Therefore, the OWD is not necessarily equal to one half of the RTT.

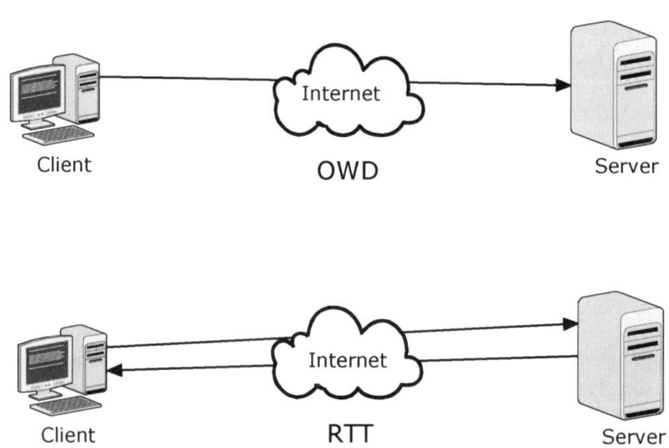

Fig. 1. OWD versus RTT.

Example 2: What is the RTT between two Internet hosts A and B, if the one-way latencies of the forward and backward paths between them are 91 ms and 92 ms? Host B takes 200 μs on average to respond to the probes.

Solution: RTT $= 91 + 92 + 0.2 = 183.2$ ms.

RTT implies the effective communication delay for applications that are request-response applications such as WWW and FTP. In comparison, OWD is a useful communication tool for applications that have one-way communication such as multicasting.

In the case of a large message transfer, the end-to-end latency of a message is higher than the packet latency. Large messages are usually disassembled into small packets and transferred to the destination. At the destination, the message is reassembled into its original form. The processes of disassembling and assembling are called fragmentation and defragmentation, respectively.

The capacity of a path to transfer a message without fragmentation depends upon its maximum transmission unit (MTU), where the MTU of a path denotes the size of the IP datagram that can be transferred. This usually varies for different networks; however for Ethernet it is equal to 1500 bytes. The end-to-end path between two Internet hosts may be composed of links with different MTUs. In this scenario, intermediate routers may perform the fragmentation according to the capacity of each link. We now describe some important latency measurement techniques.

3.1.1. *Measurement Strategies*

The measurement strategy for latency is simple. The sending host sends a packet and waits for the response. When the response is received, it subtracts the sent time stamp from the received time stamp and computes the round trip latency. For OWD, however, the destination host notes the time at which the request is received at the destination and includes it in its response to the original sender, which computes OWD by subtracting the sending time from the time at which the request was received at the destination. A major requirement for the measurement of OWD is synchronizing clocks of the two nodes. Note that the underlying protocol could be ICMP, TCP or UDP.

The methodology mentioned above is confined to active monitoring. For passive monitoring, the monitoring host can monitor the existing flows from an application and compute the RTT. For instance, a web client can compute its RTT with a web server by comparing time stamps of the HTTP request and HTTP response.

3.2. *Loss Rate*

The loss rate of a path is the rate at which packets are being dropped while traversing through the path. There could be multiple reasons for packet loss.

Most commonly, for a path with limited bandwidth, the intermediate routers buffer the packets in the queue. However, if a queue at the router approaches its storage capacity then the router drops the packet. Packet loss could also occur due to a hardware failure at a router or at the destination host. It can also happen due to the packet being corrupted because of noise in the path.

The detection of packet loss is challenging. In theory, packet loss can be detected if a response to a request is not received by the sender within a certain amount of time. However, the sender (the entity sending the request) faces a challenge in determining the duration of this timeout. A response from the destination host could be delayed for various reasons including a high RTT, a congested path, a heavily loaded server or even a low connection speed at the sender. If a sender adopts a safe passage by implementing a large timeout time then it suffers from poor performance since a lost packet might be detected earlier; on the other hand if the waiting time is small, then the sender might end up causing congestion in the network by sending multiple requests, or might erroneously conclude that a packet is lost when, in fact, the packet is just delayed. While there is no perfect answer to determine the duration of the waiting time, most distributed applications adopt a safe approach and maintain a longer waiting time. For instance, the timeout for a DNS query is 15 s.

3.2.1. *Measurement Strategies*

Packet loss is measured by initiating a timer for each probe and noting the probes for which the response is not received. Note that in such a case the direction of packet loss is unknown i.e., if the request from the sender is lost or the response from the destination has failed to reach the sender (see Fig. 2). This

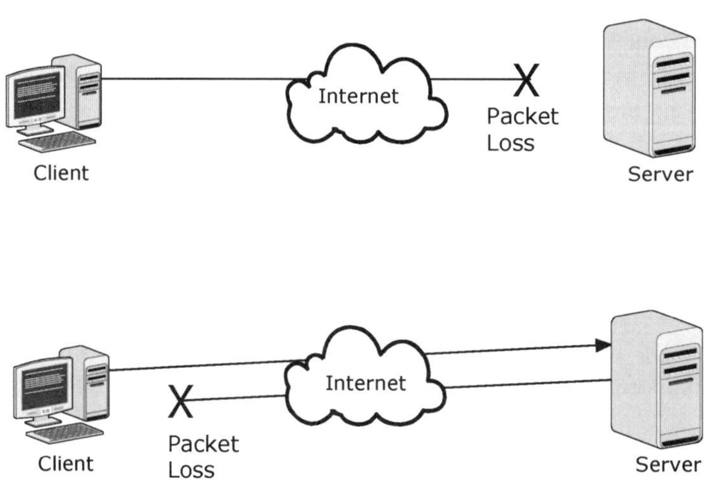

Fig. 2. Examples of packet loss.

information is important for many applications that use one-way communication such as multicasting. In Sec. 4, we will analyze the sting tool [37], which computes loss rate in both directions.

3.3. *Path Detection*

An Internet path consists of various hops connected by routers. Path detection is the process of determining information (including name and IP address) about all intermediate routers traversed when a packet is sent across an Internet path.

Note that path detection is different from topology discovery. The former is the process of determining only the intermediate routers that are traversed by a packet when it is sent along the path, whereas the latter is the process of determining all the combinations of a path between two Internet hosts. Path detection tools can be utilized to discover topology. Figure 3 illustrates a scenario where several routes exist for a path from client X to the server Y.

The computation of Internet paths is achieved through routing protocols, of which there are two broad categories: Internet gateway protocols and exterior gateway protocols. The former refers to the routing within an autonomous system,[d] while the latter is used when the routing is done across autonomous systems.

3.3.1. *Measurement Strategies*

Path detection strategies are based on using time-to-live (TTL) values in the IP header. The purpose of TTL is to avoid infinite looping (IP routing cycle) of IP packets. TTL is an 8 bit field which indicates the number of hops or routers a packet can be traversed before it must reach its destination or be discarded. When a packet traverses a path, each intermediate router examines the TTL value of the packet. If the TTL value is greater than one, then the TTL value is decremented by one and the packet is sent to the next hop, which could be another router or the final

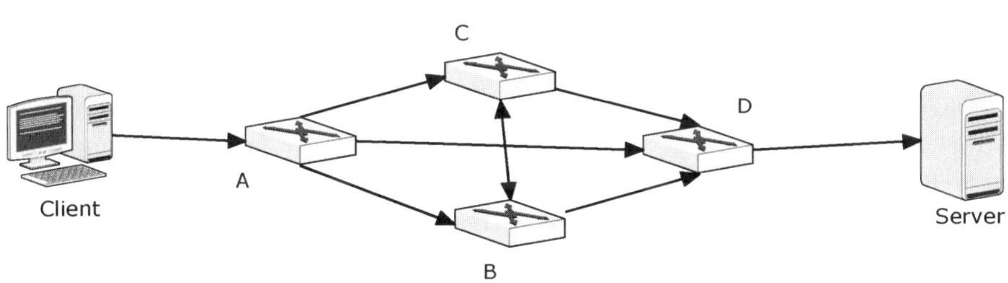

Fig. 3. Possibilities for a path.

[d]An autonomous system (AS) is a collection of networks and routers that maintains a single routing policy. An AS could be under the control of one or more entities and is uniquely identified by an AS number [35].

destination host. However, if the TTL value[e] is one, then the router discards the message and sends an ICMP "time exceeded" message to the original sender. The ICMP "time exceeded" message indicates that the TTL field has expired, the packet has failed to reach the destination and it has been discarded. The "ICMP time exceeded" message contains the address of the router that generates the message. Path detection tools work by sending a series of packets with increasing TTL to the final destination. Since the TTL value is gradually increased in the series, each intermediate router once receives a packet having TTL value equal to one and sends a reply to the original sender with the ICMP "time exceeded" message. The sender can thus obtain information about all the routers in the path.

Example 3: Can path detection tools be used to measure RTT to a specific hop?

Solution: Path detection tools can be used to measure RTT. When the original sender receives an ICMP "time exceeded," message, it can compare the send time stamp of the probing packet with the received time stamp of the ICMP message to compute RTT to a particular hop.

3.4. *Bandwidth*

Bandwidth quantifies the data rate at which a network link or a network path can transfer [31]. It is measured in bits per second (bps). Unlike latency, where the end-to-end characteristic of a path is computed by aggregating the latency of the individual links, the bandwidth of a path is the capacity of the link with the minimum bandwidth.

The term bandwidth can be used to refer to two different types of speeds. Upload speed denotes the rate at which data is being sent to the destination, while download speed refers to the rate at which data is being received. If a path has similar upload and download speed then it is called bandwidth symmetric. Most of the Internet backbone is bandwidth symmetric. However, this is not necessarily true for end users, including home users relying on cable or ADSL. The reason for this difference is that most home users are typically interested in downloading, therefore Internet Service Providers (ISPs) allocate more resources for downloading. Note that a bandwidth-symmetric path is not necessarily symmetric in route or *vice versa*. The two entities are separate and must not be confused with each other. For the measurement of bandwidth two terms are relevant: capacity and available bandwidth.

- *Capacity*: Capacity refers to the maximum data rate a link can transfer. It is measured as the number of data units (bits) transferred in a unit time (s). The capacity of a link depends upon the transmission medium and is usually

[e]When the destination host receives a packet with a TTL value of one, it delivers the packet to the application.

constant at the link layer (OSI layer 2). For instance, for a gigabit Ethernet, the capacity of a link is equal to one gigabit per second. However, this capacity refers to the capability of a link excluding any overhead. Remember, at the IP-layer (layer 3), IP packets are encapsulated in link-layer frames such as Ethernet frames, therefore the actual capacity must also consider the overhead associated in transmitting data in frames. For instance, for Ethernet the overhead consists of 38 bytes: 14 bytes for the Ethernet header, four bytes for the cyclic redundancy check (CRC),[f] eight bytes for the frame preamble,[g] and the 12 bytes for the inter frame gap[h] [31].

The actual capacity of the path considering the overhead can be expressed as

$$C = C_L \frac{L}{O - L}, \qquad (1)$$

where C is the actual capacity at the IP level, C_L is the capacity at the link level, O is the overhead needed to encapsulate the IP packet, and L is length of the Ethernet frame. Therefore, the actual capacity of a link varies with the transmission technology. Example 4 further clarifies the concept.

Example 4: Compute the capacity of a path for a 10 base T link with an Ethernet frame size of 1,400.

Solution: Given $C_L = 10\,\text{Mbps}$, $O = 38$ bytes and $L = 1{,}400$ bytes, inserting values in Eq. (1), we get $C = 9.73\,\text{Mbps}$.

The capacity of a path that consists of several links is equivalent to the capacity of the link with the minimum capacity. For this reason, the minimum capacity link is also called the *narrow link*.

- *Available bandwidth*: The available bandwidth is the unused capacity of the link. At any moment a link is either transmitting at full speed or idle [31]. Therefore, the utilization (μ) of a link is expressed as an average which is computed over a series of time intervals. Hence, the available bandwidth (A) is equal to the total capacity minus average usage, where usage is expressed as a fraction of the total capacity:

$$A = C(1 - \mu). \qquad (2)$$

[f] Checksum to detect errors in the frame.

[g] A preamble is a seven byte field, which is a combination of ones and zeros. It is used for synchronization purposes. The preamble field is followed by a one byte start of frame delimiter (SFD). The combination of both the preamble and SFD fields takes eight bytes.

[h] The interframe gap is a delay a network device must wait before it can attempt to transmit a frame. This ensures that a device which has previously transmitted a frame has reverted back to the listening mode. The interframe gap must be 96 bit times. For 10 Mbps, it takes 100 ns to transmit one bit; therefore, 96 bit times is equal to 9.6 μs, which is equal to 12 bytes.

The link with the minimum available bandwidth is known as the *tight link*. The available bandwidth of a path is equal to the available bandwidth of the tight link.

3.4.1. *Measurement Strategies*

The available bandwidth of a path can be computed by measuring the amount of data transferred over a unit time. Strauss [41] has categorized the existing bandwidth measurement tools into two models:

- *Probe Gap Model (PGM)*: The sender sends two probes that are separated by a time interval of t_1. The two probes arrive at the receiver separated by an interval of t_2. If $t_2 > t_1$, it implies that the probes have experienced a delay during their traversal. Assuming a single bottleneck that induces delay, $t_2 - t_1$ is the amount of delay experienced at the bottleneck. If the capacity (total bandwidth) of the bottleneck is known to be C, then the utilization at the bottleneck is

$$\mu = C\left(\frac{t_2 - t_1}{t_1}\right). \tag{3}$$

  Since the model assumes a single bottleneck, the utilization of the path is also equal to the utilization at the bottleneck. Therefore, the available bandwidth of the path is

$$A = C\left(1 - \frac{t_2 - t_1}{t_1}\right). \tag{4}$$

  A major limitation of the PGM is that it assumes that there is a single bottleneck with a known capacity.
- *Probe Rate Model (PRM)*: The PRM is based on the idea of creating congestion in the network. A series of packets are sent along the path. If the sending rate of packets at the sender matches with the arrival rate of packets at the receiver, then it implies no congestion. Therefore, the sending rate is increased to the point where the arrival rate becomes lower than the sending rate. At this point congestion is detected in the network, and the instance is referred to as a turning point. The sending rate just before the beginning of congestion denotes the available bandwidth. Note that the PRM has a larger overhead as compared to the PGM as it requires induction of congestion in the path.

4. Measurements Tools

This section describes some important measurement tools. The section is divided into five subsections. The first four are dedicated to each specific network characteristic, while the last subsection describes some tools that have multiple usages.

4.1. *Latency Measurements*

- *Ping*: Ping is a widely used latency measurement utility. It is built into most operating systems, including UNIX and Windows. Ping has multiple usages: it can be used to measure RTT between two hosts or to detect packet loss along a path. It works by sending ICMP "echo request" packets to the destination host and listening to the ICMP "echo reply" messages. The ICMP "echo request" is a type of message which must be replied by every host or a router via the ICMP "echo reply" message and the data of the "echo request" message must be unaltered in the "echo reply" message.

  The sending host sends a series of ping messages that are identified using probe sequence numbers and the corresponding "echo reply" messages are used to compare the time stamps of the probes and compute RTT. Ping infers a statistical summary of the path latency characteristics including minimum, maximum and average RTT and the packet loss to the destination host. Ping is an inexpensive and flexible measurement utility since it does not require the destination host to run any service or listen to any particular port.
- *Fping*: Fping [9] is an enhancement to the ping utility. Ping is limited as it can only send messages to a single destination host at a time. Fping improves upon this restriction by sending probes to multiple hosts. The hosts can be specified on the command line or through a file. However, the underlying protocol of fping is still ICMP.

  Both ping and fping may have limited accuracy as many routers or firewalls filter or rate-limit ICMP packets due to security concerns [37]. Recall that we mentioned that every host that receives "echo request" sends an "echo reply". If a firewall filters ping packets then it will drop the packet before it reaches its intended destination. Since the packet will be dropped, the destination will not receive an "echo request" message and the "echo reply" message will not be sent. In such a case, the usability of ping remains limited. Several additional tools which measure latency, as well as other network characteristics, are described in Sec. 4.5.

4.2. *Loss Rate*

Latency measurement techniques (such as ping) utilizing an active monitoring approach can be used to estimate loss rate along the path. Packet loss can be detected by using a timer. Usually, a timer is set whenever a probe request is sent, and is cancelled when the probe response is received. In this manner, a signal is raised whenever a response is not received, which indicates a lost packet. We now describe how the sting tool can be utilized to estimate loss rate in both directions.

- *Sting*: Sting [37] is a TCP-based tool which measures packet loss between two Internet hosts. It can precisely detect the direction of the packet loss, i.e., if the loss has occurred in the forward direction (from source to target) or in the reverse direction from (target to source). Sting requires the target host to run a TCP-based service such as a web or telnet server. The sting protocol is divided into two phases.

In the first phase, the source host sends a series of TCP data packets to the service running on the target host. Each packet has a sequence number[i] one greater than the sequence number of the preceding packet in the series. The target host responds with an acknowledgment for each received packet. In the second phase, the source host initially sends a data packet with a sequence number one greater than the sequence number of the last data packet sent in the first phase. The target host responds by sending a probe with an appropriate acknowledgment number such that if packet loss occurs during the first phase then the acknowledgment number indicates the sequence number of the first lost packet, otherwise the acknowledgment number indicates the next expected packet. In the case of packet loss during the first phase, the source responds by retransmitting the lost packet. The process continues until all the lost packets are retransmitted. At the end of the second phase, the loss rate can be computed using the total number of packets sent and the number of retransmitted packets.

The procedure described above is useful for computing packet loss in the forward direction. For packet loss in the reverse direction, the sender counts the number of acknowledgments received from the target. In order to ensure that the target sends an acknowledgment for each packet received from the sender and does not delay sending the acknowledgment, the sender sends the packet with some delay.

Example 5: Let sting be used to detect packet loss along a path. Given the source sends 100 packets during the first phase and three packets during the second phase, compute the packet loss in the forward direction.

Solution: In the first phase, 100 packets are sent. In the second phase, the source sends three packets. Therefore, two of the three packets must be the retransmitted packets. Therefore, $100 - 2 = 98$ packets are received at the target. Hence, the forward loss rate is $2/100 = 2\%$.

---

[i]Recall that in TCP each packet has a 32-bit sequence number and a 32-bit acknowledgment number. The sequence number uniquely identifies each packet and is used to arrange the incorrectly ordered arrival of packets at the target. The acknowledgment number is used by the target to acknowledge the receipt of the data packet. When a target host receives a packet, it sends an acknowledgment back to the sender with the acknowledgment number equal to the expected sequence number of the next packet. The acknowledgment number also implies that all the packets with the preceding sequence number have been received by the target. The acknowledgment number is not incremented if a message is received that is not in the correct order. For efficiency, many implementations of TCP delay sending the acknowledgment until they receive the next packet or a timeout occurs.

4.3. Path Detection

- *Traceroute*: Traceroute (tracert in Windows) is a path tracing utility that is used for path detection or network failure diagnosis. Traceroute works by sending a series of IP packets with incremental values of the TTL. At each step, three packets with the same TTL value are sent. For instance, the first three packets have a TTL value of one while the next three packets contain a TTL value of two, and so on. When the first series of packets (with a TTL of one) arrives at the first hop, the router discards the packet and sends an ICMP "time exceeded" message with its address as the source address to the original sender. In this manner, a series of traceroute messages are sent in which a TTL value is gradually incremented; the sending host then collects the information about each router along the path and constructs the network path. The traceroute utility prints the information about each hop-router on the screen. During this process, if a message is lost, or if a router is configured not to reply with an ICMP "time exceeded" message, then an asterisk (*) is printed.

  The choice of the underlying protocol for the traceroute is platform dependent. The original specification proposed by Jacobson [14] uses UDP packets, with UNIX utilizing the same choice. The UDP packets are destined for ports from 33434 to 33534. These ports are used by traceroute since they are unlikely to be selected by an application. Thus, when the destination receives a probe at the port at which no service is running, it responds with an ICMP "destination unreachable" message. The Windows implementation of traceroute utilizes ICMP "echo request" (similar to ping). Note that this does not alter the reply from the router when TTL reaches one, as in both the cases (UNIX or Windows), the router will send the ICMP "time exceeded" message to the original sender.

  Due to security issues, some networks block incoming traceroute packets. In such a scenario, traceroute can only display the router hops up to the firewall router of the network.
- *TCPtraceroute*: TCPtraceroute is a TCP-based implementation of traceroute. The motivation behind using TCP is to bypass firewalls that block UDP and ICMP, as most firewalls permit TCP-based inbound traffic. Unlike conventional traceroute schemes which send UDP or ICMP echo messages and wait for ICMP "time exceeded" messages, TCPtraceroute sends a TCP SYN message to the destination port 80 (since port 80 is the known port for the Web, most firewalls allow packets intended for port 80). If the target host is running any service on port 80 then it responds with a SYN ACK, otherwise it will reply with an RST message. If the sender receives a SYN ACK message then it will send an RST message to reset the connection.
- *Paris Traceroute*: Paris traceroute [1] was developed to improve the accuracy of the traceroute utility. Traceroute suffers from two major flaws: first, it can occasionally report false links between routers, and second, it can miss existing

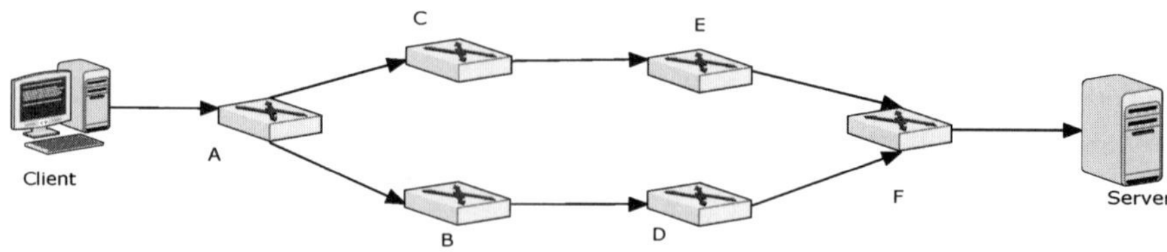

Fig. 4. Traceroute problems (based on the example mentioned in [Ref. 1]).

links between the routers. To understand these two deficiencies, consider the example illustrated in Fig. 4.

The traceroute client sends traceroute packets with increasing TTL to the server. Router A implements load balancing[j] and selects either router C or router D based on the load balancing policy. For the first traceroute packet sent by the client with a TTL value of one, router A drops the packet and replies with an ICMP "time exceeded" message. If the second packet with a TTL value of two is forwarded to router B (where it is dropped) and the third packet with TTL value of three is forwarded to router C (where it is dropped at router E), then it would appear that there is a link between router B and router E. Additionally, the link between router C and router E remains unnoticed. The first flaw is the appearance of a false link between C and D, while the second deficiency is the failure to observe the link between C and E.

Paris traceroute corrects these two problems by maintaining the probe packet header in a manner that permits all probes to follow the same path in the case of per-flow load balancing [1]. In order to achieve this, Paris traceroute modifies the packet header information such that the load balancing portion of the header remain constant. This implies that the other fields in the header are modified such that the load balancing fields remain constant and the response packets are matched with the probe packets. Paris traceroute achieves this task as follows. In the case of ICMP traceroute packets, Paris traceroute modifies the sequence number and the identifier field. For UDP packets, Paris traceroute varies the checksum field. Since checksum is used for data integrity, the payload of the packet is also modified.

However, since per-packet load balancing is random, Paris traceroute is unable to completely eliminate these problems when per-packet load balancing is used.

[j] A router has multiple interfaces. Load balancing implies that in order to route a message to the destination, a router selects an interface based on the load on the network. Load can be balanced based on per-packet, per-flow or per-destination policy [3, 16]. In per-packet balancing, each packet is balanced separately, whereas per-flow balancing works by sending all the packets of a particular flow to the same interface. A flow is identified using various fields in the IP header and the transport header. These include the source address, source port, destination address, destination port, the protocol, the type of service (TOS), the ICMP code and the checksum fields. In the per-destination policy, load is balanced according to the destination.

4.4. *Bandwidth*

- *Pathload*: Pathload [15] is a bandwidth measurement tool based on the PRM model. It induces congestion in the network and monitors the OWD between the source and the target. The moment where the OWD increases marks the start of congestion and the bandwidth can be computed. Note that in order to compute OWD, pathload does not require synchronized clocks at both ends as it is only interested in detecting changes in OWD.
- *Pathchar*: Pathchar [26] is a tool to measure capacity at each hop. Like the traceroute utility, it uses the TTL field in the packet header to get a response from each hop and measure RTT.

  The path-capacity estimation is based on the principle that the RTT to each hop consists of three components: (i) serialization delay, which is the time utilized to serialize the packet for transmission along a path, (ii) propagation delay, the time taken by a packet to traverse along the path, and (iii) queuing delay, the delay encountered by a packet while waiting in a queue at the router before being processed. Of the three delay components, the serialization delay depends upon the size of the packet (L) and the capacity (C) of the path, i.e., L/C, the propagation delay, is constant, whereas the queuing delay varies with the size of the packet and the available bandwidth of the path.

  To measure path capacity at hop n, pathchar sends a series of probes of the same packet size and with a fixed TTL value of n. The nth hop router responds by sending an ICMP "time exceeded" message for each received probe. Pathchar obtains the RTT from the ICMP response for each probe. In this manner, a series of RTT values for the nth hop are obtained. Pathchar assumes that the minimum RTT observed represents an instance in which the probe and its response did not experience any queuing delay. Therefore, the minimum RTT value consists of only two components: (i) propagation delay and (ii) serialization delay. Of the two, the latter is a function of path capacity and packet size. Since packet size is known, the path capacity can be computed via the slope of the minimum RTT up to hop n [31].

  One major limitation of pathchar is that it assumes that every router which receives an IP packet with TTL of one responds with an ICMP "time exceeded" message. This assumption works fine for layer-3 routers; however, for layer-2 routers, which operate at the link layer and route messages on MAC addresses, this is not true [32]. Layer-2 devices create serialization delays based on packet size and path capacity, but they do not respond with ICMP error messages. As a result, the estimated capacity is not accurate.
- *Spruce*: Spruce [41] is a bandwidth measurement tool that is built on the PGM model. It uses a probe pair to estimate the available bandwidth along a path. It utilizes a series of probe pair responses and computes the average.
- *TCP throughput or Bulk Transfer Capacity (BTC) measurement*: TCP throughput is the capability of the path to transfer TCP traffic in bulk. Note that

this capability may differ from the actual capacity of the path for many reasons. These include TCP flow control, packet loss, TCP congestion avoidance, and routing preferences. Since a large portion of Internet activity is made up of TCP traffic, TCP throughput provides an estimate of effective communication capacity in most cases.

Iperf [13] is a tool that measures TCP throughput over an Internet path. It works by sending bulk TCP streams over the path and measuring the amount of payload and the delay encountered for transmission. Iperf requires access to two machines that can act as a sender and a receiver. It provides various configuration options to the user.

Iperf can also be used for measuring UDP throughput. Alternatively, iperf can also be used to generate bulk amounts of TCP/UDP traffic in the network. It is available for major operating systems including UNIX and Windows and also has an available GUI interface.

4.5. *Multi-Purpose Tools*

In Sec. 4.1, we described the ping tool, which can be used to measure RTT and loss rate. We also explained traceroute in Sec. 4.3, which can be used to detect the route, measure RTT or estimate packet loss. Besides the ping and the traceroute utilities there are several other tools which have multiple usages.

- *Scriptroute*: Scriptroute [38, 39] is a public network measurement infrastructure. It allows users to run their network measurement scripts through a Web interface and measure latency, detect packet loss or estimate a path. The scriptroute facility maintains a list of active servers which run the scriptroute daemon.

  Each active server runs a web server through which it accepts user scripts via the CGI post format. The measurement scripts are written in Ruby, a user friendly scripting language. The Web server invokes the Ruby interpreter which parses the script and interacts with the scriptroute daemon to facilitate measurement in a controlled environment. The scriptroute daemon sends measurement packets via a raw socket[k] interface. Scriptroute measurement packets are generated based on the type of request submitted by the user. For instance, if a user desires to execute traceroute to the destination host then TTL-limited UDP messages will be generated. Finally, the response from the destination is matched to the probe request and the result is displayed on the web interface.

  The major advantage of scriptroute is that it aims to provide general availability to normal users. Another benefit is that the measurements are run in a controlled environment to prevent security threats such as DOS attacks.
- *Pathping*: Pathping [27] is a multi-purpose network utility. It is used to detect the route to the destination and compute hop-level RTT and loss rate, i.e., latency

[k]Raw socket is a term used to denote a socket that is delivered to an application without stripping the headers, i.e., without going through the TCP/IP stack.

and loss rate for all the intermediary hops from the source to the destination. It is built into the Windows operating system.

Pathping is a combination of traceroute (tracert) and ping. It first sends the traceroute messages to the destination host and determines all the intermediary routers. It then sends ping messages (through ICMP "echo messages") to the intermediary routers and computes latency and loss rate. The advantage of pathping is that it can detect the packet loss to intermediary routers and thus can be used for network diagnosis. Since the analysis is computed over a longer time period, the results are extensive compared to the normal ping. For this reason, pathping analysis could also take a longer time.

5. Indirect Measurements

The measurement aspects explained so far employ direct measurements, i.e., end-to-end characteristics of a path are measured directly, either through actively sending probes to the destination and reading the response, or through passively monitoring existing flows sent by some other application.

A direct mode provides a rapid and accurate mechanism for measurements. However, the schemes based on direct measurements have limited scalability. In a network of n nodes, if each node is to measure the characteristics of paths between itself and every other node then there would be $O(n^2)$ end-to-end measurements.

Therefore, often indirect measurements are utilized for improved performance. The indirect mode involves the use of heuristics or tomography to estimate the network characteristics of a path. The direct measurements from one or more components of a path are utilized to estimate end-to-end characteristics. As a result, the indirect method is not precise, but it incurs a lower overhead. In large networks and in applications where an approximate measurement is sufficient (such as locating proximity of a node), indirect measurements are utilized. Figure 5 illustrates an example of indirect measurements, where network characteristics of a path between nodes A and C can be estimated if the characteristics of paths AB and BC are known.

End-to-end path characteristics are computed through an aggregation function, which varies with the network characteristics. For instance, in the case of latency, the overall latency from node A to node C is the sum of the latencies for the paths

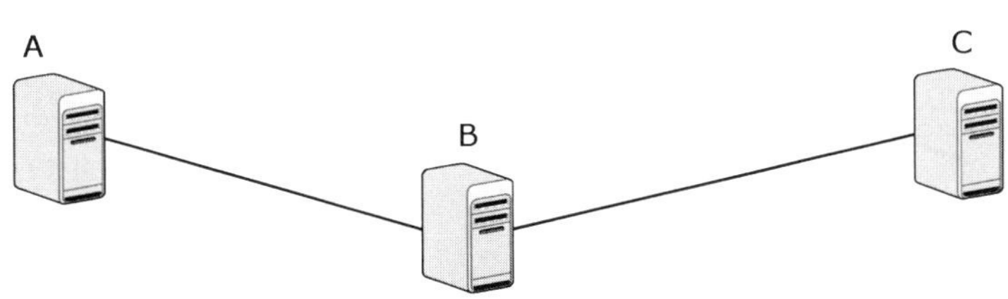

Fig. 5. Example of indirect measurement.

AB and BC. However for bandwidth, the minimum bandwidth of the paths AB and BC will be used.

An important consideration for indirect measurements is that the information about network characteristics of different paths needs to be exchanged among different nodes. For the example mentioned in Fig. 5, in order to compute the path characteristics for the path AC, node A must obtain information about the path BC.

Figure 5 is a specific example of indirect measurements. Other techniques including inference based on evidence measurements from nearby hosts also exist. A few such methods are described below.

- *King*: King [11] is a latency estimation tool that utilizes recursive DNS queries. To estimate the latency between two Internet hosts, it first finds the DNS servers that are topologically close to the two end hosts. The network latency between the two DNS servers is then computed using recursive DNS queries, which is also approximated as the latency between the two hosts.
- *IDMAPS*: The IDMAPS [8] project utilizes special hosts, called tracers, deployed widely across the Internet. Each tracer measures its distance to all the other tracers and also to a set of hosts involving nearby IP addresses. The measured distance is sent to a set of dedicated servers called HOPS, to build a virtual topology. HOPS servers estimate the latency between two end hosts as the sum of the latencies between the hosts and their nearest traces, plus the distance between the tracers. Figure 6 illustrates the concept of the IDMAPS approach.
- *Iplane*: The iplane [19] project from the University of Washington can be used to detect paths, estimate loss rate or approximate latency. It utilizes a large number of special hosts called vantage points that are distributed throughout the Internet. Vantage points send measurement probes to each other and generate an atlas of the Internet core. The iplane is built on the idea that if there are a large number of vantage points then the latency between two Internet hosts is approximately

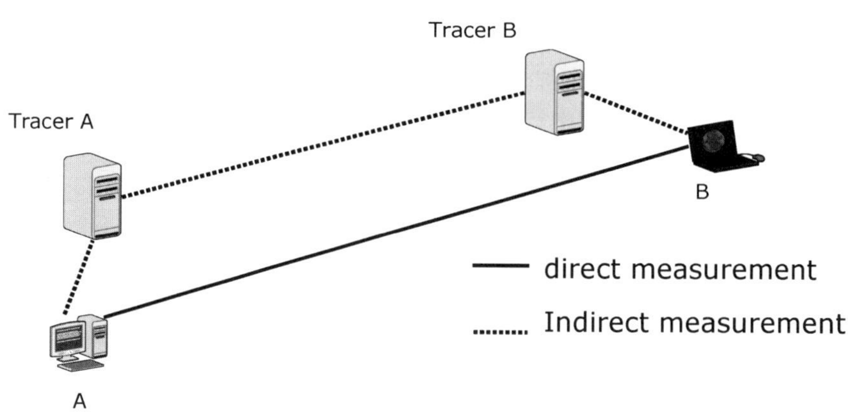

Fig. 6. Idmaps approach for latency measurement.

equal to the latency between their nearby vantage points. The atlas is utilized to predict network characteristics in this manner.

6. Thoughts for Practitioners

Whether developing a tool to measure network behavior, or using an existing technique for measurement, two factors are of particular importance. First, the accuracy of the measurements should meet the requirements of an application, and second, the measurements should bear a low cost.

Two aspects are significant for improving accuracy and reducing overhead: (i) correctness of the measurement or estimation techniques, and (ii) precise implementation of the algorithm to obtain accurate results. Sections 2–5 were related to explaining basic concepts and describing various measurement strategies. In this section, we focus on improving implementation strategies.

In general, many strategies could be significant for developing an efficient measurement utility:

- *Efficient design for the measurement tool*: This includes better utilization of the available resources such as CPU, memory and the network. For instance, selecting an appropriate number of threads and processes, ensuring mutual exclusion for the critical section, choosing suitable methods for inter-process communication, and selecting the proper mechanism for detecting timeouts, using signals and timers.
- *Selecting an efficient method for data collection*: For instance, in case of active monitoring, appropriate socket communication for sending probes and receiving responses should be used.
- Proficient strategies for analyzing network data.
- Accurate and efficient methods for clock synchronization and time stamping.

Of the four points mentioned here, the first two are related to operating system concepts and socket communication techniques. Therefore, they will not be discussed further in this chapter. The latter two points are related to network measurements and are explained below.

6.1. *Analyzing Network Traffic*

- *Tcpdump*: Tcpdump is a command line tool used to analyze network traffic. It is built into most versions of UNIX including Linux, BSD and Solaris. The Windows version of tcpdump is called WinDump. Tcpdump can be used to analyze network packets including packet header and data (pay load) information. It is a very powerful tool that can be configured for the analysis of packets that match user-specific criteria (for instance, all packets destined for port 80).

  Tcpdump utilizes the Berkeley Packet Filter (BPF) to capture packets. The BPF filter has two components: a network tap and a user-defined filter.

The network tap is used to capture packets, while the filter is used to check if the packet should be accepted, and how much of it should be delivered to the application [20]. The BPF can be used to place the network interface card in promiscuous mode. In promiscuous[1] mode, the network card captures all the packets going through the network and not just the packets destined for it. When a device driver (of the Ethernet card) senses a packet, it forwards the packet to the BPF, which passes it through the user-specific filter (the tcpdump filter in this case). The packets that match the user-specific criteria are forwarded to the user-level program. Note that in this manner any other program (such as ethereal, a network analysis tool) which uses the BPF filter can also retrieve its desired packets. To each packet forwarded to the application, BPF attaches a timestamp for the captured packet.

The use of the BPF filter by tcpdump makes it a very powerful tool. A tcpdump program running on a host can be used to analyze network traffic originating from (or destined to) a different host in the network. Note that in this manner, a network device can also be configured as a tap, or a passive monitoring device such that the packets can be copied, while the normal operation between the sender and the destination remains uninterrupted (Sec. 2.2).

Since tcpdump can be used for network analysis of any host in the network, many implementations of UNIX restrict the configuration of network devices in promiscuous mode to the superuser (root).

- *Libpcap*: The back-end of the tcpdump tool is based on libpcap, an application programming interface (API) used for capturing and analyzing packets.

Example 6: Open the device in promiscuous mode.

Solution: The tcpdump tutorial mentions the following system call for opening a device in promiscuous mode:

```
pcap_t *pcap_open_live(char *device, int snaplen, int promisc,
int to_ms, char *ebuf)
```

where

`pcap_t` is a handle returned by the function call,
`device` is the name of the Ethernet card sniff into
`snaplen` is an integer which defines the maximum number of bytes to be captured by pcap,
`promisc` is 1 (true) if the device is to be set in the promiscuous mode,
`to_ms` is the timeout in milliseconds; a 0 means no timeout, and
ebuf is for storing error messages.

[1]In non-promiscuous mode, network interfaces only capture packets destined for them or the packets that are broadcast to the whole network.

By using libpcap, a programmer can develop his or her own version of tcpdump, build a packet sniffer, or analyze captured data in several ways. Libpcap is based on the C language (the Windows version is WinPcap). For programming in other languages wrappers are provided. Example 6 shows the function call (of the pcap library) which can be used to open the device in the promiscuous mode. A detailed description and tutorial can be found at the tcpdump/libpcap website [42].

6.2. *Clock Synchronization*

Accurate CPU clock is needed for precise time stamping as well as for measuring OWD. In general, there are two clocks in a computer, a battery-powered hardware clock and a software clock. The hardware clock is used to keep track of time when the system is turned off, while the software clock (also called the CPU clock) is used to access the time when the computer is in operation. Software clock maintains a timer to generate timer interrupts and keep track of system time.

The software clock generally runs at a slightly different rate to the actual time. The rate is also affected due to temperature, aging and environmental effects, which leads to inaccurate time from the software clock. In order to correct this error, CPU clocks are generally synchronized with a timing source. The process of synchronizing the CPU clock with a reference source is called *clock synchronization*. The difference in the rate of the two clocks is called *clock drift*, whereas the difference in actual time is known as *clock skew*. The timing source for clock synchronization is generally through a time server in the network. The standard timing source for computers on the Internet is the National Institute of Standards and Technology (NIST).

Clocks can be synchronized in two ways [7]. A CPU clock is *externally synchronized* if the difference between its time and the reference time is bounded by a given constant. In a network system a set of clocks are *internally synchronized* if the difference between their times is bounded by a constant. Note that externally synchronized clocks are internally synchronized as well. However, the reverse is not necessarily true.

- *NTP*: NTP [21, 22] is the most widely and universally adopted protocol for synchronizing computer clocks across the Internet. The servers providing clock synchronization are organized in a hierarchical manner, with each level referred to as a stratum. Servers at stratum 0 (root level) are synchronized to an external reference source such as UTC (universal time coordinate) or GPS (global positioning system) and servers at the subsequent levels are synchronized with the servers at the preceding level. A client seeking clock synchronization sends NTP probes to the desired NTP server which responds with the time at the server. The NTP algorithm (at the client) compares the time of the software clock with the time at the server, computes the offset of the two clocks and adjusts the offset and rate of the software clock.

NTP offers a low cost and affordable clock synchronization mechanism for most Internet applications. However, for applications that require near-accurate clocks (such as applications measuring latency), the NTP-based clock synchronization mechanism is not acceptable [23, 24]. Due to the variable rate of the software clock, the offset of the software clock can be high, which may lead to large rate adjustments. The problem intensifies when only one-way latency is to be measured, as one-way latencies are expected to be lower than round trip latencies and an error of a few milliseconds could significantly reduce the accuracy of measurement.

- *TSC register-based clock*: To counter the limitations of NTP, a time stamp counter register (TSC) based solution has been proposed [4, 25]. The mechanism involves using a virtual clock based on the smooth oscillations of the TSC register and synchronizing the clock with a nearby NTP stratum 1 server.

6.3. *Time Stamping*

The timestamp of an event refers to the actual time of occurrence of the event. In network measurements, this normally refers to the time a probe is sent or received. Obtaining precise timestamps is pivotal for accurate network measurements.

In UNIX, the timestamp of an event is generally expressed through the C `struct timeval`, which has following members:

```
struct timeval
{
        long tv_sec; // second portion;
        long tv_usec; // micro second;
}
```

Example 7: The C `struct timeval` has microsecond (μs) precision. Is there any method available to obtain higher resolution?

Solution: The `struct timespec` provides nanosecond (ns) precision. The format is

```
struct timespec
{
        time_t tv_sec   // seconds;
        long tv_nsec    // nanoseconds;
}
```

Note that the `struct timeval` is useful for denoting the reference time (time elapsed after the occurrence of a certain event). In order to utilize this `struct` for the system time, UNIX programmers use the `gettimeofday()` system call to read the CPU clock and obtain the system time since epoch — the time elapsed since midnight UTC of January 1, 1970.

Using the `gettimeofday()` system call after receiving a probe packet or before sending a probe is not very accurate. This is because in an operating system that supports multi-tasking the processing of one task can be delayed due to scheduling of another task. If the `gettimeofday()` is called before sending a packet, the operating system (OS) could schedule another task after the `gettimeofday()` call but before sending the packet. Similarly, if the `gettimeofday()` is called after sending the packet then the OS could schedule another task after sending the packet but before calling the `gettimeofday()`. The problem persists when the response of the probe is received. There are several approaches to obtain higher accuracy.

- *RTLinux*: Since the timestamping error is associated with OS scheduling, a solution lies in minimizing the effect of OS scheduling. One such approach is to use a realtime operating system such as RT-Linux [45, 46]. The RT-Linux system runs above the hardware layer but below the Linux OS. Tasks that need deterministic processing are run as RTLinux tasks and can only be interrupted by hardware interrupt or other high priority tasks, whereas the lower priority tasks are still run by the Linux OS. RTLinux is easily available in both free and commercial versions. One major disadvantage with RTLinux is that its deployment is still limited, i.e., not many hosts on the Internet utilize RTLinux.
- *Kernel timestamps*: Even though RTLinux can correct the OS scheduling timestamping errors, using `gettimeofday()` before or after the send and receive operation is still not very accurate, as the return time from the `gettimeofday()` denotes the current system time and not the actual send or receive time of the packet. One method of obtaining packet sent or receive timestamps is to utilize kernel timestamps.

  When a network card receives a packet, the device driver (of the network card) sends an interrupt to the processor, so that kernel can pull the packet from the queue of the device driver. When Linux OS receives the packet from the driver of the network card, it also measures the timestamp. In Ref. 40, the authors have mentioned three ways of obtaining these timestamps. These are tabulated in Table 1.

Example 8: How can the `ioctl` system call be utilized to read the timestamp of a received packet?

Solution:

```
int recv_fd;
struct timeval recv_ts;
```

Create socket and receive the message using the `recv` or `recvfrom` system call

```
ioctl(recv_fd, SIOCGSTAMP, &recv_ts);
```

The `struct recv_ts` has the timestamp of the received packet.

Table 1. Kernel time stamps.

Method	Comments
`ioctl` system call	Use the `ioctl` system call with the `SIOCGSTAMP` option specified as `ioctl_type` [6]. Ping also uses `ioctl`. Only timestamps from received packets can be obtained.
`recvmsg ()`	`recv_msg` system call with `SO_TIMSTAMP`. Can be run as non-root user.
Pcap timestamps	Pcap timestamps are obtained via library libpcap [28]. The tcpdump utility in UNIX also utilizes these timestamps. One advantage is that timestamps of sent packets can also be obtained. However, the use of pcap is restricted for users with root privilege.

- *DAG cards*: So far, we have discussed improving the accuracy of timestamps by minimizing the error due to OS scheduling. However, a timestamping error can also occur by reading an inaccurate clock [25].

  The DAG card project from the University of Waikato, New Zealand solves both the problems of time stamping, i.e., error due to clock synchronization and error due to OS scheduling. The DAG card is a passive mode device that is normally connected to a hub to which the probing machine is connected.

  The internal clock of the DAG card is synchronized with the GPS time system. The DAG card can read the timestamps of sent and received packets with an accuracy of 100 ns [5], which can be obtained via tcpdump [43]. The DAG card timestamps the first bit of the probing packet, while most other network cards will timestamp only after the packet has fully arrived.

  The provision of the DAG card requires the placement of a GPS antenna on the roof of a building. This limitation, aided by the high cost of the GPS antenna, has limited its usage for end users. However, measurement facilities such as RIPE [36] use DAG cards for high accuracy.

7. Research Directions

Network measurement is an evolving topic and there are numerous directions for future research. Some of the significant trends are summarized in the following.

- The growth and expansion of the Internet has led to the proposal and deployment of new architectures and evaluation platforms such as Internet2 [12], PlanetLab [29] and GENI [10]. Many researchers are now focusing on measuring network characteristics of these architectures [17] to understand their topology and network usage. Understanding of these architectures will promote better planning for the future expansion of the Internet.
- Researchers are also utilizing network measurements to understand the usage and characteristics of popular Internet applications such as VOIP and bittorrent [30]. This will lead to improved performance from these applications.

- On the implementation side, improving clock synchronization techniques (specifically needed for OWD measurements) and better, lower cost timestamping mechanisms have also been the focus of many researchers.
- A significant amount of research proposes new techniques for indirect measurements. Since indirect measurements promote scalability, effective use of indirect measurements could promote measurements on a large scale. The focus of current research is to promote indirect measurements and estimation methods [2] that provide near-accurate measurements and have a low cost.

8. Conclusion

The growth of the Internet will continue to increase the significance of network measurements in obtaining better performance from distributed applications. In this chapter, we have explained the basic principles of network monitoring.

The chapter presents a detailed analysis of important techniques for the measurement of four important network characteristics: latency, path detection, loss rate, and bandwidth. It also describes key concepts related to network measurements, including techniques for clock synchronization, strategies for timestamping of probes, and methods for analyzing packets. The chapter also elaborates on the usefulness of different transport layer protocols (i.e., TCP, UDP and ICMP) for obtaining network measurements and describes some important measurement tools such as ping, traceroute, pathchar, sting, scriptroute, spruce and paris traceroute.

Terminology

Host: An entity that sends or receives a message. The entity could refer to an application that sends a message or the actual computer itself on which the application is deployed.

Probe: An event of capturing network information. Specifically, it involves sending message and reading its response in order to infer information about the characteristics of Internet communication between the sending and receiving host.

Probing interval: The interval between subsequent probes.

Packet: A chunk of data being transferred between two hosts. When packets are used to send information, a large message can be disassembled into packets and sent across the network. The maximum size of the packet that can be transferred across the paths is called maximum transfer unit (MTU) of the path.

Flow: A sequence of packets sent as a part of a specific application from one host to another.

Source: The host that sends a packet.

Destination: The host that is intended to receive a packet.

Hop: An intermediary host (or router) being traversed while sending a packet from source to destination. When a packet is sent from the source host to the destination host, it traverses through various intermediate hosts called routers. Each router computes the path and determines the next immediate router. The number of routers traversed from source to destination usually refers to the number of hops.

Path: The end-to-end route from source to destination. It includes all the intermediary routers that are utilized to send a packet. There could be multiple paths from source to the destination, i.e., each path could have different routers.

Queuing delay: The time spent by a packet in the queue of the router before being processed. At each hop along a path, a packet arrives at a router, which processes it and sends it to the next hop. If, at any router, the arrival rate of a packet is greater than the packet processing rate then the packets are stored in a queue. Queued packets increase the path latency. If the queue becomes full then the packets are dropped, which causes packet loss.

Congestion: The state in which the increase in the load deteriorates the quality of the network. The decrease in quality is usually observed in terms of high queuing delay, increased packet loss and denial of new connections. If the congestion lasts over a period of time then it is called persistent congestion; otherwise congestion over a short duration or spike is called transient congestion.

Timestamp: The actual time of occurrence of an event. In network measurements this normally refers to the time a probe is sent or received.

Clock synchronization: The process of synchronizing the system time with a reference source. A synchronized clock is needed in order to obtain an accurate timestamp.

Exercises

1. Suppose you modify your Web browser to obtain pcap timestamps of HTTP requests and responses. Is this an example of active or passive monitoring? Which network characteristic you can measure by using this approach?
2. What methods can be used to passively collect data?
3. What sort of problems could be yielded due to filtration of ping?
4. What is the minimum value of TTL required to send a packet from client to server, in the network configuration depicted in Fig. 4? What is the maximum number of TTL values that can be used?
5. In traceroute, how does the sending host determine not to send any further packets with increasing TTL?
6. Compute the total capacity for 100 Mbps fast Ethernet. Assume a packet size of 100 bytes.

7. Is it safe to assume that the capacity of a path remains constant? What about the available bandwidth?
8. Is the narrow link of a path the same as the tight link? Explain your answer.
9. What is the disadvantage of using TCPtraceroute?
10. As a class project you are asked to build a latency monitoring tool. Which timestamping mechanism would you use to read timestamps of sent packets?

References

1. B. Augustin *et al.*, Avoiding traceroute anomalies with Paris traceroute, *Internet Measurement Conf.* (2006).
2. Y. Chen, D. Bindel, H. H. Song and R. H. Katz, Algebra-based scalable overlay network monitoring: Algorithms, evaluation, and applications, *IEEE/ACM Trans. Network.* (2007).
3. Cisco, How does load balancing work? www.cisco.com/warp/public/105/46.html.
4. E. Corell, P. Saxholm and D. Veitch, A user friendly TSC clock, *Passive and Active Measurement Workshop* (2006).
5. DAG support documentation, www.cubinlab.ee.unimelb.edu.au/probing/docs/dag_cards.php.
6. DCROUTE an improved version of traceroute, www.cubinlab.ee.mu.oz.au/probing/dcroute.
7. C. Fetzer and F. Cristian, Integrating internal and external clock synchronization, *Real Time Systems, Special issue on global time in large scale distributed real-time systems* (1997).
8. P. Francis, S. Jamin, C. Jin, Y. Jin, D. Raz, Y. Shavitt and L. Zhang, IDMAPS: A global internet host distance estimation service, *IEEE/ACM Trans. Network.* (2002).
9. Fping measurement utility, http://fping.sourceforge.net.
10. GENI, Global Environment for Network Innovations, www.geni.net.
11. K. P. Gummadi, S. Saroiu and S. D. Gribble, King: Estimating latency between arbitrary Internet end hosts, *Internet Measurement Conf.* (2002).
12. Internet2, www.internet2.edu.
13. Iperf, The TCP/UDP bandwidth measurement tool, http://dast.nlanr.net/Projects/Iperf/.
14. V. Jacobson, Traceroute source code and documentation, available from: ftp://ftp.ee.lbl.gov/traceroute.tar.Z.
15. M. Jain and C. Dovrolis, End-to-end available bandwidth: Measurement methodology, dynamics, and relation with TCP throughput, *ACM SIGCOMM* (2002).
16. Juniper, Configuring load-balance per-packet action. www.juniper.net/techpubs/software/junos/junos70/swconfig70-policy/html/policy-actions-config11.html.
17. S. J. Lee, P. Sharma, S. Banerjee, S. Basu and R. Fonseca, Measuring bandwidth between PlanetLab nodes, *Passive and Active Network Measurement Workshop* (2005).
18. Combining active and passive network measurements to build scalable monitoring systems on the grid, *ACM Sigmetrics Performance Evaluation Review* (2003).
19. H. V. Madhyastha, T. Isdal, M. Piatek, C. Dixon, T. Anderson, A. Krishnamurthy and A. Venkataramani, iPlane: An information plane for distributed services, *Usenix OSDI* (2006).
20. S. McCanne and V. Jacobson, The BSD packet filter: A new architecture for user-level packet capture, *Winter Usenix Conf.* (1993).

21. D. Mills, Internet time synchronization: The network time protocol, *IEEE Trans. Commun.* **39**, 1482–1493 (1991).
22. D. Mills, Precisions synchronization of computer network clocks, Technical Report 93-11-1, Electrical Engineering Department University of Delaware (1993).
23. A. Pasztor and D. Veitch, High precision active probing for Internet measurement, *Proc. INET* (2001).
24. A. Pasztor and D. Veitch, PC based precision timing without GPS. *ACM SIGMETRICS Int. Conf. Measurement and Modeling of Computer Systems* (2002).
25. A. Pasztor and D. Veitch, Robust synchronization of software clocks, *Internet Measurement Conf.* (*IMC*) (2004).
26. Pathchar, www.caida.org/tools/utilities/others/pathchar.
27. Windows XP Pathping, www.microsoft.com/technet/prodtechnol/windows2000serv/reskit/cnet/cnbd_trb_vxmb.mspx.
28. Libpcap tutorial, http://www.cet.nau.edu/~mc8/Socket/Tutorials/section1.html.
29. PlanetLab, http://www.planet-lab.org.
30. J. Pouwelese, P. Garbacki, D. Epema and H. Sips, The bittorrent P2P file-sharing system: Measurements and analysis, *Inter. Workshop on Peer-to-Peer Systems — (IPTPS)* (2005).
31. Prasad, C. Dovrolis, M. Murray and K. C. claffy, Bandwidth estimation: Metrics, measurement techniques, and tools, *IEEE Network* **17**(6), 27–35 (2003).
32. R. Prasad, C. Dovrolis and B. A. Mah, The effect of layer-2 store-and-forward devices on per-hop capacity estimation, *IEEE Infocom* (2003).
33. RFC 793, Transmission Control Protocol, www.faqs.org/rfcs/rfc793.html.
34. RFC 896, Congestion Control in IP/TCP Internetworks, http://rfc.net/rfc896.html.
35. RFC 1930, Guidelines for creation, selection and registration of autonomous systems, http://tools.ietf.org/html/rfc1930.
36. RIPE Network Coordination Center, www.ripe.net.
37. S. Savage, Sting: A TCP-based network measurement tool, *USENIX Symp. Internet Technologies and Systems* (1999).
38. Scriptroute Network Measurement, www.scriptroute.org.
39. N. Spring, D. Wetherall and T. Anderson, Scriptroute: A facility for distributed Internet measurement, *USENIX Symp. Internet Technologies and Systems (USITS)* (2003).
40. N. Spring, L. Peterson, A. Bavier and V. Pai, Using PlanetLab for network research: Myths, realities, and best practices, *ACM SIGOPS Operat. Syst. Rev.* **40**(1), 17–24 (2006).
41. J. Strauss, D. Katabi and F. Kaashoek, A measurement study of available bandwidth estimation tools, *Internet Measurement Conf.* (2003).
42. Tcpdump/Libpcap Public repository, www.tcpdump.org.
43. Tcpdump FAQ, www.tcpdump.org/faq.html.
44. Unix Socket FAQ, www.unixguide.net/network/socketfaq.
45. V. Yodaiken and M. Barabanov, A real-time Linux, *Linux Applications Development and Deployment Conf. (USELINUX).* (1997).
46. V. Yodaiken, The RTLinux Manifesto, *The 5th Linux Expo* (1999).

Chapter 16

NETWORK INFORMATION FLOW AND ITS WIRELESS APPLICATIONS

JIAQING HUANG* and TEGEGNE GOBANA†

Department of Electronics and Information Engineering,
Huazhong University of Science and Technology,
Wuhan, 430074, China
**jqhuang@mail.hust.edu.cn*
†uniqute2006@yahoo.com

Network information flow (NIF) theory is a great breakthrough in information theory. The essence of NIF is that intermediate network nodes are allowed to take part in encoding and decoding. It is therefore also called network coding. One of its remarkable virtues compared with routing is that it can achieve maximum multicast capacity. This chapter describes the fundamental notions and principles of network coding as well as its typical applications, especially in wireless multi-hop scenarios. Future directions of NIF theory are discussed.

1. Introduction

In classical information theory, there are two kinds of coding (Fig. 1.): *source coding* and *channel coding*. The former aims to increase effectiveness by means of compressing source data; the goal of the latter is to enhance reliability by means of adding redundant information to detect and correct transmission errors. Note that the content addressed above concerns *end-to-end* communication.

With the increasing expansion of the Internet, network communications have to be taken into account. That is, it is necessary to consider communications from multi-point to multi-point in addition to among intermediate nodes. At the beginning of the 21st century, a brand-new theory called *network coding* was introduced [1], the pioneering work being presented in 2000 [2]. The core idea is that intermediate nodes can be allowed to do encoding and decoding (Fig. 2).

Network coding theory also showed that information flow can be compressed while commodities in classical information theory cannot [1]. In consequence, network coding theory [1] is called network information flow (NIF) theory as well. NIF is of significant enhancement of Shannon's classical information theory. In the following, two notions, network coding and network information flow, will be adopted interchangeably without specific notification.

Fig. 1. End-to-end communication.

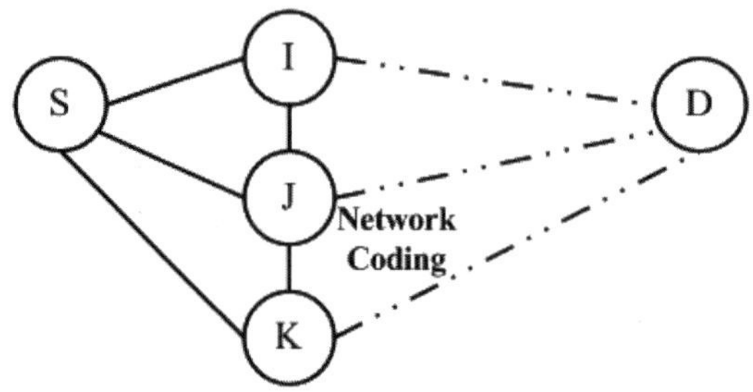

Fig. 2. Network coding: intermediate nodes can encode and decode.

The properties of network information flow and physical commodities are greatly dissimilar. Nonetheless, both obey the following two rules. In fact, information replication and coding do not increase the information content.

Theorem 1 (Law of network commodity flow [3]). *The total volume of the outflow from a non-source node cannot exceed the total volume of the inflow.*

Theorem 2 (Law of network information flow [3]). *The content of information sent out from any group of non-source nodes must be derived from the accumulated information received by the group from outside. In particular, the content of any information coming out of a non-source node must be derived from the accumulated information received by that node.*

Nevertheless, the idea of network information flow that allows coding at the intermediate nodes brings remarkable benefits. One of them is that network coding can achieve the multicast capacity. The principle will be explained by a well-known butterfly topology [1, 2] (Fig. 3) as follows.

An acyclic (directed graph without cycle) and delay-free graph with unit capacity link is given in Fig. 3(a). The source node S will send two bits a and b to sinks R_1 and R_2. Let us consider what the average maximum throughput is. Because the link UV is a bottleneck link, it can only transmit one bit at a time if only routing is allowed. Thus, as shown in Fig. 3(b), the sink R_1 can receive two bits a and b while R_2 can receive only one bit b. Likewise, as shown in Fig. 3(c), sink R_2 can receive two bits a and b while R_1 can get only one bit a. Hence, the average maximum throughput of sinks R_1 and R_2 is 1.5 bits.

On the other hand, as shown in Fig. 3(d), the average throughput can reach two bits if the intermediate node U *does* encoding (a eXtensive OR b, i.e., $a \oplus b$), and node V multicasts this encoded message to R_1 and R_2. Thus, R_1 can decode

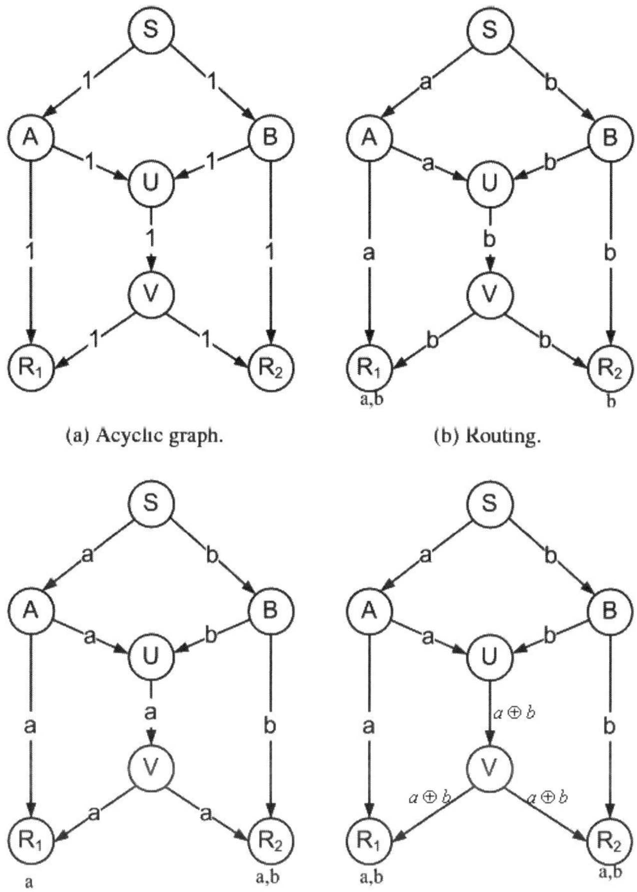

(a) Acyclic graph. (b) Routing.

(c) Routing. (d) Network coding.

Fig. 3. Butterfly topology of network coding.

to get a and b after receiving a and $a \oplus b$. Likewise, R_2 can decode to get two bits a and b after receiving b and $a \oplus b$. To sum up, the point is that the key link can transmit the coded information. In other words, the information flow is compressed.

2. Background

The brand-new notion of NIF was formally proposed by Ahlswede *et al.* [2]. It also called network coding as it allows intermediate network codes to encode. In 2003, there were several fundamental developments: Li *et al.* [3] proved that *linear network coding* suffices to achieve the optimum capacity, which is the maximum flow from the source to all sinks. Koetter and Médard [4] proposed an algebraic framework for network coding and provided an enabling tool for further research on network coding theory. Sanders *et al.* [5] and Jaggi *et al.* [6] proposed a centralized and polynomial algorithm of code construction for linear network coding. Ho *et al.* [7–9] proposed a distributed code construction algorithm for network coding, that is, *random network coding*. Chou *et al.* [10] put the idea of random network coding into practice. They took several practical factors of implementation into account, such as synchronization. The results in real networks showed the advantages of network coding. After that, network coding has been a hot area for both researchers and industrial engineers. The scope of applications covers a wide variety of areas, including peer-to-peer (P2P) networks, content distributed networks, and wireless multi-hop networks. For instance, one important application of network coding in peer-to-peer networks is called *Avalanche* [11], proposed by Gkantsidis *et al.* to apply random network coding to P2P file downloading.

3. Thoughts for Practitioners

Researchers and professionals reading this chapter should gain significant knowledge in the theory and application of network coding. Accordingly, they should consider the proper utilization of scarce network resources, especially in new emerging wireless multi-hop networks. In general, it is our hope that this chapter serves as a resource for potential researchers by providing the latest network coding concepts and practice. For a more detailed understanding of the chapter, we invite the reader to glance through reference papers indicated at the end of this chapter as well as the network coding homepage.[a]

4. Network Information Flow

In this section, the typical advantages as well as disadvantages of NIF (i.e., *network coding*) are introduced.

4.1. *Advantages of Network Information Flow*

The typical advantages of NIF are as follows.

4.1.1. *Increased Throughput*

As mentioned above in Fig. 3, NIF can increase throughput from 1.5 bits using routing to two bits using network coding. This case can be understood as increasing throughput in a multicast scenario since the source node S will send messages to two sinks R_1 and R_2.

In the following, an example of increasing throughput in the unicast scenario is demonstrated. As shown in Fig. 4(a), we consider an acyclic and delay-free graph with unity capacity link. Note that there are two sources here. Furthermore, it is a unicast scenario: source node S_1 will send one bit a to sink R_1 and the source

[a]Network coding homepage: http://www.ifp.illinois.edu/~koetter/NWC.

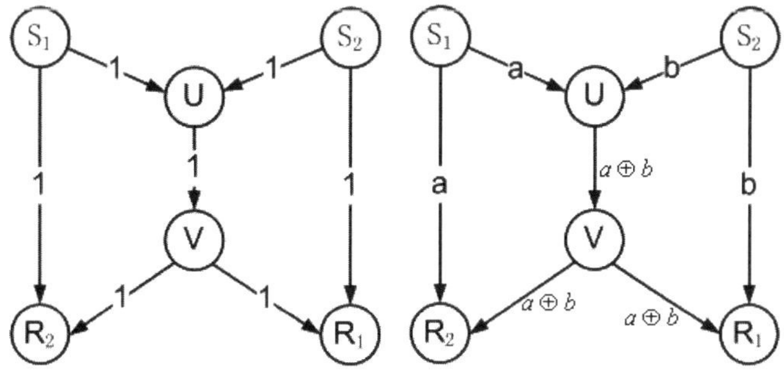

(a) Acyclic graph. (b) Network coding.

Fig. 4. Network coding in the unicast case.

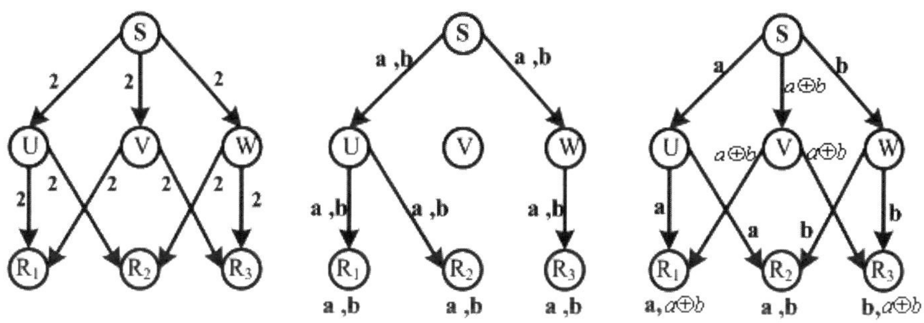

(a) Acyclic graph. (b) Multicast routing. (c) Network coding.

Fig. 5. Load balancing in network coding.

node S_2 will send one bit b to sink R_2. This aim cannot be achieved in the meantime by routing due to link UV being a bottleneck link, that is, UV can only transmit one bit at a time. However, the problem can be solved if network coding is allowed in node U. As shown in Fig. 4(b), R_1 can decode to get a from S_1 after receiving b and $a \oplus b$; at the same time, R_2 can decode to get b from S_2 after receiving a and $a \oplus b$.

4.1.2. *Load Balancing*

Network coding can perform load balancing. Consider an acyclic graph with two bits per link as in Fig. 5(a). The source node S will multicast a and b to three sinks R_1, R_2 and R_3. Let us compare between multicast routing and network coding in terms of load balancing. As shown in Fig. 5(b), S can deliver a and b to three sinks using a multicast delivery tree whose consuming bandwidth is two bits per link. Thus, the traffic concentrates on five links (SU, UR_1, UR_2, SW, WR_3) out of a total of nine links. On the other hand, network coding is adopted as shown in Fig. 5(c). The three sinks can receive a and b using nine links whose consuming bandwidth is one bit per link. As a result, traffic is uniformly distributed in all links (load balanced).

4.1.3. *Increased Bandwidth Efficiency*

Network coding can improve bandwidth efficiency. The idea can also be demonstrated in Fig. 5. Multicast routing will consume a total of ten bits by using the multicast routing tree shown in Fig. 5(b) since there are five links consuming a bandwidth of two bits per link; network coding will consume a bandwidth of only nine bits, as shown in Fig. 5(c), because it uses a total of nine links consuming a bandwidth of one bit per link. Hence, network coding can achieve the same goal while using less bandwidth. In other words, it can increase bandwidth efficiency.

4.1.4. *Reduce Number of Transmissions*

Network coding can decrease the number of transmissions. This is especially useful in wireless networks in that it can save energy. For instance, consider the scenario of the wireless network given in Fig. 6(a). There are two sources S_1 and S_2 which have one bit a and one bit b, respectively. Suppose that the two sources exchange messages with each other, that is, S_1 will send a to S_2 and S_2 will send b to S_1 through the intermediate node E.

As shown in Fig. 6(b), it requires four time slots for S_1 and S_2 to exchange messages if there is no network coding. Note that intermediate node E cannot receive a and b in the meantime because of the conflict issue in the wireless network. On the other hand, as shown in Fig. 6(c), it requires needs only three time slots if network coding is allowed at node E: S_1 sends a to node E; S_2 sends b to node E; node E network coding $a \oplus b$ and broadcasts $a \oplus b$ to S_1 and S_2; S_1 and S_2 perform a decoding to obtain what they require. Thus, network coding can save one time slot of transmission, thereby saving energy in a wireless network.

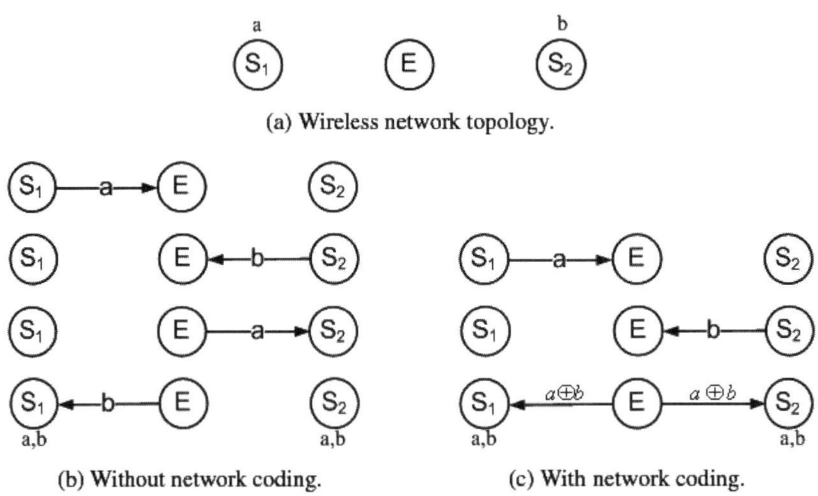

Fig. 6. Network coding can decrease the number of transmissions.

4.2. *Disadvantages of Network Information Flow*

Although network coding has many benefits, it sufferes from several problems, as outlined in the following.

4.2.1. *Increased Complexity*

Network coding will introduce a computational burden including additional memory and CPU usage since it requires intermediate network nodes to encode and decode. Also, it takes more time for network coding to transmit messages than for routing. The introduced delay will be a significant problem when network coding is applied to delay-sensitive applications, such as live broadcasting and video-on-demand.

The complexity of computation is at least $O(k)$ at the encoding node and $O(k^3)$ at the decoding nodes if k messages are transmitted [11]. At the encoding node, all available messages are combined by a linear operation with coefficient chosen in a finite *field* F. Thus, there will be an $O(k)$ operation. At the decoding node a $k \times k$ matrix of coefficients should be inverted in $O(k^3)$ and the original messages are reconstructed using Gaussian elimination.

4.2.2. *Security*

Another crucial issues with network coding is the protection against malicious nodes. As a matter of fact, when the nodes do not perform network coding, end-to-end encryption is always possible to achieve computational security against *passive* attackers, for instance, *digital signature.* However, network coding can allow an intermediate network node to combine messages from input links in addition to adding its own messages. As a result, a malicious node can introduce arbitrary messages into the system and make the reconstruction of the original messages impossible. That is termed *Byzantine active attacking* in network coding. Research is ongoing to deal with these security issues [11].

5. Linear Network Information Flow

This section describes the fundamental concepts and principles of linear network information flow (i.e., linear network coding). The reason why linear coding cooperation is of particular interest is that the coding mechanism inside a linear network code can be implemented by simple and fast circuitry.

5.1. *Global Encoding Kernel and Local Encoding Kernel*

Let S denote the source node and let R_1 and R_2 denote two sinks. For every non-source node T, let In(T) denote the set of incoming links to T and Out(T) denote the set of outgoing links from T. Let In(S) denote a set of *imaginary* links, which terminate at the source node S but are without originating nodes. The number of these *imaginary* links is denoted by ω. An acyclic network with $\omega = 2$ imaginary links appended at the source node S is given in Fig. 7(a). Let a pair of links (d, e) be called an *adjacent pair* when there is a node T with d $\in$ In(T) and e $\in$ Out(T).

Next, linear network code is formulated such that local and global encoding kernels are linear. In fact, the local and global encoding kernels are equivalent.

Definition 3 (Local encoding kernel [1]). Let F be a finite field and ω a positive integer. A ω-dimension F-valued linear network code on an acyclic network consists of a scalar $k_{\mathrm{d,e}}$, called the *local encoding kernel*, for every *adjacent* pair (d, e). In the meantime, the local encoding kernel at the node T means the $|\mathrm{In(T)}| \times |\mathrm{Out(T)}|$ matrix $K_{\mathrm{T}} = [k_{\mathrm{d,e}}]_{\mathrm{d}\in\mathrm{In(T)},\mathrm{e}\in\mathrm{Out(T)}}$.

Definition 4 (Global encoding kernel [1]). Let F be a finite field and ω a positive integer. A ω-dimension F-valued linear network code on an acyclic network consists of a scalar $k_{\mathrm{d,e}}$, called the *local encoding kernel*, for every *adjacent* pair (d, e) as well as an ω-dimension column vector f_{e} for every link e such that

$$\text{(i)}\quad f_{\mathrm{e}} = \sum_{\mathrm{d}\in\mathrm{In(T)}} k_{\mathrm{d,e}} f_{\mathrm{d}}, \quad \text{where } \mathrm{e} \in \mathrm{Out(T)}; \tag{1}$$

$$\text{(ii)}\quad \text{The vectors } f_{\mathrm{e}} \text{ for the } \omega \text{ imaginary links } \mathrm{e} \in \mathrm{In(S)} \text{ form the natural basis of the vector space } F^{\omega}. \tag{2}$$

The vector f_{e} is called the *global encoding kernel* for the link e.

Let the source generate a message x in the form of an ω-dimension row vector. A node T receives the symbols $x \cdot f_{\mathrm{d}}$,d $\in$ In(T), from which it calculates the symbol $x \cdot f_{\mathrm{e}}$ for sending onto each link e $\in$ Out(T) via the linear formula [1].

$$x \cdot f_{\mathrm{e}} = x \cdot \sum_{\mathrm{d}\in\mathrm{In(T)}} k_{\mathrm{d,e}} f_{\mathrm{d}} = \sum_{\mathrm{d}\in\mathrm{In(T)}} k_{\mathrm{d,e}} (x \cdot f_{\mathrm{d}}). \tag{3}$$

Hence, given the local encoding kernels for all the links in an acyclic network, the global encoding kernels can be calculated *recursively* in any upstream-to-downstream order by Eq. (1), while Eq. (2) provides the initial conditions.

Example 5.. Suppose the number of imaginary links is $\omega = 2$ in Fig. 7(a) and let OS and O'S denote the two imaginary links. Local and global encoding kernels are as shown in Fig. 7(b). The network code is in fact *linear*. Hence, the local encoding kernels at the nodes are the following matrices [1]:

$$K_S = \begin{bmatrix} 1 & 0 \\ 0 & 1 \end{bmatrix}, \quad K_{\mathrm{A}} = K_{\mathrm{B}} = K_{\mathrm{V}} = \begin{bmatrix} 1 & 1 \end{bmatrix}, \quad K_{\mathrm{U}} = \begin{bmatrix} 1 \\ 1 \end{bmatrix}.$$

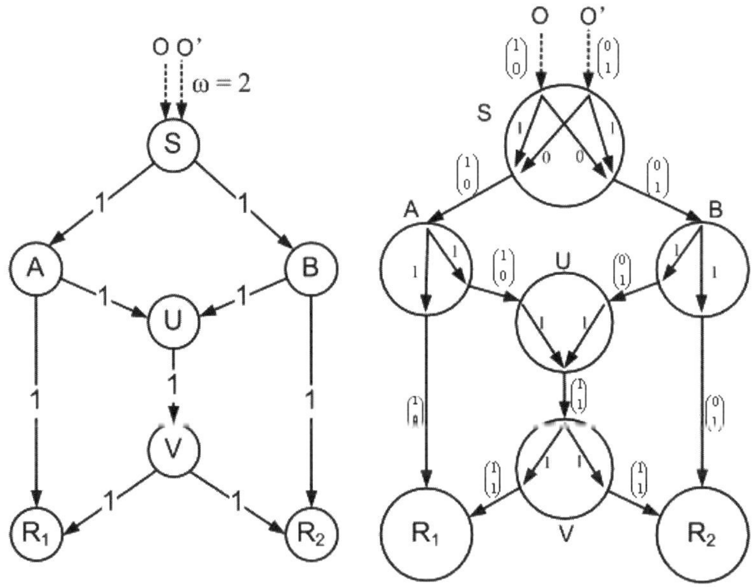

(a) Imaginary links. (b) Local/global encoding kernel.

Fig. 7. Linear network code.

The corresponding global encoding kernels are

$$f_{\mathrm{e}} = \begin{bmatrix} 1 \\ 0 \end{bmatrix} \quad \text{for e} = \mathrm{OS}, \mathrm{SA}, \mathrm{AU}, \mathrm{AR}_1,$$

$$f_{\mathrm{e}} = \begin{bmatrix} 0 \\ 1 \end{bmatrix} \quad \text{for e} = \mathrm{O'S}, \mathrm{SB}, \mathrm{BU}, \mathrm{BR}_2,$$

$$f_{\mathrm{e}} = \begin{bmatrix} 1 \\ 1 \end{bmatrix} \quad \text{for e} = \mathrm{UV}, \mathrm{VR}_1, \mathrm{VR}_2.$$

5.2. *Properties of Linear Network Coding*

Denote the maximum flow from the source node S to a non-source node T as maxflow(T). As we know, the information rate received by the node T obviously cannot exceed maxflow(T) according to the *max-flow min-cut theorem*. Similarly, denote the maximum flow from the source node S to a collection $\wp$ of non-source nodes as maxflow($\wp$). Thus, the information rate from S to the collection $\wp$ cannot exceed maxflow($\wp$) [1].

Whether this upper bound can be achieved depends on the coding scheme. In the following, three kinds of linear network codes are defined: linear multicast, linear broadcast and linear dispersion. Note: the conventional notation $\langle \cdot \rangle$ for the *linear span* of a set of vectors is employed [1].

Definition 6 (Linear multicast [1]). Let vectors f_e denote the global encoding kernels in a ω-dimension F-valued linear network code on an acyclic network. Let $V_T = \langle\{f_e : e \in \mathrm{In(T)}\}\rangle$. If $\dim(V_T) = \omega$ for every non-source node T with maxflow(T) $\geq \omega$, the linear network code qualifies as a *linear multicast.*

Definition 7 (Linear broadcast [1]). Let vectors f_e denote the global encoding kernels in a ω-dimension F-valued linear network code on an acyclic network. Let $V_T = \langle\{f_e : e \in \mathrm{In(T)}\}\rangle$. If $\dim(V_T) = \min\{\omega, \mathrm{maxflow(T)}\}$ for every non-source node T, the linear network code qualifies as a *linear broadcast.*

A linear broadcast is useful for receiving *partial* information [1]. For instance, in multi-level resolution image transmission, the image can be encoded in several resolution messages. The more messages the receiver gets, the clearer the image the reviewer will see. Thus, every non-source node T with maxflow $(T) < \omega$ receives partial information of maxflow(T) messages, which is desirable for a mobile handset when receiving a large image at a low resolution or rendering a colored image in black-and-white.

Definition 8. [Linear dispersion [1]] Let vectors f_e denote the global encoding kernels in a ω-dimension F-valued linear network code on an acyclic network. Let $V_T = \langle\{f_e : e \in \mathrm{In(T)}\}\rangle$. If $\dim(\langle U_{T\in\wp} V_T\rangle) = \min\{\omega, \mathrm{maxflow}(\wp)\}$ for every collection $\wp$ of non-source nodes, the linear network code qualifies as a *linear dispersion.*

A potential application of a *linear dispersion* is in the scalability of a two-tier broadcast system [1] as shown in Fig. 8. There is a backbone network presiding over a single source node S and a number of local area networks (LANs). Every LAN connects to the backbone network through LAN gateways. For instance, LAN1 will connect to the backbone through the gateway A; LAN2 will connect to the backbone through the gateway B. Suppose that there is a linear broadcast over the backbone network. Hence, the new LAN wants to connect to the backbone through

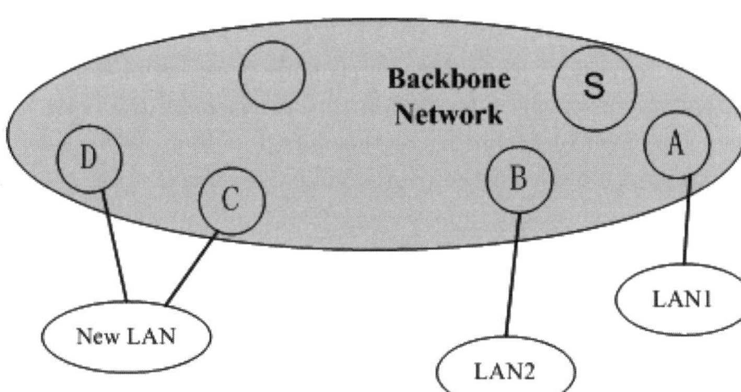

Fig. 8. Scalability of two-tier broadcast system.

a LAN gateway X with maxflow(X) $\geq \omega$. Nonetheless, it may so happen that no such node X is within the vicinity to make the connection economically feasible [1]. On the other hand, if the linear broadcast is in fact a linear dispersion, then it is sufficient to connect the new LAN gateway to any collection $\wp$ of backbone nodes with maxflow($\wp$) $\geq \omega$. That is, the new LAN can connect to gateway C and D that can be a collection {C, D} whose maximum flow is not smaller than ω, i.e., maxflow($\{C, D\}$) $\geq \omega$.

Finally, the relationships among the three properties of linear network coding are:

$$\text{Definition 6} \Leftarrow \text{Definition 7} \Leftarrow \text{Definition 8}.$$

That is, every linear dispersion is a linear broadcast, and every linear broadcast is a linear multicast. In other words, a linear broadcast is not necessarily a linear dispersion, a linear multicast is not necessarily a linear broadcast, and a linear network code is not necessarily a linear multicast. Examples can be found in detail in the book by Yeung *et al.* [1].

At last, the fourth property of linear network code, i.e. generic linear network code, is briefly introduced. An important description of this property is that ‘every collection of global encoding Kernels that can possibly be linearly independent is linearly independent [1]. Furthermore, every generic linear network code is a linear dispersion, but not vice versa. In addition to aforementioned relationship, we may conclude: generic linear network code $\rightarrow$ linear dispersion $\rightarrow$ linear broadcast $\rightarrow$ linear multicast. Thus, we call generic linear network code is the strongest property of linear of linear network code. Refer to [1] for more details.

6. Random Linear Network Information Flow

How to construct network code is one of the key problems of network coding theory. Sanders *et al.* [5] and Jaggi *et al.* [6] provided a polynomial algorithm for linear network code construction. However, it is a *centralized* scheme. In contrast, Ho *et al.* [7] proposed a *distributed* code construction scheme, called random linear network coding (RNC) [7–9], i.e., random linear network information flow, which was applied to the P2P file downloading software Avalanche by Microsoft, who claims that Avalanche will have a better performance than BitTorrent. RNC will be demonstrated in the following.

In RNC, the source will send a combination of messages to its outgoing links, while the non-source nodes will combine messages from its incoming links and forward combinations to its outgoing links. Consider the acyclic graph with unit-capacity as shown in Fig. 9. Suppose that the source node S will send a and b to two sinks (R_1 and R_2) by means of RNC. Coefficients $\gamma_1 \sim \gamma_6$ will be chosen randomly in the finite field F. The procedure is as follows: S sends combination $\gamma_1 a + \gamma_2 b$ to node A and sends combination $\gamma_3 a + \gamma_4 b$ to node B; node A sends $\gamma_1 a + \gamma_2 b$ to node U and sink R_1; node B sends $\gamma_3 a + \gamma_4 b$ to node U and sink R_2; node U combines two messages from its incoming links AU and BU, then U creates a new

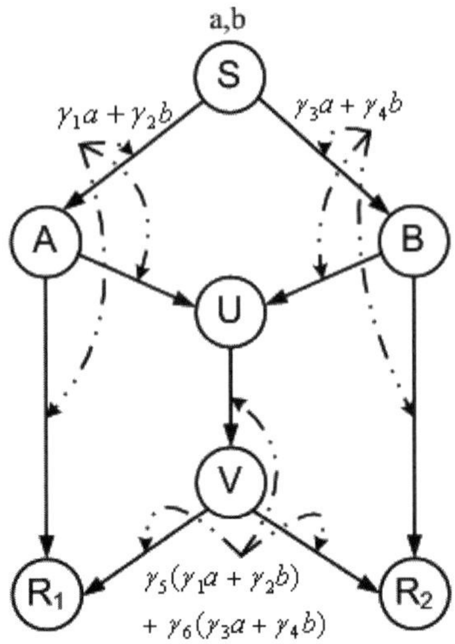

Fig. 9. Random linear network information flow.

combination $\gamma_5(\gamma_1 a + \gamma_2 b) + \gamma_6(\gamma_3 a + \gamma_4 b)$ and sends it to sink R_1 and sink R_2; R_1 receives two combinations as well as their corresponding coefficients so that R_1 can decode a and b using Gaussian elimination; R_2 can decode a and b in the same way.

It has been proved that the successful decoding probability is at least $(1 - d/q)^\eta$ for $q > d$ [7–9], where d is the number of sinks and q is the field size and η is the number of links carrying random combinations of source processes and/or incoming signals. As a matter of fact, the probability is at least $1 - 2^{-8} = 0.996$ if the field size is 2^{16} and the number of edges in the network is at most 2^8 [10].

7. Applications in Wireless Multi-Hop Networks

A wireless multi-hop network is characterized by its dynamic topological changes, limited communications bandwidth, and limited battery power of its nodes. Without prior notice, the network topology of such a network can change frequently and dramatically. The main reason for intermittent network topology is that nodes in wireless multi-hop networks are capable of moving collectively or randomly. Hence, for better utilization of network resources given such intermittent topology network coding have become an efficient algorithm.

Wireless network coding has recently gained much attention as a means to enhance overall network resources in a wireless multi-hop network that supports multiple communication flows. The basic idea is that a relay node can combine several packets intended for different destinations in a single packet that is broadcast. Each destination extracts the desired packet from the combined packet by using some previous knowledge of the other packets. Thus, the relay saves packet transmissions, which results in resource improvement. A relevant example is the network coding with the XOR operation at the relay nodes.

For many purposes, network coding is a contemporary method that can be applicable in wireless multi-hop networks such as wireless ad hoc networks, wireless sensor networks and wireless mesh networks. Network coding could improve throughput in wireless multi-hop networks by exploiting the broadcast nature of the wireless medium. In the following subsections, we detail the promising effect of network coding in different settings of wireless multi-hop networks.

7.1. *Network Coding in Wireless ad hoc Networks*

An ad hoc network is a collection of wireless mobile hosts forming a temporary network without the aid of any standalone infrastructure or centralized administration. Such networks, called mobile ad hoc networks (MANETs), are self-organizing and self-configuring multi-hop wireless networks, where the structure of the network changes dynamically. Moreover, the lifetime of an ad hoc network is constrained by each mobile node's battery capacity. In such networks network coding plays a significant role by maximizing energy efficiency, improving throughput and minimizing the number of transmissions.

The deployment of network coding in wireless ad hoc networks can help to better exploit shared resources such as wireless bandwidth, and to conserve scarce resources such as battery life. Since wireless ad hoc networks are highly dependent on the battery level of nodes participating in the network, energy efficiency could be the crucial design parameter of wireless ad hoc networks. Network coding could be interpreted as the most economical way to communicate by minimizing the energy required to transmit one bit of information through a network [12]. In fact, it has been shown that network coding can yield substantial performance gains, e.g., reduced energy consumption, in

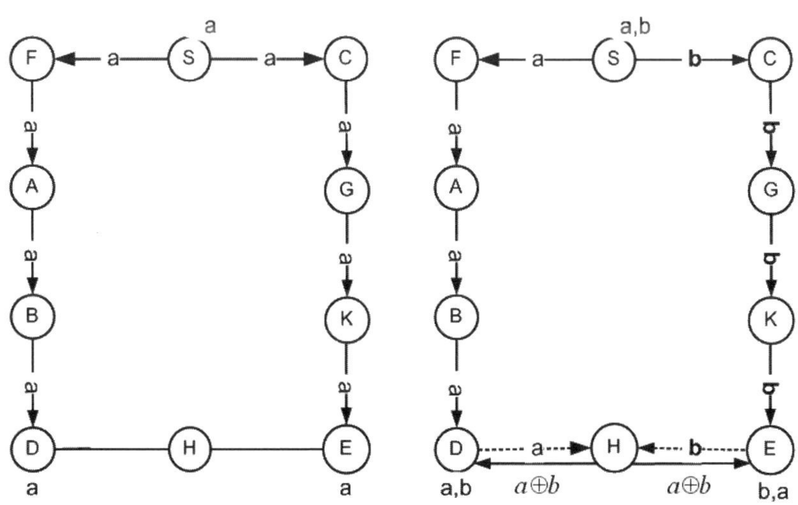

(a) With routing (transmission per bit = 7). (b) With network coding (transmission per bit = 5.5).

Fig. 10. Network coding in wireless ad hoc networks.

ad hoc networks. Figure 10 demonstrates the scenario where the minimum energy per bit can be attained by performing network coding.

For a reliable demonstration, assume that each node is equipped with a transmitter operating at a fixed transmission range, which is just sufficient to reach its lateral neighbors, but not the diagonal ones. In such conditions, each physical-layer transmission consumes a unit amount of energy.

In Fig. 10(a), the minimum amount of energy required to deliver one message from the source node S to sinks {D, E} is seven transmissions per bit using the conventional routing approach. First, S broadcasts the message a to nodes {F, C} using one transmission. Next, node F forwards it to node A; A forwards to node B and B forwards to sink D; node C forwards to node G; G forwards to node K, and K forwards to sink E.

In Fig. 10(b), the minimum amount of energy using network coding for this example network is 5.5 transmissions per bit. Suppose S has two messages, a and b. First, a is delivered to sink D with four transmissions and b is delivered to sink E with four transmissions. Next, sink D transmits a to node H and sink E transmits b to node H. The analytical step occurs at node H, which broadcasts the XOR-ed result of two messages $a \oplus b$ to sink D and sink E, consuming only one transmission. Hence, transmissions per bit amounts to 5.5 because, from 11 total transmissions of packets in a system, the decreased amount of transmissions for a single packet to reach its intended destination would be halved. Therefore, each of the two sinks can recover both a and b by solving simple linear equations. In effect, decrease in number of transmission leads into utilization of minimum energy required to transmit each bit by performing network coding.

7.2. *Network Coding in Wireless Sensor Networks*

Recent advances in wireless communications and electronics have enabled the development of low cost, low power, multifunctional sensor nodes that are small in size and communicate undeterred across short distances. These tiny sensor nodes, which consist of sensing, data processing and communicating components, leverage the idea of sensor networks. Sensor networks represent a significant improvement over traditional sensors.

Wireless sensor networks are made of small, cheap, and mostly unreliable devices equipped with limited sensing, processing and transmission capabilities, which have recently generated a fair amount of interest in communications problems involving multiple correlated sources and large-scale wireless networks. It is envisioned that an important class of applications for such networks involves a dense deployment of a large number of sensors over a fixed area, in which a physical process unfolds. The task of these sensors is then to collect measurements, encode them, and relay them to some data collection points, where this data is to be analyzed, and possibly acted upon.

Network coding has promising features applicable in wireless sensor networks, where a smart collection of tiny, dumb devices may be individually cheap, unintelligent, imprecise, and unreliable and nodes sleep most of the time to conserve energy. To make sensor network deployments economically and technologically feasible, it is necessary to considerably reduce the cost, size and energy consumption of the nodes available. Thus, the network coding mechanism has become a best-fit solution for such networks.

One hot area of research is underwater sensor networks [13, 14], which is relevant because:

(i) underwater sensor nodes are usually larger than land-based sensors and possess more computational capabilities,
(ii) the broadcast property of acoustic channels naturally renders multiple highly interleaved routes from a source to a sink, and
(iii) high error rates and long propagation delays in underwater sensor networks call for efficient error-recovery schemes.

The high error rates in underwater sensor networks imply that a certain amount of redundancy is required to recover packets at the receiver. On the other hand, the limited battery power of the sensor nodes implies that the amount of redundancy needs to be restricted to conserve their lifetimes.

Thus, network coding in underwater sensor networks needs to strike a balance between the amount of redundancy and power conservation at the sensor nodes [13, 14]. The situation is depicted in Fig. 11.

The usage of network coding in underwater wireless sensor networks is illustrated in Fig. 11(a). The source node S sends packets A, B, C and D to the sink. These packets will reach relay nodes R1, R2, R3 and R4 because of the broadcast property of the acoustic channel. Due to the high error rate in underwater environments, relay node R1 receives packets A and D and encodes them into packets Y11 and Y12; R2 receives packets A and B and encodes them into Y21 and Y22; R3 encodes its incoming packets into packets Y31 and Y32; and similarly R4 encodes into Y41, Y42, Y43 and Y44. The relay nodes then forward the encoded packets to the sink. The sink receives four encoded packets: Y11, Y21, Y31 and Y42.

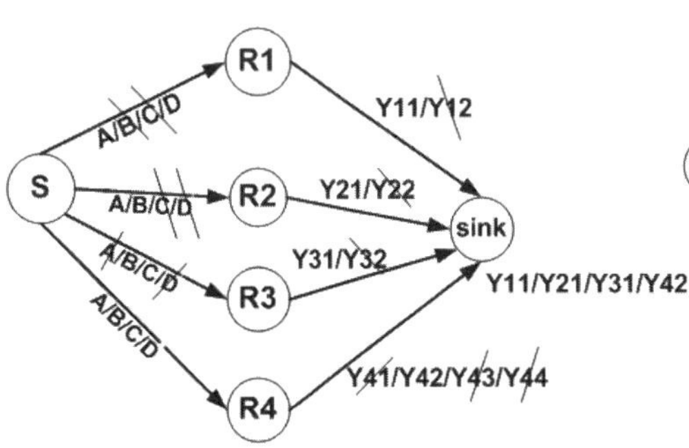

(a) With network coding.

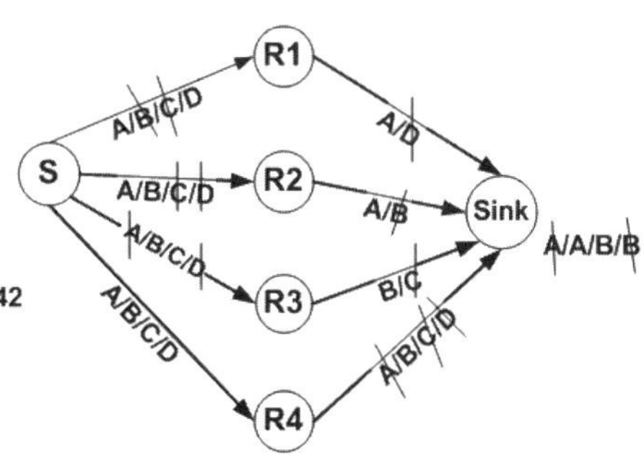

(b) Without network coding.

Fig. 11. Network coding in underwater wireless sensor networks.

When the network coding is chosen properly (e.g., using random network coding [7–9]), the sink can recover the four original packets with high probability.

As illustrated in Fig. 11(b), without the network coding scenario, when source node S sends packets A, B, C and D to the sink, due to the high error rate in the underwater environment, relay nodes R1, R2, R3 and R4 receive packets A and D; A and B; B and C; and A, B, C and D, respectively. Upon reception, without any computation, the relays then simply forward the same packets to the destination. The receiver in its counter only receives two distinct original packets A and B by omitting two redundant packets A and B [13, 14].

Therefore, applying network coding in underwater sensor networks provide efficient robustness with respect to these special conditions. Specifically, network coding is efficient in terms of both error recovery and energy consumption [13, 14].

7.3. *Network Coding in Wireless Mesh Networks*

A wireless mesh network is a mesh network created through the connection of wireless access points installed at each network user's locale. Each network user is also a provider, forwarding data to the next node. The networking infrastructure is decentralized and simplified because each node need only transmit as far as the next node. Only recently was it found that wireless mesh networks offer a fertile ground for network coding given that wireless transmissions are inherently broadcast at the physical layer and thus with coding yield better throughput even for unicast applications. Thus, in a wireless mesh network, network coding performs very well and has proven its ability at optimizing the usage of network resources.

The situation is best illustrated with COPE [15], where each node in the system snoops on the medium, learns the status of its neighbors, detects coding opportunities, and codes as long as the recipients can decode.

Let us consider the scenario illustrated in Fig. 12. Suppose that node A has a four (P5, P4, P3, P2) packet pool; node B has a three (P4, P3, P1) packet pool; node C has a three (P5, P4, P1) packet pool; node D has a three (P5, P3, P1) packet

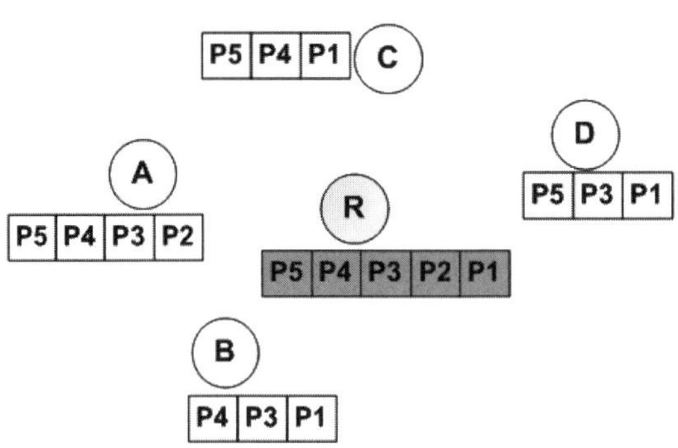

(a) Relay node R can send coded packets out.

Packets in R's queue	Next hop
P1	A
P3	C
P4	D
P5	B

(b) Next hops in R's queue.

Fig. 12. Network coding in wireless mesh network.

pool, and relay node R has a five (P5, P4, P3, P2, P1) packet pool in its output queue, and R's neighbors have overheard some of these packets. Each neighbor of node R has stored the aforementioned packets, which are depicted in Fig. 12(a). As listed in Fig. 12(b), node R can send its packets to its next hops, such as: P1 to node A, P3 to node C, P4 to node D and P5 to node B.

In such a scheme, all nodes participate in opportunistic listening [15], i.e., they listen for all communications over the wireless medium. The nodes also annotate the packets they send to tell their neighbors which packets they have heard. When a node sends, it uses its knowledge of what its neighbors have received to perform opportunistic coding [15].

Opportunistic coding [15] refers to the process of making the most efficient decision possible. The relay node (R in this example) can XOR multiple packets and send them in a single transmission if each intended receiver has enough information to decode its packet. Assuming that R knows which packets each neighbor has, it has a few coding choices that it can take, such as: (P1 $\oplus$ P3), (P1 $\oplus$ P3 $\oplus$ P4) and (P1 $\oplus$ P3 $\oplus$ P4 $\oplus$ P5). Among them, (P1 $\oplus$ P3) would be a bad coding decision for R because only two neighbors A and C can benefit from these transmissions. That is, when relay node R sends (P1 $\oplus$ P3), since node A has P3 stored, A could XOR P3 with (P1 $\oplus$ P3) to obtain the native packet, i.e., P1. Similarly, node C could XOR P1 with (P1 $\oplus$ P3) to obtain the native packet, i.e., P3. However, nodes B and D do not obtain the required packets. When relay node R sends (P1 $\oplus$ P3 $\oplus$ P4), this could be a better coding decision than the previous one because it allows nodes A, C and D to decode to obtain their respective packets that sent to them. However, node B remains a non-beneficial node, which it could not decode to obtain the required packet. Hence, relay node R should select (P1 $\oplus$ P3 $\oplus$ P4 $\oplus$ P5) because it would allow all four neighbors to receive their respective packets all at once. Thereby, it maximizes the number of packets delivered in a single transmission. It is reported that COPE could flourish the gain in throughput [15].

8. Directions for Future Research

There are many open issues concerning the emerging theory of network coding. Here, we list some interesting research directions.

(i) *Multi-source network coding.* Multi-source network coding turns out not to be a simple extension of single-source network coding [1]. Furthermore, it is a significant part of network information flow theory and there are a large number of open issues. Some current exciting areas of research include: explicitly *inner bound* and *outer bound* of *achievable information rate region*; jointly encoding and decoding between *network coding* and *source coding*, between *network coding* and *channel coding*, among *network coding*, *source coding* and *channel coding*, respectively.

(ii) *Complexity reduction of network coding* (*minimum-cost network coding*). The most common cost can be defined as the number of network coding nodes. In addition, cost can also be defined as the number of network coding operations, number of packets involved in network coding, resource cost, and so on. Many optimization tools can be adopted, e.g., graph theory, linear programming. Another significant objective is to apply delay-sensitive network coding to realtime applications, such as live broadcasting.

(iii) *Network coding in cyclic networks.* Though the problems of network coding in acyclic networks are not trivial, most results are achieved in acyclic networks due to much more complexity in cyclic networks. Nonetheless, there exist cycles in practical networks and thus it is necessary to study the properties of network coding in cyclic networks. The latest significant progress in this area is presented by Li *et al.* [16], that is, a ring-based algebraic framework of convolutional network coding is given as well as properties of convolutional multicast, convolutional broadcast, convolutional dispersion, and basic convolutional network code. Their counterparts in linear network coding are linear multicast, linear broadcast, linear dispersion, and generic linear network code. Therefore, it is reasonable to develop network coding theory in cyclic networks based on this ring algebraic framework.

(iv) *Security of network coding.* This is mentioned in Sec. 4.2.2 in detail. Solving this problem is a critical step in applying network coding to commercial applications.

(v) *Nonlinear network coding.* It is an open issue as to whether or not nonlinear network coding will provide better performance as well as lower complexity than linear network coding.

9. Conclusions

This chapter describes fundamental notions and principles of network information flow theory (network coding theory) in addition to discussing its pros and cons. Furthermore, applications in wireless ad hoc networks, wireless sensor networks and wireless mesh networks are demonstrated. We concluded by discussing the future directions of network coding.

Acknowledgments

This work is supported by the National Natural Science Foundation of China (No. 60872005), the Scientific Research Fund of Huazhong University of Science and Technology (HUST 2008), and the Fundamental Research Fund of the Department of Electronics and Information Engineering (HUST 2008). The authors are grateful to Raymond W. Yeung, Shuo-Yen Robert Li, Ning Cai and Zhen Zhang for their contributions of the book *Network Coding Theory*. The authors would also like to thank the anonymous reviewers for their constructive comments, and the editor Sudip Misra for his efforts in handling this book.

Terminology

Network information flow (NIF): A brand new theory, also called network coding compared with source coding and channel coding. Network coding allows intermediate network nodes to encode so that multicast capacity can be achieved, while routing cannot. Thus, network coding may attain better throughput performance than routing.

Network coding (NC): See *network information flow*.

Imaginary links: Denoted by $\mathrm{In}(S)$, a set of links that terminate at the source node S but are without originating nodes.

Local encoding kernel: A $|\mathrm{In}(T)| \times |\mathrm{Out}(T)|$ matrix for a given node T.

Global encoding kernel: A matrix that can be computed recursively by a local encoding kernel.

Linear multicast: One of the properties of linear network coding. Every non-source node can decode ω-dimension messages from the source if its "maxflow" is not smaller than ω.

Linear broadcast: One of the properties of linear network coding in which every non-source node T can decode $\min\{\omega, \mathrm{maxflow}(T)\}$-dimension messages from the source, where *maxflow*(T) is maxflow of node T. Every linear broadcast is a linear multicast.

Linear dispersion: One of the properties of linear network coding in which every collection $\wp$ of non-source nodes can decode $\min\{\omega, \mathrm{maxflow}(\wp)\}$-dimension messages from the source. Every linear dispersion is a linear broadcast.

Generic linear network code: One of the properties of linear network coding in which every collection of global encoding kernels that can possibly be linearly independent is linearly independent [1]. Every generic linear network code is a linear dispersion.

Random network coding (RNC): A distributed code construction method of network coding. The coefficients for linear combination are chosen randomly in a finite field. At the receive nodes, Gaussian elimination is adopted to decode the original messages.

Wireless multi-hop network: Allows stable communication with another party within an unstable network such as those used for mobile terminals. As implied by the word "multi-hop," this type of network ensures communication not only among terminals directly connected with one another, but also among terminals located further away in areas outside the range of access for radio waves by creating a relay station out of several terminals. Typical examples include mobile ad hoc networks (MANET), wireless sensor networks (WSN) and wireless mesh networks (WMN).

Mobile ad hoc network (MANET): A wireless multi-hop network that results from the cooperative engagement of a collection of mobile hosts (nodes) without any centralized access point (or an autonomous system consisting of mobile hosts connected by wireless links). It is a self-configuring network of mobile routers (and associated hosts) connected by wireless links, the union of which form an arbitrary topology. The routers are free to move randomly and organize themselves arbitrarily; thus, the network's wireless topology may change rapidly and unpredictably. Such a network may operate in a standalone fashion, or may be connected to the larger Internet.

Wireless sensor network (WSN): A network composed of a large number of sensor nodes which are densely deployed either inside the phenomenon or very close to it. Wireless sensor networks can advance many scientific pursuits while providing a vehicle for enhancing various forms of productivity, including manufacturing, agriculture, construction, and transportation. It is envisioned that an important class of applications for such networks involves a dense deployment of a large number of sensors over a fixed area, in which a physical process unfolds. The task of these sensors is then to collect measurements, encode them, and relay them to some data collection point where this data is to be analyzed, and possibly acted upon.

Wireless mesh network (WMN): A communications network made up of radio nodes in which there are at least two pathways of communication to each node. The coverage area of the radio nodes working as a single network becomes a mesh cloud. Access to this mesh cloud is dependent on the radio nodes working in harmony with one another to create a radio network. A mesh network is reliable and offers redundancy. In such wireless networks some nodes are mobile and some are fixed. When one node can no longer operate, the rest can communicate with one another directly or through one or more intermediate nodes.

Exercises

1. What are the other advantages of network coding in addition to what are mentioned in the text?
2. What is linear broadcast used for?
3. Describe a typical application of linear dispersion.
4. How are linear multicast, linear broadcast and linear dispersion related?
5. What are the practical factors that should be considered when adopting random network coding?
6. Discuss the benefits of using network coding in wireless multi-hop networks.
7. Why are other network coding options at node R (Fig. 12) in the wireless mesh network example not relevant, other than the XOR-ed packet ($\mathrm{P1} \oplus \mathrm{P3} \oplus \mathrm{P4} \oplus \mathrm{P5}$)?
8. Explain how wireless multi-hop network settings are relevant to network coding.
9. Is there any essential difference between multi-source and single-source network coding.
10. Discuss how network coding can help in overlay peer-to-peer network?

References

1. R. W. Yeung, S.-Y. R. Li, N. Cai and Z. Zhang, *Network Coding Theory, Foundation and Trends in Communications and Information Technology* (NOW Publishers).
2. R. Ahlswede, N. Cai, S. R. Li and R. W. Yeung, Network information flow, *IEEE Trans. Inform. Theor.* **46**(4), 1204–1216 (2000).
3. S.-Y. R. Li, R. W. Yeung and N. Cai, Linear network coding, *IEEE Trans. Inform. Theor.* **49**(2), 371–381 (2003).
4. R. Koetter and M. Médard, An algebraic approach to network coding, *IEEE/ACM Trans. Network.* **11**(5), 782–795 (2003).
5. P. Sanders, S. Egner and L. Tolhuizen, Polynomial time algorithms for network information flow, *Proc. 15th ACM Symp. Parallel Algorithms and Architectures (SPAA)*, San Diego, CA, June (2003), pp. 286–294.
6. S. Jaggi, P. Sanders, P. A. Chou, M. Effros, S. Egner, K. Jain and L. Tolhuizen, Polynomial time algorithms for multicast network code construction, *IEEE Trans. Inform. Theor.* **51**(6), 1973–1982 (2005).
7. T. Ho, M. Médard, J. Shi, M. Effros and D. R. Karger, On randomized network coding, *Proc. 41st Annual Allerton Conf. Communication, Control, and Computing*, October (2003).
8. T. Ho, R. Koetter, M. Médard, D. R. Karger and M. Effros, The benefits of coding over routing in a randomized setting, *IEEE Int. Symp. Information Theory*, June (2003).
9. T. Ho, M. Médard, R. Koetter, D. R. Karger, M. Effros, J. Shi and B. Leong, A random linear network coding approach to multicast, *IEEE Trans. Inform. Theor.* **52**(10), 4413–4430 (2006).
10. P. A. Chou, Y. Wu and K. Jain, Practical network coding, *Proc. Allerton Conf. Communication, Control, and Computing*, October (2003).
11. C. Gkantsidis and P. R. Rodriguez, Network coding for large scale content distribution, *IEEE INFOCOM'05* (2005).
12. Y. Wu, P. A. Chou and Sun-Yuan Kung, Minimum-energy multicast in mobile ad hoc networks using network coding, *IEEE Trans. Commun.* **53**(11), 1906–1918 (2005).
13. Z. Guo, P. Xie, J.-H. Cui and B. Wang, On applying network coding to underwater sensor networks, *Proc. 1st ACM Int. Workshop on Underwater Networks* (2006), pp. 109–112.
14. Z. Guo, B. Wang and J.-H. Cui, Efficient error recovery with network coding in underwater sensor networks. Elsevier Ad Hoc Networks, Special Issue on Underwater Networks, July (2007).
15. S. Katti, H. Rahul, W. Hu, D. Katabi, M. Médard and J. Crowcroft, XORs in the air: Practical wireless network coding, *ACM SIGCOMM* (2006).
16. S.-Y. R. Li and S.-T. Ho, Ring-theoretic foundation of convolutional network coding, *NETCOD'08*, Hong Kong, January (2008).

Chapter 17

A THEORETICAL MODEL FOR GRID, CLUSTER AND INTERNET COMPUTING

MARK BURGIN
Department of Mathematics, University of California,
Los Angeles, California 90095
mburgin@math.ucla.edu

MARC L. SMITH
Department of Computer Science, Vassar College
Poughkeepsie, New York 12604

Grid, cluster or Internet computing is essentially concurrent. There are many different models of concurrent processes, which are inherent for distributed systems. The goal of this chapter is to introduce a common formalized framework aimed at grid, cluster and Internet computing for current research in this area and to eliminate the shortcomings of existing models of concurrency. Following on from previous research, here we build a high-level metamodel event-action-process (EAP) for concurrent processes. This metamodel comprises a variety of other models of concurrent processes. We shape these mathematical models and study events, actions and processes in relation to important practical problems, such as communication in networks, concurrent programming, and distributed computations. In the third section of the chapter, a three-level algebra of events, actions and processes is constructed and studied as a new stage of algebra for concurrent processes. Relations between EAP process algebra and other models of concurrency are considered in the fourth section of this chapter.

1. Introduction: Problems of Concurrency and Related Research

The algebraic approach is a popular and effective way to study processes in multi-component systems, such as the Internet, multi-core computers and clusters of multicore computers. To efficiently deal with such problems, computer science developed a concurrency theory, which extensively and successfully utilizes algebraic structures and other mathematical techniques. Researchers have built many powerful models of concurrency: Petri nets, communicating sequential process (CSP), calculus for communicating systems (CCS), causal process algebra (CPA), event-signal-process (ESP), view-centric reasoning (VCR), synchronization trees, labeled transition systems, and grid automata, to mention but a few.

The goal of this chapter is to introduce a common formalized framework for current research in this area and to eliminate the shortcomings of existing models of concurrency. The main problem with the majority of these models is that they use an oversimplified model of time. Firstly, they consider only two types of time scales — linear time and branching time — while the system theory of time [1] implies a necessity to have a more flexible representation of temporal concurrent processes. With the advent of multi-core processors, and the prevalence of cluster and grid computing, reasoning about true concurrency is no longer an avoidable concern. Secondly, all events and actions in these models of concurrency do not have duration, while in reality to build reliable technological systems, such as computers and networks, it is necessary to take into account the duration of events and actions [2]. Thirdly, it is generally assumed that moments in time when events occur are exactly specified and distinguishable from one another, while in reality researchers and engineers have encountered the impossibility of distinguishing between two near-simultaneous events [2, 3]. As a result, the arbitration problem is one of the most important for concurrent systems [3a].

In addition, the Rice theorem [4] from computability theory restricts us to observing input/output behavior of processes to reason about properties of computation. But in concurrent systems, observable input/output behavior extends to communication between processes, and process algebras such as CSP, CCS, and the Pi-calculus are built up from elemental notions of observable events. Algebraic laws prescribe a variety of compositional possibilities, processes are composed of events and other processes, and computational histories of processes are represented by traces of their observable events. Simplifying assumptions, such as instantaneous events (events without duration) and the interleaving of parallel events in computational traces, have proven successful to date, but we may now be confronting certain limitations of such assumptions. Reasoning about composition in general, but especially concurrent composition, remains one of our greatest challenges. As experts claim, one of the reasons for this is nontrivial concurrent programs based on threads, semaphores, and mutexes are incomprehensible to humans.

The extended view-centric reasoning (EVCR) model for concurrent processes, developed by Burgin and Smith [5, 6], gives a flexible mathematical representation for temporal relations between such processes, but lacks a mathematical model of these processes as well as their system representation. Here, we enrich EVCR with such a model, constructing a high-level metamodel, event-action-process (EAP), for concurrent processes. As a basis for this new component, we take the metamodel, event-signal-process (ESP), built by Lee and Sangiovanni-Vincentelli [7]. This metamodel gives an efficient hierarchy for mathematical representation of concurrent processes and encompasses a variety of models of concurrent systems. It is demonstrated in Ref. 7 that ESP can represent Kahn process networks [8], the CSP model of Hoare [9], the CCS model of Milner [10], dataflow process networks [11], discrete event simulators [12], and Petri nets [13, 14].

EAP is inspired by CSP's observation-based reasoning capability and is aimed at modeling grid, cluster and Internet computing. It is the next step in the evolution of CSP from a model that reduces concurrency to an interleaving of sequential events, to a model of true concurrency that provides abstractions that represent degrees of interleaving. EAP is also the next step in the evolution of ESP from a model in which events happen at a moment in time (point-like events) and time is absolute, to a model that provides abstractions to represent extended events and the relativity of time. The duration of events is important for efficiency of computation and communication and thus is the base for computational complexity. As a result, a model of true concurrency should support abstractions for events whose occurrences partially overlap in time. Thus, the possibility of observed event simultaneity is not merely a Boolean proposition but rather a continuum: events A and B may overlap entirely, partially, or not at all.

Denning [2] recently described the choice uncertainty principle, a phenomenon that exists at every level of computing abstraction, from the hardware up as well as in human social situations. The choice uncertainty principle states that "it is impossible to make an unambiguous choice between near-simultaneous events under a deadline." Denning goes on to ask, "How can computations choose reliably?" We believe EAP provides one path to begin to reason about concurrency by reintroducing event duration into observation-based computational models.

EAP begins by deconstructing the notion of events, and continues by deconstructing observation itself. In Sec. 2, several event axioms are given whose truth and meaning are evident in the real world, but these are not the axioms of events that appear in classic process algebras such as CSP, CCS, and ESP. To achieve higher flexibility, in reflecting real concurrent processes and distributed systems as well as concurrent programs, at first we use semi-formal definitions which later allow several exact formalizations. For instance, initially we introduce a general concept of the temporal coordinate of an event, and only then do we give three possible mathematical realizations: the temporal coordinate as a real number for point-like events, the temporal coordinate as a real interval for extended events, and the temporal coordinate as an ordered set (tuple) of real numbers for pointed events.

Events in the real world exist in space and time, but events are more typically abstracted to occur at a single point in time, without regard for location or duration. At its most fundamental level, an event represents change. EAP considers the meaning of an event from three perspectives: the change in the process that engaged in the event, the change in the environment in which the event occurred, and the change in the relationship between a process and its environment when an event occurs. In VCR, Smith [15] considered multiple views of a computation; in EAP, we go so far as to consider different views of events themselves.

EAP deconstructs observation by considering intermediate units of event composition. Process algebras typically define processes in terms of event composition, with primitives that permit sequential composition, choice, and recursion. Traces of a process's execution take the form of traces of observable events, which provide the basis for process calculi to reason about properties of a process's computation [14]. Models such as CSP abstract away non-synchronizing concurrency by interleaving point-like events an observer perceives to have occurred simultaneously. There are several points to make here, the most important of which is a loss of entropy, which is described in detail by Smith [15]. Imposing an order of events where there was none, or where events overlap to some degree, leads to a loss of information and limits what a process calculus may reason about. Denning's choice uncertainty principle motivates us to develop process algebras and calculi that permit reasoning directly about near-simultaneous events. EAP, in addition to being a model of true concurrency, introduces intermediate units of composition, actions, which are partial traces. This implies actions do not correspond to entire processes, but also means actions are a new way to reason about infinite processes or, more significantly, threads of execution, which cross process boundaries.

EAP provides a three-level process algebra for the modeling, study, and specification of concurrent processes. It should prove especially useful for modeling and reasoning about properties of multicore and modern grid computation (cf., for example, Refs. 16 and 17). Operations in the EAP process algebra are defined in Secs. 3.3–3.5. There are unary operations, binary operations and operations of higher arity. Operations on the second and third levels of the EAP process algebra, i.e., operations, operands of which are actions and processes, are also called operators. As we show in Sec. 4, EAP process algebra operations can faithfully represent operators from many conventional process algebras, such as CSP [9, 18], ACP [19, 20], TCSP [21], and CCS [22, 23], as well as from more recent models, such as process algebras [2–7, 11] and ESP [7].

The process algebra developed in this chapter is based on a model of observation-based composition of processes, actions and events. The set of observable events is a way from the process algebra to a process calculus, the next step in the development of EAP. The motivation for VCR stemmed from a desire to preserve more information about the history of a computation by introducing lazy observation, and multiple, possibly imperfect, observers [15].

At the same time, compositions of systems and processes have become an important tool for the development of modern hardware and software systems with complex sets of requirements. Unfortunately, as Neumann [24] writes, there is a huge gap between theory and common practice: system compositions at present are typically ad hoc, based on the intersection of potentially incompatible component properties, and dependent on untrustworthy components that were not designed for interoperability — often resulting in unexpected results and risks.

The results of this chapter provide additional evidence to support this statement. The analysis of real systems and processes made possible the ability to find new types for even such a well-known operation as sequential composition. This was possible because the authors considered not only data-flow relations between systems and processes used in the conventional sequential composition but also temporal and causal relations.

In Sec. 2, we first formulate general axioms for models of concurrency and introduce a new classification of these models. Then we build the static stratum of the EAP metamodel as a unifying framework for concurrency studies. Its constructions use advanced means of modern mathematics: fiber bundles, manifolds, general algebraic systems, universal algebras and logical models. We develop the initial model in this generality to form a basis for further development because it is necessary to be able to represent in a model of concurrency not only properties of the system time and space but also properties of physical time and space. At the same time, contemporary physics uses these advanced mathematical structures to model physical objects and processes, including physical time and space (cf., for example, [25]). Besides this, some contemporary models of concurrency already use categories (cf., for example, [26]) and algebraic topology (cf., for example, [27]).

It is possible, however, to take a simplified form of this model that utilizes mathematics no more sophisticated than basic set theory. In the majority of cases, it is sufficient to employ only finite sets or, at most, countable sets. However, to properly treat complex problems of concurrent systems and computations, such as time relativity, we need sufficiently powerful mathematical tools, which we can find only in advanced mathematics.

In Sec. 3, we first develop the algebraic foundations for modeling the dynamics of multi-component systems and concurrent processes and then build the dynamic stratum of the EAP metamodel. We base our models on structures and tools from universal algebra and topology. There is a dual approach to concurrency in the framework of category theory (cf., for example, [26]). It is possible to develop the EAP metamodel in the category setting. However, the categorical formalization of the EAP metamodel is studied elsewhere. Composition of concurrent processes is based on compositions of actions that constitute these processes, and composition of actions is based on compositions of events that constitute these actions. That is why the topic of the third section is composition of events and actions in order to keep the chapter to a reasonable length. Compositions of processes are constructed and studied elsewhere. Here, we only show how processes evolve from actions and consider some simple properties of these processes.

In Sec. 4, relations between our EAP metamodel and other models of concurrent processes are considered. It is demonstrated that the EAP metamodel encompasses a variety of other models of distributed systems and concurrent processes.

For simplicity, we consider mostly point-like events and do not explicate to the full extent topological and temporal structures in systems of events, actions and processes. However, the EAP metamodel allows one to achieve a much deeper understanding of these relations and structures, and use this model for organization of concurrent processes in distributed systems.

2. Models of Events, Actions, and Processes

Models of concurrency are classified with respect to two parameters: time and substance. Traditionally (cf., for example, [28]), eight types of models are separated based on three dimensions and six types: behavior/system, interleaving/noninterleaving, and linear/branching.

The first dimension is based on substance representation of processes, while the two other dimensions are based on temporal aspects. That is to say, interleaving means a possibility of linearization of the time scale, linear model means utilization of a linear time scale, and branching model means utilization of a tree-like (branching) time scale [1].

There are two substance types of process models and thus of concurrency models: embodied (or system) and pure (or behavior) process (concurrency) models.

Definition 1. An *embodied process (concurrency) model* includes a model of the systems in which processes go on.

Petri nets [13, 29], synchronization trees [30], labeled transition systems [28], and grid automata [31, 32] are examples of embodied process (concurrency) models.

Definition 2. In a *pure process (concurrency) model* only processes are represented in more or less detail.

The CSP model of Hoare [9], the CCS model of Milner [10], the ESP model of Lee and Sangiovanni-Vincentelli [7], the VCR model of Smith [15], and the EVCR and EAP models of Burgin and Smith [33, 34] are examples of pure process (concurrency) models. Partial recursive and recursive functions are examples of pure computational models.

In turn, embodied process (concurrency) models can be divided into two classes: black box models and structural system models.

Definition 3. A *black box embodied process (concurrency) model* does not describe the structure of the system in which processes go on.

Synchronization trees [30] and labeled transition systems [28] are examples of black box embodied process (concurrency) models.

Finite automata and abstract state machines [35] are examples of black box embodied computational models.

Definition 4. A *structural system (white box) embodied process (concurrency) model* describes the structure of the system in which processes go on.

Petri nets [13, 29] and grid automata [31, 32] are examples of white box embodied process (concurrency) models.

Turing machines and inductive Turing machines are examples of white box embodied computational models [32].

2.1. *Events*

The basic elements and concepts of a theory of concurrent processes are events. To build a mathematical model of a system of events, we first formulate the main principles in the form of informal axioms that reflect fundamental properties of events. Then, we build actions from events and processes from actions, introduce operations with events, actions and processes, and formalize the obtained structures as algebras.

Note that our axioms for events are informal because informal axioms better reflect features of real events — formalization, as a rule, ignores some properties and relations. Formal axioms are used for models of events in process algebra considered as an algebraic theory to formalize and study with mathematical tools systems of concurrent processes.

Axiom E1. *Events exist in space and time and have some meaning.*

Space and time can be physical or system. Physical time means the time in a physical region (physical space) where the event takes place. System time means the inner time of the system in which the event takes place [36, 37]. Such a system can be a separate computer, a local network of computers or a global network, such as the Internet. According to the system theory of time, system time can be essentially different from physical time [1]. For instance, when we consider a theoretical model of computation, such as a Turing machine, all its operations have the same duration equal to one.

At the same time, we know that computer operations can have essentially different durations. For example, multiplication of numbers takes more time than addition of numbers, multiplication with a floating point takes more time than multiplication with a fixed point, and multiplication of matrices takes more time than multiplication of numbers.

Both kinds of time, system and physical, are used in temporal databases (cf., for example, [38, 39]), namely, the temporal aspects usually include valid time and transaction time. These attributes go together to form bitemporal data. *Valid time* is the physical time and is used to denote the time period during which a fact is true with respect to the real world. *Transaction time* is the system time of the database and is used to form the time period during which a fact is stored in the database. Physical space is the space where people live, physical processes go on, and physical (or material) systems exist. Physical space is modeled in different physical theories.

System space depends on the representation of the system(s) where events take place. For instance, the system space for such systems as finite automata or labeled transition systems [28] is the state space of a finite automaton or labeled transition system. As we take such a system as a cellular automaton A, then the system space of events in A is the corresponding grid of state spaces of individual finite automata that constitute A [40]. In a Petri net, the system space is the network in which places and transitions are situated [13, 29].

The meaning of an event is a description of what happened in this event. For instance, the meaning of one event in a computer could be "sending an e-mail", the meaning of another event in a computer could be "reading from a CD", and the meaning of an event in a printer could be "printing."

To develop semantics for events, we consider three types of events: abstract, process, and embodied or system events.

As considered at the beginning of this section, types of process models utilize five types of events: abstract or pure events, pure temporal events, and three types of embodied or system events: pure spatial events, white box embodied events and black box embodied events.

Definition 5. An *abstract or pure event* is a representation of what happened (of what is done), but no indication of when or where.

In some sense, abstract events are not events but types of events or event variables. That is why an abstract event is also called an *event label.* Others kind of event variables are events in which the name or meaning is variable.

Definition 6. A *pure temporal event* is a representation of what happened, indicating a time of occurrence, but not where it happened.

The majority of concurrency models that include time, such as timed CCP [41], use only pure temporal events or actions.

Definition 7. An *embodied or system* event is a representation of what happened, indicating both a time and place of happening.

The most popular concurrency model that uses embodied/system events is a Petri net.

Definition 8. A *black box embodied event* is a representation of what happened without a description of the system structure.

Synchronization trees [30] and labeled transition systems [28] are examples of black box embodied process (concurrency) models. Finite automata and abstract state machines [36] are examples of black box embodied computational models.

Definition 9. A *white box (structural) embodied event* is a representation of what happened without a description of the system structure.

Usually, a system belongs to some environment, while a process interacts (communicates) with other processes which form the environment of the first process. Taking into account this natural structure, we come to three categories of events that have different meaning.

Axiom E2a. *The meaning of an event in a system or in a process is a change in this system or in this process.*

Axiom E2a interprets events (in a system or process) as changes, or as reflections of changes (of the state or phase) of the system (in the process). For instance, an event in such a system as a finite automaton or finite state machine is a state transition of this automaton or machine. Sending a message is an event in a network. Printing a symbol or a text, producing a symbol on the screen of the display, and calculating "2 + 2" are events in a computer. The latter event could also be an event in a calculator.

Axiom E2b. *The meaning of an* event by a system *is a change in the environment caused by this system or process.*

For instance, when a system R sends information to another system or builds a new system or takes something from one place to another, it is an event by this system R.

Axiom E2c. *The meaning of an* event for a system *is a change in relations between this system or process and its environment.*

For instance, when a system R is connected to another system and then this connection is broken, it is an event for this system R.

Note that even in the best embodied models of concurrency, such as Petri nets [13, 29] or labeled transition systems [28], semantics represents only events in a system while in reality two other types of events are of no less importance.

To build an efficient and flexible model of concurrent processes, developing algebras and calculi for them, we need mathematical structures that allow one to deal with a diversity of situations that emerge in practice.

Let us remind ourselves of the definitions of some mathematical concepts that we need in our model.

An *algebraic system* is a set with relations (predicates) and operations in it [42].

When there are only operations, we have algebras, often called *universal algebras* [43]. When there are only relations or predicates, we have mathematical structures or models when these structures are related to corresponding logical theories [44, 45]. In mathematics, usually two types of relations are considered: relations of order, including preorder, tolerance and equivalence, and topological relations [46].

A *topological manifold* is a Hausdorff topological space X in which every point has a neighborhood homeomorphic to an open subset of Euclidean space $\mathbf{R}^n$. The integer n, called the *dimension* of X, must be the same for all points of X.

A *fiber bundle* $\boldsymbol{B}$ (also called *fibre bundle*) is a triad (E, p, B), where the topological space E is called the *total space* or simply, *space* of the fiber bundle, the topological space B the *base space* or simply, *base* of the fiber bundle, and p is a topological projection of E onto B such that every point in the base space has a neighborhood U such that $p^{-1}(b) = F$ for all points b from B and $p^{-1}(U)$ are homeomorphic to the direct product $U \times F$. The topological space F is called the *fiber* of the fiber bundle $\boldsymbol{B}$. Informally, a fiber bundle is a topological space which looks locally like a product space $U \times F$.

It is possible to find introductory information on topological manifolds, fiber bundles and other topological structures in [47–50].

A *multiset* (sometimes also called a *bag*) is a set consists of elements, but in contrast to sets each member of a multiset has a *multiplicity*, which indicates *how many* times it is present in this multiset (cf., for example, [51]). For instance, in the multiset $\{a, a, b, b, b, c\}$, the multiplicities of the members a, b, and c are respectively 2, 3, and 1.

To formally represent temporal, spatial and semantic characteristics of events, we use three algebraic systems: a naming system N of names, a semantic system V of values, and a space–time system ST of tags.

In the simplest case, N, V and ST are sets as in the ASP model [7]. Usually, systems V and ST are topological manifolds with some algebraic operations and relations, i.e., they are algebraic systems. For example, physical space–time is a four-dimensional manifold in relativity theory, a ten-dimensional manifold in string theory and an eleven-dimensional manifold in superstring theory (cf., for example, [52, 53]). Important relations for events are temporal relations, in particular, order relations, introduced and studied by the authors in [54]. The naming system N is usually a multiset [51]. Sometimes the naming system N has some operations in it.

The *naming system* N consists of names of events. A name shows the type of an event. Names can be organized in a hierarchical system.

The *semantic system* V consists of values of events. A *value* v describes (indicates) what happened (what is done), determining a transformational or operational semantics of events (cf., for example, [55–57]).

There is a function (correspondence, in a general case) *sem*: $N \rightarrow V$ from N to V that gives meaning to events, as well as to types of events.

The *space–time* (or *tag*) system ST consists of tags of events. A *tag* t shows where and when something happened (is done). It consists of time and place, determining the location of events. Topologically, the space–time manifold ST is a fiber bundle $\boldsymbol{ST}$ with the base T and the fiber S (cf., Fig. 1).

This means that $\boldsymbol{ST} = (ST, p_T, T)$, where p_T is a continuous projection and $p_T^{-1}(t) = S$ for any point t from T. In the space–time fiber bundle, T is the time manifold, which is naturally decomposed into physical time scale T_{ph} and system time scale T_{st} (cf., Fig. 2). Very often, system time does not coincide with physical time and they have different scales. It is also necessary to remark that multi-component systems often have several time scales [1].

Fig. 1. The space–time fiber bundle.

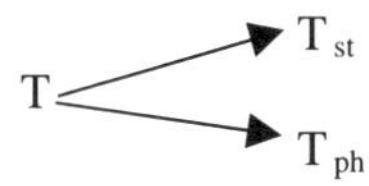

Fig. 2. Time manifold decomposition.

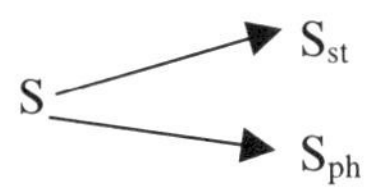

Fig. 3. Space manifold decomposition.

Usually, time in computer science is linear, implicit and discrete. However, studies of concurrency brought researchers to consider with more complex scales to be able to correctly reflect computational reality. For instance, branching time plays an important role in many computational models of concurrency (cf., for example, Refs. [58, 59]). Transitions of higher dimensional automata (cf., for example, [60]) happen in a multidimensional time.

The fiber S is the space manifold. It is naturally decomposed into physical space model S_{ph} and system space S_{st} (cf., Fig. 3).

For simplicity, we take $T_{\text{ph}} = \bigcup_{a \in S\text{st}} T_{\text{ph}a}$, where a is a node in the considered system, $T_{\text{ph}a}$ is the time scale of the physical place where a is situated, and all $T_{\text{ph}a}$ are linearly ordered. To make the time scale more transparent, we assume that each $T_{\text{ph}a}$ is a subset of the set $\boldsymbol{R}$ of all real numbers.

In a similar way, $T_{\text{st}} = \bigcup_{a \in S\text{st}} T_{\text{st}a}$, where $T_{\text{st}a}$ is the time scale of time at a node a. Time with the scale $T_{\text{st}a}$ corresponds to the concept of local time used in some theories of concurrency (cf., for example, [61]).

In this context, an event e is equal to a pair $(d,\ t)$, where d is the name of e and belongs to N, and t is the tag of e. For a *point-like* event e, its tag t belongs to ST. There are two natural mappings of events onto their names and tags, namely, if $e = (d, t)$, then $\mathbf{n}(e) = d$ and $\mathbf{t}(e) = t$. The mapping $\mathbf{n}$ allows us to define meaning (semantics) of events as Sem $e = \text{sem}(\mathbf{n}(e))$. In general, we assume that the same event may have different names, i.e., it is possible that $e = (d,\ t) = (a,\ t)$.

Note that any component of an event — the name, value, tag, time coordinate and/or space coordinate — can be a variable. In this case, i.e., when at least one component of an event e is a variable, the event e is potential.

By $\mathbf{EV}_{NV,ST}$ we denote all (point-like) events with names from N, semantics from V and tags from ST. For simplicity, the set ST is considered as the direct product of the time scale T and the abstract space S. There are two canonical projections: $p_S : ST \to S$ and $p_T : ST \to T$. Thus, the time of an event e is $p_T(\mathbf{t}(e))$ and the place of an event e is $p_S(\mathbf{t}(e))$. In the simplest case, a tag t of a point-like event is a pair $(p_S(t),\ p_T(t))$.

In computers and networks, the time scale is usually an infinite discrete set of points isomorphic to the set $\boldsymbol{N}$ of all natural numbers. The space of a network is usually some graph (cf., for example, [32]).

In addition to point-like events, there are other types of events. In *extended events*, time (that is, the projection of the tag t on the time manifold) is an interval which is represented by two points: the beginning and the end of this interval. For instance, if we assume that ST coincides with T, and T is the scale of the physical time, then an extended event $e = (d, (t_{\mathrm{b}}, t_{\mathrm{e}}))$, where t_{b} is the time of the beginning and t_{e} is the time of the end of the event e. Many models of concurrent processes ignore the space coordinate of events and assume that events take place in the physical time (cf., for example, [7]).

If we consider extended events with tags that represent both time and space, then the space of the event cannot be a single coordinate of the space manifold S but a region in (a subset of) this manifold. Thus, the possible values of extended event tags are pairs of regions (subsets): one in S and another in T. Extended events can be separated into three classes: spatial extended events, temporal extended events, and full-scale extended events.

A *temporal extension* of an event means that the temporal component of the event tag is a name of some region (usually, an interval when the time scale is one-dimensional) in the time manifold (time scale) T. Such extended events are studied in [33, 54].

A *spatial extension* of an event means that the spatial component of the event tag is a name of some region (e.g., a sphere or ball) in the space manifold S. For instance, if we assume that ST coincides with S, i.e., time is not considered, then it is natural to consider balls as values for tags because, as a rule, the space where an event occurs is not a point. In this case, an extended event may have the form $e = (d, (x, r))$, where x is the coordinate of the center of a sphere in which this event occurs and r is the radius of this sphere. An example of a system in which time of events is ignored is a finite automaton. In full-scale extended events, tags represent regions in the space manifold S and in the time manifold T.

By $\mathbf{EV}_{NV,EST}$ we denote all extended events with names from N, semantics from V, and tags from $\mathrm{P}(ST)$, which is the set of all subsets from ST.

There are also *pointed events*, which have the form $e = (d, (t_1, t_2, \ldots, t_k))$. A possible interpretation of pointed events is given by the situation when an event $e = (d, (t_1, t_2, \ldots, t_k))$ is considered in different time scales and t_i is the point-like time of e in the scale T_i ($i = 1, 2, 3, \ldots, k$). These different scales T_i may reflect physical time or system time at different places (the so-called local time [61]) or represent system time (cf., [1]) of those distributed systems in which this event takes place. Another interpretation of pointed events is given by the situation when an event $e = (d, (t_1, t_2, \ldots, t_k))$ represents an abstract event that happens at several places.

By $\mathbf{EV}_{NV,kST}$ we denote all pointed events with names from N, semantics from V, and tags from ST^k, where ST^k is the set of all subsets from ST that have k elements.

Assuming that spaces V and ST give a complete representation of all events, we have the following axiom.

Axiom E3. *An event is uniquely defined by time, space and what happened (what is done).*

In the formal model, this means that if $e_1 = (d_1, t_1), e_2 = (d_2, t_2), v_1 = v_2$, $\operatorname{sem} d_1 = \operatorname{sem} d_2$, and $t_1 = t_2$, then $e_1 = e_2$.

Axiom E3 implies that embodied or system events form a set. Abstract or pure events form, as a rule, multisets because the same abstract event can occur several times at different places or at different times.

When spaces V and ST do not give a complete representation of all events, it is also natural to consider systems of events as multisets (cf., for example, [15]). For instance, often an event is identified with its value v, while time and place are ignored. In this case, a process can contain several copies of the same event. At the same time, it is possible that two or more processes contain different copies of an event in some cases, while they have a common copy (or several common copies) of the same event. For instance, taking such an event as sending a message, we see that different copies of this event belong, as a rule, to many different processes. At the same, each copy of such an event as information (data) exchange between two processes necessarily belongs to two processes. Parallel events can coincide as abstract events.

A similar situation emerges when the space (set) ST does not give a complete representation of all events. For instance, the space of the event is not taken into consideration or the time of the event is taken as a point instead of an interval.

To study information processing (computation, communication, etc.), we consider events of two types: changes of information carriers (symbols, signals, data, knowledge, etc.) and changes of information processing systems.

Example 1. If we model information processing in such a system as a Turing machine, then events of the first type are writing and erasing symbols in cells of the machine memory. Events of the second type aremovements of the head of the Turing machine.

Definition 10. (a) Two point-like events $e_1 = (d_1, t_1)$ and $e_2 = (d_2, t_2)$ are called *parallel* or *simultaneous* if $p_T(t_1) = p_T(t_2)$. (b) Two extended events $e_1 = (d_1, ((t_{1b}, t_{1e}), s_1))$ and $e_2 = (d_2, ((t_{2b}, t_{2e}), s_2))$ are called *parallel* if $t_{1b} = t_{2b}$ and $t_{1e} = t_{2e}$.

We denote this by $e_1 || e_2$. Informally, this means that two events are parallel when they occur exactly at the same time. This agrees with one's general intuition and is represented on the abstract level by the simultaneity relation, ST_{R}, previously introduced by the authors in [33, 54].

Example 2. Let us consider information processing in such a system as a Turing machine. In the traditional representation (cf., for example, [62]), each step of a Turing machine can include two parallel operations: changing the state of the machine and either writing in a cell or erasing from a cell, or moving the head of the machine. Contemporary textbooks (cf., for example, [63]) allow the Turing machine to do three parallel operations in one step.

Note that what constitutes parallel and even simultaneous events depends on the chosen time scale. For instance, switching in multithreading can happen so fast as to give the illusion of simultaneity to an end user, that is, the computer events before and after switching look simultaneous, while to the computer where these events happen they are not simultaneous.

Proposition 1. *Parallelism of point-like (extended) events is an equivalence relation.*

Proof. Let us first consider point-like events $e_1 = (d_1, t_1)$ and $e_2 = (d_2, t_2)$. By Definition 10, any point-like event is parallel to itself. Hence, parallelism of point-like events is a reflexive binary relation. Besides, if $e_1 \parallel e_2$, then $p_T(t_1) = p_T(t_2)$. Thus, by Definition 10, $e_2 \parallel e_1$, i.e., parallelism of point-like events is a symmetric binary relation. Finally, if $e_1 \parallel e_2$ and $e_2 \parallel e_3$, then $p_T(t_1) = p_T(t_2)$ and $p_T(t_2) = p_T(t_3)$. Consequently, $p_T(t_1) = p_T(t_3)$ and by Definition 10, $e_1||e_3$. Thus, parallelism of point-like events is a transitive binary relation, and by definition, it is an equivalence relation.

Similar reasoning gives us a proof that parallelism of extended events is an equivalence relation. Proposition 1 is proved. □

In practice, it is impossible to make an unambiguous choice between near-simultaneous events under a deadline [2]. Thus, we need to introduce approximately or fuzzy parallel events. To do this, we use an arbitrary positive real number r as the parameter of this approximation or fuzziness.

Definition 11. (a) Two point-like events $e_1 = (d_1,\ t_1)$ and $e_2 = (d_2,\ t_2)$ are called *r-parallel* or *r-simultaneous* if $|p_T(t_1) - p_T(t_2)| < r$. (b) Two extended events $e_1 = (d_1,\ ((t_{1b},\ t_{1e}),\ s_1))$ and $e_2 = (d_2,\ ((t_{2b},\ t_{2e}),\ s_2))$ are called *r-parallel* if $|t_{1b} - t_{2b}| < r$ and $t_{1e} = t_{2e} < r$.

We denote this relation by $e_1||_r e_2$. Informally, this means that two events are approximately or fuzzy parallel when the difference between the times of their occurrence is less than some number r that represents the indistinguishability of event time coordinates.

For representing communication processes, we need events of four types [8]: emission, reception, reading (or information extraction), and writing (or information insertion). We introduce the following corresponding set notations:

$\mathbf{Em}_{NV,ST}$ denotes the set of all emissions from $\mathbf{EV}_{NV,ST}$.
$\mathbf{Em}_{NV,\mathrm{E}ST}$ denotes the set of all emissions from $\mathbf{EV}_{NV,\mathrm{E}ST}$.
$\mathbf{Em}_{NV,kST}$ denotes the set of all emissions from $\mathbf{EV}_{NV,kST}$.

$\mathbf{Rc}_{NV,ST}$ denotes the set of all receptions from $\mathbf{EV}_{NV,ST}$.
$\mathbf{Rc}_{NV,\mathrm{E}ST}$ denotes the set of all receptions from $\mathbf{EV}_{NV,\mathrm{E}ST}$.
$\mathbf{Rc}_{NV,kST}$ denotes the set of all receptions from $\mathbf{EV}_{NV,kST}$.
$\mathbf{Rd}_{NV,ST}$ denotes the set of all readings from $\mathbf{EV}_{NV,ST}$.
$\mathbf{Rd}_{NV,\mathrm{E}ST}$ denotes the set of all readings from $\mathbf{EV}_{NV,\mathrm{E}ST}$.
$\mathbf{Rd}_{NV,kST}$ denotes the set of all readings from $\mathbf{EV}_{NV,kST}$.

$\mathbf{Wr}_{NV,ST}$ denotes the set of all writings from $\mathbf{EV}_{NV,ST}$.
$\mathbf{Wr}_{NV,\mathrm{E}ST}$ denotes the set of all writings from $\mathbf{EV}_{NV,\mathrm{E}ST}$.
$\mathbf{Wr}_{NV,kST}$ denotes the set of all writings from $\mathbf{EV}_{NV,kST}$.

All these events are *communication events*. A general definition of a communication event is based on the classification of information operations in the general theory of information [8].

Definition 12. An event $e = (d, t)$ is called a communication event if $\mathrm{sem}\, d$ is a communication operation.

Communication operations are changes of information carriers for portions of information [34]. For instance, reading some text by a word processor from a CD changes the CD as the information carrier for this text to the screen of the computer.

Receiving some picture from a channel, e.g., a cable channel, by a TV set is a communication event in which the channel as the information carrier for this picture is changed to the screen of the TV set.

2.2. *Actions*

Usually, processes are formed from events (cf., for example, [9, 10]). However, here, following [7], we use one more level of hierarchy that consists of actions. Three levels of hierarchy reduce complexity of descriptions and make the model more flexible.

Definition 13. An *action* A is a system of related events, i.e., $A = (e_1, e_2, \ldots, e_n)$. The number n is called the *cardinality* of A and denoted by $|A|$.

It is necessary to understand that the action A is defined neither as a set of events $e_1, e_2, \ldots, e_n$ nor as a multiset of events $e_1, e_2, \ldots, e_n$ nor as a vector or n-tuple of events $e_1, e_2, \ldots, e_n$. A system is defined not only by its elements but also by relations between these elements [64]. Thus, what is A depends not only on events $e_1, e_2, \ldots, e_n$, but also on relations between these events. If there are no such relations in A, then A is a set of events. If there are only relations of indiscernibility of events in A, then A is a multiset of events. If there is a relation of linear order in A, then A is an ordered n-tuple of events. If there is a relation that connects some events in A, then A is a graph (network) with events as vertices.

Note that in some models of concurrency, such as ACP [19], actions are indivisible primitives of the model and processes are built from actions. To represent such primitive actions in EAP, we consider actions such that each consists of a single indivisible (primitive) event.

There are different interpretations of actions. In one of them, actions in the EAP are theoretical representations of threads and fibers. Threads are a way for a program to split itself into two or more simultaneously (or pseudo-simultaneously) running tasks. Fibers realize the same function as threads. The difference is that fibers use cooperative multitasking, while threads use pre-emptive multitasking. Threads and processes differ from one operating system to another, but in general, how a thread is created and shares its resources is different from the way a process does.

Multiple threads can be executed in parallel on many computer systems. This process is called multithreading. When only one processor is used, multithreading is generally organized by time slicing (similar to time-division multiplexing), wherein a single processor switches between different threads, in which case the processing is not literally simultaneous, for the single processor is really doing only one thing at a time. This is an example of interleaving of actions.

Threads form a different level from traditional multitasking operating system processes because processes are typically independent, carry considerable state information, have separate address spaces, and interact only through system-provided inter-process communication mechanisms. Threads, on the other hand, typically share the state information of a single process, and share memory and other resources directly. Threads are parts of processes. At least one thread exists within each process. If multiple threads can exist within a process, then they share the same memory and file resources. Threads are pre-emptively multitasked if the operating system's process scheduler is pre-emptive. This allows the operating system to do switching between threads in the same process faster than switching between processes. For instance, systems like Windows NT and OS/2 are said to have "cheap" threads and "expensive" processes.

Another interpretation is a signal from the metamodel ESP of Lee and Sangiovanni-Vincentelli [7]. For simplicity, we consider only point-like events in what follows. There are special classes of actions.

Definition 14. An action A is called *finite* if it consists of a finite number of events. Otherwise, A is called *infinite*.

Definition 15. An action A is called a *signal* if it consists of communication events.

For instance, writing or erasing a symbol in a cell of a Turing machine memory is a signal. Movements of the head of a Turing machine are not signals but pure actions. Changing the place of an information carrier, e.g., sending a letter by regular mail, is also a signal.

Existing tradition resulted in a situation where communication and computation processes are mostly studied separately. In reality, any computation includes some communication operations and any communication includes some computation operations. Here, we put an emphasis on communication of processes but build our model so that it allows one to represent all types of processes and operations used in practice.

Definition 16. An action A is called an *explicit communication action* if it has at least one emission and/or reception.

In an explicit communication action A, it is possible to separate three groups of events: emissions, receptions, and all other events. As a result, we represent A in the form of a triad $A = (A_{\mathrm{rc}}, A_{\mathrm{gen}}, A_{\mathrm{em}})$, where A_{rc} is the set of all receptions from A, A_{em} is the set of all emissions from A, and A_{gen} is the set of all other events from A.

Definition 17. An action A is called an *implicit communication action* if it has at least one event of reading from, and/or writing to, a shared information carrier.

For instance, two processes (or programs) have a common memory. Then writing to and reading from this memory allows these processes to communicate with one another. Such memory is a specific instance of a *communication space* introduced in Ref. 65. In general, a communication, or interaction, space is a special medium often used for human–computer interaction. Another example of such a memory is the concept of a *store* used in concurrent constraint programming [41, 66, 67].

Definition 18. An explicit communication action A is called a *pure explicit communication action* if it contains only emissions and/or receptions.

Thus, a pure explicit communication action A has the form of a dyad $A = (A_{\mathrm{rc}}, A_{\mathrm{em}})$.

Definition 19. An action A is called an *action without repetition* if all events from A have different values, i.e., if $e_i = (d_i, t_i)$ and $e_j = (d_j, t_j)$ are events from A, then $\mathrm{Sem}\, d_i \neq \mathrm{Sem}\, d_j$.

Informally, this means that nothing happens twice in an action without repetition.

Definition 20. An action A is called a *coordinated action* if all events from A have different tags, i.e., if $e_i = (d_i, t_i)$ and $e_j = (d_j, t_j)$ are events from A, then $t_i = t_j$ *implies* $e_i = e_j$.

Informally, this means that at the same place and same time only one thing can happen (be done) in a coordinated action.

Definition 21. An action A with point-like events is called *sequential* if all events from A have different times, i.e., if $e_i = (d_i, t_i)$ and $e_j = (d_j, t_j)$ are events from A, then $p_T(t_i) = p_T(t_j)$ implies $e_i = e_j$.

Informally, this means that at the same time only one thing can happen (be done) in a sequential action. In other words, a sequential action does not have parallel events. The cardinality of a sequential action A is also called the *length* of A.

Proposition 2. *Any sequential action A is coordinated.*

It is necessary to discern actions that were realized, i.e., actions that consist of events that already happened, and potential actions, which represent alternate versions of what may happen. This gives us three types of actions:

- An *actualized action* is an action for which a realization of this action includes all its events.
- A *potential action* is an action which includes all events for all possible realizations of this action.
- An *emerging action* is an action that consists of two parts (subactions): one is an actualized action; the other is a potential action. When we use the conventional linear scale, such as physical time in Newtonian mechanics, then all events from the first (actualized) part of an emerging action must precede all events from the second (potential) part of this action.

For instance, the choice operation "+", which is used in many models of concurrency for processes (cf., for example, [19]), but can also be applied to actions, transforms any two actions into a potential action.

Potential actions are schemas [5], plans or programs for realization. Any realization of a potential action is an actualized action. Possible realizations of a potential action A are determined by the following compatibility relations in A:

- Two events e_i and e_j from A are *compatible* if any realization of A that contains e_i also contains e_j.
- Two events e_i and e_j from A are *weakly compatible* if any realization of A that contains e_i can also contain e_j.
- Two events e_i and e_j from A are *strongly compatible* if any realization of A that contains e_i must also contain e_j.
- Two events e_i and e_j from A are *incompatible* if any realization of A that contains e_i does not contain e_j.

- Two events e_i and e_j from A are *strongly incompatible* if any realization of A that contains e_i cannot contain e_j.
- Two events e_i and e_j from A are *weakly incompatible* if a realization of A that contains e_i may not contain e_j.

Let us consider an action A and a set R of relations in A, i.e., relations between events from A that determine A as a system.

Definition 22. (a) Any subset B of an action A in which all relations between events in B are induced by relations from R are preserved is called an R-subaction of A. (b) An R-subaction of A is called a *complete subaction* of A if R consists of all relations in A.

When R is not specified, we call B a *subaction* of A. These definitions imply that the cardinality of any proper subaction of an action A is less than the cardinality of A.

Proposition 3. *Any subaction of a finite action A is a finite action.*

Proposition 4. *Any subaction of an actualized action A is an actualized action.*

For potential and emerging actions, this result is not true in a general case.

Proposition 5. *Any R-subaction of a signal (communication action, pure communication action) is a signal (correspondingly, communication action, pure communication action).*

Theorem 1. *A complete subaction of a coordinated action (action without repetition) A is a coordinated action (action without repetition).*

Proposition 6. *A (complete) subaction C of a (complete) subaction B of an action A is a (complete) subaction of A.*

To build parallel compositions of actions and processes, it is necessary to have a relevant and sufficiently formalized definition of parallel actions and processes. However, the relation "to be parallel" is not so simple as the relation "to be sequential." As a rule, the relation "to be parallel" is a fuzzy or valued relation (property). That is why we start with measures of parallelism.

Let us consider two actions $A = (e_{11}, e_{12}, \ldots, e_{1n})$ and $B = (e_{21}, e_{22}, \ldots, e_{2n})$.

Definition 23. *The measure $m^{\text{par}}(A, B)$ of parallelism between A and B is equal to the number of pairs $e_{1i} \parallel e_{2j}$.*

Definition 24. The measure $m^{\text{par}}(A)$ of parallelism in an action A is equal to the number of parallel pairs $e_{1i} \parallel e_{1j}$ in the action A.

Definition 25. The measure $m_{\text{par}}(A)$ of parallelism in the action A is equal to the difference between the cardinality of A and the cardinality (length) of a maximal sequential subaction of A.

Note that, in general, a maximal sequential subaction of an action is not unique. So, to show that our definition is consistent, we need to demonstrate that any two maximal sequential subactions of an action Ahave the same cardinality.

Indeed, let us consider two maximal sequential subactions B and C of an action A and assume that the length of B is larger than the length of C. Then, B has an event e that is not parallel to any event in C because B as a sequential sequence does not contain parallel events. Then, if we add the event e to the action B, we will still have a sequential subaction of A and this subaction properly contains C. This contradicts our assumption that C is a maximal sequential subaction of A and thus proves that subactions B and C have the same cardinality (length).

Lemma 1. *(a) $m_{\text{par}}(A) \leq m^{\text{par}}(A)$ for any action A. (b) $m_{\text{par}}(A) = m^{\text{par}}(A) = 0$ if and only if A is a sequential action. (c) $m_{\text{par}}(A) = m^{\text{par}}(A)$ if and only if either there are no parallel events in A or any group of parallel events in A contains only two elements.*

Definition 26. The measure $m_{\text{par}}(A, B)$ of parallelism between A and B is equal to the number of parallel pairs of events in two maximal sequential subactions of A and B.

In other words, if D is a maximal sequential subaction of A and C is a maximal sequential subaction of B, then $m_{\text{par}}(A,B) = m^{\text{par}}(D, C)$.

Lemma 2. (a) *$m_{\text{par}}(A, B) \leq m^{\text{par}}(A, B)$ for any action A.* (b) *$m_{\text{par}}(A, B) = m^{\text{par}}(A, B)$ if and only if both A and B are sequential actions.*

Proposition 7. *If D and C are subactions of actions A and B, correspondingly, then $m^{\text{par}}(D, C) \leq m^{\text{par}}(A, B)$ and $m_{\text{par}}(D, C) \leq m_{\text{par}}(A, B)$.*

Let $0 \leq k \leq 1$.

Definition 27. An action A is called *k-parallel* if $k \leq m_{\text{par}}(A)/|A|$.

Definition 28. Actions A and B are called *k-parallel* if $k \leq m_{\text{par}}(A, B)/\min\{|A|, |B|\}$.

Any action A is 1-parallel to itself.

It is possible that each of two actions$A$ and B is k-parallel to some action C, but actions A and B are not k-parallel to one another.

2.3. *Processes*

In our model, processes are built from actions as actions are built from events.

Definition 29. A *process* P is a system of actions, i.e., $P = (A_1, A_2, \ldots, A_{\mathrm{m}})$.

Systems are determined by their elements and relations between these elements [64]. Thus, a process can define some additional relations between actions that constitute this process. Relations between actions in a process determine how actions are organized in this process. For instance, actions can form a sequence (a thread), a set without any relations, an arbitrary graph, and so on.

There are temporal relations between actions (cf., for example, [33]) and inheritance relations when one action starts in a situation (state) that (may have partially) resulted from the realization of another action. Temporal relations between actions can be induced by temporal relations between events that constitute these actions. However, temporal relations between events do not always completely determine temporal relations between actions. In this case, we need additional relations. These relations can be correspondences between time scales when events with tags that have values in time scales are used in actions. Additional temporal relations can also be precedence relations indicating when one action precedes another in the given process or how some events precede other events in the actions that constitute the given process.

Similar to communication actions, we define communication processes.

Definition 30. A process P is called a *communication process* if it consists of communication actions.

Definition 31. A process P is called a *pure communication process* if it consists only of pure communication actions.

Definition 32. A process P is called *finite* if it consists of a finite number of finite actions. Otherwise, P is called *infinite.*

For a long time, computer scientists studied and accepted only finite processes. The finiteness condition was even included in definitions of the main mathematical models of algorithms, such as Turing machines. However, infinite processes become more and more important in theoretical studies and practical applications (cf., for example, [32, 68–70]).

Definition 33. Any subset of a process P in which all relations between events are induced by relations in P is called a *subprocess* of P.

Proposition 8. *Any subprocess of a subprocess of P is itself a subprocess of P.*

Proposition 9. *Any subprocess of a pure communication and/or finite process P is itself a pure communication and/or finite process.*

For communication processes, this result in general is not true.

Definition 34. Any subset Q of a process P in which relations between events include all relations induced by relations in P is called an *enhanced subprocess* of P.

Thus, any subprocess of a process is an enhanced subprocess of the same process.

Proposition 10. *Any enhanced subprocess of an enhanced subprocess of P is itself an enhanced subprocess of P.*

Proposition 11. *Any enhanced subprocess of a pure communication and/or finite process P is itself a pure communication and/or finite process.*

Similar to actions, it is necessary to discern processes that were realized, i.e., processes that consist of actions that already happened, and potential processes, which represent alternate versions of what may happen. This gives us three types of processes:

- An *actualized process* is a process that consists of actualized actions.
- A *potential process* is a process which includes all actions and events for all possible realizations of this process.
- An *emerging process* is a process that consists of two parts (subprocesses): one is an actualized process; the other is a potential process. When we use the conventional linear scale, such as physical time in Newtonian mechanics, then all events from the first (actualized) part of an emerging process must precede all events from the second (potential) part of this process.

For instance, the choice operation "+", which is used in many models of concurrency (cf., for example, [19]), transforms any two processes into a potential process.

Potential processes are schemas [5], plans or programs for realization. Any realization of a potential process is an actualized process. Note that it is possible that a potential process consists only of actualized actions. Examples of such processes give the choice operation applied to two actualized actions.

Temporal relations between events allow us to separate special classes of events.

Definition 35 ([33, 54]). A *coexisting pair of events* consists of two events where one starts before the next ends.

Definition 36 ([33, 54]). A *separable pair of events* consists of two events that are not coexisting.

To formalize the condition of action separability, we define the beginning and end of an action from some action A, namely, the beginning t_{bA} of an action A is equal to

$$t_{bA} = \min\{p_T(t); e \in A, \text{ and } t \text{ is the tag of } e\}.$$

The end t_{eA} of an action A is defined as

$$t_{eA} = \max\{p_T(t); e \in A, \text{ and } t \text{ is the tag of } e\}.$$

Definition 37. (a) Two actions are called *separable* when the end of one of them is less than or equal to the beginning of the other. (b) Two actions are called *strictly separable* when the end of one of them is less than the beginning of the other.

Definition 38. A process P is called *action sequential* if all actions from P are separable from one another in the sense of.

Definition 39. A process P is called *strictly sequential* if all actions from P are sequential and separable from one another.

Proposition 12. *Any subprocess of an action sequential (strictly sequential) process of P is an action sequential (strictly sequential) process.*

Definition 40. A process P is called *interleaving* if all events from P have different time of occurrence, i.e., if $e_i = (d_i, t_i)$ and $e_j = (d_j, t_j)$ are events from A, then $p_T(t_i) = p_T(t_j)$ implies $e_i = e_j$.

Proposition 13. *Any subprocess of an interleaving process of P is an interleaving process.*

Proposition 14. *Any interleaving process of P that has only point-like events is strictly sequential.*

For processes with extended and/or pointed events, this result in general is not true.

3. Algebras of Events, Actions and Processes

Algebras of events, actions and processes form a multi-level system of related algebraic structures. This system reflects relations between, and operations with, events, actions, and processes.

3.1. *Algebraic Foundations for Modeling Concurrency*

As in our model we have three levels of description of concurrent processes, formalization of this model brings us to three-level algebras.

Definition 41. A three-level algebra $\mathbf{M} = (\boldsymbol{A}, \boldsymbol{B}, \boldsymbol{C}, \boldsymbol{H}, \boldsymbol{K})$ consists of three horizontal algebras $\boldsymbol{A}$, $\boldsymbol{B}$, and $\boldsymbol{C}$ called *levels* and two vertical algebras $\boldsymbol{H}$ and $\boldsymbol{K}$ called *lifts*:

(i) The first level is $\boldsymbol{A} = (G_A, Op_A, A)$, where G_A is a set of generators of the algebra $\boldsymbol{A}$, Op_A is the set of all operations of the algebra $\boldsymbol{A}$, and A is the support (set of all elements) of the algebra $\boldsymbol{A}$. Operations from Op_A are called inner or internal operations of the algebra $\boldsymbol{A}$, or horizontal operations of the algebra $\mathbf{M}$.

(ii) The first lifting algebra is $\boldsymbol{H} = (A, O^p, B)$, where A is the support of the algebra $\boldsymbol{A}$, O^p is the set of all operations of the algebra $\boldsymbol{H}$, and B is the support of the algebra $\boldsymbol{B}$. Operations from O^p are called inner or internal operations of the algebra $\boldsymbol{H}$, or vertical operations of the algebra $\mathbf{M}$. Operations from O^p are applied to elements from A to build elements from B and we assume that all elements from B are built in such a way.
Vertical operations are graded operations similar to operations in graded algebras [71].

(iii) The second level is $\boldsymbol{B} = (G_B, Op_B, B)$, where G_B is a set of generators of the algebra $\boldsymbol{B}$, Op_B is the set of all operations of the algebra $\boldsymbol{B}$, and B is the support of the algebra $\boldsymbol{B}$. Operations from Op_A are called inner or internal operations of the algebra $\boldsymbol{B}$, or horizontal operations of the algebra $\mathbf{M}$.

(iv) The second lifting algebra is $\boldsymbol{K} = (B, O^{pp}, C)$, where B is the support of the algebra $\boldsymbol{B}$, O^{pp} is the set of all operations of the algebra $\boldsymbol{K}$, and C is the support of the algebra $\boldsymbol{C}$. Operations from O^p are called inner or internal operations of the algebra $\boldsymbol{H}$, or vertical operations of the algebra $\mathbf{M}$. Operations from O^{pp} are applied to elements from B to build elements from C and we assume that all elements from C are built in such a way.

(v) The third level is $\boldsymbol{C} = (G_C, Op_C, C)$, where G_C is a set of generators of the algebra $\boldsymbol{C}$, Op_C is the set of all operations of the algebra $\boldsymbol{C}$, and C is the support of the algebra $\boldsymbol{C}$. Operations from Op_A are called inner or internal operations of the algebra $\boldsymbol{C}$, or horizontal operations of the algebra $\mathbf{M}$.

We assume that all operations and, consequently, some of these algebras can be partial. However, building algebras of events, actions and processes, we do not specify when operations and the corresponding algebras are total or partial. For instance, a monoid or a group is a total algebra, while a category is a partial algebra. Often we consider total operations (total algebras) as particular cases of partial operations (partial algebras).

Note that three-level algebras, like ordinary (universal) algebras, can have additional structures, such as topology or order [46, 72].

Three levels and two lifts give us the following partially commutative diagram:

$$\begin{array}{ccc} G_A & \xrightarrow{Op_A} & A \\ O^p \downarrow & & \downarrow O^p \\ G_B & \xrightarrow{Op_B} & B \\ O^{pp} \downarrow & & \downarrow O^{pp} \\ G_C & \xrightarrow{Op_C} & C \end{array} \tag{1}$$

Taking sets Op_B^{ind} and Op_C^{ind} of operations induced by operations from Op_A and Op_B in algebras $\boldsymbol{B}$ and $\boldsymbol{C}$ instead of sets Op_B and Op_C, correspondingly, in the diagram (1), we obtain two commutative squares (2) and (3):

$$\begin{array}{ccc} G_A & \xrightarrow{Op_A} & A \\ O^p \downarrow & & \downarrow O^p \\ G_B & \xrightarrow{Op_B^{\text{ind}}} & B \end{array} \tag{2}$$

$$\begin{array}{ccc} G_B & \xrightarrow{Op_B^{\text{ind}}} & B \\ O^{pp} \downarrow & & \downarrow O^{pp} \\ G_C & \xrightarrow{Op_C^{\text{ind}}} & C \end{array} \tag{3}$$

In a natural way, homomorphisms of three-level algebras are defined.

Three-level algebras are generalizations of graded algebras in the sense of Ref. 71.

3.2. *General Principles for Compositions of Processes and Actions*

Usually, only two compositions of processes, also called operations with processes, are considered: parallel and sequential composition. In practice, for example, in concurrent programming languages more compositions have been developed. In [33, 54], it is demonstrated that there are even several kinds of sequential composition.

As our goal is to build algebras of processes, we need to determine enough compositions of processes to be able to model real situations that exist in concurrent computations, communications and networking. We start with developing a typology of process compositions. This typology will give us a plan for designing flexible and efficient constructions of process compositions. Here, we consider only binary compositions. Ternary and higher arity compositions are considered elsewhere.

- Temporal types of processes and actions compositions:
  — *sequential compositions*,
  — *concurrent compositions*,
  — *multiscale compositions.*
- Sequential compositions of processes have three subtypes:
  — *consequential compositions*,
  — *action interleaving compositions*,
  — *event interleaving compositions.*
- Concurrent compositions of processes and actions have three subtypes:
  — *free compositions*,
  — *parallel compositions*,
  — *partially parallel compositions.*
- Information types of processes and actions compositions:
  — *compositions without interactions*,
  — *interactive compositions*,
  — *transformative compositions.*

Interactive compositions are built to reflect interactions between processes and actions without taking into account substantial and informational content of interactions. Transformative compositions are built to organize interactions between processes and actions and represent not only how this interaction goes but also what is exchanged between processes and actions. In particular, information transmission and transformation is explicitly described.

According to the form, there are two types of composition, giving

- *compositions with explicit interactions*,
- *compositions with implicit interactions*, and
- *compositions with both types of interaction.*

It is necessary to remark that algebras of processes have unary operations and operations with arity more than two, i.e., applied to more than two elements (events, actions or processes), in addition to various types of binary compositions. Some operations are total, while others are partial, i.e., undefined for some elements of these algebras. Some operations that have arity of more than two are generated by binary compositions, while others cannot be reduced to binary compositions.

3.3. *Compositions of Events*

As systems V and ST have topological and algebraic structures, these structures induce corresponding structures in sets $\mathbf{EV}_{NV,ST}$, $\mathbf{EV}_{NV,EST}$, and $\mathbf{EV}_{NV,kST}$ of events. For instance, the semantic system V is usually an algebraic system. This means that there are (in general, partial) operations in V. These operations induce corresponding operations in the system of names N. This allows us to define such a partial binary operation in the space $\mathbf{EV}_{NV,ST}$ of point-like events as the direct parallel composition of point-like events.

Let m be a binary operation in N, and $e_1 = (d_1, t)$ and $e_2 = (d_2, t)$ be parallel point-like events. When the semantic function *sem* is one-to-one, operations in N are usually induced by operations in V.

Definition 42. The (direct parallel) m-composition $m(e_1, e_2)$ of events e_1 and e_2 is defined by the formula

$$m(e_1, e_2) = (m(d_1, d_2), t).$$

Example 3. Parallel composition of information processing events is used for constructing an operation of a Turing machine from such events as changing the state of the machine, writing a symbol in a cell, erasing a symbol from a cell, and moving the head of the machine.

Example 4. In the MIMD computing architecture, several functional units perform different operations on different data. Examples are a multiprocessor or transputer computer, or a network of workstations. In this case, an event is a combined operation of several functional units. This event is a composition of operations in each separate unit. Similar operations on events are organized in the SIMD computing architecture.

When both systems N and ST are metric spaces with distances $\mathbf{d}_N$ and $\mathbf{d}_{ST}$, correspondingly, it is possible to introduce a metric in $\mathbf{EV}_{NV,ST}$, making $\mathbf{EV}_{NV,ST}$ a metric space.

One way to define a metric in $\mathbf{EV}_{NV,ST}$ is to use the Euclidean extension of metrics. Thus, if we take two events $e_1 = (d_1, t_1)$ and $e_2 = (d_2, t_2)$ from $\mathbf{EV}_{NV,ST}$, then the distance between them is equal to $\mathbf{d}(e_1, e_2) = \sqrt{\mathbf{d}^2_N(d_1, d_2) + \mathbf{d}^2_{ST}(t_1, t_2)}$.

Another way to do this is to use the Shannon extension of metrics, namely, if we take two events $e_1 = (d_1, t_1)$ and $e_2 = (d_2, t_2)$ from $\mathbf{EV}_{NV,ST}$, then $\mathbf{d}(e_1, e_2) = \mathbf{d}_N(d_1, d_2) + \mathbf{d}_{ST}(t_1, t_2)$.

To develop compositions of events, we assume that the semantic system V is an algebraic system. This means that there are (in general, partial) operations in V.

Proposition 15. *(a)* $m(e_1, e_2)\|e_1\|e_2$. *(b) If* $e_1\|e_2\|e_3\|e_4$, *then* $m(e_1, e_2)\|m(e_3, e_4)$ *and* $m(e_1, e_2)\|e_3\|e_4$.

A useful operation with events is a shift.

Let $sft\colon ST \to ST$ be an arbitrary mapping and $e = (v, t)$ be an event from $\mathbf{EV}_{V,ST}$.

Definition 43. The *sft*-shift $\mathrm{F}_{sft}(e)$ of the events is equal to $(v, sft(t))$.

Proposition 16. *If two events are parallel, then the results of the sft-shift of these events are parallel.*

Let $sft\colon ST \to ST$ be a mapping such that $sft(t_1) = t_2$ and $e_1 = (v_1, t_1)$ and $e_2 = (v_2, t_2)$ be events from $\mathbf{EV}_{V,ST}$.

Definition 44. The shifted m-composition $m_{sft}(e_1,\ e_2)$ of events e_1 and e_2 is defined by the formula.

$$m_{sft}(e_1, e_2) = (m(d_1, d_2), t_2).$$

Informally, shifted m-composition means that initially we shift the first event to the same position in time and space that has the second event and then apply the direct parallel composition.

Definition 44 implies that $m_{sft}(e_1,\ e_2)$ is always parallel to e_2.

Proposition 17. *If* $e_2\|e_4$, *then* $m_{sft}(e_1,\ e_2) \parallel m_{sft}(e_3, e_4)$.

Indeed, the validity of the relation of parallelism "$\|$" depends only on the time projection of the event tags, while the shifted m-composition changes only names of events and takes the tag of the second event from this composition. This means that time projections of both compositions coincide with projections of the corresponding second arguments in these compositions and by the initial condition this time is the same for both second arguments as they are parallel.

A semantic shift of events is called *renaming* as it is possible to consider values of events as names of these events.

Let $rn : V \to V$ be an arbitrary mapping and $e = (v, t)$ be an event from $\mathbf{EV}_{V,ST}$.

Definition 45. The rn-renaming $\mathrm{R}_{rn}(e)$ of the events is equal to $(rn(v), t)$.

Proposition 18. *If* $e_1\|e_2$, *then* $\mathrm{R}_{rn}(e_1)\|\mathrm{R}_{rn}(e_2)$.

Indeed, the validity of the relation of parallelism "$\|$" depends only on the time projection of the event tags, while renaming changes only the names of events.

3.4. *Compositions of Actions*

There is a diversity of compositions of actions and an even larger diversity of compositions of processes. Many of these compositions are used in practice. Our goal here is to develop a theoretical foundation for communication and computation in technical systems and others, as well as to study these compositions with the aim of providing efficient new means for communication and computing practice.

Definition 46. The *free composition* of actions A_1 and A_2 is the action A that consists of all events from A_1 and A_2 taken without changes and without introduction of new relations.

The free composition of actions A_1 and A_2 is denoted by $A_1 \cup A_2$. Note that the free composition of actions A_1 and A_2 is not simply the union of two sets A_1 and A_2 because the free composition takes into account existing relations between events inA_1 and A_2.

Definition 47. The *meet* of actions A_1 and A_2 is defined as the action that consists of all events that are elements of both A_1 and A_2 and all relations between these events that belong both to A_1 and A_2.

The meet of actions A_1 and A_2 is denoted by $A_1 \cap A_2$. Note that the meet of actions A_1 and A_2 is not simply the intersection of two sets A_1 and A_2 because the meet takes into account existing relations between events inA_1 and A_2.

Let $\mathbf{E}$ be some set of events and $\mathrm{A}(\mathbf{E})$ be the set of all actions generated by the events from $\mathbf{E}$, i.e., the elements of action from $\mathrm{A}(\mathbf{E})$ are events from $\mathbf{E}$ and only such events.

Theorem 2. (*a*) *The free composition of actions is an idempotent, commutative and associative operation, i.e., the set $A(\mathbf{E})$ is an Abelian (commutative) monoid with the empty action as its identity element, as well as a semilattice.* (*b*) *The set $A(\mathbf{E})$ is a Boolean algebra with respect to operations $\cup$ and $\cap$.*

To build other compositions of actions, we use shifts of actions. Any *shift of an action* constitutes of the shifts of events comprised in this action.

Proposition 19. *The result of any shift of an action A without repetition is an action without repetition.*

For coordinated and sequential actions, this is not true in general. However, in some cases, we have the same result.

Definition 48. A shift of an action A is *uniform* if the shifts of all events from A are defined by the same mapping *sft*: $ST \to ST$.

Proposition 20. *The result of a uniform shift of a coordinated (sequential) action A is a coordinated (correspondingly, sequential) action.*

Proposition 21. *The result of any renaming of a sequential action A is a sequential action.*

For coordinated actions and actions without repetition, this is not true in general. However, in some cases, we have the same result.

Proposition 22. *If $rn: V \to V$ is an injection, then the result of the corresponding renaming of a coordinated action (action without repetition) is a coordinated action (correspondingly, action without repetition).*

Definition 49. A *free sequential composition* of actions A_1 and A_2 is obtained by the following operations:

(a) first, we shift, if necessary, all events in A_2 with a shift sft, so that for any events e_i from A_1 and e_j from A_2 time in the shifted event $\mathrm{F}_{sft}(e_j)$ is larger than time in the shifted event e_i;
(b) then we take the free composition of these actions A_1 and $\mathrm{F}_{sft}(A_2)$.

The free sequential composition of actions A_1 and A_2 is denoted by $A_1 \cdot A_2$.

If the first process is finite, then its free sequential composition with any other process is defined. Note that the case $i = j$ is also included in the definition.

Proposition 23. *The free sequential composition of two sequential actions is a sequential action.*

Definition 50. A *free interleaving composition* of two actions A_1 and A_2 is obtained by the following operations:

(a) first, we shift, if necessary, all events in A_2 with a shift sft, so that for any events e_1 from A_1 and e_2 from A_2 time in the shifted event $\mathrm{F}_{sft}(e_2)$ is not equal to time in the shifted event e_1;
(b) then we take the free composition of these actions A_1 and $\mathrm{F}_{sft}(A_2)$.

The free interleaving composition of actions A_1 and A_2 is denoted by $A_1 \Theta A_2$.

Proposition 24. *The free interleaving composition of two sequential actions is a sequential action.*

Let $W \subseteq V$.

Definition 51. The *W-projection* $\mathrm{Pr}_W(A)$ of an action A is obtained by excluding from A all events with values not in W.

Let $K \subseteq ST$.

Definition 52. The *K-projection* $\mathrm{Pr}_K(A)$ of an action A is by excluding from A all events with tags not in K.

Lemma 3. *Any projection of an action A is a subaction of A.*

Theorem 3. *Any projection of a coordinated action (action without repetition or sequential action) A is a coordinated action (respectively, action without repetition or sequential action).*

Definition 53. A *free parallel composition* of two actions A_1 and A_2 is obtained by the following operations:

(a) first, we shift some events in A_2 with a shift sft, so that all parallel events in A_2 preserve their parallelism and some events in $\mathrm{F}_{sft}(A_2)$ become parallel to some events in A_1;
(b) then we take the free composition of these actions A_1 and $\mathrm{F}_{sft}(A_2)$.

The free parallel composition of actions A_1 and A_2 is denoted by $\pi(A_1, A_2)$.

We remind the reader that as we consider only point-like events, their parallelism means that they happen simultaneously. Usually, parallel composition has definite restrictions. These restrictions can come from:

(i) realization of actions and events, e.g., if we have 10 processors, we cannot simultaneously perform 11 operations when each operation demands one processor;
(ii) the algorithm, e.g., we cannot simultaneously perform two operations if one of them uses the result of the other.

Proposition 25. *If π is a free parallel composition of actions A and B, then*

$$m^{\mathrm{par}}(\pi(A,B)) > \max\{m^{\mathrm{par}}(A), m^{\mathrm{par}}(B)\}$$

and

$$m_{\mathrm{par}}(\pi(A,B)) \geq m_{\mathrm{par}}(A) + m_{\mathrm{par}}(B).$$

3.5. *Compositions of Processes*

The most basic composition of processes is their free composition.

Definition 54. The *free composition* of processes P_1 and P_2 is the process P that consists of all actions from P_1 and P_2 taken without changes and introduction of new relations.

The free composition of actions processes P_1 and P_2 is denoted by $P_1 \cup P_2$.

Note that the free composition of processes P_1 and P_2 is not simply the union of two sets P_1 and P_2 because the free composition takes into account existing relations between actions in P_1 and P_2.

Definition 55. The meet of processes P_1 and P_2 is defined as the process Q that consists of all actions that are elements of both P_1 and P_2 and all relations between these actions that belong both to P_1 and P_2.

The meet of processes P_1 and P_2 is denoted by $P_1 \cap P_2$. Note that the meet of P_1 and P_2 is not simply the intersection of two sets P_1 and P_2 because the meet takes into account existing relations between events in P_1 and P_2.

Let $\mathbf{A}$ be some set of actions and $\mathrm{P}(\mathbf{A})$ be the set of all actions generated by the actions from $\mathbf{A}$, i.e., elements of action from $\mathrm{P}(\mathbf{A})$ are events from $\mathbf{A}$ and only such events.

Theorem 4. *(a) The free composition of processes is an idempotent, commutative and associative operation, i.e., the set* $\mathrm{P}(\mathbf{A})$ *is an Abelian (commutative) monoid with the empty process as its identity element, as well as a semilattice. (b) The set* $P(\mathbf{A})$ *is a Boolean algebra with respect to operations* $\cup$ *and* $\cap$.

To build other compositions of processes, we use shifts of processes. Any *shift of a process* is composed of the shifts of events comprised in this process.

Proposition 26. *The result of any shift of a process* P *without repetition is a process without repetition.*

For coordinated and sequential processes, a similar statement is not true in general. However, in some cases, we have the same result.

Definition 56. A shift of a process P is uniform if the shifts of all events from P are defined by the same mapping $sft\colon ST \to ST$.

Proposition 27. *The result of a uniform shift of a coordinated (sequential) process* P *is a coordinated (correspondingly, sequential) process.*

Proposition 28. *The result of any renaming of a sequential process* P *is a sequential process.*

For coordinated processes and processes without repetition, this is not true in general. However, in some cases, we have the same result.

Proposition 29. *If* $rn\colon V \to V$ *is an injection, then the result of the corresponding renaming of a coordinated process (process without repetition) is a coordinated process (correspondingly, process without repetition).*

Definition 57. A *free sequential composition* of processes P_1 and P_2 is obtained the following operations:

(a) first, we shift, if necessary, all events in P_2 with a shift *sft*, so that for any events e_i from P_1 and e_j from P_2, time in the shifted event $\mathrm{F}_{sft}(e_j)$ is larger than time in the shifted event e_i;
(b) then we take the free composition of these processes P_1 and $\mathrm{F}_{sft}(P_2)$.

The free sequential composition of processes P_1 and P_2 is denoted by $P_1 \cdot P_2$.

If the first process is finite, then its free sequential composition with any other process is defined. Note that the case $i = j$ is also included in the definition.

Proposition 30. *The free sequential composition of two sequential processes is a sequential process.*

Definition 58. A *free interleaving composition* of two processes P_1 and P_2 is obtained by the following operations:

(a) first, we uniformly shift, if necessary, all actions in P_2 with a shift *sft*, so that for any events e_1 from an action A_1 from P_1 and e_2 from an action A_2 from P_2, time in the shifted event $\mathrm{F}_{sft}(e_2)$ is not equal to time in the shifted event e_1;
(b) then we take the free composition of these processes P_1 and $\mathrm{F}_{sft}(P_2)$.

The free interleaving composition of processes P_1 and P_2 is denoted by $P_1 \Theta P_2$.

Proposition 31. *The free interleaving composition of two sequential processes is a sequential process.*

Let $W \subseteq V$.

Definition 59. The W-projection of a process P is obtained by excluding from A all events with values not in W.

Let $K \subseteq ST$.

Definition 60. The K-projection of a process P is by excluding from P all events with tags not in K.

Lemma 4. *Any projection of a process P is a subprocess of P.*

Theorem 5. *Any projection of a coordinated process (process without repetition or sequential process) P is a coordinated process (respectively, process without repetition or sequential process).*

Definition 61. A *free parallel composition* of two processes P_1 and P_2 is obtained by:

(a) first, shifting some events in P_2 with a shift *sft*, so that all parallel events in P_2 preserve their parallelism and some events in $\mathrm{F}_{sft}(P_2)$ become parallel to some events in P_1;
(b) then taking the free composition of these processes P_1 and $\mathrm{F}_{sft}(P_2)$.

We remind the reader that as we consider only point-like events, their parallelism means that they happen simultaneously. Usually, parallel composition has definite restrictions. These restrictions can come from:

(i) realization of processes and events, e.g., if we have 10 processors, we cannot simultaneously perform 11 operations when each operation demands one processor;
(ii) from the algorithm, e.g., we cannot simultaneously perform two operations if one of them uses the result of the other.

Proposition 32. *If π is a parallel composition of processs P and B, then*

$$m^{\text{par}}(\pi(P,Q)) > \max\{m^{\text{par}}(P), m^{\text{par}}(Q)\}$$

and

$$m_{\text{par}}(\pi(P,Q)) \geq m_{\text{par}}(P) + m_{\text{par}}(Q).$$

3.6. *Algebras of Processes*

For processes, we build the following three-level process algebra $\mathbf{Pr} = (\boldsymbol{Ev}, \boldsymbol{Ac}, \boldsymbol{Pr}, \boldsymbol{EA}, \boldsymbol{AP})$ in EAP.

(i) The first level $\boldsymbol{Ev} = (EE, Op_E, Ev)$ is an algebra of events. In it, EE is a set of elementary events in some system R, which are generators of the algebra $\boldsymbol{Ev}$, Op_E is the set of all operations of the algebra $\boldsymbol{Ev}$, and Ev is a set of events in the system R, which form the support (set of all elements) of the algebra $\boldsymbol{Ev}$. Operations from Op_E are called inner or internal operations of the algebra of events $\boldsymbol{Ev}$, or horizontal operations of the process algebra $\mathbf{Pr}$.

The system of operations in the algebra $\boldsymbol{Ev}$ contains operations on events described in the previous section: the direct parallel m-composition $m(e_1, e_2)$, strong sequential composition $e_1 \circ e_2$, and shifted m-composition $m_{sft}(e_1, e_2)$ of events, *sft*-shift $\mathrm{F}_{sft}(e)$ and *rn*-renaming $\mathrm{R}_{rn}(e)$ of an event.

(ii) The first lifting algebra is $\boldsymbol{EA} = (Ev, O^p, Ac)$, where A is the support of the algebra $\boldsymbol{A}$, O^p is the set of all operations of the algebra $\boldsymbol{H}$, and B is the support of the algebra $\boldsymbol{B}$. Operations from O^p are called inner or internal operations of the algebra $\boldsymbol{H}$, or vertical operations of the process algebra $\mathbf{Pr}$. Operations from O^p are applied to elements from Ev to build elements from Ac and we assume that all elements from B are built in such a way.

(iii) The second level $\boldsymbol{Ac} = (Ac, Op_{Ac}, Ac)$ is an algebra of actions. In it, Op_A is the set of all operations in actions and Ac is a set of actions in the system R, which form the support of the algebra of actions $\boldsymbol{Ac}$. Operations from Op_{Ac} are called inner or internal operations of the algebra of actions $\boldsymbol{Ac}$, or horizontal operations of the process algebra **Pr**.

The system of operations in the algebra $\boldsymbol{Ac}$ contains operations on actions described in the previous section: the free composition $A_1 \cup A_2$, meet $A_1 \cap A_2$, free sequential composition $A_1 \cdot A_2$, free interleaving composition $A_1 \Theta A_2$, strong sequential composition $A_1 \circ A_2$, free parallel composition $\pi(A_1, A_2)$ of actions, and W-projection $\mathrm{Pr}_W(A)$, K-projection $\mathrm{Pr}_K(A)$, *sft*-shift $\mathrm{F}_{sft}(A)$ and rn-renaming $\mathrm{R}_{rn}(A)$ of an action.

(iv) The second lifting algebra is $\boldsymbol{K} = (B, O^{pp}, Pr)$, where B is the support of the algebra $\boldsymbol{B}$, O^{pp} is the set of all operations of the algebra $\boldsymbol{K}$, and C is the support of the algebra $\boldsymbol{C}$. Operations from O^p are called inner or internal operations of the algebra $\boldsymbol{H}$, or vertical operations of the process algebra **Pr**. Operations from O^{pp} are applied to elements from B to build elements from C and we assume that all elements from C are built in such a way.

(v) The third level $\boldsymbol{Pr} = (Pr, Op_{Pr}, Pr)$ is an algebra of processes. In it, Op_{Pr} is the set of all operations in processes and Pr is a set of processes in the system R, which form the support (set of all elements) of the algebra of processes $\boldsymbol{Pr}$. Operations from Op_{Pr} are called inner or internal operations of the algebra of processes $\boldsymbol{Pr}$, or horizontal operations of the process algebra **Pr**.

The system of operations in the algebra $\boldsymbol{Pr}$ contains oprations on processes described in the previous section: the free composition $P_1 \cup P_2$, meet $P_1 \cap P_2$, free sequential composition $P_1 \cdot P_2$, free interleaving composition $A_1 \Theta A_2$, free parallel composition $\pi(A_1, A_2)$ of processes, and W-projection $\mathrm{Pr}_W(P)$, K-projection $\mathrm{Pr}_K(P)$, *sft*-shift $\mathrm{F}_{sft}(P)$ and rn-renaming $\mathrm{R}_{rn}(P)$ of a process.

Some operations in events, actions, and processes are total, while others are partial.

4. EAP and Other Concurrency Models

4.1. *Comparing EAP with ESP*

Lee and Sangiovanni-Vincentelli [7] describe a concurrency metamodel, ESP, the basic elements of which are events, signals, and processes. ESP is intended to provide a framework for comparing other existing computational models in terms of how concurrency, communication, and time are represented. In this subsection, we demonstrate that the ESP metamodel is a special case of our more general EAP metamodel. Specifically, we describe how it is possible within EAP to reason about all the models of concurrency that one can use ESP to reason about. In the process, it will become evident that EAP may also be used to reason about concurrent systems that the ESP metamodel does not readily support. This shows the greater descriptive and cognitive power of EAP in comparison with ESP.

To represent basic constructs from ESP in EAP, we start with events, namely, the set of all events in ESP corresponds to a subset $\mathrm{EV}_{\mathrm{ESP}}$ of the set $\mathbf{EV}_{NV,ST}$ of point-like events, which we defined in Sec. 2. ESP events are tag–value pairs where the value belongs to a set V and represents an observable event, while the tag belongs to a set T. In other words, $\mathrm{T} \times \mathrm{V}$, is the set of all events from ESP. The value of an event describes what happens in this event, while the tag indicates the instant in time when the corresponding event occurred. Thus, we need to take a subset $\mathrm{EV}_{\mathrm{ESP}}$ such that $N = V = \mathrm{V}$ and $ST = \mathrm{T}$, while the semantic function *sem* and the natural projection p_T are identity mappings. These conditions make the set $\mathrm{T} \times \mathrm{V}$ of all events in ESP and the set $\mathrm{EV}_{\mathrm{ESP}}$ isomorphic and provide a representation of all events from ESP in the set $\mathrm{EV}_{\mathrm{ESP}}$ from EAP.

It is necessary to remark that, as Lee and Sangiovanni-Vincentelli write [7], tags of events from ESP, in a general case, are able to indicate not only time. However, this is also true for tags in EAP, which contain the space coordinate in addition to the time coordinate and can belong to a broader structure than the space–time manifold.

Events in ESP are used to build signals, the basic construct from the next level of ESP. These signals are subsets of the direct product $\mathrm{T} \times \mathrm{V}$ and may be represented as sets or tuples of events. The set S of all signals from ESP naturally coincides with the powerset of $\mathrm{T} \times \mathrm{V}$. If n is a natural number, then the set containing all collections (or tuples) of signals of size n is denoted S^n. At the same time, the aggregations of events in EAP are actions, and the signals of ESP are one type of actions where all events are from the set $\mathrm{EV}_{\mathrm{ESP}}$ and there are no additional relations between these events in the corresponding action. As a result, these conditions and the restriction of ESP's point-like events considered above reduces EAP's actions to signals within ESP.

Signals in ESP are used to build processes, the basic construct from the top level of ESP. A process, in ESP, is an n-tuple of signals, that is, an element from S^n for some n. Signals in these processes are used for interactions between processes as Lee and Sangiovanni-Vincentelli remark [7]. Thus, any process from ESP can be represented by such a process in EAP in which all actions are signals and include only point-like events. This shows that the EAP metamodel completely encompasses the ESP metamodel.

However, EAP provides much more possibilities for modeling real concurrent processes in various systems: in computers and computer networks, in embedded systems and biological organisms, and so on. For example, the inclusion of events with duration permits actions that cannot be represented by ESP's signals. For example, ESP's signals may include only events that occur either sequentially or simultaneously, but EAP's actions may also include partially overlapping events. One more important feature of big dynamical systems (either physical systems or global networks) is time relativity. In the ESP metamodel, relativistic effects are neglected and it is assumed that time is the same everywhere. In contrast to this, the EAP metamodel bases its constructions on the space–time manifold ST, which allows one to take into account relativistic effects and others that are inherent for big dynamical systems.

Beyond the differences in temporal relationships between events that distinguish actions from signals, there is another significant difference in meaning between these two middle-tier components of ESP and EAP. Signals from ESP represent possible behaviors of a process, that is, a signal represents a possible trace of a process, and by extension, a process under ESP is defined by its set of possible behaviors, or simply, a set of signals. In contrast, the actions of EAP do not always represent behaviors of one process *per se*, but rather permit reasoning about crosscutting multi-process and sub-process behavior, e.g., threads and fibers. Thus, EAP actions permit reasoning about process interactions directly, and are more than an intermediate level of composition for processes. This crosscutting middle tier is an important contribution of EAP. In addition, three types of actions, actualized, potential and emerging, allow one not only to represent possible behaviors of a system but also to discern what really happened from what can tentatively be.

Demonstrating that EAP models all possibilities of ESP to reason about concurrent processes and taking into account transitivity of modeling relations, we have as a consequence that EAP can represent and encompass the cluster of concurrency models that comprise ESP. As is established in [7], this cluster contains such models as Kahn process networks [8], the CSP model of Hoare [9], the CCS model of Milner [10], the dataflow model [11], Petri nets [13, 14, 29], and other discrete-event simulators.

ESP's definition of process is consistent with the CSP Traces model, and the basis for the CSP's process calculus [9], that is, one can reason about properties of a process by reasoning about all possible behaviors of a process. Moreover, ESP's definition of events directly support reasoning about parallel events in the spirit of VCR by Smith [15], which itself was an extension of CSP. However, VCR goes further to provide the possibility of multiple, possibly imperfect, observers, and by extension multiple corresponding views of the same computation. These views permit reasoning about ambiguities such as occur in the Linda model when Linda predicate operations rdp() and inp() indicate a failure to match a tuple in tuple space. This scenario is discussed in greater detail in Ref. 15. Without multiple perspectives (views) of a computation's history, it is difficult to appreciate the subtlety and subsequent disambiguation of these operations in the case of failure.

4.2. *Comparing EAP with VCR*

In this section we compare EAP with VCR, which arose from the operational semantics for concurrency developed by Smith [15]. This operational semantics, in addition to providing a description of how computation proceeds for generic concurrent systems, also afforded means for constructing parallel event traces similar to Hoare's construction of event traces in CSP [9]. Thus, VCR traces are derived from an operational semantics for concurrency, while CSP traces are derived from a process algebra. We now relate the process algebra of CSP and operational semantics of VCR, and along the way provide means for comparison between VCR and EAP.

In Ref. 15, a parameterized, parallel and distributed operational semantics (paraDOS) is developed as a meta model for reasoning about concurrency. Moreover, paraDOS forms the basis for VCR. The first models of concurrency paraDOS has been instantiated for are Actors and Linda. The Actors model and the Linda model were chosen to be instantiated because they represent very different models of concurrency, and modeling both was a demonstration of the genericity of paraDOS and VCR.

Before describing the components of paraDOS in more detail, it is helpful to describe the two models that were instantiated: Actors and Linda. This will permit a better understanding of paraDOS, which provides the means of this instantiation. The Actors model is due to Agha *et al.* [73], with later development by Athes and Agha [1], Agha *et al.* [75], and Mason and Talcott [76]. The Linda model is due to Gelernter [76], with later pertinent development by Carriero and Gelernter [77]. Both models are poised to play important roles in harnessing the computational power of multicore processor architectures, which provides an added dimension of relevance to being able to reason about concurrent systems based on these models.

Let us briefly consider the Actors model. In it, an actor is represented by its mail queue, and an actor machine is an instance of an actor's behavior (i.e., of a continuation). An actor machine is bound to one (and only one) element of the actor's mail queue. An actor machine's behavior is a function of the message it receives from its mail queue. Actors communicate by sending messages (asynchronously) to another actor's mail queue. Message delivery is guaranteed (in the limit), though order of delivery is not. Thus, the Actors model is super-recursive (cf., [32]) because message delivery is guaranteed only in the limit. As a result, the time and order of message delivery are the major sources of nondeterminism in the Actors model of concurrency.

The Linda model, in contrast, is not based on message passing, but neither is it a classic shared memory model. Gelernter [76] classified the Linda model as a new communication paradigm, describing it as generative communication. Linda is noted for its communication orthogonality, with communications being decoupled in three dimensions: destination (anonymous "receivers"), space (heterogeneous communication), and time (time-disjoint interprocess communication). Linda processes share access to a distributed, associative memory called *tuple space*, where tuples may be placed, copied, and removed by the Linda language primitives out(), rd(), and in(), respectively. Linda is a coordination and coordination language that augments an existing computational language. Sources of nondeterminism in Linda arise when a single Linda process could match multiple tuples, or when multiple simultaneous processes vie for the same tuple.

In designing paraDOS as a metamodel for concurrency, Smith [15] observed that all concurrent systems could be characterized as consisting of processes and interprocess communications. The operational semantics of paraDOS required identifying the components of a system's state, and defining a transition relation between states. What resulted was a state that consists of a 4-tuple containing a set of process behaviors, a set of communication closures, a parallel event set, and, recursively, the next state to which computation proceeds. The set of process behaviors is represented by continuations. The communication closures are bound expressions, which serve as a unifying abstraction for a variety of communication paradigms, such as shared memory and message passing. The parallel event set contains the multiset of observable events that occurred in transitioning from the previous state to the current state. The parallel event set permits constructing traces of a system's computation, and it is this trace that connects paraDOS and VCR to both CSP and EAP. The final element of the 4-tuple is the recursive next state, which is lazy in that it does not exist until the transition relation elaborates it (i.e., the transition relation chooses which state to elaborate from among the set of all possible next states).

Thus, to instantiate paraDOS for Actors and Linda, one must define the components that collectively make up the state, and the transition relation between states. An important part of this instantiation process is identifying which events are observable as a system transitions from state to state. For the Actors instantiation of paraDOS, observable events are the sending and delivery of messages to an actor's mail queue. For the Linda instantiation of paraDOS, observable events include the creation, copying, and consuming of tuples in tuple space. More details on the instantiation of paraDOS for Actors and Linda are presented in [15]. In both instances of paraDOS, the observable events represent stages of communication progress.

In two theorems proved in [15] equivalence between Actors, Linda and the corresponding restricted versions of paraDOS is established, namely, the first theorem demonstrates equivalence of a restricted version of paraDOS for Actors to the *Actor Theory* operational semantics introduced by Mason and Talcott [75]; the second theorem demonstrates equivalence of a restricted version of paraDOS for Linda to the *TSspec* operational semantics developed by Jensen [78] and Ciancarini *et al.* [79]. The restriction on paraDOS for both instantiations concerns one of its parameters, transition density, which was set to one to facilitate comparison with the Actor Theory and TSspec operational semantics, which were each limited to transitions involving only a single observable event. Without this restriction, as a model of true concurrency, paraDOS is capable of transitions involving multiple processes and multiple observable events. Exact statements of these theorems and respective proofs are given in [15].

The remainder of Sec. 4.2 describes how EAP can be used to model and reason about concurrent systems based on paraDOS, VCR, and the Actors and Linda models.

Events from VCR can be represented exactly by point-like events in EAP. VCR events are instantaneous, and do not include tags, but this does not present a problem for modeling in EAP. One more feature of the EAP events that model VCR events is that tags of the EAP events represent only time and do not have space coordinates, i.e., they are pure temporal events (cf., Definition 6). In other words, equivalent EAP events occur in some sequence in time, but location information is not preserved. If this bothers the reader, one could consider events as all occurring in the same location.

VCR events constitute the observable evidence of state transitions in a particular instantiation of paraDOS. State transitions form computation. In this context, it is possible to consider VCR events as computational events. Likewise, in EAP, events describe transitions (Axiom E2a). Thus, each computational VCR event can be represented by an event in EAP by giving its description or value and its time coordinate. If necessary, it is also possible to use the space coordinate.

Processes in VCR/paraDOS are represented by their continuations. In general, it is possible to semantically represent a VCR/paraDOS process by an ordered set of computational events (not necessarily all observable). Taking actions that consist only of point-like events without space coordinates, we can represent all VCR processes by EAP processes that use only such actions. Such a representation of processes in EAP is equivalent to the use of continuations in paraDOS.

As a result, processes in VCR can be represented by processes in EAP, though we must restrict in EAP the type of events used to be point-like and without space coordinates. VCR's parallel event traces are naturally represented by EAP's actions, where parallel events from VCR are EAP point-like events with tags indicating that they occurred simultaneously.

The set of process continuations and the parallel event multiset from paraDOS induce in EAP a relation on events of being observable. Thus, being observable is a property of EAP events. We can map traces in VCR to actions in EAP by including in actions only those events that are observable. Since the act of observation of a computation affects the computation itself, it is appropriate to consider observation as an operation on events in the EAP process algebra. Such EAP actions, built from observable events, are *traceable actions*. In this way, VCR traces correspond precisely to EAP's traceable actions.

We have demonstrated how the elements of EAP can be used to represent the elements of paraDOS and VCR. Since VCR has been shown to model such diverse concurrent models of concurrency as Actors and Linda, and EAP contains elements that model the element of VCR, we conclude that EAP is also capable of modeling the Actors and Linda models of concurrency.

4.3. *Comparing Operations in EAP with Operations in Other Concurrency Models*

Some concurrency models have operators to combine processes and to form new processes from existing ones. Such operators provide representation of basic features of concurrent processes in process algebra: compositionality, concurrency, and communication [11, 12, 15]. Let us consider the main operators.

The most fundamental of algebraic operators are choice and sequential composition. The *alternative* operator "+" provides a choice between events/actions from the composed processes, and the *sequencing operator* "·" specifies the sequential ordering of events/actions in the two processes that are composed. For instance, the process $(P+Q)\cdot R$ first chooses to perform all events/actions either from the process P or from the process Q, and then performs actions/events from the process R.

To allow the representation of concurrency, the *merge*, *right-merge* and *left-merge* operators are used. The merge operator "$||$" represents the parallel composition of two processes, the individual events/actions of which are interleaved. The left-merge operator "$|\lfloor$" (also denoted by "$|\lfloor$") is an auxiliary operator with similar semantics to the merge, but a commitment to always choosing its initial step from the left-hand process. The right-merge operator "$\rfloor|$" (also denoted by "$\rfloor|$") is an auxiliary operator with similar semantics to the merge, but a commitment to always choosing its initial step from the right-hand process. For instance, if we take two processes $U=(P\cdot Q)$ and $W=(R\cdot V)$, where P, Q, R and V are actions, then the process $U \parallel W = (P\cdot Q) \parallel (R\cdot V)$ may perform the actions P, Q, R, V in any of the sequences *PQRV*, *RPQV*, *RPVQ*, *RVPQ*, *PRQV* and *PRVQ*. At the same time, the process $(P\cdot Q) \rfloor| (R\cdot V)$ may only perform the sequences *PQRV*, *PRQV* and *PRVQ* as the left-merge operator ensures that the actions of P are performed first.

Interactions and, in particular, communications between processes are represented using the binary *communication operator* $|$. For example, let us consider the action $r(d)$ of reading a data item $d\in D$ and $w(d)$ of writing a data item $d\in D$. Then, the communication composition

$$\left(\sum_{d\in D} r(d)\cdot y\right) \Bigg| (w(1)\cdot z)$$

of processes $\sum_{d\in D} r(d)\cdot y$ and $\sum_{d\in D} w(d)\cdot y$ communicates the value 1 from the right component process to the left component process (i.e., the identifier d is assigned the value 1, and free instances of d in the process y take on that value), and then behave as the merge of y and z.

The abstraction operator τ_I provides a way to "hide" certain events, actions and processes by treating them as unobservable events, actions and processes going on inside the system being modeled and thus unrepresentable in the process algebra. Abstracted actions are converted to the *silent step* action τ. In some cases, these silent steps can also be removed from the process expression. For instance, the abstraction $\tau_{\{c\}}((a+b)\cdot c)=(a+b)\cdot\tau$ allows one to reduce the result of abstraction to $a+b$ since the event c is no longer observable and has no observable effects.

Compositions of processes in EAP determined by the compatibility relations allow us to represent all operators from different models of concurrency. Let us build such representations for the basic operators of process algebras considered above: sequencing, merge, right-merge, left-merge, communication and alternative operators.

The *alternative operator* $P + Q$ of processes P and Q is obtained if we take the free composition of processes P and Q and add the compatibility relations that make possible either all actions from P or all actions from Q.

Sequencing of events, actions and processes is represented by the free sequential composition of processes because sequencing of events or actions in models of concurrency gives a process as the result.

The *merge* $P \parallel Q$ of processes P and Q is obtained if we take the free composition of processes P and Q and add the compatibility relations that make possible any interleaving of actions from P and Q, preserving all relations that exist in P and Q. Remember that when processes from other concurrency models are represented in the EAP model, any action consists of a single point-like event.

It is also possible to build the merge $P \parallel Q$ of processes P and Q by taking the free composition of all possible free interleavings of processes P and Q.

The *right-merge* $P \rfloor\!\| \; Q$ of processes P and Q is obtained from the free composition of processes P and Q in a similar way; only the compatibility relations make possible only interleavings of actions from P and Q that start with the first action from the process Q.

The *left-merge* $P \,\|\!\lfloor\, Q$ of processes P and Q is obtained from the free composition of processes P and Q in a similar way; only the compatibility relations make possible only interleavings of actions from P and Q that start with the first action from the process P.

The *communication operator* is modeled (realized) in the EAP process algebra by means of special data transition actions. These actions take some results of actions in one process and give these results as inputs (initial conditions) to events and actions of another process. To formalize communication in EAP, we need new constructions of input and output semantics, as well as a new operation of the strong sequential composition of events, actions and processes.

Let a structure D be the common domain and a structure C be the common codomain for a set events $\mathbf{E}$. If we interpret events as changes in some system R, then it is natural to interpret the common domain D as the collection of possible states of the system R before some event from $\mathbf{E}$ happens, and to interpret the common codomain C as the collection of possible states of the system R after some event from $\mathbf{E}$ occurs. For instance, we can take D equal to C and equal to the set $\mathrm{St}(R)$ of all states of R. When R is a distributed system that consists of subsystems R_i $(i \in I)$, then the set $D = C$ can be equal to the union $\bigcup_{i\in I} \mathrm{St}(R_i)$ or to the direct (Cartesian) product $\prod_{i\in I} \mathrm{St}(R_i)$, where $\mathrm{St}(R_i)$ is the set of all states of the system R_i.

Definition 62. The input semantics *InSem* is a partial mapping *InSem*: $\mathbf{E} \to D$ and the output semantics *OutSem* is a partial mapping *OutSem*: $\mathbf{E} \to C$.

Input and output semantics form the basis for functional programming languages, as well as for the logical approach to program verification [80–82].

Definition 63. The value $\mathit{InSem}(e)$ is interpreted as the input (the initial state) for an event e and the value $\mathit{OutSem}(e)$ is interpreted as the input (the initial state) for an event e.

The case when $D = C = \bigcup_{i\in I}\mathrm{St}(R_i)$ gives a local input/output semantics for events where each event changes only one subsystem R_i.

The case when $D = C = \prod_{i\in I}\mathrm{St}(R_i)$ gives a global input/output semantics for events where each event can change many subsystems R_i, and change in one of these subsystems is considered change in the whole system R.

Input and output semantics are used in different disciplines and sometimes completely represent events. For instance, in probability theory, an event is a collection of possible outcomes of an experiment. Individual outcomes comprising an event are said to be *favorable* to that event.

Terminology more consistent with reality assumes that an event is a possible trial or experiment, while all possible outcomes of this trial or experiment form the output semantics of this event. A possible trial or experiment is a potential event. An event is said to occur as a result of an experiment if it contains the actual outcome of that experiment. An experiment that occurred is an actualized event.

Transitions in finite automata, abstract state machines, higher dimensional automata [60] and labeled transition systems [28] are events that are represented by their input semantics (the initial state of the transition) and output semantics (the final state of the transition).

Definition 64. An event e is the *strong sequential composition* of events e_1 and e_2 if $\mathit{InSem}(e) = \mathit{InSem}(e_1)$, $\mathit{OutSem}(e) = \mathit{OutSem}(e_2)$, $\mathit{InSem}(e_2) = \mathit{OutSem}(e_1)$ *and* $p_T(e_1) < p_T(e_2)$.

This is denoted by $e_1 \circ e_2$.

Informally, the strong sequential composition of events e_1 and e_2 means that the result of the event e_1 is taken as the input to the event e_2. In some cases, e.g., when e_1 and e_2 are computational operations performed by different devices, the strong sequential composition demands communication (data transmission) between these devices.

Definition 65. An action A is the *strong sequential composition* of actions A_1 and A_2 if all events in A are strong sequential compositions of events from A_1 and A_2.

This is denoted by $A_1 \circ A_2$.

The strong sequential composition of actions is in some sense the opposite of the free sequential composition of actions. However, there are many compositions between these extreme cases.

Definition 66. An action A is the *mixed sequential composition* of actions A_1 and A_2 if it consists of two types of events: some events from A belong to the free sequential composition of A_1 and A_2, while all other events in A are strong sequential compositions of events from A_1 and A_2.

This is denoted by $A_1 \diamondsuit A_2$.

It is possible to introduce similar compositions for processes.

Definition 67. An process P is the *strong sequential composition* of processes P_1 and P_2 if all actions in P are strong sequential compositions of actions from P_1 and P_2.

This is denoted by $P_1 \circ P_2$.

The strong sequential composition of actions is in some sense the opposite of the free sequential composition of actions. However, there are many compositions between these extreme cases.

Definition 68. An process P is the *mixed sequential composition* of processes P_1 and P_2 if it consists of two types of actions: some actions from P belong to the free sequential composition of P_1 and P_2, while all other actions in P are strong sequential compositions of actions from P_1 and P_2.

This is denoted by $P_1 \diamondsuit P_2$.

This definition shows that the traditional sequential composition of operators, automata or algorithms requires communication between the first and the second composed operators (automata or algorithms).

Now, we can see that the communication operator from different process algebras is a kind of the mixed sequential composition $P_1 \diamondsuit P_2$ of processes in the EAP process algebra.

It is possible to represent the abstraction operator in the EAP process algebra as an operator of compression (shrinking) of the observability relation in processes. In some cases, compression of the observability relation is equivalent to deletion of some events in a process. There is another way to model abstraction, namely, it is possible to introduce silent step (unobservable) events and change some events in actions and processes for silent step (unobservable) events.

Note that constructive realization of the alternative operator demands an additional action that makes the choice between P and Q, maybe under some condition.

As time and space are represented in EAP with much more detail than in other concurrency models, representation of operators from other models, such as merge or communication, is not unique in the EAP model.

The alternative operator and sequential composition define the *basic process algebra* ACP, which satisfies the following axioms (cf., for example, [19]).

- *commutativity of the alternative operator*: $x + y = y + x$,
- *associativity of the alternative operator*: $(x + y) + z = x + (y + z)$,
- *idempotency of the alternative operator*: $x + x = x$,
- *distributivity of the sequential composition with respect to the alternative operator*:

$$(x + y) \cdot z = (x \cdot z) + (y \cdot z),$$

- *associativity of the sequential composition*: $(x \cdot y) \cdot z = x \cdot (y \cdot z)$.

It is possible to show that these realizations in the EAP process algebra of the alternative operator and sequential composition preserve all these identities. Thus, we obtain a monomorphism (faithful representation) of the process algebra ACP in the EAP process algebra.

5. Conclusion

The constructed algebra of concurrent processes has a multilayer structure. These layers are divided into three levels. The algebra of events forms the first, lower level of the algebra of processes, while the algebra of actions forms the second, intermediate level of the algebra of processes. The third, highest level is formed by operations over whole processes. Each level can consist of several layers depending on the exactness of approximation and model precision.

When construction of the process algebra is finished, the next step is to develop a logical calculus for reasoning about processes and operations with them.

The introduced construction and results obtained imply several directions for future research.

(i) It would be interesting to further develop concurrent programming based on the EAP model, to study concurrent programs, and to use such programs for developing software and firmware for computer networks and embedded networks (cf., for example, [84]].

It is important to note that concurrent programming [7, 9, 10, 16] is closely related to and has to utilize super/recursive algorithms [32]. As is emphasized in [84], continuously operating concurrent programs exhibit ongoing behavior that is ideally nonterminating.

(ii) An important problem is to build concurrent schemas based on the EAP model, to study their properties, and to use such schemas for developing hardware, software and firmware for computer networks and embedded networks, as well as for finding ways to improve utilization of such networks. Mathematical tools for representation and study of such schemas are given in mathematical schema theory [5, 6, 81a]. Some types of schemas and operations were introduced and studied in [8, 62].

(iii) It is also important to develop exact mathematical tools for comparison of different process algebras and related process calculi [14]. The theory of categories provides some such tools. However, to compare individual algebras, we need special structures from universal algebra.

Terminology

Concurrency: A property of complex systems in which several computational processes are executing at the same time, and potentially communicating with each other. The study of concurrent processes encompasses a broad range of systems, from cluster computers, to loosely-coupled, largely asynchronous distributed systems and communication networks.

Interleaving concurrency: A process when it is possible to reduce concurrency to an interleaving of sequential events.

True concurrency: Does not allow reduction of concurrency to an interleaving of sequential events and supports abstractions for events whose occurrence partially overlap in time.

Event: Something that happened.

Abstract event: Also called *event label*, a representation of what happened (of what is done), but no indication of when or where.

Pure temporal event: A representation of what happened, indicating a time of occurrence, but not where it happened.

System event: A representation of what happened, indicating both a time and place of happening.

Action: A system of related events.

Finite action: Consists of a finite number of events.

Infinite action: Consists of an infinite set of events.

Signal or communication action: An action that consists of communication events.

Free composition of actions (A_1 and A_2): The action A that consists of all events from A_1 and A_2 taken without changes and without introduction of new relations.

Process: A system of actions.

Communication process: A process that consists of communication actions.

Finite process: Consists of a finite number of finite actions.

Infinite process: Consists of an infinite set of actions.

Action sequential process: A process P where actions from A are separable from one another in the sense of.

Strictly sequential process: A process P where actions from P are sequential and separable from one another.

Interleaving process: A process P where all events from P have different times of occurrence.

Free composition of processes (P_1 and P_2): The process P that consists of all actions from P_1 and P_2 taken without changes and introduction of new relations.

Algebraic system: A set with relations (predicates) and operations in it.

Universal algebra: A set with operations in an algebraic system.

Process algebra: A universal algebra, elements of which are processes and operations with processes are defined.

Topological manifold: A Hausdorff topological space X in which every point has a neighborhood homeomorphic to an open subset of Euclidean space $\mathbf{R}^n$.

Fiber bundle $\boldsymbol{B}$ (also called fibre bundle): A triad (E, p, B), where the topological space E is called the *total space* or simply, *space* of the fiber bundle, the topological space B the *base space* or simply, *base* of the fiber bundle, and p is a topological projection of E onto B such that every point in the base space has a neighborhood U such that $p^{-1}(b) = F$ for all points b from B and $p^{-1}(U)$ is homeomorphic to the direct product $U \times F$.

Exercise

1. What is concurrency?
2. What is interleaving concurrency?
3. What is true concurrency?
4. What is an event?
5. What is an abstract event?
6. What is a pure temporal event?
7. What is a system event?
8. What is an action?
9. What is a finite action?
10. What is an infinite action?
11. What is a signal?
12. What is the free composition of actions?
13. What is a process?
14. What is a communication process?

15. What is a finite process?
16. What is an infinite process?
17. What is an action sequential process?
18. What is a strictly sequential process?
19. What is an interleaving process?
20. What is the free composition of processes?
21. What is an algebraic system?
22. What is a universal algebra?
23. What is a process algebra?
24. What is a topological manifold?
25. What is a fiber bundle?
26. What is the relation between actions and processes?
27. What is the relation between events and processes?
28. What is the relation between events and actions?
29. What is the relation between algebraic systems and universal algebras?
30. What is the relation between process algebras and universal algebras?

References

1. M. Burgin, Elements of the system theory of time, LANL, Preprint in Physics 0207055 (2002).
2. P. J. Denning, The choice uncertainty principle (column: The profession of IT), *Commun. ACM* **50**(11), 9–14 (2007).
3. L. Lamport, Buridan's principle, Technical report, http://research.microsoft.com/users/lamport/pubs/Buridan.pdf (1984).
3a. P. J. Denning, The arbitration problem, *Am. Sci.* **73**, 516–518 (1985).
4. H. G. Rice, Recursive real numbers, *Proc. AMS* **5**, 784–791 (1951).
5. M. Burgin, Mathematical schema theory for modeling in business and industry, *Proc. 2006 Spring Simulation Multi Conference (SpringSim '06)*, Huntsville, Alabama (2006), pp. 229–234,
6. M. Burgin, Operational and program schemas, *Proc. 15th Intl. Conf. Software Engineering and Data Engineering (SEDE-2006)*, ISCA, Los Angeles, California (2006), pp. 74–78.
7. E. A. Lee and A. Sangiovanni-Vincentelli, Comparing models of computation, *Proc. 1996 IEEE/ACM Intl. Conf. Computer-Aided Design*, IEEE Computer Society, Washington, DC (1996), pp. 234–241.
8. G. Kahn, The semantics of a simple language for parallel programming, *Proc. IFIP Congress 74* (North-Holland, 1974).
9. C. A. R. Hoare, *Communicating Sequential Processes*, Prentice Hall International Series in Computer Science (Prentice-Hall, UK, 1985).
10. R. Milner, *Communication and Concurrency* (Prentice-Hall, Englewood Cliffs, NJ, 1989).
11. E. A. Lee and T. M. Parks, Dataflow process networks, *Proc. IEEE*, May 1995, http://ptolemy.eecs.berkeley.edu/papers/processNets (1995).
12. G. S. Fishman, *Principles of Discrete Event Simulation* (Wiley, New York, 1978).
13. C. Petri, Kommunikation mit Automaten, Ph.D. dissertation, University of Bonn, Bonn, Germany (1962).

14. W. Reisig, *Petri Nets: An Introduction* (Springer-Verlag, 1985).
15. M. L. Smith, View-centric reasoning about parallel and distributed computation, Ph.D. thesis, University of Central Florida, Orlando, FL 32816-2362, December (2000).
16. I. Foster and C. Kesselman, *The Grid: Blueprint for a New Computing Infrastructure* (Morgan-Kaufmann, San Francisco, 1998).
17. I. Foster, The grid: A new infrastructure for 21st century science, *Physics Today*, www.physicstoday.org (2002).
18. G. M. Reed and A. W. Roscoe, A timed model for communicating sequential processes, *Theor. Comput. Sci.* **58**, 249–261 (1988).
19. J. A. Bergstra and J. W. Klop, Process algebra for synchronous communication, *Inform. Contr.* **60**(1–3), 109–137 (1984).
20. J. C. M. Baeten and J. A. Bergstra, Real time process algebra, *Form. Aspe. Comput.* **3**(2), 142–188 (1991).
21. S. D. Brooks, C. A. R. Hoare and A. W. Roscoe, A theory of communicating sequential processes, *J. ACM* **43**(3), 500–599 (1984).
22. R. Milner, *Operational and Algebraic Semantics of Concurrent Processes*, in J. van Leeuwen, editor: Handbook of Theoretical Computer Science, Chapter 19, Elsevier Science Publishers B.V. (North-Holland), pp. 1201–1242 (1990).
23. F. Moller and C. Tofts, A temporal calculus of communicating systems, in *CONCUR-90 — Theories of Concurrency: Unification and Extension*, Lecture Notes in Computer Science, Vol. 458 (Springer, 1990) pp. 401–415.
24. P. G. Neumann, Risks relating to system compositions, *Commun. ACM* **49**(1), 128 (2006).
25. D. Bleecker, *Gauge Theory and Variational Principles* (Addison-Wesley, Reading, MA, 1991).
26. M. Nielsen, V. Sassone and G. Winskel, *Relationships between Models of Concurrency*, Lecture Notes In Computer Science, Vol. 803 (Springer, 1993), pp. 425–476.
27. J. Gunawardena, Homotopy and concurrency, *Bull. EATCS* **54**, 184–193 (1994).
28. V. Sassone, M. Nielsen and G. Winskel, Models for concurrency: Towards a classification, *Theor. Comput. Sci.* **170**(1–2), 297–348 (1996).
29. J. L. Peterson, *Petri Net Theory and the Modeling of Systems* (Prentice-Hall, Englewood Cliffs, NJ, 1981).
30. G. Winskel, Synchronization trees, *Theor. Comput. Sci.* **34**, 33–82 (1985).
31. M. Burgin, From Neural Networks to Grid Automata, in *Proceedings of the IASTED International Conference "Modeling and Simulation"*, Palm Springs, California, 2003, pp. 307–312.
32. M. Burgin, *Super-Recursive Algorithms* (Springer, New York, 2005).
33. M. Burgin and M. L. Smith, From sequential processes to grid computation, *Proc. 2006 Intl. Conf. Foundations of Computer Science*, Las Vegas, Nevada, USA, 26–29 June 2006, eds. H. R. Arabnia and M. Burgin (CSREA Press, 2006), pp. 10–16.
34. M. Burgin, Cluster Computers and Grid Automata, in *Proceedings of the ISCA 17th International Conference "Computers and their Applications"*, International Society for Computers and their Applications, Honolulu, Hawaii, pp. 106–109.
35. M. Burgin and M. L. Smith, A unifying model of concurrent processes, *Proc. 2007 Intl. Conf. Foundations of Computer Science (FCS'07)*, Las Vegas, Nevada, eds. H. R. Arabnia and M. Burgin (CSREA Press, 2007), pp. 321–327.
36. Y. Gurevich and M. Spielmann, Recursive abstract state machines, *J. Univ. Comput. Sci.* **3**(4), 233–246 (1997).
37. R. M. Fujimoto, Computing global virtual time in shared-memory multiprocessors, *ACM Trans. Model. Comput. Simul.* **7**(4), 425–446 (1997).

38. A. Boukerche, S. K. Das, A. Datta and T. E. LeMaster, Implementation of a virtual time synchronizer for distributed databases on a cluster of workstations, *Parallel and Distrib. Comput. Pract.* **4**(1) (2001).
39. R. T. Snodgrass and C. S. Jensen, *Developing Time-Oriented Database Applications in SQL*, Morgan Kaufmann Series in Data Management Systems (Morgan Kaufmann, 1999).
40. C. J. Date, H. Darwen and N. Lorentzos, *Temporal Data and the Relational Model*, The Morgan Kaufmann Series in Data Management Systems (Morgan Kaufmann, 2002).
41. E. F. Codd, *Cellular Automata* (Academic, New York, 1968).
42. M. Nielsen and F. D. Valencia, *Notes on Timed CCP*, Lectures on Concurrency and Petri Nets 2003 (Springer-Verlag, 2004), pp. 702–741.
43. A. I. Malcev, *Algebraic Systems* (Nauka, Moscow, 1970) [in Russian].
44. P. M. Cohn, *Universal Algebra* (Harper & Row, New York, 1965).
45. C. C. Chen and H. J. Keisler, *Continuous Model Theory* (Princeton University Press, Princeton, 1966).
46. A. Robinson, *Introduction to Model Theory and the Metamathematics of Algebra* (North-Holland, Amsterdam, 1963).
47. N. Bourbaki, *Theorie des Ensembles* (Hermann, 1960).
48. D. B. Gauld, Topological properties of manifolds, *Am. Mathe. Month.* **81**(6), 633–636 (1974).
49. J. M. Lee, *Introduction to Topological Manifolds*, Graduate Texts in Mathematics, Vol. 202 (Springer, New York, 2000).
50. N. Steenrod, *The Topology of Fibre Bundles* (Princeton University Press, 1951).
51. D. Husemoller, *Fibre Bundles* (Springer Verlag, Berlin, 1994).
52. D. Knuth, *The Art of Computer Programming, Vol. 2: Seminumerical Algorithms* (Addison-Wesley, 1997).
53. B. R. Greene, *The Elegant Universe: Superstrings, Hidden Dimensions, and the Quest for the Ultimate Theory* (Knopf Publishing Group, 2000).
54. B. Zwiebach, *A First Course in String Theory* (Cambridge University Press, 2004).
55. M. Burgin and M. L. Smith, Compositions of concurrent processes, in *Concurrent Systems Engineering Series*, eds. F. R. M. Barnes, J. M. Kerridge and P. H. Welch (IOS Press, Amsterdam, 2006). Communicating Process Architectures, Napier University (Edinburgh, Scotland), September 17–20 (2006), pp. 281–296.
56. G. D. Plotkin, A structural approach to operational semantics, Technical Report DAIMI FN-19, Computer Science Department, Aarhus University, Aarhus, Denmark (1981).
57. C. Gunter, *Semantics of Programming Languages* (MIT Press, Cambridge, MA, 1992).
58. G. Winskel, *The Formal Semantics of Programming Languages: An Introduction* (MIT Press, 1993).
59. J. W. de Bakker, W. P. de Roever and G. Rozenberg, *Linear Time, Branching Time, and Partial Order in Logics and Models for Concurrency*, Lecture Notes in Computer Science, Vol. 35 (Springer-Verlag, 1989).
60. E. A. Emerson and J. Y. Halpern, "Sometimes" and "not never" revisited: On branching vs. linear time, *J. ACM* **33**(1), 151–178 (1986).
61. E. Goubault, Domains of higher-dimensional automata, *Proc. CONCUR '93, 4th Intl. Conf. Concurrency Theory*, Lecture Notes in Computer Science, Vol. 715 (Springer, 1993), pp. 293–307.
62. A. Mazurkiewicz, Concurrent program schema and their interpretations, Report DAIMI-PB-78, Aarhus University (1997).

63. H. Rogers, *Theory of Recursive Functions and Effective Computability* (MIT Press, Cambridge, MA, 1987).
64. J. E. Hopcroft, R. Motwani and J. D. Ullman, *Introduction to Automata Theory, Languages, and Computation* (Addison Wesley, Boston, 2001).
65. M. D. Mesarovic and Y. Takahara, *General Systems Theory: Mathematical Foundations* (Academic Press, New York, 1975).
66. M. Burgin, D. Liu and W. Karplus, The problem of time scales in computer visualization, in *Computational Science*, Lecture Notes in Computer Science, Vol. 2074, Part II (2001), pp. 728–737.
67. V. Saraswat, M. Rinard and P. Panangaden, The semantic foundations of concurrent constraint programming, in *POPL'91* (1991), pp. 333–352.
68. F. D. Valencia, Decidability of infinite-state timed CCP process and first-order LTL, *Theor. Comput. Sci.* **330**(3), 577–607 (2005).
69. D. M. R. Park, *Concurrency and Automata on Infinite Sequences*, Lecture Notes in Computer Science, Vol. 104 (Springer Verlag, 1980).
70. M. O. Rabin, Decidability of second-order theories and automata on infinite trees, *Trans. AMS* **141**, 1–35 (1969).
71. M. Y. Vardi and P. Wolper, Reasoning about infinite computations, *Inform. Comput.* **115**(1), 1–37 (1994).
72. P. J. Higgins, Algebras with a scheme of operators, *Math. Nachr.* **27**(1–2), 115–122 (1963).
73. A. G. Kurosh, *Lectures on General Algebra* (Chelsea, New York, 1963).
74. G. A. Agha, *ACTORS: A Model of Concurrent Computation in Distributed Systems*, The MIT Press Series in Artificial Intelligence (The MIT Press, Cambridge, MA, 1986).
75. G. A. Agha, I. A. Mason, S. F. Smith and C. L. Talcott, A foundation for actor computation, *J. Funct. Program.* **7**(1), 1–72 (1997).
76. I. A. Mason and C. L. Talcott, *A Semantics Preserving Actor Translation*, Lecture Notes in Computer Science, Vol. 1256 (Springer, 1997), pp. 369–378.
77. D. Gelernter, Generative communication in Linda, *ACM Trans. Program. Lang. Syst.* **7**(1), 80–112 (1985).
78. N. Carriero and D. Gelernter, Linda in Context, *Commun. ACM* **32**(4) (1989).
79. K. K. Jensen, Towards a multiple tuple space model, PhD thesis, Aalborg University (1994).
80. P. Ciancarini, K. K. Jensen and D. Yankelevich, On the operational semantics of a coordination language, in *Object-Based Models and Languages for Concurrent Systems*, Lecture Notes Computer Science, Vol. 924, eds. P. Ciancarini, O. Nierstrasz and A. Yonezawa (Springer Verlag, 1994), pp. 77–106.
81. R. W. Floyd, Assigning meanings to programs, *Proc. Symp. Applied Mathematics, Am. Math. Soc.* **19**, 19–32 (1967).
81a. M. Burgin, Mathematical models in schema theory, Preprint in Computer Science cs.AI/0512099 (2005).
82. P. Naur, Proofs of algorithms by general snapshots, *BIT* **6**, 310–316 (1966).
83. C. A. R. Hoare, An axiomatic basis for computer programming, *Commun. ACM* **12**, 576–580 (1969).
84. Z. Manna and A. Pnueli, Specification and verification of concurrent programs by ∀-automata, Computer Science Department, Stanford University, Computer Science Department, Weizmann Institute of Science (1986).
85. E. A. Emerson, The role of Buchi's automata in computing science, in *The Collected Works of J. R. Büchi*, eds. MacLane and Siefkes (Springer Verlag, Berlin, 1990), pp. 18–22.

Chapter 18

DATAFLOW COMPUTATIONS ON ENTERPRISE GRIDS

CHAO JIN* and RAJKUMAR BUYYA†
Grid Computing and Distributed System Laboratory,
Department of Computer Science and Software Engineering,
The University of Melbourne, Australia
**chaojin@csse.unimelb.edu.au*
†raj@csse.unimelb.edu.au

This chapter presents the design, implementation and evaluation of a dataflow system, including a macro-dataflow programming model, runtime system and an online scheduling algorithm, to simplify the development and deployment of distributed applications. The model provides users with a simple interface for programming applications with complex parallel patterns. The associated runtime system dispatches tasks onto distributed resources through a proposed online algorithm, called localized heterogeneous earliest-finish-time (L-HEFT), and manages failures and load balancing in a transparent manner. The system has been implemented in a .NET-based enterprise grid software platform, called Aneka. Evaluation of the scalability and fault tolerance properties of the system has been carried out. The results demonstrate that our L-HEFT scheduling algorithm is efficient compared to existing techniques as it introduces a low overhead while making mapping decisions.

1. Introduction

In recent years, parallel and distributed computing techniques have been applied to execute e-science [1] and e-business [2] applications over P2P [3] and grid computing [4] platforms. The complex nature of these distributed applications has led to research into simplifying development and deployment over large scale distributed environments. Large-scale distributed systems within an organization, also called enterprise grids or desktop grids, have been pioneered by systems such as Condor [5], XtremWeb [6] and SETI@Home [7]. However, the focus of these systems has been on executing embarrassingly parallel applications. With the increasing deployment of such systems, there is a need for simplifying and enabling the execution of complex parallel applications on enterprise grids. In this context, the well-known dataflow programming model [8] shows significant promise. We have proposed a macro-dataflow programming model [9] that (a) exploits the coarse-grained dataflow relationship in (enterprise grid) computing processes and converts the dataflow graph into a directed acyclic graph (DAG) for execution, and (b) supports namespace for data generated during the dataflow execution.

In the rest of this section, we introduce the dataflow computation model, and then discuss the advantage of supporting dataflow computation in enterprise grid environments and related scheduling of DAG tasks in grid environments.

1.1. *Dataflow Model*

The dataflow computation model [8,10] is a powerful model of parallel computation, whose inherently parallel nature can be used to freely express parallelism and avoid the single point execution bottleneck common in the traditional sequential computation model. In the dataflow model, computation can be represented as a directed graph which consists of actors connected by directed arcs. An actor can be a single instruction or a sequence of instructions, while the data required by actors flow through arcs. An actor can be fired (executed) whenever all the data it requires are ready. In a dataflow execution, many actors may be ready to fire at the same time.

Figure 1 shows a simple example of a dataflow graph for computing $C = (B * A) - (A/15)$. In this figure, circles represent actors and arrows represent arcs, and each actor consists of one instruction. The square represents a constant value. Unlike the execution in a traditional sequential model, the multiplication and division actors can be fired at the same time in a dataflow model.

When the concept of dataflow was first proposed in the 1970s, it was mainly used in the domain of computer architecture for massive parallelism, as an alternative of "von Neumann" architecture. The Dennis dataflow graph [11] uses a dataflow program graph to represent and exploit the parallelism in programs. In particular, operations are specified by actors, which are enabled for execution when all required data are produced by dependent actors. The dependency relationships between pairs of actors are defined with the arcs of graph, while conditional expressions and iterations are represented by decision and control actors, respectively. The Kahn process network [12] replaces actors in a Dennis graph with sequential

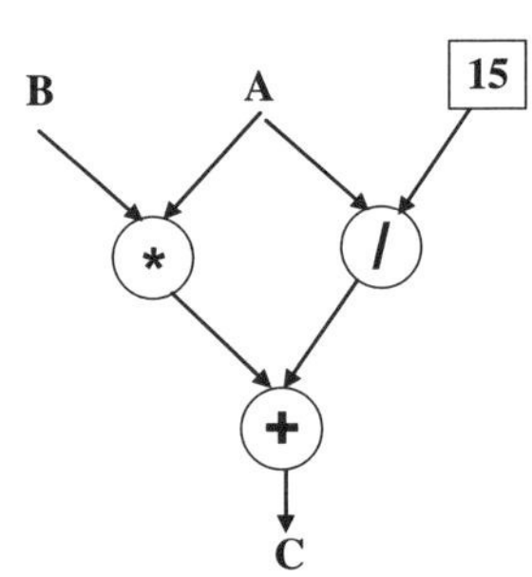

Fig. 1. A dataflow example.

processes which can communicate by sending messages through unbounded FIFO channels.

However, the parallelism used in pure dataflow computation operates at too fine a grain level, which leads to "excessive consumption of resources" in real systems and introduces unnecessary cost for sequential applications compared with the von Neumann model. To avoid the overhead from fine-grained actors in the pure dataflow model, in the 1990s the hybrid dataflow/von Neumann model was proposed to support more coarse-grained actors [13].

The hybrid dataflow model is motivated by the recognition that did not take dataflow and von Neumann techniques as two concepts that are mutually exclusive and irreconcilable. On the contrary, they can be taken as the two extremes of a continuum of possible computer architectures. From the perspective of parallelism granularity, the pure dataflow model works on a fine grain level, while the thread model over von Neumann architecture works on a comparatively coarse grain level. Sterling [14] explored the performance of different levels of granularity in dataflow machines. His results indicate that both fine-grained (in the pure dataflow model) and coarse-grained (in the sequential execution) dataflow cannot offer better parallel performance than a medium-grained approach. The hybrid model is flexible in combining the advantages of dataflow and control-flow, as well as in exposing parallelism at a desired level. Through the hybrid model, a region of actors within a dataflow graph can be grouped together as a coarse-grained thread to be executed sequentially, while the data-driven method of dataflow can be used to activate and synchronize the execution of threads. Example hybrid models include EARTH [15], P-RISC [16], and McGill dataflow architecture [17].

The recent evolution of the dataflow model is large-grained dataflow. Large-grained dataflow can begin with a fine-grained dataflow graph, which can be analyzed and partitioned into sub-graphs. The sub-graphs can be compiled into sequential von Neumann processes, which can run in a multithread environment according to dataflow scheduling principles. Normally, these processes are called *macroactors*. Recently, these macroactors have been easily programmed in an imperative language, such as C or Java, rather than derived from a fine-grained dataflow graph. Component techniques can also be used to implement macroactors. A large number of computer architectures and computational models are inspired by dataflow models as discussed in Refs. 18 and 8.

The dataflow approach has had important influences on many areas of computer science and engineering research such as programming languages, signal processing, architecture design, parallel compilation and distributed computing. Currently, dataflow as a programming model still has the advantages of having a natural parallel interface and smoothly bridging parallel applications and underlying execution environments. Especially in an epoch when large-scale parallel and distributed environments and multi-core CPUs are becoming popular, the natural parallel interface of the dataflow model shows the promise of meeting the challenge of pervasive parallelism [19].

1.2. *Enterprise Grids*

Enterprise grid computing systems are oriented towards enabling virtualization and harnessing various types of distributed IT resources within an enterprise. They are specifically focused on provisioning resources dynamically to different projects depending on their priorities, which are often driven by business goals. They need to support various types of workloads and applications. That means enterprise grids need to provide a comprehensive environment for developing various types of applications based on different parallel programming models and abstractions. They also need to embrace emerging hardware and software architectural models, such as multi-core processors and service-oriented architecture, and build on standards based platforms such as Microsoft's .NET and J2EE.

It is important to borrow mature experiences from high-end supercomputing, but the current application programming models are difficult to use for expressing, debugging and testing parallel programs [20] and they are especially not suitable for novice concurrent programmers. Parallel programs need to manage threads, locks, and explicit synchronization mechanisms. This puts limitations on the exploration of modern software development approaches such as those based on components. To enable programmers to build parallel applications easily, we need high-level constructs and abstractions which are easier to understand, express, and use than those offered by threads and locks.

The complex nature of these parallel/distributed applications has led to research into simplifying development and deployment over large-scale distributed environments. Grid computing platforms such as Condor [11,21], Entropia [22], Pegasus [7], and ASKALON [23] provide mechanisms for workflow scheduling. Condor works by considering the granularity of a single job. Existing tools, such as DAGMan, can schedule jobs with data dependencies and address the parallelism between tasks. Condor does not focus on the programming difficulties associated with data communication between tasks, but emphasizes the high level problem of matching available computing power with the requirements of jobs. For example, within each job, users mainly depend on a message passing interface for programming, such as MPI. Therefore, users must take extra care with data-sharing conflicts, deadlock avoidance, and fault tolerance. Pegasus [7] works on a higher level than DAGMan, and deploys a heuristic scheduling policy for scheduling the DAG graph of jobs rather than the *just-in-time* scheduling policy in DAGMan.

Grid Superscalar [24] aims to simplify the development of grid applications with a different method, wherein users can write sequential programs within small tasks and parallelism between tasks is discovered through analyzing the dependency of input and output files for tasks. However, scheduling and fault tolerance are not the focus of Superscalar. Kepler [25] is a scientific workflow system that allows composition of both data and control flows. It also provides a graph interface for programming.

We developed a next-generation desktop grid software system, called Aneka, that serves as a flexible and extensible software framework for realizing multiple application models, security solutions, communication protocols and persistence without affecting an existing ecosystem. Aneka was conceived with the aim of providing a set of services that make grid construction and development of applications as easy as possible without sacrificing flexibility, scalability, reliability and extensibility.

This chapter presents the realization of a macro-dataflow model and its implementation using Aneka enterprise grid software services. As a result, our macro-dataflow model works in .NET-based distributed network computing environments and supports an interface for the composition of coarse-grained dataflow graphs, which can be converted into DAG task graphs and scheduled for execution on distributed computing systems. Additional details on the macro-dataflow programming model can be found in Sec. 2.

1.3. *Dynamic Scheduling of DAG Tasks*

To efficiently execute the macro-dataflow computation in distributed environments, we need an efficient mapping algorithm that assigns tasks in the DAG graph of the dataflow to distributed resources. Furthermore, it should be robust enough to handle heterogeneity and frequent failures common in the target execution environment (shared enterprise grids) containing autonomous resources/contributors.

Meeting these requirements is a challenge [26] and has been extensively studied as DAG-based scheduling models/techniques, which are either static or dynamic in nature. Popular static scheduling algorithms, such as heuristic-based heterogeneous earliest-finish-time (HEFT) [27] and genetic search [28], map DAG tasks to distributed resources prior to execution. Such static methods do not work effectively for dynamic distributed environments where the availability of resources and their capability varies dynamically at runtime.

To effectively schedule tasks of a DAG graph to grid environments with dynamic features, many dynamic scheduling strategies have been proposed to map tasks to resources during execution. One simple choice is called *just-in-time scheduling*. For example, Condor-G [29] and Virtual Grid [30] deploy a greedy matching algorithm to decide the mapping of each task during execution. It is difficult to achieve overall optimized mapping and efficient utilization of global resources for this category of policies.

Another method is to start with a static scheduling plan and then perform iterative rescheduling for adaptation to resource changes [31]. Although these policies can potentially achieve optimized efficiency overall, they need to have detailed knowledge of the whole graph and their scheduling cost could be high for large-scale graphs with thousands of tasks [30]. The plan switching method [32] can construct a family of activity graphs beforehand and investigate the means of switching from one member to another when the execution of one activity fails. However, all of the plans are limited within the most updated information of resources, which does not take future changes into consideration. Furthermore, most heterogeneous scheduling algorithms do not pay attention to efficient failure handling.

We propose a localized heterogeneous earliest-finish-time (L-HEFT) scheduling algorithm for our macro-dataflow system within a dynamic heterogeneous environment in which failures are common. In contrast with previous methods, our adaptive scheduling algorithm focuses on optimizing the scheduling efficiency based on the available partial part of the graph, which is gradually generated during execution, and works in an online manner. Compared with iterative static mapping-based rescheduling methods, our algorithm introduces a low overhead in managing schedules and execution in a distributed environment with dynamic resources. Furthermore, it delivers nearly the same performance as the static mapping-based rescheduling methods and even outperforms rescheduling methods for dataflow applications of a large size of symmetric graph with balanced tasks distribution. In addition, our macro-dataflow system naturally supports a replication-based fault tolerance mechanism for intermediate data generated during dataflow execution, which simplifies the failure handling of our adaptive scheduling algorithm.

The rest of the chapter is organized as follows. First, we present a simple and powerful macro-dataflow programming model, which supports the composition of parallel applications for transparent deployment in a heterogeneous distributed environment, and an architecture and runtime machinery of a dataflow system. Then, we discuss an L-HEFT heuristic online scheduling algorithm and evaluate the scalability of our system and the performance of the scheduling policy with real applications in an enterprise grid environment. Performance results demonstrate that our system is effective at supporting data parallelism for real applications and our scheduling policy achieves the same performance targets as an existing dynamic policy with scheduling cost 30–50% less than existing static mapping-based rescheduling policies.

2. Macro-Dataflow Programming Model

This section describes the macro-dataflow programming model which is used to compose the coarse-grained dataflow graph for the whole execution. With this model, users can implicitly specify the dependent relationship between the data generated during execution of the application and easily edit the execution logic for each actor in the coarse-grained dataflow.

The macro-dataflow graph is represented as a DAG. Given a DAG, $\boldsymbol{G} = (\boldsymbol{V}, \boldsymbol{E})$, the set of vertices $\boldsymbol{V} = \{v_1, v_2, \ldots, v_n\}$ represents the set of tasks to be executed, and the set of directed edges $\boldsymbol{E}$ represents communication between tasks, where $e_{ij} = (v_i, v_j) \in \boldsymbol{E}$ indicates communication from task v_i to v_j. We refer to each communication data as a *stream* and users can specify a unique name for each stream. *Initial streams*, which are not generated by any tasks, are actually mapped to external files, e.g., the input for dataflow execution. *Result streams*, which have no receiver tasks, are the results of dataflow execution. With the name of each stream, users can edit execution tasks and configure its input and output streams. We call each execution task an *actor*.

2.1. *APIs*

The main APIs for composing dataflow graph are as follows:

- *Execute*. Compute (*InStream*[] *inputs, OutStream*[] *outputs*), which is inherited by users to add instructions to execute the actor.
- *Actor*. SetExecute (*Execute*) is used to specify the set of instructions of each actor.
- *Actor*. AddInput (*Stream*) is used to specify input streams for each actor.
- *Actor*. AddOutput (*Stream*) is used to specify output streams for each actor.
- SetInitialStream (*Stream, file*) is used to set the input files for the whole dataflow graph.
- SetResultStream (*Stream, file*) is used to set the output files to contain the results of dataflow execution.

Through the above APIs, it is clear that the user does not need to specify the complex dependent relationship between data generated during execution. However, our system internally composes the dataflow graph through the implicit data relationship, and also provides other APIs to make the user check the correctness of the graph.

2.2. *Namespace for Streams*

We consider a namespace to specify streams within the macro-dataflow graph. Each stream has a unique name in the dataflow graph. The name consists of three parts: *Category*, *Version* and *Space*. Thus, the name is denoted as $\langle C, T, S\rangle$. *Category* denotes the category of streams; *Version* denotes the index for the stream along the time axis during the computing process; *Space* denotes the index along the space axis during execution. In the following text, we refer to the name of the stream as *name*. In particular, *Category* is a string; *Version* is an integer and *Space* is an integer array.

We use an example to illustrate how to use the namespace to specify streams: an iterative matrix and vector multiplication, $V^t = M * V^{t-1}$. To parallelize the execution, we partition the matrix and vector into rows of m pieces with each piece being denoted as a stream. To name them, $Category = M$ denotes the matrix vertices and $Category = V$ denotes the vector vertices. For the ith vector vertex, the dependency relationship between streams should be specified as

$$\langle V, t, i\rangle \leftarrow \{\langle M, 0, i\rangle, \langle V, t-1, j\rangle\} \quad (j = 1 \ldots m).$$

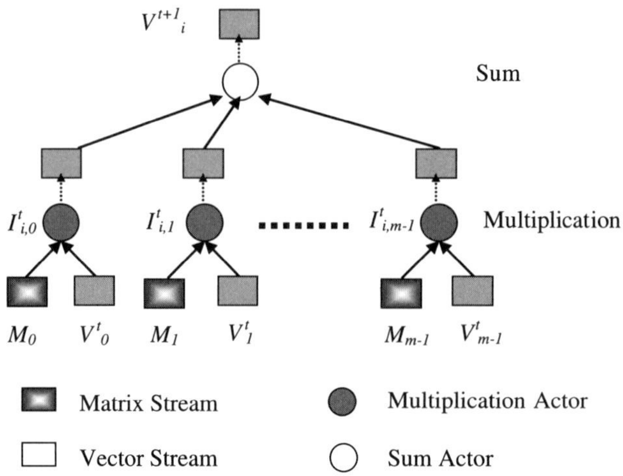

Fig. 2. Dataflow graph for the ith vector piece.

2.3. *Example*

Given the matrix vector iterative multiplication example, $V^t = M * V^{t-1}$, we partition the matrix and vector by rows into m pieces as:

$$V_i^t = \sum_{j=1}^{m} M_i * V_j^{t-1} \quad (i = 1, \ldots, m).$$

The corresponding sub-macro-dataflow graph is illustrated in Fig. 2.

For this example, users may use two basic execution modules: multiplication of the matrix and vector pieces and the sum of m multiplication results.

Given m partitions and T iterations, Fig. 3 illustrates how to compose the dataflow graph for this example.

Finally, users set the input files for the matrix and vector pieces through SetInitialStream( ). Also users need to specify to collect the result streams through SetResultStream( ).

3. Architecture and Design

This section describes the dataflow system which supports the execution of our macro-dataflow graph. The target environment of our dataflow system is a shared enterprise grid consisting of commodity PCs, where PCs can drop out of the system as soon as they are dominated, turned off or restarted by interactive users. Such nodes can rejoin the system when they are idle again. The design goal is to make our system adapt to the resource heterogeneity (including transient or static), easily incorporate new resources and handle failures. For adaptation to heterogeneity, we deploy online heuristic scheduling algorithm with the assistance of a performance prediction algorithm (Sec. 4.2) based on historical data. To handle failures, we

```
produce ComposeGraph(T, m, mulExec, sumExec)
/* T ← iteration times
 m ← partition number
 mulExec ← instructions for multiplication actor
 mulExec ← instructions for sum actor
*/
   for (t = 0; t < T; t++) {
     for (i = 0; i < m; i++) {
       matriStream = Name("M", 0, i);
          vecStream = Name("V", 0, i);
       for (j = 0; j < m; j++) {
        /*multiplication  result*/
        interStream = Name("I", t, i, j);
        mul = CreateActor("Multiplication");
        mul.SetExecute(multiExec);
        mul.AddInput(matriStream);
        mul.AddInput(vecStream);
        mul.AddOutput(interStream);
       }
       sumStream= Name("V", t, i); //sum result
       sum = CreateActor("Sum");
          sum.SetExecute(sumExec);
       for (j = 0; j < m; j++) {
        interV = Name("I", t-1, i, j);
        mul.AddInput (interStream);
       }
          mul.AddOutput(sumStream)
     }
   endfor
return
```

Fig. 3. Composition of the dataflow graph.

organize the large numbers of free disks in the PCs as a virtual storage pool and hold intermediate data generated during dataflow execution as the resuming point in handling failures.

3.1. *System Overview*

The key components of the dataflow computing system are: *coordinator* and *contributors*, as illustrated in Fig. 4. The coordinator is responsible for accepting jobs from users the organizing contributors to work cooperatively. For example, it monitors the availability of resources, sends execution requests to contributors, and handles failures of contributors. Each contributor joins the dataflow system by contributing CPU, memory and disk resources, and then passively waits for requests from the coordinator. Both coordinator and contributors are implemented as a pluggable service component in Aneka [33], which is a .NET-based enterprise grid software platform and can support the creation of an enterprise grid environment. We utilize the existing grid services such as the Resource Monitor Service supported in Aneka to simplify our implementation.

3.2. *Structure of the Coordinator*

The coordinator consists of a set of key sub-components, including *job monitor*, and *scheduler*, database of*performance history*, *performance predicator*, and *index*

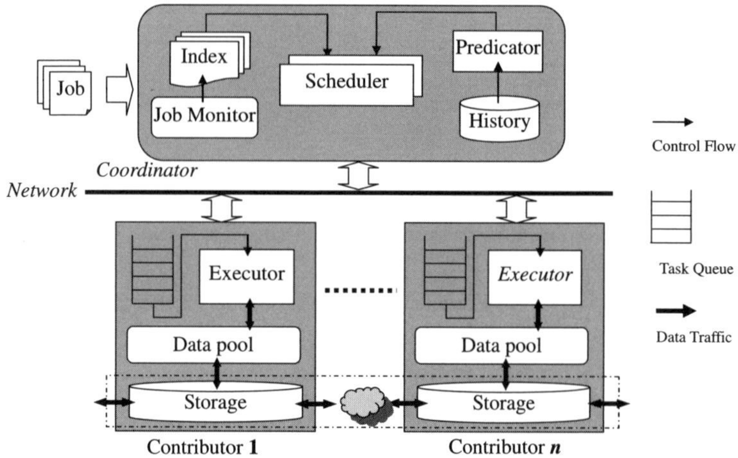

Fig. 4. Architecture of dataflow system.

of intermediate data. A *scheduler* is instantiated for each job and adopts an online scheduling policy to map ready tasks to suitable contributors for execution. The historical information on execution is recorded in the database of the performance history component, which can be used by a predicator component to predict the performance of tasks. The job monitor maintains the dataflow graph for each job, keeps track of the intermediate data generated during execution, and explores ready tasks for scheduling. The index component maintains the location for available intermediate data. Normally, each piece of intermediate data stays in memory on the contributor where it is generated. In order to improve the reliability of execution, however, the index can choose when and where to make the intermediate data persistent on disk or replicated to other contributors.

3.3. *Structure of Contributors*

Each contributor contributes local resources for dataflow computing and maintains a task queue to buffer the commands from the coordinator. Due to the large disk drive in current desktops, contributors in a dataflow system actually have a significant amount of free disk space. The free disk space available is organized by the coordinator as a virtual storage pool, which can hold the intermediate data generated during dataflow execution to improve the availability of computation and also to handle transient or permanent departure of contributors. Furthermore, there are the following important sub-components for each contributor: *executor*, *data pool* and *storage*.

- *Executor*: Fetches executing commands from the task queue, executes the tasks and puts the output data into the local *data pool*. The *executor* requests input data for tasks from the *data pool*.

- *Data pool*: Maintains the intermediate data generated by dataflow in memory, and meets the requests of input data from the executor. If a request is missed locally, the data pool will notify the storage component to fetch the requested data from other contributors according to the location in command. When the data pool finds that allocated memory is nearly full, it can swap data in memory to disks through the storage component. In order to handle failures efficiently, the data pool may also swap those data not needed by the remaining part of the dataflow execution to the storage component for persistent maintenance until the whole job is finished — rather than simply removing them.
- *Storage component*: Works as a backup cache for the data pool, and at the same time is responsible for managing persistent intermediate data, which may be generated for reliability purposes. The local storage component can communicate with the storage component of remote contributors to transfer data, which is transparent from the point view of the executor. In fact, storage components across contributors constitutes virtual storage that is specially designed for holding persistent intermediate data for dataflow with a flat namespace. To handle failures, upon request from the coordinator, a storage component can replicate the requested intermediate data on the remote side to improve reliability and availability.

3.4. *Replication Support*

With the cooperation between the index component of the coordinator and the storage components of the contributors, our dataflow system can replicate intermediate data generated during the dataflow execution to multiple contributors. The replication works in a lazy manner, just replicating the intermediate data if there are contributors found not to be busy. In order to reduce the cost of replicating intermediate data for tasks at every level (see the introduction), we replicate data associated with tasks every n levels. The replication step size, n, can be specified by users during job submission. In order to achieve execution in the face of failures, some of the intermediate data may have to be re-generated. This requires identifying the finished tasks to be re-executed to regain the lost data. Therefore, we need to explore tasks which should be re-executed to generate the intermediate data necessary to resume the execution. This exploration stops when we find replicated copies of lost intermediate data or we reach the initial tasks.

4. Scheduling Policy

This section describes in detail our dynamic scheduling algorithms with regard to mapping ready tasks of the dataflow graph to heterogeneous resources in a shared enterprise grid environment.

Our macro-dataflow programming model is aimed at scientific applications, which consist of many repetitive tasks. To support adaptation, repetitive tasks are partitioned with fine granularity, and as a result, the number of tasks is much larger than the number of resources. Taking the large number of tasks into consideration, our dynamic policy aims to efficiently map dataflow tasks onto heterogeneous resources with frequent changes. The policy optimizes the scheduling efficiency based on the available part of the graph which contains ready tasks gradually generated during the execution. Our policy works in two phases. In the first phase, it partitions the tasks in the graph into clusters and makes tasks within the same cluster independent. This partition phase can be deployed prior to the execution time or during execution. In the second phase, the policy achieves a local optimization on scheduling of ready tasks with priority on reducing data migration using our L-HEFT heuristic algorithm.

Compared with just-in-time dynamic policies, our method aims to decrease the unnecessary data movement between resources through online analysis, which is especially important for data-intensive application [34]. At the same time, it does not require the phase of complex rank assignment, which is the prerequisite for global optimization policies, and is always based on an inaccurate estimation of data transfer and computing cost. To cope with the repetition property of tasks in applications, we adopt a performance prediction algorithm to improve the efficiency of L-HEFT scheduling, which is based on historical performance information.

4.1. *DAG Execution Model*

We take the macro-dataflow graph as our execution model. With our macro-dataflow programming model, the dataflow graph is converted into a DAG. Please refer to the introduction for details on the dataflow graph. For each actor in the graph, if all of its input streams are available, it is ready to execute.

4.2. *Performance Prediction*

In dataflow execution, different tasks may share the same execution instructions. To predict execution time of *actor.Execute* on contributor r, we use Eq. (1). $E_i(r)$ is the time of ith execution of $v_i.Exec$ on contributor r and I_n is the size of the corresponding input stream. α is a value selected between 0 and 1. A larger value of α gives higher weights to recent executions and Eq. (1) also takes the weight of input size into consideration as illustrated.

$$P(v_i.Exec, r) = \left(\alpha * \frac{E_n(r)}{I_n} + (1-\alpha) * \frac{E_{n-1}(r)}{I_{n-1}} + \cdots + (1-\alpha)^i \frac{E_{n-i}(r)}{I_{n-i}} + \cdots\right) * v_i.input\_size. \qquad (1)$$

If $v_i.Exec$ has not executed on contributor r, to predict the execution time of task v_i on contributor r, we use the average of the predictions of all other contributors who have executed $v_i.Exec$, as in Eq. (2), where $S(v_i.Exec)$ is the set of contributors who have executed $v_i.Exec$ and $E(r_i)$ is the execution time of $v_i.Exec$ per byte:

$$P(v_i.Exec, r) = \left[\sum_{r_i \in S(v_i.Exec)} E(r_i) \right] * v_i.input\_size. \tag{2}$$

If $v_i.Exec$ is being executed for the first time in all of the available contributors, we use a prediction value provided by the user.

4.3. *Level-Based Clustering*

The algorithm used in the first phase is a technique for ordering the nodes based upon their precedence constraints, called *level sorting*, which has been adopted in many prior works [23, 35]. We can define the level sorting in a recursive way. Given a directed acyclic graph $\boldsymbol{G} = (\boldsymbol{V}, \boldsymbol{E})$, level 0 contains all vertices v_j such that there is no vertex v_i with $e_{ij} \in \boldsymbol{E}$ (i.e., v_j does not have any incident edges). Level k consists of all vertices v_j such that, for all $e_{ij} \in \boldsymbol{E}$, every vertex v_i has a level number less than k and at least one vertex is at level $k-1$.

The result of clustering is to partition $\boldsymbol{G}$ into L blocks numbered consecutively from 0 to $L-1$, and execution actors within each block are independent, i.e., there is no data precedence constraint between them. All tasks that send data to a task in block k must be in any of the blocks 0 to $k-1$; for each task v_j in block k, there exists at least one stream from task v_i in block $k-1$. Block 0 contains all initial tasks whose input streams are initial streams. Figure 5 shows the result of clustering for a FFT dataflow graph. This partition phase can be done during the execution of the dataflow graph.

4.4. *A Localized HEFT Algorithm*

Our aim is to minimize the execution time of tasks within each block, and as a consequence, the overall execution of the whole dataflow graph could potentially be optimized. We propose a scheduling algorithm called L-HEFT. The HEFT algorithm [27] is a static scheduling algorithm which can potentially achieve an

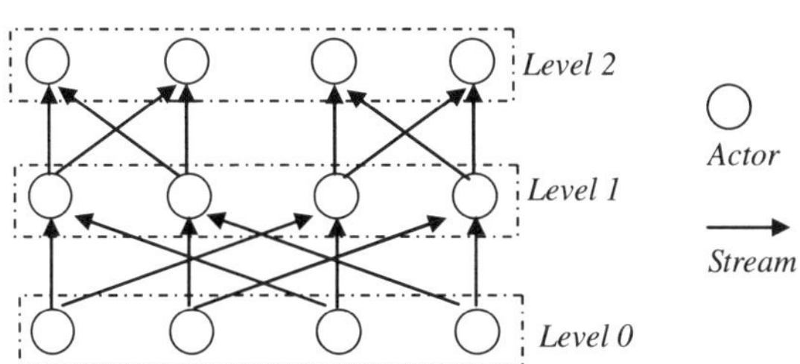

Fig. 5. The dataflow graph of FFT with four points.

overall optimized mapping with a relatively low cost. HEFT first assign a rank to each task through recursively traversing its successor tasks and computing the weight based on predicted performance and network traffic until result task is reached. After that, HEFT dispatches each task to resources which can finish it fastest according to the rank order. Therefore it needs global knowledge of the whole graph and the execution environment. In contrast, the L-HEFT algorithm does not require global knowledge for the complex ranking phase and aims to optimize the mapping of local pending tasks in a currently available partial graph.

Since we cannot optimize the scheduling in the manner of global mapping, this may lead to some unnecessary data traffic and may not give more weight to tasks on the critical path. So our policy gives a higher priority to data location as compensation and uses the increasing order of level number to ensure the priority from dependency constraints. Our algorithm attempts to decrease the data migration between resource nodes as much as possible while distributing workload across resources according to their ability. Given task t, we do not schedule it immediately when it is ready. Instead, we put it in a schedule queue. When the queue buffers enough tasks or there are contributors found to be idle, L-HEFT will be invoked.

We first assign a priority to each pending task according to level number. A task in a lower level has a higher priority than a task in a higher level. Within the same level, however, we give a higher priority to tasks which can be mapped to a contributor where execution does not require data traffic over the network. For those tasks whose execution definitely requires data communication whatever node it will be assigned to, we deploy an earliest finished time (EFT) heuristic algorithm to map them to suitable contributors. As a result, each contributor in the resource pool has a schedule queue, which holds the assigned tasks waiting for execution.

Each task is assigned a rank ID, which consists of prefix and postfix parts as illustrated in Fig. 6. The prefix part is the level number. The postfix part actually means the possible minimal traffic size if the corresponding task is executed. Equation (3) illustrates the ranking function used by L-HEFT. Given a task v_j and its predecessor task v_i, its input stream is denoted as e_{ij}. $OS(v_j)$ is the set of contributors which holds e_{ij}.

Figure 7 shows the algorithm of the L-HEFT heuristic. We assign a rank for each pending task using Eq. (3), and then we sort the pending tasks by increasing

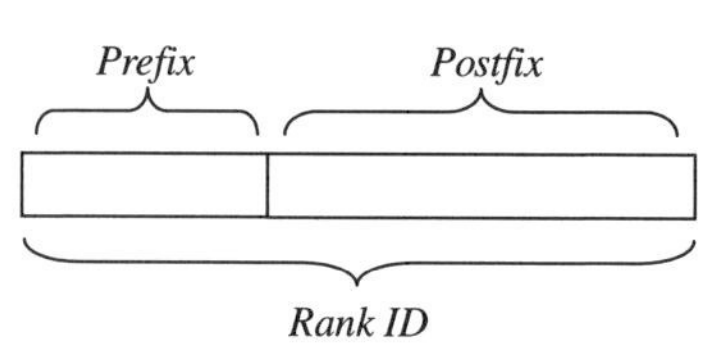

Fig. 6. Rank ID.

```
produce Level-HEFT-Schedule(T, R, F, C)
/* T ← The list of pending tasks to schedule
   R ← The list of currently available contributors
   F ← The set of prioritized tasks appending queue of
currently available contributors
   C ← Current time point
*/
 foreach t_i in T
     Compute t_i.rank with the algorithm of Eq. (3)
 endfor
 Sort each ready task, t_i, in T by increasing order of t_i.rank
 while there are unscheduled tasks in T do
   Choose the first task t_0 in T
   if(t_0.rank.postfix is zero)
    foreach r_j in R
     Compute its traffic size s_j, if t_0 is assigned to r_j
    Endfor
     Append t_0 to f_m , where s_m= max{s_j}(f_m∈ F)
     else
    foreach r_j in R
     eft[r_j] = EFT (t_0, r_j, C, f_j,R)
    endfor
    Append t_0 to f_m , where eft[r_m]= min{eft[r_j]}
   endif
 endwhile
return F
```

Fig. 7. Level-based HEFT algorithm.

order:

$$\begin{cases} rank(v_j).prefix = v_j.level\_number, \\ rank(v_j).postfix = \left[\sum_{i\in pred(v_j)} \mathrm{sizeof}(e_{ij}) - \max_{n_k\in OS(v_j)}\left(\sum_{C_{ij}.owner=n_k} \mathrm{sizeof}(e_{ij})\right)\right], \\ OS(v_j) = \bigcap_{i\in pred(v_j)} (e_{ij}.owner). \end{cases} \tag{3}$$

For tasks which have the same priority ranking, we sort them according to non-increasing predicted execution time. This phase of assigning rank and sorting tasks is totally different from the HEFT algorithm, and we do not require the phase of recursive traversing to calculate the successor's network traffic and their estimated average computation costs. In the mapping phase, we first assign tasks that may not need network traffic for execution to the contributor which holds all requested input streams, and then assign other tasks to the contributor which can finish them earliest, based on the calculated EFT.

During the execution, to compute EFT for task t on contributor r, we need to know the execution time of pending tasks on r, which are waiting for execution. As indicated in the introduction, each contributor has a prioritized task queue which contains all its assigned tasks. On the side of the coordinator, there is also a queue, f_r, for each contributor recording sent tasks and their estimated execution time.

When a task is completed on contributor r, f_r will be updated correspondingly to correct the estimated execution time of tasks on r. The time point of correction is recorded as $p(f_r)$. We use f_r to compute the EST for t on contributor r, via $\mathrm{EST}(t,r) = \mathrm{left\_time}(f_r) - (C - p(f_r))$, where C is the current time and *left_time*(f_r) is the sum of execution times for tasks in f_r. Therefore, $\mathrm{EFT}(t,r) = \mathrm{EST}(t,r) + \mathrm{Predict}(t,r)$, where $\mathrm{Predict}(t,r)$ is our algorithm to predict the execution time of task t on contributor r, which is based on the history execution information as indicated in the introduction.

During the initial phase of our scheduling model, we deploy a greedy policy on the initial tasks in block 0. During the scheduling, to prevent the worst case where some nodes hold a schedule queue with an estimated time much longer than other queues, there is a thread running in the background which frequently checks the length of the scheduling queue of each contributor. It will reassign some tasks from the tail of the longest scheduling queue to other contributors having a ligher load.

4.5. *Handling New Resources and Failed Resources*

When new resources are found in the system, the list of available resources will be updated to include them after they are ready to join the dataflow execution. Then the L-HEFT scheduling algorithm will be invoked to map pending tasks in the queue to resources, including the new resources.

When some contributors leave the system due to failures or being dominated by interactive users, it is possible that some intermediate data is lost due to the departed contributors. If these lost intermediate streams are necessary for continuing the execution, the *Job monitor* component of the coordinator will explore re-executing the corresponding actors in order to re-generate the lost intermediate streams. The tasks to be re-executed will be put into the task buffer and wait for scheduling by the L-HEFT algorithm.

5. Performance Evaluation

We have implemented our dataflow programming model, system and scheduling algorithm on the Aneka platform and deployed it in an environment consisting of desktop machines from different laboratories in Melbourne University, and shared with students and researchers. In this section, we evaluate the performance of our dataflow system and L-HEFT online scheduling algorithm through three applications. The first one is simple matrix multiplication; the other two are more complex: fast fourier translation (FFT) computation and Jacobi iteration [36].

5.1. *Environment Configuration*

The experiments are executed in an enterprise grid consisting of 33 nodes drawn from three student laboratories. During testing, one machine works as the *coordinator* and the others work as *contributors*. Each machine has a single Pentium 4 processor, 500 Mb of memory, 160 Gb IDE disk (10 Gb is contributed for dataflow storage), 1 Gbps ethernet network card and runs Windows XP.

5.2. *Sample Applications*

We implemented three sample applications using our macro-dataflow APIs indicated in the Appendix:

- *Matrix multiplication:* Each matrix consists of 4,000-by-4,000 randomly generated integers. Each matrix requires about 64 Mb and is partitioned into 250-by-250 square blocks; therefore, there is a total of 16×16 blocks with 128 Kb per block. There are 1,024 initial streams in the dataflow graph for the two matrix and 512 result streams as the result matrix.
- *FFT*: This algorithm is widely used in digital signal processing and can also be used to solve the discrete poisson equation for physical simulations. Figure 5 is a typical dataflow graph in FFT computing on a small scale. The input of the FFT example used in the experiment is a 16 M complex number, and is uniformly divided into 64 pieces. Therefore, there are a total of 1,664 actors to execute.
- *Jacobi iteration*: The Jacobi method is a simple way of solving partial differential equations (PDEs). Its iteration pattern of parallelization is shared by a large number of numerical programs and more complicated PDEs. The workspace of the Jacobi iteration in our experiment is a 16,384-by-16,384 matrix. The matrix is partitioned by rows into 64 pieces. During the experiment, we varied the ratio of computation to communication and iteration times.

5.3. *Scalability of the System*

The performance scalability evaluation does not include the time taken to send the initial data and collect the resulting data as these two actions need to transfer data across the single coordinator, which is a sequential behavior.

Figure 8 illustrates the improved performance with increasing numbers of contributors. There are two main factors that determine the execution time of the matrix multiplication: the distribution of blocks between the contributors and the overhead introduced by the transmission of blocks between the contributors. The network overhead is measured here as the ratio of the time taken for communication to the time taken for computation. As can be seen from Fig. 8, for larger numbers of contributors, while the speedup improves, the network overhead is also substantially increased. The speedup line starts diverging from the ideal when the network overhead increases to more than 10% of the execution time.

5.4. *Scheduling Policy*

This section evaluates our L-HEFT scheduling policy. We compare it with a dynamic scheduling model [31] through rescheduling on static HEFT mapping, which we

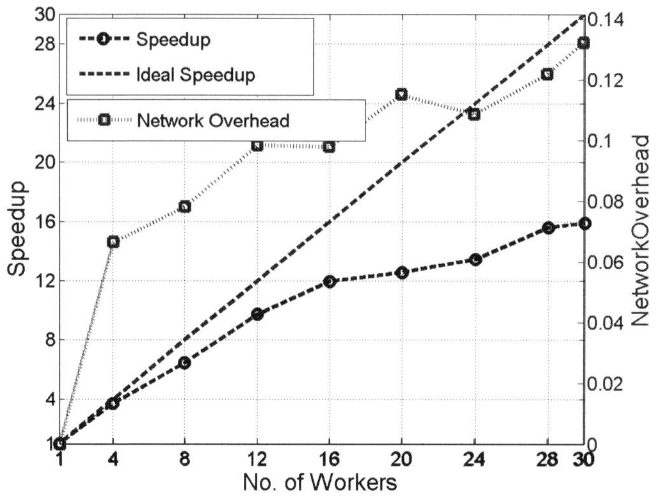

Fig. 8. Scalability of performance.

term here D-HEFT. We have implemented D-HEFT as mentioned in prior work [33], and rescheduling is triggered when the performance of resources is changing. In our implementation, rescheduling overlaps with the execution of tasks. This means that until the remapping of tasks is completely finished, they are still submitted to contributors to which they were mapped in the prior iteration of rescheduling. In this section, we compare these two scheduling models while varying the ratio of computation to communication and the size of the dataflow graphs through the Jacobi iteration and FFT benchmarks. For Jacobi iteration, every actor executes the same set of instructions. We choose α in Eq. (1) to be equal to 0.9. If the real execution time is different from the predicted value by a factor of two, we take it as a performance variation and correspondingly trigger rescheduling in D-HEFT.

First, we look at the result of these two polices on dataflow graphs of different sizes. We use a Jacobi iteration benchmark with ten iterations and 100 iterations. Therefore, the corresponding dataflow graph respectively holds 640 and 6,400 tasks. As illustrated in Fig. 9, the L-HEFT scheduling policy provides worse results than the D-HEFT policy, while in Fig. 10, L-HEFT marginally outperforms D-HEFT. The reason for this is that the scheduling cost of D-HEFT is larger than that of L-HEFT due to frequent variations in the performance availability of resources across contributors. For a large dataflow graph, the rescheduling cost of D-HEFT is even higher.

Finally, we run the FFT benchmark, whose communication pattern is more complex than that of Jacobi. The result is shown in Fig. 11. For this FFT benchmark, the ratio of computation to communication is about three. This shows that L-HEFT can compete with D-HEFT. This result is consistent with the

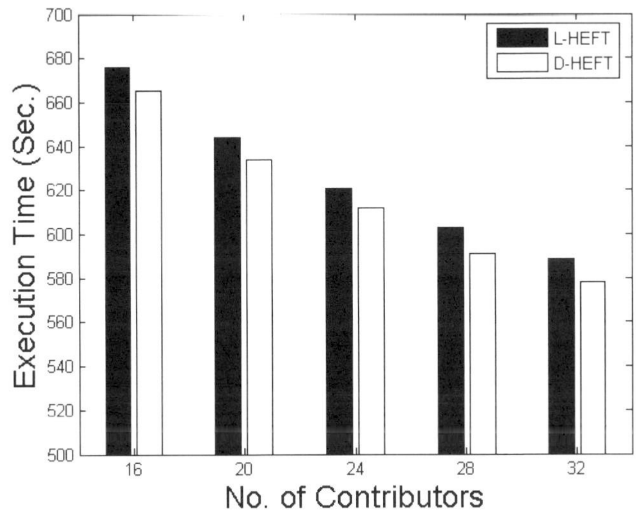

Fig. 9. Scheduling on Jacobi DAG with 640 tasks.

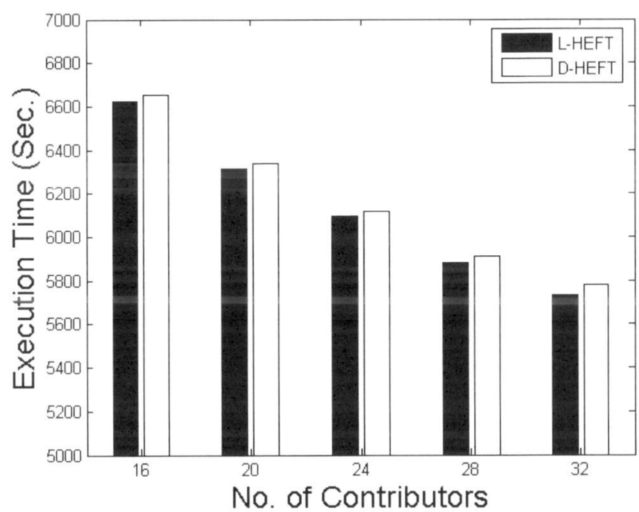

Fig. 10. Scheduling on Jacobi DAG with 6,400 tasks.

scheduling result of the Jacobi dataflow because the task number in the FFT dataflow is not large enough, only 1,664.

6. Thoughts for Practitioners

In this section, we mainly discuss the reason why L-HEFT performs better than D-HEFT and then present the effect of L-HEFT on handling the dynamics of the resources in the enterprise grid environment.

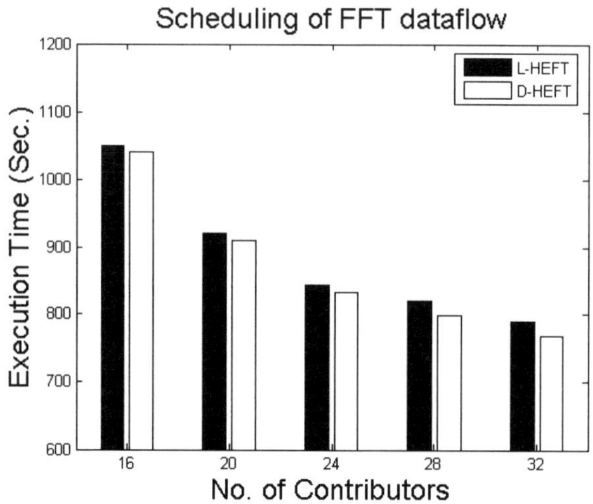

Fig. 11. Scheduling of FFT dataflow.

6.1. *Scheduling Cost*

Figures 12 and 13 illustrate the total execution time of L-HEFT and D-HEFT during the scheduling for Jacobi examples with small and large numbers of tasks, respectively. We can see that the scheduling cost of D-HEFT is much better than L-HEFT.

We use a simple model to explain why the rescheduling cost of L-HEFT is better. According to Ref. 27, the scheduling cost of the HEFT algorithm is $C_H = O(e \times q)$, where e is the average number of edges and q is the number of contributors. For

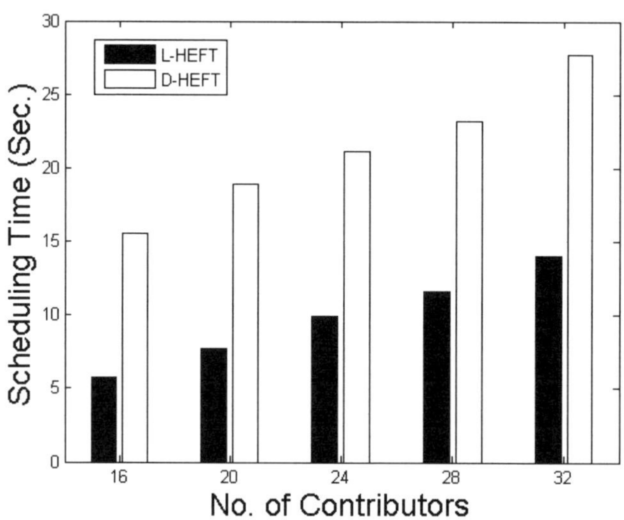

Fig. 12. Scheduling cost of Jacobi DAG with 640 tasks.

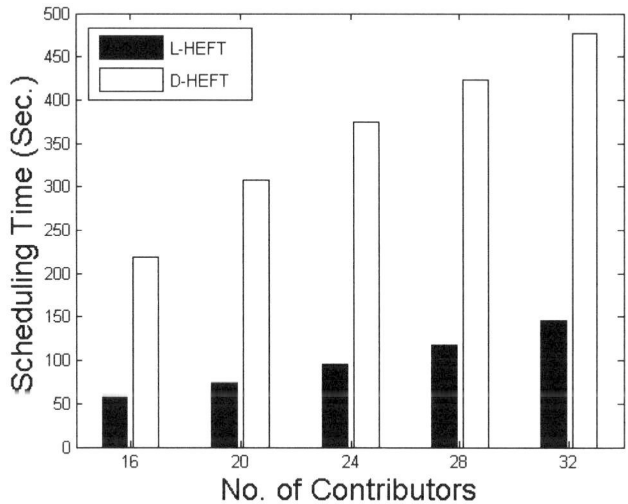

Fig. 13. Scheduling cost of Jacobi DAG with 6,400 tasks.

rescheduling, the cost depends on the size of the partial graph. We assume the size of the partial graph is half the size of the whole graph on average for each rescheduling period. Therefore, the cost of each rescheduling period is $C_r = C_H/2$. Given n_r is the number of rescheduling operations, the total cost of rescheduling is $(n_r \times C_r)$. However, for the L-HEFT algorithm, we know its cost $C_L < C_H$. From Table 1, we can see that the number of rescheduling operations is comparatively high and in each time of rescheduling, the D-HEFT algorithm needs to assign the rank for leftover tasks and then sort the tasks for re-mapping. A large amount of repeated rescheduling introduces a high scheduling cost. As a result, L-HEFT can outperform D-HEFT for large-scale dataflow graphs.

Next, we compare two scheduling polices with varied computation-to-communication ratio for a Jacobi dataflow of ten iterations. During the experiment, we adjust the ratio of computation to communication from two to 12 as illustrated in Fig. 14. We can see that for applications with a larger ratio of computation to communication, D-HEFT performs better than L-HEFT. The reason is that the rescheduling cost is gradually compensated for by the large execution time of tasks.

Finally, we compared the amount of stream data migration between contributors under the scheduling schemes of L-HEFT and D-HEFT, as shown in Fig. 15. The

Table 1. The number of rescheduling operations in D-HEFT.

Contributors#	16	20	24	28	32
640 tasks	82	102	62	58	63
6400 tasks	913	987	659	752	732

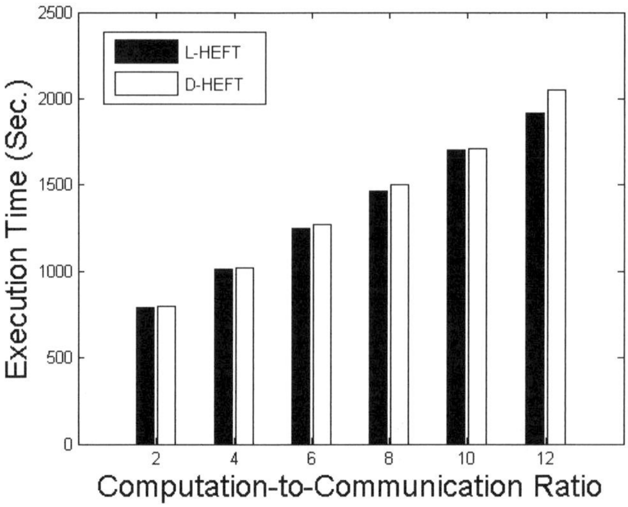

Fig. 14. Scheduling with varied ratio of computation-to-communication.

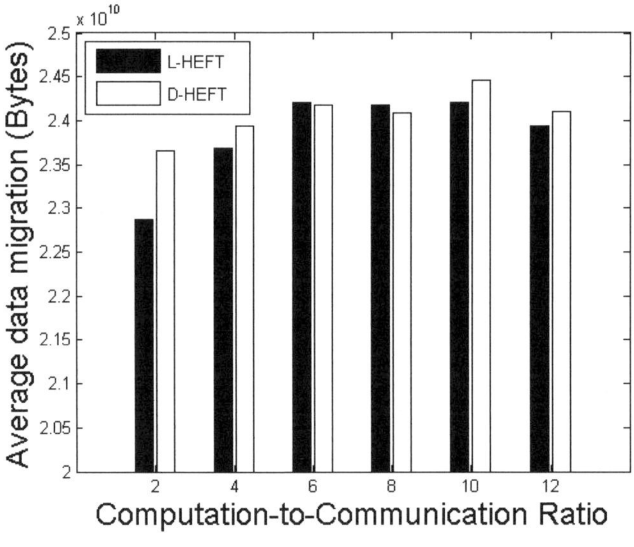

Fig. 15. Average amount of data migration between contributors.

result shows that for the Jacobi iteration application, both L-HEFT and D-HEFT generate nearly the same amount of data migration.

6.2. *Handling Joining Contributors*

This section compares the two dynamic models for handling new resources. We use a Jacobi dataflow with ten iterations and FFT dataflow. In the experiments, we first start with 16 contributors and, after three minutes, we gradually add two new

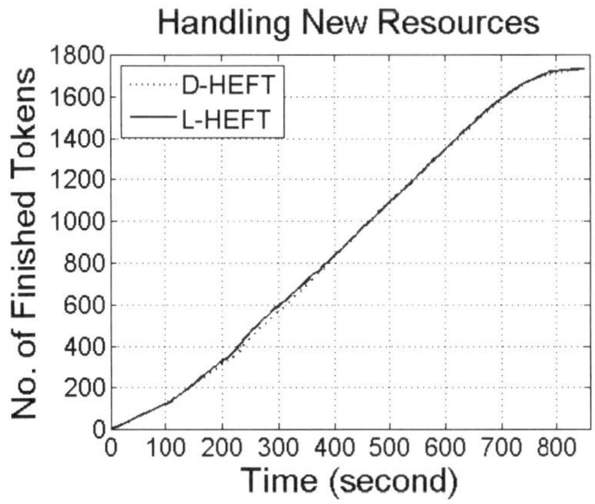

Fig. 16. Handling new resources for FFT dataflow.

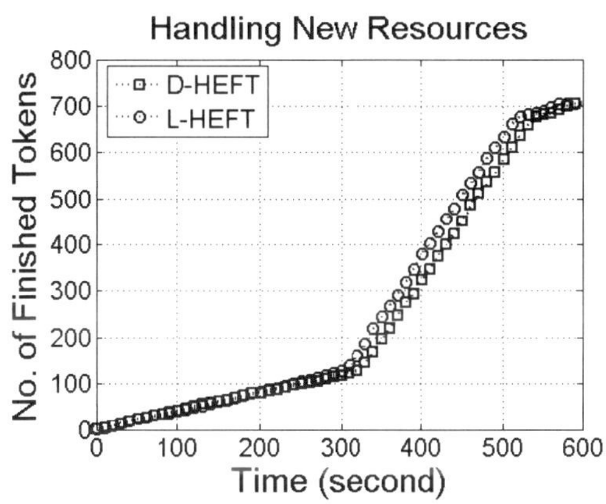

Fig. 17. Handling new resources for Jacobi dataflow.

contributors every minute. We then measured the number of finished tasks on the side of the coordinator. The slopes of the measured curves increase as more and more new resource join because more contributors can execute pending actors, as illustrated in Figs. 16 and 17. These two figures show that the response time of the L-HEFT algorithm to handling new joining resources is a bit faster than D-HEFT. The reason is the low cost of the L-HEFT algorithm.

6.3. *Handling Failures of Contributors*

This section evaluates the mechanisms dealing with failures of contributors in the dataflow system. We use the Jacobi iteration example with 40 iterations across 20 contributors. On the coordinator side, we measure the number of finished actors. If lost intermediate data needs to be re-generated by re-executing those actors due to the failure of contributors, we just reset those actors as unfinished. The L-HEFT

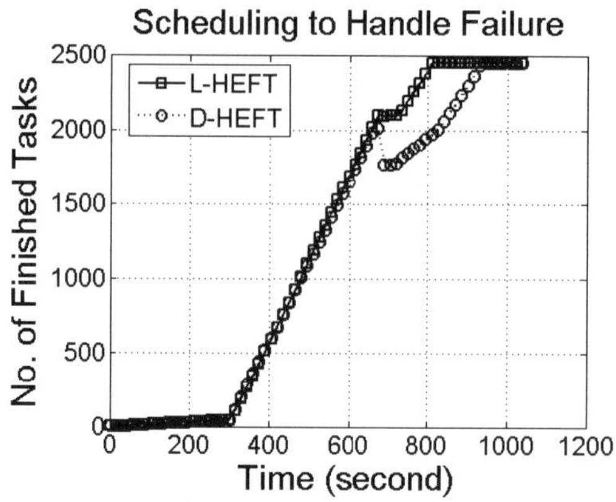

Fig. 18. Fault tolerant scheduling.

algorithm evaluated in this section is assisted by replication support with the size of replication step equal to five, while D-HEFT does not support failures through replication methods. After the system runs for 12 minutes, we manually turn off one contributor to simulate a node failure. Without replication support, D-HEFT has to re-execute all tasks to re-generate lost intermediate data in order to continue the execution. However, the number of tasks which have to be regenerated by L-HEFT is rather smaller. As Fig. 18 shows, with the failure support from the replication mechanism of the macro-dataflow system, L-HEFT outperforms D-HEFT. Hence, the overall performance of L-HEFT is better.

7. Directions for Future Research

Our macro-dataflow programming model features a DAG interface for users to compose a dataflow graph and a runtime system which can schedule the execution of the graph in an enterprise grid environment while handling and handle load balancing and fault tolerance in a transparent manner. However, meeting the quality of service (QoS) requirements remains a challenge. Our future work focuses on extending the dynamic scheduling policy to support advanced user QoS requirements by building on Aneka's advanced resource reservation and service level agreement (SLA) capabilities.

8. Conclusion

This chapter presents a dataflow computing platform within a shared enterprise grid environment. Through a macro-dataflow interface, users can freely express their parallel applications by specifying the dataflow relationship and easily deploy applications in a heterogeneous distributed environment with failures. The L-HEFT scheduling algorithm proposed for our dataflow system achieves effective mapping with fairly low cost due to greatly decreased rescheduling cost compared with static mapping-based rescheduling techniques. At the same time, it supports scalable performance and transparent fault tolerance based on the evaluation of example applications.

Acknowledgment

This work is partially supported by research grants from the Australian Research Council (ARC) and the Australian Department of Innovation, Industry, Science and Research (DIISR). We thank Srikumar Venugopal, Suraj Pandey, Charity Laplap and James Broberg for their comments on this chapter.

Terminology

1. *Dataflow model*: An inherently parallel model where the execution of instructions/operations is triggered as soon as the required input data is (made) available.
2. *Control flow model*: A traditional execution model with "von Neumann" architecture.
3. *Hybrid dataflow model*: Combines the advantages of the dataflow and control-flow models and utilizes parallelism at a desired level.
4. *Grid*: Grid computing is one of the recent paradigms for parallel and distributed computing. It provides online access to computation or storage as a service supported by a pool of distributed computing resources.
5. *Enterprise grid*: Aims to enable the virtualization and harnessing of (idle) IT resources within an enterprise.
6. *Directed acyclic graph (DAG)*: Used to express the dependency relationships between tasks within an application.
7. *DAG scheduling*: Maps the tasks in a DAG onto distributed resources.
8. *Offline DAG scheduling*: Maps the tasks in a DAG onto distributed resources prior to execution.
9. *Online DAG scheduling*: Maps the tasks in a DAG onto distributed resources during execution.
10. *Heterogeneous system:* A system consists of resources with heterogeneity in terms of architecture, capability, policies, and access interfaces, etc.

Exercises

1. What is a dataflow execution model?
2. What is the difference between the dataflow and control-flow execution models?
3. What is a hybrid data model?
4. What is grid computing?
5. What is an enterprise grid?
6. What are the advantages of an enterprise grid?
7. What is the general challenge of a DAG scheduling algorithm?

8. What are the advantages of the HEFT scheduling algorithm?
9. What are the advantages of the L-HEFT algorithm?
10. Why is the scheduling cost of the L-HEFT algorithm better than the D-HEFT algorithm?

References

1. T. Hey and A. E. Trefethen, The UK e-Science core programme and the grid, *J. Future Gen. Comput. Sys.* **18**(8), 1017–1031 (2002).
2. R. Kalakota and M. Robison, *E-business: Roadmap for Success* (Addison-Wesley and Longman 1999).
3. E. Korpela *et al.*, SETI@home-massively distributed computing for SETI, *Comput. Sci. Eng.* **3**(1), 78–83 (2001).
4. I. Foster and C. Kesselman, *The Grid Blueprint for a Future Computing Infrastructure*, (Morgan Kaufmann Publishers, 1999).
5. M. Litzkow, M. Livny and M. Mutka, Condor — A hunter of idle workstations, *Proc. 8th Int. Conf. Distributed Computing Systems (ICDCS 88)* (IEEE Computer Society Press, 1988).
6. G. Fedak *et al.*, Xtremweb: A generic global computing system, *Proc. 1st Int. Symp. Cluster Computing and the Grid, Brisbane* (2001).
7. E. Deelmana *et al.*, Pegasus: A framework for mapping complex scientific workflows onto distributed systems, *Sci. Prog. J.* **13**(3), 219–237 (2005).
8. W. M. Johnston, J. R. P. Hanna and R. J. Millar, Advances in dataflow programming languages, *ACM Comput. Surv.* **36**(1), 1–34 (2004).
9. C. Jin, R. Buyya, L. Stein and Z. Zhang, A dataflow model for .NET-based grid computing systems, *Proc. 3rd Int. Workshop Grid Computing and Applications, Singapore* (2007).
10. W. A. Najjar, E. A. Lee and G. R. Gao, *Advances In The Dataflow Computational Model*, Parallel Computing, Vol. 25 (Elsevier Press, 1999), pp. 1907–1929.
11. J. Dennis and D. Misunas, A preliminary architecture for a basic data-flow processor, *2nd IEEE Symp. Computer Architecture* (1974).
12. G. Kahn, The semantics of a simple language for parallel programming, *Proc. Int. Federation for Information Processing (IFIP) Congress 74*, Stockholm (1974).
13. C. Kim and J. L. Gaudiot, *Data-flow and Multithreaded Architectures*, Encyclopedia of Electrical and Electronics Engineering (Wiley Press, 1997).
14. T. Sterling, J. Kuehn, M. Thistle and T. Anastasis, *Studies on Optimal Task Granularity and Random Mapping*, Advanced Topics in Dataflow Computing and Multithreading (IEEE Computer Society Press, 1995), 349–365.
15. H. H. J. Hum, O. Maquelin, K. B. Theobald, X. Tian, G. R. Gao and L. J. Hendren, A study of the earth-manna multithreaded system, *J. Parall. Prog.* **24**(4), 319–347 (1996).
16. R. S. Nikhil, Arvind, Can dataflow subsume von Neumann computing? *Proc. Int. Symp. Computer Architecture (ISCA-16)*, Jerusalem, Israel (1989).
17. G. R. Gao, An efficient hybrid dataflow architecture model, *J. Parall. Distri. Comput.* **19**(4), 293–307 (1993).
18. J. L. Gaudiot and L. Bic, *Advanced Topics in Data-Flow Computing* (Prentice-Hall, 1991).
19. K. Asanovic, R. Bodik and B. C. Catanzaro, The landscape of parallel computing research: A view from Berkeley, Technical report, No. UCB/EECS-2006-183, University of Berkeley (2006).

20. H. Sutter and J. Larus, Software and the concurrency revolution, *ACM Queue* **3**(7), 54–62 (2005).
21. D. Thain, T. Tannenbaum and M. Livny, *Distributed Computing in Practice: The Condor Experience*, Concurrency and Computation: Practice and Experience, 17(2–4) (Wiley Press, 2005).
22. A. Chien, B. Calder, S. Elbert and K. Bhatia, Entropia: Architecture and performance of an enterprise desktop grid system, *J. Parall. Distrib. Comput.* **63**(5), 597–610 (2003).
23. T. Fahringer, R. Prodan, R. Duan, F. Nerieri, S. Podlipnig, J. Qin, M. Siddiqui, H.-L. Truong, A. Villazon and M. Wieczorek, ASKALON: A grid application development and computing environment, *Proc. 6th Int. Workshop Grid Computing*, Seattle, USA (2005).
24. R. M. Badia *et al.*, Programming grid applications with GRID superscalar, *J. Grid Comput.* (2004).
25. S. Bowers, B. Ludaescher, A. H. H. Ngu and T. Critchlow, Enabling scientific workflow reuse through structured composition of dataflow and control-flow, *Proc. IEEE Workshop Workflow and Data Flow for Scientific Applications*, Georgia, USA (2006).
26. A. Benoit, V. Rehn and Y. Robert, Complexity results for throughput and latency optimization of replicated and data-parallel workflows, *Proc. HeteroPar'2007: Int. Workshop Heterogeneous Computing, in conjunction with Cluster 2007 Conf.*, Austin, TX (2007).
27. H. Topcuouglu, S. Hariri and M.-Y. Wu, Performance-effective and low-complexity task scheduling for heterogeneous computing, *IEEE Trans. Parall. Distrib. Sys.* **13**(3), 260–274 (2002).
28. A. Y. Zomaya, C. Ward and B. Macey, Genetic scheduling for parallel processor systems: Comparative studies and performance issues, *IEEE Trans. Parall. Distrib. Syst.* **10**(8), 795–812 (1999).
29. J. Frey *et al.*, Condor-G: A computation management agent for multi-institutional grids, *Proc. 10th IEEE Symp. High Performance Distributed Computing*, Redondo Beach, California (2001).
30. R. Huang, H. Casanova and A. Chien, Using virtual grids to simplify application scheduling, *Proc. 20th Int. Parallel and Distributed Processing Sympo. (IPDPS'06)*, Rhodes, Greece (2006).
31. Z. Yu and W. Shi, An adaptive rescheduling strategy for grid workflow applications, *Proc. 21st Int. Parallel and Distributed Processing Symp.*, Long Beach, CA (2007).
32. H. Yu *et al.*, Plan switching: An approach to pan execution in changing environments, *Proc. 20th Int. Parallel and Distributed Processing Symp.*, Rhodes Island, Greece (2006).
33. X. Chu, K. Nadiminti, C. Jin, S. Venugopal and R. Buyya, Aneka: Next-Generation Enterprise Grid Platform for e-Science and e-Business Applications, *Proc. 3rd IEEE Int. Conf. Grid Computing*, Bangalore, India (2007).
34. J. Blythe *et al.*, Task scheduling strategies for workflow-based applications in grids, *Proc. 4th IEEE Int. Symp. Cluster Computing and Grid*, Singapore (2005).
35. M. Maheswaran and H. Siegel, A Dynamic Matching and Scheduling Algorithm for Heterogeneous Computing Systems, *Proc. 7th Heterogeneous Computing Workshop*, Florida (1998).
36. M. T. Heath, *Scientific Computing: An Introductory Survey* (McGraw-Hill, 2001).

Chapter 19

GRID-BASED COMPUTING PLATFORM FOR LARGE-SCALE ONLINE APPLICATIONS

K. L. EDDIE LAW* and Y. C. ALLEN YU†

Department of Electrical and Computer Engineering, Ryerson University, 350 Victoria Street, Toronto, Ontario, M5B 2K3, Canada

**eddie@ee.ryerson.ca*

†ayu@ee.ryerson.ca

With the vast amount of computing resources available across the Internet, basic communication and programming mechanisms have been evolving from simple client/server socket communication model to object-oriented middleware systems, and lately, to the Grid computing service system platform. Nowadays, computers can be interconnected with networks to create high-performance parallel, distributed, and clustered computing systems. From a networking design perspective, the system model has moved from a basic multiple-to-one client/server system to a peer-to-peer model. In this chapter, we review the foundation technologies that have been developed into the Grid computing. Different algorithmic designs for overlay networks are also discussed. We then investigate the design of Grid computing operating platform for serving large-scale real-time online applications. In order to validate the proposed design, which we call a massively multi-user online platform (MMOP), we design an online game to carry out thorough experiments for evaluating the overall system performance.

1. Introduction

The technological advancements in computer architectures, communications and networking have been steadily progressing in the last two decades. Each can serve as an independent area of research, and they can also be integrated and work together to provide a broad range of Internet services to assist in our daily activities. Examples include basic Web browsing and personal data transactions. Computer networking can easily be conducted through basic client/server model, that is the common way that a client Web browser is connected to a centralized Web server on the Internet. The needs and the scales of online applications have been growing rapidly with time. Today, many types of online applications (critical and non-critical, real-time and non-real-time) are available through the Internet. These applications are getting more sophisticated, more computationally intensive, and more time-dependent. It is then desirable to have a novel and reliable computing platform across the Internet to better serve these demanding applications. Grid computing [1, 2] is emerging as a distributed computing platform that offers large-scale resource sharing and executes performance demanding applications.

The term "Grid computing" has been understood by many organizations as servicing and sharing flexible, secure, coordinated resources among dynamic collections of individuals, institutional entities, and the resources themselves — virtual organizations (VOs). Currently, design, implementation, and execution of VOs are open to all designers and researchers. The definitions of Grid computing may be different for different applications and organizations. For certain types of applications, it may be more desirable if multiple application processes can work together. Ultimately, it is important to have international non-profitable organizations which can streamline and define standards and specifications for Grid computing. The Open Grid Forum (OGF) [3] is one of the standardization bodies which establish specifications for Grid computing. This has led to the creation of a set of inter-Grid protocol specifications for interoperability among different Grid computing systems.

At the inception of Grid computing, disregarding the standardization issue, there are a few common system features [1, 2]. For example, a Grid should follow an extensible Grid architecture, in which protocols, services, and application programming interfaces must be designed for sharing resources. This also indicates that Grids should be and aggregate geographically distributed resources, including personal computers, supercomputers, and storage systems, across the Internet. These resources serve as cost-effective distributed computing units for executing large-scale resource (data and computation) intensive applications in science, commerce, and industry. Grid computing is commonly conceived for running large-scale scientific and industrial applications. Examples include social networking Web services, system simulations, molecular modeling for drug design, brain analysis, weather forecasting, climate prediction, automobile modeling, structural engineering, high-energy physics, and large-scale simulations.

In general, there are two commonly accepted Grid computing models: the public and enterprise models. Public Grid computing systems take advantage of available CPU cycles of end-users' idle desktop computers at homes and at offices for distributed processing. However, computers at homes may be turned on or off depending on the users' behaviors and decisions. On the other hand, an enterprise Grid computing system only accesses pre-allocated computing resources within an enterprise organization. This can always guarantee the availability of a certain amount of computing resources for Grid applications to execute.

In the remainder of this chapter, we will discuss one specific design of an enterprise Grid-based computing platform for executing large-scale, real-time, and wide-area online applications. In general, large-scale online applications require a large amount of computing resources that can support the interactions of a large number of end-users simultaneously, for example, the massively multi-player online games (MMOGs). Grid computing should always guarantee services which offer good performance for running large-scale applications even if the platform is connecting to various quality grades of computing resources in different networks.

This situation has led to the design of a high performance enterprise Grid based computing platform, the massively multi-user online platform (MMOP), which offers system scalability, programming flexibility, and simplicity for developing large-scale distributed applications. In addition, MMOP offers dynamic addition and subtraction of computing resources during run-time, and executes applications based on policy rules. Each application should be managed separately, and multiple large-scale applications can also share a single computing architecture. In order to examine MMOP as a high-performance and scalable operating computing architecture, have created a simple 2D online game that generates a large amount of network traffic to test the functional behaviors of the proposed MMOP platform. Before going into the details of the MMOP design, we briefly review some basic networking technologies, Grid computing standards and emerging technologies.

2. Background of Networking Technologies

2.1. *Basic Technology: Socket Programming*

The simplest way to connect two computers on the Internet is to use client/server communication model. A simple setup is shown in Fig. 1. The client/server model can be facilitated using a set of programming language-specific, low-level system calls, which are commonly known as socket programming. For communications, a server should announce its Internet Protocol (IP) address or its host name, and open a local publicly known listening port number to accept clients' query messages. Similarly, a client also needs to set up a socket endpoint so as to communicate with a server. Depending on applications, the transport protocol chosen for communications may be either the User Datagram Protocol (UDP), Transmission Control Protocol (TCP), or Stream Control Transport Protocol (SCTP) in the TCP/IP protocol stack. At the moment, the standard socket application programming interfaces (APIs) are well-defined, but the implementation is programming language specific. This implies networking programs can be coded

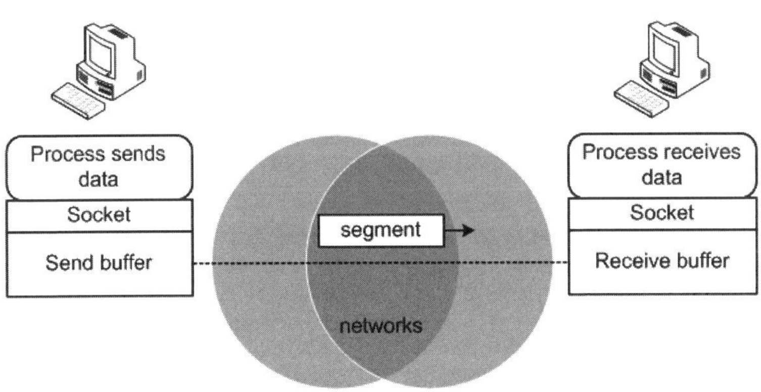

Fig. 1. Computer communications using sockets.

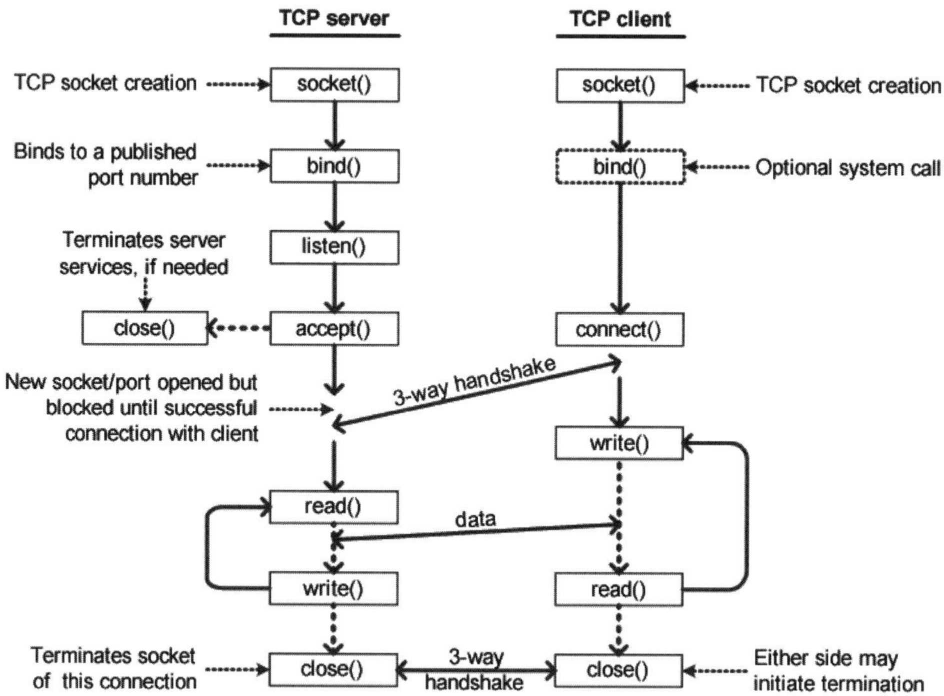

Fig. 2. TCP socket programming in C programming language.

in different programming languages and the socket calls may vary. An example of the flow of TCP socket calls in the C programming language is shown in Fig. 2. In practice, client and server programs should be able to communicate even if they are developed with different programming languages, but sometimes it may not be guaranteed. If it is portable, such as Java class files, code can also run on different operating systems. Certainly, client and server application processes in the same packages are usually coded in the same programming language using the same socket library package.

As aforementioned the socket programming is a low-level communication mechanism that usually has low overhead and offers advantage of low latency for high-speed data communications. During the early inception, networking programs were designed for establishing connections between a client and a server. However, the most recently developed applications have become complicated and large in scale with multiple components interacting in complex ways. Hence, writing low-level socket programming application has become too unproductive and time-consuming an approach.

2.2. *Object-Oriented Middleware Systems*

In order to reduce the time-consuming task of maintaining low-level network code, especially for large-scale distributed system design, higher level programming design

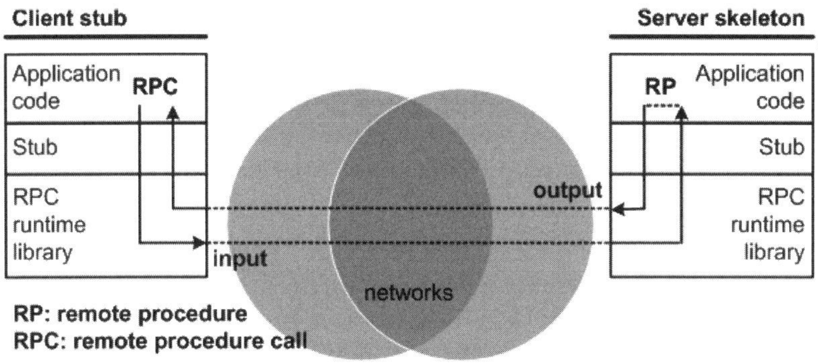

Fig. 3. Remote Procedure Call.

paradigms have been developed. For example, as shown in Fig. 3, Remote Procedure Call (RPC) [9] is a higher-level coding technique for constructing distributed client/server applications. RPC can use TCP or UDP, and is supposed to be easier to use than socket programming. RPC relies heavily on Interface Definition Language (IDL) interface to describe the remote procedures executing at the server side. From the RPC IDL interface, an RPC compiler can automatically generate a client-side stub and server-side skeleton. With the stub and skeleton, RPC hides the low-level communication and provides a high-level communication abstraction for a client to directly call a remote procedure as if the procedure were local. RPC is not object-oriented and is still difficult to code and debug for large-scale applications, but what was important was the introduction of IDL, which led to the creation of middleware systems and great improvements in computing systems.

Middleware systems are basically sets of inter-process communication APIs. They have the capability of creating larger-scale online applications. Examples include Common Object Request Broker Architecture (CORBA) [12], Sun Microsystems's Java Remote Method Invocation (RMI) [10], and Microsoft's .Net Remoting in the .Net framework, or the earlier ActiveX and Distributed Component Object Model (DCOM) [11] technology. For example, CORBA is designed for creating object-oriented middleware infrastructure. The CORBA specification was developed by the Object Management Group (OMG) [13] for handling distributed client/server applications. CORBA hides the low-level communication between client and server by automatically generating a client-side stub and a server-side skeleton through CORBA's IDL interface. CORBA uses the Internet inter-ORB protocol (IIOP) to invoke remote CORBA objects. The object request broker (ORB) is the core of CORBA; it performs data marshaling and un-marshaling between CORBA clients and objects. Figure 4 shows the component architecture of the ORB.

The design of CORBA applications can be independent of object location, executable environment, or programming language. CORBA supports both

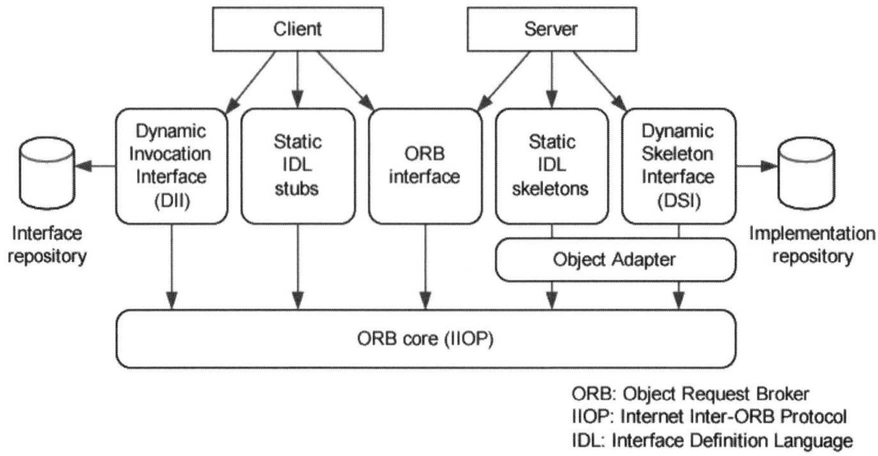

Fig. 4. Object request broker architecture.

synchronous and asynchronous communications. Its advanced directory service provides mechanisms to make the locations of objects transparent. While CORBA is a public OMG specification, Java RMI and .Net Remoting are other similar proprietary designs — although the execution environments for executing Java and .Net byte-codes are freely available. Although these designs differ in their specific implementations and features [13], they share some similarities in system design:

- An interface is required for invoking a remote object or a component.
- With an interface definition, an automatically generated client stub and server skeleton can hide the complexity of low-level communications from programmers and users.
- The interface definition is in binary format which is hard for client applications to make a query on an interface to find out, for example, the defined methods, inputs and outputs of each method to make a better use of the methods.
- Clients and objects are tightly coupled with their interfaces; changing part of a client implies that other parts of a server should also be modified.
- They may use proprietary communication protocols, for example, Java RMI uses Java Remote Method Protocol (JRMP) and CORBA uses Internet Inter-ORB Protocol (IIOP) to invoke remote objects or components.

Most of these middleware systems do not have a coherent specification for interoperability. It all depends on whether the companies developing specifications are willing to support cross-platform communications.

2.3. *Structured Peer-to-Peer (P2P) Networking*

Apart from developing new high-level programming paradigms and other computer communication technologies, system-level designs for sharing network resources should be considered. Peer-to-peer (P2P) overlays have been successfully replacing the traditional client/server model for sharing files. End-users are peers which exchange files through direct connections among one another instead of downloading from a centralized file server. In the simple client/server model, limited server bandwidth is usually the common bottleneck when there are too many clients sending requests simultaneously. The advantage of P2P file sharing is that blocks of a file can be shared without using any centralized file server. BitTorrent file sharing is an example of such a design, and the group of peers sharing the same file is called a swarm. Generally, when there are more peers sharing the same file, the total sharing network bandwidth for that particular file increases. For peers accessing the same file, they upload the missing pieces to one another, effectively sharing and contributing their bandwidth to one another. Subsequently, the problem of bandwidth bottleneck in the client/server model is mitigated. Since file sharing is based on the goodwill of peers, an insufficient number of peers participating in the file sharing process, or no seeds (the peers carrying the complete files), can result in a lower overall bandwidth and ultimately prevent the file from being downloaded if no peers are sharing it.

There are two basic classes of P2P overlay networks: structured and unstructured. Broadcasting is the common information delivery mechanism used in unstructured overlays. But for structured overlays, algorithms are designed for proper constructions of structured network overlays. One hop lookups (OHL) [14], Chord [15] and Kademlia [20] algorithms are examples of structured overlay algorithms. In the following, OHL and Chord are elaborated in detail.

Both OHL and Chord use distributed hash tables (DHTs). Hash keys can be generated for indexing files or objects, and mapping overlay nodes. A hashing algorithm provides a means of looking up any given key quickly in a structured overlay. A key can be used to determine the position of a node in the structured overlay by assigning an identifier string for each node, for example, the IP address of a node. Upon carrying out consistent hashing on the identifier string, a unique hash key can be generated to identify the node in the structured overlay. Similarly, using the hash key of the string, a data object can be virtually mapped onto a node in the overlay. A commonly used hash function is the Secure Hash Algorithm 1 (SHA1). The hashing function is known to provide a balanced load on a structured overlay, and each peer receives roughly about the same number of data objects. Furthermore, hash keys can be used extensively to enhance the availability issue of data or objects. A distributed fault tolerant design with redundancy can be constructed by adding an identifier string to a data object. Such mapping is a fundamental element of providing efficient data replications on the structured overlay [16]. Hence, replication is achievable by adding prefixes or suffixes to the identifier string. Consequently, multiple hash keys are generated upon appending a data object with an identifier string of, for example, `test`. The replica strings are `test-1`, and `test-2`, etc. This same data object is then duplicated to different nodes according to these replica strings for backup and load balancing purposes. As a result, the availability of the data object is increased.

In reality, nodes are free to join or leave an overlay at will. It is crucial for the P2P algorithm to maintain the key mappings on each node regarding these changes. When a node joins an overlay, the algorithm determines a set of keys that are the responsibilities of this node. When it leaves the overlay, the algorithm redistributes its keys to other nodes. Since hash keys should be evenly distributed on the overlay on average [17], only minimum movements of keys should be carried out when changes occur. Suppose that all hash key mappings can be treated as positive integers in the structured overlay. Then, these hash keys can be put in numerical order and wrapped around in a circle as illustrated in Fig. 5. Regarding assigning objects to nodes, for example, an object with a KEY 1 is assigned to node 1 on the structured overlay because they both have the same hash numbers. But the object with KEY 2 is assigned to its succeeding node with identity (ID) 3, and the object with KEY 6 is assigned to node 0 because keys are wrapped around the circle.

With this cyclic structure, an overlay can accommodate a maximum of N keys. This maximum number N is dependent on the hashing algorithm used. For example, for the SHA1 (160-bit) hash function, we have $N = 2^{160}$, and $0 <=$ KEY $< N$. Furthermore, this restriction also applies to the total number of nodes, because it should not exceed the maximum number of keys, N.

The P2P structured overlay is the backbone of the MMOP design. It is used to construct the VOs. Each VO is an independent structured overlay with a possibly different overlay and hashing algorithms. With different overlay algorithms, VOs may exhibit different performance and size attributes. The P2P structured overlay algorithms implemented in MMOP will be discussed later.

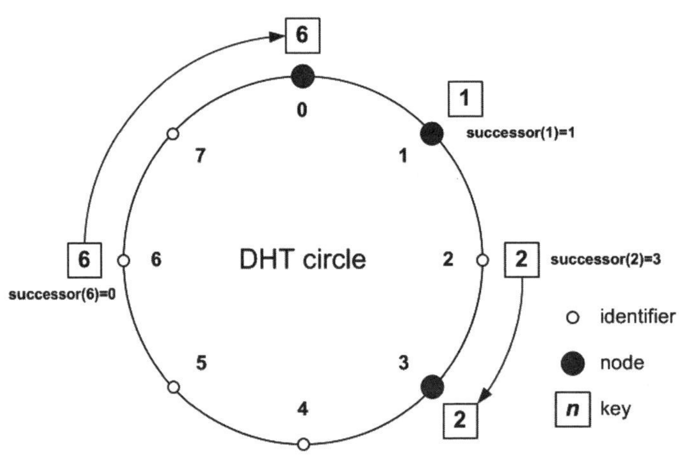

Fig. 5. P2P key distribution in a structured overlay.

2.3.1. *OHL Algorithm*

In OHL design [14], each node should have a complete view of a structured overlay. In other word, all nodes can be accessed with virtually one single hop. For logical node changes, there is a hierarchical structural information flow which is superimposed on top of the overlay for propagating changes among all nodes. An example of the superimposed OHL propagating structure is shown in Fig. 6.

The key space of OHL is divided into slices, and each slice is further subdivided into units. The configuration in Fig. 6 carries four slices (S_1, S_2, S_3, S_4) and each slice carries two units (U_1, U_2). The sizes of the units and slices are predetermined and must be able to divide the key space completely. Each node in the middle of a slice or a unit is the leader correspondingly. A slice or unit leader is denoted by a circle or a star, respectively, in the figure. The leaders have the responsibility of notifying other nodes in their slices or units regarding the membership changes of the overlay. Inter-slice messages should be aggregated and exchanged among slice leaders periodically.

When a newly arriving node is joining the overlay, it uses a bootstrap algorithm to receive a list of existing peers in order to find its successor. The successor then notifies the slice leader about the newly joined node and the notification is propagated to the other nodes, as also indicated in Fig. 6. When a node fails or leaves the overlay, a similar notification strategy is deployed. This design ensures a timely response to each node but may also require higher bandwidth consumption by the leader nodes. However, since the changes are aggregated within each slice and unit periodically, the extra bandwidth consumption is minimal.

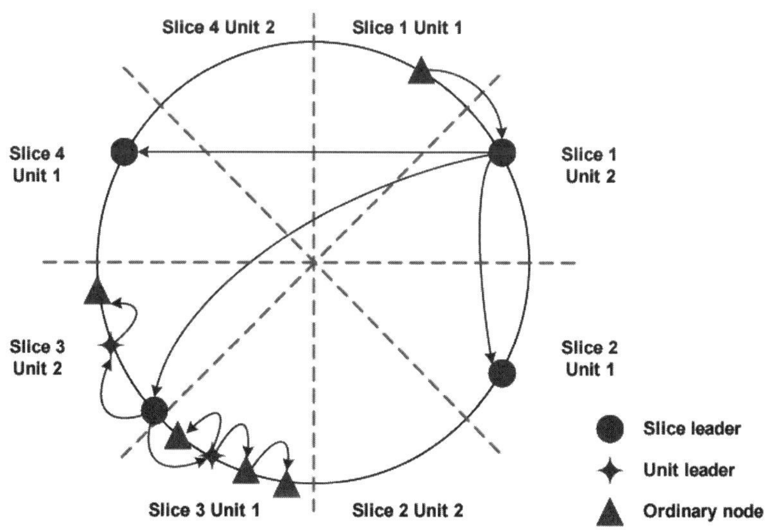

Fig. 6. Superimposed OHL structure used for membership change notification.

Table 1. Finger table of a Chord node.

Index	Node
$k + 2^0$	A node succeeds $k + 2^0$
$k + 2^1$	A node succeeds $k + 2^1$
$k + 2^2$	A node succeeds $k + 2^2$
...	...
$k + 2^{\texttt{MaxKeyBits} - 1}$	A node succeeds $k + 2^{\texttt{MaxKeyBits} - 1}$

2.3.2. *Chord Algorithm*

The Chord [15] algorithm provides each node with a finger (or index) table. As shown in Table 1, k is a key of a current node, and `MaxKeyBits` is the key size in terms of bits produced by the hashing function. The node recorded in the finger table does not necessarily pinpoint the exact location of the key. It is a rough mapping of a node that is closer to the key than the current node. The query of a key can be executed sequentially or recursively. The search size is reduced by half on each successive search. In our implementation, a sequential key lookup is implemented in order to minimize the resource consumed by the lookup queries.

Also, by implementing a bootstrap mechanism, a newly joined node can retrieve the finger table from its successor as its own finger table with updated indices. But, unlike OHL, a membership change within the Chord overlay is only noticeable by the two nodes that are directly neighboring the node that has caused it. All other nodes need to learn the changes through periodically refreshing their own finger tables' entries.

To look up a specific key, a node should initially firstly go through its finger table and find the closest successor for the key. It then contacts that node to determine if such a key is located on it. If the key is not found, the contacted node returns a closer successor from its own finger table. The originating node then restarts the query with the returned nodal location until it reaches the node that contains the key. With this approach, the algorithm can locate any key within $O(\log_2 N)$ time [15].

3. Background of Grid Computing

3.1. *Standard Tracks*

The Open Grid Forum (OGF) [3] is an organization which is responsible for establishing Grid computing specifications. The OGF was the result of merging the Global Grid Forum (GGF) and the Enterprise Grid Alliance (EGA). The Open Grid Services Architecture (OGSA) is the most important common standard developed at OGF. The specification aims at defining a common standard and open architecture for building Grid-based applications. The goal of OGSA is to standardize almost all the services that a Grid application may use, including job and resource management services, communications and security. OGSA is a service-oriented architecture (SOA) for a Grid to realize a computing system model as a set of distributed computing patterns. These patterns are then realized using Web services as the underlying technology. Basically, the OGSA standard defines service interfaces and identifies protocols for invoking these services.

Another organization, the Globus Alliance [4], focuses on developing an open software development kit, the Globus Toolkit (GT) [5], for constructing Grid applications. Many Grid systems are heterogeneous in nature, and many of them may be developed with heterogeneous protocols, which make them difficult to interoperate. At the very beginning, the Globus Toolkit was selected for developing Grid applications without regard for standards and specifications. However, Globus Toolkit has now become a popular programming platform for building distributed business related applications in heterogeneous environments.

From the networking perspective, the World Wide Web Consortium (W3C) [6] gets people connected around the world using Web browsers. Web browsing and services [7] through the Internet have made information ubiquitous. Currently, the Web Services Resource Framework (WSRF), developed at OASIS [8] and based on open standard technologies such as extensible markup language (XML) and hypertext transport protocol (HTTP) [6], is emerging as a promising infrastructure for building distributed applications. Another specification, the Web Services Resource (WS-Resource), is based on the generic SOA concept in which clients are service requestors and servers are service providers. In essence, a Web service is a loosely-coupled, encapsulated, platform-and-programming-language-neutral, integrable server-side component, and can be described, published, discovered and invoked over an internal network or on the Internet. The Globus Toolkit and the WSRF can now work together on designing various Grid applications.

3.2. *Grid Computing with OGSA*

Ultimately, it was the OGSA working group (OGSA-WG) at OGF that merged the efforts made by the Globus Alliance and OASIS. The OGSA specification was created as the architecture for building the next generation service-oriented Grid systems in a standardized way. Although OGSA is not a compulsory standard, it has become the *de facto* standard for building service-oriented Grid systems.

With the evolution of Grid computing, OGSA is using Web services to build service-oriented distributed computing systems. Hence, Grid services are Web services with certain extensions to meet some specific needs of the Grid, for example, feature designs, life cycle management of Grid services, etc. The OGSA specification only defines application programming interfaces (APIs) for Grid applications without any implementation details. The implementation technicalities are specified in detail in the Open Grid Services Infrastructure (OGSI) document. Unfortunately, the design of the OGSI specification is too complicated to work with existing Web services and XML tooling. Hence, it is the WSRF that is generally accepted for working with OGSA and modeling stateful resources with Web services. As already mentioned, OGSA is based on Web technologies such as XML, HTTP, with some extensions. Collectively, OGSA extends Web services by introducing interfaces and conventions in three main areas:

- *Interfaces*: There is a dynamic and potentially transient nature of services in a Grid. Some specific service instances may come and go as work is dispatched, as resources are configured and provisioned, and as system state changes. Grid services need interfaces to manage service creation, destruction and life cycle management.
- *States*: Grid services can have different attributes and data associated with them, and Web services need to be extended to support state information associated with Grid services.
- *Interest subscription*: Clients should be able to subscribe their interests in services. If there are changes in a service, clients should be notified through a call-back operation from services to clients.

Grid applications can be built based on OGSA-compliant services. Services in OGSA consist of two services: platform and core services. Platform services are Grid-based services related to user authentication and authorization, fault tolerance, job submission, monitoring and data access. The main core services include service creation, service destruction, life cycle management, service registration, discovery and notification.

OGSA defines various aspects related to a Grid service, e.g., the features of Grid services and what interfaces are needed, but it does not specify how these interfaces should be implemented. To identify a specific Grid service among all Grid service instances, a globally unique Grid service handle (GSH) is a URI which identifies a Grid service instance. Grid services can be upgraded during their lifetimes, for example, to support a new protocol version or to add alternative protocols. Therefore, GSH does not carry any protocol or instance-specific information, e.g., network address and supported protocol bindings. Instead, this information is encapsulated into a single abstraction called a Grid service reference (GSR), along with other instance specific information to interact with a specific service instance. Unlike the invariant GSH, GSR(s) for a Grid service instance can change over that service's lifetime. A GSR has an explicit expiration time, or it can be invalid at any time during a service's lifetime. OGSA should define proper mapping mechanisms for obtaining an updated GSR. The format of GSR is specific to the binding mechanism used by a client to communicate with the Grid service instance.

Apart from methods, each Grid service instance is associated with service data. Service data is a collection of XML elements encapsulated as service data elements (SDE), and is used to describe information about a service instance and their runtime states. Standard Web services are stateless, but the Grid services are stateful and can be introspected.

As shown in Fig. 7, a Grid service must implement a regular Grid service interface, and may implement other optional interfaces, if needed. Standard

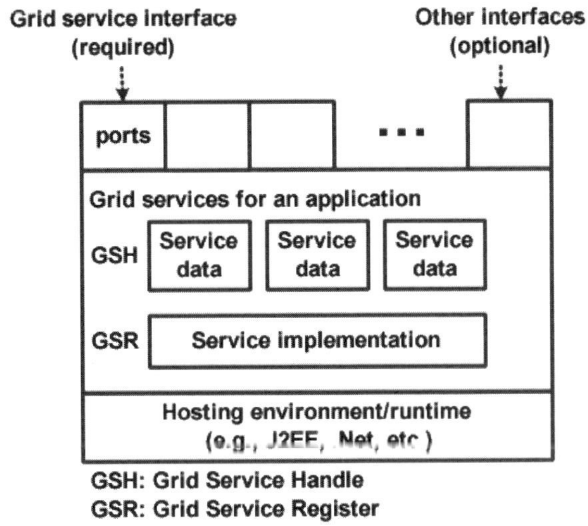

Fig. 7. Grid services in OGSA.

mechanisms for service creation, service destruction, life cycle management, service registration, discovery, and service notification should be defined. A Grid service can be a persistent or transient service instance. Each Grid service has a unique GSH and one or more GSRs to refer to implementation, which is independent of location, platform and programming language.

4. Massively Multi-User Online Platform

In this chapter, a massively multi-user online platform (MMOP) is designed to offer an online platform for executing wide-area large-scale applications on the Internet. The proposed MMOP design attempts to integrate an overlay algorithm into a Grid-based computing platform. Unfortunately, the popular Globus Toolkit could not be used for the creation of MMOP due to its current non-real-time issues. We did not follow the *de facto* OGSA design, but the concept of a Grid computing platform was followed in the proposed design and implementation of MMOP. As mentioned in Sec. 3.1, the designs of interfaces, state control, and subscription information should be investigated in the course of designing MMOP.

A Grid computing platform can be composed of different service entities, their constructions being commonly known as VOs. Grid services are offered through these VOs. An important aspect of the design of the MMOP Grid computing framework is integrating the DHT overlays into the constructions of VOs. The "virtual organization construction service" becomes the most basic internal service for other services due to its responsibility for constructing and maintaining VO system hierarchy.

The operating outline of MMOP works as follows. MMOP is aimed at setting up an environment in which application developers can program Grid services easily without much distributed computing experience. With an application-specific VO hierarchy, a Grid-to-the-Internet interface communicates through a specific group of VOs, the *Broker* VO, which masks all internal servicing VOs. In the proposed framework, a simple extensible set of application programming interfaces (APIs) has been created which should enable application developers to utilize the available computing resources easily. Certainly, the networking and servicing details are encapsulated within the MMOP. As a result, developers and users can define computational requirements and subscription information by means of policy rules. Several predefined distributed services aimed at these purposes are described in later subsections.

4.1. *Virtual Organization Construction Service*

In order to construct a Grid computing environment using structured overlays, machines are grouped into VOs. Machines in the same VO are connected through a P2P DHT overlay algorithm. In the testbed, two popular structured overlay algorithms, OHL [14] and Chord [15], are implemented and operated as modules within the VO construction service. A single machine can join multiple VOs at the same time. Consequently, it is crucial to be able to distinguish different API calls from one VO to another. All MMOP service API calls require two additional identifiers on top of regular parameters: the VO identity number (ID) and overlay key.

A VO ID is a universal identity assigned to each VO for simple API call relay purposes. For scalability, hierarchical ID space is used. In the prototype, there is one primary VO and several secondary VOs (including client VO) as illustrated in Fig. 8. The primary VO is the *Broker* VO, which stores the contact information of all secondary VOs using a distributed semaphore algorithm. Similarly, each VO may also store information of its first degree subsidiary VOs. Each VO ID is a multiple level string in the format {Primary/Secondary : 1st : 2nd:. . . :N^{th}}.

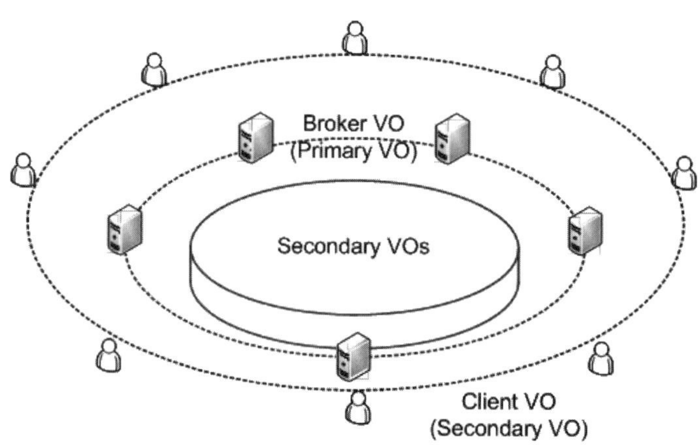

Fig. 8. VO hierarchy and encapsulation.

A prototype of MMOP has been created with the VO design discussed below. The VO hierarchy can also be extended to other topologies easily. Apart from the *Broker* VO, the application developers are free to devise other VO architectures for their applications. However, the *Broker* VO should always be present to cover the internal service architecture. Through the primary *Broker* VO, we can look up any given VO inside any hierarchical VO structures. In the prototype, as an example, we have:

- *Broker VO (primary)*: The backbone of the MMOP system which acts as a proxy and relays requests between clients and servicing VOs, and service execution information can be encapsulated.
- *Client VO (secondary)*: This VO includes all the clients, and its main purpose is to share non-critical data among clients. Direct communication between clients can be provided through this VO.
- *Application VO (secondary)*: This VO is where an application is deployed and executed. It provides computing services and resource management as defined by QoS policy of the application.
- *Module Storage VO (secondary)*: This VO provides storage services for application executables. All the data stored are split into smaller blocks, so the loads are distributed among data storage servers.
- *Free Server VO (secondary)*: This VO manages servers that have freely available resources available.

The *Broker* VO is the first VO constructed with a bootstrapping service for creating an operating MMOP system. The function of a bootstrapping service is to provide newly arriving machines with ways of joining or creating a VO. At the beginning of the formation of *Broker* VO, a single machine is set as the bootstrap master. This machine provides a bootstrap service for the initial few *Broker* machines. With more computing hosts joining the *Broker* VO, the newly arriving ones are not bound to use the bootstrap master. All computing hosts in the *Broker* VO can also initiate the bootstrapping services. When a new VO is created, the VO construction service creates subsidiary references to the new VO and stores multiple identical references using the distributed semaphore mechanism in the parent VO. The references can be extended by concatenating extra identifier strings to accommodate the new VO.

4.2. *Application Deployment Service*

The application deployment service provides application developers with a simple way of deploying their applications to specific VOs. An application is identified by the application name and version number. The name of an application should be unique within each VO while the version number is used to identify the version of the application. Combining the version and service name, the application deployment service can generate a unique key for this specific application.

Table 2. Application resource parameters.

Processor utilization	Expected processor utilization
Memory utilization	Memory required for executing the process
Spare storage	Free disk space
Network QoS	Bandwidth, latency, number of hops, etc.
Spawn threshold	A threshold is defined as any combination of the above parameters (CPU, memory utilization, storage, QoS network, etc.)

Along with each application, developers also need to specify the QoS policy requirements. A policy rule is used by the deployment service to identify the most suitable server for such a policy. The available parameters include `Policy Number`, `Real-Time`, `Priority Level`, `Expected Execution Time`, `Feedback Requirement`, and `Resources`. The `Resources` field can further be subdivided into several resource-related parameters. As shown in Table 2, these resource-related parameters are `Processor Utilization`, `Memory Utilization`, `Spare Storage`, `Network QoS`, and `Spawn Threshold`. The `Spawn Threshold` can be set to compare to, for example, a linear combination of other parameters. These parameters are monitored by the QoS monitoring service described in Sec. 4.3.1.

With these defined parameters, the application deployment service queries the QoS provisioning service entity to determine if there are in Free Server VO that can be deployed to serve the requested services. If no servers can satisfy such a query, the application which request, the corresponding application is notified. On the other hand, if the query is successful, then a selected server can join the specified *Application* VO and announce the amount of available resources. If there are no more resources available in this server, it is removed from the *Free Server* VO. Furthermore, an application may carry a preset `Spawn Threshold`. The QoS provisioning service entity should monitor the execution environment in the VO and try to spawn another process to handle new requests whenever the threshold has been reached. This enables load balancing at runtime, and increases the scalability of MMOP.

4.3. *QoS Management Service*

The QoS management service entity consists of two sub-services: (i) QoS monitoring services, and (ii) QoS provisioning services. As indicated in Sec. 4.2, the application deployment service should specify the desired type of services required when an application is being deployed. The QoS monitoring service gathers statistics of an application's execution environment, while the QoS provisioning service ensures an application's execution requirements can meet the specific requirements.

4.3.1. *QoS Monitoring Service*

Network quality and resource monitoring are important functions required for high-performance Grid computing platform. In the context of load balancing and application deployment, it is crucial to monitor the performance of service providing nodes to achieve optimal performance. The monitoring utilities provided by the MMOP should support periodic and event-driven updates. These updates are collected and aggregated by the monitoring services and relayed back to the requester. The collected data are processed by the application deployment service and QoS provisioning service in order to meet the service allocation requirement specification. Adjustment should also be made if a service performance degraded to an unacceptable predefined threshold.

To gain a reasonably accurate picture of the latest status of servicing devices, the following metrics are monitored every t_m seconds (t_m is set to 300 ms in the prototype for experiments):

- *Average CPU load*: The CPU monitoring utility takes the average of the user usage over the sum of cycles spent in user, system, and idle times.
- *Average memory load*: This is the ratio of available physical memory versus swap file in use.
- *Network statistics*: This metric can be further broken down into several sub-metrics. The statistics gathered below are for per network interface card (NIC) controller, and each of them has two components: received and sent.
  - *Throughput*: The received and sent throughput metrics indicate the bandwidth utilizations of the host.
  - *Packet error rate*: Indicator of the rate of packet integrity.
  - *Packet drop rate*: Indicator of missing packets, which occur usually due to buffer overflow in NIC.
- *Number of connections*: The total number of active clients' sessions. This is a good measure of the server loadings.
- *Available storage size*: This metric indicates the total available physical storage space.
- *Latency*: Latency parameter may be critical to applications with real-time requirements. It may be a requirement based on the decision of an application developer. The monitoring utility should send out a probing packet to the client, and calculate the network delay according to the probe acknowledgment.

4.3.2. *QoS Provisioning Service*

The QoS provisioning service entity ensures that a targeted server has sufficient resources according to the QoS requirements of an application. Associated QoS policy parameters can be found in Table 2. This service entity gathers and aggregates QoS statistics, and then compares them against the policy. All servers satisfying the requirements are reported to the application deployment service, and a deployment decision can subsequently be made. This service monitors a spawn threshold requirement for each application. If the current loading of an application reaches its predefined threshold, the QoS provisioning service notifies the application deployment service to try to offer more services. The application deployment service entity queries the provisioning service entity to find another available server to deploy more services for the application.

4.4. *Distributed Timing Service*

For gaming purposes, traditional multi-player games use the dead reckoning technique to estimate the movements of player entities. Data transmitted from a server include the position and the velocity of each player entity. When a participating client receives such data, it puts each entity at the given position specified by the positioning data. It then estimates a path for each entity from the current position based on the local clock. However, this projection can be inaccurate due to the network latency between server and client. When network delay increases, the inaccuracy may increase substantially and render the game unplayable in the worst case.

In order to minimize the impact on performance due to the network delays at a client, a distributed synchronized timing service is designed to enable the client to render different accurately. Experiments conducted in Ref. 18 show significant quantitative improvement in accuracy when minimum delay requirements are exceeded between the sender–receiver pairs. This introduces and appreciable qualitative improvement in game playing experience. In MMOP, we implement a simple distributed clock approximation as described in Ref. 19. The algorithm periodically sends packets back and forth between client and server to measure the round-trip time (RTT). By removing network latency spikes, we can provide a distributed time synchronization service that is accurate on the order of 150 ms or better in the prototype. A client of the service can also easily turn itself into a server by providing another client with the synchronized clock instead of its own local clock. In this way, a distributed timing service can be achieved and all sub-servers/clients are synchronized to the clock of the main server.

5. Performance Evaluation

To evaluate the performance of the MMOP platform, we designed a simple distributed shooting game on a 2D plane. In the next section, the design of the game and the provision of MMOP services are discussed.

5.1. *2D Shooting Game Design*

For the experiments, a shooting game is designed to run on a flat, infinite 2D plane. Each player controls his or her own aircraft, and launches missiles against other players continuously. This generates a large amount of network traffic in the testbed. When a missile hits an aircraft, the server removes the missile and decrements the shield value of the aircraft. Each aircraft has five shields and is removed once its shield value reaches zero. Each missile hit scores 100 points for the missile owner.

5.2. *Experiments and Results*

The MMOP platform have been implemented and deployed in a networking testbed. Nodes in the testbed are meshed together. The testbed can be configured into different network topologies upon needed. In the testbed, a computer operates as a router and connects via 100 Mbps Ethernet links to other routers in network. Each computing node may host several simulation nodes in the MMOP. In order to better simulate Internet traffic conditions, Pareto distribution traffic generators are deployed to create self-similar background traffic. Two types of background traffic loads (10% and 60%) are generated in experiments on all network interfaces. For different settings of background traffic, the online games are also set up with different VO topologies and various numbers of simulated players.

In order to demonstrate the flexibility of MMOP to run in different VO structures, three different VO setups are evaluated. The first VO setup is to place all game quadrant servers within one single application VO. This setup is similar to the cluster computing setup, where all the servers are co-located within a single administrative domain. The second VO setup creates two tiers of application VOs. The game plane is partitioned into four quadrants. The four quadrant servers run on four different subsidiary application VOs, as shown in Fig. 9. For the third VO setup, each quadrant application VO into four more independent subsidiary VOs. Hence, there are a total of sixteen VOs on the third tier.

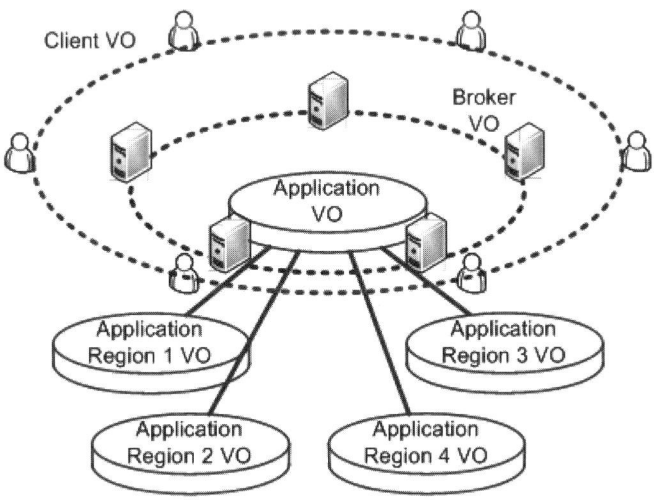

Fig. 9. Setup for four subsidiary application VOs.

5.2.1. *Selection of Overlay Algorithm*

The first set of experiments evaluates the impact of different overlay algorithms. Both the OHL and Chord are implemented for VO deployments and experiments. The overhead introduced by the overlay network is measured. Since the total number of simulated nodes is known in the OHL design, stabilization implies that the total node entries at each node should be equal to the total number of simulated nodes. For Chord, the stabilization process takes the approach of periodically refreshing indices within a finger table until no more updates are needed. For this set of experiments, a single *Application* VO configuration with no other secondary VOs is used. A *Broker* node requests to update a variable on the *Application* once every 500 ms. The updates are carried out one thousand times. The average latency is recorded in Fig. 10.

From the plotted results, OHL has a noticeable advantage over Chord. This is due to the fact that Chord uses fingers to index the storage nodes, and, in the worst case, it may take $\log_2 N$ requests to find the data. For OHL, all indices are stored locally and hence actual indexing has a shorter latency. The drawback is that OHL takes longer to stabilize the indices. For the subsequent simulations, OHL is selected to provide a better performance of the MMOP implementation in the testbed.

5.2.2. *Session Durations*

In this subsection, the time durations required to complete games are measured under different background traffic conditions. All simulations could be completed normally without any errors. However, upon observing the game execution, we found that the simulated players appear to turn left and right excessively instead of aiming directly at the target. This might be due to a combination of several factors, such as predefined angle, latency, and value rounding. However, artificial intelligence in

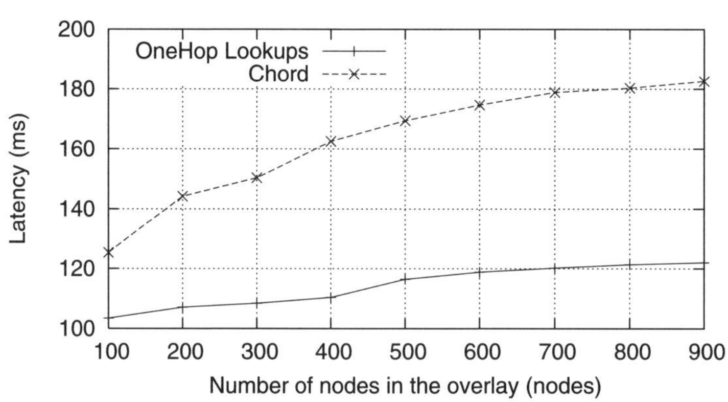

Fig. 10. Latency of three replicas on the overlay versus number of nodes.

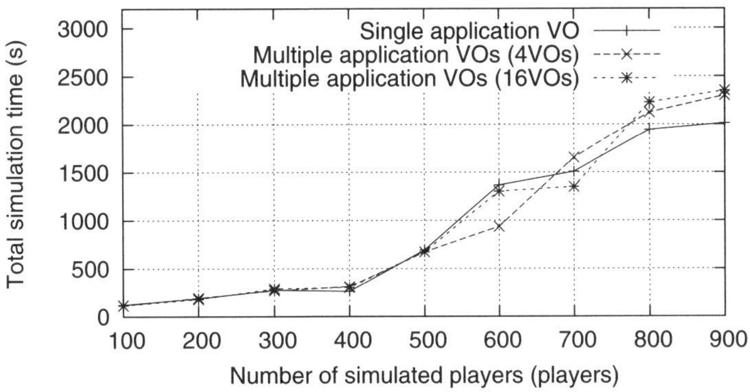

(a) 10% background traffic.

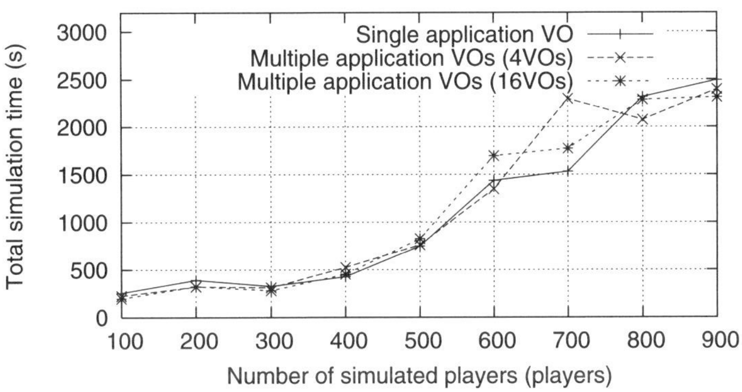

(b) 60% background traffic.

Fig. 11. Total game durations under different VO setups versus number of simulated players.

the game is not part of our research focus. Investigation in this area could certainly improve the gaming experience for online players.

In Figs. 11(a) and 11(b), the differences between total execution times among different VO setups are measured under different traffic loadings for the same number of players. The differences are not significant, and this implies that the network traffic and VO configuration do not have a huge impact in terms of actual game performance. Besides, the completion times increase roughly linearly with respect to the number of players, that is, the game completion times change from a few hundred seconds to two thousand seconds when the number of players increases from 100 to 900. This shows that the MMOP is capable of offering a transparent platform for a large number of simultaneous active players. However, the performance degrades slightly when the background traffic increases, as shown in the minor differences with 700-player cases in Fig. 11(b) for 60% background traffic loading. Again, the MMOP provides consistently high system throughput performance in the experiments.

6. Thoughts for Practitioners

The proposed MMOP suceeds in handling large numbers of users under heavy network traffic loads. In fact, Grid and cloud computing have already been generally accepted as the platform for performing large-scale and computationally intensive applications. A wide-area Grid computing system is being created in Europe for scientific research. In North America, Open Grid exists and is available for Grid-based research operations. Commercially, IBM has recently created a Grid computing platform for the social networking application Second Life to operate on the Internet. We can foresee that the numbers of Grid platforms and applications will only increase in future. For practitioners, although OGSA and the Globus Toolkit may not be the perfect platforms for creating new Grid applications, they offer a simple way to understand and design Grid computing applications.

7. Directions for Future Research

MMOP is one architectural design based on the concepts of Grid and cloud computing. Integrating Grid computing and overlay algorithms has become one of the most active research areas. The potential research areas include load balancing and sharing, load and application admissions with different policy rules, scaling of VOs, APIs, interface and semantic designs, etc. Is Globus Toolkit the best choice for creating Grid applications? Or should MMOP be generalized for building different types of Grid applications? Effective mapping of Grid applications to VO hierarchy will also be an important research area.

8. Conclusion

Emerging large-scale online applications are presenting challenges to many application developers. In Grid computing, the main issues are the huge variance in computer resources and the dynamics of server memberships with respect to the structures of different virtual organizations. In order to provide a high performance service-oriented distributed architecture, it is required that the underlying system platform should provide means of developing distributed application efficiently. This is exactly the design goal of the massively multi-user online platform (MMOP). MMOP offers a virtual organization construction service, a distributed semaphore atomic data access service, an application deployment service, a QoS management service, and a distributed timing service. A set of easy-to-use service APIs can be deployed. Through experiments, MMOP has shown itself to be a practical, efficient and fault-tolerant platform that takes advantages of structured overlays. Our simulation results demonstrate that the MMOP can offer a high performance distributed architecture for large-scale applications.

Terminology

Socket programming: The basic programming technique to connect computing hosts in networks.

Peer-to-peer overlays: There is no centralized server to access; file sharing is achieved through direct connection between two peers.

One hops lookups (OHL): An algorithm that can be used to create an overlay network. A file or object can be retrieved one virtual on the overlay.

Chord: Another algorithm that can be used to create overlays. It may take $O(\log_2 N)$ steps to get the file or object.

Grid computing: The widely accepted computing platform to handle large-scale applications.

Virtual organization (VO): An operating entity in Grid computing.

Open Grid Forum (OGF): An organization that provides recommendations for setting up Grid computing systems.

Globus Toolkit: A programming software toolkit developed at Globus Alliance for building Grid applications.

Massively multi-player online games (MMOGs): The widely popular games that run online on the Internet, for example, the World of Warcraft (WoW) from Bizarre Entertainment. Inc. Another commonly used name is massively multi-player role playing online games (MMRPGs).

Massively multi-user online platform (MMOP): The proposed large-scale wide-are online computing platform for applications on the Internet. MMOG can run on this platform.

Exercises

1. What is the common interpretation of Grid computing?
2. Find online the commonly used system calls in the C programming language for setting up a UDP connection.
3. Grid computing is a computation intensive platform requiring programming skill. Starting from the basics, search online and try to write simple client and server code for setting up a TCP connection using C.
4. Features can be added more easily with a higher level programming language. Search online and try to write a network server and client in the Java programming language.
5. What is the main contribution of Remote Procedure Call (RPC) in subsequent technology advancements?
6. What are the three algorithms mentioned for constructing structured P2P overlays?
7. Which organization is working on defining specifications on Grid computing?
8. Which software toolkit is the popularly selected toolkit for constructing Grid applications?

9. For the example design given, what are the virtual organizations (VOs) created for the games? Which one is the compulsory VO in the MMOP design?
10. What is the traditional method for estimating the movements of players in games?

References

1. I. Foster, C. Kesselman and S. Tuecke, The anatomy of the Grid enabling scalable virtual organizations, *Int. J. Supercomput. Appl.* **15**(3), (2001).
2. I. Foster, C. Kesselman, J. Nick and S. Tuecke, *The Physiology of the Grid: An Open Grid Services Architecture for Distributed Systems Integration*, June 2002.
3. Open Grid Forum, www.ogf.org.
4. The Globus Alliance, www.globus.org.
5. I. T. Foster, Globus toolkit version 4: Software for service-oriented systems, in NPC, Lecture Notes in Computer Science, Vol. 3779 (Springer, 2005), pp. 2–13.
6. World Wide Web Consortium, www.w3.org.
7. Web Services, www.w3.org/2002/ws.
8. Advancing Open Standards for the Information Society, www.oasis-open.org.
9. A. D. Birrell and B. J. Nelson, Implementing remote procedure calls, *ACM Trans. Comput. Syst.* **2**(1), 39–59 (1984).
10. Remote Method Invocation, http://java.sun.com/javase/technologies/core/basic/rmi/index.jsp.
11. Distributed Component Object Model, www.microsoft.com/com.
12. Common Object Request Broker Architecture, www.corba.org.
13. The Object Management Group, www.omg.org.
14. A. Gupta, B. Liskov and R. Rodrigues, One hop lookups for peer-to-peer overlays, *9th Workshop on Hot Topics in Operating Systems (HotOS-IX)*, Lihue, Hawaii, May (2003), pp. 7–12.
15. R. Morris, D. Karger, F. Kaashoek and H. Balakrishnan, Chord: A scalable peer-to-peer lookup service for Internet applications, *ACM Sigcomm 2001*, San Diego, September (2001).
16. R. Bhagwan, S. Savage and G. Voelker, Understanding availability, *Proc. 2nd Int. Workshop Peer-to-Peer Systems (IPTPS '03)*, February (2003).
17. D. Karger, E. Lehman, T. Leighton, M. Levine, D. Lewin and R. Panigrahy, Consistent hashing and random trees: Distributed caching protocols for relieving hot spots on the world wide Web, *ACM Symp. Theory of Computing*, May (1997), pp. 654–663.
18. S. Aggarwal, H. Banavar, A. Khandelwal, S. Mukherjee and S. Rangarajan, Accuracy in dead-reckoning based distributed multi-player games, *Proc. 3rd ACM Sigcomm Workshop on Network and System Support for Games (NetGames'04)*, New York, USA (ACM Press, 2004), pp. 161–165.
19. Z. B. Simpson, A stream-based time synchronization technique for networked computer games, www.mine-control.com/zack/timesync/timesync.html, 1 March (2000).
20. P. Mymounkov and D. Mazieres, Kademlia: A peer-to-peer information system based on the XOR metric, *Proc. 1st Int. Workshop Peer-to-Peer Systems (IPTPS'02)*, Cambridge, USA, 7–8 March (2002).

Chapter 20

ADAPTIVE MULTIMEDIA TRANSMISSION OVER THE INTERNET

CHRISTOS BOURAS* and APOSTOLOS GKAMAS†
Computer Engineering and Informatics Department,
University of Patras, GR26500, Greece
Research Academic Computer Technology Institute,
N. Kazantzaki, University of Patras Campus, GR26500, Greece
**bouras@cti.gr*
†gkamas@cti.gr

The Internet is a heterogeneous network environment and the network resources that are available to multimedia applications can be modified very quickly. Multimedia applications must have the capability to adapt their operation to network changes. In order to add adaptation characteristics to multimedia applications, we can use techniques both at the network and application layers. Adaptive multimedia transmission techniques have the capability to transmit multimedia data over heterogeneous networks and adapt media transmission to network changes. In order to provide adaptive multimedia transmission, mechanisms to monitor the network conditions and mechanisms to adapt the transmission of the data to the network changes must be implemented. This chapter concentrates on the architecture and design issues of adaptive multimedia techniques that provide the capability to transmit multimedia data over heterogeneous networks and adapt the transmission of the multimedia data to the network changes.

1. Introduction

The Internet is a heterogeneous network environment and the network resources that are available to realtime applications can be modified very quickly. Realtime applications must have the capability to adapt their operation to network changes. In order to add adaptation characteristics to realtime applications, we can use techniques both at the network and application layers. Adaptive realtime applications have the capability to transmit multimedia data over heterogeneous networks and adapt media transmission to network changes. In order to implement an adaptive multimedia transmission application, mechanisms to monitor the network conditions and mechanisms to adapt the transmission of the data to the network changes must be implemented.

Today, the underlying infrastructure of the Internet does not sufficiently support quality of service (QoS) guarantees. The new technologies that are used for the implementation of networks provide capabilities to support QoS in one network domain but it is not easy to implement QoS among various network domains, in order to provide end-to-end QoS to the user. In addition, some researchers believe that the cost of providing end-to-end QoS is too heavy, and it is better to invest in careful network design and careful network monitoring, in order to identify and upgrade the congested network links [1].

In this chapter, we concentrate on the architecture of an adaptive realtime application that has the capability to transmit multimedia data over heterogeneous networks and adapt the transmission of the multimedia data to the network changes. The chapter covers both unicast and multicast transmission of multimedia data.

The heterogeneous network environment that the Internet provides to realtime applications, as well as the lack of sufficient QoS guarantees, often forces applications to employ adaptation schemes in order to work efficiently. In addition, any application that transmits data over the Internet should not adversely affect the other flows that exist, especially the transmission control protocol (TCP) flows that comprise the majority of flows. We define as *TCP friendly flow* a flow that consumes no more bandwidth than a TCP connection which is traversing the same path as that flow [2].

During multimedia transmission over the Internet, several aspects need to be considered:

- *Transmission rate adaptation*: The sender must adapt the transmission rate based on the current network conditions.
- *TCP friendliness*: During the multimedia transmission over the Internet, the multimedia flows must be TCP-friendly.
- *Scalability*: The performance of the adaptation scheme must not deteriorate with increasing numbers of receivers.
- *Heterogeneity*: The adaptation scheme needs to take into account the heterogeneity of the Internet and must aim at satisfying the requirements of a large part of the receivers if not all possible receivers.

The remainder of this chapter is structured as follows. The next section reviews the various international contributions to research on adaptive multimedia transmission over the Internet. Section 3 presents some thoughts for practitioners. Section 4 describes unicast multimedia adaptive transmission over the Internet, while Section 5 tackles multicast multimedia adaptive transmission. Section 6 considers the future trends in the field, and Section 7 draws conclusions.

2. Background

The subject of adaptive transmission of multimedia data over networks has engaged researchers all over the world for many years [1]. During the design and implementation of an adaptive application special attention must be paid to the following critical modules:

- the module responsible for the transmission of the multimedia data,
- the module responsible for monitoring the network conditions and determines the changing the network conditions,
- the module responsible for the adaptation of the multimedia data to the network changes,
- the module responsible for handling transmission errors during the transmission of the multimedia data.

A common approach for the implementation of adaptive applications is the use of the user datagram protocol (UDP) for the transmission of the multimedia data and the use of the Transmission Control Protocol (TCP) for the transmission of control information [3]. Another approach for the transmission of the multimedia data is the use of RTP over UDP [4, 5]. Most adaptive applications use (Realtime Transmission Protocol/Realtime Control Transmission Protocol (RTP/RTCP) [6]) for the transmission of multimedia data. RTP seems to be the *de facto* standard for the transmission of multimedia data.

For the implementation of the network monitoring module a common approach is to use packet loss as an indication of congestion in the network [4, 5, 7]. Another approach for monitoring the network conditions is the use of the client buffer [8]. An important factor that can be used for monitoring the network conditions, and especially for an indication of network congestion, is the delay jitter.

For the implementation of the adaptation module some common approaches are the use of rate shaping [4, 9], layered encoding, and frame dropping [8], or a combination of the above techniques [10]. The implementation of the adaptation module depends on the encoding method used. For example, to employ the frame dropping technique for the adaptation of an MPEG video stream, a selective frame dropping technique must be used since MPEG video uses inter-frame encoding and some frames contain information relative to other frames.

It is important for adaptive realtime applications to have "friendly" behavior towards the dominant transport protocols (TCP) [11].

For multimedia transmission over the Internet both unicasting and multicasting can be used. In unicast multimedia transmission a separate multimedia stream is transmitted by the sender for each of the receivers. When the number of receivers is large unicasting is not effective (in terms of the required bandwidth) and multicasting can be used. In multicast multimedia transmission a single multimedia stream serves many receivers.

When multimedia data are multicast over the Internet, receivers with heterogeneous data reception capabilities must be accommodated. To accommodate heterogeneity, the sender application may transmit one multicast stream and determine the transmission rate that best satisfies most of the receivers, it may transmit multiple multicast streams with different transmission rates and allocate receivers at each stream, or it may use layered encoding and transmit each layer to a different multicast stream. A detailed survey of adaptive video multicasting over the Internet is given in [12].

The single multicast stream approach has the disadvantage that clients with a low bandwidth link will always get a high bandwidth stream if most of the other members are connected via a high bandwidth link and *vice versa.* This problem can be overcome with the use of a multistream multicast approach. Single multicast stream approaches have the advantages of easy encoder and decoder implementation and simple protocol operation since during the single multicast stream approach there is no need for synchronization of receivers' actions (as is required for the multiple multicast streams and layered encoding approaches).

The methods proposed for the multicast transmission of multimedia data over the Internet can generally be divided into three main categories, depending on the number of multicast streams used:

- *The sender uses a single multicast stream for all receivers* [4]. This results in the most effective use of network resources, but gives rise to the fairness problem among the receivers, especially when the receivers have very different capabilities. The sender application must select the transmission rate that satisfies most of the receivers under the current network conditions. Three main approaches can be found in the literature: equation based [2], network feedback based [13, 14] or a combination of the two approaches [15].
- *Simulcast: The sender transmits different versions of the same video encoded with varying degrees of quality.* This results in the creation of a small number of multicast streams with different transmission rates [12, 16]. The different multicast streams carry the same video information but in each one the video is encoded with different bit rates, and even different video formats. Each receiver joins the stream that carries the video quality, in terms of transmission rate, that it is capable of receiving. The main disadvantage here is that the same multimedia information is replicated over the network, but recent research has shown that under some conditions simulcasting has a better behavior than multicast transmission of layered encoded video [17].
- *The sender uses layered encoded video.* This is video that can be reconstructed from a number of discrete data layers, the basic layer and more additional layers. The sender transmits each layer in different multicast streams [18–20]. The basic layer provides the basic quality and the quality improves with each additional layer. Receivers subscribe to one or more multicast streams depending on the available bandwidth of the network path to the source. A survey of adaptive layered video multicasting over the Internet is given in [21].

A comparison of simulcast and layered encoded approaches can be found in [5].

3. Thoughts for Practitioners

The deployment of adaptive transmission applications has the benefit that there is not need for network device changes or any extra configuration of network devices because adaptation takes place to the end points (sender and receiver applications) and not within the network. Adaptive unicast transmission applications require only the presence of an IP network, and adaptive multicast transmission applications require only the presence of an IP multicast network. Even when a part of the network used for adaptive multicasting does not support IP multicasting, the IP tunneling approach can be used to overcome this limitation (something that has been done many times in the MBONE network). This is very important when comparing approaches based on the QoS concept (either InteServ or DiffServ), where network device changes and extra configuration of network devices is needed.

Especially for the unicast adaptive transmission and the single multicast stream adaptive transmission approaches, deployment is narrowed to only the sender application end point since all the required modules for the implementation are located on the sender side alone. This means that any application which is compatible with the transmission of multimedia data through RTP sessions (for example, MBONE tools [10] can access the adaptive transmission service and benefit from its adaptive transmission characteristics.

In implementing adaptive transmission applications, Java technology can be used and, in particular, Java Media Framework (JMF) application programmable interface (API). JMF provides capabilities for importing in Java applications and applets time-based media like video and audio. JMF supports the most common audio and video formats like AIFF, AU, AVI, GSM, MIDI, MPEG, QuickTime, RMF and WAV. In addition, JMF supports the transmission of realtime data (i.e., multimedia) with the use of RTP/RTCP. Moreover, JMF has capabilities for elaboration of audio and video data during transmission over the network with the use of RTP/RTCP. All the above characteristics of JMF make it an attractive platform for the implementation of adaptive transmission mechanisms. More information about JMF can be found in Ref. 22.

The implementation of multistream adaptive multicasting (simulcast and layered encoded approaches) is based on complicated video encoding and decoding mechanisms. The current state-of-the-art technology in such video encoders/decoders is the H.264 video coding standard with the AVC [3] and the SVC [23] extensions. The H.264 AVC extension can be used for the implementation of simulcast multimedia transmission, and the H.264 SVC extension can be used for the implementation of layered encoded multimedia transmission.

4. Unicast Multimedia Adaptive Transmission Over the Internet

4.1. *The Architecture of an Adaptive Streaming Application*

This section presents a typical architecture for a unicast adaptive multimedia transmission application based on the client–server model. (Fig. 1).

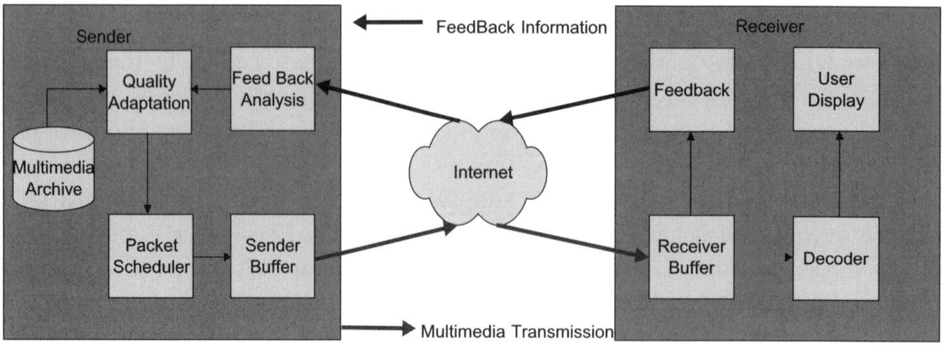

Fig. 1. System architecture.

The sender comprises the following modules:

- *Multimedia archive*: A set of hard disks in which the multimedia files are stored. The adaptive transmission application may support various multimedia formats (e.g., MPEG, JPEG, H.263). It is possible for one multimedia file to be stored in the multimedia archive in more than one format in order to serve different target user groups. For example, it is possible to store the same video in MPEG format in order to serve users of a local area network (who have faster network connections to the sender) and in H.263 format in order to serve distant users with slower network connections.
- *Feedback analysis*: Responsible for the analysis of feedback information from the network. The role of this module is to determine the network conditions mainly based on packet loss rate and delay jitter information, which are provided by RTCP receiver reports. After the examination of the network conditions, the feedback analysis module informs the quality adaptation module in order to adapt the transmission of the video to current conditions.
- *Quality adaptation*: Responsible for the adaptation of the multimedia transmission quality in order to match with the current network conditions. This module can be implemented using various techniques (rate shaping, layered encoding, frame dropping, etc.).
- *Packet scheduler/sender buffer*: Responsible for the encapsulation of multimedia information in the RTP packets. In addition, this module is responsible for the transmission of the RTP packets in the network. In order to smooth out glitches in the transmission of the multimedia data from the sender to the network, an output buffer is used on the sender.

The receiver of a unicast adaptive multimedia transmission architecture comprises the following modules:

- *Receiver buffer*: The use of a buffer on the receiver in the implementation of such applications is very important. The receiver application stores the incoming data to the buffer before starting to present data to the user. The presentation of the multimedia data to the user starts only after the necessary amount of the data is stored in the buffer. The capacity of the receiver buffer depends to the delay jitter during the transmission. In any case, the capacity of the receiver buffer must be greater than the maximum delay jitter during the transmission of the data (we suppose that we measure the buffer capacity and the delay jitter in the same units, for example, in seconds).

- *Feedback*: Responsible for monitoring the transmission quality of the multimedia data and informing the sender. The monitoring of the transmission quality is based on the RTCP receiver reports, which the receiver sends to the sender. RTCP receiver reports include information about the packet loss rate and the delay jitter during the transmission of the data. With the above information the feedback analysis module of the sender determines network conditions.
- *Decoder*: Reads the data packets from the receiver buffer and decodes the encoded multimedia information. Depending on the packet losses and the delay during the transmission of the packets, the quality of the multimedia presentation can vary. The decoding and the presentation of the multimedia data can stop if the appropriate amount of data does not exist in the buffer.
- *User display*: Responsible for the presentation of the multimedia data to the user.

In the following subsections we provide a detailed description of the most important modules in the above architecture.

4.2. *Transmission of Multimedia Data*

The *de facto* protocols currently used for the transmission of multimedia data on the Internet are RTP and RTCP. RTP is used for the transmission of the multimedia data from the sender to the receiver, and the receiver uses the RTCP protocol, to inform the sender of the transmission quality. RTCP is the control protocol of RTP.

RTP and RTCP were designed for the transmission of multimedia data like video and audio. Although they were initially designed for multicast transmission, they have also been used for unicast transmissions. RTP/RTCP can be used for one-way communication like video on demand or for two-way communication like videoconferencing. RTP/RTCP offers a common platform for the representation of the synchronization information that realtime applications need.

RTP is a protocol that offers end-to-end transport services with realtime characteristics over packet-switching networks like IP networks. RTP packet headers include information about the payload type of the data, numbering of the packets and time stamping information.

RTCP offers the following services to applications:

- *QoS monitoring*: Providing — feedback to applications about transmission quality is one of the primary services of RTCP. RTCP uses sender and receiver reports, which contain useful statistical information like total transmitted packets, packet loss rate and delay jitter. This statistical information is very useful because it can be used for the implementation of congestion control mechanisms.

- *Source identification*: RTCP source description packets can be used for identification of the participants in an RTP session. In addition, source description packets provide general information about the participants in an RTP session. The service is useful for multicast conferences with many members.
- *Inter-media synchronization*: In realtime applications, it is common to transmit audio and video in different data streams. RTCP provides services like time stamping, which can be used for inter-media synchronization of different data streams (for example, synchronization of audio and video streams).

More information about RTP/RTCP can be found in RFC 3550 [6].

4.3. *Feedback from the Network*

The presentation quality of multimedia data depends on the packet loss rate and the delay jitter during transmission over the network. In addition, packet losses or rapid increases in delay jitter may be considered an indication of problems during transmission. In such cases, the multimedia transmission application must adapt the transmission of the data in order to avoid phenomena like network congestion. Multimedia applications have upper bounds to the packet loss rate and the delay jitter. If packet loss rate or jitter exceeds these upper bounds, transmission of realtime data cannot be continued.

Packet loss rate is defined as the fraction of the total transmitted packets that did not arrive at the receiver. Usually, the main reason for packet losses is congestion.

It is difficult to define delay jitter. Some researchers define delay jitter as the difference between the maximum and the minimum delay during the transmission of packets over a period of time. Other researchers define delay jitter as the maximum difference between the delays of the transmissions of two sequential packets over a period of time. According to RFC 3550 [6] delay jitter is defined as the mean deviation (smoothed absolute value) of the difference in packet spacing at the receiver compared to the sender for a pair of packets. This is equivalent to the difference in the "relative transit time" for the two packets. The relative transit time is the difference between a packet's timestamp and the receiver's clock at the time of arrival. If S_i is the timestamp from packet i and j is the time of arrival for this packet, then for two packets i and j, D is defined as

$$D(i,j) = (R_j - R_i) - (S_j - S_i) = (R_j - S_j) - (R_i - S_i). \qquad (1)$$

The delay jitter is calculated continuously as each packet i arrives, using the difference D for that packet and the previous packet, according to the following formula:

$$J_i = J_{i-1} + (|D(i-1,j)| - J_{i-1})/16. \qquad (2)$$

The above formula states that the new value of delay jitter depends on the previous value of the delay jitter and on a gain parameter, which gives good noise reduction.

Delay jitter occurs when sequential packets encounter different delays in the queues of the network devices. The different delays are related to the server model of each queue and the cross traffics in the transmission path.

Sometimes delay jitter occurs during the transmission of multimedia data that does not originate from the network but from the transmission host (host included delay jitter). This is because during the encoding of the multimedia data the encoder places a timestamp in each packet, which gives information about the time that the packet's information must be presented to the receiver. In addition, this timestamp is used for the calculation of the delay jitter during the transmission of the multimedia data. If a notable time passes from the encoding of the packet and transmission of the packet in the network (because the CPU of the transmitter host is busy), the calculation of the delay jitter is not valid. Host included delay jitter can lead to erroneous estimations of the network conditions.

We can conclude that delay jitter cannot by itself lead to reliable estimations of network conditions. Delay jitter has to be used in combination with other parameters like packet loss rate in order to allow reliable estimations of the network conditions to be made. Thus, the combination of packet loss rate and delay jitter can be used for reliable indications of network congestion [4].

4.4. *Quality Adaptation*

One popular approach for quality adaptation is the rate shaping technique. According to this technique, if we change some parameters of the encoding procedure, we can control the amount of the data that the video encoder produces (either increase or decrease the amount of the data) and as a result we can control the transmission rate of the multimedia data.

The implementation of rate shaping techniques depends on the video encoding used. Rate shaping techniques change one or more of the following parameters:

- *Frame rate*: The rate of the frames that are encoded by the video encoder. Decreasing the frame rate can reduce the amount of the data that the video encoder produces but will reduce the quality.
- *Quantizer*: Specifies the number of DCT coefficients that are encoded. Increasing the quantizer decreases the number of encoded coefficients and reduces image quality.
- *Movement detection threshold*: Used for inter-frame coding, where the DCT is applied to signal differences. The movement detection threshold limits the number of blocks which are detected to be "sufficiently different" from the previous frames. Increasing this threshold decreases the output rate of the encoder.

4.5. *Error Control/Packet Loss*

The packet loss rate depends on various parameters and adaptive multimedia transmission applications must adapt to changes in packet loss. Two approaches are available to reduce the effects of packet loss:

- Automatic repeat request (APQ): APQ is an active technique where the receiver asks the sender to retransmit lost packets.
- Forward error correction (FEC): FEC is a passive technique where the sender transmits redundant information. This redundant information is used by the receiver to correct errors and lost packets.

5. Multicast Multimedia Adaptive Transmission Over the Internet

5.1. *Introduction*

As we have already mentioned, for multimedia transmission over the Internet the unicast approach does not scale well. In unicast multimedia transmission a separate multimedia stream is transmitted by the sender to each of the receivers. When the number of receivers is large, the unicast transmission is not effective (in terms of the required bandwidth) and multicasting can instead be used. During multicast transmission of data, a multicast stream traverses a network node as long as at least one receiver behind that node is listening to that stream. As result, if a receiver stops listening to a multicast stream, the transmission will stop only if that receiver was the only receiver listening to that multicast stream behind that node.

During multicast transmission, receivers with heterogeneous data reception capabilities must be accommodated. To accommodate heterogeneity, the sender application may transmit one multicast stream and determine the transmission rate that best satisfies most of the receivers, it may transmit at multiple multicast streams with different transmission rates and allocate receivers at each stream, or it may use layered encoding and transmit each layer to a different multicast stream.

5.2. *Single Stream Multicasting*

In this scenario, a sender application transmits multimedia data to a group of n receivers with the use of one multicast stream. The sender application uses RTP/RTCP for the transmission of the multimedia data. Receivers receive the multimedia data and inform the sender application about the quality of the transmission with the use of RTCP receiver reports. The sender application collects the RTCP receiver reports, analyzes them and determines the transmission rate that satisfies most receivers given the current network conditions.

During a single stream adaptive multicast transmission, the sender usually runs two algorithms:

- *Feedback analysis algorithm*: Analyzes the feedback information that the receivers send to the sender application (most mechanisms use the RTCP receiver reports

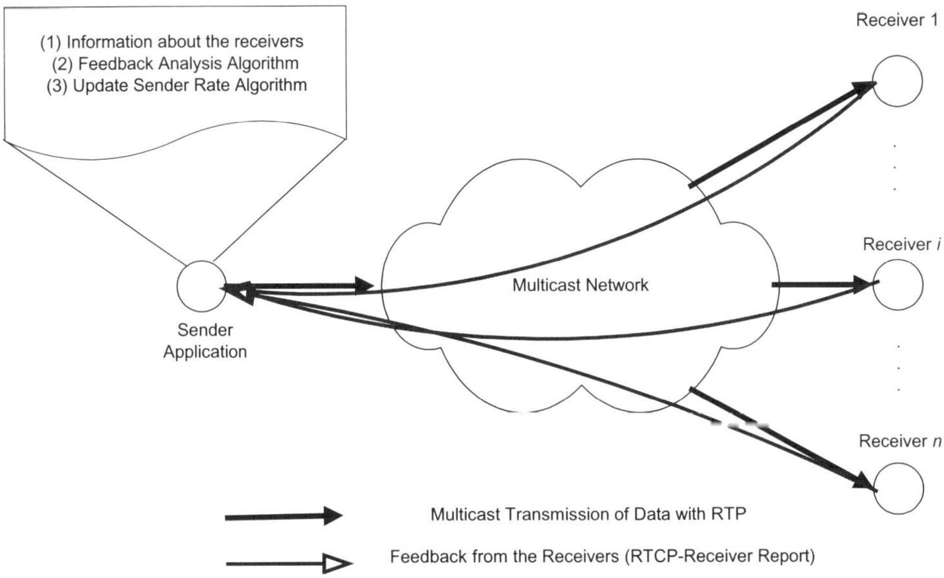

Fig. 2. Architecture of a single stream adaptive multicast transmission mechanism.

for this purpose) concerning the transmission quality of the multimedia data. Every time the sender application receives feedback from a receiver, it runs the feedback analysis algorithm in order to estimate the preferred transmission rate that will satisfy that receiver. The receiver's preferred transmission rate represents the transmission rate that this receiver would prefer if it were the only receiver receiving the multimedia data.

- *Update sender rate algorithm*: The sender application in repeated time periods estimates the transmission rate with the use of this algorithm. The estimation is aimed at increasing the satisfaction of the group of receivers for the given network conditions.

The receiver of a single stream multicast multimedia transmission behaves like the corresponding receiver of the unicast multimedia transmission and via RTCP reports provides the sender with feedback on the quality of the multimedia transmission.

5.3. *Simulcasting*

In the simulcast approach, the sender transmits different versions of the same video encoded with varying degrees of quality. This results in the creation of a small number of multicast streams with different transmission rates [4]. The different multicast streams carry the same video information but in each one the video is encoded with different bit rates, and even different video formats. Each receiver joins the stream that carries the video quality, in terms of transmission rate, that it is capable of receiving.

In such a mechanism the sender is unique and responsible for:

- creating the n different multicast streams (generally a small number of multicast streams, usually three or four are enough),
- setting each stream's bandwidth limits,
- tracking if there are any receivers that are not handled fairly, and
- providing the mechanisms to the receivers to switch streams whenever they consider that they should be in another stream closer to their capabilities.

Figure 3 shows the organisation and the architecture of the sender entity. The sender generates n different stream managers. In each stream manager, an arbitrary number of receiver managers are assigned. Each receiver manager corresponds to a unique receiver that has joined the stream controlled by this stream manager. The synchronization server is responsible for the management, synchronization and intercommunication between stream managers.

The stream manager entity is responsible for the maintenance and the monitoring of one of the n different multicast streams. Also the stream manager entity has all the intra-stream adaptation mechanisms for the adjustment of the transmission rate. The stream manager gathers the states reported by all receiver managers belonging to it at specific, fixed time intervals. It then uses an appropriate algorithm that tries to improve fairness between receivers by determining whether a lower or a higher bit rate is more appropriate. Whenever a receiver cannot be satisfied by a stream because most of the other receivers have much higher or much

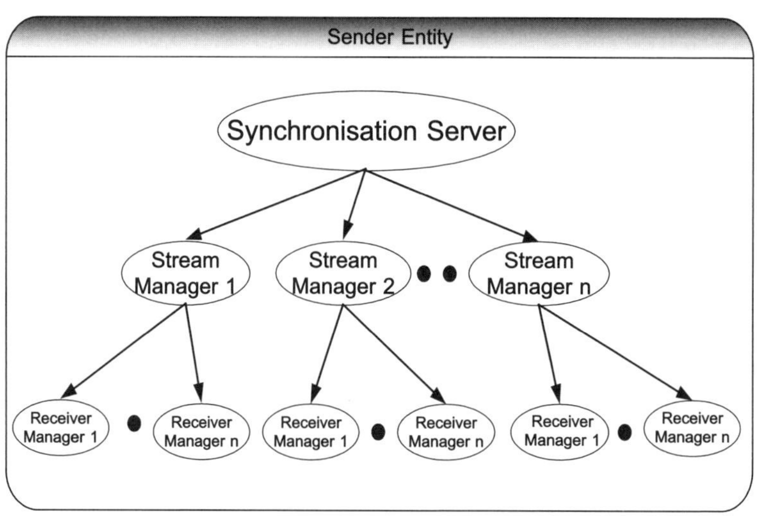

Fig. 3. The architecture and the data flow of the sender for simulcasting.

lower reception capabilities, the stream manager informs it that it has to move to a lower or higher quality stream.

Each receiver manager corresponds to a unique receiver (for scalability reasons a small representative group of receivers may have a corresponding receiver manager). The receiver manager processes the RTCP reports generated by the receiver and can be considered as a representative of the receiver at the side of the sender. It can interact only with one stream manager at a given time, the stream manager controlling the stream from which the receiver is receiving the video. The receiver manager receives the RTCP reports from the receiver and processes them based on packet loss rate and delay jitter information. It then makes an estimation of the state of the receiver based on the current report and a few previous reports that it stores in a buffer.

Receivers join the appropriate streams that better suit their requirements (available bandwidth between the sender and the receiver, etc.) and if during the transmission of multimedia data the network conditions to the path between them and the sender change, the receivers have the capability to change stream in order to better fulfil their requirements. Each receiver measures the characteristics of the path which connects it with the sender and informs the sender with the use of RTCP receiver reports. The communication between the sender and the receivers is based on RTP/RTCP sessions. The sender uses RTP to transmit the video streams and the participants (the sender and the receivers) use RTCP to exchange control messages.

5.4. *Layered Encoding*

In this mechanism the sender transmits multimedia data to a group of m receivers with the use of multicast. The sender uses the layered encoding approach, and transmits the video information in n different layers (the basic layer and $n-1$ additional layers). The sender transmits each layer in a different RTP/RTCP multicast session. The transmission rate within each layer adapts within its limits (each layer has an upper and lower limit in its transmission rate) according to the capabilities of the receivers. Receivers join the appropriate number of layers which better suit their requirements (available bandwidth between the sender and the receiver, etc.) and if during the transmission of multimedia data the network conditions to the path between them and the sender change, the receivers have the capability to receive more or fewer video layers in order to better fulfill their requirements. The communication between the sender and the receivers is based on RTP/RTCP sessions. The sender again uses the RTP to transmit the video layers and the participants (the sender and the receivers) use RTCP to exchange control messages.

Figure 4 shows the organization and the architecture of the sender entity. The sender generates n different layer managers. Each layer manager is responsible for the transmission of a video layer. The sender creates a new receiver manager

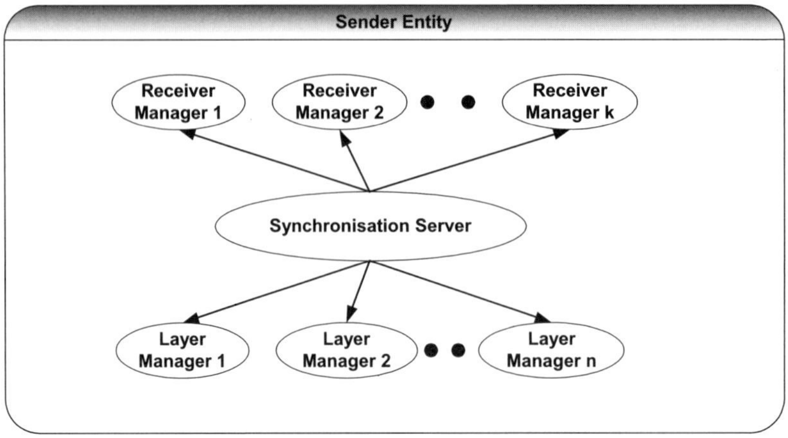

Fig. 4. The architecture and the data flow of the sender for layered encoding.

every time it receives an RTCP report from a new receiver. Each receiver manager corresponds to a unique receiver (for scalability reasons a small representative group of receivers may have a corresponding receiver manager). The receiver manager processes the RTCP reports generated by the receiver and can be considered as a representative of the receiver at the side of the sender. In addition, the synchronization server is responsible for the management, synchronization and intercommunication between layer managers and receiver managers. If a receiver manager does not receive RTCP reports from the receiver which it represents for a long time, it stops its operation and releases its resources.

Each receiver measures the characteristics of the path which connects it with the sender and informs the sender with the use of RTCP receiver reports.

The receivers join the appropriate layers that better suit their requirements (available bandwidth between the sender and the receiver, etc.) and if during the transmission of multimedia data the network conditions to the path between them and the sender change, the receivers have the capability to receive more or fewer video layers in order to better fulfill their requirements.

5.5. *Evaluation Parameters*

The following criteria are used to evaluate the approaches discussed:

- *Network congestion*: The goal of the adaptive transmission mechanisms is to increase the usage of the available bandwidth and decrease the packet losses of all the applications that transmit data in the same network path carrying the multicast data.
- *Scalability*: During transmission, the multimedia data may be received by a large number of receivers. The performance of the selected mechanism must not be degraded as the number of the receivers increases. This means that the complexity

and the performance of the mechanism used must be acceptable even when there are a large number of receivers.

- *Adaptation speed*: This refers to the time taken from the beginning of the multicast transmission until the selected mechanism achieves a stable operation. The smaller this time, the higher the performance of the mechanism.
- *TCP friendliness*: Most of the Internet traffic is TCP traffic. Any application that transmits data over the Internet should not adversely affect the other flows that exist and should be especially friendly towards TCP flows.
- *User satisfaction*: It is difficult to measure user satisfaction. For example, studies have show that during the transmission of MPEG video, just 3% packet loss can result in an up to 30% reduction in the presentation quality. As a result the satisfaction of the end user is influenced greatly by packet loss.

6. Directions for Future Research

The mechanisms described in this chapter have been proposed for installation and operation over the Internet. One interesting extension is tailoring these mechanisms to operate over mobile networks. The adaptive transmission of multimedia data over mobile networks is a challenge because one of their basic characteristics is the continuously changing environment. In order to tailor the above mechanisms for usage over mobile networks various issues must be considered, including:

- designing effective TCP models for wireless/mobile environments,
- creating more efficient encoding /decoding techniques, and
- power consumption.

As wireless communications and networking are quickly occupying centre stage of research and development activity in the area of communication networks, the suitability of the layered protocol architecture is coming under close scrutiny from the research community. Although layered protocol architectures have served wired networks well, they are not suitable for wireless networks. To illustrate this point, researchers usually present what they call a cross-layer design proposal. Thus, there have been a large number of cross-layer design proposals in the literature recently, with some of them focusing on multimedia transmission. Generally speaking, cross-layer design refers to actively exploiting the dependence between protocol layers to obtain performance gains. This is unlike layering, where the protocols at the different layers are designed independently.

7. Conclusion

Multimedia transmission is an important component of many current and future Internet applications, but high quality transmission is challenging because of the heterogeneous environment of the Internet. Multimedia transmission must be adapted to the various network changes due to the heterogeneous group of multimedia receivers and the lack of end-to-end QoS.

Many researchers have suggested that due to the use of new technologies that offer QoS guarantees, adaptive multimedia transmission applications will not be used in the future. We believe that this will not be the case for the following reasons:

- Users may not always want to pay the extra cost for a service with specific QoS guarantees, when they have the capability to access a service with good adaptive behavior.
- Some networks may never be able to provide specific QoS guarantees to users.
- Even if the Internet eventually supports reservation mechanisms or differentiated services, it is more likely to be on a per-class than a per-flow basis. Thus, flows are still expected to perform congestion control within their own class.
- With the use of the differential services network model, networks can support services with QoS guarantees together with best-effort services and adaptive services.

Terminology

Adaptive multimedia applications: Applications that have the capability to transmit multimedia data over heterogeneous networks and adapt media transmission to network changes.

Quality of service (*QoS*): The capability of a network to provide better service to selected network traffic.

Multimedia data: Data that consist of various media types like text, audio, video and animation.

RTP/RTCP: Protocols which are used for the transmission of multimedia data. RTP performs the actual transmission and RTCP is the control and monitoring Protocol.

Transmission Control Protocol (*TCP*): A connection-oriented, reliable protocol of the TCP/IP protocol suite used for managing full-duplex transmission streams.

TCP-friendly flow: A flow that consumes no more bandwidth than a TCP connection which is traversing the same path as that flow.

User Datagram Protocol (*UDP*): A connectionless, unreliable protocol of the TCP/IP protocol suite used for sending and receiving datagrams over an IP network.

Multicast: Transmitting data simultaneously to many receivers without the need to replicate the data.

Simulcast: Transmission of the same multimedia data in multiple multicast streams with different transmission rates.

Layered encoding: Transmission of the multimedia data in n different layers the basic layer and $n - 1$ additional layers.

Frame rate: The rate of the frames that are encoded by a video encoder.

Exercise

1. What is the difference between unicast and multicast multimedia transmission?
2. Which protocols are the *de facto* protocols for multimedia transmission and what are their services?
3. What is delay jitter and how is it calculated?
4. What are the most common approaches to handling packet loss during multimedia transmission?
5. What modules comprise the sender in a unicast adaptive multimedia transmission architecture?
6. What are the different approaches for multicast multimedia adaptive transmission over the Internet?
7. What is the difference between the simulcast and layered encoding approaches?
8. What is the most effective approach (in terms of bandwidth consumption) for multicast multimedia adaptive transmission over the Internet?
9. What is the most complicated approach (in terms of encoding and decoding issues) for multicast multimedia adaptive transmission over the Internet?
10. What are the evaluation parameters for multicast multimedia adaptive transmission over the Internet?

References

1. Ch. Diot, Ch. Huitema and Th. Turletti, Multimedia applications should be adaptive, *Proc. HPCS'95*, Mystic, CN (1998).
2. J. Pandhye, J. Kurose, D. Towsley and R. Koodli, A model based TCP-friendly rate control protocol, *Proc. Inter. Workshop Network and Operating System Support for Digital Audio and Video*, Basking Ridge, NJ (1999).
3. B. Vandalore, W. Feng, R. Jain and S. Fahmy, A survey of application layer techniques for adaptive streaming of multimedia, *J. Real Time Syst.* (Special Issue on Adaptive Multimedia), (1999).
4. Ch. Bouras and A. Gkamas, A mechanism for multicast multimedia data with adaptive QoS characteristics, *Protocols for Multimedia Systems 2001*, Enschede, The Netherlands, 17–19 October (2001).
5. J. Byers, M. Frumin, G. Horn, M. Luby, M. Mitzenmacher, A. Roetter and W. Shaver, FLID-DL: Congestion control for layered multicast, *Proc. NGC 2000* November (2000), pp. 71–81.
6. H. Schulzrinne, S. Casner, R. Frederick and V. Jacobson, RTP: A Transport Protocol for Real-Time Applications, RFC 3550, IETF (2003).
7. J. Korhonen, Adaptive multimedia streaming for heterogeneous networks, *Wired/Wireless Internet Communications (WWIC) 2004*, Lecture Notes in Computer Science, Vol. 2957 (Springer, 2004), pp. 248–259.
8. J. Walpole, R. Koster, S. Cen, C. Cowan, D. Maier, D. McNamee, C. Pu, D. Steere and L. Yu, A player for adaptive MPEG video streaming over the Internet, *Proc. 26th Applied Imagery Pattern Recognition Workshop (AIPR-97)*, SPIE, Washington DC, October (1997).
9. J. Liu, B. Li and Y. Zhang, Adaptive video multicast over the Internet, **10**(1), 22–33 (2008).

10. R. Ramanujan, J. Newhouse, M. Kaddoura, A. Ahamad, E. Chartier and K. Thurber, Adaptive streaming of MPEG video over IP networks, *Proc. 22nd IEEE Conf. Computer Networks (LCN'97)*, November (1997).
11. S. Floyd and K. Fall, Promoting the use of end-to-end congestion control in the Internet, *IEEE/ACM Trans. Network* (1998).
12. J. Liu, B. Li and Y. Zhang, Optimal stream replication for video simulcasting, *IEEE Trans. Multimedia* **8**(1), 162–169 (2006).
13. T. Jiang, M. Ammar and E. Zegura, Inter-receiver fairness: A novel performance measure for multicast ABR sessions, *SIGMETRICS* (1998), pp. 202–211.
14. D. Sisalem, Fairness of adaptive multimedia applications, *IEEE Inter. Conf. Communications* (1988).
15. D. Sisalem and A. Wolisz, LDA+ TCP-friendly adaptation: A measurement and comparison study, *10th Inter. Workshop Network and Operating Systems Support for Digital Audio and Video*, Chapel Hill, NC (2000).
16. Ch. Bouras, A. Gkamas, An. Karaliotas and K. Stamos, Architecture and performance evaluation for redundant multicast transmission supporting adaptive QoS, in *Multimedia Tools and Applications* (Kluwer Academic Publishers, 2005), pp. 85–110.
17. T. Kim and M. Ammar, A comparison of layering and stream replication video multicast schemes, *Proc. NOSSDAV'01*, Port Jefferson, NY (2001).
18. C. Bouras and A. Gkamas, SRAMT: A hybrid sender and receiver-based adaptation scheme for TCP friendly multicast transmission, *Comput. Net. J.* **47**(4), 551–575 (2005).
19. A. Legout and E. Biersack, PLM: Fast convergence for cumulative layered multicast transmission schemes, *Proc. ACM SIGMETRICS'2000*, Santa Clara, CA (2000).
20. D. Sisalem and A. Wolisz, MLDA: A TCP-friendly congestion control framework for heterogeneous multicast environments, *8th Inter. Workshop Quality of Service*, Pittsburgh, PA (2000).
21. A. Mayer and H. Linder, A survey of adaptive layered video multicast using MPEG-2 streams, *IST Mobile & Wireless Telecommunication Summit 2005*, Dresden, Germany (2005).
22. JMF, Java Media Framework, http://java.sun.com/products/java-media/jmf/index.html, accessed 07 November (2007).
23. H. Schwarz, *et al.*, Overview of the scalable H.264/MPEG4-AVC extension, *Proc. IEEE ICIP* (2006).
24. C. Bouras and A. Gkamas, Multimedia transmission with adaptive QoS based on real time protocols, *Int. J. Communi. Syst.* **16**(2), 225–248 (2003).
25. P. Cuetos, D. Saparilla and K. Ross, Adaptive streaming of stored video in a TCP-friendly context: Multiple versions or multiple layers?, *Proc. Int. Packet Video Workshop*, Kyongju, Korea, April (2001).
26. K. Savetz, N. Randall and Y. Lepage, *MBONE: Multicasting Tomorrow's Internet* (John Wiley & Sons, 1996).
27. J. Widmer and M. Handley, Extending equation-based congestion control to multicast applications, *Proc. ACM SIGCOMM*, San Diego, CA, August (2001).
28. T. Wiegand, *et al.*, Overview of the H.264/AVC video coding standard, *IEEE Trans. Circuits Syst. Vid. Techno.* **13**, 560–576 (2003).

Chapter 21

ANALYZING BANDWIDTH USAGE IN A DISTRIBUTED PROCESSING ENVIRONMENT

DENNIS GUSTER*, MARK B. SCHMIDT, RENAT SULTANOV and CHARLES HALL

Business Computing Research Laboratory, St. Cloud State University, CH 367C St. Cloud, MN 56301, USA

**dcguster@stcloudstate.edu*

Theoretically packet inter-arrival patterns will follow a Poisson distribution. In practice they do not. Further, in a distributed processing environment, there are often different protocols involved which may exacerbate the inter-arrival pattern variability. This chapter uses four examples to provide thoughts for practitioners. In the first example, there is evidence to suggest that the efficiency of the inter-processor communication decayes as the complexity of the matrix increases. The next example uses a better designed algorithm. The improved algorithm allows for a decrease in the time it takes to solve the problem as additional nodes are added; however, the decrease is not a linear one. In the third example, a performance gain is seen with up to 12 processors. In the final example, performance of a password cracking experiment increases with each additional processor. The low cost and performance of distributed computing makes it a popular option to solve complex problems. Perhaps this environment will replace the supercomputer at some point in the future.

1. Introduction

Forecasting packet inter-arrival patterns and their influence on network performance has been a challenging problem for many years [1]. This can be explained in part by the failure of the packet distribution to follow the theoretically expected Poisson distribution. Several studies confirm that the actual inter-arrival distribution of packets is not exponential as might be expected in the classical model [1–5]. Some feel that the variation in protocols from site to site may have some influence on the fact that the theoretical distribution across a system is not realized and the resulting lack of predictability.

Specifically, the data analyzed in the previously cited studies were taken from general purpose networks that served a wide variety of applications and hence required a large number of different protocols, each with their own workload profiles. The variation of protocols has been studied by Guster, Safonov and Sundheim [6] and they found the service used and its interaction with the employed protocol may tend to vary significantly. For example, http and ssh both use Transmission Control Protocol (TCP) on the transport layer, but http does a better job of maximizing payloads so it tends to generate fewer packets with larger payloads. Therefore, the configuration of a system used to support distributed processing will be influenced by the protocols present on that system. Obviously, a system dedicated specifically to parallel applications has the potential to function more efficiently than if the parallel processing were done on a general purpose system. This in part could be attributed to optimizing the protocol stack and eliminating some of the management traffic required in most general systems. For example, layer 3 address resolution could be handled only by a hosts file (instead of DNS) thereby reducing some of the domain traffic (port 53).

The low cost and availability of workstation based LANs as a parallel processing environment has been recognized for many years [7]. At first there was a concern that the LAN environment had inadequate bandwidth to support inter-process communication [8]. A number of studies have shown that workstation clusters if interconnected via a high-speed LAN can be an effective parallel processing environment [9–11]. Although the hardware available to support workstation-based LANs continues to improve, many feel that relying on hardware alone may not ensure adequate performance for the demanding applications of the future [12, 13].

One method to address performance optimization on the network protocol level is to look at the overhead related to the data transfer logic [14]. This approach has merit in studying the efficiency of the network connectivity in a distributed computer grid. There are several methods that can be applied to optimizing performance on the network protocol level such as optimizing the buffers, minimizing management traffic and scheduling applications. In most cases the planning and implementation of such methods can be improved by examining historical network traffic data observed on the system in question. Truong and Fahringer [15] are proponents of such methodology and suggest that more research is needed. A good place to start this research is with the analysis of experimental data. They further state that such research will require better planning in regard to how to capture, store and analyze such data. In following that premise, this chapter will analyze four different systems of varying efficiency. Both successes and failures are included to show what can happen if the parallelization strategy is not well thought out.

Often the wrong assumptions are made about the effectiveness of parallel processing. This is especially true of students, users or network managers who have few observations to base their expectations upon. Too often a *linear mindset* is applied, in which it is expected that adding a second processor to help solve the problem should reduce the solution time by one half. In reality, parallel processing is a complex environment in which a one-to-one direct relationship is seldom observed. There are many different classes of problems in a parallel processing environment, some of which provide a near linear gain, but many others do not enjoy such a degree of improvement as they take longer to solve in a parallel than in a *serial environment*.

In some cases, such ineffectiveness can be traced to the algorithm, but in others it is related to the network interconnectivity. Analyzing the effectiveness of any loosely coupled solution logically should begin with the network. The literature emphasizes the need for adequate bandwidth so that inter-processor communication is effective. That analysis is fairly easy to accomplish by just using a simple packet sniffer such as TCPDUMP. By looking at packet inter-arrival and throughput, it is fairly easy to determine if the network is the bottleneck. If it is known that in fact the network is the bottleneck then focus can be placed on network performance and remediation aimed at the algorithm can be focused on the inter-processor communication strategy. In an effort to help students, users, and network managers understand the problem and be able to perform the required network analysis, a series of cases will be synthesized to provide the core material for such an analysis. These will include instances where almost a linear gain occurred, where improvement was realized up to 12 processors, where CPU time improved but elapsed time increased, and where the problem could be solved quicker in serial than parallel. The analysis will feature data collected from a live system on the packet level.

2. Background

Inter-processor communication is a queuing theory problem, and the relationship between how quickly the server can process the information and how long information must wait in queue are critical to a successful implementation. Often it is difficult to get people (especially students) to understand the importance of this relationship. In a loosely coupled environment, network performance is critical. Most loosely coupled environments feature an Ethernet network architecture which uses a packet switched strategy. In other words, variable blocks of data are sent out from around 50 to 1,500 bytes. Each packet contains management/addressing information in headers and a payload which contains the actual data. How quickly the packets arrive and the size of the payload determine the throughput of data. The higher the throughput, the less likely a processor being used as part of a parallel processing team will have to wait to perform its assigned function. Basic packet traffic might look as follows:

```
17:15:18.003256      00:07:e9:11:c7:1c    >  00:d0:01:de:80:00, length 166:
199.17.59.234.22 > 71.87.46.90.3231: [|tcp]
17:15:18.029776      00:d0:01:de:80:00    >  00:07:e9:11:c7:1c, length  60:
71.87.46.90.3231 > 199.17.59.234.22: [|tcp]
17:15:18.029831      00:07:e9:11:c7:1c    >  00:d0:01:de:80:00, length 342:
199.17.59.234.22 > 71.87.46.90.3231: [|tcp]
17:15:18.030064      00:07:e9:11:c7:1c    >  00:d0:01:de:80:00, length 230:
199.17.59.234.22 > 71.87.46.90.3231: [|tcp]
17:15:18.030256      00:07:e9:11:c7:1c    >  00:d0:01:de:80:00, length 230:
199.17.59.234.22 > 71.87.46.90.3231: [|tcp]
```

In the five packets displayed above, the first field is the timestamp. It is followed by the source physical address and a ">" that points to the destination physical address. The length of the entire packet follows in bytes. The numeric IP (Internet) addresses follow. Last the transport protocol used, in this case TCP (reliable delivery), is displayed. Using the timestamp from this simple output, one can determine how quickly the packets are being transferred (inter-arrival rate). Further, the size of each packet is also contained in this dump so metrics like throughput can be determined as well. Generally, the more closely the packet size is to the maximum allowed (1,514) the more efficient the transmission. In the data above, the packet sizes range from a minimum of 60 to a maximum of 342 bytes. In the case of the 60-byte packet, the function is probably entirely management, such as a request to connect, or acknowledgment, meaning there is no data payload. In the larger packets the data payload is roughly the size less a 60-byte overhead. That overhead would be contained in headers that would contain such things as source/destination address, checksums for error detection, and flags to control segmentation/connections.

In the example above, secure shell (port 22) was the service monitored. To illustrate the different characteristics of services in regard to maximizing the packet size described in the introduction section, a five-packet sample of http (port 80) is displayed below:

```
17:39:14.072466      00:07:e9:11:c7:1c          > 08:00:20:f0:59:8c, length   66:
199.17.59.234.26314 > 199.17.59.247.80:      [|tcp]
17:39:14.082541      00:07:e9:11:c7:1c          > 08:00:20:f0:59:8c, length  656:
199.17.59.234.26314 > 199.17.59.247.80:      [|tcp]
17:39:14.083008      08:00:20:f0:59:8c          > 00:07:e9:11:c7:1c, length   66:
199.17.59.247.80    > 199.17.59.234.26314: [|tcp]
17:39:14.084629      08:00:20:f0:59:8c          > 00:07:e9:11:c7:1c, length 1514:
199.17.59.247.80    > 199.17.59.234.26314: [|tcp]
17:39:14.084692      00:07:e9:11:c7:1c          > 08:00:20:f0:59:8c, length   66:
199.17.59.234.26314 >  199.17.59.247.80:     [|tcp]
17:39:14.084753      08:00:20:f0:59:8c          > 00:07:e9:11:c7:1c, length 1514:
199.17.59.247.80    > 199.17.59.234.26314:  |tcp]
```

It is clear from comparing the two outputs that http does in fact offer higher efficiency. In fact, in two of the packets observed the maximum size of 1,514 bytes was realized. Although the few observations above make it difficult to compare inter-arrival time, a quick look shows varying degrees of intensity within both protocol types. However, it is the sum of all different types of activity that needs to be considered when trying to predict network performance. Figure 1 below depicts a common traffic pattern. It should be noted that the data are from an isolated dedicated network. In other words, it is not supporting a wide variety of different applications, but is dedicated to a single purpose such as grid or cluster computing. If applications are run on a general purpose network, the application must compete with other applications and the background noise caused by the

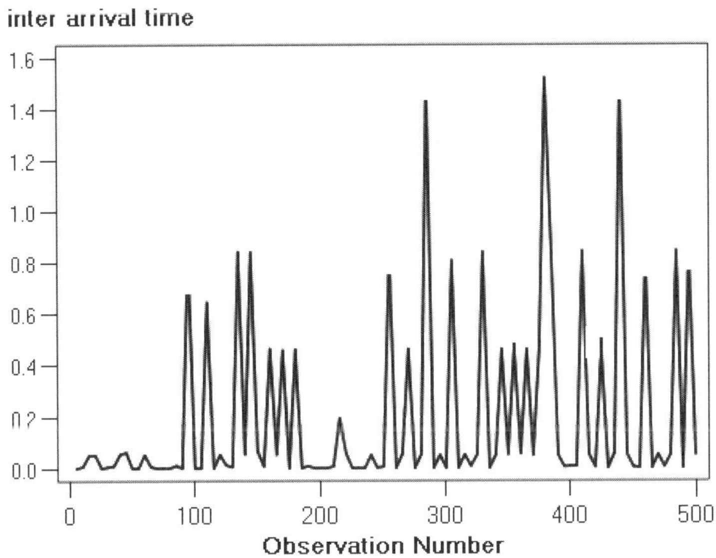

Fig. 1. Inter-arrivals in multiple TCP sessions.

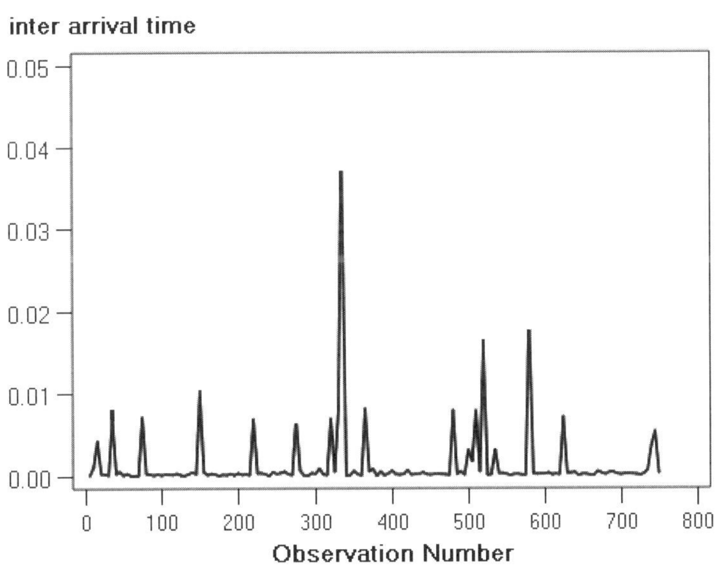

Fig. 2. Inter-arrivals in multiple TCP sessions with background noise.

management package traffic (such as arp, icmp, domain) required on such networks. Figure 2 provides some idea how much additional load background noise can place on a network. A comparison of the figures reveals that with background noise almost no spikes occur. It is those spikes which indicate a lengthening of the time between packet arrivals. One could view those spikes as recovery time, so that queue length does not get excessive and response time for any application remains within a two second target. From the figures provided, it is clear that the packet intensity is definitely greater when the background noise is present.

The output that is sent over the network can be generated by a single processor or by several processors. These processors can be loosely or tightly coupled. In the output below, CPU usage data from a single computing unit that contains four processors is displayed (tightly coupled). In the iostat (input/output statistics) output the CPU usage for the entire unit is displayed. In this case there is 10% user, 2% system, 0% wait and 88% idle. The output from the mpstat (multiprocessor statistics) command provides detailed information in regard to the usage of each of the four processors, which are numbered 0 to 3. Note that the same user usage is observed but it is split between processors 0 and 3. Further, processors 1 and 2 are performing no user activity but yet are still exhibiting system activity. This in part provides some insight into the problem of attaining a linear gain in performance. In fact for multiple processors to work as a team to solve applications they must constantly communicate with one another. This communication may be management in nature to support the exchange of pieces of data required to enact the total solution of the application. In this case the communication is across the bus of the computer system.

```
-bash-3.00$ iostat
 tty        md0             md1        md2          md20        cpu
tin tout kps tps serv kps tps serv kps tps serv kps tps serv us sy wt id
 0    0 1    0   19   1   0   16   1   0   17   0   0   13 10  4  0 86
```

```
-bash-3.00$ mpstat
CPU minf mjf xcal  intr ithr csw icsw migr smtx srw syscl usr sys wt idl
 0     2   0  304   400  300  218   0   13   16   0    96   2   1  0  97
 1     1   0    3   104  103  332   0   31   16   0   179   0   1  0  99
 2     1   0    3   111  110  257   0   40    8   0   190   0   1  0  99
 3     1   0    3   134  133  219   0   35    5   0   199   8   1  0  91
```

There are commands that allow the processors within loosely coupled environments to be displayed as well. In the output below a cluster that uses *message passing interface* (MPI) for inter-processor communication is described. The nodes within the cluster n0 to n3 are assigned to hostnames hp05 to hp08. Each one of the hosts has but a single slot (processor), hence the ":1". The command was run on host hp05 and the cluster was initiated by host hp08. The grid output below describes a grid that contains 34 processors [four in clotho (the master node) and one each in the 30 netras]. It treats each node as an independent part of the team and uses the operating system to link them together by their Internet address (English in the output below). The network communication is accomplished via rsh (remote shell) or ssh (secure shell) depending upon whether encryption is desired.

- *MPI nodes*:

```
mpiuser@HP05:~$ lamnodes
n0   hp05:1:this_node
n1   hp06:1:
n2   hp07:1:
n3   hp08:1:origin
```

- *Sun grid nodes*:

```
# qconf -sh
clotho.bcrl.stcloudstate.edu
netra1.bcrl.stcloudstate.edu
netra10.bcrl.stcloudstate.edu
netra11.bcrl.stcloudstate.edu
netra12.bcrl.stcloudstate.edu
netra13.bcrl.stcloudstate.edu
netra14.bcrl.stcloudstate.edu
netra15.bcrl.stcloudstate.edu
netra16.bcrl.stcloudstate.edu
netra17.bcrl.stcloudstate.edu
netra18.bcrl.stcloudstate.edu
netra19.bcrl.stcloudstate.edu
netra2.bcrl.stcloudstate.edu
netra20.bcrl.stcloudstate.edu
netra21.bcrl.stcloudstate.edu
netra22.bcrl.stcloudstate.edu
netra23.bcrl.stcloudstate.edu
netra24.bcrl.stcloudstate.edu
netra25.bcrl.stcloudstate.edu
netra26.bcrl.stcloudstate.edu
netra27.bcrl.stcloudstate.edu
netra28.bcrl.stcloudstate.edu
netra29.bcrl.stcloudstate.edu
netra3.bcrl.stcloudstate.edu
netra30.bcrl.stcloudstate.edu
netra4.bcrl.stcloudstate.edu
netra5.bcrl.stcloudstate.edu
netra6.bcrl.stcloudstate.edu
netra7.bcrl.stcloudstate.edu
netra8.bcrl.stcloudstate.edu
netra9.bcrl.stcloudstate.edu
```

Now that the environment and the metrics have been described, it is possible to proceed with some examples of how that environment might be used. In addition the relative efficiency of each case will be delineated. The examples are designed to illustrate varying levels of efficiency and drive home the point that putting additional processors on the job will not necessarily result in a linear increase in performance.

3. Thoughts for Practitioners

In the literature, it is easy to find successful research studies in which this inter-processor communication is adequate and the time to solve drops as processors are added to the mix. There have been some that were not so successful as well [16]. However, when teaching distributed parallel processing, it may be also useful to look at an occurrence in which the process inter-communication went bad and the time to solve increased as processors were added to the problem. Some of any application's efficiency can be traced to the software used to distribute the information between/among the processors. The two most common software options are MPI and private virtual machine (PVM).

In the past several years, many applications have been written using both MPI and PVM, but many programmers writing distributed applications were not aware of the potential performance difference between the two. PVM was the initial standard for distributed computing and MPI, although introduced later, became the dominant message passing standard [17]. This came about partly because, from a security perspective, its use of TCP on the transport layer made it safer to implement across WANs and it offered reliability delivery. While using TCP to support inter-processor communication methods does provide reliability, it comes with the cost of increased overhead. This choice, which is based on a *de facto* standard, can drastically reduce the efficiency of the network packet flow [18]. In this example, MPI is used with disastrous results from a performance perspective; although PVM might help to some degree, the parameters from this example (network speed, efficiency of the algorithm and the load placed on the network) are such that it would probably have a limited effect.

There has been research undertaken in both PVM and MPI performance levels, but this example concentrates more on network overhead and processing time performance and is focused toward illustrating what happens if the supporting network infrastructure cannot process the communications overhead in a timely manner. For students and professionals trying to understand network overhead and its relationship to processor efficiency, analysis of an ineffective system can be a very important learning aid. Whenever applications are shared in a distributed environment, it is very important to use an effective communication algorithm. If the algorithm is not effective, the time to solve will increase rather than decrease. The goal of this example was to provide baseline metrics while describing the overhead encountered. The research was done with a selected parallel matrix multiplication program, which was run in a distributed environment in order to illustrate what happens when the communications channel is not adequate.

3.1. *Example 1: Faster in Serial then Parallel*

Specifically in this research example (a replication of Ref. 16), a parallel matrix multiplication program was used to generate random values in order to calculate time ratios between two different processor configurations using MPI. This program was run on both a three-node cluster and a 20-processor cluster and then, thereafter, the performance characteristics were compared.

The matrix multiplication algorithm created random values in two initial matrices and then calculated the product of those matrices. The matrix sizes (RC) always had the same dimensions. The following example illustrates the first iteration of a 3×3 matrix. The actual experiments involved 75 iterations and two place numbers.

$$\begin{matrix} 3 & 1 & 0 \\ 1 & 3 & 2 \\ 0 & 1 & 0 \end{matrix} \times \begin{matrix} 2 & 1 & 1 \\ 1 & 1 & 2 \\ 0 & 2 & 1 \end{matrix} = \begin{matrix} 7 & 4 & 5 \\ 5 & 8 & 9 \\ 1 & 1 & 2 \end{matrix}$$

To add to the structure of this example several research questions were devised:

(i) What happens to the time needed to solve the matrix multiplication problem as additional processors are added?

(ii) What happens to the efficiency of the data transfer methodology as additional processors are added?

(iii) What happens to the accuracy of the data flow when additional processing nodes are added?

These questions can be can be modified to provide three-null hypotheses, which were tested through experimentation:

Hypothesis 1. There will be no difference in a session's elapsed time in solving MPI matrix multiplication as nodes are added.
Hypothesis 2. There will be no significant differences in payload size as nodes are added.
Hypothesis 3. There will be no considerable difference in lost packets as nodes are added.

The computer nodes were connected to an Ethernet 100BASETX switched network. Each computer contained two 500 MHZ Intel Pentium 3 processors with 256 MB of memory and a 100 Mbs Ethernet card. The matrix sizes and run parameters were as shown in Table 1.

To determine performance, a TCPSTAT log recorded the performance for each array multiplication. This TCPSTAT program stored the session's total time,

Table 1. Matrix size.

Matrix size	Number of nodes on the first run	Number of nodes on the second run	Number of processors
57 × 57	3	20	2
75 × 75	3	20	2
99 × 99	3	20	2
165 × 165	3	20	2
255 × 255	3	20	2
510 × 510	3	20	2

number of packets, number of bytes, number of TCP packets, standard deviation of packet size, average packet size, and number of bytes per second. The tables that follow contain the data that was collected from TCPDUMP and filtered using the TCPSTAT command. In Table 2 three computer nodes were used, and in Table 3 20 computer nodes were used, to solve the matrix multiplication problem.

When evaluating Tables 2 and 3, the information that is most noteworthy is the second column, total time (elapsed time). As might be expected, the elapsed times increased significantly as the size of the matrices were increased. However, when adding additional processors to the problem, the time to solve did not decrease but rather increased. Specifically, increasing the number of nodes from three to 20 increased, by a factor of three, the elapsed time. The frequency of packets and the scaling of throughput are about what would be expected as the size of the matrices increases. Also, as might be expected, the number of packets/bytes increased as the number of nodes increased from three to 20. The magnitude of this increase, approximately one and a half times, is perhaps smaller than might be expected based on the elapsed times observed herein. Both tables report that the average packet size followed a similar pattern in which the size continued to drop. This may indicate that the efficiency of the inter-processor communication decayed as the complexity of the matrix increased. More simply stated, it took more packets and each packet contained less data as the matrix complexity increased. This relationship is explained further by the last column, bytes per second transferred. The transfer rate dropped as the matrix complexity increases and, therefore, the transfer efficiency was better with three nodes when compared to the 20-node model. The conclusions related to these data follow.

Hypothesis 1 can be rejected while the data provide evidence to fail to reject Hypotheses 2 and 3:

- *Hypothesis 1*: There is no difference in a session's elapsed time in solving MPI matrix multiplication as nodes are added. Elapsed time is definitely greater across all matrix categories for the 20-node experiment when compared to the three-node data; however, this is not true in the desired directions.
- *Hypothesis 2*: There is no significant difference in payload size as nodes are added. For both the three- and 20-node experiments, the packet size will remain relatively close within matrix size categories.

Table 2. Tcpstat results with three nodes.

Matrix size_# of processors	Total time	Number of packets	Number of bytes offered	Number of lost packets	Standard deviation of each packet	Average packet size	Number of bytes transferred per second
57 × 57_3	3.854543	37,432	3,632,356	1,032	205.34	98.35	446756.23
75 × 75_3	5.923543	58,634	5,154,343	301	181.43	86.38	476755.35
99 × 99_3	8.264300	108,935	8,934,564	149	116.69	81.65	534945.48
165 × 165_3	16.354552	217,564	17,345,713	423	102.71	74.32	463832.43
255 × 255_3	33.925376	502,254	36,321,043	437	74.85	72.75	499521.31
510 × 510_3	125.91634	1,753,955	134,374,532	1,614	57.16	72.05	493754.37

Table 3. Tcpstat results with twenty nodes.

Matrix size_# of processors	Total time	Number of packets	Number of bytes offered	Number of lost packets	Standard deviation of each packet	Average packet size	Number of bytes transferred per second
57 × 57_20	11.14323	57,756	5,423,476	679	175.99	95.40	244364.46
75 × 75_20	15.83548	83,735	7,337,546	964	149.25	88.74	233475.54
99 × 99_20	22.35476	125,437	10,247,437	234	127.60	87.48	228359.37
165 × 165_20	51.24500	279,154	20,983,465	197	88.04	78.27	211948.14
255 × 255_20	103.83600	522,567	39,936,457	289	79.42	77.34	196437.63
510 × 510_20	376.3546	1,984,538	143,534,764	1,803	49.74	73.64	194267.11

- *Hypothesis 3*: There is no considerable difference in lost packets as nodes are added. There is not a consistent pattern of packet loss when the three- and 20-node data are compared.

The data above allow us to conclude that the inter-processor communication channel must be adequate or it may very well take more time to solve a given problem in parallel than in serial. As might be expected, the complexity of the matrix multiplication influences the intensity of the packet exchange as does the number of nodes used to solve the problem. In Example 1, the additional overhead prevented the problem from being solved more quickly on 20 instead of just three nodes. There are several factors that might be evaluated and changed to improve performance within the experimental computer configuration utilized herein:

- *Faster bus size machine*: The cluster of machines used for this study had about 100 MHz bus speed. During the data transmission, the 100 MHz bus speed was oversubscribed and the computer node ended up dropping packets due to the lack of resources. If the bus speed could be increased to 1 GHz or more, the dropped packet ratio could be reduced as well as the total time.
- *An algorithm better suited to the computer environment*: The volume of data transmitted across the cluster also depends on the algorithm used. If a more efficient message passing algorithm was used herein, there is a distinct possibility the volume of packets transferred over the network could be reduced.
- *Faster network connection*: Upgrading the network from 100 Mbs Ethernet to 1 Gbs Ethernet (1000BASE-T) could be explored, thereby increasing the data transmitting flow by a factor of 10. Bus size of the machine would need to match the connection speed or else the data transmission would be limited to the slower speed.
- *Computer memory*: Because of the nature of complex multiplication, it is critical to have enough memory on the machine. Otherwise, due to hardware delay, the total time will increase. In the problems used herein, this value should at the very least be doubled.

3.2. *Example 2: CPU Time Decreases, but Elapsed Time Increases*

In spite of the performance obtained in Example 1, there are other applications that are better designed and use resources more effectively. The second example still uses a cluster in which the inter-processor communication is handled though MPI, but the algorithm is better designed. However, in this example the network is marginal at best so the desired scaling is not obtained.

In this example workload performance data were collected from a live network in which parallel molecular modeling software was used to generate the network workload; this is a replication of Ref. 19. The MOLDY software ([20]) was used to generate the inter-processor traffic via MPI. This example was selected because the source code was readily available and the output dealt with three-dimensional graphics, an area that the authors have used successfully to solve complex hydrogen fuel storage problems in a timely manner. With this program the number of server machines can be programmed and thereby the intensity can be varied. TCPDUMP was used to collect the performance data. The number of servers was varied so that performance scaling can be evaluated. The following information was reported for each test run: CPU time in seconds, elapsed time in seconds, number of packets in sample, mean inter-arrival time, mean throughput in bytes, and packet intensity in packets per second.

Specifically in this problem a computer simulation methodology is used to determine the characteristics of water using first physical principles. In the parallel algorithm each processor stores a complete set of dynamic variable arrays for all defined molecules. This problem was selected to demonstrate some practical issues in parallel computing, and focuses on molecular dynamic simulations used to study the statistical mechanics of condensed phase matter composed of small molecules.

The simulations were carried out for water molecules while using the 4-site model of Jorgensen. In this case, only the oxygen site interacts via the Lennard–Jones potential, and the charge site is displaced by 0.15 Å from the oxygen molecule. An interesting point in these simulations is the fact that the applied algorithm generates intensive communication between all parallel processors included in the system. It is a challenging problem and would be useful if further research replicated these investigations and compared speed-up values for this type of calculation. The MOLDY software provides quite intensive interaction between computers during the simulation process. It is hoped that investigation of this type of problem will supplement the understanding of how different types of algorithms influence the performance of parallel applications. More specifically, the area in which the particles will collide is defined through a three-dimensional matrix. To support parallelization, that space is broken into N subparts based in the number of processors used. Inter-processor communication is required whenever a particle collision occurs and a particle moves from the space associated with one processor to the space area of another processor. That particle movement is relayed by the MPI protocol using TCP packets. The status of the movement of particles is updated within the simulation every millisecond, which results in a high intensity of packet exchange between/among processors.

The basic configuration of network follows. Two to 12 Intel-based hosts were used to run the experiment. Each host was configured with two 550 MHz CPUs that utilized symmetric multi-processing as supported by the Linux operating system. Each unit ran its part of the MOLDY program as required and housed the TCPDUMP program which collected packet traffic. Each unit was connected to a Force 10, E300 switch (a high-end Enterprise level switch) at 100 Mbs.

The parallel computing environment was programmed using the MOLDY software. TCPDUMP was run on each unit and therefore traffic for each unit was collected locally. The various files were later linked together by combining the files from each unit and then sorting by timestamp. The times on each unit were synchronized via a time server. Once combined the resulting file could be analyzed and the inter-arrival times and throughput statistics were available from two to twelve units. Two different trials were run: one defined the number of steps to reach convergence in the problem at 10,000 and the other at 25,000. Both trials were designed to solve the same problem but with different levels of accuracy/reliability. Obviously, the 25,000-step trial offers the higher reliability. Step one was to obtain performance data on the live network for a range of different numbers of processors. Therefore, each problem was solved multiple times and the number of units were varied from two to 12. The results are depicted in Tables 4 and 5.

The data displayed in the two tables is strikingly similar, except the number of packets in the sample and CPU/elapsed times in Table 4 are about twice the values

Table 4. Timings and means for packet arrival, throughput and intensity (10,000 iterations).

	2 concurrent hosts	4 concurrent hosts	6 concurrent hosts	8 concurrent hosts	10 concurrent hosts	12 concurrent hosts
CPU time	142.58	92.23	68.36	58.49	50.37	50.09
Elapsed time	246.37	201.39	224.39	262.84	259.84	262.27
Packets in sample	201,477	191,414	470,836	469,672	602,936	603,114
Inter-arrival time	0.00119	0.00102	0.000490	0.000559	0.000427	0.000441
Throughput	575,710	707,219	1,265,537	1,091,023	1,396,104	1,337,576
Packet intensity	818.58	961.26	2069.89	1772.46	2326.37	2232.35

Table 5. Timings and means for packet arrival, throughput and intensity (25,000 iterations).

	2 concurrent hosts	4 concurrent hosts	6 concurrent hosts	8 concurrent hosts	10 concurrent hosts	12 concurrent hosts
CPU time	353.47	216.58	169.27	151.10	134.70	129.39
Elapsed time	629.74	509.49	576.17	667.74	651.48	665.69
Packets in sample	503,099	474,467	1,175,002	1,176,104	1,506,024	1,506,174
Inter-arrival time	0.00118	0.00103	0.000479	0.000557	0.000429	0.000437
Throughput	569,034	703,067	1,244,678	1,089,365	1,391,658	1,342,003
Packet Intensity	805.58	952.92	2023.38	1774.47	2312.63	2229.04

observed in Table 5. This is logical because the number of iterations was increased from 10,000 to 25,000. While the CPU time required to solve the problems decreases as additional units are added, there is not a linear decrease. In fact, the decrease from two units to 12 units is only about three times. The variable elapsed time also exhibited similar traits within the two samples. In both cases it was reduced when four units were used, but increased steadily as additional units were added. A look at the packet patterns in the sample provides a clue as to why the elapsed time increases when more than four units are utilized. When the number of units is increased from four to six, the number of packets required about doubles in both samples, which results in significant communication overhead. Average packet inter-arrival times in both samples are similar, with the values observed in Table 2 being slightly higher. Throughput and packet intensity were also similar in the two samples, which indicates the data in both tables had a similar profile, but the 25,000 iteration sample simply took longer to run.

In terms of providing an advantage in solving the problems in less time this method fails when more than four units are utilized. While the resulting reduction in the CPU time as more units are added is encouraging, the increase in network traffic offsets this advantage. Therefore, to optimize the algorithm it needs to be re-evaluated in terms of the massive amount of inter-processor communication utilized. However, if the problem was run on a cluster that was not dedicated only to solving this problem but had several other parallel problems running at the same time, the saving observed in CPU time herein would be attractive.

It appears that there are several other things to consider besides a redesign of the distribution algorithm. A network speed-up to 1 Gbs would have minimal effect because the average throughput observed did not exceed 1.4 MBs. Also noteworthy is the loss in packet payload efficiency as units are added. The packet mean is about 700 bytes in the two- and four-unit tests, but drops off to about 600 bytes in the 12-unit experiments. This may in part be explained by the extra work of setting up and maintaining the additional reliable TCP connections used by MPI. There may be some promise in adapting the software to use PVM that is based on UDP, which is connectionless. Guster *et al.* [18] found that PVM could greatly reduce the communications overhead when compared to MPI. Also, perhaps a supercomputer would help in this regard because the processors would all be tightly coupled in the same box and connected via a high-speed bus. However, an analysis of the number of management packets (such as TCP syn) in the data stream revealed that they typically accounted for only 0.05% of the total packet flow, which may negate the potential of PVM. A further analysis of the packet sizes revealed that there were frequently a large number of small packets. In fact the number of packets less than 100 bytes (payload less than 40 bytes) averaged around 36% within the data stream and in some cases exceeded 48% within a single trial. These values help explain why the transfer rates observed were well below Ethernet's maximum of 1,514 bytes.

Although a reduction in elapsed time was obtained up to the four-unit level, the scaling beyond that point was not in the desired direction. Even though the decrease in CPU time is encouraging, it is the elapsed time that counts on the end-user level. For this particular problem the effectiveness of using a CPU distributed across a LAN is negated by the network communication overhead. It appears this problem is quite complex and is a function of the time any CPU has to wait for a piece of the "puzzle" from another CPU. Speeding up the network may have some slight effect, but the transfer rates never exceed 1.6 MBs (12 Mbs) on a 100 Mbs network. Therefore, more research is needed that addresses alternatives to MPI (such as PVM and Open MP) and re-evaluates the algorithm that was used to distribute the workload among the CPUs. In regard to trying to transfer this basic parallel logic to other three-dimensional graphics applications, there would be little advantage given the configuration used herein. However, if the inter-processor communication problem can be resolved and the scaling potential based on the CPU times observed can be realized then it is worth attempting to transfer the basic parallel logic.

3.3. *Example 3: Performance Gain up to 12 Processors*

In this example we will delineate the efficiency of a fairly well-designed loosely coupled parallel system that is replicated from Ref. 21. Specifically, the results of intensive parallel calculations from a problem in the field of molecular dynamics simulation will be described. This problem involves the calculation of molecular hydrogen–hydrogen and hydrogen–hydrogen isotopes energy transfer collisions, which are deemed important in astrophysical applications, astro-chemistry, and in hydrogen fuel storage problems. Elapsed times to solve at different processor levels are presented and the scaling of the algorithms is described for this example.

The data are distributed to the various processors according to the value of the momentum quantum number J and its projection M. The majority of the work is local to each processor. It is important to note that in this parallel algorithm calculations for specific values of J and M are essentially independent.

In the PMP MOLSCAT program the parallelization is performed across the loop on values J and M. The parallel software distributes the required JM pairs across the available processors. The computational work distribution is depicted schematically in Fig. 3.

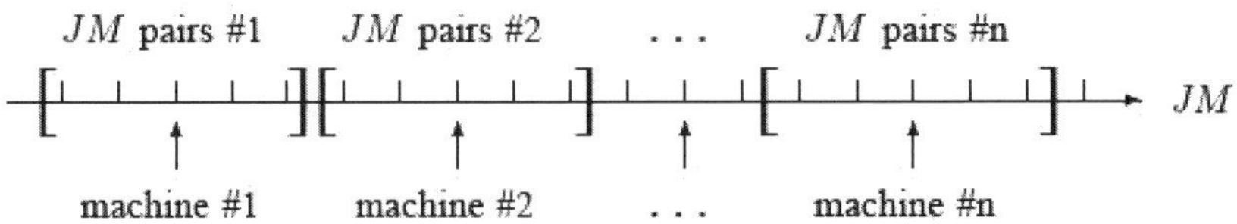

Fig. 3. Computational workload.

The machines and the loosely coupled parallel computational environment were as follows:

- Netra X1 (UltraAX-i2) with 128 Mb RAM,
- 512 Mb Swap,
- 500 Mhz UltraSPARC-IIe processor,
- Master computer: SunFire v440 with 8 Gb RAM,
- Four 1.062 Ghz UltraSPARC-III processors,
- LAM/MPI to provide parallel environment.

Figure 4 graphically illustrates this environment. The main computer is the SunFire v440 whereas the satellite computers are the Netras. In the actual run the number of processors was varied from two to 12.

The scaling results are shown in Table 6. The results indicate that although an advantage is realized by using multiple processors it is not a linear gain. Further, the improvement does not continue beyond 12 processors. Specifically, the speed-up reaches a maximum of about 3.4 times and in terms of time reduction results in a minimum of about 49 seconds. This value is definitely an improvement over the time of 167 seconds that was achieved when this problem was run on a single processor of the same type used in the parallel configuration.

Several observations can be made from analyzing this example. First, parallel processing can certainly be effective. While a linear gain was not obtained, a

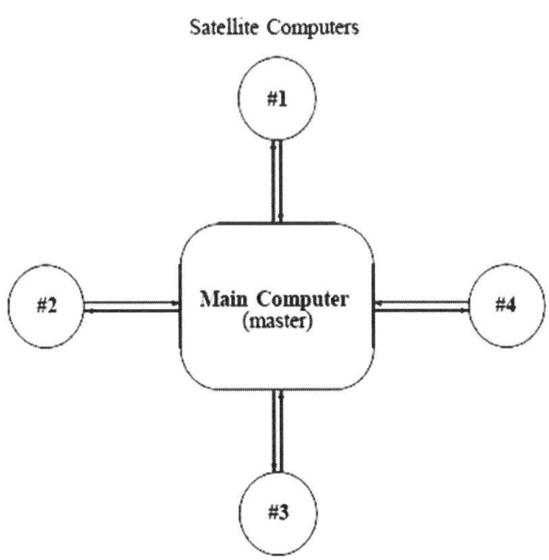

Schematic diagram of the topology of interprocessor communication: an example of a star-type cluster with one main and four satellite computers.

Fig. 4. The coupled parallel computational environment.

Table 6. Scaling results for molecular simulations of water using the MOLDY program.

Number of processors	Run time (s)	Speed-up (tl/tnp)
1	167	na
2	143	1.2
3	106	1.6
4	93	1.8
5	72	2.3
6	68	2.5
7	61	2.7
10	49	3.4
12	49	3.4

speed-up of 3.4 times can contribute greatly to productivity. A program that took a month to run in serial can be reduced to about eight days, meaning that it can be run, tested and tweaked 45 times in a year instead of just 12. Second, while adding additional processors is the primary methodology, optimizing the system first before parallelization is critical. To get the 3.4 speed-up factor, the application was optimized first in the following areas: the OS, compilers, scratch files, internal bus, disk I/O, network, and algorithm used. Not all applications are appropriate for parallelization. However, in this case the molecular modeling program was an excellent candidate for parallelization due to its computationally intensive nature and its inherent ability to effectively subdivide the problem based on the independent pairs *J* and *M*.

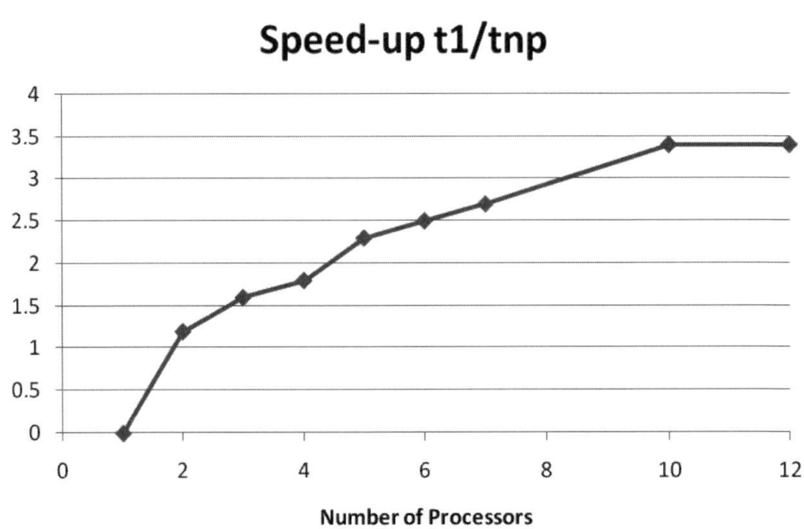

Fig. 5. Computation of speed-up based on the number of processors.

3.4. *Example 4: An Almost Linear Decrease in Elapsed Time is Obtained*

It is somewhat ironic that the example used in this chapter that exhibits the highest degree of success is based on cracking passwords. It should be pointed out that this research was not undertaken to break and misuse passwords, but rather to illustrate how vulnerable poor passwords could be if attacked by a hacker using distributed processing. It is the method (replicated from Ref. 22) used in this example that provides such striking results and scaling. Therefore, a brief overview of the software design follows.

Because the software design had to incorporate a large number of different processing elements, a modular design was selected to enhance flexibility. Also, there was a desire to achieve that same flexibility on the hardware level so the project could be successfully carried out on single workstations, clusters with MPI, as well as on random workstation groups. The password evaluation procedure was easy to incorporate in a parallel computational environment, since it is possible to break passwords independently from one another on various nodes of a given cluster. In other words, synchronization within the computations is not necessary. The reason being, the generation of random passwords is independent and any given password guess (based on a dictionary search) can be generated on any node within the cluster utilized. This type of computational task is referred to as single instruction, multiple data (SIMD).

To provide an overview of functionality, a small data set of 10 passwords was chosen and processed on a single machine. The results are displayed below. Five of the 10 passwords were guessed in 8.22 s. The other five were not determined because the cracking logic used in the cracker program used was not capable of breaking them. Therefore, even if the cracker program were run for a much longer time no additional passwords would be broken.

```
-- Test with 1 machine --
Cluster5 --
Loaded 10 passwords with 10 different salts (Standard DES [24/32 4K)
Ache                    (person3)
aChed                   (person4)
aCoRn                   (person7)
AcQuAiNt                (person8)
Arch                    (person9)

guesses: 5 time: 0:00:08:219 c/s: 34867 trying: Arches -- SNOITISI
```

To obtain performance data that would depict the performance advantages that might be realized when the program was split between two machines, a subsequent experiment was run. Once again as expected since the same cracking algorithm was used a total of five passwords were guessed (note AcQuAiNt was guessed on both machines). The total time to solve was reduced from about the eight minute range down to the four minute range. This is the case because when there are two independent machines running in parallel, the greater of the two execution times reported becomes the time to solve.

```
-- Test with 2 machines --
cluster1 --
the cluster size is 2 nodes
run on node 0
Loaded 10 passwords with 10 different salts (Standard DES [24/32 4K)
Ache                (person3)
aCoRn               (person7)
AcQuAiNt            (person8)
guesses: 3 time: 0:00:03:25 c/s: 50121 trying: NOITIsIu - NOITISIU

cluster2 --
the cluster size is 2 nodes
run on node 1
Loaded 10 passwords with 10 different salts (Standard DES [24/32 4K)
aChed               (person4)
AcQuAiNt            (person8)
Arch                (person9)
guesses: 3 time: 0:00:04:12 c/s: 34949 trying: SNOITIsi -- SNOITISI
```

To provide a more realistic idea of how this system would perform in parallel on a typical UNIX host password file, a file containing 194 accounts with encrypted passwords from a discontinued host was subjected to an entire dictionary search (in the previous example it was just "A"). An array of homogenous Sun Microsystems Netras running at 500 Mhz hosted this test. A simple attempt was tried with no dictionary word modifiers. The results are displayed in Table 7. The resulting data indicate that the majority of the passwords were not a basic dictionary word. In fact, only about 20% of the passwords were cracked when using the basic routine. The effectiveness of the distribution algorithm is quite promising. In fact, all throughout

Table 7. Performance metrics of the complex password cracking problem.

Number of nodes	Number of passwords guessed	Time (h:mm:ss)
1	40	3:19:23
2	40	1:57:58
4	40	0:49.46
8	40	0:23:16
16	40	0:12:85
32	40	0:08:24

the table doubling the number of processors almost reduces the time to solve by one half.

The scaling results are the most promising observed in this chapter. First, as the number of processors is increased the time to solve continues to decrease. What would happen beyond 32 processors is not known, but based on the ratios observed so far one would expect the point of diminishing returns to be a much higher number than 32. The speed-up is most encouraging; while not quite linear it is still substantial. Specifically, a speed-up of about 24 times is obtained when increasing the number of processors from 1 to 32. Also of note, in other experiments, using this same class of software with more complex cracking algorithms the authors observed a time reduction from about a year to solve on a single processor reduced down to about 12 days when 32 processors were used, which is a speed-up of about 30 times and therefore very close to linear.

4. Directions for Future Research

Distributing processing has made a major impact on high performance computing and its use (perhaps taking the place of a supercomputer) is well accepted. Its low cost and performance potential make it a very popular option in solving complex problems [23]. The low cost of hardware coupled with the ease of network configuration through self-configuring switching technology such as Ethernet have made it easy to get a cluster up and running. However, the next frontier may be optimizing that cluster so the workload is balanced throughout [24]. For example, it is not unusual to find 10% utilization on one part of the system while 65% is observed elsewhere. This balancing act not only needs to take place within the cluster and IT network fabric, but across the backbone on which the cluster may be connected to other computing and storage resources.

Perhaps one would expect the first improvements/changes to occur on the hardware level. Certainly, one expects significant improvements in both CPU and network capabilities, but perhaps it is the continual advancement of the Ethernet architecture that offers the greatest promise on the network level particularly for users that do not want to use specialized network architecture and wish to integrate their cluster into a standard high-speed Ethernet LAN [25]. Reference 26 envisions a 64-bit CPU technology that includes fewer denser cluster nodes, is more flexible in memory allocation, uses hierarchical technologies, and uses and integrated storage design. It is one thing to extend the capabilities on the physical level, but the other layers need to be extended as well. To take advantage of this improvement, for example, the TCP/IP stack needs to be improved as well and this problem is being addressed by research such as in Ref. 27.

The basic potential of any parallel application is based on the efficiency of its parallelization algorithm. Optimizing these algorithms will be a key area in the future. A question of concern for years has been whether a general purpose algorithm such as symmetric multi-processing or a customized algorithm that might get invoked from C code which is multithreaded and uses MPI is the most effective [28], and this will continue to be an issue. The customized algorithm typically has the higher performance potential, but a much higher development cost so it must exhibit significant performance advantages to be cost effective. Further, beyond just trying to split the problem efficiently into subparts some of the newer algorithms also have a load balancing mechanism built into the code so that the inter-processor traffic attains equality among the destinations [29]. More emphasis needs to be placed on multithreading and hence training present and future programmers to implement multithreaded code. Also, analysts need to think about parallelization during the design phase rather than waiting until an application runs too slow and needs a quick fix through "parallelization." IT providers are making available the tools to support this [30], but deployment plans need to be carefully thought out.

With the added performance potential of distributed cluster computing comes added concerns about users finding/gaining access to resources. Instead of finding one host and getting authenticated by it, there is a need to find/gain access to multiple hosts. This requires some type of global authentication system or the user will have to "login" and "provide a password" to each host. Research such as in Ref. 31 addresses these concerns and also addresses the concept of wireless nodes being part of the distributed environment.

Although clusters have been placed and been accessible via WANs for years, bandwidth limitations have limited the type of applications that are practical across distributed clusters. As Internet infrastructure continues to improve, it can be expected that more types of applications will become practical. Projects such as the Albatross Project have dealt with this problem and strive to advance the practicality of clusters distributed across a WAN [32].

The last area of note is expected improvements in the way traffic is managed. This logically starts with sound design and sound policy. This policy must not only deal with optimizing network flows but doing it in a secure manner, which due to the added overhead of security tools such as encryption and global authentication becomes very challenging. The work of Sacks *et al.* [33] provides a great starting point in the evaluation of these concepts. One of the problems apparent in Table 8, lost packets, is also being addressed. Work integrating the management logic into the network level is underway so that time-sensitive data such as inter-processor

Table 8. Performance metrics of the four distributed processing examples.

Example number	Speed-up CPU	Elapsed ratio	Scaling	Inter-arrival rate	Network throughput	Performance lost packets	Packet size
1	1.1	8	none	0.0002	100,000s	hundreds	~ 100
2	2.5	1.2	4	0.001	100,000s	a few	~ 700
3	3.97	3.65	12	0.001	100,000s	a few	~ 600
4	26.4	23.7	32+	0.01	10,000	none	~ 200

communication will less likely be compromised [34]. Often to obtain the optimum computing power it may be necessary to link multiple clusters together. Work such as Ref. 35 addresses model development for optimizing/managing packet traffic in such diverse network environments.

5. Conclusions and Outlook

The examples provided herein definitely indicated that the advantage gained through distributed parallel processing may vary on a case-by-case basis. Further, they indicated that, although possible, a linear gain is probably the exception rather than the rule. In several of the examples it is clear that inter-processor communication across the network is a major limiting factor. Specifically, in Example 2, beyond four processors the elapsed time continued to increase in spite of a reduction in CPU time. Table 8 is designed to provide numeric data that can be used to gain a greater understanding of the relationship between available bandwidth and actual speed-up.

This table illustrates that there is a direct relationship between the characteristics of the implemented algorithm and the available bandwidth. In Example 1 the implemented algorithm only provides a slight increase. When this slight advantage is served across a network, the communication overhead not only negates the advantage but is so great it takes longer in parallel than in serial. The inter-arrival rate coupled with the high volume would of course slow down inter-processor communication, but the number of lost packets (which in TCP need to be recovered via retransmission) slows things down even further. The small packet size may contribute to this problem as well. Perhaps, the algorithm could be redesigned to send out fewer packets with larger payloads. In Example 2 not only is a useable performance gain realized but it is passed on across the network, although the scaling is disappointing in that the gain is only realized up to four processors. While the network performance is not as dismal as that observed in Example 1, it is still not ideal. In fact, the 100,000-byte range is close to capacity of a 100 Mbs network. In the case of the 0.0002 inter-arrival rate in Example 1 a backlog occurs, things slow down and packets get lost. In Example 2, the system can just about keep up with the arriving data and few packets are lost.

Example 3 provides the first practical use of distributed parallel processing within the four examples. A speed-up of 3.4 is probably worth the extra effort of parallelization, although the limitation of scaling is disturbing. The network performance observed in Example 3 is very similar to Example 2. One might hypothesize that improving network performance might lead to an improvement in overall performance. It should also be noted that improving only the network may not be enough. The authors observed in several of their experiments that the bus of the processing nodes could often be the source of the bottleneck and it along with the network needed to be sped up if better performance was to be realized. Example 4 illustrates a situation where all of the components appear to be working well together. There is an excellent gain in performance and based on the data available no scaling limitations. It is also clear that there is adequate network performance based on the inter-arrival rate and no packet loss.

Given the data above one can certainly conclude that distributed processing under the right conditions can provide enormous processing advantages. However, completely tuning the system becomes paramount. The methodology used to split the problem and the means to provide effective communication between/among the processors is critical. If this communication does not take place fast enough then it may well take longer to solve the problem in parallel than it did in serial. To ascertain the efficiency of the data flow, it is important to collect and analyze data which can be accomplished fairly efficiently with a simple packet sniffer such as TCPDUMP. This analysis can determine if the network is the bottleneck or if the bottleneck is elsewhere such as the CPU bus or the design of the algorithm. It is hoped that the four examples delineated herein provide a basic foundation of the process and alert the potential analyst as to what can go wrong as well as what an efficient application might look like.

Terminology

Inter-arrival distribution: The probability density function which describes likely and unlikely inter-arrival times for packets.

Inter-arrival time: The amount of time that elapses after the receipt of a packet until the next packet arrives.

Inter-processor communication: The movement of packets between/among the various processors in a computer grid/cluster required so information can be shared in relation to solving a common problem.

Loosely coupled parallel processing: A processing array in which the processors reside in different computer cabinets and a network serves as the physical path for inter-processor communication.

M/M/1 queuing model (*exponential/exponential with one server*): The queuing model which assumes an exponential distribution for inter-arrival times, an exponential distribution for service times, and a single server.

Packet: A finite stream of bits sent in one block with header/and trailer bits to perform routing and management functions which contains headers (management/ addressing information) and a payload (the actual data).

Scaling: The degree to which a parallel application's performance improves as additional processors are added to the processor array.

(*Transmission control protocol/Internet protocol* (*TCP/IP*)): A suite of protocols used on the Internet that are used to route packets, direct data to a program and provide services.

TCPDUMP: A packet sniffing program that allows individual packets to be recorded and evaluated as they pass through a computer interface or to be logged for future reference.

TCPSTAT: A statistical evaluation filter for data captured via TCPDUMP.

Exercises

1. What is the relationship of packet payload size to performance? How is this related to services such as ssh and http?
2. How does management/address resolution traffic affect network performance?
3. Why is it difficult to obtain linear scaling in loosely coupled parallel processing?
4. Why is a loosely coupled solution cheaper than a supercomputer?
5. What is an ethical use of a packet sniffer?
6. Why might CPU time improve, but not elapsed time?
7. Why are packet sizes variable?
8. How are MPI nodes linked together in a common processor array?
9. What factors might lead to a speed up within and MPI cluster?
10. In analyzing Table 4, why does the throughput generally increase as processors are added, but the inter-arrival time decreases?

References

1. C. Partridge, The end of simple traffic models (Editor's Note), *IEEE Network* **VII**(5) (1993).
2. D. Guster, D. Robinson and M. Richardson, The application of the power law process in modeling the inter-arrival times of packets in a computer network, *Proc. Midwest Decision Sciences Institute*, Springfield, IL, 22–24 April (1999).
3. D. Guster, D. Robinson and P. Safonov, Packet inter-arrival distributions in computer network workloads, *Encyclopedia of Information Science and Technology* (IRMA, Hersey, 2005).
4. K. Krzenski, The effect of varying the packet interarrival distribution in the simulation of Ethernet computer networks, Unpublished graduate research project, St. Cloud State University (1998).
5. B. Vandolore, G. Babic and R. Jain, Analysis and modeling of traffic in modern data communications networks, submitted to the *Applied Telecommunication Symposium* (1999).
6. D. Guster, P. Safonov and R. Sundheim, Analysis of end-user services and their potential load on the network, *J. Acad. Busi. Econ.* **V**(3) (2005).
7. J. Vila-Sallent, J. Sole-Pareta, T. Jove and J. Torres, Potential performance of distributed computing systems over ATM networks, *INFOCOM'97* (1997).
8. R. Fatoohi and S. Weeratunga, Performance evaluation of three distributed computing environments for scientific applications, *Proc. Supercomputing'94* (1994), pp. 400–409.

9. T. Fahringer and R. Prodan, ZENTURIO: An experiment management system for cluster and grid computing, *4th Int. APART Workshop, Euro-Par* (2002).
10. T. Luckenbach, R. Ruppelt and F. Schulz, Performance experiments within local ATM networks, GMD-FOKUS, Berlin, Germany (1994).
11. L. Mengjou, J. Hsiehn, H. C. Du, J. P. Thomas and J. MacDonald, Distributed network computing over local ATM networks, Technical report TR-94-17, Computer Science Department University of Minnesota, Computer Science Department (1994).
12. M. Courson, A. Mink, M. Marcais and B. Traverse, An automated benchmarking toolset, *HPCN Europe* (2000), pp. 497–506.
13. A. Popescu, A parallel approach to integrated multi-Gbit/s communication over multiwavelength optical networks, Ph.D. dissertation, Royal Institute of Technology, Stockholm (1994).
14. G. Riley, *et al.*, Performance improvement through overhead analysis: A case study in molecular dynamics, *Proc. 11th ACM Int. Conf. Supercomputing* (1997), pp. 36–43.
15. H. Truong and T. Fahringer, On utilizing experiment data repository for performance analysis of parallel applications. *9th Int. Europar Conf.* (*EuroPar 03*), Lecture Notes in Computer Science, Klagenfurt, Austria (Springer-Verlag, 2003).
16. D. Guster, U. Millathe, M. Nordby and B. Jansen, Analysis of inter-processor overhead and its importance in using distributed processing to solve computationally intensive applications, *proc. Int. Academy of Business and Economics Symposium*, Las Vegas, NV, 14–17 October (2007).
17. G. Geist, J. Kohl and P. Papadopulos, PVM and MPI: A comparison of features, *Calculator Paralleles* **VIII**(2) (1996).
18. D. Guster, A. Al-Hamamah, P. Safonov and E. Bachman, Computing and network performance of a distributed parallel processing environment using the MPI and PVM communication methods, *J. Comput. Sci. Colleg.* **XVIII**(4), 248–253 (2003).
19. D. Guster, R. Sultanov, M. Nordby and T. Slattery, Managing a computer cluster: Tradeoffs and scalability, *Proc. Int. Academy of Business and Economics Symposium*, Las Vegas, NV, 14–17, October (2007).
20. K. Refson, Moldy: A portable molecular dynamics simulation program for serial and parallel computers, *Comput. Phys. Commun.* **CXXVI**(310) (2000).
21. R. Sultanov, M. Nordby and D. Guster, Molecular dynamics in the framework of parallel computing techniques, *Proc. Int. Conf. Scientific Computing* (*World Comp*), Las Vegas, NV, 25–28, June (2007).
22. D. Guster, D. Podkorytov, P. Safonov and A. Rudenko, Business computer information systems security against hacking attacks: Application of distributed processing and software modifiers in defense of password files, *Proc. Academy of Business Administration Conference*, Las Vegas, NV, 15–19 March (2004).
23. B. Moxon, High performance computing: Past, present and future — Storage networking, *Comput. Tech. Rev.*, January (2004).
24. NETXEN, The data center network of the future: 10 gigabit Ethernet converged, agile and secure, White paper, www.netxen.com (2006).
25. P. Sokolowski and D. Grosu, Performance consideration for network switch fabric on Linux clusters, *Proc. Parallel and Distributed Computer Systems Conf.* (2004).
26. SGI, The future of cluster computing, White paper Silicon Graphic Corporation (2005).
27. A. Nomura, H. Matsuba and Y. Ishikawa, Network performance model for TCP/IP based cluster computing, *Cluster* September, 194–203 (2007).
28. P. Czarnul, A. Ciereszko and M. Fraczak, Towards efficient parallel image processing on cluster grids using GIMP, *J. Fut. Gen. Comput. Syst.* **13**, 351–360 (1998).

29. A. AL-Dubai, M. Ould-Hhaoua and L. MacKenzie, On balancing network traffic in path-based multicast communication, *Fut. Gen. Comput. Syst.* **22**(7), 805–811 (2007).
30. SUN, Sun dramatically accelerates network performance, www.sun.com/aboutsun/pr/2007-02/sunflash.20070220.1.xml (2007).
31. B. Lim, K. Choi and D. Shin, An architecture for lightweight service discovery protocol in MANET, in *Lecture Notes in Computer Science*, Vol. 3516 (Springer, 2005), pp. 963–966.
32. H. Bal, A. Plaat, T. Kielmann, J. Maassen, R. Nieuwpoort and R. Veldema, Parallel computing on wide-area clusters: The Albatross Project, www.cs.vu.nl/~rob/papers/el99.ps.gz (1999).
33. L. Sacks, O. Prnjat, L. Ioannis, T. Olukemi, A. Ching, M. Fisher, P. McKee, N. Georgalas and H. Yoshi, Active robust resources management in cluster computing using policies, *J. Net. Syst. Manage.* **11**(3) (2003).
34. G. Jin and H. Tang, Control transmission pace at IP layer to avoid packet drop, *Proc. IEEE IPOM Conf.*, Beijing, 11–13 October (2004).
35. B. Javadi, J. Abawajy and M. Akbari, Performance analysis of interconnection networks for multi-cluster systems, in *Lecture Notes in Computer Science*, Vol. 3516 (Springer, 2005), pp. 205–212.

Chapter 22

INTRUSION DETECTION IN NETWORKS AND APPLICATIONS

KAPIL KUMAR GUPTA*, BAIKUNTH NATH†
and KOTAGIRI RAMAMOHANARAO‡

Department of Computer Science and Software Engineering,
NICTA Victoria Research Laboratory,
University of Melbourne, Australia
**kgupta@csse.unimelb.edu.au*
†bnath@csse.unimelb.edu.au
‡rao@csse.unimelb.edu.au

Detecting intrusions in networks and applications has become one of the most critical tasks to prevent the misuse of network resources by attackers. The cost involved in protecting these valuable resources is often negligible when compared with the actual cost of a successful intrusion. This is one of the motivating factors for developing more powerful intrusion detection systems. In this chapter, we describe the problem of intrusion detection in detail and discuss various methods that have been used for building intrusion detection systems. We also discuss some of the emerging methods, such as conditional random fields, which can detect a wide variety of attacks with relatively higher accuracy.

1. Introduction

The abundance of information and the popularity of services offered over the Internet have raised serious concerns regarding network and information security. Present networks contain valuable information which can be exploited for financial gains [1, 2]. According to one study, the size of the Internet was estimated to be 532,897 Tb in the year 2002 [3]. The increasing dependence of businesses on the services over the Internet, though, has led to their rapid growth; it has also made the networks (and applications) a prime target for attacks. This is primarily attributed due to vulnerabilities in software which are exploited by the attackers who launch powerful attacks such as the denial of service (DoS) [4] and information attacks [5, 6]. The rise in the number of vulnerabilities discovered in software has resulted in an exponential rise in the number of attacks. According to the Computer Emergency Response Team (CERT), the number of vulnerabilities reported for the year 2007 increased to 7,236 [7], many of which were in highly deployed software. Considering that it is near to impossible to build "perfect" software, it has become critical to build effective intrusion detection systems that can detect attacks reliably and at early stages so that appropriate intrusion response mechanisms can be activated to mitigate their impact.

In this chapter, we explore the problem of security in an interconnected environment with emphasis on intrusion detection. We describe the problems associated with intrusion detection in detail, classify them, and discuss the associated challenges. We then discuss methods which have been used for developing intrusion detection systems, including their strengths and limitations, suggest better methods, and give directions for future research. There have been a number of surveys which give the taxonomy, classify different intrusion detection methods and compare different systems [5, 8–12]. Very often, the focus of the surveys is to compare a few commercial products, and as a result the core issues are not discussed in detail. Our focus is not to survey or to analyze different products, but to provide a comprehensive study of the area of intrusion detection which will help the reader to better understand the problem and the associated core issues.

2. Background

In this section, we explore the problem of intrusion in a network. We discuss basic security principles and why the problem of intrusion exists. We define the key terms and highlight the importance of intrusion detection in the overall security framework. We then discuss some current attack trends as well as possible future attacks, which will guide us in building robust and efficient intrusion detection systems.

2.1. *Basic Security Principles*

Present networks are increasingly based on the concept of resource sharing as it is a necessity for collaboration and provides an easy means of communication. However, the need to communicate and share resources increases the complexity of the system. The systems are becoming larger with more and more add-on features increasing complexity. This results in vulnerabilities in software and configuration errors in networks and deployed applications. The ease of access of resources in addition to vulnerabilities in software and poor management of resources can be exploited to launch attacks [13]. Further, features intended for some specific usage in many applications may also be exploited by attackers. A typical example of this is the response generated by the SQL server which is often exploited in SQL injection attacks. Regardless of the size and complexity of a network, it must provide and ensure basic security features such as authentication and authorization, availability, integrity, confidentiality and non-repudiation [6, 14]. We now give their definitions and explain various terms that will be helpful in understanding the remaining chapter.

2.1.1. *Definitions*

(i) *Authentication*: Validating the identity of a user or application accessing a system [14]. The most common method for authentication is the use of a user ID and a password. However, passwords can be guessed using tools which are available freely. Hence, authentication methods, which are relatively difficult to guess and forge, including biometric and multifactor authentication mechanisms, such as the use of a security token in addition to the password, have gained significance. Such methods require the physical presence of a human or the device and are hence more secure than a simple password mechanism [15]. However, the password mechanism is still the most preferred method for authentication and systems have been updated to only accept strong passwords based on a combination of letters, numbers and special characters, making them very difficult to guess.

(ii) *Authorization*: A process that infers whether an authenticated user or application has the privilege to access a particular resource [14]. Authorization is often implemented by creating the access control matrix which defines the level of access of a resource to a user or application [16]. An authenticated user is granted or denied access depending upon the access rights defined in the access control matrix.

Authentication, therefore, identifies the source while authorization determines whether the identified source is allowed access to the resource.

(iii) *Availability*: The property of a system which must ensure that any resource (data or service) must be available to an authenticated and authorized entity upon request [14]. Many services are offered on the Internet and their uninterrupted availability is critical for many businesses. DoS attacks [4] target the availability of a resource thereby rendering it unavailable to legitimate users.

(iv) *Integrity*: Ensuring that the data is free from modification by an unauthenticated and/or unauthorized entity [14].

(v) *Confidentiality*: Protecting the disclosure of data to an unauthenticated and/or unauthorized entity [14]. Networks and applications store a wide variety of information such as credit card details and medical histories of individuals. Such personal information must not be disclosed to unauthorized users. Any such malicious attempt to access the confidential information must be detected by the installed security systems.

(vi) *Non-repudiation*: The property which ensures accountability by preventing an entity from denying when it accessed a particular resource [14]. This property is important for most applications and particularly for banking applications, which require tamper-proof logging of every transaction on write-once only media. The logs can then be analyzed in case of any dispute. Similarly, law enforcement agencies also require non-repudiation so that their actions can also be audited.

To ensure complete security, the communication channel must also be secure, i.e., the communication channel should be available to transmit data without interruption, there should be no modification of data in the channel, the data must not be intercepted by any other user or application, and the data itself should not be fabricated by any illegitimate source which may be masquerading as a true source [6]. All of these security features are significant and must be considered together to define a security policy for an entire network.

(vii) *Security policy*: A policy document that defines the rules applicable to access any resource (data or service) in a network [16]. The security policy must define these rules in a form which clearly states the acceptable and/or unacceptable usage of every single resource and how to respond to any security incident.

(viii) *Attack (or intrusion)*: An attack can be defined as a violation of the security policy [17]. An attack generally exploits software vulnerability or a configuration error in the system, resulting in violation of the defined security policy. However, if we consider an attack as a violation of security policy, we assume that such a policy exists and clearly states the complete acceptable and/or unacceptable use of every resource.

An attack can also be considered as an event which aims to compromise the confidentiality, integrity and/or availability (*the CIA triad*) of a resource. However, every event must be analyzed with regard to a metric which can qualify it either as normal or as an attack. A security policy is one such metric. Further, the security policy is often different for different networks and it is important to note that one policy may qualify an event as normal while another policy may qualify the same event as an attack.

(ix) *Intrusion detection*: Given that an attack is a violation of a security policy, intrusion detection is defined as the process of identifying such violations. We will discuss a number of methods that have been used for building intrusion detectors in various intrusion detection systems. These methods include pattern matching approaches, statistical methods, and data mining and machine learning approaches.

(x) *Intrusion detection system*: A system which includes processes to detect, identify and respond to attacks. The processes include audit data collection, data pre-processing, data analysis and decision-making followed by recovery and response mechanisms. An intrusion detector is one of the core components of an intrusion detection system. Thus, an intrusion detection system must collect audit patterns and present them in a form which can be analyzed by the intrusion detector. The intrusion detection system also has the capability to react to an intrusion, once it is detected, either by blocking the source of attack or by activating other response mechanisms. Processes that are necessary to recover after an attack may also be initiated depending upon the defined security policy.

2.2. *Overall Security Infrastructure and Intrusion Detection*

Security is often implemented as a multi-layer infrastructure. Different approaches for providing security fall into any one of the six areas which are discussed next [18].

(i) *Attack deterrence*: Persuading an attacker not to launch an attack by increasing the perceived risk of negative consequences for the attacker. Having a strong legal system may be helpful in attack deterrence. However, it would require strong evidence against the attacker in the case an attack were launched. Research in this area focuses on methods such as those discussed in Ref. 19, which can effectively trace the true source of attack as very often the attacks are launched with spoofed source IP address. Spoofing refers to sending IP packets with modified source IP address such that the true sender of the packet cannot be traced [20].

(ii) *Attack prevention*: Aims to prevent an attack by blocking it before it can reach the target. However, it is very difficult to prevent all the attacks. This is because, to prevent an attack, the system requires complete knowledge of all possible attacks as well as the complete knowledge of all the allowed normal activities, which is not always available. An example of an attack prevention system is a firewall, which aims to prevent an attack from reaching the target by blocking the source based on some preconfigured rules [18, 21].

(iii) *Attack deflection*: Tricking an attacker by making him/her believe that the attack was successful though, in reality, the attacker was trapped by the system and deliberately made to reveal the attack. Research in this area focuses on attack deflection systems such as "honey pots" [10, 22].

(iv) *Attack avoidance*: Aims to make the resource unusable by an attacker even though the attacker is able to illegitimately access that resource. An example of a security mechanism for attack avoidance is the use of cryptography [18, 23]. Encrypting data may render the data useless to the attacker, thus avoiding the possible threat of misuse of information.

(v) *Attack detection*: The process of detecting an attack while the attack is still in progress or to detect an attack which has already occurred in the past. Detecting an attack is significant for two reasons: first the system must recover from the damage caused by the attack, and second it allows the system to take measures to prevent similar attacks in the future. Research in this area focuses on building robust and efficient intrusion detection systems [52].

(vi) *Attack reaction and recovery*: Once an attack is detected, the system must react to an attack and perform the recovery mechanisms as defined in the security policy.

Tools available to perform attack detection followed by reaction and recovery are known as intrusion detection systems and have become a critical requirement in the network security arsenal. However, the difference between intrusion prevention and intrusion detection is slowly diminishing as the present intrusion detection systems increasingly focus on realtime attack detection and blocking an attack before it reaches the target. Such systems are better known as Intrusion Prevention Systems.

2.3. *Need of Intrusion Detection*

The simplest way to ensure complete security, provided we can ensure hardware level security, is to disable communication between any two computers and to disable resource sharing, such as the sharing of the same node by multiple users. However, this is in no way a solution for securing today's highly networked computing environment.

The need for security was first identified with the emergence of time sharing systems in the 1960s [9]. One solution for this was the introduction of access control, which gave rise to the concept of ownership. In this model, every user has access to only those processes and data which are either owned by a user or are explicitly made accessible to the user. Access control lists and access control matrices are defined to implement access control [24]. However, with the emergence of more and more interconnected networks and ultimately the Internet, the problem of providing security has scaled many fold and moved from implementing access control for a limited number of users accessing a single system to securing the entire Internet with millions of interconnected computers accessible to several million users which are spread over a wide geographical area. With the ever-increasing size and complexity of networks, there is a need to develop methods which can detect attacks efficiently and effectively. The prospect of huge financial gains, as a result of a successful attack, diminish the threat of legal convictions. The inability to prevent attacks furthers the need for intrusion detection. The problem becomes more profound since authorized users can misuse their privileges and attackers can masquerade as authentic users by exploiting vulnerable applications.

2.3.1. *Attack Trends and Emerging Attacks*

The first major attack over the Internet was the Morris Worm of 1988, which is estimated to have cost between US $10–100M [25]. Since then, the number of attacks has been on a rise and in the year, 2008, the number of viruses, worms and trojans in circulation crossed one million [68]. The vulnerabilities in software, which are exploited in order to launch an attack, are also on a rise. Further, the time required to prepare for an attack has drastically reduced as a number of tools are available

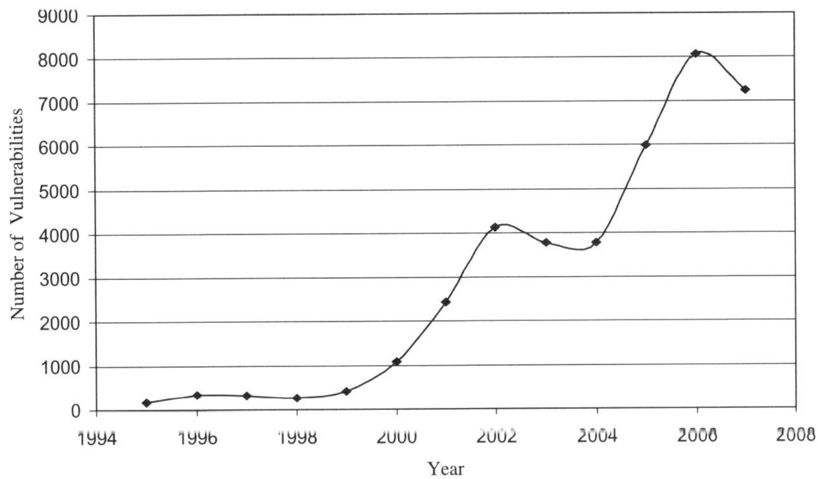

Fig. 1. Number of vulnerabilities versus year [7].

which can automate the entire attack process [1]. The number of reported incidents surpassed 100,000 in the year 2003 and since then the CERT stopped keeping track of the number of incidents [7]. Rather, they only track the reported vulnerabilities. Figure 1, represents how the number of reported vulnerabilities in software has increased over the years [7]. These vulnerabilities result in huge losses which amount to billions of dollars [26].

The authors in Ref. 56 identify two major threats, the DoS and the information attacks, which must be addressed. All the other types of attacks can be classified as belonging to either of the two. They also identify the challenges and discuss possible approaches for detecting the two attacks. It is important to note that the methods which are applicable for detecting DoS attacks are insufficient to detect information attacks. Similarly, methods which work well for detecting information attacks cannot detect DoS attacks reliably.

The purpose of attacks has also undergone a drastic change. Earlier, the attacks were frequently launched by individuals who disrupted services over the Internet that affected a large number of legitimate users in order to gain popularity and make themselves known to a larger group of people. However, with the rise in services and maturity of businesses over the Internet, the attackers have become more focused and engage in criminal activity which is driven by the goal of making money [1, 26]. This has not only resulted in increasing the severity of attacks, but the attacks have become more focused and isolated, targeting only a few nodes often in a single network. Such attacks are very difficult to detect using generic systems and hence the network administrators may be completely unaware of the ongoing malicious activities in their networks. We now give an example of one such possible attack, which is described in Ref. 1.

The authors in Ref. 1 describe a scenario in which a software agent can be used to attack a specific target without affecting any other network with the aim of searching for and transmitting confidential and sensitive information without authorized access. The authors explain that the attack can be carried out by experts with the goal of hiding the entire attack and preventing their identity from being discovered. Further, since the attack targets only a single network, it would not be detected by large-scale cooperative intrusion detection systems. The most significant part of the entire attack is that none of the present systems can detect such attacks and the agent can destroy itself when the attack is successful without leaving traces of its activities. Unlike worms, the replication in the case of an intruding agent is limited and it does not degrade performance at the target. The authors also compare their intruding agent with other well-known malware such as the worms and spyware and show that the intruding agent has different characteristics which make it unique and very difficult to detect. The authors point out that such attacks are possible and suggest some possible methods which can help in their detection. We shall discuss various methods for detecting intrusions and compare their relative advantages and disadvantages in the following sections. As discussed in Ref. 1, we illustrate the behavior of the intruding agent in Fig. 2 with a flow diagram.

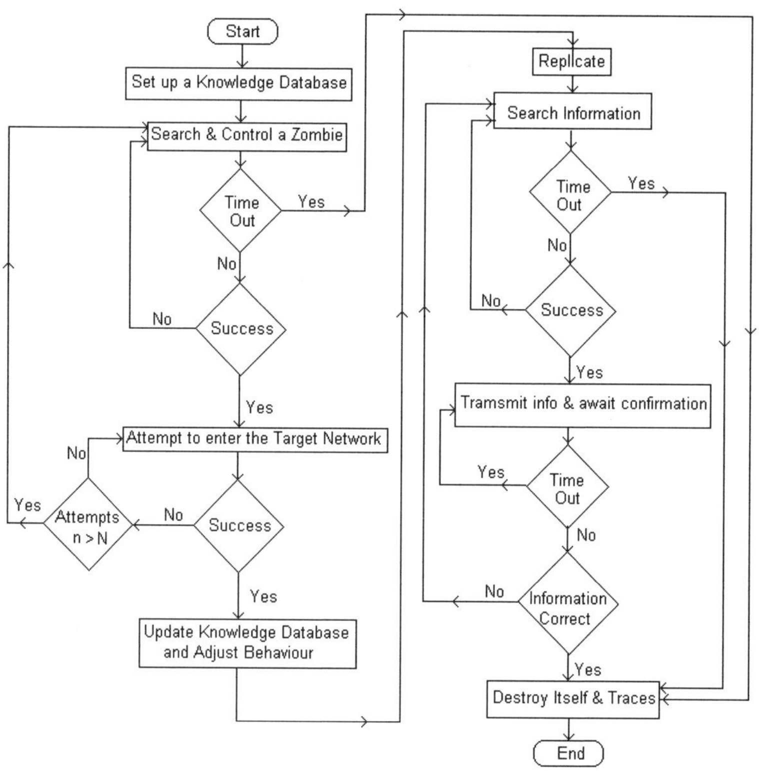

Fig. 2. Flow diagram of an intruding agent [1].

3. Intrusion Detection and Intrusion Detection Systems

Given the need for an intrusion detection system in the present networks, we will now describe the components and requirements for building such systems. We shall also discuss the principles and assumptions involved in building intrusion detection systems, which will give a deeper insight and help the reader to understand them better. Finally, we will provide a classification.

3.1. *Components of an Intrusion Detection System*

An intrusion detection system (IDS) typically consists of three sub-systems or components:

(i) *Data pre-processor*: Responsible for collecting and providing the data (in a specified form) that will be used by the next component (analyzer) to make a decision. The data pre-processor is, therefore, concerned with collecting the data from the desired source and converting it into a form that is comprehensible by the analyzer.

The data that can be used for detecting intrusions range from user access patterns (for example, the sequence of commands issued at the terminal and the resources requested) to network packet level features (such as the source and destination IP addresses, type of packets and rate of occurrence of packets) to application and system level behavior (which includes the sequence of system calls generated, and many more). From now onwards, we refer to this data as audit patterns.

(ii) *Analyzer (intrusion detector)*: The core component which analyzes the audit patterns to detect attacks. This is a critical component and one of the most researched. Various pattern matching, machine learning, data mining and statistical techniques can be used as intrusion detectors and are discussed in the following sections. The capability of the analyzer to detect an attack often determines the strength of the overall system.

(iii) *Response engine*: Determines how to react when the analyzer detects an attack. The system may decide either to raise an alert without taking any action against the source or may decide to block the source for a predefined period of time. Such an action depends upon the predefined security policy of the network.

In Ref. 27 the authors define the Common Intrusion Detection Framework (CIDF), which recognizes a common architecture for all the intrusion detection systems. The CIDF defines four components that are common to any intrusion detection system: event generators (E-boxes), event analyzers (A-boxes), event databases (D-boxes) and the response units (R-boxes). The additional component, D-boxes, is optional and can be used for later analysis.

3.2. *Principles and Assumptions in Intrusion Detection*

Denning [28] defines the principle for characterizing a system under attack. The principle states that for a system that is not under attack, the following three conditions hold true:

(i) Actions of users conform to statistically predictable patterns.
(ii) Actions of users do not include sequences which violate the security policy.
(iii) Actions of every process correspond to a set of specifications which describes what the process is allowed to do.

Systems under attack do not meet at least one of these three conditions. Further, intrusion detection is based upon some assumptions which are true regardless of the detection method adopted by the intrusion detection system. These assumptions are:

(i) There exists a security policy which defines the normal and/or the abnormal usage of a resource.
(ii) The patterns generated during the abnormal system usage are different from the patterns generated during the normal usage of the system, i.e., the normal and abnormal usage of a system results in different system behavior, which can be used to detect intrusions [29].

As we will discuss, different methods can be used as intrusion detectors which make a number of assumptions that are specific only to the method concerned. Hence, in addition to the definition of the security policy and the access patterns which are used in the learning phase of the detector, the detection capability of an intrusion detector is also dependent upon the assumptions made by individual approaches for analysis of the audit patterns.

3.3. *Challenges and Requirements for Intrusion Detection Systems*

The purpose of an intrusion detection system is to detect attacks. However, it is equally important to detect attacks at an early stage in order to minimize their impact. We now give the challenges and requirements for building intrusion detection systems.

(i) The system must be able to detect attacks reliably without giving false alarms. It is very important that the false alarm rate is low as in a live network with large amount of traffic the number of false alarms may exceed the total number of attacks detected correctly, thereby decreasing the confidence in the attack detection capability of the system. Ideally, the system must detect all intrusions with no false alarms. The challenge is to build a system which has broad attack detection coverage, i.e., it can detect different kinds of attacks and at the same time result in very few false alarms.

(ii) The system must be able to handle a large amount of data without affecting performance and without dropping data, i.e., the rate at which data is processed and a decision is made must be greater than or equal to the rate of arrival of data. Hence, the speed of operation is critical for systems deployed in high-speed networks. In addition, the system must be capable of operating in real time by initiating a response mechanism once an attack is detected. The challenge is to prevent an attack rather than simply detecting it.

(iii) A system that can link an alert generated by the detector to the actual security incident is desirable. Such a system would help in quick analysis of the attack and may also provide effective response to intrusion as opposed to a system which provides no after attack analysis capability. Hence, it is not only necessary to detect an attack, but it is also important to identify the attack.

(iv) It is desirable to develop a system which is resistant to attacks since a system which can be exploited during attack may not be able to detect attacks reliably.

3.4. *Classification of Intrusion Detection Systems*

To understand the capabilities and limitations of different types of intrusion detection systems, it is very important to classify them. We provide this classification in Fig. 3.

From Fig. 3, we observe that for any intrusion detection system, the security policy and audit patterns are the two prime information sources. Audit patterns are analyzed to detect an attack and the security policy defines the acceptable and unacceptable usage of a resource and helps to qualify whether an event is normal or an attack. *Hence, based on the given classification, an example of an intrusion detection system can be a centralized system deployed on a network with sliding window based data collection which operates in real time and is based on signature analysis with active response to intrusion.*

3.4.1. *Classification Based Upon Security Policy Definition*

(i) Security policy defines the normal and abnormal usage of every resource. Consider a set U, which represents the complete domain (universe) for a resource R. The set U consists of both normal and abnormal usage of R, which is represented in Fig. 4(a). Hence, $U = \{U_{R\text{-normal}}, U_{R\text{-attack}}\}$. The problem is to identify the set U such that it is complete and unambiguous. However, in most practical situations it is very difficult to identify and define the complete set U and only a small portion of this set is available, which can be denoted as S. Hence, the security policy is defined with only the knowledge contained in the subset S, which is defined as $S = \{S_{R\text{-normal}}, S_{R\text{-attack}}\}$. This is represented in Fig. 4(b).

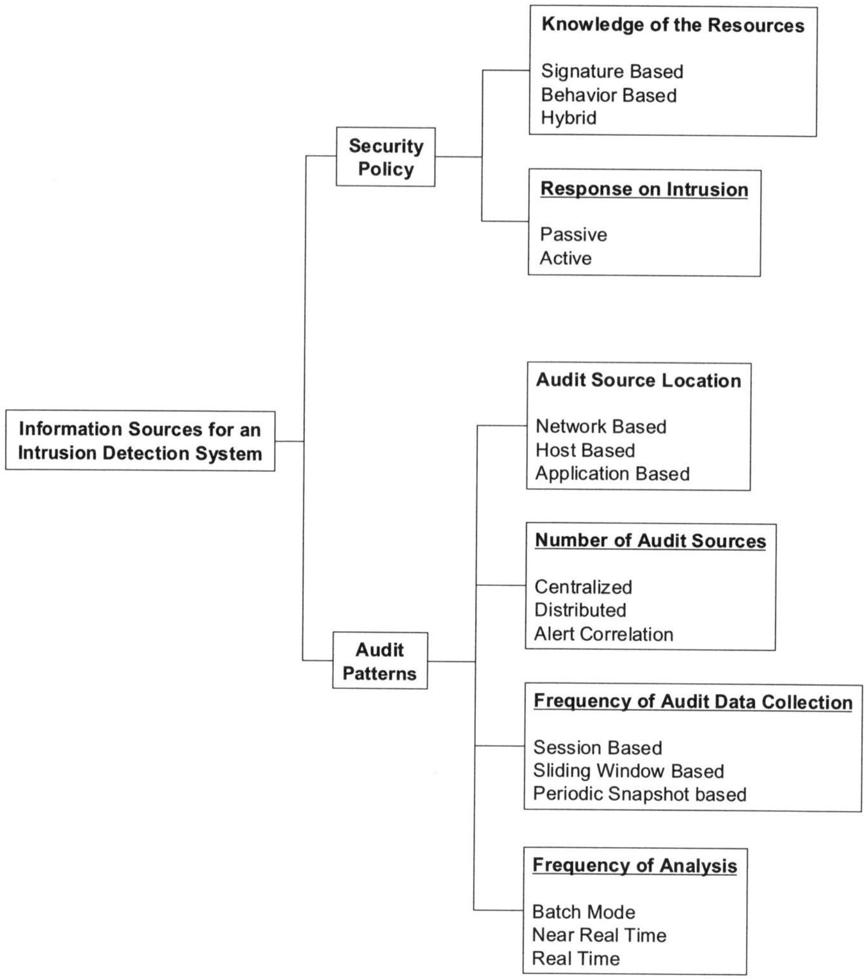

Fig. 3. Classification of intrusion detection systems.

Based upon the elements of subset S, an intrusion detection system can be classified as:

(a) *Signature (misuse) based*: When the set S only contains the events which are known to be anomalous, the system focuses on detecting known misuses and is known as a signature or misuse based system [10]. A signature based system is represented in Fig. 5.

Signature based systems employ pattern matching approaches to detect attacks. They can detect attacks with very few false alarms but have limited attack detection capability since they cannot detect new and unseen attacks. Their attack detection capability is directly proportional to the available knowledge of attacks in the

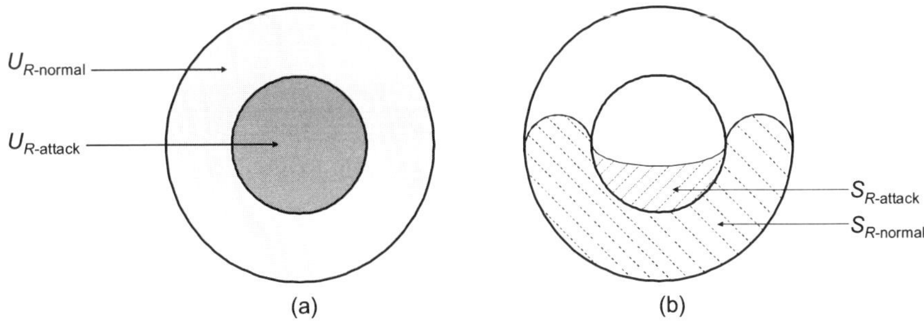

Fig. 4. Representation for a resource R: (a) complete knowledge, and (b) available knowledge, where $|U_{R-\text{normal}}| \geq |S_{R-\text{normal}}|$ and $|U_{R-\text{attack}}| \geq |S_{R-\text{attack}}|$.

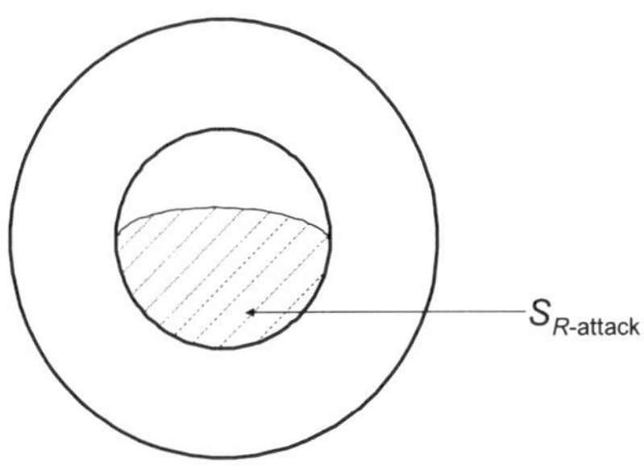

Fig. 5. Representation of a signature based system.

set S, i.e., knowledge of $S_{R-\text{attack}}$. For such a system to be effective, complete knowledge of attacks is required, i.e., $S_{R-\text{attack}}$ should be equal to $U_{R-\text{attack}}$, which is not always possible.

(b) *Behavior (anomaly) based*: When the set S only consists of events which are known to be normal, the goal of the intrusion detection system is to identify significant deviations from the known normal deviations [10]. They are represented in Fig. 6.

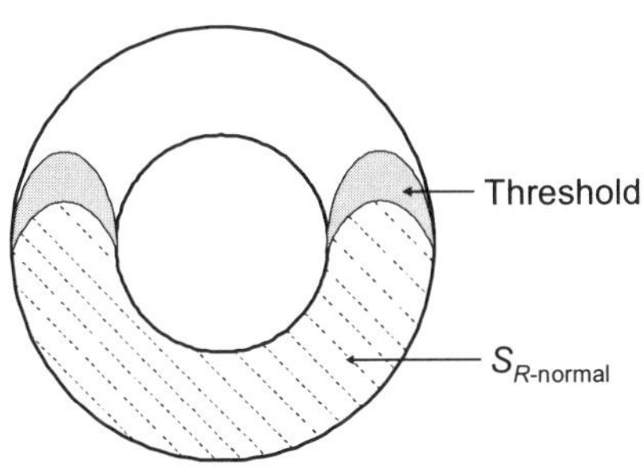

Fig. 6. Representation of a behavior based system.

For behavior based systems to be effective, complete knowledge of normal behavior of a resource is required, i.e., the set $S_{R\text{-normal}}$ should be equal to the set $U_{R\text{-normal}}$. Very often a threshold is used which gives some flexibility to the system when complete knowledge of normal behavior is not available. Events which lie beyond the threshold are detected as an attack. Behavior based systems, in general, suffer from a large false alarm rate.

(c) *Hybrid*: In most environments, it may not be possible to completely define either the normal or the abnormal behavior. As a result, the systems may result in large false alarms or may be specific in detecting only a few types of attacks. Hence, a hybrid system uses the partial knowledge of both, i.e., $S_{R\text{-normal}}$ and $S_{R\text{-attack}}$, to detect attacks, often resulting in fewer false alarms and detecting more attacks. Such systems generally employ machine learning approaches. A hybrid system is shown in Fig. 7.

(ii) The security policy also defines how the system must respond when an attack is detected, based upon which the intrusion detection systems can be classified as:

  (a) *Passive response systems*: In a passive response system, the system does not take any measure to respond to an attack once an attack is detected. It simply generates an alert which can be analyzed by the administrator at some later stage [10, 18].
  (b) *Active response systems*: In active response systems, the system responds to attacks by various possible approaches which may include blocking the source of the attack for a predefined time [10, 18].

3.4.2. *Classification Based Upon Audit Patterns*

(i) The source from which the audit patterns are collected affects the attack detection capability of a system. For example, when network statistics are used as the audit patterns, they cannot provide any detail about the user and

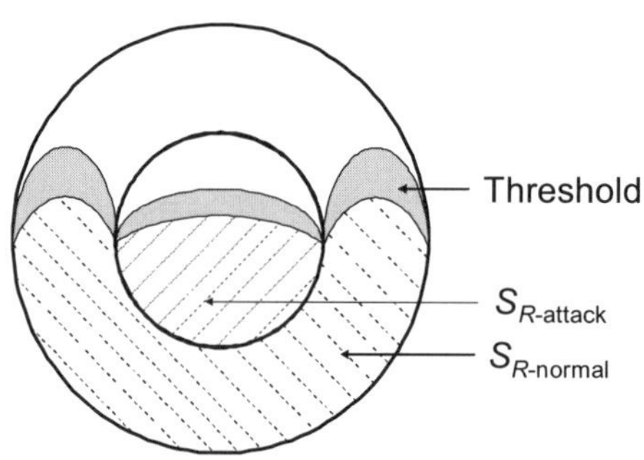

Fig. 7. Representation of a hybrid system.

system interaction. Based on this, intrusion detection systems are classified as follows:

(a) *Network based*: In a network based system, the audit patterns collected at the network level are used by the intrusion detector. Though a single system (or a few strategically placed systems) often suffice for the entire network and is easy to manage, the attack detection capability of a network based system is limited. This is because it is hard to infer meaningful contextual information directly from the network audit patterns. Further, the audit patterns may be encrypted rendering them unusable by the intrusion detector at the network level. In addition, large amount of audit patterns at the network level may also affect the total attack detection accuracy. This is for of two reasons: first, a significant portion of the total incoming patterns may be allowed to pass into the network without any analysis, and second, in high-speed networks it may be practical to analyze only the summary statistics collected at regular time intervals. These statistics may include features such as the total number of connections, amount of incoming and outgoing traffic. Such features may only provide a high level summary and may not be able to detect attacks reliably [10].

(b) *Host based*: The intrusion detector in a host based system analyzes the audit patterns generated at the kernel level of the system, which include system access logs and the error logs [10]. The audit patterns collected at the individual host contain more specific information than the network level audit patterns, which may be used to detect attacks reliably. However, it becomes difficult to manage a large number of host based systems in a big network. Additionally, host based systems can themselves be victims of attack and can be manipulated as part of an attack.

(c) *Application based*: Host based systems analyze the system level logs; however, the application based systems are concerned only with a single application and detect attacks directed at a particular application or a privileged process [10]. Application based systems can analyze either the application transaction logs or the system calls generated by the processes to detect anomalous activities [30]. The application based systems can be very effective as they can exploit the complete knowledge of the application and can be used even when encryption is used. They can also analyze the user and application interactions, which can significantly improve the attack detection accuracy.

(ii) In order to detect intrusions, the audit patterns can be collected from a single source or from a number of sources. When the patterns are collected from more than one source, the decision can be made individually or by aggregating the audit patterns at a single point and then analyzing them together.

Based upon this property, the intrusion detection systems can be classified as follows:

(a) *Centralized systems*: In a centralized system, the audit patterns are collected either from a single source or from multiple sources but are processed at a single point where they are analyzed together to determine the global state of the network [10]. However, they may themselves become a target of attack.
(b) *Distributed system*: In contrast to centralized systems, distributed systems can make local decisions close to the source of the audit patterns and may report only a small summary of activities to a higher level in the system. The advantage of a distributed system for intrusion detection is that an immediate response mechanism can be activated based upon local decisions. Additionally, global monitoring can be done by analyzing the summary report which can be generated by individual intrusion detectors in a distributed system. However, distributed systems can be less accurate due to a lack of global knowledge. Agent based systems are examples of distributed intrusion detection systems [10].
(c) *Alert correlation*: Alert correlation based systems analyze the alerts generated by a number of cooperating intrusion detection systems [18]. The individual systems may themselves be centralized or decentralized. Alert correlation systems can only be effective when multiple networks are attacked with similar attacks such as in the case of a worm outbreak. However, when the attacks are network specific, alert correlation systems will not be effective even though a few target networks may detect some anomalous activities which may be discarded as false alarms due to a lack of global consensus.

(iii) Regardless of the source and the number of audit patterns, intrusion detection systems can be classified depending upon the frequency at which the audit patterns are collected. Based on this, they are classified as follows:

(a) *Session based*: Audit patterns can be collected at the end of every session by summarizing different features. Methods can be used which analyze the summary of every session once the session is terminated.
(b) *Sliding window based*: In the case of sliding window based collection of audit patterns, events are recorded using a moving window of fixed or variable width. The width of the window defines the number of events recorded together and the step size for sliding the window determines how fast the window is advanced forward.
(c) *Periodic snapshot based*: Instead of recording every event or summarizing a session at its termination, snapshots of different states of the entire system can be taken at regular intervals, which can be analyzed to detect intrusions.

(iv) Depending upon the frequency of analysis of audit patterns, intrusion detection systems can be classified as follows:

(a) *Batch mode*: In batch mode intrusion detection, patterns are aggregated at a central repository. The patterns are then analyzed for intrusions at predefined time intervals. Such systems cannot provide any immediate response to intrusion and can only perform the recovery task once an attack is detected.

(b) *Near real time*: An intrusion detection system is said to perform in near real time when the system cannot detect an intrusion when it commenced, but can detect it at some later stage during the attack or immediately at the end of an attack. In a near realtime system, there is some delay before the patterns are made available to the intrusion detector. Patterns collected by taking periodic snapshots or using moving window with step size greater than one can be used in a near realtime intrusion detection system.

(c) *Real time*: A realtime intrusion detection system must detect an attack as soon as it has commenced, i.e., the system is said to perform in real time if and only if, for an event x when the attack commenced, the attacker cannot succeed with the event $x + 1$. Hence, for a realtime intrusion detection system, the system must detect and react immediately when the attack commences. However, in practice it is very difficult to build such a system given the constraint that it should have low false alarms and high detection accuracy. Realtime intrusion detection systems can be implemented using a moving window with a step size of one. Network based signature detection systems, which perform pattern matching, can also perform in real time by checking every event for known attacks. However, they are limited in detecting only previously known attacks. A typical example is the Snort [31] intrusion detection system.

4. Evaluation Metrics

Evaluating different methods for detecting intrusions is important. The intrusion detection problem is an example of a problem with imbalanced classes, i.e., the number of instances in the two classes "normal" and "attack" are not equally distributed. The number of attacks is very low when compared with the total number of normal events. Note that in the case of the DoS attacks, the amount of attack traffic is extremely large compared to the normal traffic. Hence, evaluating intrusion detection systems using a simple accuracy metric may result in very high accuracy even if no attacks are detected and the system simply predicts all the events as normal [54]. Hence, other metrics such as the precision, recall and F-measure must

Table 1. Confusion matrix.

	Predicted normal	Predicted attack
True normal	True negative	False positive
True attack	False negative	True positive

be used for evaluating intrusion detectors. These are defined below with the help of a confusion matrix which is represented in Table 1.

$$Precision = \frac{Number\ of\ true\ positives}{Number\ of\ true\ positives + Number\ of\ false\ positives},$$

$$Recall = \frac{Number\ of\ true\ positives}{Number\ of\ true\ positives + Number\ of\ false\ negatives}.$$

Hence, a system must have high precision (i.e., it must detect only attacks) and high recall (i.e., it must detect all attacks). The two metrics can be combined and a single metric, F-measure, can be used, which is defined as

$$F\text{-}measure = \frac{(1+\beta^2) * Precision * Recall}{\beta^2(Precision + Recall)},$$

where β is the relative importance of precision and recall and is usually set to 1.

Instead of the F-measure, a receiver operating characteristic (ROC) curve [55] can also be used to evaluate an intrusion detector. The ROC curve is a plot of the attack detection rate versus the false alarm rate. The ROC curve can be represented as shown in Fig. 8.

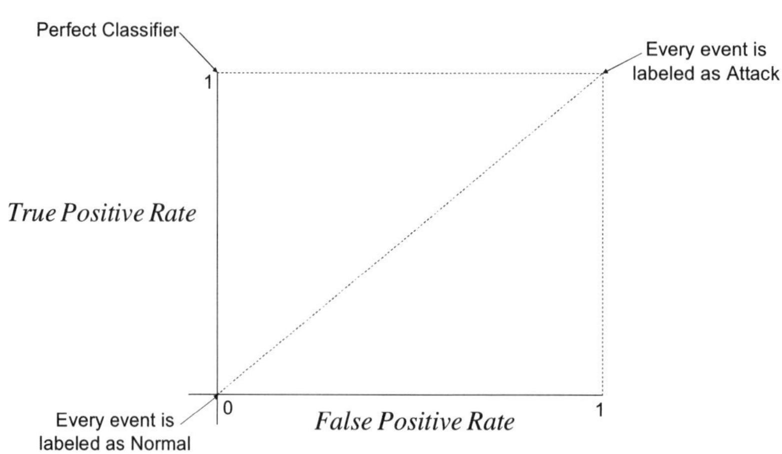

Fig. 8. ROC curve.

The *False Positive Rate* and *True Positive Rate* are defined as follows:

$$\textit{False Positive Rate} = \frac{\textit{Number of false positives}}{\textit{Number of false positives} + \textit{Number of true negatives}},$$

$$\textit{True Positive Rate} = \frac{\textit{Number of true positives}}{\textit{Number of true positives} + \textit{Number of false negatives}}.$$

In addition to evaluating the attack detection capability of the detector, the time taken to detect an attack is also significant. The time performance is generally measured for the time taken by the intrusion detector to detect an attack from the time the audit patterns are fed into the detector. This is sufficient for comparison when different methods use exactly the same data for analysis; however, it does not represent the efficiency of the intrusion detection system as the time taken in collecting and pre-processing the audit patterns is not considered. Hence, total time must be measured, which is the time from the point when intrusion actually started to the point in time when the response mechanism is activated.

5. Representation of Audit Patterns and Methods for Intrusion Detection

In this section, we first discuss the features of data patterns and their representation, which will help to decide which method should be used for building a intrusion detector. We shall then discuss various methods which can be used for detecting intrusions.

5.1. *Representation of Audit Patterns*

The raw patterns must be pre-processed before they can be analyzed by the intrusion detector. The audit patterns can be represented in various forms and those are discussed below.

5.1.1. *Properties of Audit Patterns Useful for Intrusion Detection*

The authors in Ref. 32 describe three properties which can be used to detect intrusions:

(i) *Frequency of event(s)*: This determines how often an event occurs in a predefined time interval. A threshold can be used to define the limit. When the frequency crosses this limit, an alarm can be raised. Properties such as the number of invalid login attempts and the number of rows accessed in a database can be used as the frequency measure.

(ii) *Duration of event(s)*: Rather than counting the number of times an event occurs, the duration property determines the acceptable time duration for a particular event. This is also based upon selecting a threshold which defines an acceptable range for a particular event. For example, a large number of invalid login attempts for a single user ID in a very short time span can be considered as an attempt to guess a password and hence an attack.

Systems analyzing the frequency and duration property for the events can perform efficiently but they suffer from a large false alarm rate as it is often difficult to determine the correct threshold for the events.

(iii) *Ordering of events*: Analyzing the order in which events occur can improve the attack detection accuracy and reduce false alarms. This is because very often intrusion is a multi-step process in which a number of events must occur sequentially in order to launch a successful attack. However, to avoid detection from the systems which are based on analyzing the ordering of events, the attacks can be spread over a long period of time such that the events cannot be correlated unless a long history is maintained by the intrusion detection system.

5.1.2. *Univariate or Multivariate*

The audit patterns that are collected (such as from the routers and switches for network audit patterns) may either be univariate or multivariate. When only one feature is analyzed, in the case of univariate audit patterns, the analysis is much simpler compared to when many features are analyzed together, as in the case of multivariate analysis. However, a single feature itself may not be the complete representation and, hence, insufficient to detect attacks. For example, when the sequence of system calls of a privileged process are analyzed for detecting abnormal behavior, discarding other features such as the parameters of the system calls can affect the detection capability of the system. Hence, it is important to decide how many and what features must be selected for representing the audit patterns.

5.1.3. *Relational or Sequential Representation*

Very often the audit patterns collected are sequential, where one or more events are recorded continuously. However, the raw audit patterns may be processed into a relational form and a number of new features can be added. These features often give a high level representation of the audit patterns in a summarized form. Examples of such features include total amount of data transferred in a session and duration of a session. Frequency and duration properties of events can easily be represented in a relational form. Converting the audit patterns from sequential to relational form has two advantages. First, more features can be added, and second, efficient methods can be used for analysis of audit patterns in the relational form. However, this may result in affecting the attack detection capability since in the relational form the ordering of events, and hence the relationship among sequential events, is lost. When the audit patterns are represented sequentially, event ordering can be exploited in favor of higher attack detection accuracy. However, in general, sequence analysis is slower when compared to relational analysis.

5.2. *Methods for Intrusion Detection*

The field of intrusion detection and network security has been around since the late 1980s. Since then a number of methods and frameworks have been proposed and many systems have been built to detect intrusions. Various techniques such as association rules, clustering, naive Bayes classifiers, support vector machines, genetic algorithms, artificial neural networks, and others have been applied to detect intrusions. Given the features of the audit patterns and their representation, we now describe various methods which can be used for building intrusion detection systems. We shall focus on the audit patterns that are analyzed by different methods, and the assumptions made by them, and compare their advantages and disadvantages. These methods can be broadly divided into the three categories outlined in the following subsections.

5.2.1. *Pattern Matching*

Pattern matching techniques search for a predefined set of patterns (known as signatures) from the audit patterns to detect intrusions. Pattern matching approaches are often employed on the audit patterns represented in relational form which do not have any state information. Hence, they assume that every event is independent of every other event. However, this assumption may not always hold as a single intrusion may span multiple events which are correlated. The prime advantage of pattern matching approaches is that they are very efficient and trigger alarms only when an exact match of an attack signature is found, i.e., they result in very few false alarms. They can, however, detect attacks only if the corresponding pattern (signature) exists in the signature database. As a result, they cannot detect new unseen attacks for which there are no signatures [33]. The snort intrusion detection system [31] is based upon a pattern matching technique.

5.2.2. *Statistical Methods*

Statistical methods based on modeling the monitored variables as independent Gaussian random variables and methods such as those based on the Hotelling T^2 test statistic can be used to determine attacks by calculating deviations in the profile from the stored normal profile [33]. Statistical methods are based upon modeling the underlying process which generates the audit patterns. Such methods exploit the frequency and duration property of events. They often analyze properties such as the overall system load and statistical distribution of events, which represent a summary measure. When the deviations exceed a predefined threshold, the system triggers an alarm. Determining this threshold is a critical issue. When the threshold is low, the system raises a large number of (false) alarms and when the threshold is high, the system may not detect attacks reliably. Though these methods can handle multiple features in the audit patterns, very often in order to reduce complexity and improve system performance only a single variable is considered, as in the Intrusion-Detection Expert System (IDES) [34], or the variables are assumed to be independent, as in the Haystack system [35]. This, however, affects the attack detection accuracy. The statistical methods can be implemented to run either in batch mode (such as in the Haystack system) or in realtime mode (such as in the IDES).

5.2.3. *Data Mining and Machine Learning*

Data mining and machine learning methods focus on analyzing the properties of the audit patterns rather than identifying the process which generated them [33]. These methods include approaches for mining association rules, classification and cluster analysis. As we shall discuss, classification methods are one of the most researched and include methods like decision trees, Bayesian classifiers, artificial neural networks, k-nearest neighbor classification, support vector machines, and many others.

In contrast to the rule based classification methods, clustering methods are based upon calculating the numeric distance of a test point from different cluster centers and adding the point to the closest cluster. The most important issue when applying any clustering method is to select the distance measure as different distance measures result in clusters with different shapes and sizes. Frequently used distance measures are the Euclidian distance and the Mahalanobis distance [33]. Clustering can also be performed in case only the normal audit patterns are available. In such cases, density based clustering methods can be used and are based on the assumption that intrusions are rare and dissimilar to the normal events. In this case, the clustering operation is similar to identifying the outlier points which can be considered as intrusions.

- *Data mining*: Data mining approaches for intrusion detection [36–38] include association rules and frequent episodes and are based on building classifiers by discovering relevant patterns of program and user behavior. Association rules [39] and frequent episodes are used to learn the record patterns that describe user behavior. They can deal with symbolic features and the features can be defined in the form of packet and connection details. However, mining of features is limited to the entry level of the packet and requires the number of records to be large and sparsely populated; otherwise they tend to produce a large number of rules, which increases the complexity of the system [40].
- *Clustering*: Clustering of data has been applied extensively for intrusion detection using various methods such as k-means, fuzzy c-means, and others [41, 42]. However, one of the main drawbacks of the clustering technique is that it is based on calculating the numeric distance between the observations and hence

the observations must be numeric. Observations with symbolic features cannot be easily used for clustering, resulting in inaccuracy. In addition, they consider the features independently and are unable to capture the relationship between different features of a single record, which results in lower accuracy.

- *Bayesian classifiers*: Naive Bayes classifiers are also proposed for intrusion detection in Ref. 43. However, the authors make a strict independence assumption between the features in an observation resulting in lower attack detection accuracy when the features are correlated, which is often the case for intrusion detection. Bayesian networks can also be used for intrusion detection [44]. However, they tend to be attack specific and build a decision network based on special characteristics of individual attacks. Thus, the size of a Bayesian network increases rapidly as the number of features and the type of attacks modeled by the Bayesian network increases.
- *Decision trees*: Decision trees have also been used for intrusion detection [43]. Decision trees select the best features for each decision node during the construction of the tree based on some well-defined criteria. One such criterion is the gain ratio, which is used in C4.5. Decision trees generally have a very high speed of operation and high attack detection accuracy.
- *Artificial neural networks*: The use of artificial neural networks is discussed for network intrusion detection in Refs. 45 and 46. Though the neural networks can work effectively with noisy data, they require a large amount of data for training and it is often hard to select the best possible architecture for the neural network.
- *Support vector machines*: Support vector machines, which map real valued input feature vectors to higher-dimensional feature space through non-linear mapping, have also been used for detecting intrusions [47]. They can provide realtime detection capability, deal with large dimensionality, and can be used for binary-class as well as multi-class classification.

Other approaches include the use of genetic algorithms and autonomous and probabilistic agents for intrusion detection [10]. These methods are generally aimed at developing a distributed intrusion detection system.

For data mining and machine learning approaches, the accuracy of the trained system also depends upon the amount of audit patterns available during training. Generally, more data during training results in a better model. Very efficient methods have been developed for intrusion detection which deal with audit patterns in relational form. However, intrusion detection has not been much explored with sequential representation of audit patterns even though methods for mining continuous data streams and learning data sequences are available. The prime reason for working with the relational form is that the systems tend to be simple, efficient and give fairly good attack detection accuracy. Similar to the pattern matching and statistical methods, methods based upon relational representation of audit patterns assume independence among consecutive events and hence do not consider the order of events for attack detection. They generally deal with summary patterns and may analyze multiple features which are often considered independently depending upon the individual method.

Mining association rules for intrusion detection has the advantage that they are easy to interpret. However, they are based upon building a database of rules of normal and frequent items during the training phase. During testing, rules from the test data are extracted and various classification methods can be used to classify the test data. The detection accuracy suffers as the database of rules is not a complete representation of the normal audit patterns. Additionally, once the rules are extracted they are considered independently by the classifier, which further decreases the attack detection accuracy [33].

•*Markov models*: Markov chains and hidden Markov models can be used when dealing with sequential data. References 48–50 describe the use of hidden Markov models for modeling normal sequences of system calls of a privileged process, which can then be used to detect anomalous traces. However, modeling the system calls alone may not always provide accurate classification as in such cases various connection level features are ignored. Further, hidden Markov models cannot model long-range dependencies between the observations [51]. Very often the sequence is itself a vector and has many correlated features. However, in order to gain computational efficiency the multivariate data analysis problem is broken down into multiple univariate data analysis problems and the results are combined using a simple voting mechanism or by assigning weights to individual features to get an overall score [33]. This, however, results in inaccuracy as the correlation among the features is lost. The authors in Ref. 32 show that modeling the ordering property of events in addition to the duration and frequency can result in higher attack detection accuracy. The only drawback with modeling the ordering of events is that the complexity of the system increases, which affects the performance of the system. Hence, there is a trade-off between detection accuracy and the time required for attack detection.

To overcome the weakness of a single intrusion detection system, a number of frameworks have been proposed which describe the collaborative use of intrusion detection systems. A combination of network based and host based systems is proposed in Ref. 57. Systems which employ both signature based and behavior based techniques are discussed in Refs. 58 and 59. In Ref. 38, the authors describe a data mining framework for building adaptive intrusion detection models. A distributed intrusion detection framework based on mobile agents is discussed in Ref. 60.

5.2.4. *Our Approach*

As we discussed before, the two desirable properties for building intrusion detection systems are attack detection accuracy and performance of operation. We also discussed that the audit patterns which are analyzed by the intrusion detector affect the attack detection capability of the detector. Further, the patterns are collected as continuous streams which consist of multiple features. In most situations, these features are interdependent and correlated. Present sequence based methods consider only one feature, or consider the features to be independent, resulting in reduced accuracy. We propose using conditional random fields [51], which can be used to analyze multiple data streams without making any assumption about the independence of features, resulting in higher attack detection accuracy [66].

5.2.5. *Conditional Random Fields for Intrusion Detection*

Conditional random fields [51] offer us the required framework to build robust intrusion detection systems [52]. The prime advantage of conditional random fields is that they are discriminative models which directly model the conditional distribution $p(y \mid x)$. Further, conditional random fields are undirected models and are free from label bias and observation bias, which are present in other graphical models.

Generative models such as Markov chains, hidden Markov models, naive Bayes and the joint distribution have two disadvantages. First, the joint distribution is not required since the observations are completely visible and the interest is in finding the correct class which is the same as the conditional distribution $p(y|x)$. Second, inferring conditional probability $p(y|x)$ from the modeled joint distribution, using the Bayes rule, requires marginal distribution $p(x)$. Estimating this marginal distribution is difficult as the amount of training data is often limited and the observation, x, contains highly dependent features which are difficult to model, and hence strong independence assumptions are made to simplify the task, resulting in reduced accuracy. Instead, conditional random fields predict the label sequence, y, given the observation sequence, x, allowing them to model arbitrary relationships among different features in the observations without making independence assumptions. The graphical structure of a conditional random field is represented in Fig. 9, where $x_1x_2x_3x_4$ represents an observed sequence of length four and every event in the sequence is correspondingly labeled $y_1y_2y_3y_4$.

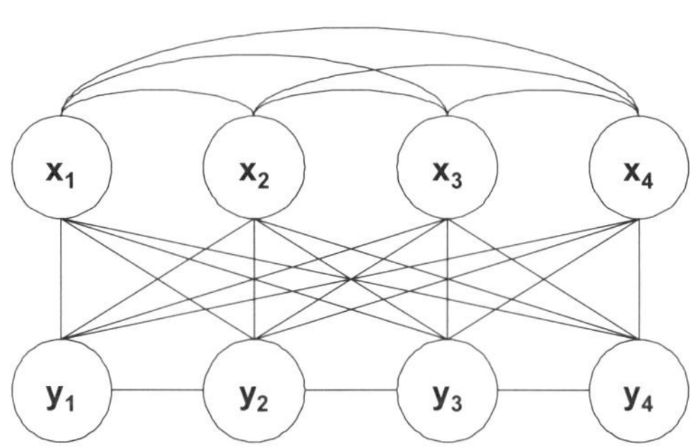

Fig. 9. Graphical representation of conditional random field.

The following mathematical description of a conditional random field is motivated by the work in Ref. 51. Given X and Y, the random variables over the data sequence to be labeled and the corresponding label sequences, let $G = (V, E)$ be a graph with vertices V and edges E such that $Y = (Y_v)$, where $v \in V$ and Y is represented by the vertices of the graph G; then, (X, Y) is a conditional random field; when conditioned on X, the random variables Y_v obey the Markov property with respect to the graph: $p(Y_v|X, Y_w, w \neq v) = p(Y_v|X, Y_w, w \sim v)$, where $w \sim v$ means that w and v are neighbors in G, i.e., a conditional random field is a random field globally conditioned on X. For a simple sequence (or chain) modeling, as in our case, the joint distribution over the label sequence Y given X has the form:

$$p_\theta(y|x) \propto \exp\left(\sum_{e \in E,k} \lambda_k, f_k(e, y|_e, x) + \sum_{v \in V,k} \mu_k, g_k(v, y|_v, x) \right)$$

where x is the data sequence, y is a label sequence, and $y|_s$ is the set of components of y associated with the vertices or edges in sub-graph S. The features f_k and g_k are assumed to be given and fixed.

In Ref. 52, the authors show that conditional random fields work very well for intrusion detection. Their system analyzes the connection summary between two communicating hosts, which is represented as a single record with multiple features. We first describe this model and then extend it to model multiple events as sequences [61] rather than considering a summarized record.

5.2.6. *Relational Representation of Audit Patterns*

Network monitoring is one of the common and widely applied methods for detecting malicious activities in an entire network. However, realtime monitoring of every single event in even a moderate size network may not be feasible, simply due to the large amount of network traffic. As a result, it is only possible to perform pattern matching using attack signatures which may at best detect only previously known attacks. Anomaly based systems result in dropping data when they are used to analyze every event. Hence, they are often based upon monitoring the summary statistics. The summary statistics may include features of a single TCP session between two IP-addresses or may include network level features such as the load on a server and number of incoming connections per unit time among others. These statistics are represented in the KDD 1999 dataset [62]. The dataset represents the summary of an IP connection between two well-known IP addresses in a relational form each having 41 features. Every record in the dataset is either labeled as "normal" or as an "attack" and belongs to one of the four classes: Probe, denial of service (DoS), remote to local (R2L) and user to root (U2R). For our experiments we used the conditional random field toolkit, CRF++ [63] and the Weka tool [64]. We developed python and shell scripts for data formatting and implementation was on a desktop running on Intel(R) Core(TM) 2, CPU 2.4 GHz and 2 GB RAM. We performed every experiment ten times under exactly the same conditions and report their average.

As described in Ref. 52, we discuss how conditional random fields can be used for detecting attacks effectively and compare them with other methods such as the decision trees and naive Bayes which are known to perform very well. We performed experiments to separately detect all four attack classes when they are mixed with normal data. Additionally, we note that different attacks can be detected by using only a small set of features instead of using all 41 features. Hence, we performed feature selection using our domain knowledge for all four attack classes. We selected five features for Probe, nine features for DoS, 14 features for R2L and eight features for U2R. For more details about the experiments refer to Ref. 52. We present the results in Table 2.

The results clearly suggest that conditional random fields perform better than decision trees and naive Bayes. The reason for the better attack detection capability for the conditional random fields is explained as follows.

Consider for example, when classifying network connections as either "normal" or as "attack," a system may consider features such as "logged in" and "number of file creations". When these features are analyzed individually, they do not provide any information that can aid in detecting attacks. However, when these features are analyzed together they, can provide meaningful information for the task of classification. Taking another example, the connection level feature such as the "service invoked" at the destination provides some information about the class label (in the case an attacker sends a request to a service that is not available). This information becomes more concrete and aids in classification when analyzed with other features such as "protocol type" and "amount of data transferred" between source and destination (in the case the client connects to an available service such as FTP and performs data transfer). Such relationships between different features in the observed data, if considered during classification, can significantly decrease classification error. Conditional random fields do not consider these features to be independent and hence this results in higher attack detection accuracy.

However, higher attack detection accuracy comes at the cost of performance. The time complexity for training a linear chain conditional random field is $O(TL^2NI)$ where T is the length of the sequence, L is the number of labels, N is the number of training instances, and I is the number of iterations. For inference (testing), the Viterbi algorithm is employed, which has a complexity of $O(TL^2)$.

Table 2. Comparison of F-measure [52].

	F-measure (%)			
	Probe	DoS	R2L	U2R
Conditional random fields	92.73	98.50	42.08	58.19
Naive Bayes	31.22	98.19	11.98	41.97
Decision trees	91.93	98.50	18.43	43.70

Table 3. Comparison of time complexity.

	Test time per instance (10^{-5} s)			
	Probe	DoS	R2L	U2R
Conditional random fields	3.15	5.22	7.75	4.40
Naive Bayes	1.74	2.24	3.89	3.02
Decision trees	1.54	1.33	1.86	1.53

Training can be performed offline and is not a major concern. However, the quadratic complexity for testing is significant when the number of labels is large, as in language tasks. However, for intrusion detection there are only two labels "normal" and "attack" and thus the system is very efficient. Additionally, methods such as discussed in Ref. 53 can be used to improve performance by reducing the length of the sequence T. We compare the test time performance of the three methods in Table 3.

We observe that conditional random fields are not prohibitively more expensive than decision trees and naive Bayes. Considering both the attack detection accuracy and the test time performance, we conclude that conditional random fields are a better choice for detecting attacks. It is important to note that for decision-making the system uses summary statistics, which are unavailable until the end of the session. Hence, the system may, at best, react to an attack only immediately at the end of the session, which may be sufficient for many but not all situations. However, to detect attacks in realtime, it is important to analyze every event instead of analyzing the summary statistics. In the next section, we describe how conditional random fields can be used for detecting attacks in continuous multiple data streams.

5.2.7. *Sequential Representation of Audit Patterns*

Network monitoring is often restricted to monitoring summary statistics due to an excessive amount of network traffic and is further affected due to network address translation and encryption, making it unsuitable for providing high level of security. Thus, it becomes necessary to extend network monitoring and focus on data and applications, which are often the targets of attacks. Present systems which focus on application and data monitoring either only focus on analyzing every data access query [65] or only monitor sequences of system calls for privileged processes neglecting other features. Earlier, we also discussed that for realtime detection, multiple events must be analyzed together as sequences where every event in a sequence itself has multiple features. The audit patterns are thus similar to continuous multiple data streams. Hence, we need a method which can consider these multiple sequences together rather than considering them individually.

However, there are no publicly available datasets which can be used for such experiments. Unfortunately, getting real-world data, for example a bank website data, is very hard, if not impossible. Hence, we have collected such datasets locally, which can be downloaded from Ref. 67. The collected patterns represent individual user sessions which were labeled either as "normal" or as "attack." We performed experiments using a moving window to analyze sequential events in a session. To make the intrusion detection task realistic, we disguised the attack sessions within normal sessions. For this, we define the disguised attack parameter p as follows:

$$p = \frac{number\ of\ \text{``}Attack\text{''}\ events}{number\ of\ \text{``}Normal\text{''}\ events + number\ of\ \text{``}Attact\text{''}\ events}$$

where the number of "Attack" events > 0 and number of "Normal" events ≥ 0.

The value of p lies in the range $(0,1]$. The attacks are not disguised when $p = 1$, since the number of normal events is 0. As the value of p decreases, when the number of normal events is large, the attacks are disguised. To create disguised attack data, we randomly add a variable number of attack events at random locations in normal sessions and label all the events as anomalous.

We present some results in Fig. 10, where we set the value of p as 0.60 and vary the size of the moving window from 1 to 20. More details on the experimental procedure can found in Ref. 61.

We observe that conditional random fields perform best, and are robust in detecting disguised attacks. Their attack detection capability increases as the size of the window S increases, i.e., their detection capability increases as the number of sequential events analyzed together in a session increases. Support vector machines, decision trees and naive Bayes do not perform well when the audit patterns are disguised with normal events. Nonetheless, there is a trade-off between disguise attack parameter and window size. In general, for better attack detection, S must be increased when p decreases. The advantage of conditional random fields is that higher attack detection occurs at lower values of S, which is desirable.

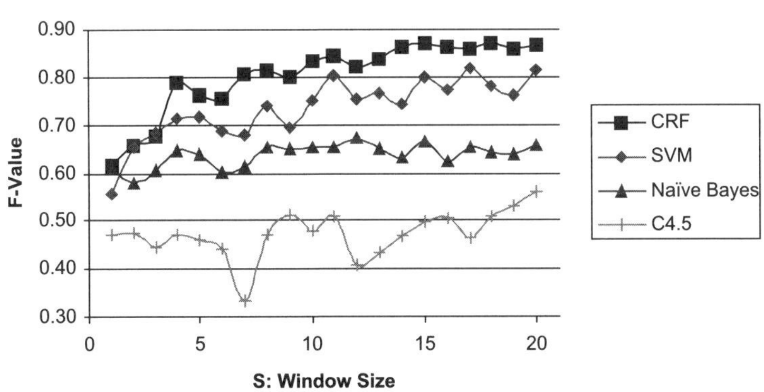

Fig. 10. Comparison of F-measure at $p = 0.60$.

6. Thoughts for Practitioners

Given the description of the problem of intrusion detection, a number of issues must be addressed before we can develop an intrusion detection system with all the desired properties. We give a brief description of such issues, which are discussed in detail in Ref. 56.

(i) Many attacks are successful because the attackers enjoy anonymity and can launch attacks from spoofed sources making it very hard to trace back the true source of the attack. However, if there were a reliable method to trace back packets to their actual source, many of the attacks could be prevented. Solutions are available for this such as adjusted probabilistic packet marking and others [19], but they require a global effort, which is not very easy to ensure. The problem is to identify the true source of attack without affecting the performance of the system.

(ii) Security policy plays an important role in a network and describes the acceptable and unacceptable usage of the resources. There are two major issues in defining the security policy: first, the security policy must be complete, and second, the policy must be clear and unambiguous. Hence, the problem is to clearly define the acceptable and the unacceptable usage of every resource.

(iii) The Internet is an aggregation of individual networks which are owned and managed separately. Since every network is different from any other network, a single intrusion detection system may not be suitable for every network. Signature based systems have common signatures which can be updated regularly. However, custom signatures must be defined as per the requirements of the network concerned. This means that there is no single solution that can be sufficient for all networks. Hence, the problem is how to customize intrusion detection systems automatically to cater to the requirements of individual networks.

(iv) An intrusion detection system issues an alert when it detects abnormal behavior. However, the alert may represent a change in behavior rather than an intrusion. The problem is to correlate alerts with attacks such that the alerts are easily comprehensible.

(v) Many systems are based upon authenticating a user. However, authentication mechanisms such as the use of login and password are weak and can be compromised. Multifactor authentication and use of biometric methods have been introduced, but they can also be cracked. The problem is how to link the supplied credentials with the actual human user. There are methods based on user profiling, which learns the normal user profile to detect significant deviations from the learnt profile. However, they are based upon thresholds which are selected by empirical analysis rather than analytical study. The problem is how to determine the thresholds analytically instead of empirically.

7. Directions for Future Research

The field of intrusion detection has been around since the 1980s and a number of approaches have been introduced. However, to keep pace with the ever-changing networks, research on intrusion detection must be in step with network improvements. The present networks increasingly support wireless technologies, removable and mobile devices. Intrusion detection systems must integrate with these networks and provide support for such advances in a comprehensive manner.

Another promising area for future work in the field of intrusion detection is to focus on detecting data breaches. Intrusion detection systems must move a step forward from monitoring networks and focus on applications which store critical data.

There is ample scope and need to build systems which aim at preventing attacks rather than simply detecting them. Further, integrating intrusion detection systems with the security policy in individual networks would help to minimize false alarms and qualify the alarms raised by the systems.

8. Conclusions

In this chapter, we have identified the need for intrusion detection systems in the present networks and explored the problem of intrusion detection in detail. We have discussed the components and principles of an intrusion detection system and have classified them. We have then discussed various methods which have been used for detecting intrusions, their underlying assumptions and their strengths and limitations with regard to their attack detection capability. We have also suggested better methods that are more effective at detecting intrusions. Finally, we discussed some open questions and gave directions for future research.

Terminology

Attack (or Intrusion): An attack can be defined as a violation of the security policy.

Authentication: Authentication refers to validating the identity of a user or application accessing a system.

Authorization: Authorization refers to a process to infer whether an authenticated user or an application has the privilege to access a particular resource.

Availability: Availability refers to the property of a system which must ensure that any resource (data or service) must be available to an authenticated and authorized entity upon request.

Conditional Random Fields: Conditional random fields are undirected and discriminative graphical models which directly model the conditional distribution of the labels, y, given the observation sequence x.

Confidentiality: Confidentiality refers to protecting the disclosure of data to unauthenticated and/or unauthorized entity.

Data Mining: Data mining is the process of finding patterns, automatically, generally from a very large data set.

Integrity: Integrity refers to ensuring that the data is free from modification by unauthenticated and/or unauthorized entity.

Intrusion Detection: Given, an attack is a violation of a security policy; intrusion detection is defined as the process of identifying such violations.

Intrusion Detection System: An intrusion detection system is a system which includes processes to detect, identify and respond to attacks. The processes include audit data collection, data pre-processing, data analysis and decision making followed by recovery and response mechanisms.

Machine Learning: Machine learning refers to the ability of a machine (usually a computational system) to learn from the data in order to build a system which can then be used for understanding underlying process that generated the data, classification of new instances, clustering and other artificial intelligence tasks.

Non-Repudiation: Non-Repudiation refers to the property which ensures accountability by preventing an entity from denying when it accessed a particular resource.

Pattern Matching: Pattern matching refers to the capability of a system to identify distinctive features which constitute a well known pattern.

Security Policy: A security policy is a policy document which defines the rules applicable to access any resource (data or service) in a network.

Exercises

1. What are the two most significant requirements for any intrusion detection system?
2. Explain the difference between authentication and authorization.
3. Explain the "CIA Triad" with respect to information security.
4. Briefly describe the three main components of an intrusion detection system.
5. State the principle for characterizing a system under attack.
6. How can intrusion detection systems be classified depending upon security policy definition?
7. How can intrusion detection systems be classified depending upon audit patterns?
8. What are the three properties of audit patterns that can be used to detect intrusions?
9. Compare network-based intrusion detection systems with host-based intrusion detection systems.

10. Describe the evaluation metrics that can be used for better evaluation of intrusion detection systems. Explain why simple accuracy must not be used for the same.

References

1. K. K. Gupta, B. Nath, K. Ramamohanarao and A. U. Kazi, Attacking confidentiality: An agent based approach, *Proc. IEEE Int. Conf. Intelligence and Security Informatics*, Lecture Notes in Computer Science, Vol. 3975 (Springer Verlag, 2006), pp. 285–296.
2. T. A. Longstaff, J. T. Ellis, S. V. Hernan, H. F. Lipson, R. D. Mcmillan, L. H. Pesante and D. Simmel, Security of the Internet, The Froehlich/Kent Encyclopedia of Telecommunications, Vol. 15, CERT Coordination Center report (1997), pp. 231–255.
3. P. Lyman and H. R. Varian, How much information, http://www2.sims.berkeley.edu/research/projects/how-much-info-2003, accessed 29 November (2007).
4. V. D. Gligor, A note on denial-of-service in operating systems, *IEEE Trans. Software Eng.* **10**(3), 320–324 (1984).
5. M. T. Siponen and H. Oinas-Kukkonen, A review of information security issues and respective research contributions, *SIGMIS Database* **38**(1), 60–80 (2007).
6. W. Stallings, *Network Security Essentials — Applications and Standards* (Prentice Hall, 2000).
7. CERT Statistics, www.cert.org/stats, accessed 27 November (2007).
8. S. Axelsson, Intrusion detection systems: A survey and taxonomy, Technical report 99-15, Department of Computer Engineering, Chalmers University of Technology (2000).
9. J. S. Sherif and T. G. Dearmond, Intrusion detection: Systems and models, *11th IEEE Int. Workshops on Enabling Technologies: Infrastructure for Collaborative Enterprises (WETICE'02)* (2002).
10. R. Bace and P. Mell, Intrusion detection systems, Computer Security Division, Information Technology Laboratory, National Institute of Standards and Technology, Gaithersburg, MD (2001).
11. E. Lundin and E. Jonsson, Survey of intrusion detection research, Technical report, Chalmers University of Technology (2002).
12. T. Peng, C. Leckie and K. Ramamohanarao, Survey of network-based defense mechanisms countering the DoS and DDoS problems, *ACM Comput. Surv.* **39**(1), 3 (2007).
13. C. E. Landwehr, A. R. Bull, J. P. McDermott and W. S. Choi, A taxonomy of computer program security flaws, *ACM Comput. Surv.* **26**(3), 211–254 (1994).
14. S. Northcutt, *Network Intrusion Detection — An Analyst's Handbook* (New Riders, 1999).
15. Authentication, http://en.wikipedia.org/wiki/Authentication, accessed 29 November (2007).
16. A. S. Tanenbaum and M. van Steen, *Distributed Systems: Principles and Paradigms* (Prentice Hall, 2002).
17. S. Lodin, Intrusion detection product evaluation criteria (1998).
18. C. Kruegel, F. Valeur and G. Vigna, *Intrusion Detection and Correlation: Challenges and Solutions* (Springer, 2005).
19. T. Peng, C. Leckie and K. Ramamohanarao, Adjusted probabilistic packet marking for IP traceback, *Proc. 2nd IFIP Networking Conf. (Networking 2002)* (2000), pp. 697–708.
20. IP address spoofing, http://en.wikipedia.org/wiki/IP_address_spoofing, accessed 29 November (2007).

21. W. R. Cheswick and S. M. Bellovin, *Firewalls and Internet Security* (Addison-Wesley, 1994).
22. Honeypot (computing), http://en.wikipedia.org/wiki/Honeypot_(computing), accessed 29 November (2007).
23. B. Schneier, *Applied Cryptography* (John Wiley & Sons, 1996).
24. B. W. Lampson, Protection, *Proc. 5th Princeton Conf. Information Sciences and Systems*, Princeton (1971).
25. M. Worm, http://en.wikipedia.org/wiki/Morris_worm, accessed 29 November (2007).
26. 11th annual CSI/FBI Computer Crime and Security Survey, http://www.sis.pitt.edu/~jjoshi/IS2150/Fall07/FBI2006.pdf, accessed 29 November (2007).
27. P. Porras, D. Schnackenberg, S. Staniford-Chen, M. Stillman and F. Wu, The common intrusion detection framework architecture, http://gost.isi.edu/cidf/drafts/architecture.txt, accessed 29 November (2007).
28. D. E. Denning, An intrusion-detection model, *IEEE Trans. Software Eng.* **13**(2), 222–232 (1987).
29. J. P. Anderson, Computer security threat monitoring and surveillance, http://csrc.nist.gov/publications/history/ande80.pdf, accessed 29 November (2007).
30. S. Forrest, S. A. Hofmyer, A. Somayaji and T. A. Longstaff, A sense of self for UNIX processes, *Proc. IEEE Symp. Research in Security and Privacy* (IEEE Computer Society Press, 1996), pp. 120–128.
31. Snort, A network based intrusion detection system, http://www.snort.org/, accessed 28 November (2007).
32. N. Ye, X. Li, Q. Chen, S. M. Emran and M. Xu, Probabilistic techniques for intrusion detection based on computer audit data, *IEEE Trans. Sys. Man Cybern. A* **31**(4) (2001).
33. A. Patcha and J.-M. Park, An overview of anomaly detection techniques: Existing solutions and latest trends, *Computer Networks*, accepted manuscript, http://dx.doi.org/10.1016/j.comnet.2007.02.001, accessed 29 November (2007).
34. H. S. Javitz and A. Valdes, The SRI IDES statistical anomaly detector, *Proc. IEEE Symp. Security and Privacy* (IEEE Press, 1991), pp. 316–326.
35. S. E. Smaha, Haystack: An intrusion detection system, *IEEE 4th Aerospace Computer Security Applications Conf.* (1988), pp. 37–44.
36. W. Lee and S. Stolfo, Data mining approaches for intrusion detection, *Proc. 7th USENIX Security Symp.* (1998), pp. 79–94.
37. W. Lee, S. Stolfo and K. Mok, Mining audit data to build intrusion detection models, *Proc. 4th Int. Conf. Knowledge Discovery and Data Mining* (AAAI Press, 1998), pp. 66–72.
38. W. Lee, S. J. Stolfo and K. W. Mok, A data mining framework for building intrusion detection model, *Proc. IEEE Symp. Security and Privacy* (IEEE Press, 1999), pp. 120–132.
39. R. Agrawal, T. Imielinski and A. Swami, Mining association rules between sets of items in large databases, *Proc. Int. Conf. Management of Data (SIGMOD)*, Vol. 22, Issue 2 (ACM Press, 1993), pp. 207–216.
40. T. Abraham, IDDM: intrusion detection using data mining techniques, http://www.dsto.defence.gov.au/publications/2345/DSTO-GD-0286.pdf, accessed 29 November (2007).
41. L. Portnoy, E. Eskin and S. Stolfo, Intrusion detection with unlabeled data using clustering, *ACM Workshop on Data Mining Applied to Security (DMSA)* (ACM Press, 2001).

42. H. Shah, J. Undercoffer and A. Joshi, Fuzzy clustering for intrusion detection, *12th IEEE Int. Conf. Fuzzy Systems*, Vol. 2 (IEEE Press, 2003), pp. 1274–1278.
43. N. B. Amor, S. Benferhat and Z. Elouedi, Naive Bayes vs. decision trees in intrusion detection systems, *Proc. ACM Symp. Applied Computing* (ACM Press, 2004), pp. 420–424.
44. C. Kruegel, D. Mutz, W. Robertson and F. Valeur, Bayesian event classification for intrusion detection, *19th Annual Computer Security Applications Conf.* (IEEE Press, 2003), pp. 14–23.
45. H. Debar, M. Becke and D. Siboni, A neural network component for an intrusion detection system, *Proc. IEEE Computer Society Symp. Research in Security and Privacy* (1992), pp. 240–250.
46. Z. Zhang, J. Li, C.N. Manikopoulos, J. Jorgenson and J. Ucles, HIDE: A hierarchical network intrusion detection system using statistical preprocessing and neural network classification. *Proc. IEEE Workshop on Information Assurance and Security United States Military Academy* (2001), pp. 85–90.
47. D. S. Kim and J. S. Park, Network-based intrusion detection with support vector machines, *Proc. Information Networking: Networking Technologies for Enhanced Internet Services Int. Conf. ICOIN*, Lecture Notes in Computer Science (Springer-Verlag, 2003), pp. 747–756.
48. Y. Du, H. Wang and Y. Pang, A hidden markov models-based anomaly intrusion detection method, *5th World Congress on Intelligent Control and Automation (WCICA)*, Vol. 5 (IEEE Press, 2004), pp. 4348–4351.
49. W. Wang, X. H. Guan and X. L. Zhang, Modeling program behaviors by hidden markov models for intrusion detection, *Proc. Int. Conf. Machine Learning and Cybernetics*, Vol. 5 (IEEE Press, 2004), pp. 2830–2835.
50. C. Warrender, S. Forrest and B. Pearlmutter, Detecting intrusions using system calls: alternative data models, *Proc. IEEE Symp. Security and Privacy* (IEEE Press, 1999), pp. 133–145.
51. J. Lafferty, A. McCallum and F. Pereira, Conditional random fields: Probabilistic models for segmenting and labeling sequence data, *Proc. 18th Int. Conf. Machine Learning (ICML)* (2001), pp. 282–289.
52. K. K. Gupta, B. Nath and K. Ramamohanarao, Layered approach using conditional random fields for intrusion detection, *IEEE Trans. Depend. Secur. Comput.*, in press.
53. K. K. Gupta, B. Nath and K. Ramamohanarao, Network security framework, *Int. J. Comput. Sci. Net. Sec.* **6**(7B), 151–157 (2006).
54. P. Dokas, L. Ertoz, A. Lazarevic, J. Srivastava and P. -N. Tan, Data mining for network intrusion detection, *Proc. NSF Workshop on Next Generation Data Mining* (2002), pp. 21–30.
55. Receiver operating characteristic, http://en.wikipedia.org/wiki/Receiver_operating_characteristic, accessed 29 November (2007).
56. K. Ramamohanarao, K. K. Gupta, T. Peng and C. Leckie, The curse of ease of access to the internet, *Proc. 3rd Int. Conf. Information Systems Security (ICISS)*, Lecture Notes in Computer Science, Vol. 4812 (Springer Verlag, 2007), pp. 234–249.
57. Y.-S. Wu, B. Foo, Y. Mei and S. Bagchi, Collaborative intrusion detection system (CIDS): A framework for accurate and efficient IDS, *Proc. 19th Annual Computer Security Applications Conf.* (IEEE Press, 2003), pp. 234–244.
58. L. Ertoz, A. Lazarevica, E. Eilertson, P. -N. Tan, P. Dokas, V. Kumar and J. Srivastava, Protecting against cyber threats in networked information systems, *Proc SPIE: Battlespace Digitization and Network Centric Systems III* (2003), pp. 51–56.

59. E. Tombini, H. Debar, L. Me and M. Ducasse, A serial combination of anomaly and misuse IDSes applied to HTTP traffic, *Proc 20th Annual Computer Security Applications Conf.* (IEEE Press, 2004), pp. 428–437.
60. D. Boughaci, H. Drias, A. Bendib, Y. Bouznit and B. Benhamou, Distributed intrusion detection framework based on mobile agents, *Proc. Int. Conf. Dependability of Computer Systems* (IEEE Press, 2006), pp. 248–255.
61. K. K. Gupta, B. Nath and K. Ramamohanarao, User session modeling for effective application intrusion detection, *Proc. 23rd Int. Information Security Conf.* (Lectures Notes in Computer Science, Vol. 278 (Springer Baston, 2008), pp. 269–283.)
62. KDD Cup 1999 intrusion detection data, http://kdd.ics.uci.edu/databases/kddcup99/kddcup99.html, accessed 5 February (2008).
63. T. Kudo, CRF++ yet another CRF toolkit, http://crfpp.sourceforge.net/, accessed 9 February (2008).
64. I. H. Witten and E. Frank, *Data Mining: Practical Machine Learning Tools and Techniques* (Morgan Kaufmann, 2005).
65. W. L. Low, J. Lee and P. Teoh, DIDAFIT: Detecting intrusions in databases through fingerprinting transactions, *Proc. 4th Int. Conf. Enterprise Information Systems (ICEIS)* (2002), pp. 264–269.
66. K. Ramamohanarao, K. K. Gupta and B. Nath, Sequence labeling for effective intrusion detection, *Proc. Computer Security Conf.* (2008).
67. K. K. Gupta, B. Nath and K. Ramamohanarao, Application based intrusion detection dataset, http://www.csse.unimelb.edu.au/~kgupta, accessed 10 May (2008).
68. Computer viruses hit one million, http://news.bbc.co.uk/2/hi/technology/7340315.stm, accessed 14 May (2008).

Chapter 23

SECURITY IN MOBILE AD HOC NETWORKS

VENKAT BALAKRISHNAN*, VIJAY VARADHARAJAN† and UDAY TUPAKULA‡

Information Networked System Security (INSS) Research Group, Department of Computing, Macquarie University, North Ryde, Sydney, NSW 2109, Australia

*venkat@ics.mq.edu.au

†vijay@ics.mq.edu.au

‡uday@ics.mq.edu.au

Security is paramount in mobile ad hoc networks (MANETs) since a MANET is neither conducive to centralized authorities nor suitable for inheriting the solutions that have been proposed for wired networks. Given that end-to-end communication between applications relies on the self-organized characteristics of MANETs, most if not all the proposed security solutions concentrate on securing communication through multi-hop trustworthy nodes. In this chapter, we present state-of-the-art security in MANETs and the survey comprises MANET-based secure routing, key management, and trust management systems. However, we confine ourselves to a few well-regarded proposals due to the exhaustive list of proposals available in each of the above-mentioned categories. First, we discuss the features inherent in MANETs and their impact on the design of security mechanisms, in addition to the threats and attacks that are common in MANETs. Second, we describe a few well-known solutions in the area of secure routing and key management to demonstrate their role as a prevention system. We then discuss the limitations of those systems such as their inability to react to dynamically changing attack patterns and their assumption that nodes will cooperate for routing and network management. Finally, we address the recent advancements in security systems, where a defense-in-depth approach is adopted to incorporate trust management systems as the second layer of defense to prevention systems. Trust management systems complement prevention systems by measuring the trustworthiness of nodes and promptly react to dynamically changing attack patterns. We then detail the limitations of trust management systems and discuss possible research directions to address those limitations.

1. Introduction

The advent of wireless communication, the proliferation of wireless devices, and the significance of nomadic computing have led to the growth of mobile ad hoc networks (MANETs). In these networks, any two nodes that are beyond their radio transmission range can communicate with each other through intermediate nodes and hence they are capable of establishing communications on the fly without relying on any infrastructure. This has influenced the development of various types of similar networks such as wireless sensor, ubiquitous, peer-to-peer, mesh and vehicular ad hoc networks. Nevertheless, features such as (a) wireless communication, (b) mobility, (c) lack of infrastructure, and (d) power cables, which serve as the substratum for the development of MANETs, also hinder their successful deployment. Thus, these features translate into the following issues: (a) promiscuous communication channels, (b) dynamically changing topology leading to broken links and sporadic connections, (c) difficulty in achieving cooperation among nodes, which is a prerequisite for self-organized networks, and (d) battery constrained nodes. Security is paramount in such networks since the above-mentioned issues are neither conducive to the assumption of centralized or distributed trusted authorities online, nor suitable for inheriting the solutions proposed for wired networks. In other words, mobile nodes struggle to enlist trusted intermediaries due to the self-organized characteristics of MANETs. It is noted that trusted intermediaries are a prerequisite for allowing a mobile node to forward information to various destinations and also to ensure that the forwarded information is free from modifications. This has encouraged researchers to develop security solutions for the routing layer so that secure end-to-end services between applications can be achieved over a trustworthy and secure routing layer.

In this chapter, we survey the major security issues in MANETs. We consider the security systems that have been proposed to mitigate those security issues, as well as their limitations. In the following, we detail the features inherent in MANETs and their impact on the design of security systems. We then briefly outline the attacks that are common in MANETs and also the basic security concepts to establish the background for our survey. Section 3 presents a few well-regarded secure routing and key management systems to demonstrate their role in protecting multi-hop communications against traditional attacks. We end the section with a detailed discussion on the limitations of secure routing and key management systems. Section 4 presents the defense-in-depth approach adopted in security systems, where trust management systems are used to address the shortcomings of prevention systems. We introduce the concepts and methodology relevant to traditional trust management systems and then describe various trust management systems that have been proposed for MANETs. Finally, we discuss the limitations of trust management systems and present possible research avenues for the development of efficient trust management systems. Section 6 summarizes the chapter.

2. Background

2.1. *Issues in MANETs*

Although features such as wireless communication, mobility, lack of infrastructure and power cables serve as the substratum for the development of MANETs, they open the door to issues such as promiscuous communication channels, dynamically changing topology, cooperation as a prerequisite for the existence networks, and battery constrained resources. These issues severely impact the design of security systems in MANETs and hence prevent them from inheriting the security solutions that have been proposed for wired networks.

2.1.1. *Wireless Medium — Promiscuous Communication*

In comparison with wired networks, mobile nodes communicate flexibly because MANETs eliminate the need for wired cables. However, the promiscuous wireless medium is prone to eavesdropping, while in wired networks an adversary can eavesdrop only by gaining physical access. Hence, the lack of a clear line of defense demands an efficient security system at every node. Using such security systems, mobile nodes can defend against adversaries that take advantage of the promiscuous wireless medium by injecting modified or spoofed packets.

2.1.2. *Mobility — Broken Links and Dynamically Changing Topology*

Mobility introduces flexibility into MANETs by facilitating nodes to locate potential network services. Mobility when combined with a wireless medium allows nodes to enter and leave the network with ease. This has led to the development of a dynamically changing topology and produced networks which have no fixed shape and size. Although mobility has been shown to increase the capacity of MANETs [1], it is irrefutable that mobility-induced dynamically changing topology causes broken links and sporadic connections. This opens the door for adversaries to report genuine links as broken links and there by disrupt communications. Also, the lightweight and portable characteristics of mobile nodes make them vulnerable to capture and compromise.

2.1.3. *Self-organization and Lack of Infrastructure — Prerequisite Cooperation for Network Operation*

Since self-organized, infrastructureless and multi-hop communication precludes the deployment of centralized servers and dedicated nodes for routing and network management, all mobile nodes are required to cooperate for the correct execution of routing and network management. This is necessary to establish and sustain the network. Such an intrinsic requirement makes MANETs vulnerable to adversaries, and several simulations [2, 3] have shown how adversaries can degrade the network performance dramatically by exploiting non-cooperation. Also, MANET-based security systems have to address the fact that a centralized authority (CA) is infeasible in self-organized and infrastructureless MANETs.

2.1.4. *Battery Powered Devices — Constrained Resources*

Battery powered nodes eliminate the use of power cables to complement nomadic communication. However, the heterogeneity that prevails in networks inspires adversaries to maximize their resources or network utility by either not forwarding packets for other nodes or forwarding only self-generated packets. This has a profound effect on network performance, and under extreme conditions it may lead to a partitioned or inoperative network. Also, heterogeneous battery, storage and computational resources in MANETs present challenges to the designers of security systems.

2.2. *Attacks and Adversaries*

In general, based on their origin, attacks can be broadly classified into *internal* and *external*. External attacks are launched by nodes that are not part of the network, while internal attacks are originated by malicious or compromised nodes that are within the network. In comparison with external attacks, it is difficult to defend against internal attacks. Attacks can also be classified as either *passive* or *active* depending on their nature. In this chapter, we concentrate on security systems that have been proposed to defend against routing layer specific active attacks. However, for completeness, we briefly discuss the scope of passive attacks and the security solutions proposed to defend against them.

2.2.1. *Passive Attacks and Anonymous Routing*

In Ref. 4, Kong *et al.* demonstrate the effect of passive attacks performed by both external and internal adversaries. External adversaries can launch passive attacks even in the presence of end-to-end encryption since the routing headers have to remain plain for routing purposes. They passively analyze the flow timings when group encryption is employed. However, such restrictions do not hold for internal attackers and group encryption only levies an additional overhead. Passive eavesdropping allows an adversary to trace the motion pattern and the location of monitored nodes. In addition, it also allows an adversary to analyze multiple routes and partially visualize the dynamic topology of a network. Further, when adversaries collude, they can effectively understand (a) where the monitored nodes are heading to and at what rate they are moving, (b) how many nodes are stationary relative to them and list of their neighbors, (c) the rate at which they communicate with destination through their neighbors, (d) to which destinations they target the communications, (e) how far destinations are positioned from adversaries and monitored nodes, and (f) what types of monitored communications are being used. The situation worsens if adversaries can integrate geographical information into their analyses. Note that such analyses are critical especially if MANETs are deployed for defense related applications.

Passive attacks are traditionally mitigated by anonymous communications. However, security systems deploying anonymous communications rely on well-established cryptographic and robust key management mechanisms, and demand one-time valid routing information to defend against traffic analysis. In general, most of the solutions that have been proposed for MANETs are inspired by

Chaum's *mix-net technique* [5, 6] or public-key based protocols. In mix-net, the traffic from a source to a destination is passed through one or more *mixes*. Unlike traditional routers, a mix reorders and re-encrypts incoming packets to separate the relation between incoming and outgoing packets. In Ref. 7, Jiang *et al.* extended the concept of mixes to MANETs, while an *Anonymous On Demand Routing (ANODR)* protocol [8] assigns pseudonyms using mixes to conceal the identities of communicating nodes. In Ref. 9, Shokri *et al.* established a framework such that nodes in a path are virtually bound to their immediate neighbors like a chain. Hence, they are not required to know any other information about the source, destination and other parts of the chain. They have deployed an on-demand routing protocol known as *Chain-based Anonymous Routing (CAR)* over an established framework to discover untraceable routes. However, the computational overhead levied by CAR makes it impractical for MANETs. The *Anonymous Secure Routing (ASR)* protocol [10] is similar to the *Dynamic Source Routing (DSR)* protocol [11], except that ASR neither contains source nor destination address. In addition, intermediary nodes do not append their identities to messages; however, they retain the state information of messages in order to respond to them later. Pairing-based key agreements [12] have been employed in Ref. 13 for an anonymous neighborhood authentication protocol allowing neighbors to authenticate one another without revealing their identities. Secret keys and pseudonyms that are established during the neighborhood authentication protocol are then used to perform anonymous on-demand routing known as MASK. In Ref. 14, Seys and Preneel have proposed an *Anonymous Routing Protocol for Mobile Ad hoc Networks (ARM)*, which provides higher efficiency than ANODR and ASR, and addresses the drawbacks of MASK (i.e., the tight synchronization of keys and pseudonyms between neighboring nodes) using random padding and time-to-live values.

2.2.2. *Active Attacks*

We classify active attacks into three broad categories: modification, fabrication and interruption of routing packets.

- *Modification*: An adversary alters the contents of routing messages and injects them back into the network to disrupt either the routing or data flow phase (e.g., injecting a route request packet with maliciously increased sequence number).
- *Fabrication*: An adversary originates routing messages that contain the identities of other nodes and injects them into the network to disrupt the routing phase (e.g., injecting spoofed packets).
- *Interruption*: An adversary interrupts the routing or network management without altering or originating spoofed routing or data messages (e.g., packet dropping).

Depending on the objective of an adversary, active attacks can also be alternatively classified as follows, and it usually tends to be a combination of modification, fabrication or interruption attacks. We refer to mobile nodes that perform active attacks as *malicious nodes* and collectively active attacks as *misbehaviors.*

- In a *routing loop attack*, an adversary modifies route discovery messages so that intermediate nodes can be driven to dissipate valuable battery resources by forwarding the modified routing messages along a loop.
- Adversaries may also alter routing messages to attract all the packets in order to drop those packets. Otherwise, they may selectively drop packets to conceal themselves from being identified. The former is known as a *blackhole attack*, while the later is known as a *grayhole attack.*
- *A spoofing attack*, one of the most malicious attacks, permits a node to become an authorized entity in network and allows it to take advantage of authorized services.
- *A detour attack* routes packets along a suboptimal path to make sure that one set of nodes are never reached. In a *gratuitous attack* (a variation of a detour attack), an adversary modifies the routing header to lengthen the route so that the lengthened route is not chosen for data flow. Such attacks allow an adversary to flee from forwarding packets for other nodes.
- In hop-count based on-demand routing protocols such as the Ad hoc On-Demand Vector Routing Protocol (AODV) [15], an adversary can suppress the propagation of valid route requests by quickly propagating a route request whose hop-count has not been incremented. Since the adversary rushes the modified route request ahead of valid route requests by not incrementing the hop count, it is known as a *rushing attack.*
- In the absence of authentication, an adversary can corrupt another node's legitimate information by performing a *blackmail attack.*
- *A wormhole attack* refer to tunneling attacks in which an adversary tunnels routing messages to another adversary positioned at the other end of network. The latter then disseminates received routing messages (which has shorter routes or reduced hop count) to corrupt the routing table of its downstream neighbors and there by prevent those neighbors from discovering valid routes.
- *A route salvaging attack* allows an adversary to invoke falsified route salvations and hence to disrupt the network functioning.
- Similarly, a *falsified route error generation attack* causes a source node to re-initiate route discovery by generating route errors that falsely report valid links as broken links. A *valid route error suppression attack* is a variation of an earlier attack, where valid route errors are suppressed from reaching a source node given a link along the route is actually broken.

- *A flooding attack* causes intermediate nodes to burn their battery resources by driving them to forward flooded packets. In some cases, it also blows out the routing table as a result of overflow.
- *Packet dropping* is similar to blackhole and grayhole attacks, except the adversary does not modify routing headers to attract packets.

Apart from malicious nodes, there is another type of adversary known as *selfish nodes* in a MANET which result from the heterogeneity in battery, computational, and storage resources. Selfish nodes that are powered with low power resources attempt to save their resources by not forwarding packets on the behalf of other nodes (i.e., drop the packets of other nodes), while selfish nodes that are powered with high power resources aim to hijack the wireless medium by boycotting the Medium Access Control (MAC-LL) protocol's contention resolution mechanism. A second type of selfish nodes maximizes the network utility by propagating only self-generated packets. Although selfish nodes differ from malicious nodes in terms of their objective, the effect is synonymous with the behavior of malicious nodes.

2.2.3. *Security Concepts*

Similar to traditional wired networks, a MANET requires security services such as confidentiality, integrity, authentication, non-repudiation, availability, and authorization to defend against adversaries.

- *Confidentiality* ensures the privacy of information such that the information is delivered only to the intended recipient. This is generally achieved by employing symmetric and asymmetric key based cryptographic mechanisms.
- *Integrity* maintains the information intact and assures a recipient that the information is free from modification. Although symmetric and asymmetric key based cryptographic mechanisms can be employed, a one-way hash based cryptographic mechanism is preferred over other mechanisms.
- *Authentication* enables a node to verify the identity of the claimant and hence prevents an adversary from masquerading as a trusted mobile node.
- *Non-repudiation* ensures that a mobile node cannot deny a forwarded message in the future. Public-key based certificates are traditionally employed to render non-repudiation services.
- *Authorization policies* at the routing layer are not as comprehensive as at the application layer. For instance, they assist a source node in shortlisting intermediate nodes according to the sensitivity and type of communications. Trust management systems incorporate such policies to enhance routing decisions.
- *Availability* assures that network services are available to mobile nodes even in the case of (a) faulty mobile nodes, (b) limitations of the MANET, and (c)

adversaries. Trust management systems measure the trustworthiness of nodes based on their behavioral pattern and hence efficiently route around nodes that disrupt the availability of network service.

3. Prevention Systems

3.1. *Secure Routing Systems*

Given that routing protocols [16] do not (a) authenticate intermediate nodes, (b) verify routing messages, and (c) protect data transmissions, the routing layer opens the door to a wide range of passive and active attacks. Secure routing protocols [17–29] step in to defend against active attacks that correspond to modification and fabrication of routing messages. They heavily rely on robust key management so that they can (a) utilize the secret associations established between mobile nodes to define appropriate protocol steps, and (b) thereby employ suitable cryptographic mechanisms to authenticate intermediate nodes and/or verify the integrity of routing messages. Therefore, secure routing protocols are able to assist mobile nodes in discovering secure paths and hence to protect data transmissions by employing end-to-end encryption using those established secret associations. In the following, we detail a few well-known secure routing protocols for completeness.

3.1.1. *ARAN: Authenticated Routing for Ad Hoc Networks*

In ARAN [24], certificates are used to bind a node's Internet Protocol (IP) address to its public key. The source node provides authenticity and freshness to the route request by signing (a) the IP address of the destination, (b) the nonce, and (c) the timestamp. At every hop, intermediate nodes wrap their signature over the signature provided by the source node before re-broadcasting the route request. Hence, intermediate nodes accept a route request only after verifying their previous hop's signature and then verifying the authenticity and freshness of the route request using the signature provided by the source node. For example, in Fig. 1 node C broadcasts the route request received from its previous hop B only after verifying the authenticity of B, and then the authenticity and freshness of the route request using the signature provided by *Src*. An exception to this rule is the intermediate node that is next to the source which verifies only the authenticity and freshness of the route request.

The same procedure is carried out in reverse for route reply, except that the route request is a broadcast and the route reply is a unicast. The main drawback in ARAN is that it fails to address how a CA is deployed in a self-organized MANET. ARAN also bypasses addressing the establishment, refreshment and revocation of certificates.

Route request phase:

$$Src \rightarrow *: \{(RREQ, Dest, Cert_{Src}, Nonce, Timestamp)_{K^-_{Src}}\},$$

$$NodeA \rightarrow *: \{((RREQ, Dest, Cert_{Src}, Nonce, Timestamp)_{K^-_{Src}})_{K^-_{NodeA}}, Cert_{NodeA}\},$$

$$NodeB \rightarrow *: \{((RREQ, Dest, Cert_{Src}, Nonce, Timestamp)_{K^-_{Src}})_{K^-_{NodeB}}, Cert_{NodeB}\},$$

$$NodeC \rightarrow *: \{((RREQ, Dest, Cert_{Src}, Nonce, Timestamp)_{K^-_{Src}})_{K^-_{NodeC}}, Cert_{NodeC}\}.$$

Route reply phase:

$$Dest \rightarrow NodeC: \{(RREP, Src, Cert_{Dest}, Nonce, Timestamp)_{K^-_{Dest}}\},$$

$$NodeC \rightarrow NodeB: \{((RREP, Src, Cert_{Dest}, Nonce, Timestamp)_{K^-_{Dest}})_{K^-_{NodeC}}, Cert_{NodeC}\},$$

$$NodeB \rightarrow NodeA: \{((RREP, Src, Cert_{Dest}, Nonce, Timestamp)_{K^-_{Dest}})_{K^-_{NodeB}}, Cert_{NodeB}\},$$

$$NodeA \rightarrow Src: \{((RREP, Src, Cert_{Dest}, Nonce, Timestamp)_{K^-_{Dest}})_{K^-_{NodeA}}, Cert_{NodeA}\}.$$

Fig. 1. Secure route discovery from *Src* to *Dest* using ARAN.

3.1.2. *SAODV: Secure Ad-Hoc On-Demand Distance Vector*

SAODV [27–29] achieves authentication, integrity, confidentiality and non-repudiation using public-key based certificates. Hence, source and destination mobile nodes are able to verify and authenticate each other by signing the mutable fields of route request and route reply, respectively. The signature also contains the seed of the one-way hash-chain in order to prevent the modification of hop count. At every hop, intermediate nodes increase the hop count by hashing the previous value of the hash-chain, and hence, the one-way nature of the hash-chain prevents intermediate nodes from reducing the hop count. For instance, if the hash-chain values $h_0, h_1, \ldots, h_i, \ldots, h_N$ are generated such that $h_i = H[h_{i+1}]$, then the hop-count authenticator h_i corresponds to a hop count of $N - i$, and this can be verified using the values (a) hash-chain anchor h_0 and (b) length N that is embedded in the signature. Let us consider the route request phase in Fig. 2. Node B verifies the hop count using the hash-chain authenticator h_{N-2}, anchor h_0, and length N because $h_0 = H_{N-2}[h_{N-2}]$.

SAODV struggles to address the issues related to public-key based certificates. It is also prone to *same distance fraud*, where a forwarding node fails to increment the hop count in order to make the route appear shorter in length. Also, it is vulnerable to malicious incrementing of the hop count, which may be carried out by selfish nodes to discourage the route from being chosen for data flow.

Route request phase:

$$
\begin{aligned}
&Src \rightarrow *: && \{(RREQ, RouteId, Src, Seq_{Src}, Dest, OldSeq_{Dest}, h_0, N)_{K_{Src}^-}, 0, h_N\},\\
&NodeA \rightarrow *: && \{(RREQ, RouteId, Src, Seq_{Src}, Dest, OldSeq_{Dest}, h_0, N)_{K_{Src}^-}, 1, h_{N-1}\},\\
&NodeB \rightarrow *: && \{(RREQ, RouteId, Src, Seq_{Src}, Dest, OldSeq_{Dest}, h_0, N)_{K_{Src}^-}, 2, h_{N-2}\},\\
&NodeC \rightarrow *: && \{(RREQ, RouteId, Src, Seq_{Src}, Dest, OldSeq_{Dest}, h_0, N)_{K_{Src}^-}, 3, h_{N-3}\}.
\end{aligned}
$$

Route reply phase:

$$
\begin{aligned}
&Dest \rightarrow NodeC: && \{(RREP, Dest, Seq_{Dest}, Src, lifetime, h'_0, N)_{K_{Dest}^-}, 0, h'_N\},\\
&NodeC \rightarrow NodeB: && \{(RREP, Dest, Seq_{Dest}, Src, lifetime, h'_0, N)_{K_{Dest}^-}, 1, h'_{N-1}\},\\
&NodeB \rightarrow NodeA: && \{(RREP, Dest, Seq_{Dest}, Src, lifetime, h'_0, N)_{K_{Dest}^-}, 2, h'_{N-2}\},\\
&NodeA \rightarrow Src: && \{(RREP, Dest, Seq_{Dest}, Src, lifetime, h'_0, N)_{K_{Dest}^-}, 3, h'_{N-3}\}.
\end{aligned}
$$

Fig. 2. Secure route discovery from *Src* to *Dest* using SAODV.

3.1.3. *Ariadne*

Ariadne [20] secures DSR by employing a broadcast based authentication mechanism known as TESLA [30], which relies on loosely synchronized clocks and delayed key disclosures. TESLA allows intermediate nodes to authenticate other intermediate nodes that are enlisted in the route. Ariadne calculates *Message Authentication Code (MAC)* against the identities of the source and destination nodes, and the route request's sequence number using the secret key shared between source and destination nodes. MAC defends against the modification of routing messages.

Route requests are broadcast by source nodes with an expected time of arrival to destinations and subsequently intermediate nodes authenticate the nodes that are listed in the route using their valid TESLA key. Intermediate nodes drop a route request only if they have either seen the route request in the past or failed to confirm the validity of a TESLA key. Otherwise, they append themselves to the route and add the MAC value of the header to the MAC list in the route request. In addition, they also replace the previous hash value (i.e., $h_i = H[ID_i, h_{i-1}]$) with the hash value generated from their identity. The hash value and MAC list prevent intermediate nodes from altering the route. As shown in Fig. 3, destination D accepts a route request only after verifying the hash value $h_i = H[ID_i, H[ID_{i-1}, H[ID_{i-2}, \ldots, H[h_0]\ldots]]]$, where h_0 is the MAC generated by the source. This process has been called as *per-hop hashing* since no single intermediate node is omitted from the route request. Optionally, the destination may also wait for intermediate nodes to release their TESLA keys before responding back with a route reply. The route reply along with the MAC list is unicast through the reverse path to source.

Route request phase:

$$
\begin{aligned}
&Src \rightarrow * : \{RREQ, Src, Dest, Id, time, h_0, (\ ), (\ )\},\\
&\qquad h_0 = MAC_{K_{Src-Dest}}(RREQ, Src, Dest, Id, time);\\
&NodeA \rightarrow * : \{RREQ, Src, Dest, Id, time, h_1, (NodeA), (M_A)\},\\
&\qquad h_1 = H[NodeA, h_0],\\
&\qquad M_A = MAC_{K_{A_{time}}}(RREQ, Src, Dest, Id, time, h_1, (NodeA), (\ ));\\
&NodeB \rightarrow * : \left\{\begin{matrix} RREQ, Src, Dest, Id, time, h_2, \\ (NodeA, NodeB), (M_A, M_B) \end{matrix}\right\},\\
&\qquad h_2 = H[NodeB, h_1],\\
&\qquad M_B = MAC_{K_{B_{time}}}\left(\begin{matrix} RREQ, Src, Dest, Id, time, h_2, \\ (NodeA, NodeB), (M_A) \end{matrix}\right);\\
&NodeC \rightarrow * : \left\{\begin{matrix} RREQ, Src, Dest, Id, time, h_3, \\ (NodeA, NodeB, NodeC), (M_A, M_B, M_C) \end{matrix}\right\},\\
&\qquad h_3 = H[NodeC, h_2],\\
&\qquad M_C = MAC_{K_{C_{time}}}\left(\begin{matrix} RREQ, Src, Dest, Id, time, h_3, \\ (NodeA, NodeB, NodeC), (M_A, M_B) \end{matrix}\right).
\end{aligned}
$$

Route reply phase:

$$
\begin{aligned}
&Dest \rightarrow NodeC : \left\{\begin{matrix} RREP, Dest, Src, time, (NodeA, NodeB, NodeC), \\ (M_A, M_B, M_C), M_D, (\ ) \end{matrix}\right\},\\
&\qquad M_D = MAC_{K_{Dest-Src_{time}}}\left(\begin{matrix} RREP, Dest, Src, time, \\ (NodeA, NodeB, NodeC), (M_A, M_B, M_C) \end{matrix}\right);\\
&NodeC \rightarrow NodeB : \left\{\begin{matrix} RREP, Dest, Src, time, (NodeA, NodeB, NodeC), \\ (M_A, M_B, M_C), M_D, (K_{C_{time}}) \end{matrix}\right\};\\
&NodeB \rightarrow NodeA : \left\{\begin{matrix} RREP, Dest, Src, time, (NodeA, NodeB, NodeC), \\ (M_A, M_B, M_C), M_D, (K_{C_{time}}, K_{B_{time}}) \end{matrix}\right\};\\
&NodeA \rightarrow Src : \left\{\begin{matrix} RREP, Dest, Src, time, (NodeA, NodeB, NodeC), \\ (M_A, M_B, M_C), M_D, (K_{C_{time}}, K_{B_{time}}, K_{A_{time}}) \end{matrix}\right\}.
\end{aligned}
$$

Fig. 3. Secure route discovery from *Src* to *Dest* using Ariadne.

The authors of Ariadne claim that TESLA remains secure irrespective of the end-to-end delay. However, the delay parameter and assumption in TESLA that a node should be able to determine which keys a sender might have already published impacts the network performance. Further, it has been shown that solutions based on loosely synchronized clocks, which require re-synchronization to avoid clock drifts are prone to a special type of denial of service (DoS) attack known as a *desynchronization attack* [31].

The authors have also proposed a solution known as *packet leashes* [19] to defend against wormhole attacks by using a similar technique.

Route request phase:

$$Src \rightarrow * : \{RREQ, Q_{Dest_{Seq}}, Q_{ID}, Src, Dest, (\,), M_{Src}\},$$
$$M_{Src} = HMAC_{K_{Src-Dest}}(RREQ, Q_{Dest_{Seq}}, Q_{ID}, Src, Dest, (\,));$$
$$NodeA \rightarrow * : \{RREQ, Q_{Dest_{Seq}}, Q_{ID}, Src, Dest, (A), M_{Src}\};$$
$$NodeB \rightarrow * : \{RREQ, Q_{Dest_{Seq}}, Q_{ID}, Src, Dest, (A, B), M_{Src}\};$$
$$NodeC \rightarrow * : \{RREQ, Q_{Dest_{Seq}}, Q_{ID}, Src, Dest, (A, B, C), M_{Src}\}.$$

Route reply phase:

$$Dest \rightarrow NodeC : \{RREP, Q_{Dest_{Seq}}, Q_{ID}, Dest, Src, (A, B, C), M_{Dest}\},$$
$$M_{Dest} = HMAC_{K_{Src-Dest}}(RREP, Q_{Dest_{Seq}}, Q_{ID}, Dest, Src, (A, B, C));$$
$$NodeC \rightarrow NodeB : \{RREP, Q_{Dest_{Seq}}, Q_{ID}, Dest, Src, (A, B, C), M_{Dest}\};$$
$$NodeB \rightarrow NodeA : \{RREP, Q_{Dest_{Seq}}, Q_{ID}, Dest, Src, (A, B, C), M_{Dest}\};$$
$$NodeA \rightarrow Src : \{RREP, Q_{Dest_{Seq}}, Q_{ID}, Dest, Src, (A, B, C), M_{Dest}\}.$$

Fig. 4. Secure route discovery from *Src* to *Dest* using SRP.

3.1.4. *SRP: Secure Routing Protocol*

SRP [23] delivers a secure path from source to destination based on the assumption that source and destination have a secure association prior to deployment. Unlike other secure routing protocols, SRP does not levy heavy computations at intermediate nodes. As shown in Fig. 4, the source node maintains a pair of identifiers for each route request: (a) a query sequence number, and (b) a random query identifier. The message authentication code (HMAC) computed against the source, destination and two query identifiers using the secure association is then utilized to verify the integrity and authenticity of the route request. The query sequence number ensures the freshness of the route request and the random query identifier assists the intermediate nodes in identifying already forwarded queries. If the route request is valid, the destination then responds with a route reply in a similar manner.

3.1.5. *BISS: Building Secure Routing out of an Incomplete Set of Security Association*

BISS [17] extends Ariadne to networks where there is an incomplete set of security associations by using the certificates obtained from an offline authority. The rate of convergence depends on various factors such as node density, mobility, and connectivity.

As shown in Fig. 5, BISS facilitates a source node in establishing a secure association with any destination using the source node's certificate, provided there is a secure association between every intermediate node and destination. Destination and intermediate nodes utilize the certificate appended by the source node to

Roqte request phase (nodes A, B and C have secret association with Dest):

$$Src \rightarrow * : \{RREQ, Src, Dest, Id, (\ ), (\sigma_{Src}), (Cert_{Src})\},$$
$$\sigma_{Src} = (RREQ, Src, Dest, Id, (\ ))_{K_{Src-private}};$$
$$NodeA \rightarrow * : \{RREQ, Src, Dest, Id, (A), (\sigma_{Src}, M_A), (Cert_{Src})\},$$
$$M_A = MAC_{K_{NodeA-Dest}}(RREQ, Src, Dest, Id, (A));$$
$$NodeB \rightarrow * : \{RREQ, Src, Dest, Id, (A, B), (\sigma_{Src}, M_A, M_B), (Cert_{Src})\},$$
$$M_B = MAC_{K_{NodeB-Dest}}(RREQ, Src, Dest, Id, (A, B));$$
$$NodeC \rightarrow * : \{RREQ, Src, Dest, Id, (A, B, C), (\sigma_{Src}, M_A, M_B, M_C), (Cert_{Src})\},$$
$$M_C = MAC_{K_{NodeC-Dest}}(RREQ, Src, Dest, Id, (A, B, C)).$$

Roqte reply phase (node B has a secret association with Src):

$$Dest \rightarrow NodeC : \{RREP, Src, Dest, Id, (A, B, C), (\sigma'_{Dest}), (Cert_{Dest})\}$$
$$\sigma'_{Dest} = (RREP, Src, Dest, Id, (A, B, C))_{K_{Dest-private}};$$
$$NodeC \rightarrow NodeB : \{RREP, Src, Dest, Id, (A, B, C), (\sigma'_{Dest}, \sigma'_C), (Cert_{Dest}, Cert_C)\},$$
$$\sigma'_C = (RREP, Src, Dest, Id, (A, B, C))_{K_{C-private}};$$
$$NodeB \rightarrow NodeA : \{RREP, Src, Dest, Id, (A, B, C), (\sigma'_{Dest}, \sigma'_C, M'_B), (Cert_{Dest}, Cert_C)\},$$
$$M'_C = MAC_{K_{NodeB-Src}}(RREP, Src, Dest, Id, (A, B, C));$$
$$NodeA \rightarrow Src : \{RREP, Src, Dest, Id, (A, B, C), (\sigma'_{Dest}, \sigma'_C, M'_B, \sigma'_A), (Cert_{Dest}, Cert_C, Cert_A)\},$$
$$\sigma'_A = (RREP, Src, Dest, Id, (A, B, C))_{K_{A-private}}.$$

Fig. 5. Secure route discovery from *Src* to *Dest* using BISS.

authenticate the route request. In addition, the destination authenticates the intermediate nodes using the secret associations established with them in the past. On successful authentication of source and intermediate nodes, the destination responds with a signature-protected route reply. In addition, the intermediate nodes that do not have secure associations with the source append their certificates to the route reply. The source node authenticates the destination and intermediate nodes using the integrity fields provided in the route reply. Although BISS increases the security associations, it also increases the overall network overhead.

3.2. *Key Management Systems*

From our discussions it is evident that secure routing protocols are heavily reliant on the secret associations established between mobile nodes so that they can bootstrap protected network services. Hence, a robust key management service is required to establish secret associations between nodes such that the service is — (a) established on the fly without exposing the keying material to unauthorized nodes or compromised nodes, (b) capable of performing key refreshment and revocation dynamically, and (c) able to scale well with varying network sizes and densities. It is noted that the self-organized feature of MANETs opposes CA based key management service. Alternatively, the need for one-to-many verification of broadcast routing messages discourages pair-wise keys so that a unique signature for each receiver can be avoided. Therefore, we confine ourselves to solutions that are based on public-key systems.

3.2.1. *Partially Distributed Public Key System*

Zhou and Hass [32] distribute the private key of CA only to a set of nodes known as *server nodes*, but they publish the public key of CA to all nodes in network. Server nodes are capable of generating partial certificates using their own share of CA's private key, and k such partial certificates can generate a valid certificate based on *threshold cryptography.* One of the server nodes combines these partial certificates to generate the certificate and is hence known as a *combiner.* Server nodes possess their own separate public/private key pair and are assumed to know the public key of other servers so that they can communicate the shares of CA's private key among themselves. Also, server nodes are responsible for refreshing the shares and storing the certificate of all nodes.

A mobile node possesses a valid certificate when it joins the network and this certificate is valid only for a certain period of time. Once the certificate expires, the mobile node has to renew its certificate by obtaining shares from k servers and then submitting them to a combiner. The combiner, after joining the partial certificates, checks the validity of generated certificate in order to avoid the inclusion of an invalid partial signature generated by any compromised server. Since k shares of CA's private key are used to generate the certificate, threshold cryptography can tolerate up to $k - 1$ compromised servers.

Yi and Kravets [33] extended the above proposal by delegating the role of certificate construction to mobile nodes and specifying a certification protocol for retrieving the shares of CA's private key from server nodes which are known as the *MObile Certificate Authority* (MOCA). Hence, they eliminate the need for combiner nodes in the network. Similar to DSR, the certification protocol involves a broadcast which is initiated by a mobile node, and known as *certification request (CREQ). Certification reply (CREP)* is the corresponding message generated by MOCAs. A mobile node unicasts *β-specific* MOCAs based on cached routing in order to reduce the flooding of CREQ. The value of β is chosen as $\beta = (k + \alpha)$ such that the probability of receiving at least k responses is increased. If a mobile node fails to collect enough shares, then it resorts to default flooding. SEKM [34] forms a multicast group using MOCAs, in which a mobile node forwards CREQ to a MOCA, and the MOCA in turn forwards CREQ to additional $k + \alpha$ MOCAs. However, SEKM fails to state how a MOCA is aware that it is the first server to receive the CREQ.

The major issue in distributed CA based solutions is the difficulty in achieving synchronization among distributed CAs. Although the strength of threshold cryptography (n, k) rests on the choice of k, it is unclear how to choose the parameter (n, k) because it is a trade-off between the security and availability of distributed CAs. Generic factors that can be considered in choosing (n, k) include bandwidth, mobility, node density, nature of wireless connectivity, and physical security of the nodes.

3.2.2. *Completely Distributed Public-Key System*

Luo *et al.* [35] and Kong *et al.* [36] extend the capability of server nodes to all mobile nodes. Thus, the private key of CA is shared among all mobile nodes and a valid signature is generated by combining k such shares based on threshold cryptography. Authors limit share requests to one-hop nodes, and in parallel enforce mobile nodes to monitor the behavior of their neighbors so that those mobile nodes can decide whether to provide a share or not to their neighbors. Although the proposed design saves bandwidth and accommodates scalability, it is unrealistic to assume that each mobile node has k neighbors in order to renew a certificate. Likewise, solutions based on distributed CAs also suffer from the above-mentioned issues.

3.2.3. *Identity Based Public-Key System*

In identity based public-key systems, the *identity* serves as the *public key* to remove the necessity for certificates, and to eliminate overhead and scalability. Identity based cryptography consists of a *private-key generator* (PKG) to generate the private-key signatures corresponding to the user identities, i.e., the public keys. A detailed description of identity based cryptography can be found in Ref. 37. In Ref. 38, Khalili *et al.* divide the PKG of identity based cryptography into k thresholds based on the concept of threshold cryptography. Hence, a mobile node can construct a private key for its identity from the PKG by collecting k shares from PKG nodes. However, the proposal fails to demonstrate how identity based cryptography can work with threshold cryptography, and also struggles to address how to update the PKG and the issues specific to public-key systems.

3.2.4. *Transitive Chain Based Public-Key System*

In Ref. 39, Capkun *et al.* suggest an approach similar to *Pretty Good Privacy* (PGP) [40]. Mobile nodes generate their own public/private key pairs and issue certificates to trustworthy nodes as in PGP. However, they store certificates rather than publishing the certificates in a centralized repository. When two mobile nodes wish to validate each other's certificate, they merge their local certificate repositories to find a legitimate certificate chain. Therefore, the strength of this proposal rests on the construction of local repositories. In Ref. 39, the authors propose various algorithms to construct local repositories and to analyze the performance of their proposed algorithms. In the *maximum degree algorithm*, the certificates contained in the local repository of each node lead to directed and mutually disjoint paths such that each path consists of nodes that have the highest number of disjoint paths of certificates. In the *shortcut hunter algorithm*, certificates that have a short chain to other nodes are stored in local repositories. Although this proposal addresses simple certification revocation and renewal, it is unclear how synchronization is achieved among mobile nodes. The main advantage of the approach is that it suits the self-organized characteristics of MANETs by not assuming the existence of an offline CA for bootstrapping. Nevertheless, the approach is only probabilistic and not deterministic, and only as strong as its weakest link. If any one of the mobile nodes is compromised in the chain then it leads to false authentication. Otherwise, the chain itself is open to the issues of trust transitivity, where there is no requirement for a mobile to trust a recommended node in the same manner it trusts the recommender. Researchers have also shown how mobility can be taken advantage of establish secret associations [41].

4. Thoughts for Practitioners

Although public key based systems eliminate the limitations of CA, they struggle to address key refreshment and revocation, and certificate synchronization. This needs to be addressed in MANETs since nodes are prone to physical capture and compromise. Perhaps the difficulty arises due to broken links and sporadic connections induced by dynamically changing topology, and also the autonomous structure of the network whereby nodes are allowed to enter and leave the network at will. Hence, any vulnerability in the key management service can permit adversaries to reduce the strength of secure routing protocols. Further, key management and secure routing systems are incapable of defending against adversaries that disrupt either key refreshment or revocation through the execution of packet dropping or flooding attacks. Similarities can be observed in key management and secure routing systems when a genuine link is reported as a broken link. Since secure routing protocols are only designed to prevent against predefined attacks and assume that all available nodes carry out routing and network management, they overlook the correct execution of critical network functions such as packet forwarding. For this reason, secure routing protocols also fail to enforce cooperation among nodes. Hence, they allow a separate category of adversary known as selfish nodes to maximize their utility in resource constrained MANETs.

Incentive based systems [42–46] have been proposed to stimulate cooperation among nodes. In Ref. 42, virtual currencies known as Nuglets are used to stimulate cooperation among nodes in two ways: (a) the packet purse model (PPM) in which a packet's source is charged and (b) the packet trade model (PTM) in which packet's destination is charged. The proposal assumes tamper-resistant hardware at each node to assure a fair use of Nuglets. In PPM, the source node propagates a packet with sufficient Nuglets so that intermediate nodes can debit Nuglets from the packet for forwarding it. However, if the packet runs out of Nuglets then it is dropped. The key advantage of this approach is that it forces the source node to pay for each propagated packet thereby defending against illegitimate transmissions. The main drawback is the need for the source node to predetermine the count of Nuglets. In PTM, each intermediate node buys the packet and sells it to the next hop. If the receiving node could not sell a packet, it tries for another node; otherwise, it drops the packet. The main advantage is that there is no need for the source node to predict the required count of Nuglets before transmission, but on the other hand the approach fails to prevent the network from being overloaded. Sprite [45] eliminates the use of tamper-resistant hardware by providing incentives to stimulate cooperation among selfish nodes. However, the proposed approach relies on the presence of a CA known as a *credit clearance service* (CCS) in order to charge mobile nodes that generate packets and credit intermediate nodes that produce receipts for forwarding those packets. Hence, they discourage the destination from paying for the propagation of the packet so that DoS attacks can be defended and the collusion of the source with intermediate nodes can be discouraged. In general, incentive-based systems assume nodes to be economically rational, and consider tamper-proof hardware or trusted third parties (TTP) to make incentives unforgeable. Further, incentive based systems struggle to address the issue of pricing [47], and other related issues such as how to deal with deprivation of incentives. They express poor insight with respect to boundary nodes, especially when boundary nodes are willing to cooperate with other nodes to earn incentives but are unable to do so due to lack of opportunities. In addition, most of the incentive based systems limit themselves only to selfish nodes that attempt to retain battery resources by not forwarding packets for other nodes. They fail to defend against malicious nodes that disrupt the transmissions of other nodes through the execution of packet dropping or flooding attacks.

5. Trust Management Systems

The history of security has shown that a completely intrusion-free system is infeasible [26] no matter how carefully the prevention mechanism is designed. The main reason for the shortcomings of secure routing and incentive based systems is that they fail to measure the trustworthiness of nodes based on the dynamically changing behaviors of those nodes. Hence, it is necessary for secure routing and incentive based systems to react to those dynamically changing behaviors accordingly. These considerations have encouraged a defense-in-depth strategy in MANETs and eventually led to the growth of *trust management systems* [48–82], which are synonymously referred to as *detection reaction* and *reputation systems* in the literature. Since trust management systems proactively detect and reactively isolate (select) malicious (benign) nodes, these systems are also known as *self-policing systems* [56, 75]. Although these systems lack consensus on the definition of *trust* at a more fundamental level, they adhere to all or some of the following steps. First, these systems tend to collect evidence for the behaviors of other nodes through passive monitoring, acknowledgments, or intrusion detection systems (IDS) [83, 84].

They may also consider evidence from other nodes and define suitable approaches for evidence distribution. Such evidence is often regarded as recommendations. Second, trust management systems subjectively evaluate and rate the evidence, and then utilize those ratings to predict the future behavior of other nodes. Finally, they make decisions based on the (a) policies defined for contexts, and (b) behavior anticipated for those nodes involved in the context. In the following subsections, we investigate the concepts of *trust* and *reputation*, and the methodology adopted in trust management systems from the perspective of distributed computing. These allow us to establish the groundwork for our analysis and present the significance of trust management systems in MANETs.

5.1. *Overview*

Trust management and trustworthy computing are becoming increasingly significant in a distributed environment as they assist in making sensible interactions with unknown parties by providing a basis for more detailed and automated decisions [85]. The concepts of *trust* and *reputation* are closely related in trust management systems [86] and they are firmly rooted in sociology and psychology. Although there is no universal definition for these concepts due to their rich connections to different disciplines, we confine ourselves to their meaning within the computing discipline.

In traditional trust management systems, trust enables a trustor to reduce uncertainty in the trustor's future interactions with a trustee, who is beyond the control of the trustor but whose actions are of interest to the trustor and affect the state of trustor. In other words, trust is a subjective probability which enables the trustor to make a binary decision by balancing between known risks and the opinion held about the trustee. Only known risks are considered for making decisions since it is difficult to prove unknown risks, and the opinion presents trustor's relationship with the trustee based on the trustor's experiences. Other factors influencing the decision are time and context, where context accounts for the type of interaction between trustor and trustee, and the nature of application.

In reputation systems, reputation is defined as an opinion held by the trustor about the trustee depending on the trustor's past experiences with the trustee [86]. In other words, reputation represents the trustor's direct relationship with the trustee. Similarly, the trustor's relationship with a second trustee based on its direct relationship with a first trustee and the first trustee's direct relationship with the second trustee is known as an indirect relationship. These relationships are established by enabling nodes to share their opinions in the network.

Although trust and reputation are used interchangeably in MANETs, we define them as follows since they complement each other as inferred above. Hence, trust can be defined as the prediction of a node's future actions in a context such as forwarding routing messages without modification, while reputation then becomes the opinion held about the node based on the node's past actions and the one that influences the prediction [68]. For this reason, we consider the trust definition in Ref. 87 to be more appropriate and timely: "Trust is the firm belief in the competence of an entity to act as expected such that this firm belief is not a fixed value associated with the entity but rather subject to the entity's behavior (reputation held for the entity) and applies only within the context and at a given time."

Trust management systems are characterized by the following components: (a) an evidence manager to collect and classify evidence, (b) a mathematical model to formulate the evidence into opinions and then to apply them to predict the result of future interactions, and (c) a policy manager to define decision policies for making decisions. Traditional trust management systems were monotonic as they were only designed to authenticate users for granting access to services using digital certificates. Such a simple trust management system may be warranted in a closed organization with CA, but the same fails to hold in a distributed system where no hierarchical relationship exists between entities. Although policy systems [88, 89] later expanded significantly, the decisions were still based on the credentials presented by the user. In the meantime, the development of IDS to tackle the shortcomings of prevention systems has led researchers to consider IDS for contributing behavioral evidence to trust management systems [85]. The reason for merging IDS and trust management systems is that IDS is not sufficiently flexible to take full advantage of behavioral evidence and trust management systems struggle to adapt to peer-to-peer distributed networks. Accordingly, Lin and Varadharajan [90] refer to such behavioral evidence as *soft evidence* and the credentials used for authentication as *hard evidence*.

5.2. *Significance in MANETs*

After briefly discussing the concepts and methodologies in trust management systems, let us now consider the significance of trust management systems in MANETs. The majority of MANET-based trust management systems [48–56, 58, 59, 61–63, 66–73, 75–82] are decentralized and deployed at every node to make subjective decisions. Most of these systems consider only behavioral evidence, and collect them through passive monitoring, acknowledgments, or IDS [83, 84]. The behavioral evidence collected by passive monitoring is based on the assumption that this evidence is observable and classifiable. Alternatively, the feature to accommodate IDS to collect behavioral evidence facilitates trust management systems to handle new type of attacks in MANETs. This is in contrast to secure routing and incentive-based payment systems, where the protocol design has to be changed for every new type of attack. Further, a few trust management systems [48–54, 75] consider the evidence resulting from system failure as malicious behavior in order to realize a reliable and trustworthy MANET. Most of these systems [48–58, 61–64, 66–70, 72–77, 79–82] also exchange opinions as reputation ratings with other nodes in order to enhance their decisions, but they neither rely on higher authorities nor are they forced to reach consensus with other nodes. The reputation ratings that are disseminated to communicate opinions with other nodes are referred to as *recommendations* and they facilitate the establishment of indirect relationships.

MANET-based trust management systems employ various mathematical models such as graph theory based models [61], entropy based models [80], and Bayesian logic based models [55] to quantify evidence into opinion and represent the resulting opinion as a relationship between nodes. These systems execute simple decision policies such as (a) accepting or rejecting a newly discovered route, (b) sending or forwarding a packet on behalf of other nodes, (c) accepting or ignoring a recommendation from another node, (d) deleting or retaining those paths that contain misbehaving nodes, (e) abstaining or warning other nodes about misbehaving nodes, and (f) choosing which path for communication. A few systems [91, 92] attempt to model trust management systems based on human behavior; however, it is not certain whether such systems will meet requirements as humans do not seem to always make fully rational decisions regarding trust [93]. Several trust management systems [48–82] have been proposed for MANETs in recent years, and we choose a few recently proposed [69, 74, 77, 79–82] and some established systems [50–52, 54, 55, 70–72, 94] for analysis. In our analysis, we use the terms *opinion*, *reputation* and *relationship* interchangeably based on the hypothesis established in Sec. 3.1.

5.2.1. *Quantifying Trust in MANETs*

Virendra *et al.* [79] have proposed a trust model in which trust relationships are utilized to enable nodes to establish keys with other nodes. In their proposal, they eliminate assumptions such as (a) a centralized trusted authority to establish keys, and (b) nodes are non-malicious at the time of key establishment.

The decentralized trust model at every node adopts a five-phase approach to establish and maintain trust relationships with other nodes. The phases are: (a) initiate and monitor, (b) query and evaluate, (c) update, (d) restructure, and (e) re-establish. The model implements a metric to represent opinions or relationships in the range from 0 to 1, and further subdivides the range into three regions: bad, uncertain, and good, respectively. However, the model lacks sound mathematical proof for the chosen metric.

During the initiation and monitoring phase, a node fixes its relationship with other nodes to the median of the uncertain region. It promiscuously monitors the packet transmissions of neighbors to collect evidence of trustworthiness for the benign and malicious behaviors of those neighbors. Also, it abstains from sending sensitive data to neighbors until keys are established with them, for which its relationship with them has to be in the good region. The query and evaluation phase facilitates the node to collect recommendations from neighbors. However, recommendations are collected only from neighbors with whom the node has a good relationship. Also, recommendations are treated secondarily to the evidence collected from promiscuous monitoring. The update phase regularly evaluates a relationship depending on the incoming evidence through promiscuous monitoring and recommendations. As the relationship shifts towards the good region, the periodicity of evaluation is reduced. The restructure phase addresses the uncertainty that may creep into the relationship when neighbors move out of the node's transmission range, and when neighbors who had previously moved out are now back into the node's transmission range. When neighbors are out of range, the node exponentially decays its relationship to the floor of the region (bad, uncertain or good) to which the trust relationship belongs. Alternatively, the decayed relationship is resumed when neighbors come back into the node's vicinity. Finally, the re-establishment phase is an optional phase in which a malicious neighbor re-establishes a relationship with a node by exhibiting a linear benign behavior.

The node then utilizes its trust relationship to establish pair-wise and group keys, where keys are established with neighbors for whom the trust relationship is in the good region. Pair-wise keys are established with neighbors using a mechanism such as *duckling* [95]. In group key establishment, one of the nodes in the group invites all the other neighbors to form a cluster based on its trust relationship with those neighbors, such clusters are known as *physical logical trust domains (PLTD)*. The neighbors may accept the invitation to join the group or in turn invite the node to join their PLTD. The model also permits a node to participate in more than one PLTD.

The model's novelty rests on its scheme to employ behavioral and recommendation based trust relationships to establish pair-wise and group keys among nodes. However, it is unclear how the model defends against nodes that perform malicious attacks by spoofing packets with the identities of other nodes before the key establishment phase. Other drawbacks are the model's inability to handle recommendation issues such as honest-elicitation,[a] free-riding,[b] and recommender's bias. Finally, during the re-establishment phase, it is unclear how nodes select a malicious node for forwarding packets while trustworthy neighbors exist in neighborhood.

5.2.2. *Establishing and Propagating Trust in Pure Ad-Hoc Networks*

Pirzada and McDonald [71] have proposed a trust model to improve reliability in pure MANETs.[c] The model performs three tasks, namely *trust derivation*, *trust*

---

[a]A node is subject to honest-elicitation when it forwards a high recommendation for a malicious node in order to avoid itself from being labeled with a low recommendation by the malicious node. A malicious node may also exhibit honest-elicitation by forwarding high recommendations for colluding malicious nodes.

[b]A node is subject to free-riding when it accepts recommendations from other nodes, but fails to reciprocate with recommendations when requested by them.

[c]A network in which centralized authority is absent for managing network services and establishing secure associations.

quantification, and *trust computation*. Trust derivation is synonymous with the evidence manager mentioned in Sec. 5.1 and collects evidence for each type of packet (e.g., route request and route reply packets) in all the categories such as forwarding data packets, forwarding routing packets without modification, providing gratuitous route replies, and salvaging route errors. Here, the opinion is referred to as trust and measured in continuous values between −1 and +1. Similar to Ref. 79, the model fails to provide a sound mathematical proof for the chosen trust metric. Trust quantification formulates the opinion for each category by combining the trust metric held for different packet types within the category. To achieve this, the operation assigns a weight for each packet type, where the weight summarizes the factors *utility* and *importance*, suggested by Marsh in Ref. 96. The value for weight ranges from 0 (unimportant) to +1 (important). Here, utility refers to the cost and benefits associated with the context, and importance refers to the significance of context based on time. Finally, trust computation is responsible for computing the trustworthiness of a node by combining the trust quantified for each category. For this, the model adopts the same strategy of assigning weights to each category before combining them together.

Unlike the previous model [79], the system is composed of only the evidence manager and weak computational logic. It overlooks one of the trust management components, i.e., the decision manager, since it fails to take advantage of the trust relationships established between nodes. It is not clear how the accuracy of gratuitous route replies and salvaged route errors are verified, especially in a pure MANET where there is no pre-established relationship among nodes. This is because nodes can maliciously report a genuine link as a broken link and introduce tampered routes through gratuitous route replies and salvaged route errors. Similar to Ref. 79, Pirzada and McDonald also fail to demonstrate the strengths and limitations of their proposed models through simulation results.

However, Pirzada *et al.* enhanced their earlier trust model 71 in Ref. 70 to address the questions of the decision manager and recommendations. In their recent model, they incorporate their previous model as a trust agent in order to collect behavioral evidence and to subsequently compute the *direct trust* of a node. A reputation agent is responsible for sharing direct trust values with other nodes as recommendations, and the opinion derived from recommendations is known as *derived trust*. To achieve this, the recommendation is scaled with the direct trust held about the recommender. In order to keep fallacious recommendation requests and recommendations at bay, the authors suggest HashCash.[d] The combiner then combines direct and derived trusts from trust and reputation agents respectively to arrive at *aggregate trust*. Finally, trustworthy routes are chosen by assigning weights

[d]A CPU cost function that computes a proof-of-effort token using a cryptographic hash function. The requester tries different combinations of trial string to find a token, and then sends the token to the recommender, which can easily verify the token by performing a single hash operation.

to each link in the route based on the aggregate trust and then employing shortest path algorithm using the assigned weights.

Pirzada *et al.* further extended their current model in Ref. 72 to elaborate the dissemination of recommendations and demonstrated the effectiveness of their extended model through simulation results. In the extended model, mobile nodes disseminate recommendations by appending their direct trust of other nodes along with data packets. This successfully reduces the overhead that may otherwise occur as a result of forwarding separate packets to disseminate recommendations. Simulation results show that DSR coupled with their trust model performs 10% better than normal DSR.

Since the model excludes malicious nodes by resorting to only trustworthy routes, it is interesting to know how the model will include repenting malicious nodes in the future. Also, it is speculative whether a node appends the direct trust rating of *all nodes* or *few selected nodes* along with the data packet. Finally, the notion of disseminating recommendations opens the door to honest-elicitation, free-riding, and recommender's bias.

5.2.3. *Performance Analyses of the CONFIDANT Protocol*

Buchegger and Boudec have adopted a defense-in-depth strategy to enhance the strength of the prevention mechanism by proposing a trust management system known as *CONFIDANT* (Cooperation Of Nodes: Fairness In Dynamic Ad-hoc NeTworks) [50, 51]. Their trust model defends against attacks such as traffic deviation, route salvaging, unusual frequent route updates, silent route tampering, lack of error messages, and suppression of control or data packets. Their motivation derives from Richard Dawkins' book, *The Selfish Gene* [97], in which *suckers* and *cheaters* are demonstrated as losers, while *grudgers* are winners.

CONFIDANT collects evidence from direct experience and recommendations. Trust relationships are established based on the collected evidence and then used for trust decisions. These operations are achieved through four interdependent modules: (a) a monitor, (b) a reputation system, (c) a path manager, and (d) a trust manager. The monitor collects evidence by passively monitoring the transmission of neighbors after forwarding a packet to them. It then reports to the reputation system, which consists of a rating list and a blacklist, only if the collected evidence represents a malicious behavior. The reputation system changes the rating of a node if the evidence collected for a node's malicious behavior exceeds the pre-defined threshold value. It is important to note that the evidence collected from direct experience has more influence than the evidence collected from recommendations. Thereafter, the path manager makes a decision to delete the malicious node from the path. Also, path manager assists a node in making a decision such as whether to forward a received packet by cross-checking the upstream node's identity (previous hop) against the blacklist. The reputation system calls for a time-out operation to handle false accusations, fault rating and list blow-up. Finally, the trust manager takes the responsibility of forwarding and receiving recommendations to and from trustworthy nodes. Here, recommendations are known as ALARM messages and trustworthy nodes are referred to as *friends*. The ALARM messages received from friends are evaluated for trustworthiness before being sent to the reputation system. Trust decisions pertaining to the trust manager are: (a) providing and accepting routing information, (b) accepting a node as part of route, and (c) taking part in a route originated by some other node. The authors demonstrate the effectiveness of their model through extensive simulation results. Interestingly, CONFIDANT nodes drop around 100 packets in the presence of 90% malicious nodes, while DSR nodes drop 10,000 packets in the presence of 10% malicious nodes. Also, CONFIDANT nodes deliver 75% of data packets in the presence of 60% malicious nodes.

Similar to the models discussed earlier, a friend's ALARM message may not reflect the actual status since the friend may be biased. In order to address honest-elicitation, researchers have extended the model in Refs. 54 and 55 to accommodate recommendations that are in agreement with their opinions and accepted from friends whose trustworthiness is measured separately for forwarding honest recommendations. However, a disagreement would fail to consider recommendations that may report unusual behavior. Further, the model fails to handle free-riding behavior. The notion of refreshing the rating list and blacklist using timeouts are reconsidered in their later revision [52] to avoid the re-entry of malicious nodes.

5.2.4. *Information Theoretic Framework of Trust Modeling and Evaluation for Ad Hoc Networks*

Yan Lindsay *et al.* have developed a trust model for improving the security of MANET routing protocols in Ref. 80. Similar to related models, their proposed trust model establishes trust relationships using the evidence collected through monitoring and recommendations. Established trust relationships are then used to choose trustworthy routes and to isolate malicious nodes. The model differs from related models by laying axioms for measuring, propagating, and combining trust. This is due to the belief that it is hard to compare trust metrics from various trust models and also that the fundamental definition of trust is incomplete. Similar to Ref. 94, the authors define trust as uncertainty and measure uncertainty using entropy. The evidence collected for malicious and benign behaviors is then probabilistically mapped by following a modified Bayesian approach. All these allow the model to give low importance to past evidence and more importance to recent evidence. Finally, the probabilistic estimate of the Bayesian approach is mapped to entropy.

In the case of recommendations, the authors ascertain that the trust established through a recommendation should not be more than the trust held for the recommender or the recommendation. Also, they state that the trust built using multiple recommendations received from the same node should not be greater than the trust built using recommendations received from independent nodes. To prevent other nodes from knowing a requesting node's favorite recommenders, the requesting node disseminates a trust recommendation request (TRR), which contains a favorite list of recommenders for which its recommendation trust is greater than a threshold, and also includes few more other recommenders for which it is keen to update its recommendation trust. The requesting node receives recommendations only from the list of recommenders that are specified in the TRR packet. Note that it is up to the recommender to respond to the TRR. Later, the recommendation trust of recommenders is updated by the requesting node depending on the requesting node's interaction with the recommended node.

The authors have performed intensive simulations using (a) malicious nodes that drop packets, (b) malicious nodes that forward wrong recommendations, and (c) malicious nodes that perform both the actions. Simulation results show that malicious nodes do not form clusters because once nodes are identified for malicious behaviors then there will be no more routes through them. In the case of selective malicious behaviors, a few benign nodes are mistakenly considered as malicious nodes. Finally, mobility has been observed to report benign nodes as packet dropping nodes. However, mobility is believed to decrease the overhead of requesting more recommendations due to the tendency of nodes to move around and meet other nodes frequently.

Interestingly, Yan Lindsay's work lays the groundwork for the definition of trust and specifies the properties for propagating trust. However, recommendations are prone to recommender's bias, honest-elicitation and free-riding problems. In addition, it is unclear how TRR and TTL are protected against modification attacks.

5.2.5. *Trust Enhanced Secure Ad Hoc Network Routing*

In Refs. 81 and 82, we have proposed a trust model known as *Secure MANET Routing with Trust Intrigue* (SMRTI) to enhance the security decisions in MANETs. The decisions include (a) accepting or rejecting a route from a route discovery, (b) recording or ignoring a route from a forwarded packet, (c) forwarding or discarding a packet, (d) forwarding a packet from a previous hop, (e) sending a packet to the next hop, (f) refreshing or revoking a key of other nodes, and (g) choosing the route for communication. Note that these decisions are based on the trust relationships established between nodes. The model enables a node to establish trust relationships with other nodes using three types of reputations: direct, observed, and recommended. Direct reputation is formulated from the evidence collected during one-to-one interactions with a node. Observed reputation is unique to this model because nodes observe the interactions between its neighbors to formulate an opinion. Finally, recommended reputation establishes an indirect trust relationship between two nodes through positive recommendations derived from the recommender.

Similar to the majority of trust models, here trust relationships are measured in continuous values between $[-1, +1]$. SMRTI sets precise rules to map specific values to the collected evidence. For example, the evidence is mapped either to a positive or negative value within [−1, +1] depending on whether the evidence represents either malicious or benign behavior. The magnitude of the positive value is proportional to the type of event (route request, route reply, route error or data flow). In contrast, the magnitude of the negative value is a function of both the type of event and the malicious behavior (flooding, packet dropping, modification of route sequence number, addition or deletion of routes, and fabrication). Once a node has been identified for a malicious behavior, SMRTI excludes it from the corresponding communication flow until the completion of the flow, regardless of the relationship maintained with the node.

The main feature of SMRTI is its ability to prevent a node's opinion from being corrupted by the recommender, and hence forces the node to rely only on its opinion. Therefore, it better resolves the issues concerned with recommender's bias. Further, it adopts a novel approach to communicating recommendations between nodes that eliminates the need to disseminate explicit packets as recommendations. This prevents recommenders from exhibiting both honest-elicitation and free-riding behaviors. Let us now consider the approach for deriving recommendations. For clarify, the node that provides a recommendation is referred to as the *recommender* and the recommended node is referred to as the *recommendee*. SMRTI derives recommendations from a recommender for a recommendee using the route contained in a data packet. It deduces a node's intention to forward or discard an upstream packet received from its previous hop as the node's opinion for its previous hop. It then derives the deduced opinion as the node's recommendation for its previous hop. Since recommendations are derived from the route of a received packet, the trustworthiness of the previous hop, next hop, source, destination, and route are evaluated before deriving recommendations. For example, let us consider the scenario where node X unicasts a packet to node N, which contains the route $S \rightarrow O \rightarrow X \rightarrow N \rightarrow C \rightarrow D$. Node N will forward the received packet, only if X, C, S, D, and the route are trustworthy. N derives X's willingness to forward the packet on behalf of O, as X's recommendation for O. Similarly, N derives O's willingness to forward the packet on behalf of S, as O's recommendation for S. The process of deriving recommendations terminates at S as there is no previous hop for S.

In the absence of secure routing protocols, SMRTI demonstrates efficient performance in the presence of up to 70% malicious nodes; however, it is hard for SMRTI to produce similar performance against spoofed packets in the absence of secure routing protocols. Similar to very few related models, SMRTI takes advantage of secure routing protocols to authenticate intermediate nodes and to verify the integrity of routing messages. The main shortcoming of SMRTI is a lack of sound mathematical proof for its evidence mapping into trust relationships. However, it stands out from other trust models in proposing a novel approach to eliminating honest-elicitation, free-riding, and recommender's bias.

6. Directions for Future Research

In this section, we summarize our analysis of various trust models that have been discussed above. Although trust management systems in MANETs have introduced a defense-in-depth strategy to enhance the security of communications, they are still incomplete due to some limitations and shortcomings. Here we discuss those limitations and shortcomings and present possible future directions.

6.1. *Behavioral Evidence*

Most of the MANET-based trust management systems consider only behavioral evidence since it is observable and classifiable. However, it is not possible to collect evidence for all observable behaviors or the collected evidence may not be accurate due to ambiguous collisions, receiver collisions, and limited transmission power. Ambiguous collisions occur when a node receives a packet while it passively monitors the transmission of another node. Alternatively, receiver collision occurs when a passively monitored node transmits a packet to its next hop at the same time the next hop is receiving another packet from some other node. In such situations, even if the passively monitored node fails to retransmit the packet, it can increase its reputation at the monitoring node. Finally, a selfish node can circumvent the monitoring node by varying its transmission power such that the signal reaches the monitoring node but not the selfish node's next hop. In such instances, the selfish node requires to know the transmission power range of its neighbors.

The severity increases when trust management systems collect only behavioral evidence and fail to consider credentials or secret associations to authenticate nodes. In the absence of authentication, evidence may be collected from a spoofed packet and hence the corresponding trust relationships and resulting decisions may be inaccurate. This clearly advocates the need to authenticate intermediate nodes and to verify routing messages using secure routing protocols and only a few models [81, 82, 94] acknowledge such requirements. For this reason, it is necessary to collect both *hard* and *soft evidence* [90] so that trust management systems can also be employed to assist secure routing protocols in enlisting only trustworthy nodes to routes.

6.2. *Recommendations*

In MANETs, if nodes happen to rely only on the evidence collected from direct interactions, then they can defend against malicious nodes only after having interactions with them. For this reason, nodes exchange their opinion of other nodes with their neighbors in the form of recommendations. In this way they partially avoid encounters with malicious nodes even without an interaction with those malicious nodes. However, recommendations are effective only if the trust model is capable of deploying some strategies to eliminate or at least cope with the following: (a) false accusations or false praise, which we collectively refer to as honest-elicitation, (b) free-riding in which neighbors fail to reciprocate with recommendations, and (c) recommender's bias resulting from recommender's subjective evaluation of evidence.

A straightforward defense against honest-elicitation is to agree on the received recommendations (consensus) so that valid recommendations are differentiated from falsified recommendations. However, this approach is vulnerable to collusion attacks, if recommendations are generated by colluding malicious neighbors and those recommendations surpass the recommendations disseminated by benign neighbors. Hence, it becomes important not to penalize any recommender since honest recommendations may fail to emerge due to the consensus approach. Alternatively, a node may defend against honest-elicitation by only considering recommendations that are in agreement with its belief. Such an approach overlooks recommendations that may otherwise report the infrequent malicious behavior of a neighbor. *Recommender's bias* is another issue pertaining to recommendations. Unlike honest-elicitation, here the recommender may disseminate an honest recommendation which is derived from either an optimistic or pessimistic evaluation of collected evidence. Such recommendations are critical in transitive trust relationships, where a node receiving a recommendation believes that the recommender has evaluated the trustworthiness of the recommended node in the same manner it evaluates the trustworthiness of the recommender. Free-riding confronts the advantages of recommendations as it adheres to the specifications of the routing protocol for forwarding packets but fails to follow the specifications outlined for the trust model. One of the solutions to thwart free-riding is to opt for a recursive design so that nodes are forced to communicate recommendations with other nodes as they are forced to forward packets for other nodes. Finally, propagation of recommendation opens the door to many design questions such as whether to restrict recommendations to single or multiple hops, and whether to attach opinions for all nodes or report only malicious nodes. The answers to such questions rest on the balance between the overhead incurred in disseminating recommendations and the importance of informing other nodes regarding malicious nodes.

These issues have motivated us to question whether recommendations have to be considered at all in MANET-based trust management systems. However, the benefit of defending against malicious nodes even without having interactions with them prioritizes the need to consider recommendations in MANETs. Perhaps, the direction to look for solutions is to investigate the trade-off between the advantage of considering recommendations to establish trust relationships with unknown nodes and the benefit of ignoring recommendations as a result of their vulnerabilities. Among related trust models, our model [81, 82] establishes the balance by addressing those issues pertaining to recommendations and at the same time taking advantage of the benefits of communicating recommendations.

6.3. *Modeling Ignorance in Trust Relationships*

Most, if not all, trust models often fail to represent the aspect of ignorance and thereby the associated uncertainty, which are intrinsic to the establishment of trust relationships in MANETs. Hence, a trust relationship between two nodes may not always reflect the actual relationship and consequently the executed decision may not always be accurate. For instance, consider a new node joining the network, where existing nodes may not have a record of past evidence to trust or distrust a newly joining node. Assigning an arbitrary level of trust to the new node poses several issues. Trust models address this issue either by pessimistically assigning a low level of trust or by optimistically assigning a neutral or high level of trust to the new node. The purpose of a pessimistic approach is to compel the new node to exhibit a consistently benign behavior from the point it enters the network. However, in some of these models, it is not always clear as to how the less trusted new node is selected for communications when nodes with high trust values exist in the network. If a new node is not preferred due to its low level of trust, then it lacks the opportunity to gain trust with existing nodes. Alternatively, with an optimistic approach, the aim is to promptly identify whether the new node exhibits malicious behavior from the point it enters into network. Prompt identification is feasible since the neutral or high level of trust assigned for a new node decreases rapidly as any malicious behavior increases. However, an optimistic approach may favor existing malicious nodes to re-enter the network with a new identity. These issues arise as trust models explicitly fail to represent an existing node's ignorance about a newly joining node's behavior. The issue also extends to nodes that have already established trust relationship with one another depending on their interactions and recommendations. For example, when a node moves away from a neighbor (due to mobility), it is unclear whether to consider the neighbor with the same level of trust or distrust during the next interaction (when it returns). It may be that the neighbor could retain its current behavior which may be either benign or malicious. Considering the neighbor to be benign, there is a chance for the neighbor to be compromised prior to the next interaction. Alternatively, if the neighbor is considered to be malicious, then it may be repenting and expecting an interaction to improve its relationship. Another possibility is that the neighbor may be malicious as a result of compromise, and it may be redeemed prior to the next interaction. These issues are often addressed by either increasing or decreasing the trust or distrust of nodes in proportion to the duration for which they are out of communication. The seriousness of this approach is that a node's ignorance of other nodes is represented by either increasing or decreasing its trust or distrust for them, which indeed denotes their benign or malicious behavior, respectively. Hence, the failing to represent the notion of ignorance and the associated uncertainty has a fundamental impact on trust models. Recently, a few trust models [74, 80, 94] have considered this issue by modeling ignorance in established trust relationships.

6.4. *Selective Malicious Behaviors*

The majority of trust models consider nodes to exhibit persistent malicious or benign behaviors. This is not true in MANETs where nodes are either prone to capture and compromise or redeemed after being compromised. Modeling trust management systems to handle such selective malicious behaviors enable prompt detection and isolation of compromised benign nodes. Alternatively, it enables the detection of malicious nodes that may perform benign behaviors to remain unidentified or to gain trustworthiness in a node's neighborhood for a future objective. A similar approach can be employed to detect selfish nodes that aim for maximum utility by selectively dropping the packets received from neighbors. Although a few models [50–52, 54, 55] measure the relative rate of such selective malicious behaviors, they fail to take advantage of their measurement by policing such nodes in a separate category. By defining efficient policies, these nodes can then be included in a communication only if there is no available path through other nodes and provided it is an insensitive communication.

6.5. *Evidence-to-Opinion Mapping*

Only a few models [50–52, 54, 55, 69, 74, 80, 94] are built on strong mathematical proofs that map evidence to opinion. The remaining models provide a weak basis for evidence-to-opinion mapping and also fail to provide valid reasoning for the continuous or discrete values chosen for trust metrics. As a consequence, this leads to inconsistencies in evaluations and makes it difficult to compare results with other models. The other issue in managing opinions is whether to give more weight to recent or past behaviors. Past behaviors are given more weight in order to avoid recent wrong observations to overshadow past benign behaviors; however, it is also important to prevent nodes from leveraging of past benign behaviors. Since trust evolves continuously in a dynamically changing MANET, it is advantageous to give more importance to recent behaviors. Even if a benign node's behavior has been mistakenly evaluated as malicious, the model should be designed to allow benign nodes to regain their reputation through future benign behaviors. In other words, the logic should not reverse the existing opinion upside down. Another important factor that needs consideration while choosing the mathematical logic is the ability of the logic to prioritize different types of opinion. For example, opinion formulated from one-to-one interactions should have more weight than opinion formulated from recommendations.

Finally, not many models [83] enable nodes to call for a strict decision to exclude malicious nodes in their communication and to deny the requests received from malicious nodes. Such models have to be designed to take advantage of established trust relationships so that they can efficiently make decisions including (a) accepting or rejecting a discovered route, (b) recording or ignoring a route from a forwarded packet, (c) forwarding or discarding a packet, (d) forwarding a packet for a previous hop, (e) sending a packet to the next hop, (f) refreshing or revoking a secret association with a node, and (g) choosing the route for communication. In summary, dynamic and efficient trust management systems can be realized only if decision policies evolve with the evidence manager, which also has to evolve by accommodating an IDS to detect new type of attacks.

7. Conclusion

In this chapter, we have presented the state of the art in security for MANETs. Initially, we have discussed the features inherent to MANETs, their impact on the design of security mechanisms and the threats and attacks that are common to MANETs. Second, we have described a few well-known solutions to present the role of secure routing and key management systems as prevention systems and their limitations in MANETs. In addition, we have also briefly discussed the significance of incentive-based payment systems in MANETs. Finally, we have addressed the recent advancements in security systems where the defense-in-depth approach is adopted to incorporate trust management systems as the second layer of defense to prevention systems. We have detailed the context for trust management systems in MANETs by exploring the concepts and methodology prevalent in traditional trust management systems. We have also shown the relationship between trust management and IDS as part of our study. Various trust models including those recently proposed and a few well-known ones have also been analyzed and compared. Finally, we have presented an analysis of those trust models and discussed their limitations and shortcomings. In addition, we have also highlighted the recent research directions towards the development of efficient trust management systems.

Terminology

Mobile ad-hoc network (MANET): A network in which nodes are mobile and capable of establishing wireless communication with other mobile nodes (which are beyond their transmission range) in the absence of any infrastructure.

Security: The process of denying access to unauthorized users and preventing unauthorized access to data.

Secure routing system: A system that deploys a security mechanism to authenticate and verify the integrity of communication.

Intrusion detection system (IDS): A non-intrusive system that detects malicious or abnormal actions.

Trust: A subjective belief that an entity will act as expected, which depends on the opinion held about the entity.

Reputation: The opinion held about an entity based on the credentials collected or presented by the entity and those credentials include behavioral evidence, certificates, etc.

Trust management system: A system that decides whether an entity can perform an action depending on the policies defined and the opinion derived using the credentials presented by entity.

Trust enhanced security system: A security system that enhances its actions based on the decisions provided by a trust management system.

Self-policing system: A system in which evidence is reactively collected and decisions are proactively executed without the intervention of any higher authority.

Detection reaction system: A system which collects evidence by persistently monitoring actions and then reacts depending on the policies defined for handling an anomaly.

Exercises

1. What are the inherent issues in MANETs?
2. What are the various security trends in MANETs?
3. Why do secure routing protocols not serve as a complete security solution for MANETs?
4. Why are centralized authority based key management systems not conducive to MANETs?
5. Why do incentive based systems fail to complement secure routing protocols?
6. What are the differences between malicious and selfish nodes?
7. Why are trust management systems necessary for MANETs?
8. What are the shortcomings and limitations of trust management systems in MANETs?
9. Why is behavioral evidence not sufficient to establish trust relationships?
10. Why does ignorance have to be represented in trust relationships?
11. Why is past evidence given more weight than recent evidence and why is it important to give more weight to recent evidence?

References

1. M. Grossglauser and D. N. C. Tse, Mobility increases the capacity of ad hoc wireless networks, *IEEE/ACM Trans. Network.* **10**(4), 477–486 (2002).
2. P. Michiardi and R. Molva, Simulation-based analysis of security exposures in mobile ad hoc networks, *Proc. European Wireless Conf.*, Florence, Italy (2002).
3. P. Ning and K. Sun, How to misuse AODV: A case study of insider attacks against mobile ad-hoc routing protocols, *Proc. IEEE Workshop on Information Assurance United States Military Academy*, West Point, NY, USA (2003), pp. 60–67.
4. J. Kong, X. Hong and M. Gerla, A new set of passive routing attacks in mobile ad hoc networks, *IEEE Military Communications Conference* (*MILCOM 2003*), Boston, MA, USA (2003), pp. 796–801.
5. D. Chaum, Untraceable electronic mail return address, and digital pseudonyms, *ACM Commun.* **24**(2), 84–88 (1981).

6. D. Chaum, The dining cryptographers problem: Unconditional sender and recipient untraceability, *J. Cryptogr.* **1**(1), 65–75 (1988).
7. S. Jiang, N. Vaidya and W. Zhao, A dynamic mix method for wireless ad hoc networks, *IEEE Military Commun. Conf.* (*MILCOM 2001*), Washington (2001), pp. 873–877.
8. J. Kong and X. Hong, ANODR: Anonymous on demand routing with untraceable routes for mobile adhoc networks, *4th ACM Int. Symp. Mobile Ad hoc Networking and Computing* (*MobiHoc'03*), Annapolis, MD (2003), pp. 291–302.
9. R. Shokri, N. Yazdani and A. Khonsari, Chain-based anonymous routing for wireless ad hoc networks, *4th IEEE Consumer Communications and Networking Conf.* (*CCNC 2007*), Las Vegas, NV, USA (2007), pp. 297–302.
10. B. Zhu, Z. Wan, M. S. Kankanhalli, F. Bao and R. H. Deng, Anonymous secure routing in mobile ad-hoc networks, *29th Annual IEEE Int. Conf. Local Computer Networks* (*LCN 2007*), Tampa, FL, USA (2004), pp. 102–108.
11. D. B. Johnson, D. A. Maltz and J. Broch, DSR: The dynamic source routing protocol for multihop wireless ad hoc networks, in *Ad Hoc Networking*, ed. C. E. Perkins (Addison-Wesley Longman Publishing Co., Boston, MA, 2001).
12. D. Balfanz, G. Durfee, N. Shankar, D. Smetters, J. Staddon and H.-C. Wong, Secure handshakes from pairing-based key agreements, *IEEE Symp. Security & Privacy*, Oakland, CA, May (2003), pp. 180–196.
13. Y. Zhang, W. Liu and W. Lou, Anonymous communications in mobile ad hoc networks, *24th Annual Joint Conf. IEEE Computer and Communications Societies* (*INFOCOM 2005*), Miami, FL (2005), pp. 1940–1951.
14. S. Seys and B. Preneel, ARM: Anonymous routing protocol for mobile ad hoc networks, *20th IEEE Int. Conf. Advanced Information Networking and Applications* (*AINA 2006*), Vienna, Austria (2006), pp. 133–137.
15. C. E. Perkins, E. M. Royer, S. R. Das and M. K. Marina, Performance comparison of two on-demand routing protocols for ad hoc networks, *IEEE Pers. Commun.* **8**(1), 16–28 (2001).
16. M. Abolhasan, T. Wysocki and E. Dutkiewicz, A review of routing protocols for mobile ad hoc networks, *Ad Hoc Networks* **2**(1), 1–22 (2004).
17. S. Capkun and J.-P. Hubaux, BISS: Building secure routing out of an incomplete set of security associations, *Proc. 2003 ACM Workshop on Wireless Security*, San Diego, CA (2003), pp. 21–29.
18. Y.-C. Hu and A. Perrig, A survey of secure wireless ad hoc routing, *IEEE Security Privacy* **2**(3), 28–39 (2004).
19. Y.-C. Hu, A. Perrig and D. B.Johnson, Packet leashes: A defense against wormhole attacks in wireless networks, *INFOCOM 2003: 22nd Annual Joint Conf. IEEE Computer and Communications Societies* (2003), pp. 1976–1986.
20. Y.-C. Hu, A. Perrig and D. B. Johnson, Ariadne: A secure on-demand routing protocol for ad hoc networks, *Int. Conf. Mobile Computing and Networking*, Atlanta, Georgia (2002), pp. 12–23.
21. Y.-C. Hu, A. Perrig and D. B. Johnson, Efficient security mechanisms for routing protocols, *Network and Distributed System Security Symposium* (*NDSS '03*), San Diego, CA (2003), pp. 57–73.
22. Y.-C. Hu, A. Perrig and D. B. Johnson, Rushing attacks and defense in wireless ad hoc network routing protocols, *Proc. 2003 ACM Workshop on Wireless security*, San Diego, CA (2003), pp. 30–40.
23. P. Papadimitratos and Z. J. Haas, Secure routing for mobile ad hoc networks, *SCS Communication Networks and Distributed Systems Modeling and Simulation Conf.*, San Antonio, TX (2002).

24. K. Sanzgiri, B. Dahill, B. N. Levine, C. Shields and E. M. Belding-Royer, A secure routing protocol for ad hoc networks, *10th IEEE Int. Conf. Network Protocols (ICNP'02)*, Paris, France (2002), pp. 78–89.
25. V. Varadharajan, R. Shankaran and M. Hitchens, Security for cluster based ad hoc networks, *Comput. Commun.* **27**(5), 488–501 (2004).
26. H. Yang, X. Meng and S. Lu, Self-organized network-layer security in mobile ad hoc networks, *Proc. ACM Workshop on Wireless Security, Int. Conf. Mobile Computing and Networking*, Atlanta, GA (2002), pp. 11–20.
27. M. G. Zapata, Secure ad hoc on-demand distance vector (SAODV) routing, *IETF Internet Draft (Work in Progress)* (2001).
28. M. G. Zapata, Secure ad hoc on-demand distance vector routing, *ACM SIGMOBILE Mob. Comput. Commun. Rev.* **6**(3), 106–107 (2002).
29. M. G. Zapata and N. Asokan, Securing ad hoc Routing Protocols, *Proc. ACM Workshop on Wireless security, Int. Conf. Mobile Computing and Networking*, Atlanta, GA (2002), pp. 1–10.
30. A. Perrig, R. Canetti, D. Song and J. D. Tygar, Efficient and secure source authentication for multicast, *Network and Distributed System Security Symposium (NDSS '01)* (2001), pp. 35–46.
31. A. D. Wood and J. A. Stankovic, Denial of service in sensor networks, *IEEE Computer* **35**(10), 54–62 (2002).
32. L. Zhou and Z. J. Haas, Securing ad hoc networks, *IEEE Network* **13**(6), 24–30 (1999).
33. S. Yi and R. Kravets, Key management for heterogeneous ad hoc wireless networks, *Proc. 10th IEEE Int. Conf. Network Protocols*, Paris, France (2002), pp. 202–205.
34. B. Wu, J. Wu, E. B. Fernandez, M. Ilyas and S. Magliveras, Secure and efficient key management in mobile ad hoc networks, *J. Net. Comput. Appl.* **30**(3), 937–954 (2007).
35. H. Luo, P. Zerfos, J. Kong, S. Lu and L. Zhang, Self-securing ad hoc wireless networks, *Proc. 7th Int. Symp. Computers and Communications (ISCC 2002)*, Taormina, Italy (2002), pp. 567–574.
36. J. Kong, P. Zerfos, H. Luo, S. Lu and L. Zhang, Providing robust and ubiquitous security support for mobile ad-hoc networks, *Proc. 9th IEEE Int. Conf. Network Protocols (ICNP 2001)*, Riverside, CA (2001), pp. 251–260.
37. D. Boneh and M. Franklin, Identity-based encryption from the Weil pairing, *SIAM J. Compu.* **32**(3), 586–615 (2003).
38. A. Khalili, J. Katz and W. A. Arbaugh, Toward secure key distribution in truly ad-hoc networks, *Proc. Symp. Applications and the Internet Workshops (SAINT 2003)*, Orlando, FL (2003), pp. 342–346.
39. S. Capkun, L. Buttyán and J.-P. Hubaux, Self-organized public-key management for mobile ad hoc networks, *IEEE Trans. Mob. Comput.* **2**(1), 52–64 (2003).
40. P. R. Zimmermann, *The Official PGP User's Guide* (MIT Press, 1995).
41. S. Capkun, J.-P. Hubaux and L. Buttyán, Mobility helps security in ad hoc networks, *Proc. 4th ACM Int. Symp. Mobile Ad Hoc Networking & Computing*, Annapolis, MD (2003), pp. 46–56.
42. L. Buttyan and J. Hubaux, Nuglets: A virtual currency to stimulate cooperation in self-organized ad hoc networks. Technical report (DSC/2001/001), Swiss Federal Institute of Technology (2001).
43. J. Crowcroft, R. Gibbens, F. Kelly and S. Östring, Modelling incentives for collaboration in mobile ad hoc networks, *Perform. Evaluation* **57**(4), 427–439 (2004).
44. Q. He, D. Wu and P. Koshla, A secure incentive architecture for ad-hoc networks. *Wireless Commun. Mob. Comput.* (Special Issue: Wireless Networks Security) (2006).

45. S. Zhong, J. Chen and Y. R. Yang, Sprite: A simple, cheat-proof, credit-based system for mobile ad-hoc networks, *IEEE 22nd Annual Joint Conference of the IEEE Computer and Communications Societies* (*INFOCOM 2003*) (2003), pp. 1987–1997.
46. N. B. Salem, L. Butty'an, J.-P. Hubaux and M. Jakobsson, A charging and rewarding scheme for packet forwarding in multi-hop cellular networks, *Proc. 4th ACM Int. Symp. Mobile Ad Hoc Networking & Computing*, Annapolis, MD (2003), pp. 13–24.
47. E. Huang, J. Crowcroft and I. Wassell, Rethinking incentives for mobile ad hoc networks, *Proc. ACM SIGCOMM Workshop on Practice and Theory of Incentives in Networked Systems* (*SIGCOMM'04 Workshops*), Portland, OR (2004), pp. 191–196.
48. S. Buchegger and J.-Y. L. Boudec, Nodes bearing grudges: Towards routing security, fairness, and robustness in mobile ad hoc networks, *Proc. 10th Euromicro PDP* (*Parallel, Distributed and Network-based Processing*), Gran Canaria, Spain (2002), pp. 403–410.
49. S. Buchegger and J.-Y. L. Boudec, Cooperative routing in mobile ad-hoc networks: current efforts against malice and selfishness, *Proc. Mobile Internet Workshop* (*Informatik 2002*), Dortmund, Germany (2002).
50. S. Buchegger and J.-Y. L. Boudec, Performance analysis of the CONFIDANT protocol, *Proc. 3rd ACM Int. Symp. Mobile Ad Hoc Networking & Computing*, Lausanne, Switzerland (2002), pp. 226–236.
51. S. Buchegger and J.-Y. L. Boudec, Performance analysis of the CONFIDANT protocol: Cooperation of nodes — fairness in dynamic ad-hoc networks, Technical report (IC/2002/01), EPFL I&C (2002).
52. S. Buchegger and J.-Y. L. Boudec, Coping with false accusations in misbehavior reputation systems for mobile ad-hoc networks, Technical report (IC/2003/31), EFPL (2003).
53. S. Buchegger and J.-Y. L. Boudec, The effect of rumor spreading in reputation systems for mobile ad-hoc networks, *Proc. Modeling and Optimization in Mobile, Ad Hoc and Wireless Networks* (*WiOpt 2003*), Sophia-Antipolis, France (2003).
54. S. Buchegger and J.-Y. L. Boudec, A robust reputation system for mobile ad-hoc networks, Technical report (IC/2003/50), EPFL-IC-LCA, Lausanne, Switzerland (2003).
55. S. Buchegger and J.-Y. L. Boudec, A robust reputation system for P2P and mobile ad-hoc networks, *Proc. 2nd Workshop on the Economics of Peer-to-Peer Systems* (*P2PEcon 2004*), Harvard University, Cambridge, MA (2004).
56. S. Buchegger and J.-Y. L. Boudec, Self-policing mobile ad-hoc networks, in *Mobile Computing Handbook*, eds. M. Ilyas and I. Mahgoub (CRC Press, 2004).
57. P. Lamsal, Requirements for modeling trust in ubiquitous computing and ad hoc networks, Technical report (HUT TML — Course T-110.557 — ISBN 951-22-6309-2 — ISSN 1456-7628 TML-C8), Helsinki University of Technology (2002).
58. P. Michiardi and R. Molva, Core: A collaborative reputation mechanism to enforce node cooperation in mobile ad hoc networks, *IFIP — Communication and Multimedia Security Conf.* (2002).
59. S. Bansal and M. Baker, Observation-based cooperation enforcement in ad hoc networks, Technical report (CoRR cs.NI/0307012), Stanford University (2003).
60. T. Hughes, A. Muckelbauer, J. Denny and J. Etzl, Dynamic trust applied to ad hoc network resources, *6th Int. Workshop on Trust, Privacy, Deception, and Fraud in Agent Societies: Proc. Autonomous Agents & Multi-Agent Systems Conf.* (*AAMAS 2003*), Melbourne, Australia (2003), pp. 1–7.

61. Y. Liu and Y. R. Yang, Reputation propagation and agreement in mobile ad-hoc networks, *Proc. IEEE Wireless Communications and Networking* (*WCNC 2003*), New Orleans, LA (2003), pp. 1510–1515.
62. D. Senn, Reputation and trust management in ad hoc networks with misbehaving nodes, Diploma thesis. Information Security, Swiss Federal Institute of Technology Zurich (2003).
63. P. Dewan, P. Dasgupta and A. Bhattacharya, On using reputations in ad hoc networks to counter malicious nodes, *Proc. 10th IEEE Int. Conf. Parallel and Distributed Systems* (*ICPADS 2004*), California, CA (2004), pp. 665–672.
64. L. Eschenauer, V. D. Gligor and J. Baras, On trust establishment in mobile ad-hoc networks, *Proc. 10th Int. Security Protocols Workshop*, Cambridge, UK (2004), pp. 47–66.
65. A. Fernandes, E. Kotsovinos, S. Ostring and B. Dragovic, Pinocchio: Incentives for honest participation in distributed trust management, *Proc. 2nd Int. Conf. Trust Management* (*iTrust 2004*), Oxford, UK (2004), pp. 63–77.
66. Q. He, D. Wu and P. Khosla, SORI: A secure and objective reputation-based incentive scheme for ad-hoc networks, *Proc. IEEE Wireless Communications and Networking Conf.* (*WCNC 2004*), Atlanta, GA (2004), pp. 825–830.
67. T. Jiang and J. S. Baras, Ant-based adaptive trust evidence distribution in MANET, *Proc. 24th Int. Conf. Distributed Computing Systems Workshops* (*ICDCSW 2004*), Tokyo, Japan (2004), pp. 588–593.
68. J. Liu and V. Issarny, Enhanced reputation mechanism for mobile ad hoc networks, *2nd Int. Conf. Trust Management* (*iTrust 2004*), Oxford, UK (2004), pp. 48–62.
69. Z. Liu, A. W. Joy and R. A. Thompson, A dynamic trust model for mobile ad hoc networks, *Proc. 10th IEEE Int. Workshop on Future Trends of Distributed Computing Systems* (*FTDCS 2004*), Suzhou, China (2004), pp. 80–85.
70. A. A. Pirzada, A. Datta and C. McDonald, Propagating trust in ad-hoc networks for reliable routing, *Proc. IEEE Int. Workshop on Wireless Ad-Hoc Networks*, Oulu, Finland (2004), pp. 58–62.
71. A. A. Pirzada and C. McDonald, Establishing trust in pure ad-hoc networks, *Proc. 27th Conf. Australasian Computer Science*, Dunedin, New Zealand (2004), pp. 47–54.
72. A. A. Pirzada, C. McDonald and A. Datta, Dependable dynamic source routing without a trusted third party, *Proc. 28th Australasian Conf. Computer Science*, Newcastle, Australia (2005), pp. 79–85.
73. N. Pissinou, T. Ghosh and K. Makki, Collaborative trust-based secure routing in multihop ad hoc networks, *3rd Int. IFIP-TC6 Networking Conf.*, Athens, Greece (2004), pp. 1446–1451.
74. G. Theodorakopoulos and J. S. Baras, Trust evaluation in ad-hoc networks, *Proc. ACM Workshop on Wireless Security* (*WiSe'04*), Philadelphia, PA (2004), pp. 1–10.
75. S. Buchegger and J.-Y. Le Boudee, Self-policing mobile ad hoc networks by reputation systems, *IEEE Commun. Mag.* **43**(7), 101–107 (2005).
76. J. Mundinger and J.-Y. Le Boudec, Analysis of a reputation system for mobile ad-hoc networks with liars, *3rd Int. Symp. Modeling and Optimization in Mobile Ad Hoc and Wireless Networks* (*WIOPT 2005*), Trentino, Italy (2005), pp. 41–46.
77. Y. Rebahi, V. E. Mujica-V and D. Sisalem, A reputation-based trust mechanism for ad hoc networks, *Proc. 10th IEEE Symp. Computers and Communications* (*ISCC 2005*), Cartagena, Spain (2005), pp. 37–42.

78. M. T. Refaei, S. Vivek, L. DaSilva and M. Eltoweissy, A reputation-based mechanism for isolating selfish nodes in ad hoc networks, *Proc. 2nd Annual Int. Conf. Mobile and Ubiquitous Systems: Networking and Services* (*MOBIQUITOUS 2005*), Washington, DC (2005), pp. 3–11.
79. M. Virendra, M. Jadliwala, M. Chandrasekaran and S. Upadhyaya, Quantifying trust in mobile ad-hoc networks, *Proc. Int. Conf. Integration of Knowledge Intensive Multi-Agent Systems* (*KIMAS*), Waltham, MA (2005), pp. 65–70.
80. S. Yan Lindsay, Y. Wei, H. Zhu and K. J. R. Liu, Information theoretic framework of trust modeling and evaluation for ad hoc networks, *IEEE J. Sel. Area. Commun.* **24**(2), 305–317 (2006).
81. V. Balakrishnan, V. Varadharajan, P. Lucs and U. Tupakula, Trust enhanced secure mobile ad hoc network routing, *2nd IEEE Int. Symp. Pervasive Computing and Ad Hoc Communications* (*PCAC 2007*), *Proc. 21st IEEE Int. Conf. Advanced Information Networking and Applications Workshops* (*AINAW 2007*), Niagara Falls, Canada (2007), pp. 27–33.
82. V. Balakrishnan, V. Varadharajan, U. Tupakula and P. Lucs, Trust and recommendations in mobile ad hoc networks, *Proc. 3rd Int. Conf. Networking and Services* (*ICNS 2007*), Athens, Greece (2007), pp. 64–69.
83. S. Marti, T. J. Giuli, K. Lai and M. Baker, Mitigating routing misbehavior in mobile ad hoc networks, *Proc. 6th Annual Int. Conf. Mobile Computing and Networking* (*MOBICOM*), Boston, MA (2000), pp. 255–265.
84. Y.-A. Huang and W. Lee, A cooperative intrusion detection system for ad hoc networks security, *Conf. Computer and Communications, Proc. 1st ACM Workshop on Security of Ad Hoc and Sensor Networks*, Fairfax, VI (2003), pp. 135–147.
85. S. Ruohomaa and L. Kutvonen, Trust management survey, *Proc. 3rd Int. Conf. Trust Management* (*iTrust 2005*), Rocquencourt, France (2005), pp. 77–92.
86. L. Mui, M. Mohtashemi and A. Halberstadt, A computational model of trust and reputation, *Proc. 35th Annual Hawaii Int. Conf. System Sciences* (*HICSS 2002*), Hawaii (2002), pp. 2431–2439.
87. F. Azzedin and M. Maheswaran, Evolving and managing trust in grid computing systems, *IEEE Canadian Conf. Electrical & Computer Engineering* (*CCECE '02*) (2002), pp. 1424–1429.
88. M. Blaze, J. Feigenbaum and J. Lacy, Decentralized trust management, *Proc. IEEE Symp. Security and Privacy*, Oakland, CA (1996), pp. 164–173.
89. M. Blaze, J. Feigenbaum and A. D. Keromytis, KeyNote: Trust management for public-key infrastructures (Position Paper), *Proc. 6th Int. Workshop on Security Protocols*, Cambridge, UK (1998), pp. 59–63.
90. C. Lin and V. Varadharajan, Modelling and evaluating trust relationships in mobile agents based systems, *Int. Conf. Applied Cryptography and Network Security*, Kunming, China (2003), pp. 176–190.
91. L. Capra, Towards a human trust model for mobile ad-hoc networks, *Proc. 2nd UK-UbiNet Workshop*, London, UK (2004).
92. L. Capra, Engineering human trust in mobile system collaborations, *Proc. 12th Int. Symp. Foundations of Software Engineering* (*SIGSOFT*), Newport Beach, CA (2004), pp. 107–116.
93. C. M. Jonker, J.J.P. Schalken, J. Theeuwes and J. Treur, Human experiments in trust dynamics, *Proc. 2nd Int. Conf.* (*iTrust 2004*), Oxford, UK (2004), pp. 206–220.

94. L. Xiaoqi, M. R. Lyu and L. Jiangchuan, A trust model based routing protocol for secure ad hoc networks, *Proc. IEEE Aerospace Conf.* Big Sky, MT (2004), pp. 1286–1295.
95. F. Stajano and R. J. Anderson, The resurrecting duckling: Security issues in ad-hoc wireless networks, *Proc. 7th Security Protocols Workshop*, Berlin, Germany (2000), pp. 172–182.
96. S. Marsh, Formalizing trust as a computational concept, Ph.D. thesis. Department of Computer Science, University of Stirling (1994).
97. R. Dawkins, *The Selfish Gene*, 1989 Edition (Oxford University Press, 1976).

Chapter 24

IDENTITY MANAGEMENT IN MOBILE COMMUNICATION SYSTEMS

SILKE HOLTMANNS
Nokia Research Center, Itämerenkatu 11–13,
00180 Helsinki, Finland
Silke.Holtmanns@nokia.com

GUENTHER HORN* and WOLF-DIETRICH MOELLER†
Nokia Siemens Networks GmbH & Co. KG,
St.-Martin-Str. 76, 81541 München, Germany
**Guenther.Horn@nsn.com*
†*wolf-dietrich.moeller@nsn.com*

Identity management in mobile communication systems has the advantage that it can be bound not only to something that the user knows, but also to something that he possesses, i.e., it provides two-factor authentication. In converging communication networks the smart card can support a generic user identity management. These considerations led to the development of the Generic Bootstrapping Architecture (GBA) by the mobile standardization body 3rd Generation Partnership Project (3GPP) presented in this chapter. We describe existing mobile identity management approaches, introduce the Liberty Alliance Framework and outline how the mobile GBA can be utilized together with the Liberty Alliance Identity Federation Framework and the Web Services Framework for single sign-on or authentication services. Finally, we highlight the latest network convergence aspects in the area of identity management and outline the latest research questions and activities for meta-identity management systems.

1. Introduction

1.1. *Service Access*

Many services, especially on the World Wide Web, come for free, and top layer access is not restricted. But the situation is more restrictive when more valuable information is given or more functionality is provided. Also, access to many other services is controlled by the service provider because, for example,

- the service provider wants to ensure he gets paid for the service,
- the information offered by the service is personalized or confidential,

- the service provider wants to ensure that the user has a serious interest in the service, and
- the service allows modification of data (e.g., accounts, posting of data).

Therefore, in order to be able to access a controlled service, a service user has to present appropriate credentials or login details. It may suffice that the user can prove his ability to pay for the service, e.g., by using cash; then it does not matter who he or she is. But often, access to a service requires the user to be verifiably identified, i.e., authenticated, by the service provider. This is because:

- payment for the service is ensured by a subscription tied to a user,
- access to confidential information is only permitted for specific users,
- only the user themselves is allowed to modify records in their account, and
- permanent user identifiers allow continuous service experience, e.g., reviewing of previous transactions.

Most service systems use some form of user identity for service access control and most users own a mobile phone. Therefore, we focus on identity-based service access control and how mobile network identities and credentials can be leveraged to provide identity management for service access. The web-based identity management framework of the Liberty Alliance Project is a well-known approach to identity management for service access. We therefore also show how this approach and identity management based on mobile network identities can be combined to exploit the strengths of both.

1.2. *Key Features of Service Access Control Mechanisms*

In most cases, it is a desirable feature of service access systems that the user can log in to one service and move on from there to other "connected services" in the same service domain without further authentication. The user is in many cases not identified by his real name, but just by a pseudonym. Also the communication between the user and the service provider is, depending on the service, often secured with cryptographic credentials. The key features of an identity-based service access control mechanism include:

- authentication,
- single sign-on,
- protection of communication and distribution of cryptographic keys,
- support for pseudonymity,
- federation of identities and user profiles,
- independence of communication networks, and
- applicability to a wide range of services.

We address these features one-by-one in the following.

Authentication: By definition, authentication is fundamental to identity-based service access control — both authentication of the user and of the service provider. The importance of the latter is demonstrated, for example, by phishing attacks. Authentication of large groups of users is costly, and strong authentication is difficult to guarantee. It is therefore economically advantageous to avoid the building and maintenance of separate authentication infrastructures for different purposes. One strong authentication infrastructure with a huge footprint of over a billion users is provided by the smart cards in users' mobile phones and the authentication centers in the mobile communication systems GSM and UMTS. The authorization of the user to allow access to a requested service is often achieved by checking the validity of an entry or profile in the user database.

The idea to leverage this existing infrastructure to provide identity-based service access control lies at the heart of the development of the Generic Bootstrapping Architecture (GBA) by the 3rd Generation Partnership Project (3GPP) [1], the body responsible for GSM and UMTS specifications. The idea has been picked up by other standardization bodies for communication systems such as the 3rd Generation Partnership Project 2 [2], aiming at developing the North American CDMA standards further [3]; the Open Mobile Alliance (OMA); Telecoms & Internet Converged Services & Protocols for Advanced Networks [4]; and CableLabs [5]. These extensions allow the application of GBA based on credentials other than SIM or USIM, e.g., passwords more typically used for fixed network access, as the basis for bootstrapping. The GBA and its functionality are described in more detail in the following sections. In communications security, the loosely defined term "bootstrapping" has come to mean something like "initializing security for a particular feature by tying it to a pre-existing security infrastructure," cf., also, e.g., Ref. 6. For service providers, it is important that the usage of the GBA-based identity does not require expensive changes and additions to their systems, e.g., the re-usage of the same interfaces and databases for GBA-based authentication and legacy authentication methods.

Single sign-on: It is not only costly to maintain separate authentication infrastructures, but it is also bothersome for the user to use different means of authentication for different purposes. One example is the well-known problem of having to remember many different passwords for access to different web servers, and having to repeatedly type them into a small key pad in the mobile environment is not improving the user experience either. Another example is the fact that we have to carry different security tokens: a mobile phone with a Subscriber Identity Module (SIM) or some other smart card, a Secure ID card for corporate access, credit cards, debit cards with chips for electronic purses, and so on. This leads to the concept of single sign-on, which is to ensure that a user has to key in a password only once for access to several services, that one security token may be used for many purposes, etc. Single sign-on may also reduce the performance requirements for the security infrastructure provider and allows the usage of off-the-shelf libraries, standardized interfaces and messages.

Protection of communication and distribution of cryptographic keys: It is often not enough to mutually authenticate user and service provider. If the links between the two are open to attack then encryption and/or integrity protection are required, e.g., for payment transactions. These, in turn, require the availability of cryptographic keys which may need to be distributed by the service access control mechanism as, in general, a user and a service provider will not share keys at the start of their communication.

Support for pseudonymity: A user may have to reveal who he is to a mobile operator with whom he has a subscription, e.g., for the purpose of correct billing. But the user may not want to reveal his permanent identity to all service providers for privacy reasons, e.g., to avoid spam. Therefore, support for the use of temporary pseudonyms should be provided. One-time pseudonyms may be used to provide anonymity. Some legislations may require the possibility for a user to access a service with a pseudonym, especially if from a technical point of view no permanent identifier is needed. This protects the user's privacy against matching of user profiles from different service providers.

Federation of identities and user profiles: The different identities which a user uses with different service providers may all be federated. The same holds for different accounts held by a user with the same service provider. The federation can be provided by a separate entity, the identity provider. The identity provider and service providers are then associated in one or more circles of trust, as all service providers must trust the identity of the user which is provided by the identity provider. A circle of trust is the basis for single sign-on. This idea lies at the heart of the specifications of the Liberty Alliance Project. We will only give a brief introduction later in this chapter to the Identity Federation Framework and the Web Services Framework of the Liberty Alliance, since further detailed reading can be found on the Liberty Alliance Project web page [7].

Independence of communication networks: This requirement is crucial for a service access control mechanism suitable for next-generation networks (NGN) as the combined use of a multitude of heterogeneous networks with IP connectivity as the common denominator is a defining property of NGN. This means that it should not be required for service providers or application developers to use a particular communications system and protocol for transporting the data between the user and the service provider. The same service access mechanism should apply no matter whether IP connectivity is provided, for example, by the packet service of a mobile communications system or by a public WLAN hotspot. This requirement does not preclude the use of, for example, SIM or other smart cards originally issued to enable access to mobile telephony services for other purposes.

Applicability to a wide range of services: The usefulness of this requirement is self evident. It would be useful, for instance, to have a service access control mechanism which is applicable to both HTTP-based and non-HTTP-based services (although the overwhelming importance of HTTP-based services is readily acknowledged).

1.3. *Key Features of Generic Bootstrapping Architecture and Liberty Alliance Project Frameworks*

1.3.1. *Generic Bootstrapping Architecture*

The GBA provides smartcard-based two-factor authentication (the user holds the smart card token and knows the PIN required to activate the smart card) between a user and a corresponding network entity called the Bootstrapping Server Function (BSF), cf., the next section. The GBA also distributes cryptographic keys to service providers and provisions the user with data needed for local application specific key generation. The generated keys may then be used in turn to mutually authenticate service provider and user and protect the communication between them. This form of server authentication may provide better practical security than the usual server authentication by certificates in HTTPS, which are often blindly accepted by users even if unknown, expired or self-signed. The user may derive cryptographically separated keys for many service providers from one master service key obtained from the BSF. This is a big improvement on the currently typical service access scenario where users tend to re-use their username/passwords for a large range of services. In this sense, GBA also provides single sign-on since it builds the application specific keys upon one authentication to the BSF. Furthermore, logging on to an application does not require explicit user interaction as the GBA is an automatic procedure in the terminal. This property is also often associated with single sign-on. In addition, the GBA provides support for pseudonymity through its concept of User Security Settings (USS), which contain a collection of identities used with different services, cf., the next section.

Another kind of pseudonymity, or rather anonymity, offered by GBA is the assertion that the user is an authorized user of the service. In this case no user identity is transmitted to the service provider from the network, but the user is just known to the mobile network, and the service provider only knows this user has been authenticated by the network. For most services, this kind of pseudonymity is sufficient for service provisioning; only services that require service continuity, e.g., mobile TV, technically require a permanent identifier to be able to provide a service experience to the user without interruptions for security purposes.

The GBA alone only provides a limited form of identity federation. The USS allow the storage of different user identities for different service types. The GBA does not, however, provide a federation of user profiles. In other words, service providers cannot use the USS to store user profile data or common storage of user profiles for several services to use. It should be noted that the mobile network operator and the IdP are assumed to be trustworthy. The GBA is independent of the communications network in which the service resides in spite of the fact that the user credentials are provided by a smart card with SIM, User Services Identity Module (USIM, the UMTS version of SIM), IP Multimedia Subsystem Identity Module (ISIM) or Removable-User Identity Module (R-UIM), which are typically considered to be associated only with mobile networks. Only IP connectivity is required for using the GBA. The GBA is applicable to any type of service which allows transporting the GBA-specific temporary session identifiers. In particular, the GBA is also applicable to non-HTTP-based services such as 3GPP Mobile Broadcast Multicast Service (MBMS) [8] or OMA Broadcast [9].

1.3.2. *Liberty Alliance Project frameworks*

The Liberty Alliance Project (LAP) frameworks include the concept of authentication between a user and an identity provider. The identity provider serves as a point of authentication for the user and relays the information of the successfully performed authentication to the service provider. The LAP specifications are intended to be used in a wide range of scenarios; hence the particular authentication method and the credentials used are deliberately left outside the specifications to enable easy integration of existing systems. LAP does not provide the distribution of cryptographic keys, but rather relies on a protection mechanism for the communication between user and service provider outside the scope of the framework, e.g., HTTPS. LAP offers an identity management framework that enables providing authentication as a web service to other web-based services in their Web Services Framework (WSF). This includes the federation of identities and user accounts with support for pseudonymity. The LAP frameworks are independent of particular communication networks. The usage of the Simple Object Access Protocol (SOAP) [10] in LAP currently points to the use of HTTP-based services and builds on SOAP over HTTP, but in principle LAP does not exclude the use of other protocols.

1.3.3. *How Do GBA and LAP Frameworks Fit Together?*

From the above comparison, it may seem at first that GBA and LAP frameworks are two competing concepts as they both fulfil many of the key features discussed above. However, this would mean overlooking the fact that their relative strengths lie in different areas. While the Liberty Alliance Project is agnostic about the authentication method, GBA is able to make strong smart card-based authentication integrated with existing mobile communication systems and usable for service access control for a very large user base. On the other hand, LAP has very elaborate mechanisms for federation of identities and user profiles which are not present in GBA. This observation suggests combining the relative strengths of the two approaches. How this can be achieved is explained in the remainder of this chapter. It should be noted that both systems were developed independently and were designed to be deployed without a dependence on each other.

2. Background — The GBA

2.1. *Evolution Towards the GBA*

The idea to leverage the mobile communications infrastructure and, in particular, SIM or other smart cards, e.g., UICC, to provide identity-based service access control is not new [11]. It goes back to the times when Wireless Access Protocol [12] (WAP) was developed. WAP provides slimmed down HTTP-services to users of mobile phones. At least in later versions of WAP, WAP messages were transported over GPRS, the packet service of the GSM mobile system. In GPRS, the user is given an IP address, which is securely bound, through the GPRS security mechanisms, to his permanent mobile identity. To achieve this the user is identified by the International Mobile Subscriber Identity (IMSI) and authenticated by means of the SIM card. Service providers would only see the user's IP address, but the mobile operator would be able to resolve this IP address to the user's IMSI. In this way, the mobile operator can provide authentication and charging services to the service provider. A similar IP-binding approach was taken in the Early IP Multimedia Subsystem (IMS) Security [13]. An even more recent publication using this approach can be found in Ref. 14. The IP-binding approach works reasonably well under certain assumptions.

These assumptions, however, are too restrictive even in many current deployments. With the proliferation of Network Address Translation (NAT) also in large networks or home networks, different users may share the same public IP address. Additionally, the access network has to ensure that no other user can spoof the IP address of the authenticated user. These assumptions may be even more restrictive for converging networks which build the fundament of the NGN environment where the tight binding of one user to an IP address no longer works and where a NAT device may be present. Also, converging networks may introduce risks like IP address spoofing to this solution approach. In addition, usage of IP address binding assumes that the user uses a particular access network, violating the key feature of independence of communication networks discussed in the previous section.

2.2. *GBA — Requirements and Design Criteria*

The GBA [1] developed by 3GPP provides a service provider and a user equipment (UE) with a dedicated shared secret. (A UE is a terminal with a smart card.) The service specific dedicated shared secret is based on the user's credentials stored in the user's smart card, e.g., SIM, USIM, ISIM or R-UIM application on a smart card, and in the authentication centre (AuC) in the home subscriber system (HSS) or (in older systems) in the home location register (HLR). It should be noted that no new secret is provisioned to the smart card, but the existing stored secret between the operator and the UE is used to derive new application specific keys. To enable this, the UE communicates with a key distribution server (Bootstrapping

Server Function or BSF) as specified in Ref. 15. The BSF authenticates the user using the Authentication and Key Agreement Protocol (AKA) and derives the application specific keys from the existing shared secret; it also serves as a policy enforcement point for the mobile network operator. The network-internal communication between BSF, service providers and HSS/HLR is specified in Refs. 1 and 16. For security reasons, the BSF is always located in the home network, as it has direct access to the HSS/HLR, while the services may be provided in visited networks or by third parties. The interface between the service provider and the BSF network node that acts as a credential server can use DIAMETER or Web services [16]. If the service is provided by an operator, then the DIAMETER protocol might be more applicable; if the service provider is an Internet service provider, then Web services may suit better.

An important design criterion for GBA was to minimize the number of contacts with the AuC in the HSS/HLR, which is a particularly valuable resource in a mobile system since it stores and manages the database containing the users' subscriptions. Hence, it has to be avoided that every instance of a service access causes a call to the AuC, which may overload the AuC and deny service to other users. This led to the approach that, in a first step involving the AuC, an intermediate master shared key is established between UE and BSF, from which service specific keys are derived without any further involvement of the AuC. The BSF has obtained all the needed data and policy information in the first step and does not need to contact the AuC again, when the service provider key request message comes in.

Another design criterion was to reduce the communication between UE and network as far as possible because the corresponding link may be slow (e.g., low bit rate radio) and expensive (e.g., roaming). Therefore, the GBA was designed so that a user simply includes a transaction identifier pointing to the intermediate shared key in the first request to the service provider, and the remaining work (i.e., fetching the service-specific key) is done entirely in the network. This contrasts with the approach taken, for example, in Kerberos [17] where, for each service provider, the service-specific key is sent from the key distribution server to the service provider through the client.

Another requirement is to prevent a security breach in one service provider using GBA from affecting other service providers. A refinement of this requirement is to guarantee that a weakness in one application protocol run between user and service provider does not affect other protocols, even with the same service provider. These two requirements are realized by appropriate derivation of service- and protocol-specific keys from the intermediate shared key. Hence, even if a service provider offers different services (using different protocols), then the keys used would be different. It should be noted that commonly the wording "service-specific key" or "application-specific key" is used, but actually the derived keys are also always protocol specific. One typical case is that a news service server has a commenting blog, where it requires user authentication, and additionally the server has a news streaming service. In this case, we would have the same service provider identification, but then different protocol identifiers for the different protocols used.

2.3. *GBA*

The purpose of the GBA is to provision a shared service-specific secret to an application server residing in an IP-based network and a UE. This key provisioning is based on the AKA authentication of the UE [18]. AKA is the authentication and key agreement protocol used in 3GPP-defined mobile networks. The basic steps of GBA are outlined in Ref. 1 and can be summarized as follows (see also Fig. 1):

(i) The UE requests a service by contacting an application server. This application server is called Network Application Function (NAF) in the GBA system. The GBA-specific functionality that an application server has to provide can in practice be realized through a specific NAF library that is added to the application server to handle the communication with the BSF.

(ii) The NAF indicates to the UE that GBA shall be used for authentication (see, e.g., Refs. 19 and 20).

(iii) After the UE receives the request to use GBA for authentication, the NAF client application in the UE requests NAF specific GBA credentials from a GBA function (also called BSF client or GBA module) in the UE. The NAF client application in the UE is, for example, a browser or a streaming application. In closed platforms or fully proprietary environments, this distinction may not be that strict.

(iv) The GBA function in the device that is responsible for the GBA credential related communication with the smart card and the BSF communicates with the BSF (that acts as a credential server to the NAF) to establish GBA credentials [15]. The BSF interacts with the HSS/HLR to obtain the needed smart card based secret for the master key derivation and the user security related information stored in the GBA User Security Settings (GUSS) [16]. The GUSS can contain data about the relationship between the operator and the NAF in the *NAFgroup* field, i.e., the operator may indicate that NAFs from a specific NAF group are more trusted than others. If the BSF client already has valid GBA keys, then it will re-use those.

(v) The GBA function in the UE then derives a service provider-specific session key from the GBA master session key that is directly based on the credentials stored in the device smart card. In a smart card centric variant of GBA, called GBA_U, the key derivation part of the GBA function resides on the smart card (cf. Refs. 1 or 21 and more detailed discussion below). The GBA function returns the service specific session key, bootstrapping transaction identifier (B-TID, which serves as an identifier for the key), and key lifetime to the NAF application in the UE. Examples of the interaction details between the

NAF client and the GBA function in the terminal for trusted open platforms can be found in Ref. 22.

(vi) The NAF client in the UE uses the NAF-specific keys as instructed, e.g., for authentication. The UE calculates the authentication response to the authentication challenge received from the NAF server in Step (ii).

(vii) The UE responds to the authentication challenge by sending the authentication response to the NAF server.

(viii) The NAF server requests the NAF-specific session key from the BSF [16] using the transaction ID received from the UE in the authentication response. The BSF finds the user's GBA credentials from its databases using the transaction ID, and calculates the NAF server-specific session key.

(ix) The BSF returns the NAF server-specific session key and key lifetime to the NAF server. The BSF may also return user identities, e.g., an application specific username or authorization flags of the user. These are contained in the service type-specific USS, which are part of the GUSS received from BSF. At this point both UE and application server are holding an application server-specific shared secret. This can then be used for user authentication or other communication related security functions (e.g., service protection for mobile TV streaming/broadcast). In the following, we will focus on the user authentication use case.

(x) The NAF validates the usage of the NAF-specific keys, e.g., if the keys were used for authentication then the NAF verifies that the authentication response is correct using the NAF server- and protocol-specific session key received from the BSF.

(xi) The NAF and the UE use the NAF-specific keys as outlined by the service. In the most common case of authentication, if authentication was successful, then the NAF server allows the UE to access the requested service.

Figure 1 outlines a simple architecture. If an HSS is used, then the HSS holding the subscriber data can be located by the BSF by contacting a Subscriber Locator Function (SLF). Also, if an HLR is deployed, then the Message Application Part (MAP) protocol is used instead of DIAMETER, and the interface is called Zh' instead of Zh.

2.4. *Handling of GBA Keys in the Terminal*

The application server-specific credentials, also called NAF-specific session keys, are derived based on the result of the authentication protocol run. For this there are three GBA variants in 3GPP which were specified to handle different requirements:

- *GBA_ME*: This is the basic variant which is designed to work with any USIM and ISIM out in the field. It only requires the mobile equipment (ME, normally the terminal) to be GBA aware.

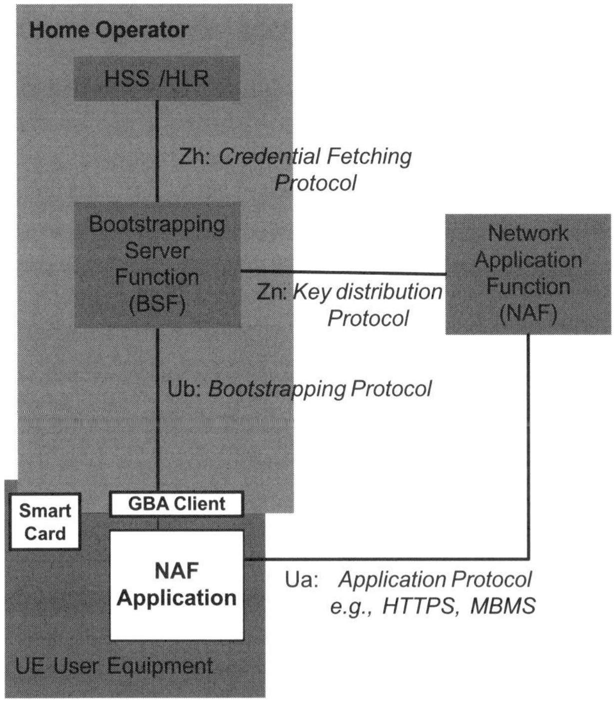

Fig. 1. Generic bootstrapping architecture.

The terminal stores the key resulting from the authentication AKA protocol run as received from the USIM or ISIM application on the smart card inside the terminal (the ME, hence the name "GBA_ME"). The terminal provides security for the stored key through the operating system and the platform. This variant is mainly meant for applications that do not require the usage of a special tamper-resistant smart card.

If the user accesses a GBA-enabled service, the service-specific key is derived in the GBA function in the ME based on the stored key and given to the NAF application in the terminal for further usage. This API is protected by the terminal platform.

- *GBA_U*: In this variant the key resulting from the authentication protocol run never leaves the UICC smart card, hence the name "GBA_U." To provide compatibility with GBA_ME enabled applications, two keys are derived from this resulting key: one internal key stored inside the UICC and used only for functions residing on the same smart card (UICC), and one external key stored in the GBA function of the ME as in GBA_ME. The internal key is not accessible to the user or the terminal, even if the terminal is somehow compromised. Thus, this and any derived service specific internal key also stored in the UICC cannot be given away outside the smart card. For the external key that is given out to the terminal the same security measures apply as for the GBA_ME case, and the key is protected by the operating system and the platform security. For usage of GBA_U the UICC smart cards must be GBA_U enabled and support this special functionality [21]. Currently, they are not yet commercially available in the market.

If the user accesses a service, the application server, depending on the local policy, may indicate that it only accepts GBA_U based keys for authentication and/or communication security. Then, the terminal has to access the related key derivation function and use the respective key. The application server can check from the data it receives from the BSF if the terminal really used a GBA_U derived key, and can deny access if not.

- *SIM (2G) GBA* or *legacy GBA*: This is an early implementation feature in Release 7 of 3GPP allowing GBA-based services to be offered to the large range of users that hold a SIM card. Here also the terminal derives an application-specific key, based on the credentials received from the SIM card [23] (or Annex I of Ref. 1).

  This variant is different from a security point of view as it is based on a SIM, and not a USIM or ISIM. It should be noted that even if 2G GBA uses a SIM card, the known weaknesses of the SIM card are mitigated by additional security measures. The owner of a service which normally requires GBA_ME or GBA_U for access to the service must decide if the service should also accept 2G GBA based keys with reduced security, at least for a transitional period until most subscribers are provided with a USIM or ISIM.

Additionally, CDMA-specific variants for GBA were defined by 3GPP2, but we will not elaborate further here.

3. Thoughts for Practitioners — Usage of the GBA

The GBA is a generic enabler and has been taken up by many applications and standardization forums. The most mature use cases can be found in presence list management for IP Multimedia Subsystem (IMS) [20], Mobile Broadcast Multicast Service (MBMS) [8], provisioning of subscriber certificates [24] and the usage of GBA for HTTP TLS or pre-shared key TLS [19]. Other use cases include the Open Mobile Alliance (OMA) Presence Specification, and OMA Broadcast [9, 25].

The propagation of GBA into other areas outside of 3GPP produced the need for further dedicated extensions to GBA, like the GBA Push specification [26], which enables network triggered credential generation, or some smart card based GBA features. GBA also plays a role in the future converging networks, since future networks like the ones specified by TISPAN or CableLabs have taken up GBA into their ongoing work. In most cases GBA is used for authentication to a service or authentication proxy together with the possibility to provide a shared secret for communications security to both parties.

4. Background — The LAP

In this section we introduce briefly the LAP Identity Federation Framework (ID-FF) and the Web Services Framework (ID-WSF), but only to the degree to which it is applicable to the identity interworking between GBA and LAP architecture. The ID-FF and the ID-WSF have been designed for a wide range of potential Internet service providers. Therefore, the most commonly used underlying protocol is HTTP. Mobile network considerations were taken into account (e.g., in the authentication context specification), but basically LAP is network-agnostic.

4.1. *ID-FF*

The LAP ID-FF is a system that enables user identity federation, i.e., mapping of several user identities to each other and management through features such as identity or account linkage, simplified single sign on (SSO), and simple SSO session management [27]. For the interworking between LAP and the 3GPP GBA, the Identity Provider (IdP) is the most interesting role in the ID-FF concept. The IdP is an entity that manages identity information on behalf of the user and provides assertions of the user authentication to other providers, e.g., other service providers or other identity providers acting as identity proxies.

4.2. *WSF*

The LAP WSF is a system that provides the framework for building interoperable identity based services, permission based attribute sharing, identity service description and discovery, and the associated security profiles. The WSF also offers other services, but those are not relevant for the interworking with the mobile network authentication infrastructure. The LAP specified a single sign–on service (SSOS) [28] and an authentication service, which are the most relevant Web services from an interworking point of view.

5. Architecture for Liberty Alliance and Generic Bootstrapping Architecture Interworking

5.1. *Collocated Identity Provider — Network Application Function Architecture*

In the LAP ID-FF system we have the user (called "principal" in LAP), the IdP and the service provider (SP). The user wants to access a service at the SP using his UE. This service request is normally HTTP based, but this architecture is not restricted to a single protocol. If necessary, the SP and the IdP use the Simple Object Access Protocol (SOAP) [10] for direct Web service communication as outlined in Fig. 2.

Interworking of the GBA and ID-FF means that authentication based on GBA credentials is used within the LAP framework, i.e., the specifications are then complementing each other. Thus, in the LAP ID-FF the role of the IdP is collocated with a GBA entity. There are two basic design choices concerning which GBA

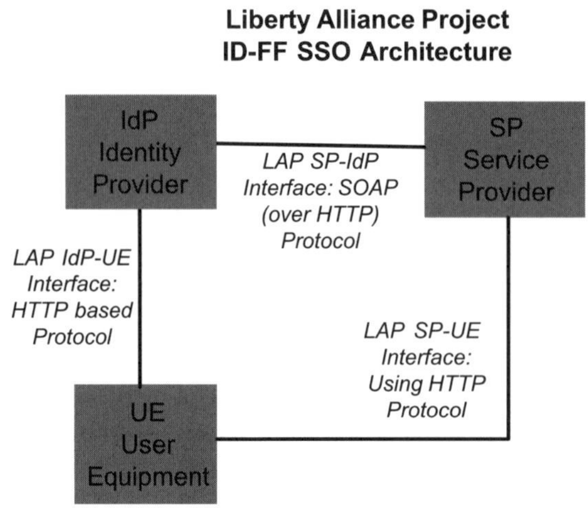

Fig. 2. LAP identity federation framework.

entity to collocate with the IdP. One choice is to collocate the IdP very close to the operator's subscriber database and collocate the IdP with the BSF, cf, the next section. However, the easiest way to accomplish interworking of LAP and GBA without major adaptations of both worlds is to collocate the IdP with the NAF. The IdP/NAF collocation also allows that an operator outsources the IdP to a trusted partner or, in large affiliation networks, that one operator hosts and IdP/NAF for several other affiliated operators. The IdP/NAF authenticates the UE using GBA credentials. In this collocation scenario, there is only one interface carrying both LAP [27, 29] and GBA related information, i.e., the reference point between the IdP/NAF and the UE. The architecture for a collocated IdP/NAF together with GBA and LAP ID-FF architecture is outlined in Fig. 3. Note that the NAF in this case is not the Liberty Alliance SP, but that the NAF takes the role of the IdP. The dashed lines indicate the interfaces specified by 3GPP and the solid lines indicate the LAP ID-FF interfaces.

5.2. *Collocation of IdP and BSF*

This recently added alternative is also feasible and has been specified in Ref. 30.

Collocation of IdP and BSF has the advantage that it needs fewer round-trips than the variant with collocated NAF and IdP. However, it also comes with a number of drawbacks. There is a large impact on the generic interface to the terminal to transport Liberty related information. Furthermore, the interface to the service provider has to be modified and extended to support the Liberty SSO use case. Also, the security guarantees are somewhat weaker: the communication between the client and the collocated IdP-NAF is protected using a key derived from GBA which is specific to this communication, using either HTTPS with HTTP Digest for

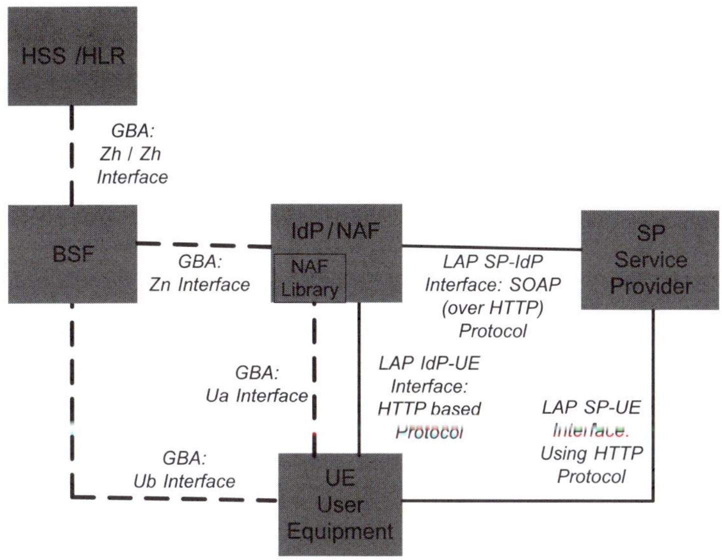

Fig. 3. Collocated architecture for IdP/NAF.

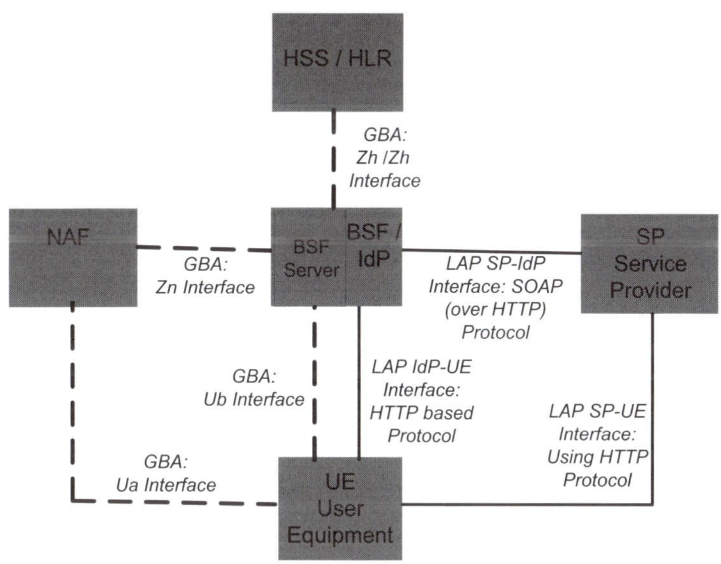

Fig. 4. Combined LAP ID-FF and GAA architecture with BSF/IdP collocation.

client authentication or pre-shared key TLS. From the architectural point of view, the generic BSF has to support specific functionality for the IdP (see Figure 4). For other applications the BSF is agnostic to the actual usage of the keys and no specific functionality is needed for the BSF to support, e.g., HTTPS, mobile TV security or presence security. If many SPs connect to the IdP it may also be desirable for load reasons not to collocate the BSF with the IdP. Note that the IdP/BSF collocation implies that the IdP is part of the home network (i.e., no outsourcing or affiliated operator IdP is possible). For details, see Ref. 30. On the other hand, the BSF/IdP collocation scenario presents a security vulnerability under certain circumstances (i.e., a MitM attack over the Ub interface may become possible as the GBA bootstrapping over Ub is not cryptographically bound to the Liberty procedures). The attack becomes very difficult to implement (and, therefore, almost negligible) if the Ub procedures are run end-to-end over the operator administrated network which is properly encrypted. (UE initiates the bootstrapping procedure directly with the preconfigured BSF-address, and if all the communication runs over the properly encrypted operator administrated network, there is in practice little chance for the MitM to actually get "in the middle" during this Ub procedure). In this case, the security of the solution is basically ensured by relying on the trustworthiness and non-vulnerability of the operator's routing infrastructure.

5.3. *User Identity Data Management*

The IdP commonly needs some persistent user identity for authentication. This stems from the fact that the IdP must have a "root of identity" of the user, which is authenticated, and which is the basis for any federation. The mobile environment in turn has knowledge of the user identity and can provide the IdP with persistent subscriber-specific data. This will normally be the identity under which the user is persistently known at the IdP. This identity may be the IMPI (IP Multimedia Private Identity) of the user. If the IdP is not within the network domain of the operator, or if there is a need for different identities of the user, or if required by general privacy rules, then instead of the IMPI a service type-specific identity from user's USS is provided to the IdP. For this purpose 3GPP specified a service type "GBA-LAP-interworking." If necessary, the operator may also store some interworking-specific authorization data (flags) in the user's USS, which is under operator control. Also, the temporary GBA user identifier (Bootstrapping Transaction Identifier) is not suited as a persistent user identifier since it changes with every bootstrapping run between UE and BSF.

One special case of user authentication shall also be mentioned. If the service provider does not require a user identity on access, but only a certain attribute, e.g., he wants it to be asserted that the user belongs to some predefined group, such as to the subscribers of a specific operator, then the IdP does not need a user identity. Using the GBA feature of asserting that the user is authorized, but anonymous, the IdP may provide the service provider with an anonymous user identity, which still asserts the correct attribute of the user.

To make most use of the specific advantages of GBA and LAP, it can normally be assumed that most of the LAP related user data is stored within IdP or some user profile services. In addition, the IdP must store the persistent user identity which is authenticated by GBA as the root of federation and identity assertion (except if anonymous user access is desired).

From the user's perspective there are several options to register and manage his identity in a combined LAP GBA architecture. The user may register with his home operator, and then there are two procedural choices.

The user explicitly subscribes to GBA-LAP interworking, where he may provide the additional data needed. This may be useful if the subscriber has an existing relation to the LAP IdP and wants to use his mobile subscription for authentication there. Alternatively, the user may automatically be provided with access to GBA-LAP interworking, e.g., by his mobile network operator. This requires either providing each subscriber at the start of the subscription with interworking-specific data, like user identity, or alternatively only using data for interworking which exists for the subscriber anyway (e.g., IMPI).

The user may also register directly at his IdP, the "Internet" way, e.g., being redirected from a service provider. The registration to participate in LAP federation in general may be independent of the usage of the interworking service. If the IdP does not offer the interworking with GBA as part of the initial registration, then the interworking may be provided by the IdP as a system extension later on.

If the IdP is not hosted by the user's home operator, then the user has to indicate to the IdP the GBA-related identity (IMPI or public user identity) which shall be used as the root of authentication for LAP or to request the root from the BSF. In addition the user has to prove to the IdP that he is entitled to use the GBA-related identity. This is best accomplished by using a GBA-authenticated communication for the registration procedure at IdP also. This proves the legitimate use of the identity given by the current user by comparison with the GBA-related identity provided to IdP/NAF over the credential fetching interface Zn. The IdP/NAF may receive multiple public user identities, of which the user may indicate one to be used as the root for federation within LAP federation. In special cases, different "LAP root identities" may also be bound to one subscriber, which requires that the IdP selects the correct root identity based on the federation data with the requesting service provider.

5.4. *Interworking for GBA and LAP Web Services Framework*

The architecture for the interworking between the GBA and the LAP Web Services Framework (ID-WSF) is applicable for the Web service based authentication service (AS) [28] or the single sign-on service (SSOS). In LAP ID-WSF (deploying a Liberty enabled client) the AS is the counterpart of GBA. Here, as with interworking with ID-FF, only the authentication step is influenced by the interworking, as the LAP ID-FF and ID-WSF specifications do not make assumptions about how authentication is performed. But if authentication data is carried within the same communication path as the LAP ID-WSF SOAP messages between UE and AS, then Liberty Alliance mandates the use of the Simple Authentication and Security

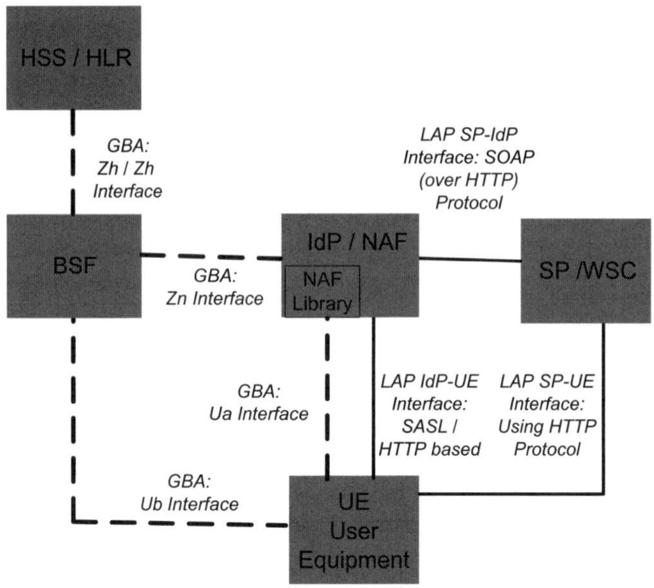

Fig. 5. Combined LAP ID-WSF and GBA with collocated NAF and AS.

Layer (SASL) protocol [31]. Therefore, 3GPP specified "HTTP Digest over SASL" as a new protocol for the Ua interface. Figure 5 shows the architecture for the collocated AS/NAF scenario. In the case that there is a SSOS, then the SSOS takes the role of the Web Service Consumer (WSC)/SP in Fig. 4.

6. Directions for Future Research — Interworking of GBA and Other Identity Management Systems

Other identity management systems that could be using GBA are the Organization for the Advancement of Structured Information Standards (OASIS) Web Services Secure Exchange (WS-SX) [32]. In OASIS WS-SX the client application has to be aware of the identity management system used, and the identity mechanism needs to be integrated. Another identity management solution that may utilize GBA is OpenID 2.0 [33]. In the case, the client in the terminal would be a browser.

The requirement to support legacy databases and systems and also the realization that different identity management systems will exist also in the future in parallel resulted in the creation of Meta Identity Systems. These are designed to allow the plugging in of different identity management systems and provide a user interface for selection of the appropriate information for the intended purpose. The GBA can also be integrated here as one identity management system based on HTTP Digest authentication [19]. One popular example of a Meta Identity System is Microsoft CardSpace [34], formerly known as InfoCard. This is part of the .NET framework and is pre-installed on Windows Vista. In Microsoft CardSpace the user has a range of identity cards to choose from that provide the appropriate identity information to the requesting service using other systems underneath. It should be noted that meta identity systems provide much more than pure authentication, by helping users to manage all their identity related information. Another example is the open source project Bandit, which also has a user-centric identity data management approach. It runs on Linux and Mac OS X. Bandit supports role-based access control and common identity [35].

The actual details of integration of GBA into those systems is a task for future research and development.

7. Conclusion

User identity management in the mobile environment, as described in this chapter, has the advantage that it can be bound to an existing cryptographic token, the smart card that binds the user to his mobile subscription. The user has to not only provide something he knows, but also something he possesses, i.e., the identity management described in this chapter provides two-factor authentication. This approach is realized using the GBA developed by 3GPP. The wide adoption of GBA and the convergence between mobile and Internet environments for next-generation networks has resulted in the specification of interworking between the procedures defined by the LAP and the GBA procedures. This interworking covers the identity federation framework, the single sign-on service and the authentication service of the LAP WSF.

Terminology

Access control: The restriction of service access by a service provider based on the presented user credentials.

Bootstrapping: Initializing security for a particular feature by tying it to a pre-existing security infrastructure.

Bootstrapping Server Function: A credential distribution server in the Generic Bootstrapping Architecture.

Generic Bootstrapping Architecture (GBA): A 3GPP architecture that allows provisioning of a shared secret to a user device and an application server.

GBA_ME: Terminal specific variant of GBA, where one service-specific key is derived and stored in the terminal protected by the platform and operating system.

GBA_U: Smart card variant for GBA, where one service-specific key stays in the GBA-enabled smart card.

Identity provider (IdP): Validates the presented user identity and relays the result to the service providers.

Legacy GBA: The shared secret in GBA is derived based on the secret shared in the legacy SIM card; additionally, extra security measures are applied in the GBA protocols for this variant.

Network Application Function (NAF): A GBA server that provides one or several applications to the user.

Subscriber database: A database in the operator network that stores the cryptographic shared secret that is also on the smart card handed out to the subscriber.

Exercises

1. What is the meaning of the term "bootstrapping" in communication security?
2. Why do some services exercise access control?
3. What are the key features of the service access control mechanism?
4. Outline the basic GBA architecture.
5. Which basic GBA variants exist in 3GPP?
6. Outline the Liberty Alliance ID-FF architecture.
7. What design choices do we have to collocate the identity provider in a joint GBA/LAP architecture?
8. Outline the architectures for ID-FF with NAF/IdP and BSF/IdP collocation.
9. Outline the architecture for ID-WSF with NAF/IdP collocation.
10. What are the areas of future work for GBA and identity management interworking?

References

1. 3rd Generation Partnership Project 2 (3GPP2), www.3gpp2.org.
2. 3rd Generation Partnership Project (3GPP), Technical report TR 33.905, Recommendations for trusted open platforms, Version 7.0.0, www.3gpp.org (2007).
3. 3rd Generation Partnership Project (3GPP), Technical report TR 33.920, SIM card based generic bootstrapping architecture (gba), early implementation feature, Version 7.1.0, www.3gpp.org (2006).
4. 3rd Generation Partnership Project (3GPP), Technical report TR 33.978, Security aspects of early IP multimedia subsystem, Version 7.0.0, www.3gpp.org (2007).
5. 3rd Generation Partnership Project (3GPP), Technical report TR 33.980, Liberty alliance and 3GPP security interworking, Interworking of Liberty Alliance Identity Federation Framework (ID-FF), Identity Web Services Framework (ID-WSF) and Generic Authentication Architecture (GAA), Version 7.4.0, www.3gpp.org (2007).
6. 3rd Generation Partnership Project (3GPP), Technical specification TS 24.109, Bootstrapping interface (Ub) and network application function interface (Ua), Protocol details, Version 7.5.0, www.3gpp.org (2006).
7. 3rd Generation Partnership Project (3GPP), Technical specification TS 29.109, Generic Authentication Architecture (GAA); Zh and Zn interfaces based on the Diameter protocol; Stage 3, Version 7.5.0, www.3gpp.org (2006).

8. 3rd Generation Partnership Project (3GPP), Technical specification TS 31.102, Characteristics of the Universal Subscriber Identity Module (USIM) application, Version 7.8.0, www.3gpp.org (2007).
9. 3rd Generation Partnership Project (3GPP), Technical specification TS 33.141, Presence Service, Security, Version 7.1.0, www.3gpp.org (2006).
10. 3rd Generation Partnership Project (3GPP), Technical specification TS 33.220, Generic Authentication Architecture (GAA), Generic Bootstrapping Architecture, Version 7.7.0, www.3gpp.org (2007).
11. 3rd Generation Partnership Project (3GPP), Technical specification TS 33.221, Generic Authentication Architecture (GAA), Support for subscriber certificates, Version 6.3.0, www.3gpp.org (2006).
12. 3rd Generation Partnership Project (3GPP), Technical specification TS 33.222, Generic Authentication Architecture (GAA), Access to network application functions using Hypertext Transfer Protocol over Transport Layer Security (HTTPS), Version 7.2.0, www.3gpp.org (2006).
13. 3rd Generation Partnership Project (3GPP), Technical specification TS 33.223, Generic Authentication Architecture (GAA), Generic Bootstrapping Architecture (GBA), Push Function, Version 0.5.0, Release 8, www.3gpp.org (2007).
14. 3rd Generation Partnership Project (3GPP), Technical specification TS 33.246, 3G Security, Security of Multimedia Broadcast/Multicast Services (MBMS), Version 7.3.0, www.3gpp.org (2007).
15. Bandit Project, www.bandit-project.org (2007).
16. M. Bonifati, P. De Lutiis, C. Moiso, E. Morello and L. Sarchi, Identity federation for services in convergent networks, *ICIN 2006*, Bordeaux (2006).
17. CableLabs, www.cablelabs.com.
18. Internet Engineering Task Force (IETF), RFC 1510, The Kerberos network authentication service (V5), www.ietf.orf/rfc/rfc1510.txt (1993).
19. Internet Engineering Task Force (IETF), RFC 2222, Simple Authentication and Security Layer (SASL), www.ietf.org/rfc/rfc2222.txt (1997).
20. Internet Engineering Task Force (IETF), RFC 3310, Hypertext Transfer Protocol (HTTP) digest authentication using Authentication and Key Agreement (AKA), www.ietf.org/rfc/rfc3310.txt (2002).
21. Internet Engineering Task Force (IETF), RFC4640, Problem statement for bootstrapping mobile IPv6 (MIPv6), www.ietf.org/rfc/rfc4640.txt (2006).
22. V. Gerstenberger, P. Lahaije and M. Schuba, Internet ID — Flexible re-use of mobile phone authentication security for service access, NordSec, Helsinki (2004).
23. Liberty Alliance Project (LAP), http://www.projectliberty.org.
24. Liberty Alliance Project (LAP), ID-FF v1.2: Liberty ID-FF architecture overview, www.projectliberty.org.
25. Liberty Alliance Project, ID-WSF v2.0 Liberty ID-WSF authentication service specification and single sign-on service, www.projectliberty.org.
26. Microsoft CardSpace, cardspace.netfx3.com.
27. Open Mobile Alliance (OMA), www.openmobilealliance.org.
28. Open Mobile Alliance (OMA), BCAST Working Group, Broadcast service and content protection for mobile broadcast services. Version 1.0, www.openmobilealliance.org/tech/wg_committees/bac.html.
29. Open Mobile Alliance (OMA), Presence Working Group, www.openmobilealliance.org/tech/wg_committees/pag.html.
30. OpenID, openid.net.

31. Organization for the Advancement of Structured Information Standards (OASIS), Bindings and profiles for the OASIS Security Assertion Markup Language (SAML) v2.0.
32. Organization for the Advancement of Structured Information Standards (OASIS), Web Service Secure Exchange (WS-SX) Technical Committee, www.oasis-open.org/committees/ws-sx.
33. Telecoms & Internet Converged Services & Protocols for Advanced Networks (TISPAN), www.etsi.org/tispan.
34. Wireless Application Protocol (WAP), now part of OMA, www.openmobilealliance.org.
35. World Wide Web Consortium (W3C), Simple Object Access Protocol (SOAP), www.w3.org/TR/soap (2007).

Chapter 25

PROACTIVE MODELS FOR MITIGATING INTERNET DENIAL-OF-SERVICE/DISTRIBUTED DENIAL-OF-SERVICE ATTACKS

H. R. NAGESH* and K. CHANDRA SEKARAN
Department of Computer Engineering,
National Institute of Technology, Karnataka,
Surathkal 575025, India
**hrnagesh2001@rediffmail.com*
†kchnitk@gmail.com

The enormous growth of the Internet has had a huge impact on users' daily lives, providing us with a wealth of information easily and conveniently. At the same time, this accessibility has made the Internet an easy target for users who wish to disrupt the flow of information or exploit the Web for personal gain. Those who compromise the flow of information or access information in an unauthorized manner are called attackers. Many tools are now available for attackers to test the vulnerability of Internet.

One form of attack is denial-of-service (DoS). A DoS attack is launched by sending a stream of packets to a victim (affected system or destination system). This consumes some key resources of the victim and renders them unavailable to legitimate users, or it provides an attacker with unlimited access to the victim so that the attacker can inflict arbitrary damage. If DoS attacks are generated from different places then it is called distributed denial-of-service (DDoS). Attackers deploy multiple systems to attain this goal. DoS/DDoS attacks are one of the major threats to the Internet. The normal functions of popular servers on the Internet are disturbed due to this. In both cases, the attackers hide their identity by spoofing their Internet Protocol (IP) addresses. The mitigation of a DoS attack is a reactive countermeasure that is actually initiated by the victim after detecting an attack. The main challenges in DoS mitigation is to accurately identify attack packets and filter them without causing collateral damage to legitimate traffic destined for the victim. Two models have been proposed for mitigating DoS/DDoS attacks: *secure overlay services* and *server hopping using distributed firewalls*. In this chapter, the effectiveness of these approaches is assessed for different types of DoS/DDoS attacks. The simulation results of DoS/DDoS that without any defense models shows the packet delivery time increases and the packet delivery to the server is delayed. In the secure overlay services defense model for DoS/DDoS attacks, the variation in packet delivery time remains almost constant with the actual packet delivery time. The server hopping using distributed firewalls model also maintains a constant packet delivery time. However, the amount of variation in packet delivery time in secure overlay services is greater than with server hopping using distributed firewalls. Through simple analytical models, it is shown that DoS/DDoS attacks directed against any part of the secure overlay services infrastructure have a negligible probability of disrupting the communication between two parties. Furthermore, the resistance of a secure overlay services network to DoS/DDoS attacks increases greatly with the number of nodes that participate in the overlay. The secure overlay services and server hopping using distributed firewalls architectures provide a range of defenses that can severely limit the damage caused by DDoS attacks.

1. Introduction

A denial-of-service (DoS) attack [1–3] is an attempt to prevent legitimate users of a service or network resource from accessing that service or resource. DoS attacks usually make use of software to crash or freeze a service or a network resource, or exploit bandwidth limits by making use of a flood attack to saturate the network. The intention is to overrun the components of network resources such as bandwidth, memory or CPU so that service to a legitimate group of members is denied. A DoS attack can be either a single-source attack, originating at only one host, or multi-source, where multiple hosts coordinate to flood the victim with a barrage of attack packets. The latter is called a distributed Dos attack. Very few approaches have been proposed [4–7] to solve the problem of DoS attacks. The solutions can be either proactive (they prevent the attack) or reactive (they react to stop the attack after it has begun). To actually stop the attack, they usually require human intervention and cooperation between different administrative domains. The administrator's desire is to use proactive protection in order to prevent the attack. The Internet Indirection Infrastructure (I3) [4, 5] and "capabilities" [7] are the two important protection architectures recently proposed. These solutions make some assumptions about network vulnerabilities. A crucial idea put forward by the I3 proposal is that its model should not introduce new vulnerabilities. However, many of I3's weaknesses arise from the ability of anyone using any identifier to launch an attack. Better infrastructure can be a combination of the strengths of an overlay network and the capabilities infrastructure, with multiple credential generation or authorization points. Hence, there is a need for new models to be designed and developed to mitigate DoS/DDoS attacks.

2. Background

DoS attacks are invoked by flooding the target network and its computers with a large amount of traffic from a computer which is under the attacker's control. In DoS attacks, the packets are routed correctly but the destination becomes the target of the attackers [8]. DoS attacks are very easy to generate and are very difficult to detect. In a typical DoS attack, the attacker node spoofs its Internet Protocol (IP) address and uses multiple intermediate nodes to overwhelm other nodes with traffic. DoS attacks are typically used to take important servers out of action for a few hours, resulting in denial-of-service to all the users served by the server. It can also be used to disrupt the services of intermediate routers. Often, the source address of these packets is spoofed, making it difficult to locate the real source of the attack.

2.1. *DDoS Attack*

When the traffic of a DoS attack comes from multiple sources, we call it a distributed denial-of-service (DDoS) attack. In a DDoS attack, there might still be a single attacker, but the effect of the attack is greatly multiplied by the use of attack servers known as agents. The attack not only disables that server but denies access to legitimate users. Routing table positioning and packet mistreaming attacks are capable of causing denial-of-service. Such attacks are among the toughest to address because they are simple to implement, hard to prevent, and difficult to trace. Figure 1 shows a DDoS attack scenario.

2.2. *DoS Attack Methods*

Smurf attacks: Smurf attacks are one of the most devastating DoS attacks. In the Smurf (ICMP Packet Magnification) attack, the attacker sends an ICMP echo request (ping) to a broadcast address [4]. The source address of the echo request is the IP address of the victim (the IP address of the victim is used as the return address). After receiving the echo request, all the machines in the broadcast domain send echo replies (responses) to the victim's IP address, as shown in Fig. 2. The victim's machine will crash or freeze when receiving a flood of larger-sized packets from many machines. A Smurf attack uses bandwidth consumption to disable a victim system's network resources. Smurf attacks can also use UDP echo packets.

SYN flood: This method uses resource starvation to achieve the DoS attack by exploiting the vulnerabilities of TCP. Figure 3 shows a normal TCP handshake,

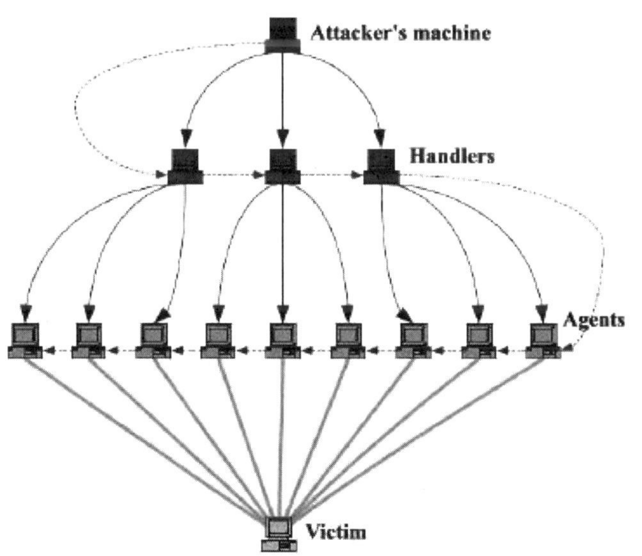

Fig. 1. DDoS attack model.

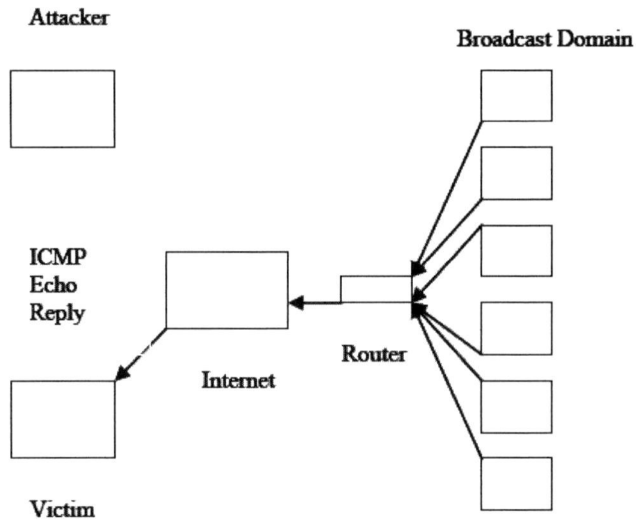

Fig. 2. Smurf attack.

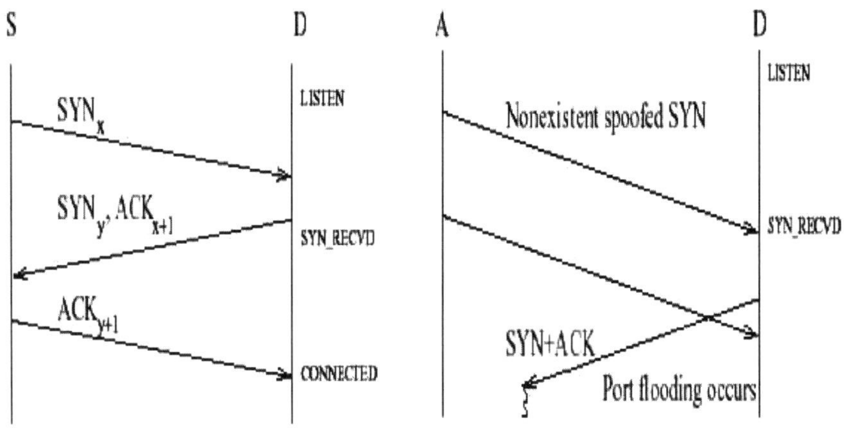

Fig. 3. SYN flood attack.

where a client sends a SYN request to the server. The server responds with an ACK/SYN to the client, and the client sends a final ACK back to the server. But in a SYN flood attack, the attacker sends multiple SYN requests to the victim server with spoofed source addresses for the return address. The spoofed addresses are nonexistent on the network. The victim server then responds with an ACK/SYN back to the nonexistent address. Because no address receives this ACK/SYN, the victim server just waits for the ACK from the client. The ACK never arrives, and the victim server eventually times out. If the attacker sends SYN requests often enough, the victim server's available resources for setting up a connection will be consumed waiting for these bogus ACKs. These resources are usually low in number, so relatively few bogus SYN requests can create a DoS event.

DNS hacking attacks: Attacks of this type have illustrated the lack of authenticity and integrity of the data held within the DNS as well as in the protocols that use host names as an access control mechanism. The DNS, being a critical infrastructure, is contacted by all hosts when accessing servers and starting connections [4]. The DNS consists of a distributed database that lends to its robustness but also leads to various types of vulnerabilities, which can be categorized into three main types [4]:

- *Cache poisoning*: Generally, to enhance the process of query response, DNS servers store common information in a cache. If the DNS server is made to cache bogus information, the attacker can redirect traffic intended for a legitimate site to a site under the attacker's control.
- *Server compromising*: Attackers can compromise a DNS server, thus giving them the ability to modify the data served to the users. These compromised servers can be used for cache poisoning or DoS attacks on some other server.
- *Spoofing*: In this type of attack, the attacker masquerades as a DNS server and feeds the client wrong and/or potentially malicious information. This type of attack can also redirect the traffic to a site under the attacker's control.

2.3. *DoS Architectures*

DoS protection architectures can be either proactive or reactive. For stopping the attack, they usually require human intervention and cooperation between different administrative domains. Administrators use proactive protection to prevent attacks. The existing proactive protection architectures are Internet Indirection Infrastructure [4, 5], and "capabilities" [6, 7]. Each architecture includes some kind of "credential" in each packet. Each strategy also makes changes or additions to the Internet's infrastructure. The infrastructure looks at packets as they cross the network, filtering them based on their credentials. Packets that do not have the proper credentials are dropped and do not reach their destination.

2.3.1. *Comparison of Distributed Denial-of-Service Architectures*

The existing architectures for distributed denial-of-service attacks can be compared with respect to incremental deployment, traffic analysis and infrastructure attacks [4–7]. Table 1 lists the merits and demerits of different architectures with respect to incremental deployment.

An attacker performs a traffic analysis attack when it observes the traffic passing through a router or on an infrastructure link. It can see the packet headers and the packet contents (if they are not encrypted). Table 2 lists the merits and demerits of different architectures with respect to traffic analysis attacks.

Attacks on the Internet infrastructure can lead to enormous disruption. Just as an attacker can compromise individual hosts to create a zombie army, it can use

Table 1. Incremental deployment analysis.

	Merits of I3. capabilities, and SOS
I3	Very simple to add and organize servers.
Capabilities	Very simple to add and organize servers.
	Easy to add clients by inserting new capabilities server at BGP server. No client modification required.
	Centrally deployed verification points can moderate traffic.
	Provides protection to the implemented. Strong protection available, if capabilities scheme is enforced on all communicators.
SOS	Very simple to add and organize servers.
	With local filtering, protection is very strong as there is a limited list of approved senders.
	Demerit of I3, capabilities, and SOS
I3	All clients must be modified to use pseudonyms or a proxy must be inserted to capture and modify all traffic. Without near-complete deployment, IP addresses will still be used. Once a critical segment has adopted I3, a server may be able to insist on compliance from the remainder of clients for service. Until then, it is still vulnerable.
SOS	Clients must be modified to send to SOS or a proxy must be inserted.

Table 2. Traffic analysis.

	Merits of I3, capabilities, and SOS
I3	Recovers by switching IP address and creating new triggers.
Capabilities	Attacker with a forged credential can only disrupt one sender/receiver pair. High-rate traffic will be dropped quickly and will not affect the other communicators. Automatic recovery at set intervals is possible.
SOS	Receiver driven recovery by choosing new secret servlets.
	Demerits of I3, capabilities, and SOS
13	On the path between receiver and I3 node, IP addresses are easy to learn. The receiver can be attacked directly using the IP address: this can disrupt all ongoing connections.
	Can learn the trigger/IP address relation by observing traffic euteriug and leaving an I3 node.
Capabilities	A close proximity attacker cau insert additional traffic to use up the permitted bandwidth of all communicators.
SOS	The credential can be clearly observed on the path between SOS and the receiver. Packets forged with this information can overwhelm all connections in progress.

other vulnerabilities to compromise infrastructure routers. Once an attacker has complete control over the router, it can observe all information passing through the router as well as modify or delete it. Table 3 lists the merits and demerits of different architectures with respect to infrastructure attacks.

Every model makes some assumptions about the vulnerabilities of the network. A crucial idea made clear by the I3 proposal is that any model should not

Table 3. Infrastructure attacks.

	Merits of I3, capabilities, and SOS
I3	Receivers avoid a misbehaving router through trigger selection.
	No one node is critical to any particular operation. The functionality of the failed node will be provided elsewhere.
Capabilities	Connections can always maintain valid capabilities.
	RTS servers can filter traffic efficiently as they should only communicate with their local clients and local BGP routers. All other traffic can be discarded. DoS attack requires close physical proximity.
SOS	No one node is critical to any particular operation. The functionality of the failed node will be provided elsewhere. If a beacon is attacked the protocol will choose a new beacon.
	Demerits of I3, capabilities, and SOS
I3	Malignant routers can amplify traffic, send it to genuine triggers, and overwhelm the destination. The pseudonym is not bound to the sender.
Capabilities	Can forge packets with locally stored capabilities. Uses up the bandwidth for each connection.
	Enables a DoS attack by enlarging all outgoing capabilities from local clients.
SOS	If the compromised node is the beacon, it can reveal the secret servlets' identities allowing attackers to send unfilterable traffic.

introduce new vulnerabilities. However, many of I3's weaknesses arise from the ability of anyone using any identifier to launch an attack. Better infrastructure can be a combination of the strengths of an overlay network and the capabilities infrastructure, with multiple credential generation or authorization points. This protects against the dangers of a DDoS attack on the infrastructure. A design might include a credential that is valid for any sender but impose strict limits on its use. Capabilities should have varying length validities. Ideally, they should be short lived and new ones should be acquired. They should also be able to be withdrawn in the case of an attack, or automatically expire. Better DDoS models require trade-offs between overhead and security.

3. Main Focus

Every solution presented in the literature [1–7], as discussed in earlier sections, makes some assumptions about the vulnerabilities of the network. A crucial idea made clear by the I3's [4, 5] proposal is that any solution should not introduce new vulnerabilities. However, many of I3's weaknesses arise from the ability of anyone using any identifier to launch an attack. Better infrastructure can be a combination of the strengths of an overlay network and the capabilities infrastructure, with multiple credential generation or authorization points. This protects against the dangers of a DoS or DDoS attacks on the infrastructure. A design might include a credential that is valid for any sender but impose strict limits on its use. Capabilities should have varying length validities. Ideally, they should be short lived and new ones should be acquired. They should also be able to be withdrawn in the case of an attack, or automatically expire. Better DoS/DDoS solutions require trade-offs between overhead and security.

3.1. *Design and Development*

Analysis of existing techniques reveals that the major challenges of defending against DoS and DDoS attack are how to identify the attack traffic accurately and efficiently, and how to locate attack sources and filter attack traffic close to the source. In the SOS architecture, we address the problem of securing communication in today's existing IP infrastructure from DoS and DDoS attacks, where the communication is between a predetermined location and a set of well-known users, located anywhere in the wide-area network, who have authorization to communicate with that location. We focus our efforts on protecting a site that stores information that is difficult to replicate due to security concerns or due to its dynamic nature.

In the server hopping using distributed firewalls architecture, the proxy server changes its location among a pool of servers to defend against unpredictable and likely undetectable attacks. Only legitimate clients will be able to follow the server as it roams. The main strength of the mechanism lies in the simplification of both the detection and filtering of malicious attack packets. In this technique, the proxy server's location changes dynamically as a function of time and a cryptographic key is shared between the server and the client. Authorized clients who have the key will be able to determine the current location used by the server, whereas the malicious users will not know the current location. The firewall can then easily filter illegitimate packets by inspecting the headers.

The following sections describe two proposed models: *secure overlay services (SOS)* and *server hopping using distributed firewalls* to mitigate DDoS attacks in group communication.

3.1.1. *Secure Overlay Services*

The proposed architecture for SOS uses a combination of routing via consistent hashing, and filtering. The forwarding of a packet within the SOS architecture, depicted in Fig. 4, proceeds through five stages:

- A source point that is the origin of the traffic forwards a packet to a special overlay node called a SOAP, which receives and verifies that the source point has a legitimate communication for the target.
- The SOAP routes the packet to a special node in the SOS architecture that is easily reached, called the beacon.
- The beacon forwards the packet to a "secret" node, called the secret servlet, whose identity is known to only a small subset of participants in the SOS architecture.
- The secret servlet forwards the packet to the target.

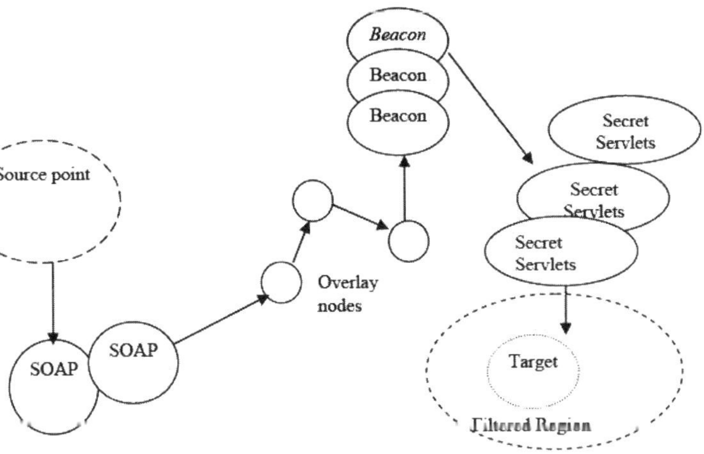

Fig. 4. Secure overlay services architecture.

- The filter around the target stops all traffic from reaching the target except for traffic that is forwarded from a point whose IP address is the secret servlet.

In the above proposed architecture, allowing a large number of overlay nodes to act as SOAPs increases the bandwidth resources that an attacker must obtain to prevent legitimate traffic from accessing the overlay. Effectively, SOS becomes a large distributed firewall that discriminates "good" (authorized) traffic from "bad" (unauthorized) traffic. By using a large number of topologically distributed firewall instances, we can increase the amount of resources (bandwidth) an attacker has to spend to deny connectivity to legitimate clients. This will severely limit the damage caused by DDoS attacks.

3.1.2. *Server Hopping using Distributed Firewalls*

Traditional data networks passively transport bits from one end system to another. Ideally, the user data is transferred opaquely, i.e., the network is insensitive to the bits it carries and they are transferred between end systems without modification [1]. The role of computation within such networks is extremely limited, e.g., header processing in packet-switched networks and signaling in connection-oriented networks. Active networks [10–16] break with tradition by allowing the network to perform customized computations on the user data. For example, a user of an active network could send a customized compression program to a node within the network (e.g., a router) and request that the node execute that program when processing their packets. These networks are "active" in two ways:

(i) Switches/routers perform computations on the user data flowing through them.
(ii) Individuals can inject programs into the network, thereby tailoring the node processing to be user- and application-specific.

The active network replaces the passive packets of present-day architectures with active "capsules." Capsules are the miniature programs that are executed at each router they traverse. This change in architectural perspective, from passive packets to active capsules, simultaneously addresses both of the "active" properties described above.

In active networks, every message is a program. Every message, or capsule, that passes between nodes contains a program fragment (of at least one instruction) that may include embedded data. When a capsule arrives at an active node, its contents are evaluated. Figure 5 provides a conceptual view of how an active node is organized. Bits arriving on incoming links are processed by a mechanism that identifies capsule boundaries, possibly using the framing mechanisms provided by traditional link layer protocols. The capsule's contents are dispatched to a transient execution environment where they can be safely evaluated. The programs are composed of "primitive" instructions that perform basic computations on the capsule contents, and can also invoke external "methods," which may provide access to resources external to the transient environment. The execution of a capsule results in the scheduling of zero or more capsules for transmission on the outgoing links and may change the non-transient state of the node. The transient environment is destroyed when capsule evaluation terminates.

The effectiveness of the framework relies on how the legitimate clients know where the active server is and how we migrate the in-process connections, as shown in Fig. 6. To be able to know the active server location, a client needs to have at least two sets of information: the server address and the time that the server will be active. This information can simply be obtained by using a series of communications. To avoid the DoS attacks on the Internet, however, clients and servers need a secure communication that provides privacy and integrity to protect the information.

The main issue is to provide the framework for moving one end point of a live connection from one location and reincarnating it at another location having

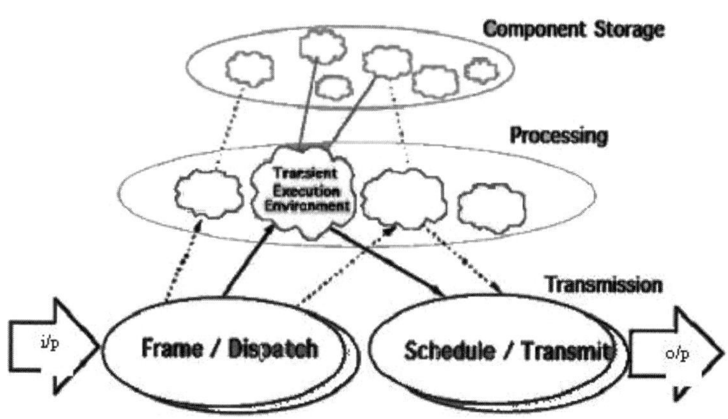

Fig. 5. Active node organization.

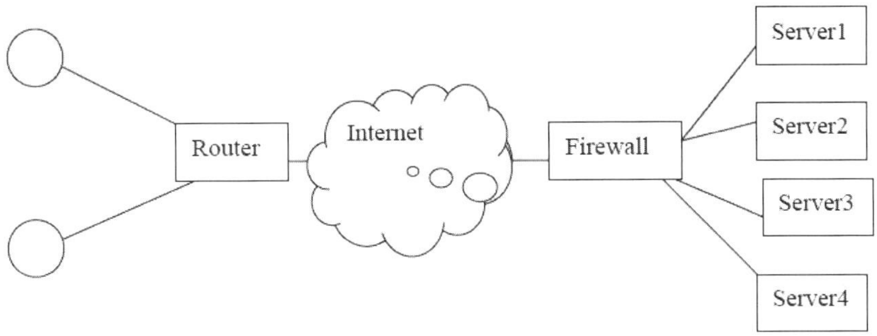

Fig. 6. Server hopping using distributed firewalls architecture.

a different IP address and/or a different port number. The mechanism must deal with four issues:

- how the connection is continued between the new end points,
- the impact on the network stack and application layer on both the server and the client sides,
- how to recover both connection and application states, and
- when to trigger the migration mechanism.

The migration model is simplified for our simulation. The active server is scheduled to roam among the servers in the pool in a certain time interval. We call this interval the *roaming interval.*

3.2. *Experiments and Results*

The architectures are implemented in the NS-2 network simulator. The visual simulations are facilitated by the network animator NAM. The results are plotted using the XGraph package.

3.2.1. *Implementation of Agents*

Agents are the programs in our implementation that do the processing at the intermediate components in our proposed models. The following are the agents we have implemented in our proposed models.

- *Secure overlay services model*:
  - PacketGenerate at "Source Point",
  - ValidateClient at "SOAP",
  - BeaconForward at "SOAP",
  - SecretForward at "Beacon",
  - BeaconVerify at "Secret Servlet",
  - TargetConnect at "Secret Servlet".

- *Server hopping using distributed firewalls model*:
  - — PacketGenerate at "Source Point",
  - — TimeGenerate at "Source Point",
  - — ForwardtoFirewall at "Source Point",
  - — SourceVerify at "Firewall",
  - — DestinationVerify at "Firewall",
  - — TargetConnect at "Firewall".

The IP packet header is modified to include various additional parameters in the active architecture. The structure of the modified IP packet header is shown in Fig. 7.

The send and receive modules of the active agent are designed to identify active packets and forward normal IP packets. The structure of the module is shown in Fig. 8.

```
struct hdr_active
{                                                    //header structure
 int num;
 int stage;
 static int offset_;
 inline static int& offset()
 {
         return offset_;
 }
 inline static hdr_active* access(const Packet* p)
 {
         return(hdr_active*)p->access(offset_);
 }
};
```

Fig. 7. Structure of modified IP packet header.

```
void ActiveAgent::recv(Packet* pkt,Handler*)                    //packet receiving
module
{
        hdr_ip* hdrip = HDR_IP(pkt);
        //active header
        hdr_active* hdr = (hdr_active*)pkt->access(off_active_);
        char out[100];
        int num;
        int stage = hdr->stage;
                num = decrypt(hdr->num);
                sprintf(out , "%s recv %d %d" , name(), num, stage);
                Tcl& tcl = Tcl::instance();
                //eval(out) ports it to exec of ns
                tcl.eval(out);
                //Discard packet
                Packet::free(pkt);
}
```

Fig. 8. Module for active agent.

```
#Define a 'recv' function for the class 'Agent/Active'
Agent/Active instproc recv {num stage} {
        global ns p0 p1 p2 p3 p4 n2 sysout
        set current_time [$ns now]
        $self instvar node_
        puts " @  node [$node_ id]  value of num is $num stage is $stage."
        If {$stage == 1} {
                $p1 2send5
        } elseif {$stage == 2} {
                $p2 3send5
        } elseif {$stage == 3} {
                $p3 4send5
        } elseif {$stage == 4} {
                $p0 1send5
        } elseif {$stage == 10} {
                $ns at [expr $current_time + 0.1] "$p0 1send5"
        }       puts $sysout "$curent_time $stage"

                                Active agent module
```

Fig. 9. Active agent module.

The nodes are attached to the active agents. The active agent communication module is shown Fig. 9.

3.2.2. *Implementation of Secure Overlay Services*

The following are the modules that are used in the implementation of the proposed SOS architecture:

- *Send*(): Packet generation at "source point" with information about current time and addressed to a SOAP in its network.
- *Recv*(): At the SOAP the packet is received and the header information is extracted.
- *Validate*(): At the SOAP the "source point" is validated to verify the authenticity of the client.
- *Forward*(): The packets from the SOAP must be forwarded to the beacons without revealing information about the source and destination.
- *Filter*(): At the beacons the incoming packets are filtered in such a way as to allow only packets originating at SOAPs.
- *Hash*(): The packets arriving at the beacons are authenticated and hashed to a fixed set of proxy servers (secret servlets).
- *SecretPass*(): The beacons hash the packets and forward them to "secret servlets." The packet forwarding is over a secure network, and source and target shielding is important.
- *Authenticate*(): At the "secret servlet" the packets are authenticated and verified that they are arriving from the allowed set of beacons.
- *Forward*(): The data in the packet is extracted and forwarded to the target.

- *Filter*(): The target has a very restrictive set of secret servlets, which are the only nodes from which the target accepts packets.

3.2.3. *Implementation of Server Hopping using Distributed Firewalls*

The following are the modules that are used in the implementaion of the proposed server hopping using distributed firewalls architecture.

- *Hop*(): The server migration is based on time hashing.
- *Filter*(): The filter is distributed around the target. The filter allows only those packets which address the currently active server.
- *Find*(): The client and the server both have an identical hashing function to decide the server migration. The authentic clients can identify the current location of the server from the hash function.
- *Connect*(): The distributed firewalls connect to the server only when the particular instance of the respective active server is active.

3.2.4. *Construction of Simulation Networks*

The networks that are used for simulating the proposed architectures are shown in the following figures. Figure 10 shows the network used to simulate the SOS architecture for DoS attack.

The simulated network shows the traffic generated at client and attacker. In the figure, node 1 represents the SOAP, node 2 represents overlays, node 3 represents the beacon, and node 4 contains the secret servlet and server.

The network used to simulate the SOS architecture for DDoS attack is shown in Fig. 11.

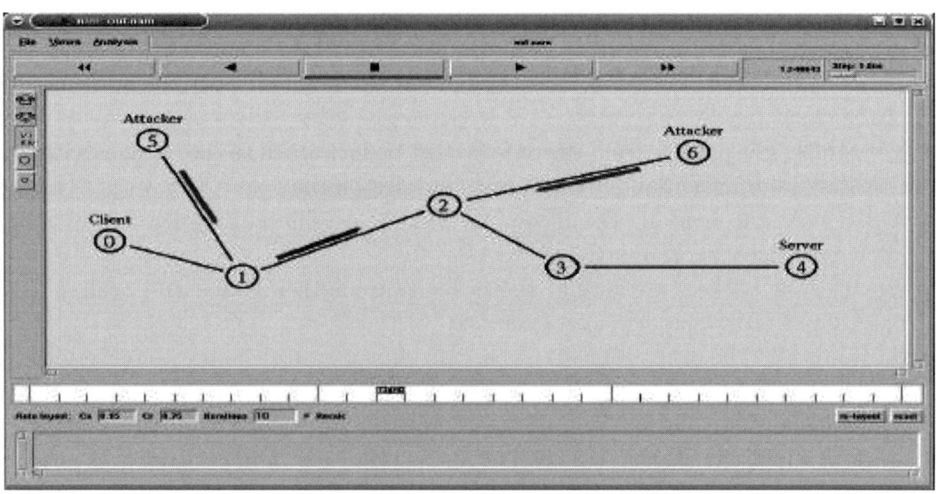

Fig. 10. Network used to simulate the SOS architecture for DoS.

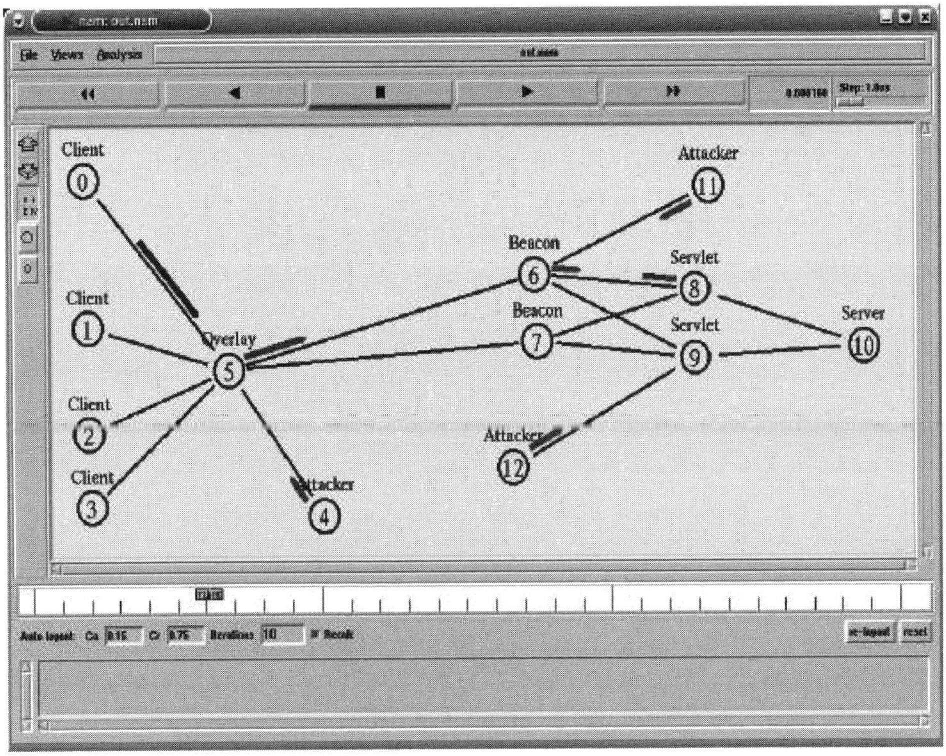

Fig. 11. Network used to simulate SOS architecture for DDoS.

In Fig. 11, nodes 0–3 represent source points where the network traffic is generated. Node 5 contains both SOAP and overlay. Nodes 6 and 7 represent the beacons of the proposed architecture. Nodes 8 and 9 represent the secret servlets. Node 10 is the server or the target of the architecture.

Figure 12 shows the network used for simulating the server hopping architecture for DoS. In the figure, node 0 represents the client, and node 1 represents the router which discriminates "good" (authorized) traffic from "bad" (unauthorized) traffic.

Figure 13 shows the network used for simulating server hopping using the distributed firewalls architecture for DDoS attacks. Node 0 represents the client and node 1 represents router. Node 5–7 represent the distributed firewalls that connect to the server only when the particular instance of the respective active server is active. Node 8–10 represent the server or targets that are active only during a specified interval of time.

3.2.5. *Evaluation and Comparison*

To evaluate the performance of the proposed models for mitigating DoS/DDoS attacks for messages exchanged between group members, we first measure the packet delivery time for the attacked network without our defense models. We also measure

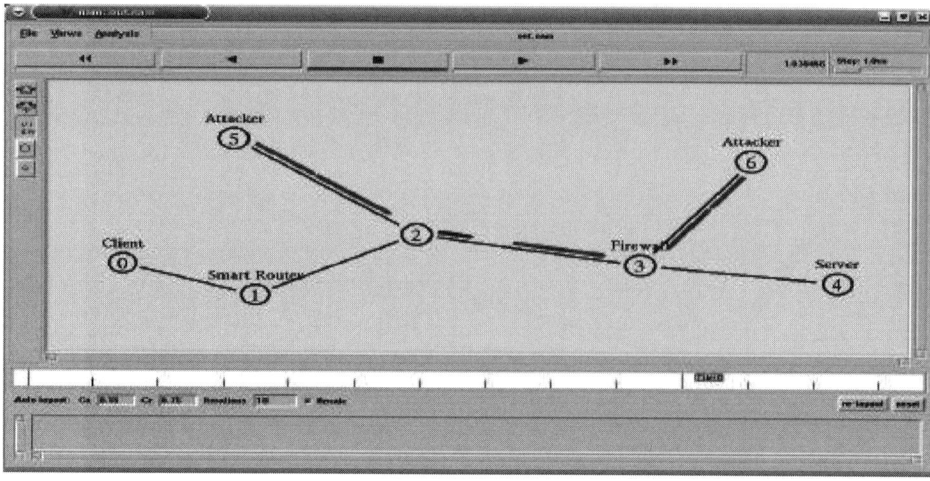

Fig. 12. Network used to simulate the server hopping architecture for DoS.

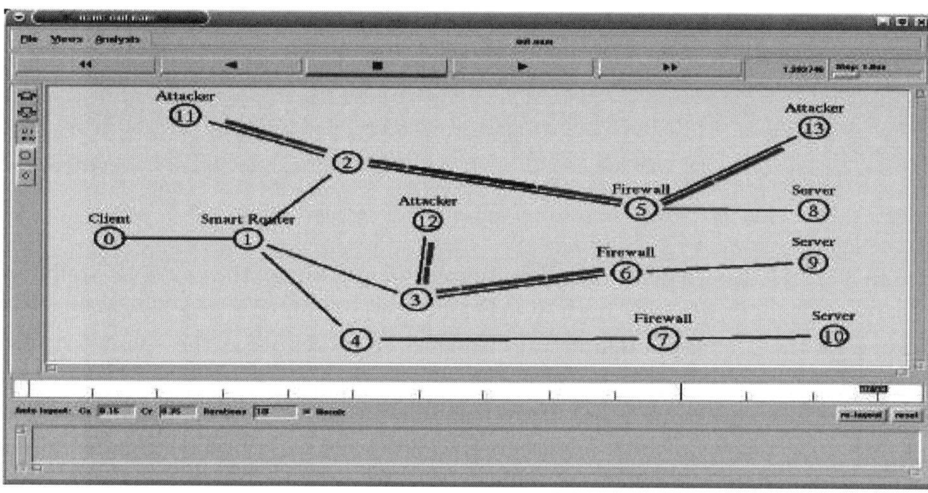

Fig. 13. Network used to simulate the server hopping architecture for DDoS.

the packet delivery times for the attacked network with each of our two defense models. We then compare the performance of the proposed models with the other existing models for DDoS attacks.

In Fig. 14 the x-axis represents the actual time when running the simulation. The simulation is started at 0.0000 seconds and the DDoS attack is started at 10.0000 seconds. After 10.0000 seconds the attack decays the packet delivery time. The y-axis shows the time taken by the sample packet to reach the server. During a normal simulation (i.e., without the DoS attack) it takes 6.000 seconds. As the attack begins, the delivery time increases from 6.000 seconds to infinity at infinite time.

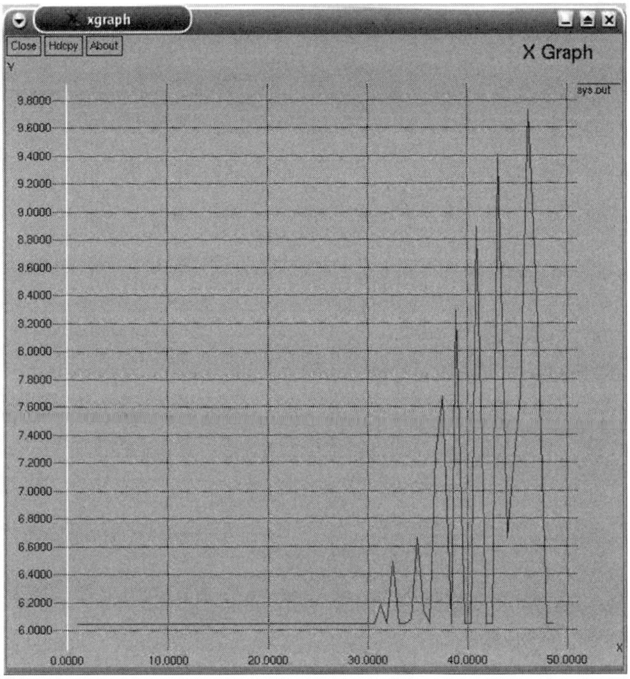

Fig. 14. Analysis of DoS.

This means that without the defense model the packet delivery to the destination will be delayed.

The graph shown in Fig. 15 depicts the variation in packet delivery time between an attacked network and the network with the SOS model. The upper line in the graph shows the constant increase in delivery time as the attack progresses. The lower line in the graph shows the initial increase in packet delivery time when the attack begins and the active node is registering the attack. As the attack progresses, the smart routers can detect the attacking packets and eliminate them from the network. This results in the downward slope of the graph. As time progresses, the delivery time approaches the actual delivery time with no attack.

The graph shown in Fig. 16 depicts the packet delivery time variation between an attacked network and the network with the server hopping defense model for DoS attack. The upper line in the graph shows the constant increase in delivery time as the attack progresses. The lower line in the graph shows the initial increase in packet delivery time when the attack begins and the active node is registering the attack. Again, as the attack progresses, the smart routers can detect the attacking packets and eliminate them from the network. This results in the downward slope of the graph, and as time progresses, the delivery time approaches the actual delivery time with no attack.

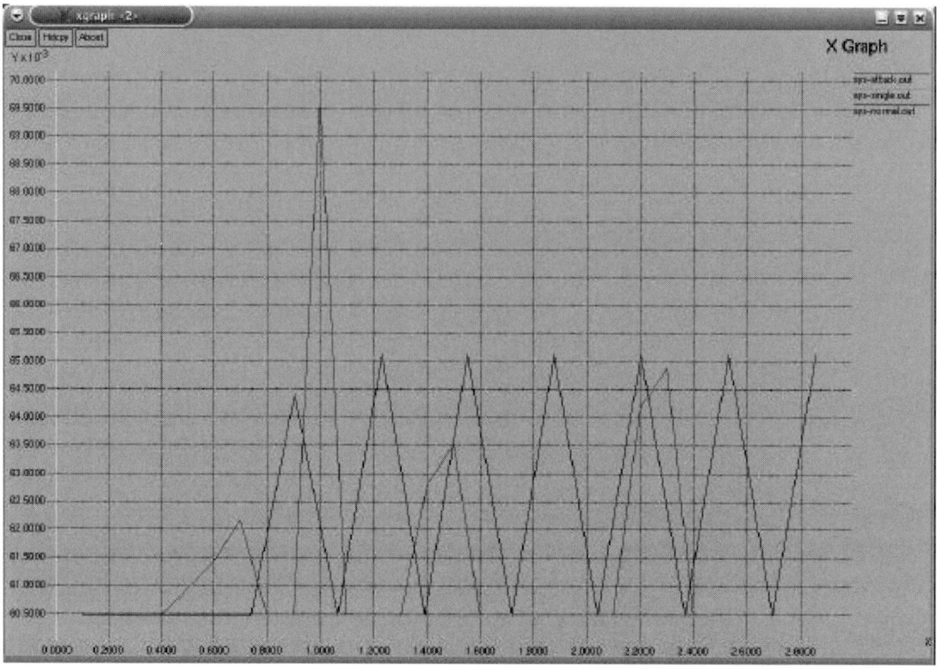

Fig. 15. Packet delivery time without DoS defense and with DoS defense for SOS.

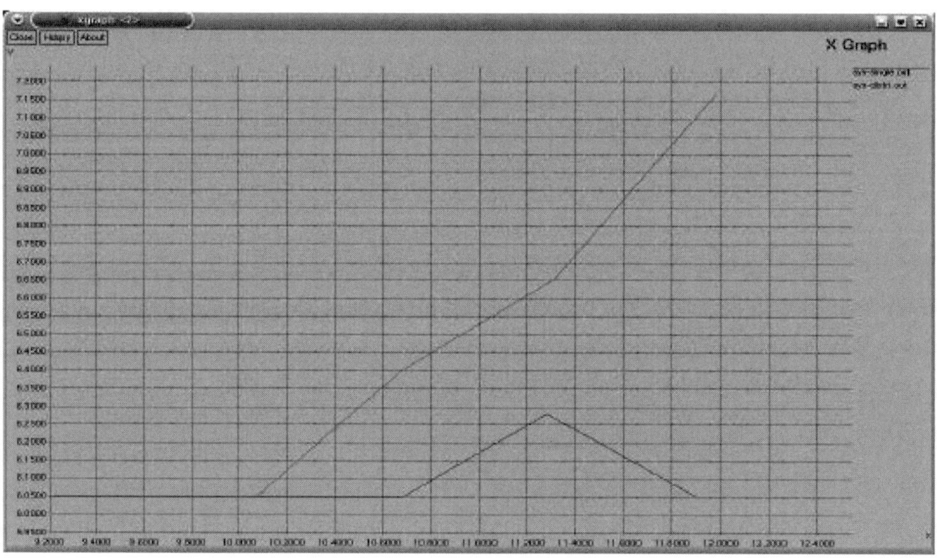

Fig. 16. Packet delivery time without DoS defense and with DoS defense for server hopping.

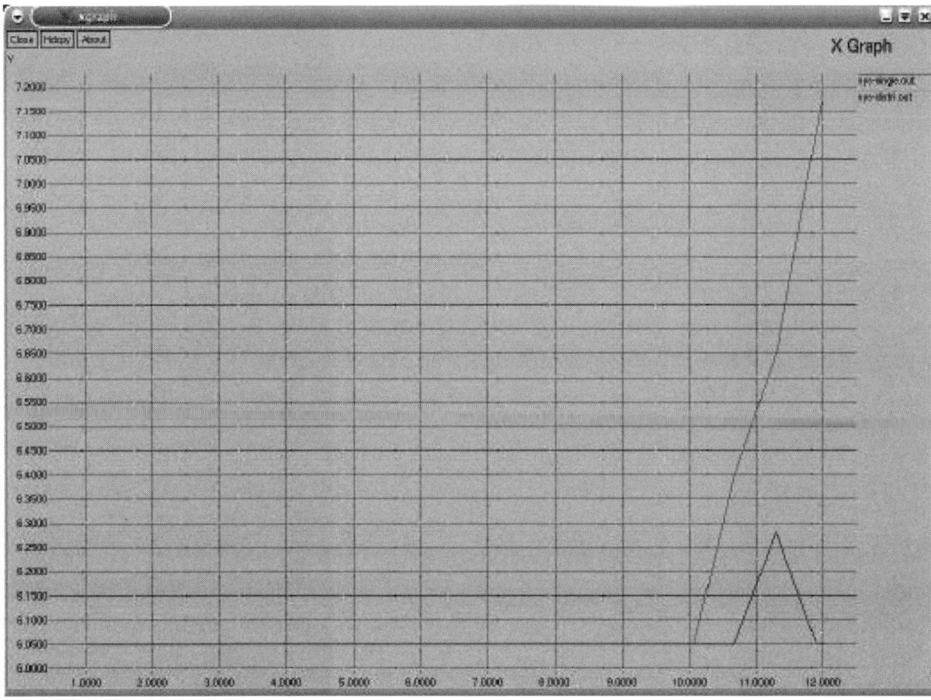

Fig. 17. Packet delivery time without DDoS defense and with DDoS defense for server hopping.

The graph shown in Fig. 17 depicts the packet delivery time variation between an attacked network and the network with the server hopping defense model for DDoS attack. The characteristics of the graph are similar to those of Figs. 15 and 16.

From the above experimental plots, it is clear that the developed architectures for defending against DoS/DDoS attacks maintain almost the same packet delivery time as that in the absence of DoS/DDoS attacks.

4. Directions for Future Research

DoS/DDoS is a serious problem that requires a complex solution. Moreover, DDoS requires a distributed solution. A crucial building block of this solution is to implement systems that provide a selective and dynamic response.

We believe that our approach is a novel way of countering DoS attacks, especially in service-critical environments. It maintains good service to legitimate traffic during the attack, which is the ultimate goal of DDoS defense.

These architectures provide a range of defenses that can severely limit the damage caused by DoS attacks. This in itself is a significant step forward in providing robust Internet services that can be confidently used for electronic commerce and other on-line services.

The basic assumption for all the schemes is that there are a limited number of attack paths, and not all legitimate traffic shares a path with the attacking traffic. The assumption fails when the attacking traffic is uniformly distributed. All intermediate network reaction schemes are vulnerable to a large-scale reactor attack. Our next step is to develop architectures focusing on distributed reflector DoS attacks.

In the case of server hopping using distributed firewalls, our next step for the simulation is to develop better and more practical attack and roaming models. Some heuristic techniques are needed. We plan to search for attack patterns in the real world and design experiments to improve our models. Additionally, we could deploy other well-known network applications, such as a Web server and domain name servers, as attacked services to explore different attack behaviors and the roaming strategies to thwart them.

5. Conclusions

The proposed models, the secure overlay services model and the server hopping model using distributed firewalls, mitigate DDoS attacks in group communication but provide defense in different parts of the network and have different resource requirements. The simulation results of DDoS shows that without any defense models the packet delivery time increases and the packet delivery to the server will be delayed. In the SOS defense model for DDoS, the variation in packet delivery time remains almost the same as the actual packet delivery time. The server hopping model also maintains the constant packet delivery time, but the amount of variation in packet delivery time for SOS is more than for the server hopping model.

Through simple analytical models, it is shown that DDoS attacks directed against any part of the SOS infrastructure have a negligible probability of disrupting the communication between two parties due to the constant packet delivery time. Furthermore, the resistance of an SOS network to DDoS attacks increases greatly with the number of nodes that participate in the overlay. The SOS and server hopping architectures provide a range of defenses that can severely limit the damage caused by DDoS attacks. This is a significant step forward in providing robust Internet services that can be used with confidence for electronic commerce and other on-line services.

Terminology

Authentication: A principle of security which identifies a user or a computer system so that it can be trusted.

Capsules: Miniature programs that are executed at each router they traverse.

Denial-of-service (DoS) attack: An attempt by an attacker to disallow authorized users from accessing a resource/computer system.

Distributed denial-of-service (DDoS) attack: A DoS attack that occurs when multiple compromised systems flood the bandwidth or resources of a targeted system, usually one or more Web servers.

Firewall: Special type of router which can perform security checks and allows rule-based filtering.

Integrity: A principle of security which specifies that the contents of a message must not be altered during its transmission from the sender to the receiver.

Proxy server: A type of firewall that filters packets at the application layer of the TCP/IP stack.

Smurf attack: A Smurf attack is a DoS attack where a large number of innocent hosts respond to ICMP echo-request packets that contain a spoofed source IP address.

Spoofing: A method whereby a user with complete control over a device's software modifies the device's protocols in order to place an arbitrary IP into a datagram's source address field.

SYN flooding attack: An attempt made by an attacker to deluge a server with TCP SYN packets, each having a spoofed IP source addresses.

Exercises

1. Differentiate between denial-of-service and distributed denial-of-service attacks. How can attackers hide their identity in these attacks?
2. What is meant by mitigating denial-of-service attacks? What are the main challenges?
3. What are the differences between secure overlay services and server hopping in using distributed firewall models for mitigating denial-of-service and distributed denial-of-service attacks?
4. Define the following terms: Smurf attack, SYN flooding and spoofing.
5. What is the difference between proactive and reactive protection architectures for denial-of-service?
6. How do the existing architectures for denial-of-service attacks filter traffic?
7. Differentiate between passive and active networks.
8. Define roaming interval.

References

1. D. L. Tennenhouse and D. J. Wetherall, Towards an active network architecture, *ACM SIGCOMM Computer Communi. Rev.* **26**(2), 5–17 (1996).
2. Y. Xiang, Y. Lin, W. L. Lei and S. J. Huang, Detecting DDOS attack based on network self similarity, *IEEE Proc. Commun.* **151**(3) (2004).
3. E. Y. Chen and A. Yonezawa, Practical techniques for defending against DDoS attacks, *Computer Systems and Applications*: *3rd ACS/IEEE Int. Conf.* (2005).

4. A. Chakrabarthi and G. Manimaran, Internet infrastructure security: A taxonomy, *IEEE Network*, November/December (2002).
5. I. Stoica, D. Adkins, S. Zhuang, Shenkarm and S. Surana, Internet indirection infrastructure, *Proc. ACM SIGCOMM* (2002).
6. T. Anderson, T. Roscoe and D. Wetherall, Preventing Internet denial-of-service with capabilities, *Proc. Hotnets-II*, Cambridge, MA, November (2003).
7. A. Keromytis, V. Misra and D. Rubenstein, SOS: Secure overlay services, *Proc. ACM SIGCOMM* (2002).
8. www.cert.org/archive/pdf/DoS_trends.pdf.
9. E. Y. Chen and A. Yonezawa, Practical techniques for defending against DDoS attacks, *Computer Systems and Applications: 3rd ACS/IEEE Int. Conf.* (2005).
10. www.sds.lcs.mit.edu/darpa-activenet.
11. D. L. Tennenhouse, J. M. Smith, W. D. Sincoskie, D. J. Wetherall and G. J. Minden, A survey of active network research, *IEEE Commun. Mag.* **35**(1), 80–86 (1997).
12. V. Van, A defense against address spoofing using active networks, Master's thesis, MIT, Cambridge, MA, May (1997).
13. D. L. Tennenhouse, S. J. Garland, L. Shrira and M. F. Kaashoek, From Internet to ActiveNet, January (1996).
14. D. Wetherall and D. Tennenhouse, The ACTIVE IP option, *Proc. 7th ACM SIGOPS European Workshop*, Connemara, Ireland, September (1996).
15. U. Legedza, D. J. Wetherall and J. Guttag, Improving the performance of distributed applications using active networks, *IEEE INFOCOM'98* (1998).
16. D. J. Wetherall, U. Legedza and J. Guttag, Introducing new Internet services: Why and how, *IEEE Network Magazine*, July/August (1998).
17. Computer Crime and Intellectual Property Section (CCIPS) of the U.S. Department of Justice, http://usdoj.gov/criminal/cybercrime/compcrime.html. http://www.cnn.com/2000/TECH/computing/02/09/cyber.attacks.01/index.htm.
18. E. Y. Chen and A. Yonezawa, Practical techniques for defending against DDoS attacks, *Computer Systems and Applications: 3rd ACS/IEEE Int. Conf.* (2005).
19. S. Savage, D. Wetherall, A. R. Karlin and T. Anderson, Practical network support for IP traceback, *In SIG COMM* (2000).
20. Y. Xiang, Y. Lin, W. L. Lei and S.J. Huang, Detecting DDOS attack based on network self similarity, *IEEE Proc. Commun.* **151**(3) (2004).
21. E. Y. Chen and A. Yonezawa, Practical techniques for defending against DDoS attacks, *Computer Systems and Applications: 3rd ACS/IEEE Int. Conf.* (2005).

SOLUTIONS

Chapter 1

1. Low level tasks: Terminal, mode and ad hoc. High level tasks: Personal, session and service.
2. Using the cosine law for a triangle with sides a, b, and c and the angle μ opposite the side c, $c^2 = a^2 + b^2 - 2ab\cos(\mu)$.

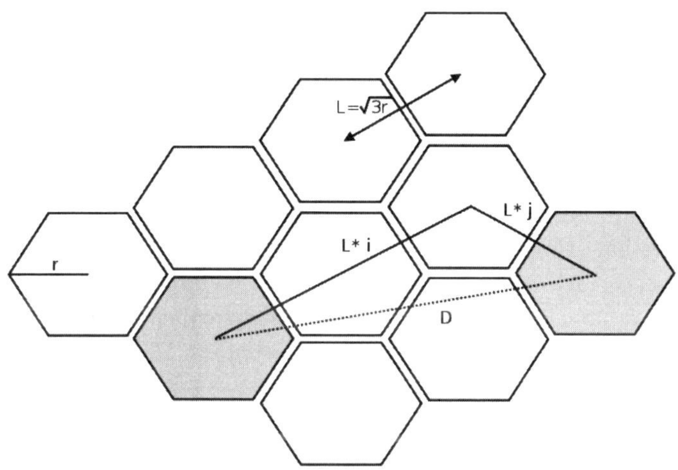

$$\begin{aligned} D^2 &= (L \times i)^2 + (L \times j)^2 - 2(L \times i)(L \times j)\cos(2\pi/3) \\ &= L^2 \times i^2 + L^2 \times j^2 - 2 \times L^2 \times i \times j \times (-0.5) \\ &= L^2(i^2 + j^2 + ij), \\ \frac{D}{r} &= \sqrt{3(i^2 + j^2 + ij)} = \sqrt{3N}. \end{aligned}$$

3. (i) Conversational, streaming, interactive and background. (ii), (iii) Conversational — Preserve time relation between information entities, stringent and low delay (< 150 ms);
streaming — Preserve time relation between information entities (delay <400 ms);

interactive — Request response pattern; preserve payload;
Background — Destination not expecting data within a certain time; preserve data load.

4. Terminal mobility handles and tracks the movement of the mobile device in the network for both idle and active users. If active devices are mobile then the network needs to hand over the user to a new cell. If the cell size in a location area is small ($r < 1\,\text{km}$) and the mobile device is highly mobile ($> 100\,\text{km/h}$), then the number of handovers will be high. Proper network planning of cells would be needed for this scenario along with directional antennas. If the user's mobility is low then the handover level will be acceptable.
5. Each idle mobile is required to regularly report its location at a set time interval using a periodic location update procedure. Whenever a mobile moves from one location area to the next while not on a call, a random location update is required. This is also required of a stationary mobile that reselects coverage from a cell in a different location area, because of signal fading.
6. GSM systems use a combination of TDMA and FDMA. Each BS is assigned a number of frequencies for the uplink and downlink communication and these frequencies are separated to avoid interference. With GSM the mobile device's antenna can only communicate on one frequency at any time. When handing over from one BS to another it must change frequency and therefore break the connection. However, with the CDMA system a special coding scheme is used where each transmitter is assigned a code. With CDMA the device's antenna does not need to change transmitting frequency when communicating with several BSs, so soft handover can be achieved.
7.

QoS	Characteristics	Applications
0	Realtime, jitter sensitive, highly interactive	Interactive gaming
1	Realtime, jitter sensitive, interactive	Voice calls, video conferencing
2	Transaction data, highly interactive	Instant messaging
3	Transaction data, interactive	E-mail, web browsing
4	Low loss only (short data, bulk data)	FAX, FTP, Torrent
5	Traditional applications of default IP networks	Telnet, background traffic

8. First, we calculate the path loss by substituting Eqs. (11)–(14) into Eq. (3), obtaining

$$\begin{aligned}L_E &= 63.35 + (27.72 - 1.1h_m)\log_{10}(f_c) + 44.9\log_{10}(d)\\ &\quad - (13.82 + 6.5\log_{10}(d))\log_{10}(h_B) + 0.7h_m - 2(\log_{10}(f_c/28))^2.\end{aligned}$$

Substituting the values of h_m, d and f_c, we obtain

$$L_E = 150.72 - 15.78\log_{10}(h_B).$$

The link budget equation in (10) is now

$$-85 = 33 + 12 + 0 - 150.72 + 15.78 \log_{10}(h_B),$$

which leads to

$$\log_{10}(h_B) = 1.31,$$

and finally $h_B = 10^{1.31} = 20.42\,\text{m}$.

9. A user agent sends a REGISTER message to its registrar with its new contact location(s) in the "contact" header field and the "via" header field also reflects the change in location as shown in the illustration and the REGISTER message. The REGISTER message informs the registrar of the new location and the old location becomes invalid when the registration timer expires — after 120 seconds at most in this example. The user agent could also send a registration message for the old location with an expiry time of "0" to de-register the old location.

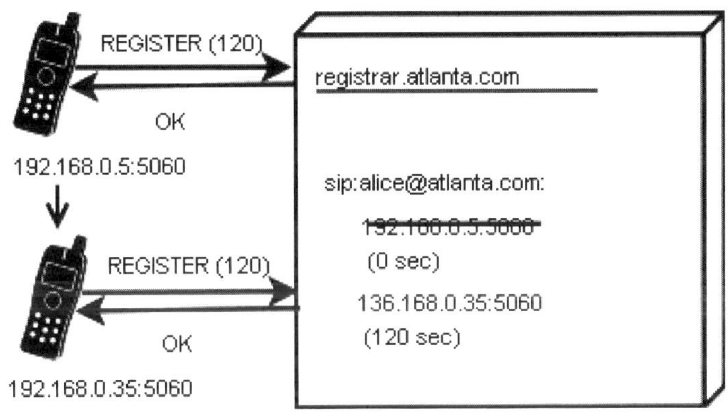


```
         REGISTER sip:registrar.atlanta.com SIP/2.0
Via:SIP/2.0/UDP192.168.0.35:5060;branch=z9hG4bKnashes7
         Max-Forwards: 70
         To: Alice <sip:alice@atlanta.com>
         From: Alice <sip:alice@atlanta.com>;tag=456248
         Call-ID: 843817638423O@998sdasdh09
         CSeq: 1826 REGISTER
         Contact: <sip:alice@192.168.0.35>;expires=120
         Expires: 7200
         Content-Length: 0
```

10. The "expires" parameter indicates the lifetime for which the contact data is valid. After this timer expires, the contact location should no longer be assumed to be valid by the location service (registrar) or the user agent.

Chapter 2

1. Although UMTS networks offer high capacity, the expected demand will certainly overcome the available resources. Actually, the major factor for

integrating MBMS into UMTS networks was the rapid growth of mobile communications technology and the massive spread of wireless data and wireless applications. The increasing demand for communication between one sender and many receivers led to the need for PTM transmission. Therefore, MBMS was introduced as a downlink service in order to satisfy the need for optimal usage of radio and network resources and provide rich multimedia services to a large users' popularity (for more information refer to Sec. 3).

2. The broadcast mode requires no subscription or activation from the users' point of view, while on the other hand, in the multicast operation mode, data is transmitted solely to users that explicitly request such a service (for more information refer to Sec. 3.1).
3. MBMS multicast efficiency improvement in UMTS networks can be derived from the fact that only one single stream per MBMS service of identical data is essential for the delivery of the multicast data. On the other hand, without the MBMS enhancement, multicast data should be replicated in all interfaces as many times as the total number of multicast users. In this way, a bottleneck would emerge when the number of users increased significantly, leading in turn, to a heavy overload of all interfaces (for more information refer to Sec. 3.3).
4. DCHs can support fast power control, while FACH can not. Consequently, transmission power in DCH is variable, while in FACH a fixed power allocation level is considered. More specifically, DCH power depends on many factors, such as the number of serving users, their location in the cell, the bit rate of the MBMS session and the experienced signal quality E_b/N_0 for each user. On the other hand, in FACH the fixed power should be high enough to ensure the requested QoS in the desired coverage area of the cell, where the users are located (for more information refer to Secs. 4.1 and 4.2).
5. MBMS Counting Mechanism constitutes a mechanism that decides whether it is more economic to use PTP or PTM MBMS transmission mode. Actually, this mechanism aims to maximize radio resource efficiency through a threshold for switching between the two different transmission modes (for more information refer to Sec. 4.3).
6. Conventional MBMS Counting Mechanism uses a threshold for switching between PTP and PTM modes, based on the number of simultaneous users receiving the same multicast content. This scheme, though, can not always ensure resource efficiency, since it does not consider the dynamic nature (i.e., users' mobility, etc.) of a MBMS-enabled UMTS network. Therefore, the current form of this mechanism may lead to an erroneous threshold determination that, in turn, may result to inefficient utilization of the network resources. The fundamental criterion for maximizing resource efficiency should be the Node B's total downlink MBMS transmission power (for more information refer to Sec. 4.3).

7. Several techniques have been proposed in order to reduce the power requirements during a MBMS session. Such techniques are:

   - Dynamic power setting
   - Macro diversity combining
   - Rate splitting
   - Mixed usage of multiple DCHs and FACH

   (for more information refer to Sec. 4.4).
8. According to DPS technique, the transmission power of the FACH is allocated dynamically, based on the worst user's path loss. To perform DPS, the MBMS users need to turn on measurement report mechanism while they are on the Cell_FACH state. Based on such measurement reports, the Node B can adjust the transmission power of the FACH (for more information refer to Sec. 4.4.1)
9. The MBMS power control mechanism consists of five distinct operation phases. These are:

   - the initialization phase
   - the parameter retrieval phase
   - the power computation phase
   - the radio bearer selection phase and
   - the event scheduling phase

   (for more information refer to Sec. 5.1).
10. An interesting issue that can further improve MBMS power efficiency and capacity is the transmission of MBMS multicast data over the HS-DSCH transport channel. HS-DSCH offers improved spectral efficiency and increases peak data rates. MBMS over HS-DSCH can offer significant power savings and enhancements on total MBMS capacity, thus enabling the mass market delivery of higher bit rate multimedia services to end users. Therefore, HS-DSCH can play an instrumental role in positioning MBMS services as a key enabler for true "Mobile Broadband" (for more information refer to Sec. 6).

Chapter 3

1. QPSK: 2 bits; 16-QAM: 4 bits; 64-QAM: 6 bits.
2. Order: QPSK, 16-QAM, 64-QAM; data bursts are sent in increasing degree of sophistication. Hence, an MS may only receive the burst up to its reception capacities and ignore the bursts it cannot demodulate.
3. Bandwidth share of each channel: 1/32 (also accept $64 \times 187\,\text{kHz} = 12\,\text{MHz}$). Bandwidth per channel: $64 \times 187\,\text{kHz} = 12\,\text{MHz}$ (also accept 48 on downlink, or 53 on uplink, instead of 64). Downlink bandwidth used for control: $(64–48) \times 32 \times 187\,\text{kHz} = 96\,\text{MHz}$. Uplink bandwidth used for control: $(64–53) \times 32 \times 187\,\text{kHz} = 65\,\text{MHz}$.

4.

	Advantages	Disadvantages
Centralized	Global picture Optimized schedule	More communication Heavier load on scheduler
Distributed	Local decisions Fewer communications Lighter load on scheduler	Possible non-optimal schedules Channel contention

5. Each form of authentication is required because device authentication verifies the identity of the hardware and blocks access to non-authorized devices (e.g. stolen or lost devices), user authentication verifies the identity of the person using the hardware and blocks access to non-authorized people. Message authentication verifies that the message's payload comes from the message's sender and prevent message spoofing or tampering.

   Device authentication is based on digital certificates assigned to devices by manufacturers or network providers. User authentication is username- and password-based. Message authentication is done by attaching each message to a cryptographic signature.
7. (a) **Hint**: There are four intersections.
   (b) **Hint**: Find the area delimited by the union of the three circles as well as the corresponding intersections. Observe that the desired probability is equal to the proportion of area covered by the frequency.
   (c) **Hint**: Compute $E(f_1, f_2, f_3)$ for the regions depicted in Fig. 17.
8. **Hint**: Give an example of three circles of unequal size.
9. **Hint**: The expected number of steps until successful connection is established is

$$E(f_1, f_2) = \Pr[F_1] + 2(\Pr[F_2] - \Pr[F_2 \cap F_1])$$
$$E(f_2, f_1) = \Pr[F_2] + 2(\Pr[F_1] - \Pr[F_1 \cap F_2])$$

   in the two cases respectively. This leads to us selecting the most likely frequency.
10. **Hint**: Given that $\Pr[F_1] \geq \Pr[F_2]$, we can easily find an upper bound on the competitive ratio between the worst and best choices

$$\frac{E(f_2, f_1)}{E(f_1, f_2)} = \frac{\Pr[F_2] + 2\Pr[F_1] - 2\Pr[F_1 \cap F_2]}{\Pr[F_1] + 2\Pr[F_2] - 2\Pr[F_2 \cap F_1]} \leq 2.$$

   In other words, in the worst case, the mobile user will take at most twice as long as the best case.

Chapter 4

1. A
2. C
3. A, C
4. B, C

5. C
6. A
7. A
8. A
9. A
10. A

Chapter 5

1. The output of a DANN may be written as
   The equation represents a hyper plane with increasing dimensionality with the order of differential feedback.
2. Differential feedback provides increased stability and predictability for the output, making it autoregressive.
3. The long-range dependency and degree of self-similarity in the output depend upon the time scales. They influence QoS parameters such as cell loss ratio, delay, etc. Bursty traffic over short time scales flood the resources, leading to increased cell loss and delays.
4. The output in both cases happens to be the sum of the scaled version of previous outputs.
5. In the feedback path, with appropriate characteristics matching with the forward traffic.
6. Multipath results in superposition of scaled versions of time-shifted signals and imparts LRD.
7. Intelligent element learning based on experience and working with unforeseen circumstances are required to handle ad hoc traffic.
8. Shifting and prediction of feedback or the control signal provides sufficient time for data sources and routers to adjust the rates and shape the traffic. It improves the QoS.
9. Simulation of network traffic is important for understanding the issues and fine-tuning design parameters.
10. Unsupervised learning is preferred because of the non-availability of sufficient data and crisp changes in the patterns.

Chapter 6

1. Let there be a function f and it needs to be guessed out. Hypothesis about function to be learned is denoted by h. Both f and h are functions of a vector valued input $X = (x_1, x_2, \ldots, x_z, \ldots, x_n)$, which has n components. We have h as being implemented by a device that has X as input and $h(X)$ as output. Both f and h themselves may be vector-valued. We assume *a priori* that the hypothesized function h, is selected from a class of functions $\mathcal{H}$. Sometimes, we know that f also belongs to this class or to a subset of this class. We select based on a training set S of m input vector examples.

In supervised learning, we know (sometimes only approximately) the values of f for the m samples in the training set S. We assume that if we can find a hypothesis, h that closely agrees with f for the members of S, then this hypothesis will be a good guess for f, especially if S is large.

In the other setting termed unsupervised learning, we simply have a training set of vectors without function values for them. The problem in this case, typically, is to partition the training set into subsets $S_1, \ldots, S_R$ in some appropriate way. We can still regard the problem as one of learning a function, the value of the function is the name of the subset to which an input vector belongs.

2. Problem of inference basically implies gaining knowledge, making predictions, making decisions or constructing models from a set of data. Statistical learning theory provides a statistical framework where inputs are being taken as the parameters used to generate the data, or in other words, the way in which data is being generated. For example, in case of location fingerprinting, statistical framework takes received signal strength as the input to generate regression model.

   Let $\mathcal{L}$ be the set of location informations, i.e. the space of tuples representing information about physical location. Two cases shall be considered:

   (a) ***Regression problem***: Location data can be expressed as a d-uple of real coordinates where d, the dimension of physical space, may vary from 1 (e.g. position along a corridor) to 5 (position in three-dimensional space and orientation expressed in spherical coordinates), $\mathcal{L} = R^d$.
   (b) ***Decision or classification problem***: Location data is a single variable from a two-valued set, usually $\{-1, 1\}$, the values meaning "outside" and "inside" a given area; in this case, $d = 1$ and $\mathcal{L} = \{-1, 1\}$. In both cases, r independent radio access points are located in the working area and send continuous beaconing signals. The collected data can be seen as a sequence of tuples, each tuple representing the measurement of all radio signals from a single location.

   $$(y_1, x_1), \ldots, (y_1, x_1) \in \mathcal{L} \times R^d,$$

   where x_1 represents the radio component, and y_1 the spatial component of the measurement. This set of tuples shall be called the training set. A training set consists of an input vector and an *answer* vector, and is used together with a supervised learning method to *train* a knowledge database (e.g. a neural net or a naive bayes classifier) used by an AI machine.

3. In case of linearly separable data, then the following equality will hold,

$$||w||^2 = \sum_{i=1}^{i} \alpha_i = \sum_{i \in SV_s} \alpha_i = \sum_{i \in SV_s} \sum_{j \in SV_s} \alpha_i \alpha_j y_i y_j (x_i, x_j).$$

This shows that all the SV will lie on the margin and hence the number of SV can be very small. Consequently the hyperplane is determined by a small subset of the training set; the other points could be removed from the training set and recalculating the hyperplane would produce the same answer. Hence SVM can be used to summarize the information contained in a data set by the SV produced. However, in case of non-separable data, slack variables ξ_i accountable for misclassification errors are incorporated and the equality gets modified to

$$\max_{\alpha} w(\alpha) = \max_{\alpha} -\frac{1}{2}\sum_{i=1}^{i}\sum_{j=1}^{i} \alpha_i\alpha_j y_i y_j (x_i, x_j) - \sum_{k=1}^{i} \alpha_k.$$

4. Kernel is used to construct a mapping into high-dimensional feature space by the use of reproducing kernels. The idea of the kernel function is to enable operations to be performed in the input space rather than the potentially high-dimensional feature space. Hence, the inner product does not need to be evaluated in the feature space. This provides a way of addressing the curse of dimensionality. However, the computation is still critically dependent upon the number of training patterns and to provide a good data distribution for a high dimensional problem will generally require a large training set.

   The kernel function $K(\ldots)$ is a convolution of the canonical inner product in the feature space. Common kernels for use in a SVM are the following:

   (a) **Dot Product**: $K(x, y) = x \cdot y$; in this case no mapping is performed, and only the optimal separating hyperplane is calculated.
   (b) **Polynomial functions**: $K(x, y) = (x \cdot y + 1)^d$, where the *degree* d is given.
   (c) **Radial Basis Functions** (RBF): $K(x, y) = e^{-\gamma\|x-y\|^2}$ with parameter γ.
   (d) **Sigmoid (or neural) kernel**: $K(x, y) = \tanh(ax \cdot y + b)$ with parameters a and b.
   (e) **ANOVA kernel**: $K(x, y) = (\sum_{i=1}^{n} e^{-\gamma(x_i - y_i)})^d$, with parameters γ and d.

5. A Location Fingerprinting localization system consists of two phases, the offline (training phase) and online (location phase). During the offline phase, a site survey is performed by measuring the Received Signal Strength (RSS) values from multiple access points (APs). The floor is divided into predefined grid points. The RSS values are measured at predefined locations on the grid. In the online phase, the system simply measures the RSS values and matches the measured value to the closest location in the database. The drawback here is the extensive training values that have to be predetermined, depending on the indoor environment.

   Let us say, a training data set of ℓ tuples is considered, where each tuple is of the form $(y_i, x_i), i = 1, \ldots, \ell, x_i$ being an array of r radio signal intensity values and Y_i the location information, either a pair of coordinates (regression problem) or $= 1$ (classification problem). Now, for each input x, y is determined on the basis of SVM for regression/classification on training data set.

6. In statistics it is quite possible that we are trying to over fit the data to a certain model. Now as the dimensions increase we need to take into more and more points to justify the model and this exponential increase in test points needed for justifying a model with increase in dimensions is called "Curse of Dimensionality". One example is that 100 evenly-spaced sample points generally suffice to sample a unit interval with no more than 0.01 distance between points. An equivalent sampling of a 10-dimensional unit hypercube with a lattice with a spacing of 0.01 between adjacent points would require 1020 sample points. Thus, in some sense, the 10-dimensional hypercube can said to be a factor of 1018 larger than the unit interval.
   Question: Where do we need to use Empirical Risk Minimization Induction Principle?
   Answer: If we are dealing with an unknown probability measure, then we use ERM Induction Principle to minimize the same. The ERM principle is quite general. The classical methods for solving a specific learning problem, such as the least squares method in the problem of regression estimation or the maximum likelihood method in the problem of density estimation are realizations of the ERM principle for the specific loss functions $L(y, f_\lambda(x))$ are given below:-

$$L(y, f_\lambda(x)) = \begin{cases} 0 & \text{if } y = f_\lambda(x) \\ 1 & \text{otherwise.} \end{cases}$$

7. The risk associated with a function f is defined as the expectation of the loss function, as follows:

$$R(f) = \sum_i L(f(x_i), g(x_i))p(x_i),$$

   if the probability distribution p is discrete. The goal is to find a function f^* among a fixed subclass of functions for which the risk $R(f^*)$ is minimal.
   However, since the behavior of g is generally only known for a finite sequence of points $(x_1, y_1), \ldots, (x_n, y_n)$, one can only approximate the true risk, for example with the empirical risk

$$\widetilde{R_n}(f) = \frac{1}{n}\sum_{i=1}^{n} L(f(x_i), y_i).$$

   Selecting the function f^* that minimizes the empirical risk is known as the principle of empirical risk minimization. Statistical learning theory investigates the conditions under which empirical risk minimization is admissible and how good the approximations can expect to be.

   Structural risk minimization (SRM) comes into play here as it is an inductive principle for model selection used for learning from finite training data sets. It describes a general model of capacity control and provides a trade-off between hypothesis space and the quality of fitting the training data.

8. The Vapnik–Chervonenkis dimension is a measure of the capacity of a statistical classification algorithm, defined as the cardinality of the largest set of points that the algorithm can shatter. Class C of sets is said to shatter a set A if, for each subset T of A, there is some element U of C such that

$$U \cap A = T$$

Equivalently, C shatters A when the power set $P(A)$ is the set $\{U \cap A | U \in C\}$.

Thus VC dimension tells the capacity of the model taken into account and helps in minimizing empirical error along with reducing the "curse of dimensionality" by putting a cap on the capacity.

9. The procedure for SRM is outlined below:

- Using *a priori* knowledge of the domain, choose a class of functions, such as polynomials of degree n, neural networks having n hidden layer neurons, a set of splines with n nodes or fuzzy logic models having n rules.
- Divide the class of functions into a hierarchy of nested subsets in order of increasing complexity. For example, polynomials of increasing degree.
- Perform empirical risk minimization on each subset (this is essentially parameter selection).
- Select the model in the series whose sum of empirical risk and VC confidence is minimal.

Chapter 7

1. Power management and transmission power control. They are performed on the wireless interface of the node.
2. Energy conservation is achieved by putting a node in the doze state for as long as possible to reduce power consumption.
3. TPC is divided into classes: topology control and per-packet control. In turn, per-packet is divided into two categories: energy-oriented and throughput-oriented.
4. A node transmits senses if the channel is idle (i.e., the noise power in its surroundings is below its carrier sensing threshold). This is termed physical carrier sensing mechanism. It also checks its network allocation vector for any recorded ongoing transmission from its neighbor. This is termed virtual carrier sensing. If both PCS and VCS are clear, a node transmits its packet.
5. The exposed terminal problem and the hidden terminal problem.
6. Here, the SINR is calculated according to the following equation:

$$SINR = G \cdot \frac{P_r}{P_n + I},$$

where P_r is the good received signal, P_n is the average noise power, and I is the interference from other communicating nodes. Since the two-ray channel model is used, the received power at a receiver from a sender transmitting at a power P_t is modeled as

$$P_r = \frac{P_t \cdot G_r \cdot G_t \cdot h_t \cdot h_r}{d^4},$$

where G_t, G_r, h_t, and h_r are the antenna gains and heights of the transmitter and receiver, respectively, which are equal to one.

(i) Now we analyze the case when no power control is implemented. The *SINR* at Node B when it receives a packet from Node A is calculated as

$$SINR_B = \frac{10 \cdot \frac{250}{95^4}}{10^{-10} + \frac{250}{65^4}} = 2.046.$$

Convert to dB:

$$SINR_B = 10\log(2.046) = 3.109\,\text{dB}.$$

Here the interference I results from the ongoing communication between C and D. Since $SINR_B \leq 10$ dB, the connection between A and B is not established.

Similarly, the SINR at Node D is

$$SINR_D = \frac{10 \cdot \frac{250}{57^4}}{10^{-10} + \frac{250}{98^4}} = 87.375.$$

Convert to dB:

$$SINR_D = 10\log(87.375) = 19.41\text{dB}.$$

Here, the connection is established between C and D since $SINR_D > 10\,\text{dB}$. The average transmitting power in this case is 250 mW.

(ii) Alternatively, if we apply power control, repeating the same steps as before we obtain

$$SINR_B = \frac{10 \cdot \frac{100}{95^4}}{10^{-10} + \frac{20}{65^4}} = 10.957.$$

Convert to dB:

$$SINR_B = 10\log(10.957) = 24.538\,\text{dB}.$$

Also,

$$SINR_D = \frac{10 \cdot \frac{20}{57^4}}{10^{-10} + \frac{100}{98^4}} = 17.4741.$$

Convert to dB:

$$SINR_D = 10\log(17.4741) = 10.3969\,\text{dB}.$$

Now, both connections are established with the target SINR. The average power transmitted is 60 mW.

7. According to Eq. (1.2.2), the transmission ranges for Nodes A and B are simply

$$r_{t,A} = r_{t,B} = \left(\frac{0.0281}{7.1936 \times 10^{-12}}\right)\left(\frac{1}{4}\right) = 250\,\text{m}.$$

According to Eq. (1.2.2), the carrier sensing ranges for Nodes A and B are simply

$$r_{c,A} = r_{c,B} = \left(\frac{0.0281}{3.0708 \times 10^{-13}}\right)\left(\frac{1}{4}\right) = 550\,\text{m}.$$

Nodes C and E lie in the carrier sensing zone of Nodes A and B, respectively. Node A sends an RTS to Node B, so Node C is silenced for EIFS; Node C replies with a CTS, and Node E is silenced for EIFS. The minimum power with which Node A is going to send its DATA packet is

$$P_{\text{min}} = 7.1936 \times 10^{-12} \times 70^4 = 1.7272 \times 10^{-4}\,\text{W}.$$

Moreover, the new carrier sensing ranges for Nodes A and B are simply

$$r_{c,A} = r_{c,B} = \left(\frac{1.7272 \times 10^{-4}}{3.0708 \times 10^{-13}}\right)\left(\frac{1}{4}\right) = 154.0007\,\text{m}.$$

The duration of the DATA packet T_{DATA} from Node C is calculated as follows:

$$T_{\text{DATA}} = \frac{\text{packetsize}}{\text{channelrate}} = \frac{1000 \times 8}{2} = 4,000\,\mu s,$$
$$T_{\text{DATA}} > \textit{EIFS}.$$

Nodes C and E are no longer within the carrier sensing zone of Nodes A and B, respectively. After EIFS, Node C contends for the channel and compares the current interference with its carrier sensing threshold after checking its NAV. Since Node A is transmitting its DATA packet, the current noise $P_{n,C}$ at Node C will be

$$1.7272 \times 10^{-4}/450^4 = 4.212 \times 10^{-15}\,\text{W}.$$

Thus, Node C can transmit since its carrier sensing threshold $CS_{\text{th}} > P_{n,C}$.

Node C will send its RTS packet with a power of 0.0281 W. The transmission from Node C to Node D will interfere with the DATA packet reception at Node B. The interference from Node C at Node B is $\frac{0.0281}{520^4} = 3.8432 \times 10^{-13}$.

So now Node E after EIFS duration elapsed from the time CTS packet is received at Node will contend for the channel access; the current noise at Node E will be that resulting from the DATA packet reception at Node B. The current noise at Node E is $\frac{1.7272 \times 10^{-4}}{570^4} = 1.6362 \times 10^{-15}$.

Node E will be able to transmit too since its CS_{th} is greater than the current noise around it. Node E interferes with the DATA packet reception at Node B. The interference from Node C at Node B is $\frac{0.0281}{500^4} = 4.496 \times 10^{-13}$.

Thus, the total interference at node B is simply $3.8432 \times 10^{-13} + 4.496 \times 10^{-13} + 10^{-16} = 8.3492 \times 10^{-13}$ W.

The SIR at node B is calculated as $\frac{7.1936\times10^{-12}}{8.3492\times10^{-13}} = 8.616$, which is around $9.3531 < 10$ dB; thus, the transmission of DATA packet will be corrupted.

8. The worst case scenario is that the interfering node is transmitting at maximum power $P_{\max}$. In BASIC, the DATA packet is transmitted at minimum power $P_{\min}$. Then, we have

$$r_i = 1.78 \times \frac{P_{\max}}{P_{\min}} \times r.$$

However, using the path-loss model we have: $\frac{P_{\max}}{P_{\min}} = \frac{r_{\max}}{r}$, and hence we have

$$r_i = 1.78 \times r_{\max}.$$

9. The transmission range of the CTS packet from Eq. (1.2.2) is

$$r_{t,CTS} = \left(\frac{0.02818}{3.652 \times 10^{-12}}\right)(0.25) = 166.6681\,\text{m}.$$

Since the DATA packet duration is more than EIFS, Node C will interfere with the DATA packet reception at node B.

(a) IEEE 802.11: All the packets are transmitted at maximum power. Thus, the *SINR* at Node B is $SINR_B = (\frac{180}{50})^4 = 167.9616$, which is 16.5989 dB. The packet is received correctly.
(b) BASIC: The RTS and CTS packet are transmitted at the minimum power whereas DATA and ACK packets are transmitted at the minimum power $= P_{\min} = 3.652 \times 10^{-12} \times 50^4 = 0.0023$ W. The $SINR_B = \frac{3.652\times10^{-12}}{\frac{0.02818}{180^4}} = 1.3604$, which is 1.337 dB. The packet is corrupted.
(c) CAPC: RTS and CTS are transmitted at maximum power and the DATA packet will be assigned a power such that the transmission range of CTS equals the interference range of the DATA packet. Thus, the interference range [Eq. (1.7)] of the DATA packet receiver is equal 166.6681 m. Node C lies outside the interference range and hence it will not corrupt the DATA packet; we can verify that by calculating the DATA power value $P_{t,\text{DATA}} = 0.0228$ W using Eq. (1.18). Accordingly, $SINR_B = \frac{0.0228}{50^4}/\frac{0.02818}{130^4} = 13.5895$, which is 11.332 dB. The packet is received correctly.

10. DATA rate adaptation, tuning the physical carrier sensing threshold, and using directional antennas.

Chapter 8

1. Physical carrier sensing threshold, power control, and rate adaptation.
2. Collisions due to contention, i.e., nodes transmit their packets at the same time slot; collisions due to interference from hidden terminals (also termed packet error).
3. Collision due to contention: Use temporal approaches [dynamically adjusting the contention window size (CW)]. Collisions due to interference from hidden terminals: Use either one or a combination of the physical attributes (carrier sensing threshold, power control, rate adaptation).
4. Transmission power control.
5. By setting its physical carrier sensing range r_c to cover the interference range r_i (1.6), the interference impact from hidden terminals is eliminated, i.e., $r_c = r_i + r$. r is the distance between the sender and the receiver.
6. Here, the SINR is calculated according to the following equation:

$$SINR = G \times \frac{P_r}{P_n + I},$$

where P_r is the good received signal, P_n is the average noise power, and I is the interference from other communicating nodes. Since the two-ray channel model is used, the received power at a receiver from a sender transmitting at a power P_t is modeled as

$$P_r = \frac{P_t \cdot G_r \cdot G_t \cdot h_t \cdot h_r}{d^4},$$

where G_t, G_r, h_t, and h_r are the antenna gains and heights of the transmitter and receiver, respectively, which are equal to one.

(i) Now we analyze the case when no power control is implemented. The *SINR* at node B when it receives a packet from node A is calculated as

$$SINR_B = \frac{10 \times \frac{250}{95^4}}{10^{-10} + \frac{250}{65^4}} = 2.046.$$

Convert to dB:

$$SINR_B = 10 \log(2.046) = 3.109\,\text{dB}.$$

Here the interference I results from the ongoing communication between C and D. Since $SINR_B \leq 10\,\text{dB}$, the connection between A and B is not established.

Similarly, the SINR at node D is

$$SINR_D = \frac{10 \times \frac{250}{57^4}}{10^{-10} + \frac{250}{98^4}} = 87.375.$$

Convert to dB:

$$SINR_D = 10 \log(87.375) = 19.41 \, \text{dB}.$$

Here, the connection is established between C and D since $SINR_D >$ 10 dB. The average transmitting power in this case is 250 mW.

(ii) Alternatively, if we apply power control, repeating the same steps as before we obtain:

$$SINR_B = \frac{10 \times \frac{100}{95^4}}{10^{-10} + \frac{20}{65^4}} = 10.957.$$

Convert to dB:

$$SINR_B = 10 \log(10.957) = 24.538 \, \text{dB}.$$

Also,

$$SINR_D = \frac{10 \times \frac{20}{57^4}}{10^{-10} + \frac{100}{98^4}} = 17.4741.$$

Convert to dB:

$$SINR_D = 10 \log(17.4741) = 10.3969 \, \text{dB}.$$

Now, both connections are established with the target SINR. The average power transmitted is 60 mW.

7. The interference ranges for a node receiving at 1, 2, 5.5 and 11 Mbps are respectively from Eq. (1.6) assuming the current noise equals zero:

$$\begin{cases} r_{i,1\,\text{Mbps}} = 1.43\,d = 143\,\text{m}, \\ r_{i,2\,\text{Mbps}} = 1.78\,d = 178\,\text{m}, \\ r_{i,5.5\,\text{Mbps}} = 1.99\,d = 199\,\text{m}, \\ r_{i,11\,\text{Mbps}} = 2.37\,d = 237\,\text{m}. \end{cases}$$

So 2 Mbps is the optimum rate.

8. ILARI will use the RTS/CTS scheme with 11 Mbps since the transmission range, which is 250 m, covers the interference range $r_{i,11\,\text{Mbps}} = 2.37\,d = 237$ m.

9. The RCRC approach since the interference range $r_{i,11\,\text{Mbps}} = 2.37d = 474$ m.

The CTS carrier sensing range is 550 m, which covers the interference range. Nodes inside the CTS carrier sensing range will be silenced for EIFS. Here, the EIFS duration is larger than the data packet time duration.

10. The transmission range of the CTS packet from Eq. ?? is

$$r_{t,CTS} = \left(\frac{0.02818}{3.652 \times 10^{-12}}\right)(0.25) = 166.6681\,\text{m}.$$

Since the DATA packet duration is more than EIFS, node C will interfere with the DATA packet reception at node B.

(a) IEEE 802.11: All the packets are transmitted at maximum power and thus the SINR at node B is $SINR_B = (\frac{180}{50})^4 = 167.9616$, which is 16.5989 dB. The packet is received correctly.

(b) CAPC: RTS and CTS are transmitted at maximum power and the DATA packet will be assigned a power such that the transmission range of CTS equals the interference range of the DATA packet. Thus, the interference range [Eq. (1.6)] of the DATA packet receiver is equal to 166.6681 m. Node C lies outside the interference range and hence it will not corrupt the DATA packet; we can verify that by calculating the DATA power value $P_{t,DATA} = 0.0228\,\text{W}$ using Eq. (1.9). Accordingly, $SINR_B = (\frac{0.0228}{50^4}/\frac{0.02818}{130^4}) = 13.5895$, which is 11.332 dB. The packet is received correctly. So with CAPC, the DATA power transmitted is diminished by a factor of 12.3596.

Chapter 9

1. Waypoint routing is a linearly hierarchical routing protocol. Linearly hierarchical means that if any link breaks, it affects only the nodes of the routes which use this link. In hierarchical routing, on the other hand, if a link breaks, the information has to be disseminated within the cluster, if the node is not a cluster head; if node is a cluster head, it has to be disseminated to all other nodes.
2. CDOA considers queuing delay, interference and bandwidth for routing decisions. During the calculation of ETX, the probe is transmitted between nodes periodically, every second. To transmit a probe, first it has to be placed in the queue. This is how queuing delay is considered for routing decisions. When multiple nodes try to send a packet (including the one which has to send a probe) simultaneously, then no-one can transmit successfully. Again each node waits and retransmits the packets. In a very dense network, there are more nodes trying to transfer packets, leading to a long delay in the transfer of the probe packet from the node. In a sparse network, the probe is transmitted faster. This is how interference is taken consideration. Bandwidth is either fixed for a node, or it is calculated using SNR from the channel and is calculated whenever required.
3. The CDOA routing protocol is more scalable compared to DSR. As CDOA data packets only store waypoint node addresses in the source route option field, more addresses can be accommodated and thus, even if network size increases, longer

routes can also be supported. The CDOA routing protocol also has less control packet overhead compared to the AODV routing protocol. In the CDOA there are exchanges of control information only between nodes on the route whereas in the AODV there are exchanges among all its neighbors whenever change occurs in its table. Thus, as the network size increases, the control information exchange becomes very large in AODV. The packet delivery ratio is also high compared to the DSR routing protocol. This is because broken links are repaired locally, which is very fast, and thus packet loss due to broken links is very low and hence packet delivery ratio is high.

4. CDOA is a waypoint approach. Mobile nodes generally have a higher packet loss rate. Thus, the ETT value is greater on these nodes, and the segments containing mobile nodes will be very small, so that if the node moves out, it can repair faster through some other path.
5. (a) The packet loss probability (forward) in the direction AB is $p_f = (10 - 9)/10 = 0.1$. The packet loss probability (reverse) in the direction BA is $p_r = (10 - 10)/10 = 0$. The probability of successful transmission of a packet is

$$\begin{aligned} p &= (1 - p_f) * (1 - p_r) \\ &= (1 - 0.1) * (1 - 0) \\ &= 0.9. \end{aligned}$$

Thus, ETX $= 1/0.9 = 1.1$ (approximately 1), i.e., no retransmission is required on average.

6. The packet loss probability in the direction AB is $p_f = (10 - 6)/10 = 0.4$. The packet loss probability in the direction BA is $p_r = (10 - 8)/10 = 0.2$. The probability of successful transmission of a packet is

$$\begin{aligned} p &= (1 - p_f) * (1 - p_r) \\ &= (1 - 0.4) * (1 - 0.2) \\ &= 0.6 * 0.8 \\ &= 0.48. \end{aligned}$$

Thus, ETX $= 1/0.48 = 2.083$.

Then, ETT $= 2.083 \times (20/2\,\text{Mbps}) = 19.86\,\mu\text{s}$.

The packet loss probability in the direction AC is $p_f = (10 - 5)/10 = 0.5$. The packet loss probability in the direction CA is $p_r = (10 - 10)/10 = 0$. The probability of successful transmission of a packet is

$$\begin{aligned} p &= (1 - p_f) * (1 - p_r) \\ &= (1 - 0.5) * (1 - 0) \\ &= 0.5. \end{aligned}$$

Thus, ETX $= 1/0.5 = 2$.

Then, $\text{ETT} = 2 \times (20/2\,\text{Mbps}) = 19.07\,\mu\text{s}$.

Since the ETT values of both links AB and AC are nearly the same, both are of equal quality and thus either one of them can be selected for transmission.

7. Given that the path is A-B-C-D-E-F-G-H-I-J-K-L-M and the corresponding ETT values are 7, 5, 7, 5, 8, 6, 8, 4, 10, 6, 4, 9 and 6,

$$\begin{aligned} p_f &= p_r = 0.5, \\ p &= 0.25, \\ \text{ETX} &= 1/p = 1/0.25 = 4, \\ \text{ETT} &= 4 \times 10/2\,\text{Mbps} = 19.07\,\mu\text{s}. \end{aligned}$$

Based on these ETT values, the waypoint nodes are D, G, I, K and the source A and destination X.

The respective segment costs are AD = 19, DG = 19, GI = 12, IK = 16, and KX = 19.

8. Routing cache:

Destination	Source Route	Cost
F	F	16
K	FK	31

Routing table:

Destination	Next Hop Node	Hop Count
F	E	2

9. (a) Whenever a broken link is repaired during the intersegment route repair process, and the repaired link has got new waypoint nodes, then the route cache entries in all the tables of the nodes storing these paths have to be changed accordingly. This message is sent in reverse direction towards the source from the node where the route repair process was started, updating the table entries in the route cache and forwarding to the next node till it is received by the source.

   (b) If a loop is detected in the route, which might have been created during the route discovery or route repair process, then the loop is removed. If the removal of the loop from the route removes any waypoint node in the route, then this message is sent towards the direction of the source. Whenever a node receives this message, it updates routes in the route cache accordingly, and forwards to next node on the route till it is received by the source node.

   (c) If the broken link is not repaired by the intrasegment route repair process as well as the intersegment route repair process, then the node sends a message towards the source stating that the route is broken and thus starts a new global route discovery. Whenever a node receives this message, it deletes the entries in the route cache associated with this route and forwards it to the next node till it is received by the source node.

(d) This message is sent by the node towards the start node of its segment, whenever it finds the link is broken. All the nodes that receive this message will remove the entry of this route from the route table and forward the message towards the start node of that segment. Whenever the start node receives this message, it starts an intrasegment route repair process.

10. In order to let the end node and forwarding nodes on the segment know the sequence number of and the hop count to the start node, the start node sends a route activate (RACT) message to the end node. The RACT message contains two values, namely, start_seq and start hop_count.

Chapter 10

1. Pervasive computing is a computation embedded in an environment and is available everywhere to assist users in accomplishing their tasks.
2. Locating and interacting with services is the job of service discovery. It can be broken down into the tasks of description, dissemination, selection, and interaction.
3. An important property that an ad hoc network should exhibit is organizing and maintaining the network by itself. The major activities that an ad hoc network is required to perform for group management include neighbor discovery, topology organization, and topology reorganization. During neighbor discovery, every node in the network gathers information about their neighbors and maintains that information in appropriate data structures. In topology organization, every node in the network gathers information about the entire network or a part of the network in order to maintain topological information. In topology reorganization, the ad hoc network is required to update topology information by incorporating the topological changes occurring in the network due to the mobility and failure of nodes.
4. The major requirements of a routing protocol in an ad hoc network are the following:

   - *Minimum route acquisition delay*: The route acquisition delay for a node that does not have a route to a particular destination node should be as minimal as possible. This delay may vary with the size of the network and the network model.
   - *Quick route reconfiguration*: The unpredictable changes in the topology of the network require that the routing protocol be able to quickly perform route reconfiguration in order to handle path breaks and subsequent packet losses.

- *Loop-free routing*: This is a fundamental requirement of any routing protocol to avoid unnecessary wastage of network bandwidth. In ad hoc networks, due to the random movement of nodes, transient loops may be formed in the routes that are established. A routing protocol should detect such transient routing loops and take corrective action.
- *Distributed routing approach*: An ad hoc wireless network is a fully distributed wireless network and the use of centralized routing approaches in such a network may consume a large amount of bandwidth.

5. The major issues in designing multicast routing protocols are as follows:

   - *Robustness*: A multicast routing protocol must be able to recover and reconfigure quickly from link breaks thus making it suitable for highly dynamic environments.
   - *Efficiency*: A multicast protocol should make a minimum number of transmissions to deliver a data packet to all the group members.
   - *Efficient group management*: Group management refers to the process of accepting multicast session members and maintaining the connectivity among them until the session expires. This process of group management needs to be performed with the minimal exchange of control messages.
   - *Scalability*: The multicast routing protocol should be able to scale for a network with a large number of nodes.

6. Energy management can be classified into the following categories: Transmission power management, battery energy management, processor power management and device power management.
7. Beacons are short messages transmitted over the network to indicate the presence of a device or an access point. They are useful for discovering neighbors in an ad hoc network.
8. Load sharing is the technique of sharing the load (work) of a device among the other types of compatible devices. It is implemented when the load of the device is maximum or crosses the threshold limit. For example, in the Pervasive Service Discovery protocol, power utilization is the major issue. When a device gets loaded, irrespective of the other devices providing the same service, it is in an active state for a long period and its power consumption is high. This is not suitable for mobile devices, so the loaded device will share its work among the other devices to optimize the available power.
9. If the service requested by the device is not present in L1 then it checks in L2. If the service is present in the remote cache then it directly connects to the remote device. If the service is not present in the remote cache then it multicasts the service request to the network. Then, the other devices in the network, if matched with the service request, will respond by acknowledging the requested message.

10. (a) Service access time $= (X/100 \times a1) + [(Y/100 \times a1) + (Y/100 \times h2 + a2)] + (Y/100 \times (1 - h2) \times RTD)$, where RTD is round-trip delay.
    (b) (i) $30/100 \times 5 \times 10^{-9}$ ns;
    (ii) $(30/100 \times 5 \times 10^{-9}) + [(70/100 \times 5 \times 10^{-9}) + (70/100 \times 0.65 \times 10 \times 10^{-9}) + [70/100 \times (1 - 0.65) \times 120 \times 10 \times 10^{-3}]$ ns.

Chapter 11

1. The coverage problem is heavily dependent on the coverage model of individual sensors and the locations of the deployed sensor nodes. The *sensor coverage model* can be considered as a measure of the quality of service of the sensor's sensing function and is subject to a wide range of interpretations due to a large variety of sensors and applications.The *network sensing coverage*, on the other hand, can be considered as a collective measure of the quality of service provided by sensor nodes at different geographical locations. In many cases, we may interpret the coverage concept as a non-negative mapping between the *space points* (of a sensor field) and the sensor nodes (of a deployed sensor network).
2. From the viewpoint of signal detection, the most commonly used sensing disk model can be interpreted as one in which a sensor can detect an event that occurred within its covered disk area; or, in other words, such a disk is covered by the sensor. Another implication of this sensing disk model is that each sensor node makes its decision independent other sensors. The definition of information coverage, on the other hand, considers measurement correlations to exploit sensing spatial diversity from geographically distributed sensors.
3. The design issues for coverage problems include: coverage type, coverage degree, coverage ratio, deployment method, sensor heterogeneity, activity scheduling, network connectivity, and performance metrics.
4. Before network deployment, one may want to know how many nodes are needed to cover all the points of a sensor field. For deterministic deployment, the basic objective is to use the least number of nodes as possible. For random deployment, the basic objective is to determine the critical sensor density: whenever the number of the deployed nodes is equal to or larger than this critical density times the area of the sensor field, all points of the sensor field can be covered almost surely in every random deployment.
5. The analysis of CSD normally starts by providing bounds for the complete coverage probability of a square region with finite area and then uses asymptotical analysis to provide the relationship between the CSD and the area (or the side length) of the square. Two approaches have been used to bound for the probability of no vacancy. One is to exploit the property of the sensing disk model; the other is based on a grid approach.
6. After sensor nodes have been deployed, there might be some redundant sensors whose covered area can also be covered by other sensors. Node activity

scheduling can therefore be used to schedule nodes to be activated alternatively such that the network operation time may be prolonged and certain area coverage requirements can still be met. Sensor activity scheduling has been intensively researched in the literature. Although these scheduling schemes are different in terms of their assumptions, objectives and approaches, they all need to answer the following question of how to determine which sensors should be active at what time and for how long.

7. One approach to sensing activity scheduling is to use a grid approach and divide the sensors into different sensor coverage sets, which are activated sequentially. This normally requires a centralized algorithm. The other approach is to apply some properties of the sensing disk model and determine redundant sensors. After the redundancy check, a distributed sensor activity scheduling protocol can be established. For example, one can allow all sensors to be active initially and then let each sensor perform its redundancy check. After a sensor has determined its own redundancy, it may choose to go into a sleep state.
8. Tian and Georganans propose the concept of the *sponsored sector* for checking redundancy. Huang *et al.* propose using *perimeter coverage* to check field complete coverage and sensor redundancy. Xing *et al.* propose a coverage configuration protocol (CCP) that applies *crossing coverage* to determine redundant sensors. Carbunar proposes using *Voronoi diagram vertices and intersections* to check redundancy.
9. After an initial random deployment, coverage holes may exist if the number of deployed sensors is not larger than that required by the critical sensor density. We can also use mobile sensor nodes which are equipped with mobile platforms to adjust their positions to improve network coverage after the initial deployment.
10. Wang *et al.* propose using Voronoi diagrams for hole detection and hole size estimation. A sensor can determine the existence of coverage holes by examining whether there are uncovered Voronoi vertices in its own Voronoi cell. Furthermore, they propose using the distance from the sensor to its farthest uncovered Voronoi vertex to estimate the size of a coverage hole and that vertex is also considered as the target position for a mobile sensor to reside.

Chapter 12

1. Use the Software factory design pattern.
2. Use ESC/Java (Ref. 46) to verify your program.
3. Lab project.
4. False. The modality $\Diamond$ does not distribute over conjunction. A counterexample is: consider a finite state machine having a path starting from an initial state along which ϕ holds on some states and ψ holds on some states; however $\phi \wedge \psi$ does not hold for any state. Such a state machine would satisfy $\Diamond\phi \wedge \Diamond\psi$ while it does not satisfy $\Diamond(\phi \wedge \psi)$.

5. No. For example, consider the situation in which σ always remains true. In this case the agent with nominal I never comes to know that σ has changed from false to true.
6. The formula is valid. The proof by natural deduction is as follows (assumption)
   $p \to p$ (assumption)
   p (implication elimination)
   $\overline{p \to p}$ (implication introduction)
   $\overline{p \to p} \to p \to p$ (implication introduction)
7. Consider a program as a game between a protagonist and an antagonist (the environment)
8. Lab Project.
9. Lab Project.
10. Lab Project.
11. See Ref. 8.

Chapter 13

1. Performance measures of routing techniques:
   Criterion
   Description

   - *Correctness/reliability*: A routing algorithm should find correct paths for packets to their intended destinations.
   - *Complexity/efficiency*: A good routing algorithm must have low overhead in terms of the number of control messages exchanged among routers, size of routing tables, and processing time. The bottom line is to use resources efficiently.
   - *Optimality*: A good routing algorithm must have the ability to determine optimal routes in reasonable time based on some routing metric which is determined to optimize the objectives of a network operator.
   - *Adaptability*: In real networks, unexpected things can happen such as link and/or router failure. A good routing algorithm must have the ability to quickly adapt to changes in the network topology. Also, it must have the capability to adapt to fluctuations in traffic loads.
   - *Robustness/resilience*: A good routing algorithm must be capable of rerouting packets away from heavily overloaded and/or failed links or routers. The routing tables need to be updated automatically and quickly when there is a link/node failure without the need to reboot the router.
   - *Stability/convergence*: A good routing must be stable, i.e., ensures loop-free paths to avoid routing loops or oscillation. This also requires quick routing table updates when there is a change in the network.
   - *Scalability*: A good routing must be capable of being used in complex and heterogeneous networks that have a large number of nodes.

- *QoS support*: A good routing must be capable of supporting the QoS required by different applications or individual users.

2. Distance vector versus link state routing:

Distance vector routing	Link state routing
Optimal route calculation is decentralized using distributed Bellman–Ford algorithm	Optimal route calculation is centralized by running Dijkstra's algorithm at each node
Does not require a global map of the network	Global map is needed before calculating optimal paths
Advertize to neighbors only known distances to all other nodes (i.e., distance vector)	Advertize to all nodes (by flooding) the cost to its neighbors only (i.e., LSPs)
Use hop count as a cost metric	Allows other more sophisticated metrics to be used, including delay, load, reliability and bandwidth.
Share information at regular intervals if an update occurs	Share information only if there is a change in the network (update triggered)
Suffers from routing loop problem	Loop-free routing
Suffers from count-to-infinity problem	Quick convergence

3. The count-to-infinity problem is one of the problems that faces distance vector routing, which occurs when a link or a router goes down or when the cost of a link increases. The distance vector routing will suffer from slow convergence until the routers eventually realize the change. Two partial solutions for this problem are: *split horizon*, and *split horizon with poisoned reverse.*
4. OLSR is a proactive routing technique for MANETs. OLSR uses a technique called *multipoint relaying for optimized message flooding*. In this technique, each node selects a set of its neighbor nodes as multi-point relays (MPRs); see Fig. 21. The nodes which are selected as MPRs periodically announce reachability information about the nodes which have selected them to the network in their control messages. Thus, unlike pure link state protocols, the technique declares only a subset of links and reduces flooding of control messages using only nodes within the MPR set (instead of the entire network).
5. *Random early detection* (RED): This is an active queue management technique that keeps the average queue length low while allowing occasional bursts of packets in the queue. It detects congestion early before the queue overflows by computing the average queue length (Q_{avg}) at each packet arrival. Then, it compares the average queue length with two pre-specified thresholds: minimum threshold ($th_{\min}$) and maximum threshold ($th_{\max}$). If the average queue length is below the minimum threshold, the arriving packet is admitted to the queue. However, if the average queue length is greater than the maximum threshold, the packet is dropped or marked. This ensures that the average queue length does not significantly exceed the maximum threshold. Finally, when the average queue length is between the minimum and maximum

thresholds, then the packet is dropped or marked with a probability p that is a function of the average queue size, $th_{\min}$ and $th_{\max}$. The performance of RED depends on how the average queue length and the dropping probabilities are computed.

Leaky bucket: This is a simple traffic shaping technique that operates in a similar manner to a bucket with a hole at the bottom. The water enters the bucket and leaks through the hole at a constant rate as long as the bucket is not empty, i.e., the output rate remains fixed even if the input rate is varying; see Fig. 22. A simple leaky bucket implementation in a network router is through a finite buffer FIFO queue discipline that holds arriving packets then processes them at a constant rate; see Fig. 23. If the arriving packets exceed the buffer size, the extra packets will be dropped. Otherwise, packets are buffered and served/transmitted from the queue at a constant rate.

Deficit weighted round robin (DWRR): This is a scheduling technique that was proposed to guarantee QoS with respect to delay and bandwidth for realtime bursty traffic. DWRR was proposed to address the limitations of WFQ and an earlier algorithm known as weighted round robin (WRR). Similar to WFQ, packets are first classified into various service classes, assigned to separate queues and then serviced in a round-robin order. However, each queue maintains a deficit counter that specifies the total number of bytes that the queue is permitted to transmit. Each time a queue is visited by the scheduler, the deficit counter is first increased by a quantum of service proportional to its weight. Then, the scheduler transmits the packets at the head of the queue and decrements the deficit counter by the size of the transmitted packet as long as the size of the packet is not greater than the deficit counter. If the queue becomes empty, the deficit counter is set to zero. Then, the scheduler moves to the next non-empty queue.

6. A router is composed of several modules: line cards [including network interfaces, traffic manager (TM), and ingress/egress port buffers], forwarding engines, a routing processor, an interconnection unit, routing/forwarding tables, and management components. See Fig. 5 and Sec. 3 for a detailed description.
7. Two techniques for controlling the traffic generated during flooding are: (a) using sequence number controlled flooding implemented in the Gnutella P2P application (see Sec. 4.1.), and (b) using multi-point relaying as in OLSR; see Sec. 7.2.
8. Traffic shaping is a traffic management technique that regulates the traffic rate entering the network and thus smoothes out bursty traffic. Traffic policing is a traffic management technique that monitors the adherence of incoming traffic characteristics to the service contract specifications and takes appropriate action accordingly (e.g., discard, delay, or mark packets/flows violating the contract).

9. ADOV takes a reactive approach: the route is established only on demand to cope with the frequent changes in the topology. AODV maintains information only about the active routes and thus has less overhead. However, it suffers from route discovery delay. On the other hand, OLSR is a proactive approach that maintains information about the entire network at all the times. Hence, OLSR suffers from increased overhead but to alleviate this problem it uses multi-point relaying to optimize message flooding.
10. Five examples of applications for multicast routing: Online video conferencing, video on demand, software update distribution, distance learning, and distributed interactive simulation.
11. In each iteration of the main loop of the algorithm, we search for a node that has the minimum cost; then, the costs of its neighbors are updated. Roughly, in the first iteration, we check N nodes. In the second iteration, we check $N - 1$ nodes and so on. Thus, the total number will be $N + (N-1) + (N-2) + \cdots + 2 + 1 = n(n+1)/2 \Rightarrow O(N2)$.
12. The total rate of packets that enter the switch = 10 + 20 + 30 = 60 packets/s. The overall average packet service time = 100((10/60) + 200((20/60) + 300((30/60) = 233.333 ms. The average number of packets that will be in the switch = 60(233.333(10 − 3 = 14 packets (by applying Little's law of queueing theory).
13. The shortest paths from node a to all other nodes are shown in the following graph by thick arcs and the steps are as shown in the table below.

Chapter 14

1. Network management refers to the management of the network, which comprises nodes and links. Systems management refers to the management of a system's resources, such as central processor usage, disk usage and application processes. As an extension of network and systems management, service management deals with the services provided by organizations to customers.
2. At one end of the spectrum, OSI-SM is considered the most powerful management technology in theoretical terms. However, it is complicated and expensive to implement, and relies on OSI protocols, which have gone out of fashion. At the other end of the spectrum, SNMP has been the most widely deployed management framework in practice, particularly in IP environments. However, since its information modeling capabilities are rudimentary and it does not support configuration management well due to its lack of transaction capabilities, its simplicity is its biggest weakness.
3. The OSI network model is an ISO standard and the best of all the models proposed. It is well-structured and addresses all aspects of management. An OSI network management architecture comprises four models: the organization model, the information model, the communication model and the functional model.

4. SNMP-based manager-agent management solutions are the *de facto* standards, which are still widely used in the industry. SNMP provides inadequate coverage of the five functional areas of network management as specified by OSI and has a scalability problem as network size increases. Policy-based solutions offer a more flexible management concept than traditional ones, but are still not widely applied due to their complexity. A promising approach is distributed network management including CORBA-based solutions and mobile agent-based solutions. Web-based solutions are a new direction for distributed network management, but distributed technologies and network management technologies are still far from being perfectly combined. XML-based solutions focus on the improvement of SNMP in terms of configuration management and integration with SNMP. But these solutions still lack standardization. A promising path toward standardization is an integrated application of NETCONF and Web services. Event correlation techniques are limited in capability due to the large number of events generated by network devices. Thus, alert evaluation techniques have been introduced to reduce false positives and this has become an important prerequisite for gaining good correlation results.
5. Some current requirements include: inter-domain cooperative management for highly distributed networks; integration for multiple network management solutions; vendor-proprietary network management solutions; mature technologies for convenient application in the field of network management to promote automation.
6. The current trends in the field include: standardization, automation and integration. Web services are now under review with a view to improving the standardization process of XML-based network management. Meanwhile, the semantic approach with the use of ontologies seems promising in the field of automatic network management. Other approaches have also been applied, such as integrated network management, improved root cause analysis techniques, and active network management.
7. It has become necessary to put forward an evaluation framework for data modeling languages in order to leverage their capabilities in adapting to the requirements of network management. It seems that a well-designed framework for evaluation will play an important role in studying data modeling for network management.
8. The application of an integrated approach based on NETCONF and Web services has become a promising way for standardization of XML-based network management.
9. Topics include management for new networks, P2P-based network management, predictive network management, autonomic networks with intelligent self-managing devices, and research on management information models.

Chapter 15

1. This is an example of passive monitoring. The timestamps can be used to measure round-trip time (RTT) from the client to the Web server. However, the RTT measurements may not be accurate if the server is heavily loaded or if it processes queries (such as database queries) based on the client's requests.
2. In order to collect data in a passive mode, a hub, a tap or port-mirroring can be used.
3. Many routers or networks filter ping. Ping filtration could lead to inaccurate estimates of packet loss or inference of service unavailability by the client.
4. In the network configuration of Fig. 4, the minimum value of TTL required is 3, which is a path through routers A and D. The maximum TTL is more complicated. Since both routers B and C have links to each other, a packet can traverse between them indefinitely. However, the purpose of TTL is to avoid infinite loops; therefore, the maximum TTL is the maximum value allowed. For an 8-bit field the maximum value allowed is 255.
5. The procedure of deciding not to send any further packets with increasing TTL depends upon the underlying protocol. If traceroute is utilizing UDP, then the destination host will send an ICMP *destination unreachable* message to the original sender, indicating that the destination host is not running any service on the particular port. However, in the case of ICMP (Windows implementation), the traceroute message is not destined for any particular port, and an ICMP *echo reply* (type 0) message will be sent. In either case, the original sender will recognize that the final destination host is reached.
6. The interframe gap must be 96 bit times, which is equal to 12 bytes. The overhead is 38 bytes, i.e., 14-byte Ethernet header, 4-byte CRC, 8 bytes for preamble and 12 bytes for interframe gap. Therefore, the capacity $C = 100(100/138) = 72.46\,\text{Mbps}$.
7. The capacity of a path may remain constant over a long period. However, in the case of a route change or path upgrade, the capacity of the path could change. In comparison, the available bandwidth of a path may change abruptly. A link may experience a sudden change in its utilization, resulting in change in the available bandwidth.
8. The narrow link is not necessarily the same as the tight link. For instance, consider an example where a link between two Internet routers A and B is included in several Internet paths. At a given moment, the link AB may appear as a narrow link for a path, even though it may not be the tight link for the path.
9. The principal disadvantage of TCPtraceroute is that it requires an extra message. Conventional traceroute schemes utilize two messages: a UDP or ICMP echo message from the sender, and an ICMP time exceed message from the target. By comparison, in TCPtraceroute, a sender has to send an RST message if it receives a SYN ACK from the target.

10. Sent timestamps can be obtained via the PCAP utility. A precise mechanism is to use DAG cards. If a DAG card is not available then you can obtain timestamps from the PCAP library.

Chapter 16

1. Other advantages include: increases robustness, helps in network monitoring, helps in distributed caching, and so on. Interested readers may refer to the network coding homepage for detailed information.
2. One usage of linear broadcast is for receiving partial information. For instance, in multi-level resolution image transmission, the image can be encoded in several messages with different resolutions. The more messages the receiver gets, the clearer the image the viewer sees. Thus, every non-source node T with maxflow(T) $<$ receives partial information of maxflow(T) messages, which is desirable for a mobile handset when receiving a large image at a low resolution or rendering a colored image in black-and-white.
3. One typical application of linear dispersion is in the scalability of a two-tier broadcast system as shown in Fig. 8. If the linear broadcast is in fact a linear dispersion, then it is sufficient to connect the new LAN gateway to any collection of backbone nodes with maxflow(), that is, the new LAN can connect to gateways C and D, which will be a collection {C, D} with maxflow({C, D}).
4. Every linear dispersion is a linear broadcast, and every linear broadcast is a linear multicast. In other words, a linear broadcast is not necessary a linear dispersion, a linear multicast is not necessarily a linear broadcast, and a linear network code is not necessarily a linear multicast.
5. The main practical factors include: the synchronization problem and the buffering solution, the flushing mechanism of buffers, the overhead to transmit the coefficients, and the interleaving mechanism. More details can be found in the literature [10].
6. Network coding significantly improves the forwarding performance in challenging wireless networks. The most outstanding gains in different settings are throughput optimization, energy conservation and efficient error recovery in underwater sensor networks. In general terms, in wireless networks, network coding can increase energy efficiency in broadcast/multicast scenarios, and network coding can increase throughput by leveraging the broadcast nature of the wireless medium in unicast scenarios.
7. If relay node R sends ($\mathrm{P1} \oplus \mathrm{P3}$), nodes A and C can decode to obtain the respective native packets sent to them. However, node B and D are non-beneficial nodes. If relay node R sends ($\mathrm{P1} \oplus \mathrm{P3} \oplus \mathrm{P4}$), nodes A, C and D can decode to obtain the respective native packets sent to them. However, node B remains a non-beneficial node. If relay node R sends ($\mathrm{P3} \oplus \mathrm{P4} \oplus \mathrm{P5}$), nodes B, C and D can decode to obtain the respective native packets sent to them. However, node A remains a non-beneficial node. Consequently, relay

node R should select the ($P1 \oplus P3 \oplus P4 \oplus P5$) because it would allow all four neighbors to receive their respective packets all at once. In this way, the number of packets delivered in a single transmission is maximized.

8. In fact, wireless networks are a very natural setting for network coding because the characteristics of wireless links that complicate routing (namely, their unreliability and broadcast nature) are the very characteristics for which coding is a natural solution.
9. Yes. In fact, multi-source network coding turns out not to be a simple extension of single-source network coding. For single-source network coding, the maximum information rate is considered. Moreover, in multicast scenarios the maximum information rate can be achieved by the maxflow min-cut theorem. In multi-source network coding, the achievable information rate region is addressed. The latter is actually an open issue.
10. There are many debates between Avalanche and BitTorrent, which are typical examples of network coding and routing, respectively. In fact, theoretical analysis shows that the theoretical capacity of both network coding and routing are the same in overlay peer-to-peer networks. However, random network coding (in Avalanche) can increase variety, which result in better performance than the rarest first policy (in BitTorrent), possibly resulting in long download times if the peer with the rarest piece leaves the P2P group occasionally.

Chapter 17

1. Concurrency is a property of complex systems in which several computational processes are executing at the same time, and potentially communicating with each other. The study of concurrency encompasses a broad range of systems, from cluster computers, to loosely-coupled, largely asynchronous distributed systems, and communication networks.
2. Interleaving concurrency is a process whereby it is possible to reduce concurrency to an interleaving of sequential events.
3. True concurrency does not allow reduction of concurrency to an interleaving of sequential events and supports abstractions for events whose occurrences partially overlap in time.
4. An event is something that happened.
5. An abstract event, also called event label, is a representation of what happened (of what is done), but no indication of when or where.
6. A pure temporal event is a representation of what happened, indicating a time of occurrence, but not where it happened.
7. A system event is a representation of what happened, indicating both a time and place of occurrence.
8. An action is a system of related events.
9. A finite action consists of a finite number of events.
10. An infinite action consists of an infinite set of events.

11. An action is called a signal or communication action if it consists of communication events.
12. The free composition of actions A_1 and A_2 is the action A that consists of all events from A_1 and A_2 taken without changes and without introduction of new relations.
13. A process is a system of actions.
14. A process is called a communication process if it consists of communication actions.
15. A process is called finite if it consists of a finite number of finite actions.
16. An infinite process consists of an infinite set of actions.
17. A process P is called action sequential if all actions from P are separable from one another in the sense of.
18. A process P is called strictly sequential if all actions from P are sequential and separable from one another.
19. A process P is called interleaving if all events from P have different times of occurrence.
20. The free composition of processes P_1 and P_2 is the process P that consists of all actions from P_1 and P_2 taken without changes and introduction of new relations.
21. An algebraic system is a set containing relations (predicates) and operations.
22. A universal algebra is a set containing operations.
23. A process algebra is a universal algebra, elements of which are processes and operations where processes are defined.
24. A topological manifold is a Hausdorff topological space X in which every point has a neighborhood homeomorphic to an open subset of Euclidean space $\mathbf{R}^n$.
25. A fiber bundle $\boldsymbol{B}$ (also called fibre bundle) is a triad (E, p, B) where the topological space E is called the total space, or simply space of the fiber bundle; the topological space B the base space, or simply base of the fiber bundle; and p is a topological projection of E onto B such that every point in the base space has a neighborhood U such that $p^{-1}(b) = F$ for all points b from B and $p^{-1}(U)$ is homeomorphic to the direct product $U \times F$.
26. Processes consist of actions.
27. Events are elements of actions, which are elements of processes.
28. Actions consist of events.
29. Universal algebras are particular cases of algebraic systems.
30. Process algebras are particular cases of universal algebras.

Chapter 18

1. A dataflow execution model is an inherently parallel model which can be used to freely express parallelism with a dataflow graph.
2. Normally, in a control flow model programs are executed sequentially, while with the dataflow model programs can be expressed as a dataflow graph in

a natural parallel manner, which can be used to avoid the bottleneck in the control flow model.

3. The hybrid model is flexible in combining the advantages of dataflow and control-flow, as well as in exposing parallelism at a desired level. Through the hybrid model, a region of actors within a dataflow graph can be grouped together as a coarse-grained thread to be executed sequentially, while the data-driven method of dataflow can be used to activate and synchronize the execution of threads.
4. Grid computing is one of the recent paradigms for parallel and distributed computing. It provides online access to computation or storage as a service supported by a pool of distributed computing resources.
5. Enterprise grid computing systems aim to enable virtualization and harnessing of various types of distributed IT resources within an enterprise.
6. Enterprise grids are specifically focused on provisioning resources dynamically to different projects depending on their priorities with idle resources in an enterprise.
7. A scheduling is a process that maps and manages the execution of interdependent tasks in a DAG onto distributed resources, which is known as an NP-complete problem.
8. The HEFT (heterogeneous earliest-first-time) algorithm is effective in scheduling tasks in a DAG onto heterogeneous distributed resources.
9. The L-HEFT algorithm is effective in rescheduling of DAG tasks in the case of failures or new resources.
10. L-HEFT reschedules the DAG tasks just for partial graphs, while the D-HEFT algorithm reschedules the whole graph. This means that the rescheduling cost of D-HEFT is higher than L-HEFT.

Chapter 19

1. Grid computing has been understood by many organizations as servicing and sharing flexible, coordinated resources among dynamic collections of individuals, institutional entities, and the resources themselves distributed on the Internet.
2. The commonly used system calls are: `socket()`, `bind()`, `recvfrom()`, `sendto()`, `close()`.
3. Example: Simple TCP server in C on the Linux platform:

```
#include <stdio.h>
#include <sys/types.h>
#include <sys/socket.h>
#include <netinet/in.h>
#include <arpa/inet.h>
#define BUFSIZE 1024             // set 1 Kbytes receive data buffer
int main(int argc, char ** argv) {
 struct sockaddr_in my_address, remote_address;
 int s, fd, len, sin_size;
```

```
  char buf[BUFSIZE];
  memset(&my_address, 0, sizeof(my_address));   // set my_address to 0
  my_address.sin_family = AF_INET;              // Internet address
  my_address.sin_addr.s_addr = INADDR_ANY;    // any incoming address
  my_address.sin_port = htons(9000);        // local port number is 9000
  if ((s = socket(AF_INET, SOCK_STREAM, 0)) < 0) { // create TCP socket
    perror("socket");
    return 1;
  }
  if (bind(s, (struct sockaddr *)&my_address, \
   sizeof(struct sockaddr)) < 0) {        // bind socket to local port, OK?
    perror("bind");
    return 1;
  }
  listen(s, 5);   // accepts incoming requests
  sin_size = sizeof(struct sockaddr_in);
  if ((fd=accept(s, (struct sockaddr *)&remote_address, \
   &sin_size)) < 0) {     // accept a request, OK?
    perror("accept");
    return 1;
  }
  printf("accepted client %s\n", \
   inet_ntoa(remote_address.sin_addr));
  len = send(fd, "Server X\n", 9, 0);
  while ((len = recv(fd, buf, BUFSIZE, 0)) > 0) {
   buf[len] = '\0';
   printf("%s\n", buf);
  if (send(fd, buf, len, 0) < 0) {
    perror("write");
    return 1;
   }
  }
  close(fd); close(s); return 0;
}
/* Example: Simple TCP client in C on Linux platform */
#include <stdio.h>
#include <sys/types.h>
#include <sys/socket.h>
#include <netinet/in.h>
#include <arpa/inet.h>
#include BUFSIZE 1024
int main(int argc, char ** argv) {
  struct sockaddr_in remote_address;
  int s, len;
  char buf[BUFSIZE];
  memset(&remote_address, 0, sizeof(remote_address));
  remote_address.sin_family = AF_INET;
  remote_address.sin_addr.s_addr = inet_addr("127.0.0.1"); //
      local host
  remote_address.sin_port = htons(9000);
  if ((s = socket(AF_INET, SOCK_STREAM, 0)) < 0) {
    perror("socket"); return 1;
```

```
  }
  if (connect(s, (struct sockaddr *)&remote_address, \
   sizeof(struct sockaddr)) < 0) {
    perror("connect"); return 1;
  }
  printf("Connected to server X\n");
  len = recv(s, buf, BUFSIZE, 0);
  buf[len] = '\0';
  printf("%s", buf);
  while(1) {
   printf("Write your sentence to send: ");
   scanf("%s", buf);
   if (!strcmp(buf, "exit")) break; // quit program upon receiving ``exit''
   len = send(s, buf, strlen(buf), 0);
   len = recv(s, buf, BUFSIZE, 0);
   buf[len] = '\0';
   printf("Received: %s\n", buf);
  }
  close(s); return 0;
}
```

4.
```
// Example: echo server in Java
package test;
import java.io.BufferedReader;
import java.io.IOException;
import java.io.InputStreamReader;
import java.io.PrintWriter;
import java.net.ServerSocket;
import java.net.Socket;
public class EchoServer implements Runnable {
 private Socket socket;
 public EchoServer(Socket socket) {
  this.socket = socket;
 }
 public void run() {
  try {
    BufferedReader bufread = new BufferedReader(new \
     InputStreamReader(socket.getInputStream()));
    PrintWriter out = new PrintWriter(socket.getOutputStream());
    // print a welcome message
    out.println("This is the Echo Server.");
    out.println("\tThings typed will be returned. Press '!' to terminate.");
    out.println();
    out.println();
    out.flush();
    int currChar = 0;
    while ((currChar = bufread.read()) != -1) {
     char c = (char) currChar;
     if (c == '!') break;    // if '!' is typed, close the connection
     out.print(c);
     out.flush();
    }
```

```
      } catch (IOException ioe) {
       ioe.printStackTrace();
      } finally {
       try {
        if (socket != null) {
         socket.close();
        }
       } catch (IOException ex) {
        ex.printStackTrace();
       }
      }
     }
     public static void main(String[] args) {
      int port = 9000;    // set a default port number
      if (args.length >= 1) {
       try {
        port = Integer.parseInt(args[0]);
       } catch (NumberFormatException nfe) {
        System.out.println("Error: port must be a number -- use 9000.");
       }
      }
      try {
       ServerSocket serverSocket = new ServerSocket(port);
       System.out.println("Echo server is running.");
       int counter = 0;
       while (true) {
        Socket client = serverSocket.accept();
        System.out.println("Accepted a connection from " + \
         client.getInetAddress().getHostName());
         // use multiple threads to handle simultaneous connections
         Thread t = new Thread(new EchoServer(client));
         t.setName(client.getInetAddress().getHostName()+":"+counter++);
         t.start();
        }
       } catch (IOException ioe) {
        ioe.printStackTrace();
       }
      }
     }

     // Example: HTTP client in Java
     package test;
     import java.io.BufferedReader;
     import java.io.File;
     import java.io.FileOutputStream;
     import java.io.IOException;
     import java.io.InputStream;
     import java.io.InputStreamReader;
     import java.io.PrintWriter;
     import java.net.InetSocketAddress;
     import java.net.MalformedURLException;
     import java.net.Socket;
```

```
import java.net.URL;
import java.util.StringTokenizer;
public class saveHTTP {
 public static void main(String[] args) {
  try {
   if (args.length < 2) {
     System.out.println("Usage");
     System.out.println("\tsaveHTTP <URL> <file to save>");
     System.out.println("\tExample: saveHTTP \
      http://www.abc.com/ abc.html");
     System.out.println(1);
    }
    URL url = new URL(args[0]);
    File outFile = new File(args[1]);
    Socket socket = new Socket();
    int port = url.getPort();
    if (port == -1) port = url.getDefaultPort();
    InetSocketAddress remoteAddress = new \
     InetSocketAddress(url.getHost(), port);
    socket.connect(remoteAddress);
    PrintWriter out = new PrintWriter(socket.getOutputStream());
    // print client's request
    out.println("GET " + url.getFile() + " HTTP/1.0");
    out.println("User-Agent: saveHTTP");
    out.println("Host: " + url.getHost());
    out.println();
    out.flush();
    // read remote server's response
    InputStream in = socket.getInputStream();
    boolean responseOK = true;
    BufferedReader bufread = new BufferedReader(\
     new InputStreamReader(in));
    String currLine = null;
    // get HTTP response code from the first line of result
    currLine = bufread.readLine();
    if (currLine != null) {
      System.out.println(currLine);
      StringTokenizer st = new StringTokenizer(currLine, "\t");
      st.nextToken();
      String responseCode = st.nextToken();
      int httpResponseCode = Integer.parseInt(responseCode.trim());
      if (httpResponseCode != 200) {
       responseOK = false; // response fails
      }
     } else {
      System.err.println("Server returned no response!");
      System.exit(1);
     }
     while ((currLine = bufread.readLine()) != null) { // read headers
      System.out.println(currLine);
      // done with headers, break the loop
      if (currLine.trim().equals("")) break;
```

```
        }
        if (responseOK) {
        FileOutputStream fout = new FileOutputStream(outFile);
        int currByte;
        while ((currByte = bufread.read()) != -1) fout.write(currByte);
        fout.close();
        System.out.println("** File saved to " + args[1]);
       } else {
        System.out.println("Bad HTTP response -- file is not saved");
       }
       socket.close();
      } catch (MalformedURLException me) {
       me.printStackTrace();
      } catch (IOException ioe) {
       ioe.printStackTrace();
      }
     }
    }
```

5. The use of Interface Definition Language (IDL).
6. The three algorithms are: one hop lookups, Chord, and Kademlia.
7. The Open Grid Form (OGF) defines specifications on grid computing.
8. Globus Toolkit is popularity selected for constructing grid applications.
9. In the MMOP design stated, we have the Broker VO, the Client VO, the Application VO, the Module Storage VO, and the Free Server VO. The primary VO, i.e., the Broker VO, must exist in a grid-based computing platform such as MMOP.
10. The dead reckoning technique is the traditional method.

Chapter 20

1. During unicast multimedia transmission a separated multimedia stream is transmitted by the sender for each of the receivers. During multicast multimedia transmission a single multimedia stream serves many receivers. During the multicast transmission of data, a multicast stream transverses a network node as long as at least one receiver behind that node is listening to that stream. As result, if a receiver stops listening to a multicast stream, the transmission of the multicast stream will stop only if that receiver was the only receiver listening to that multicast stream behind that node. For more information, see Sec. 2.
2. The *de facto* protocols that are currently used for the transmission of multimedia data on the Internet are RTP and RTCP. RTP is used for the transmission of multimedia data from the sender to the receiver, and the receiver uses the RTCP protocol to inform the sender of the transmission quality. RTCP offers the following services to applications: QoS monitoring, source identification and inter-media synchronization. For more information, see Sec. 4.2.
3. According to RFC 3550 [20], delay jitter is defined to be the mean deviation (smoothed absolute value) of the difference D in packet spacing at the receiver

compared to the sender for a pair of packets. This is equivalent to the difference in the "relative transit time" for the two packets. The relative transit time is the difference between a packet's timestamp and the receiver's clock at the time of arrival. If S_i is the timestamp from packet i and R_i is the time of arrival for this packet, then for two packets i and j, D is defined as

$$D(i,j) = (R_j - R_i) - (S_j - S_i) = (R_j - S_j) - (R_i - S_i).$$

The delay jitter is calculated continuously as each packet i arrives, using the difference D for that packet and the previous packet, according to

$$J_i = J_{i-1} + (|D(i-1,j)| - J_{i-1})/16.$$

For more information, see Sec. 4.3.

4. Two approaches are available to reduce the effects of packet loss during multimedia transmission:
   - *APQ (automatic repeat request)*: An active technique where the receiver asks the sender to retransmit some lost packets.
   - *FEC (forward error correction)*: A passive technique where the sender transmits redundant information. This redundant information is used by the receiver to correct errors and lost packets.

   For more information, see Sec. 4.5.
5. The sender in a unicast adaptive multimedia transmission architecture consists of the following modules: the multimedia archive, feedback analysis, quality adaptation and packet scheduler/sender buffer. For more information, see Sec. 4.1.
6. During the multicast transmission of multimedia data over the Internet receivers with heterogeneous data reception capabilities must be accommodated. To accommodate heterogeneity, the sender application may transmit one multicast stream. By determining the transmission rate that better satisfies most of the receivers, it may transmit multiple multicast streams with different transmission rates and allocate receivers to each stream (simulcast approach) or may use layered encoding and transmit each layer to a different multicast stream. For more information, see Sec. 5.1.
7. In the simulcast approach, the sender entity transmits the same multimedia data in multiple multicast streams with different transmission rates and the receiver entity receives the appropriate multicast stream depending on its capabilities. In the layered encoding approach, the sender entity encodes the multimedia data in layers (basic and more enhanced layers) and transmits each layer in a different multicast stream, and the receiver entity receives the basic and zero, one or more enhanced layers depending on its capabilities. For more information, see Sec. 5.
8. The most effective approach in terms of bandwidth consumption is the single stream multicast approach due to the fact that only one multicast stream is

used in order to serve the entire group of receivers. The other two approaches need more bandwidth: the simulcast approach uses many multicast streams to replicate the same multimedia over the network and the layer encoding approach introduces overhead (due to the encoding of multimedia in layers). Of course, the single multicast stream approach suffers from fairness problems. For more information, see Sec. 5.

9. The most complicated approach is the layered encoding approach due to the complex encoding and decoding mechanisms which are needed to encode and decode the multimedia data in layers. The other two approaches (single stream and simulcast) use less complicated encoding and decoding mechanisms. For more information, see Sec. 5.
10. During multicast multimedia adaptive transmission over the Internet, the overall target is the optimal usage of the network resources and for this reason an appropriate mechanism must be used. In order to evaluate such mechanisms, the following criteria are used: network congestion, scalability, adaptation speed, TCP friendliness and user satisfaction. For more information, see Sec. 5.5.

Chapter 21

1. Generally speaking the larger the payload, the more efficient the packet stream. Interactive services such as ssh often send payloads of one byte which, after the size of the headers are factored in, results in a packet of 67 bytes and an overhead percentage of about 98%. In contrast, http often boasts payloads in the 1,450-byte range resulting in an overhead percentage of only about 4%.
2. Performance management/address resolution increases the load on the network and tends to make the packet inter-arrival times more intense.
3. The overhead of inter-processor communication requires that "pieces of the puzzle" be transferred across a network which may be slower and more spread out than an internal bus. Due to these speed differences and length of travel, a given processor may have to wait for a required piece, thereby negating the possibility of the ideal linear solution.
4. Often a workstation connected to a network can serve a dual purpose. In most cases their utilization seldom exceeds 30% for an extended period of time. Therefore, it is easy to leverage these unused CPU cycles.
5. An ethical use of a packet sniffer is analyzing packet flows to get a better understanding of workload intensity and distribution so that network parameters can be tuned to offer better performance.
6. The algorithm that splits the problem is efficient but the algorithm that directs the inter-processor communication is not, or the network is under the required capacity.
7. Packet sizes are variable to optimize network performance. If they were fixed, say at 1,000 bytes, if only 200 bytes needed to be sent, the packet would still be

1,000 bytes in length (200 actual bytes and 800 bytes of filler). With variable packets, the packet in the example above would in fact be only 200 bytes, a saving of 800 bytes.

8. MPI nodes are linked via a table that links an IP address to a node name and defines a master node.
9. The factor include: faster node bus size, more efficient parallel algorithms, a faster computer network and more and faster computer memory.
10. The number of packets required increases because they need to be sent among more nodes. Hence, there is a higher inter-arrival intensity (shorter arrival values) and more bytes being transferred.

Chapter 22

1. The system must be able to detect attacks reliably without giving false alarms. It is very important that the false alarm rate is low as in a live network with a large amount of traffic, the number of false alarms may exceed the total number of attacks detected correctly, thereby decreasing the confidence in the attack detection capability of the system. Ideally, the system should detect all intrusions with no false alarms.

   The system must be able to handle large amounts of data without affecting performance and without dropping data, i.e., the rate at which patterns are processed and decisions are made must be greater than or equal to the rate of arrival of the audit patterns. Hence, the speed of operation is critical for systems deployed in high-speed networks. The system must be capable of operating in real time by initiating a response mechanism once an attack is detected.
2. Authentication refers to validating the identity of a user or application accessing a system. The most common method for authentication is the use of a user ID and a password. However, passwords can be guessed using tools which are freely available. Hence, authentication methods which are relatively difficult to guess and forge, including biometric and multifactor authentication mechanisms such as the use of a security token in addition to the password, have gained significance. Such methods require the physical presence of a human or the device and are hence more secure than a simple password mechanism. However, the password mechanism is still the most preferred method for authentication, and systems have been updated to accept only strong passwords based on a combination of letters, numbers and special characters, making them very difficult to guess.

   Authorization refers to a process of inferring whether an authenticated user or an application has the privilege to access a particular resource. Authorization is often implemented by creating the access control matrix which defines the level of access of a resource to a user or application. An authenticated user is granted or denied access depending upon the access rights defined in the access control matrix.

Authentication thus identifies the source and authorization determines whether the identified source is allowed access to the resource.

3. With respect to information security, the CIA triad refers to ensuring confidentiality, integrity and availability of data and services. They are defined as follows:

   (i) *Confidentiality* refers to protecting the disclosure of data to unauthenticated and/or unauthorized entity.
   (ii) *Integrity* refers to ensuring that the data is free from modifications by unauthenticated and/or unauthorized entity.
   (iii) *Availability* refers to the property of a system which must ensure that any resource (data or service) must be available to an authenticated and authorized entity upon request.

4. Three components of any intrusion detection system are:

   (i) *Data pre-processor*: The data pre-processor is responsible for collecting and providing the data (in a specified form) that will be used by the next component (analyzer) to make a decision. Hence, the data pre-processor is concerned with collecting the data from the desired source and converting it into a form that is comprehensible by the analyzer.

   The data that can be used for detecting intrusions range from the user access patterns (for example, the sequence of commands issued at the terminal and the resources requested) to the network packet level features (such as the source and destination IP addresses, type of packets and rate of occurrence of packets) to the application and system level behavior (which includes the sequence of systems of system calls generated and many more).
   (ii) *Analyzer* (*intrusion detector*): The analyzer or the intrusion detector is the core component which analyzes the audit patterns to detect attacks. This is a critical component and one of the most researched. Various pattern matching, machine learning, data mining and statistical techniques can be used as intrusion detectors. The capability of the analyzer to detect an attack often determines the strength of the overall system.
   (iii) *Response engine*: The response engine determines how to react when the analyzer detects an attack. The system may decide either to raise an alert without taking any action against the source or decide to block the source for a predefined period of time. Such an action depends upon the predefined security policy of the network.

5. The principle states that for a system that is not under attack, the following three conditions hold true:

   (i) Actions of users conform to statistically predictable patterns.
   (ii) Actions of users do not include sequences which violate the security policy.

(iii) Actions of every process correspond to a set of specifications which describes what each process is allowed to do.

6. (i) Based on the available knowledge of the resources, as defined in the security policy, intrusion detection systems are classified as signature based, anomaly based, or hybrid.
   (ii) Based on the type of response defined in the security policy when an intrusion is detected, intrusion detection systems are classified as passive response systems, or active response systems.
7. (i) Based on the source of audit patterns, intrusion detection systems are classified as network based, host based, or application based.
   (ii) Audit patterns can be collected from a single source or from a number of sources. When the patterns are collected from more than one source, the decision can be made individually or by aggregating them at a single point and then analyzing the entire set of patterns together. Based upon this property, intrusion detection systems can be classified as centralized systems, distributed systems, or alert correlation based systems.
   (iii) Based on the frequency of audit pattern collection, intrusion detection systems are classified as session based, sliding window based, or periodic snapshot based.
   (iv) Depending upon the frequency of analysis of the audit patterns, intrusion detection systems are classified as batch mode, near real time, or real time.
8. Three properties of the audit patterns which can be used for detecting intrusions are:

   (i) Frequency of events,
   (ii) Duration of events, and
   (iii) Ordering of events.

9. *Network based systems*: In a network based system, the audit patterns collected at the network level are used by the intrusion detector. Though a single system (or a few strategically placed systems) often suffice for the entire network and is easy to manage, the attack detection capability of a network based system is limited. This is because it is hard to infer meaningful contextual information directly from the network audit patterns. Further, the audit patterns may be encrypted rendering them unusable by the intrusion detector at the network level. In addition, large number of audit patterns at the network level may also affect the total attack detection accuracy. This is for two reasons: first, a significant portion of the total incoming patterns may be allowed to pass into the network without any analysis, and second, in high-speed networks it may be practical to analyze only the summary statistics collected at regular time intervals. These statistics may include features such as the total number of connections, and the amount of incoming and outgoing traffic. Such features

may only provide a high level summary and may not be able to detect attacks reliably.

Host based systems: The intrusion detector in a host based system analyzes the audit patterns generated at the kernel level of the system, which include system access logs and the error logs. The audit patterns collected at the individual host contain more specific information than the network level audit patterns, which may be used to detect attacks reliably. However, it becomes difficult to manage a large number of host based systems in a big network. Additionally, host based systems can themselves be victims of attack and can be manipulated as part of an attack.

10. Evaluation metrics which are used for better evaluation of intrusion detection systems are Precision, Recall and F-measure. These are defined below with the help of a confusion matrix:

	Predicted normal	Predicted attack
True normal	True negative	False positive
True attack	False negative	True positive

$$Precision = \frac{Number\ of\ true\ positives}{Number\ of\ true\ positives + Number\ of\ false\ positives},$$

$$Recall = \frac{Number\ of\ true\ positives}{Number\ of\ true\ positives + Number\ of\ false\ negatives}.$$

Hence, a system must have high precision (i.e., it must detect only attacks) and high recall (i.e., it must detect all attacks). The two metrics can be combined and a single metric, F-measure, can be used, which is defined as

$$F\text{-}measure = \frac{(1+\beta^2) * Precision * Recall}{\beta^2(Precision + Recall)},$$

where β is the relative importance of Precision and Recall and is usually set to one.

The intrusion detection problem is an example of a problem with imbalanced classes, i.e., the number of instances in the two classes "normal" and "attack" are not equally distributed. The number of attacks is very low when compared with the total number of normal events. Note that in the case of DoS attacks the amount of attack traffic is extremely large compared to the normal traffic. Hence, evaluating intrusion detection systems using a simple accuracy metric may result in very high attack detection accuracy even if no attacks are detected and the system simply predicts all the events as normal. Thus, other metrics such as the Precision, Recall and F-measure must be used for evaluating intrusion detectors.

Chapter 23

1. The inherent issues are: promiscuous communication channels; dynamically changing topology resulting in broken links and sporadic connections; difficulty in achieving cooperation among nodes, which is a prerequisite for self-organized networks; and battery constrained nodes.
2. The security trends are: secure routing, key management, incentive-based payment, intrusion detection and trust management systems.
3. Since secure routing protocols are only designed to prevent against predefined attacks and assume all available nodes carry out routing and network management, they fail to counteract new types of attacks such as packet dropping and flooding.
4. Mobility induced dynamically changing topology, self-organized and autonomous characteristics of MANETs lead to a single point of failure.
5. A shortcoming of incentive based systems is that they fail to measure the trustworthiness of nodes based on the dynamically changing behavior of those nodes so that they could react to those dynamically changing behaviors accordingly.
6. Malicious and selfish nodes may exhibit similar malicious behavior such as dropping the packets received from neighbors or flooding the network with packets. Malicious nodes are capable of performing other types of attacks such as modification of routing messages and generating spoofed packets. However, selfish nodes differ from malicious nodes since they attempt to save their resources by dropping the packets of neighbors or try to maximize the utility of network services by forwarding only self-generated packets.
7. Trust management systems are required to enhance the strength of prevention mechanisms. They are capable of adapting to evolving attacks and responding to them accordingly.
8. The shortcomings and limitations are: reliance only on behavioral evidence; recommendations subject to honest-elicitation; free-riding and recommender's bias; poor evidence-to-opinion mapping logic; failing to model ignorance in trust relationships; and falling short when trying to handle selective malicious behaviors.
9. Since a trust management system do not employ any mechanism to authenticate intermediate nodes in a path, the behavioral evidence may be collected from spoofed packets and hence the established trust relationships may be inaccurate.
10. For example, in the case of a newly joining node, existing nodes in the network may not have a record of past evidence to trust or distrust a newly joining node.
11. Past evidence is given more weight in order to avoid recent incorrect observations from overshadowing past benign behaviors. It is important to prevent nodes from leveraging past benign behaviors and this is necessary in dynamically changing self-organized MANETs.

Chapter 24

1. Bootstrapping means initializing security for a particular feature by tying it to a pre-existing security infrastructure.
2. Services exercise access control for the following reasons:
   - Payment for the service is ensured by a subscription tied to a user.
   - Access to confidential information is only permitted for specific users.
   - Only the user himself is allowed to modify records in his account.
   - Permanent user identifiers allow continuous service experience, e.g. reviewing of previous transactions.
3. The key features are:
   - authentication,
   - single sign-on,
   - protection of communication and distribution of cryptographic keys,
   - support for pseudonymity,
   - federation of identities and user profiles,
   - independence of communication networks, and
   - applicability to a wide range of services.
4. The basic GBA variants are: GBA_ME, GBA_U and 2G GBA.
5. The design choices are: NAF/IdP and BSF/IdP.
6. A future area is the integration of GBA into meta-identity systems like Microsoft CardSpace or Bandit.

Chapter 25

1. A denial-of-service (DoS) attack is caused by sending a stream of packets to a victim (affected system or destination system). It consumes some key resources of the victim, thus rendering it unavailable to legitimate users, or it provides an attacker with unlimited access to the victim so that the attacker can inflict arbitrary damage on it. If DoS attacks are generated from different places then it is called a distributed denial-of-service (DDoS) attack. Attackers deploy multiple systems to attain this goal. In both cases, attackers hide their identity by spoofing their IP addresses.
2. Mitigating a DoS attack is a reactive countermeasure that is actually initiated by the victim after detecting an attack. The main challenges in DoS mitigation is to accurately identify attack packets and filter them without causing collateral damage to legitimate traffic destined for the victim.
3. The SOS architecture addresses the problem of securing communication in today's existing IP infrastructure from DoS and DDoS attacks, where the communication is between a pre-determined location and a set of well-known users, located anywhere in the wide-area network, who have authorization to communicate with that location. In server hopping, using distributed firewall

architecture, the proxy server changes its location among a pool of servers to defend against unpredictable and likely undetectable attacks. Only legitimate clients will be able to follow the server as it roams.

4. A *Smurf attack* is a DoS attack where a large number of innocent hosts respond to ICMP echo-request packets that contain a spoofed source IP address. **SYN flooding attack** is a attempt made by an attacker to deluge a server with TCP SYN packets, each having a spoofed IP source address. **Spoofing** is when a user with complete control over a device's software modifies the device's protocols to place an arbitrary IP into a datagram's source address field.
5. DoS protection architectures can be either proactive (they prevent the attack), or reactive (they react in order to stop the attack after it has begun).
6. Existing architectures for DoS attacks include some kind of "credential" in each packet. Each strategy also makes changes or additions to the Internet's infrastructure. The infrastructure looks at packets as they cross the network, filtering them based on their credentials. Packets that do not have the proper credentials are dropped and do not reach their destination.
7. Traditional data networks passively transport bits from one end system to another. Ideally, the user data is transferred opaquely, i.e., the network is insensitive to the bits it carries and they are transferred between end systems without modification. The role of computation within such networks is extremely limited, e.g., header processing in packet-switched networks and signaling in connection-oriented networks. Active networks break with tradition by allowing the network to perform customized computations on the user data. For example, a user of an active network could send a customized compression program to a node within the network (e.g., a router) and request that the node execute that program when processing its packets.
8. An active server is scheduled to roam among the servers in the pool in a certain time interval. This is called the *roaming interval.*